INSIDE MACINTOSH

Text

Addison-Wesley Publishing Company

Reading, Massachusetts   Menlo Park, California   New York
Don Mills, Ontario   Wokingham, England   Amsterdam   Bonn
Sydney   Singapore   Tokyo   Madrid   San Juan
Paris   Seoul   Milan   Mexico City   Taipei

Apple Computer, Inc.
20525 Mariani Avenue
Cupertino, CA 95014
408-996-1010

ISBN 0-201-63298-5
1 2 3 4 5 6 7 8 9-MU-9796959493
First Printing, March 1993

The paper used in this book meets the EPA standards for recycled fiber.

Contents

| Chapter 4 | **Font Manager**   4-1 |

Chapter 5   Text Utilities   5-1

Chapter 6	**Script Manager** 6-1

Chapter 7	**Text Services Manager** 7-1

Chapter 8

Dictionary Manager 8-1

Appendix A	**Built-in Script Support** A-1

Appendix C

Keyboard Resources   C-1

Figures, Tables, and Listings

Chapter 4

Font Manager   4-1

Chapter 5   Text Utilities 5-1

Chapter 7   Text Services Manager   7-1

Appendix D

Renamed and Relocated Text Routines   D-1

About This Book

Among personal computers, the Macintosh computer is foremost in the areas of desktop publishing, page layout, high-end graphical word processing, and international text presentation. The Macintosh computer's capabilities in these areas is due in large part to its unique and powerful support for text handling. *Inside Macintosh: Text* describes how you can use that support to put superior text capabilities into your software.

This book documents the parts of Macintosh system software that allow you to generate and manipulate text, including text in multiple languages. It includes introductory material on the Macintosh approach to text handling, as well as a complete technical reference to each of the text-handling managers in the system software.

What to Read

Whatever your text needs are, you should first read the chapter "Introduction to Text on the Macintosh." It describes Macintosh text concepts, outlines the kinds of text features addressed by the system software, and describes the organization and workings of script systems—collections of resources that give the Macintosh its multiple-language text capabilities.

If your text-handling needs are minor, the only other chapter you may need to read is "TextEdit," which describes a simple, multiple-language text-processing service provided by Macintosh system software. TextEdit is used by the system software to present text and accept user input in dialog boxes and alerts, and its capabilities are available for your application to use as well.

If you are planning a text-handling application with capabilities beyond those of TextEdit, read the remaining chapters of this book in any order. "QuickDraw Text" describes how to lay out and draw text to the screen or printer. "Font Manager" describes how to access Macintosh fonts and specify text characteristics. "Text Utilities" describes a collection of text-handling routines that allow you to specify, sort, format, search, and otherwise manipulate text strings. "Script Manager" describes how to access and manipulate script systems.

If you want your application to work efficiently with Japanese, Korean, or Chinese text input, or if you are designing an input method for those languages, read the chapter "Text Services Manager." It describes how to make your application work with multiple input methods in multiple languages, and how to create an input method that provides multiple-language input for any application. If you are creating an input method, read also the chapter "Dictionary Manager" to find out how to create and use input dictionaries that are portable across input methods and applications.

If you are planning to add specific language capabilities to an application, or need to modify the system software's text-handling for a given language, read the chapter "Script Manager" and the appendixes "Built-in Script Support," "International Resources," and "Keyboard Resources." They describe the organization of script systems on the Macintosh, and show you how to modify parts of a script system in order to obtain the exact text-handling characteristics you need.

If you are designing a font or a font editor, read the parts of the chapter "Font Manager" that describe the data structures and tables that make up Macintosh fonts. In addition, you will need information contained in the *TrueType Font Format Specification*, available from APDA.

If you are already familiar with Macintosh system software and with previous versions of *Inside Macintosh*, you may notice that in this book the organization of some managers and the names of some routines have changed. You can refer to the appendix "Renamed and Relocated Text Routines" for information on how the new organization and terminology relate to previous presentations.

Format of a Typical Chapter

Most chapters in this book follow a standard structure. For example, the chapter "TextEdit" contains these sections:

- "About TextEdit." This section provides an overview of the features provided by TextEdit.

- "Using TextEdit." This section describes the tasks you can accomplish using TextEdit. It describes how to use the most common routines, gives related user interface information, provides code samples, and supplies additional information.

- "TextEdit Reference." This section provides a complete reference to TextEdit by describing the constants, data structures, and routines that it uses. Each routine description also follows a standard format, which gives the routine declaration and description of every parameter of the routine. Some routine descriptions also give additional descriptive information, such as assembly-language information or result codes.

- "Summary of TextEdit." This section provides the Pascal interface and the C interface to TextEdit, defining the constants, data structures, routines, and result codes associated with TextEdit. It also includes relevant assembly-language interface information.

Some chapters contain additional main sections that provide more detailed discussions of certain topics. For example, in the chapter "Font Manager," the sections "About Fonts" and "About Font Resources" describe the capabilities and structure of the fonts that the Font Manager supports.

Conventions Used in This Book

Inside Macintosh uses various conventions to present information. Words that require special treatment appear in specific fonts or font styles. Certain information, such as parameter blocks, use special formats so that you can scan them quickly.

Special Fonts

All code listings, reserved words, and the names of actual data structures, constants, fields, parameters, and routines are shown in Courier (`this is Courier`).

Words that appear in **boldface** are key terms or concepts and are defined in the Glossary.

Types of Notes

There are several types of notes used in this book.

Note
A note like this contains information that is interesting but possibly not essential to an understanding of the main text. (An example appears on page 1-5.) ◆

IMPORTANT
A note like this contains information that is essential for an understanding of the main text. (An example appears on page 2-63.) ▲

▲ **WARNING**
Warnings like this indicate potential severe problems that you should be aware of as you design your application. Failure to heed these warnings could result in system crashes and loss of data. (An example appears on page 4-17.) ▲

Development Environment

The system software routines described in this book are available using Pascal, C, or assembly-language interfaces. How you access these routines depends on the development environment you are using. This book shows system software routines in their Pascal interface, C interface, or assembly language using the Macintosh Programmer's Workshop (MPW).

Code listings in this book are shown in MPW Pascal or MPW C or MPW Assembler. They suggest methods of using various routines and illustrate techniques for accomplishing particular tasks. Most code listings have been compiled and tested, although in some cases only fragments of the full listings are shown. However, Apple Computer does not intend that you use exactly these code samples in your application.

Developer Products and Support

APDA is Apple's worldwide source for over 300 development tools, technical resources, training products, and information for anyone interested in developing applications on Apple platforms. Customers receive the quarterly *APDA Tools Catalog* featuring all current versions of Apple development tools and the most popular third-party development tools. Ordering is easy; there are no membership fees, and application forms are not required for most of our products. APDA offers convenient payment and shipping options including site licensing.

To order products or to request a complimentary copy of the *APDA Tools Catalog*, contact

APDA
Apple Computer, Inc.
P.O. Box 319
Buffalo, NY 14207-0319
U.S.A.

Telephone	800-282-2732 (United States)
	800-637-0029 (Canada)
	716-871-6555 (International)
Fax	716-871-6511
AppleLink	APDA
America Online	APDA
CompuServe	76666,2405
Internet	APDA@applelink.apple.com

If you provide commercial products and services, call 408-974-4897 for information on the developer support programs available from Apple.

For information on obtaining Macintosh Technical Notes, and for other technical information, contact

Macintosh Developer Technical Support
Apple Computer, Inc.
20525 Mariani Avenue, M/S 75-3T
Cupertino, CA 95014-6299

Introduction to Text on the Macintosh

Contents

This chapter is an overview of Macintosh text handling. It is meant to help you get started by introducing the concepts described in detail throughout the rest of *Inside Macintosh: Text.*

The chapter contains four major sections. The first presents high-level concepts, and the following three develop those concepts further and give important programming suggestions and hints:

- "Macintosh Text Overview" summarizes what text means for Macintosh programmers, including how to support text in multiple languages. It concludes with suggestions for planning your application's level of text handling.

- "Writing Systems and Script Systems" surveys the issues that must be addressed by any computer-based text-handling system, and then describes the organization of the Macintosh script management system, the set of software managers and resources that help you support text-handling capabilities across many languages.

- "How Script Systems Work" describes the approach taken by the script management system to provide multi-language capabilities in areas such as text display, text input, and string manipulation.

- "Script Systems in Use" describes how the computer user interacts with script systems, including installing script systems, switching text input and display from one language to another, and controlling script-system configuration.

If you are developing a text-handling application, read this chapter's first section, "Macintosh Text Overview," before reading any other parts of this book. You can then either read the remainder of this chapter before going on, or start immediately on the other chapters, returning to this chapter as needed for further explanation of script-system concepts and for specific programming suggestions. The chapters that are most important for general application development are "TextEdit," "QuickDraw Text," "Font Manager," "Text Utilities," and "Script Manager." The chapters that are most important for applications that use input methods, or for developers of input methods, are "Text Services Manager" and "Dictionary Manager."

If you are developing or modifying a script system, read this chapter completely before turning to other chapters and appendixes. Those that are most important for understanding script-system design are "Script Manager," "Built-in Script Support," "International Resources," and "Keyboard Resources."

Valuable information related to the topics discussed in this chapter can be found in *Guide to Macintosh Software Localization.* That book discusses features of individual script systems and gives specific techniques for software localization.

Macintosh Text Overview

Text handling on the Macintosh is fundamentally different from the way it is approached on some common text-based computer systems. There is no hardware-based character generator to put text on the screen; there is no standard input/output window (and no `Writeline` command) for easy generation of text messages.

To draw any text, you first must create a window to draw in. In that window, you can then draw shapes, including the shapes of letters. See the Window Manager chapter in *Inside Macintosh: Macintosh Toolbox Essentials* for a discussion of how to create a window.

In accepting text input and storing text in memory, you cannot assume any particular hardware (keyboard) configuration, you should not assume a particular language for input, you should not assume that characters are always represented by ASCII codes, and you should not even assume that a single character is always represented by 1 byte of storage.

This section paints a broad picture of how text processing works on the Macintosh, and presents some fundamental terminology. It also introduces script systems and briefly discusses two components of system software of special interest for text processing. The section concludes with suggestions on how to give your application the level of text-handling sophistication it requires.

Separation of Tasks

The Macintosh approach separates text handling tasks into three fundamental categories, each relatively independent of the others:

- Text input
- Text storage and manipulation
- Text display

See Figure 1-1. In the discussions in this chapter and elsewhere in this book, keep in mind which category of task is under discussion, to avoid misunderstanding.

Figure 1-1   Separation of input, storage, and display in Macintosh text handling

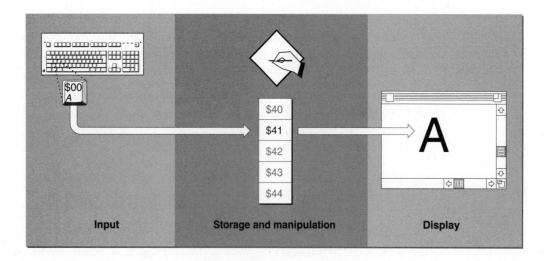

Through text input, your application obtains representations of text characters. It starts with the user pressing keys on a keyboard. Text input is aided by specialized parts of system software that allow input of text in many languages. Text input is completely independent of text display.

Your application stores character representations in memory, as numeric codes. The main focus of your application is on storing, tracking the characteristics of, and manipulating these codes in memory. How those codes got into memory, and how you will display or print them, are mostly separate issues. For much of your processing, you will be concerned with codes in a memory buffer, rather than keypresses on a keyboard or pixel locations on a screen. The system software has many routines that aid in manipulating text of many languages in memory.

Note
In Figure 1-1 and throughout this book, text in computer memory is drawn as a vertical table of codes, representing sequential (downward) storage of text characters in a buffer. Some diagrams also include byte offsets in the buffer, and even miniature representations of the characters themselves in a given language. See, for example, Figure 1-3 on page 1-8. ◆

Though text display, your application makes visible the characters it has stored and manipulated in memory. The end result of the display process is a sequence of text shapes drawn on a display device. As is shown later in this chapter, the displayed form of text often has a complex relationship to the way it is stored. In most cases you can consider text display as an independent task, handled in large part by system software, that you call after you have finished receiving, storing, or otherwise processing characters in memory. It is only during display, for example, that the concept of a font has meaning. (Preparation for text display, such as width measurement and line-breaking, falls on the boundary between storage and display, and is in general a cooperative effort between your application and system software.)

If your application is a word processor that is drawing characters to the screen as the user enters them, all three of these tasks are closely coupled in time. Nevertheless, they are still independent of each other and can be understood best as separate processes.

Text Is Graphics

Your application draws graphic shapes on the Macintosh screen by making calls to QuickDraw, the graphics manager of Macintosh system software. The graphics components of QuickDraw are described in the chapter "QuickDraw," in *Inside Macintosh: Imaging*.

Drawing text is fundamentally the same as drawing graphics. The application makes QuickDraw calls to write text to the screen or to a printer. Those parts of QuickDraw that are concerned specifically with drawing text are documented in the chapter "QuickDraw Text" in this book.

When QuickDraw draws text, it places bitmapped shapes on a display device. Those shapes are the forms of individual letters in a particular font. A **font** is a resource that contains a complete set of character representations in a particular typeface, such as Times® or Geneva. Without a font, QuickDraw cannot draw text.

When you ask QuickDraw to draw text, it draws it according to the settings of the window (specifically, of the current **graphics port** record) that you are drawing into. The text's screen location, font, size, color, and style are all implied by the current state of the graphics port; they are not explicit parameters of your text-drawing call.

For example, when QuickDraw draws a character, it draws it at the current **pen position,** the screen position at which drawing occurs, in the current window. The character's origin (usually its left edge) is placed with respect to that location, with the rest of the character extending to the right of the origin. After drawing, QuickDraw automatically updates the pen location by the width of the character, so that the next character drawn will be automatically placed the correct distance to the right of the first. See Figure 1-2.

Likewise, when QuickDraw draws a string of text, it keeps advancing the pen location as it draws, so that the current location ends up at the right end of the string. This left-to-right orientation of QuickDraw is fundamental, and applies whether or not the text being drawn is meant to be read left-to-right (such as English) or right-to-left (such as Arabic).

Figure 1-2   How QuickDraw draws text

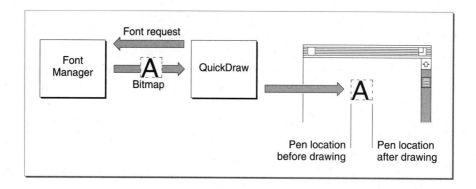

QuickDraw's text-measuring capabilities are as important as its drawing capabilities. In many cases, before you draw a line of text, you first need to know its length in pixels, so that you can correctly place it on the screen and be assured that it does not overrun its allotted space. Pixels are screen dots, and are nominally equal to one point, or approximately 1/72 inch, in size. You often make two sets of QuickDraw calls when drawing a string; the first to measure it, and the second to actually draw it.

The **Font Manager** supports QuickDraw by providing the character bitmaps that QuickDraw needs, in the typefaces, sizes, and **styles** (such as bold or italic) that QuickDraw requests. The Font Manager keeps track of all fonts available to an application. If QuickDraw requests a typeface that is not represented in the available fonts, the Font Manager substitutes one that is; if QuickDraw requests a size that is not available, the Font Manager scales an available size and returns the bitmaps to QuickDraw; if QuickDraw requests a style that is not available, the Font Manager returns an unstyled set of bitmaps and QuickDraw applies a style to them (by slanting for italic, or darkening extra pixels for boldface, and so on). In general, the Font Manager does the calculations and creates the bitmaps; QuickDraw transfers those bitmaps to the screen.

Fonts are strongly language-dependent. A font is the manifestation of the character set—the body of meaningful characters—of a language or group of languages, called a **writing system.** Fonts also implement additional symbols and forms, such as ligatures, needed by that writing system. The Font Manager provides for fonts in many writing systems; fonts are identified by a numbering scheme with which the writing system of a font can be determined from its number.

Macintosh fonts come in two basic kinds: **bitmapped** and **outline** (such as TrueType). Each bitmapped font is a set of character bitmaps of a given typeface in a single size; each outline font is a set of templates from which bitmaps of any size can be generated. All Macintosh text-handling routines work with both types of fonts.

Fonts can also be classified by the sizes of the character sets they implement. The typical Macintosh fonts, suitable for most languages of the world, are called 1-byte fonts; each contains fewer than 256 characters. Fonts for some East Asian languages, however, need thousands of characters; they are called 2-byte fonts. The Macintosh text-handling routines can work with both 1-byte and 2-byte fonts, although special techniques may be required for character handling with 2-byte fonts. Bitmapped and outline fonts are described in the chapter "Font Manager" in this book and in *TrueType Font Format Specification*, available from APDA. For more information on how fonts are used on the Macintosh, see "Fonts" beginning on page 1-44, and "Font Handling" beginning on page 1-60.

The text measuring and drawing routines in QuickDraw and the Text Utilities operate under certain assumptions, based principally on the fact that Macintosh system software was originally developed for the left-to-right Roman writing system of the English language, and that the system software provides line-layout, but not page-layout, capabilities. Remember these points:

- QuickDraw draws all text from left to right. Whether your text has a left-to-right or right-to-left **line direction**—the direction in which the text is read—QuickDraw places its left edge at the current location in your window and draws its characters in order from the leftmost to the rightmost character. QuickDraw and the Text Utilities provide routines that allow you to order and draw your text properly regardless of its line direction or directions.

- On a line of text, screen position is in terms of pixel offset from the *left* edge of the text-drawing area, regardless of the line direction of the text being drawn.

- The text-measuring routines in this book help you calculate and lay out individual lines; it is up to you to track where a line starts, both in terms of vertical screen position and in terms of offset in your text run.

Characters, Glyphs, Character Codes, and Bytes

In memory, applications store text as numerical representations of characters. On the screen, QuickDraw draws text as bitmapped representations of those characters, generated from a particular font. To clarify how numbers in memory are converted to letters on the screen, keep the following terms in mind. See also Figure 1-3.

A writing system's alphabet, numbers, punctuation, and other writing marks consist of **characters.** A character is a symbolic representation of an element of a writing system; it is the concept of, for example, "lowercase a" or "the number 3". It is an abstract object, defined by custom in its own language.

As soon as you write a character, however, it is no longer abstract but concrete. The exact shape by which a character is represented is called a **glyph.** A font, then, is a collection of glyphs, all of similar design, that constitute one way to represent the characters of the language. The "characters" that QuickDraw places on the screen are really glyphs.

In memory, text is stored as **character codes,** where each code is a number that defines a particular (abstract) character. The "characters" that an application reads into or out of a buffer, sorts, and searches for are really numeric codes. One purpose of a Macintosh font is to provide glyphs that the system software can associate with character codes; different fonts for the same language will typically have different glyphs, all representing the same character, for a specific character code. Thus no matter which font you use, an English "C" is always a "C" (character code $43), though it may be Garamond or Chicago font, italic or bold style, and 7 points or 72 points in size. (Note that fonts in certain languages may have more than one glyph per character, and may have special glyphs for various combinations of characters.)

Figure 1-3   Bytes, character codes, characters, and glyphs

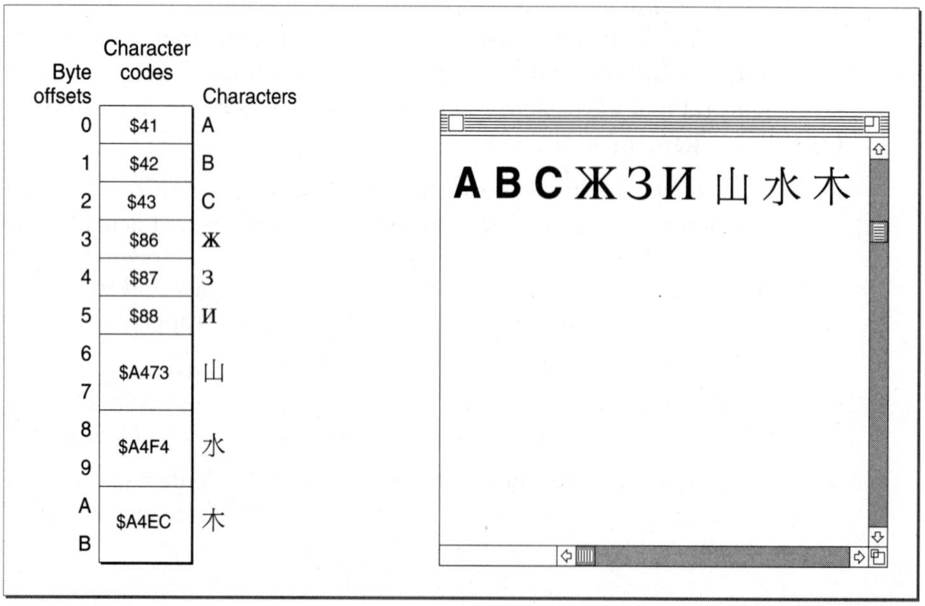

In computer memory, 1 byte (8 bits) is commonly used to store a single character code. For most languages that is sufficient: the standard **ASCII character set** (also called **low ASCII**) requires only 7 bits per character code, and the Apple Standard Roman character set (an extended ASCII character set derived from the original Macintosh character set) requires only 1 byte per character code. In many other languages, such as Russian, Arabic, and Thai, each character code is also 1 byte in size. But in some East Asian languages such as Japanese, Chinese, and Korean, the character set is so large that most character codes must be 2 bytes long. Macintosh system software provides routines to help you recognize and manipulate 2-byte characters; if your application is to be useful throughout the world, *you must be prepared to deal with 2-byte characters.*

The left side of Figure 1-3 shows a portion of a text buffer in memory. Byte offsets into the buffer are shown down the left side of the column. The character codes the buffer contains are shown within the column; note that some codes are a single byte, whereas others are 2 bytes in size. (For clarity, miniature representations of the characters defined by those character codes are shown down the right side of the column.)

The right side of Figure 1-3 shows what happens when QuickDraw draws the contents of the buffer. The character codes define which glyphs are placed on the screen, and in what order. The character codes do not define the style or size of the glyphs, however.

Character codes are only numbers; the meaning of each character code is different in different writing systems. In Figure 1-4, for example, the same four bytes are interpreted very differently if they are considered to be two Japanese character codes than if they are considered to be four English (= Roman writing system) character codes.

Figure 1-4   Four bytes displayed in Japanese and in English

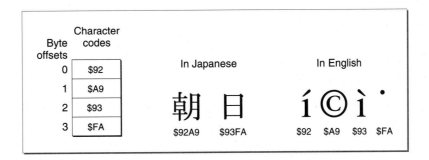

Text Storage

In considering how to store text in buffers, strings, and files, it may be clearer if you understand the assumptions that the Macintosh text managers make about your text-storage method. The discussions throughout this book assume that your text is stored and accessed according to these conventions:

■ Your program stores text as a simple sequence of character codes. The character codes may be 1-byte or 2-byte codes, but there is nothing else in the text stream except for those codes. Using font information that your program stores separately,

Script Manager routines can help you determine whether a character is 1 or 2 bytes, and other managers allow you to work with either character size.

■ Character location within a text sequence in memory is in terms of byte offset (not character offset) from the beginning of the text. Offset is zero-based; the first byte in the sequence has an offset of 0.

■ The **storage order** of your text—the sequence in memory in which the character codes occur—is the same as its logical order. It is the order in which the characters would be read or pronounced in the language of the text. Because text of different languages may be read either left-to-right or right-to-left, storage order is not always the same as the left-to-right **display order** of the text when it is drawn. In Figure 1-5, for example, note that the Hebrew characters are displayed in reverse order from the order in which they are stored.

Figure 1-5   Storage order and display order

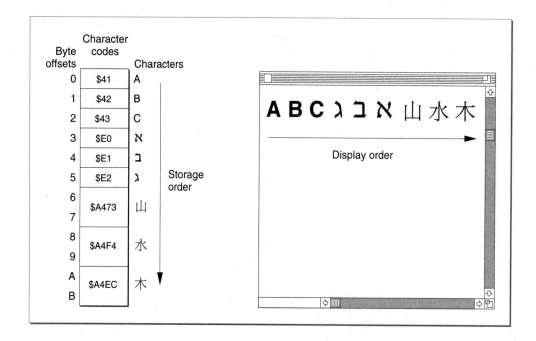

■ All writing-system, font, size, color, and style information about each part of your text is stored separately from the text, and it is your application's responsibility to maintain that information. The text stream itself carries no information about what writing system or font it was created with or is meant to be drawn with; you need to keep track of and supply that information before making a drawing or measuring call.

■ Text is divided into **runs.** There are text runs, direction runs, script runs, font runs, and style runs. A **style run** is a continuous sequence of text that is all of the same writing system, font, size, color, style, and scaling factors (if the text is scaled). Figure 1-6 shows four style runs on a single line. Because of the way many drawing and measuring routines work, it is important to track all the individual style runs in your text. Runs are described in more detail under "Style Runs, Font Runs, Script Runs, Direction Runs" beginning on page 1-70.

Figure 1-6   Style runs in text

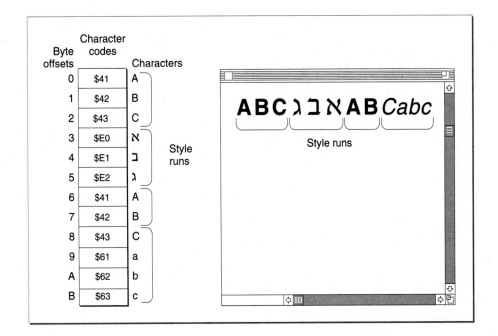

- Drawing involves converting character codes in memory to glyphs on the screen. When drawn, some characters in some writing systems change their shape, size, or position depending on their contextual position, that is, on what other characters surround them. See "Contextual Forms and Character Reordering" beginning on page 1-26. Using information in a set of **international resources,** the Macintosh text-measuring and drawing routines can automatically perform these contextual transformations for you.

- For text that is contextual, you do not store the transformed, ready-to-draw version; what you store in memory are the codes for the fundamental characters that make up the text. That makes searching, sorting and other manipulation more straightforward. Each time the text is drawn it is re-transformed as appropriate.

Keyboards and Input Methods

By means of keyboard input, the user can create text that your application stores as character codes and displays as glyphs. At first glance this may seem a difficult task: your application should be able to handle input from at least 13 different hardware types of Apple keyboards, as listed in the appendix "Keyboard Resources" in this book. Furthermore, it must be able to derive the proper character codes for any writing system from each of the keyboards and recognize the states of the **modifier keys** (Shift, Caps Lock, Command, Option, and Control).

The system software and the **keyboard resources** make this relatively easy for you. The Event Manager uses the keyboard resources to convert keypresses into the correct character codes for the current writing system, for whatever keyboard is used. Your application receives the codes directly and needn't keep track of the specific keyboard in use.

Figure 1-7 is a simplified view of **key translation,** the process by which character codes are generated. Each keyboard has a particular physical arrangement of keys, and each keypress generates a value called a **raw key code,** which indicates which key was pressed. The keyboard driver that handles the keypress uses the **key-map resource** to map these raw key codes to keyboard-independent **virtual key codes.** It then uses the Event Manager and the **keyboard-layout resource** to convert a virtual key code into a character code, and passes it to your application in the event record generated by the keypress. See "Keyboards and Key Translation" beginning on page 1-87 for a more complete description of key translation; see the Event Manager chapter in *Inside Macintosh: Macintosh Toolbox Essentials* for a description of events and event records.

Figure 1-7   Key translation (simplified)

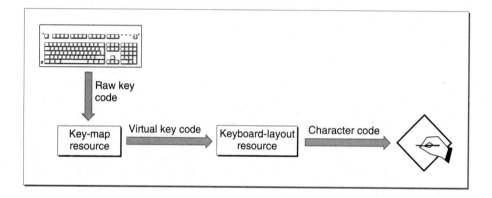

Keyboard layout can be considered the overall relationship between the physical arrangement of keys on a keyboard and the glyphs produced when those keys are pressed. It is what the Key Caps desk accessory shows; see Figure 1-8.

Figure 1-8   Key Caps display of Thai keyboard layout (no modifier keys pressed)

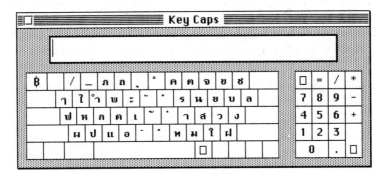

Changing the physical keyboard, changing the keyboard-layout resource, pressing modifier keys, and changing the font can all change the relationship between keypresses and glyphs. Figure 1-9 is a Key Caps display for the same physical keyboard as that in Figure 1-8, but the writing system has been changed from Thai to Cyrillic. For the purposes of this book, however, the keyboard-layout resource is the critical item in determining keyboard layout; *changing the keyboard layout means changing the keyboard-layout resource.* Because keyboard layouts are independent of the physical keyboard attached to the computer, your application has the flexibility of changing text input from one writing system to another by simply using a different keyboard-layout resource.

Figure 1-9   Key Caps display of Cyrillic keyboard layout (Caps Lock key pressed)

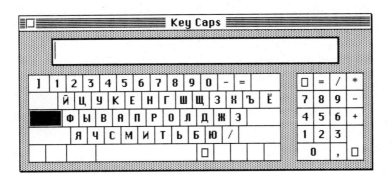

For languages with large character sets, it is impractical to manufacture keyboards with keys for every possible character. In such a case, it is usually the job of an input method, working in conjunction with a keyboard, to handle text input. An **input method** is a software module, often independent of the application it serves, that converts character codes that can be entered from the keyboard into character codes that cannot. Japanese and Chinese input methods commonly display a small window, into which the user types a sequence of phonetic characters; the input method converts them into one or more ideographic character codes and sends them to the application. A more sophisticated input method is **inline input,** in which entry and conversion of text occur directly in the window of the text document being edited. See "Input Methods" beginning on page 1-91 and the chapter "Text Services Manager" in this book for more information on input methods and inline input.

In most cases, your application does not need to do anything special related to keyboard input. You can use the character codes returned by the Event Manager function `WaitNextEvent`—whether generated directly from keypresses or through an input method—and handle the text appropriately for the language being used for input. Remember, however, that keyboard input is independent of text display; it is your responsibility to keep the two synchronized when necessary. If the user switches language for text input, you must switch the language for text display accordingly. The Font Manager and Script Manager provide routines that help you with that; see "Font and Keyboard Synchronization" beginning on page 1-90, and further discussion in the chapter "Script Manager" in this book.

Writing Systems and Script Systems

Localization is the process of adapting software to local use. When a version of Macintosh system software is created for a particular country or region, its text strings usually must be translated and it must support the writing system of that region. To facilitate the localization of Macintosh system software around the world, much of Macintosh text-handling is concerned with proper presentation in multiple languages. Macintosh computers are sold worldwide, and Macintosh system software is currently available in over 30 localized versions, allowing computer users in many parts of the world to use the Macintosh in their native languages. Macintosh system software likewise provides your application with the capability of simultaneously supporting multiple writing systems.

IMPORTANT

Even if you do not plan to localize your application, it should still support multiple writing systems. Users in your own target region may have capability for more than one writing system on their computers, and may want your application to support that capability. ▲

In this book, a **writing system** denotes a method used to depict words visually. It consists of a character set and a set of rules for displaying, ordering, and formatting those characters. Writing systems can differ in **line direction,** the direction in which their characters are read; the size of the character set used to represent the writing system; and whether or not they are contextual—whether a character changes its form depending on its position relative to other characters. Writing systems have specific requirements for text display, text editing, character set, and fonts. A writing system, of which one example is Roman, can serve more than one language, of which two examples are French and Spanish. A single language such as French can have regional variations with slightly different requirements, such as Swiss French and Canadian French. Writing systems and their features are described under "Features of the World's Writing Systems" beginning on page 1-21.

On the Macintosh computer, a **script system** (or **script** for short) is a collection of resources that provides for the representation of a particular writing system. A script's **keyboard resources** define the character codes and keyboard layout for the writing system, and its **international resources** provide a host of formatting and ordering rules for the writing system. A script system requires one or more fonts designed specifically for the writing system. The script system is accessed through the Script Manager, the Text Utilities, the script extensions WorldScript I and WorldScript II, and the other text-related software managers described in this book. Together, these software components make up the **Macintosh script management system.** The files, managers, and resources that make up the script management system are described under "Components of the Macintosh Script Management System" beginning on page 1-35.

A script system on the Macintosh is identified primarily by number, its **script code.** And just as writing systems can serve several languages, script systems can have variations for different languages, specified by **language code.** Each language code "belongs" to a particular script code. Regional variations can also be reflected in script systems, by **region code.** Each region code "belongs" to a particular language code. See, for example, Figure 1-34 on page 1-49.

More than one script system may be **enabled,** or present and available, on the Macintosh. Script systems may be installed either as **auxiliary scripts,** which just provide writing-system support, or as the *system script*, which affects system defaults such as the default font, keyboard layout, line direction, and so forth, and is typically the writing system used for localized dialog boxes, menus, and alerts. All other scripts are secondary to the system script. The **font script,** also called the *current script,* is the script system currently being used to draw text. The **keyboard script** is the script system currently being used for text input.

The Roman script system is always available, either as the system script or as an auxiliary script. Furthermore, the low-ASCII Roman characters are always available in any script system; they are a standard part of every script system's character set.

Macintosh system software routines that take into account the script system of the text they manipulate are called **script-aware** routines. Likewise, applications that use those routines to properly handle text according to its script system are also called script-aware. Your applications should be script-aware.

More details about script systems and how they work are found under "Components of a Script System" beginning on page 1-40, "How Script Systems Are Classified" beginning on page 1-45, and "How Script Systems Work" beginning on page 1-52.

Macintosh Text Utilities

The Text Utilities are a broad collection of text-manipulation routines provided by Macintosh system software. With Text Utilities calls, you can

- specify strings for various purposes

- sort strings, including strings in any writing system and combinations of strings in different writing systems

- convert case or strip diacritical marks from text for sorting purposes

- format numbers and currency

- format dates and times

- search and replace text

- find word boundaries and line breaks when laying out lines of text

Some Text Utilities routines function with the Roman script system only, but many are script-aware and work properly with all script systems. Script-aware Text Utilities routines rely on a script system's international resources to define the specific behavior in that script system.

The Text Utilities are described in the chapter "Text Utilities" in this book.

TextEdit, a Text-Processing Service

Macintosh system software provides a simple text-processing service, used by the Dialog Manager and other parts of system software, and available for your use also. TextEdit handles certain basic text-handling tasks for small (less than 32 KB) amounts of text.

TextEdit maintains a text buffer, provides line breaks, tracks the selection range and insertion point for text, handles insertions and deletions from the buffer, and tracks style information for all its text. TextEdit formats and draws text properly in multiple styles and different script systems—even multiple scripts on a single line. TextEdit handles mixed-directional text, synchronizes fonts and keyboards, handles 2-byte characters, determines word boundaries, and matches text alignment with line direction. TextEdit even allows you to customize several of its features, such as word selection and text measurement.

If you want multiscript text handling, and you do not need to manipulate large files and do not need formatting other than font styles, TextEdit is a convenient alternative to writing your own text processor. You can use TextEdit at different levels of complexity:

- For the very simplest text handling (in dialog boxes), you needn't even call TextEdit directly. Use the Dialog Manager, which in turn uses TextEdit, to correctly edit and display text in either the system script or Roman script. For example, the Save As dialog box shown in Figure 1-10 handles mixed-directional text (in this case, Arabic) correctly. The Dialog Manager is described in *Inside Macintosh: Macintosh Toolbox Essentials*.

Figure 1-10   TextEdit edits and displays mixed-directional text in a dialog box

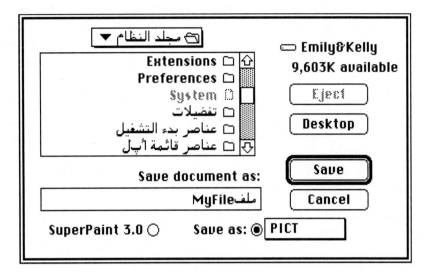

■ If you simply want to display one or more lines of static (non-editable) text, you can call the TextEdit `TETextBox` procedure. `TETextBox` draws your text at the location you specify with the alignment you specify. You need not make any other TextEdit calls or allocate any data structures if you use `TETextBox`.

■ Other than dialog boxes and static text display, if your application requires very basic text handling, in which neither styled text nor multiple fonts are needed (as in many desk accessories), you may need only monostyled TextEdit. You can use monostyled TextEdit with the application font (if you don't allow the user to select a font) or with any single available font (if you do allow user selection) in any version of Roman or non-Roman Macintosh system software.

■ If your application requires a somewhat higher level of text handling (allowing the user to set the font, size, and style of text, for example), you can use multistyled TextEdit. You can use multistyled TextEdit with any combination of available fonts, in any version of Roman or non-Roman Macintosh system software.

TextEdit does have limitations; it is not powerful or efficient enough for use as a general text editor. For example, TextEdit

■ can only handle up to 32 KB of text

■ is not highly optimized for speed

■ contains data structures that can be inefficiently large for multistyled text

Nevertheless, TextEdit's convenience and multiscript capabilities make it an attractive alternative to writing your own text processor. TextEdit is described in the chapter "TextEdit" in this book.

Planning Your Text Handling Capabilities

The Macintosh system of text handling—with its graphic approach to text drawing, separation of text storage from text rendering, ability to handle many writing systems, event-controlled text input, large library of utility routines, and availability of a simple text-handling service—is general and powerful. But you may not need all of its power, and the simpler your needs are the less you will have to do to meet them.

It may appear difficult at the outset to generalize your text-handling capabilities so that they can work across all script systems around the world. You may instead wish to customize your application to work with a specific regional variation or script system in a target market that interests you. Either approach is possible; you can use the Macintosh script management system to build in language-independence or language customization, as you wish. There are three general approaches you can take:

- **Globalization** is the preparation of a culturally neutral application that provides the technical underpinnings for script-specific, linguistic, and regional variations, and that is capable of running with any script system. Globalization involves careful design and writing of the application and its textual and graphic resources.

- **Localization** is the adaptation of an application to a particular language or region, to achieve proper formats for dates, times, currency, measurement, calendars, and numbers, proper text sorting, and acceptable forms of other culturally specific material. Localization involves translation of textual resources, modification of graphic resources such as icons, and possibly creation of a customized set of script-system resources. The better globalized an application is, the easier it is to localize.

- **Customization** is the inclusion of script-specific, linguistic, or regional capabilities supporting features that are not otherwise supported by Macintosh system software (for instance, vertical text direction or special underlining modes for the Japanese writing system).

This book supports and describes the process of globalization; it helps you prepare your application to support all writing systems and regions. The process of localization is discussed in *Guide to Macintosh Software Localization*. This book does not discuss customization, beyond the few suggestions presented at the end of this section.

To achieve globalization, localization, or customization, the level of work required is related to the level of text-handling sophistication you need. There are three general levels to consider—rudimentary, moderate, and highly sophisticated.

Rudimentary Text Handling

Rudimentary text handling means that the user either cannot set fonts at all (the lowest level of sophistication) or that the user can set fonts and styles but not alignment (a slightly higher level). In either case large amounts of text and sophisticated formatting are not required.

If your application requires only rudimentary handling, use TextEdit—either directly or through the Dialog Manager—to handle user input and editing. TextEdit exhibits the correct behavior for editing and displaying text in multiple styles and different script systems.

In addition, at an absolute minimum, design your application so that it can display its own Roman text properly when operating with a non-Roman script system. For text in dialog boxes, menus, alert boxes, and so on, if you do not plan to translate the text for localization use only the low-ASCII character codes that are the same on all script systems. High-ASCII character codes may map to incomprehensible characters in another script. The ellipsis in menu items, for example, maps to other characters when displayed in other system scripts. Instead of using the ellipsis, a high-ASCII character code, you can use three periods, a low-ASCII string; the ellipsis is displayed regardless of the system script. (A better approach, however, is to use the script management system to retrieve the appropriate form of the ellipsis character for whatever script system you are running under. See the discussion of retrieving text from tokens in the chapter "Script Manager" in this book.)

Moderate Text Handling

Moderate text-handling sophistication means an application allows users to set font, style, alignment, tabs, writing direction, keyboard, input method, and so forth, across script systems. It handles large amounts of text and offers greater formatting sophistication than TextEdit provides.

The Macintosh script management system and all the text managers documented in this book are designed to support this level of sophistication. You can use these managers and the rest of Macintosh system software to include basic word-processing capabilities in your application, capabilities that work across the entire range of worldwide writing systems supported by Macintosh system software.

Within the range of moderate text handling, the level of complexity is largely a function of the number and types of script systems that are currently enabled. You may wish to structure your application's text-handling algorithms to allow for categories of increasing complexity, based on conditions such as the following four. (The item in parentheses following each condition is a selector or flag that tests for that condition. See the discussion of selectors for Script Manager variables and script variables in the chapter "Script Manager" in this book.)

■ Only one script system is present (`smEnabled` = 1). If there is only one script system, it is Roman; you can assume all text-handling follows the built-in Roman rules, and you do not need to account for or test for the script system of any text.

■ More than one script system is present (`smEnabled` > 1). You need to track the script system associated with each run of text. You need to use script-aware routines for text handling. You need to synchronize the font script with the keyboard script.

■ A bidirectional script system is present (`smBidirect` = TRUE). You need to allow for the possibility of right-to-left text, right alignment of text, discontinuous highlighting, and a display order for style runs that is different from storage order. You need to allow for contextual behavior in drawing; you cannot use font width tables for measuring text.

■ A 2-byte script system is present (`smDoubleByte` = TRUE). You need to allow for the presence of 2-byte character codes in searching, drawing, and line-breaking. You should also support inline input of text whenever the keyboard script is a 2-byte script system.

These probably represent the major divisions in text-handling complexity that you address, although you may want to account for others. For example, you may want to test each individual script system to see if it is contextual (`smsfContext` set), 1-byte (`smsfSingByte` set), or bidirectional (`smScriptRight` = TRUE) before deciding how to handle its text.

With the moderate level of text-handling supported by the Macintosh script management system as documented in this book, your application can be powerful enough and general enough for worldwide acceptance.

Sophisticated Text Handling

Highly sophisticated text processing might be employed by a very powerful word processor that works across many script systems. If you write such a program, you will probably need to go beyond the capabilities provided by the Macintosh script management system.

Areas that may need special attention include specialization or customization of delimiters, higher-level grammatical structures, word selection, sorting, arrow keys, and line direction. All of these issues are addressed by the current Macintosh script management sytem, but if your needs go beyond what the system is now capable of, you may need to write your own code to accomplish them. Here are a few examples:

■ Your application may require the implementation of functions not supported by the Macintosh script management system but needed by certain languages—for example, text with a vertical line direction.

■ Your application may mark text by language, and allow users to limit searching, sorting, or spell-checking to specific languages.

■ Your application may want to display characters in a more sophisticated manner than is supported—such as *furigana*, also called *rubi*, a Japanese text display in which small Kana characters are placed adjacent to a Kanji character to indicate its pronunciation or to explain it if it is rare.

If you do write your own code to replace one or more of the Macintosh script management capabilities, make sure you do it in a modular fashion, so that you can work with current Macintosh text managers and also be prepared to take advantage of possible future enhancements to system software.

Writing Systems and Script Systems

The first section of this chapter, "Macintosh Text Overview," has given an overview to all of Macintosh text handling. This section and the rest of the chapter develop many of those concepts in more detail, to give you the background necessary to work with the routines documented throughout the remainder of this book.

This section presents the language features that must be addressed by system software if it is to properly handle the world's writing systems. It also describes the organization of the Macintosh script management system and the structure and classification of the Macintosh script systems that implement that international text handling.

Features of the World's Writing Systems

In order to understand the structure and workings of Macintosh text handling, it is useful to first consider the range of text features that need to be represented on the computer. This section presents the principal text-related features, taken from writing systems around the world, that the Macintosh addresses.

A **writing system** is a set of characters and the basic rules for their use in creating a visual depiction of language. There are more than 30 active writing systems in the world today, used to represent the official written languages of one or more regions and countries. Examples of writing systems are Roman, Chinese, Japanese, Hebrew, and Arabic. Color Plate 1 shows the world distribution of some of the principal writing systems.

Each writing system has distinct attributes. Simple systems such as Roman, Greek, and Cyrillic usually have fewer than 200 characters; Japanese, a complex writing system, theoretically contains more than 40,000. Printed Roman characters are relatively independent of each other; Arabic characters change shape depending on the characters that surround them. Some writing systems use spaces to separate words; others do not separate words at all. Some writing systems, such as Japanese, actually include multiple subsystems, each with its own set of characters and rules for how they are combined.

Figure 1-11 shows the names of various languages and regions, written in the appropriate writing system for each language.

Figure 1-11   Writing-system examples

The variety of writing-system attributes presents difficult, though not insurmountable, challenges to their representation on the Macintosh computer. This section discusses the principal attributes that the Macintosh script management system addresses.

Character Representation

Writing systems differ in the kind and number of characters required to create words as the basic components of language. Some writing systems, such as Roman and Cyrillic, are basically alphabetic: the characters in the writing system symbolize, more or less, the discrete phonemic elements in the languages represented by that writing system. Other writing systems, such as Japanese Kana, are syllabic: the characters stand for syllables in the language.

Some writing systems—namely, Japanese **Kanji**, Chinese **Hanzi**, and Korean **Hanja**— include **ideographic** characters. These characters do not represent pronunciation alone, but are also related to the component meanings of words. A typical character set for ideographic writing systems is quite large, ranging from 7,000 to 30,000 characters.

Figure 1-12 shows examples of alphabetic, syllabic, and ideographic representations of characters.

Figure 1-12   Words with alphabetic, syllabic, and ideographic characters

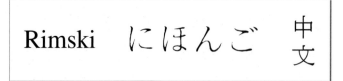

Several writing systems, including Hebrew, Thai, and Korean, contain character clusters. A **character cluster** is a collection of alphabetic characters.

■ In some systems, character clusters consist of a principal character plus attachments in memory. For example, in Hebrew, a cluster may be composed of a consonant, a vowel, a dot to soften the pronunciation of the consonant, and a cantillation mark.

■ In other systems, character clusters occur as alphabetic blocks made of 2 to 5 component parts. For example, in Korean, consonant and vowel components called Jamo are combined into blocks called Hangul. See Figure 1-39 on page 1-60 for an example. In Thai (as shown in Figure 1-13), consonants are combined with vowel marks and tone marks to make clusters.

On the computer, character clusters pose difficulties in the treatment of word demarcation, the movement of the caret, deletion, and highlighting.

Figure 1-13   Thai character cluster

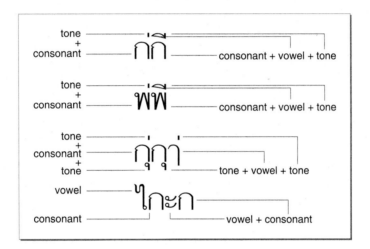

Line Direction and Alignment

Writing systems also vary in the direction in which characters are written:

■ In Roman writing systems, characters are written from left to right, with horizontal lines of text filling the page from top to bottom.

■ Arabic and Hebrew writing systems have most characters written from right to left, with horizontal lines of text filling the page from top to bottom.

■ In Japanese and Chinese, characters are traditionally written from top to bottom, with vertical lines (columns) of characters filling the page from right to left. There are no spaces between words. In modern China and Japan, technical documents and academic journals are written in standard left-to-right horizontal lines, while text for newspapers and magazines is written mostly in vertical columns.

■ In Mongolian, the characters are written in a vertical column, with spaces between words, and the lines fill the page from left to right.

Figure 1-14 shows several text directions. These three writing directions—left-right top-bottom, right-left top-bottom, and top-bottom right-left—are the most common of the eight possible combinations of line direction and fill direction.

Figure 1-14   Line directions in text

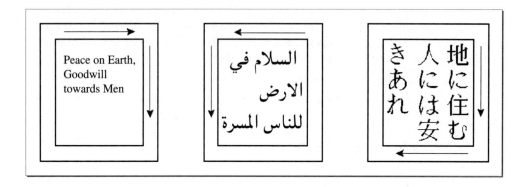

More than one line direction can exist within a single writing system. For example, numbers in Arabic and Hebrew are commonly written left to right, even though nonnumeric text is written from right to left. Furthermore, commonly interspersed foreign words from the Roman writing system are also written from left to right. Thus the Hebrew and Arabic writing systems are actually **bidirectional,** even though their primary line direction is right-to-left.

The Macintosh script management system supports the ability to write text from left to right and from right to left, and to mix text with different directions within lines and blocks of text. Your application can add the ability to handle vertical text, if desired.

Alignment is the horizontal placement of lines of text with respect to the left and right edges of the text area. Alignment can be left-aligned (also called *flush left* or *ragged right*), right-aligned (also called *flush right* or *ragged left*), centered, or **justified** (that is, aligned to both left and right edges of the text area). See Figure 1-15.

Figure 1-15   Text alignment

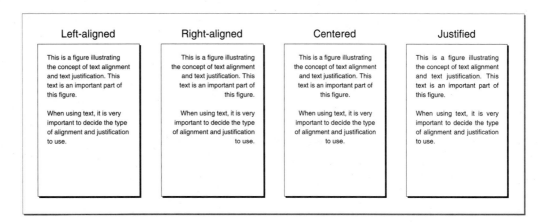

Note

Although the term *justified* is sometimes used as a synonym for *aligned*, as in "left-justified" or "right-justified" text, this book considers *justified* to be equivalent only to *fully justified*, and uses *aligned* exclusively when referring to text that is left-aligned, right-aligned, or centered. ◆

Alignment is related to line direction in that text with a left-to-right line direction is usually left-aligned, whereas text with a right-to-left line direction is usually right-aligned.

Justification is achieved by spreading or compressing printed text to fit a given line width. It can be performed in Roman text by altering the widths of interword spaces alone, or by altering both interword and intercharacter spaces. Writing systems that don't use interword spaces typically justify text by modifying the intercharacter spacing alone. See Figure 1-16.

Figure 1-16   Justification through interword (Hebrew) and intercharacter (Japanese) spacing

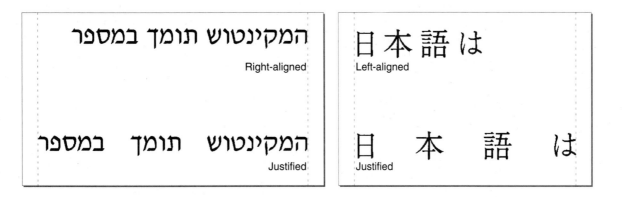

Arabic text, however, is justified by extending characters themselves. Printed or displayed text is justified by inserting extension bar characters (**kashida**) between joined characters, and by widening blank characters to fill any remaining gaps. See Figure 1-17.

Figure 1-17   Justification with Arabic extension bar characters

The Macintosh script management system can take all of these justification methods into account when drawing, measuring, or selecting text.

Contextual Forms and Character Reordering

In writing systems, *contextuality* or *context dependence* means that character forms may be modified by the values of preceding and following characters in the input stream. In Arabic, the displayed form of many characters changes depending on their position in a word or on what other characters are nearby.

The displayed form that represents a character in printed English does not usually depend on bordering characters. This is not the case for many writing systems. Even in cursive English, for example, when one letter is joined to the preceding letter, the connecting line varies according to which letters are being joined. Characters may also have considerably different shapes depending on where they occur within a word, for example, at the beginning (initial form) or elsewhere in the word (noninitial form). Figure 1-18 illustrates two of these variations in cursive English, which are called *contextual forms.*

Figure 1-18   Contextual forms in cursive English

Introduction to Text on the Macintosh

The ability to represent contextual forms is required for the proper display of Arabic text. Figure 1-19 shows standalone and contextual forms in Arabic.

Figure 1-19   Standalone and contextual forms in Arabic

Independent	Final	Medial	Initial
؞	ܢ	؞	؞

Furthermore, certain character forms may be combined into a new form when they occur together. Figure 1-20 provides an example of how characters combine to form **ligatures** or *conjunct characters* in Roman text.

Figure 1-20   A ligature in Roman text

f + i ⟶ fi ⟶ fi

The composition rules for Arabic text, for example, are very complex. The use of ligatures can be highly developed, and some ligatures are required for proper display. Each character can have up to four contextual forms, and the precise form depends upon a varying number of characters that precede and follow it. Figure 1-21 shows an example of a simple ligature in Arabic text.

Figure 1-21   A ligature in Arabic text

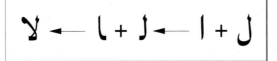

Dozens of Arabic characters form ligatures. As Figure 1-22 illustrates, in some cases, more than two characters can join together into a completely different form, although usually there are only two characters per ligature.

Figure 1-22   A complex ligature in Arabic text

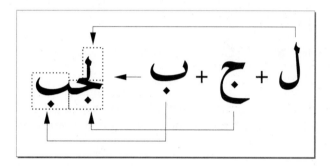

Character reordering is another form of contextuality. Principles of text ordering differ according to the type of writing system under consideration. In most writing systems (including Roman, Greek, Cyrillic, Arabic, and Hebrew), phonetic and writing order are synonymous except for vowel signs and other marks. With certain South Asian writing systems, however, there may be significant differences between phonetic and writing order.

Figure 1-23 shows an example of the reordering of vowels for the word *hindi* in the Devanagari writing system. The left side of the figure shows, in order, the characters that make up the word; the right side shows how the word is actually written. Where there is no explicit vowel sign, consonants take a default vowel sound "a". To cancel the default vowel, you add a vowel marker (*virama*). Some vowel markers are written to the right of the consonant they modify; others are written to the left, above, or below. In this example, the consonant "h" is followed by a vowel sign, which appears on the *left* when displayed. The consonant "n" is followed by a virama; together they make a small contextual form when displayed. The consonant "d" is followed by a vowel sign, which appears in normal order (on the right).

Figure 1-23   Character reordering in the Devanagari writing system

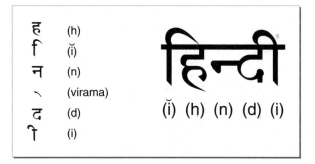

Diacritical Marks

Many writing systems use **diacritical marks,** signs that modify the implicit sound or value of the characters with which they are associated. Some diacritical marks are often referred to as *accents* in Roman writing systems: the acute accent in "é", for instance. Others, such as certain Vietnamese diacritical marks, may indicate pitch, while certain Arabic diacritical marks, such as *shadda* (shown in Figure 1-24), specify extra emphasis on a consonant sound.

Figure 1-24   Arabic text with diacritical mark to specify extra emphasis on a consonant

Hebrew text can contain optional vowel and cantillation marks. Vowel marks are shown in Figure 1-25.

Figure 1-25   Vowel marks in Hebrew text

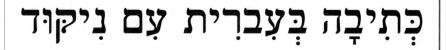

Uppercase and Lowercase Characters

English speakers are familiar with uppercase and lowercase characters in the Roman writing system; however, the majority of the world's writing systems do not have separate uppercase and lowercase forms. The implications for computer applications are primarily in the areas of searching, sorting, and proofreading (for example, spell-checking).

Note

In the Roman writing system, different languages (and even different regions or countries that use the same language) can have different conventions for the treatment of accents and diacritical marks on uppercase characters. These differences are accounted for in individual localized versions of the Roman script system. ◆

Word Demarcation

Words in Roman writing systems are generally delimited by spaces and punctuation marks as shown in Figure 1-26. Note also that word demarcation for word selection may follow different rules from word demarcation for line breaking.

Figure 1-26   Word demarcation in the Roman writing system

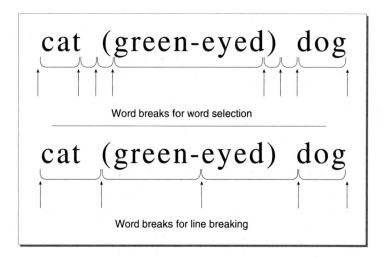

Bidirectional writing systems provide extra challenges to word selection and line breaks. Figure 1-27 shows a single English phrase ("Writing systems including bidirectional") embedded within Hebrew text. The first line breaks within the English text. Note that the line break itself occurs, not at the right or left edge of the first line, but in its interior; and the continuation of the English phrase occurs in the interior of the following line.

Figure 1-27 Line breaking in a bidirectional writing system

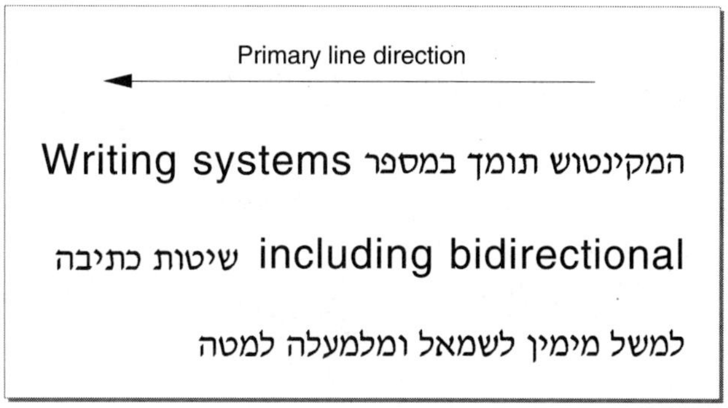

Primary line direction ←

המקינטוש תומך במספר Writing systems

שיטות כתיבה including bidirectional

למשל מימין לשמאל ומלמעלה למטה

In contrast, many Asian writing systems (such as Japanese and Thai) typically have no word delimiters, so the Macintosh script management system provides a more sophisticated method of finding word boundaries. Figure 1-28 shows word demarcation in Japanese.

Figure 1-28 Word demarcation in Japanese

The definition of a word can be an extremely complex issue. Word boundaries are not always well-defined, and native writers of a language may not agree on where particular word boundaries occur.

Styles

Style for a writing system means the systematic alteration of a set of glyphs of a given typeface, to uniformly change their appearance while preserving the overall sense of the typeface. Boldfacing, italicizing, underlining, lining-through, and outlining are possible styles that can be applied to text. Not all styles are appropriate or conventional for all writing systems; for example, underlining may not be meaningful for text that is written in vertical columns, and italicizing may not be appropriate for text that should not be slanted.

Figure 1-29 provides some examples of the application of styles to several writing systems.

Figure 1-29   Selected valid styles in various writing systems

	Roman	Japanese	Arabic	Hebrew
Plain	WorldScript	日本語は	ماكنتوش	מקינטוש
Bold	**WorldScript**		**ماكنتوش**	**מקינטוש**
Italic	*WorldScript*	*日本語は*		
Underline	<u>WorldScript</u>	<u>日本語は</u>		<u>מקינטוש</u>
Outline	WorldScript	日本語は	ماكنتوش	מקינטוש
Shadow	WorldScript	日本語は	ماكنتوش	מקינטוש
Double strike through		~~日本語は~~		

Numbers, Currencies, and Dates

Each language—or in many cases each regional variation of a language—includes a set of conventions for presentation of numbers. For example, in many European countries the decimal character is a comma (,), and the thousands separator is a period (.). In some other areas, western numbers (1…9, 0) are not even used.

Each nation has its own currency format, including the symbol used to denote money. The symbol may be one or more characters, and may precede or follow the numeric amount. Negative monetary values are shown differently in different countries.

Date and time formats vary with language and region. The order in which days, months, and years are written, the words and common abbreviations for days and months, and the separators used in writing dates and times can all differ from region to region.

Figure 1-30 shows some common differences in number, currency, and date formats among the United States, European countries, and Japan.

Figure 1-30   Standard international formats

	Numbers List separators	Currency	Time	Short date	Long date (unabbreviated) Long date (abbreviated)
United States	1,234.56 ;	$0.23 ($0.45) $345.00	9:05 AM 11:20 PM 11:20:09 PM	12/22/85 2/1/85	Wednesday, February 1, 1985 Wed., Feb 1, 1985
Great Britain	1,234.56 ,	£ 0.23 (£ 0.45) £ 345	09:05 23:20 23:20:09	22/12/1985 1/02/1985	Wednesday, February 1, 1985 Wed., Feb 1, 1985
Germany	1.234,56 ;	0,23 DM -0,45 DM 345 DM	09:05 Uhr 23:20 Uhr 23:20:09 Uhr	22.12.1985 1.02.1985	Mittwoch, 1. Februar 1985 Mit, 1. Feb 1985
France	1 234.56 ;	0,23 F -0,45 F 345 F	09:05 23:20 23:20:09	22.12.1985 1.02.1985	Mercredi 1 Février 1985 Mer 1 fev 1985
Greece	1 234.56 ,	*0,23 (0.45) *345	09:05 23:20 23:20:09	22-12-85 1-02-85	Τετάρτη 1 Φερουαρίου 1985 Τετά 1 Φερο 1985
Japan	1 234.56 ;	¥0.23 (¥0.45) ¥345.00	09:05 AM 11:20 PM 11:20:09 PM	85.12.22 85.2.1	1985年2月1日水曜日 1985年2月1日(水)

Even the calendar itself is not the same around the world. The standard **Gregorian calendar** used in Europe and the Americas is not universally accepted:

■ In Japan, the Emperor's year is sometimes used instead of the standard Gregorian calendar. The rest of the Japanese calendar system is similar to the Gregorian calendar.

■ The Arabic calendar is used extensively throughout the Middle East. It is lunar rather than solar. The months are alternately 29 and 30 days long, so the Arabic calendar year is about 11 days shorter than the Gregorian year. The months have no fixed relation to the sun, so they slowly rotate through all of the seasons of the year (that is, every three years the months shift forward by one Gregorian calendar month).

There are actually two Arabic calendars in common use: the astronomical lunar calendar, based on the moon's phases as actually observed at each location around the world; and the civil lunar calendar, a statutory version of the astronomical calendar. To compute a date correctly for the astronomical lunar calendar requires calculating not only the orbits of the sun and moon, but also knowing the exact latitude, longitude, and time difference from Greenwich mean time.

■ Other calendars in common use include the Coptic, Jewish, and Persian calendars.

Character Order and Text Sorting

In most writing systems a need exists for ordering lists of characters, words, or lines of text—such as for writing an alphabet or arranging a dictionary, encyclopedia, or telephone book. Each writing system has its own rules and conventions for sorting text into a meaningful order.

In Roman writing systems, sorting is usually based on alphabetic order, which is fairly simple. However, complications arise when sorting text that includes mixed uppercase and lowercase letters, letters with diacritical marks, ligatures, abbreviations, characters that should be grouped, and characters that should be ignored for sorting purposes.

One important concept for Roman systems is the distinction between primary sorting order and secondary sorting order. Text items that are equivalent in terms of primary sorting characteristics are first grouped, and then differentiated according to secondary sorting characteristics. This allows all variations of a character (uppercase and lowercase, with or without diacritical marks, and so on) to be grouped together in sorted lists.

Nonalphabetic writing systems, such as Chinese or Japanese, can have more complex and less standardized sorting conventions than Roman. Some sorting algorithms for ideographic characters are based on the number of strokes per character. Others are based on *radicals,* standard character subcomponents with a defined sorting order. Others consider the phonetic spelling of the character with Roman or other types of characters (such as Kana), and sort according to Roman alphabetic order or standard Kana order.

Macintosh support for sorting of text is fully described in the chapter "Text Utilities" and the appendixes "International Resources" and "Built-in Script Support" in this book. Tables of specific sorting orders for individual script systems are given in *Guide to Macintosh Software Localization.*

Variations Among Languages and Regions

A writing system by itself may not be enough to define how a language is written. For example, the Roman writing system is used for both the English and French languages. A written **language** refers to the whole body of written words and of methods of combining words, including their meanings, used by a particular group of people. A single writing system may be used by multiple languages. Languages within a writing system can modify the sorting order and word boundaries defined by the writing system, and can define minor modifications to its character set.

Conversely, some languages are written in more than one writing system. The official language of Malaysia, for example, may be written in either the Roman or the Arabic writing system, but the spoken language is called Malay in either case. Romanian and Moldovan are essentially the same spoken language; however, in Romania this language is written in the Roman writing system, whereas in the adjacent republic of Moldova, it is written in the Cyrillic writing system.

A language in itself may not be enough to define all the conventions for written communication in a particular region. A **region** is a linguistic or cultural entity, not necessarily a nation or geographic area, whose written language or other text features are unique enough to be treated separately from other regions. A single language, such as French, may have several regional versions. For example, the French language is used in France, in parts of Belgium, Switzerland, and Canada, and in other countries such as Luxembourg, Haiti, Mali, Zaïre, Tahiti, and Vanuatu. Such different areas that use the same language may have different conventions for time, date, and number formats, as well as rules for case conversion or placement of diacritical marks. Some differences may also occur in the behavior of the written language. For example, in France, accents on most characters are generally omitted if the character is written in uppercase; in Québec, the accents are usually preserved.

The Macintosh script management system can account for multiple languages and regional variations within script systems. See "Script Codes, Language Codes, and Region Codes" beginning on page 1-48.

Components of the Macintosh Script Management System

This section describes the organization of the Macintosh script management system, those parts of the system software that provide support for the writing-system features described in the previous section, "Features of the World's Writing Systems."

The Macintosh script management system makes it possible to represent many writing systems and languages on the Macintosh computer. With the Macintosh script management system, your application's text-manipulation capabilities can extend far beyond the Roman writing system and its languages. If you use its features your application can have a much wider market worldwide. You can implement text-handling capabilities that work properly with any supported writing system, or you can tailor your application to work correctly with any specific writing system or any regional variation of a writing system.

The script management system supplies much of the same basic capability for entering and displaying text as does a multi-language word processor—but on a system level. Since the capability is built into the system, you do not have to duplicate the code necessary to support each writing system; instead, you can devote your efforts to the primary functions of your application.

As Figure 1-31 shows, the script management system consists of

- routines in various components (managers) of system software
- two WorldScript extensions (optional)

■ one or more script systems

■ one or more fonts

The text managers and the script extensions are mostly code; they execute the script-aware calls your application makes when handling text. The script systems and fonts are mostly data; they consist largely of tables of script-specific information used by the text routines, and glyph descriptions.

Figure 1-31   Components of the script management system for text display

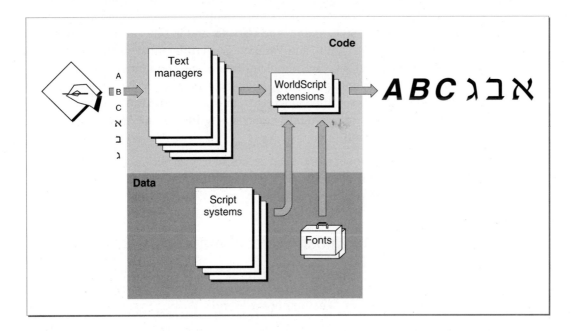

The Macintosh Text Managers

Several parts of Macintosh system software work together to provide specific text-handling services to your application. These text-related managers include the Script Manager, the text-handling components of QuickDraw, the Font Manager, the Text Utilities, the Text Services Manager, and the Dictionary Manager.

The Script Manager

The Script Manager is at the center of the Macintosh script management system. It initializes script systems and makes them available to applications; it maintains important data structures and provides a standard application interface to script systems; it supports switching text input among different script systems; and it provides several text-manipulation services.

The Script Manager works closely with the Text Utilities and with QuickDraw. Your program typically makes calls to all three managers in the course of text-handling, and in many cases a call to one of these managers results in internal calls among them. TextEdit also relies on the Script Manager, Text Utilities, and QuickDraw to make sure that it handles text correctly in any script system.

The Script Manager provides routines with which you can

- control the values of many script-related settings, including the *system direction* and the keyboard script

- get information about script systems, such as script codes, character-type information, and direct access to a script's international resources

- modify text through lexical conversion to tokens or phonetic conversion within a script system

- modify script systems by replacing international resources or routines

In particular, the Script Manager gives you access to *Script Manager variables*, which control many overall settings of the text environment, and *script variables*, which control settings specific to each enabled script system.

QuickDraw

QuickDraw is the graphics manager of Macintosh system software. The graphics components of QuickDraw are described in the QuickDraw chapters in *Inside Macintosh: Imaging*; the text-handling components of QuickDraw are described in the chapter "QuickDraw Text" in this book.

Your application makes QuickDraw calls to write text to the screen or to a printer. When QuickDraw draws text, it places bitmapped shapes on the display device that represent the characters it is drawing. The characters are drawn according to the settings of the currrent window's graphics port record, which includes the location at which to draw and a specification of the font and character attributes with which to draw.

For text in various script systems, the QuickDraw text routines allow you to

- set the characteristics of the drawing environment

- draw text

- measure the width of text

- lay out lines of text

- determine caret positions and highlight text

Font Manager

QuickDraw cannot draw text without a font. The Font Manager supports QuickDraw by providing the character bitmaps that QuickDraw needs, in the typefaces, sizes, and styles that QuickDraw requests. The Font Manager keeps track of all fonts available to an application. The Font Manager supports fonts in many languages, for both bitmapped and outline fonts, and for both 1-byte and 2-byte fonts.

Besides providing QuickDraw with the bitmaps it needs, the Font Manager provides routines with which you can

■ determine the characteristics of a font

■ change certain font settings, such as fractional widths or scaling

■ favor outline fonts over bitmapped fonts

■ manipulate fonts in memory

Text Utilities

The Text Utilities are an integrated collection of routines for performing a variety of operations on text, ranging from sorting strings to formatting dates and times to finding word boundaries. The Text Utilities work in conjunction with the Macintosh script management system and can take into account the differences in text-handling among script systems. If you use these routines you can handle text operations in a manner that is transportable to different parts of the world.

Many of the Text Utilities routines are script-aware; they work in conjunction with the Script Manager and with QuickDraw to determine the script-system characteristics of text and to prepare the text for drawing to the screen or printing.

The Text Utilities provide routines that, for text in any script system, allow you to

■ define strings in various ways

■ compare and sort strings

■ modify the contents of strings by truncation, stripping of diacritical marks, case conversion, or replacement

■ find boundaries of words, lines, and runs of Roman characters

■ convert and format date and time strings

■ convert and format numeric strings

Text Services Manager

The Text Services Manager is the part of Macintosh system software that provides an environment for applications to use text services such as input methods. The Text Services Manager handles communication between client applications and text service components. **Text service components** are specialized software modules for entry, processing, or formatting of text.

Client applications can use the Text Services Manager to

■ make text services available to the user

■ search for and communicate with text service components

■ accept text input or other information from text service components

■ ask for a special floating input window service

Text service components can use the Text Services Manager to

- make their text service available to an application

- act on events involving their windows, menus, or cursor

- pass text input or other information to an application

- display floating utility windows

Dictionary Manager

The Dictionary Manager is the part of Macintosh system software that allows you to create dictionaries for input methods and other text services that let the user enter, format, and process text. A dictionary is a data file with information essential to the conversion of text from one form to another. Most input methods provide both a **main dictionary,** which contains standard information for conversion between forms, and a **user dictionary,** which allows users to add custom information.

The Dictionary Manager defines a uniform and public dictionary format that you can apply to your text service's dictionaries. The Dictionary Manager provides routines with which you can

- create and access a dictionary

- locate, insert, or delete records in a dictionary

- compact data in a dictionary

The WorldScript Extensions

The Roman script system, always available on every Macintosh, needs only the previously mentioned managers to function correctly. Several other similar script systems also need no other software. However, for those 1-byte script systems that have contextual characters or right-to-left line direction, additional code is needed so that the Script Manager, Text Utilities, and QuickDraw routines can work properly. Likewise, 2-byte script systems need code extensions in order to properly handle the thousands of characters they use.

Although each writing system has unique requirements and procedures for presenting, sorting, and formatting text, in many cases separate script systems can use similar algorithms. Therefore, to avoid inconsistencies and unnecessary duplication of code, the script management system supplies two system extension files—WorldScript I and WorldScript II—that support 1-byte complex script systems and 2-byte script systems, respectively (see "Types of Script Systems" on page 1-46). They contain code that implements many script-aware text-manipulation routines, eliminating the need for each script system to maintain its own code extensions. Script-specific behavior is encoded in resource-based tables accessed by the extensions.

WorldScript I and WorldScript II are described in the appendix "Built-in Script Support" in this book.

WorldScript I

WorldScript I is the script extension that implements table-driven text measuring and drawing behavior for all 1-byte complex script systems (such as Hebrew, Arabic, Thai, and Devanagari). Using tables in each script system's international resources, WorldScript I performs text manipulation properly for all supported scripts. WorldScript I is a single file located in the Extensions folder within the System Folder on the user's Macintosh. It installs all compatible 1-byte script systems that are present in the System file, and provides them with a standard set of script-aware text-manipulation routines.

WorldScript I implements **script utilities,** the low-level routines through which an individual script system implements script-aware Text Utilities, QuickDraw, and Script Manager routines. WorldScript I also implements patches to certain QuickDraw and Font Manager text-handling routines.

The Script Manager provides routines that allow you to modify or replace a 1-byte complex script system's script utilities and QuickDraw patches. See the chapter "Script Manager" in this book.

WorldScript II

WorldScript II is the script extension that implements table-driven text measuring and drawing behavior for all 2-byte (Chinese, Japanese, Korean) script systems. Using tables in each script system's international resources, WorldScript II performs text manipulation properly for all supported scripts. WorldScript II is a single file located in the Extensions folder within the System Folder on the user's Macintosh. It installs all compatible 2-byte script systems that are present in the System file, and provides them with a standard set of script-aware text-manipulation routines.

Like WorldScript I, WorldScript II implements script utilities that implement script-aware Text Utilities, QuickDraw, and Script Manager routines. Unlike WorldScript I, WorldScript II does not support the Script Manager routines that allow replacement of script utilities.

Components of a Script System

The Macintosh script management system, as described in the previous section, is designed to manipulate text according to information contained in script systems. This section describes how script systems are organized.

A Macintosh script system is a collection of resources, mostly tables of data, that defines the behavior of a particular writing system. The script system specifies the character set, sorting orders, date and number formats, line direction, character reordering, accent placement, and other writing-system-specific features. Your application uses the information in a script system when it makes a script-aware text-handling call, and it can also access the resources of a script system directly, to inspect or modify its behavior.

Each Macintosh script system consists of a set of international resources and a set of keyboard resources. In addition, a script system requires one or more fonts in order to display its text. A script system may also have a control panel device through which the user can configure the individual characteristics of the script at any time.

Resources in general are described in the chapter "Resource Manager," in *Inside Macintosh: More Macintosh Toolbox.*

International Resources

The international resources are a set of Macintosh resources that specify text handling and display information for a particular writing system, language, or region. Such information includes number and currency formats, long and short date formats, preferred sorting order, character type, case conversion, and word-boundary information.

Table 1-1 lists the international resources, shows their resource types, and summarizes their contents.

Table 1-1   The international resources

Name	Resource type	Content
International configuration	`'itlc'`	Configuration of the system script, plus Script Manager flags, and the region code for the system script
Script sorting	`'itlm'`	Tables showing sorting order and mapping among script systems, languages, and regions
International bundle	`'itlb'`	IDs of all required resources for a script system, plus bit flags, default language, and other settings
Numeric format	`'itl0'`	Number and currency formats, short date and time formats, unit of measurement for a script system, plus a region code
Long-date format	`'itl1'`	Long date and time formats, names of days and months for a script system, plus a region code
String manipulation	`'itl2'`	Sorting routines, tables for character type, case conversion, and word boundaries for a script system
Tokens	`'itl4'`	Tables and code for converting characters to tokens and back in a script system, and for formatting numbers
Encoding/rendering	`'itl5'`	Tables for character rendering (for 1-byte script systems); tables for character encoding (for 2-byte script systems)
Transliteration	`'trsl'`	Tables for phonetic conversion among subscripts of a 2-byte script system

International resources reside in the resource fork of the Macintosh System file. However, not every installed script system requires a complete set of them:

- There is only one international configuration resource for each Macintosh System file, and its resource ID is 0. It configures the system and defines the system script.

- There is only one script-sorting resource for each Macintosh System file, and its resource ID is 0. It does not belong to any script system.

- Each installed script has one international bundle resource. Its resource ID is the script code of the script system it implements.

- Each installed script system has one or more numeric-format, long-date-format, string-manipulation, and tokens resources. Their resource IDs are in a range that defines the script system they belong to; see Figure 1-35 on page 1-50.

- A script system may have one or more optional encoding/rendering and transliteration resources.Their resource IDs are also in a range that defines the script system they belong to.

A single script system may have multiple localized versions of its 'itl0', 'itl1', 'itl2', 'itl4', 'itl5', and 'trsl' resources, in order to represent different languages or regional variations of the script. You can manipulate text in different formats within that script system by switching among the multiple versions of the resources. See "Installing Modifications to a Script System" beginning on page 1-103.

See the appendix "International Resources" in this book for more information on international resources.

Keyboard Resources

The keyboard resources are a set of Macintosh resources that specify how keyboard input is converted to text for a particular writing system, language, or region. The Event Manager, the Script Manager, and the Menu Manager use the information in these resources to convert keypresses to character codes, to switch input among different script systems, and to display the icon of the current keyboard in the Keyboard menu. The Resource Manager, the Event Manager and the Menu Manager are described in *Inside Macintosh: Macintosh Toolbox Essentials*; the Resource Manager is described in *Inside Macintosh: More Macintosh Toolbox*.

Table 1-2 lists the keyboard resources, shows their resource types, and summarizes their purpose.

Table 1-2   The keyboard resources

Name	Resource type	Content
Key map	`'KMAP'`	Maps hardware-dependent raw key codes to hardware-independent virtual key codes
Key remap	`'itlk'`	Remaps some virtual key codes from certain keyboards for use by some keyboard-layout resources
Keyboard layout	`'KCHR'`	Maps virtual key codes to character codes; represents the character set for a script system
Keyboard icons	`'kcs#'`	Keyboard icon list for black-and-white icon display in the Keyboard menu
	`'kcs4'`	Keyboard icon list for 4-bit color/gray-scale icon display in the Keyboard menu
	`'kcs8'`	Keyboard icon list for 8-bit color/gray-scale icon display in the Keyboard menu
Keyboard swap	`'KSWP'`	Specifies modifier-plus-key combinations to let the user change keyboard layout, keyboard script, or input method
Key caps	`'KCAP'`	Determines keyboard display for a given physical keyboard (in Key Caps desk accessory)

Keyboard resources reside in the resource fork of the Macintosh System file. Some are script-related, but others are hardware-related and script-independent:

■ There is only one keyboard-swap resource per Macintosh System file. Because it specifies how to switch among script systems, it does not belong to any script system. Its resource ID is 0.

■ There is one key-map resource that supports most types of physical keyboards. Some keyboards need their own key-map resource, in which case the key-map resource ID is equal to the ID number of the keyboard it is associated with.

■ There is one key-caps resource for each type of physical keyboard available. It is independent of any script system. Its resource ID is equal to the ID number of the keyboard it is associated with.

■ There are one or more keyboard-layout resources per script system. There are one or more families of keyboard icon resources per script system (one per keyboard layout resource or input method). The resource ID for each keyboard-layout resource is in a range that defines the script system it belongs to; see Figure 1-35 on page 1-50. The resource ID for each keyboard icon family is equal to the ID of its associated keyboard-layout resource.

■ There is one key-remap resource for each keyboard-layout resource that needs one. Its resource ID is equal to the ID number of its associated keyboard-layout resource.

See the appendix "Keyboard Resources" in this book for more information.

Fonts

A font is not technically part of a script system. The script's international bundle resource does not have to specify any particular font resource IDs, and even if it does, their presence is not guaranteed. Nevertheless, no script system can be used unless one or more fonts accompany it.

A Macintosh font implements the character set and other written forms such as ligatures for a given script system. Each font contains a particular set of glyphs that share certain design characteristics. Those glyphs constitute a typeface, and the typeface has a name, such as Times, Helvetica®, or Kyoto. A font may be a plain implementation of a typeface, or it may be styled—such as bold or italic. (QuickDraw can also *produce* styled versions of the characters of a typeface from a plain font.)

Glyphs in a font represent each of the characters of a character set. Additional glyphs may be present to represent ligatures, and other contextual forms. In some fonts there may be more contextual glyphs than character glyphs.

A font maps character codes to glyphs, and may contain tables that map special glyph codes to the glyphs of contextual forms. When laying out and drawing text, the script management system uses information in the font to convert character codes in memory to a properly formatted series of glyphs on the screen or on the page.

Macintosh fonts are either bitmapped (meaning that each glyph is a single bitmap) or outline (meaning that each glyph is a mathematical outline that is size-independent). A bitmapped font contains a single set of glyphs at a fixed size, whereas one outline font can produce glyphs of any size.

Fonts are either 1-byte—meaning that they have glyphs for 256 or fewer characters—or 2-byte, meaning that they can have glyphs for thousands of characters. The 1-byte fonts represent character codes that are 1 byte long, and include all fonts of the Roman script system. The 2-byte fonts represent character codes that are 1 byte or 2 bytes long, and include fonts of the Chinese, Japanese, and Korean script systems. The script management system supports 2-byte fonts, and can correctly handle mixtures of 1-byte and 2-byte characters in text.

Each font is a Macintosh resource. For ease of reference, fonts are grouped into **font families** (resource type `'FOND'`). Each family consists of all the available sizes and styled variations of a single named typeface. For example, "Courier 10", "Courier 12 Italic", and "Courier Semibold" could be two bitmapped fonts and one outline font belonging to the single font family "Courier". Whenever you supply a font ID to a script management call, it is the `'FOND'` resource ID that you supply (unless you supply the special font designators 0 or 1; see page 1-61).

As with other script-related resources, the ID numbers for fonts are in a range that defines the script system they belong to. See, for example, Figure 1-35 on page 1-50. In fact, the script management system relies fundamentally on font family ID to determine the script system associated with any text that is to be manipulated or drawn.

See the section "Font Handling" beginning on page 1-60 of this chapter for more information and programming suggestions involving fonts. See the chapter "Font Manager" for more specific information on font structure and use. For more complete information on both 1-byte and 2-byte TrueType fonts, see *The TrueType Font Format Specification*, available from APDA.

How Script Systems Are Classified

Different kinds of script systems function differently. The previous section, "Components of a Script System," described the components of all script systems; this section describes the different ways of classifying script systems. The following section, "How Script Systems Work," describes how to use script systems for your text handling needs.

Script systems are typed in general by the size of their character set and by their relative similarity to Roman. The Roman script system is used widely in North America, South America, Australia, Europe, and Africa, and in parts of Asia and Oceania. The Roman script system is standard on all Macintosh system software versions 4.1 and higher, but the Macintosh also supports all types of non-Roman script systems—simple or complex, and with small or large character sets.

Script systems are individually classified by code numbers. Resources associated with a script system have ID numbers that are related to the script's code. Languages and regional variations are subsets of script systems and have their own code numbers.

On an individual computer, more than one script system can be available at a time; different scripts are classified by their function. The most important script system is the *system script*; other script systems are secondary. The script system currently being used for text display is the *font script*; the script currently being used for text input is the *keyboard script*.

Note
Because the Roman script system is always installed, you can always manipulate Roman text, no matter what other script systems are present. ◆

Types of Script Systems

Because of its historical support for the Roman writing system, and because Roman text layout is fairly simple, the Macintosh computer most easily supports script systems that are like Roman. Other script systems can add complications like right-to-left line direction, contextual character forms, and large character sets.

As shown in Figure 1-32, script systems are divided into three groups, based on the size of their character set and their relative complexity compared to Roman:

- The **1-byte simple script systems** have character sets of 256 characters or fewer. They are called 1-byte because their character codes are one byte long. They are called simple because they are similar to Roman: they have a uniform left-to-right line direction and are noncontextual. The 1-byte simple script systems support variations within the Roman writing system and among Roman-like writing systems such as differences of character set, keyboard layout, sorting order, word boundaries, and the formatting of dates, times, and numbers. The 1-byte simple script systems include Roman, Greek, and Cyrillic.

- The **1-byte complex script systems** also have character sets of 256 characters or fewer. They are complex because they may have left-to-right or right-to-left line direction, and may be contextual. The 1-byte complex script systems support the more difficult formatting required for bidirectional writing and the extensive use of ligatures, cursive fonts, character reordering, and other contextual features. The 1-byte complex script systems include Thai, Devanagari, Hebrew, and Arabic.

- The **2-byte script systems** have character sets so large that most character codes are two bytes long. The 2-byte script systems require sophisticated methods for character input, as well as an independent font mechanism for display and printing. The 2-byte script systems include Traditional Chinese, Simplified Chinese, Japanese, and Korean.

Figure 1-32   Types of script systems

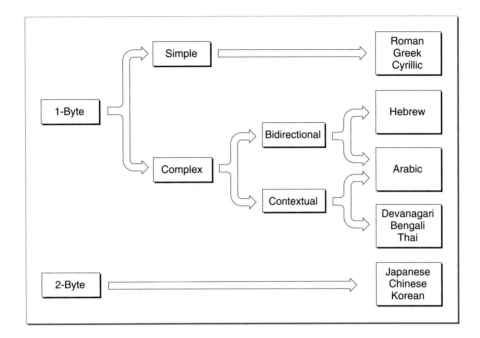

Figure 1-33 shows which parts of the Macintosh script management system are involved in handling text from the different types of script systems:

■ Roman text is handled with code and resources largely built into system software.

■ Text of 1-byte simple script systems is handled with the same built-in Roman code and resources, supplemented by minor additional resources such as alternate keyboard layouts and fonts.

■ Text of 1-byte complex script systems is handled by WorldScript I, which may use, modify, or completely replace any of the built-in code. The complex 1-byte script systems may replace much of the Roman resources with their own international and keyboard resources and fonts.

■ Text of 2-byte script systems is handled by WorldScript II, which may use, modify, or completely replace any of the built-in code. The 2-byte script systems may replace much of the Roman resources with their own international and keyboard resources and fonts; they also provide special input methods for text entry.

Figure 1-33   How the script management system handles different types of scripts

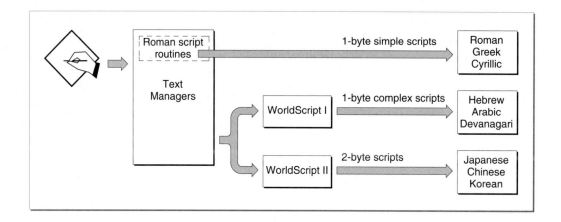

Script Codes, Language Codes, and Region Codes

The Macintosh script management system accommodates the international differences within writing systems by defining languages and regional variations for script systems, and organizing them into a classified hierarchy. Script systems are identified by **script codes,** languages by **language codes,** and regions by **region codes.** A spoken language that may be written in more than one writing system is treated on the Macintosh computer as several languages, each belonging to a different script system.

Three general concepts underlie the hierarchy of script, language, and region.

■ A script system is often differentiated by its character encoding, the specification of the characters that compose the writing system and their numeric representations. Different character encodings usually have different script codes. (This is not always true within the Roman script system; see "The Standard Roman Character Set" on page 1-54.)

■ Each language belongs to a particular script system. Every language code thus implies a particular script code. Several languages may be associated with a single script system; in such a case, they share the same character set.

■ A region code designates an area that may be smaller or larger than a single country (for example, *French Swiss* or *Arabic*), in which a specific variation of a single script system and language is used. Each region belongs to a particular language. Several regions may be associated with a single language. A region code typically represents a localized version of the system software for a particular language in a particular country or region.

Figure 1-34 illustrates the script, language, and region hierarchy. Note, for example, that the regions of France, Québec, and French Swiss are associated with the French language, which is part of the Roman script system.

Figure 1-34   The script, language, and region hierarchy

Script	Language	Region
Cyrillic	Russian	Russia
	Azerbaijani	Azerbaijan
Arabic	Persian	Iran
	Arabic	Arabic world
Japanese	Japanese	Japan
Roman	French	France
		French Canada
		French Swiss
	English	United Kindom
		United States

You can use language codes and region codes to specify multiple subsets of the international resources for a single script system. That way you can implement regional variations to a writing system without having to create an entirely new script system each time. See "Installing Modifications to a Script System" beginning on page 1-103.

See the chapter "Script Manager" in this book for a complete list of the constant names that define the codes for all scripts, languages, and regional versions.

Script Codes and Resource ID Numbers

Each script system is assigned a unique script code. The script codes currently defined are in the range 0–32, although the Script Manager can support 64 script systems at the same time. All the resources related to a script system, including its fonts, have resource ID numbers related in some way to the script ID:

■ The resource ID number for a script system's international bundle (`'itlb'`) resource is the same as the script code.

■ The resource ID numbers for most other resources associated with a script are in a range specific to that script. You can use these ID ranges to determine the script system associated with a font or other resource. Likewise, even when a font is missing, the Font Manager can use the ID range to substitute a font of the same script.

☐ For Roman (script code = 0), this range is 0–16383.

☐ Scripts with script codes in the range 1–32 have a range of 512 resource ID numbers each. For example, the script code for Japanese is 1, so Japanese resources can have any of the first 512 ID numbers beyond the Roman range, that is, 16384–16895. The script code for Korean is 3, so Korean resources can have resource IDs in the range 17408–17919.

Figure 1-35 illustrates the resource ID ranges for script systems with script codes between 0 and 32. The ranges for the Roman, Japanese, Chinese, Korean, and Devanagari scripts are noted. A full table of resource ID ranges is provided in the appendix "International Resources" in this book.

Note

The Script Manager provides routines for determining the script system based on the value of a font family ID. ◆

Figure 1-35   Distinguishing scripts by resource ID range (for script codes 0–32)

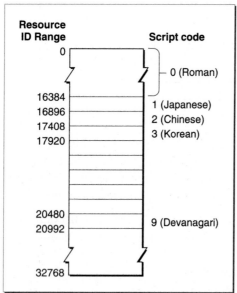

IMPORTANT

The special font designators *0* and *1,* although in the range of the Roman script system, specify the Macintosh *system font* and *application font,* respectively; they do *not* necessarily indicate a Roman font and the Roman script system. See the section "Font Handling" beginning on page 1-60 for more information. ▲

The System Script and Auxiliary Scripts

A script system may be installed either as an **auxiliary script** (also called a *secondary script*), which only provides support for a particular writing system, or as the **system script** (also called the *primary script*), which is the script system associated with the currently running version of Macintosh system software. The system script affects system defaults such as the default font, keyboard layout, and primary line direction. The system script defines which writing system is used for dialog boxes, menus, and alerts. Therefore, most text displayed by the Finder and other parts of the system is in the language of the system script.

The system script is specified in the System file's international configuration (`'itlc'`) resource. All other script systems are secondary to the system script. In non-Roman versions of system software, Roman is an auxiliary script.

Some versions of Macintosh system software, such as the Turkish or French, are simply variations of the U.S. system software (which includes the Roman script system). Their script system is a modified version of the standard U.S. Roman script system, and they do not include a second script system. When a non-Roman script system is installed, however, at least two script systems are always present. For example, the Japanese system software is a combination of U.S. system software and the Japanese script system, all of which are localized for Japan. Thus it contains both Roman and Japanese script systems.

Font Script and Keyboard Script

In every version of Macintosh system software, the system script is always enabled and is the principal script system for determining how text is presented and handled in the Finder and other parts of system software. But if there are auxiliary scripts present, the system script is not always the script system that controls text-handling.

The text-manipulation and drawing routines in the Macintosh script management system work with individual character codes or strings of character codes, manipulating them or converting them to glyphs. A character code by itself carries no identifier as to what script system should be used to interpret it; the script management system uses other information to decide what script system to use for presenting or processing a given run of text.

Many of the routines use the script system associated with the font of the current graphics port to perform their tasks. The font is specified by the `txFont` field of the graphics port that is identified by the global variable `thePort`. The script system associated with that font is called the **font script.** Therefore, to manipulate text in a given script system, you typically first set the current port with a call to the QuickDraw `SetPort` procedure, and then set the current font with a call to the QuickDraw `TextFont` procedure, and then call the series of text-manipulation routines you need. (For those routines that take a script code as an explicit parameter, you need not set the current font before making the call.)

Text input by the user involves the conversion of keypresses to character codes. Because every script system has its own character set, the character codes produced depend explicitly on the script system used for keyboard input. That script system is called the **keyboard script.** It is not automatically the same as the script used for display of text; your application must keep the keyboard script and the font script synchronized if characters are to be displayed correctly as they are typed in. Synchronization of the font script and keyboard script is further described on page 1-90 in this chapter and in the chapter "Script Manager" in this book.

What is the "current" script?

As just stated, the font script is usually the script system that is used by a script-aware text routine when the identity of the script or its resources is not an explicit parameter of the call. However, if the font script is not enabled, the routine uses the system script by default. Furthermore, some script-aware routines may use the system script instead of the font script, depending on the values of two Script Manager flags: the **font force flag** and the **international resources selection flag.**

The font force flag, when TRUE, specifies that fonts with ID numbers in the Roman range are to be considered as fonts of the system script rather than Roman fonts. The international resources selection flag, when TRUE, specifies that resources of the system script are to be used by those Text Utilities routines that format dates, times, and numbers. The font force flag is supported only by some non-Roman 1-byte scripts for special purposes, and is typically FALSE. The international resources selection flag is typically TRUE.

The font force flag and the international resources selection flag are described in the chapter "Script Manager" in this book. ◆

How Script Systems Work

The previous sections, "Components of a Script System" and "How Script Systems Are Classified," described the organizational aspects of script systems. This section explains how Macintosh script systems function in support of the world's writing systems. It discusses how script systems represent the multitude of characters in the world's languages, how they format and draw those characters in the context of surrounding text, how they support user input of text, and how they handle text-manipulation such as sorting and searching across many languages.

Character Encoding

Character encoding is the organization of the set of numeric codes that represent all the meaningful characters of a script system in memory. Each character is stored in memory as a number. When a user enters characters, the user's keypresses are converted to character codes; when the characters are displayed onscreen, the character codes are converted to the glyphs of a font.

There are two fundamental classes of character encodings supported by Macintosh system software: 1-byte and 2-byte. A 1-byte encoding represents every character with a 1-byte number; a 2-byte encoding (actually a mixed encoding) represents characters with either 1-byte or 2-byte numbers. There can be up to 256 characters in a character set that has 1-byte encoding, whereas there can be over 28,000 characters in a character set that has the currently supported 2-byte encoding. Roman and many other script systems use 1-byte encodings; Chinese, Korean, and Japanese script systems use 2-byte encodings.

The meaning of each character code is unique only within its script system. In an Arabic font, the code $CC represents the character *jiim*, and in a standard Roman font, the code $CC represents the character Ã. The traditional Chinese and simplified Chinese script systems are two different script systems and use different character encodings; the Chinese characters used in the Japanese and Korean script systems have still different character encodings.

Much of a script system's behavior, including sorting and composition rules for drawing and measuring, is encoded in tables that rely on a particular order of character codes. Therefore, the character encoding is fixed; it cannot be changed without significant consequences. Ideally, each script system is consistent in its character encoding; all fonts within a script system should have identical font layouts that reflect that encoding. This is largely true, with the exception of some Roman fonts; Symbol font, for example, is a Roman font but its glyphs are completely different from those of other Roman fonts.

The character set of a script system can include the characters of one or more subscripts. A **subscript** is a portion of a script system that has its own character set and conventions for use. Subscripts within the Japanese script system, for example, include the **Katakana** and **Hiragana** syllabic characters. All non-Roman script systems include Roman as a subscript. The parts of a script system's character set that implement its natural writing system are called **native** characters. In the Arabic script system, Arabic characters are native and Roman characters constitute a subscript.

The Unicode standard

Unicode is an ISO standard for 16-bit universal worldwide character encoding. It has been developed by a consortium that includes Apple Computer, Inc. In the future, Unicode will replace individual script systems' character encodings with one complete 16-bit character encoding applicable worldwide to all characters in all languages. The script systems described in this book do not yet use Unicode encodings.

With a universal character encoding such as Unicode, the character sets of separate writing systems do not overlap; there is no need to define script systems, because each character code by itself determines which writing system the character is part of. Furthermore, Unicode takes care of the problem of conflicting character encodings within a single writing system; for example, in Unicode, there is no overlap between Roman character codes and the codes of the symbols in Symbol font. ◆

The Standard Roman Character Set

The Apple **Standard Roman character set** is the 1-byte character encoding for the Roman script system. It is the fundamental character set for the Macintosh computer, and is built into every Macintosh throughout the world.

This character set (see Figure 1-36) uses all character codes from $00–$FF, and includes uppercase versions of all of the lowercase accented Roman characters, a number of symbols, and other forms. A complete set of glyphs for all characters is available in most outline fonts, but not all characters are represented in the Apple bitmapped versions of Chicago, Geneva, New York, and Monaco.

The Standard Roman character set is an extended version of the original **Macintosh character set**, as described in Volume I of the original *Inside Macintosh*. It adds characters with codes from $D9–$FF, which are empty in the original Macintosh character set. Like the original Macintosh character set, the Standard Roman character set is an extended version of the **ASCII character set**. The ASCII character set, sometimes called *low ASCII*, is the traditional but limited character encoding for English-language computer systems. It uses character codes from $00–$7F only, and includes uppercase and lowercase letters, numerals, a few symbols, and a set of control (nonprinting) characters. The Standard Roman character set includes all the ASCII character codes and adds the characters (sometimes called *high ASCII*) with codes from $80–$FF.

The Standard Roman character set is implemented by the U.S. keyboard-layout resource (type = 'KCHR', ID = 0) and other Roman keyboard layouts. The Standard Roman character set and its sorting and formatting rules form a baseline which other script systems adopt, modify, or replace as their needs align with or diverge from the Roman conventions.

Figure 1-36   The Standard Roman character set

	0x	1x	2x	3x	4x	5x	6x	7x	8x	9x	Ax	Bx	Cx	Dx	Ex	Fx
x0	nul	dle	sp	0	@	P	`	p	Ä	ê	†	∞	¿	–	‡	
x1	soh	DC1	!	1	A	Q	a	q	Å	ë	°	±	¡	—	·	Ò
x2	stx	DC2	"	2	B	R	b	r	Ç	ì	¢	≤	¬	"	‚	Ú
x3	etx	DC3	#	3	C	S	c	s	É	î	£	≥	√	"	„	Û
x4	eot	DC4	$	4	D	T	d	t	Ñ	ï	§	¥	ƒ	'	‰	Ù
x5	enq	nak	%	5	E	U	e	u	Ö	ï	•	µ	≈	'	Â	ı
x6	ack	syn	&	6	F	V	f	v	Ü	ñ	¶	∂	Δ	÷	Ê	ˆ
x7	bel	etb	'	7	G	W	g	w	á	ó	ß	Σ	«	◊	Á	˜
x8	bs	can	(	8	H	X	h	x	à	ò	®	Π	»	ÿ	Ë	¯
x9	ht	em	)	9	I	Y	i	y	â	ô	©	π	…	Ÿ	È	˘
xA	lf	sub	*	:	J	Z	j	z	ä	ö	™	∫	nbsp	⁄	Í	˙
xB	vt	esc	+	;	K	[	k	{	ã	õ	´	ª	À	¤	Î	˚
xC	ff	fs	,	<	L	\	l	|	å	ú	¨	º	Ã	‹	Ï	¸
xD	cr	gs	-	=	M	]	m	}	ç	ù	≠	Ω	Õ	›	Ì	˝
xE	so	rs	.	>	N	^	n	~	é	û	Æ	æ	Œ	ﬁ	Ó	˛
xF	si	us	/	?	O	_	o	del	è	ü	Ø	ø	œ	ﬂ	Ô	ˇ

In Figure 1-36, note that each character code is represented by a two-digit hexadecimal number. The first digit is determined by the column, and the second by the row. For example, the character code for ¶ is $A6 (from column *Ax* at row *x6*).

Inconsistencies in Roman Character Encoding

For historical reasons, Roman character encoding has not always been consistent. The Roman script system in particular contains many fonts with unique glyphs that are not part of the Standard Roman character set. Since the character encoding is limited to 256 values, fonts such as Symbol, ITC Zapf Dingbats®, and other specialized fonts override the standard Roman character encoding.

For example, in the standard Roman character set $70 corresponds to lowercase "p", but it is the numeric symbol for pi ("π") in the Symbol font, an outlined square ("□") in ITC Zapf Dingbats, and the musical symbol pianissimo for *play quietly* in the Sonata font. Hence, be aware that a Roman character code may have different interpretations in different fonts.

Furthermore, different variations of the Roman script system can have slightly different character encodings to allow for their slightly different character sets. This situation occurs only in the Roman script system; other script systems have uniform character encodings. The Roman character set and its variations are described in more detail in the appendix "Built-in Script Support" in this book.

Other 1-Byte Character Encodings

All 1-byte simple script systems have character encodings that can be thought of as simple substitutions for parts of the standard Roman character set. As noted previously, some encodings, such as Croatian or Turkish, replace or relocate relatively few characters, and are still considered Roman scripts.

Other encodings for 1-byte simple script systems, such as Central European or Cyrillic, replace much of the high-ASCII range of the Standard Roman character set (code values from $80 to $FF) with a different alphabet.

The 1-byte complex script systems replace the same general range of Roman characters as do the 1-byte simple script systems, but they also define additional text forms in order to accommodate extensive use of ligatures or other contextual variations.

For all 1-byte script systems, the character sets include the standard low-ASCII control characters (code values from $00 to $1F) and Roman characters (code values from $20 to $7F). This allows users to enter Roman text, including western numbers, without having to switch script systems. It also allows applications to display low-ASCII Roman text regardless of the font in the current graphics port. It also means that control characters are interpreted as control characters in any script system. Figure 1-37 shows the general scheme of character encoding for 1-byte script systems.

Those 1-byte complex script systems that need more contextual forms than can fit in the high-ASCII range solve the problem through associated fonts and fonts with special glyph codes, rather than by changing any of the low-ASCII character encoding. See the discussion of associated fonts in "Font Handling" beginning on page 1-60.

Figure 1-37   Character encodings for 1-byte script systems

	0x	1x	2x	3x	4x	5x	6x	7x	8x	9x	Ax	Bx	Cx	Dx	Ex	Fx
x0	nul	dle	sp	0	@	P	`	p								
x1	soh	DC1	!	1	A	Q	a	q								
x2	stx	DC2	"	2	B	R	b	r								
x3	etx	DC3	#	3	C	S	c	s								
x4	eot	DC4	$	4	D	T	d	t								
x5	enq	nak	%	5	E	U	e	u								
x6	ack	syn	&	6	F	V	f	v								
x7	bel	etb	'	7	G	W	g	w								
x8	bs	can	(	8	H	X	h	x								
x9	ht	em	)	9	I	Y	i	y								
xA	lf	sub	*	:	J	Z	j	z								
xB	vt	esc	+	;	K	[	k	{								
xC	ff	fs	,	<	L	\	l	|								
xD	cr	gs	-	=	M	]	m	}								
xE	so	rs	.	>	N	^	n	~								
xF	si	us	/	?	O	_	o	del								

Low ASCII range — High ASCII range

Control Codes — Roman characters — Script-specific characters

2-Byte Character Encodings

Worldwide, the majority of script systems have character encodings that can fit within the limits set by the size of a byte, which permits up to 256 distinct characters. However, Asian scripts with ideographic characters, such as Chinese and Japanese, require thousands to tens of thousands of characters. The Korean script system, which is not ideographic, nevertheless requires at least 2,000 characters; furthermore, ideographic Chinese-derived characters are often included in Korean text.

To define that many characters requires 2-byte character codes. The Macintosh script management system is designed to handle 2-byte codes correctly. The use of script-aware routines permits your application to handle text without having to know whether each character code is 1 byte or 2 bytes, as long as the application allows for the possibility of 2-byte codes. Basically, that means not assuming that one byte equals one character, and not breaking or truncating text in the middle of a 2-byte character.

As with 1-byte script systems, the character encoding for each 2-byte script system includes the standard ASCII control characters (code values from $00 to $1F) and the low-ASCII Roman characters (code values from $20 to $7F) as a subscript. But in addition, a 2-byte script system may include a second set of Roman characters with 2-byte character codes, and character encodings for several other subscripts besides that of its native writing system. Figure 1-38 shows one example of a 2-byte encoding scheme.

IMPORTANT

2-byte scripts use a mixture of 1-byte and 2-byte encodings to represent characters. You cannot use the terms *byte* and *character* interchangeably, nor can you assume that every character is 2 bytes long. Obtaining character-type information about characters is discussed in the chapter "Script Manager" in this book. ▲

Japanese

Japanese is one of the most intricate writing systems in the world, containing four individual subscripts: Romaji (alphabetic Roman letters), Katakana and Hiragana (syllabic characters), and Kanji (ideographic characters). For example, the word *Japan* can be written in these four ways, as

Romaji,

N i h o n

Katakana,

ニホン

Hiragana,

にほん

or Kanji:

日本

Romaji, Katakana, and Hiragana each have relatively few characters, but a minimal set of Kanji contains over 3,000 characters.

The Japanese character encoding can be thought of as an extension of a typical 1-byte character encoding. Control codes and low-ASCII Roman characters are in the range $00–$7F; script-specific 1-byte characters and the first bytes of 2-byte characters are in the range $80–$FF. Additional 256-byte tables contain the second bytes of the 2-byte characters.

Figure 1-38   Character encoding for a 2-byte script system (Japanese)

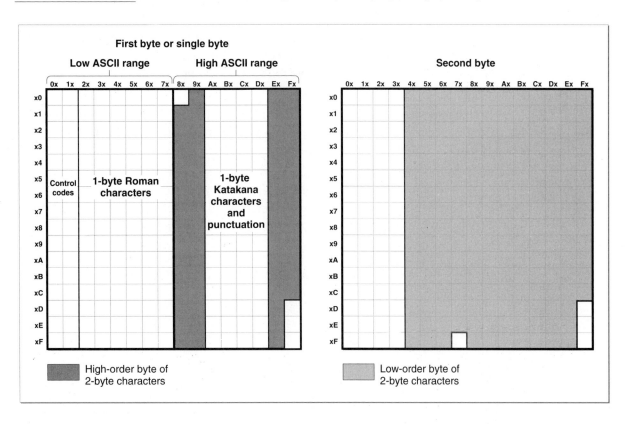

In Figure 1-38, each 2-byte character code is represented by a four-digit hexadecimal number. The first two digits (the high-order byte) come from the *First byte* table, and specify which of the many *Second byte* tables contains the character. The second two digits (the low-order byte) come from the appropriate *Second byte* table. For example, the character code for 日 is $93FA (from column *Fx* at row *xA* in the *Second byte* table whose location is specfied by the value at column *9x* at row *x3* in the *First byte* table).

Chinese

The Macintosh script management system supports two separate Chinese script systems: Simplified Chinese and Traditional Chinese. Simplified Chinese consists of approximately 8,000 ideographic characters, about 2,000 of which have been simplified from their traditional presentation for ease of learning. Traditional Chinese consists of approximately 13,000 of the traditional Chinese ideographic characters, called Hanzi.

Simplified Chinese and Traditional Chinese use incompatible character encodings; the same character may have different character codes in the two scripts.

Korean

The Korean script system is based on characters of the Hangul subscript, devised in 1443. Chinese characters, called Hanja, are often mixed with Hangul, but their use is gradually declining. The Korean Standard Hangul Coding Scheme for Communications (KS5601) defines 2,350 Hangul characters for Korean writing, which form the basic character set of the Korean script system.

Hangul characters are syllabic blocks composed of component elements called **Jamo.** Jamo can be simple or double consonants and vowels. There are 24 simple Jamo elements and 27 double elements.

The first sound in a Hangul block is a simple or double consonant, the second is a simple or complex vowel, and the third (optional) sound is a simple, double, or complex consonant. Figure 1-39 shows an example. Each Hangul character (on the right) can have two or three elements (first sound and middle sound, plus optional last sound).

Figure 1-39   Constructing blocks (Hangul) from elements (Jamo) in Korean

Font Handling

As discussed under "Fonts" on page 1-44, a Macintosh font provides a specifically designed set of glyphs that implement the character set and other written forms that belong to a given script system. Fonts can be classified as 1-byte and 2-byte, and as bitmapped or outline. Some fonts provide plain (unstyled) glyphs, whereas others provide styled variations, such as bold or italic. This section summarizes some of the basic font issues to keep in mind when working with text, and especially multiscript text.

Font Availability and Selection

You cannot display text in a given script system without a font for that script system. A font is available only if its file resides in the Fonts folder within the System Folder, or if its resources are installed in the System file itself.

In terms of font availability and font selection for text, remember these points:

- The script management system uses font family ID (the ID number of the font resource of type 'FOND') to refer to fonts. That is the ID you supply as a parameter to text-handling calls. However, do not store font family ID numbers in your text files; store font names instead, and redetermine the ID numbers at run time with Font Manager calls. Font family IDs are not unique, and the system can renumber fonts between executions of your application.

- Every font family has an ID number in a range that identifies the script system it belongs to. Identifying the font family used to write text is equivalent to identifying the script system of that text. See Figure 1-35 on page 1-50 for an illustration of resource ID ranges. A text string in a font with a font family ID of 200 is interpreted as Roman text, while the same text string in a font whose ID is 17000 is interpreted as Chinese text and displayed accordingly. You can use the Script Manager to convert font IDs into script codes.

- Because the script management system uses the font associated with a given range of text to determine the script system of that text, store your text in such a way that, for each run of text, you track the font to be used to display it.

- Because the script system can be determined from just the font family ID, the Font Manager can use that information to substitute a font of the proper script system, even when an entire font family is missing.

- Because the Roman script system is present in all Macintosh systems, at least two Roman fonts are always available: 12-point Chicago and 12-point Geneva.

System Font and Application Font

Macintosh system software recognizes two special fonts that should always be present: the **system font** and the **application font.** The system font is the font used for menus, dialog boxes, and other messages to the user from the Finder or Operating System. The application font is the suggested default font for use by monostyled TextEdit and by applications that do not support user selection of fonts. In all unmodified Roman versions of Macintosh system software, the system font is 12-point Chicago and the application font is 12-point Geneva.

In all localized versions of Macintosh system software, whether Roman or not, the system font has a *special font designator* of 0, and the application font has a special designator of 1. These special designators are not actual font family resource ID numbers and cannot be used as such in Resource Manager calls; however, you can use them in place of a font family ID in the txFont field of the graphics port, and in text-related calls that take a font family ID, such as FontToScript. The system maps the special designators to the actual font family IDs for the system font and application font. You can use the Font Manager to determine the actual ID numbers of the system font and application font for any system script.

Remember these points about the system font and the application font, in relation to Chicago font, Geneva font, and the special designators:

■ On localized versions of system software in which the system script is Roman, Chicago is the system font and it has a font family ID of 0. The special designator 0 also refers to Chicago font.

■ When the system script is non-Roman, Chicago has a different font family ID (usually 16383), and the special font designator 0 refers to the system font for the non-Roman system script. On system software in which Japanese is the system script, for example, a value of 0 in the txFont field means the Osaka font, which has a font family ID of 16384.

■ When the system script is Roman, Geneva is the application font and it has a font family ID of 3. The special designator 1 also refers to Geneva font.

■ When the system script is non-Roman, Geneva has the same font family ID of 3, but the special font designator 1 refers to the application font for the non-Roman system script. On system software in which Thai is the system script, for example, a value of 1 in the txFont field means the Thonburi font, which has a font family ID of 26625.

■ The actual font family ID of the system font is specified in the low-memory global variable SysFontFam; the actual font family ID of the application font is specified in the low-memory global variable AppFontID. You can get the actual font family ID of the system font or the application font by making Font Manager calls; see the chapter "Font Manager" in this book. You can also get the actual font family ID of the preferred system font or application font for a script system by making Script Manager calls; see the discussion of script variables in the chapter "Script Manager" in this book.

Perhaps the most common mistake developers make in adapting their applications to global markets is to assume that the application font is always Geneva. *Do not assume that different script systems have the same system and application fonts.*

Roman Characters and Associated Fonts

All Macintosh script systems include the low-ASCII Roman characters and control characters as part of their character sets. Most non-Roman fonts provide glyphs for those low-ASCII Roman characters. If the font itself does not contain those characters, the script system substitutes characters from an **associated font**—a Roman font that is associated with that script system—for character codes (mostly in the low-ASCII range) that the script system determines are Roman. Some contextual script systems must use associated fonts because they need more glyphs than can fit into the high-ASCII range normally available for native glyphs.

Note

A script system specifies the associated font for its system font and application font, but may allow the user to select a single Roman font to associate with all other fonts of the script system. ◆

In most cases your application does not have to account for associated fonts; glyphs from the associated font are substituted automatically when you draw text that contains Roman characters. However, keep in mind that font measurements (such as the results of the `GetFontInfo` and `FontMetrics` procedures) always account for the width and height characteristics of *both* the current font and the associated font. This can sometimes cause unexpected results, such as a line height that is greater than the current font's expected line height. The `GetFontInfo` procedure is described in the chapter "QuickDraw Text" in this book; font measurement and the `FontMetrics` procedure are further described in the chapter "Font Manager" in this book.

There are several other issues to keep in mind related to Roman characters and Roman fonts:

■ Remember that the presence of Roman glyphs in displayed or printed text does not necessarily imply that they were created with a Roman font. The Text Utilities can help you locate Roman characters in a text buffer and explicitly change them to the Roman script system, if you wish.

■ As noted on page 1-56, the Roman script system does not have a consistent character set across all fonts. For example, character codes in the Symbol font map to different glyphs from the same character codes in the Geneva font. Conversely, identical symbols can have different character codes in different fonts. The division sign (÷) is located at $D6 in the Helvetica font and $B8 in the Symbol font.

■ Inconsistent character codes for symbols other than letters and numbers can also be a problem across script systems. For instance, in the Roman script system the division sign (÷) is located at $D6 in most fonts, whereas in the Arabic script system the division sign (÷) is at $9B.

Other Font Issues

In general, when drawing text, you set the font characteristics before you make a call, and the script management system makes sure that the font you specify is used. However, there are some issues and complications to keep in mind:

■ If a particular size or styled variation (such as bold or italic) of a font is not available on the computer, the Font Manager can scale an existing size and QuickDraw can apply a style to an existing plain version of a font. Certain styles may be disabled in scripts where they are inappropriate. You can use the Script Manager to determine all of the valid styles for a given script system.

■ The setting of the font force flag is controlled by the user when a script system that supports it is the system script. If the font force flag is `TRUE`, text written with a Roman font is considered instead to be text of the system script; any character codes corresponding to native characters of the system script are drawn in the system font rather than in the specified Roman font. If you do not want that to happen in your application, you must monitor the state of the font force flag and change it temporarily whenever necessary.

■ The font force flag exists to permit multiple-language support by applications that expect a single font. It is only a partial solution to the problem. *Do not hardcode your application to require any single font.*

- If your application needs to have a font whose characters should never be interpreted as system script characters (for example, symbol fonts used for paint program palettes), you can assign the font an ID in the reserved range $7E00 to $7FFF (uninterpreted symbols) rather than in the Roman range. Then, even if the font force flag is set to TRUE, your symbols are not re-interpreted as system-script characters.

- When displaying characters as they are typed in by the user, you must make sure that the font for text display belongs to the same script system that is used for text input. See "Font Script and Keyboard Script" beginning on page 1-51.

- Many fonts—particularly those associated with non-Roman writing systems—do not draw legibly unless they are at least 12 point. However, you cannot assume that the system font size is always 12 point. Use QuickDraw, Font Manager, and Menu Manager calls to get the default size for the system font, default size for the current font, and required menu bar height for the system font.

- Do not assume that the application font exists in a 9-point size. Use the Script Manager to determine the application font family and size for legible small text.

- Diacritical marks (such as the acute accent over the "E" in "École") may extend above or below the normal limits for character height. The Font Manager allows you to either extend the spacing between lines or shrink the marked characters to make sure that the characters are not cut off at the top or bottom.

- If you use your own menu-definition ('MDEF') resource to draw a Font menu in your application, be sure it can draw all font names correctly. It should use the font itself, or a font of the same script system, to display the font name. See the Menu Manager chapter of *Inside Macintosh: Macintosh Toolbox Essentials* for more information on creating menus.

- A 2-byte font can be very large; outline fonts for 2-byte script systems can contain single resources over 6 MB in size. Large numbers of 2-byte fonts can be a storage problem for the user. Furthermore, because the Resource Manager limits the size of a file's resource fork to 16 MB, it may be difficult to include 2-byte fonts with your application or document files.

Character Rendering and Text Display

The process of properly preparing characters for display is called *character rendering*. When QuickDraw draws a character, string, or line of text, it takes the stored character codes you supply it and processes them if necessary to take into account line direction, contextual substitution, or character reordering. It uses the rules of the font script (the script system of the current font of the active graphics port) to make these calculations. QuickDraw then gets the glyphs for the resulting characters from the Font Manager, and draws the glyphs in order on the screen, starting at the current pen location.

IMPORTANT

A fundamental assumption of the Macintosh script management system is that contextual analysis, character reordering, and the formation of ligatures should occur during the *display* of text, not its storage. That way the stored version of text can be much simpler; it contains only the basic characters of its writing system. Searching and other text-manipulation tasks are much more straightforward that way. It is the Macintosh script management system that has the job of handling differences between storage order and display order, and differences between stored codes and displayed glyphs. ▲

The 1-byte simple script systems and all 2-byte script systems currently have no individual character-rendering specifications; QuickDraw's built-in ability to draw characters sequentially in a given font, style, and size is sufficient.

The 1-byte complex script systems carry character-rendering information in line-layout tables in their encoding/rendering ('itl5') resources. WorldScript I performs the rendering based on specifications in those tables.

The section "Features of the World's Writing Systems" beginning on page 1-21 shows examples from writing systems that require the kinds of rendering abilities provided by the Macintosh script management system. Your application should not have to explicitly perform any of these tasks; you merely store character codes, and the script management system renders those characters properly whenever you need to display them.

Storage Order and Display Order

QuickDraw draws glyphs and lines of text from left to right only. This left-to-right orientation of QuickDraw is fundamental, and applies whether or not the text being drawn is meant to be read left-to-right or right-to-left. Each character is drawn with its origin (usually its left edge) placed at the current pen location, and after it is drawn QuickDraw moves the pen location rightward by the width of the glyph. Likewise, when QuickDraw draws a string of text, it keeps advancing the location as it draws, so that the pen location ends up at the right end of the string.

Display order is this left-to-right order in which QuickDraw draws glyphs on a display device. For example, QuickDraw draws a string of Hebrew text in reverse order from the way the string is read: the glyph for the last (= leftmost) character in the string is drawn *first*, and the glyph for the first (= rightmost) character in the string is drawn *last*. Figure 1-40 is an example showing a line of mixed Arabic and Roman text. The glyphs are drawn as shown, from left to right in the sequence labeled *Display order*, even though the primary line direction is right-to-left.

Figure 1-40   Storage order and display order

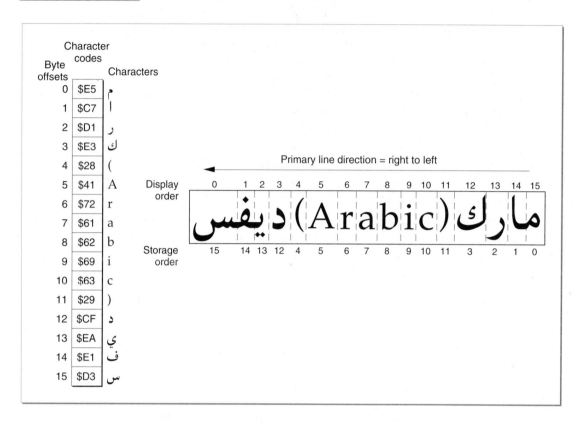

Storage order is the sequence of character codes in memory. The Macintosh script management system assumes that your application stores characters in the order in which they would be typed in—that is, with the first character code in a string at a lower address than subsequent character codes in that string. Storage order is different from display order for text with a right-to-left line direction.

In Figure 1-40, for example, the line of numbers labeled *Storage order* shows the byte offset in the buffer of the character for each glyph. Note that the glyphs for the Hebrew characters are drawn in reverse sequence from the order in which they are stored, whereas the glyphs for the Roman characters are drawn in the same sequence as their storage order.

If your application stores its text in the expected storage order, the script management system properly orders all characters within each style run that you draw.

Storage order can differ from display order not only in the sequence of individual characters within a run of text, but also in the order in which entire runs of text are drawn on the screen. See Figure 1-41 on page 1-67 for an example. If multiple scripts with different line directions occur on a single line, determining the order in which to draw the individual runs can be complex. The Macintosh script management system helps you with that determination; see the discussion of the GetFormatOrder procedure in the chapter "QuickDraw Text" in this book.

Line Direction and Alignment

Writing systems exist with several different line directions, as shown in Figure 1-14 on page 1-24. The Macintosh script management system supports two of them: left-to-right (used for Roman and most other writing systems), and right-to-left (used for Arabic and Hebrew). As noted earlier in this chapter, Arabic and Hebrew systems are considered bidirectional rather than purely right-to-left because numbers and commonly intermixed foreign words are written from left to right. And although Japanese and Chinese are traditionally written vertically, the Japanese and Chinese script systems currently support only a left-to-right line direction.

The Macintosh script management system supports multiscript text, including text with mixed directions, in a single line. The layout, measurement, and drawing routines can help you correctly render text—even justifed text—from multiple script systems.

Primary Line Direction

When text with different line directions is mixed on a single line, the **primary line direction** is the principal, controlling direction for display of that text. The concept of primary line direction is important because it affects the order in which text elements are drawn. For example, suppose a block of Hebrew text follows (in storage order) a block of Roman text. If the primary line direction is left-to-right—equivalent to saying that the Hebrew text is embedded within a line of Roman text—the Hebrew text is drawn after and to the right of the Roman text. If the primary line direction is right-to-left—equivalent to saying that the Roman text is embedded within a line of Hebrew text—the Roman text is drawn after and to the right of the Hebrew text. Figure 1-41 illustrates the concept.

Figure 1-41   How primary line direction affects display order

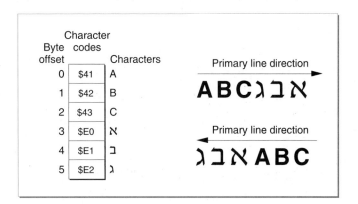

Your application controls the primary line direction of its text by specifying it in parameters to certain text-layout calls such as the QuickDraw `GetFormatOrder` procedure. You can set your primary line direction independently of any system settings, but TextEdit and many text-processing applications tie their primary line direction to the current value of the system direction.

The **system direction** is a global setting, used by all parts of system software to control the alignment of text elements in dialog boxes, menus, and so on. TextEdit sets the primary line direction of its text to the system direction. Some script-aware routines assume that the primary line direction for the text they manipulate is equal to the system direction; see, for example, the description of the `CharToPixel` function in the chapter "QuickDraw Text" in this book.

System direction is determined by the value of the low-memory system global variable `SysDirection`. At startup, `SysDirection` is initialized to the line direction specified by the system's international configuration (`'itlc'`) resource. That value is commonly localized to correspond to the primary line direction of the system script, but if a bidirectional script system is enabled the user can control the system direction from the Text control panel; see "User Control of Script Settings" beginning on page 1-107.

Your application (and other applications) can also control the system direction with Script Manager routines. Do not simply assume a value for system direction.

The right-to-left primary line direction of bidirectional script systems has several further implications for program design. In working with bidirectional text, remember these points:

■ Characters are read from right to left. Numerals are read from left to right. A word processor must therefore implement two sets of tabs and two ruler directions.

■ Mathematical expressions are read from left to right in Hebrew and from right to left in Arabic. If in Hebrew one writes "6 + 4 = 10", in Arabic the same expression in the same order would be written "10 = 4 + 6".

■ The concepts of **leading edge** and **trailing edge** of a glyph are important for mouse-down event testing, caret positioning, and highlighting. In left-to-right text, a glyph's leading edge is its left edge; in right-to-left text, a glyph's leading edge is its right edge. See "Caret Handling" beginning on page 1-74.

■ Some punctuation marks and numerals from the Standard Roman character set are duplicated at different locations in bidirectional character sets in order to account for this. For example, the exclamation point (!) is at $21 in the Standard Roman character set, but Hebrew and Arabic add a second, right-to-left version of it, at $A1.

■ Despite the fact that a single style run in a bidirectional script system can contain two directions of text, your application can treat it as a unit. See the note on bidirectional style runs on page 1-71.

Alignment

Alignment is the horizontal placement of lines of text with respect to the left and right edges of the text area or page. Text is typically left-aligned, right-aligned, centered, or justified—aligned to both the left and right margins. See Figure 1-15 on page 1-25.

A script system's default text alignment usually follows its line direction. The system global variable `SysDirection`, which controls line direction, also controls the default alignment for text and other items in dialog boxes, alerts, and menus. For example, in Arabic system software (and in applications localized to the Arabic script system) menu items are right-aligned, and radio buttons and checkboxes are modified so that the boxes or buttons themselves are on the right. The user controls the system alignment by controlling the system direction with the Text control panel. See "User Control of Script Settings" beginning on page 1-107.

TextEdit uses the value of `SysDirection`, to set the default alignment for text in its windows.

You should anticipate that right alignment might occur in your application's text elements. Be sure to allow for it:

■ Do not assume that, once you have measured the length of a line of text, you can always place it at the left margin. For right-aligned text, you need to indent the pen location from the left margin by an appropriate amount so that the right end of the text line falls on the right margin.

■ Do not allow a text item in a dialog box to extend to the right of the dialog-box boundary; the right edge of a line of text in that item will be truncated if text is right-aligned. See Figure 1-42 for an illustration of this.

Figure 1-42   Dialog items truncated at dialog-box boundary

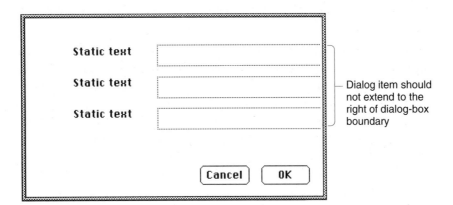

■ When creating a column of checkboxes or radio buttons, make the text boxes all the same length. This ensures that when the line direction and alignment are reversed, the checkboxes or radio buttons remain correctly aligned.

If you are specifically formatting right-aligned text in a bidirectional script system, remember these additional alignment issues:

■ Text is typically right-aligned. It breaks near the left margin and continues at the right margin of the following line. However, the "last" character on a line is not always the leftmost; see, for example, Figure 1-27 on page 1-31.

■ Headers, footers, and footnotes are typically right-aligned.

■ In a table or list, the first column is the rightmost.

■ Line indentation is measured from the right margin.

■ Odd pages are on the left in a book, and even pages are on the right. The inside front cover is on the right when a book is opened, and page 1 is on the left.

Justification

Justified text, which is aligned to both the left and right margins of the text area, is a special form of alignment that poses particular challenges to multiple-language formatting. The Macintosh script management system provides an entire set of routines for measuring, laying out, and drawing lines of justified text. See, for example, the descriptions of the `PortionLine` and `DrawJustified` routines, and the discussions of measuring and drawing lines of justified text in the chapter "QuickDraw Text" in this book.

Style Runs, Font Runs, Script Runs, Direction Runs

When QuickDraw draws a character or string of text, it examines the current graphics port record to determine how the text should be drawn. The font (and therefore the script system), the point size, and the style of the text are all determined by fields in the current graphics port.

This feature of QuickDraw has several consequences. First, it means that you must be sure to set the graphics port fields properly before calling QuickDraw. Second, it means that each call to QuickDraw must be restricted to a run of text that has uniform values for all those fields.

This finest division of the runs of text in your document is called a **style run.** A style run comprises the set of contiguous characters that all share the same font, size, and style characteristics. Because they share the same font, they naturally share the same script system. *The style run is the most important organizational unit for script-aware text handling,* and your application should always maintain style-run information for all its text. For many script-aware calls, you first set up the graphics port record appropriately and then make the call, passing it a single style run of text (or even less than a single style run, if the style run spans more than one line of text).

A larger division than style run is the **font run;** it consists of those characters that share the same font (and therefore the same script), but do not all share the same size or style attributes. You need not reset the `txFont` field of the graphics port between calls that involve text within a single font run.

The next larger division is the **script run;** it consists of all contiguous characters that belong to a given script system, regardless of their individual fonts. Within a script run, all the text's formatting and text-manipulation specifications are constant; there is no need to load different resources or validate the existence of another script system between calls involving a single script run. If your application does not support multiple script systems, all of your text is a single script run.

The largest division is the **direction run.** A direction run consists of all contiguous characters with the same line direction, regardless of what script system they belong to. (However, see the note on bidirectional style runs page 1-71.) Within a direction run, the display order of characters and style runs has a very simple relation to their storage order. If all of your text consists of a single direction run, your text-layout tasks are simplified.

Figure 1-43 shows a line of text and its separation into style runs, font runs, script runs, and direction runs.

Figure 1-43   Style runs, font runs, script runs, and direction runs in text

TEXT:	small Large العربي עברית *Hebrew* Nihongo 火曜日						
Direction run	⟶	⟵		⟶			
Script run	Roman	Arabic	Hebrew	Roman			Japanese
Font run	Times	Baghdad	Ramat Gan	Geneva	New York		Ryobi Hon Mincho
Style run	Times 10	Times 14	Baghdad 16	Ramat Gan 16	Geneva 10 italic	New York 10	Ryobi Hon Mincho 10

Runs of Roman characters in text of a non-Roman script system are *not* necessarily considered separate style runs, and may be displayed (as Roman characters) in the non-Roman font of that script system. For greater formatting control, however, you may want to explicitly separate out those Roman characters into style runs of their own. You can use a Text Utilities routine to do so.

Bidirectional styie runs

Bidirectional script systems have a unique concept of a style run. Numerals and Roman characters in a bidirectional style run have a different direction from the rest of the native text, but your application needn't consider them as separate style runs. The script management system handles all the special formatting, highlighting, and character location for you in these cases, so you can treat such a mixed-direction sequence just as you would any other single style run. ◆

Text Layout

Laying out lines of text—calculating how many characters fit on a line, determining the order of drawing of all the elements, performing all contextual formatting, and drawing the text—is a standard task in word processing. It can be a challenging task in a single language, but it is especially difficult to write a text-layout routine that is general enough to work with text in any script system. Even more complex is the laying out of text from several script systems in a single line. Add to that the complications of trying to draw justified lines of multiscript text, and the task can appear daunting.

The Macintosh script management system includes several groups of routines that ease the task by helping you write very generalized text-layout code that can handle multiscript lines of text, and can even justify those lines appropriately for the script systems involved. Routines from the Script Manager, the Text Utilities, and QuickDraw cooperate to analyze, arrange, format, measure, and draw the text.

There are two main principles that control how text layout occurs on the Macintosh:

■ There is no system support for layout of more than a single line at a time. You are responsible for knowing where in memory your line starts and where on the screen to start drawing it.

■ (Nearly) all text-layout routines operate on a single style run at a time. Therefore, to handle text with potentially multiple styles or scripts on a single line, you may need to call a routine repeatedly, once for each style run on the line.

Therefore, if a syle run extends beyond the boundaries of the current line, you call the routine for *only that portion of the style run that is on the line*. The part of a style run that exists on a single line is called a **text segment** in the chapter "QuickDraw Text" in this book.

In general, text layout involves taking the following steps, in order, for each line you intend to draw:

1. Starting with the buffer location of the first character on the line, and knowing the width of your display line in pixels, calculate the byte offset of the character at which to break the line. There are several ways to do this, using both QuickDraw and Text Utilities routines. The routines give proper results for any script system.

2. Determine the order in which to draw the individual style runs on the line, using a QuickDraw routine. If the line contains mixed-directional text, the left-to-right order in which you draw style runs may not be the same as the order in which they occur in memory. See, for example, Figure 1-41 on page 1-67.

   If you are drawing justified text, take these additional steps:

   ☐ Eliminate trailing spaces at the end of the rightmost or leftmost (depending on the primary line direction) style run on your display line, so your justified text will line up properly. You can use a QuickDraw routine for this purpose (remember that a space character may not have the ASCII value $20 in a non-Roman script system).

   ☐ Calculate the **slop value,** the extra amount of space that needs to be distributed throughout your line of text. Do that by measuring the total pixel width of all the style runs on the line and subtracting that from the display line width.

   ☐ Calculate how to distribute that slop value among the style runs on your line, using a QuickDraw routine.

3. Position the QuickDraw pen both vertically and horizontally. The horizontal position must be at the left end of the text to be drawn on the line, regardless of the primary line direction. The vertical position is your responsibility; if you are drawing multiple lines in sequence, you can use QuickDraw or Font Manager routines to obtain font-height information to help you position the pen.

4. Draw the text, a style run at a time, using QuickDraw calls. For justified text, pass the amount of slop you calculated for each style run when you call the drawing routine for that run.

You can also use QuickDraw and Text Utilities calls to draw explicitly *scaled* multiscript text, in which the character are enlarged, shrunk, or distorted from their normal shapes; and you can even draw justified, scaled, multiscript text. For more information on text measurement and drawing, see the chapter "QuickDraw Text" in this book. For more information on line breaking, see the chapter "Text Utilities" in this book.

Remember these points when laying out and drawing lines of text:

- There are tables available that help you measure text before drawing it. The **global width table** is a table constructed in memory every time FMSwapFont is called; it can be used to calculate the pixel width of each glyph in a font, and it is helpful in determining line lengths. Each font family resource may have an optional width table with normalized glyph widths. Bitmapped fonts have tables that give the actual integer widths for their glyphs. For more information on these tables and on the FMSwapFont call, see the chapter "Font Manager" in this book.

- Don't break text into arbitrary chunks before formatting it for display: the second byte of a 2-byte character can be lost, or improper contextual formatting can result. If you need to truncate the displayed text at a location that is not a style run boundary or a valid line break or word boundary, use the QuickDraw clipping facility rather than truncating the string.

- Roman characters within style runs of a non-Roman font may display better if converted to the Roman script system and formatted as Roman text. You can use the Text Utilities to locate sequences of such characters.

If you are measuring the pixel width of a line of text before drawing it, keep these cautions in mind:

- Do not assume that a glyph for a given character code always has the same width. With certain scripts, using the Font Manager global width tables may give inaccurate results. The QuickDraw text-measuring routines return correct results for all script systems.

- Do not assume that specifying a fixed-width font in a graphics port always produces monospaced text. For example, the printed versions of some glyphs in some fixed-width fonts (such as "®" in Courier) have widths different from other glyphs in the font. Furthermore, when the Script Manager font force flag is set, the user might, for example, insert a wide Japanese character within a line of Monaco text. See the description of the font force flag in the chapter "Script Manager" in this book.

- Some characters, such as diacritical marks, may have zero width. A zero-width character should never be divided from the previous character in the text when you partition text. When truncating a string to fit into a horizontal space, the correct algorithm is to truncate from the end of the string toward the beginning, one character at a time, until the total width is small enough. This prevents cutting text before a zero-width character. You can also call Text Utilities functions to perform the truncation correctly.

■ Do not set the `chExtra` field of the graphics port to a nonzero value with text containing connected glyphs or text that may include zero-width characters. Diacritical marks are placed incorrectly in relation to their base characters, and connected glyphs have white space inserted improperly, like this:

chExtra = 0   **chExtra nonzero**

العربي   ا لعر بي

हिन्दी   हि न्दी

Caret Handling

By standard word-processing convention, the **selection range** is the sequence of zero or more characters—contiguous in memory—where the next editing operation is to occur. A selection range of zero characters is called an **insertion point.**

Highlighting a selection range and marking the insertion point both involve converting offsets of characters in a text buffer into pixel positions on a display device. In multiscript text, expecially text that has mixed line directions and contextual formatting, this can be a complex task.

The Macintosh script management system provides a routine that helps you draw carets properly for text in any combination of script systems. The QuickDraw function `CharToPixel` returns the onscreen pixel position corresponding to a given offset in your text buffer. The function returns the horizontal offset (in pixels) from the left margin of the text you pass it to the proper caret position corresponding to the character at the specified byte offset in your text buffer.

Caret and cursor

By convention in this book, the **caret** is defined as the blinking bar that marks the insertion point in text. The **cursor,** on the other hand, is the arrow, I-beam, spinning disk, or other small icon that marks screen position and moves with the mouse. ◆

This section discusses the conventions underlying the relationship of text offset to caret position. For more information on conversion of text offset to screen position, see the description of the `CharToPixel` function in the chapter "QuickDraw Text" in this book.

The Caret

A **caret position** is a location on the screen that corresponds to an insertion point in memory. It lets the user know where in the text file the next insertion (or deletion) will occur. A caret position is always *between* glyphs on the screen, usually on the leading edge of one glyph and the trailing edge of another. The **leading edge** of a glyph is the edge that is encountered first when reading text of that glyph's script system; the **trailing edge** is opposite from the leading edge. In left-to-right text, a glyph's leading edge is its left edge; in right-to-left text, a glyph's leading edge is its right edge.

In most situations for most text applications, the caret position is on the leading edge of the glyph corresponding to the character at the insertion point in memory; see Figure 1-44. When a new character is inserted, it displaces the character at the insertion point, shifting it and all subsequent characters in the buffer forward by one character position. (That shift may be one or two bytes, depending on the size of the inserted character.)

Figure 1-44   Caret position and insertion point

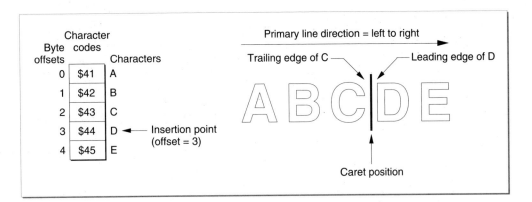

The caret position is unambiguous in text with a single line direction. In such a case, the caret position is on the trailing and leading edges of characters that are contiguous in the text buffer; it thus corresponds directly to a single offset in the buffer. This is not always the case in mixed-directional text, as described next.

Caret Positions at Direction Boundaries

In determining caret position, an ambiguous case occurs at direction boundaries because the byte offset in memory can map to two different glyph positions on the screen—one for text in each line direction. In Figure 1-45, for example, the insertion point is at byte offset 4 in the buffer. If the next character to be inserted is Arabic, the caret should be drawn at caret position 4 on the screen; if the next character is English, the caret should be drawn at caret position 12.

Figure 1-45   Caret positions at direction bondaries

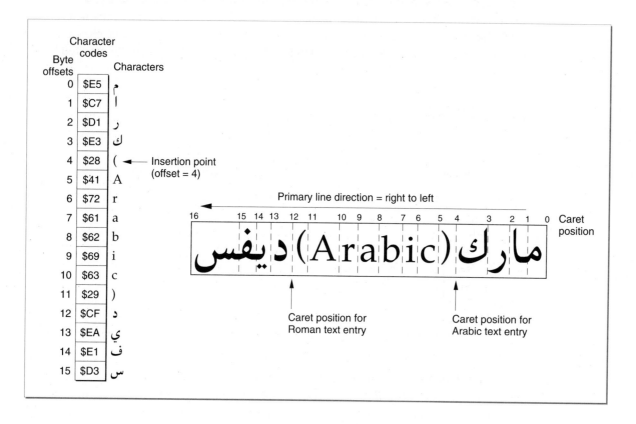

The Macintosh script management system codifies this relationship between text offset and caret position as follows:

- For any given offset in memory, there are two potential caret positions:
    - □ the *leading edge* of the glyph corresponding to the character *at that offset*
    - □ the *trailing edge* of the glyph corresponding to the *previous (in memory) character*

    (The first and last characters of a text segment are special cases; see the discussion of the `CharToPixel` function in the chapter "QuickDraw Text" in this book.)

- In unidirectional text, the two caret positions coincide: the leading edge of the glyph for one character is at the same location as the trailing edge of the glyph for the previous character. In Figure 1-44, the offset of 3 yields caret positions on the leading edge of "D" and the trailing edge of "C", which are the same unambiguous location.

- At a boundary between text of opposite directions, the two caret positions do not coincide. Thus, in Figure 1-45, for an offset of 4 there are two caret positions: 12, on the leading edge of "("; and 4, on the trailing edge of "ك". Likewise, an offset of 12 yields two caret positions (also 12 and 4, but on the edges of two different glyphs).

    At an ambiguous character offset, the current line direction (the presumed direction of the *next character to be inserted*) determines which caret position is the correct one:

    - □ If the current direction equals the direction of the character at that offset, the caret position is the leading edge of that character's glyph. In Figure 1-45, if Roman text is to be inserted at offset 4 (occupied by a Roman character), the caret position is on the leading edge of that character's glyph ("(")—that is, at caret position 12.
    - □ If the current direction equals the direction of the previous (in memory) character, the screen position is on the trailing edge of the glyph corresponding to that previous (in memory) character. In Figure 1-45, if Arabic text is to be inserted at offset 4, the caret position is on the trailing edge of the glyph of the character at offset 3 ("ك")—that is, at caret position 4.

Two common approaches for drawing the caret at direction boundaries involve the use of a dual caret and a single caret. A **dual caret** consists of two lines, a high caret and a low caret, each measuring half the text height; see Figure 1-46. The high caret is displayed at the primary caret position for the insertion point; the low caret is displayed at the secondary caret position for that insertion point. Which position is primary, and which is secondary, depends on the primary line direction:

- The **primary caret position** is the screen location associated with the glyph that has the same direction as the primary line direction. If the current line direction corresponds to the primary line direction, inserted text will appear at the primary caret position. A **primary caret** is a caret drawn at the primary caret position.

■ The **secondary caret position** is the screen location associated with the glyph that has a different direction from the primary line direction. If the current line direction is opposite to the primary line direction, inserted text will appear at the secondary caret position. In Figure 1-46, the display of the Roman keyboard icon shows that the current line direction is not the same as the primary line direction, so the next character inserted will appear at the secondary caret position. A **secondary caret** is a caret drawn at the secondary caret position.

Figure 1-46   Dual caret at direction boundaries in mixed-directional text

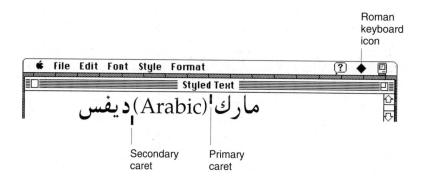

A **single caret** (or **moving caret**) is simpler than a dual caret; see Figure 1-47. It is a single, full-length caret that appears at the screen location where the next glyph will appear. At direction boundaries, its position depends on the keyboard script. At a direction boundary, the caret appears at the primary caret position if the current line direction corresponds to the primary line direction; it appears at the secondary caret position if the current line direction is opposite to the primary line direction. The moving caret is also called a *jumping caret* because its position "jumps" between the primary and secondary caret positions as the user switches the keyboard script between the two text directions represented.

Figure 1-47   Single carets at direction boundaries in mixed-directional text

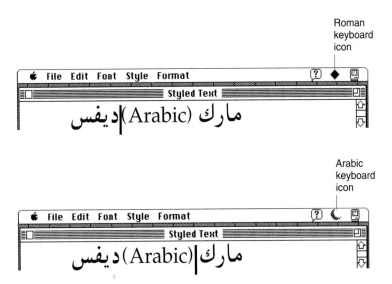

The script management system permits the user to select a preference between dual carets and a single (moving) caret; your text application should support both. TextEdit employs both types of carets; see the chapter "TextEdit" in this book.

Caret Movement With Arrow Keys

Most text applications allow the user to move the caret through displayed text with the arrow keys. In general, using the Right or Left Arrow key should move the caret uniformly right or left, regardless of the line direction of the text in which the caret appears. To do this means that your application needs to take the current line direction into consideration, rather than simply advancing the insertion point through the text buffer in response to presses of, say, the Right Arrow.

When the caret moves through a direction boundary (or any style run boundary) in response to a series of arrow keypresses, you need to set the keyboard script (and graphics port settings) to match the characteristics of the text that the caret is in. By convention, you should change the keyboard script and port characteristics after the caret has *passed* the boundary, not when it first reaches it.

For a discussion of how TextEdit handles the complications that occur at direction boundaries and within runs of bidirectional text, see the chapter "TextEdit" in this book.

Highlighting

When displaying a selection range, an application typically marks it by **highlighting,** drawing the glyphs in inverse video or with a colored or outlined background. As part of its text-display tasks, your application is responsible for knowing what the selection range is and highlighting it properly—as well as for making the necessary changes in memory that result from any cutting, pasting, or editing operations involving the selection range.

Discontinuous selection

A selection range as defined in this book always consists of characters contiguous in memory. Some word processors allow for **discontinuous selection,** in which the characters that constitute the selection range are not necessarily contiguous in memory. You can think of discontinuous selection as the simultaneous existence of several selection ranges of the type described here. Discontinuous selection is not discussed further in this book. In particular, keep in mind that the discontinuous *highlighting* shown in this section is not an example of discontinuous selection; all selection ranges shown here are single, contiguous ranges in memory. ◆

Unidirectional Text

In text with a single line direction, the selection range always appears on screen as a continuous range of highlighted glyphs; see Figure 1-48.

Figure 1-48   Highlighting a selection range in unidirectional text

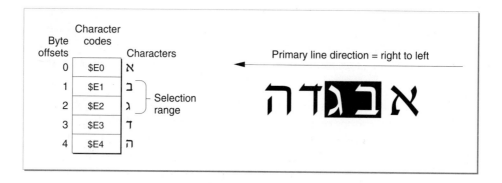

The Macintosh script management system measures the limits of highlighting rectangles in terms of caret position. Thus, in Figure 1-48, in which the selection range consists of the characters at offsets 1 and 2 in memory, the ends of the highlighting rectangle correspond to caret positions for offsets 1 and 3. It's equivalent to saying that the highlighting extends from the leading edge of the glyph for the character at offset 1 to the leading edge of the glyph for the character at offset 3.

Highlighting for word selection

If your application supports word selection by double-clicking, it involves three steps. First, use a QuickDraw call to locate the offset in memory corresponding to the double-click. Second, use a Text Utilities call to locate the offsets of the word boundaries on either side of the double-click. Third, use QuickDraw calls to determine the boundaries of the rectangle to highlight. ◆

Mixed-Directional Text

If the displayed text has mixed direction runs, the selection range may appear as discontinuous highlighted text. This is because the characters that make up the selection range are always contiguous in memory, but characters that are contiguous in memory may not be contiguous on screen.

Figure 1-49 is an example of text whose selection range consists of a contiguous sequence of characters in memory, whereas the highlighted glyphs are displayed discontinuously.

Figure 1-49   Highlighting a selection range in mixed-directional text

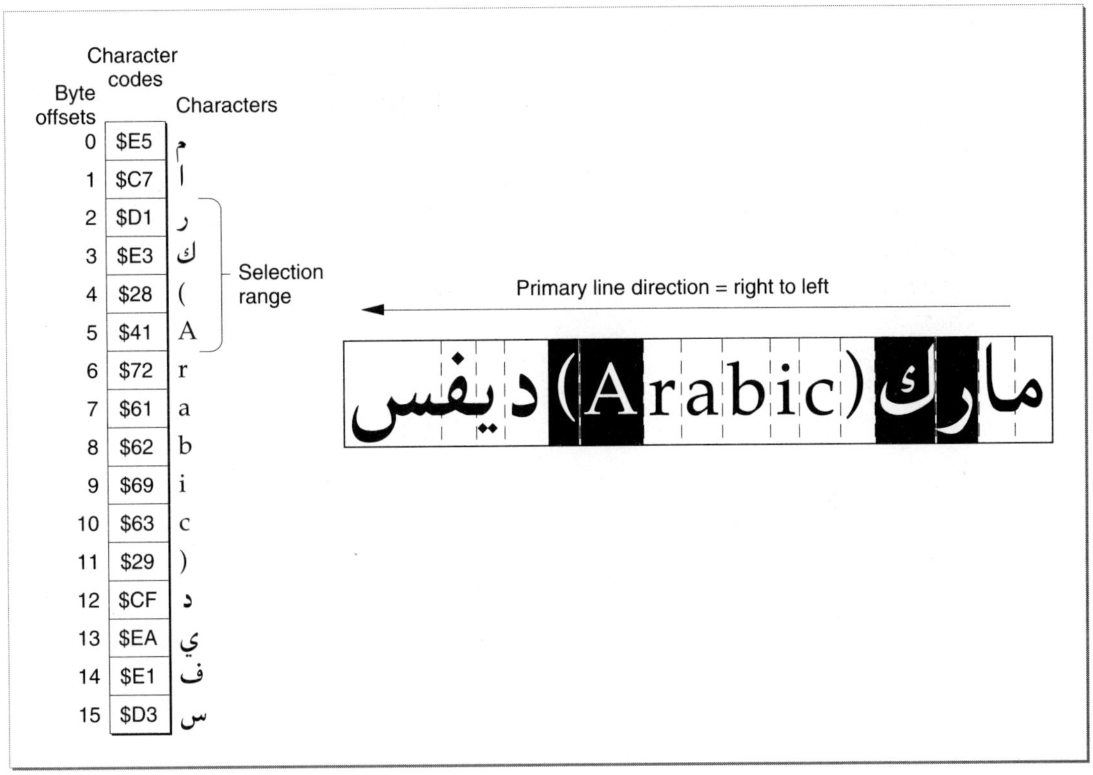

In describing the boundaries of the highlighting rectangles in terms of caret position, note that for Figure 1-49 it is not possible to simply say that the highlighting extends from the caret position of offset 2 to the caret position of offset 6. Using the definitions of caret position given earlier, however, it is possible to define it as two separate rectangles, one extending from offset 4 to offset 2, and another extending from offset 12 to offset 6 (assuming for the ambiguous offsets—4 and 12—that the current text direction equals the primary line direction).

The QuickDraw function `HiliteText` makes those kinds of calculations and is especially useful for determining the correct caret positions when highlighting a selection range in mixed-directional text. See the discussion of `HiliteText` in the chapter "QuickDraw Text" in this book for more details.

Converting Screen Position to Text Offset

Caret handling and highlighting, as just discussed, require conversion from text offset to screen position. But that is only half the picture; it is just as necessary to be able to convert from screen position to text offset. For example, if the user clicks the cursor within your displayed text, you need to be able to determine the offset in your text buffer equivalent to that mouse-down event. You can then use that information to set the insertion point or selection range.

The script management system does most of this work for you. It provides routines that convert a screen position to the byte offset of a character code in memory (and vice versa); those routines function correctly with multiscript text, even text that has been rendered with ligatures and contextual forms.

Determining the character associated with a screen position requires first defining the caret position associated with a given screen position. Once that is done, the previously defined relationship between caret position and text offset can be used to find the character.

Figure 1-50 shows the cursor positioned within a line of text at the moment of a mouse click. A mouse-down event can occur anywhere within the area of a glyph, but the caret position that is to be derived from that event must be an infinitesimally thin line that falls between two glyphs.

Figure 1-50   Interpreting caret position from a mouse-down event

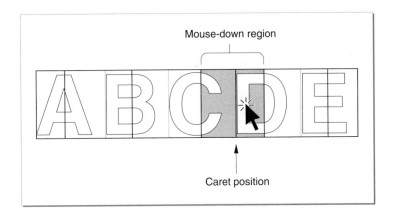

A line of displayed glyphs is divided by the script management system into a series of mouse-down regions. A **mouse-down region** is the screen area within which any mouse click will yield the same caret position. For example, a mouse click that occurs anywhere between the leading edge of a glyph and the center of that glyph results in a caret position at the leading edge of that glyph. For unidirectional text, mouse-down regions extend from the center of one glyph to the center of the next glyph (except at the ends of a line), as Figure 1-50 shows. A mouse click anywhere within the region results in a caret position between the two glyphs.

At line ends, and at the boundaries between text of different line directions, mouse-down regions are smaller and interpreting them is more complex. As Figure 1-51 shows, the mouse-down regions at direction boundaries extend only from the leading or trailing edges of the bounding glyphs to their centers. Note that the shaded part of Figure 1-50 is a single mouse-down region, whereas *each* of the shaded parts of Figure 1-51 is two mouse-down regions.

Figure 1-51   Mouse-down regions and caret positions in mixed-directional text

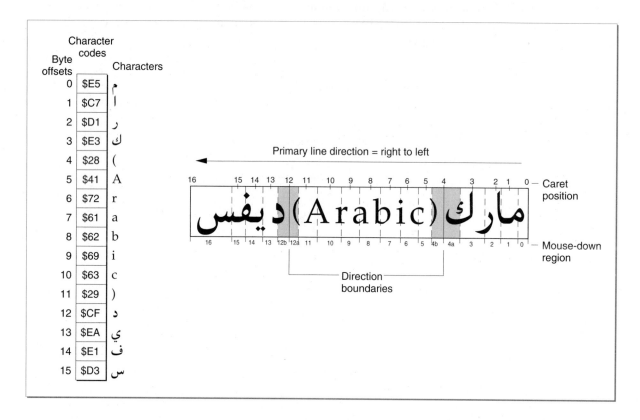

How do mouse-down regions relate to text offset? Referring to Figure 1-51, and remembering that the primary line direction is right-to-left, consider the two mouse-down regions 4a and 12a:

■ A mouse click within region 4a is associated with the trailing edge of the Arabic character "ك". In response, your application might make the keyboard script Arabic, draw a primary caret (or single caret) at caret position 4, and place the insertion point at offset 4 in the buffer, to insert Arabic text following "ك". (If you are drawing a dual caret, the secondary caret should be at caret position 12, which also corresponds to an insertion point at offset 4 in the buffer.)

■ A mouse click within region 12a is associated with the leading edge of the Roman character "(". In response, your application might make the keyboard script Roman, draw a secondary caret (or single caret) at caret position 12, and place the insertion point at offset 4 in the buffer, to insert Roman text preceding "(". (If you are drawing a dual caret, the primary caret should be at caret position 4, which also corresponds to an insertion point at offset 4 in the buffer.)

Thus mouse clicks in two widely separated areas of the screen can lead to an identical caret display and to a single insertion point in the text buffer. One, however permits insertion of Roman text, and the other Arabic text, and the insertions occur at different screen locations.

Mouse clicks in regions 4b and 12b in Figure 1-51 would lead to just the opposite situation: a primary caret at caret position 12, a secondary caret at caret position 4, and an insertion point at offset 12 in the text buffer. Either Roman text would be inserted after the Roman character ")", or Arabic text would be inserted before the Arabic character " ﺩ".

The QuickDraw function `PixelToChar` helps you make these calculations; it returns the byte offset in your text buffer corresponding to the character associated with a particular distance (in pixels) from the left margin of the displayed text. It even handles the special cases of pixel locations outside (to the left or right of) the margins of the displayed text. For more information on conversion of screen position to text offset, see the description of the `PixelToChar` function in the chapter "QuickDraw Text" in this book.

Printing

At the application level, printing on the Macintosh computer is not fundamentally different from drawing to the screen. A printer is considered a display device, and your application prints by creating a printing graphics port (a graphics port with a few extra fields for printing), setting the port's fields, and drawing in the port with calls to QuickDraw. General procedures for printing are described in the Printing Manager chapter of *Inside Macintosh: Imaging*. However, printing text, and especially contextual text, can pose extra challenges.

A very common complication results from the difference in resolution and pixel size between screen and printer. QuickDraw measurements are theoretically in terms of **points,** which are nominally equivalent to screen pixels at normal resolution. High-resolution printers have very much smaller pixel sizes, although printer drivers are expected to take this into account so that the same QuickDraw calls will produce text lines of the same width on the screen and on a printer. Nevertheless, this higher resolution, and the fact that printers can use different fonts from those used for screen display, can result in some loss of fidelity from the screen to the printed page:

- QuickDraw places text glyphs on the screen at whole screen-pixel intervals, whereas a high-resolution printer has much smaller pixels and can therefore provide much finer placement on the printed page. If your application specifies the use of fractional glyph widths, the spacing of the text on the screen can be awkward but it more accurately reflects the optimum layout of the printed text. Alternatively, specifying integer glyph widths gives more pleasing screen results because the characters are drawn with regular pixel spacing, but the results on the page can be typographically unacceptable. See the discussions of fractional glyph width in the chapters "QuickDraw Text" and "Font Manager" in this book for more information.

- Printer drivers attempt to reproduce faithfully the text formatting as drawn by QuickDraw on the screen, including keeping the same intended character spacing, line breaks, and page breaks. However, because printers can have resident fonts that are different from the fonts that QuickDraw uses, because the drivers may handle text layout somewhat differently than QuickDraw, and because font metrics do not always scale linearly, fidelity may not always be achieved. Typically, identical line breaks and page breaks can be maintained, but character spacing can be noticeably different.

Other complications result from the fact that high-resolution printers use *deferred printing,* in which the document to be printed is first converted into a spool file in picture-file format, and it is the picture file rather than the original document that is printed. This can result in loss of certain display features that picture files do not support, such as the following:

■ The `grayishTextOr` transfer mode cannot be used for printing. See the discussion of transfer modes in the chapter "QuickDraw Text" in this book.

■ You cannot pass `DrawText` (or `StdText`) more than 255 bytes of text at a time when printing. `DrawText` and `StdText` are documented in the chapter "QuickDraw Text" in this book.

Some of the most difficult problems result from the fact that printer drivers replace the QuickDraw bottleneck routines `StdText` and `StdTxMeas` (by changing the `grafProcs` field of the printing graphics port) to allow printing to function with QuickDraw calls, whereas certain script systems use different modifications (trap patches) to those same routines to perform contextual formatting. Printer drivers that print from spool files can then interact with QuickDraw in several ways that may cause complications:

■ Some drivers call QuickDraw twice: once to create a spool file for printing, and once again to unwind the spooling. If the text is contextually transformed during spooling, the transformation must not be repeated during unwinding.

■ Some drivers may not call QuickDraw at all, meaning that necessary contextual transformations might not be made at all.

■ Some drivers may call QuickDraw re-entrantly, such as when displaying a status message during printing.

To avoid these problems, printer drivers should call the Script Manager Print Action routine whenever they change the `grafProcs` field. For more information on the Print Action routine, see the discussion on writing device drivers in *Inside Macintosh: Devices.*

To accommodate the special contextual formatting needs of 1-byte complex script systems, WorldScript I patches the QuickDraw routines `StdText`, `StdTxMeas`, `MeasureText`, and the Font Manager procedure `FontMetrics`. There are Script Manager routines that allow you to modify or replace those patches if your text has additional needs not met by the WorldScript I routines. To allow for the extra complications that may occur during printing, WorldScript I allows you to define separate entry points or even separate routines for printing as opposed to screen display. See the discussion on replacing a script system's default routines in the chapter "Script Manager" in this book, and the description of WorldScript I in the appendix "Built-in Script Support."

Text Input

Typically, your application accepts text input from the user through the keyboard. The Macintosh script management system allows you to accept text input in any script system, and to switch easily among input script systems.

Keyboard input is a complex process that involves conversion of hardware keypresses to software **raw key codes,** then to **virtual key codes,** and finally to character codes. Subsequent display of those input characters on the screen involves conversion of character codes to the glyphs of a font, and the drawing of those glyphs on the screen. As noted under "Separation of Tasks" beginning on page 1-4, text input and text display are completely independent of each other.

The conversion of keypresses to character codes is complex because the Macintosh computer has to support many different physical keyboards and many script systems. The conversion of raw key codes to virtual key codes accommodates the spectrum of keyboards; the conversion of virtual key codes to character codes accommodates the spectrum of script systems.

For 1-byte script systems, characters are generated directly from keypresses. For 2-byte script systems, the large number of characters makes direct keyboard input impractical; those systems provide input methods to make text input more convenient.

Keyboards and Key Translation

Every Macintosh keyboard has a specific physical arrangement of keys. An example is shown in Figure 1-52. The figure shows the physical arrangement of keys on the domestic (U.S.) layout of the Apple Keyboard II. It also shows the virtual key codes produced when each key is pressed, as well as the character generated (for U.S. system software) by each key.

Figure 1-52   Apple Keyboard II (domestic layout)

Other keyboards produce a similar set of virtual key codes, although the keys and their codes may be arranged differently. Apple supports at least 13 separate physical keyboards, listed in the appendix "Keyboard Resources" in this book. All can produce a set of hardware-independent virtual key codes, which translate directly into the characters of any script system. That process is called **key translation.**

As far as the application is concerned, text input for all keyboards and for all script systems is hardware-independent. Except for a few minor hardware-specific characteristics, the function of the keyboard is completely determined by a script system's keyboard-layout ('KCHR') resources. Tables within the keyboard-layout resource specify the characters produced by each key in combination with each modifier key (Command, Shift, Caps Lock, Control, and Option).

Figure 1-53 illustrates the process of key translation. A keypress initially produces a raw key code. The keyboard driver uses the hardware-dependent key-map ('KMAP') resource to map the raw key code into a hardware-independent virtual key code and to set bits indicating the state (up or down) of the modifier keys. It then calls the Event Manager KeyTranslate function.

If the optional key-remap ('itlk') resource is present, KeyTranslate uses it to remap certain key combinations on certain keyboards before performing additional processing. The key-remap resource transforms this information based on which keyboard is in use. It reintroduces hardware dependence because certain writing systems, languages, and regions need subtle differences in layout for specific keyboards. Generally, the key-remap resource affects only a few keys.

The KeyTranslate function then uses the current script's keyboard-layout resource to map the virtual key code and modifier state into a character code. KeyTranslate returns the character code, and the keyboard driver posts the key-down event into the event queue. The application receives the original virtual key code and a character code in the message field of the event record, and modifier-key information in the modifiers field of the event record.

Figure 1-53   Key translation

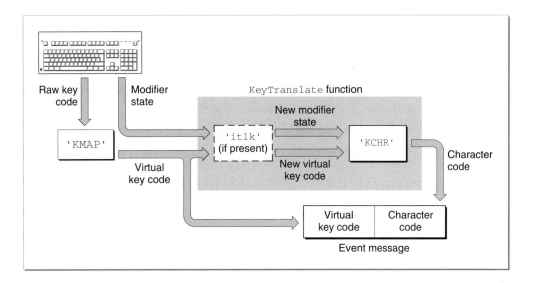

The `KeyTranslate` function is described in the chapter "Event Manager" in *Inside Macintosh: Macintosh Toolbox Essentials.* For additional information on the `KeyTranslate` function and the keyboard-layout resource, see the appendix "Keyboard Resources" in this book.

Dead keys

The keyboard-layout resource also handles dead keys, by means of additional subtables. A **dead key** is a key combination that has no immediate effect, but sets a state that affects the results of the next keypress (typically, the generation of one or two characters). Dead keys are commonly used to generate accents and accented characters. Dead-key processing is discussed in more detail in the appendix "Keyboard Resources" in this book. ◆

Font and Keyboard Synchronization

Whenever your application displays text as it is being entered at the keyboard, it needs to keep the font script coordinated with the keyboard script (see "Font Script and Keyboard Script" beginning on page 1-51). The upper half of Figure 1-54 shows an example of font and keyboard synchronization with the user entering the characters for *Nihongo* when the font script corresponds to the keyboard script, which is Japanese. The lower half of Figure 1-54 provides an example of the characters that are displayed when the user enters the same characters when the font script does not match the keyboard script. If the two scripts don't match, the results are meaningless to the user.

Figure 1-54   Font script and keyboard script synchronization

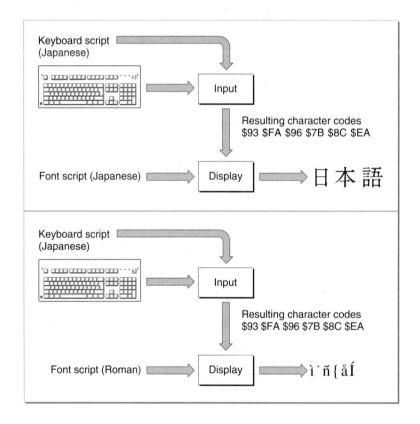

You use the Script Manager KeyScript procedure to set the keyboard script when, for example, the user chooses a new font from your Fonts menu or when the user clicks in an area of text that has a font different from the current one. The Operating System automatically changes the keyboard script (or keyboard layout or input method) when the user chooses a new one from the Keyboard menu (see Figure 1-62 on page 1-106). When that happens you need to set the font script to equal the keyboard script.

The Operating System also automatically changes the keyboard script (or keyboard layout or input method) when the user presses certain key combinations, as specified by the keyboard-swap ('KSWP') resource. When that happens you should set the font script to equal the keyboard script.

You can force a particular keyboard layout to be used with your application by using the Script Manager to define the default keyboard layout for a script system and then calling KeyScript.

For more information on setting the font script and keyboard script, see the discussion on making keyboard settings and the description of the KeyScript procedure in the chapter "Script Manager" in this book. For more information on the keyboard-swap resource, see the appendix "Keyboard Resources" in this book.

Handling Keyboard Equivalents

Many applications support keyboard commands or keyboard equivalents to menu commands. This can be a problem in a multiscript environment. Be careful of these issues in the keyboard equivalents that you allow:

- Avoid keyboard equivalents that use the Space bar in combination with the Command key and other modifier keys. Command–Space bar and Command–Option–Space bar are already commonly used for switching among script systems and keyboard layouts. See the discussion of the KeyScript procedure in the chapter "Script Manager" and the description of the keyboard-swap resource in the appendix "Keyboard Resources" in this book.

- When the Command key is pressed, some characters—such as the period or question mark—cannot be produced on certain keyboard layouts. To make Command-key handling work in these cases, it may be necessary to use the virtual key code to determine which character code *would have been produced* if the Command key had not been pressed. For more information, see the discussion of special uses for the KeyTranslate function in the appendix "Keyboard Resources" in this book.

- If your application extends the set of standard Macintosh modifier-plus-key combinations for specific purposes, your keyboard equivalents might not function properly in all script systems. Be sure to supply alternative methods—such as menu or dialog-box items—for gaining access to such features.

Input Methods

Script systems for ideographic writing systems such as Japanese cannot simply use a larger keyboard or multiple dead keys for effective text input. The sheer numbers of their characters demand a more complex solution, such as providing ways to convert phonetic text into ideographic text and vice versa. Most script systems with large character sets provide for the complex parsing of phonetic sequences to produce ideograms and character clusters.

Automatic conversion of phonetic glyphs into final representations is performed by an input method. For example, the Japanese script system supplements the keyboard by providing software for transcribing Kana (phonetic Japanese) into ideographic Kanji. Each Kanji character can correspond to more than one possible Kana sequence, and vice versa. The input method must grammatically parse sentences or phrases of Kana text (which has no word separations), and select the best combination of Kanji and Kana characters to represent that text.

Entry and Conversion

When a user types a character, one kind of input method opens a window (called a **floating input window** or **bottomline input window**) at the bottom of the screen for text entry; see Figure 1-55. In Japanese, the user can type using either Roman or Kana characters. When the converted glyphs are in the window, the user can freely cut and paste or convert them to any of the other subscripts.

Figure 1-55   Bottomline input window for Japanese input method

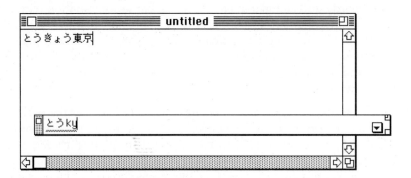

The Text Services Manager supplies an interface for input methods that use **inline input.** In inline input, the user types directly into an **active input area** within a document, as shown in Figure 1-56. Conversion then occurs within the active input area.

Figure 1-56   Active input area (underlined) for inline input

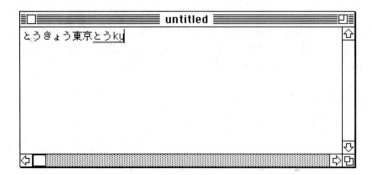

Input methods are often extended so that glyphs may be converted in extremely precise ways. For example, in the Japanese script system, when the text is converted to Kanji, the user has the option of changing any individual phrase: lengthening it, shortening it, or selecting different possible interpretations. All of the commands that perform these changes have both mouse and keyboard equivalents. Once the user presses the Return key, the text is entered as if it had been typed directly from the keyboard.

Differences Among Script Systems

In Japanese and Chinese input methods, the principal conversion is from Roman or other phonetic input to **Han** (Chinese) characters. In Japanese the input can be Romaji (Roman), Hiragana (phonetic), or Katakana (phonetic); the output is Kanji (Chinese characters). In Chinese the input can be **Pinyin** (Roman) or **Zhuyinfuhao** (phonetic; also called **Bopomofo**), and the output is Hanzi (Chinese characters). Chinese and Japanese use a semi-automatic conversion to Han characters that requires user confirmation.

The Korean script system's input method converts from Jamo (phonetic) to Hangul (clusters of Jamo). Transcription to Hanja (Chinese characters) is optional. Furthermore, the Korean input method uses a completely automatic conversion from Jamo to Hangul; user confirmation is not required.

Figure 1-57 illustrates the process of constructing Hangul from Jamo during bottomline input. Note that an added Jamo can appear in various positions (beside, beneath, and so on) relative to the Jamo or Hangul that it is added to.

Figure 1-57   Bottomline input in Korean

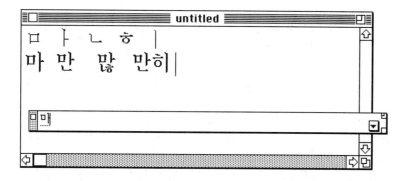

To gain the greatest acceptance worldwide, your application should support text input, and preferably inline input, in 2-byte script systems. For additional information on input methods, inline input, and input-method dictionaries, see the chapters "Text Services Manager" and "Dictionary Manager" in this book.

Text Manipulation

The Macintosh Operating System and Macintosh script management system implement certain script features transparently. For example, your application may not need to know that its dialog boxes can accept Japanese text. However, if your application actually manipulates the text of any language—as any word processor certainly does—it needs access to text-handling information that varies from script system to script system.

For example, to perform word selection and line-breaking, your application may need routines to determine word boundaries in any language. To sort text, it may need routines that sort acording to language-specific rules, and possibly also routines that perform case conversion or strip diacritical marks according to language-specific rules. Do not assume that all languages or regions have the same rules or conventions; use Text Utilities and Script Manager routines to handle different conventions.

Note that the user can affect which of the available script-system resources are used to control text manipulation such as sorting, number formatting, and date and time formatting. See "User Control of Script Settings" beginning on page 1-107.

This section discusses routines that perform a variety of script-aware text manipulations including sorting strings; formatting dates, times, and numbers; analyzing characters; searching and modifying text; and finding word boundaries and line breaks. Most of these topics are described more fully in the chapters "Text Utilities" and "Script Manager" in this book.

Note

The script management system does not address all possible localizable text issues. There is other information, not covered in a script's international resources, that may vary from locale to locale—such as formats for addresses, postal zone codes, and telephone numbers. You should place all such information in resources for ease of localization. ◆

Sorting Strings

Comparing strings can be an intricate operation that involves subtle issues. Even for English, determining the sorting order cannot be done by a simple table look-up or comparison of character-code values. Furthermore, sorting rules vary not just among script systems but among the individual languages or regions within a script system.

Every script system—and every language-specific variation of a script system—has information specifying how its text is to be sorted. That information is in the script's string-manipulation (`'itl2'`) resource. The Text Utilities provides routines for comparing two strings for sorting purposes. Some routines work with Pascal strings, others with generalized **text strings** (defined by pointer and length). Some are script-aware, some are not. The script-aware routines take into account the sorting rules of the current script system or any script system that you explicitly specify, and can address these sorting factors:

- primary and secondary sorting order

- expansion and contraction of characters

- ignorable characters

- case-conversion and stripping of diacritical marks

Other special cases, such as expansion of abbreviations that requires dictionary lookup, may be beyond the capability of the script management system.

In sorting lists of strings that may be from more than one script system, keep these points in mind:

- If you are sorting strings from different script systems into a single list, the ordering relationship among the scripts as well as the sorting rules within each script are important. The script-sorting (`'itlm'`) resource that is part of system software contains tables that define the sorting relationship among all defined script systems. Text Utilities functions use that information to help you create a sorted list of strings in more than one script system.

- If you are sorting strings from different languages within a single script system, you may or may not want to sort the strings into groups by language. If you do, you can determine the ordering relationship between the languages from the the script-sorting resource. Text Utilities functions use that information to help you create a sorted list of strings in more than one language.

- If you need to sort strings in exactly the same way that the Macintosh file system does, there are Text Utilities routines that perform that type of sorting. The sorting order is fixed, and it is independent of any script system or language. It should be used only for operations internal to your application, not for user display of sorted filenames or other text strings.

- Uppercase characters and diacritical marks affect sorting and searching, and conventions for their handling vary among script systems and languages. Text Utilities routines allow you to sort according to the rules of each script or language, and to take into account or disregard case and diacritical marks.

Introduction to Text on the Macintosh

Formatting Dates, Times, Numbers, and Symbols

Dates, times, numbers, and symbols are common types of specialized strings whose formats vary widely around the world. Each script system defines how its times, dates, numbers, and other symbols are to be defined and formatted in its numeric-format ('itl0'), long-date-format ('itl1'), and tokens ('itl4') resources.

Dates and Times

Figure 1-58 shows two different Finder displays of the same filenames and modification dates. The upper display uses Arabic date formats, Arabic month names (with theGregorian calendar), Arabic numerals, and a right-to-left primary line direction. The lower display is exactly the same, except with U.S. date formats, English month names, western numerals, and a left-to-right primary line direction. (The changes were made with control panel selections; see "User Control of Script Settings" beginning on page 1-107.)

Figure 1-58   Filenames and dates in Arabic and U.S. formats (Arabic system script)

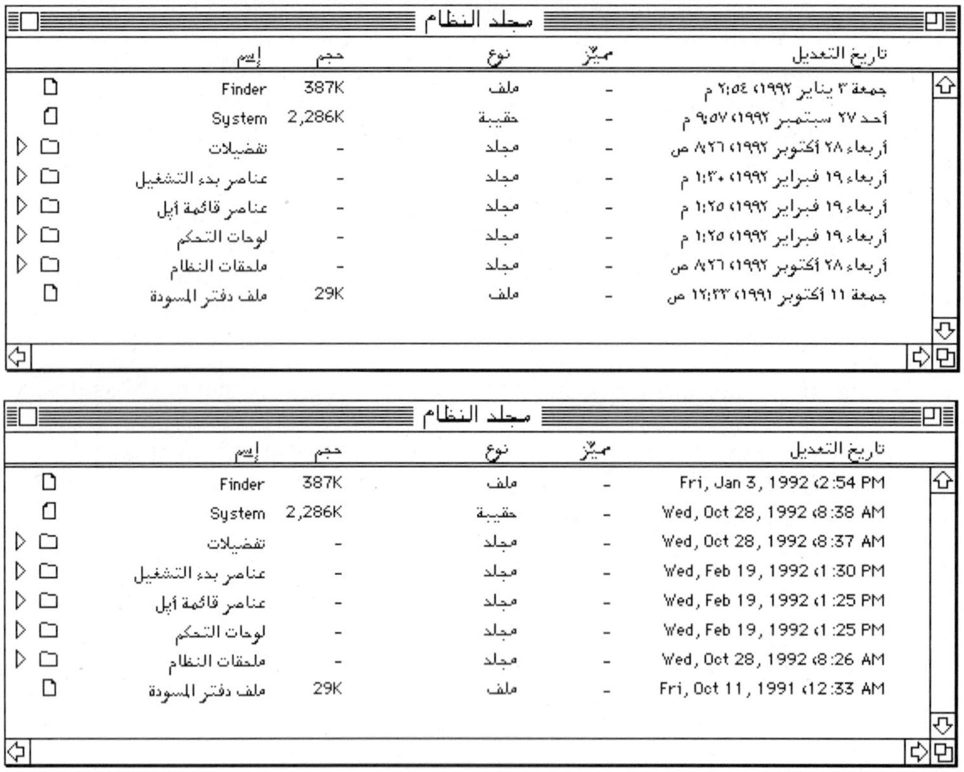

The Text Utilities include a number of routines for converting and formatting date and time strings on the Macintosh. These routines allow you to specify each element of the date and time formats, including the number of digits used for each numeric element (for example, 3/01/90 or 3/1/90), the names of the months and the days of the week, and other characteristics such as the order of the elements and the use of a.m. and p.m. instead of a 24-hour clock.

Be careful about abbreviating the names of the weekdays (for instance, in English *S, M, T, W, Th, F,* and *S*). In Hebrew, for example, the names all begin with the same character, so the English convention would not be useful. Use instead the Text Utilities routines that give you the abbreviated versions provided by each script system.

Multiple calendars may be available on some Macintosh systems. The time-formatting and date-formatting routines in the Text Utilities are generalized enough that they can handle other calendar systems. The Gregorian calendar is the standard Macintosh calendar that is used in most of the world, but other calendars are also supported. See the description of the long-date-format resource in the appendix "International Resources" in this book for a list of defined calendar types.

Numbers and Symbols

Western numerals (*1, 2, 3,* and so forth) are not universal, and the decimal separator is not always the period. The formats of numbers vary widely. The Japanese writing system, for instance, uses the standard ASCII Western digits, 2-byte encodings of the same Western digits, and 2-byte Japanese number characters in two forms.

To accommodate differences in number and currency formats around the world, the Text Utilities provide routines that separate the presentation of numeric values from their internal representation. They allow a script system or your application to define separately how positive numbers, negative numbers, and zero values are presented. They allow you to specify what separators, digits, text annotations, marks (such as +), and literals (such as brackets or parentheses) can appear in numbers, and what kinds of padding can be used. In addition, they allow you to define how to represent positive and negative exponents for scientific notation. Each script system's numeric-format (`'itl0'`) and tokens (`'itl4'`) resources contain information used for formatting numbers.

Currency formats include the specification of the currency symbol (for example, $, £, or DM) and whether it precedes or follows the value. Each script system's numeric-format resource specifies formats for currency.

Use the regional forms of symbols such as the bullet (center dot, •). Tokens that allow you to define these symbols in a language-independent fashion are found in each script system's international resources; use the Script Manager to gain access to those tokens.

Note

Units of measure should be appropriate for the region you are targeting. For example, *lines per inch* is meaningless in the metric world. Units of measurement can be specified as metric or imperial (inches and miles). Each script system's numeric-format resource indicates the preferred measurement unit. You can use the Operating System Utilities function `IsMetric` to determine the appropriate unit of measure for the current script system. See *Inside Macintosh: Operating System Utilities.* ◆

Analyzing Characters

Analyzing characters is another common type of text-manipulation task. The Script Manager provides functions that let you analyze the size and type of individual characters. For example, with script systems that use 2-byte characters, you may need to determine what part of a character a single byte represents. In either 1-byte or 2-byte systems, you may need to know what type of character a particular character code represents. Character-type information is contained in a script system's string-manipulation ('itl2') or encoding/rendering ('itl5') resource.

For example, when searching for a single 1-byte character in text that may contain 2-byte characters, it is important not to mistake part of a 2-byte character for the character you are seeking. You can also determine whether a particular character is a letter, number, or punctuation mark, or whether or not it is uppercase. This information can be useful, for example, to filter input into specialized text fields. Also, for example, because several uppercase letters in the Cyrillic and Roman script systems are identical in appearance, you can detect an unwanted mixture of Cyrillic and Roman characters.

The Text Utilities provide a function that locates sequences of Roman characters (or characters of any other subscript) within non-Roman text. Use this routine when you want to separate out Roman characters into their own style runs, so that they can be formatted independently of the surrounding non-Roman text.

Searching, Modifying, and Converting Text

The Text Utilities provide several script-aware routines that you can use to modify the contents of strings or convert text from one form to another. You can use these routines on strings of any script system; the script-specific information they need is in the script's string-manipulation ('itl2'), tokens ('itl4'), encoding/rendering ('itl5'), or transliteration ('trsl') resource.

For modifying strings, there are routines to

- convert case and strip diacritical marks from characters (such as for sorting)

- truncate a string to make it fit into a specified area on the screen

- search for a character sequence in a string and replace it with a different sequence (accounting for both 1-byte and 2-byte characters)

When searching, note that the text of some script systems can have accents or other diacritical marks that are considered optional. In Hebrew, for example, you may want to give the user the option to have search procedures ignore vowel and cantillation marks, because they are infrequently used in everyday writing. Note, however, that your application would have to provide this capability on its own; the Text Utilities stripping routines do not strip vowel or cantillation marks.

Different script systems have their own rules for dictionaries and hyphenation references. In searching text, your routines must be able to ignore text from script systems other than those to which the dictionaries and hyphenation references apply. As usual, it is your application's responsibility to track the script system of the text you manipulate; the script management system does not.

If you need to truncate a string, use the regional form of the ellipsis to indicate the truncation; different symbols may be expected in different languages. The Script Manager and the Text Utilities have routines that help you truncate strings and insert the proper symbol for an ellipsis.

Macintosh Human Interface Guidelines has guidelines for implementing intelligent cut-and-paste in your application. If the user cuts an entire word and pastes it in another location or document, you should make sure that the pasted word has proper word delimiters at its new location, and that extra word delimiters are not left at the location it was cut from. Applying intelligent cut-and-paste across all script systems requires complete understanding of word delimiters for each one. The Macintosh script management system does not provide support for this. However, the guidelines presented in *Macintosh Human Interface Guidelines* can work for any script system that uses spaces as word delimiters, and each script system sets a flag that you can access to determine whether it uses spaces. See the descriptions of script-variable selectors in the chapter "Script Manager" in this book.

Compilers, assemblers, and scripting-language interpreters usually parse sequences of characters to **tokens,** abstract entities that stand for variables, symbols, and quoted literals. Each script system provides tokenizing information in its tokens resource, for use by the Script Manager. Using the Script Manager you can create tokens recognizable by a parser in any script system.

The Script Manager also provides support for **transliteration,** the automatic conversion of text from one phonetic form or subscript to another within a single script system. In the Roman script system, this simply means case conversion. In Japanese, Chinese, and Korean script systems, it means the phonetic conversion of characters from one subscript to another. Script-specific information for transliteration is in a script's string-manipulation or transliteration resource. With the Script Manager you can convert, for example, from Hiragana to Romaji and Romaji to Katakana in Japanese; from Bopomofo to Roman in Chinese; and from Roman to Jamo, Jamo to Hangul, Hangul to Jamo, and Jamo to Roman in Korean.

Finding Word Boundaries and Line Breaks

Finding word boundaries for word-selection and for line-breaking is a common, though often difficult, text-manipulation task. Word-selection methods differ among script systems. For example, the Thai script does not use spaces between words; the Thai system must detect word boundaries by parsing. The Text Utilities provide a procedure that you can use to determine word boundaries, in order to support double-clicking, highlighting of search targets, and so on. You can also use the same procedure to find word boundaries for line breaking; see "Text Layout" on page 1-71. The procedure works for all script systems and uses information in the script's string-manipulation (`'itl2'`) resource.

Script Systems in Use

When a version of Macintosh system software is created for a particular country or region, its system script supports the writing system of that country or region. In addition, the system software's text strings are usually translated, and its icons and other graphical elements may be altered to fit the cultural conventions of the region. This process of adapting software to local use is called *localization*.

Localization of system software is performed by Apple Computer, Inc. In constructing a localized system, many different combinations of script capability and text translation are possible. For example, one localized version of Hebrew system software might use Hebrew text strings and Israeli currency, date, and calendar formats. Another might leave all text strings in English and use Roman formatting. In both, of course, the system script would be Hebrew. In another example, localized system software for India might possibly use Gurmukhi (an Indic script system) as the system script but leave all text strings in English, using the low-ASCII characters in the Gurmukhi character set.

This final section of the chapter discusses how a localized system is presented to a user. It shows the locations of the files and resources that make up the system script and any auxiliary scripts. It then describes how you can modify existing script systems or make additional auxiliary script systems available to the user. The section then summarizes how the user can switch among the available script systems. Finally, it shows how the user can alter the configurations of the script systems on the computer, including possibly selecting as script-system defaults resources that you provide.

More information on localization and localized versions of system software can be found in *Guide to Macintosh Software Localization.*

Installing and Enabling Script Systems

A user receives a script system in one of two forms: as a system script, already installed in the user's System file and System Folder; or as a secondary script consisting of a set of files that, if not present in the System file already, need to be installed before they can be used.

Initialization

The Operating System initializes the Script Manager at startup, and the Script Manager, along with WorldScript I and WorldScript II, initializes all installed script systems. If a script system is properly installed and successfully initialized, it becomes **enabled** (made available for use by the Script Manager and applications). For more information, see the discussion on testing for the Script Manager and script systems in the chapter "Script Manager." ◆

Components of the System Script

Because localization of system software involves more than installing script-system resources—for example, system and Finder text strings need to be translated—the user typically does not install a system script. However, if the user has two separate systems with two different localized versions of system software, the user can change system scripts by using the "Update Install" command in the installer to completely replace one localized version's system script (and all other localized resources) with those of the other localized version.

Once installed, the system script and associated files and resources are organized in the System Folder as follows (see Figure 1-59):

■ The essential resources that make up the system script are in the System file. This includes the script's 'itlb' resource and any of the following resources specified by the 'itlb' resource: 'itl0', 'itl1', 'itl2', 'itl4', 'itl5', 'trsl', 'itlk', 'KCHR', 'kcs#', 'kcs4', and 'kcs8'.

■ The System file also contains an international configuration resource ('itlc') and a script-sorting resource ('itlm').

■ The Keyboard resources needed for each type of supported keyboard ('KMAP' and 'KCAP'), though not considered part of any script system, are in the System file.

■ If the system script is a 1-byte complex script system or a 2-byte script system, the Extensions folder contains a script extension: either WorldScript I or WorldScript II, respectively.

■ If the system script is a 2-byte script system, the Extensions folder contains one or more input-method files. The Extensions folder may also contain one or more dictionary files needed by the input method.

■ Depending on its individual needs or version, the system script may also have an extension file of its own, a file of type 'scri' in the Extensions folder.

■ The Fonts folder contains the fonts needed by the system script.

■ If the system script provides a control panel for the user, its control panel file is in the Control Panels folder. If the control panel allows the user to save script settings, there is a script preferences file in the Preferences folder to hold those settings. (The file is created the first time the user changes any settings.) Note that this control panel and preferences file are separate from the Text, Numbers, and Date & Time control panels described under "User Control of Script Settings" beginning on page 1-107.

■ If the system script needs additional files, they are in the System Folder.

Figure 1-59 System-script components in the System Folder

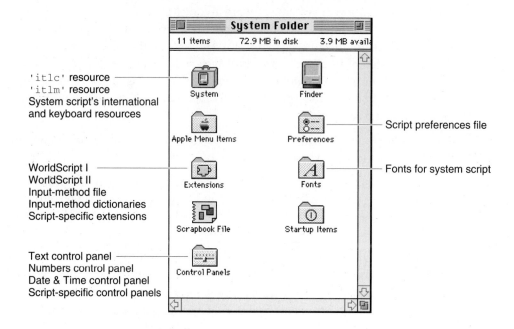

Components of Auxiliary Scripts

Auxiliary scripts consist of a set of resources and files mostly similar to those of a system script. The essential resources that make up the auxiliary script—an international bundle resource and any other international and keyboard resources needed by the script—may have been installed in the System file during system localization or may be contained in a file that is shipped separately from system software or applications. Other files are parallel to the files associated with a system script, as shown in Figure 1-59. (The closer a script system is to the U.S. version of the Roman script system, the fewer resources and files it has.)

To install a separately shipped secondary script from the Finder, the user can simply drag the contents of a folder containing the script's resources and files to the System Folder. The Finder automatically installs the files and resources properly, as follows:

■ The Finder installs the resources from the script file into the System file. That includes the script's 'itlb' resource and any of the following resources specified by the 'itlb' resource: 'itl0', 'itl1', 'itl2', 'itl4', 'itl5', 'trsl', 'itlk', 'KCHR', 'kcs#', 'kcs4', and 'kcs8'.

■ The Finder places all system extension files, including input-method files, dictionary files, and files of type 'scri', into the Extensions folder. This includes the WorldScript I or WorldScript II script extensions, if included.

- The Finder places all fonts for the script system into the Fonts folder.

- The Finder places any control panel documents for the script system into the Control Panels folder. (Once the user saves any new settings, a script preferences file is created in the Preferences folder.)

- The Finder places all other files into the System Folder.

If a script system has been installed but not yet enabled (if the computer has not been restarted), the user can take the script system's resources back out of the System file. (When the System file is opened, the Finder displays any script files that can be moved out of the System file.) Once the script system has been enabled, its resources can no longer be removed from the System file with the Finder.

Disabling script systems at startup

Holding down the Option–Space bar key combination at startup disables all (non-Roman) auxiliary scripts. This allows the user to remove auxiliary scripts from the System file that would normally have been enabled and thus impossible to remove from the Finder.

Holding down the Shift key at startup prevents system extension files from executing—including WorldScript I and WorldScript II. If the system script requires a script extension, system messages may not display properly. ◆

Apart from installing a script system itself, users can always move fonts into and out of the Fonts folder, and input methods into and out of the Extensions folder.

Installing Modifications to a Script System

Applications that are written to take advantage of the Macintosh script management system function correctly regardless of the localized version of Macintosh system software under which they run. However, it is also possible to tailor an individual application for a specific script system or set of scripts, or for a specific regional variation of the system script or other script.

To do so may require installing a new script system or a modified set of resources to replace those of a currently installed script system. (This is especially true if your target region is not already supported by a localized version of system software.) Either way usually involves modifying the System file. The Apple Computer system software licensing policy forbids shipping a modified System file, so you cannot install your replacement resources in a System file and ship it with your application. However, there are three other approaches you can take:

- If you create individual modified versions of an installed script system's resources—in order to implement region-specific sorting or formatting conventions—you can attach those resources to your application and have them replace the existing script system's resources whenever your application is running.

This method requires no modifications to the System file at all. For specific instructions, see the discussion on replacing a script system's default international resources in the chapter "Script Manager" in this book.

■ If you want individual resources permanently installed in the System file, you can have the user run the Installer to install your resources. Contact Macintosh Developer Technical Support for information on how to use the Installer. The user will then be able to select or deselect your resources as defaults through the Text, Numbers, and Date & Time control panels. See "User Control of Script Settings" beginning on page 1-107.

■ If you want to provide a complete script system with your application, you can ship it as a separate file in a folder along with fonts and any other assocated files. The user can then install it as an auxiliary script as described earlier, under "Components of Auxiliary Scripts."

Your script system must be complete or it will not be enabled at startup. What constitutes a complete script system is described under testing for script systems in the chapter "Script Manager" in this book. The formats of the resources you need to include are described in the appendixes "International Resources" and "Keyboard Resources" in this book.

In general, it is not feasible to replace a system script, except by doing an "Update Install" from another complete localized system, as described on page 1-101. Although the user can replace individual resources in the System file by using a resource editor such as ResEdit, it is not possible to directly replace a system script with an auxiliary script because a system script requires an international configuration ('itlc') resource, which is not part of any auxiliary script. Furthermore, replacing the system script is not the same as localizing all of the system software. A system script should support the system software it is shipped with, meaning that the language and icons of system menus, dialog boxes, and messages should reflect the system script. Merely replacing the system script does not accomplish that.

How the User Switches Among Script Systems

The script system for display of text is controlled by the application or by the system, based on which graphics port is active, which font is the current font, and what the states of the font force flag and international resources selection flag are.

The script system for text input, the keyboard script, is controlled by the user, either explicitly through a menu selection, or implicitly through choosing a font or selecting or clicking in displayed text of a particular script system. This section summarizes how the keyboard script is selected; for more complete information, see the discussions of keyboard settings and synchronization in the chapter "Script Manager" in this book.

In any localized version of system software in which more than one script system is present, a small icon called a **keyboard icon** appears on the right side of the menu bar. Figure 1-60 shows the keyboard icon for the Korean script system, to the left of the application icon and to the right of the Help menu icon.

Figure 1-60   Menu bar with keyboard icon

This symbol indicates which keyboard script, as represented by a keyboard layout or input method, is currently being used for text input. For example, the Arabic keyboard is represented by a crescent, the Hebrew keyboard by a Star of David, and common European keyboards by flags or other appropriate symbols. The Japanese input method is represented by an Apple icon in front of a rising sun; Chinese by a coin (Simplified) or a pot called a *Ding* (Traditional); Korean by the circular yin-yang symbol. The default Roman keyboard is represented by a blue diamond, except on versions of system software localized for the United States, in which it is represented by a U.S. flag. Figure 1-61 gives some examples of keyboard icons and input-method icons. Color Plate 4 shows a larger set of keyboard icons in color.

Figure 1-61   Keyboard icons and input-method icons

The keyboard icon serves as the title for the Keyboard menu; the user can click the keyboard icon to pull down the Keyboard menu. The Keyboard menu shows all keyboard layouts and input methods for all available keyboard scripts. The user makes a selection from the Keyboard menu in order to change the keyboard script, or to select among different keyboard layouts or input methods within a given script. See Figure 1-62.

Figure 1-62   Keyboard menu

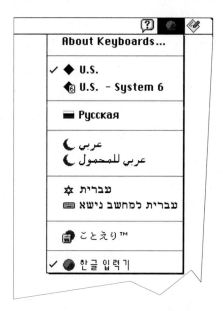

The Operating System provides keyboard equivalents for switching among script systems. In system software localized for the U.S., for example, if the user presses Command–Space bar, the Operating System switches the keyboard script to the "next" script system, meaning the default keyboard layout or input method for the next script system listed (down) the Keyboard menu. If the user presses Command–Option–Space bar, the Operating System switches to the next keyboard layout or input method within the current script system.

To see how the current keyboard layout functions, the user can select the Key Caps desk accessory. Whenever the keyboard script or keyboard layout changes, the Key Caps display changes to reflect the new character set and its arrangement on the keyboard. See Figure 1-63.

Figure 1-63   Arabic Key Caps

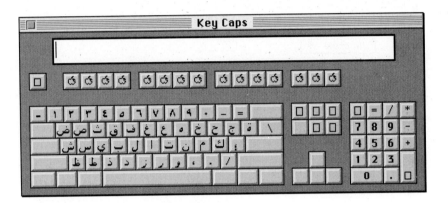

Application-Controlled Switching

Your application must synchronize the current font with the keyboard script whenever you are displaying characters as the user enters them. If the user changes fonts, you need to automatically change the keyboard script to correspond to the new font. Conversely, if the user changes keyboard scripts, you need to change the font appropriately before displaying the next character typed. Failure to do so can lead to incorrect text display. See "Font and Keyboard Synchronization" on page 1-90. ◆

User Control of Script Settings

The script management system provides three control panels that allow the user to change the settings of certain script-system features and to save the settings across system restarts.

The **Text control panel**, shown in Figure 1-64, is available on non-U.S. versions of system software. It allows users to set the text behavior of any enabled script system, and may allow the user to set the system direction, the state of the font force flag, the caret style, and the rate of caret blinking. (Some of the settings are not available unless certain script systems are present.)

The appearance of the dialog box varies with the version of localized system software; Figure 1-64 represents a Text control panel for Hebrew system software localized to have all text strings in English.

Figure 1-64　　Text control panel

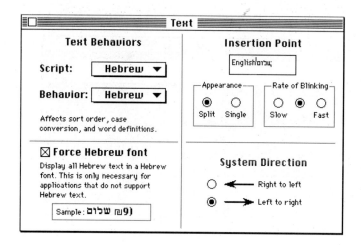

- The Text Behaviors settings control which string-manipulation ('itl2') resource is used for sorting, case conversion, and word selection for the selected script system (including the system script). The choices are limited to the installed string-manipulation resources for the enabled script systems (including the Roman string-manipulation resource, which is always present). If more than one choice is available and the user changes this setting, the new setting is saved in the itlbSort field of the script's international bundle resource.

- The System Direction setting controls the primary line direction and alignment for all text and interface elements controlled by the system. The system direction may be set to either left to right or right to left. The user's selection is immediately reflected in the alignment of elements in all system and Finder dialog boxes and in all menus. It changes the setting of the system global variable SysDirection. The setting is also saved in the itlcSysFlags field of the system's international configuration resource. (This control appears only if at least one bidirectional script system is enabled.)

- The font force flag may be set to either TRUE or FALSE, which affects the setting of the Script Manager variable accessed through the smFontForce selector for the GetScriptManagerVariable function. The font force flag allows display of non-Roman text in an application that normally supports Roman text only. See the chapter "Script Manager" in this book. The setting made by the user is saved in the itlcFontForce field of the system's international configuration resource. (This control appears only if the system script supports font forcing.)

■ The Insertion Point setting sets the caret style. The caret may appear either as a single caret or as a dual (split) caret (see Figure 1-46 on page 1-78 for an example). The setting made by the user is reflected in the value of the Script Manager general flags, accessed through the smGenFlags selector for the GetScriptManagerVariable function. See the chapter "Script Manager" in this book. The setting made by the user is saved in the itlcFlags field of the system's international configuration resource. (This control appears only if at least one bidirectional script system is installed.)

The rate of caret blinking (slow, medium, or fast) affects the insertion point in text fields. The user's setting is saved in parameter RAM.

The **Numbers control panel,** shown in Figure 1-65, allows users to specify the basic number and currency formats for the system script. User settings made through this control panel are saved in the system script's numeric-format ('itl0') resource.

Figure 1-65   Numbers control panel

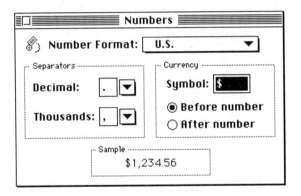

■ The Number Format setting controls which numeric-format ('itl0') resource is used for default number, currency, and short-date formats. The choices are limited to the installed numeric-format resources for the system script. If the user changes any of the default settings, a new setting called *custom* is created in the Number Format popup menu, and is saved as a new numeric-format resource for the system script; its ID is then saved in the itlbNumber field of the system script's international bundle resource.

■ The Separators settings allow the user to override the default decimal separator and thousands separator for the system script. Suggested separators are presented in the popup menus for the settings, although the user can enter any 1-byte character for either separator. The settings made by the user are saved in the decimalPt and thousSep fields of the system script's custom numeric-format resource.

■ The Currency settings allow the user to specify a currency symbol of up to three 1-byte characters or a single 2-byte character, and to choose whether the symbol precedes or follows a currency number. The settings made by the user are saved in the currSym1 through currSym3 fields of the system script's custom numeric-format resource.

The **Date & Time control panel,** shown in Figure 1-66, allows users to set the current date and time and to specify formatting preferences for both. The settings made with this control panel affect the display of dates and times by the system and Finder and by the Text Utilities date- and time-formatting routines, when the resources of the system script are used (that is, as long as the international resources selection flag is TRUE).

Figure 1-66   Date & Time control panel

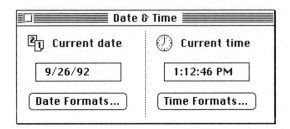

Format settings are made with individual Date Formats and Time Formats dialog boxes. Custom user settings made through these dialog boxes are saved as new numeric-format ('itl0') and long-date-format ('itl1') resources for the system script.

The Date Formats dialog box sets date formats, as shown in Figure 1-67.

Figure 1-67   Date Formats dialog box (from Date & Time control panel)

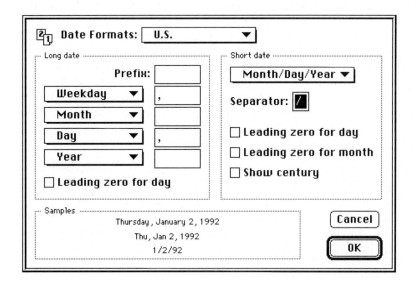

■ The Date Formats setting allows the user to select a long-date-format ('itl1') and numeric-format ('itl0') resource to be used for date formatting. The choices are limited to the installed pairs of numeric-format and long-date-format resources for the system script. If the user changes any of the default settings, a new setting called "custom" is created in the Date Formats popup menu, and is saved as a new pair of numeric-format and long-date-format resources for the system script; their IDs are then saved in the itlbNumber field and itlbDate field of the system script's international bundle resource.

■ The Long date settings allow the user to select what elements to include in a long date, what order they should be in, and what separators should be between them. The Long date settings also allow the user to specify the use of a leading zero for the day number in a long date. The settings made by the user are saved in the days, months, suppressDay, lngDateFmt, st0 through st4, and dayLeading0 fields of the system script's custom long-date-format resource.

■ The Short date settings allow the user to select the order of date elements in a short date, and to specify a single (1-byte) character as separator. The Short date settings also allow the user to specify whether to use a leading zero for day number or month number, and whether to show the century. The settings made by the user are saved in the dateOrder, dateSep, and shortDateFmt fields of the system script's custom numeric-format resource.

The Time Formats dialog box sets time formats, as shown in Figure 1-68.

Figure 1-68   Time Formats dialog box (from Date & Time control panel)

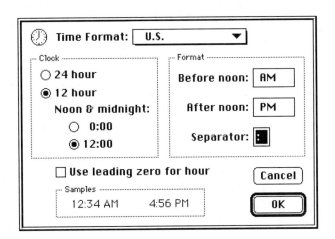

■ The Time Format setting allows the user to select a numeric-format ('itl0') resource to be used for time formatting. The choices are limited to the installed numeric-format resources for the system script. If the user changes any of the default settings, a new setting called "custom" is created in the Time Formats popup menu, and is saved as a new pair of numeric-format and long-date-format resources for the system script; their IDs are then saved in the itlbNumber field and itlbDate field of the system srcipt's international bundle resource.

■ The Clock settings allow the user to choose a 12- or 24-hour time cycle, and to specify whether midnight (and noon, if a 12-hour cycle) is considered to be hour 0 or hour 12. The settings made by the user are saved in the `timeCycle` field of the system script's custom numeric-format resource.

■ The Format settings allow the user to specify a 1-byte character as separator for the time elements, and to specify morning and evening trailing strings (such as *AM* and *PM*) for the 12-hour cycle. The current separators and trailing strings are presented in the fields for the settings, but the user can enter any 1-byte character for the separator and any string of up to 4 bytes for either trailing string. The settings made by the user are saved in the `timeSep`, `mornStr`, and `eveStr` fields of the system script's custom numeric-format resource.

Script-specific control panels

In addition to the control panels described in this section, individual script systems may provide their own control panels for other purposes, such as allowing a user to select a custom calendar system, an associated font, or a set of numerals (ASCII or non-ASCII). The results of those selections may be kept in a script preferences file. ◆

TextEdit

2

Contents

TextEdit

TextEdit is a collection of routines and data structures that give your application basic text formatting and editing capabilities, including text display in multiple scripts. TextEdit manages fundamental text processing tasks on text limited to 32 KB. You can use the TextEdit routines in many kinds of applications, such as spreadsheets, online (data-entry) forms, online advertising programs, simple programming-language or text-file text editors, electronic mail programs, drawing and painting programs with simple text-editing features, and electronic note cards. However, TextEdit was not designed to be used to implement word-processing applications with complex support that manipulate lengthy documents.

To use TextEdit and the information provided in this chapter, you should be familiar with the basic concepts and structures behind QuickDraw and how it handles text—particularly points, rectangles, graphics ports, fonts, and character style—the Event Manager, the Window Manager—particularly update and activate events—the Font Manager, the Script Manager, and Text Utilities.

For information on non-text features of QuickDraw, see *Inside Macintosh: Imaging*. For information on the Event Manager and the Window Manager, see *Inside Macintosh: Macintosh Toolbox Essentials*.

This book includes chapters that cover the Font Manager, Text Utilities, the Script Manager, and QuickDraw Text. Although these chapters pertain to TextEdit, the only chapter in this book that you need to read as a prerequisite to TextEdit is "Introduction to Text on the Macintosh."

This chapter describes how to use TextEdit to perform a range of editing and formatting capabilities including

- inserting new text

- selecting and highlighting ranges of text

- deleting selected text and possibly inserting it elsewhere, or copying text without deleting it

- replacing selected text

- translating mouse activity into text selection

- scrolling text within a window, including automatically scrolling text that is not visible but is affected by the editing activity

- changing the characteristics of text, including font family, style, and size

- customizing some TextEdit behavior

About TextEdit

TextEdit was originally designed to handle editable text items in dialog boxes and other parts of the system software. Although TextEdit has been enhanced to provide more text-handling support since its inception, especially in its handling of multi-script text, it retains some of its original limitations. TextEdit was not originally intended to manipulate lengthy documents or text requiring more than rudimentary formatting. For example, TextEdit does not handle tabs. (Your application can provide support for tabs to supplement TextEdit.)

However, TextEdit handles some of the cumbersome tasks that a text processor needs to perform, and provides you with an alternative to writing your own text processor. For example, when you use TextEdit routines to edit text, your application does not need to allocate memory for blocks of text that change dynamically during the editing session because TextEdit takes care of this for you. When the user selects a range of displayed text of a TextEdit edit record, TextEdit recognizes this and responds by highlighting the text.

TextEdit relies on the Script Manager, QuickDraw, and Text Utilities to handle text correctly, and eliminates the need for your application to call these routines directly. Because TextEdit supports text from more than one script system and manages scripts having different primary line directions, you can use its routines and features to develop applications that support multiple languages.

TextEdit uses Text Utilities routines: the `FindWordBreaks` procedure for determining word breaks and the `StyledLineBreak` function for determining line breaks. TextEdit also allows you to customize how word boundaries and line breaks are defined.

TextEdit and Standard Macintosh Features

Because TextEdit routines follow the Macintosh user interface guidelines, using them ensures the presentation of a consistent user interface in your application. Your application can rely on TextEdit to support these standard features instead of having to implement them directly:

- selecting text by clicking and dragging with the mouse

- double-clicking to select words, which are defined according to the rules of the script system in which they are written

- line breaking, which prevents a word from being split inappropriately between lines when text is drawn

- extending or shortening a selection range by Shift-clicking
- highlighting of the current text selection, or display of a blinking vertical bar at an insertion point
- cutting, copying, and pasting within and between applications
- the use of more than one font, size, color, and stylistic variation from character to character within a single block of text
- display of text in more than one language on a single line

Multistyled and Monostyled Text

Text is rendered in a certain font, style, size, and color. These aspects of text are collectively referred to as **character attributes.** TextEdit supports the display of text in various character attributes (different fonts, styles, sizes, and colors) within the context of a single edit record.

Text that uses a variety of fonts, styles, sizes, or colors is referred to in this chapter as *multistyled text* to distinguish it from text that uses a single font, style, size, and color, which is referred to as *monostyled text*.

TextEdit lets you boldface, italicize, underline, outline, condense, extend, and shadow text. Using TextEdit routines, you can change the font family and type size of the entire text of an edit record (or a selected range of text that the user has chosen or the application has set). You can even increase the type size incrementally across a range of text containing various sizes, for example, so that all 10 point text is changed to 12 point and all 12 point text is changed to 14 point. If your application uses multistyled TextEdit and allows users to select fonts, TextEdit displays text correctly in all scripts. Apart from the TextEdit routines that deal with multistyled text exclusively, you can use all of the TextEdit routines to simplify and manage your application's text editing tasks for both multistyled and monostyled text.

Note
In the original *Inside Macintosh* documentation that describes TextEdit, the term *face* is used to refer to the following text style attributes: bold, italic, underline, outline, condense, extend, and shadow. The term *style* is now used instead of face to refer to these attributes. ◆

TextEdit organizes multistyled text into style runs. The characters comprising a **style run** are contiguous in memory and are all displayed in the same font, size, color, and script as well as style. TextEdit tracks style runs in the data structures that are allocated for a multistyled edit record and uses this information to correctly display multistyled text.

Figure 2-1 shows four style runs in a line of text.

Figure 2-1   Style runs in a line of text

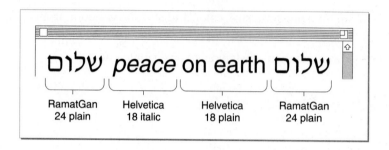

TextEdit supports **mixed-directional text:** the combination of scripts with left-to-right and right-to-left directional text within a single line. Figure 2-2 shows an example of Hebrew and Roman text on the same line. The two runs of Hebrew text have a right-to-left direction, and the Roman text direction is left to right.

Figure 2-2   Mixed-directional text display

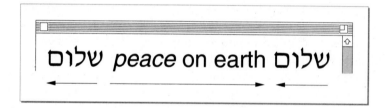

Font and Keyboard Script Synchronization

TextEdit handles synchronization of the **font script,** the script system that corresponds to the font of the current graphics port, and the **keyboard script,** the script system used for keyboard input, for multistyled and monostyled text.

For monostyled text, the primary script system determines whether or not TextEdit synchronizes the font script and the keyboard script, based on the value of a flag in the script system's international bundle resource (`'itlb'`). TextEdit uses this flag, without requiring any action on the part of your application.

For multistyled text, TextEdit always synchronizes the font script and the keyboard script. (If the font script at the selection range or insertion point is the same as the keyboard script, then this font is used.) The following sections explain the conditions that determine whether TextEdit matches the keyboard script to the font script or vice versa. TextEdit synchronizes *the keyboard script with the font script* under the following conditions:

■ When your application calls a TextEdit routine to change the font of a text selection or to process a mouse-down event in text as either an insertion point or a selection. This means, for example, that if a user types Arabic text followed by Roman text and clicks in the Arabic text, the keyboard adjusts and changes to Arabic without the user's needing to change the keyboard manually. Similarly, if a user clicks in the Roman text, the keyboard changes to Roman without the user's altering the keyboard.

■ If the selection range encompasses text—if it is not an insertion point—then TextEdit uses the font corresponding to the first character of the selected text to determine the keyboard script. When an insertion point falls on a script boundary, the keyboard is synchronized to the font of the character preceding the boundary (in storage order). (A **selection range** is a series of characters, selected by the user or the application, where the next editing operation is to occur. Although the character representations are contiguous in memory, they can be discontinuous on the display screen when the text is bidirectional. For more information, see "The Selection Range, the Insertion Point, and Highlighting in TextEdit" on page 2-10.)

TextEdit synchronizes *the font script with the keyboard script* under the following condition:

■ When your application calls a TextEdit routine to input a character and if the keyboard script is different from the font script at the selection range (or insertion point). If a font was selected and never used, thus remaining in the scrap that TextEdit uses for character attributes (null scrap) and if the font script coincides with the keyboard script, then this font is used. Otherwise, TextEdit searches through the preceding fonts in the style run table until it locates a font that corresponds to the keyboard. If one does not exist, then it uses the application font. For more information about the null scrap, see "The TextEdit Private, Null, and Style Scraps" on page 2-15.

Cutting, Copying, and Pasting Text

TextEdit provides routines that let you cut, copy, and paste text

■ within a single edit record

■ between edit records within an application

■ between an application and a desk accessory

■ across applications

You use the same routines to cut and copy monostyled and multistyled text. There are, however, separate routines for pasting monostyled and multistyled text. For multistyled text, the TextEdit routines preserve any stylistic variation along with the cut or copied text in order to restore it when you paste the text.

The TextEdit User Interface

This section describes the TextEdit user interface, that is, how TextEdit displays text on the screen and the methods it uses to communicate information about that text to an application user. It explains some of the processes that TextEdit performs automatically for your application, including how TextEdit uses highlighting or a caret to identify where the next editing operation is to occur, how TextEdit handles line measurement for your application, and how TextEdit uses buffering to handle 2-byte characters. This section also covers some aspects of the user interface that your application can control through TextEdit routines, such as the kind of text alignment and the use of buffering to enhance performance.

The Selection Range, the Insertion Point, and Highlighting in TextEdit

Depending on the purpose of an application, a user might select a range of text to be edited or the application might set the selection range. In either case, the selected text becomes the current selection range. TextEdit uses a byte offset to identify the position of a character in the text buffer of an edit record, and an edit record includes fields that specify the byte offsets of the characters in the text buffer that correspond to the beginning and the end of the current selection range in the displayed text. (See "An Overview of the Edit Record" on page 2-16 for more about edit records.)

When the byte offset values for the beginning and the end of the selection range are the same, the selection range is an **insertion point.** TextEdit marks an insertion point with a blinking **caret** in the form of a vertical bar (|).

TextEdit uses highlighting to display a selection range. Because TextEdit supports mixed-directional text, the selection range can appear as discontinuous text. Displayed text is highlighted according to the storage order of the characters. When multiple script systems having different line directions are installed, a continuous sequence of characters in memory may appear as a discontinuous selection when displayed. Figure 2-3 shows how TextEdit highlights a range of text whose displayed glyphs are not contiguous, although their corresponding byte offsets are contiguous in memory. In this example, the primary line direction is left to right.

Figure 2-3   Discontinuous highlighting display

About TextEdit

TextEdit provides a function that lets you to turn **outline highlighting,** the framing of text in a selection range, in an inactive window, on or off. See Figure 2-4. (For more information about outline highlighting, see "TEFeatureFlag" on page 2-107.)

Figure 2-4   Outline highlighted text selection in background window

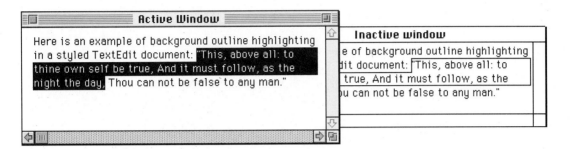

Caret Position and Movement

This section describes how TextEdit displays and moves a caret. For more information, see the discussion of caret handling in the chapter "Introduction to Text on the Macintosh" in this book.

TextEdit marks the position in the displayed text where the next editing operation is to occur with a caret. When TextEdit pastes text into a record, it positions a caret after the newly pasted text on the screen. TextEdit uses a single caret for text that does not include mixed directions. When TextEdit displays a single caret in unidirectional text and the user presses an arrow key to move the caret left or right across the text, TextEdit moves the caret in the direction of the arrow key.

When the text includes mixed directions, TextEdit uses either a moving caret or a dual caret, depending on the value of a Script Manager flag. For example, if this flag specifies a moving caret, TextEdit displays the caret at the screen location where the next glyph is to appear, based on the text direction of the keyboard script.

If this flag specifies a dual caret, TextEdit displays a high caret and a low caret, each measuring half the line's height. The high caret is displayed at the screen location associated with the glyph that has the same direction as the primary line direction, and the low caret is displayed at the screen location associated with the glyph that has a different direction from the primary line direction.

When TextEdit displays a dual caret on a direction boundary, only the primary caret moves in the direction of the arrow. Figure 2-5 shows a sequence of two Right Arrow keypresses and their impact on caret display and movement in a line containing mixed-directional text. In this example, the primary line direction is right to left.

Figure 2-5   Caret movement across a direction boundary

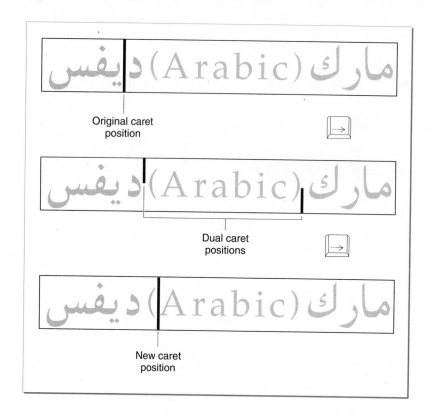

In the first instance of the text segment, the caret is positioned within the Arabic text. When the user presses the Right Arrow key once, the insertion point is positioned on a direction boundary and the caret splits into a dual caret. When the user presses the Right Arrow key again, TextEdit displays a single, full caret after the parenthesis in the Roman text. Because the caret position is again in the middle of a style run, TextEdit no longer uses the dual caret.

Note

TextEdit currently deviates from this model for caret movement in monostyled left-to-right text (displayed in a non-Roman font) on any primary right-to-left script system. On the Arabic script system, for example, it is possible to display the low-ASCII Roman characters from an Arabic font. If a user presses the arrow keys to move through these characters, the caret moves in the opposite direction of the arrow. ◆

Vertical movement of the caret is less complex. When the user presses the Up Arrow key, the caret moves up by one line, even in lines of text containing fonts of different sizes. When the caret is positioned on the first line of an edit record, and the user presses the Up Arrow key, TextEdit moves the caret to the beginning of the text on that line, at primary caret position 0. (This position corresponds to the visible right end of a line when the primary line direction is right to left and to the left end of the line when the primary line direction is left to right.)

Similarly, when the user presses the Down Arrow key, the caret moves down one line. When the caret is positioned on the last line of an edit record, and the user presses the Down Arrow key, TextEdit moves the caret to the end of the text on that line (that is, the visible left end of a line when the primary line direction is right to left and to the right end of a line when the primary line direction is left to right).

Note

TextEdit does not support the use of modifier keys, such as the Shift key or the Option key, in conjunction with the arrow keys. ◆

If spaces at the end of a text line extend beyond the view rectangle, TextEdit draws the caret at the edge of the view rectangle, not beyond it. Whether TextEdit displays a caret at the beginning or end of a line when a mouse-down event occurs at a line's end depends on the current caret position and the value in a field (`clikStuff`) of the edit record. TextEdit sets this field to reflect whether the most recent mouse-down event occurred on the leading or trailing edge of a glyph.

For example, if the mouse-down event occurs on the leading edge of a glyph, TextEdit displays the caret at the caret position corresponding to the leading edge of that glyph. If the mouse-down event is on the trailing edge of a glyph, TextEdit displays the caret at the beginning of the next line. For more information about determining a caret position, see the sections that discuss caret handling in the chapters "Introduction to Text on the Macintosh" and "QuickDraw Text" in this book.

Text Alignment

TextEdit allows you to specify the alignment of the lines of text, that is, their horizontal placement with respect to the left and right edges of the text area or destination rectangle. The different types of alignment that TextEdit supports accommodate script systems that are read from right to left, as well as those that are read from left to right. The types of alignment supported are

- default alignment (positions the text according to the line direction of the system script. It can be either left or right. Line direction is the direction in which text in a particular language is written and read. The English language has a rightward, or left-to-right, line direction. Arabic and Hebrew have a [primarily] leftward, or right-to-left, line direction.)

- center alignment (centers each line of text between the left and right edges of the destination rectangle)

- right alignment (positions the text along the right edge of the destination rectangle)

- left alignment (lines up the text with the left edge of the destination rectangle)

If your application requires justified alignment, you can use the QuickDraw routines that support full justification; TextEdit does not support justified alignment. See the chapter "QuickDraw Text" in this book for more information.

Line Measurement

TextEdit measures a line of text appropriately for all script systems by removing any trailing white space from the end of it, taking the line direction into account. It uses the QuickDraw `VisibleLength` function to exclude trailing white space, based on the script system, the text direction, and the primary line direction. For more information about the behavior of `VisibleLength` for various script systems, see the chapter "QuickDraw Text" in this book.

An anomaly exists, however, in the way TextEdit draws at the end of a line. When the primary line direction of a script system is right to left (for instance, on a Hebrew system), when the alignment is left or center, and when spaces are entered in a right-to-left font, TextEdit measures spaces at the end of the line and therefore may draw the text beyond the edge of the view rectangle. The caret, however, remains in view and is pinned to the left edge of the view rectangle.

This anomaly also exists when the primary line direction of a script system is left to right and the alignment is center. In this instance, TextEdit measures spaces at the end of the line, and as more spaces are added (and, therefore, measured), the visible text in the line is drawn out of view beyond the left edge of the view rectangle. The caret, however, remains in view and is pinned to the right edge of the view rectangle.

Text Buffering

TextEdit uses two methods of text buffering; one method, which is automatic, is used to handle 2-byte characters properly. The other method, which you can enable or disable, improves performance in relation to how TextEdit handles input of 2-byte characters.

For the first method, which is automatic, TextEdit relies on the Script Manager. The Script Manager handles 2-byte characters properly, and TextEdit takes advantage of this. If a 2-byte character, such as a Kanji character, is typed, TextEdit buffers the first byte until it processes the second byte, at which time it displays the character. The internal buffer that TextEdit uses for a 2-byte character is unique to each edit record. For example, TextEdit can buffer the first byte of a 2-byte character in a record, then the application can call the TextEdit `TEKey` procedure for another edit record. While `TEKey` processes the character for the second edit record, the first byte of the 2-byte character remains in the first edit record's buffer until TextEdit processes the second byte of that 2-byte character, and then displays the character.

The second method of text buffering enhances performance, and you can turn it on or off through the TextEdit function, `TEFeatureFlag`. In this case, TextEdit uses a global buffer—it differs from the `TEKey` procedure's internal 2-byte buffer—that is used across all active edit records. These records may be in a single application or in multiple applications. Because of this, you should exercise care when you enable the text-buffering capability in more than one active record; otherwise, the bytes that are buffered from one edit record may appear in another edit record.

■ Ensure that buffering is not turned off in the middle of processing a 2-byte character. To guarantee the integrity of your record, it is important that you wait for an idle event before you disable buffering or enable buffering in a second edit record.

■ When text buffering is enabled, ensure that `TEIdle` is called before any pause of more than a few ticks—for example, before `WaitNextEvent`. A possibility of a long delay before characters appear on the screen exists—especially in non-Roman systems. If you do not call `TEIdle`, the characters may end up in the edit record of another application.

If you enable text buffering for performance enhancement on a non-Roman script system and the keyboard has changed, TextEdit flushes the text of the current script from the buffer before buffering characters in the new script.

The TextEdit Private, Null, and Style Scraps

There are three scrap areas that TextEdit uses exclusively: the TextEdit private scrap, the TextEdit null scrap, and the TextEdit style scrap. The TextEdit routines use all of these scraps to hold transient information.

TextEdit uses the **private scrap** for all cut, copy, and paste activity whether the text is multistyled or monostyled. The private scrap belongs to the application. When the text is multistyled, TextEdit also copies the text to the Scrap Manager's desk scrap.

TextEdit uses the **null scrap** to store character attribute information associated with a null selection (an insertion point) or text that is deleted when the user backspaces over it. The null scrap belongs to the multistyled edit record. Character attribute information stored in the null scrap is retained until it is used, for example, when applied to newly inserted text, or until some other editing action renders it unnecessary, such as when TextEdit sets a new selection range. A number of routines that deal with multistyled text check the null scrap for character attribute information and, if there is any, apply it to newly inserted text when character attributes for that text are not available.

When you cut or copy multistyled text, memory is allocated dynamically for the **style scrap** and the character attribute information is copied to it. Your application can also use the style scrap for other purposes. For example, to save and restore multistyled text both the text and the associated character attribute information must be preserved; you can save character attributes associated with a range of text in the style scrap. Also, you can create a style scrap record and store character attribute information in it to be applied to inserted text. Your application can create as many style scraps as it needs. For more information, see the discussion of the style scrap record under "Data Structures" on page 2-64.

As part of TextEdit initialization, `TEInit` creates the private scrap and allocates a handle to it. TextEdit creates and initializes a null scrap for a multistyled edit record when an application calls `TEStyleNew` to create the edit record. (The null scrap remains throughout the life of the edit record: it is disposed of when the application calls `TEDispose` to destroy the edit record and release the memory allocated for it.) TextEdit allocates memory used for the style scrap dynamically when your application calls a routine that uses it.

Note
Because these scraps are in RAM, they are volatile, and a power failure can cause the data in a scrap to be lost. ◆

An Overview of the TextEdit Data Structures

To edit text on the screen, TextEdit maintains information about where the text is stored, where to display it, and the text style. This information is contained in a record that defines the complete editing environment. You can allocate a **monostyled edit record** to contain text that is set in a single font, size, and style, or you can allocate a **multistyled edit record** to contain text with attributes that can vary from character to character.

An Overview of the Edit Record

An edit record, which is the primary data structure that TextEdit uses, carries text storage, display, and editing information. When you allocate an edit record, you specify where the text is to be drawn and where it is to be made visible. The **destination rectangle** is the area in which the text is drawn, and the **view rectangle** is that portion of the window within which the text is actually displayed. (For a complete discussion of destination and view rectangles, see the QuickDraw chapters in *Inside Macintosh: Imaging*.) Figure 2-6 shows two sets of destination and view rectangles. The view rectangles are shaded and defined by dotted lines. The text is drawn in the destination rectangle; the part of it that is displayed is defined by the view rectangle.

Figure 2-6   Destination and view rectangles

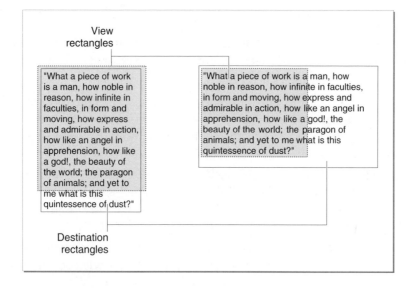

The edit record includes fields that point to these rectangles. In addition to the two rectangles, the edit record also contains

- a handle to the text to be edited

- the current selection range that determines exactly which characters are to be affected by the next editing operation

- the alignment of the text, as left, right, or center

- for multistyled edit records, a handle to a subsidiary record, the style record, containing the character attributes used to portray the text. This style record, itself, contains subsidiary data structures.

Related Data Structures

Stemming from the main TextEdit edit record, relationships exist among the rest of the TextEdit data structures.

When TextEdit creates an edit record, the record contains a field that stores the handle to the dispatch record. The dispatch record is an internal data structure whose fields, referred to as hook fields or hooks, contain the addresses of routines that TextEdit uses internally, for example, to measure and draw text, or to determine a character's position on a line. These routines, called hook routines, determine the way TextEdit behaves. You can use a TextEdit customization routine to replace the address of a default hook routine with the address of your own customized routine. For example, you can provide a routine to be used for word selection that defines word boundaries more precisely for any script system.

When you allocate a monostyled edit record, the edit record, a handle to the text, and a single subsidiary internal data structure, the dispatch record, are created. However, when you allocate a multistyled edit record, a number of additional subsidiary data structures are created to support the text styling capabilities and the display of text in multiple languages.

For a multistyled edit record, the edit record contains a handle to the style record. The style record stores the character attribute information for the text, and contains a handle to the style table, which has one entry for each distinct set of character attributes. Each entry in the style table is a style element record. The style record also contains a style run table, which is an array that gives the start of each style run, and an index into the style table. The style run table array identifies the byte offset of the starting character to which the character attributes, stored in the style table, apply.

The style record contains two other handles: a handle to the line-height table and a handle to the null style record. The line-height table provides vertical spacing and line ascent information for the text to be edited with one element for each line of an edit record. A line number is a direct index into this array. The null style record consists of a reserved field and a handle to the style scrap record.

The style scrap record, which is part of the null scrap, stores character attribute information associated with a null selection to be applied to inserted text. It also holds character attribute information associated with a selected range of multistyled text when the character attributes are to be copied, or the text and its attributes are to be cut or copied.

Part of the style scrap record is the scrap style table which has a separate element for each style run in the style scrap record. The character attribute information for each of these elements is stored in a scrap style element record.

Several TextEdit routines use a text style record to pass character attribute information between the application and the routine.

Figure 2-7 shows the two data structures that TextEdit creates for monostyled text. Figure 2-8 shows the data structures that TextEdit creates for multistyled text and how they are related; these data structures consist of the two records that TextEdit also creates for monostyled text plus additional structures needed to store character attribute information. See Figure 2-15 on page 2-66 for a version of the data structures including fields.

Figure 2-7   Relationship between the TextEdit data structures for monostyled text

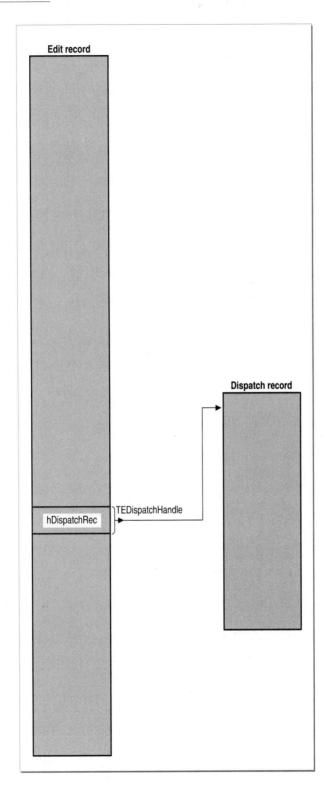

Figure 2-8   Relationships among the TextEdit data structures for multistyled text

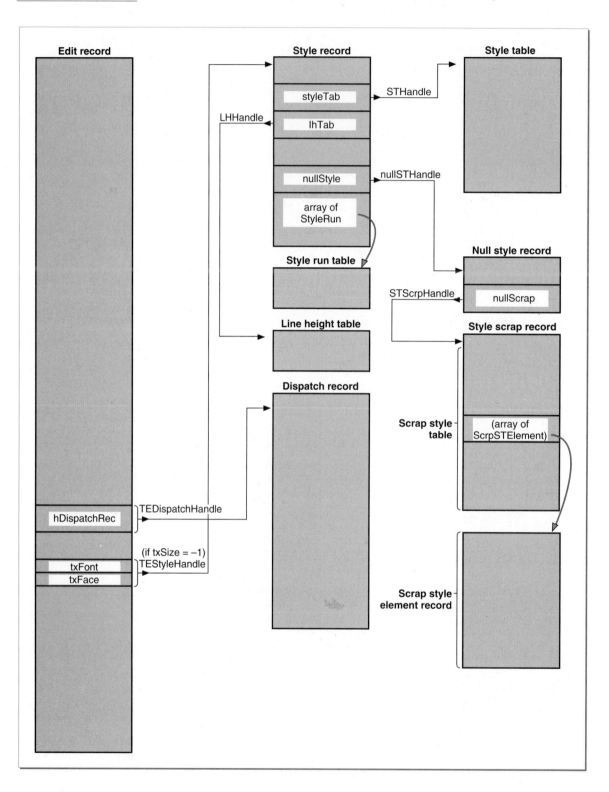

Using TextEdit

This section describes how to initialize TextEdit and use the TextEdit routines and data structures to display text and implement editing features in an application. It also describes how to customize the behavior of TextEdit, for example, to better suit the requirements of your application and the script systems it supports.

- "Getting Started With TextEdit" describes how to display static text in a box, create an edit record for modifiable text, set the text of an edit record and scroll it, set its insertion point, and dispose of the edit record.

- "Responding to Events Using TextEdit" describes how to handle mouse-down, key-down, and idle events.

- "Moving Text In and Out of Edit Records" describes how to cut, copy, and paste text and its character attributes within or across applications, or between an application and a desk accessory.

- "Text Attributes" describes how your application can check the current attributes of a range of text to determine which ones are consistent across the text. It also describes how you can manipulate the font, style, size, and color of a range of text.

- "Saving and Restoring a TextEdit Document, and Implementing Undo" describes how to save to disk the contents of a document created using TextEdit, and restore it when the user opens the document.

- "Customizing TextEdit" describes how to replace the default end-of-line, drawing, width-measuring, and hit test hook routines, use the multi-purpose low-memory global variable `TEDOText` hook routine, customize word selection and automatic scrolling, and determine the length of a line of text.

This section includes sample application-defined routines and code fragments that show some of the ways you can use TextEdit. These examples are provided for illustrative purposes only; they are not meant to be used in applications you write.

Note
For both monostyled and multistyled edit records, the text is limited to 32 KB. Whenever you insert or paste text, you need to ensure that adding the new text does not exceed the 32 KB limit. Your application can check for this limit before you insert or paste text. ◆

Getting Started With TextEdit

You can use TextEdit to display static text, for example, in a dialog box; the TextEdit procedure that you use to do this creates its own edit record. You can use TextEdit to display and manipulate modifiable text, for which purpose you must first create an edit record. This section discusses these two uses of TextEdit. It describes how you create an edit record and bring existing text into its text buffer, then set the text selection range or insertion point, scroll the text, and, finally, release the memory allocated for the edit record when you are finished with it. The topics are described in the following order:

- preparing to use TextEdit
- displaying static text
- creating an edit record
- setting the text of an edit record
- setting the selection range or the insertion point
- scrolling text
- disposing of an edit record

Preparing to Use TextEdit

This section describes two basic tasks that your application needs to perform before using TextEdit. It must

- determine the installed version of TextEdit
- initialize other managers and TextEdit

To determine the installed version of TextEdit, you use the Gestalt Manager, which is fully documented in the chapter "The Gestalt Manager" in *Inside Macintosh: Operating System Utilities*.

You can get information about the current version of TextEdit using the `Gestalt` function with the `Gestalt` selector `gestaltTextEditVersion`, which returns one of the values listed and described below. In this list, a new feature is shown only when it is first introduced in the software, although it is part of TextEdit in succeeding versions. For system software version 6.0.4, different patches were made to TextEdit for different hardware platforms. In these cases, unique values are returned that also identify the hardware.

Returned value	New features	System software/hardware
gestaltUndefSelectorErr	Multistyled TextEdit	Systems before 6.0.4/all hardware
gestaltTE1		System 6.0.4 Roman script system/IIci-family hardware
gestaltTE2	New width measurement hook Script Manager compatible	System 6.0.4 non-Roman script system/IIci-family hardware
gestaltTE3		System 6.0.4 non-Roman script system/all non-IIci family hardware
gestaltTE4	TEFeatureFlag	System 6.0.5/all hardware
gestaltTE5	Text width measurement hook	System 7.0/all hardware

You need to initialize other managers and TextEdit before your application calls any TextEdit routines, including TEInit. First, you initialize QuickDraw, the Font Manager, and the Window Manager, and then TextEdit, in that order. To do this, call the following routines from an initialization procedure that is called from your application's main routine.

```
BEGIN
    InitGraf(@thePort);
    InitFonts;
    InitWindows;
    InitMenus;
    TEInit;
    . . . .
```

In addition to initializing miscellaneous global variables, such as TEDoText and TERecal, the TEInit procedure sets up the private scrap and allocates a handle to it.

Note
You should call TEInit even if your application doesn't use TextEdit so that desk accessories and dialog and alert boxes, which use TextEdit routines, work correctly. ◆

Displaying Static Text

TextEdit provides an easy way for your application to display static text whether or not it uses other TextEdit features to implement editing services. The `TETextBox` procedure displays unchanging text that you cannot edit. You don't create an edit record because the `TETextBox` procedure creates its own edit record, which it deletes when it's finished with it.

The `TETextBox` procedure draws the text in a rectangle whose size you specify in the local coordinates of the current graphics port. You can also specify how text is aligned in the box. Text can be right aligned, left aligned, or centered.

You can use any of the following constants to specify how text is aligned in the box that `TETextBox` creates.

Constant	Description
`teFlushDefault`	Default alignment according to the primary line direction
`teCenter`	Center for all scripts
`teFlushRight`	Right for all scripts
`teFlushLeft`	Left for all scripts

Listing 2-1 shows how to use `TETextBox`. The first parameter is a pointer to the text to be drawn, which is a Pascal string. Because Pascal strings start with a length byte, you need to advance the pointer one position past the beginning of the string to point to the start of the text.

Listing 2-1 Using `TETextBox` to draw static text

```
str    := 'String in a box';
SetRect(r,100,100,200,200);
TETextBox(POINTER(ORD(@str)+1),LENGTH(str),r,teCenter);
FrameRect(r);
```

Creating an Edit Record

To use all other TextEdit routines in your application except the `TETextBox` procedure, first you need to create an edit record. This section discusses how to create an edit record. It also describes

- which type of edit record to use, monostyled or multistyled, and why

- some ways to store the edit record handle that the function returns when you create an edit record

- what to consider when you specify values for the destination and view rectangles when you create an edit record

- how TextEdit initializes those edit record fields that are used differently for monostyled and multistyled edit records, and those that are used the same

The `TEStyleNew` function allocates a multistyled edit record which contains text with character attribute information that can vary from character to character. The `TENew` function allocates a monostyled edit record which contains text in a single font, face, and size. (Before your application calls either of these functions, the window must be the current graphics port.)

If your application supports only monostyled text, use `TENew` to avoid the unnecessary allocation of additional data structures used to store character attribute information for multistyled edit records. You can use `TEStyleNew` in this case also, although it is not recommended.

Both `TENew` and `TEStyleNew` return a handle to the newly created record. Most TextEdit routines require you to pass this handle as a parameter, so your application needs to store it using any of the following methods:

- You can store the edit record handle in a private data structure whose handle is stored in your application window's `refcon` field.

- You can create a record in which to store information about the window, and include a field to store the edit record handle. Listing 2-2 provides an example of this method.

- You can define a variable in your application for each edit record handle, and then use the variable to store the handle.

Listing 2-2 shows a sample document record declaration for an application that handles text files. The document record is an application-specific data structure that contains the handle to the edit record, and any controls for scroll bars.

Listing 2-2   A sample document record

```
TYPE
    MyDocRecHnd  =   ^MyDocRecPtr;
    MyDocRecPtr  =   ^MyDocRec;
    MyDocRec     =
    RECORD
        editRec:       TEHandle;       {handle to TextEdit record}
        vScrollBar:    ControlHandle; {vertical scroll bar}
        hScrollBar:    ControlHandle; {horizontal scroll bar}
    END;
```

To associate an application-defined document record with a particular window, you can set a handle to that record as the reference constant of the window by using the Window Manager procedure `SetWRefCon`. This technique is described further in the chapter "Introduction to File Management" in *Inside Macintosh: Files*.

When you create an edit record, you specify the area in which the text is drawn as the destination rectangle, and the portion of the window in which the text is actually displayed as the view rectangle.

To ensure that the first and last characters in each line are legible in a document window, you can inset the destination rectangle at least four pixels from the left and right edges of the graphics port (20 pixels from the right edge if the window contains a scroll bar or size box).

The destination rectangle must always be at least as wide as the first character drawn. The view rectangle must not be empty; for example, if you do not want any text visible, specify a rectangle off the screen—don't make its trailing edge less than its leading edge.

Editing operations may lengthen or shorten the text. The bottom of the destination rectangle can extend to accommodate the end of the text. In other words, you can think of the destination rectangle as bottomless. The sides of the destination rectangle determine the beginning and the end of each line of text, and its top determines the position of the first line.

Your program should not have a destination rectangle that is wider than the view rectangle if you are displaying mixed-directional text. For example, the Dialog Manager makes the destination rectangle extend twice as far on the right as the view rectangle, so that horizontal scrolling can be used in normal dialog boxes. When the Arabic script system is installed, this extension is disabled, because the text may be right aligned, and therefore out of view. Your application can include the following code to check that the destination and view rectangles have the same width.

```
IF scriptsInstalled > 1 THEN
   IF GetEnvirons (smBidirect)<>0 THEN
      BEGIN
      {make the rectangles the same width}
      END;
```

When you create an edit record, TextEdit initializes the record's fields, based on values in the current graphics port record and the kind of edit record you create. Although most edit record fields are initialized similarly for both monostyled and multistyled edit records, there are some fields that are used differently, and their initial values depend on how they are used.

For a monostyled edit record that you create by calling TENew, the txSize, lineHeight, and fontAscent fields of the edit record hold actual values reflecting the text size, the line height, and the font ascent. Because the text is monostyled, these values apply to all of the text of the edit record.

- The txSize field is set to the value of the current graphics port's text size (txSize) field, which indicates that all text is set in a single font, size, and face.

- The value of the lineHeight field specifies the fixed vertical distance from the ascent line of one line of text down to the ascent line of the next. The line height corresponds to the ascent plus descent for the font and leading to create single-spacing for the lines in the new edit record.

■ The value of the `fontAscent` field specifies how far above the base line the pen is positioned to draw the caret or to highlight the text. For single-spaced text, this is the ascent of the text in pixels (the height of the tallest characters in the font from the base line). The font ascent corresponds to the ascent of the font indicated by the `txFont` and `txSize` fields of the current graphics port.

Note

To adjust the spacing for a monostyled edit record, you can alter the values in the `fontAscent` and `lineHeight` fields of the edit record. ◆

For more information, see the discussion of font measurements in the chapter "Font Manager" in this book.

For a multistyled edit record, `TEStyleNew` initializes the `txSize`, `lineHeight`, and `fontAscent` fields of the edit record to –1. A value of –1 in each of these fields means:

■ `txSize`

The edit record contains associated character attribute information and the `txFont` and `txFace` fields combine to contain the text style record handle for the character attribute information.

■ `lineHeight`

The vertical distance from the ascent line of one line of text down to the ascent line of the next is calculated independently for each line, based on the maximum value for any individual character attribute on that line. These values are stored in the line height table (`LHTable`).

■ `fontAscent`

The font ascent is calculated independently for each line, based on the maximum value for any individual character attribute on that line. These values are stored in the line height table (`LHTable`).

For both multistyled and monostyled records, the following fields are initially set to the same values:

■ The record initially contains no text. The text handle (`hText`) points to a zero-length block in the heap, and the text length field (`teLength`) of the edit record is set to 0. To furnish text to be edited, you use the `TESetText` procedure if you are incorporating existing text and the `TEKey` procedure if the user is entering text.

■ The value of the `just` field determines the alignment of text in the edit record. The default value is `teFlushDefault`, indicating that the alignment is to follow the primary line direction. For languages that are read from left to right, the default value is left; for languages that are read from right to left, the default value is right. To change the alignment of text in the record, you use the `TESetAlignment` procedure.

■ The `selStart` and `selEnd` fields are initially set to 0; this places the insertion point at the beginning of the text.

■ The edit record uses the drawing environment of the graphics port specified by the `destRect` and `viewRect` parameters. These parameters contain the local coordinates of rectangles within the current graphics port, which becomes the graphics port for the new edit record. The text in the new edit record is to have the characteristics of the current graphics port.

Listing 2-3 shows the `MyAddTE` function, which is a sample application-defined function that creates a new multistyled edit record for an existing window. The `TEStyleNew` function call returns a handle to the edit record that it creates. The code stores the handle in the `docTE` variable. The `TEAutoView` procedure call turns on automatic scrolling for the newly created edit record. For a complete discussion of scrolling, see the chapter "Control Manager" in *Inside Macintosh: Macintosh Toolbox Essentials.*

Listing 2-3   Creating a multistyled edit record

```
FUNCTION MyAddTE (myWindow: WindowPtr): TEHandle;
VAR
    destRect, viewRect:  Rect;
    docTE:               TEHandle;
    CONST
    kMaxDocWidth = 576;
BEGIN
    MyGetTERect(myWindow, viewRect); {get TextEdit rectangle}
    destRect := viewRect;
    destRect.right := destRect.left + kMaxDocWidth;
    docTE := TEStyleNew(destRect, viewRect);
    IF docTE <> NIL THEN
        BEGIN
            TEAutoView(TRUE, docTE);
            docTE^^.clikLoop := @AsmClikLoop;
        END;
    MyAddTE := docTE;
END;
```

Specifying the Destination and View Rectangles

When you create an edit record, whether monostyled or multistyled, you specify the area in which the text is drawn as the destination rectangle, and the portion of the window in which the text is actually displayed as the view rectangle.

To ensure that the first and last glyphs in each line are legible in a document window, you can inset the destination rectangle at least four pixels from the left and right edges of the graphics port (20 pixels from the right edge if the window contains a scroll bar or size box).

The destination rectangle must always be at least as wide as the first glyph drawn. The view rectangle must not be empty; for example, if you do not want any text visible, specify a rectangle off the screen—don't make its trailing edge less than its leading edge.

Editing operations may lengthen or shorten the text. The bottom of the destination rectangle can extend to accommodate the end of the text. In other words, you can think of the destination rectangle as bottomless. The sides of the destination rectangle determine the beginning and the end of each line of text, and its top determines the position of the first line.

Your program should not have a destination rectangle that is wider than the view rectangle if you are displaying mixed-directional text. For example, the Dialog Manager makes the destination rectangle extend twice as far on the right as the view rectangle, so that horizontal scrolling can be used in normal dialog boxes. When the Arabic script system is installed, this extension is disabled, because the text may be right aligned, and therefore out of view. Your application can include the following code to check that the destination and view rectangles have the same width.

```
IF scriptsInstalled > 1 THEN
    IF GetEnvirons (smBidirect)<>0 THEN
        BEGIN
        {make the rectangles the same width}
        END;
```

Setting the Text of an Edit Record

When you create an edit record, it doesn't contain any text until either the user enters text through the keyboard or opens an existing document. This section describes how to specify *existing* text to be edited. "Accepting Text Input Through Key-Down Events" on page 2-36 discusses how to insert text that the user enters through the keyboard.

When a user opens a document, your application can bring the document's text into the text buffer of an edit record by calling TESetText. If the text has associated character attribute information, your application also needs to manage it.

There are two ways to specify existing text to be edited. The easier method is to use TESetText, which creates a copy of the text and stores the copy in the existing handle of the edit record's hText field. One of the parameters that you pass to TESetText specifies the length of the text. The TESetText procedure resets the teLength field of the edit record with this value and uses it to determine the end of the text; it sets the selStart and selEnd fields to the last byte offset of the text so that the insertion point is positioned at the end of the displayed text. The TESetText procedure calculates line breaks, eliminating the need for your application to do this.

You can use the second method to save space if you have a lot of text. Using this method, you can bring text into an edit record by directly changing the hText field of the edit record, replacing the existing handle with the handle of the new text. When you do this for a monostyled edit record, you need to modify the teLength field to specify the length of the new text, and then call TECalText to recalculate the lineStarts array and nLines values to match the new text.

Using the second method is somewhat more complicated for multistyled text because TECalText does not update the style run table (StyleRun) properly. To compensate for this, your application needs to perform the following tasks:

■ Before changing the edit record's hText field, reduce the style run table to one entry. Do this by setting the edit record's selStart field to 0 and its selEnd field to 32767, then call TESetStyle.

■ Before calling TECalText, set the start character (startChar) field of the style run table to the length of the new text plus one, that is:

```
TEStyleRec.runs[1] to length(hText)+1
```

Using the same edit record for different pieces of text

Rather than allocate a new edit record for each piece of text you want to edit, you can use the same record to edit different pieces of text. For example, you can create an edit record and either accept user input or call TESetText to incorporate existing text. If you know that you'll want to edit the text again whose handle is currently stored in the hText field, first you need to save the text before you call TESetText, because TESetText uses the same handle, resizing it for the new text, if necessary. ◆

The TESetText procedure doesn't affect the text drawn in the destination rectangle, so call the Window Manager's InvalRect procedure afterward, if necessary. For more information about the InvalRect procedure, see the chapter "Window Manager" in *Inside Macintosh: Macintosh Toolbox Essentials*.

Setting the Selection Range or the Insertion Point

You can use the TESetSelect procedure to specify the selection range or the position of the insertion point as determined by the application. For example, you can use TESetSelect to highlight an initial default value in an application such as an online data-entry form, or to position the caret at the start of the field where you want the user to enter a value. You can also use it to implement a Select All menu command.

You can set the selection range (or insertion point) to any character positions within the text of the edit record corresponding to byte offsets 0 through 32767. To select a range of text, you pass TESetSelect the handle to the edit record along with the byte offsets corresponding to the beginning and the ending characters of the text to be highlighted. The TESetSelect procedure modifies the selStart and selEnd fields of the edit record.

To display a caret at an insertion point, specify the same value for both the selStart and selEnd parameters. To encompass the edit record's entire text block as the selection range, specify 0 as the value of selStart and 32767 as the value of selEnd. You can implement a Select All menu command by specifying the edit record's entire range of text, as shown in the following code fragment, by using the teLength field.

```
iSelectAll:
    TESetSelect(0, myTERec^^.teLength, myTERec);
```

Scrolling Text

Using TextEdit routines, your application can allow the user to control text scrolling through the scroll bars; in this case, you scroll the text by calling a TextEdit procedure. It can also automatically scroll the text of an edit record into view when the user clicks in the view rectangle, and then drags the mouse outside of it, if you enable automatic scrolling through another TextEdit procedure.

To scroll the text when a mouse-down event occurs in a scroll bar, your application needs to determine how far to scroll the text. For example, to vertically scroll the text of a monostyled edit record, you can use the lineHeight field of the edit record to calculate the number of pixels to scroll; you multiply every click in the scroll bar by the number of pixels in the lineHeight field and by the number of lines displayed in the view rectangle. For multistyled text, you need to use the value of the lhHeight field of the line height table for each line in the view rectangle because line height can vary from line to line.

To scroll the text, you call either TEScroll or TEPinScroll specifying the number of pixels to scroll. The only difference between TEScroll and TEPinScroll is that TEPinScroll stops scrolling when the last line is scrolled into the view rectangle.

When the user clicks in the scroll arrow pointing down, you scroll the text up. When the user clicks in the scroll arrow pointing up, you scroll the text down. Passing a positive value to either routine moves the text right and down, passing a negative value moves the text left and up. The destination rectangle is offset by the amount you scroll. For example, the following call scrolls the text of a monostyled edit record up one line.

```
TEScroll(0, -hTE^^.lineHeight, hTE)
```

There are two ways to enable or disable automatic scrolling for an edit record. You can use the TEAutoView procedure or the teFAutoScroll feature of the TEFeatureFlag function. However, neither of these routines actually scrolls the text. To ensure that the selection range is always visible, your application should call TESelView. When automatic scrolling is turned on, TESelView scrolls the selection range into view, if necessary.

Listing 2-3 on page 2-28 creates a multistyled edit record and turns on automatic scrolling for it. It saves the address of the default click loop procedure installed in the edit record's clikLoop field, then replaces it with the address of its own customized click loop routine.

The clikLoop field of the edit record contains the address of a click loop procedure that is called continuously as long as the mouse button is held down. When automatic scrolling is turned on, the default click loop routine determines if the mouse has been dragged out of the view rectangle; if it has, the default click routine scrolls the text using TEPinScroll. For example, if the user clicks in the text and drags the mouse outside of it to the right, the text is automatically scrolled left.

How much the text is scrolled vertically is determined by the lineHeight field of the edit record for a monostyled edit record and by the lhHeight field of the line height table for a multistyled edit record.

Scroll bars are not scrolled automatically with the text if the default click loop routine is used. However, you can replace the default click loop routine with a routine that updates scroll bars. For more information about customizing scrolling, see "Customizing Automatic Scrolling" on page 2-61. For a complete discussion of scrolling, see the chapter "Control Manager" in *Inside Macintosh: Macintosh Toolbox Essentials.*

Disposing of an Edit Record

When your application is completely finished with an edit record, you should release any memory allocated for it by calling `TEDispose`. To continue to refer to the text once you've destroyed the edit record, use the Operating System Utilities `HandToHand` function before you call `TEDispose`. It copies the text (whose handle is stored in the edit record's `hText` field), and returns a new handle to it. (See *Inside Macintosh: Operating System Utilities* for more information.) For a multistyled edit record, you also need to save the character attribute information. If your program retains the original handle to the text stored in the `hText` field after you call `TEDispose`, the handle becomes invalid because the text is removed—the memory used for it is deallocated.

Responding to Events Using TextEdit

This section discusses some of the TextEdit routines that your application can call in response to event notification. You can use TextEdit routines to

- handle idle processing in response to null events (`TEIdle`)
- identify the active edit record in response to an activate event (`TEActivate` and `TEDeactivate`)
- handle mouse-down events (`TEClick`)
- update the destination rectangle in response to an update event (`TEUpdate`)
- handle key-down events (`TEKey`)

Handling a Null Event

Your program needs to call `TEIdle` whenever it receives a null event. If there is more than one edit record associated with an active window, make sure you pass `TEIdle` the handle to the currently active edit record. (See "Activating an Edit Record" in the following section for more information.)

If you have turned on text buffering through the `TEFeatureFlag` function, you should call `TEIdle` before any pause of more than a few ticks—for example, before `WaitNextEvent`. A possibility of a long delay before characters appear on the screen exists—especially in non-Roman systems. Blinking the caret alerts the user to this delay.

To blink the caret at a constant frequency, you should call `TEIdle` at least once through your main event loop—otherwise, the caret blinks irregularly. No matter how often you call `TEIdle`, the time between blinks is never to be less than the minimum interval.

Listing 2-4 shows a sample application-defined procedure, `MyDoIdle`, that calls `TEIdle` to handle a null event.

Listing 2-4   An idle-processing procedure

```
PROCEDURE MyDoIdle(myWindow: WindowPtr);
VAR
    myData:     MyDocRecHnd;     {handle to a document record}
    myTERec:    TEHandle;        {handle to TextEdit record}
BEGIN
    myData    := MyDocRecHnd(GetWRefCon(myWindow));
    IF myData <> NIL THEN
        BEGIN
            myTERec   := myData^^.editRec;
            IF myTERec <> NIL THEN
                TEIdle(myTERec);
        END;
END;
```

Note

The value stored in the low-memory global `CaretTime` determines the blinking time for the caret. (The user can also set the minimum interval through the General Controls control panel.) You can use the Event Manager's `GetCaretTime` function to retrieve this value. For more information, see the chapter "The Event Manager" in *Inside Macintosh: Macintosh Toolbox Essentials.* ◆

Activating an Edit Record

When a window becomes active or inactive, the Window Manager updates the frames of the windows on the screen, and then informs the Event Manager that an activate event has occurred. The next time `WaitNextEvent` is called from your main event loop, the Event Manager notifies your application that an activate event has occurred. (An activate event can have a flag set indicating that a window is to be deactivated.) When your application receives this notification, it needs to call `TEActivate` for an activate event and `TEDeactivate` for a deactivate event. When you call `TEActivate`, you pass it the handle to the edit record to be activated; when you call `TEDeactivate`, you pass it the handle to the currently active edit record.

An application can have more than one edit record associated with it. The active edit record is the one where the next editing operation is to take place. The `TEActivate` procedure identifies an edit record as the active one by either highlighting the selection range or displaying a caret at the insertion point. The `TEDeactivate` procedure changes an edit record's status from active to inactive and removes the highlighting or the caret. If outline highlighting is on, `TEDeactivate` frames the selection range or displays a dimmed caret.

Note

The `TEActivate` procedure does not set the selection range; it uses the current values in the `selStart` and `selEnd` fields of the edit record to highlight the specified text or display a caret at the insertion point. The `TEDeactivate` procedure does not affect the current settings of these fields. ◆

Before you can activate an edit record, you need to deactivate the currently active edit record, if there is one. If your application has a routine which it calls to activate and deactivate its own windows, you can include processing in that routine to make an edit record the active one or make the currently active record inactive. Because deactivate events happen before activate events, these events occur in the proper order when the user switches from one window to another.

If there is more than one edit record associated with a window, you'll probably want to call `TEDeactivate` whenever the mouse button is clicked in an edit record other than the active one. In this case, each `TEDeactivate` call not associated with a window deactivate event would be coupled with a call to `TEActivate`.

You can modify the text of an edit record associated with a background window; however, to do so, you need to call `TEActivate` for that edit record before you call any other TextEdit routines.

Note

When you use `TEClick` and `TESetSelect` to set the selection range or insertion point, the selection range is not highlighted nor is a blinking caret displayed at the insertion point until the edit record is activated through `TEActivate`. However, if you had already turned on outline highlighting (through the `TEFeatureFlag` function), the text of the selection range is framed or a gray, unblinking caret is displayed at the insertion point. ◆

Handling Mouse-Down Events

When your application receives notification of a mouse-down event that it determines TextEdit should handle, it needs to pass the click on to the `TEClick` procedure. Before calling `TEClick`, your application needs to perform the following steps:

1. Convert the mouse location that is passed in the event record from global to local coordinates, so that it can pass those local coordinates to `TEClick`. To perform the conversion, you can use the `GlobalToLocal` QuickDraw procedure. (For more information, see *Inside Macintosh: Imaging*.)

2. Determine if the Shift key was held down at the time of the click to extend the selection. The behavior of `TEClick` depends on the user's actions.

   □ If the Shift key was down, `TEClick` extends the current selection range.

   □ If the Shift key was not held down, `TEClick` removes highlighting of the current selection range and positions the insertion point as close as possible to the location where the mouse click occurred.

□ When the mouse is moved or dragged, TEClick expands or shortens the selection range a character at a time. The TEClick procedure keeps control until the user releases the mouse button.

□ If the mouse button is clicked twice (a double-click), TEClick extends the selection to include the entire word where the cursor is positioned.

Note

As long as the mouse button is held down, TEClick repeatedly calls the click loop routine pointed to from the clikLoop field of the edit record. ◆

Listing 2-5 shows an application-defined procedure, MyDoContentClick, that calls TEClick, passing it a mouse-down event.

Listing 2-5   Passing a mouse-down event to TextEdit

```
PROCEDURE MyDoContentClick (myWindow: WindowPtr; event: EventRecord);
VAR
    myData:  MyDocRecHnd;          {handle to a document record}
    myTERec: TEHandle;             {handle to TextEdit record}
    mouse:   Point;
BEGIN
    myData   := MyDocRecHnd(GetWrefCon(myWindow));  {get window's data record}
    IF myData = NIL THEN
        exit(MyDoContentClick);
    myTERec  := myData^^.editRec;                    {get TERec}
    IF myTERec = NIL THEN
        exit(MyDoContentClick);
    SetPort(myWindow);
    mouse := event.where;                            {get the click position}
    GlobalToLocal(mouse);                            {convert to local coordinates}
    IF PtInRect(mouse, myTERec^^.viewRect) THEN
        BEGIN
            shiftDown := BAnd (event.modifiers, shiftKey) <> 0;
                             {extend if Shift is down}
            TEClick(mouse, shiftDown, myTERec);
        END;
END;
```

When TEClick is called, the clickTime field of the edit record contains the time when TEClick was last called. When TEClick returns, it sets the clickTime field, adjusting the current tick count. The default click loop procedure uses this value.

Responding to an Update Event

After changing any fields of the edit record that affect the appearance of the text or after any editing or scrolling operation that alters the onscreen appearance of the text, you need to call TEUpdate.

Your application needs to call TEUpdate every time the Event Manager function WaitNextEvent reports an update event for a text editing window—after you call the Window Manager procedure BeginUpdate, and before you call the EndUpdate procedure. You call the following routines when an update event occurs:

```
BeginUpdate(myWindow);
EraseRect(myWindow^.portRect);
TEUpdate(myWindow^.portRect, hTE);
EndUpdate(myWindow);
```

If you don't include the EraseRect procedure, the caret may sometimes remain visible when the window is deactivated. For more information about responding to events, see the chapter "Event Manager" in *Inside Macintosh: Macintosh Toolbox Essentials*. For more information about the Window Manager, see the chapter "Window Manager" in *Inside Macintosh: Macintosh Toolbox Essentials*.

Accepting Text Input Through Key-Down Events

When the user enters text through the keyboard, your application needs to call the TEKey procedure to accept the keyboard input a byte at a time or to delete a character when the user backspaces over it. Call TEKey every time the Event Manager function WaitNextEvent reports a key-down event that your application determines TextEdit should handle.

Because TEKey accepts every character it is passed, your application needs to first filter out Command-key equivalents, special keys, and nonprinting characters as appropriate, such as Enter or Tab, and only pass TEKey a text, a Return key character, an arrow key character, or a backspace key character.

Note
If you want to display the text as multiple paragraphs, don't filter out Return key characters. ◆

Listing 2-6 shows the MyHandleKeyDown procedure which calls TEKey to accept text a character at a time. First MyHandleKeyDown filters out special characters. For example, it treats the Tab key as a special character, and calls an application-defined routine, MyDoTab, to handle this character appropriately for the document. Then it checks to make sure that inserting the character won't exceed the maximum text length allowed. It does not count the Delete or arrow keys because they are not text characters.

If the maximum text length is not exceeded, the code passes the character to TEKey. Otherwise, it calls an application-defined routine, MyAlertUser, to notify the user that the character is not inserted, and that inserting it would exceed the edit record text limitation. In this example listing, the maximum text length is set to the highest possible value; you can specify a lower limit.

Listing 2-6   Inserting text in a document

```
PROCEDURE MyHandleKeyDown(myWindow: WindowPtr; event: EventRecord);
CONST
    kMaxTELength = 32767;
    kTab = $09;
    kDel = $08;
    kRightArrow = $1D;
    kLeftArrow = $1C;
    kDownArrow = $1F;
    kUpArrow = $1E;
VAR
    myData:      MyDocRecHnd;        {handle to a document record}
    myTERec:     TEHandle;           {handle to TextEdit record}
    key:         CHAR;
BEGIN
    myData    := MyDocRecHnd(GetWRefCon(myWindow));  {get window's data record}
    IF myData = NIL THEN
        exit(MyDoContentClick);
    myTERec   := myData^^.editRec;                   {get TERec}
    IF myTERec = NIL THEN
        exit(MyDoContentClick);
    key := CHR(BAnd(event.message, charCodeMask));
    IF key = char(kTab) THEN {handle special characters}
        MyDoTab(event)
    ELSE
        BEGIN
            IF (key = CHR(kDel)) | (key = CHR(kRightArrow)) |
            (key = CHR(kLeftArrow)) | (key = CHR(kUpArrow)) |
            (key = CHR(kDownArrow)) | {don't count deletes or arrow keys}
            (LongInt(myTERec^^.teLength - MyGetTESelLength(myTERec) + 1 <
             kMaxTELength)
            THEN
                BEGIN
                    TEKey(key, myTERec); {insert character in document}
                    MyAdjustScrollbars(window, FALSE);
                END
            ELSE
```

```
          MyAlertUser(eExceedChar);
      END;
  END;
```

Before testing to ensure that the input character does not exceed the edit record's text limitation, the code subtracts the length of the selection range, which the inserted character is to replace, from the current length of the text. To get the length of the selection range, the code calls an application-defined function, `MyGetTESelLength`. Listing 2-7 shows this function. Several other sample application-defined routines in this chapter also call this function.

Listing 2-7   Getting the selection range length

```
FUNCTION MyGetTESelLength (myTERec: TEHandle): Integer;
   Begin
      MyGetTESelLength := myTERec^^.selEnd - myTERec^^.selStart;
   END;
```

If the selection range is an insertion point and the key is not an arrow key character or a Backspace key character, `TEKey` inserts the character before the insertion point. When the character direction is right-to-left, the character is inserted to the right of the insertion point. When the character direction is left-to-right, the character is inserted to the left of the insertion point.

When you call `TEKey` and the keyboard script is different from the font script, TextEdit changes the font script to correspond to the keyboard script. If the font at the insertion point is the same as the keyboard script, then this font is used. If a font was written to the TextEdit style scrap record (in the null scrap) and never used and that font script coincides with the keyboard script, then it is used. Otherwise, TextEdit searches through the fonts in the style table until it locates a font that corresponds to the keyboard. If one does not exist, then it uses the application font.

When the user backspaces over characters of a multistyled edit record, `TEKey` deletes the characters but it saves the character attributes associated with the last character deleted in order to apply it to any new characters that the user might enter; the character attributes are saved in the null scrap's style scrap record. As soon as the user clicks in another area of the text, `TEKey` clears the attributes from the null scrap.

Moving Text In and Out of Edit Records

This section describes how to cut, copy, and paste text, and insert and delete it. Because TextEdit manages the varying character attribute information associated with multistyled text, you use separate routines for monostyled and multistyled text to perform some of these tasks; this section explains those differences. If your application supports both monostyled and multistyled text, you need to handle these cases separately.

Using TextEdit to Cut, Copy, and Paste Text

You can use TextEdit to cut, copy, and paste text within a single edit record, between edit records, or across applications, and to handle menu commands that let the user perform these actions. You use the `TECut` and `TECopy` procedures to cut and copy both monostyled and multistyled text. To paste monostyled text, you use the `TEPaste` procedure. To paste multistyled text, you use the `TEStylePaste` procedure. To move monostyled text across applications or between an application and a desk accessory, you use the `TEFromScrap` and `TEToScrap` functions. This section describes how to use these routines and what they do.

Note

This section and those that follow do not describe how to create menus and their commands. For guidelines and a complete discussion of how to create and manage the menus in your application, see the chapter "The Menu Manager" in *Inside Macintosh: Macintosh Toolbox Essentials*. ◆

The `TECut` procedure removes and transfers the selected text. The `TECopy` procedure copies the selected text, leaving the original text intact. To implement cut-and-paste or copy-and-paste services, you can couple either of these calls with `TEPaste` or `TEStylePaste` to overlay a text selection or insert the text to be pasted at an insertion point.

To cut, copy, and paste text within the same edit record or between two edit records within the same application, you do not need to write the text to and from the desk scrap, although this is always done automatically for multistyled text. However, to carry text across applications or between an application and a desk accessory, whether the text is multistyled or monostyled, you must write it to and from the desk scrap.

For monostyled text, `TECut` and `TECopy` write the text to the private scrap only. The `TEPaste` procedure pastes the monostyled text from the private scrap to the edit record. To determine the length of the text to be pasted, you can call the `TEGetScrapLength` function which returns the size in bytes of the text in the private scrap, or you can check the value of the global variable `TEScrapLength`.

To move monostyled text across applications or between an application and a desk accessory, you need to use the `TEFromScrap` and `TEToScrap` functions, which write text to and from the desk scrap.

For multistyled text, `TECut` and `TECopy` always write both the text and its associated character attribute information to the Scrap Manager's desk scrap under scrap types `'TEXT'` and `'styl'`. For more information, see the chapter "Scrap Manager" in *Inside Macintosh: More Macintosh Toolbox*.

The `TEStylePaste` procedure reads both the text and its attributes back from the desk scrap and writes the multistyled text into the edit record's text buffer at the current selection range or insertion point.

You can use these procedures to move multistyled text across two applications or between an application and a desk accessory; you don't need to call `TEFromScrap` and `TEToScrap` for multistyled text. To either copy or move the text selection from the text buffer to the desk scrap, `TECut` and `TECopy` write the text to the private scrap and to the Scrap Manager's desk scrap. To copy or move the attributes along with the text, `TECut` and `TECopy` write the character attribute information stored in the style table to both the style scrap and the Scrap Manager's desk scrap. Figure 2-9 shows what happens when you cut multistyled text using `TECut`.

Figure 2-9   Cutting text from a multistyled edit record

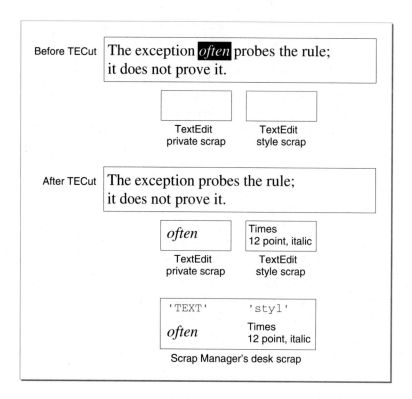

The `TEStylePaste` procedure either pastes the text from the desk scrap at the insertion point or replaces the current selection range with the text to be pasted. Along with the text, `TEStylePaste` writes the character attribute information to the style record's style table and applies it to the inserted text.

For multistyled text, text is pasted from the desk scrap. Therefore, before you call `TEStylePaste`, use the Scrap Manager's `GetScrap` procedure to check the size of the text (`'TEXT'` data) to be pasted.

TextEdit

To calculate the amount of memory required for the style scrap before you cut or copy multistyled text, you can use the information returned by the TENumStyles function. This function returns the number of attribute changes contained in a range of text. Since the style scrap is linear in structure, with one element for each attribute change, you can multiply the number returned by TENumStyles by SizeOf(ScrpSTElement) and add 2 to get the number of bytes needed.

Listing 2-8 shows a sample application-defined procedure that handles cut, copy, and paste menu commands. Before the application pastes the multistyled text into the edit record's text at the current selection range, it calls the Scrap Manager's GetScrap function to get the size of the text to be pasted. The code adds the returned value to the size of the text in the edit record, subtracts the size of the selection range, then compares the result against the maximum length of the edit record text to make sure that pasting the text won't exceed it. (To get the selection range length, the code calls the application-defined function MyGetTESelLength, as shown in Listing 2-7 on page 2-38.)

To avoid copying the data when you want only the length of the text returned, pass a value of NIL for the hDest parameter to GetScrap. For more information about GetScrap, see the chapter "Scrap Manager" in *Inside Macintosh: More Macintosh Toolbox*.

Listing 2-8   Handling Cut, Copy, and Paste commands on an Edit menu

```
PROCEDURE MyHandleEditMenu (myWindow: WindowPtr; menuItem: Integer);
CONST
   kMaxTELength = 32000;
   kTESlop  = 1024;
      {kTESlop provides some extra security when preflighting edit commands.}
VAR
   myData:            MyDocRecHnd;      {handle to a document record}
   myTERec:           TEHandle;         {handle to TextEdit record}
   myErr:             OSErr;
   offset:            LONGINT;
   aHandle:           Handle;
   oldSize, newSize:  LONGINT;
   saveErr:           OSErr;
BEGIN
   myData   := MyDocRecHnd(GetWrefCon(myWindow));   {get window's data record}
   IF myData = NIL THEN
      exit(MyDoContentClick);
   myTERec  := myData^^.editRec;                     {get TERec}
   IF myTERec = NIL THEN
      Exit(MyDoContentClick);
   CASE menuItem OF
      iCut:
```

```
            BEGIN
                IF ZeroScrap = noErr THEN
                    BEGIN
                        PurgeSpace(total, contig);
                        IF MyGetTESelLength(myTERec) + kTESlop >
                         contig THEN
                            MyAlertUser(eNoSpaceCut)
                        ELSE
                            TECut(myTERec);
                    END;
            END;
        iCopy:
            BEGIN
                IF ZeroScrap = noErr THEN
                    TECopy(myTERec);
            END;
        iPaste:
            BEGIN
                IF GetScrap(NIL, 'TEXT', offset) +
                    (myTERec^^.teLength - MyGetTESelLength(myTERec)) >
                    kMaxTELength
                THEN
                    MyAlertUser(eExceedPaste)
                ELSE
                    BEGIN
                        aHandle := Handle(TEGetText(myTERec));
                        oldSize := GetHandleSize(aHandle);
                        newSize := oldSize + GetScrap + kTESlop
                        SetHandleSize(aHandle, newSize);
                            {see if handle can be resized}
                        saveErr := MemError;
                        SetHandleSize(aHandle, oldSize);
                        IF saveErr <> noErr THEN
                            MyAlertUser(eNoSpacePaste)
                        ELSE
                            TEStylePaste(myTERec);
                    END;
                END;
            END;
    END;
```

Inserting and Deleting Text

You can use TextEdit routines to delete and insert text. You use `TEInsert` to insert monostyled text into the edit record's text buffer if the current selection range is an insertion point. If the current selection range is a range of text, `TEInsert` replaces it with the text to be inserted. You use `TEStyleInsert` to insert multistyled text in the same way; however, the text *and* its associated character attribute information are inserted.

To delete text, your application calls the same routine whether the text is multistyled or monostyled. The `TEDelete` procedure removes the text of the current selection range. When the text is multistyled, `TEDelete` saves the character attributes in the null scrap to be applied to characters that the user might enter following the deletion. After each editing procedure, TextEdit redraws the text if necessary from the insertion point to the end of the text.

You can handle a Clear command using `TEDelete`; you call `TEDelete` with the handle to the edit record containing the text you want to eliminate. The `TEDelete` procedure removes the selected text without transferring it to the scrap.

```
iClear:
   TEDelete(myTERec);
```

Text Attributes

This section describes how your application can check the current attributes of a range of text to determine which ones are consistent across the text. It also describes how you can manipulate the font, style, size, and color of a range of text; the text selection can consist of a segment of text, the entire text of the edit record, a single character, or even an insertion point.

You use the `TEContinuousStyle` function to determine the current attributes for a range of text, and you use the `TESetStyle` procedure to change them. You can change character attributes singly, collectively, or in any combination using `TESetStyle`. For example, you can change the font style to bold or italic, and you can underline, outline, or shadow the selected text. You can increase or decrease the type size incrementally, or change the color in which the text is displayed. You use the `TESetAlignment` procedure to change the alignment of the entire text of an edit record.

This section describes these tasks in this order:

■ checking the text attributes across a selection range

■ toggling an attribute

■ handling a font menu that lets the user change the font family

■ handling a font size menu that lets the user change the text size

■ handling a style menu that lets the user change the style of the text

■ changing the text alignment

Some general information about TESetStyle that applies to many of the tasks for which you can use it is discussed here. If you call TESetStyle for an insertion point, TextEdit stores the input character attribute information in the null scrap's style scrap record. If the user then enters text (pastes without attributes, inserts, or types it), the attributes are written to the style record and applied to that text.

There are many ways in which you can use TESetStyle to handle menu commands that let the user modify text attributes. If your application allows a user to change any or all the text attributes from a single format menu before redrawing the text, you can make one call to TESetStyle specifying the particular attributes to be changed. If your application provides separate menus to let a user manipulate different aspects of the text, you can make separate calls to TESetStyle specifying the discrete text attribute to be changed.

Note
A field in the text style record is only valid if the corresponding bit is set in the mode parameter; otherwise, the field contains invalid information. ◆

The value of mode specifies which existing character attributes are to be changed to the new character attributes specified by newStyle.

Constant	Value	Description
doFont	1	Sets the font family ID
doFace	2	Sets the character style
doSize	4	Sets the type size
doColor	8	Sets the color
doAll	15	Sets all attributes
addSize	16	Increases or decreases the type size
doToggle	32	Modifies the mode

Checking the Text Attributes Across a Selection Range

When a particular attribute is set for an entire selection range, that attribute is said to be *continuous* over the selection. For example, in the selected text in Figure 2-10, the bold attribute is continuous over the selection range and italic is not.

Figure 2-10   Continuous attributes over a selection range

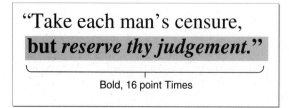

To determine the actual values for continuous attributes, you can use the
`TEContinuousStyle` function. This function takes two variable parameters: `mode` and
`aStyle`. For its input value, `mode` specifies the attributes to be checked; for its output
value, `mode` specifies those attributes that are continuous over the selection range. For
the input value of `aStyle`, you pass a pointer to a text style record (of type
`TextStyle`); for those attributes that are continuous, the text style record fields contain
the actual values when `TEContinuousStyle` returns.

A field in the text style record is only valid if the corresponding bit is set in the `mode`
parameter; otherwise, the field contains invalid information. Possible values for the
`TEContinuousStyle` mode parameter are defined by the following constants.

Constant	Value	Description
doFont	1	Specifies the font family number
doFace	2	Specifies the character style
doSize	4	Specifies the type size
doColor	8	Specifies the color
doAll	15	Specifies all the attributes

Listing 2-9 illustrates how to use the `TEContinuousStyle` function to determine the
font, style, size, and color of the current selection range. The code sets the `mode`
parameter. Then it calls `TEContinuousStyle`, passing it the text style record. When
`TEContinuousStyle` returns, it checks each bit of the `mode` parameter to see which
attributes are continuous across the selection.

Listing 2-9   Determining the font, style, size, and color of the current selection range

```
PROCEDURE MyGetCurrentSelection (VAR mode: Integer;
        VAR continuous: Boolean; VAR astyle: TextStyle;
        myTERec: TEHandle);
BEGIN
    mode := doFont + doFace + doSize + doColor;
    continuous := TEContinuousStyle(mode, aStyle, myTERec);
    IF BitAnd(mode, doFont) <> 0 THEN
        {font for selection = aStyle.tsFont}
    ELSE
        {more than one font in selection};
    IF BitAnd(mode, doFace) <> 0 THEN
        {aStyle.tsFace contains the text faces (or plain) that }
        { are common to the selection.}
    ELSE
        {No text face is common to the entire selection.};
    IF BitAnd(mode, doSize) <> 0 THEN
        {size for selection = aStyle.tsSize}
```

```
    ELSE
        {more than one size in selection};
    IF BitAnd(mode, doColor) <> 0 THEN
        {color for selection = aStyle.tsColor}
    ELSE
        {more than one color in selection}
END;
```

Toggling an Attribute

Once you know what attributes are continuous across a selection range, you can use `TESetStyle` to toggle an attribute on and off. For example, if you specify a `mode` parameter for `TESetStyle` that includes both `doToggle` and `doFace`, and an attribute that has been set in the `tsFace` field of the text style record exists across the current selection range, then `TESetStyle` removes that attribute. However, if the attribute isn't continuous over the current selection, then all of the selected text is set to include it.

For example, in the selected text shown in Figure 2-11, the bold style is continuous over the selection range and the italic style is not.

Figure 2-11   An initial selection before `TESetStyle` is called

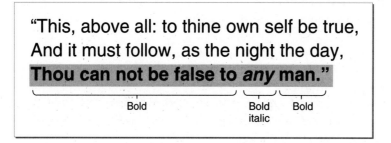

If you call `TESetStyle` with a `mode` of `doFace + doToggle` and a text style record parameter with its `tsFace` field set to `bold`, the resulting selection is no longer bold, as shown in Figure 2-12.

Figure 2-12   The result of calling `TESetStyle` to toggle to bold

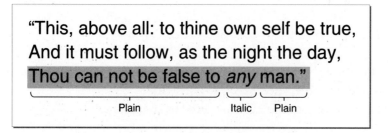

On the other hand, if instead you call TESetStyle with a mode of doFace + doToggle and a text style record with its tsFace field set to italic, the resulting selection is all bold italic as shown in Figure 2-13.

Figure 2-13   The result of calling TESetStyle to toggle italics

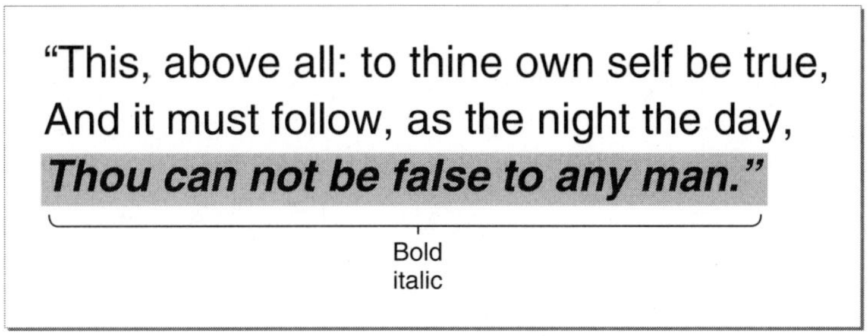

"This, above all: to thine own self be true,
And it must follow, as the night the day,
Thou can not be false to any man."

Bold
italic

Handling a Font Menu

You can use TESetStyle to handle a Font menu that allows the user to change the font family for a text selection. The user might select the entire text of an edit record or a portion of it, then choose a different font family from your menu to be used to render the text. Listing 2-10 shows how to handle a Font menu that allows the user to do this. The code determines which font the user has selected from the menu. Next, it calls the Font Manager's GetFNum procedure to get the font family ID for the font of the selected text. Then it calls TESetStyle passing it the text style record with the tsFont field set to the font ID. Because the redraw parameter is set to TRUE, the current selection range is redrawn immediately in the new font.

Listing 2-10   Handling the Font menu

```
PROCEDURE MyHandleFontMenu (myWindow: WindowPtr; myTERec: TEHandle;
                            menuItem: Integer);
VAR
    txStyle:    TextStyle;    {holds style selected}
    fontName:   Str255;       {name of font selected}
    fontID:     Integer;      {ID of font selected}
BEGIN
    GetItem(GetMenuHandle(mFont), menuItem, fontName);
    GetFNum(fontName, fontID);
    txStyle.tsFont := fontID;
    TESetStyle(doFont, txStyle, true, myTERec);
    MyAdjustScrollBars(window, FALSE);
END;
```

Handling a Font Size Menu

If your application includes a menu that allows users to change the font size of the selected text, you can use the TESetStyle procedure to handle this modification. The code in Listing 2-11 sets the tsSize field of the text style record to the font size that the user selects; then it calls TESetStyle to apply the new font size immediately. The doSize mode parameter value forces all the text to the new size.

Listing 2-11   Handling the Size menu

```
PROCEDURE MyHandleSizeCommand (myTERec: TEHandle; menuItem: Integer);
VAR
    txStyle:    TextStyle;
BEGIN
    MyGetSize(GetMenuHandle(mSize), menuItem, sizeChosen);
    txStyle.tsSize := sizeChosen;
    TESetStyle(doSize, txStyle, TRUE, myTERec);
    MyAdjustScrollBars(window, FALSE);
END;
```

Handling a Style Menu

Your application can also use TESetStyle to handle Style menu commands. For example, you can set the mode parameter to doFace and set the tsFace field of the text style record to any of the font attributes that the user selects. If your menu supports a Plain option to remove all attributes from the text selection, you need to explicitly set tsFace. Because of the behavior of TESetStyle, you cannot implement a Plain selection by passing a null (empty set) text style record to remove the current attributes. Listing 2-12 shows how to use TESetStyle to change the text attributes, including how to render plain text.

Listing 2-12   Handling a Style menu

```
PROCEDURE MyHandleStyleMenu (myWindow: WindowPtr; myTERec: TEHandle;
                            menuItem: Integer);
VAR
    txStyle:    TextStyle;
    anIntPtr:   Integer;
BEGIN {mStyle}
    WITH txStyle DO BEGIN
        CASE menuItem OF
            plainItem:
                BEGIN
                    anIntPtr := @txStyle.tsFace;
```

```
            anIntPtr^ := 0;
            tsFace := [ ];
        END;
    boldItem:
     tsFace := [bold];
    italicItem:
     tsFace := [italic];
    underlineItem:
     tsFace := [underline];
    outlineItem:
     tsFace := [outline];
    shadowItem:
     tsFace := [shadow];
END; {case}


IF menuItem <> 1 THEN
    TESetStyle(doFace + doToggle, txStyle, TRUE, myTERec)
        {if we don't select plain then use doToggle}
ELSE
    TESetStyle(doFace, txStyle, TRUE, myTERec);
        {TESetStyle has problems with plain and doToggle }
        { has no effect!so we need to special case it.}
    MyAdjustScrollBars(window, FALSE);
    END;
END;
```

If you set redraw to TRUE, TextEdit redraws the current selection with the new attributes, recalculating line breaks, line heights, and font ascents. If you call TESetStyle with a value of FALSE for the redraw parameter, TextEdit does not redraw the text or recalculate line breaks, line heights, and font ascents until the next update event occurs. Consequently, when your application calls a routine that uses any of this information, such as TEGetHeight (which returns a total height between two specified lines), the routine uses the old character attribute information that existed before you called TESetStyle to change it. To be certain that the new information is always reflected immediately, call the TESetStyle procedure with a redraw parameter of TRUE.

Listing 2-13 shows a sample procedure that calls TEContinuousStyle to check the character attributes of the current selection range; it determines whether the style is plain, bold, or italic. For each style that is continuous across the text, the MyAdjustStyleNew procedure marks the item on the style menu. In this case, if TEContinuousStyle returns a mode parameter that contains doFace and the text style record tsFace field is bold, it means that the selected text is all bold, but may contain other text styles, such as italic, as well. Italic does not apply to all of the selected text, or it would have been included in the tsFace field. If the tsFace field is an empty set, then all of the selected text is plain.

_____ **Listing 2-13**   Checking the style and marking Style menu items to reflect
                                     the current selection range

```
PROCEDURE MyAdjustStyleNew (myTERec: TEHandle);
VAR
styleMenu:   MenuHandle;
aStyle:      TextStyle;
mode:        Integer;
BEGIN
   mode := doFace;
   styleMenu := GetMenuHandle(mStyle);
   IF TEContinuousStyle(mode, aStyle, myTERec) THEN
      BEGIN
         {There is at least one style that is continuous over }
         { the selection. Note that it might be plain, which is }
         { actually the absence of all styles.}
         CheckItem(styleMenu, plainItem, aStyle.tsFace = []);
         CheckItem(styleMenu, boldItem, bold IN aStyle.tsFace);
         CheckItem(styleMenu, italicItem, italic IN aStyle.tsFace);
         {Set other menu items appropriately.}
      END

   ELSE
      BEGIN
         {No text face is common to the entire selection.}
         CheckItem(styleMenu, plainItem, FALSE);
         CheckItem(styleMenu, boldItem, FALSE);
         CheckItem(styleMenu, italicItem, FALSE);
         {Set other menu items appropriately.}
      END;
END;
```

Changing the Text Alignment

Your application can change the alignment of the entire text of an edit record by calling
the TESetAlignment procedure. The default alignment used to display the text of an
edit record is based on the primary line direction of the system script. For example, when
the system script is Arabic or that of any language that is read from right to left, the
default line direction is right to left and the text is right aligned.

For a script system whose primary line direction is right to left, you can force left
alignment of the text by specifying teFlushLeft as the value of the align parameter,
as shown in the following example:

```
TESetAlignment (teFlushLeft, myTERec);
```

You can use any of the following constants to specify how text is aligned.

Constant	Description
teFlushDefault	Default alignment according to the primary line direction
teCenter	Center for all scripts
teFlushRight	Right for all scripts
teFlushLeft	Left for all scripts

Make sure that you call the Window Manager's `InvalRect` procedure after you change the alignment so the text is redrawn with the new alignment. For more information about `InvalRect`, see the chapter "Window Manager" in *Inside Macintosh: Macintosh Toolbox Essentials*.

Saving and Restoring a TextEdit Document, and Implementing Undo

This section describes how to save to disk the contents of a document created using TextEdit, and restore it when the user opens the document. For both monostyled and multistyled text, you need to save and restore the text and its character attribute information. This section also discusses how to implement an Undo feature.

Saving a TextEdit Document

To save the contents of a document created using TextEdit and a monostyled edit record, you store the text. You can also save the text characteristics, such as the font and its size and style, and the text margins; you can store this information in a resource. (Save the font name, not the font number.)

To save the contents of a document created using TextEdit and a multistyled edit record, you need to save all of the associated character attribute information in addition to the text. Because the text format of the character attribute information in the style scrap is easier to export than the style record itself—it uses the Desk Manager's `'styl'` format— you should use the TextEdit routines that use the style scrap for moving character attribute information: `TEGetStyleScrapHandle` and `TEUseStyleScrap`. For example, you can use the following steps to save a multistyled text document to disk:

1. Create a text file, select all the text of the edit record, and save it in the text file's data fork.

2. Call `TEGetStyleScrapHandle` to get a handle to the style scrap record. This creates the style scrap record and uses it to store the character attribute information.

3. Save the character attribute information in the resource fork of the file.

The application-defined procedure `MyDoSaveAsTextEdit` shown in Listing 2-14 uses this method. Notice that this procedure avoids using `TESetSelect` to select all of the edit record's text. The `TESetSelect` procedure sets and highlights the selection range that you specify. Because you are selecting the text to save it, you don't want it to be highlighted. (Highlighting the text before saving it can mislead a user to presume that some other action is required.)

However, if you want to use TESetSelect, you can circumvent highlighting of the selection range if you first render the edit record inactive; before you call TESetSelect, call TEDeactivate. Also, if you have outline highlighting turned on through the TEFeatureFlag function's teFOutlineHilite feature, turn it off. When the edit record is not the active one, TESetSelect can set the selection range without causing it to be highlighted.

Listing 2-14   Saving a multistyled text edit record to disk

```
PROCEDURE MyDoSaveAsTextEdit(textToSave: TEHandle);
    CONST
    kFileType   = 'TEXT'; {file type of text file}
    kFileCreator = 'NIIM'; {creator code of text file}

VAR
    reply: StandardFileReply;
        {location, name of file to save text to}
    styles:    StScrpHandle; {contains all character }
                            { attributes in text}
    dataLength: LongInt; {number of bytes of text to write}
    dataRefNum: Integer; {ref number of text file's data fork}
    rsrcRefNum: Integer; {ref number of text file's rsrc fork}
    savedStart: Integer; {saves offset of start of selection}
    savedEnd:   Integer; {saves offset of end of selection}
    error:      OSErr;   {error code from toolbox}

BEGIN
    StandardPutFile( '', '', reply);
    IF reply.sfGood THEN
        BEGIN
        {save the current starting and ending offsets of selection}
            savedStart := textToSave^^.selStart;
            savedEnd := textToSave^^.selEnd;

        {select all text; don't use TESetSelect because it }
            { draws selection}
                textToSave^^.selStart := 0;
                textToSave^^.selEnd := textToSave^^.teLength;

        {get a list of all the attributes in the text}
                styles := TEGetStyleScrapHandle(textToSave);
```

```
        {reset the selection back to what it was}
            textToSave^^.selStart := savedStart;
            textToSave^^.selEnd := savedEnd;

        {create the text file if it didn't exist before}
            IF NOT reply.sfReplacing THEN
                BEGIN
                    error := FSpCreate(reply.sfFile,
                            kFileCreator, kFileType, reply.sfScript);
                    FSpCreateResFile(reply.sfFile, kFileCreator,
                            kFileType, reply.sfScript);
                    error := ResError;
                END;

        {open the text file}
        error := FSpOpenDF(reply.sfFile, fsCurPerm, dataRefNum);
        rsrcRefNum := FSpOpenResFile(reply.sfFile, fsCurPerm);
        error := ResError;

        {write the text to the file}
        dataLength := textToSave^^.teLength;
        error := FSWrite(dataRefNum, dataLength,
                        textToSave^^.hText^ );

        {Write the attributes to the file}
        AddResource(Handle(styles), 'styl', 0, '');
        WriteResource(Handle(styles));
        ReleaseResource(Handle(styles));

        {close the text file}
        error := FSClose(dataRefNum);
        CloseResFile(rsrcRefNum);
        error := ResError;
        END;
END;
```

Restoring an Existing TextEdit Document

You can restore the text of an edit record when a user opens a document that was created using TextEdit. One way to do this is to read the text from the data fork into a handle, then write the handle to the hText field of the edit record; call TECalText after you do this. Before you write the new handle to the hText field, dispose of the existing handle, if there is one. For a multistyled edit record, you need to reinstate both the text and the character attribute information for it. (For information about how to open a file, see *Inside Macintosh: Files.*)

You can use a method similar to the one shown in Listing 2-14 on page 2-52 to save a multistyled text document. However, to restore the text, you retrieve the data from the file's data fork and write it to a buffer, then call `TESetText` to make a copy of the text and set the `hText` field of the edit record to point to it. The `MyDoOpenTextEdit` procedure shown in Listing 2-15 shows an example of this. Before copying the text to a buffer, the `MyDoOpenTextEdit` procedure checks to ensure that the text length does not exceed the 32 KB limit; if it does, TextEdit truncates the text before it copies it.

The `MyDoOpenTextEdit` procedure retrieves the character attribute information from the resource fork of the disk file and reinstates it in the edit record's style record by calling `TEUseStyleScrap`.

Listing 2-15   Restoring a document that uses multistyled TextEdit

```
PROCEDURE MyDoOpenTextEdit(textToOpen: TEHandle);
   CONST
      kFileType = 'TEXT'; {file type of text file}

   VAR
      reply:      StandardFileReply; {location, name of file to get text from}
      typeList:   SFTypeList;    {specifies 'TEXT' files in SF dialog}
      dataRefNum: Integer;   {ref number of text file's data fork}
      rsrcRefNum: Integer;   {ref number of text file's rsrc fork}
      textBuffer: Handle;   {holds text from file}
      textLength: LongInt;   {number of bytes of text to read}
      styles:     StScrpHandle;  {contains all character attributes in text}
      error:      OSErr;       {error code from toolbox}
      savedState: SignedByte; {saves state of 'styl' resource}

BEGIN
   typeList[0] := kFileType;
   StandardGetFile(NIL, 1, typeList, reply);
   IF reply.sfGood THEN
      BEGIN
         {open the data fork of the text file}
         error := FSpOpenDF(reply.sfFile, fsCurPerm, dataRefNum);
         error := SetFPos(dataRefNum, fsFromStart, 0);
         {get the number of bytes of text in the file; limit to 32KB}
         error := GetEOF( dataRefNum, textLength );
         IF textLength > 32767 THEN
            textLength := 32767;
         {allocate a buffer for the text}
         textBuffer := NewHandle(textLength);
         {read the text into the buffer}
```

```
error := FSRead( dataRefNum, textLength, textBuffer^ );
{put the text into the TextEdit record}
LockHHi(TextBuffer);
TESetText(textBuffer^, textLength, textToOpen);
HUnlock(textBuffer);
{get rid of the text buffer}
DisposeHandle(textBuffer);
{close the data fork of the text file}
error := FSClose(dataRefNum);
{open the resource fork of the text file}
rsrcRefNum := FSpOpenResFile(reply.sfFile, fsCurPerm);
error := ResError;
{get the style scrap}
styles := StScrpHandle(GetResource('styl', 0));
error := ResError;
IF styles <> NIL THEN
    BEGIN
        savedState := HGetState(Handle(styles));
        {apply the character attributes to the TextEdit record}
        TEUseStyleScrap(0, textLength, styles, true, textToOpen);
        {restore state of 'styl' resource}
        HSetState(Handle(styles), savedState);
    END;
{close the forks of the text file}
error := FSClose(dataRefNum);
CloseResFile(rsrcRefNum);
error := ResError;
END;
END;
```

Handling Undo

Application users find Undo an especially useful feature. Users might accidently choose Clear from the Edit menu instead of Cut, or they might backspace over more words than intended. In these and cases like them, Undo is invaluable.

If you are implementing Undo for multistyled text, you need to save the character attribute information along with the text. Although this section discusses one method, there are a number of ways that you can do this. For example, when you want to save the current attributes of the selected text to allow the user to revert to them, your application calls the `TEGetStyleScrapHandle` function, which returns a handle to the style scrap's style record containing the attributes used for the selected text. To restore the style later, you call the `TEUseStyleScrap` procedure. You also need to save the offsets into the edit record's text buffer of the first and last characters to which the character attribute information is to be applied.

If your application supports any 2-byte script systems, your Undo operations needs to check for 2-byte characters. Normal cut or paste operations do not present a problem, but be careful when undoing a backspace. When TextEdit backspaces over single characters, it checks CharByte to determine if the character to be removed is a 2-byte character. If it is, it removes 2 bytes. (For more information about the CharByte function, see the chapter the "Script Manager," in this book.) When an application program maintains a buffer of characters that have been backspaced over in order to support Undo, it needs to make a test similar to that in Listing 2-16.

Listing 2-16 Checking for 2-byte characters when backspacing

```
IF myChar = BS then aTeHandle^^ do begin
   {support backspace undo}
   IF selStart <> selEnd then begin
   {not an insertion point save the selection}
   END
   ELSE begin
      i := selStart;
      IF i > 0 then begin
            repeat i := i - 1
            until CharByte(hText^, i) <= 0;
      {Note: Guarantees that CharByte(x,0) <= 0}
      {Also, CharByte does not touch the heap}
      {Put bytes from i to selStart into buffer}
      END;
   END;
END;
```

Customizing TextEdit

This section describes how to customize TextEdit using the TECustomHook routine to replace the end-of-line, drawing, width-measuring, and hit test default hook routines. It also describes the multi-purpose low-memory global variable TEDoText hook routine that displays, highlights, and hit-tests characters, and positions the pen to draw a caret. Finally, this section discusses how to customize word selection, automatic scrolling, and how to determine the length of a line of text in order to justify it. (For a brief discussion of hook fields and hook routines, see "Related Data Structures" on page 2-17.)

The next four sections describe how to customize TextEdit using the TECustomHook procedure. Information about the use of TECustomHook that is common to all four sections is provided here.

You can customize TextEdit's behavior by replacing any of the default hook routines with those of your own. You use the TECustomHook procedure to replace a routine installed in a hook field of the dispatch record (TEDispatchRec). Initially, each hook field of the dispatch record contains the address of the default hook routine that TextEdit uses.

The TECustomHook procedure returns the address of the default routine that it replaces so that your application-supplied routine can call the default routine, daisy-chaining it, if you want it to. For example, your routine can add additional functionality, then call the default routine instead of replicating all of its behavior. If you replace the address of a default hook routine with that of your own customized version, the next time you call TECustomHook for that hook field, TECustomHook will return the address of your routine. (For more information, see "TECustomHook" on page 2-110.) To ensure future compatibility, use the TextEdit customization routines to modify hooks rather than write directly to these fields.

If you replace a default hook routine with a customized version that you write in a high-level language, such as Pascal or C, you need to provide assembly-language glue code that utilizes the registers for your high-level language routine. Refer to "TECustomHook" on page 2-110 for a description of the register contents on entry and return for each of the hook routines.

If you replace a default routine, take the following precautions:

- Before placing the address of your routine in the TextEdit dispatch record, strip the addresses, using the Operating System Utilities StripAddress function, to guarantee that your application is 32-bit clean. For more information, see *Inside Macintosh: Operating System Utilities*.

- Before replacing a TextEdit routine with a customized one, determine whether more than one script system is installed, and, if so, ensure that your customized routine accommodates all of the installed script systems. This avoids the problem of your customized routine producing results that are incompatible with the Script Manager.

- When you use assembly language, note that all registers must be preserved except those specified as containing return values. Register A3 contains a pointer to the edit record and Register A4 contains a handle to it. You can obtain line start positions from the lineStarts array in the edit record. Register A5 is always valid. Refer to TECustomHook in the TextEdit Reference section for complete coverage of the register content requirements for all hook routines.

Replacing the End-of-Line Routine

You can replace the address of the default end-of-line hook routine with the address of your own routine that determines an end-of-line character if you want the end-of-line to be defined by a character other than the carriage return.

The default routine compares a given character with $0D (a carriage return) to determine whether it is an end-of-line character, and returns with the appropriate status flags (either TRUE or FALSE) in the status register.

Replacing the Drawing Routine

TextEdit calls the draw hook routine any time the various components of a line are drawn. The appropriate font, face, and size characteristics have already been set into the current graphics port by the time this routine is called.

If your application uses an outline font, the default behavior of the Font Manager ensure's that glyphs fit within the font's ascent and descent. Glyphs that extend beyond the ascent or descent, such as certain accented fonts, are scaled down to fit.

If your application has set the preserveGlyph parameter of the Font Manager's SetPreserveGlyph procedure to TRUE to preserve the original unscaled shape of the glyph, note that TextEdit sets it to FALSE before it calls the draw hook to perform any drawing. This is to guarantee that the glyphs whose bounding boxes exceed the font's ascent or descent are scaled down to prevent them from colliding with other glyphs on the lines above or below. TextEdit then restores the preserveGlyph parameter to its previous value before proceeding.

Replacing the Width-Measuring Routines

A width measurement hook routine measures portions of a line of text, and TextEdit calls one each time the width of various components of a line is calculated. There are three width measurement hooks: the width measurement hook, the new width measurement hook, and the text width measurement hook. Default hook routines of the same name as the hook field are installed in each of these hooks.

The width measurement hook, which TextEdit used in the past, now exists to provide backward compatibility for applications that have replaced the default routine with a customized one. TextEdit uses the routine whose address is installed in this field only when both of the following conditions exist: when only the Roman script system is installed and the field contains the address of a customized routine.

In all other cases—when more than one script system is installed or when the width measurement hook has not been customized—TextEdit calls the routine whose address is installed in the new width measurement hook field to measure text.

Figure 2-14 shows a flow chart illustrating when the width measurement hook and the new width measurement hook routines are used.

Figure 2-14   Determining when to use `WIDTHHook` and `nWIDTHHook`

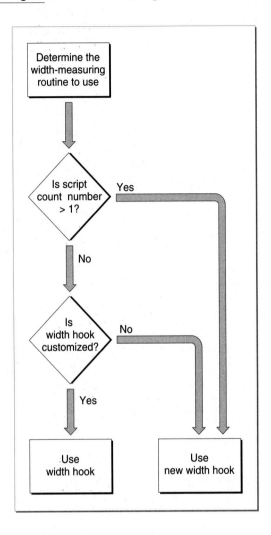

The new width measurement hook routine is called to measure text for both Roman and non-Roman script systems. If you replace this routine, make sure that your customized routine is script-aware.

The default action for the new width measurement hook routine is to call the QuickDraw Manager's `CharToPixel` function or `TextWidth` procedure to measure for non-Roman scripts. By default, the `TextWidthHook` field contains the address of the QuickDraw `TextWidth` function. You can use this hook to replace TextEdit's use of the QuickDraw `TextWidth` function with your own measuring routine. If you replace this hook routine with a customized version, when the routine whose address is installed in the new width measurement hook field makes a call to `TextWidth`, your customized routine is invoked.

To test for the availability of the width-measuring hooks, you can call the `Gestalt` function with the `gestaltTextEditVersion` selector. A result of `gestaltTE2` or greater returned in the `response` parameter indicates that the new width measurement hook is available, and a result of `gestaltTE5` or greater indicates that `TextWidthHook` is available.

Replacing the Hit Test Routine

TextEdit calls the hit test hook routine to determine the glyph position in a line, given the pixel width from the left edge of the view rectangle. For versions of software earlier than 7.0, the default action is to call the `TextWidth` function to determine if the pixel width of the measured text is greater than the input width. If it is, then the hit test hook routine calls the QuickDraw `PixelToChar` function and returns. For system software version 7 and later, the default action is to call the QuickDraw `PixelToChar` function. In addition to the values defined by the register contents on entry, when TextEdit calls the `PixelToChar` function, it passes a value of `OnlyStyleRun` for the `styleRunPosition` parameter and scaling factors of 1/1 for the `numer` and `demon` parameters. See "Hit Test Hook Registers" on page 2-113.

Customizing Word Selection

A word-selection break routine determines which word is highlighted when the user double-clicks in the text. It also determines where TextEdit breaks the text at the end of a line. You can use `TESetWordBreak` to replace the default routine, installed in the edit record's `wordBreak` field, that is used for word selection and line breaking under certain circumstances. Whether or not TextEdit uses the word break hook routine installed in this field is determined by the algorithm implemented in the default `TEFindWord` routine, which is described below.

When you replace the `wordBreak` field hook routine, your customized word-selection break routine is used instead of the default one. The default routine breaks words at any character with an ASCII value of $20 or less (the space character or nonprinting control characters).

Before non-Roman script systems were supported, TextEdit used the word-selection break routine referenced by the `wordBreak` field for all word selection and line breaking. However, in order to support both Roman and non-Roman script systems, TextEdit now uses the routine referenced by the low-memory global variable `TEFindWord`. The default `TEFindWord` hook routine determines which hook TextEdit should use for word selection and line breaking—the `wordBreak` hook or the Text Utilities `FindWordBreaks` procedure—based on what script systems are installed and some other factors. You can replace the `TEFindWord` hook routine with a customized version.

The `TEFindWord` hook routine is a higher level routine than `wordBreak`. Because of this, when you customize the `TEFindWord` hook you are completely changing how TextEdit handles word selection and line breaking. However, when you replace `wordBreak`, you are only impacting those aspects of word selection and line breaking that are normally handled by the `wordBreak` routine.

The TEFindWord hook routine gives your application more control over the breaking process and allows you to write more efficient routines. However, unless you include explicit tests for scripts in your customized routine, the algorithms you provide may be incorrect for non-Roman scripts. If you replace TEFindWord, you should understand the behavior of the default routine.

Here's how the default TEFindWord routine works:

- TextEdit initially determines whether a non-Roman script system is installed. If more than the Roman script system is installed, TextEdit always uses the Text Utilities FindWordBreaks procedure for line breaking and word selection.

- When TextEdit determines that only the Roman script system is installed and the TEFindWord routine is being called for line breaking (not word selection), TextEdit calls the wordBreak hook.

- If TEFindWord is called for word selection for system software with only the Roman script system installed, TextEdit checks to see if your application has placed the address of a customized word-selection breaks routine in the wordBreak field of the edit record. If so, TextEdit calls your word-selection breaks routine. Otherwise, if the wordBreak field contains the address of TextEdit's internal word-selection breaks routine, TextEdit uses the Text Utilities FindWordBreaks procedure to determine word-selection breaks.

When TextEdit calls the Text Utilities FindWordBreaks procedure, it uses information in the edit record to provide the necessary parameters. TextEdit determines the current script boundaries from the Text Utilities FindWordBreaks procedure by using the font run information in the style record (of type TEStyleRec). TextEdit also determines the length of the script run and the offset within the script run from which to begin searching for a word boundary. TextEdit uses the value in the clikStuff field of the edit record to determine the leading edge flag for the FindWordBreaks procedure. You must use similar information to replace TEFindWord correctly for non-Roman scripts.

Customizing Automatic Scrolling

Scroll bars associated with the text are not automatically scrolled with the text unless you replace the address of the default click loop routine with that of a customized routine that updates the scroll bars. You can write your own click loop routine that includes code to update the scroll bars along with the text and install its address in the clikLoop field. To replace the default click loop routine with your customized version, you call the TESetClickLoop procedure.

You can write a routine that manages the scroll bars, then calls the default click loop routine, rather than replicating its behavior in your routine. However, if your routine scrolls the text and updates scroll bars, you should consider what the default click loop routine does. It adjusts the value in the clickTime field of the edit record to allow for slower scrolling.

When TEClick is called, the clickTime field contains the time when TEClick was last called. TextEdit sets the clickTime field with the current tick count on exit from the TEClick procedure and uses the new value at reentry the next time TEClick is called.

If you code a click loop routine in Pascal, it should have no parameters and it should return a Boolean value. You can declare a click loop routine named MyClickLoop like this:

```
FUNCTION MyClickLoop: Boolean;
```

The function should return TRUE. Returning FALSE from your click loop routine tells the TEClick procedure that the mouse button has been released, which aborts TEClick.

Installing a customized default click loop routine

If you code a click loop routine in Pascal, then call the TESetClickLoop procedure to install the Pascal routine in the clikLoop field, TESetClickLoop installs a glue code routine in the clikLoop field because clikLoop expects a routine that uses assembly-language conventions. Because of this, you must always use TESetClickLoop to install a Pascal routine, while you must always directly install an assembly routine in the clikLoop field. ◆

If you code a click loop routine in assembly, it should set register D0 to 1 and preserve register D2. Returning 0 in register D0 aborts TEClick.

You can write a routine that manages the scroll bars, then calls the default click loop routine, rather than replicating its behavior in your routine. If your customized routine calls the default click loop routine, it must use assembly-language calling convention.

Determining the Line Length

This section describes how to determine the length of a line. You can use this information, for example, to justify a line of text; although TextEdit aligns text with the right or left margins, or centers it, it does not justify it.

To determine the length of a line, you use the information contained in the edit record's line starts array and nLines field. The line starts array is a variable-length field in the edit record that contains the byte offset for the first character of each line. This array has the following boundary conditions:

- The first entry has index 0 and value 0.

- The last entry in the array has index nLines and value teLength (therefore, there are nLines + 1 entries).

- The beginning of the first line is given by lineStarts[0], and the beginning of the second line is given by lineStarts[1]; therefore, the length of the first line is given by lineStarts[1] – lineStarts[0].

- The maximum number of entries is 16,000.

For example, if you want to determine the length of the line *n* (where *n* = 0 for the first line), subtract its start location (contained in the array entry with index *n*) from its end location (contained in the array with index *n* + 1):

```
lengthOfLineN := myTE^^.lineStarts[n+1] — myTE^^.lineStarts[n];
```

The terminating condition for this measurement is when *n* is equal to `nLines` plus 1.

IMPORTANT

Do not change the information contained in the `lineStarts` array. ▲

Advanced Customization

The low-memory global variable `TEDoText` is a hook which contains the address of a multi-purpose text editing routine that advanced programmers may find useful. It lets you display, highlight, and hit-test characters, and position the pen to draw the caret. Hit-testing is the process of determining where to place the insertion point when the user clicks the mouse button; the point selected with the mouse is in the `SelPoint` field. The registers contain the following values.

Registers on entry

A3   Pointer to the locked edit record

D3   Position of the first character (word)

D4   Position of the last character; used as defined below (word)

D7   Selectors for `TEDoText` (word)

teFind	EQU	0	to hit-test the character specified in D3
teHighlight	EQU	1	to highlight the text range specified in D3 and D4
teDraw	EQU	−1	to display the range of text specified in D3 and D4
teCaret	EQU	−2	to draw the caret at the position specified in D3
teFind	EQU	0	to hit-test the character specified in D3

Registers on exit

A0   Pointer to current graphics port

D0   If hit-testing, byte offset where hit, or −1 for none (word)

Note

You need to use the value stored in the edit record `selPoint` field for hit-testing if you replace the routine pointed to by the global variable `TEDoText`. (The assembly-language offset for this field is named `teSelPoint`.) ◆

TextEdit Reference

This section describes the data structures and routines that comprise TextEdit. The "Data Structures" section shows the Pascal data structures including the edit record and subsidiary structures that allow for text styling and customization of TextEdit. Together with the TextEdit private scrap and the TextEdit style scrap, these data structures define the TextEdit environment.

The "Routines" section describes the routines that provide applications with the means of creating edit records and accessing, editing, and displaying multistyled and monostyled text, including text highlighting and scrolling.

The constants that define values for some of the parameters used in several of these routines are listed in the "Summary of TextEdit" on page 2-118.

Data Structures

This section describes the data structures and their contents which provide information to the TextEdit routines. Both monostyled and multistyled edit records have a 32 KB maximum text size.

The TextEdit data structures are defined as follows:

- The edit record, defined by the `TERec` data type, stores the display and editing information for TextEdit.

- Along with various subsidiary data structures, the style record, defined by the `TEStyleRec` data type, stores the character attribute information for the text of the edit record.

- The style run table, defined by the `StyleRun` data type, is an array that contains the boundaries of each style run and an index to its character attribute information in the style element array.

- The style table, defined by the `TEStyleTable` data type, contains one entry for each distinct set of character attributes used in the text of the edit record.

- The line-height table, defined by the `LHTable` data type, provides an array of line heights to hold the vertical spacing information for a given edit record. It also contains line ascent information.

■ The null style record, defined by the `NullStRec` data type, contains the null scrap which is used to store character attribute information for a null selection.

■ The style scrap record, defined by the `StScrpRec` data type, is used by routines to store character attribute information temporarily.

■ The scrap style table, defined by the `scrpStyleTab` data type, is contained in the style scrap record.

■ The scrap style element record, defined by the `ScrpSTElement` data type, contains the character attribute information for an element in the scrap style table. One scrap style element record exists for each sequential attribute change in the associated text.

■ The TextEdit dispatch record, defined by the `TEDispatchRec` data type, contains the internal addresses of the TextEdit routines for the end-of-line hook, the draw hook, the width measurement hook, the new width measurement hook, and the text width measurement hook, unless you replace them with the addresses of your own customized versions of these routines.

■ The text style record, defined by the `TextStyle` data type, is used by several routines to pass character attribute information between the application and a routine. The record is passed as a variable or reference parameter.

Figure 2-15 shows the TextEdit data structures and their fields to help you understand how the TextEdit data structures are organized and related. (For a monostyled edit record, TextEdit creates only the `TERec` and `TEDispatchRec` data structures.) To read from and write to these data structures, use the TextEdit routines rather than modifying these fields directly. This practice ensures future compatibility.

For most operations, you do not need to know the exact structure of an edit record; TextEdit routines gain access to the record for you. However, when manipulating character attribute information, you might find it helpful to understand how the data structures used to contain and track character attribute information are organized.

Note
The space beyond the hooks in the TextEdit dispatch record is reserved for internal use. If you attempt to use this private area, you may corrupt TextEdit data. ◆

Figure 2-15   The TextEdit data structures and fields

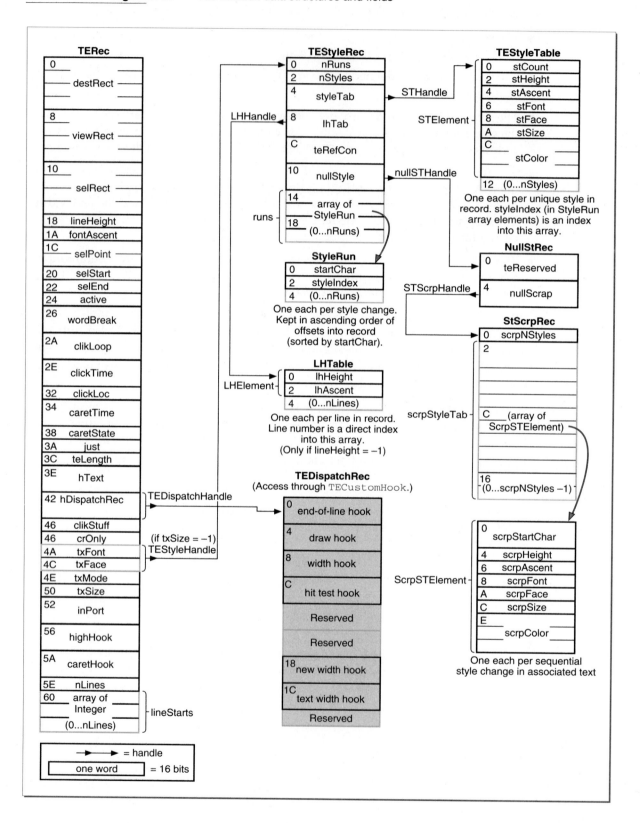

The Edit Record

The edit record contains display, storage, styling, and other information related to editing that TextEdit requires. Although some fields are used differently for multistyled edit records and monostyled edit records, the structure of an edit record is the same whether the text is multistyled or monostyled.

```
TYPE  TERec =
      RECORD
            destRect:    Rect;      {destination rectangle}
            viewRect:    Rect;      {view rectangle}
            selRect:     Rect;      {the selection rectangle}
            lineHeight:  Integer;   {used for vertical spacing of lines}
            fontAscent:  Integer;   {used for caret/highlighting }
                                    { position}
            selPoint:    Point;     {point selected with the mouse}
            selStart:    Integer;   {start of selection range}
            selEnd:      Integer;   {end of selection range}
            active:      Integer;   {set when record is activated or }
                                    { deactivated}
            wordBreak:   ProcPtr;   {word break hook}
            clikLoop:    ProcPtr;   {click loop hook}
            clickTime:   LongInt;   {used internally}
            clickLoc:    Integer;   {used internally}
            caretTime:   LongInt;   {used internally}
            caretState:  Integer;   {used internally}
            just:        Integer;   {alignment of text}
            teLength:    Integer;   {length of text}
            hText:       Handle;    {handle to text to be edited}
            hDispatchRec: Handle;   {handle to TextEdit dispatch record}
            clikStuff:   Integer;   {used internally}
            crOnly:      Integer;   {if <0, new line at Return only}
            txFont:      Integer;   {text font.Otherwise, if txSize is }
                                    { -1, combines with txFace to hold }
                                    { a handle to the style record.}
            txFace:      Style;     {character style; unpacked byte. }
                                    { Otherwise, if txSize is -1, }
                                    { combines with txFont to hold a }
                                    { handle to the style record}
            txMode:      Integer;   {pen mode}
            txSize:      Integer;   {tells if multistyled }
                                    { edit record; if not, font size}
            inPort:      GrafPtr;   {a pointer to the graphics port }
                                    { for this TERec}
```

```
                     highHook:    ProcPtr; {used for text highlighting}
                     caretHook:   ProcPtr; {used for caret appearance}
                     nLines:      Integer; {number of lines}
                     lineStarts:  ARRAY[0..16000] OF Integer;
                                             {positions of line starts}
                END;

          TYPE  TEPtr    = ^TERec;
                TEHandle = ^TEPtr
```

Field descriptions

destRect	The destination rectangle, in local coordinates.
viewRect	The view rectangle, in local coordinates.
selRect	The selection rectangle, whose boundaries are defined in local coordinates. This value is the current selection range or insertion point.
lineHeight	The vertical spacing of lines of text. Vertical spacing may be fixed or it may vary from line to line, depending upon specific text attributes. If the value of lineHeight is greater than 0, this field specifies the fixed vertical distance from the ascent line of one line of text down to the ascent line of the next.
	If the value of lineHeight is less than 1, then this field specifies the vertical distance from the ascent line of one line of text down to the ascent line of the next calculated independently for each line, based on the maximum value for any individual character attribute on that line.
fontAscent	The font ascent line. If the value of fontAscent is greater than 0, this field specifies how far above the base line the pen is positioned to begin drawing the caret or highlighting.
	For single-spaced text, this is the height of the text in pixels (the height of the tallest characters in the font from the base line). If the value of fontAscent is less than 1, this field specifies the font ascent calculated independently for each line, based on maximum value for any individual character attribute on that line.
selPoint	The point selected with the mouse, in the local coordinates of the current graphics port. The assembly-language offset for this field is named teSelPoint.
selStart	The byte offset of the beginning of a selection range. Note that byte offset 0 refers to the first byte in the text buffer.
selEnd	The byte offset of the end of a selection range. To include that byte, this value must be 1 greater than the position of the last byte offset of the text.
active	This field is used internally by TextEdit. It is set when an edit record is activated through TEActivate and then reset when the edit record is rendered inactive through TEDeactivate. To ensure future compatibility, use TEActivate or TEDeactivate to access this field.

wordBreak	The record's word selection break routine. This routine determines the word that is highlighted when the user double-clicks in the text and the position at which text is wrapped at the end of a line.
clikLoop	The pointer to the click loop routine. The specified click loop routine is called repeatedly by the TEClick procedure as long as the mouse button is held down within the text.
clickTime	This field is for internal use only.
clickLoc	This field is for internal use only.
caretTime	This field is for internal use only.
caretState	This field is for internal use only.
just	The type of text alignment: default (according to primary line direction), left, center, or right.
teLength	The number of bytes in the text to be edited. For two-byte systems, potentially twice the number of characters. Initially set to zero. The maximum length is 32767 bytes.
hText	A handle to the text. Initially, it points to a zero-length block of text in the heap.
hDispatchRec	The handle to the TextEdit dispatch record. This field is for internal use only; do not modify this field, or copy it to another edit record. Each edit record has its own dispatch record. Attempting to use the dispatch record of one edit record with another edit record can cause TextEdit to crash.
clikStuff	This field is for internal use only. TextEdit sets this field to reflect whether the most recent mouse-down event occurred on the leading or trailing edge of a glyph. TextEdit uses this value in determining a caret position.
crOnly	A value specifying whether or not text wraps at the right edge of the destination rectangle. If crOnly is positive, text does wrap.
	If crOnly is negative, new lines are specified explicitly by Return characters only; text does not wrap at the edge of the destination rectangle. (This is useful in an application similar to a programming-language editor, where you may not want a single line of code to be split onto two lines.)
txFont	The font of all the text in the edit record if the txSize field of this edit record ≥ 0. If you change this value, the entire text of this edit record has the new characteristic when it is redrawn; also, remember to change the lineHeight and fontAscent fields as well.
	If the txSize field is –1, this field combines with txFace to hold a handle to the associated style record.
txFace	The character attributes of all the text in an edit record if the txSize field of this edit record ≥ 0. If you change this value, the entire text of this edit record has the new characteristic when it is redrawn; also, remember to change the lineHeight and fontAscent fields as well.
	If the txSize field is –1, this field combines with txFont to hold a handle to the associated style record.

txMode   The pen mode of all the text in the edit record. If you change this
                value, the entire text of this edit record has the new characteristic
                when it is redrawn; also, remember to change the lineHeight and
                fontAscent fields as well.

txSize   Depending on its value, txSize either contains the point size of all
                of the text or it acts as a flag indicating whether or not there is
                associated character attribute information. If txSize ≥ 0, this is a
                monostyled edit record, that is, all text is set in a single font, size,
                and face, and the value of txSize is the size of the text. If txSize
                is –1, the edit record contains associated character attribute
                information and the txFont and txFace fields combine to form a
                handle to the style record.

inPort   A pointer to the graphics port associated with this edit record.

highHook   A pointer to the routine that deals with text highlighting. In
                assembly language, the highHook field is located at the offset
                teHiHook. For more information, see the following section, "The
                High Hook and Caret Hook Fields."

caretHook   A pointer to the routine that controls the appearance of the caret. In
                assembly language, the caretHook field is located at the offset
                teCarHook. For more information, see the following section, "The
                High Hook and Caret Hook Fields."

nLines   The number of lines in the text.

lineStarts   An array containing the character position of the first character in
                each line. It is declared to have 16001 elements to comply with
                Pascal range checking. This is a dynamic data structure having only
                as many elements as needed. TextEdit calculates these values
                internally, so do not change the elements of the lineStarts array.
                Because this data structure grows and shrinks, the size of the edit
                record changes.

The High Hook and Caret Hook Fields

The highHook and caretHook fields—at the offsets teHiHook and teCarHook in
assembly language—contain the addresses of routines that deal with text highlighting
and the caret. These routines pass parameters in registers; if you replace these routines,
your application must save and restore the registers' contents.

If you store the address of a routine in teHiHook, that routine is used instead of the
QuickDraw procedure InvertRect, which is called by default, whenever a selection
range is to be highlighted. Your routine can destroy the contents of registers A0, A1, D0,
D1, and D2. On entry, A3 is a pointer to a locked edit record; the stack contains the
rectangle enclosing the text being highlighted. (Use of the A3 register is equivalent to the
InvertRect r parameter of type RECT. See the QuickDraw chapters in *Inside Macintosh:
Imaging* for more information about the InvertRect procedure.) For example, if you
store the address of the following routine in teHiHook, selection range is underlined
instead of inverted.

```
UnderHigh
    MOVE.L    4(SP),A0              ;get address of rectangle to be
                                    ;highlighted
    MOVE      bottom(A0),top(A0)    ;make the top coordinate equal to
    SUBQ      #1,top(A0)           ;the bottom coordinate minus 1
    _InverRect                     ;invert the resulting rectangle
    RTS
```

The routine whose address is stored in `teCarHook` acts exactly the same way as the `teHiHook` routine, but on the caret instead of the selection range, allowing you to change the appearance of the caret. The routine is called with the stack containing the rectangle address that encloses the caret.

The Style Record

The style record stores the character attribute information for the text of a multistyled edit record. If an edit record has associated character attribute information, its `txFont` and `txFace` fields combine to hold a style handle, of type `TEStyleHandle`, to its style record. The text is divided into style runs, summarized in the style run table, of type `StyleRun`, which is part of the style record. Each entry in the style run table gives the starting character position of a run and an index into the style table, of type `TEStyleTable`.

The style table element pointed to by the style run index describes the character attributes for that run.

To determine the length of a run, you subtract its start position from that of the next entry in the style run table. A dummy entry at the end of the style run table delimits the length of the last run; its start position is equal to the overall number of characters in the text, plus 1. The `TEStyleRec` data type defines the style record.

```
TYPE  TEStyleRec =
    RECORD
        nRuns:     Integer;       {number of style runs}
        nStyles:   Integer;       {size of style table}
        styleTab:  STHandle;      {handle to style table}
        lhTab:     LHHandle;      {handle to line-height table}
        teRefCon:  LongInt;       {reserved for application use}
        nullStyle: NullStHandle;  {handle to style set at }
                                  { null selection}
        runs:      ARRAY [0..8000] OF StyleRun;
    END;

TEStylePtr = ^TEStyleRec;
TEStyleHandle = ^TEStylePtr;
```

```
StyleRun = RECORD
    startChar:  Integer;          {starting character position}
    styleIndex: Integer;          {index in style table}
END;
```

Field descriptions

nRuns	The number of style runs in the text.
nStyles	The number of distinct sets of character attributes used in the text; this forms the size of the style table.
styleTab	A handle to the style table.
lhTab	A handle to the line height table.
teRefCon	A reference constant for use by applications. The application can use this 32-bit field to suit its needs.
nullStyle	A handle to the style scrap record used to store the character attribute information for a null selection.
runs	A table of style runs that is of indefinite length.

```
TEStylePtr = ^TEStyleRec;
TEStyleHandle = ^TEStylePtr;

StyleRun = RECORD
    startChar:  Integer;          {starting character position}
    styleIndex: Integer;          {index in style table}
END;
```

The Style Table

The style table contains one entry for each distinct set of character attributes used in the text of an edit record. Each entry is defined in a style element record. The size of the table is given by the nStyles field of the style record. There is no duplication; each set of character attributes appears exactly once in the table. A reference count tells how many times each set of attributes is used in the table. The TEStyleTable data type defines the style table. The STElement data type defines the style element record.

```
TYPE  STElement =
      RECORD
          stCount:    Integer;     {number of runs in this style}
          stHeight:   Integer;     {line height}
          stAscent:   Integer;     {font ascent}
          stFont:     Integer;     {font family ID}
          stFace:     Style;       {character style}
          stSize:     Integer;     {size in points}
          stColor:    RGBColor;    {absolute RGB color}
      END;
```

```
STHandle = ^STPtr;
STPtr    = ^TEStyleTable;


TEStyleTable = ARRAY [0..1776] OF STElement;
```

Field descriptions

stCount	A reference count of character runs using this set of character attributes.
stHeight	The line height for this run, in points.
stAscent	The font ascent for this run, in points.
stFont	The font family ID.
stFace	The character style (bold, italic, and so forth). This field consists of two bytes. The low-order byte contains the character style. TextEdit uses the high bit (bit 15) of the high-order byte to store the style run direction: it uses 0 for left-to-right text, and 1 for right-to-left text.
stSize	The text size, in points.
stColor	The RGB (red, green, blue) color.

The Line Height Table

The line height table holds vertical spacing information for the text of an edit record. This table parallels the lineStarts array in the edit record itself. Its length equals the edit record's nLines field plus 1 for a dummy entry at the end, just as the lineStarts array ends with a dummy entry that has the same value as the length of the text. The table's contents are recalculated whenever the line starting values are themselves recalculated with the TECalText routine or whenever an editing action causes recalibration.

The line height table is used only if the lineHeight and fontAscent fields in the edit record are negative; positive values in those fields specify fixed vertical spacing, overriding the information in the table. The line height table is of type LHTable, which is an array of elements of LHElement.

```
TYPE LHElement =
   RECORD
      lhHeight:     Integer;     {maximum height in line}
      lhAscent:     Integer;     {maximum ascent in line}
   END;

LHPtr = ^LHTable;
LHHandle = ^LHPtr;


LHTable = ARRAY [0..8000] OF LHElement;
```

Field descriptions

lhHeight   The line height in points. This is the maximum value for any individual character attribute in the line.

lhAscent   The font ascent in points; this is the maximum value for any individual character attribute in a line.

The Null Style Record

The null style record contains the null scrap, which is used to store the character attribute information for a null selection (insertion point). A number of routines either write this character attribute information to the null scrap or read it from this scrap (to be applied to inserted text). The null scrap is created and initialized when an application calls TEStyleNew to create a multistyled edit record. The null scrap is retained for the life of the edit record; it is destroyed when TEDispose destroys the edit record and releases the memory allocated for it.

The NullSTRec data type defines the null style record.

```
TYPE NullStRec =
    RECORD
        teReserved:    LongInt; {reserved for future expansion}
        nullScrap:     StScrpHandle;  {handle to the style scrap }
                                      { record}
    END;


NullStPtr = ^NullStRec;
NullStHandle = ^NullStPtr;
```

Field descriptions

teReserved   This field is reserved for future expansion.

nullScrap   A handle to the style scrap record.

The Style Scrap Record

The style scrap is used for storing character attribute information associated with the current text selection or insertion point, character attribute information to be applied to text, or multistyled text that is cut or copied. When multistyled text is cut or copied, the character attribute information is written to both the style scrap and the desk scrap.

In most cases, the style scrap is created dynamically as needed by routines. However, a style scrap record can be created directly without using the TEGetStyleScrapHandle function; the character attribute information written to it can be applied to inserted text through TEStyleInsert or to existing text through TEUseStyleScrap.

The format of the style scrap is defined by a style scrap record of type STScrpRec.

```
TYPE   StScrpRec =
       RECORD
           scrpNStyles:   Integer;   {number of sets of }
                                     { character attributes in scrap}
           scrpStyleTab:  ScrpSTTable; {table of attributes for }
                                     { scrap}
       END;

StScrpPtr = ^StScrpRec;
StScrpHandle = ^StScrpPtr;
```

Field descriptions

scrpNStyles   The number of style runs used in the text. This determines the size
                of the style table. When character attribute information is written to
                the null scrap, this field is set to 1; when the character attribute
                information is removed, this field is set to 0.

scrpStyleTab   The scrap style table containing an element for each style run.

The Scrap Style Table

The style scrap record contains the scrap style table. Unlike the main style table for an edit record, the scrap style table may contain duplicate elements; the entries in the table correspond one-to-one with the style runs in the text. The scrpStartChar field of each entry gives the starting position for the run.

The scrpStyleTab data type defines the scrap style table data structure, which is an array of scrap style element records. The ScrpSTElement data type defines each scrap style element record.

```
TYPE   ScrpSTElement =
       RECORD
           scrpStartChar: LongInt;    {offset to start of style}
           scrpHeight:    Integer;    {line height}
           scrpAscent:    Integer;    {font ascent}
           scrpFont:      Integer;    {font family ID }
           scrpFace:      Style;      {character style}
           scrpSize:      Integer;    {size in points}
           scrpColor:     RGBColor;   {absolute (RGB) color}
       END;

ScrpSTTable = ARRAY[0..1600] OF ScrpSTElement;
```

Field descriptions

scrpStartChar   The offset to the beginning of a style record in the scrap.

scrpHeight	The line height. You can determine the line height and the font ascent using the QuickDraw routine `GetFontInfo` described in the chapter "QuickDraw Text" in this book.
scrpAscent	The font ascent. See `scrpHeight`.
scrpFont	The font family ID.
scrpFace	The style (such as plain, bold, underline).
scrpSize	The size in points.
scrpColor	The RGB (red, green, blue) color for the style scrap.

Text Style Record

Text style records are used for communicating character attribute information between the application and several TextEdit routines, such as `TEContinuousStyle` and `TEReplaceStyle`. They carry the same information as the style element records in the style table, but without the reference count, line height, and font ascent.

The `TextStyle` data type defines a text style record.

```
TYPE   TextStyle =
       RECORD
           tsFont:  Integer;      {font family number}
           tsFace:  Style;        {character style}
           tsSize:  Integer;      {size in points}
           tsColor: RGBColor;     {absolute RGB color}
       END;


TextStylePtr = ^TextStyle;
TextStyleHandle = ^TextStylePtr;
```

Field descriptions

tsFont	The font family number.
tsFace	The character style (bold, italic, plain, and so forth).
tsSize	The text size in points.
tsColor	The RGB (red, green, blue) color.

Routines

This section describes the TextEdit routines that an application can call to

- initialize TextEdit and create an edit record

- activate and deactivate an edit record

- set and get the text and character attribute information of an edit record

- set the caret and selection range

- display and scroll text

- modify the text of an edit record

- manage the TextEdit private scrap

- check, set, and replace character attributes

- use byte offsets and corresponding points

- toggle automatic scrolling, outline highlighting, and text buffering on and off

- customize TextEdit

Each routine description defines a Pascal interface, provides related assembly-language information, and lists possible result codes, if any are returned.

Initializing TextEdit, Creating an Edit Record, and Disposing of an Edit Record

Preparation of a window for text editing involves setting up TextEdit's internal data structures by calling the `TEInit` procedure and creating an edit record for the window with the `TEStyleNew` function or the `TENew` function.

The `TEStyleNew` function creates a new multistyled edit record. A multistyled edit record contains text whose attributes, including font, size, and style, can vary from character to character. The `TENew` function creates a new monostyled edit record. A monostyled edit record contains text that is set in a single font, size, and style. Before either of these functions is called, the window must be in the current graphics port.

The `TEDispose` procedure destroys an edit record and releases the memory used for it. For a complete description of the edit record and its fields, see "An Overview of the TextEdit Data Structures" on page 2-16 and "Data Structures" on page 2-64.

TEInit

The `TEInit` procedure initializes TextEdit.

```
PROCEDURE TEInit;
```

DESCRIPTION

In addition to initialization of miscellaneous global variables, such as `TEDoText` and `TERecal`, the `TEInit` procedure sets up the private scrap and allocates a handle to it. Call `TEInit` at the beginning of your program after you initialize QuickDraw, the Font Manager, and the Window Manager, in that order, and before you initialize the Dialog Manager. You should call `TEInit` even if your application doesn't use TextEdit, so that desk accessories and dialog and alert boxes, which use TextEdit routines, work correctly.

TEStyleNew

The TEStyleNew function creates a multistyled edit record and allocates a handle to it.

```
FUNCTION TEStyleNew (destRect: Rect; viewRect: Rect): TEHandle;
```

destRect   The destination rectangle for the new edit record, specified in the local coordinates of the current graphics port. This is the area in which text is laid out.

viewRect   The view rectangle for the new edit record, specified in the local coordinates of the current graphics port. This is the area of the window in which text is actually displayed.

DESCRIPTION

Always use the TEStyleNew function to create an edit record for text that uses varying character attributes. The TEStyleNew function sets the txSize, lineHeight, and fontAscent fields of the edit record to –1, allocates a style record, and stores a handle to the style record in the txFont and txFace fields. The TEStyleNew function creates and initializes a null scrap that is used by TextEdit routines throughout the life of the edit record.

Call TEStyleNew once for every edit record you want allocated. Your application needs to store the handle to the edit record that is returned; many routines require it as an input parameter.

If your application contains more than one window where text editing occurs, you need to create an edit record for each window.

TENew

The TENew function creates and initializes a monostyled edit record and allocates a handle to it.

```
FUNCTION TENew (destRect,viewRect: Rect): TEHandle;
```

destRect   The destination rectangle for the new edit record, specified in the local coordinates of the current graphics port. This is the area in which text is laid out.

viewRect   The view, or visible, rectangle for the new edit record, specified in the local coordinates of the current graphics port. This is the area of the window in which text is actually displayed.

DESCRIPTION

A monostyled edit record is one in which all text is restricted to a single font, size, and style. Use TENew when the text is to be rendered in attributes that are consistent from character to character. Otherwise, use TEStyleNew.

Call TENew once for every edit record you want allocated. Your application should store the handle to the edit record that is returned; many routines require it as an input parameter. The edit record assumes the drawing environment of the graphics port.

If your application contains more than one window where text editing occurs, you need to create an edit record for each window.

TEDispose

The TEDispose procedure removes a specified edit record and releases all memory associated with it.

```
PROCEDURE TEDispose (hTE: TEHandle);
```

hTE   A handle to the edit record for which the allocated memory should be
             released.

DESCRIPTION

Call the TEDispose procedure only when you're completely through with an edit record.

Note that if your program retains a handle to text associated with the edit record that you are destroying with TEDispose, the handle becomes invalid because the TEDispose procedure disposes of it, as well as the dispatch record handle. If the record is multistyled, TEDispose also disposes all of the style-related handles: STHandle, LHHandle, STScrpHandle, nullSTHandle, and TEStyleHandle.

To continue to refer to the text after you've destroyed the edit record, you need to make a copy of the handle in the hText field of the edit record using the Operating System Utilities HandToHand function before you call TEDispose. (See *Inside Macintosh: Operating System Utilities* for more information.)

In addition to disposing of the edit record, the edit record handle, and the dispatch record handle, the TEDispose procedure destroys the null scrap associated with the edit record and releases the memory used for it.

Activating and Deactivating an Edit Record

When your application receives notification of an activate event, it can call the TEActivate procedure, which activates an edit record and highlights the selection range or displays a caret at the insertion point. When the activate event flag is set to deactivate the window, your application can call the TEDeactivate procedure, which changes an edit record's status from active to inactive and removes the selection range highlighting or the caret. (When outline highlighting is on, TEDeactivate frames the text or displays a dimmed caret.)

TEActivate

The TEActivate procedure activates the specified edit record.

```
PROCEDURE TEActivate (hTE: TEHandle);
```

hTE   A handle to the specified edit record.

DESCRIPTION

When you call TEActivate for an edit record, the selection range is highlighted. If the selection range is an insertion point, TEActivate displays a caret there.
Call this procedure every time the Event Manager function WaitNextEvent reports that the window containing the edit record has become active.

If you do not call TEActivate before you call TEClick, TEIdle, or TESetSelect, the selection range is not highlighted, or, if the selection range is set to an insertion point, a caret is not displayed at the insertion point. However, if you have turned on outline highlighting through the TEFeatureFlag function for the edit record, the text of the selection range is framed or a dimmed or an unblinking caret is displayed at the insertion point.

SEE ALSO

For a description of the WaitNextEvent function, see the chapter "Event Manager" in *Inside Macintosh: Macintosh Toolbox Essentials*.

TEDeactivate

The TEDeactivate procedure deactivates an edit record.

```
PROCEDURE TEDeactivate (hTE: TEHandle);
```

hTE   A handle to the specified edit record.

DESCRIPTION

When you call `TEDeactivate` for an edit record, the highlighted selection range is no longer displayed. If the selection range is an insertion point, `TEDeactivate` no longer displays the caret. However, if you turned on outline highlighting through the `TEFeatureFlag` function for the edit record, the text of the selection range is framed or a dimmed or an unblinking caret is displayed at the insertion point when the record is deactivated.

Call this procedure every time the Event Manager function `WaitNextEvent` reports that the window containing the edit record has become inactive.

SEE ALSO

For a description of the `WaitNextEvent` function, see the chapter "Event Manager" in *Inside Macintosh: Macintosh Toolbox Essentials*.

Setting and Getting an Edit Record's Text and Character Attribute Information

The TextEdit procedure `TEKey` allows you to handle key-down events and enter text input through the keyboard. The procedure `TESetText` lets you incorporate existing text into the text buffer of an edit record. Once an edit record contains text, you can use the `TEGetText` function to get a handle to the text itself. For a multistyled edit record, you can get a handle to the style record by calling `GetStyleHandle`. You can set the handle to the style record using the `TESetStyleHandle` procedure. This section describes these routines.

TEKey

The `TEKey` procedure replaces the selection range in the text of the specified edit record with the input character and positions the insertion point just past the inserted character.

```
PROCEDURE TEKey (key: Char; hTE: TEHandle);
```

key   The input character.

hTE   A handle to the edit record in whose text the character is to be entered.

DESCRIPTION

If the selection range is an insertion point, `TEKey` inserts the character. (Two-byte characters are passed one byte at a time.) If the `key` parameter contains a backspace character, the selection range or the character immediately before the insertion point is deleted. When the primary line direction is right-to-left, the character to the right of the insertion point is deleted. When the primary line direction is left-to-right, the character to the left of the insertion point is deleted.

When the user deletes text up to the beginning of a set of character attributes, TEKey saves the attributes in the null scrap's style scrap record. The attributes are saved temporarily to be applied to characters inserted after the deletion. As soon as the user clicks in another area of the text, TEKey removes the attributes. TEKey redraws the text as necessary.

Call TEKey every time the Event Manager function WaitNextEvent reports a keyboard event that your application determines should be handled by TextEdit.

Because TEKey inserts every character passed in the key parameter, your application must filter all characters which aren't actual text, such as keys typed in conjunction with the Command key.

SEE ALSO

For a description of the WaitNextEvent function, see the chapter "Event Manager" in *Inside Macintosh: Macintosh Toolbox Essentials*.

TESetText

The TESetText procedure incorporates a copy of the specified text into the designated edit record.

```
PROCEDURE TESetText (text: Ptr; length: LongInt; hTE: TEHandle);
```

text   A pointer to the text to be copied and incorporated.

length   The number of characters in the text to be incorporated.

hTE   A handle to the edit record into which the text is to be copied.

DESCRIPTION

The TESetText procedure copies the specified text into the existing hText handle of the edit record, resizing the buffer, if necessary; it doesn't bring in the original text. The copied text is wrapped to the destination rectangle, and its lineStarts and nLines fields are calculated accordingly. The selection range is set to an insertion point at the end of the incorporated text. The TESetText procedure does not display the copied text on the screen. To do this, call TEUpdate.

TEGetText

The `TEGetText` function returns a handle to the text of the specified edit record.

```
FUNCTION TEGetText (hTE: TEHandle): CharsHandle;
```

hTE   A handle to the edit record containing the text whose handle you want
             returned. You pass this handle as an input parameter.

CharsHandle
             A handle to the text of the edit record.

DESCRIPTION

The `TEGetText` function doesn't make a copy of the text. Rather, it returns the handle to the text which is stored as a packed array of characters. (This handle belongs to TextEdit; your application must not destroy it.) The `teLength` field of the edit record contains the length of the text whose handle is returned.

The handle of type `CharsHandle` that is returned by `TEGetText` corresponds to the `hText` field of the edit record, but the data type is defined as follows:

```
TYPE   CharsHandle = ^CharsPtr;
       CharsPtr    = ^Chars;
       Chars       = PACKED ARRAY[0..32000] OF CHAR;
```

TESetStyleHandle

The `TESetStyleHandle` procedure sets an edit record's style handle, which is stored in the `txFont` and `txFace` fields.

```
PROCEDURE TESetStyleHandle (theHandle: TEStyleHandle;
                            hTE: TEHandle);
```

theHandle   The style handle to be set in the combined `txFont` and `txFace` fields of
             the specified edit record.

hTE   A handle to the edit record.

DESCRIPTION

The `TESetStyleHandle` procedure has no effect on monostyled edit records.

Your application should always use `TESetStyleHandle` rather than manipulate the fields of the edit record directly.

TEGetStyleHandle

The `TEGetStyleHandle` function returns the style handle stored in the designated edit record's `txFont` and `txFace` fields. The style handle points to the associated style record.

```
FUNCTION TEGetStyleHandle (hTE: TEHandle): TEStyleHandle;
```

hTE   A handle to the multistyled edit record containing the style handle to be returned.

DESCRIPTION

The `TEGetStyleHandle` function returns a handle to the style record (of type `TEStyleRec`), not a copy of it. Because only multistyled edit records have style records, `TEGetStyleHandle` returns `NIL` when used with a monostyled edit record. To ensure future compatibility, your application should always use this function rather than manipulate the fields of the edit record directly.

Setting the Caret and Selection Range

Your application can call `TEIdle` to blink a caret at an insertion point during idle processing, the `TEClick` procedure to control the placement and highlighting of the text selection range in response to mouse-down events generated when a user clicks the mouse button, and the `TESetSelect` procedure to set the text selection range to be edited next or denote the insertion point. This section describes these routines.

TEIdle

When called repeatedly, the `TEIdle` procedure displays a blinking caret at the insertion point, if any exists, in the text of the specified edit record of an active window.

```
PROCEDURE TEIdle (hTE: TEHandle);
```

hTE   A handle to the edit record.

DESCRIPTION

You need to call `TEIdle` only when the window containing the text is active; the caret is blinked only then. TextEdit observes a minimum blink interval, initially set to 32 ticks. No matter how often you call `TEIdle`, the time between blinks is never less than the minimum interval. (The user can adjust the minimum interval setting with the General Controls control panel.)

To maintain a constant frequency of blinking, you need to call `TEIdle` at least once each time through your main event loop. Call it more than once if your application does an unusually large amount of processing each time through the loop.

Call the Event Manager's `GetCaretTime` function to get the blink rate. (See the chapter "Event Manager" in *Inside Macintosh: Macintosh Toolbox Essentials*.)

TEClick

The `TEClick` procedure controls placement and highlighting of the selection range as determined by mouse events.

```
PROCEDURE TEClick (pt: Point; extend: Boolean; hTE: TEHandle);
```

pt   The mouse location in local coordinates at the time the mouse button was pressed, obtainable from the event record (in global coordinates).

extend   A flag denoting the state of the Shift key at the time of the click as indicated by the Event Manager. If the Shift key was held down at the time of the click to extend the selection, pass a value of TRUE.

hTE   A handle to the edit record whose text is displayed in the view rectangle where the click occurred.

DESCRIPTION

Call `TEClick` whenever a mouse-down event occurs in the view rectangle of the edit record and the window associated with that edit record is active. The `TEClick` procedure keeps control until the mouse button is released. Use the QuickDraw procedure `GlobalToLocal` to convert the global coordinates of the mouse location given in the event record to the local coordinate system for `pt`.

The `TEClick` procedure removes highlighting of the old selection range unless the selection range is being extended. If the mouse moves, meaning that a drag is occurring, `TEClick` expands or shortens the selection range accordingly a character at a time. In the case of a double-click, the word where the cursor is positioned becomes the selection range.

SEE ALSO

For more information about the `GlobalToLocal` procedure, see the QuickDraw chapters in *Inside Macintosh: Imaging*.

TESetSelect

The `TESetSelect` procedure sets the selection range within the text of the specified edit record.

```
PROCEDURE TESetSelect (selStart, selEnd: LongInt; hTE: TEHandle);
```

selStart   The byte offset at the start of the text selection range.

selEnd   The byte offset at the end of the text selection range.

hTE   A handle to the edit record.

DESCRIPTION

The `TESetSelect` procedure removes highlighting of the old selection range and highlights the new one. If `selStart` equals `selEnd`, the new selection range is an insertion point, and a caret is displayed. If `selEnd` is anywhere beyond the last character of the text, `TESetSelect` uses the first position past the last character. The `selEnd` and `selStart` fields can range from 0 to 32767.

SPECIAL CONSIDERATIONS

When only the Roman script system is used, the selection range is always displayed and highlighted as a continuous range of text. However, when one or more script systems requiring mixed-directional display of text are installed, a continuous sequence of characters in memory may appear as a discontinuous selection when displayed.

Displaying and Scrolling Text

The routines that this section describes let you control how text is displayed. `TESetAlignment` lets you specify whether text is to be right aligned, left aligned, or centered. `TEUpdate` draws the text, updating the text editing window. `TETextBox` lets you draw static text in a box, such as a dialog box, without requiring that you first create an edit record. `TECalText` recalculates line breaks. `TEGetHeight` returns the height of all the lines of text between two lines. `TEScroll` scrolls the text by the amount you specify. `TEPinScroll` scrolls the text, automatically stopping when it scrolls the last line into view. `TEAutoView` lets you turn automatic scrolling on or off. `TESelView` automatically scrolls the text into view, if automatic scrolling is turned on through `TEAutoView`.

TESetAlignment

The `TESetAlignment` procedure sets the alignment of the specified text in an edit record so that it is centered, right aligned, or left aligned, or aligned according to the line direction.

```
PROCEDURE TESetAlignment (align: Integer; hTE: TEHandle);
```

align   The alignment for the specified text.

hTE   A handle to the edit record containing the text.

DESCRIPTION

You can use the following constants to specify the text alignment through the `align` parameter.

Constant	Value	Description
teFlushDefault	0	Align according to primary line direction
teCenter	1	Centered for all scripts
teFlushRight	−1	Right aligned for all scripts
teFlushLeft	−2	Left aligned for all scripts

For compatibility, the previous names of these constants are still supported. They are `teJustLeft`, `teJustCenter`, `teJustRight`, and `teForceLeft`.

The default value of the `just` field of the edit record is `teFlushDefault`. This means that text alignment is based on the primary line direction which is set by default according to the system script.

For languages that are read from right to left, text is right aligned by default. For languages that are read from left to right, text is left aligned by default. If you change the alignment, call the `InvalRect` procedure after `TESetAlignment` to redraw the text with the new alignment.

TextEdit does not support justified alignment. To draw justified text, use the QuickDraw Text routines.

SEE ALSO

For more information about the `InvalRect` procedure, see the chapter "Window Manager" in *Inside Macintosh: Macintosh Toolbox Essentials*. For more information about drawing justified text, see the chapter "QuickDraw Text" in this book.

TEUpdate

The TEUpdate procedure draws the specified text within a given update rectangle.

```
PROCEDURE TEUpdate (rUpdate: Rect; hTE: TEHandle);
```

rUpdate   The update rectangle, given in the coordinates of the current graphics
            port, where the specified text is to be drawn.

hTE   A handle to the edit record containing the text to be drawn.

DESCRIPTION

Call TEUpdate every time the Event Manager function WaitNextEvent reports an
update event for a text editing window—after you call the Window Manager procedure
BeginUpdate, and before you call the EndUpdate procedure. You also need to erase
the update region with the EraseRect procedure. If you don't the caret can sometimes
remain visible when the window is deactivated.

SEE ALSO

For a description of the WaitNextEvent function, see the chapter "Event Manager" in
Inside Macintosh: Macintosh Toolbox Essentials. For more information about the
BeginUpdate and EndUpdate procedures, see the chapter "Window Manager" in
Inside Macintosh: Macintosh Toolbox Essentials.

TETextBox

The TETextBox procedure draws the indicated text in a given rectangle with the
specified alignment.

```
PROCEDURE TETextBox (text: Ptr; length: LongInt; box: Rect;
                     align: Integer);
```

text   A pointer to the text to be drawn.

length   The number of bytes comprising the text.

box   The rectangle where the text is to be drawn. The rectangle is specified in
            local coordinates (of the current graphics port) and must be at least as
            wide as the first character drawn. (A good rule of thumb is to make the
            rectangle at least 20 pixels wide.)

align   The kind of alignment for the specified text.

DESCRIPTION

The TETextBox procedure provides you with an easy way to display static text to a user. It creates its own monostyled edit record, which it deletes when finished with it, so you cannot edit the text it draws. The TETextBox procedure breaks a line of text correctly. You can specify how text is aligned in the box using any of the following alignment constants:

Constant	Description
teFlushDefault	Aligned according to primary line direction
teCenter	Centered for all scripts
teFlushRight	Right aligned for all scripts
teFlushLeft	Left aligned for all scripts

TECalText

The TECalText procedure recalculates the beginnings of all lines of text in the specified edit record.

```
PROCEDURE TECalText (hTE: TEHandle);
```

hTE   A handle to the edit record whose text lines are to be recalculated.

DESCRIPTION

The TECalText procedure updates elements of the lineStarts array in an edit record. Call TECalText if you've changed the destination rectangle, the hText field, or any other property of the edit record that pertains to line breaks and the number of characters per line—for example, font, size, style, and so on.

ASSEMBLY-LANGUAGE INFORMATION

The low-memory global variable TERecal contains the address of the routine called by TECalText to recalculate the line starts and set the first and last characters that need to be redrawn. The TERecal default hook routine calls the Text Utilities StyledLineBreak function. If you replace the default TERecal hook routine with a customized version and your application supports non-Roman script systems, make sure that your customized hook routine is script-aware. The registers on entry and exit for this hook routine are:

Registers on entry

A3   Pointer to the locked edit record

D7   Change in the length of the record (word)

Registers on exit

D2   Line start of the line containing the first character to be redrawn (word)

D4   Position of last character to be redrawn (word)

TextEdit uses the low-memory global variable `WordRedraw` widely, but primarily for line calculations and to determine how much of a line to redraw after the user types in a character. TextEdit sets the correct value for `WordRedraw` in `TEInit` based upon the installed script systems. If a 2-byte script is installed, `TEInit` performs an OR operation on `WordRedraw` with a 1; if a right-to-left script is installed, `TEInit` performs an OR operation on `WordRedraw` with an $FF. The size of this global is one byte.

TextEdit interprets the final value of `WordRedraw` as follows:

Value	Description
0	Redraws the character before the entered character.
1	Redraws the word before the entered character.
$FF	Redraws the whole line.

TEGetHeight

The `TEGetHeight` function returns the total height of all of the lines in the text between and including the specified starting and ending lines.

```
FUNCTION TEGetHeight (endLine, startLine: LONGINT;
                      hTE: TEHandle): INTEGER;
```

endLine   The number of the last line of text whose height is to be included in the total height. You can specify a value that is greater than or equal to 1 for this parameter.

startLine   The number of the first line of text whose height is to be included in the total height. You can specify a value that is greater than or equal to 1 for this parameter.

hTE   A handle to the edit record containing the lines of text whose height is to be returned.

DESCRIPTION

For monostyled text, the `TEGetHeight` function uses the value of the edit record's `lineHeight` field. For multistyled text, it uses the line height element (`LHElement`) of the line height table (`LHTable`). Note that `TEGetHeight` does not take into account the height of any blank lines at the end of the text. You need to consider this when scrolling text.

TEScroll

The TEScroll procedure scrolls the text within the view rectangle of the specified edit record by the designated number of pixels.

```
PROCEDURE TEScroll (dh,dv: Integer; hTE: TEHandle);
```

dh   The distance in pixels that the text is to be scrolled horizontally. A positive value moves the text to the right; a negative value moves the text to the left.

dv   The distance in pixels that the text is to be scrolled vertically. A positive value moves the text down; a negative value moves the text up.

hTE   A handle to the edit record whose text is to be scrolled.

DESCRIPTION

The TEScroll procedure updates the text on the screen automatically to reflect the new scroll position. The destination rectangle is offset by the amount scrolled. The TEScroll and TEPinScroll procedures behave the same, except that TEPinScroll stops scrolling when the last line of text is scrolled into view.

TEPinScroll

The TEPinScroll procedure scrolls the text within the view rectangle of the specified edit record by the designated number of pixels. Scrolling stops when the last line of text is scrolled into view.

```
PROCEDURE TEPinScroll (dh: Integer; dv: Integer; hTE: TEHandle);
```

dh   The distance in pixels that the text is to be scrolled horizontally. A positive value moves the text to the right; a negative value moves the text to the left.

dv   The distance in pixels that the text is to be scrolled vertically. A positive value moves the text down; a negative value moves the text up.

hTE   A handle to the edit record whose text is to be scrolled.

DESCRIPTION

The TEPinScroll procedure updates the text on the screen automatically to reflect the new scroll position, as does the TEScroll procedure. The destination rectangle is offset by the amount scrolled. When the edit record is longer than the text it contains, TEPinScroll displays up to the last line of text inclusive, and not beyond it.

TEAutoView

The TEAutoView procedure enables and disables automatic scrolling of the text in the specified edit record.

```
PROCEDURE TEAutoView (fAuto: Boolean; hTE: TEHandle);
```

fAuto   A flag indicating whether to enable or disable automatic scrolling. A value of TRUE enables automatic scrolling. A value of FALSE disables automatic scrolling.

hTE   A handle to the edit record for which automatic scrolling is to be enabled or disabled.

DESCRIPTION

The TEAutoView procedure does not actually scroll the text automatically: TESelView does. However, when fAuto is set to FALSE, a call to TESelView has no effect.

If there is a scroll bar associated with the edit record, your application must manage scrolling of it. You can replace the default click loop routine, which scrolls the text only, with a customized version that also updates the scroll bar.

You can also enable or disable automatic scrolling for an edit record through the teFAutoScroll feature of the TEFeatureFlag function.

SEE ALSO

For more information, see "TEFeatureFlag" on page 2-107.

TESelView

Once automatic scrolling has been enabled by a call to the TEAutoView procedure or through the TEFeatureFlag function, the TESelView procedure ensures that the selection range is visible and scrolls it into the view rectangle if necessary.

```
PROCEDURE TESelView (hTE: TEHandle);
```

hTE   A handle to the edit record containing the text selection range.

DESCRIPTION

The top left part of the selection range is scrolled into view. If the text is displayed in a rectangle that is not high enough, automatic scrolling can cause text to appear to flicker. If automatic scrolling is disabled, TESelView has no effect.

SEE ALSO

For more information, see "TEFeatureFlag" on page 2-107.

Modifying the Text of an Edit Record

Although all of the TextEdit routines provide and support editing capabilities, the set of routines described in this section implement the standard Macintosh editing features. An application can use these routines to delete, insert, cut, copy, or paste multistyled or monostyled text. The routines that you use for these purposes are `TEDelete` to remove a selected range of text, `TEInsert` to insert text, `TECut` to remove the text, but save it to be inserted, `TECopy` to copy the selected text with affecting the selection range, `TEPaste` to replace the selected text with the text in the private scrap, without applying character attribute information, `TEStylePaste` to replace the selected text with text and its character attribute information from the desk scrap, and `TEToScrap` and `TEFromScrap` to move monostyled text across applications or between applications and a desk accessory.

TEDelete

The `TEDelete` procedure removes the selected range of text from the text of the designated edit record and redraws the remaining text as necessary.

```
PROCEDURE TEDelete (hTE: TEHandle);
```

hTE   A handle to the edit record containing the text to be deleted.

DESCRIPTION

When the `TEDelete` procedure deletes a selected range of text, it does not transfer the text to either the private scrap or the Scrap Manager's desk scrap.

For multistyled records, when you use `TEDelete` to delete a selected range of text, the associated character attributes are saved in the null scrap to be applied to characters entered after the text is deleted. When the user clicks in some other area of the text, the character attributes are removed from the null scrap. You can use `TEDelete` to implement the Clear command. The `TEDelete` procedure recalculates line starts and line heights.

TEInsert

The TEInsert procedure inserts the specified text immediately before the selection range or the insertion point in the text of the designated edit record, redrawing the text as necessary.

```
PROCEDURE TEInsert (text: Ptr; length: LongInt; hTE: TEHandle);
```

text   A pointer to the text to be inserted.

length   The number of characters to be inserted.

hTE   A handle to the edit record containing the text buffer into which the new text is to be inserted.

DESCRIPTION

When you call the TEInsert procedure and a range of text is selected, TEInsert doesn't affect the selection range. The TEInsert procedure does not check for a 32 KB limit, so your application must ensure that the inserted text does not exceed this text size limit of 32 KB. The TEInsert procedure recalculates line starts and line heights to adjust for the inserted text.

TECut

The TECut procedure removes the current selection range from the text of the designated edit record, redrawing the text as necessary.

```
PROCEDURE TECut (hTE: TEHandle);
```

hTE   A handle to the edit record containing the text to be cut.

DESCRIPTION

For monostyled text, the TECut procedure writes the cut text to the private scrap.

For multistyled text, TECut writes the cut text to the private scrap and its character attributes to the style scrap; it also writes both to the Scrap Manager's desk scrap. For multistyled text, the TECut procedure removes the character attributes from the style record's style table when the text is cut.

For both monostyled and multistyled text, if the selection range is an insertion point, TextEdit deletes everything from the private scrap. When the selection range is an insertion point and the text is multistyled, TECut has no effect on the style scrap or the Scrap Manager's desk scrap.

SEE ALSO

For more information about the desk scrap, see the chapter "Scrap Manager" in
Inside Macintosh: More Macintosh Toolbox.

TECopy

The `TECopy` procedure copies the text selection range from the edit record, leaving the
selection range intact.

```
PROCEDURE TECopy (hTE: TEHandle);
```

hTE   A handle to the edit record containing the text to be copied.

DESCRIPTION

The `TECopy` procedure copies the text to the private scrap. For text of a monostyled edit
record, the text is written to the private scrap only. For text of a multistyled edit record,
the text is written to the TextEdit private scrap, the character attribute information is
written to the TextEdit style scrap, and both are written to the Scrap Manager's desk
scrap. Anything previously in the private scrap is deleted before the copied text is
written to it.

For both multistyled and monostyled text, if the selection range is an insertion point,
TECopy empties the TextEdit private scrap. When the selection range is an insertion
point and the text is multistyled, `TECopy` has no effect on the null scrap, the style scrap,
or the Scrap Manager's desk scrap.

SEE ALSO

For more information about the desk scrap, see the chapter "Scrap Manager" in
Inside Macintosh: More Macintosh Toolbox.

TEPaste

The `TEPaste` procedure replaces the edit record's selected text with the contents of the
private scrap and leaves an insertion point after the inserted text. If the selection range is
an insertion point, `TEPaste` inserts the contents of the private scrap there.

```
PROCEDURE TEPaste (hTE: TEHandle);
```

hTE   A handle to the edit record into which the text is to be pasted.

DESCRIPTION

When you call `TEPaste`, after it pastes the text from the private scrap, it redraws all of the text as necessary. If the private scrap is empty, `TEPaste` deletes the selection range. If you call `TEPaste` for a multistyled edit record, it pastes only the text in the private scrap. In this case, `TEPaste` ignores any associated character attribute information stored in the style scrap; instead, it applies the character attributes of the first character of the selection range being replaced to the text. If the selection range is an insertion point, `TEPaste` applies the character attributes of the character preceding the insertion point.

TEStylePaste

The `TEStylePaste` procedure pastes text and its associated character attribute information from the desk scrap into the edit record's text at the insertion point—if the current selection range is an insertion point—or it replaces the current selection range.

```
PROCEDURE TEStylePaste (hTE: TEHandle);
```

hTE   A handle to the edit record into which the text is to be pasted.

DESCRIPTION

When you call `TEStylePaste` and there is no character attribute information associated with text in the desk scrap, `TEStylePaste` first checks the null scrap. If the null scrap contains character attribute information, this is used. If the null scrap is empty, `TEStylePaste` gives the text the same attributes as those of the first character of the replaced selection range or that of the preceding character if the selection is an insertion point.

For a monostyled edit record, `TEStylePaste` pastes the text only; there is no associated character attribute information because all the text uses the same attributes.

TEToScrap

The `TEToScrap` function copies the contents of the TextEdit private scrap to the desk scrap.

```
FUNCTION TEToScrap: OSErr;
```

DESCRIPTION

You use the `TEToScrap` function to move monostyled text across applications or between an application and a desk accessory. Call the Scrap Manager function `ZeroScrap` to initialize the desk scrap or clear its contents before calling `TEToScrap`.

ASSEMBLY-LANGUAGE INFORMATION

Copy the contents of the private scrap to the desk scrap by calling the Scrap Manager function `PutScrap`; you can get the values you need from the global variables `TEScrpHandle` and `TEScrpLength`.

RESULT CODES

noErr	0	No error
noScrapErr	−100	Desk scrap isn't initialized

SEE ALSO

For more information about the `PutScrap` function, the `ZeroScrap` function, and the desk scrap, see the chapter "Scrap Manager" in *Inside Macintosh: More Macintosh Toolbox*.

TEFromScrap

The `TEFromScrap` function copies the contents of the desk scrap to the TextEdit private scrap.

```
FUNCTION TEFromScrap: OSErr;
```

DESCRIPTION

You use this function to move monostyled text across applications or between an application and a desk accessory.

ASSEMBLY-LANGUAGE INFORMATION

You can store a handle to the desk scrap in the global variable `TEScrpHandle` and the size of the desk scrap in the global variable `TEScrpLength`; get the desk scrap's handle and size by calling the Scrap Manager's `InfoScrap` function.

RESULT CODE

noErr   0   No error

SEE ALSO

For more information about the `InfoScrap` function and the desk scrap, see the chapter "Scrap Manager" in *Inside Macintosh: More Macintosh Toolbox*.

Managing the TextEdit Private Scrap

This section describes the routines that you use to manage the private scrap. You use the `TEScrapHandle` function get a handle to the private scrap, the `TEGetScrapLength` function to determine its size, and the `TESetScrapLength` procedure to set its size.

TEScrapHandle

The `TEScrapHandle` function returns a handle to the TextEdit private scrap.

```
FUNCTION TEScrapHandle: Handle;
```

ASSEMBLY-LANGUAGE INFORMATION

You can get the handle to the private scrap from the global variable `TEScrpHandle`.

TEGetScrapLength

The `TEGetScrapLength` function returns the size of the TextEdit private scrap in bytes.

```
FUNCTION TEGetScrapLength: LongInt;
```

ASSEMBLY-LANGUAGE INFORMATION

You can get the size of the private scrap in bytes from the global variable `TEScrpLength`.

TESetScrapLength

The `TESetScrapLength` procedure sets the size of the TextEdit private scrap to the specified number of bytes.

```
PROCEDURE TESetScrapLength (length: LongInt);
```

length   The size of the private scrap in bytes.

ASSEMBLY-LANGUAGE INFORMATION

You can set the global variable `TEScrpLength` to the size of the private scrap.

Checking, Setting, and Replacing Styles

The routines described in this section let you manipulate the character attribute information associated with a range of text. You can use the following routines to set, replace, or copy character attribute information, or to check aspects of the text's character attributes. These routines are `TESetStyle`, `TEReplaceStyle`, `TEContinuousStyle`, `TEStyleInsert`, `TEGetStyleScrapHandle`, `TEUseStyleScrap`, and `TENumStyles`.

Note

In the original *Inside Macintosh* documentation the term *style* was used to refer to the text font, size, style (face), and color. In this chapter the term *character attributes* is used instead. This is so that the term *style* can be used consistently throughout all of the documentation to refer to the following text style attributes: bold, italic, underline, outline, condense, extend, and shadow. In the past, the term *face*, which is now obsolete, was used to refer to these attributes instead of *style*. ◆

TESetStyle

The `TESetStyle` procedure sets new character attributes for the current selection range in the specified edit record.

```
PROCEDURE TESetStyle (mode: Integer; newStyle: TextStyle;
                      redraw: Boolean; hTE: TEHandle);
```

mode   A selector that specifies which character attributes are to be changed. The value for `mode` can be any additive combination of the `mode` constants for font, style, type size, color, and so forth.

newStyle   A record of type `TextStyle` that specifies the new attributes to be set. This record contains the character attributes to be applied to the current selection range based on the value of `mode`.

redraw   A flag that specifies whether or not TextEdit should immediately redraw the affected text to reflect the new character attribute changes. A value of TRUE causes the text to be redrawn immediately. Line breaks, line heights, and line ascents are recalculated. A value of FALSE delays redrawing until another event forces the update.

hTE   A handle to the multistyled edit record containing the selected text.

DESCRIPTION

The TESetStyle procedure has no effect on a monostyled record. You can use any combination of the following constants to specify a value for the mode parameter. The value of mode specifies which existing character attributes are to be changed to the new character attributes specified by newStyle.

Constant	Value	Description
doFont	1	Sets the font family ID
doFace	2	Sets the character style
doSize	4	Sets the type size
doColor	8	Sets the color
doAll	15	Sets all attributes
addSize	16	Increases or decreases the current type size
doToggle	32	Modifies the mode

If doToggle is specified along with doFace and if an attribute specified in the given newStyle parameter exists across the entire selected range of text, then TESetStyle removes that attribute. Otherwise, if the attribute doesn't exist across the entire selection range, all of the selected text is set to include that character attribute.

If the redraw parameter is set to TRUE, TextEdit redraws the current selection range using the new character attributes, recalculating line breaks, line heights, and line ascents. If the redraw parameter is set to FALSE, TextEdit does not redraw the text or recalculate line breaks, line heights, and line ascents. Consequently, when you call a routine that uses any of this information, such as TEGetHeight (which returns a total height between two specified lines), it does not reflect the new character attributes set with TESetStyle. Instead, the routine uses the information that was available before TESetStyle was called. To update this information, call the TECalText procedure. (See "TECalText" on page 2-89 for more information.) To be certain that the new information is always reflected, call the TESetStyle procedure with the redraw parameter set to TRUE.

If you call the TESetStyle routine when the value of the selStart field of an edit record equals the value of the selEnd field (specifying an insertion point), TextEdit stores the input character attributes in the null scrap record pointed to by the null style handle.

TEReplaceStyle

The TEReplaceStyle procedure replaces any character attributes in the current selection range that match the specified existing character attributes with the specified new character attributes.

```
PROCEDURE TEReplaceStyle (mode: INTEGER;
                          oldStyle,newStyle: TextStyle;
                          redraw: BOOLEAN; hTE: TEHandle);
```

mode   A selector that specifies which attributes to replace. It corresponds to any additive combination of the mode constants for font, character style, type size, color, and so forth.

oldStyle   A pointer to a text style record that specifies the current character attributes to search for in the selected text.

newStyle   A pointer to a text style record that specifies the new attributes to be set. This record contains the character attributes to be applied to the current selection range based on the value of mode.

redraw   A flag that specifies whether or not TextEdit should immediately redraw the text to reflect the attribute changes. A value of FALSE delays redrawing until another event forces the update. A value of TRUE causes the text to be redrawn immediately using the new character attributes.

hTE   A handle to the multistyled edit record containing the text selection whose character attributes are to be changed.

DESCRIPTION

The TEReplaceStyle procedure replaces any attribute in the current selection range that matches the attribute specified by oldStyle with that given by newStyle. Only the character attributes specified by mode are affected.

Attribute changes are made directly to the style elements (STElement) within the style table itself (TEStyleTable). If you specify the value doAll for the mode parameter, newStyle replaces oldStyle outright. Possible values for the mode parameter are defined by the following constants. The TEReplaceStyle procedure has no effect on a monostyled edit record.

Constant	Value	Description
doFont	1	Sets the font family ID
doFace	2	Sets the character style
doSize	4	Sets the type size
doColor	8	Sets the color
doAll	15	Sets all attributes
addSize	16	Increases or decreases the current type size

TEContinuousStyle

The TEContinuousStyle function determines whether a given character attribute is continuous over the current selection range.

```
FUNCTION TEContinuousStyle (VAR mode: Integer;
                            VAR aStyle: TextStyle;
                            hTE: TEHandle): Boolean;
```

mode   On input, a selector specifying the attributes to be checked. On output, mode identifies only those attributes determined to be continuous over the selection range.

aStyle   On input, a text style record. On output, this record contains the values for the mode attributes determined to be continuous over the selection.

hTE   A handle to the edit record containing the selected text whose attributes are to be checked.

DESCRIPTION

This function does not modify the text selection. Possible values for the mode parameter are defined by the following constants.

Constant	Value	Description
doFont	1	Specifies the font family ID
doFace	2	Specifies the character style
doSize	4	Specifies the type size
doColor	8	Specifies the color
doAll	15	Specifies all the attributes

The TEContinuousStyle function returns TRUE if all of the attributes to be checked are continuous and returns FALSE if none or some are continuous.

If the current selection range is an insertion point, TEContinuousStyle first checks the null scrap. If the null scrap contains character attributes, then they are used based on the value of the mode parameter. Otherwise, if the null scrap is empty, TEContinuousStyle returns the attributes of the character preceding the insertion point. The TEContinuousStyle function always returns TRUE in this case, and each field of the text style record is set if the corresponding bit in the mode parameter is set.

If the value of hTE is a handle to a monostyled edit record, TEContinuousStyle returns the set of character attributes that are consistent for the entire record.

Note that fields in the text style record specified by aStyle are only valid if the corresponding bits are set in the mode variable.

How the tsFace field of the aStyle record is used requires some consideration. For example, if TEContinuousStyle returns a mode parameter that contains doFace and the text style record tsFace field is bold, it means that the selected text is all bold, but may contain other text styles, such as italic, as well. Italic does not apply to all of the selected text, or it would have been included in the `tsFace` field. If the `tsFace` field is an empty set, then all of the selected text is plain.

TEStyleInsert

The `TEStyleInsert` procedure inserts the specified text immediately before the selection range or the insertion point in the edit record's text and applies the specified character attributes to the text, redrawing the text if necessary.

```
PROCEDURE TEStyleInsert (text: Ptr; length: LongInt;
                         hST: STScrpHandle; hTE: TEHandle);
```

text   A pointer to the text to be inserted.

length   The length in bytes of the text to be inserted.

hST   A handle to the style scrap record containing the character attribute information to be applied to the inserted text.

hTE   A handle to the edit record into which the text is to be inserted.

DESCRIPTION

You should create your own style scrap record, specifying the character attributes to be inserted and applied to the text, and pass its handle to `TEStyleInsert` as the value of the hST parameter. The character attributes are copied directly into the style record's (`TEStyleRec`) style table.

The `TEStyleInsert` procedure does not affects the current selection range.

TEGetStyleScrapHandle

The `TEGetStyleScrapHandle` function creates a style scrap record, copies the character attributes associated with the current selection range into it, and returns a handle to it.

```
FUNCTION TEGetStyleScrapHandle (hTE: TEHandle): STScrpHandle;
```

hTE   The handle to the edit record containing the text selection range whose character attributes are to be copied.

DESCRIPTION

The `TEGetStyleScrapHandle` function creates a style scrap record of type `StScrpRec` and copies the character attributes associated with the current selection range of the designated edit record into it. If the current selection range is an insertion point, TEGetStyleScrapHandle first checks the null scrap. If the null scrap contains character attributes, they are written to the newly created style scrap record. If the null scrap is empty, the attributes associated with the character preceding the insertion point are copied to the style scrap record.

The TEGetStyleScrapHandle function has no impact on the Scrap Manager's desk scrap. The TEGetStyleScrapHandle function returns a NIL value if called with a handle to a monostyled record.

TEUseStyleScrap

The TEUseStyleScrap procedure assigns new character attributes to the specified range of text in the designated edit record.

```
PROCEDURE TEUseStyleScrap (rangeStart: LongInt; rangeEnd: LongInt;
                           newStyles: STScrpHandle; redraw: Boolean;
                           hTE: TEHandle);
```

rangeStart
: The offset of the first character in the text of the edit record to which the character attributes are to be applied.

rangeEnd
: The offset of the last character in the text of the edit record to which the character attributes are to be applied.

newStyles
: A handle to a style scrap record. The style scrap record contains the attributes to be applied to the specified range of text. If the value of newStyles is NIL, no action is performed.

redraw
: A flag that specifies whether TextEdit should immediately redraw the selection range using the new character attributes.

hTE
: A handle to the edit record containing the range of text to which the character attributes are to be applied. If the handle points to a monostyled edit record (created using TENew), no action is performed.

DESCRIPTION

The TEUseStyleScrap procedure writes the character attribute information into the style record's style table and updates the style run table. If the redraw parameter is set to TRUE, the attributes are applied immediately to the specified range of text, and line breaks, line heights, and line ascents are recalculated. If redraw is set to FALSE, the new character attributes are not reflected in the view rectangle until the next update event occurs.

Regardless of whether the text is redrawn, the current selection range is not changed; if characters are highlighted before TEUseStyleScrap is called, they remain highlighted after it is called. However, if characters within the current selection range also fall within the specified range of text, they are rendered in the new character attributes when the text is redrawn.

Each element in the style scrap record contains a field that is the offset of the beginning of the element's character attributes. This field (`scrpStartChar`) defines the boundaries for the scrap's style runs.

The `TEUseStyleScrap` procedure applies the first element's attributes to the characters from `rangeStart` up to the `scrpStartChar` field of the next element. The `TEUseStyleScrap` procedure terminates without error if it prematurely reaches the end of the range or if there are not enough scrap style elements to cover the whole range. In the latter case, `TEUseStyleScrap` applies the last set of character attributes in the style scrap record to the remainder of the range.

Depending on the requirements of your application, you can create a style scrap record directly and pass its handle to `TEUseStyleScrap` as the value of `newStyles` or you can use a style scrap record created by `TEGetStyleScrapHandle`.

TENumStyles

The `TENumStyles` function returns the number of character attribute changes contained in the specified range, counting one for the start of the range.

```
FUNCTION TENumStyles (rangeStart: LongInt; rangeEnd: LongInt;
                      hTE: TEHandle): LongInt;
```

rangeStart
:   The beginning of the range of text for which the number of style runs (sets of character attributes) or changes is counted and returned.

rangeEnd
:   The end of the range of text for which the number of style runs (sets of character attributes) or changes is counted and returned.

hTE
:   A handle to the edit record containing the range of text.

DESCRIPTION

The number of character attribute changes that `TENumStyles` returns does not necessarily represent the number of unique sets of attributes for the range because some sets of attributes may be repeated. For monostyled edit records, `TENumStyles` always returns 1.

Using Byte Offsets and Corresponding Points

You can use the `TEGetOffset` function to convert a point to its corresponding byte offset and the `TEGetPoint` function to convert a byte offset to its corresponding point. These functions are discussed in this section.

TEGetOffset

The TEGetOffset function finds the byte offset of a character in an edit record's text that corresponds to the specified point.

```
FUNCTION TEGetOffset (pt: Point; hTE: TEHandle): Integer;
```

pt   A point in the displayed text of the specified edit record.

hTE   A handle to the edit record containing the text.

DESCRIPTION

The TEGetOffset function works for both monostyled and multistyled edit records. The TEGetOffset function returns the byte offset of the first byte for a 2-byte character.

TEGetPoint

The TEGetPoint function determines the point that corresponds to the specified byte offset of a character and returns the coordinates of that point.

```
FUNCTION TEGetPoint (offset: Integer; hTE: TEHandle): Point;
```

offset   A byte offset into the text buffer of an edit record.

hTE   A handle to the edit record containing the text.

DESCRIPTION

The TEGetPoint function returns a valid result even when the edit record does not contain any text. The point returned is based on the values in the record's destination rectangle. In the case of an offset being equal to a line end, which is also the start of the next line, TEGetPoint returns a point corresponding to the line start of the next line. In the case of a dual caret, the primary caret position, the one corresponding to the primary line direction, is returned.

The line height, taken either from the lineHeight field for a monostyled edit record or from the line-height array, LHElement, for a multistyled edit record, is also used to determine the vertical component. Both the text direction and the primary line direction are used to determine the horizontal component.

The TEGetPoint function works for both monostyled and multistyled edit records.

Additional TextEdit Features

The TEFeatureFlag function lets you check the status of additional TextEdit features and enable or disable them. It is described in this section.

TEFeatureFlag

The TEFeatureFlag function turns a specified feature on or off or returns the current status of that feature. Features supported are automatic scrolling, text buffering, outline highlighting, inline input, and text services.

```
FUNCTION TEFeatureFlag (feature: Integer; action: Integer;
                        hTE: TEHandle): Integer;
```

feature   The feature for which the action is to be performed.

action   A selector stipulating that the feature, specified by the feature
            parameter, is to be turned on or off, or that the current status of the
            feature is to be returned.

hTE   A handle to the edit record for which the action should be performed.

DESCRIPTION

You can use the TEFeatureFlag function to check the status of additional TextEdit features—automatic scrolling, outline highlighting, and text buffering—and to enable or disable the feature. You can also use this function to disable inline input in a particular edit record and to enable several features that have been provided so that inline input works correctly with TextEdit.

To identify a feature, you specify one of the following constants as the value of the feature parameter.

Constant	Value	Description
teFAutoScroll	0	Automatic scrolling
teFTextBuffering	1	Text buffering
teFOutlineHilite	2	Outline highlighting
teFInlineInput	3	Inline input
teFUseTextServices	4	Use inline input service

You specify the action to be performed on a feature through the following constants.

Constant	Value	Description
teBitClear	0	Disables the specified feature
teBitSet	1	Enables the specified feature
teBitTest	−1	Returns the current setting of the specified feature

If `teBitTest` returns `teBitSet`, the feature is enabled; if it returns `teBitClear`, it is disabled.

You can use the `TEFeatureFlag` function to turn automatic scrolling on and off as an alternative to calling `TEAutoView`. The effect is the same.

The `teFOutlineHilite` selector specifies outline highlighting as the feature for which an action is to be performed. If a highlighted region exists in an edit record and the window is inactive, then the highlighted region is outlined or framed.

In the case that outline highlighting is enabled and the current selection range is an insertion point, the caret is then drawn in a gray pattern so that it appears dimmed. To do the framing and caret dimming, TextEdit temporarily replaces the current address in the `highHook` and `caretHook` fields of the edit record, redraws the caret or the highlighted region, and then immediately restores the hooks to their previous addresses.

The `teFTextBuffering` selector enables or disables text buffering for performance improvements of 2-byte scripts. This is a global buffer, as opposed to the `TEKey` procedure's internal 2-byte buffer, and it is used across all active edit records. When using text buffering, take the following precautions:

■ Exercise care when you enable the text-buffering capability in more than one active record; otherwise, the bytes that are buffered from one edit record may appear in another edit record.

■ Ensure that buffering is not turned off in the middle of processing a 2-byte character. To guarantee the integrity of your record, it is important that you wait for an idle event before you disable buffering or enable buffering in a second edit record.

■ When text buffering is enabled, ensure that `TEIdle` is called before any pause of more than a few ticks—for example, before the Event Manager procedure `WaitNextEvent`. A possibility of a long delay before characters appear on the screen exists, especially in non-Roman systems. If you do not call `TEIdle`, the characters can end up in the edit record of another application. For more information, see "TEIdle" on page 2-84.

If text buffering is enabled on a non-Roman script system and the keyboard has changed, TextEdit flushes the text of the current script from the buffer before bringing characters of the new script into the buffer.

If your application follows the guidelines for inline input available from Macintosh Developer Technical Support, then you should set the `useTextEditServices` flag in the Size resource in your application. This allows inline input to work with your application. **Inline input** is a keyboard input method (often used for double-byte script systems) in which conversion from a phonetic to an ideographic representation of a character takes place at the current line position where the text is intended to appear. This allows the user to type text directly in the line as opposed to a special conversion window. If inline input is installed and the `useTextEditServices` flag in the Size resource is set, inline input sets TextEdit's `teFUseTextServices` feature bit whenever an edit record is created. TextEdit does not use this bit.

Inline input checks the `teFUseTextServices` bit during text editing to determine if an inline session should begin. If you want to disable inline input for a particular edit record, your application can clear this bit after the edit record is created. You can also clear this bit to disable inline input temporarily and then restore it, but the edit record must always be deactivated before the state of the bit is changed.

IMPORTANT

You *must* deactivate an edit record (using `TEDeactivate`) before changing the state of the feature bits or any fields in the edit record. ▲

In the future, other text services may use this same mechanism. If you follow the guidelines specified here, your application should also work with future text services. When an inline edit session begins, inline input also sets the `teFInlineInput` bit to provide the following features so that inline input works correctly with TextEdit:

- disabling font and keyboard synchronization

- forcing a multiple-line selection to be highlighted line by line using a separate rectangle for each line rather than using a minimum number of rectangles for optimization

- highlighting a line only to the edge of the text rather than beyond the text to the edge of the view rectangle

IMPORTANT

The `teFInlineInput` bit is cleared by inline input when an inline session ends. Use the `teFInlineInput` constant in the feature parameter of `TEFeatureFlag` to include these features in your application even when inline input is not installed. Be careful about changing the state of this bit if the `teFUseTextServices` bit is set. Again, the edit record should always be deactivated before you change the state of the `teFInlineInput` bit. If you clear the `teFUseTextServices` bit and you set the `teFInlineInput` bit, inline input is disabled, but your application retains the features listed above. ▲

To test for the availability of these features, you can call the `Gestalt` function with the `gestaltTextEditVersion` selector. A result of `gestaltTE4` or greater returned in the response parameter indicates that outline highlighting and text buffering are available. A result of `gestaltTE5` or greater returned in the response parameter indicates that the two inline input features are available.

The inline input features are also available on version 6.0.7 systems with non-Roman script systems installed. However, there is no Gestalt constant that indicates this availability.

SEE ALSO

For a description of the `WaitNextEvent` function, see the chapter "Event Manager" in *Inside Macintosh: Macintosh Toolbox Essentials*.

Customizing TextEdit

The TextEdit `TECustomHook`, `TESetWordBreak`, and `TESetClickLoop` routines described in this section let you customize the behavior of TextEdit. You can use these routines to replace the default hook routines with your customized versions.

However, if you use any of the TextEdit hooks to override default TextEdit behavior, the results may no longer be Script Manager–compatible. Before replacing TextEdit routines, you should determine whether more than one script system is installed, and, if so, ensure that the replacement routine you provide is script-aware.

TECustomHook

The `TECustomHook` procedure replaces a default TextEdit hook routine with a customized routine and returns the address of the replaced routine.

```
PROCEDURE TECustomHook (which: TEIntHook; VAR addr: ProcPtr;
                        hTE: TEHandle);
```

which   The hook whose default routine is to be replaced.

addr   On input, the address of your customized procedure.

             On output, the `addr` parameter contains the address of the routine that was previously installed in the field identified by the `which` parameter. This address is returned so that you can daisy-chain routines.

hTE   A handle to the edit record to be modified.

DESCRIPTION

The `TECustomHook` procedure lets you alter the behavior of TextEdit to better suit your application's requirements and those of the script systems installed. If you replace a default hook routine with a customized version that you write in a high-level language, such as Pascal or C, you need to provide assembly-language glue code that utilizes the registers for your high-level language routine. The register contents for each of the hook routines are described in this section under "Assembly-Language Information."

The end-of-line hook, width measurement hook, new width measurement hook, text width measurement hook, draw hook. and hit test hook fields are hook fields in the TextEdit dispatch record. The `which` parameter identifies the hook whose default routine is to be replaced; you use the following constants to specify a value for this parameter.

Constant	Value	Description
`intEOLHook`	0	End-of-line hook
`intDrawHook`	1	Draw hook
`intWidthHook`	2	Width measurement hook
`intHitTestHook`	3	Hit test hook
`intNWidthHook`	6	New width measurement hook
`intTextWidthHook`	7	Text width measurement hook (low-memory global width measurement hook)

ASSEMBLY-LANGUAGE INFORMATION

The end-of-line hook, width measurement hook, new width measurement hook, text width measurement hook, draw hook, and hit test hook fields are hook fields in the TextEdit dispatch record. When you use `TECustomHook` to replace the default routines installed in these hook fields with customized ones, remember that the replacement routine must preserve all registers except those specified as containing return values.

End-of-Line Hook Registers

You specify the `intEOLHook` constant as the value of the `which` parameter to identify the end-of-line hook routine as the one you want to replace. This hook routine determines whether an incoming character is an end-of-line character. It tests the character, sets the appropriate status flags in the status register, and returns. The default action is to compare the character with $0D (a carriage return).

Registers on entry

D0	Character to compare (byte)
A3	Pointer to the edit record
A4	Locked handle to the edit record

Registers on exit

Z	(Zero) flag in the status register clear if end-of-line character; set otherwise.

Draw Hook Registers

You specify the intDrawHook constant as the value of the which parameter to identify the drawing hook routine as the one you want to replace. The draw hook routine is called any time the components of a line are drawn. The appropriate font, style, and size characteristics have already been set into the current port by the time this routine is called. By default, the address of the QuickDraw DrawText procedure is stored in the draw hook field.

If your application is using outline (TrueType) fonts, TextEdit has also set the preserveGlyph parameter of the Font Manager's SetPreserveGlyph procedure to FALSE, so your customized hook procedure may need to reset this parameter if your application depends on it.

Registers on entry

D0   Offset into text (word)

D1   Length of text to draw (word)

A0   Pointer to text to draw

A3   Pointer to the edit record

A4   Locked handle to the edit record

Width Measurement Hook Registers

You specify the intWidthHook constant as the value of the which parameter to identify the width measurement hook routine as the one you want to replace. The width measurement hook routine measures portions of a line of text. It is used when only the Roman script system is installed and the field contains the address of a customized routine. It is supported for backward compatibility. In all other cases, when more than one script system is installed or when the width measurement hook field has not been customized, TextEdit calls the routine whose address is installed in the new width measurement hook field.

Registers on entry

D0   Length (in bytes) of text to measure (word)

D1   First byte of text to measure (word)

A0   Pointer to text buffer

A3   Pointer to the edit record

A4   Locked handle to the edit record

Registers on exit

D1   Pixel width of measured text (word)

Hit Test Hook Registers

You specify the `intHitTestHook` constant as the value of the `which` parameter to identify the hit test hook routine as the one you want to replace. The hit test hook routine determines the glyph position in a line given the pixel width from the left edge of the view rectangle. For system software before System 7, the default action is to call the QuickDraw `TextWidth` function to determine if the pixel width of the measured text is greater than the input width. If it is, then the hit test hook routine calls the QuickDraw `PixelToChar` function and returns. For System 7, the default action is to call the QuickDraw `PixelToChar` function.

Registers on entry

D0   Length of text block (style run) to measure (word)

D1   Pixel width from start of text block (word)

D2   Slop (should equal 0) (word)

A0   Pointer to start of text block

A3   Pointer to the edit record

A4   Locked handle to the edit record

Registers on exit

D0   Pixel width to character offset in text block (low word)

A Boolean that is `TRUE` if a character offset corresponding to the given pixel width was found (high word). Otherwise, `FALSE`.

D1   Character offset (word)

D2   A Boolean that is `TRUE` if the pixel width falls within the leading edge of the character (low word). Otherwise, `FALSE`.

TextEdit also uses the least significant bit of the high word. If the hit test hook routine calls `PixelToChar`, TextEdit sets this bit. If it uses `TextWidth`, TextEdit clears this bit. Your customized routine needs to do the same if you call either `PixelToChar` or `TextWidth` (high word). See the chapter "QuickDraw Text" in this book for more about these routines.

Note

In earlier versions of TextEdit, the value in register D2 on entry was not always used. If you daisy-chain in a routine and then call the hit test hook routine, D2 must be 0 (on entry). ◆

New Width Measurement Hook Registers

You specify the `intNWidthHook` constant as the value of the `which` parameter to identify the new width measurement hook routine as the one you want to replace. The new width measurement hook routine measures portions of a line of text when a non-Roman script system is installed. It is also used when only a Roman script system is installed and the width hook field does not contain the address of a customized routine.

The default procedure calls `CharToPixel` or `TextWidth`, depending on the primary line direction. The appropriate font, style, and size characteristics have already been set into the current graphics port by the time this routine is called.

The new width measurement hook routine is called to measure text for both Roman and non-Roman script systems, so make sure that your customized routine is script-aware.

Registers on entry

D0	Overall style run length, bounded by the line end (word)
D1	Offset position within style run on the current line (word)
D2	Slop (low word); direction flag (high word)
A0	Pointer to text buffer
A2	Pointer to current line start (from TextEdit's `lineStarts` array)
A3	Pointer to the edit record
A4	Locked handle to the edit record

Registers on exit

D1	Pixel width of measured text (word)

Text Width Measurement Hook Registers

You specify the `intTextWidthHook` constant as the value of the `which` parameter to identify the low-memory global text width measurement hook routine as the one you want to replace. By default, this hook field contains the address of the QuickDraw `TextWidth` function and provides a way to replace TextEdit's use of `TextWidth`. The new width measurement hook routine uses the routine whose address is installed in this field.

Registers on entry

D0	Length (in bytes) of text to be measured (word)
D1	Offset in text of first byte to measure (word)
A0	Pointer to text to measure
A3	Pointer to the edit record
A4	Locked handle to the edit record

Registers on exit

D1	Pixel width of measured text (word)

SEE ALSO

For more information about the `SetPreserveGlyph` procedure, see the chapter "Font Manager" in this book. For more information about `DrawText`, `TextWidth`, `PixelToChar`, and `CharToPixel`, see the chapter "QuickDraw Text" in this book.

SPECIAL CONSIDERATIONS

Take the following precautions if you replace a default routine:

■ Before placing the address of your routine in the TextEdit dispatch record, strip the addresses, using the Operating System Utilities `StripAddress` function, to guarantee that your application is 32-bit clean. For more information, see *Inside Macintosh: Operating System Utilities.*

■ Before replacing a TextEdit routine with a customized one, determine whether more than one script system is installed, and, if so, ensure that your customized routine accommodates all of the installed script systems. This avoids the problem of your customized routine producing results that are incompatible with the Script Manager.

■ When you use assembly language, note that all registers must be preserved except those specified as containing return values. Registers A3 contains a pointer to the edit record and Register A4 contains a handle to it. You can obtain line start positions from the `lineStarts` array in the edit record. Register A5 is always valid. Refer to `TECustomHook` in the "TextEdit Reference" section for complete coverage of the register content requirements for all hook routines.

TESetWordBreak

The `TESetWordBreak` procedure installs the address of a customized word-selection break routine in the `wordBreak` field of the specified edit record.

```
PROCEDURE TESetWordBreak (wBrkProc: ProcPtr; hTE: TEHandle);
```

wBrkProc   A pointer to the customized word-selection break routine.

hTE   A handle to the edit record containing the `wordBreak` field to be modified.

DESCRIPTION

A word break routine determines which word is highlighted when the user double-clicks in the text. It also determines where TextEdit breaks the text at the end of a line. You can use `TESetWordBreak` to replace the default routine in the `wordBreak` field that is used for word selection and line breaking under certain circumstances. Whether or not TextEdit uses the word-selection break routine referenced by this field is determined by the algorithm implemented in the default `TEFindWord` routine. For a description of this algorithm, see "Customizing Word Selection" on page 2-60; this section also describes what to consider if you replace the `TEFindWord` hook routine.

When you replace the `wordBreak` field hook routine, your customized word break routine is used instead of the default one. The default routine breaks words at any character with an ASCII value of $20 or less (the space character or nonprinting control characters). Your routine can use a different value.

Before non-Roman script systems were supported, TextEdit used the word break hook routine installed in the `wordBreak` field for all word selection and line breaking.

However, in order to support both Roman and non-Roman script systems, TextEdit now uses the routine installed in the low-memory global variable TEFindWord. The default TEFindWord hook routine determines which hook TextEdit should use for word selection and line breaking—the wordBreak hook or the Text Utilities FindWordBreaks procedure—based on what script systems are installed and some other factors. You can replace the TEFindWord hook routine with a customized version.

ASSEMBLY-LANGUAGE INFORMATION

You must directly set the wordBreak field to point to your own word break routine; do not use the TESetWordBreak procedure. The registers for the word break routine must contain the following values.

Registers on entry

A0   Pointer to text

D0   Character position (word)

Register on exit

Z bit (zero flag)   Condition code:

status register   0 to break at specified character

1 not to break there

If you replace TEFindWord, be careful to set the correct values in the appropriate registers. For TEFindWord, the registers are set on entry as specified below, and TextEdit depends on the registers being set at exit as specified below.

Registers on entry

D0   Current position (the value of selStart field in edit record) (word)

D2   Identifier of routine that called FindWordBreaks (word)

Identifier	Value	Explanation
teWordSelect	4	called for word selection
teWordDrag	8	called for extending word selection
teFromFind	12	called for determining new line breaks
teFromRecal	16	called for word breaking in line recalculation

A3   Pointer to the edit record

A4   Locked handle to the edit record

Registers on exit

D0   Word start (word)

D1   Word end (word)

SEE ALSO

For more information about the FindWordBreaks procedure, see the chapter "Text Utilities" in this book.

TESetClickLoop

The TESetClickLoop procedure installs in the clikLoop field of the edit record the address of the application-supplied click loop routine.

```
PROCEDURE TESetClickLoop (clickProc: ProcPtr; hTE: TEHandle);
```

clickProc   A pointer to the customized click loop routine.

hTE   A handle to the edit record whose clikLoop field is to be modified.

DESCRIPTION

The TESetClickLoop procedure lets you replace the default click loop routine. The TEClick procedure repeatedly calls the routine that the click loop field points to as long as the user holds down the mouse button within the text of the view rectangle. The default click loop routine scrolls only the text. However, you can provide a customized click loop procedure that scrolls the text and the scroll bars in tandem.

If automatic scrolling is enabled, the default click loop routine checks to see if the mouse has been dragged out of the view rectangle; if it has, the routine scrolls the text using TEPinScroll. (For more information, see "TEPinScroll" on page 2-91.) The amount by which TEPinScroll scrolls the text vertically is determined by the lineHeight field of the edit record for monostyled text and the LHTable for multistyled text.

ASSEMBLY-LANGUAGE INFORMATION

You can directly set the click loop (clikLoop) field; you don't need to use the TESetClickLoop procedure. Your routine should set register D0 to 1 and preserve register D2. Returning 0 in register D0 terminates TEClick.

Summary of TextEdit

Pascal Summary

Constants

```
CONST
      {Gestalt returned values}

      gestaltUndefSelectorErr {Systems before 6.0.4, multistyled TextEdit }
                              { on all hardware}
      gestaltTE1 = 1;         {System 6.0.4 Roman script system on }
                              { IIci-family hardware}
      gestaltTE2 = 2;         {Script Manager-compatible. System 6.0.4 }
                              { non-Roman script systems on all }
                              { IIci family hardware.New measuring hook }
                              { nWIDTHHook.}
      gestaltTE3 = 3;         {Script Manager—compatible. System 6.0.4 }
                              { non-Roman script systems on all non-IIci }
                              { family hardware.}
      gestaltTE4 = 4;         {Script Manager-compatible. System 6.0.5 on }
                              { all hardware. New TEFeatureFlag function.}
      gestaltTE5 = 5;         {Script Manager—compatible. System 7.0 on all }
                              {hardware}

      {alignment styles: new constant names for the align parameter }
      { of TESetAlignment and TETextBox}
      teFlushDefault =  0;          {flush according to system direction }
      teCenter       =  1;          {centered for all scripts }
      teFlushRight   = -1;          {flush right for all scripts}
      teFlushLeft    = -2;          {flush left for all scripts}

      {alignment styles; old constant names supported for }
      { backward-compatibility}
      teJustLeft            =  0;
      teJustCenter          =  1;
      teJustRight           = -1;
      teForceLeft           = -2;
```

```
{values for TEFeatureFlag feature parameter}
teFAutoScroll        = 0;        {automatic scrolling
teFAutoScr           = 0;        {old constant for automatic scrolling}
teFTextBuffering     = 1;        {text buffering}
teFOutlineHilite     = 2;        {outline highlighting}
teFInlineInput       = 3;        {inline input}
teFUseTextServices   = 4;        {use inline input service}


{values for TEFeatureFlag action parameter}
teBitClear           = 0;        {clear TEFeatureFlag features}
teBitSet             = 1;        {set TEFeatureFlag features}
teBitTest            = -1;       {test TEFeatureFlag features: return }
                                 { the current setting}


{selectors for identifying the routine that called TEFindWord }
teWordSelect         = 4;        {called for determining new }
                                 { line breaks}
teWordDrag           = 8;        {called for extending word selection}
teFromFind           = 12;       {called for word selection}
teFromRecal          = 16;       {called for word breaking in line }
                                 { recalculation}


{values for TESetStyle/TEContinuousStyle/TEReplaceStyle modes}
doFont               = 1;        {set font family number}
doFace               = 2;        {set character style}
doSize               = 4;        {set type size}
doColor              = 8;        {set color}
doAll                = 15;       {set all attributes}
addSize              = 16;       {adjust type size }
doToggle             = 32;       {toggle mode for TESetStyle}


{selectors for TECustomHook}
intEOLHook           = 0;        {end-of-line hook}
intDrawHook          = 1;        {drawing hook}
intWidthHook         = 2;        {width measurement hook}
intHitTestHook       = 3;        {hit-test hook}
intNWidthHook        = 6;        {nWIDTHHook measurement hook}
intTextWidthHook     = 7;        {TextWidth measurement hook}
```

Data Types

```
TYPE  TERec =
      RECORD
          destRect:    Rect;           {destination rectangle}
          viewRect:    Rect;           {view rectangle}
          selRect:     Rect;           {the selection rectangle}
          lineHeight:  Integer;        {used for vertical spacing of lines}
          fontAscent:  Integer;        {used for caret/highlighting position}
          selPoint:    Point;          {point selected with the mouse}
          selStart:    Integer;        {start of selection range}
          selEnd:      Integer;        {end of selection range}
          active:      Integer;        {set when record is }
                                       { activated/deactivated}
          wordBreak:   ProcPtr;        {word break hook}
          clikLoop:    ProcPtr;        {click loop hook}
          clickTime:   LongInt;        {used internally}
          clickLoc:    Integer;        {used internally}
          caretTime:   LongInt;        {used internally}
          caretState:  Integer;        {used internally}
          just:        Integer;        {alignment of text}
          teLength:    Integer;        {length of text}
          hText:       Handle;         {handle to text to be edited}
          hDispatchRec: LongInt;       {handle to TextEdit }
                                       { dispatch record}
          clikStuff:   Integer;        {used internally}
          crOnly:      Integer;        {if <0, new line at Return only}
          txFont:      Integer;        {text font}
          txFace:      Style;          {character style; unpacked byte}
          txMode:      Integer;        {pen mode}
          txSize:      Integer;        {value indicates either a multistyled }
                                       { edit record or a font size}

          inPort:      GrafPtr;        {a pointer to the grafPort for this TERec}
          highHook:    ProcPtr;        {used for text highlighting }
          caretHook:   ProcPtr;        {used for the caret appearance}
          nLines:      Integer;        {number of lines}
          lineStarts:  ARRAY[0..16000] OF Integer;
                                       {positions of line starts}
      END;

      TEPtr    = ^TERec;
      TEHandle = ^TEPtr;
```

```
    Chars= PACKED ARRAY[0..32000] OF CHAR;

    CharsHandle = ^CharsPtr;
    CharsPtr    = ^Chars;


TEStyleRec =
RECORD
    nRuns:      Integer;        {number of style runs}
    nStyles:    Integer;        {size of style table}
    styleTab:   STHandle;       {handle to style table}
    lhTab:      LHHandle;       {handle to line-height table}
    teRefCon:   LongInt;        {reserved for application use}
    nullStyle:  NullStHandle;   {handle to style set at }
                                { null selection}
    runs:       ARRAY [0..8000] OF StyleRun;
                                {ARRAY [0..8000] OF StyleRun}
END;

TEStylePtr = ^TEStyleRec;
TEStyleHandle = ^TEStylePtr;

StyleRun =
RECORD
    startChar:  Integer;        {starting character position}
    styleIndex: Integer;        {index in style table}
END;

STElement =
RECORD
    stCount:    Integer;        {number of runs in this style}
    stHeight:   Integer;        {line height}
    stAscent:   Integer;        {font ascent}
    stFont:     Integer;        {font (family) number}
    stFace:     Style;          {character style}
    stSize:     Integer;        {size in points}
    stColor:    RGBColor;       {absolute RGB color}
END;

STPtr    = ^TEStyleTable;
STHandle = ^STPtr;

TEStyleTable = ARRAY [0..1776] OF STElement;
```

```
LHElement =
RECORD
   lhHeight:        Integer;       {maximum height in line}
   lhAscent:        Integer;       {maximum ascent in line}
END;

LHPtr = ^LHTable;
LHHandle = ^LHPtr;

LHTable = ARRAY [0..8000] OF LHElement;

ScrpSTElement =
RECORD
   scrpStartChar:       LongInt;       {offset to start of style}
   scrpHeight:          Integer;       {line height}
   scrpAscent:          Integer;       {font ascent}
   scrpFont:            Integer;       {font (family) number}
   scrpFace:            Style;         {character style}
   scrpSize:            Integer;       {size in points}
   scrpColor:           RGBColor;      {absolute (RGB) color}
END;

ScrpStyl2Tab = ARRAY[0..1600] OF ScrpSTElement;

StScrpRec =
RECORD
   scrpNStyles:     Integer;           {number of styles in scrap}
   scrpStyleTab:    ScrpSTTable;       {table of styles for scrap}
END;

StScrpPtr = ^StScrpRec;
StScrpHandle = ^StScrpPtr;

NullStRec =
RECORD
   teReserved:          LongInt;       {reserved for future expansion}
   nullScrap:           StScrpHandle;  {handle to scrap style table}
END;

NullStPtr = ^NullStRec;
NullStHandle = ^NullStPtr;

TextStyle =
RECORD
```

```
    tsFont:  Integer;      {font (family) number}
    tsFace:  Style;        {character Style}
    tsSize:  Integer;      {size in points}
    tsColor: RGBColor;     {absolute (RGB) color}
END;

TextStylePtr = ^TextStyle;
TextStyleHandle = ^TextStylePtr;

TEIntHook = Integer;
```

Routines

Initializing TextEdit, Creating an Edit Record, and Disposing of an Edit Record

PROCEDURE TEInit;	
FUNCTION TEStyleNew	(destRect: Rect; viewRect: Rect): TEHandle;
FUNCTION TENew	(destRect, viewRect: Rect): TEHandle;
PROCEDURE TEDispose	(hTE: TEHandle);

Activating and Deactivating an Edit Record

PROCEDURE TEActivate	(hTE: TEHandle);
PROCEDURE TEDeactivate	(hTE: TEHandle);

Setting and Getting an Edit Record's Text and Character Attribute Information

PROCEDURE TEKey	(key: Char; hTE: TEHandle);
PROCEDURE TESetText	(text: Ptr; length: LongInt; hTE: TEHandle);
FUNCTION TEGetText	(hTE: TEHandle): CharsHandle;
PROCEDURE TESetStyleHandle	(theHandle: TEStyleHandle; hTE: TEHandle);
FUNCTION TEGetStyleHandle	(hTE: TEHandle): TEStyleHandle;

Setting the Caret and Selection Range

PROCEDURE TEIdle	(hTE: TEHandle);
PROCEDURE TEClick	(pt: Point; extend: Boolean; hTE: TEHandle);
PROCEDURE TESetSelect	(selStart, selEnd: LongInt; hTE: TEHandle);

Displaying and Scrolling Text

PROCEDURE TESetAlignment	(align: Integer; hTE: TEHandle);
PROCEDURE TEUpdate	(rUpdate: Rect; hTE: TEHandle);

```
PROCEDURE TETextBox        (text: Ptr; length: LongInt;
                            box: Rect; just: Integer);
PROCEDURE TECalText        (hTE: TEHandle);
FUNCTION TEGetHeight       (endLine, startLine:LONGINT;
                            hTE: TEHandle): INTEGER;
PROCEDURE TEScroll         (dh,dv: Integer; hTE: TEHandle);
PROCEDURE TEPinScroll      (dh: INTEGER; dv: INTEGER; hTE: TEHandle);
PROCEDURE TEAutoView       (fAuto: Boolean; hTE: TEHandle);
PROCEDURE TESelView        (hTE: TEHandle);
```

Modifying the Text of an Edit Record

```
PROCEDURE TEDelete         (hTE: TEHandle);
PROCEDURE TEInsert         (text: Ptr; length: LongInt; hTE: TEHandle);
PROCEDURE TECut            (hTE: TEHandle);
PROCEDURE TECopy           (hTE: TEHandle);
PROCEDURE TEPaste          (hTE: TEHandle);
PROCEDURE TEStylePaste     (hTE: TEHandle);
FUNCTION TEToScrap: OSErr;
FUNCTION TEFromScrap: OSErr;
```

Managing the TextEdit Private Scrap

```
FUNCTION TEScrapHandle:     Handle;
FUNCTION TEGetScrapLength:  LongInt;
PROCEDURE TESetScrapLength  (length: LongInt);
```

Checking, Setting, and Replacing Styles

```
PROCEDURE TESetStyle       (mode: Integer; newStyle: TextStyle;
                            redraw: Boolean; hTE: TEHandle);
PROCEDURE TEReplaceStyle   (mode: INTEGER; oldStyle, newStyle: TextStyle;
                            redraw: BOOLEAN; hTE: TEHandle);
FUNCTION TEContinuousStyle (VAR mode: Integer; VAR aStyle: TextStyle;
                            hTE: TEHandle) : Boolean;
PROCEDURE TEStyleInsert    (text: Ptr; length: LongInt;
                            hST: STScrpHandle; hTE: TEHandle);
FUNCTION TEGetStyleScrapHandle
                           (hTE: TEHandle): StyleScrpHandle;
PROCEDURE TEUseStyleScrap  (rangeStart: LongInt; rangeEnd: LongInt;
                            newStyles: STScrpHandle; redraw: Boolean;
                            hTE: TEHandle);
```

```
FUNCTION TENumStyles        (rangeStart: LongInt; rangeEnd: LongInt;
                             hTE: TEHandle): LongInt;
```

Using Byte Offsets and Corresponding Points

```
FUNCTION TEGetOffset        (pt: Point; hTE: TEHandle): Integer;
FUNCTION TEGetPoint         (offset: Integer; hTE: TEHandle): Point;
```

Additional TextEdit Features

```
FUNCTION TEFeatureFlag      (feature: Integer; action: Integer;
                             hTE: TEHandle) : Integer;
```

Customizing TextEdit

```
PROCEDURE TECustomHook      (which: TEIntHook; VAR addr: ProcPtr;
                             hTE: TEHandle);

PROCEDURE TESetWordBreak    (wBrkProc: ProcPtr; hTE: TEHandle);
PROCEDURE TESetClickLoop    (clickProc: ProcPtr; hTE: TEHandle);
```

C Summary

Constants

```
enum {
/*alignment styles of TESetAlignment and TETextBox*/
teFlushDefault    = 0,        /*flush according to system direction*/
teCenter          = 1,        /*centered for all scripts*/
teFlushRight      = -1,       /*flush right for all scripts*/
teFlushLeft       = -2,       /*flush left for all script*/

/*alignment styles; old names supported for backward-compatibility*/
teJustLeft        = 0,
teJustCenter      = 1,
teJustRight       = -1,
teForceLeft       = -2,

/*feature or bit definitions for TEFeatureFlag feature parameter*/
teFAutoScroll     = 0,        /*automatic scrolling*/
teFAutoScr        = 0,        /*old constant for automatic scrolling*/
teFTextBuffering  = 1,        /*text buffering*/
teFOutlineHilite  = 2,        /*outline highlighting*/
```

```
teFInlineInput     = 3,          /*inline input*/
teFUseTextServices  = 4,         /*use inline input service*/

/* action for the new bit (un)set interface,TEFeatureFlag */
teBitClear         = 0,          /*set the selector bit*/
teBitSet           = 1,
};
enum {
teBitTest          = -1, /*no change; just return the current setting*/
teBitClear         = 0,
teBitSet           = 1,  /*set the selector bit*/
teBitTest          = -1, /*no change; just return the current setting*/

/*constants for identifying the routine that called TEFindWord */
teWordSelect       = 4,      /*clickExpand to select word*/
teWordDrag         = 8,      /*clickExpand for extending word selection*/
teFromFind         = 12,     /*FindLine called it ($0C)*/
teFromRecal        = 16,
    /*called for word breaking in line recalculation*/

/*values for TESetStyle/TEContinuousStyle/TEReplaceStyle modes*/
doFont   = 1,      /*set font family number*/
doFace   = 2,      /*set character style*/
doSize   = 4,      /*set type size*/
doColor  = 8,      /*set color*/
doAll    = 15,     /*set all attributes*/
addSize  = 16,     /*adjust type size*/
};
enum {
  doToggle = 32,     /*toggle mode for TESetStyle*/

  /*selectors for TECustomHook*/
  intEOLHook      = 0,      /*end-of-line hook*/
  intDrawHook     = 1,      /*drawing hook*/
  intWidthHook    = 2,      /*width measurement hook*/
  intHitTestHook = 3,       /*hit-test hook*/
  intNWidthHook  = 6,       /*nWIDTHHook measurement hook*/
  intTextWidthHook = 7,   /*TextWidth measurement hook*/
};
```

Types

```
typedef pascal Boolean (*WordBreakProcPtr)(Ptr text, short charPos);
typedef pascal Boolean (*ClikLoopProcPtr)(void);

struct TERec {
  Rect destRect;          /*destination rectangle*/
  Rect viewRect;          /*view rectangle*/
  Rect selRect;           /*the selection rectangle*/
  short lineHeight;       /*used for vertical spacing of lines*/
  short fontAscent;       /*used for caret/highlighting position*/
  Point selPoint;         /*point selected with the mouse*/
  short selStart;         /*start of selection range*/
  short selEnd;           /*end of selection range*/
  short active;           /*set when record is activated/deactivated*/
  WordBreakProcPtr wordBreak;   /*word break hook*/
  ClikLoopProcPtr clikLoop;     /*click loop hook*/
  long clickTime;         /*used internally*/
  short clickLoc;         /*used internally*/
  long caretTime;         /*used internally*/
  short caretState;       /*used internally*/
  short just;             /*alignment of text*/
  short teLength;         /*length of text*/
  Handle hText;           /*handle to text to be edited*/
  long hDispatchRec;      /*handle to TextEdit dispatch record*/
  short clikStuff;        /*used internally*/
  short crOnly;           /*if <0, new line at Return only*/
  short txFont;           /*text font*/
  Style txFace;           /*character style; unpacked byte*/
  char filler;
  short txMode;           /*pen mode*/
  short txSize;
     /*value indicates either a multistyled edit record or a font size*/
  GrafPtr inPort;         /*a pointer to the grafPort for this TERec*/
  ProcPtr highHook;       /*used for text highlighting and the caret appearance*/
  ProcPts caretHook;      /*used from assembly language*/
  short nLines;           /*number of lines*/
  short lineStarts[16000];/*positions of line starts*/
};

typedef struct TERec TERec;
typedef TERec *TEPtr, **TEHandle;
```

```
typedef char Chars[32001];
typedef char *CharsPtr, **CharsHandle;

struct StyleRun {
  short startChar;  /*starting character position*/
  short styleIndex; /*index in style table*/
};

typedef struct StyleRun StyleRun;

struct STElement {
  short stCount;      /*number of runs in this style*/
  short stHeight;     /*line height*/
  short stAscent;     /*font ascent*/
  short stFont;       /*font family number*/
  Style stFace;       /*character style*/
  char filler;        /*stFace is unpacked byte*/
  short stSize;       /*size in points*/
  RGBColor stColor;   /*absolute Red Green Blue color*/
};

typedef struct STElement STElement;

typedef STElement TEStyleTable[1777], *STPtr, **STHandle;

struct LHElement {
  short lhHeight;     /*maximum height in line*/
  short lhAscent;     /*maximum ascent in line*/
};

typedef struct LHElement LHElement;

typedef LHElement LHTable[8001], *LHPtr, **LHHandle;
  /* ARRAY [0..8000] OF LHElement */

struct ScrpSTElement {
  long scrpStartChar; /*starting character position*/
  short scrpHeight;     /*line height*/
  short scrpAscent;
  short scrpFont;
  Style scrpFace;     /*unpacked byte*/
  char filler;        /*scrpFace is unpacked byte*/
  short scrpSize;
```

```
  RGBColor scrpColor;
};

typedef struct ScrpSTElement ScrpSTElement;

typedef ScrpSTElement ScrpSTTable[1601]; /*ARRAY [0..1600] OF ScrpSTElement*/

struct STScrpRec {
  short scrpNStyle;          /*number of styles in scrap*/
  ScrpSTTable scrpStyleTab;  /*table of style for scrap*/
};

typedef struct StScrpRec StScrpRec;
typedef StScrpRec *StScrpPtr, **StScrpHandle;

struct NullSTRec {
  long teReserved;           /*reserved for future expansion*/
  StScrpHandle nullScrap;    /*handle to scrap style table*/
};

typedef struct NullStRec NullSTRec;
typedef NullSTRec *NullStPtr, **NullStHandle;

struct TEStyleRec {
  short nRuns;            /*number of style runs*/
  short nStyles;         /*size of style table*/
  STHandle styleTab;    /*handle to style table*/
  LHHandle lhTab;       /*handle to line-height table*/
  long teRefCon;         /*reserved for application use*/
  NullSTHandle nullStyle; /*handle to style set at null selection*/
  StyleRun runs [8001];   /*ARRAY [0..8000] OF StyleRun*/
};

typedef struct TEStyleRec TEStyleRec;
typedef TEStyleRec *TEStylePtr, **TEStyleHandle;

struct TextStyle {
  short tsFont;      /*font family number*/
  Style tsFace;      /*character Style*/
  char filler;       /*tsFace is unpacked byte*/
  short tsSize;      /*size in points*/
  RGBColor tsColor; /*absolute red, green, and blue color*/
};
```

```
typedef struct TextStyle TextStyle;
typedef TextStyle *TextStylePtr, **TextStyleHandle;

typedef short TEIntHook;
```

Routines

Initializing TextEdit, Creating an Edit Record, and Disposing of an Edit Record

```
pascal void TEInit          (void);
pascal TEHandle TEStyleNew  (const Rect *destRect,const Rect *viewRect);
pascal TEHandle TENew       (const Rect *destRect, const Rect *viewRect);
pascal void TEDispose       (TEHandle hTE);
```

Activating and Deactivating an Edit Record

```
pascal void TEActivate      (TEHandle hTE);
pascal void TEDeactivate    (TEHandle hTE);
```

Setting and Getting an Edit Record's Text and Character Attribute Information

```
pascal void TEKey           (short key, TEHandle hTE);
pascal void TESetText       (const void *text, long length, TEHandle hTE);
pascal CharsHandle TEGetText
                            (TEHandle hTE);
pascal void TESetStyleHandle
                            (TEStyleHandle theHandle, TEHandle hTE);
pascal TEStyleHandle TEGetStyleHandle
                            (TEHandle hTE);
```

Setting the Caret and Selection Range

```
pascal void TEIdle          (TEHandle hTE);
pascal void TEClick         (Point pt, Boolean fExtend, TEHandle hTE);
pascal void TESetSelect     (long selStart, long selEnd, TEHandle hTE);
```

Displaying and Scrolling Text

```
pascal void TESetAlignment  (short just, TEHandle hTE);
pascal void TEUpdate        (const Rect *rUpdate, TEHandle hTE);
pascal void TETextBox       (const void *text, long length, const Rect *box,
                             short just);
pascal void TECalText       (TEHandle hTE);
pascal long TEGetHeight     (long endLine, long startLine, TEHandle hTE);
```

```
pascal void TEScroll          (short dh, short dv, TEHandle hTE);
pascal void TEPinScroll       (short dh, short dv, TEHandle hTE);
pascal void TEAutoView        (Boolean fAuto, TEHandle hTE);
pascal void TESelView         (TEHandle hTE);
```

Modifying the Text of an Edit Record

```
pascal void TEDelete          (TEHandle hTE);
pascal void TEInsert          (const void *text, long length, TEHandle hTE);
pascal void TECut             (TEHandle hTE);
pascal void TECopy            (TEHandle hTE);
pascal void TEPaste           (TEHandle hTE);
pascal void TEStylePaste      (TEHandle hTE);
pascal OSErr TEToScrap        (void);
pascal OSErr TEFromScrap      (void);
```

Managing the TextEdit Private Scrap

```
#define TEScrapHandle()       (* (Handle*) 0xAB4)
#define TEGetScrapLength()    ((long) * (unsigned short *) 0x0AB0)
pascal void TESetScrapLength
                              (long length);
```

Checking, Setting, and Replacing Styles

```
pascal void TESetStyle        (short mode, const TextStyle *newStyle, Boolean
                                 fRedraw, TEHandle hTE);
pascal void TEReplaceStyle    (short mode, onst TextStyle *oldStyle,
                                 const TextStyle *newStyle, Boolean fRedraw,
                                 TEHandle hTE);
pascal Boolean TEContinuousStyle
                              (short *mode, TextStyle *aStyle, TEHandle hTE);
pascal void TEStyleInsert     (const void *text, long length,
                                 STScrpHandle hSt, TEHandle hTE);
pascal StScrpHandle TEGetStyleScrapHandle
                              (TEHandle hTE);
pascal void TEUseStyleScrap   (long rangeStart, long rangeEnd, StScrpHandle
                                 newStyles, Boolean fRedraw, TEHandle hTE);
pascal long TENumStyles       (long rangeStart, long rangeEnd, TEHandle hTE);
```

Using Byte Offsets and Corresponding Points

```
pascal short TEGetOffset      (Point pt, TEHandle hTE);
pascal Point TEGetPoint       (short offset, TEHandle hTE);
```

Additional TextEdit Features

```
pascal short TEFeatureFlag    (short feature, short action, TEHandle hTE);
```

Customizing TextEdit

```
pascal void TECustomHook      (TEIntHook which, ProcPtr *addr, TEHandle hTE);
pascal void TESetWordBreak    (WordBreakProcPtr wBrkProc, TEHandle hTE);
pascal void TESetClickLoop    (ClikLoopProcPtr clickProc, TEHandle hTE);
```

Assembly-Language Summary

Trap Macros

Trap Macro Names

Pascal name	Trap macro name
TEContinuousStyle	_TEContinuousStyle
TEUseStyleScrap	_TEUseStyleScrap
TECustomHook	_TECustomHook
TENumStyles	_TENumStyles
TEFeatureFlag	_TEFeatureFlag
TEStylePaste	_TEStylePaste
TEReplaceStyle	_TEReplaceStyle
TEGetStyleHandle	_TEGetStyleHandle
TESetStyleHandle	_TESetStyleHandle
TEReplaceStyle	_TEReplaceStyle
TEGetStyleScrap	_TEGetStyleScrap
TEGetStyleHandle	_TEGetStyleHandle
TEGetStyleScrapHandle	_TEGetStyleScrapHandle
TEStyleInsert	_TEStyleInsert
TEGetPoint	_TEGetPoint
TEGetHeight	_TEGetHeight

Global Variables

`WordRedraw`	Used for line calculations to determine how much of a line must be redrawn after a character is entered.
`TEFindWord`	TextEdit's word selection and line breaking routine.
`TERecal`	The address of the routine called by `TECalText` to recalculate the line starts and set the first and last characters that need to be redrawn.
`TEDoText`	The address of a multi-purpose text editing routine used to display, highlight, and hit-test characters, and position the pen to draw the caret.
`TEScrpHandle`	A handle to the TextEdit private scrap.
`TEScrapLength`	The size of the TextEdit scrap in bytes.

QuickDraw Text

Contents

This chapter describes the text-handling components of QuickDraw. You can use the QuickDraw text routines to measure and draw text ranging in complexity from a single glyph to a line of justified text containing multiple languages and styles. In addition to measuring and drawing text, the QuickDraw text routines also help you to determine which characters to highlight and where to position the caret to mark the insertion point. These routines translate pixel locations into byte offsets and vice versa.

Read this chapter if you are writing an application that draws static text in a box, such as a dialog box, or draws and manipulates text of any length in one or more languages. Before you use the routines described in this chapter, read the chapter "Introduction to Text on the Macintosh" in this book. To understand the concepts and routines described in this chapter, you must be familiar with the other parts of QuickDraw described in *Inside Macintosh: Imaging*.

Read this chapter along with the chapter "Font Manager," in this book, because of the close relationship between QuickDraw and the Font Manager. For help in understanding the tasks involved in text layout, refer to the chapters "Text Utilities" and "Script Manager," also in this book.

This chapter explains how to set up the text-drawing environment and lay out and draw text, including how to

- draw and measure a single character, a text segment, or a line of text

- determine where to break a line of text

- determine the order in which to draw text segments for a line of text containing multiple styles and mixed directions

- eliminate trailing space characters

- distribute extra space throughout a line of text to justify it appropriately for the script system

- draw and measure scaled text

- identify caret positions for marking an insertion point and highlighting text

About QuickDraw Text

Text on the Macintosh is graphical. This section provides an overview of how to draw text using the text-handling components of QuickDraw. These routines let you direct how the text is to be rendered and drawn, while insulating your application from the low-level implementation details.

Whether for onscreen display or to be printed, you always draw text in the context of a graphics port. To draw the text, QuickDraw displays the bitmap of each glyph on the display device. Although QuickDraw displays the text, you define how the text is to be rendered by setting the text-drawing parameters in the graphics port record. Text rendering is the process of portraying the text according to its character attributes, such as the font, font size, and style. You use the character attribute information associated with the text to set up the drawing environment each time you draw a segment of text that begins a new style run. A **style run** is a sequence of text that is all in the same script system, font, size, and style.

QuickDraw routines let you accept keyboard input or gain access to existing text stored in memory. In general, the tasks that you need to perform to draw text on the Macintosh are easier if your store the text as a simple sequence of character codes separate from all the character attribute information that describes how QuickDraw is to render the stored text. (For an example of how to define data structures to store the character attribute information, you can look at the TextEdit data structures used for this purpose; see the chapter "TextEdit" in this book.)

Graphics Ports and Text Drawing

You draw text on the Macintosh in the current graphics port according to the graphics environment defined by the graphics port record. A **graphics port** defines where and how graphic and text drawing operations are to take place. QuickDraw treats the graphics port information as its primary set of global information.

You can define many graphics ports on the screen, each with its own complete drawing environment, and easily switch between them. Because QuickDraw always draws in the current graphics port, it is essential that you keep track of which one this is.

Each graphics port is tied to a window. To draw in the graphics port of a window, you first need to make the port the current one. (You do this using the `SetPort` procedure, described in *Inside Macintosh: Imaging*.) The window whose port you want to draw in does not have to be active or the frontmost window. QuickDraw draws to the **current graphics port** identified by `SetPort`. You can draw to a background window or an inactive window by making its port the current one.

There are two types of graphics ports: the original version (`GrafPort`) that supports mainly black-and-white drawing with some rudimentary color capabilities and the color graphics port (`CGrafPort`), which supports all of the characteristics of the original graphics port, plus additional features including color facilities.

Both types of graphics port records contain fields that specify the colors to be used for the foreground (`fgColor`) and the background (`bkColor`) of a glyph. You can think of the **foreground** as the pixels that constitute the glyph, and the **background** as the pixels that surround the glyph. In terms of a black-and-white screen, the foreground pixels of a glyph are black, and the surrounding background pixels are white.

The original graphics port provides eight colors—black, white, red, green, blue, cyan, magenta, and yellow; however, on a black-and-white screen nonwhite colors appear as black. A color graphics port provides a wide range of possible colors that allow you to portray all aspects of the user interface in color, including the representation of text. Both types of graphics ports maintain the fractional horizontal pen position, so that a series of text-drawing calls accumulates the fractional position. For the color graphics port, this value is maintained in a graphics port record field. For the original graphics port, this value is maintained in a `grafGlobal`, which is reset whenever you reposition the pen.

There is only one QuickDraw text-handling procedure that requires a color graphics port, `CharExtra`. (Although you can call `CharExtra` for an original graphics port without causing the system to crash, `CharExtra` produces no result.) You can use all the other QuickDraw text routines with either an original graphics port or a color graphics port.

Fields in the graphics port record determine which font QuickDraw is to use to portray the text, the font style, the font size, and how the bits forming the glyph are to be placed in the bit image. You control how the text is to be rendered by setting each of these fields *before* you measure or draw a segment of text that begins a new style run. QuickDraw provides procedures that let you set each field. To ensure future compatibility, you should always use these procedures rather than directly modify a field. You use the appropriate QuickDraw procedure to set the graphics port field for the style run to be drawn, if the current value of a field differs from the characteristic that you want QuickDraw to use. The following sections describe what each of these field values represents.

Font, Font Style, and Font Size

This section provides an overview of how QuickDraw and the Font Manager interact to provide the font that you specify in the graphics port to be used to render the text.

The Font Manager keeps track of detailed font information, such as the glyphs' character codes, whether fonts are fixed-width or proportional, and which fonts are related to each other by name. When you make a call to QuickDraw to measure or draw text, QuickDraw passes the font request, including the font's size and style that you have set in the current graphics port, to the Font Manager, and the Font Manager satisfies the request as best as possible, returning to QuickDraw a bitmap of the glyph of the font, along with some information that QuickDraw uses for stylistic variation and layout. When QuickDraw receives the bitmap, it transfers the bitmap to the screen. If necessary, QuickDraw first scales the bitmap, or applies stylistic variation to it if the requested style was not intrinsic to the font.

The Macintosh supports two types of fonts: bitmapped and outline. A **font** is a complete set of glyphs in a specific typeface and style—and in the case of bitmapped fonts, a specific size. Outline fonts consist of outline glyphs in a particular typeface and style with no size restriction. The Font Manager can generate thousands of point sizes from the same TrueType outline font. For example, a single outline Courier font can produce Courier 10-point, Courier 12-point, and Courier 200-point. (You can read more about these two types of fonts and the relationship between QuickDraw and the Font Manager in the chapter "Font Manager" in this book. How the Font Manager responds to a QuickDraw font request is also explained in detail in the chapter "Font Manager," and summarized later in this chapter.)

When multiple fonts of the same typeface are present in system software, the Font Manager groups them into font families. Each font in a font family can be bitmapped or outline. Bitmapped fonts in the same family can be different styles or sizes.

A font has a name and a *font family ID* number. A font name is usually the same as the typeface from which it is derived, such as Courier. If an intrinsic font is not in plain style, its style becomes part of the font's name, for example, Courier Bold. A font family ID is a resource ID for a font family that identifies the font and also reveals the script system to which the font belongs. When you set the graphics port font field (`txFont`) for a style run, you specify the font family ID. The font family ID identifies to the Font Manager both the font and the script system to be used.

Some fonts are designed and supplied with stylistic variations integral to the font. If the Font Manager does not return a font with the requested style integral to the font design, QuickDraw applies the style. A font designer can design a font in a specific style, such as Courier Bold, or QuickDraw can add styles, such as bold or italic, to bitmaps.

A **style** is a specific variation in the appearance of a glyph that can be applied consistently to all the glyphs in a typeface. A font is described as *plain* when no styles are specified for it. The styles that QuickDraw supports include bold, italic, underline, outline, shadow, extend, and condense.

When QuickDraw requests a font in a specific style, such as Courier Bold, if the Font Manager has the font whose design includes the style, the Font Manager returns that font to QuickDraw; QuickDraw does not need to apply the stylistic variation when drawing the font, in this case. If the Font Manager does not have the font with the stylistic variation intrinsic to it, the Font Manager returns the plain font to QuickDraw, and QuickDraw applies the style when drawing the glyphs. When QuickDraw requests a font with multiple styles, if the Font Manager does not have a font with all of the styles intrinsic to it, but it has a font with one intrinsic style, the Font Manager returns that font, and QuickDraw applies the additional style or styles when drawing the glyphs. The Font Manager does not apply stylistic variations to a font.

Figure 3-1 illustrates the styles that QuickDraw supports as applied to the Helvetica font. There are many other stylistic variations not explicitly supported by QuickDraw, such as strikethrough, that you can implement.

Figure 3-1   Stylistic variations

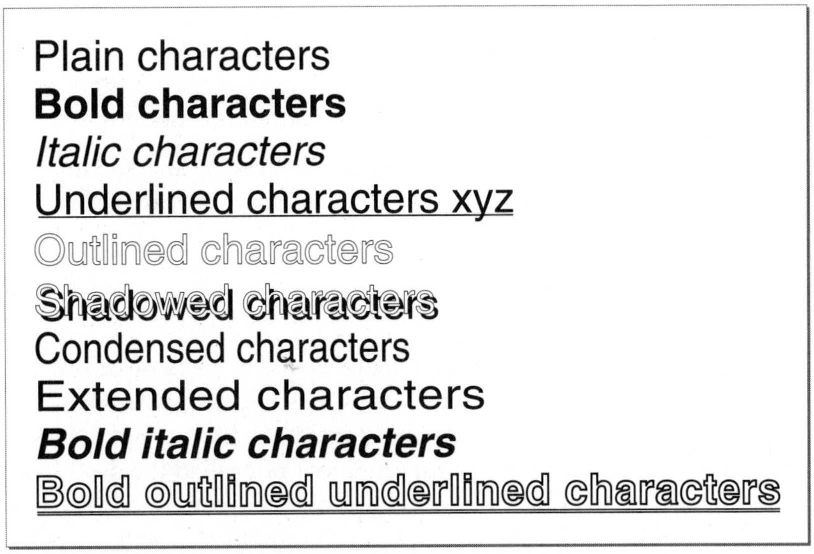

Plain characters
Bold characters
Italic characters
<u>Underlined characters xyz</u>
Outlined characters
Shadowed characters
Condensed characters
Extended characters
Bold italic characters
Bold outlined underlined characters

You can specify stylistic variations alone or in combination. (Certain styles may be disabled in some script systems.) Most combinations usually look good only for large font sizes. Here are the results of specifying any of the styles that QuickDraw supports:

■ Bold increases the thickness of a glyph. It causes each glyph to be repeatedly drawn one bit to the right for extra thickness.

■ Italic adds an italic slant to the glyphs. Glyph bits above the base line are skewed right; bits below the base line are skewed left.

■ Underline draws a line below the base line of the glyphs. If part of a glyph descends below the base line (as does the y shown in the fourth line of text in Figure 3-1), generally, the underline isn't drawn through the pixel on either side of the descending part. However, when printing to a PostScript™ LaserWriter printer, the line is drawn through the descenders.

■ Outline makes a hollow, outlined glyph rather than a solid one. If you specify bold along with outline, the hollow part of the glyph is widened.

■ Shadow also makes an outlined glyph, but the outline is thickened below and to the right of the glyph to achieve the effect of a shadow. If you specify bold along with shadow, the hollow part of the glyph is widened.

■ Condense affects the horizontal distance between all glyphs, including spaces. Condense decreases the distance between glyphs by the amount that the Font Manager determines is appropriate.

■ Extend affects the horizontal distance between all glyphs, including spaces. Extend increases the distance between glyphs by the amount that the Font Manager determines is appropriate.

The style underline draws the underline through the entire text line, from the pen starting position through the ending position, plus any offsets from the font or italic kerning. QuickDraw text clips the right edge of the underline to the ending pen position, causing outlined or shadowed underlines to match imperfectly when you draw text in sections. If the underlined text is outlined or shadowed, the ends aren't capped, that is, consecutively drawn pieces of text maintain a continuous underline.

Note that the outline and shadow styles cause the outline and shadow of the glyph to be drawn in the foreground color. The inside of the glyph, if drawn at all, is drawn in the background color.

Transfer Modes

A **transfer mode** specifies the interaction between what is to be drawn with what already exists on the screen. When you draw text, QuickDraw uses the foreground and background colors to determine how the text to be drawn, called the source, interacts with text already drawn in the current graphics port, called the destination. You define how this interplay is to occur by specifying a transfer mode, which is a value consisting of two parts. The first part is the kind of transfer mode. It specifies whether the graphic to be drawn is a pattern or text. The second part is the operation. It is a Boolean value that defines the type of interaction that is to occur, resulting in the text display.

There are two basic kinds of transfer modes in QuickDraw: pattern (`pat`), which is used to draw lines or shapes in a pattern, and source (`src`), which is used to draw text. There are four basic types of operations, totaling eight including their opposites. They are: `Copy`, `Or`, `Xor`, and `Bic`. In addition to the basic operations, there are arithmetic drawing mode operations designed specifically for use with color.

When you draw text, for each bit in the text, the corresponding bit in the destination bitmap is identified, the specified Boolean operation is performed on the pair of bits, and the resulting bit is stored into the destination bit image. The basic operations produce the following results.

The `Copy` operation replaces the pixels in the destination with the pixels in the source, painting over the destination.

For black-and-white images, the `Or`, `Xor`, and `Bic` operations leave the destination pixels under the white part of the source unchanged. These operations differ in how they affect the pixels under the black part.

- `Or` replaces those pixels with black pixels, overlaying the destination with the black part of the source; it combines the destination with the source.

- `Xor` inverts the pixels under the black part. (The `Xor` mode inverts black in the source image at all destination depths, including 16-bit and 32-bit direct pixels.)

- `Bic` (bit clear) erases the pixels under the black part, leaving it white.

Figure 3-2 shows how each of the basic transfer modes affects the source and destination images resulting in what is displayed on the screen.

Figure 3-2   Effect of the basic transfer modes for black-and-white images

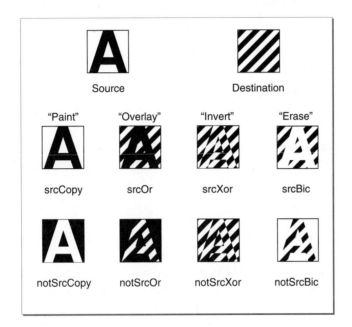

These transfer modes work with color images as follows:

- `Copy` replaces the destination with the colored source.

- `Or` mode results in the source image, regardless of the destination depth.

- `Bic` mode causes the foreground color in the source image to erase, resulting in the background color in the destination image.

- `Xor` inverts the foreground color in the source image, but not the background color, at all destination depths, including 16-bit and 32-bit direct pixels. (Inversion is not well defined for color pixels.)

The initial transfer mode for drawing text is `srcOr`. This text drawing mode is recommended for all applications because it uses the least memory and draws the entire glyph in all cases. The `srcOr` mode only affects other parts of existing glyphs if the glyphs overlap.

Note
The center of shadowed or outlined text is drawn in a graphics port in `srcBic` transfer mode if text mode is `srcOr`, for compatibility with old applications. (For color graphics ports, the center isn't drawn at all.) This allows black text with a white outline on an arbitrary background. ◆

QuickDraw Text, Script Systems, and Other Managers

Although QuickDraw provides the routines that are pivotal to drawing text on the Macintosh, it uses the services of other managers including the Font Manager and the Script Manager. To draw text consisting of multiple lines and mixed directions, you also need to use routines that belong to these managers, as well as some Text Utilities services. This section describes the relationship between QuickDraw and the Script Manager. It also provides an overview of the line-layout and text-drawing processes. For specific discussion of the routines that you use to perform the tasks inherent in these processes, see "Measuring and Drawing Lines of Text" on page 3-29.

When you draw text using QuickDraw, the Script Manager interacts with QuickDraw to provide the script-specific support. To do this, the Script Manager needs to know which script you are using. It determines this from the font that you specify in the graphics port txFont field. For example, if the font is Geneva, the font script is Roman. The script specified by the current graphics port font is referred to as the **font script.**

Although you can use most QuickDraw routines with all script systems, some QuickDraw routines entail restrictions. For example, you use one QuickDraw procedure to draw the glyph of a single character in a 1-byte script system, but you must use a different procedure to draw the glyph of a single character in a 2-byte script or a script system that contains zero-width characters. Some script systems contain fonts that have only 1-byte characters and some script systems contain fonts that have a mix of 1-byte and 2-byte characters. Some fonts have zero-width characters; these are usually overlapping diacritical marks which typically follow the base character in memory. With 2-byte characters, all but the first (high-order, low-address) byte are measured as zero width.

Most fonts, whatever script system they belong to, contain Roman characters, typically consisting of the 128 low-ASCII character set. The inclusion of Roman characters within another script system allows the user to enter Roman text without having to switch script systems. For script systems whose text has a left-to-right direction, such as Roman and Japanese, the direction of the text is uniform within a single style run. However, a single script system that portrays text read from right to left, such as Hebrew or Arabic, can also contain left-to-right text, such as numbers within the language of the script system or Roman-based text such as English. A single style run can also contain *bidirectional text.*

Some script systems that include the 128 low-ASCII character set include an **associated font** that is used to portray these characters. Use of an associated font is handled by the script management system without requiring any action on the part of your application. The way QuickDraw treats Roman space characters within a script system that supports bidirectional text differs from how it handles them otherwise. This behavior is explained later in this chapter in relation to eliminating trailing spaces from the end of a line.

QuickDraw Text

For those script systems that support it, the existence of bidirectional text in a text range does not violate the concept of a single style run because QuickDraw uses the same text-related values in the graphics port record fields to draw all the glyphs of the entire segment of text; you do not need to change any of these values in order to draw the complete segment of bidirectional text as a single style run.

Figure 3-3 shows mixed Hebrew and Chinese text on a single line. There are three style runs. Only the first style run includes bidirectional text.

Figure 3-3   Multiple style runs on a single line

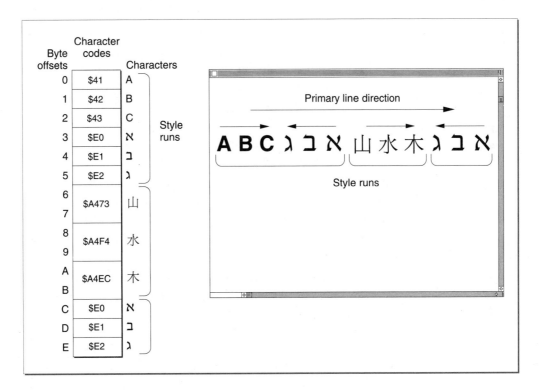

For all script systems, you measure and draw text a single style run at a time, whether the text consists of a single character, a Pascal string, or a segment of characters. A **text segment,** as used in this chapter, means the portion of a style run that you may pass to a single QuickDraw call. It may be a complete style run or any portion of a style run, as long as it fits on a single line. If a style run extends across a line break, you must make separate calls for the separate segments of the style run.

Whether you draw the glyph of a single character or a line of text, it is up to you to track where the text begins, both in terms of vertical and horizontal screen position and offset into your text stream. With the help of either a Font Manager function (`OutlineMetrics`) or a QuickDraw procedure (`GetFontInfo`), you can assess the line height based on the measurements of the script system font, and the associated font, if one exists, used to render the text, then determine the vertical screen position.

In most cases, you also need to know the width of the display area where the text is to be drawn. For a line of text, you can think of this area as the display line. A **display line** is the horizontal length in pixels of the screen area where you draw a line of text; the left and right ends of the display line constitute its left and right margins. You define the display line length in pixels and uses this value to determine how much text will fit on the display line.

You specify where QuickDraw is to begin drawing by setting the current pen location of the graphics port. Within a single line of text, QuickDraw takes care of correctly advancing the pen position after it draws each glyph or text segment.

For text that exceeds a single display line, you must control where a line ends and the next one begins. For unidirectional text, this task essentially constitutes the line layout process. For mixed-directional text, the order in which you display the style runs may be different from their storage order. In this case, you also need to determine the drawing order in the line layout process.

To draw a line of text, you can loop through the text, laying it out first, then loop through the drawing process. A line-layout loop measures the text and determines where to break it. In most cases, you can use a Text Utilities function (`StyledLineBreak`) for this purpose.

To lay out justified text, a loop needs to include several additional steps that determine how to distribute the extra space among the text of the line. This process entails eliminating trailing spaces from the end of the line, then distributing the remaining extra space among the text. How the distribution of extra space is expressed throughout a line of text is dependent on the script system. For example, some script systems add additional width to space characters that are used as word delimiters; some script systems, which use connecting glyphs, stretch certain glyphs to encompass the additional width. See the next section, "Text Formatting and Justification," for more information.

Before you call a QuickDraw measuring routine, you need to set the graphics port text-related fields to those of the style run that the text is part of. You set these fields only for each new style run.

Once you have laid out a line of text, drawing it is fairly simple. An application can have a text-drawing loop that positions the pen at the beginning of a new line, sets the text-related fields of the current graphics port to the text characteristics for that style run if the text string begins a new style run, then draws the text, using one of the QuickDraw drawing routines to draw aligned text, justified text, or scaled text.

Text Formatting and Justification

When you lay out text, you can change its width and its alignment. You change the width of text to format it for special purposes, or to justify the text to fit a display area or a given line. To justify text, you spread or condensed it so that any white space is distributed evenly throughout the display area or line.

You can draw text that is aligned with either the right margin of the display area or line, which produces ragged-left text, or the left margin, which produces ragged-right text. You align text by positioning the pen appropriately so that the first glyph of the text line is flush against the margin.

There are several ways to change the width of text. You can

- use the QuickDraw justification routines that measure and draw text, automatically changing the width of the text appropriately for each script system

- set the graphics port `txFace` field to condense or extend the text

- set the graphics port `spExtra` and `chExtra` fields to narrow or widen space and nonspace characters by a specific number of pixels

You can even justify text that includes special formatting. For example, you can extend or condense the width of space and nonspace characters, while justifying the text line overall.

Of these methods, the easiest way to justify text for all script systems is to use the QuickDraw justification routines. These routines handle the script system requirements for your application. For example, because the text of some script systems, such as Arabic and Devanagari, is drawn as connected glyphs, the justification routines do not add width to or remove it from nonspace characters.

The justification routines assume that a slop value specified in pixels is to be distributed throughout the text. The **slop value** is the difference between the width of the text and the width of the display area or line. You can pass the justification routines a positive or negative slop value. To extend text to fit the display area or line, you specify a positive slop value. To justify a line of text more smoothly by condensing it when it only slightly exceeds the display area or line length, you can use a negative slop value.

How the justification routines distribute this extra space within a style run depends on the script system.

- For Roman script systems, text justification is performed by altering the size of the space characters. You can think of this as interword spacing. (Every space in a style run is allocated the same amount of extra width and thus is the same size, whether or not it is at the beginning or end of the line or the style run.)

- For Arabic, the justification routines insert extension bar glyphs between joined glyphs and widen space characters to fill any remaining gaps.

- For scripts that don't use spaces to delimit words, these routines usually modify the intercharacter spacing to achieve justification.

Figure 3-4 shows a line of text in the Roman script system containing three style runs and how extra space is distributed among the space characters within a style run.

Figure 3-4   Justification of Roman text

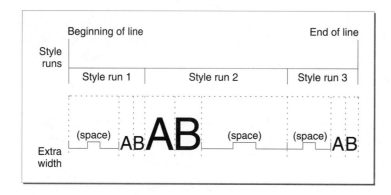

To correctly handle spacing between multiple style runs on a line, the justification routines take a parameter that specifies the position of the style run on the line. The style run position parameter is meaningful only for those script systems that use intercharacter spacing for justification. For all other script systems, the parameter exists for future extensibility. Although the style run position parameter is not used, for example, for justifying text in the Roman script system, to allow for future compatibility, you should always specify the appropriate value for it for all calls that take it.

For those script systems that do use intercharacter spacing, space between styles is allocated differently depending upon whether the style is leftmost, rightmost, or between two other style runs. For example, if a style run occurs at the beginning or end of a line, extra space is *not* added to the outer edge of the outermost glyph, whereas if a style run is interior to a line, all of the glyphs of the text are treated the same: extra space is allocated to both sides of every glyph including those at either end of the style run.

Note

The text justification routines do not automatically eliminate trailing spaces from the last style run on the line. However, QuickDraw provides a routine (`VisibleLength`) that does not include trailing spaces in the byte count of the last style run on the line. ◆

If you do not want to justify a range of text, you can change the width of the text for onscreen display, for example, to format an advertisement by setting the graphics port `spExtra` and `chExtra` fields to an amount by which space and nonspace characters are to be widened or narrowed. If you use `SpaceExtra` and `CharExtra` to widen or narrow text, you are responsible for handling them properly for the script system.

The original graphics port does not have a `chExtra` field, so you can only change the width of nonspace characters if you use a color graphics port. Although line breaks are maintained, spacing defined by these values is not preserved when you print to a LaserWriter printer.

Scaling

Text scaling is the process of changing glyphs from one size or shape to another. This section discusses two kinds of scaling: implicit and explicit. This section also summarizes how the Font Manager handles scaling requirements when scaling is disabled. The chapter "Font Manager" in this book describes disabling scaling in greater detail.

Implicit scaling is performed automatically by QuickDraw when the Font Manager cannot supply a bitmapped font in the size that you request. In this case, the Font Manager returns to QuickDraw a bitmapped font that is the closest approximation, along with scaling factors. QuickDraw uses these values to scale the text when drawing it. This process is transparent to your application. Because the Font Manager can always satisfy a font request completely when outline fonts are installed, no scaling is necessary.

Explicit scaling is performed in essentially the same way as implicit scaling, but you specify how the text is to be scaled. Several QuickDraw routines include parameters that let your application specify (explicitly) how text is to be scaled. You might want to scale text explicitly, for example, to create unusual glyph shapes, or to increase or decrease the size of text when a user clicks in a zoom box. You can use the high-level QuickDraw justification routines to explicitly scale text. Alternatively, you can use the low-level standard measuring and drawing routines, referred to as *bottleneck* routines. See "Using Scaled Text" on page 3-44. To explicitly scale text, you specify values that let you stretch or shrink a glyph horizontally or vertically. You can change a glyph from a familiar point size to one that is unusual—for example, a glyph that is 12 points high but as wide as the entire page.

The same rules apply to the interaction between the Font Manager and QuickDraw whether scaling is implicit or explicit. However, for explicit scaling, QuickDraw passes the scaling factors that you specify as routine parameters to the Font Manager in an input record (`FMInput`) along with the standard information, which includes the font family ID number, the size, and the stylistic variation of the font request. Taking the requested scaling factors into account, the Font Manager follows a standard path looking for an available font that best satisfies the request, and returns the bitmap information to QuickDraw via an output record (`FMOutput`), which contains a handle to the requested font resource and, among other information, the scaling factors that now apply, if any. The returned scaling factors describe how QuickDraw is to draw the text to fulfill the input scaling factors request.

If you use the low-level bottleneck procedure or the higher-level justification procedure to *draw* the scaled text and the Font Manager returns scaling factors to be applied to the text, QuickDraw applies the additional scaling.

The low-level bottleneck *measuring* function lets you specify scaling factors in reference parameters. If only bitmapped fonts are installed and a font does not exist that matches the scale you specify, the Font Manager uses the font that best approximates the request, and measures the text using that font. The Font Manager returns scaling factors in the reference parameters, along with the width of the text based on the supplied font. In this case, QuickDraw does not apply the necessary additional scaling to the text to give you the correct text measurement including scaling. To measure the text correctly, you need to apply the additional scaling to the text width of the font that the Font Manager returns.

For example, suppose only bitmapped fonts are installed and you request a point size of 24 with a horizontal scaling factor of 2/1 and a vertical scaling factor of 1/1. The Font Manager returns the most optimal matching font that it has, which is 12, say, with a horizontal scaling factor of 4/1 and a vertical scaling factor of 2/1. Now, you must apply these scaling factors to the text width and height metrics in the 12-point font to get the correct text measurement.

You can use the Font Manager `SetFScaleDisable` procedure to enable or disable font scaling of bitmapped glyphs. When you disable scaling, the Font Manager finds the closest, smaller-sized font to the one that you request, and adjusts the width table associated with the font to match the requested size. As a result, the height of the glyphs is smaller than you requested, but the spacing compensates for it. When scaling is disabled, the Font Manager returns 1/1 scaling in response to the request.

For a complete discussion of how the Font Manager determines which font to return to QuickDraw to satisfy a font request, see the chapter "Font Manager" in this book. This chapter also describes the `SetFScaleDisable` procedure and the width table.

Carets and Highlighting

Highlighting a selection range and marking the insertion point with a caret both involve converting offsets of characters in a text buffer to pixel locations on a display screen. This task is prerequisite to both drawing a caret and highlighting text. See the chapter "Introduction to Text on the Macintosh" in this book for a discussion of the conventions underlying the relationship of a character at a byte offset to a caret position for unidirectional text and text at a direction boundary.

When the text is unidirectional, performing these tasks is uncomplicated because storage order and display order are the same. For unidirectional text, a caret position always falls between the corresponding glyphs of these characters—on the leading edge of one and the trailing edge of the other. When the text is bidirectional, it can contain characters that occur on direction boundaries; although the characters are stored contiguously in memory, the leading edge of one character's glyph does not constitute the trailing edge of the other in display order. Consequently, two physically separate caret positions exist on the display screen, one associated with each glyph.

There are a number of situations in which you need to know a caret position, and they fall within two categories: drawing a caret to mark the insertion point, and using a caret position to denote an endpoint for highlighting a text selection. For a discussion of marking an insertion point with either a single caret or a dual caret, and caret movement with arrow keys, see the chapter "Introduction to Text on the Macintosh."

You need to know the caret positions marking the endpoints of a text selection to highlight it when the user selects either a word or a range of text, and for other features that the application supports, such as a search operation. Generally, you know the byte offsets of the characters that begin and end a selection range for tasks such as search operations. However, when the user clicks in or selects a range of text to be highlighted, usually you first need to convert the pixel locations marking the cursor locations to the corresponding characters' byte offsets in memory, and then convert the characters' byte offsets to caret positions.To encompass all of the characters within the text segment to be highlighted, you use caret positions that mark endpoints which include the beginning and ending characters of the text.

On a black-and-white screen, highlighting a selection is simple; white pixels turn black and vice versa. In a color environment, the inversion of multibit pixel values usually yields many different colors, which is unsuitable for highlighting text. To highlight text rendered in color, QuickDraw lets you specify a highlight value that it uses instead of the current graphics ports background color. Generally the user sets the highlighting color, but your application can change the color. When you use highlight mode, all pixel values of the current background color are replaced with the value of the highlighting color.

Using QuickDraw Text

This section describes how to

- initialize QuickDraw

- set up the text drawing environment

- specify the text characteristics, such as the font, style, spacing, and transfer mode

- measure and draw text ranging from a single character to a line containing multiple styles and mixed directions

Preparing to Use QuickDraw

The QuickDraw text-handling routines rely on both QuickDraw and the Script Manager. Therefore, before you call any of these routines, you need to determine what versions of QuickDraw and the Script Manager are installed, and initialize QuickDraw. For more information about determining the version of the Script Manager, see the chapter "Script Manager" in this book.

Determining the Version and Initializing QuickDraw

To determine the current version of QuickDraw, you call the Gestalt function with the gestaltQuickdrawVersion selector. The gestaltQuickdrawVersion selector returns a 2-byte value indicating the version of QuickDraw currently present. The high-order byte of that number represents the major revision number, and the low-order byte represents the minor revision number. These are the currently defined values for the QuickDraw selector.

Constant	Value
gestaltOriginalQD	$000
gestaltOriginalQD1	$001
gestalt8BitQD	$100
gestalt32BitQD	$200
gestalt32BitQD11	$210
gestalt32BitQD12	$220
gestalt32BitQD13	$230

Gestalt returns a 4-byte value in its response parameter; the low-order word contains QuickDraw version data. In that low-order word, the high-order byte gives the major revision number and the low-order byte the minor revision. Major revisions currently defined are the original QuickDraw, the original Color QuickDraw, and the current 32-Bit QuickDraw with direct-pixel capability.

Values having a major revision number of 1 or 2 indicate that Color QuickDraw is available in either the 8-bit or 32-bit version. These results do not, however, indicate whether a color monitor is attached to the system. You need to use high-level QuickDraw routines to obtain that information.

Many Macintosh applications don't care what version of QuickDraw is available on the user's system: they don't use color at all, use only the basic QuickDraw color model, or specify all their colors abstractly, in RGB form. If your application does depend on a specific version of QuickDraw, you can check the version at run time and adapt to make best use of the available hardware (or at least inform the user gracefully that your program's graphics needs aren't being met).

For more information about the Gestalt function, see the chapter "Gestalt Manager" in *Inside Macintosh: Operating System Utilities*.

Initialize QuickDraw at the beginning of your program before any other parts of the Toolbox. To do so, call the InitGraf procedure. For more information about the InitGraf procedure, see *Inside Macintosh: Imaging*.

Setting Up the Text-Drawing Environment

You draw text in the current graphics port. You create a distinct graphical environment for every window on the screen by specifying values for the graphics port. Each graphics port has its own complete drawing environment—including its own coordinate system, drawing location, font set, and character attributes.

Because your application can have more than one window open at the same time, QuickDraw routines access the data structures within the current graphics port only. You must keep track of the current graphics port and identify it to QuickDraw when you change windows.

You can use the QuickDraw SetPort procedure, which operates on both types of graphics ports (GrafPort and CGrafPort), to identify the current graphics port. You use the global variable thePort to indicate the current port. In the following example, SetPort identifies the port pointed to by thePort as the current one.

```
SetPort(thePort);
```

For more information about the SetPort procedure, see *Inside Macintosh: Imaging*.

Each time you draw text in a window's graphics port, you need to set the text-related fields of the graphics port to the characteristics of the text that you want to draw, if they differ from the current ones. A graphics port record contains three fields that determine how text is drawn—the font, style, and size of glyphs—and one that specifies how it will be placed in the bit image, the transfer mode. In addition to these fields, a graphics port record contains two fields that let you specify character widths to define how text is to be formatted on a line.

Specifying Text Characteristics

Each time you measure or draw text that begins a new style run and whose characteristics differ from those of the current graphics port, first you need to set the graphics port text-related fields to match those of the text. Here is how the text-related graphic port fields are initialized:

Field	Value	Explanation
txFont	0	System font
txFace	[ ]	Plain style of the current font
txSize	0	Size of the system font used to draw text
spExtra	0	Standard width of the space character for the font
chExtra	0	Standard width of nonspace characters for the font
txMode	srcOr	Combines the destination with the source

Do not modify any of these fields directly. Instead, always use the QuickDraw routines to change their values: `TextFace`, `TextFont`, `TextMode`, `TextSize`, `SpaceExtra`, and `CharExtra`. Using these routines ensures that your application will benefit from any future improvements to QuickDraw.

Listing 3-1 shows a simple sequence of QuickDraw calls. These routines set the current port, set the graphics port text fields, then draw a text string. The calls render the text in 12-point Geneva font using the styles bold and italic, and widen the spaces between words by 3 pixels to format the text. QuickDraw text-handling procedures that set these fields are discussed later in this section.

Listing 3-1   Using QuickDraw to set the graphics port text-related fields

```
SetPort(thePort);
TextFont(geneva);
TextFace([bold, italic]);
TextSize(12);
SpaceExtra(3);
```

If you must directly change the values of any of the graphics port fields, call the QuickDraw `PortChanged` procedure to notify QuickDraw of the change after you modify the field. For more information about `PortChanged`, see the QuickDraw chapters in *Inside Macintosh: Imaging*.

Setting the Font

You use the `TextFont` procedure to set the font for the text. The value that you specify for this field is either the font family ID or a predefined constant.

If you know the font name, you can get the font family ID by calling the `GetFNum` procedure, passing it the font name. You can get a font's name if it has a font family ID by calling the Font Manager `GetFontName` procedure. For more information about these procedures and the predefined font constants, see the chapter "Font Manager" in this book.

If you do not know either the font family ID or the name of the font, you can use the Resource Manager's `GetIndResource` function followed by the `GetResInfo` procedure to determine the fonts that are available and what their names and IDs are. See the chapter "Resource Manager" in *Inside Macintosh: More Macintosh Toolbox* for more information.

The values 0 and 1 have special significance. When a graphics port is created, the `txFont` field is initialized to 0, which specifies the system font. This is the font that the system uses to draw text in system menus and system dialog boxes. You can use a font that is defined by the system—to do so, it sets this field to 1; 1 always specifies the application font.

Note

Do not use the font family ID 0 or the constant `'chicago'` to specify the Chicago font because the ID can vary on localized systems. To specify the Chicago font, use the following calls.

```
GetFNum('Chicago', theNum);
TextFont(theNum);
```

The variable `theNum` is an integer. ◆

Storing a font name in a document

Always store a font name, rather than its font family ID, in a document to avoid problems that can arise because IDs are not unique—many font families share the same font family ID—or because one font family may have different IDs on different computer systems. ◆

You use `TextFont` to set the `txFont` field of the current graphics port for a new style run that uses a font different from the current one, and in response to a user's actions, for example, when a user selects a new font from a menu.

Note

Whenever a user changes the keyboard script, you are responsible for setting the `txFont` field to the new font, so that the keyboard script and the font script are synchronized. ◆

Modifying the Text Style

When you create a graphics port, the `txFace` field value is initially an empty set (`[ ]`), which specifies the plain style of the current font.

To change the text style, you call `TextFace`, using any combination of the following constants to specify the text style: `bold`, `italic`, `underline`, `outline`, `shadow`, `condense`, and `extend`. In Pascal, you specify the value or values within square brackets. For example:

```
TextFace([bold]);          {bold}
TextFace([bold,italic]);   {bold and italic}
```

You can also add another style to the current text style, or remove a style. For example:

```
TextFace(thePort^.txFace+[bold]); {existing style plus bold}
TextFace(thePort^.txFace-[bold]); {existing style minus bold}
```

To reset the style to plain, you specify an empty set. For example:

```
TextFace([]);   {plain text}
```

If you want to restore the existing value after you draw the text in another style, save it before you call `TextFace`. For a description of how QuickDraw renders text in each of these styles, see "Font, Font Style, and Font Size" on page 3-5.

Changing the Font Size

When you create a graphics port, the value of the `txSize` field is 0, which specifies the size of the font to be used to draw system text, such as menus. The size of the system font is usually 12 points. You use the `TextSize` procedure to set the `txSize` field of the current graphics port to the font's point size. Text drawn on the QuickDraw coordinate plane can range from 1 point to 32,767 points.

Changing the Width of Characters

When you create a graphics port, the `spExtra` and `chExtra` fields are set to 0, which specifies the standard width for space and nonspace characters in the font. You change the width of space characters and nonspace characters using the `SpaceExtra` and `CharExtra` procedures, respectively.

Widening or narrowing space and nonspace characters lets you meet special formatting requirements that are not satisfied by simply justifying the text. If you want to change only the width of the space characters in a line of text for onscreen typographical formatting, you can set the `spExtra` field value before you draw each style run, narrowing spaces in some style runs and widening those in others. To change the width of nonspace characters, either extending them or narrowing them, you set the `chExtra` field value before you draw a style run.

You use the `SpaceExtra` procedure to set the `spExtra` field of the current graphics port to the number of pixels to be added to or subtracted from the standard width of the space character in the style run. (A value specified in the `spExtra` field is ignored by script systems that do not use space characters, so don't to set it for 2-byte script systems that use only intercharacter spacing.) The text measuring and drawing routines apply the `spExtra` field pixel value to every space in the text string, regardless of whether the space occurs at the beginning or the end of a style run or between words within a style run. You can use the `SpaceExtra` procedure, for both a color graphics port (`CGrafPort`) and an original graphics port (`GrafPort`).

You use the `CharExtra` procedure to set the `chExtra` field of the current graphics port to the number of extra pixels to be added to or subtracted from the width of all nonspace characters in a style run. Because only the color graphics port record has a `chExtra` field, use of `CharExtra` is limited to color graphics ports. The measuring and drawing routines apply the pixel value that you set in the `chExtra` field to the right side of the glyph of each nonspace character.

You can use `SpaceExtra` and `CharExtra` together, for example, to format text consisting of multiple style runs with different fonts in order to create a smooth visual effect by causing the fonts to measure the same or proportionally.

Note
Although printing on a LaserWriter preserves the line's endpoints, it alters the line layout in between. Any formatting internal to the line that you set through `SpaceExtra` and `CharExtra` is lost when you print. ◆

If you do not want to use the justification routines to draw justified text, you can justify a line of text using `SpaceExtra` and `CharExtra` to widen each glyph (space and nonspace characters) by the same amount of pixels for onscreen display. Here is how you do this:

1. Determine the slop value to be applied to the text to justify it.
   - □ Measure the width in pixels of each style run in the line of text using `TextWidth`.
   - □ Sum the values.
   - □ Subtract the total from the display line length.

2. Count the total number of characters (both space characters and nonspace characters) that the text contains.

3. Divide the slop value by the number of characters minus 1. Round the slop value to a whole number.

4. Call the `SpaceExtra` procedure, passing it the result of step 3.

5. Call the `CharExtra` procedure, passing it the result of step 3.

6. Call `DrawText` or `DrawString` to draw each style run on the line.

Use of `CharExtra` entails some restrictions. You cannot use intercharacter spacing for 1-byte complex script systems or 1-byte simple script systems that include zero-width characters, such as diacritical marks, because of the way extra width is applied to a glyph. For example, for 1-byte simple script systems with diacritical marks, intercharacter space is added to all glyphs separating the diacritical mark from the glyph of the character.

Using Fractional Glyph Widths

Fractional glyph widths are measurements of a glyph's width that can include fractions of a pixel. Using fractional glyph widths allows QuickDraw to place glyphs on the screen in a manner that will closely match the eventual placement of glyphs on a page printed by a LaserWriter. Fractional glyph widths make it possible for the LaserWriter printer to print with better spacing. You can use the Font Manager's `SetFractEnable` procedure to turn the use of fractional glyph widths on or off.

Because screen glyphs are made up of whole pixels, QuickDraw cannot draw a fractional glyph. To compensate, QuickDraw rounds off the fractional parts resulting in uneven spacing between glyphs and words. Although the text is somewhat distorted on the screen, it is correctly proportioned and shows no distortion when printed on a page using a LaserWriter.

However, to avoid screen distortion, your application can disable the use of fractional widths. A consequence of this it that placement of text on the printed page is less than optimal. For more information about fractional glyph widths, see the chapter "Font Manager" in this book.

Specifying the Transfer Mode

The value of the current graphics port transfer mode (txMode) field determines the way glyphs are placed in the bit image and how the text is to appear. It defines the way text to be drawn interacts with text and graphics already drawn. (When a glyph is drawn, QuickDraw does a bit-by-bit comparison based on the mode and stores the resulting bits into the bit image.) You set the text mode by calling the TextMode procedure.

By default, the transfer mode field is set to srcOr, which specifies that text to be drawn should overlay the existing graphics. The srcOr transfer mode produces the best results for drawing text because it writes only those bits that make up the actual glyph. In most situations, when drawing text with the basic transfer modes, you should use only srcOr or srcBic; all other modes can result in clipping of glyphs by adjacent glyphs. For example, the Copy operation paints over what already exists on the destination, replacing it entirely.

Basic Transfer Mode Operations

For each type of drawing mode, there are four basic kinds of operations: Copy, Or, Xor, and Bic (bit clear). For Color QuickDraw, there are additional arithmetic drawing mode operations designed specifically for use with color. They are discussed later in this section, and fully in *Inside Macintosh: Imaging*.

The transfer mode operation determines how the text is to be displayed: for each bit in the item to be drawn, the corresponding bit in the destination bitmap is identified, the specified Boolean operation is performed on the pair of bits, and the resulting bit is stored into the destination bit image. When you work with color pixels, transfer modes produce different results on indexed and direct devices.

In addition to drawing the entire glyph in all cases, the srcOr mode is recommended for all applications because it uses the least memory. The srcOr mode only affects other parts of existing glyphs if the glyphs overlap. In srcOr mode the color of the glyph is determined by the foreground color.

The maximum stack space required for a text drawing operation can be considerable. Text drawing uses a minimum amount of stack if the following conditions are true:

- The transfer mode is srcOr.
- The foreground color is black.
- The destination of the text is contained within a rectangular portion of the region of the graphics port that is actually visible on the screen.
- The text is not scaled.
- The text does not have to be italicized, outlined, or shadowed by QuickDraw.

Otherwise, the amount of stack space required to draw all of the text at once depends most on the size and the width of the text and the depth of the destination.

If QuickDraw can't get enough stack space to draw an entire text segment at once, it draws the segment in pieces. This can produce unusual results in modes other than srcOr or srcBic if some of the glyphs overlap because of kerning or italicizing. If the mode is srcCopy, overlapping glyphs are clipped by the last drawn glyph. If the mode is srcXor, pixels where the glyphs overlap are not drawn at all. If the mode is one of the arithmetic modes, the arithmetic rules are followed, ignoring that the destination may include part of the text being drawn.

The stack space required for a drawing operation in Color QuickDraw is roughly estimated by the following calculation.

```
(text width) * (text height) * (font depth) / (8 bits per byte) + 3K
```

Pixel depth normally equals the screen depth. If the amount of stack space available is small (less than 3.5K), QuickDraw instead uses a pixel depth of 1, which is slow, but uses less stack space.

For the original QuickDraw, the required stack space is roughly estimated by the following calculation.

```
(text width) * (text height) / (8 bits per byte) + 2K
```

Arithmetic Transfer Mode Operations

Arithmetic transfer modes calculate pixel values by adding, subtracting, or averaging the RGB components of the source and destination pixels. The arithmetic modes change the destination pixels by performing arithmetic operations on the source and destination pixels.

Each drawing routine converts the source and destination pixels to their RGB (red, green, and blue) components, performs an operation on each pair of components to produce a new RGB value for the destination, and then assigns the destination to a pixel value close to the calculated RGB value. The arithmetic drawing modes are addOver, addPin, subOver, subPin, adMax, adMin, and blend. To specify an arithmetic mode, you pass the operation to be used to the TextMode procedure. For example, the following calls save the current state of the text mode field, then set it to the transfer mode blend.

```
oldTextMode := theport.^txMode;
TextMode(blend);
```

The arithmetic modes were designed for use with color. They are most useful for 8-bit color, but they work on 4-bit and 2-bit color also. When the destination bitmap is one bit deep, the mode reverts to the basic transfer mode that best approximates the arithmetic mode requested. For more information about arithmetic mode operations, see the QuickDraw chapters in *Inside Macintosh: Imaging*.

Note

To help make color work well on different screen depths, Color QuickDraw does some validity checking of the foreground and background colors. If your application is drawing to a `CGrafPort` with a depth equal to 1 or 2, and if the RGB values of the foreground and background colors aren't the same, but both of them map to the same pixel value, then the foreground color is inverted. This ensures that, for instance, red text drawn on a green background doesn't map to black on black. ◆

The grayishTextOr Transfer Mode

You can use the text drawing mode, `grayishTextOr`, to draw dimmed text on the screen. It is especially useful for displaying disabled user interface items. If the destination device is color and `grayishTextOr` is the transfer mode, QuickDraw draws with a blend of the foreground and background colors. If the destination device is black and white, the `grayishTextOr` mode dithers black and white. **Dithering** is a technique that creates the effect of additional colors, if the destination device is color. If the destination device is black-and-white, dithering creates the effect of levels of gray.

Note that `grayishTextOr` is not considered a standard transfer mode because currently it is not stored in pictures, and printing with it is undefined. (It does not pass through the QuickDraw bottleneck procedure.) The following calls show how to use `grayishTextOr`. They save the current state of the text mode field, then set it to `grayishTextOr`.

```
oldTextMode := theport.^txMode;
TextMode(grayishTextOr);
```

Text Mask Mode

You can add the `mask` constant to another transfer mode to cause only the glyph portion of the text to be applied in the current transfer mode to the destination. If the text font contains more than one color or if the drawing mode is an arithmetic mode, the mask mode causes only the portion of the glyphs not equal to the background to be drawn.

The arithmetic transfer modes apply the glyph's background to the destination; this can lead to undesirable results if you draw the text in pieces. QuickDraw draws the leftmost part of a piece of text on top of a previous piece if the font kerns to the left. Using `maskMode` in addition to these modes causes only the foreground part of the glyph to be drawn.

Because the rightmost glyph is clipped, to kern to the right in text mask mode, you should use srcOr, or add trailing spaces. The following call sets the transfer mode to blend with mask mode.

```
TextMode(blend + mask);
```

Transparent Transfer Mode

The transparent mode replaces the destination pixel with the source pixel when the source pixel isn't equal to the background color. For a complete description of the transparent mode, see the QuickDraw chapters in *Inside Macintosh: Imaging*.

The arithmetic transfer modes apply the glyph's background to the destination; this can produce undesirable results if you draw the text in pieces. QuickDraw draws the leftmost part of a piece of text on top of a previous piece if the font kerns to the left. If you use the mask mode (maskMode) in addition to these modes, QuickDraw draws only the foreground part of the glyph. Because the rightmost glyph is clipped, to kern to the right in text mask mode, you should use srcOr. For an explanation of kerning, see the chapter "Font Manager" in this book.

Transfer Modes and Multibit Fonts

Multibit fonts can have a specific color. Some transfer modes may not produce the desired results with a multibit font. However, the arithmetic mode and transparent mode work equally well with single bit and multibit fonts.

Unlike single bit fonts, multibit fonts draw quickly in srcOr mode only if the foreground is white. Single bit fonts draw quickly in srcOr mode only if the foreground is black. Grayscale fonts produce a spectrum of colors, rather than just the foreground and background colors.

Measuring and Drawing Single Segments of Text

This section describes how to draw a single glyph or a series of glyphs that share the same font and character attributes. Because you usually measure text before you draw it to determine if it fits on the display area, this section describes the measuring and drawing routines in pairs. These pairs are CharWidth and DrawChar to measure and draw the glyph of a single character, StringWidth and DrawString to measure and draw Pascal strings, and TextWidth and DrawText to measure and draw text segments.

You are responsible for tracking and specifying the memory location and the character attributes of the text to be drawn. This is true whether you are working with a single glyph, a Pascal string, or a text string. For a single glyph, you pass the character code to the procedure; for a Pascal string, you pass the string.

Note
Before you call a QuickDraw measuring or drawing routine, you need to set the graphics port text-related fields to those of the character. ◆

Individual Glyphs

You measure text a character at a time by calling the `CharWidth` function, and you draw text a character at a time by calling the `DrawChar` procedure. These routines only work with 1-byte simple script systems.

Although this section describes how to use these routines, you should understand their limitations, and avoid using `CharWidth` and `DrawChar` for applications drawing sequences of more than one character. Nevertheless, you may want to use `DrawChar` for special purposes, such as including a glyph in a book's index, to show a single glyph as it exists apart from contextual transformations.

The `CharWidth` function takes into account all of the text characteristics defined in the current graphics port, so make sure these values reflect the attributes that you intend to draw with. You can draw a sequence of individual glyphs by placing the pen at the beginning of the leftmost glyph, and making a succession of calls to `DrawChar`.

Always use `CharWidth` to measure the width of a sequence of glyphs that you intend to draw using `DrawChar`, instead of using `StringWidth`; `StringWidth` and `DrawString` accumulate fractional portions, while `CharWidth` and `DrawChar` do not. Making successive calls to `CharWidth` to measure a segment of text and calling `StringWidth` to measure the same segment of text produce different results.

In general, you should measure and draw text in segments, rather than as individual glyphs. In Roman fonts, if you measure fractional-width glyphs singly using `CharWidth`, you can get incorrect results, because `CharWidth` doesn't accumulate fractional-width positions. Also, it takes longer to measure the widths of several glyphs one at a time than it does to measure them together using `TextWidth`.

For contextual 1-byte fonts, `CharWidth` and `DrawChar` do not correctly measure or draw ligatures, reversals, or other contextual forms. You cannot use `CharWidth` and `DrawChar` for 2-byte fonts, because they take a 1-byte character code as a parameter.

Pascal Strings

You can call the `StringWidth` function to measure the screen pixel width of a Pascal string to determine how many glyphs will fit on the screen, and you can call the `DrawString` procedure to draw a Pascal string with the text characteristics of the current graphics port. The `DrawString` procedure accumulates the fractional portion as it draws each glyph and positions the next glyph correctly.

You cannot use the `DrawString` and `StringWidth` routines to draw or measure a Pascal string that is justified or explicitly scaled. If you want to do this, you must separate the string from its length byte, and call `MeasureJustified` or `StdTxMeas` to measure it, and then `DrawJustified` to draw it, passing the text and the text length separately. Note that a Pascal string is limited to 255 characters. The following code fragment shows how to adjust for the length byte.

```
myTextPtr := Ptr(Ord(@myString) + 1);
myTextLength := Ord(myString[0]);
```

Text Segments

You can call the `TextWidth` function to measure a segment of text to see if it fits on a single line; if it does, then you can the `DrawText` procedure to draw it.

You pass `DrawText` a pointer to the text buffer, the byte offset into the text buffer of the first character to be drawn, and the length of the text segment you want to draw. QuickDraw draws the text at the current pen position with the text characteristics of the current graphics port.

Measuring and Drawing Lines of Text

This section describes how to lay out and draw a line of text consisting of a single style run or multiple style runs. A line of text all in the same font, script, and character attributes constitutes a single style run. A new style run begins when any of these textual characteristics change. QuickDraw relies on the construct of style runs to track these text attribute changes throughout a line of text. Before you measure or draw a text segment that constitutes a new style run, you need to set the text-related graphics port fields for that style run.

This section also describes how to draw text lines that are right or left aligned, or justified. Finally, it explains how to draw explicitly scaled text, whether the lines of text are justified or not.

To draw a line of text, you first need to lay it out. If the text does not contain mixed directions, the text layout process consists of a single step: determining where to break the line. If the text contains mixed directions, the order in which you display the style runs may be different from their storage order, so you also need to determine the drawing order.

Moreover, if you want to draw a line of justified text, the process entails additional steps: you need to determine the total amount of extra pixels that remains to be distributed throughout the line of text and how to distribute these extra pixels throughout the style runs.

If you want to draw a line of text that is not justified, you can position the pen according to its alignment. You align text by positioning the pen appropriately so that the first glyph of the text line is flush against the display line's margin: at the left margin for left-aligned text, or at the right margin for right-aligned text.

Your application loops through these steps for each style run and each line of text that it measures and draws, and it needs to track the text in memory as it proceeds through each loop. Each time you measure or draw a text segment, you need to pass the beginning byte offset and its length to the QuickDraw routine. Before you call a QuickDraw measuring or drawing routine, you need to set the graphics port text-related fields to reflect the new style run's values.

These steps summarize the line layout and drawing process:

1. Determine where to break the line.

2. Determine the display order of the style runs (mixed-directional text).

3. Eliminate trailing spaces (justified text).

4. Calculate the slop value (justified text).

5. Distribute the slop (justified text).

6. Position the pen.

7. Draw the text.

Each step covers the basics, plus any additional information you need to know to perform the step for justified or scaled text. The following sections elaborate these steps.

Determining Where to Break the Line

For text that spans multiple lines, you are responsible for controlling where a text line starts and ends. To determine where to break a line of text, first you need to know the screen pixel width of the display line. Then, taking into account all the text characteristics, you need to assess how much of the text you can display on the line, and the appropriate point to break the text.

You should always break a line on a word boundary. To allow for text in different languages, use the QuickDraw and the Text Utilities routines that identify the appropriate place to break a line in any script system.

The two routines you use for unscaled text are the `StyledLineBreak` and `TextWidth` functions; `StyledLineBreak` is described in the chapter Text Utilities in this book. Each time you call `StyledLineBreak` for a style run, first you need to set the graphics port text characteristics for that style run.

Saving the screen pixel width of each style run

To draw justified text, you need to determine the amount of extra pixels to allocate to each style run in the text line. To determine this value, you need to know the screen pixel width of each style run. You can avoid having to measure the width of each style run twice in the text-layout process by using the `textWidth` parameter of the `StyledLineBreak` function to get and save the screen pixel width of each style run. The `StyledLineBreak` function maintains the value of the `textWidth` parameter, which you initially set to the length of the display line. When you call `StyledLineBreak` for each style run in the script run, it decrements this value by the width of the style run. You can calculate the screen pixel width of a style run by subtracting the current value of `textWidth` from the display line length each time through your `StyledLineBreak` loop, and save the value to be used later. ◆

If you do not want to use `StyledLineBreak`, you can use the `TextWidth` function to measure each style run, adding the returned values until the sum exceeds the display line length. You can next use the Text Utilities `FindWordBreaks` procedure on the last style run to identify the ending location of the appropriate word in the style run, then break the text accordingly.

If a space character occurs at a line's end, and more space characters follow it in memory, `StyledLineBreak` breaks the line after the final space character in memory. This obviates the need for you to check for space characters in memory, when you lay out the next line of text. However, if you do not use `StyledLineBreak`, you need to check for space characters at the beginning of a line of text, and increment the memory pointer beyond these space characters. You can use the `CharacterType` function to identify space characters. For more information about `CharacterType`, see the chapter "Script Manager" in this book.

Listing 3-2 calculates line breaks using `StyledLineBreak`. The procedure sets the local variables, the display line length, and a value to control the line-breaking loop. Then it iterates through the text for each style run, setting the graphics port text fields for the style run and calling `StyledLineBreak` to identify where to break the line.

Listing 3-2   Calling `StyledLineBreak` to identify where to break the text line

```
PROCEDURE MyBreakTextIntoLines (window: WindowPtr);
VAR
    thetextPtr: Ptr;
    thetextLength: LongInt;
    pixelWidth: Fixed;
    textOffset: LONGINT;
    StartOfLine: Point;
    index: Integer;
    tempRect: Rect;
    lineData: myLineArray;
    lineIndex: Integer;
    theBreakCode: StyledLineBreakCode;
    theStartOffset: Integer;
BEGIN
    thetextPtr := gText.textPtr;
    index := 0;
    SetPort(window);
    tempRect := window^.portRect;
    InsetRect(tempRect, 4, 4);
    SetPt(StartOfLine, 10, 4);
    MoveTo(StartOfLine.h, StartOfLine.v);
        {Set up our local flags and variables.}
    lineIndex := 0;   {This is the index into the line data.}
```

```
index := 0;          {This is the index into the style data.}
WITH gText.runData[index] DO
BEGIN
   thetextPtr := Ptr(ORD(gText.textPtr) + runStart);
   thetextLength := gText.textLength;
   theStartOffset := 0;
END;

   {Start walking through the textblock.}
REPEAT
      {For the first style run in a line, textOffset must be non-zero.}
   textOffset := -1;
      {smBreakOverFlow means that the whole style run fits on the }
      { line with space remaining. The routine uses that condition to }
      { control the loop.}
   theBreakCode := smBreakOverflow;
      {StyledLineBreak expects the width of the display area }
      { to be expressed as a fixed value.}
   pixelWidth := BSL((tempRect.right - tempRect.left), 16);
   WITH gText DO
      BEGIN
         WHILE (theBreakCode = smBreakOverflow) DO
            BEGIN WITH gText.runData[index] DO
               BEGIN
                     {set the port}
                  TextFont(font);
                  TextFace(face);
                  TextSize(size);
                     {call StyledLineBreak to break the line}
                  theBreakCode := StyledLineBreak(thetextPtr,
                              thetextLength, theStartOffset,
                              runEnd, 0, pixelWidth, textOffset);
                     {now remember the information returned}
   lineData[lineIndex].textStartOffset := theStartOffset;
         {remember the beginning of this run}
   lineData[lineIndex].textLength := textOffset - theStartOffset;
         {and the length of this run length}
   lineData[lineIndex].styleIndex := index;
         {since the style information is global, just remember }
         { the index to that information}
   lineIndex := lineIndex + 1;
   END;
```

```
                {If textoffset == the end of the run, increment the }
                { rundata index and set theStartOffset to be the beginning }
                {of the next run.}
        IF (textOffset = gText.runData[index].runend) THEN
            BEGIN
                index := index + 1;
                theStartOffset := gText.runData[index].runStart;
            END
        ELSE
                {If textOffset <> the end of the run, the routine splits }
                { a run, so set theStartOffset appropriately}
            theStartOffset := theStartOffset + (textOffset - theStartOffset);
                {If there is more text, reset the offset value }
                { returned by StyledLineBreak}
            IF textOffset = thetextLength THEN LEAVE
                {if textOffset == the textLength there is no more}
                { text, so jump out of the loop}
            ELSE
                textOffset := 0;
                    {we haven't found the line break yet, }
                    { textOffset must be zero for all runs after }
                    { the first in a line}
    END; {of while loop}
END;
```

If the text is explicitly scaled, you cannot use `StyledLineBreak` to determine where to break the line. This is because the `StyledLineBreak` function does not accept scaling factors. To determine where to break a line of scaled text, you can directly call the routines that `StyledLineBreak` uses. The section "Using Scaled Text" on page 3-44 describes these steps.

Determining the Display Order for Style Runs

Now that you know where to break the line, you need to determine the display order of the style runs that constitute the line when the text contains mixed directions; if your text does not contain mixed directions, you can skip this step.

You draw style runs in their display order, which may be different from how the text is stored if it contains mixed directions. (For more information about storage order and display order, see the chapter "Introduction to Text on the Macintosh" in this book.) To determine the correct order, use `GetFormatOrder`; this procedure returns the order, from left to right, in which to draw the style runs on a line.

To use `GetFormatOrder`, you must have organized your style runs sequentially in storage order. You pass `GetFormatOrder` the numbers of the first and last style runs on the line, and the primary line direction of the text to be drawn. If you do not explicitly define the primary line direction, you can base it on the value of the `SysDirection` global variable. (The `SysDirection` global variable is set to –1 if the system direction is right to left, and 0 if the system direction is left to right.)

You pass `GetFormatOrder` a pointer to an application-defined Boolean function that calculates the correct direction for each style run and a pointer to an application-defined information block, containing font and script information, that the Boolean function uses to determine the style run direction. The `GetFormatOrder` procedure calls your Boolean function for each style run on the line.

Listing 3-3 shows an example Boolean function that calculates the line direction of a style run. Here is the type declaration for the `MyLineDrawingInfo` records, which are created as the application calculates line breaks:

```
TYPE MyLineDrawingInfo =
RECORD
    textPtr: Ptr;
    textLength: Integer;
    styleIndex: Integer:
END;

MyLineArray = ARRAY[0 ..MaxNumberofStyleRuns] OF
    MyLineDrawingInfo;
myLineDrawingInfoPtr = ^MyLineDrawingInfo;
```

The `styleIndex` field of each record of type `MyLineDrawingInfo` points to an entry in an array of style run records of type `MyStyleRun`. A style run record contains style information including font, size, style, and scaling factors. The declaration for `MyStyleRun` follows:

```
MyStyleRun =
RECORD
    runStart: Integer;
    runEnd: Integer;
    size: Integer;
    font: Integer;
    face: Style;
    numer: Point;
    denom: Point;
END;

{This sample program uses a static array to store style run }
{ information. Typically, a program would use a dynamic }
{ data structure.}
```

The `MyDirectionProc` function checks the font of the style run to determine if the font belongs to a right-to-left script system. If it does, the function returns `TRUE`; otherwise it returns `FALSE`. When `GetFormatOrder` calls `MyDirectionProc`, it passes an integer identifying the style run and a pointer to an application-defined parameter block. In Listing 3-3, the pointer indicates the `MyLineArray` array. The `MyDirectionProc` function uses the style run identifier and the size of a `MyLineDrawingInfo` record to find the right `MyLineDrawingInfo` record in the array. It uses the `styleIndex` field of the `MyLineDrawingInfo` record to locate the right style run record in the array of `MyStyleRun` records. The font field of the style run record contains a font family ID that the function uses to determine the script code. The function calls the Script Manager with the script code to determine the script direction

Listing 3-3   An application-defined run direction function called by `GetFormatOrder`

```
FUNCTION MyDirectionProc(theFormat: Integer;
                         myDirectionParam: Ptr):Boolean;
    VAR
        scriptCode:     Integer;
        p:              myLineDrawingInfoPtr;
        offset:         LongInt;
BEGIN
    offset := SIZEOF(MyLineDrawingInfo) * theFormat;
    p := myLineDrawingInfoPtr(ORD(myDirectionParam) + offset);
    scriptCode := FontToScript(gText.runData[p^.styleIndex].font);
    IF Boolean(GetScriptVariable(scriptCode, smScriptRight)) = TRUE
        THEN MyDirectionProc := TRUE
    ELSE
        MyDirectionProc := FALSE;
END;
```

You reference the format order array to determine the display order when you draw the text. To draw a line of text that is not justified, after you determine the display order of the style runs, you can position the pen and draw the text. (To draw a line of text that is not justified, see "Drawing the Line of Text" on page 3-42.) To draw text that is scaled, you can skip ahead to "Using Scaled Text" on page 3-44. If you are drawing a line of justified text, you must complete some additional steps before positioning the pen and actually drawing the text. These steps are described in the next three sections.

Listing 3-4 shows an application-defined procedure that declares a format order array; it passes a pointer to that array when it calls GetFormatOrder for a line of text containing style runs with mixed directions. Using the information that GetFormatOrder returns in the format order array, the procedure iterates through the style runs in display order, setting the graphics for each style run, then drawing the text.

Listing 3-4 Determining the style run display order and drawing the line

```
PROCEDURE MyGetDisplayOrderAndDrawLine (theLineData: myLineArray; VAR
                                        index: Integer);
VAR
   FormatOrderArray: ARRAY[0..kMaximumNumberOfStyleRuns] OF Integer;
   I: Integer;
BEGIN
   GetFormatOrder(FormatOrderPtr(@FormatOrderArray), 0, index,
               Boolean(GetSysDirection), @DirectionProc, @theLineData);
      {we know the display order, now we are ready to draw}
   FOR I := FormatOrderArray[0] TO FormatOrderArray[index] DO
      BEGIN
      {Set the port.}
            WITH gText.runData[theLineData[i].styleIndex] DO
               BEGIN
                  TextFont(font);
                  TextFace(face);
                  TextSize(size);
               END;
            DrawText(theTextPtr, lineData[i].textStartOffset,
                  theLineData[i].textLength);
      END;
      index := 0;
         {we found a line, so bump the index into the line data}
   END;
```

Eliminating Trailing Spaces (for Justified Text)

If you are justifying text, after you know the line break and display order for your text, you must determine the total amount of extra pixels that remain to be distributed throughout the line, and how to spread the extra pixels throughout the style runs. To get the correct total number of extra pixels, first you need to eliminate any trailing spaces from the last style run in memory order.

The VisibleLength function returns the length in bytes of the style run minus any trailing spaces; this is the byte length that you must use for the style run in any calculations necessary to determine the line layout, and for drawing the text.

The VisibleLength function behaves differently for various script systems. For simple script systems, such as Roman and Cyrillic, and 2-byte script systems, such as Japanese, VisibleLength does not include in the byte count it returns trailing spaces that occur at the display end of the text segment. For 2-byte script systems, VisibleLength does not count them, whether they are 1-byte or 2-byte space characters.

Figure 3-5 shows that VisibleLength eliminates trailing spaces at the right end of Roman text when the primary line direction is left to right. However, if you change the primary line direction, VisibleLength assumes the left end as the display end of the text, and does not eliminate the spaces on the right.

Figure 3-5   Calling VisibleLength for a Roman style run

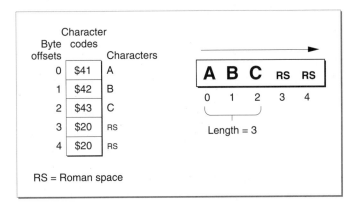

For 1-byte complex script systems, VisibleLength does not include in the byte count that it returns spaces whose character direction is the same as the primary line direction. The primary line direction is determined by the SysDirection global variable. By default, the value of SysDirection is the direction of the system script. You can change this value. Some word processors that allow users to change the primary line direction, for example, to create a document entirely in English when the system script is Hebrew, change the value of SysDirection. If you modify the SysDirection global value, be sure to first save the original value and restore it before your program terminates.

Figure 3-6 shows a Hebrew style run with trailing spaces at the left end, which VisibleLength eliminates. In this case, the primary line direction is right to left; if it were left to right, VisibleLength would return 5.

Figure 3-6   Calling `VisibleLength` for a Hebrew style run

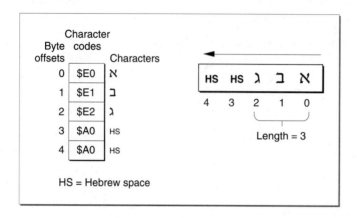

For those 1-byte complex script systems that support bidirectional text, Roman spaces take on a character direction based on the primary line direction. If the Roman spaces then fall at the end of the text, `VisibleLength` does not include them in the returned byte count. Figure 3-7 shows Roman spaces following Hebrew text in storage order. In the first part of the example, the Roman spaces take on the primary line direction of right to left, and follow the Hebrew text in display order also. Because they fall at the end of the display line, `VisibleLength` does not count them. The second part of the example shows what happens when the primary line direction is changed to left to right: the Roman spaces fall at the end of the line again and are not counted.

Figure 3-7   Calling `VisibleLength` for Hebrew text with Roman space characters

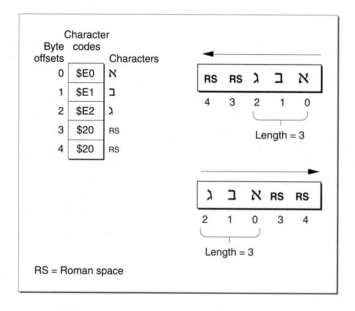

Calculating the Slop Value (for Justified Text)

To draw justified text, after you eliminate trailing spaces from the line's last style run in memory order, you need to determine the amount of remaining extra space to be distributed throughout the line. This is called the *slop value*; it is measured in pixels, and is the difference between the width of the text and the width of the display line. After you add the widths of all the style runs on the line to get the total width of the text, you can use the following statement to determine the slop value. Be sure to use the value returned by `VisibleLength` for the last style run in memory order when you add the style run widths.

```
TotalSlop := DisplayLineLength — SumofStyleRunWidths
```

If you saved the screen pixel width of each style run when you called `StyledLineBreak`, then all you need to do is sum the total of the style run widths and subtract that total from the display line length to get the total slop value.

If you did not use `StyledLineBreak` or you did not save the screen pixel width of each style run when you called `StyledLineBreak`, first measure the width of each style run, using `TextWidth`, then add the widths to get the total. (Remember that each time you measure a style run, first you need to set the text-related graphics port fields for that style run.)

The `TextWidth` function returns the width in pixels of a style run. You pass `TextWidth` the number of bytes of the text to be measured. For script systems containing 2-byte characters, be certain that you pass the correct number of bytes; 2-byte script systems can contain a mix of one-byte and two-byte characters.

For scaled text, you cannot use the `TextWidth` function to get the screen pixel width of a style run. Instead, you can call the `StdTxMeas` function, which accepts and returns scaling parameters. Whenever you call `StdTxMeas` directly, first you must check the graphics port `grafProc` field to determine if the bottleneck routines have been customized, and if so, use the customized version. See "Low-Level QuickDraw Text Routines" on page 3-98 for more information.

Using a negative slop value
You can pass the justification routines a positive or negative slop value. Word processing programs can use a negative slop value to justify a line of text more smoothly by condensing it, when it only slightly exceeds the display line length. ◆

Allocating the Slop to Each Style Run (for Justified Text)

Once you have assessed the total amount of slop to be distributed throughout the line of text, you need to determine the portion to apply to each style run. When you draw a style run that is part of a line of justified text, you pass this number as the value of the slop parameter.

To determine the actual number of pixels for each style run, first you determine the percentage of slop to attribute to the style run, and then apply that percentage to the total slop to get the number of pixels. To get the percentage of slop for a style run, you compute what percentage each portion is of the sum of all portions.

The following steps summarize this process:

1. Call `PortionLine` for each style run on the line. The `PortionLine` function returns a "magic number" which is the correct proportion of extra space to apply to a style run.

2. Add the returned values together.

3. For each style run, divide the value returned by `PortionLine` for that style run by the sum of the values returned for all of the style runs on the line.

4. For each style run, multiply the result of step 3 by the total slop value for the line.

For example, suppose that there are three style runs on a line: style run A, style run B, and style run C. The total slop = 11; the line needs to be widened by 11 pixels to be justified. If you call `PortionLine` for each of the style runs, it produces the following results:

Style run	Value returned by `PortionLine`
A	5.4
B	7.3
C	8.2

Summing the three values together produces a total of 20.9. Now you need to convert the values into percentages by dividing each by the total. This produces the following results:

Style run	Proportion	Percentage of total
A	5.4/20.9	25.84%
B	7.3/20.9	34.93%
C	8.2/20.9	39.23%

The final step is to multiply the total slop value—11 pixels—by each percentage and round off to compute the actual number of pixels (slop) allocated to each style run. (To correct for the roundoff error, add the remainder to the pixels for the final style run.) This produces these results:

Style run	Amount of slop (in pixels)
A	3
B	4
C	4

Listing 3-5 provides a code fragment that illustrates how you can use the `PortionLine` function to do this. The application-defined `MyCalcJustAmount` routine expects an array of the following type of records.

```
Type RunRecord =
     Record
          tPtr:           Ptr;                {ptr to the text}
          tLength:        LongInt;            {length of run}
          tFace:          style;              {txFace of run}
          tFont:          Integer;            {font family ID}
          tSize:          Integer;            {pt size}
          tPlaceOnLine:   JustStyleCode;
          tnumer,tdenom:  Point;              {scaling factors}
          tJustAmount:    Fixed;              {this value }
                                             { calculated here}
     END;
RunArray = ARRAY[1..MaxRuns] OF RunRecord;
```

The `MyCalcJustAmount` routine also takes as a parameter a count of the total number of records that the array contains. Finally, the extra screen pixel width to be distributed is passed in as the `TotalPixelSlop` parameter. The routine calculates the amount of slop to be allocated to each run, and assigns that value to the field `tJustAmount`.

Listing 3-5   Distributing slop value among style runs

```
PROCEDURE MyCalcJustAmount(rArray: RunArray; NRuns: Integer;
                           TotalPixelSlop: Integer);
VAR
   I:                  Integer;
   TotalSlopProportion: Fixed;
   PixelSlopRemainder:  Fixed;

BEGIN
{Find the proportion for each run, temporarily storing}
{ it in the tJustAmount field, and sum the }
{ returned values in TotalSlopProportion.}
   TotalSlopProportion := 0;
   FOR I := 1 TO NRuns DO
      WITH rArray[I] DO BEGIN
         {Set the graphics port's fields for each style run}
         { to this style run}
         TextFace(tFace);
         TextFont(tFont);
         TextSize(tSize);
```

```
                tJustAmount :=
PortionLine(tPtr,tLength,tstyleRunPosition,tnumer,tdenom);
            TotalSlopProportion := TotalSlopProportion + tJustAmount;
            END;
{ Normalize the slop to be allocated to each run }
{ ( runportion / totalportion), and then convert that value to }
{ UnRounded Pixels: }
{ (runportion / totalportion) * TotalPixelSlop ).}
    PixelSlopRemainder := Fixed(TotalPixelSlop);
        IF NRuns > 1 THEN
            FOR I := 1 TO NRuns-1 DO
                WITH rArray[I] DO BEGIN
                    {Use the FixRound routine to round this value.}
                    tJustAmount := FixMul(FixDiv(tJustAmount,
                            TotalSlopProportion),TotalPixelSlop);
                    PixelSlopRemainder := PixelSlopRemainder -
                                        tJustAmount;
                END;
        rArray[NRuns].tJustAmount := PixelSlopRemainder;
END;
```

Drawing the Line of Text

Once you have laid out a line of text, drawing it is fairly simple. Your application's text-drawing routine needs to loop through the text, following these steps:

1. To position the pen correctly at the beginning of a new line, set the pnLoc graphics port field to the local coordinates representing the point where you want to begin drawing the text. You use the QuickDraw MoveTo or Move procedure to reposition the pen. (For more information about Move or MoveTo, see the QuickDraw chapters in *Inside Macintosh: Imaging*.) Within a line of text, after you draw a text segment, QuickDraw increments the pen location for you and positions the pen appropriately for the next text segment.

2. Before you draw each text run, set the text-related fields of the current graphics port to the text characteristics for that style run, if the text segment begins a new style run.

3. Draw the text segment.

   □ If your text is not justified, use DrawText or StdText to draw it. The StdText procedure also allows you to draw scaled text that is not justified. If you use StdText, first you must determine whether the standard routine has been customized. If so, you must use the customized version. For more information, see "Low-Level QuickDraw Text Routines" on page 3-98.

Listing 3-4 on page 3-36 shows how to draw the text using `DrawText` after determining the display order.

□ If your text is justified, use the `DrawJustified` procedure to draw it. This procedure takes a parameter, `styleRunPosition`, that identifies the location of the style run in the line of text. You must specify the same value for this parameter that you used for it when you called the `PortionLine` function for this style run. The `DrawJustified` and `PortionLine` routines also take `numer` and `denom` parameters for scaling factors. For unscaled text, specify values of 1, 1 for both of these parameters.

4. After you draw each text segment, increment the pointer in memory to the beginning of the next text segment to be drawn.

To position the pen horizontally, remember that QuickDraw always draws text from left to right:

- For left-aligned text, position the pen at the left margin of the display line.

- For right-aligned text, indent the pen from the left margin by the difference between the display line length and the total width of all the style runs. If you have set a `CharExtra` value, after you sum the total width of all the style runs, subtract the value that you passed to `CharExtra` from the total so that the rightmost character will be flush against the right margin.

- For justified text, set the pen at the left margin.

To determine the vertical coordinate of the pen position when you draw lines of text rendered in varying fonts and styles, you need to assess the required line height for each new style. You base this on the style run that requires the greatest number of vertical pixels. You can use the `GetFontInfo` procedure, which fills a record with information describing the current font's ascent, descent, and the width measurements of the largest glyph in the font, and leading. You can determine the line height by adding the values of these fields. For outline fonts, you can use the `OutlineMetrics` function to get the font measurements. For more information about `OutlineMetrics`, see the chapter "Font Manager" in this book. Listing 3-6 shows how to call `GetFontInfo`, and use the information it returns in the font information record to determine the line height.

Listing 3-6   Calling `GetFontInfo` to determine the line height

```
FUNCTION MyGetMaximumLineHeight (VAR mylineData: myLineArray;
                                     lastStyleIndex: Integer): Integer;
   VAR
      info: fontInfo;
      I: Integer;
      ignore: Integer;
      maxHeight: Integer;
   BEGIN
      maxHeight := 0;
      FOR i := 0 TO lastStyleIndex DO
         WITH gText.rundata[mylineData[i].styleIndex] DO
```

```
    BEGIN
        {set the grafport up}
        TextFont(font);
        TextFace(face);
        TextSize(size);
        {Get the vertical metrics}
        GetFontInfo(info);
        {If this style run is taller than any others measured, }
        { remember the height.}
            WITH info DO
                IF (ascent + leading > maxHeight) THEN
                    maxHeight := ascent + leading;
        END;
    MyGetMaximumLineHeight := maxHeight;
END;
```

Using Scaled Text

This section describes how to determine where to break a line of scaled text. Then it describes how to draw scaled text, whether aligned or justified.

You cannot call StyledLineBreak for scaled text. To determine where to break a line of scaled text, you can directly call the routines that StyledLineBreak uses. The StyledLinedBreak function uses the PixelToChar function to locate the byte offset that corresponds to the pixel location marking the end of the display line.

The primary use of PixelToChar is to locate a caret position associated with a mouse-down event. For this purpose, the PixelToChar function reorders the text when the text belongs to a right-to-left script system; this ensures that PixelToChar returns the correct byte offset associated with the pixel location of a mouse-down event.

If right-to-left text is reordered when you use PixelToChar to determine where to break a line, it returns the wrong byte offset. For right-to-left text, the end of a line in memory order can occur either at the left end of a display line or in the middle of one. To get the correct result, StyledLineBreak turns off reordering before it calls PixelToChar. Your application must also do this.

You can define a routine that turns off reordering if the font's script system is right to left, and call your routine just before you call PixelToChar. Remember to restore reordering after you have determined where to break the line.

Listing 3-7 shows an application-defined routine that turns off reordering of text in a right-to-left script system. It tests to determine whether the reordering bit is on or off so that the application can restore it to its current state, then it clears the reordering bit (smsfReverse), and sets the script flag with the SetScriptVariable function. See the chapter "Script Manager" in this book for more information.

Listing 3-7   Turning off reordering of right-to-left text before calling `PixelToChar` for line-breaking

```
FUNCTION MySetReordering(font: integer): Boolean
    VAR
        flags: LongInt;
        err:   OSErr;
BEGIN
    flags := GetScriptVariable(smCurrentScript, smScriptFlags);
    MySetReordering := BTST(flags, smsfReverse);
    BCLR(flags, smsfReverse);
    err := SetScriptVariable(smCurrentScript, smScriptFlags,
                                    flags);
END;
```

Here are the steps you take to determine where to break a line of scaled text:

1. Call `PixelToChar` to determine the byte offset that corresponds to the pixel location where you want to break the line. You pass the pixel location of the end of the display line to `PixelToChar` as the value of the `pixelWidth` parameter. The `PixelToChar` function returns the byte offset corresponding to the pixel location of the end of the display line, if the corresponding byte offset falls with the style run that you call `PixelToChar` for.

   If the byte offset corresponding to this pixel location does not fall within the style run, on return the `widthRemaining` parameter contains the number of pixels from the right edge of the text string for which you called `PixelToChar` to the end of the display line. You can loop through your text, calling `PixelToChar` for each style run until you encounter the byte offset that corresponds to the pixel location of the end of the display line.

2. Call the Text Utilities `FindWordBreaks` procedure with an `nbreaks` parameter of –1 to determine the boundaries of the word containing the byte offset that corresponds to the pixel location of the end of the display line. If the byte offset that `PixelToChar` returns is the beginning boundary or interior to the word, you should break the text before this word, or after the preceding word.

3. If the byte offset that falls at the end of the display line is a space character, you should check to determine if there are succeeding space characters in memory; `StyledLineBreak` does this. You can use the Script Manager's `CharType` function for this purpose. If there are additional space characters, increment the text pointer beyond them in memory to determine the starting offset for the next line of text.

The steps that you follow to draw scaled text are the same as those for unscaled text, described under "Drawing the Line of Text" on page 3-42. However, you perform some steps differently for scaled text. The steps are summarized here, and the differences are elaborated.

1. Set the pnLoc graphics port field to the local coordinates representing the point to begin drawing the text. You use StdTxMeas to get the font metrics for scaled text in order to determine the line height, instead of using GetFontInfo, which doesn't support scaling. Using the information that StdTxMeas returns, you can scale the vertical metrics. Listing 3-8 shows one way to do this.

2. Before you draw each style run, set the text-related fields of the current graphics port to the text characteristics for that style run. This step is the same as for drawing unscaled text.

3. Use DrawJustified or StdText to draw the scaled text a style run at a time. To draw scaled text that is not justified, you call StdText or you can call DrawJustified and pass in onlyStyleRun for the styleRunPosition parameter.

Listing 3-8 shows how to measure scaled text using StdTxMeas, and use the information returned in the font information (fontInfo) record to determine the line height. The gText global variable is initialized before the routine is called.

The application of which this routine is a part stores style runs in a text block, which is defined by the TextBlock data type.

```
TextBlock = RECORD
    textPtr: Ptr;
    textLength: Integer;
    runData: StyleRunArray;
END;
```

Listing 3-8   Using StdTxMeas to get the font metrics for determining the line height of scaled text

```
FUNCTION MyGetMaximumLineHeight(VAR lineData: LineArray;
                    lastStyleIndex: Integer): Integer;
    VAR
    info: fontInfo;
    i: Integer;
    ignore:Integer;
    MaxHeight:Integer;
    localNumer, localDenom: Point;
    size, font: Integer;
    face: Style;
```

```
BEGIN
   MaxHeight := 0;
   FOR i := 0 TO lastStyleIndex DO
    WITH gText.runData[lineData[i].styleIndex] DO BEGIN
   {Set up the graphics port}
      TextFont(font);
      TextFace(face);
      TextSize(size);
   {measure the text}
      localNumer := numer;
      localDenom := denom;
      ignore := StdTxMeas(lineData[i].textlength,
       lineData[i].textPtr, localNumer, localDenom, info);
   {scale the vertical metrics based on the StdTxMeas }
         { returned values of numer and denom}
      info.ascent := FixRound(FixMul(BSL(info.ascent, 16),
            FixRatio(localNumer.v, localDenom.v)));
      info.leading := FixRound(FixMul(BSL(info.leading, 16),
            FixRatio(localNumer.v, localDenom.v)));
      WITH info DO
         IF (ascent + leading > maxHeight) THEN
            maxHeight := ascent + leading;
   END;
```

Drawing Carets and Highlighting

This section discusses how to determine a caret position to be used to mark an insertion point or endpoint for highlighting a range of text. This section describes how to

■ determine the byte offset of a character whose glyph is closest to an onscreen pixel location where a mouse-down event occurred

■ determine a caret position from a byte offset, and draw a caret to mark an insertion point

■ locate the endpoints for a selection range in order to highlight it, using the byte offsets at characters that begin and end the segment of text to be highlighted

For a discussion of the conventions underlying the relationship of a character at a byte offset to a caret position for unidirectional text and text at a direction boundary, see the treatment of caret handling and highlighting in the chapter "Introduction to Text on the Macintosh" in this book.

Generally, an application draws and blinks the caret in an active document window from its idle-processing procedure in response to a null event. If your application uses TextEdit, you can call the TEIdle procedure to do this. If your application does not use TextEdit, you are responsible for drawing and blinking the caret.

You should check the keyboard script and change the onscreen pixel location where you draw the caret, if necessary, to synchronize the caret with the keyboard script. The caret marks the insertion point where the next character is to be entered, and when the user changes the keyboard script, the caret location can change. (For more information, see "Synchronizing the Caret With the Keyboard Script" on page 3-59.)

You call `PixelToChar` from within a loop that iterates through the style runs on a line of text until you locate the byte offset of the character associated with the input pixel location. Once you have the byte offset, you call `CharToPixel` to get the pixel location of the caret position. If you already have the byte offset, you do not need to call `PixelToChar`. The `CharToPixel` function returns the length in pixels from the left edge of the text segment to the caret position corresponding to that character. (The text segment that you pass to `CharToPixel` can be a complete style run or the portion of a style run that fits on the line.)

Once you have the pixel location of the caret position within the context of the text segment, you must convert it to a pixel location relative to the entire display line's left margin. To get the correct display line pixel location, you lay out the line of text, measuring the screen pixel width of each style run from left to right up to the text segment that contains the caret position, then add the screen pixel width of the caret position to the sum of all the preceding style runs. Once you have the pixel location relative to the display line's left margin, you can draw the caret. Figure 3-8 shows Hebrew text between two runs of English text on a line. `CharToPixel` and `PixelToChar` recognize the pixel location in the Hebrew text relative to the left edge of the Hebrew style run, although the left margin of the display line begins with the English text.

Figure 3-8   What pixel position means for `CharToPixel` and `PixelToChar`

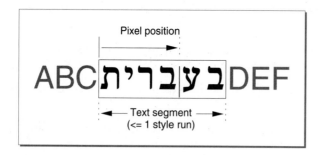

Converting an Onscreen Pixel Location to a Byte Offset

You need to find the byte offset and the text direction of the character that corresponds to a glyph onscreen in order to display the caret correctly. You need this information to mark an insertion point with a caret, select words, determine the endpoints for highlighting a range of text, and determine where to break a line of text. You can use the `PixelToChar` function to get this information.

The `PixelToChar` function returns a byte offset and a Boolean value. The Boolean flag tells you whether the input pixel location is on the leading edge or the trailing edge of the glyph.

- When the input pixel location is on the leading edge of the glyph, `PixelToChar` returns the byte offset of that glyph's character and a `leadingEdge` flag of `TRUE`. (If the glyph represents multiple characters, it returns the byte offset of the first of these characters in memory.)

- When the input pixel location is on the trailing edge of the glyph, `PixelToChar` returns the byte offset of the first character in memory *following* the character or characters represented by the glyph, and a `leadingEdge` flag of `FALSE`.

- When the input pixel location is *before* the leading edge of the first glyph in the displayed text segment, `PixelToChar` returns the byte offset of the first character in the text segment and a `leadingEdge` flag of `FALSE`.

- When the input pixel location is *after* the trailing edge of the last glyph in the displayed text segment, `PixelToChar` returns the next byte offset in memory, the one after the last character in the text segment, and a `leadingEdge` flag of `TRUE`.

If the primary line direction is left to right, *before* means to the left of all the glyphs for the characters in the text segment, and *after* means to the right of all these glyphs. If the primary line direction is right to left, before and after hold the opposite meanings.

Finding a Caret Position and Drawing a Caret

Once you have a byte offset, you need to convert it to a caret position. The `PixelToChar` and `CharToPixel` functions work together to help you determine a caret position. You use the byte offset that `PixelToChar` returns as input to `CharToPixel`. The `CharToPixel` function requires a `direction` parameter to determine whether to place the caret for text with a left-to-right or right-to-left direction. You base the value of the `direction` parameter on the `leadingEdge` flag that `PixelToChar` returns.

When a mouse-down event in text occurs, if `PixelToChar` returns a `leadingEdge` flag of `TRUE`, you pass `CharToPixel` the text direction of the character whose byte offset `PixelToChar` returns. Figure 3-9 illustrates a simple case. The user clicks on the leading edge of the glyph of character D; `PixelToChar` returns byte offset 3 and a `leadingEdge` flag of `TRUE`. You then call `CharToPixel`, passing it byte offset 3 and a `direction` parameter of `leftCaret`, based on the text direction of the character D. The `CharToPixel` function returns the pixel location equivalent to the caret position; now you can draw the caret as shown, on the leading edge of D.

Figure 3-9   Caret position for a leading-edge mouse-down event

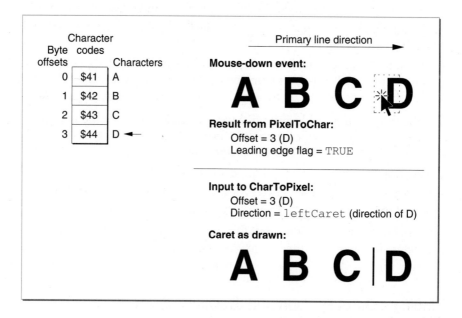

If `PixelToChar` returns a `leadingEdge` flag of `FALSE`, it returns the *next* byte offset in memory, not the one on whose trailing edge the mouse-down event occurred. You still base the value of the `direction` parameter on the character of the glyph at whose trailing edge the mouse-down event occurred, but this character is the one in memory that is *before* the byte offset that `PixelToChar` returned.

Figure 3-10 illustrates this for the same simple case. The user clicks on the trailing edge of the glyph of character C; PixelToChar returns byte offset 3, the byte offset of the next character (D) in memory, and a leadingEdge flag of FALSE. You then call CharToPixel, passing it byte offset 3 and a direction parameter of leftCaret, based on the text direction of the character C. The CharToPixel function returns the pixel location equivalent to the caret position; now the application can draw the caret as shown, on the trailing edge of C, which is the same position as the leading edge of D.

Figure 3-10   Caret position for a trailing-edge mouse-down event

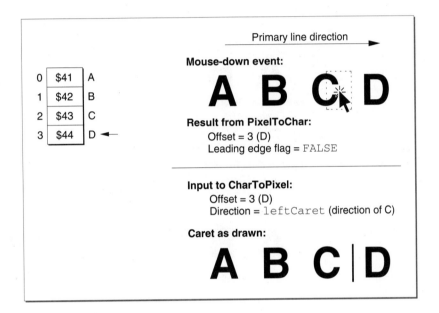

When a character falls on a direction boundary, the case is more complicated. In display order, a direction boundary can occur on the trailing edges of two glyphs, the leading edges of two glyphs, or at the beginning or end of a text segment. The same rules apply for calling PixelToChar and CharToPixel, but the results can be different.

Figure 3-11 shows what happens when the user clicks on the leading edge of the glyph א, whose character falls on a direction boundary; PixelToChar returns a leadingEdge flag of TRUE and a byte offset of 3. You pass this byte offset and a direction of rightCaret, the text direction for *Hebrew*, to CharToPixel. The CharToPixel function returns the caret position on the leading edge of א, and you draw the caret there.

Figure 3-11   Caret position for a leading-edge mouse-down event at a direction boundary

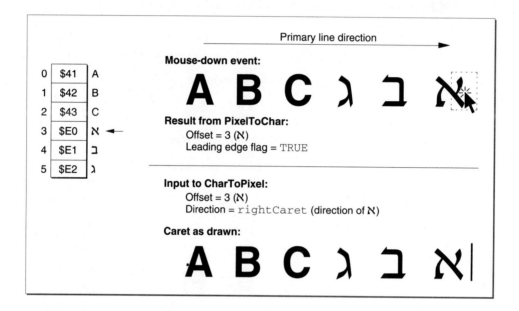

Figure 3-12 shows what happens when the user clicks on the trailing edge of the glyph C (byte offset 2). The PixelToChar function returns byte offset 3 (the Hebrew character א) and a leadingEdge flag of FALSE. You pass this byte offset and a direction parameter of leftCaret, the text direction for *English*, to CharToPixel. In this case, CharToPixel returns a caret position on the trailing edge of C, which is where you draw the caret.

Figure 3-12   Caret position for a trailing-edge mouse-down event at a direction boundary

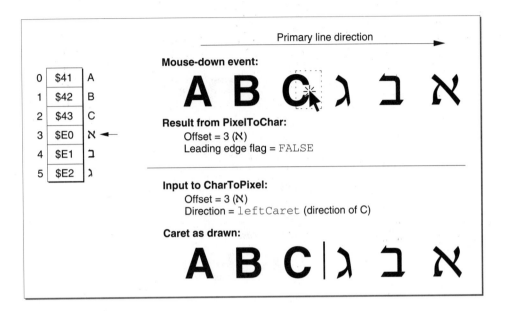

Using a dual caret

If your application is configured to use a dual caret, you must call
CharToPixel twice to draw the caret. For example, in Figure 3-12, you
would call it once with a leftCaret direction and again with a
rightCaret direction, both times for byte offset 3. You always draw
the high (primary) caret at the caret position obtained when the
direction parameter equals the primary line direction. For more
information, see the discussion of caret positions at direction boundaries
in the chapter "Introduction to Text on the Macintosh" in this book. ◆

Figure 3-11 and Figure 3-12 show how one offset can yield two caret positions.
Figure 3-13, when compared with Figure 3-12, shows how two offsets can yield one
caret position. In Figure 3-13, the user clicks on the trailing edge of the glyph ג. The
PixelToChar function returns byte offset 6 and a leadingEdge flag of FALSE.
(Although there is no character code associated with byte offset 6, it is the memory
position of the next character to be entered.) You then call CharToPixel, passing it byte
offset 6 and a direction parameter of rightCaret, the text direction for Hebrew. The
CharToPixel function returns the pixel location on the trailing edge of the glyph ג.

Figure 3-13   Caret position for a trailing-edge mouse-down event at a direction boundary

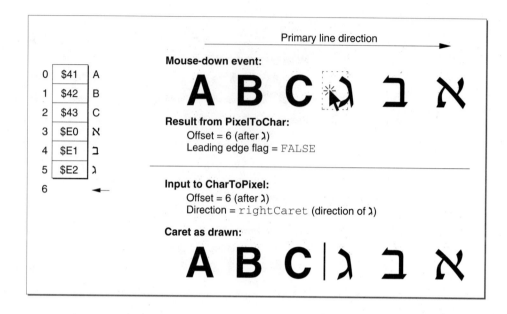

There is one additional complication that occurs at the ends of a text segment that is the only style run on a line, and at the outer end of a text segment that is the rightmost or leftmost style run on a line. Again, the rules for calling `PixelToChar` and `CharToPixel` are the same. Here is how they are interpreted for these cases. If a user clicks the mouse *before* the text segment that is at the beginning of a line, `PixelToChar` returns a leading edge value of `FALSE` and a byte offset of 0. (The first character of a text segment that you pass to `PixelToChar` is always at byte offset 0.)

If a user clicks the mouse *after* the text segment that is at the end of a line, `PixelToChar` returns a leading edge value of `TRUE` and the next byte offset in memory, following the last character in the text segment.

Figure 3-14 shows what happens when a mouse-down event occurs beyond the last glyph of the text segment. The `PixelToChar` function returns byte offset 3 and a `leadingEdge` flag of `TRUE`. You pass this byte offset and a `direction` parameter of `leftCaret` to `CharToPixel`. In this case, the direction parameter is based on the value of `SysDirection` because there isn't a character in memory associated with byte offset 3. The `CharToPixel` function returns a caret position on the trailing edge of C, which also marks the insertion point of the next character to be entered. This is where you draw the caret.

Figure 3-14   Caret position for a mouse-down event beyond the last glyph of the text segment

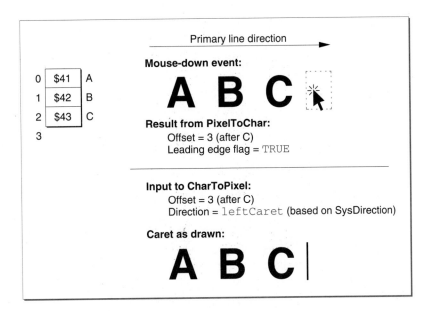

Listing 3-9 is a sample routine that converts mouse clicks to caret positions for drawing the caret or for highlighting a selection range. It determines a text offset (`charLoc`) from a mouse-down position and turns it into caret positions or ends of highlighting rectangles (`leftSide`, `rightSide`). It tracks the mouse and dynamically draws highlighting as the cursor is moved across the text. The routine calls `HiliteText` to determine selection ranges. It calls `CharacterType` to determine the primary and secondary caret positions for mixed-directional text. It draws the caret or highlighting rectangles by calling the application routine `MyAddSelectionArea`.

Listing 3-9   Drawing the caret and highlighting a selection range

```
PROCEDURE MyDoTextClick(w: WindowPtr; where: POINT;
                        cmdKeyIsDown, shiftKeyIsDown,
                        optionKeyIsDown: BOOLEAN);
VAR
    txLineH:                TextLineHandle;
    horizontalPosition:     FIXED;
    leadingEdge:            BOOLEAN;
    widthRemaining:         FIXED;
    charLoc:                INTEGER;
    selectionOffsets:       OffsetTable;
    c:                      INTEGER;
    leftSide, rightSide:    INTEGER;
```

```
        prevMouseLoc:           POINT;
        direction:              INTEGER;
BEGIN
   txLineH := TextLineHandle(GetWRefCon(w));      {get the text}
   IF txLineH <> NIL THEN BEGIN
      LockHandleHigh(txLineH);

      WITH txLineH^^ DO BEGIN
         {initialize character offsets to invalid values}
         IF NOT shiftKeyIsDown THEN
            leftOffset := -1;
         rightOffset := -1;

         {initialize mouse position to invalid values}
         SetPt(prevMouseLoc, kMaxInteger, kMaxInteger);
         {track mouse and display text selection or caret }
         REPEAT
            IF DeltaPoint(where, prevMouseLoc) <> 0 THEN BEGIN
               {mouse has moved:}
               prevMouseLoc := where;

               {adjust mouse position relative to lineStart, }
               { convert mouse position's INTEGER to FIXED, }
               { assume style run position doesn't matter, }
               { assume no scaling (1: 1 ratio)}
               charLoc := PixelToChar(@textBuffer, textLength, 0,
                           BitShift(where.h - lineStart.h, 16),
                           leadingEdge, widthRemaining,
                           smOnlyStyleRun,
                           POINT(kOneToOneScaling),
                           POINT(kOneToOneScaling));

               IF charLoc <> rightOffset THEN BEGIN
                  {character location has changed:}
                  IF leftOffset = -1 THEN
                     {anchor position hasn't been set yet:}
                     leftOffset := charLoc;   {set anchor position}
                  rightOffset := charLoc;     {save new caret pos.}

                  {erase previous selection; note that it }
                  {would be more optimal to erase only the }
                  { difference between old and new selection}
                  MyDeleteSelectionAreas(w, txLineH);
```

```
{now get the selection ranges to highlight}
HiliteText(@textBuffer, textLength, leftOffset,
          rightOffset, selectionOffsets);


{check whether a range of text is selected, }
{ or if it's only an insertion point}
IF selectionOffsets[0].offFirst <>
selectionOffsets[0].offSecond THEN BEGIN
    {it's a selection range:}
    c := 0;        {offsetPairs are zero-based}
    REPEAT
        leftSide := CharToPixel(@textBuffer,
                textLength, 0,
                selectionOffsets[c].offFirst,
                smHilite, smOnlyStyleRun,
                POINT(kOneToOneScaling),
                POINT(kOneToOneScaling));
        rightSide := CharToPixel(@textBuffer,
                textLength, 0,
                selectionOffsets[c].offSecond,
                smHilite, smOnlyStyleRun,
                POINT(kOneToOneScaling),
                POINT(kOneToOneScaling));

        {put rectangle ends in right order}
        IF rightSide < leftSide THEN
            SwapIntegers(leftSide, rightSide);

        {now draw the rectangle}
        MyAddSelectionArea(txLineH, leftSide,
                lineStart.v - caretHeight,
                rightSide,lineStart.v,
                TRUE);
        c := c + 1;
    UNTIL (selectionOffsets[c].offFirst =
    selectionOffsets[c].offSecond) OR (c = 3);
END
ELSE BEGIN
    {it's a caret position, not a range:}
    { calculate caret and draw it}

    {position of caret depends on character's }
    { direction; call CharacterType to find it}
```

```
IF BAND(CharacterType(@textBuffer,
selectionOffsets[0].offFirst),
smCharRight) <> 0 THEN
   direction := smRightCaret
ELSE
   direction := smLeftCaret;
leftSide := CharToPixel(@textBuffer,
            textLength, 0,
            selectionOffsets[0].offFirst,
            direction, smOnlyStyleRun,
            POINT(kOneToOneScaling),
            POINT(kOneToOneScaling));
{if user has specified dual caret, call }
{ CharToPixel again with the opposite }
{ value for the direction parameter}
IF documentSettings.useDualCaret THEN BEGIN
   IF direction = smRightCaret THEN
      direction := smLeftCaret
   ELSE
      direction := smRightCaret;
   rightSide := CharToPixel(@textBuffer,
            textLength, 0,
            selectionOffsets[0].offFirst,
            direction, smOnlyStyleRun,
            POINT(kOneToOneScaling),
            POINT(kOneToOneScaling));
END
ELSE
   rightSide := leftSide;

IF leftSide = rightSide THEN
   {it's only a single caret:}
   MyAddSelectionArea(txLineH, leftSide,
            lineStart.v - caretHeight,
            leftSide + kCaretWidth,
            lineStart.v, TRUE)
ELSE BEGIN
   {it's a split-caret: assume upper caret }
   { is left-to-right text, lower caret is }
   { right-to-left text}
   IF direction = smRightCaret THEN BEGIN
      {rightSide is right-to-left: }
      { use upper caret for leftSide}
```

```
                              MyAddSelectionArea(txLineH, leftSide,
                                      lineStart.v - caretHeight,
                                      leftSide + kCaretWidth,
                                      lineStart.v -
                                      (caretHeight DIV 2), TRUE);
                              MyAddSelectionArea(txLineH, rightSide,
                                      lineStart.v -
                                      (caretHeight DIV 2),
                                      rightSide + kCaretWidth,
                                      lineStart.v, TRUE);
                    END
                    ELSE BEGIN
                        {rightSide is left-to-right: }
                        { use lower caret for leftSide}
                        MyAddSelectionArea(txLineH, rightSide,
                                lineStart.v - caretHeight,
                                rightSide + kCaretWidth,
                                lineStart.v -
                                (caretHeight DIV 2), TRUE);

                        MyAddSelectionArea(txLineH, leftSide,
                                lineStart.v -
                                (caretHeight DIV 2),
                                leftSide + kCaretWidth,
                                lineStart.v, TRUE);
                    END;
                END;
              END
            END;
          END;

        GetMouse(where);
      UNTIL NOT WaitMouseUp;
    END;

    HUnlock(Handle(txLineH));
  END
END;                              {MyDoTextClick}
```

Synchronizing the Caret With the Keyboard Script

If the user changes the keyboard script, you can call the CharToPixel function to
determine the caret position, specifying the direction parameter based on the
keyboard script. However, the user may change the keyboard script between the time

QuickDraw Text

you draw and erase the caret. You can save the position where you drew the caret, then invert (erase) at that position again. To do this, save the direction of the keyboard script, the screen pixel width, or even the whole rectangle.

Highlighting a Text Selection

To display a selection range, you typically highlight the text. This process entails converting the offsets to their display screen pixel locations, and then calling the `InvertRect` procedure to display the text selection in inverse video or with a colored or outlined background.

When a range of text to be highlighted is unidirectional, it is contiguous in both memory order and display order; the highlighted text constitutes a single range. When the text is bidirectional, however, it can contain characters that occur on direction boundaries. Although the characters are stored contiguously in memory, the leading edge of one character's glyph does not constitute the trailing edge of the other in display order. A range of mixed-directional text that is contiguous in memory can produce up to three physically separate ranges of displayed text to be highlighted. For example, Figure 3-15 shows two separate ranges of highlighted text whose characters are contiguous in memory.

Figure 3-15   Highlighting mixed-directional text

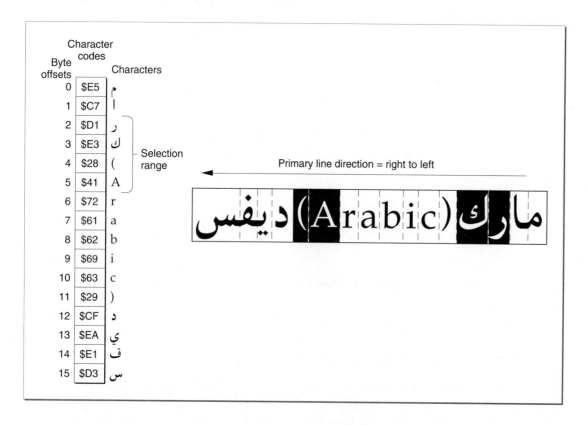

To highlight a selection range, you need the beginning and ending byte offsets of the selected text. From these offsets, you determine one or more pairs of offsets of the displayed text. Once you have the pairs of offsets, you determine the pixel locations that mark the beginning and the end of the displayed text of each pair. You can include the following steps in the inner loop of your highlighting routine to determine these values.

1. You call `HiliteText` to get the individual pairs of byte offsets that encompass the onscreen ranges of text to be highlighted. The `HiliteText` procedure always returns three pairs of offsets. This is because if a text selection contains mixed-directional text, it can consist of up to three distinct ranges of text when displayed. For unidirectional text, `HiliteText` returns one pair that contains the beginning and ending byte offsets whose text is to be highlighted, and two pairs that each include the same numbers. You can ignore any pair of duplicate numbers.

2. Using the offset pairs that `HiliteText` returns, you convert each byte offset of a pair to its equivalent onscreen pixel location. You call `CharToPixel` once each for the beginning and ending offsets of a pair. You might call `CharToPixel` up to 6 times. You must pass the `CharToPixel` function a direction parameter of `hilite`, which signals it to use the primary line direction to determine the correct caret position. When you specify `hilite`, `CharToPixel` returns the correct caret position for the glyph based on the text direction of its character.

Once you have the pixel locations corresponding to the ends of each range of text, you must convert them to display line pixel locations that are relative to the line's left margin. (The `CharToPixel` function returns the pixel location relative to the left edge of the text range for which you called it.) If you saved the line layout information and you have the screen pixel widths of the preceding style runs in display order, you can sum the widths of these style runs and add the screen pixel width that `CharToPixel` returns to the total. You must do this for the beginning and ending pixel locations that mark the text. If you did not save the screen pixel widths of the preceding style runs on the display line, you must lay out the text line again to get these values. When you have the pixel locations relative to left margin of the display line, you can highlight the text.

For text that is rendered in black and white, you call the `InvertRect` procedure to highlight each distinct text range; the background color is exchanged with the foreground color. For text that is rendered in color, all pixel values of the current background color are replaced with the value of the highlighting color.

Generally, the user chooses the highlighting color from the Color control panel, and the application uses this color. However, you can reset this color using the QuickDraw `HiliteColor` procedure. If a monitor is black-and-white and a highlighting color is specified, the highlighting color reverts to black.

Before you call `InvertRect` for colored text, first you must clear the `HiliteMode` low-memory global. By default the highlight mode bit of the low-memory global variable is set to 1. You clear it by setting it to 0. After you highlight the text, you don't need to reset the bit; `InvertRect` resets it automatically.

The easiest way to clear the highlight mode bit is to call the Toolbox Utilities' `BitClr` procedure, for example:

```
BitClr(Ptr(HiliteMode), pHiliteBit);
```

just before calling `InvertRect` using `srcXor` mode. (Do not alter the other bits in `HiliteMode`.)

Note

Routines that formerly used `Xor` inversion, such as `InvertRect` and the text drawing routines, will use highlight mode if the `hilite` bit is clear. ◆

From assembly language, you must call the `pHiliteBit` selector for highlight mode when you use the `BitClear` trap: BCLR must use the assembly-language equate `hiliteBit`. For example:

```
BCLR #hiliteBit, hiliteMode
```

Customizing QuickDraw's Text Handling

The QuickDraw bottleneck routines are procedures that perform the fundamental tasks associated with QuickDraw drawing operations. For each type of object that QuickDraw can draw, including text, there is a low-level routine which the higher-level routines call that actually performs the operation. These low-level routines, called bottlenecks because so many of the higher-level routines use them, carry out the actual work of measuring and drawing text.

The QuickDraw text routines use two of the bottleneck routines extensively—one to measure text (`StdTxMeas`) and one to draw it (`StdText`). Most of the high-level QuickDraw text routines call the low-level routines. The use of bottleneck routines provides flexibility to QuickDraw and applications that need to alter or augment the basic behavior of QuickDraw.

The graphics port record contains a field (`grafProcs`) which is set by default to `NIL`, indicating that QuickDraw should use the standard low-level bottleneck routines. You can modify this field to point to a record, `QDProcs`, which holds the addresses of customized routines for QuickDraw to use instead of the standard ones. For more information about the `QDProcs` record, see the QuickDraw chapters in *Inside Macintosh: Imaging*.

You can set some of the fields of this record to point to the standard bottleneck routines, and some to point to your customized routines. Your customized bottleneck routine can augment the standard bottleneck routine by calling it directly, either before or after performing its own operations, or it can replace a standard routine. If you replace either of the two standard bottleneck routines used for measuring (`StdTxtMeas`) and drawing

(StdText) text, the routines you install must have the same calling sequences as the standard routines. See "Low-Level QuickDraw Text Routines" on page 3-98 for these routines and their parameters. For the major discussion of how to customize the QuickDraw bottleneck routines, see *Inside Macintosh: Imaging*.

Note

Before replacing a bottleneck routine, consider the possibility that to do so could jeopardize the future compatibility of the application. If you replace either StdTxMeas or StdText, you change the behavior of the high-level routines that call them. ◆

You can also customize QuickDraw's text drawing and measuring capabilities by writing high-level routines that do additional processing, but call the standard bottleneck routines.

Note

If you need to call either StdText or StdTxMeas directly, you must first check the graphics port grafProc field to determine whether the bottleneck routines have been customized, and if so, you must call the customized routine instead of the standard one. The bottleneck routines are always customized for printing. ◆

Text in QuickDraw Pictures

This section describes aspects of how text is stored in picture files, including related limitations and restrictions, such as the following:

- The grayishTextOr transfer mode is not stored in pictures files, and therefore you cannot use it for printing.

- Inside a picture definition, DrawText cannot have a byteCount greater than 255.

Fonts

Whenever you record text in a picture file, QuickDraw stores the name of the current font and uses it when playing back the picture. This is true for pictures drawn in both the original and color graphics ports. The opcode that QuickDraw uses to save this information is $002C. Here is its data type:

```
PictFontInfo   =  Record
                  length:  Integer; {length of data in bytes}
                  fontID:  Integer; {ID in the source system}
                  fontName:STR255;
               End;
```

QuickDraw saves this information only one time for each font used in a picture. The code in Listing 3-10 generates a picture file containing the font information that Listing 3-11 shows.

Listing 3-10   Generating a picture file with font information

```
GetFNum ('Venice', theFontID); {Set a font before opening PICT}
TextFont (theFontID);

pHand2    := OpenPicture (pictRect);
     MoveTo(20,20);
     DrawString(' Better be Venice');

     GetFNum('Geneva', theFontID);
     TextFont(theFontID);
     MoveTo(20,40);
     DrawString('Geneva');

     GetFNum('Geneva', theFontID);
     TextFont(theFontID);
     MoveTo(20,60);
     DrawString('Geneva');
   ClosePicture;
```

When QuickDraw plays back a picture, it uses the font family ID (fontID) as a reference into the list of font names which are used to set the correct font on the target system.

Listing 3-11   A picture file with font information

```
OpCode 0x002C {9,
   "0005 0656 656E 6963 65"} /* save current font */
TxFont 'venice'
DHDVText {20, 20, " Better be Venice"}
OpCode 0x002C {9,               /* save next font name */
   "0003 0647 656E 6576 61"}
TxFont 'geneva'
DVText {20, "Geneva"}
OpCode 0x002C {11,      /* ditto        */
   "0002 084E 6577 2059 6F72 6B"}
TxFont 'geneva'                 /* second Geneva does not need
                                   another $002C */
DVText {20, "Geneva"}
```

Text With Multiple Style Runs

If you used the `GetFormatOrder` procedure to determine the correct order in which to draw text consisting of multiple style runs, the style runs are stored in display order when you record the text in a picture file. To reconstruct the storage order of the text from the picture file, an application that reads the style runs into memory from the picture file must then use the `GetFormatOrder` procedure to reverse the display order to storage order. Finally, the application must write the text into memory again, following the order that `GetFormatOrder` returns.

For example, suppose you have a a text string consisting of three style runs with different text directions—A (right-to-left), B (left-to-right), and C (left-to-right)—in storage order. You number them: A=1, B=2, C=3.

You call `GetFormatOrder` for these style runs with a line direction of right to left, and it returns 2, 3, 1. When you draw the style runs in display order and record them in a picture file, they are written to the picture file in display order. Suppose that after you record the picture file, an application cuts and pastes the text. Now the style runs are written to memory in display order: B, C, A.

To get the proper storage order, you call `GetFormatOrder` again, with the same line direction that you used the first time you called `GetFormatOrder` to determine the display order, and it produces the original storage order: A, B, C.

QuickDraw Text Reference

This section describes the data structures, routines, and an application-defined routine that provide the text-handling components of QuickDraw.

In addition to the graphics port record, which all of the routines use and which is defined in the QuickDraw chapters of *Inside Macintosh: Imaging*, these routines use two additional data structures: the font information record and the `Style` data type. They are described in the "Data Structures" section.

The "Routines" section describes the QuickDraw routines that you use to define the text drawing environment, measure and draw text, and identify what glyphs to highlight and where to position the cursor in a range of text.

The constants that you use to identify the text direction and to specify where a style run occurs within a line of text are listed in the "Summary of QuickDraw Text." The constants that you use to identify a font are listed in the chapter "Font Manager" in this book. Equivalent declarations in the C language for the declarations and routines described in this section are listed in the "C Summary."

Data Structures

This section describes the data structures that you use to provide information to the text-handling routines of QuickDraw. The font information record returns measurement information about the font or fonts used. The `Style` data type defines the styles that you use to set the text style.

For more information about QuickDraw pictures, see the QuickDraw chapters in *Inside Macintosh: Imaging*.

The Font Information Record

The `GetFontInfo` procedure uses the font information record to return measurement information based on the font of the current graphics port. If the current font has an associated font, as do Arabic and Hebrew, `GetFontInfo` returns information based on both fonts. The font information record contains the ascent, the descent, the width of the largest glyph, and the leading for a given font. The `StdTxtMeas` function also uses a record of type `FontInfo` to return information about the current font. The `FontInfo` data type defines a font information record.

```
TYPE FontInfo = RECORD
    ascent:   Integer; {ascent}
    descent:  Integer; {descent}
    widMax:   Integer; {maximum glyph width}
    leading:  Integer; {leading}
    END;
```

Field descriptions

ascent	The measurement in pixels from the baseline to the ascent line of the font.
descent	The measurement in pixels from the baseline to the descent line of the font.
widMax	The width in pixels of the largest glyph in the font.
leading	The measurement in pixels from the descent line to the ascent line below it.

The Style Data Type

The `Style` data type defines the styles that you specify as values to the `TextFace` procedure to set the text style in the current graphics port's `txFace` field. QuickDraw draws the glyph in this style.

```
StyleItem   = (bold, italic, underline, outline,
                shadow, condense, extend);
    Style   = SET OF StyleItem;
```

Routines

This section describes the routines that you use to set the text characteristics of the graphics port drawing environment, measure and draw text, lay out lines of text, and determine where to position the caret and which glyphs to highlight in a range of text. It also describes two low-level routines that you can use to measure and draw text.

Four parameters that are common to a number of routines are described in detail here. These parameters are also listed and defined briefly in the each routine.

The slop Parameter

The `DrawJustified`, `MeasureJustified`, `PixelToChar`, and `CharToPixel` routines take a `slop` parameter. The value of this parameter is the number of pixels by which the width of the text segment is to be changed, after the text has been scaled. The `slop` is a signed value that specifies how much the text is to be extended or condensed. The `slop` is derived from the calculations made using the proportion returned from the `PortionLine` function for a style run. To measure or draw text that is not to be extended or condensed, pass a `slop` value of 0.

The styleRunPosition Parameter

The `PortionLine`, `MeasureJustified`, `DrawJustified`, `PixelToChar`, and `CharToPixel` routines take a `styleRunPosition` parameter. This parameter specifies the position of the style run on the display line, and is used to

- determine the proportion of total slop to apply to a style run

- measure or draw a line of justified text

- identify where to break a line of text

- determine the caret position to mark an insertion point or highlight text.

The style run position parameter is meaningful only for those script systems that use intercharacter spacing for justification. For all other script systems, the parameter exists for future extensibility. Although the style run position parameter is not used, for example, for justifying text in the Roman script system, to allow for future compatibility, you should always specify the appropriate value for it for all calls that take it.

For those script systems that do use intercharacter spacing, space between style runs may be allocated differently depending upon whether the style run is leftmost, rightmost, or between two other style runs. For example, depending on the script system, if a style run occurs at the beginning or end of a line, extra space *may not* be added to the outer edge of the outermost glyph, whereas if a style run is interior to a line, all of the glyphs of the text may be treated the same: extra space is allocated to both sides of every glyph including those at either end of the style run.

Note

The current implementations of simple script systems such as Roman and Cyrillic do not justify a line of text by changing the width of nonspace characters. Instead, they rely solely on the use of space characters: the same amount of extra width is added to (or subtracted from) every space whether the space is at the beginning or end of the line or interior to it. ◆

Use one of the following constants (defined as type `JustStyleCode`) in the `styleRunPosition` parameter.

Constant	Value	Meaning
onlyStyleRun	0	Only style run on the line
leftStyleRun	1	Leftmost of multiple style runs on the line
rightStyleRun	2	Rightmost of multiple style runs on the line
middleStyleRun	3	Interior style run: neither leftmost nor rightmost

The numer and denom Parameters

The `PortionLine`, `DrawJustified`, `MeasureJustified`, `PixelToChar`, `CharToPixel`, `StdText`, and `StdTxMeas` routines take numer and denom parameters. Both numer and denom are point values: numer specifies the numerator for the horizontal and vertical scaling factors, and denom specifies the denominator for the horizontal and vertical scaling factors. Together, these values specify the scaling factors for the text: `numer.v` over `denom.v` gives the vertical scaling (height), and `numer.h` over `denom.h` gives the horizontal scaling factors (width). For routines that take these parameters, you need to specify values for numer and denom even if you are not scaling the text. For unscaled text, you can specify scaling factors of 1, 1.

For all routines except `StdTxtMeas` that take these parameters, numer and denom are input parameters only. For `StdTxtMeas`, numer and denom are reference parameters. On output, these parameters contain additional scaling to be applied to the text. Use of the output values is explained in the description of "StdTxMeas" on page 3-99.

Setting Text Characteristics

The routines in this section set values in the text-related fields of the current graphics port (`GrafPort` or `CGrafPort`). You also use these routines to set text characteristics that vary from style run to style run. You use these routines to set the graphics port fields to values equivalent to a new style run's text characteristics before you call other QuickDraw routines to measure and draw the text.

- The `TextFont` procedure specifies the font to be used.

- The `TextFace` procedure specifies the glyph style.

- The `TextMode` procedure specifies the transfer mode.

- The `TextSize` procedure specifies the font size.

■ The `CharExtra` procedure specifies the amount of pixels by which to widen or narrow each space character in a range of text.

■ The `SpaceExtra` procedure specifies the amount of pixels by which to widen or narrow each glyph other than the space characters in a range of text (`CharExtra`).

Note
To ensure future compatibility and benefit from any future enhancements, always use these routines to modify the text fields of the graphics port record, rather than directly change the field values. ◆

TextFont

The `TextFont` procedure sets the font of the current graphics port in which the text is to be rendered.

PROCEDURE TextFont (font: Integer);

font   The font family ID.

DESCRIPTION

The `TextFont` procedure sets the value of the graphics port text font (`txFont`) field. The initial font family ID is 0, which represents the system font. The value that you specify for this field is either an integer or a constant. The range of integers currently defined are from 0 to 32767. Currently, negative font family IDs are not supported, although they may be supported in the future.

For more information about `TextFont`, see "Setting the Font" on page 3-20.

SPECIAL CONSIDERATIONS

The system font and application font have different font IDs and sizes on various script systems. However, the special designators 0 and 1 always map to the system font and the application font for the system script, respectively.

TextFace

The `TextFace` procedure sets the style of the font in which the text is to be drawn in the current graphics port.

PROCEDURE TextFace (face: Style);

face   The style for text to be drawn in the current graphics port.

DESCRIPTION

The TextFace procedure sets the value for the style of the font in the text face (txFace) field of the current graphics port. The Style data type allows you to specify a set of one or more of the following predefined constants: bold, italic, underline, outline, shadow, condense, and extend. In Pascal, you specify the constants within square brackets. For example:

```
TextFace([bold]);          {bold}
TextFace([bold,italic]);   {bold and italic}
```

The style is set to the empty set ([ ]) by default, which specifies plain. For more information, see "Modifying the Text Style" on page 3-21.

ASSEMBLY-LANGUAGE INFORMATION

In assembly language, the style set is stored as a word whose low-order byte contains bits representing the style. The bit numbers are specified by the following global constants.

Constant	Bit	Meaning
bold	0	Bold style
italicBit	1	Italic style
ulineBit	2	Underlined style
outlineBit	3	Outlined style
shadowBit	4	Shadowed style
condense	5	Condensed style
extendBit	6	Extended style

If all bits are 0, the low-order byte represents the plain glyph style.

TextMode

The TextMode procedure sets the transfer mode for drawing text in the current graphics port.

PROCEDURE TextMode (mode: Integer);

mode   The transfer mode to be used to draw the text.

DESCRIPTION

The TextMode procedure sets the transfer mode in the graphics port txMode field. The transfer mode determines the interplay between what an application is drawing (the source) and what already exists on the display device (the destination), resulting in the text display.

There are two basic kinds of modes: pattern (pat) and source (src). Source is the kind that you use for drawing text. There are four basic Boolean operations: Copy, Or, Xor, and Bic (bit clear), each of which has an inverse variant in which the source is inverted before the transfer, yielding eight operations in all. Original QuickDraw supports these eight transfer modes. Color QuickDraw enables your application to achieve color effects within those basic transfer modes, and offers an additional set of transfer modes that perform arithmetic operations on the RGB values of the source and destination pixels. See the chapter "Color QuickDraw" in *Inside Macintosh: Imaging* for a complete discussion of the arithmetic transfer modes. Other transfer modes are grayishTextOr, transparent mode, and text mask mode.

Table 3-1 shows the eight basic transfer modes and their effects on the destination pixels.

Table 3-1   Effects of the basic transfer modes

Source	Action on the destination pixel	
	If black source	If white source
srcCopy	Force black	Force white
srcOr	Force black	Leave alone
srcXOr	Invert	Leave alone
srcBic	Force white	Leave alone
NotSrcCopy	Force white	Force black
NotSrcOr	Leave alone	Force black
NotSrcXOr	Leave alone	Invert
NotSrcBic	Leave alone	Force white

This is how color affects these transfer modes when the source pixels are either all black (all 1's) or white (all 0's).

Copy

The Copy mode applies the foreground color to the black part of the source (the part containing 1's) and the background color to the white part of the source (the part containing 0's), and replaces the destination with the colored source.

Or

The Or mode applies the foreground color to the black part of the source and replaces the destination with the colored source. The white part of the source isn't transferred to the destination. If the foreground is black, the drawing will be faster. Copying to a white background always reproduces the source image, regardless of the pixel depth.

Xor

The Xor mode complements the bits in the destination corresponding to the bits equal to 1 in the source. When used on a colored destination, the color of the inverted destination isn't defined.

Bic

The Bic mode applies the background color to the black part of the source and replaces the destination with the colored source. The white part of the source isn't transferred to the destination. The black part of the source is erased, resulting in white in the destination.

NotCopy

The NotCopy mode applies the foreground color to the white part of the source and the background color to the black part of the source, and replaces the destination with the colored source. It thus has the effect of reversing the foreground and background colors.

NotOr

The NotOr mode applies the foreground color to the white part of the source and replaces the destination with the colored source. The black part of the source isn't transferred to the destination. If the foreground is black, the drawing will be faster.

NotXor

The NotXor mode inverts the bits that are 0 in the source. When used on a colored destination, the color of the inverted destination isn't defined.

NotBic

The NotBic mode applies the background color to the white part of the source and replaces the destination with the colored source. The black part of the source isn't transferred to the destination.

The arithmetic transfer modes are addOver, addPin, subOver, subPin, adMax, adMin, and blend. For color, the arithmetic modes change the destination pixels by performing arithmetic operations on the source and destination pixels. Arithmetic transfer modes calculate pixel values by adding, subtracting, or averaging the RGB components of the source and destination pixels. They are most useful for 8-bit color, but they work on 4-bit and 2-bit color also. When the destination bitmap is one bit deep, the mode reverts to the basic transfer mode that best approximates the arithmetic mode requested.

The grayishTextOr transfer mode draws dimmed text on the screen. You can use it for black-and-white or color graphics ports. The grayishTextOr transfer mode is not considered a standard transfer mode because currently it is not stored in pictures, and printing with it is undefined. (It does not pass through the QuickDraw bottleneck routines.)

The transparent mode replaces the destination pixel with the source pixel if the source pixel isn't equal to the background color. This mode is most useful in 8-bit, 4-bit, or 2-bit color modes.

Note
Multibit fonts may have a specific color. Some transfer modes may not produce the desired results with a multibit font. However, the arithmetic modes, transparent mode, and hilite mode work equally well with single bit and multibit fonts. Multibit fonts draw quickly in srcOr mode only if the foreground is white. Single bit fonts draw quickly in srcOr mode only if the foreground is black. Grayscale fonts produce a spectrum of colors, rather than just the foreground and background colors. The following table shows transfer mode constants and their selectors. ◆

Table 3-2   Transfer mode constants and selectors

Transfer mode	Selector	Transfer mode	Selector
srcCopy	0	addPin	33
srcOr	1	addOver	34
srcXor	2	subPin	35
srcBic	3	transparent	36
notSrcCopy	4	adMax	37
notSrcOr	5	subOver	38
notSrcXor	6	adMin	39
notSrcBic	7	grayishTextOr	49
blend	32	mask	64

For more information about transfer modes, see the chapters "QuickDraw Drawing" and "Color QuickDraw" in *Inside Macintosh: Imaging*.

TextSize

The TextSize procedure sets the font size for text drawn in the current graphics port to the specified number of points.

```
PROCEDURE TextSize (size: Integer);
```

size   The font size in points. If you specify 0, the system font size (normally 12 points) is used.

DESCRIPTION

The TextSize procedure sets the font size in the text size (txSize) field of the current graphics port record. The initial setting is 0, which specifies that the font size of the system font is to be used. You may specify a value from 0 up to 32,767. For more information, see "Changing the Font Size" on page 3-22.

SpaceExtra

The SpaceExtra procedure specifies the number of pixels by which to widen (or narrow) each space in a style run to be drawn in the current graphics port.

```
PROCEDURE SpaceExtra (extra: Fixed);
```

extra   The amount (in pixels or binary fractions of a pixel) to widen (or narrow) each space in a style run on a line.

DESCRIPTION

The SpaceExtra procedure sets the value of the extra space (spExtra) field in the current graphics port record. The initial setting is 0. You can pass a negative value for the extra parameter, but be careful not to narrow spaces so much that the text is unreadable. The value you specify is added to the width of each space character in the style run. For those script systems that do not use spaces, any value set in the extra space field is ignored. For those script systems that use spaces as delimiters, if you do not want to justify a line of text using DrawJustified, you can use the SpaceExtra procedure to set a fixed number of pixels to be added to each space character, then call DrawText or DrawString.

When you use the justification routines (MeasureJustified, DrawJustified) to measure or draw justified text, they temporarily reset the extra space value. They add to the current value of the field, if any, the amount of extra space to be added to space characters in the specified text in order to justify the text, based on calculations that take into account the slop value for the range of text and all of the text characteristics. On exit, these routines restore the original value.

For more information about SpaceExtra, see "Changing the Width of Characters" on page 3-22.

SPECIAL CONSIDERATIONS

For a color graphics port (CGrafPort), you can use SpaceExtra by itself or in conjunction with the CharExtra procedure to format a line of text in the 1-byte simple or 2-byte script systems. You should not use CharExtra for 1-byte complex script systems.

CharExtra

For a color graphics port (CGrafPort), the CharExtra procedure specifies the number of pixels by which to widen (or narrow) the glyphs of each nonspace character in a style run.

```
PROCEDURE CharExtra (extra: Fixed);
```

extra   The amount (in pixels or decimal fractions of a pixel) to widen (or narrow) each glyph other than the space character in a range of text.

DESCRIPTION

The CharExtra procedure sets the value of the chExtra field of the color graphics port record. This field contains a number that is in 4.12 fractional notation: four bits of signed integer followed by 12 bits of fraction. The CharExtra procedure uses the value of the txSize field, so you must call TextSize to set the font size of the text before you call CharExtra.

The initial setting is 0. You can pass a negative value for the extra parameter, but be careful not to narrow glyphs so much that the text is unreadable. The measuring and drawing routines use the value in this field when an application calls them to measure or draw text. The CharExtra procedure is available only for color graphic ports.

SPECIAL CONSIDERATIONS

Do not use CharExtra for script systems that include zero-width characters, such as diacritical marks, because intercharacter space is added to all glyphs, separating the diacritical mark from the glyph of the character. Do not use it for script systems that include contextual forms, such as ligatures or conjunct characters, which would not be represented properly were intercharacter space added to these glyphs. For example, you should not use CharExtra for the Devanagari or Arabic languages, whose text is drawn as connected glyphs, or with the Sonata font because it includes zero-width characters.

The 2-byte script systems use the chExtra field value properly.

GetFontInfo

The GetFontInfo procedure returns information about the current graphics port's font, taking into account the style and size in which the glyphs are to be drawn.

```
PROCEDURE GetFontInfo (VAR info: FontInfo);
```

info   A font information record that contains the font measurement information, in integer values.

DESCRIPTION

The GetFontInfo procedure returns the ascent, descent, leading, and width of the largest glyph of the font in the text font, size, and style specified in the current graphics port. If the script system specified by the current graphics port txFont field has an associated font, as do Hebrew and Arabic, GetFontInfo returns combined information based on both fonts. This is to accommodate text written in the Roman script when the primary script system is non-Roman. However, even if all of the text is written in a non-Roman script, if there is an associated font, GetFontInfo always bases its information on the combined fonts. You can determine the line height, in pixels, by adding the values of the ascent, descent, and leading fields.

The GetFontInfo procedure is similar to the Font Manager's FontMetrics procedure, except that the GetFontInfo procedure returns integer values. See "The Font Information Record" on page 3-66 for a description of the record and its fields.

Drawing Text

QuickDraw provides routines that allow you to draw a single character, a Pascal string, or an arbitrary sequence of text. You can also draw a text sequence made narrower or wider using these routines; this technique is commonly used to justify a line of text. These routines draw text in the font, style, and size of the current graphics port. Consequently, you can draw only a single style run at a time using these routines.

- The DrawChar procedure draws the glyph of a single 1-byte character.

- The DrawString procedure draws the text of a Pascal string.

- The DrawText procedure draws the glyphs of a sequence of characters.

- The DrawJustified procedure draws a sequence of text that is widened or narrowed by a specified number of pixels.

Whether the text to be drawn has a left-to-right direction, a right-to-left direction, or is bidirectional, QuickDraw always draws text starting at the current pen location and always advances the pen to the right by the width of the glyph or glyphs it has just drawn. Before drawing text that has a right-to-left direction, QuickDraw reorders the glyphs for display so that they can be read correctly, even though it draws them from left to right.

DrawChar

The DrawChar procedure draws the glyph for the specified character at the current pen location in the current graphics port.

```
PROCEDURE DrawChar (ch: CHAR);
```

ch   The character code whose glyph is to be drawn.

DESCRIPTION

The `DrawChar` procedure draws a single character's glyph and then advances the pen by the width of the glyph. If the glyph isn't in the font, the font's missing symbol is drawn. For more information, see "Individual Glyphs" on page 3-28.

Note

If you're drawing more than one character, it's faster to make one `DrawString` or `DrawText` call rather than a series of `DrawChar` calls. ◆

SPECIAL CONSIDERATIONS

Because it takes a single-byte value as the `ch` parameter, `DrawChar` works only for 1-byte script systems. If you want to draw the glyph of a single character in a 2-byte script, call either `DrawText`, `DrawString`, or `DrawJustified`.

However, a series of calls to `DrawChar` in a 1-byte complex script system can give incorrect results because a text string is not always a simple concatenation of a series of characters. In a contextual script, two different glyphs may be used to represent a single character in its contextual form and alone. To draw a sequence of text in a 1-byte complex script system, use `DrawText`, `DrawString`, or `DrawJustified` instead.

However, for 1-byte complex scripts, you can use `DrawChar` for special purposes, such as to include the isolated glyph of a character in a book's index, for example, to show a single glyph as it exists apart from contextual transformations.

DrawString

The `DrawString` procedure draws the specified Pascal string at the pen location in the current graphics port (`GrafPort` or `CGrafPort`).

```
PROCEDURE DrawString (s: Str255);
```

s   A Pascal string consisting of the text to be drawn.

DESCRIPTION

The `DrawString` procedure draws the string with its left edge at the current pen location, extending right. The final position of the pen location, after the text is drawn, is to the right of the rightmost glyph in the string. QuickDraw does not do any formatting, such as handling of carriage returns or line feeds.

Note that you can use `DrawString` only for a Pascal string containing a single style run.

Drawing text visible on the screen

QuickDraw temporarily stores on the stack all of the text you ask it to draw, even if the text is to be clipped. When drawing large font sizes or complex style variations, draw only what is visible on the screen. You can determine the number of characters whose corresponding glyphs actually fit on the screen by calling the StringWidth function to determine the length of the string before calling DrawString. ◆

If you specify values in the graphics port spExtra or chExtra fields to change the width of space or nonspace characters, DrawString takes these values into account.

SPECIAL CONSIDERATIONS

For right-to-left text, such as Hebrew or Arabic, QuickDraw draws the final (leftmost) glyph first, then moves to the right through all the glyphs, drawing the initial (rightmost) glyph last.

Note that you should not change the width of nonspace characters for 1-byte simple script systems with zero-width characters or 1-byte complex script systems. For more information, see "CharExtra" on page 3-75.

For contextual script systems, DrawString substitutes the proper ligatures, reversals, and compound characters as needed.

Note

Inside a picture definition, DrawString can't have a byteCount greater than 255. ◆

DrawText

The DrawText procedure draws the specified text at the current pen location in the current graphics port.

```
PROCEDURE DrawText (textBuf: Ptr; firstByte, byteCount: Integer);
```

textBuf   A pointer to a buffer containing the text to be drawn.

firstByte   An offset from the start of the text buffer (textBuf) to the first byte of the text to be drawn.

byteCount   The number of bytes of text to be drawn.

DESCRIPTION

The DrawText procedure draws the text with the leftmost glyph at the current pen location, extending right. After QuickDraw draws the text, it sets the pen location to the right of the rightmost glyph. For more information, see "Text Segments" on page 3-29.

Drawing text visible on the screen

QuickDraw temporarily stores on the stack all of the text you ask it to draw, even if the text is to be clipped. When drawing a range of text, it's best to draw only what is visible on the screen. If an entire text string does not fit on a line, truncate the text at a word boundary. If possible, avoid truncating within a style run. You can determine the number of characters whose glyphs actually fit on the screen by calling the `TextWidth` function before calling `DrawText`. ◆

If you specify values in the graphics port `spExtra` and `chExtra` fields to change the width of nonspace and space characters, both `TextWidth` and `DrawText` take these values into account.

SPECIAL CONSIDERATIONS

For 1-byte complex script systems, `DrawText` substitutes the proper ligatures, reversals, and compound characters as needed.

For right-to-left text, such as Hebrew or Arabic, QuickDraw draws the final (leftmost) glyph first, then moves to the right through all the characters, drawing the initial (rightmost) glyph last.

For 2-byte script systems, note that `byteCount` is the number of *bytes* to be drawn, not the number of glyphs. Because 2-byte script systems also include characters consisting of only 1 byte, do not simply multiply the number of characters by 2 to determine this value; you must determine and specify the correct number of bytes.

Note

Inside a picture definition, `DrawText` cannot have a `byteCount` greater than 255. ◆

DrawJustified

The `DrawJustified` procedure draws the specified text at the current pen location in the current graphics port, taking into account the adjustment necessary to condense or extend the text by the slop value, appropriately for the script system.

```
PROCEDURE DrawJustified (textPtr: Ptr; textLength: LongInt;
                         slop: Fixed;
                         styleRunPosition: JustStyleCode;
                         numer, denom: Point);
```

textPtr   A pointer to the memory location of the beginning of the text to be drawn.

textLength
             The number of bytes of text to be drawn.

slop   The amount of slop for the text to be drawn. A positive value extends the
                    text segment; a negative value condenses the text segment.

styleRunPosition
                    The position on the line of this style run. The style run can be the only one
                    on the line, the leftmost on the line, the rightmost on the line, or one
                    between two other style runs.

numer   A point giving the numerator for the horizontal and vertical
                    scaling factors.

denom   A point giving the denominator for the horizontal and
                    vertical scaling factors.

DESCRIPTION

The DrawJustified procedure is similar to the DrawText procedure, except that you
use it to draw text that is expanded or condensed by the number of pixels specified by
slop. The DrawJustified procedure is most commonly used to draw a line of
justified text.

The DrawJustified procedure draws the specified text in the font, size, and style of
the current graphics port, taking into account any scaling factors, and it distributes the
slop appropriately for the script system. Regardless of the line direction of the text to be
drawn, you place the pen at the left edge of the line before calling DrawJustified for
the first style run. For all subsequent style runs on that line, QuickDraw advances the
pen appropriately.

If DrawJustified changes the width of spaces, it temporarily resets the space extra
(spExtra) value. It adds to the current value of the field, if any, the amount of extra
space to be applied to each space character within the range of text in order to justify the
text, based on calculations that take into account the slop value and all of the text
characteristics. On exit, DrawJustified restores the original value.

For the slop parameter, pass DrawJustified the value assessed for this style run based
on the proportion returned for it from PortionLine. For more information, see "The
numer and denom Parameters" on page 3-68.

Note
Be sure to pass the same values for styleRunPosition and the scaling
factors (numer and denom) to DrawJustified that you pass to
PortionLine. ◆

See "The styleRunPosition Parameter" on page 3-67 for a description of this parameter
and the values it takes. See "The slop Parameter" on page 3-67 for more information
about the slop parameter.

For more information about how to use DrawJustified in conjunction with the other
routines used to prepare to draw a line of justified text, see"Measuring and Drawing
Lines of Text," beginning on page 3-29.

SPECIAL CONSIDERATIONS

The DrawJustified procedure works with text in all script systems. For example, to depict justified Arabic text, DrawJustified uses extension bars to create the additional width that is distributed as slop within a style run.

For 1-byte complex script systems, DrawJustified substitutes the proper ligatures, reversals, and compound characters as needed.

For 2-byte script systems that do not use space characters to delimit words, DrawJustified distributes the slop value in a manner appropriate to the script system. For script systems, such as Japanese, that use ideographic characters, DrawJustified distributes the additional screen pixel width appropriately for the text representation.

Note that textLength is the number of *bytes* to be drawn, not the number of characters. Because 2-byte script systems also include characters consisting of only 1 byte, do not simply multiply the number of characters by 2 to determine this value; you must determine and specify the correct number of bytes.

The DrawJustified procedure may move memory; do not call this procedure at interrupt time.

Measuring Text

Laying out text to determine how much of it fits on the display line entails measuring the text. QuickDraw provides five high-level routines that let you do this:

- The CharWidth function returns the horizontal extension of a single glyph.

- The StringWidth function returns the width of a Pascal string.

- The TextWidth function returns the width of the glyphs of a text segment.

- The MeasureText procedure fills an array with an entry for each character identifying the width of each character's glyph as measured from the left side of the entire text segment.

- The MeasureJustified procedure fills an array with an entry for each character in a style run identifying the width of each character's glyph as measured from the left side of the text segment.

These routines measure text in the font, style, and size of the current graphics port. Consequently, you need to call them once for each individual style run in any line of text that contains multiple style runs.

CharWidth

The CharWidth function returns the width in pixels of the specified character.

```
FUNCTION CharWidth (ch: CHAR): Integer;
```

ch   The character whose width is to be measured.

DESCRIPTION

The CharWidth function includes the effects of the stylistic variations for the text set in the current graphics port. If you change any of these attributes after determining the glyph width but before actually drawing it, the predetermined width may not be correct. For a space character, CharWidth also includes the effect of SpaceExtra. For a nonspace character, CharWidth includes the effect of CharExtra. For more information, see "Individual Glyphs" on page 3-28.

SPECIAL CONSIDERATIONS

Because it takes a single-byte value as the ch parameter, CharWidth works only for 1-byte simple script systems.

A series of calls to CharWidth in a contextual 1-byte font may give incorrect results, because the width of a text segment may be different from the sum of its individual character widths. In that case, to measure a line of text you should call TextWidth.

Do not use the CharWidth function for 2-byte script systems. If you want to measure the width of a single glyph in a 2-byte font, you should use TextWidth.

StringWidth

The StringWidth function returns the length in pixels of the specified Pascal string.

```
FUNCTION StringWidth (s: Str255): Integer;
```

s   A pascal string containing the text to be measured.

DESCRIPTION

You should not call StringWidth to measure scaled text. Although StringWidth takes into account the graphics port record settings, it does not accept scaling parameters, and therefore cannot determine the correct text width result for text to be drawn using scaling factor parameters. For more information, see "Pascal Strings" on page 3-28.

If you specify values in the graphics port spExtra or chExtra fields to change the width of space or nonspace characters, StringWidth takes these values into account. The StringWidth function works with all script systems.

TextWidth

The TextWidth function returns the length in pixels of the specified text.

```
FUNCTION TextWidth (textBuf: Ptr;
                    firstByte, byteCount: Integer): Integer;
```

textBuf   A pointer to a buffer that contains the text to be measured.

firstByte   An offset from textBuf to the first byte of the text to be measured.

byteCount   The number of bytes of text to be measured.

DESCRIPTION

You can use TextWidth to measure the screen pixel width of any text segment that has uniform character attributes. You can use it to measure the style runs in a line of text, whether you intend to draw the line using DrawText or DrawJustified. The TextWidth function takes into account the character attributes set in the graphics port. If you change any of these attributes after determining the text width but before actually drawing the text, the predetermined width may not be correct. For a space character, TextWidth also includes the effect of SpaceExtra. For a nonspace character, TextWidth includes the effect of CharExtra.

The TextWidth function works with text in all script systems because the script management system modifies the routine if necessary to give the proper results.

Note

To draw justified lines of text that include multiple style runs, you calculate the amount of extra pixels, or slop, that remains to be distributed throughout the line. This process entails measuring the screen pixel width of each style run on the line: you can use TextWidth for this purpose. For a complete discussion of how to use TextWidth to prepare to draw a line of justified text, refer to "Measuring and Drawing Lines of Text" beginning page 3-29. ◆

SPECIAL CONSIDERATIONS

For 1-byte complex script systems, TextWidth calculates the widths of any ligatures, reversals, and compound characters that need to be drawn.

Note that byteCount is the number of bytes to be measured, not the number of characters. Because 2-byte script systems also include characters consisting of only one byte, you should not simply multiply the number of characters by 2 to determine this value; you must determine and specify the correct number of bytes.

MeasureText

The MeasureText procedure provides an array version of the TextWidth function. For each character in the specified text, MeasureText calculates the width of the character's glyph in pixels from the left edge of the text segment.

```
PROCEDURE MeasureText (count: Integer; textAddr, charLocs: Ptr);
```

count   The number of bytes to be measured.

textAddr   A pointer to the memory location of the beginning of the text to be measured. The value of textAddr must point directly to the first character whose glyph is to be measured.

charLocs   A pointer to an application-defined array of count + 1 integers.

DESCRIPTION

The MeasureText procedure calculates the onscreen pixel width of the glyph of each character beginning from the left edge of the text segment. On return, the first element in the charLocs array contains 0 and the last element contains the total width of the text segment, when the primary line direction is left to right and the text is unidirectional. When the primary line direction is right to left and the text is unidirectional, the first element in the array contains the total width of the text segment, and the last element in the array contains 0. When the text is bidirectional, at a direction boundary, MeasureText selects the character whose direction maps to that of the primary line direction.

The MeasureText procedure returns the same results that an application would get if it called CharToPixel for each character with a direction parameter value of hilite. Using MeasureText to find the pixel location of a character's glyph is less efficient than using the CharToPixel function because the application must define the array pointed to by charLocs, and then walk the array after MeasureText returns the results.

For more information about MeasureText, contact Developer Technical Support.

SPECIAL CONSIDERATIONS

Some fonts in 1-byte script systems may have zero-width characters, which are usually overlapping diacritical marks that typically follow the base character in memory. In this case, MeasureText measures both the glyph of the base character (the high-order, low-address byte) and the width of the diacritical mark. The charLoc array includes an entry for each, but both entries contain the same value.

For 1-byte complex script systems, MeasureText calculates the widths of any ligatures, reversals, compound characters, and character clusters that need to be drawn. For example, for an Arabic ligature, the entry that corresponds to the trailing edge of each character that is part of the ligature is the trailing edge of the entire ligature.

Note that count is the number of *bytes* to be measured, not the number of characters. Because 2-byte script systems also include characters consisting of only one byte, do not simply multiply the number of characters by 2 to determine this value; you must determine and specify the correct number of bytes. For 2-byte characters, the charLocs array contains two entries—one corresponding to each byte—but both entries contain the same pixel-width value.

MeasureJustified

For text that is expanded, condensed, or scaled, the MeasureJustified procedure calculates the onscreen width in pixels from the left edge of the text segment to the glyph of the character.

```
PROCEDURE MeasureJustified (textPtr: Ptr; textLength: LongInt;
                            slop: Fixed; charLocs: Ptr;
                            styleRunPosition: JustStyleCode;
                            numer, denom: Point);
```

textPtr   A pointer to the memory location of the beginning of the text to be measured.

textLength
               The number of bytes of text to be measured. The text length should equal the entire visible part of the text on a line, including trailing spaces if and only if they are displayed. Otherwise, the results for the last glyph on the line may be invalid.

slop   The amount of slop for the text to be drawn. A positive value extends the text segment; a negative value condenses the text segment.

charLocs   A pointer to an application-defined array of textLength + 1 integers.

styleRunPosition
               The position on the line of this style run. The style run can be the only one on the line, the leftmost on the line, the rightmost on the line, or one between two other style runs.

numer   A point giving the numerator for the horizontal and vertical scaling factors.

denom   A point giving the denominator for the horizontal and vertical scaling factors.

DESCRIPTION

The MeasureJustified procedure is similar to the MeasureText procedure, except that it is used to find the pixel location of a character's glyph in text that is expanded or condensed.

The `MeasureJustified` procedure calculates the onscreen pixel width of the glyph of each character beginning from the left edge of the text segment, taking into account `slop` value, scaling, and style run position.

On return, the first element in the `charLocs` array contains 0 and the last element contains the total width of the text segment, when the primary line direction is left to right and the text is unidirectional. When the primary line direction is right to left and the text is unidirectional, the first element in the array contains the total width of the text segment, and the last element in the array contains 0. When the text is bidirectional, at a direction boundary, `MeasureJustified` selects the character whose direction maps to that of the primary line direction.

The `MeasureJustified` procedure returns the same results that an application would get if it called `CharToPixel` for each character with a direction parameter value of `hilite`. Using `MeasureJustified` to find the pixel location of a character's glyph is less efficient than using the `CharToPixel` function because the application must define the array pointed to by `charLocs`, and then walk the array after `MeasureText` returns the results.

The `MeasureJustified` procedure temporarily resets the space extra (`spExtra`) value, adding to the current value of the field, if any, the amount of extra space to be added to space characters in order to fully justify the text, based on calculations that take into account the slop value and all the text characteristics. On exit, `MeasureJustified` restores the original value.

Because `MeasureJustified` measures text in only the current font, style, and size, you need to call it once for each individual style run.

For more information about the scaling factors, see "The numer and denom Parameters" on page 3-68. See "The styleRunPosition Parameter" on page 3-67 for a description of the `styleRunPosition` parameter and the values it takes. See "The slop Parameter" on page 3-67 for more information about the `slop` parameter.

For additional information about `MeasureJustified`, contact Developer Technical Support.

SPECIAL CONSIDERATIONS

The `MeasureJustified` procedure works properly for text in all script systems. For 1-byte complex script systems, `MeasureJustified` calculates the widths of any ligatures, reversals, and compound characters that would need to be drawn.

Note that `textLength` is the number of *bytes* to be drawn, not the number of characters. Because 2-byte script systems also include characters consisting of only one byte, you should not simply multiply the number of characters by 2 to determine this value; the application must determine and specify the correct number of bytes.

Some 1-byte script system fonts may have zero-width characters, which are usually overlapping diacritical marks that typically follow the base character in memory. In this case, `MeasureJustified` measures both the glyph of the base character (the high-order, low-address byte) and the width of the diacritical mark. The `charLoc` array includes an entry for each, but both entries contain the same value.

For 1-byte complex script systems, `MeasureJustified` calculates the widths of any ligatures, reversals, compound characters, and character clusters that need to be drawn. For example, for an Arabic ligature, the entry that corresponds to the trailing edge of each character that is part of the ligature is the trailing edge of the entire ligature.

The `MeasureJustified` procedure may move memory; do not call this procedure at interrupt time.

Laying Out a Line of Text

In addition to the routines that measure text, QuickDraw text provides additional routines that help you perform the tasks involved in laying out a line of text.

■ The `GetFormatOrder` procedure determines the display order of style runs for a line of text containing multiple style runs with mixed directions.

■ The `VisibleLength` function eliminates trailing spaces from the last style run on the line.

■ The `PortionLine` function determines how to distribute the total slop value for a line among the style runs on that line.

GetFormatOrder

The `GetFormatOrder` procedure determines the display order of multiple style runs with mixed directions.

```
PROCEDURE GetFormatOrder (ordering: FormatOrderPtr;
                          firstFormat: Integer;
                          lastFormat: Integer;
                          lineRight: Boolean;
                          rlDirProc: Ptr; dirParam: Ptr);
```

ordering
: A pointer to a format order array. Upon completion of the call, the format order array contains the numbers identifying the style runs in display order. This is its type declaration:

```
TYPE
    FormatOrder = ARRAY [0..0] OF Integer;
    FormatOrderPtr = ^FormatOrder;
```

firstFormat
: A number greater than or equal to 0 identifying the first style run in storage order that is part of the line for which you are calling `GetFormatOrder`.

lastFormat
: A number greater than or equal to 0 identifying the last style run in storage order that is part of the line for which you are calling `GetFormatOrder`.

lineRight   A flag that you set to TRUE if the primary line direction is right-to-left.

rlDirProc   A pointer to an application-supplied function that calculates the correct direction, given the style run identifier. The GetFormatOrder procedure calls the application-defined rlDirProc function for each identifier from firstFormat to lastFormat. The interface to this function looks like this:

```
FUNCTION MyRlDirProc(theFormat: Integer;
                     dirParam: Ptr ): Boolean;
```

This function returns TRUE for right-to-left text direction and FALSE for left-to-right. Given dirParam and a style run identifier, the application-defined rlDirProc routine should be able to determine the style run direction.

theFormat   A number identifying the style run and its associated attribute information in the information block pointed to by dirParam.

dirParam   A pointer to a parameter block that contains the font and script information for each style run in the text. This parameter block is used by the application-supplied routine.

DESCRIPTION

The GetFormatOrder procedure helps you determine how to draw text that contains multiple style runs with mixed directions. For mixed-directional text, after you determine where to break the line, you need to call GetFormatOrder to determine the display order. When you call GetFormatOrder, you supply a Boolean function, and reference it using the rlDirProc parameter. This function calculates the direction of each style run identified by number. Do not call GetFormatOrder if there is only one style run on the line.

You must index the style runs in storage order. You pass GetFormatOrder numbers identifying the first and last style runs of the line in storage order and the primary line direction. The GetFormatOrder procedure returns to you an equivalent sequence in display order.

If you do not explicitly define the primary line direction of the text, base the lineRight parameter on the value of the SysDirection global variable. (The SysDirection global variable is set to -1 if the system direction is right to left, and 0 if the system direction is left to right.)

The ordering parameter points to an array of integers, with (lastFormat — firstFormat + 1) entries. The GetFormatOrder procedure fills an array (the size of the number of the style runs) with the display order of each style run. On exit, the array contains a permuted list of the numbers from firstFormat to lastFormat. The first entry in the array is the number of the style run to draw first; this is the leftmost style run in display order. The last entry in the array is the number of the entry to draw last, the rightmost style run in display order. For more information about how to use the GetFormatOrder procedure, see "Determining the Display Order for Style Runs," which begins on page 3-33. For more information about the rlDirProc function, see "Application-Supplied Routine" on page 3-100.

VisibleLength

The `VisibleLength` function calculates the length in bytes of a given text segment, excluding trailing white space.

```
FUNCTION VisibleLength (textPtr: Ptr;
                        textLength: LongInt): LongInt;
```

textPtr   A pointer to a text string.

textLength
              The number of bytes in the text segment.

DESCRIPTION

The `VisibleLength` function determines how much of a style run to display, without displaying trailing spaces. You call `VisibleLength` for the last style run of a line *in memory order*. The last style run in memory order of the text constituting the line is not always the last style run in display order. For a line of unidirectional left-to-right text, the last style run in memory order is the rightmost style run in display order. For a line of unidirectional right-to-left text, the last style run in memory order is the leftmost style run in display order. However, if the text contains mixed directions, the last style run in memory order may be an interior style run in display order.

The text justification routines do not automatically exclude trailing spaces, so you pass them the value that `VisibleLength` returns as the length of the last style run in memory order.

The `VisibleLength` function behaves differently for various script systems.

■ For simple script systems, such as Roman and Cryllic, and for 2-byte script systems, `VisibleLength` does not include in the byte count it returns trailing spaces that occur at the display end of the text segment. For 2-byte script systems, `VisibleLength` does not count them, whether they are 1-byte or 2-byte space characters.

■ For 1-byte complex script systems, `VisibleLength` does not include in the byte count that it returns spaces whose character direction is the same as the primary line direction. For 1-byte complex script systems that support bidirectional text, Roman spaces take on a character direction based on the primary line direction. If the Roman spaces then fall at the end of the text, `VisibleLength` does not include them in the returned byte count.

Advancing the pointer in memory in response to VisibleLength

The purpose of `VisibleLength` is to trim off white space at the display end of the line. The `VisibleLength` function does not eliminate the white space by removing its character code from memory. Rather, it does not include white space characters in the count that it returns as the length of the range of text for which you call it. ◆

For more information about VisibleLength, see the task description "Eliminating Trailing Spaces (for Justified Text)" on page 3-36.

PortionLine

The PortionLine function determines the correct proportion of extra space to apply to the specified style run in a line of justified text.

```
FUNCTION PortionLine(textPtr: Ptr; textLen: LongInt;
                     styleRunPosition: JustStyleCode;
                     numer: Point; denom: Point) : Fixed;
```

textPtr   A pointer to the style run.

textLen   The number of bytes in the text of the style run.

styleRunPosition
             The position on the line of this style run. The style run can be the only one on the line, the leftmost on the line, the rightmost on the line, or one between two other style runs.

numer   A point giving the numerator for the horizontal and vertical scaling factors.

denom   A point giving the denominator for the horizontal and vertical scaling factors.

DESCRIPTION

You use PortionLine in formatting a line of justified text. It helps you determine how to distribute the slop for a line among its style runs. When you know the total slop for a line of text, you need to determine what portion of it to attribute to each style run. To do this, you call the PortionLine function once for each style run on the line. The PortionLine function computes the portion of extra space for a style run, taking into account the font, size, style, and scaling factors of the style run. It returns a number that represents the portion of the slop to be applied to the style run for which it is called. You use the value that PortionLine returns to determine the percentage of slop that you should attribute to a style run.

To determine the percentage of slop to allocate to each style run, you compute what percentage each portion is of the sum of all portions. To determine the actual slop value in pixels for each style run, you apply the percentage to the total slop value. The following steps summarize this process:

1. Call PortionLine for each style run on the line.

2. Add the returned values together.

3. Calculate the percentage of the slop value for each style run using the ratio of the value returned by PortionLine for that style run and the total of the values returned for all of the style runs on the line.

4. Calculate the number of pixels to be added to each style run by multiplying the percentage of the slop for each style run by the total number of pixels.

For more information about the scaling factors, see "The numer and denom Parameters" on page 3-68. See "The styleRunPosition Parameter" on page 3-67 for a description of the `styleRunPosition` parameter and the values it takes.

Note
Be sure to pass the same values for `styleRunPosition` and the scaling factors (`numer` and `denom`) to `PortionLine` that you pass to any of the other justification routines for this style run. ◆

Determining the Caret Position, and Selecting and Highlighting Text

To mark an insertion point you need to know where to draw the caret. To highlight text, you need to know the caret positions that begin and end the text range. This section describes routines that you use to locate a caret position for marking an insertion point or highlighting text. You can also use the `PixelToChar` function to determine where to break a line, and the `CharToPixel` function to find the screen pixel width of a text segment.

- The `PixelToChar` function converts a pixel location associated with a glyph in a range of text to a byte offset within the style run.

- The `CharToPixel` function converts a byte offset to a pixel location. The pixel location is measured from the left edge of the style run.

- The `HiliteText` procedure returns three pairs of offsets marking the endpoints of ranges of text to be highlighted.

PixelToChar

The `PixelToChar` function returns the byte offset of a character in a style run, or part of a style run, whose onscreen glyph is nearest the place where the user clicked the mouse.

```
FUNCTION PixelToChar (textBuf: Ptr; textLen: LongInt;
                      slop: Fixed; pixelWidth: Fixed;
                      VAR leadingEdge: Boolean;
                      VAR widthRemaining: Fixed;
                      styleRunPosition: JustStyleCode;
                      numer: Point; denom: Point): Integer;
```

textBuf   A pointer to the start of the text segment.

textLen   The length in bytes of the entire text segment pointed to by `textBuf`. The `PixelToChar` function requires the context of the complete text segment in order to determine the correct value.

slop   The amount of slop for the text to be drawn. A positive value extends the text segment; a negative value condenses the text segment.

pixelWidth

The screen location of the glyph associated with the character whose byte offset is to be returned. The screen location is measured in pixels beginning from the left edge of the text segment for which you call PixelToChar.

leadingEdge

A Boolean flag that, upon completion of the call, is set to TRUE if the pixel location is on the leading edge of the glyph, and FALSE if the pixel location is on the trailing edge of the glyph. The leading edge is the left side if the direction of the character that the glyph represents is left-to-right (such as a Roman character), and the right side if the character direction is right-to-left (such as an Arabic or a Hebrew letter).

widthRemaining

Upon completion of the call, contains –1 if the pixel location (specified by the pixelWidth parameter) falls within the style run (represented by the textLen bytes starting at textBuf). Otherwise, contains the amount of pixels by which the input pixel location (pixelWidth) extends beyond the right edge of the text for which you called PixelToChar.

styleRunPosition

The position on the line of this style run. The style run can be the only one on the line, the leftmost on the line, the rightmost on the line, or one between two other style runs.

numer   A point giving the numerator for the horizontal and vertical scaling factors.

denom   A point giving the denominator for the horizontal and vertical scaling factors.

DESCRIPTION

You can use the information that PixelToChar returns for highlighting, word selection, and identifying the caret position. The PixelToChar function returns a byte offset and a Boolean value that describes whether the pixel location is on the leading edge or trailing edge of the glyph where the mouse-down event occurred. When the pixel location falls on a glyph that corresponds to one or more characters that are part of the text segment, the PixelToChar function uses the direction of the character or characters to determine which side of the glyph is the leading edge. (A glyph can represent more than one character, for example, for a ligature. Generally, if a glyph represents more than one character, all of the characters have the same text direction.)

If the pixel location is on the leading edge, PixelToChar returns the byte offset of the character whose glyph is at the pixel location. (If the glyph represents multiple characters, it returns the byte offset of the first of these characters in memory.) If the pixel location is on the trailing edge, PixelToChar returns the byte offset of the first character in memory *following* the character or characters represented by the glyph. If the pixel location is on the trailing edge of the glyph that corresponds to the last character in the text segment, `PixelToChar` returns a byte offset equal to the length of the text segment.

When the pixel location is *before* the leading edge of the first glyph in the displayed text segment, `PixelToChar` returns a leading edge value of `FALSE` and the byte offset of the first character. When the pixel location is *after* the trailing edge of the last glyph in the displayed text segment, `PixelToChar` returns a leading edge value of `TRUE` and the next byte offset in memory, the one after the last character in the text segment. If the primary line direction is left to right, *before* means to the left of all of the glyphs for the characters in the text segment, and *after* means to the right of all these glyphs. If the primary line direction is right to left, before and after hold the opposite meanings.

You also use the value of the `leadingEdge` flag to help determine the value of the `direction` parameter to pass to `CharToPixel`, which you call to get the caret position. If the `leadingEdge` flag is `FALSE`, you base the value of the `direction` parameter on the direction of the character at the byte offset in memory that precedes the one that `PixelToChar` returns; if `leadingEdge` is `TRUE`, you base the value of the `direction` parameter on the direction of the character at the byte offset that `PixelToChar` returns. If there isn't a character at the byte offset, you base the value of the `direction` parameter on the primary line direction as determined by the `SysDirection` global variable.

You specify a value for `textLen` that is equal to the entire visible part of the style run on a line and includes trailing spaces if and only if they are displayed. They may not be displayed, for example, for the last style run in memory order that is part of the current line.

For more information about the scaling factors, see "The numer and denom Parameters" on page 3-68. See "The styleRunPosition Parameter" on page 3-67 for a description of the `styleRunPosition` parameter and the values it takes. See "The slop Parameter" on page 3-67 for more information about the `slop` parameter.

Note
Be sure to pass the same values for `styleRunPosition` and the scaling factors (`numer` and `denom`) to `PixelToChar` that you pass to any of the other justification routines for this style run. ◆

You pass `PixelToChar` a pointer to the byte offset of the character in the text buffer that begins the text segment or style run containing the character whose glyph is at the pixel location. If you do not know which style run on the display line contains the character whose glyph is at the pixel location, you can loop through the style runs until you find the one that contains the pixel location. If the style run contains the character, `PixelToChar` returns its byte offset. If it doesn't, you can use the `widthRemaining` parameter value to help determine which style run contains the glyph at the pixel location.

If you pass PixelToChar the pixel width of the display line, you can use the returned value of widthRemaining to calculate the length of a style run. The widthRemaining parameter contains the length in pixels from the end of the style run for which you call PixelToChar to the end of the display line, in this case, if the style run for which you call it does not include the byte offset whose glyph corresponds to the pixel location. You subtract the returned widthRemaining value from the screen pixel width of the display line to get the style run's length.

To truncate a line of text, you can use PixelToChar to find the byte offset of the character where the line should be broken. To return the correct byte offset associated with the pixel location of a mouse-down event when the text belongs to a right-to-left script system, the PixelToChar function reorders the text. If right-to-left text is reordered when you use PixelToChar to determine where to break a line, it returns the wrong byte offset. To get the correct result, you must turn off reordering before you call PixelToChar. Remember to restore reordering after you have determined where to break the line. See "Using Scaled Text" beginning on page 3-44 for more information.

SPECIAL CONSIDERATIONS

The PixelToChar function works with text in all script systems, and for text that is justified or not. For contextual script systems, PixelToChar takes into account the widths of any ligatures, reversals, and compound characters that were created when the text was drawn.

Because 2-byte script systems also include characters consisting of only one byte, you should not simply multiply the number of characters by 2 to determine this value; you must determine and specify the correct number of bytes.

The PixelToChar function may move memory; do not call this procedure at interrupt time.

CharToPixel

The CharToPixel function returns the screen pixel width from the left edge of a text segment to the glyph of the character whose byte offset you specify.

```
FUNCTION CharToPixel (textBuf: Ptr; textLen: LongInt;
                      slop: Fixed; offset: LongInt;
                      direction: Integer;
                      styleRunPosition: JustStyleCode;
                      numer: Point; denom: Point): Integer;
```

textBuf   A pointer to the beginning of the text segment.

textLen   The length in bytes of the entire text segment pointed to by textBuf. The CharToPixel function requires the context of the complete text in order to determine the correct value.

slop   The amount of slop for the text to be drawn. A positive value extends the text segment; a negative value condenses the text segment.

offset   The offset from textBuf to the character within the text segment whose display pixel location is to be measured. For 2-byte script systems, if the character whose position is to be measured is 2 bytes long, this is the offset of the first byte.

direction   This parameter specifies whether CharToPixel is to return the caret position for a character with a direction of left-to-right or right-to-left. A direction value of hilite indicates that CharToPixel is to use the caret position for the character direction that matches the primary line direction as specified by the SysDirection global variable.

styleRunPosition
    The position on the line of this style run. The style run can be the only one on the line, the leftmost on the line, the rightmost on the line, or one between two other style runs.

numer   A point giving the numerator for the horizontal and vertical scaling factors.

denom   A point giving the denominator for the horizontal and vertical scaling factors.

DESCRIPTION

You use CharToPixel to find the onscreen pixel location at which to draw a caret and to identify the selection points for highlighting. The CharToPixel function returns the horizontal distance in pixels from the start of the range of text beginning with the byte offset at textBuf to the glyph corresponding to the character whose byte offset is specified by the offset parameter. The pixel location is relative to the beginning of the text segment, not the left margin of the display line. To get the actual display line pixel location of the glyph relative to the left margin, you add the pixel value that CharToPixel returns to the pixel location at the end of the previous style run (on the left) in display order. In other words, you need to know the length of the text in pixels on the display line up to the beginning of the range of text that you call CharToPixel for, and then you add in the screen pixel width that CharToPixel returns.

You specify a value for textLen that is equal to the entire visible part of the style run on a line and includes trailing spaces if and only if they are displayed. They may not be displayed, for example, for the last style run in memory order, which is part of the line. Do not confuse the textLen parameter with the offset, which is the byte offset of the character within the text segment whose pixel location CharToPixel is to return.

If you use CharToPixel to get a caret position to mark the insertion point, you specify a value of leftCaret or rightCaret for the direction parameter. You can use the value of the PixelToChar leadingEdge flag to determine the direction parameter value.

If the leadingEdge flag is FALSE, you base the value of the direction parameter on the direction of the character at the byte offset in memory that precedes the one that PixelToChar returns; if leadingEdge is TRUE, you base the value of the direction parameter on the direction of the character at the byte offset that PixelToChar returns. If there isn't a character at the byte offset, you base the value of the direction parameter on the primary line direction as determined by the SysDirection global variable.

You can use the following constants to specify a value for direction.

Constant	Value	Meaning
leftCaret	0	Place caret for left-to-right text direction.
rightCaret	−1	Place caret for right-to-left text direction.
hilite	1	Specifies that the caret position should be determined according to the primary line direction, based on the value of SysDirection.

For more information about the scaling factors, see "The numer and denom Parameters" on page 3-68. See "The styleRunPosition Parameter" on page 3-67 for a description of the styleRunPosition parameter and the values it takes. See "The slop Parameter" on page 3-67 for more information about the slop parameter.

Note
Be sure to pass the same values for styleRunPosition and the scaling factors (numer and denom) to CharToPixel that you pass to any of the other justification routines for this style run. ◆

For more information about CharToPixel see "Drawing Carets and Highlighting" on page 3-47.

SPECIAL CONSIDERATIONS

The CharToPixel function works with text in all script systems. For 1-byte contextual script systems, CharToPixel calculates the widths of any ligatures, reversals, and compound characters that need to be drawn.

Note that textLen is the number of *bytes* to be drawn, not the number of characters. Because 2-byte script systems also include characters consisting of only one byte, do not simply multiply the number of characters by 2 to determine this value; you must determine and specify the correct number of bytes.

The CharToPixel function may move memory; do not call this procedure at interrupt time.

HiliteText

The `HiliteText` procedure finds all the characters between two byte offsets in a text segment whose glyphs are to be highlighted.

```
PROCEDURE HiliteText (textPtr: Ptr;
                      textLen, firstOffset, secondOffset: Integer;
                      VAR offsets: OffsetTable);
```

`textPtr`   A pointer to a buffer that contains the text to be highlighted.

`textLen`   The length in bytes of the entire text segment pointed to by `textPtr`.

`firstOffset`
            The byte offset from `textPtr` to the first character to be highlighted.

`secondOffset`
            The byte offset from `textPtr` to the last character to be highlighted.

`offsets`   A table that, upon completion of the call, specifies the boundaries of the text to be highlighted.

DESCRIPTION

The `HiliteText` procedure returns three pairs of byte offsets that mark the onscreen ranges of text to be highlighted. This is because for bidirectional text, although the characters are contiguous in memory, their displayed glyphs can include up to three separate ranges of text.

The `HiliteText` procedure takes into account the fact that to highlight the complete range of text whose beginning and ending byte offsets you pass it, it must return byte offsets that encompass the glyphs of the first and last characters in the text segment. To determine the correct offset pairs, `HiliteText` relies on the primary line direction as specified by the `SysDirection` global variable.

Before calling `HiliteText`, you must set up an offset table (of type `OffsetTable`) in your application to hold the results. You can consider the offset table a set of three offset pairs:

```
TYPE OffPair =
   RECORD
      offFirst:   Integer;
      offSecond:  Integer;
   END;

   OffsetTable = ARRAY [0..2] of OffPair;
```

If the two offsets in any pair are equal, the pair is empty and you can ignore it. Otherwise the pair identifies a run of characters whose glyphs are to be highlighted.

SPECIAL CONSIDERATIONS

The offsets that `HiliteText` returns depend on the primary line direction as defined by the `SysDirection` global variable. If you change the value of `SysDirection`, `HiliteText` returns the offset that is meaningful according to the primary line direction for ambiguous offsets on the boundary of right-to-left and left-to-right text.

The `HiliteText` procedure may move memory; do not call this procedure at interrupt time. For more information, see "Highlighting a Text Selection" on page 3-60.

Low-Level QuickDraw Text Routines

The QuickDraw text routines use two bottleneck routines extensively—one to draw text, and one to measure it. This section describes the `StdText` procedure that is used to draw text and the `StdTxMeas` function that is used to measure text. Although the high-level QuickDraw text routines provide most of the functionality needed to measure and draw text under most circumstances, you can call these low-level routines directly when necessary. However, if you need to call either `StdText` or `StdTxMeas` directly, you must first check the graphics port `grafProc` field to determine whether the bottleneck routines have been customized, and if so, you must call the customized routine instead of the standard one. The bottleneck routines are always customized for printing.

If the `grafProcs` field contains `NIL`, the standard bottleneck routines have *not* been customized. If the `grafProcs` field contains a pointer, the standard bottleneck routines have been replaced by customized ones. A pointer (of type `QDProcsPtr`) in the `grafProc` field points to a `QDProc` record. This record contains fields that point to the bottleneck routine to be used for a specific drawing function. If the standard bottleneck routine has been customized, your application needs to use the customized routine indicated by the `QDProcs` record field.

The QuickDraw standard low-level bottleneck routines work properly for all script systems. For more information about replacing or customizing the bottleneck routines, see "Customizing QuickDraw's Text Handling" on page 3-62 and the QuickDraw chapters in *Inside Macintosh: Imaging*.

StdText

The `StdText` procedure is the standard low-level routine for drawing text. It draws text from an arbitrary structure in memory specified by `textBuf`, starting from the first byte and continuing for `count` bytes.

```
PROCEDURE StdText (count: Integer; textBuf: Ptr;
                   numer, denom: Point);
```

count   The number of bytes to be counted.

textBuf   A pointer to the beginning of the text in memory.

numer	A point giving the numerator for the horizontal and vertical scaling factors.
denom	A point giving the denominator for the horizontal and vertical scaling factors.

DESCRIPTION

The StdText procedure is a QuickDraw bottleneck routine that the QuickDraw text drawing routines use extensively. However, you can call the StdText routine directly to draw text that is scaled or unscaled. For more information about the scaling factors, see "The numer and denom Parameters" on page 3-68.

SPECIAL CONSIDERATIONS

The StdText procedure gives the correct results for all script systems. The count parameter is the number of bytes of the text to be drawn, not characters. When specifying this value, consider that 2-byte script systems also include characters consisting of only one byte.

StdTxMeas

The StdTxMeas function measures the width of scaled or unscaled text.

```
FUNCTION StdTxMeas (byteCount: Integer; textAddr: Ptr;
                    VAR numer, denom: Point;
                    VAR info: FontInfo): Integer;
```

byteCount	The number of bytes to be counted.
textAddr	A pointer to the beginning of the text in memory.
numer	A point giving the numerator for the horizontal and vertical scaling factors.
denom	A point giving the denominator for the horizontal and vertical scaling factors.
info	A font information record that describes the current font.

DESCRIPTION

The StdTxMeas function is a QuickDraw bottleneck routine that the QuickDraw text-measuring routines use extensively. The StdTxMeas function returns the width of the text stored in memory beginning with the first character at textAddr and continuing for byteCount bytes. You can call the StdTxMeas function directly, for example, to measure text that you want to explicitly scale, but not justify. You can also use StdTxMeas to get the font metrics for scaled text in order to determine the line height, instead of using GetFontInfo, which doesn't support scaling.

On input, you need to specify values for numer and denom, even if you are not scaling the text. You can specify 1,1 scaling factors, in this case, so that no scaling is applied. On return, numer and denom contain the additional scaling to be applied to the text. For more information about the input scaling factors, see "The numer and denom Parameters" on page 3-68.

The StdTxtMeas function returns output scaling factors that you need to apply to the text to get the right measurement if the Font Manager was not able to fully satisfy the scaling request. You can use the Toolbox Utilities' FixRound and FixRatio functions to help with this process. For more information, see "Using Scaled Text" on page 3-44.

SPECIAL CONSIDERATIONS

The StdTxMeas routine gives the correct results for all script systems. The byteCount parameter is the number of bytes of the text to be drawn, not characters. When specifying this value, consider that 2-byte script systems also include characters consisting of only one byte.

Application-Supplied Routine

One of the QuickDraw text routines, GetFormatOrder, requires an application-supplied routine, which is described in this section.

MyRlDirProc

The MyRlDirProc function is a callback routine that you supply for use by the GetFormatOrder procedure. The MyRlDirProc function is a Boolean function that calculates, for a style run identified by number, the direction of that style run. Your routine returns TRUE for right-to-left text direction, FALSE for left-to-right. MyRlDirProc is pointed to by the rlDirProc parameter of GetFormatOrder.

```
FUNCTION MyRlDirProc (theFormat: Integer;
                      dirParam: Ptr): Boolean;
```

theFormat   A value that identifies the style run whose direction is needed.

dirParam   A pointer to an application-defined parameter block that contains the font and script information for each style run in the text. The contents of this parameter block are used to determine the direction of the style run. Because of the relationship between the font family ID and the script code, the font family ID can be used to determine the text direction.

DESCRIPTION

To fill the ordering array (type `FormatOrder`) for style runs on a line, the `GetFormatOrder` procedure calls `MyRlDirProc` for each style run numbered from `firstFormat` to `lastFormat`. `GetFormatOrder` passes `MyRlDirProc` a number identifying the style run in storage order, and a pointer to the parameter information block, `dirParam`, that contains the font and style information for the style run. Given `dirParam` and a style run identifier, the application-defined `MyRlDirProc` routine should be able to determine the style run direction.

You should store your style run information in a way that makes it convenient for `MyRLDirProc`. One obvious way to do this is to declare a record type for style runs that allows you to save things like font style, font family ID, script number, and so forth. You then can store these records in an array. When the time comes for `GetFormatOrder` to fill the ordering array, `MyRlDirProc` can consult the style run array for direction information for each of the numbered style runs in turn.

For more information, see "GetFormatOrder" on page 3-87.

Summary of QuickDraw Text

Pascal Summary

Constants

```
CONST
   {CharToPixel directions}
   leftCaret   =  0;    {Place caret for left block}
   rightCaret  = -1;    {Place caret for right block}
   hilite      =  1;    {Direction is SysDirection}

   {constants for styleRunPosition parameter in PortionLine, DrawJustified, }
   { MeasureJustified, CharToPixel, and PixelToChar}
   onlyStyleRun   = 0;    {This is the only style run on the line.}
   leftStyleRun   = 1;    {This is the leftmost of multiple style runs on }
                          { the line.}
   rightStyleRun  = 2;    {This is the rightmost of multiple style runs }
                          {  on the line.}
   middleStyleRun = 3;    {There are multiple style runs on the line }
                          {  and this one is interior; neither }
                          {  leftmost nor rightmost.}
```

Data Types

```
TYPE
   {Type declaration for GetFontInfo info VAR parameter}
   FontInfo =  RECORD
      ascent:  Integer;
      descent: Integer;
      widMax:  Integer;
      leading: Integer;
      END;
```

```
{GetFormatOrder ordering array}
FormatOrder = ARRAY  [0..0] OF Integer;
FormatOrderPtr =  ^FormatOrder;
FormatStatus   =  Integer;


{Type declaration for TextFace face parameter}
StyleItem   =  (bold,italic,underline,outline,shadow,condense,extend);
Style       =  SET OF StyleItem;
```

Routines

Setting Text Characteristics

```
PROCEDURE TextFont          (font: Integer);
PROCEDURE TextFace          (face: Style);
PROCEDURE TextMode          (mode: Integer);
PROCEDURE TextSize          (size: Integer);
PROCEDURE SpaceExtra        (extra: Fixed);
PROCEDURE CharExtra         (extra: Fixed);
PROCEDURE GetFontInfo       (VAR info: FontInfo);
```

Drawing Text

```
PROCEDURE DrawChar          (ch: CHAR);
PROCEDURE DrawString        (s: Str255);
PROCEDURE DrawText          (textBuf: Ptr; firstByte, byteCount: Integer);
PROCEDURE DrawJustified     (textPtr: Ptr; textLength: LongInt;slop: Fixed;
                             styleRunPosition: JustStyleCode;
                             numer: Point; denom: Point);
```

Measuring Text

```
FUNCTION CharWidth          (ch: CHAR): Integer;
FUNCTION StringWidth        (s: Str255) : Integer;
FUNCTION TextWidth          (textBuf: Ptr;
                             firstByte, byteCount: Integer): Integer;
PROCEDURE MeasureText       (count: Integer; textAddr, charLocs: Ptr);
PROCEDURE MeasureJustified  (textPtr: Ptr; textLength: LongInt;
                             slop: Fixed; charLocs: Ptr;
                             styleRunPosition: JustStyleCode;
                             numer: Point; denom: Point);
```

Laying Out a Line of Text

```
PROCEDURE GetFormatOrder    (ordering: FormatOrderPtr; firstFormat: Integer;
                             lastFormat: Integer; lineRight: Boolean;
                             rlDirProc: Ptr;dirParam: Ptr);
FUNCTION VisibleLength       (textPtr: Ptr; textLength: LongInt): LongInt;
FUNCTION PortionLine         (textPtr: Ptr; textLen: LongInt;
                             styleRunPosition: JustStyleCode;
                             numer: Point; denom: Point): Fixed;
```

Determining the Caret Position, and Selecting and Highlighting Text

```
FUNCTION PixelToChar         (textBuf: Ptr; textLen: LongInt;
                             slop: Fixed; pixelWidth: Fixed;
                             VAR leadingEdge: Boolean;
                             VAR widthRemaining: Fixed;
                             styleRunPosition: JustStyleCode;
                             numer, denom: Point): Integer;
FUNCTION CharToPixel         (textBuf: Ptr; textLen: LongInt;
                             slop: Fixed; offset: LongInt;
                             direction: Integer;
                             styleRunPosition: JustStyleCode;
                             numer: Point; denom: Point): Integer;
PROCEDURE HiliteText         (textPtr: Ptr;textLength, firstOffset,
                             secondOffset: Integer;
                             VAR offsets: OffsetTable);
```

Low-Level QuickDraw Text Routines

```
PROCEDURE StdText            (count: Integer; textAddr: Ptr;
                             numer, denom: Point);
FUNCTION StdTxMeas           (byteCount: Integer; textAddr: Ptr;
                             VAR numer, denom: Point;
                             VAR info: FontInfo): Integer;
```

Application-Supplied Routine

```
FUNCTION MyRlDirProc         (theFormat: Integer; dirParam: Ptr) Boolean;
```

C Summary

Constants

```
enum{
   /*CharToPixel directions*/
   leftCaret   =  0,     /*Place caret for left block*/
   rightCaret  = -1,     /*Place caret for right block*/
   hilite      =  1,     /*Direction is SysDirection*/

   /*constants for styleRunPosition parameter in PortionLine,*/
   /*DrawJustified, MeasureJustified, CharToPixel, and PixelToChar*/
   onlyStyleRun   =  0,     /*This is the only style run on the line.*/
   leftStyleRun   =  1,     /*This is the leftmost of multiple style */
                            /*runs on the line.*/
   rightStyleRun  =  2,     /*This is the rightmost of multiple style runs */
                            /* on the line.*/
   middleStyleRun =  3,     /*There are multiple style runs on the line */
                            /* and this one is interior: neither */
                            /* leftmost nor rightmost.*/
```

Types

```
TYPE
   /*Type declaration for GetFontInfo info VAR parameter*/
   struct FontInfo {
      short ascent;
      short descent;
      short widMax;
      short leading;
   };
   typedef struct FontInfo FontInfo;

   /*GetFormatOrder ordering array*/
   typedef short FormatOrder[1];
   typedef FormatOrder *FormatOrderPtr;
   typedef short FormatStatus;

   /*Type declaration for TextFace face parameter*/
   ??StyleItem =  (bold,italic,underline,outline,shadow,condense,extend);
   Style       =  SET OF StyleItem;??
```

Routines

Setting Text Characteristics

```
pascal void TextFont       (short font);
pascal void TextFace       (short face);
pascal void TextMode       (short mode);
pascal void TextSize       (short size);
pascal void SpaceExtra     (extra: Fixed);
pascal void CharExtra      (Fixed extra);
pascal void GetFontInfo    (FontInfo *info);
```

Drawing Text

```
pascal void DrawChar       (short ch);
pascal void DrawString     (ConstStr255Param s);
pascal void DrawText       (const void *textBuf, short firstByte,
                             short byteCount);
pascal void DrawJustified  (Ptr textPtr, long textLength, Fixed slop,
                             JustStyleCode styleRunPosition,
                             Point numer, Point denom);
```

Measuring Text

```
pascal short CharWidth     (short ch);
pascal short StringWidth   (ConstStr255Param s);
pascal short TextWidth     (const void *textBuf, short firstByte,
                             short byteCount);
pascal void MeasureText    (short count, const void *textAddr,
                             void *charLocs);
pascal void MeasureJustified
                           (Ptr textPtr, long textLength, Fixed slop,
                             Ptr charLocs, JustStyleCode styleRunPosition,
                             Point numer, Point denom);
```

Laying Out a Line of Text

```
pascal void GetFormatOrder (FormatOrderPtr ordering,
                             short firstFormat, short lastFormat,
                             Boolean lineRight,
                             Ptr rlDirProc, Ptr dirParam);
pascal long VisibleLength   (Ptr textPtr, long textLen);
pascal Fixed PortionLine     (Ptr textPtr, long textLen, JustStyleCode
                             styleRunPosition, Point numer, Point denom);
```

Determining the Caret Position, and Selecting and Highlighting Text

```
pascal short PixelToChar      (Ptr textBuf, long textLen, Fixed slop,
                               Fixed pixelWidth, Boolean *leadingEdge,
                               Fixed *widthRemaining, JustStyleCode
                               styleRunPosition, Point numer, Point denom);

pascal short CharToPixel      (Ptr textBuf, long textLen, Fixed slop,
                               long offset, short direction, JustStyleCode
                               styleRunPosition, Point numer, Point denom);

pascal void HiliteText        (Ptr textPtr, short textLength,
                               short firstOffset, short secondOffset,
                               OffsetTable offsets);
```

Low-Level QuickDraw Text Routines

```
pascal void StdText           (short count, const void *textAddr,
                               Point numer, Point denom);

pascal short StdTxMeas        (short byteCount, const void *textAddr,
                               Point *numer, Point *denom, FontInfo *info);
```

Application-Supplied Routine

```
pascal Boolean MyRlDirProc    (short theFormat,Ptr dirParam);
```

Assembly-Language Summary

Trap Macros

Trap Macro Names

Pascal name	Trap macro name
DrawJustified	_DrawJustified
MeasureJustified	_MeasureJustified
GetFormatOrder	_GetFormatOrder
VisibleLength	_VisibleLength
PortionLine	_PortionLine
CharToPixel	_CharToPixel
PixelToChar	_PixelToChar
HiliteText	_HiliteText

Trap Macros With Trap Words

Trap macro name	Trap word
_MeasureText	$A837
_StdText	$A882
_DrawChar	$A883
_DrawString	$A884
_DrawText	$A885
_TextWidth	$A886
_TextFont	$A887
_TextFace	$A888
_TextMode	$A889
_TextSize	$A88A
_GetFontInfo	$A88B
_StringWidth	$A88C
_CharWidth	$A88D
_SpaceExtra	$A88E
_StdTxMeas	$A8ED
_CharExtra	$AA23

Global Variables

HiliteMode	Flag used for color highlighting
SysDirection	System direction; the primary line direction and alignment for text
thePort	The currently active graphics port

Font Manager

Contents

Font Manager

The Font Manager is a collection of routines and data structures that you can use to manage the fonts your application uses to display and print text. The Font Manager takes care of reading font data from font resources and creating the bitmap images that QuickDraw uses to display text.

This chapter describes how your application can use the Font Manager to find specific fonts and to get font display information, such as the size of the letters, the amount of space between letters, and how sizing and spacing change if the user decides to apply a style such as bold or italic. It also describes how the Font Manager keeps track of fonts and font families.

You need to read this chapter if you are designing a font or if your application uses different font families or allows the user to choose from a variety of fonts. Two types of fonts can be used on the Macintosh computer: bitmapped fonts and TrueType outline fonts. Your application should be able to handle both types. The information in this chapter about outline fonts applies only to TrueType fonts on the Macintosh, and not to other kinds of outline fonts or to TrueType fonts on any other platform.

Almost half of the information in this chapter describes the tables that make up the resources that are used to define fonts on the Macintosh. Unless you are writing an application, such as a font editor, that needs access to these details, you can skip over most of the material in the "The Bitmapped Font ('NFNT') Resource," "The Outline Font ('sfnt') Resource," and "The Font Family ('FOND') Resource" sections of the Reference portion of the chapter.

Before reading this chapter, read the chapter "Introduction to Text on the Macintosh" in this book. General font-related information and programming suggestions are found in the discussion of font handling in that chapter. You should also be familiar with the information in the chapter "QuickDraw Text" in this book. If you are writing a font editor for TrueType fonts, you also need to read the *TrueType Font Format Specification*, available from APDA.

This chapter begins with an overview of the terminology used throughout *Inside Macintosh* to describe fonts and basic Font Manager concepts, including

■ characters, character codes, and glyphs

■ bitmapped and outline fonts

■ font families, font names, and font IDs

■ system and application font usage

■ font measurements such as left-side bearing, advance width, base line, leading, and kerning

The chapter then describes

- how font resources are used to store fonts
- how the Font Manager finds the information your application or QuickDraw requests
- how the Font Manager and QuickDraw work together to create or alter glyph bitmaps for displaying and printing
- how to use the Font Manager routines to manipulate information about fonts
- the data structures and font resources used by the Font Manager

About Fonts

This section describes the terminology used throughout this chapter to refer to the individual elements of a font, different types of fonts, and the different functions a font can have. Even if you are already familiar with the basic terminology of fonts and typography, you need to know the specific Font Manager concepts described in this section in order to understand the functions of all the Font Manager resources, data structures, and routines.

Characters, Character Codes, and Glyphs

The smallest element in any character set is a **character,** which is a symbol that represents the concept of, for example, a lowercase "b", the number "2", or the arithmetic operator "+". You do not ever see a character on a display device. What you actually see on a display device is a **glyph,** the visual representation of the character. One glyph can represent one character, such as a lowercase "b"; more than one character, such as the "fi" ligature, which is a single glyph that could represent two characters; or a nonprinting character, such as the space character.

When you want to print or display text, you generally refer to characters rather than glyphs. The Font Manager identifies an individual character by a **character code** and provides the glyph for that character to QuickDraw. Character codes for most character sets are single byte values between $00 and $FF; however, the character codes for some large character sets, such as the Japanese character set, are two bytes long. A font designer must supply a **missing-character glyph**—usually an empty rectangle (□)—for characters that are not included in the font. QuickDraw displays this glyph whenever the user presses a key for a character that is not in the font. The Font Manager does not use the missing-character glyph for nonprinting characters, such as the space character, that are included in the 'FONT', bitmapped font, and outline font resources.

Although most fonts assign the same glyphs to character code values $00 to $7F, there are differences in which glyphs are assigned to the remaining character codes. For example, the glyph assigned to byte value $F0 (⌘) in the Apple Standard Roman character set is not typically included in a font defined for a non-Apple software system. And different regions of the world require different glyphs for their typography, which makes it impossible for any one standard to be complete.

The **character-encoding** scheme was developed to manage the assignment of different glyphs to character codes in different fonts. It names each character and then maps that name into a character code in each font. PostScript fonts that use an encoding scheme that differs from the standard Apple encoding scheme can specify their glyph assignments in the encoding table of the font family resource, which is described in the section "The Style-Mapping Table," beginning on page 4-99. This table contains a collection of assignments of glyph names to character codes. For example, the PostScript name of the character "ñ" is "ntilde"; a font designer can specify in the encoding table that this character is assigned to character code $B9.

The Font Manager uses two types of glyphs: bitmapped glyphs and glyphs from outline fonts. A **bitmapped glyph** is a bitmap—a collection of bits arranged in rows and columns—designed at a fixed point size for a particular display device, such as a monitor or a printer. For example, after deciding that a glyph for a screen font should be so many pixels tall and so many pixels wide, a font designer carefully chooses the individual pixels that constitute the bitmapped glyph. A pixel is the smallest dot the screen can display. The font stores the bitmapped glyph as a picture for the display device.

A glyph from an outline font is a model of how a glyph should look. A font designer uses lines and curves rather than pixels to draw the glyph. The outline, a mathematical description of a glyph from an outline font, has no designated point size or display device characteristic (such as the size of a pixel) attached to it. The Font Manager uses the outline as a pattern to create bitmaps at any size for any display device.

Kinds of Fonts

Each glyph has some characteristics that distinguish it from other glyphs that represent the same character: for example, the shape of the oval, the design of the stem, or whether or not the glyph has a serif. If all the glyphs for a particular character set share certain characteristics, they form a typeface, which is a distinctly designed collection of glyphs. Each typeface has its own name, such as New York, Geneva, or Symbol. The same typeface can be used with different hardware, such as typesetting machines, monitors, or laser printers.

A **style** is a specific variation in the appearance of a glyph that can be applied consistently to all the glyphs in a typeface. Styles available on the Macintosh computer include plain, bold, italic, underline, outline, shadow, condensed, and extended. QuickDraw can add styles such as bold or italic to bitmaps, or a font designer can design a font in a specific style (for instance, Courier Bold).

A **font** refers to a complete set of glyphs in a specific typeface and style—and, in the case of bitmapped fonts, a specific size. **Bitmapped fonts** are fonts of the bitmapped font ('NFNT') resource type or 'FONT' resource type that provide an individual bitmap for each glyph in each size and style. Courier plain 10-point, Courier bold 10-point, and Courier plain 12-point, for example, are considered three different fonts. If the user requests a font that is not available in a particular size, QuickDraw can alter a bitmapped font at a different size to create the required glyphs. However, this generated bitmap often appears to be irregular in some way.

Outline fonts are fonts of the outline font ('sfnt') resource type that consist of glyphs in a particular typeface and style with no size restriction. TrueType outline fonts are outline fonts that use the Apple TrueType format. The Font Manager can generate thousands of point sizes from the same TrueType outline font: a single outline Courier font can produce Courier 10-point, Courier 12-point, and Courier 200-point.

Identifying Fonts

When multiple fonts of the same typeface are present in system software, the Font Manager groups them into **font families** of the font family ('FOND') resource type. Each font in a font family can be bitmapped or outline. Bitmapped fonts in the same family can be different styles or sizes. For example, an outline plain font for Geneva and two bitmapped fonts for Geneva plain 12-point and Geneva italic 12-point might make up one font family named Geneva, to which a user could subsequently add other sizes or styles.

A font has a **font name,** which is stored as a string such as "Geneva" or "New York". The font name is usually the same name as the typeface from which it was derived. If a font is not in plain style, its style becomes part of the font's name and distinguishes it from the plain style of that font: for example, "Palatino" and "Palatino Bold".

A **font family ID** is the resource ID for a font family. Because there are so many font families available for the Macintosh, many families have the same font ID. Therefore, to avoid confusion, when your application stores font references in a document, it should refer to fonts by name and not by number.

Font Measurements

Font designers use specific terms for the measurements of different parts of a glyph, whether outline or bitmapped. Figure 4-1 shows the terms used for the most frequently used measurements.

Figure 4-1   Terms for font measurements

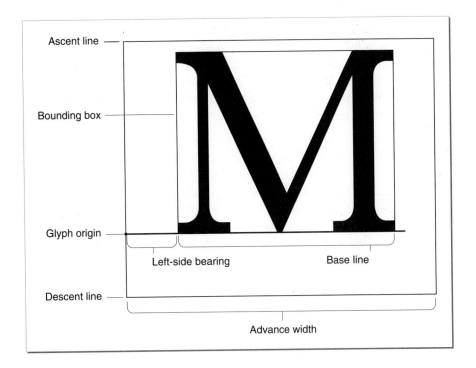

Note

The terms given here are based on the characteristics of the Roman script system, which is associated with most European languages and uses fonts that are meant to be read from left to right. Some other script systems use different definitions for some of these terms. However, QuickDraw always draws glyphs using the glyph origin and advance width measurement, even if the font is read from right to left. ◆

As shown in Figure 4-1, the bounding box of a glyph is the smallest rectangle that entirely encloses the pixels of the bitmap. The **glyph origin** is where QuickDraw begins drawing the glyph. Notice that there is some white space between the glyph origin and the visible beginning of the glyph: this is the left-side bearing of the glyph. The left-side bearing value can be negative, which lessens the spacing between adjacent characters. The **advance width** is the full horizontal measurement of the glyph as measured from its glyph origin to the glyph origin of the next glyph on the line, including the white space on both sides.

If all of the glyph images in the font were superimposed using a common glyph origin, the smallest rectangle that would enclose the resulting image is the **font rectangle.**

The glyphs of a **fixed-width font** all have the same advance width. Fixed-width fonts are also known as **monospaced fonts.** In Courier, a fixed-width font, the uppercase "M" has the same width as the lowercase "i". In a **proportional font,** different glyphs may have different widths, so the uppercase "M" is wider than the lowercase "i". For example, the proportionally spaced text "iMaGe" has a different appearance from the fixed-width version of the same string "iMaGe".

Most glyphs in a font appear to sit on the **base line,** an imaginary horizontal line. The **ascent line** is an imaginary horizontal line chosen by the font's designer that corresponds approximately with the tops of the uppercase letters in the font, because these are generally the tallest commonly used glyphs in a font. The ascent line is the same distance from the base line for all glyphs in the font. The **descent line** is an imaginary horizontal line that usually corresponds with the bottoms of descenders (the tails on glyphs like "p" or "g"), and it's the same distance from the base line for every glyph in the font. The ascent and descent lines are part of the font designer's recommendations about line spacing as measured from base line to base line. All of these lines are horizontal because Roman text is read from left to right, in a straight horizontal line.

For bitmapped fonts, the ascent line marks the maximum y-value and the descent line marks the minimum y-value used for the font. The y-value is the location on the vertical axis of each indicated line: the minimum y-value is the lowest location on the vertical axis and the maximum y-value is the highest location on the vertical axis. For outline fonts, a font designer can create individual glyphs that extend above the ascent line or below the descent line. The integral sign in Figure 4-2, for example, is much taller than the uppercase "M". In this case, the maximum y-value is more important than the ascent line for determining the proper line spacing for a line containing both of these glyphs. You can have the Font Manager reduce such oversized glyphs so that they fit between the ascent and descent lines. See "Preserving the Shapes of Glyphs," which begins on page 4-35, for details.

Figure 4-2 The ascent line and maximum y-value

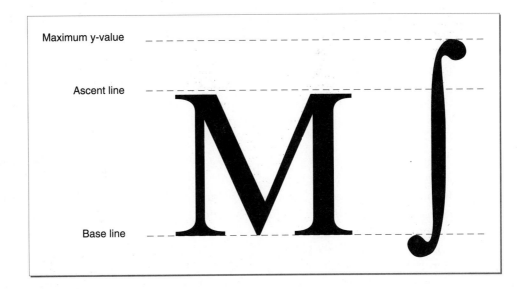

Font size (or *point size*) indicates the size of a font's glyphs as measured from the base line of one line of text to the base line of the next line of single-spaced text. In the United States, font size is traditionally measured in **points**, and there are 72.27 traditional points per inch. However, QuickDraw and the PostScript language define 1 point to be $1/72$ of an inch, so there are exactly 72 points per inch on the Macintosh.

Previously, the Font Manager required fonts to be less than or equal to 127 points in size, but this restriction no longer applies to any type of font. All bitmaps must fit on the QuickDraw coordinate plane; on a 72-dpi display device, fonts have an upper size limit of 32,767 points.

There is no strict typographical standard for defining a point size: it is often, but not always, the sum of the ascent, descent, and leading values for a font. Point size is used by a font designer to indicate the size of a font relative to other fonts in the same family. Glyphs from fonts with the same point size are not necessarily of the same height. This means that a 12-point font can exceed the measurement of 12 points from the base line of one line of text to the base line of the next.

Note
The Font Manager does not force fonts that are specified as having a certain point size to be of that size. This can have an impact when laying out text in your application, so you need to take it into account. You may need to determine the actual height of the text that you are displaying by using the QuickDraw routine `MeasureText` (which is described in the chapter "QuickDraw Text" in this book) rather than relying on the point size of the font. ◆

Leading (pronounced "LED-ing") is the amount of blank vertical space between the descent line of one line of text drawn using a font and the ascent line of the next line of single-spaced text drawn in the same font. The Font Manager returns the font's suggested leading, which is in pixels, in the `FontMetrics` procedure for both outline and bitmapped fonts. QuickDraw returns similar information in the `GetFontInfo` procedure. Although the designer specifies a recommended leading value for each font, you can always change that value if you need more or less space between the lines of text in your application. The **line spacing** for a font can be calculated by adding the value of the leading to the distance from the ascent line to the descent line of a single line of text.

Although each glyph has a specific advance width and left-side bearing measurement assigned to it, you can change the amount of white space that appears between glyphs. **Kerning** is the process of drawing part of a glyph so that it overlaps another glyph. The period in the top portion of Figure 4-3 stands apart from the uppercase "Y". In the bottom portion of the figure, the word and the period have been kerned: the period has been moved under the right arm of the "Y" and the glyphs of the word are closer. Kerning data—the distances by which pairs of specified glyphs should be moved closer together—is stored in the kerning tables of the different font resources. The kerning table of the outline font resource is described on page 4-84. The kerning table of the font family resource is described on page 4-106.

Figure 4-3   Unkerned text (top) and kerned text (bottom)

About Font Resources

This section provides a general description of the resources used for font management on the Macintosh, including

- an overview of each of the font resource types

- a brief history of the evolution of font resource use on the Macintosh

- information about font family IDs

Font Resource Types

Although the display of different fonts has always been an important aspect of using the Macintosh computer, the need for increased font availability and flexibility has expanded significantly since the introduction of the Macintosh. The built-in font management software has increased in power and complexity to accommodate the expanded needs of users. There used to be only one font resource type, of type 'FONT', but it is now out of date. There are now three additional font resource types.

- Bitmapped font ('NFNT') resources describe bitmapped fonts. These bitmapped font resources have an identical structure to the earlier 'FONT' resources, which they have replaced, but the bitmapped font resources add a more flexible font ID number scheme. This chapter assumes that you are working with bitmapped font resources rather than 'FONT' resources. The fields of the bitmapped font resource are described in the section "The Bitmapped Font ('NFNT') Resource," which begins on page 4-66.

- Outline font ('sfnt') resources describe outline fonts. The fields and tables of the outline font resource are described in the section "The Outline Font ('sfnt') Resource," which begins on page 4-72.

- Font family ('FOND') resources describe font families, including information such as which fonts are included in the family and the recommended width for a glyph at a given point size. The fields and tables of the font family resource are described in the section "The Font Family ('FOND') Resource," which begins on page 4-90.

Each font that you use is represented by either a bitmapped font or outline font resource (or a 'FONT' resource, in some cases), and each is part of a font family. A single font family can contain a mixture of bitmapped and outline fonts. The font association table in the font family resource refers to the font resources that the family includes.

Handles to font resources, found in data structures such as the global width table and the FMOutput record, can point to either kind of font.

A Brief History of Font Resource Use

The use of font resources has evolved considerably since the early days of the Macintosh computer. Knowing how the changes have evolved can help you understand their use in current software.

The earliest versions of Macintosh system software stored and created all font data in 'FONT' resources. Font families were created by storing a unique family ID in bits 7–14 of the resource ID of each font in the family. To name a font family, a designer included a 'FONT' resource with a point size of zero. This method severely restricted the range of both family IDs and point sizes.

With the introduction of the 128K ROM, there were two new resource types: the font family ('FOND') resource, which stores size-independent information for a font family, and the bitmapped font ('NFNT') resource, which has the same internal format as the 'FONT' resource, but can use any resource ID. Each font family resource names the family and contains a font association table, which consists of a number of individual font entries. Each entry contains a word for the font style, a word for the font size, and a word for the 'FONT' resource ID or bitmapped font resource ID of the font. This new scheme expanded the range of both font sizes and font family IDs to allow values from 0 to 32,767.

When TrueType outline font support was added for System 7, a new font resource type was added: the outline font resource, the internal format of which is substantially different from that of the bitmapped font resources.

Note

Because of the way that 'FONT' resources were originally constructed, a 'FONT' resource can exist independently of a font family resource. This is not true of bitmapped font and outline font resources, each of which must be associated with a font family resource. ◆

Font Family IDs

Several of the Font Manager routines and data structures make use of a font ID value, which is actually a font family ID value. The valid values for font family IDs, like the resource IDs of all script-specific resources, are subdivided into ranges for each script system, with half of the total range allocated for Roman font families and 512 IDs allocated for each other script system. The ranges for each non-Roman script system are listed in the appendix "International Resources" in this book.

The system software keeps track of two font family IDs. It uses the **system font** for drawing items such as system menus and system dialog boxes. The **application font** is the font that your application will use for text unless specified otherwise by you or the user. In Roman script systems, the system font is Chicago, the system font size is 12 points, and the application font is Geneva. In other script systems, the system and application fonts are defined in the international resources. The Script Manager variables smScriptSysFond, smScriptAppFond, smScriptSysFondSize, and smScriptAppFondSize, which define the system and application fonts and font sizes for each script system, are described in the "Script Manager" chapter in this book.

Font family ID values 0 and 1 are reserved. The system software always maps the system font to font 0 and the application font to font 1. The Roman font family ID range is itself subdivided as shown in Table 4-1.

Table 4-1   Subdivisions of Roman font family IDs

ID range	Use
2–255	Mostly older font families that use the 'FONT' resource numbering method. Do not use these IDs.
256–1023	Reserved numbers that should not be used for family IDs. The Font/DA Mover program uses this range of IDs to resolve font conflicts.
1024–16382	Commercial fonts. This is the range of IDs that all Roman font families should use.
16383	Reserved. Do not use.

The Font Manager defines constants for the system font and the application font, as well as for several of the older font IDs in the range from 2 to 255. These constants are presented here; however, you need to use the older font ID constants with caution, since most of them have become obsolete.

```
CONST
    systemFont = 0;         {the system font}
    applFont = 1;           {the application font}
    newYork = 2;            {hard-coded New York font ID}
    geneva = 3;             {hard-coded Geneva font ID}
    monaco = 4;             {hard-coded Monaco font ID}
    venice = 5;             {hard-coded Venice font ID}
    london = 6;             {hard-coded London font ID}
    athens = 7;             {hard-coded Athens font ID}
    sanFran = 8;            {hard-coded San Francisco font ID}
    toronto = 9;            {hard-coded Toronto font ID}
    cairo = 11;             {hard-coded Cairo font ID}
    losAngeles = 12;        {hard-coded Los Angeles font ID}
    times = 20;             {hard-coded Times Roman font ID}
    helvetica = 21;         {hard-coded Helvetica font ID}
    courier = 22;           {hard-coded Courier font ID}
    symbol = 23;            {hard-coded Symbol font ID}
    mobile = 24;            {hard-coded Mobile font ID}
```

The Script Manager provides functions that allow you to determine which script a font belongs to. For more information, see the chapter "Script Manager" in this book.

Restrictions on the Use of 'FONT' Resources

Since some older applications only work with 'FONT' resources, you might need to create a 'FONT' resource to retain compatibility. If this is necessary, you need to follow these restrictions on 'FONT' resources that are part of a font family.

■ The font name and family name must be identical.

■ The font ID and font family ID must be identical.

■ The resource ID of the font must equal the number produced by concatenating the font ID times 128 with the font size. Remember that fonts stored in 'FONT' resources are restricted to a point size of less than 128 and to a font ID in the range 0 to 255. The resource ID is computed by the following formula:

```
resourceID := (font ID * 128) + font size;
```

These restrictions ensure that both the 64K ROM found in older Macintosh computers and the newer 128K ROM versions of the Font Manager will associate the font family ID and point size with the proper corresponding 'FONT' resource ID, whether or not there is a family resource.

Font Resource Tables

The Font Manager takes care of the details of how fonts are stored in resources, reading the resource files when required and building internal representations of the data stored in them. The Font Manager provides routines to interact with fonts, meeting the font-manipulation needs of most application developers.

However, if you are developing an application that requires you to work directly with font resource data, you may need to understand how the font data is stored in resource files. Each font resource consists of a number of tables, each of which has a specific structure. Some of these tables are described in the section "Font Manager Reference" beginning on page 4-39, while others are described in the *TrueType Font Format Specification*.

About the Font Manager

QuickDraw draws text to the screen and, sometimes, to a printer. For its purposes, the glyphs that make up text are simply little images that make up a large, albeit well-ordered, image. QuickDraw uses size information, such as height and width, as it might use that information when arranging any graphic image.

The Font Manager, by contrast, keeps track of detailed font information such as the glyphs' character codes, whether fonts are fixed-width or proportional, and which fonts are related to each other by name.

When QuickDraw needs to draw some text in a particular font, it sends a request for that font to the Font Manager. The Font Manager finds the font or the closest match to it that is available, and sends the font back to QuickDraw with some information that QuickDraw uses for stylistic variations and layout.

Note
Although the terms *glyph* and *character code* have different meanings, QuickDraw routines and data structure fields often use the word *character* for both. Review the purpose of the routine or data structure you're using before deciding whether it handles character codes or glyphs. ◆

How QuickDraw Requests a Font

When your application calls a QuickDraw routine that does anything with text (for example, `DrawText` or `TextFont`), QuickDraw gets information from the Font Manager about the font specified in the current graphics port record and the individual glyphs of that font. The Font Manager performs any necessary calculations and returns the requested information to QuickDraw.

QuickDraw makes its request for font information using a font input record (of data type `FMInput`), which is described on page 4-40. This record contains the font family ID, the size, the style, and the scaling factors of the font request.

QuickDraw makes a font request by filling in a font input record and calling the `FMSwapFont` function. If your application needs to make a font request in the same way that QuickDraw does, you can call `FMSwapFont`. Since responding to a font request can be a lot of work, `FMSwapFont` has been optimized to return as quickly as possible if the request is for the same font as was most recently requested. Building the global width table, which is described in "How the Font Manager Calculates Glyph Widths" on page 4-23, is one of the more time-consuming tasks in this process, which is why the Font Manager maintains a cache of up to 12 width tables.

The Font Manager looks for the font family resource of the requested font and from that determines information about which font it can use to meet the request. If necessary, the Font Manager calls the Resource Manager to read the font.

For certain types of devices, such as a screen or the ImageWriter printer, the Font Manager uses the font characterization table from the device driver to determine any additional information that QuickDraw may need. The font characterization table contains information about the dots per vertical inch and dots per horizontal inch for that device, along with information about the different styles that the device can produce. Non-QuickDraw devices, such as the LaserWriter printer, return an error when the Font Manager requests their font characterization table.

▲ **WARNING**
Never assume that the font resource is a bitmapped font resource or outline font resource. If you need to read information from the resource, you should first call the Resource Manager `GetResInfo` procedure with the handle to the resource. The `GetResInfo` procedure is described in the Resource Manager chapter in *Inside Macintosh: More Macintosh Toolbox*. ▲

How the Font Manager Responds to a Font Request

The Font Manager returns the needed information to QuickDraw in a font output record (of data type `FMOutput`), which is described on page 4-41. This record contains a handle to the font resource that the `FMInput` record requested, information on how different stylistic variations affect the display of the font's glyphs, and the scaling factors.

When the Font Manager gets a request for a font in a font input record, it attempts to find a font family resource for the requested font family by following these steps:

1. The Font Manager checks the global variable `LastFOND`, which contains a handle to the last font family resource used.

2. If the last font family resource used is not the one requested, the Font Manager checks its memory cache, in which it keeps the last 12 width tables used.

3. If the font family resource is not in the cache, the Font Manager calls the Resource Manager `GetResource` function to get the resource.

If the font family resource is available, the Font Manager looks in the font family resource for the ID of the appropriate font resource to match the request. If a font family resource isn't available, the Font Manager follows these steps:

1. The Font Manager looks for a 'FONT' resource, since such resources can exist without being associated with a font family resource.

2. If it can't find a 'FONT' resource, the Font Manager looks for the application font.

3. If it can't find the application font, the Font Manager looks for a **neighborhood base font**, which is the font with the lowest font ID for that script system. For fonts numbered below 16384, this is font 0. For fonts above 16384, the Font Manager looks for the nearest font resource that is a multiple of 512 and less than the specified font value.

4. If it can't find a neighborhood font, the Font Manager gets the system font.

5. If it can't find the system font, the Font Manager always uses Chicago 12.

When responding to a font request, the Font Manager first looks for a font family resource of the specified size. It then looks for the stylistic variation that was requested. It does this by assigning weights to the various styles (for example, a weight of 8 for italic, 4 for bold) and then choosing the font whose style weight most closely matches the weight of the requested style.

If the Font Manager cannot find the exact font style that QuickDraw has requested, it uses the closest font style that it does find for that font and QuickDraw then applies the correct style to that font. For example, if an italic version of the requested font cannot be found, the Font Manager returns the plain version of the font and QuickDraw will slant the characters as it draws them. The QuickDraw styles are given in the QuickDraw data type Style, which includes the values bold, italic, underline, outline, shadow, condense, and extend.

With the additional complication of having both outline and bitmapped fonts available, this process can sometimes produce results other than those that you expected. The Font Manager can be set to favor either outline or bitmapped fonts when both are available to meet a request, as described in "Favoring Outline or Bitmapped Fonts" on page 4-35. The following scenario is one example of how the font that is selected can be a surprise:

1. You have specified that bitmapped fonts are to be preferred over outline fonts when both are available in a specific size.

2. The system software on which your application is running has the bitmap font Times 12 and the outline fonts Times, Times Italic, and Times Bold.

3. The user requests Times Bold 12.

4. The Font Manager chooses the bitmapped version of Times 12 and QuickDraw algorithmically smears it to create the bold effect.

There's not much that you can do about such situations except to be aware that telling the Font Manager to prefer one kind of a font over another has implications beyond what you might initially expect.

How the Font Manager Scales Fonts

Font scaling is the process of changing a glyph from one size or shape to another. The Font Manager and QuickDraw can scale bitmapped and outline fonts in three ways: changing a glyph's point size, modifying the glyph (but not its point size) for display on a different device, and altering the shape of the glyph.

For bitmapped fonts, the Font Manager does not actually perform scaling of the glyph bitmaps. Instead, the Font Manager finds an appropriate font and computes the horizontal and vertical scaling factors that QuickDraw must apply to scale the bitmaps. QuickDraw performs all modifications of bitmapped font glyphs.

The simplest form of scaling occurs when the Font Manager returns scaling factors for QuickDraw to change a glyph from one point size to another on the same display device. If the glyph is bitmapped and the requested font size is not available, there are certain rules the Font Manager follows to create a new bitmapped glyph from an existing one (see "The Scaling Process for a Bitmapped Font" on page 4-22). If the glyph is from an outline font, the Font Manager uses the outline for that glyph to create a bitmap.

Figure 4-4 shows how the Font Manager and QuickDraw scale a bitmapped font and an outline font from 9 points to 40 points for screen display. The sizes of the bitmapped fonts available to the Font Manager to create all 32 sizes were 9, 10, 12, 14, 18, and 24 points. A single glyph outline produces a smoother bitmap in all point sizes.

Figure 4-4   A comparison of scaled bitmapped and outline fonts

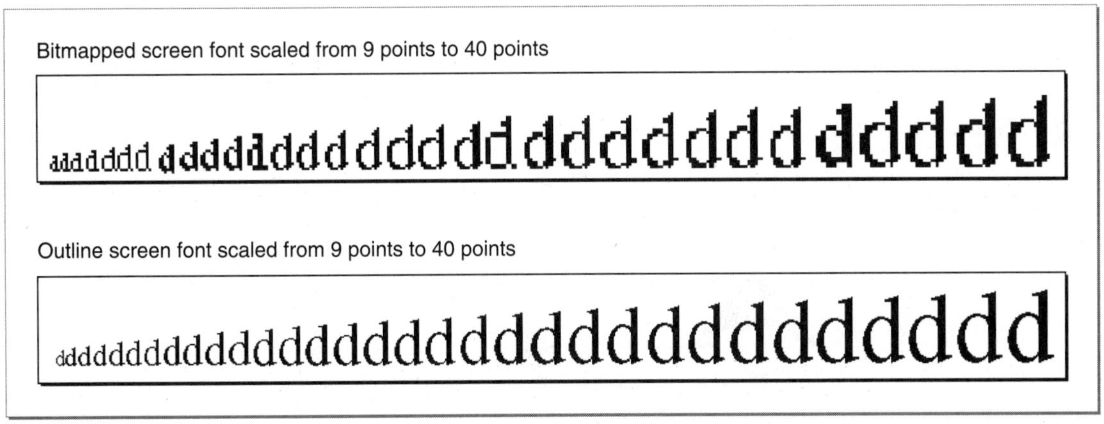

The Font Manager produces better results by scaling glyphs from outline fonts, because it changes the font's original outline to the new size or shape, and then makes the bitmap. Outlines give better results than bitmaps when scaled, because the outlines are intended for use at all point sizes, whereas the bitmaps are not.

The Font Manager also determines that a glyph must be scaled when moving it from one device to another device with a different resolution: for instance, from the screen to a printer. A bitmap that is 72 pixels high on a 72-dpi screen measures one inch, but on a 144-dpi printer it measures a half inch. In order to print a figure the same size as the original screen bitmap, QuickDraw needs a bitmap twice the size of the original. If there are no bitmaps available in twice the point size of the bitmap that appears on the screen, the Font Manager returns the proper scaling factors, and QuickDraw scales the original bitmap to twice its original size in order to draw it on the printer.

With some QuickDraw calls, your application can also use the Font Manager to explicitly scale a glyph by stretching or shrinking it, which changes the glyph from a familiar point size to something a little stranger—for example, a glyph that is 12 points high but as wide as a whole page of text. Your application tells the Font Manager how to scale a glyph using **font scaling factors,** which are represented as proportions or fractions that indicate how the Font Manager should scale the glyph in the vertical and horizontal directions. The ratio given by the font scaling factors determines whether the glyph grows or shrinks: if the ratio is greater than one, the glyph increases in size, and if it is less than one, the glyph decreases in size. If the font scaling factors are 1-to-1 (1/1) for both horizontal and vertical scaling, the glyph does not change size.

In some circumstances, the Font Manager finds a font and returns different scaling factors to QuickDraw. The scaling factors in a QuickDraw font request tell the Font Manager how much QuickDraw wants to scale the font, and the scaling factors returned by the Font Manager tell QuickDraw how much to actually scale the glyphs before drawing them.

In Figure 4-5, the font scaling factors are 2/1 in the horizontal direction and 1/1 in the vertical direction. The glyph stays the same height, but grows twice as large in width.

Figure 4-5   A glyph stretched horizontally

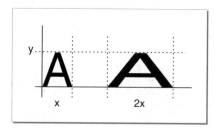

In Figure 4-6, the font scaling factors are 2/1 in the vertical direction and 1/1 in the horizontal direction. The glyph stays the same width, but grows to twice its original height.

Figure 4-6   A glyph stretched vertically

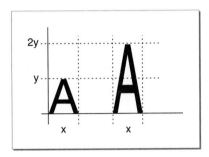

In Figure 4-7, the font scaling factors are 1/1 in the vertical direction and 1/2 in the horizontal direction. The glyph stays the same height but retains only half its width.

Figure 4-7   A glyph condensed horizontally

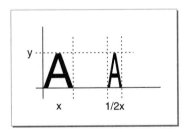

If the font scaling factors are 2/1 in both directions and the font is an outline font, then the Font Manager computes the size of the glyph as twice the specified size and QuickDraw draws the glyph. With bitmapped fonts, QuickDraw first looks for a bitmap at twice the size of the original before redrawing the glyph at the new point size.

Many routines use the value of the font scaling factors in order to calculate the best measurements for text in the current graphics port record. You can find the current horizontal and vertical scaling factors in the global variables `FScaleHFact` and `FScaleVFact`. The exact value of the font output scaling factors can be found by multiplying the value of the global width table's `hOutput` and `vOutput` fields by the values of the `hFactor` and `vFactor` fields, also of the global width table, respectively. The description of the global width table begins on page 4-43.

Font Manager

4

The Scaling Process for a Bitmapped Font

Although the Font Manager does not scale the glyph bitmaps of a bitmapped font, it does compute the scaling factors that QuickDraw uses to perform the scaling. The Font Manager computes scaling factors other than 1/1 when the exact point size requested is not available. Font scaling is the default behavior; however, you can disable it, as described below. When the Font Manager cannot find the proper bitmapped font that QuickDraw has requested and font scaling is enabled, it uses the following procedure:

1. The Font Manager looks for a font of the same font family that is twice the size of the font requested. If it finds that font, the Font Manager computes and returns to QuickDraw factors to scale it down to the requested size.

2. The Font Manager looks for a font of the same font family that is half the size of the font requested. If it finds that font, the Font Manager computes and returns to QuickDraw factors to scale it up to the requested size.

3. The Font Manager looks for a font of the same font family that is the next larger size of the font requested. If it finds that font, the Font Manager computes and returns to QuickDraw factors to scale it down to the requested size.

4. The Font Manager looks for a font of the same font family that is the next smaller size of the font requested. If it finds that font, the Font Manager computes and returns to QuickDraw factors to scale it up to the requested size.

5. If the Font Manager cannot find any size of that font family, it returns the application font, system font, or neighborhood base font, as described in the section "How the Font Manager Responds to a Font Request" beginning on page 4-17. The Font Manager computes and returns to QuickDraw the factors to scale that font to the requested size.

You can disable the scaling of bitmapped fonts in your programs by calling the `SetFScaleDisable` procedure. When the Font Manager cannot find the proper bitmapped font that QuickDraw has requested and font scaling is disabled, the Font Manager looks for a different font to substitute instead of scaling. The `SetFScaleDisable` procedure is described on page 4-59.

With scaling disabled, the Font Manager looks for a font with characters with the correct width, which may mean that their height is smaller than the requested size. The Font Manager returns this font and returns scaling factors of 1/1, so that QuickDraw does not scale the bitmaps. QuickDraw draws the smaller font, the widths of which produce the spacing of the requested font. This is faster than font scaling and accurately mirrors the word spacing and line breaks that the document will have when printed, especially if fractional character widths are used. Disabling and enabling of font scaling are described in the section "Using Fractional Glyph Widths and Font Scaling" on page 4-38.

Note
A font request made with scaling disabled does not necessarily return the same result as an identical request with scaling enabled. The widths are sure to be the same only if fractional widths are enabled, the font does not have a glyph-width table, and the font is a member of a family record with a family character-width table. Fractional widths and width tables are discussed in "How the Font Manager Calculates Glyph Widths" on page 4-23. ◆

The Scaling Process for an Outline Font

The Font Manager always scales an outline font in order to produce a bitmapped glyph in the requested size, regardless of whether font scaling for bitmapped fonts is enabled or disabled. An outline font is considered to be the model for all possible point sizes, so the Font Manager is not scaling it from one "real" size to a "created" size, the way it does with a bitmapped font; it is drawing the outline in the requested point size, so that it can then create the bitmapped glyph.

How the Font Manager Calculates Glyph Widths

Integer glyph widths are measurements of a glyph's width that are in whole pixels. Fractional glyph widths are measurements that can include fractions of a pixel. For instance, instead of a glyph measuring exactly 5 pixels across, it may be 5.5 pixels across. Fractional glyph widths allow the sizes of glyphs as stored by the Font Manager to be closer in proportion to the original glyphs of the font than integer widths allow. Fractional widths also make it possible for high-resolution printers to print with better spacing.

You can enable or disable the use of fractional glyph widths in your application, as described in "Using Fractional Glyph Widths and Font Scaling" on page 4-38. As a default, fractional widths are disabled to retain compatibility with older applications.

When using fractional glyph widths, the Font Manager stores the locations of glyphs more accurately than any actual screen can display: since screen glyphs are made up of whole pixels, QuickDraw cannot draw a glyph that is 5.5 pixels wide. The placement of glyphs on the screen matches the eventual placement of glyphs on a page printed by the high-resolution printers more closely, but the spacing between glyphs and words is uneven as QuickDraw rounds off the fractional parts. The extent of the distortion that is visible on the screen depends on the font point size relative to the resolution of the screen.

The Font Manager communicates fractional glyph widths to QuickDraw through the **global width table,** which is a data structure that is allocated in the system heap. The Font Manager fills in this table by accessing data from one of several places:

■ Integer glyph widths are taken from the width/offset table of the bitmapped font resource and the horizontal device metrics table of the outline font resource.

■ Fractional glyph widths are taken from the glyph-width table in the bitmapped font resource, the horizontal metrics table in the outline font resource, and the family glyph-width table in the font family resource.

The Font Manager looks for width data in the following sequence:

1. For a bitmapped font, it first looks for a font glyph-width table in the font record, which is the record used to represent in memory the data in a bitmapped font resource. For an outline font, it first looks for data in the horizontal metrics table. The width table for bitmapped fonts is described in the section "The Bitmapped Font ('NFNT') Resource," which begins on page 4-66. The width table for outline fonts is described in "The Horizontal Device Metrics Table" on page 4-78.

2. If it doesn't find this table, the Font Manager looks in the font family record for a family glyph-width table. The font family record is used to represent in memory the data in a font family resource. This is described in "The Family Glyph-Width Table" on page 4-98.

3. If the Font Manager doesn't find a family glyph-width table, it derives the global character widths from the integer widths contained in the width/offset table in the bitmapped font record, as described in "The Bitmapped Font ('NFNT') Resource" on page 4-66.

Note
If you need to use different widths than those returned by the global width table, you should change the values in the global width table only. You should never change any values in the font resources themselves. ◆

To use fractional glyph widths effectively, your application must get accurate widths when laying out text. Your application should obtain glyph widths either from the QuickDraw procedure `MeasureText` or by looking in the global width table. The `MeasureText` procedure is described in the chapter "QuickDraw Text" in this book. You can get a handle to the global width table by calling the `FontMetrics` procedure, which is described on page 4-54.

Synthetic Fonts

You may want your application to handle fonts that have a font depth greater than the normal 1-bit depth. (The font depth is the number of bits per pixel; it is specified in bits 2 and 3 of the `fontType` field of the bitmapped font resource, which is described beginning on page 4-70. The Font Manager supports font depths of 1, 2, 4, and 8 bits.) An advantage of using fonts with a larger font depth is that the Font Manager draws bitmapped fonts to the screen considerably faster if the font depth matches the screen depth specified by the user in the Monitors control panel.

The Font Manager can create a **synthetic font** from a `'FONT'` or bitmapped font resource (but not from an outline font resource) by expanding the 1-bit font into a font that matches the current screen depth. The Font Manager creates and maintains synthetic fonts internally, for performance reasons. However, if there is not enough memory to support synthetic fonts, the Font Manager displays a font at 1-bit depth, no matter what the current screen depth is. Font manufacturers can specify that the Font Manager should not expand a font by setting bit 14 of the `fontType` field of the bitmapped font resource.

How the Font Manager Renders Outline Fonts

Outline fonts are stored in an outline font (`'sfnt'`) resource as a collection of outline points. (Don't confuse these outline points with the points that determine point size, or the `Point` data type, which specifies a location in the QuickDraw coordinate plane.) The Font Manager calculates lines and curves between the points, sets the bits that make the bitmap, and then sends the bitmap to QuickDraw for display.

There are two types of outline points: **on-curve points** define the endpoints of lines, and **off-curve points** determine the curve of the line between the on-curve points. Two consecutive on-curve points define a straight line. To draw a curve, the Font Manager needs a third point that is off the curve and between the two on-curve points.

The Font Manager uses this parametric Bézier equation to draw the curves of the glyph from an outline font:

```
F(t) = (1 - t)² * A + 2t(1 - t) * B + t² * C
```

where t ranges between 0 and 1 as the curve moves from point A to point C. A and C are on-curve points; B is an off-curve point.

Font Manager

Figure 4-8 shows two Bézier curves. The positions of on-curve points A and C remain constant, while off-curve point B shifts. The curve changes in relation to the position of point B.

Figure 4-8   The effect of an off-curve point on two Bézier curves

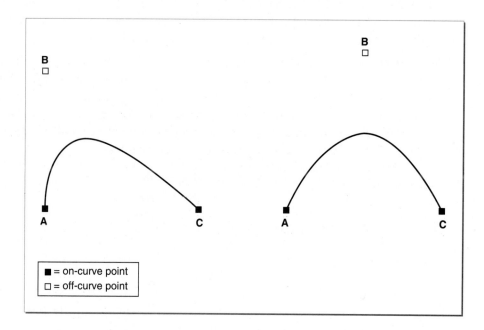

A font designer can use any number of outline points to create a glyph outline. These points must be numbered in a logical order, because the Font Manager draws lines and curves sequentially. This process produces a glyph such as the lowercase "b" in Figure 4-9.

Figure 4-9   An outline with points on and off the curve

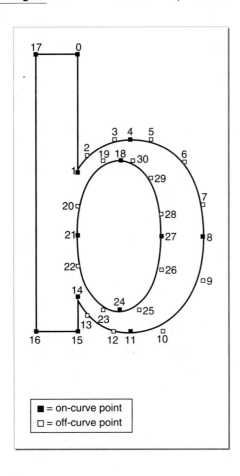

Font Manager

There are several groups of points in Figure 4-9 that include two consecutive off-curve points. For instance, points 2 and 3 are both off-curve. In this case, the Font Manager interpolates an on-curve point midway between the two off-curve points, thereby defining two Bézier curves, as shown in Figure 4-10. Note that this additional on-curve point is used for creation of the glyph only; the Font Manager does not alter the outline font resource's list of points.

Figure 4-10   A curve with consecutive off-curve points

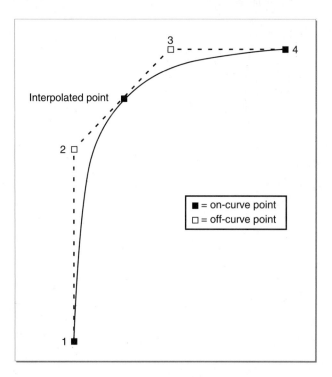

When the Font Manager has finished drawing a closed loop, it has completed one contour of the outline. The font designer groups the points in the outline font resource into contours. In Figure 4-9, the Font Manager draws the first contour in the glyph from point 0 to point 17, and the second contour from point 18 to the end, creating the glyph in Figure 4-11.

Figure 4-11   A glyph from an outline font

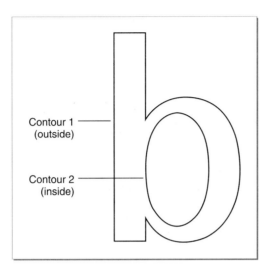

At this stage, the glyph does not have a fixed point size. Remember that point size is measured as the distance from the base line of one line of text to the base line of the next line of single-spaced text. Because the Font Manager has the measurements of the outline relative to the base line and ascent line, it can correlate the measurements with the requested point size and calculate how large the outline should be for that point size.

The Font Manager uses the contours to determine the boundaries of the bitmap for this glyph when it is displayed. For example, the Macintosh computer's screen is a grid made of pixels. The Font Manager fits the glyph, scaled for the correct size, to this grid. If the center of one section of this grid—comparable to a pixel or a printer dot—falls on a contour or within two contours, the Font Manager sets this bit for the bitmap.

Because there are two contours for the glyph in Figure 4-11, the Font Manager begins with pixels at the boundary marked by contour 1 and stops when it gets to contour 2. Some glyphs need only one contour, such as the uppercase "I" in some fonts. Others have three or more contours, such as the ✍ glyph from the ITC Zapf Dingbats font.

If the pixels (or dots) are tiny in proportion to the outline (when resolution is high or the point size of the glyph is large), they fill out the outline smoothly, and any pixels that jut out from the contours are not noticeable. If the display device has a low resolution or the point size is small, the pixels are large in relation to the outline. You can see in Figure 4-12 that the outline has produced an unattractive bitmap. There are gaps and blocky areas that would not be found in the high-resolution versions of the same glyph.

Figure 4-12 An unmodified glyph from an outline font at a small point size

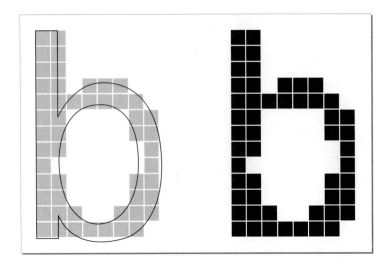

Because the size of the pixels or dots used by the display device cannot change, the outline should adapt in order to produce a better bitmap. To achieve this end, font designers include instructions in the outline font resource that indicate how to change the shape of the outline under various conditions, such as low resolution or small point size. The lowercase "b" outline in Figure 4-13 is the same one depicted in Figure 4-12, except that the Font Manager has applied the instructions to the figure and produced a better bitmapped glyph. These instructions are equivalent to "move these points here" or "change the angle formed by these points." A font designer includes programs consisting of these instructions in certain outline font resource tables, where the Font Manager finds them and executes them under specified conditions. Most applications do not need to use instructions; however, if you want to know more about them, see the book *TrueType Font Format Specification*.

Once the Font Manager has produced the outline according to the design and instructions, it creates a bitmap and sends the bitmap to QuickDraw, which draws it on the screen. The Font Manager then saves the bitmapped glyph in memory (caches it) and uses it the next time the user requests this glyph in this font at this point size.

Figure 4-13   An instructed glyph from an outline font

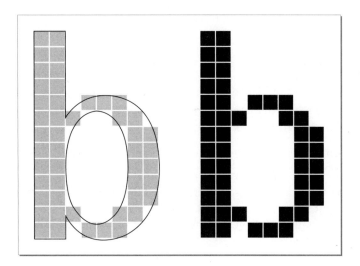

Using the Font Manager

You can use the Font Manager to take full advantage of the information that fonts contain about their widths and scaling possibilities and present this information to the user. The Font Manager provides routines that give your application control over selecting fonts and measuring the individual glyphs of the font. It also helps you to handle the coexistence of bitmapped and outline versions of fonts.

This section describes how to use the capabilities of the Font Manager in your program to handle tasks, including

- initializing the Font Manager
- adding font names and sizes to the Font menu
- storing font names in your documents
- getting font measurement information
- setting the Font Manager to favor outline or bitmapped fonts
- preserving or scaling the shapes of glyphs
- using the font tables
- getting the system or application font ID
- enabling and disabling font scaling and fractional width use

To initialize the Font Manager, you must call the `InitFonts` procedure. Before calling `InitFonts`, you need to initialize QuickDraw by calling the `InitGraf` procedure, which is described in *Inside Macintosh: Imaging*.

Adding Font Sizes and Names to the Menu

When you use the Menu Manager to add font sizes to a menu, make sure that you construct the menu so that it displays appropriate sizes for both bitmapped and outline fonts. Keep the following guidelines in mind:

■ Support all possible font sizes. The maximum point size on the QuickDraw coordinate plane is 32,767 points.

■ Provide a short list of the most useful font sizes. For the menu that your application uses to display font sizes, you shouldn't predefine a static list of sizes available to the user or allow the default to be every possible font size, because outline fonts can produce thousands of sizes.

■ Provide a method of increasing or decreasing the font size by one point at a time. You can add Larger and Smaller commands, which make choosing slightly different sizes for outline fonts easier for the user. Also, the user should be able to choose any possible point size at any time in a simple manner.

■ Place a check next to the current size.

■ Display available font sizes in outline style. For a bitmapped font, the `RealFont` function returns `TRUE` if the font is available in the requested point size and `FALSE` if the font is not; you can thereby determine which bitmapped fonts are available. For outline fonts, the `RealFont` function returns `TRUE` for almost any size. The font's designer may decide that there is a lower limit to the point sizes at which the font looks acceptable. The `RealFont` function returns `FALSE` for an outline font if the size requested is smaller than this lower limit.

Figure 4-14 shows one possible method for accomplishing these goals in a menu.

Figure 4-14   A sample Size menu and font size dialog box

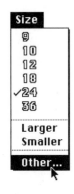

To create a menu that displays font names, use the `AddResMenu` procedure. This procedure ensures that any changes to the Font Manager do not affect your application

and that the menu that displays font names is not dependent on how fonts are stored in system software. The `AddResMenu` procedure is documented in the chapter "Menu Manager" in *Inside Macintosh: Macintosh Toolbox Essentials*.

Storing a Font Name in a Document

When presenting a font to a user, you should always refer to a font by name rather than by font family ID; this prevents several problems that can arise if you use the font family ID. One problem with identifying fonts by font family ID rather than by name is the plethora of font families available for the Macintosh computer. Many share the same font family ID, and even though the font the user wants is present in the System file, another font with the same ID may appear in a font menu. Another problem is that one font family may have different IDs on different computer systems, so that when the application opens the document using this font family on a different computer system, it can't find the proper font, even though it is available, and substitutes another.

If you've stored the name of the font in the document, you can find its font family ID by calling the `GetFNum` procedure, which is described on page 4-52. However, if the font isn't present in the system software when the user opens the document, `GetFNum` returns 0 for the ID. Since 0 is also the system font ID (or the neighborhood base font for the active script system), you need to double-check the name of the font from the document against the name of the system font, as illustrated in Listing 4-1.

Listing 4-1   Checking a font name against the system font name

```
FUNCTION MyGetFontNumber(fontName: Str255;
                         VAR fontNum: Integer): Boolean;
     {MyGetFontNumber returns in the fontNum parameter the number for }
     { the font with the given font name. If there's no such font, }
     { it returns FALSE.}

VAR
   systemFontName: Str255;

BEGIN
   GetFNum(fontName, fontNum);
   IF fontNum = 0 THEN
      BEGIN {either the font was not found, or it is the system font}
      GetFontName(0, systemFontName);
      GetFontNumber := EqualString(fontName, systemFontName, FALSE, FALSE);
      END{ if theNum was not 0, the font is available }
   ELSE
      GetFontNumber := TRUE;
END;
```

Storing a font's name rather than its ID is a more reliable method of finding a font, because the name, unlike the font family ID, does not change from one computer system to another. You may also want to store the checksum of a font (the sum of the values of the bytes in the font data) with its name, to be sure that the version of the font is the same on different computer systems. Listing 4-2 on page 4-76 provides a function for computing a checksum.

If the font versions are different—that is, if the checksums don't match—you should offer users the option of substituting for the font temporarily (until they can find the proper version of the font) or permanently (with another font that is currently available).

If you are developing software for use with non-Roman fonts and the font is not found (by a function such as MyGetFontNumber above), you can use the neighborhood base font rather than the system font. The neighborhood base font is the lowest font ID for a particular script.

Getting Font Measurement Information

You sometimes need to get font measurement information for the text font in the current graphics port. The Font Manager provides two routines for this purpose: FontMetrics and OutlineMetrics. In addition, QuickDraw provides font measurement information in the GetFontInfo procedure. You can use this information when arranging the glyphs of one font or several fonts on a line or to calculate adjustments needed when font size or style changes.

The FontMetrics procedure can be used on any kind of font, whether bitmapped or outline. It returns the ascent and descent measurements, the width of the largest glyph in the font, and the leading measurements. The FontMetrics procedure returns these measurements in a font metrics record (of data type FMetricRec), which allows fractional widths, whereas QuickDraw's GetFontInfo procedure returns a font information record (of data type FontInfo), which uses integer widths. In addition to these four measurements, the font metrics record includes a handle to the global width table, which in turn contains a handle to the font family resource for the current text font. The GetFontInfo procedure and the font information record are described in the chapter "QuickDraw Text" in this book. The global width table is described on page 4-36. The FontMetrics procedure and the font metrics record are described on page 4-54.

The OutlineMetrics function returns measurements for glyphs to be displayed in an outline font. The function returns an error if the text font in the current graphics port is any other kind of font. These measurements include the maximum y-values, minimum y-values, advance widths, left-side bearings, and bounding boxes. (For the definitions of these terms, see the section "About Fonts," which begins on page 4-6.) The OutlineMetrics function is described beginning on page 4-56.

For a font of a non-Roman script system that uses an associated font, the font measurements reflect combined values from the current font and the associated font. This is to accommodate the script system's automatic display of Roman characters in the associated font instead of the current font. See the discussion of associated fonts in the chapter "Introduction to Text on the Macintosh" in this book.

Favoring Outline or Bitmapped Fonts

When a document uses a font that is available as both an outline font and a bitmapped font, the Font Manager has to decide which kind of font to use. Its default behavior is to use the bitmapped font when your application opens the document. This behavior avoids problems with documents that were created on a computer system on which outline fonts were not available. See "How the Font Manager Responds to a Font Request" on page 4-17 for more information.

You can change this default behavior by calling the `SetOutlinePreferred` procedure. If you call `SetOutlinePreferred` with the `outlinePreferred` parameter set to `TRUE`, the Font Manager chooses outline fonts over bitmapped fonts when both are available.

The `GetOutlinePreferred` function returns a Boolean value that indicates which kind of font the Font Manager has been set to favor. You should call this function and save the value that it returns with your documents. Then, when the user opens a document in your application, you can call `SetOutlinePreferred` with that value to ensure that the same fonts are used.

If only one kind of font is available, the Font Manager chooses that kind of font to use in the document, no matter which kind of font is favored. You can determine whether the font being used in the current graphics port is an outline font by using the `IsOutline` function, which is described on page 4-61.

Preserving the Shapes of Glyphs

Most glyphs in an alphabetic font fit between the ascent line and the descent line, which roughly mark (respectively) the tops of the lowercase ascenders and the bottoms of the descenders. Bitmapped fonts always fit between the ascent line and descent line. One aim of outline fonts is to provide glyphs that are more accurate renditions of the original typeface design, and there are glyphs in some typefaces that exceed the ascent or descent line (or both). An example of this type of glyph is an uppercase letter with a diacritical mark: "N" with a tilde produces "Ñ". Many languages use glyphs that extend beyond the ascent line or descent line.

However, these glyphs may disturb the line spacing in a line or a paragraph. The glyph that exceeds the ascent line on one line may cross the descent line of the line above it, where it may overwrite a glyph that has a descender. You can determine whether glyphs from outline fonts exceed the ascent and descent lines by using the `OutlineMetrics` function. `OutlineMetrics` returns the maximum and minimum y-values for whatever glyphs you choose. You can get the values of the ascent and descent lines using the `FontMetrics` procedure. If a glyph's maximum or minimum y-value is greater than, respectively, the ascent or descent line, you can opt for one of two paths of action: you can change the way that your application handles line spacing to accommodate the glyph, or you can change the height of the glyph.

The Font Manager's default behavior is to change the height of the glyph, providing compatibility with bitmapped fonts, which are scaled between the ascent and descent lines. Figure 4-15 shows the difference between an "Ñ" scaled to fit in the same amount of space as an "N" and a preserved "Ñ". The tilde on the preserved "Ñ" clearly exceeds the ascent line.

Figure 4-15   The difference between a scaled glyph and a preserved glyph

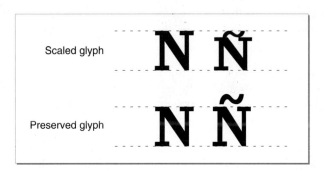

You can change this default behavior by calling the `SetPreserveGlyph` procedure. If you call `SetPreserveGlyph` with the `preserveGlyph` parameter set to `TRUE`, the Font Manager preserves the shape of the glyph intended by the font's designer.

The `GetPreserveGlyph` function returns a Boolean value that indicates whether or not the Font Manager has been set to preserve the shapes of glyphs from outline fonts. You should call this function and save the value that it returns with your documents. Then, when the user opens a document in your application, you can call `SetPreserveGlyph` with that value to ensure that glyphs are scaled appropriately.

Using Width Tables

When the Font Manager responds to a request to make a font available, the font resource is loaded into memory and the Font Manager allocates memory for various tables that are needed to use the font. To make font usage more efficient, the Font Manager maintains a cache of the tables for the most recently used fonts, so that it does not have to reread the resources and rebuild the tables more often than necessary. The Font Manager can cache the tables for up to 12 fonts. For outline fonts, the cached information includes the width tables and any bitmaps that have been created from the outlines.

The global width table contains the widths of all the glyphs of one font. If you are measuring text to be displayed on the screen, you can use the QuickDraw procedure `MeasureText` to determine glyph widths; however, if you are printing text and need to determine glyph widths, you have to use widths from the global width table. The `OutlineMetrics` function returns the individual widths of glyphs for an outline font and the `FontMetrics` procedure returns the width of the largest glyph in a bitmapped font. You can also directly access the global width table, which is defined by the `WidthTable` data type. This data type is described in the section "The Global Width Table" beginning on page 4-43.

To use the global width table, you can get a handle to it from the `FontMetrics` procedure, or you can use the handle stored in the global variable `WidthTabHandle`. The global variable `WidthPtr` contains a pointer to the global width table; however, this variable is reliable only immediately after a call to `FMSwapFont`. Like all pointers to data in handles, `WidthPtr` may become invalid after a call to the Memory Manager. In general, use the `WidthTabHandle` global variable instead of the `WidthPtr` global variable.

The global variable `WidthListHand` is a handle to a list of up to 12 handles to recently used width tables. You can scan this list and look for width tables that match the font family ID, size, and style of the font you wish to measure. If you reach a width-table handle that contains –1 in the `tabFont`, `fID`, and `aFID` fields, that width table is invalid. When you reach a handle that is equal to `NIL`, you have reached the end of the list.

IMPORTANT

Do not use the values from the global width table if your application is running on a computer on which non-Roman script systems are installed. You can check to see if a non-Roman script system is present by calling the `GetScriptManagerVariable` function with a selector of `smEnabled`; if the function returns a value greater than 0, at least one non-Roman script system is present and you need to call `MeasureText` to measure text that is displayed on the screen. Measuring text from a non-Roman script system for printing is handled by the printer driver. ▲

If your application directly manipulates data in a font resource (for example, if your application edits fonts), you may need to flush the Font Manager's cache, so that the cached information reflects any changes that your application makes. The `FlushFonts` function, which is described on page 4-66, erases all of the Font Manager's caches. The Font Manager then rebuilds the cache as new fonts are called into use again.

Normally, fonts are purgeable, which means that the space used for each font's resource information can be released from memory. You can temporarily prevent a font from being purged by locking it with a call to the `SetFontLock` procedure. A subsequent call to `SetFontLock` unlocks the font, allowing the Font Manager to purge it from memory. The `SetFontLock` procedure is described on page 4-65.

If you are calculating the amount of extra width that is added to a glyph as a result of adding a font style, you can choose how you want the Font Manager to determine the extra pixels needed. It can find the information in the style property field of the font family resource or from the style extra field in the Font Manager's internal tables. If the value of the global variable `FDevDisable` is 0, the Font Manager uses the style extra value from its internal tables; if `FDevDisable` is any other value, the Font Manager uses the value from the style property field, which is described on page 4-93.

Getting the System or Application Font ID

When your application does not allow the user to change the font, your application has to tell the Font Manager to use either the system font or the application font. You do this by passing either the systemFont constant or the applFont constant to the TextFont procedure, which is described in the chapter "QuickDraw Text" in this book. The Font Manager maps fonts with other resource IDs to these values, as described in the chapter "Script Manager" in this book.

If you need to know the true font family ID of the system font, you can call the GetSysFont function, which checks the global variable SysFontFam and returns that resource ID. Similarly, if you want to know the true font family ID of the application font, you can call the GetAppFont function or check the global variable ApFontID.

The global variable SysFontSize contains the point size of the current system font. If you call the TextSize procedure (which is described in the chapter "QuickDraw Text" in this book) with a value of 0, the default application font size is used. You can find the default system font size value by calling the GetDefFontSize function. If the default system font point size is set to 0, the Font Manager uses 12 as its value.

You can read more about the system and application fonts in the chapter "Introduction to Text on the Macintosh" in this book.

Using Fractional Glyph Widths and Font Scaling

Using fractional glyph widths allows the Font Manager to place glyphs on the screen in a manner that closely matches the eventual placement of glyphs on a page printer by high-resolution printers. (See "How the Font Manager Calculates Glyph Widths" on page 4-23.)

You can enable the use of fractional glyph widths with the SetFractEnable procedure. If you set the parameter fractEnable to TRUE, the Font Manager uses fractional glyph widths. If you set it to FALSE, the Font Manager uses integer glyph widths. The Font Manager sets the global variable FractEnable to FALSE by default. You can find out whether the Font Manager has used fractional widths in the calculations for the global width table or other tables by checking the value of the UsedFWidths global variable; if the value is nonzero, the Font Manager used fractional widths.

When a bitmapped font is not available in a specific size, the Font Manager can compute scaling factors for QuickDraw to use to create a bitmap of the requested size. You can set the Font Manager to compute scaling factors for bitmapped fonts by using the SetFScaleDisable procedure, which sets the value of the FScaleDisable global variable. If you set the fontScaleDisable parameter of this procedure to TRUE, the Font Manager disables font scaling.

When font scaling is disabled, the Font Manager responds to a request for a font size that is not available by returning a bitmapped font with the requested widths, which may mean that their height is smaller than the requested size. If you set it to FALSE, the Font Manager computes scaling factors for bitmapped fonts and QuickDraw scales the glyph bitmaps. The Font Manager sets the global variable FScaleDisable to FALSE by default. If the value of this global variable is FALSE, scaling is enabled. (See "The Scaling Process for a Bitmapped Font" on page 4-22.) If scaling is enabled, you can get the current horizontal and vertical scaling factors from the global variable FScaleHFact and FScaleVFact, respectively.

The Font Manager always scales an outline font, regardless of the value of the FScaleDisable global variable.

Fractional glyph widths and font scaling are also described in the chapter "QuickDraw Text" in this book.

Font Manager Reference

This section describes the data structures, routines, and resources provided by the Font Manager.

The "Data Structures" section shows the Pascal data structures used by the bitmapped font resource, the font family resource, and the Font Manager routines. Many, but not all of the tables in these resources have corresponding high-level data structures and detailed descriptions of the tables in each resource type are found in the sections dedicated to each resource.

The "Routines" section describes the routines you can use to get information about the font in the current graphics port record—such as its name, ID, and measurements for layout—or to get a handle to a specific font.

The resources sections describe the resources used by the Font Manager: the bitmapped font ('NFNT') resource, the outline font ('sfnt') resource, and the font family ('FOND') resource. You only need to understand most of the information in this section if you are writing an appliction, such as a font editor, that works directly with font resource data.

Equivalent declarations in the C language for the data structures and routines presented here can be found in the "Summary of the Font Manager" section at the end of this chapter.

Data Structures

This section describes the data structures that you use to provide information to the Font Manager.

You use the font input record to request a font that matches the specified characteristics. The actual characteristics of the font that the Font Manager chooses for the request are returned in a font output record.

You use the global width table record to find the widths of all glyphs in a font.

You use the font record to access the contents of a bitmapped font ('NFNT') resource and a font family record to access the contents of a font family ('FOND') resource. The font family resource includes a number of other tables, each of which has a corresponding data structure, including the font association table record, the bounding-box table record, the family glyph-width table record, the style-mapping table record, and the family kerning table record.

Although some of the resource tables have corresponding data types, many of them do not. If you need to define a data type for a table that does not yet have one defined for it, the resources sections contain pictures of each table, including the length of each table element.

The Font Input Record

The font input record, of data type FMInput, is used by QuickDraw to request a font from the Font Manager, as described in the section "How QuickDraw Requests a Font" on page 4-16. You can also use this data type to request a font with the FMSwapFont function, which is described on page 4-64.

```
TYPE FMInput =
PACKED RECORD
    family:    Integer;    {font family ID}
    size:      Integer;    {requested point size}
    face:      Style;      {requested font style}
    needBits:  Boolean;    {if bitmaps need to be constructed}
    device:    Integer;    {device driver ID}
    numer:     Point;      {scaling factor numerators}
    denom:     Point;      {scaling factor denominators}
END;
```

Field descriptions

family   The font family ID of the requested font.

size   The point size of the requested font.

face   The requested font style. The defined QuickDraw styles are bold, italic, underline, outline, shadow, condense, and extend.

needBits   Indicates whether QuickDraw draws the glyphs. If QuickDraw does not draw the glyphs, as is the case for measurement routines such as MeasureText, then the glyph bitmaps do not have to be read or constructed. If QuickDraw draws the glyphs and the font is contained in a bitmapped font resource, all of the information describing the font, including the bit image, is read into memory.

device   The high-order byte contains the device driver reference number. The low-order byte is reserved.

numer   The numerators of the vertical and horizontal scaling factors. (For more information about font scaling, see "How the Font Manager Scales Fonts" on page 4-19.) The `numer` field is of type `Point` and contains two integers: the first is the numerator of the ratio for vertical scaling and the second is the numerator of the ratio for horizontal scaling.

denom   The denominators of the vertical and horizontal scaling factors. (For more information about font scaling, see "How the Font Manager Scales Fonts" on page 4-19.) The `denom` field is of type `Point` and contains two integers: the first is the denominator of the ratio for vertical scaling and the second is the denominator of the ratio for horizontal scaling.

The Font Output Record

The font output record, of data type `FMOutput`, contains a handle to a font and information about font measurements. It is filled in by the Font Manager upon responding to a font request. You can request a font using the `FMSwapFont` function, which is described on page 4-64.

```
TYPE FMOutput =
PACKED RECORD
    errNum:     Integer;     {reserved for internal use}
    fontHandle: Handle;      {handle to font}
    bold:       Byte;        {for drawing of bold style}
    italic:     Byte;        {for drawing of italic style}
    ulOffset:   Byte;        {for drawing of underline style}
    ulShadow:   Byte;        {for drawing of underline shadow style}
    ulThick:    Byte;        {for drawing of underline thickness}
    shadow:     Byte;        {for drawing of shadow style}
    extra:      SignedByte;  {# of pixels added for styles}
    ascent:     Byte;        {ascent measurement of font}
    descent:    Byte;        {descent measurement of font}
    widMax:     Byte;        {maximum width of glyphs in font}
    leading:    SignedByte;  {leading value for font}
    fOutCurStyle:
                Byte;        {actual output font style}
    numer:      Point;       {scaling factor numerators}
    denom:      Point;       {scaling factor denominators}
END;
```

Field descriptions

errNum   Reserved for use by Apple Computer, Inc.

`fontHandle`	A handle to the font resource requested by the font input record, which may either be a bitmapped font or outline font resource. The bitmapped font is described in the section "The Bitmapped Font ('NFNT') Resource," which begins on page 4-66. The outline font is described in the section "The Outline Font ('sfnt') Resource," which begins on page 4-72.
`bold`	Modifies how QuickDraw applies the bold style on the screen and on raster printers. Other display devices may handle styles differently.
`italic`	Modifies how QuickDraw applies the italic style on the screen and on raster printers. Other display devices may handle styles differently.
`ulOffset`	Modifies how QuickDraw applies the underline style on the screen and on raster printers. Other display devices may handle styles differently.
`ulShadow`	Modifies how QuickDraw applies the underline shadow style on the screen and on raster printers. Other display devices may handle styles differently.
`ulThick`	Modifies how QuickDraw applies the thickness of the underline style on the screen and on raster printers. Other display devices may handle styles differently.
`shadow`	Modifies how QuickDraw applies the shadow style on the screen and on raster printers. Other display devices may handle styles differently.
`extra`	The number of pixels by which the styles have widened each glyph.
`ascent`	The ascent measurement of the font. Any algorithmic styles or stretching that may be applied to the font are not taken into account for this value.
`descent`	The descent measurement of the font. Any algorithmic styles or stretching that may be applied to the font are not taken into account for this value.
`widMax`	The maximum width of the font. Any algorithmic styles or stretching that may be applied to the font are not taken into account for this value.
`leading`	The leading assigned to the font. Any algorithmic styles or stretching that may be applied to the font are not taken into account for this value.
`fOutCurStyle`	The actual style being made available for QuickDraw's text drawing, as opposed to the requested style.
`numer`	The numerators of the vertical and horizontal scaling factors. (For more information about font scaling, see "How the Font Manager Scales Fonts" on page 4-19.) The `numer` field is of type `Point` and contains two integers: the first is the numerator of the ratio for vertical scaling and the second is the numerator of the ratio for horizontal scaling.

denom The denominators of the vertical and horizontal scaling factors. (For more information about font scaling, see "How the Font Manager Scales Fonts" on page 4-19.) The denom field is of type Point and contains two integers: the first is the denominator of the ratio for vertical scaling and the second is the denominator of the ratio for horizontal scaling.

The bold, italic, ulOffset, ulShadow, ulThick, and shadow values are all used to communicate to QuickDraw how to modify the way it renders each stylistic variation. Each byte value is taken from the font characterization table of the printer driver and is used by QuickDraw when it draws to a screen or raster printer.

The ascent, descent, widMax, and leading values can all be different in this record than the corresponding values in the FontInfo record that is produced by the GetFontInfo function in QuickDraw. This is because GetFontInfo takes into account any algorithmic styles or stretching that QuickDraw performs, while the Font Manager routines do not.

The numer and denom values are used to designate how font scaling is to be done. The values for these fields in the font output record can be different than the values specified in the font input record. For more information about font scaling, see the section "How the Font Manager Scales Fonts," which begins on page 4-19.

The Global Width Table

The global width table record, of data type WidthTable, contains the widths of all the glyphs of one font. The font family, point size, and style of this font are specified in this table. Your application should use the widths found in the global width table for placement of glyphs and words both on the screen and on the printed page. You can use the FontMetrics procedure, described on page 4-54, to get a handle to the global width table. However, you should not assume that the table is the same size as shown in the record declaration; it may be larger because of some private system-specific information that is attached to it.

```
Type WidthTable =
PACKED RECORD
    tabData: ARRAY [1..256] OF Fixed;
                            {character widths}
    tabFont:    Handle;     {font record used to build table}
    sExtra:     LongInt;    {extra line spacing}
    style:      LongInt;    {extra line spacing due to style}
    fID:        Integer;    {font family ID}
    fSize:      Integer;    {font size request}
    face:       Integer;    {style (face) request}
    device:     Integer;    {device requested}
    inNumer:    Point;      {scale factors requested}
    inDenom:    Point;      {scale factors requested}
    aFID:       Integer;    {actual font family ID for table}
```

```
       fHand:      Handle;       {family record used to build up table}
       usedFam:    Boolean;      {used fixed-point family widths}
       aFace:      Byte;         {actual face produced}
       vOutput:    Integer;      {vertical scale output value}
       hOutput:    Integer;      {horizontal scale output value}
       vFactor:    Integer;      {vertical scale output value}
       hFactor:    Integer;      {horizontal scale output value}
       aSize:      Integer;      {size of actual font used}
       tabSize:    Integer;      {total size of table}
   END;
```

Field descriptions

tabData	The widths for the glyphs in the font, in standard 32-bit fixed-point format. If a glyph is missing in the font, its entry contains the width of the missing-character glyph.
tabFont	A handle to the font resource used to build this table.
sExtra	The average number of pixels by which QuickDraw widens each space in a line of text.
style	The average number of pixels by which QuickDraw widens a line of text after applying a style.
fID	The font family ID of the font represented by this table. This is the ID that was used in the request to build the table. It may be different from the ID of the font family that was used, which is indicated by the aFID field.
fSize	The point size that was originally requested for the font represented by this table. The actual size used is specified in the aSize field.
face	The font style that was originally requested for the font represented by this table. The actual style used is specified in the aFace field.
device	The device ID of the device on which these widths may be used.
inNumer	The numerators of the vertical and horizontal scaling factors. The numer field is of type Point and contains two integers: the first is the numerator of the ratio for vertical scaling and the second is the numerator of the ratio for horizontal scaling.
inDenom	The denominators of the vertical and horizontal scaling factors. The denom field is of type Point and contains two integers: the first is the denominator of the ratio for vertical scaling and the second is the denominator of the ratio for horizontal scaling.
aFID	The font family ID of the font family actually used to build this table. If the Font Manager could not find the font requested, this value may be different from the value of the fID field.
fHand	The handle to the font family resource used to build this table.
usedFam	Set to TRUE if the fixed-point family glyph widths were used rather than integer glyph widths.
aFace	The font style of the font whose widths are contained in this table.

`vOutput`	The factor by which glyphs are to be expanded vertically in the current graphics port. This is a 16-bit fixed-point number, with the integer part in the high-order byte and a fractional part in the low-order byte.
`hOutput`	The factor by which glyphs are to be expanded horizontally in the current graphics port. This is a 16-bit fixed-point number, with the integer part in the high-order byte and a fractional part in the low-order byte.
`vFactor`	The factor by which widths of the chosen font, after a style has been applied, have been increased vertically in the current graphics port. This is a 16-bit fixed-point number, with the integer part in the high-order byte and a fractional part in the low-order byte. The value of the `vFactor` field is not used by the Font Manager.
`hFactor`	The factor by which widths of the chosen font, after a style has been applied, have been increased horizontally in the current graphics port. This is a 16-bit fixed-point number, with the integer part in the high-order byte and a fractional part in the low-order byte.
`aSize`	The size of the font actually used to build this table. Both the point size and the font used to build this table may be different from the requested point size and font. If font scaling is disabled, the Font Manager may use a size different from the size requested and add more or less space to approximate the appearance of the font requested. See "The Scaling Process for a Bitmapped Font" on page 4-22 for more information.
`tabSize`	The total size of the global width table.

Multiplying the values of the `hOutput` and `vOutput` fields by the values of the `hFactor` and `vFactor` fields, respectively, gives the font scaling. (Because the value of the `vFactor` field is ignored, the Font Manager multiplies the value of the `vOutput` field by 1.) The product of the value of the `hOutput` field and an entry in the global width table is the scaled width for that glyph.

The Font Manager gathers data for the global width table from one of three data structures:

1. The Font Manager looks in the font resource for a table that stores fractional glyph widths. For bitmapped fonts, the Font Manager uses the glyph-width table of the bitmapped font resource (described on page 4-70). For outline fonts, the Font Manager uses the advance width and left-side bearing values in the horizontal metrics table of the outline font (described on page 4-83). In both cases, the values are stored in 16-bit fixed format, with the integer part in the high-order byte and the fractional part in the low-order byte.

2. If there is no glyph-width table in the font resource, the Font Manager looks for the font family's glyph-width table in the font family resource, which contains fractional widths for a hypothetical 1-point font. The Font Manager calculates the actual values by multiplying these widths by the requested font size. The font family's glyph-width table is described in "The Family Glyph-Width Table" on page 4-98.

3. If there is no glyph-width table in the font family resource, and if the font is contained in a bitmapped font resource, the Font Manager derives the glyph widths from the

4

Font Manager

integer widths contained in the glyph-width table of the bitmapped font resource, which is described on page 4-70. There is no corresponding table for the outline font resource.

Your application should obtain glyph widths either from the global width table or from the QuickDraw procedure MeasureText. The MeasureText procedure works only with text to be displayed on the screen, not with text to be printed. You can get the individual widths of glyphs of an outline font using the OutlineMetrics function. The FontMetrics procedure returns only the width of the largest glyph in a font contained in a bitmapped font resource.

IMPORTANT

Do not use the values from the global width table if your application is running on a computer on which non-Roman script systems are installed. You can check to see if a non-Roman script system is present by calling the GetScriptManagerVariable function with a selector of smEnabled; if the function returns a value greater than 0, at least one non-Roman script system is present and you need to call MeasureText to measure text that is displayed on the screen. Measuring text from a non-Roman script system for printing is handled by the printer driver. ▲

For more information about the MeasureText procedure, see the chapter "QuickDraw Text" in this book. The FontMetrics procedure is described on page 4-54 and the OutlineMetrics function is described on page 4-56.

The Font Record

The font record, of data type FontRec, describes the format of the bitmapped font ('NFNT') resource (and, likewise, the 'FONT' resource). It is shown here as a guide to the format of the resource. The font record is not used directly by any Font Manager routines.

```
TYPE FontRec =
RECORD
    fontType:    Integer;    {font type}
    firstChar:   Integer;    {character code of first glyph}
    lastChar:    Integer;    {character code of last glyph}
    widMax:      Integer;    {maximum glyph width}
    kernMax:     Integer;    {maximum glyph kern}
    nDescent:    Integer;    {negative of descent}
    fRectWidth:  Integer;    {width of font rectangle}
    fRectHeight: Integer;    {height of font rectangle}
    owTLoc:      Integer;    {offset to width/offset table}
    ascent:      Integer;    {maximum ascent measurement}
    descent:     Integer;    {maximum descent measurement}
    leading:     Integer;    {leading measurement}
    rowWords:    Integer;    {row width of bit image in 16-bit wds}
END;
```

The fields of the font record are described in the section "The Bitmapped Font ('NFNT') Resource," beginning on page 4-66.

The Font Family Record

The font family record, of data type `FamRec`, describes the format of the font family (`'FOND'`) resource. It is shown here as a guide to the format of the resource. The font family record is not used directly by any Font Manager routines.

```
TYPE FamRec =
RECORD
    ffFlags:    Integer;    {flags for family}
    ffFamID:    Integer;    {family ID number}
    ffFirstChar:Integer;    {ASCII code of first character}
    ffLastChar: Integer;    {ASCII code of last character}
    ffAscent:   Integer;    {maximum ascent for 1-pt font}
    ffDescent:  Integer;    {maximum descent for 1-pt font}
    ffLeading:  Integer;    {maximum leading for 1-pt font}
    ffWidMax:   Integer;    {maximum glyph width for 1-pt font}
    ffWTabOff:  LongInt;    {offset to family glyph-width table}
    ffKernOff:  LongInt;    {offset to kerning table}
    ffStylOff:  LongInt;    {offset to style-mapping table}
    ffProperty: ARRAY [1..9] OF Integer;
                            {style properties info}
    ffIntl:     ARRAY [1..2] OF Integer;
                            {for international use}
    ffVersion:  Integer;    {version number}
END;
```

The fields of the font family record are described in the section "The Font Family ('FOND') Resource," beginning on page 4-90.

The Font Association Table Record

The font association table record, which is part of the font family resource, maps a point size and style to a specific font that is part of the family. The table record, of data type `FontAssoc`, consists of a count of the entries in the table and is followed by the entry records.

```
TYPE FontAssoc =
RECORD
    numAssoc:   Integer;    {number of entries - 1}
    {entries:   ARRAY[0..n] of AsscEntry;}
END;
```

Each entry in the font association table is a font association entry record, of data type `AsscEntry`.

```
TYPE AsscEntry =
RECORD
    fontSize:   Integer;    {point size of font}
    fontStyle:  Integer;    {style of font}
    fontID:     Integer;    {font resource ID}
END;
```

The fields of the font association table and font association table entry record are described in the section "The Font Association Table," beginning on page 4-95.

The Family Glyph-Width Table Record

The font family glyph-width table record, which is part of the font family resource, is used to specify glyph widths for the font family on a per-style basis. The table record, of data type `WidTable`, consists of a count of the entries in the table and is followed by the entry records.

```
TYPE WidTable =
RECORD
    numWidths:  Integer;    {number of entries - 1}
END;
```

Each entry in the family glyph-width table is a family glyph-width table entry record, of data type `WidEntry`, which specifies a style and a variable length array of glyph-width values.

```
TYPE WidEntry =
RECORD
    widStyle:   Integer;    {style code}
    {widths:    ARRAY[0..n] of Fixed;}
END;
```

The fields of the family glyph-width table and family glyph-width table entry records are described in the section "The Family Glyph-Width Table," beginning on page 4-98.

The Style-Mapping Table Record

The style-mapping table record, which is part of the font family resource, provides information that is used by printer drivers to implement font styles. Each font family can have its own character encoding and its own set of font suffix names for style designations. Each style of a font has its own name, typically created by adding a style suffix to the base name of the font, as described in the section "The Style-Mapping Table" beginning on page 4-99. The table record, of data type `StyleTable`, provides information about the font class and is followed by the font name suffix subtable and the font glyph-encoding subtable.

```
TYPE StyleTable =
RECORD
    fontClass:  Integer;      {font class of this font family}
    offset:     LongInt;      {offset to glyph-encoding subtable}
    reserved:   LongInt;      {reserved}
    indexes:    PACKED ARRAY [0..47] OF SignedByte;
                              {indexes into the font suffix name }
                              { table that follows this table}
END;
```

The font suffix name subtable record, of data type `NameTable`, contains the base name and suffixes for a font family.

```
TYPE NameTable =
RECORD
    stringCount:   Integer;   {string count}
    baseFontName:  Str255;    {base font name}
    {suffix strings}          {strings}
END;
```

The fields of the style-mapping table and font suffix name subtable are described in the section "The Style-Mapping Table," beginning on page 4-99.

The Font Family Kerning Table Record

The font family kerning table record, which is part of the font family resource, contains a number of kerning subtable entries, with different subtables for different stylistic variations. The table record, of data type `KernTable`, consists of a count of the entries in the table and is followed by the entry records.

```
TYPE KernTable =
RECORD
    numKerns:  Integer;       {number of subtable entries}
    {kernPairs: ARRAY[0..n] of KernEntry}
END;
```

Each kerning subtable record entry, of data type `KernEntry`, contains kerning pair records for a specific stylistic variation of the font family. It is followed by the kerning pair records.

```
TYPE KernEntry =
RECORD
    kernStyle:  Integer; {kern style}
    kernLength: Integer; {entry length}
    {kernRec:   ARRAY[0..n] of kernPair}
                            {the kerning data records}
END;
```

Each kerning pair record, of data type `KernPair`, specifies a kerning value for a pair of glyphs. Each glyph in the pair is specified by its ASCII character code.

```
TYPE KernPair =
RECORD
    kernFirst:  CHAR;    {Code of 1st character of kerned pair}
    kernSecond: CHAR;    {Code of 2nd character of kerned pair}
    kernWidth:  Integer; {kerning value in 1pt fixed format}
END;
```

The fields of the kerning table, kerning subtable entry, and kerning pair records are described in the section "The Font Family Kerning Table," beginning on page 4-106.

Routines

This section describes the routines you use to initialize the Font Manager and to get information about a font, such as its name, ID, or measurements. It also describes the routines you use to get a handle to a font and to control aspects of the way the Font Manager manipulates fonts, such as font scaling and fractional widths.

▲ **WARNING**
Do not change any data in a font or in any of the font data structures or global variables (except where expressly noted). ▲

Initializing the Font Manager

Typically, the Font Manager has already been initialized when your application opens. However, you should call the `InitFonts` procedure before you call any Font Manager or QuickDraw text routines, just to be sure.

InitFonts

The `InitFonts` procedure initializes the Font Manager.

```
PROCEDURE InitFonts;
```

DESCRIPTION

If the system font isn't already in memory, the `InitFonts` procedure reads it into memory. Call this procedure once, after calling the `InitGrafs` procedure and before calling any other Font Manager routines or any Toolbox routine that calls the Font Manager.

ASSEMBLY–LANGUAGE INFORMATION

The trap macro for the `InitFonts` procedure is

Trap macro

`_InitFonts`

Getting Font Information

The Font Manager provides three routines that allow you to get basic information about a font. The `GetFontName` procedure gets the name of a font family with a specified ID, and the `GetFNum` procedure gets the font family ID for a font with a specified name. The `RealFont` function tells you whether a font is available in a specific point size.

GetFontName

The `GetFontName` procedure gets the name of a font family that has a specified family ID number.

```
PROCEDURE GetFontName (familyID: Integer; VAR theName: Str255);
```

familyID   The font family ID.

theName   On output, this parameter contains the font family name for the font family specified in `familyID`.

DESCRIPTION

Given a font family ID, the `GetFontName` procedure returns, in the parameter `theName`, the name of the font family. If the font specified in the `familyID` parameter does not exist, `theName` contains an empty string.

The trap macro for the GetFontName procedure is

Trap macro

_GetFontName

GetFNum

The GetFNum procedure gets the font family ID for a specified font family name.

```
PROCEDURE GetFNum (theName: Str255; VAR familyID: Integer);
```

theName   The font family name.

familyID   On output, this parameter contains the font family ID for the font family
             specified in theName.

DESCRIPTION

Given a font name, the GetFNum procedure returns, in the familyID parameter, the
font family ID for the font family. If the font specified in the parameter theName does
not exist, familyID contains 0.

ASSEMBLY-LANGUAGE INFORMATION

The trap macro for the GetFNum procedure is

Trap macro

_GetFNum

RealFont

The RealFont function determines whether a font is available or is intended for use in a
specified size.

```
FUNCTION RealFont (fontNum: Integer; size: Integer): Boolean;
```

fontNum   The font family ID.

size   The font size requested.

DESCRIPTION

The RealFont function returns TRUE if the requested size of a font is available. RealFont first checks for a bitmapped font from the specified family. If one is not available, RealFont checks next for an outline font. If neither kind of font is available, RealFont returns FALSE.

If an outline font exists for the requested font family, RealFont normally considers the font to be available in any requested size; however, the font designer can include instructions in the font that outlines should not be used at certain point sizes, in which case the RealFont function will consider the font unavailable and return FALSE. The Font Manager determines whether the size is valid by testing the value of the smallest readable size element of the font family header table, which is described in "The Font Header Table," beginning on page 4-79.

ASSEMBLY–LANGUAGE INFORMATION

The trap macro for the RealFont function is

Trap macro

_RealFont

Using the Current, System, and Application Fonts

The GetDefFontSize, GetSysFont, and GetAppFont functions return the current values of the global variables that contain the default size of the system font, the ID number of the system font, and the ID number of the application font.

GetDefFontSize

The GetDefFontSize function determines the default size of the system font.

```
FUNCTION GetDefFontSize: Integer;
```

DESCRIPTION

The GetDefFontSize function returns the current value of the global variable SysFontSize if that value is not 0. If the value of SysFontSize is 0, GetDefFontSize returns 12 as the default font size.

At system startup, the value of SysFontSize is set to 0.

SEE ALSO

You can determine the preferred size for either the system font or the application font of any enabled script system by calling the GetScriptManagerVariable function. See the chapter "Script Manager" in this book.

GetSysFont

The `GetSysFont` function determines the font family ID of the current system font.

```
FUNCTION GetSysFont: Integer;
```

DESCRIPTION

The `GetSysFont` function returns the current value of the global variable `SysFontFam`, which is the font family ID of the current system font. This is the font family ID that has been mapped to 0 by the system software.

GetAppFont

The `GetAppFont` function returns the font family ID of the current application font.

```
FUNCTION GetAppFont: Integer;
```

DESCRIPTION

The `GetAppFont` function returns the current value of the global variable `ApFontID`, which is the font family ID of the current application font. This is the font family ID that has been mapped to 1 by the system software.

Getting the Characteristics of a Font

The `FontMetrics` procedure and the `OutlineMetrics` function both return font measurement information. The `FontMetrics` procedure returns the ascent and descent measurements, width of the largest glyph, and leading measurements for either a bitmapped or an outline font. The `OutlineMetrics` function returns measurements for text to be written in an outline font.

FontMetrics

The `FontMetrics` procedure gets fractional measurements for the font, size, and style specified in the current graphics port.

```
PROCEDURE FontMetrics (VAR theMetrics: FMetricRec);
```

`theMetrics`
> A font metrics record that contains the font measurement information, in fractional values.

DESCRIPTION

The FontMetrics procedure returns measurements for the ascent, descent, leading, and width of the largest glyph in the font for the font, size, and style specified in the current graphics port. FontMetrics returns this information in a font metrics record.

The font metrics record (of data type FMetricRec) contains a handle to the global width table, which in turn contains a handle to the associated font family resource for the current font (the font in the current graphics port). It also contains the values of four measurements for the current font.

```
Type FMetricRec =
RECORD
    ascent: Fixed;      {baseline to top}
    descent: Fixed;     {baseline to bottom}
    leading: Fixed;     {leading between lines}
    widMax: Fixed;      {maximum glyph width}
    wTabHandle: Handle; {handle to global width table}
END;
```

Field descriptions

ascent	The measurement from the baseline to the ascent line of the font.
descent	The measurement from the baseline to the descent line of the font.
leading	The measurement from the descent line to the ascent line below it.
widMax	The width of the largest glyph in the font.
wTabHandle	A handle to the global width table.

You can determine the line height, in pixels, by adding the values of the ascent, descent, and leading fields of the font metrics record.

The FontMetrics procedure is similar to QuickDraw's GetFontInfo procedure, except that FontMetrics returns fractional values for greater accuracy in high-resolution printing. FontMetrics also does not take into account any additional widths that are added by QuickDraw when it applies styles to the glyphs in a font.

ASSEMBLY–LANGUAGE INFORMATION

The trap macro for the FontMetrics procedure is

Trap macro

_FontMetrics

SEE ALSO

The GetFontInfo procedure is described in the chapter "QuickDraw Text" in this book.

4

Font Manager

OutlineMetrics

The OutlineMetrics function gets font measurements for a block of text to be drawn in a specified outline font.

```
FUNCTION OutlineMetrics (byteCount: Integer; textPtr: UNIV Ptr;
                         numer,denom: Point;
                         VAR yMax: Integer; VAR yMin: Integer;
                         awArray: FixedPtr; lsbArray: FixedPtr;
                         boundsArray: RectPtr): OSErr;
```

byteCount   The number of bytes in the block of text that you want measured.

textPtr   A pointer to the block of text that you want measured.

numer   The numerators of the vertical and horizontal scaling factors. The numer parameter is of type Point, and contains two integers: the first is the numerator of the ratio for vertical scaling, and the second is the numerator of the ratio for horizontal scaling. The Font Manager applies these scaling factors to the current font in order to calculate the measurements for glyphs in the block of text.

denom   The denominators of the vertical and horizontal scaling factors. The denom parameter is of type Point, and contains two integers: the first is the denominator of the ratio for vertical scaling, and the second is the denominator of the ratio for horizontal scaling. The Font Manager applies these scaling factors to the current font in order to calculate the measurements for glyphs in the block of text.

yMax   On output, this is the maximum y-value for the text. Pass NIL in this parameter if you don't want this value returned.

yMin   On output, this is the minimum y-value for the text. Pass NIL in this parameter if you don't want this value returned.

awArray   A pointer to an array that, on output, is filled with the advance width measurements for the glyphs being measured. These measurements are in pixels, based on the point size and font scaling factors of the current font. There is an entry in this array for each glyph that is being measured.

The awArray parameter is of type FixedPtr. The FixedPtr data type is a pointer to an array, and each entry in the array is of type Fixed, which is 4 bytes in length. Multiply byteCount by 4 to calculate the memory you need in bytes.

If the FractEnable global variable has been set to TRUE through the SetFractEnable procedure, the values in awArray have fractional character widths. If FractEnable has been set to FALSE, the Font Manager returns integer values for the advance widths, with 0 in the decimal part of the values.

lsbArray A pointer to an array that is, on output, filled with the left-side bearing measurements for the glyphs being measured. The measurements are in pixels, based on the point size of the current font. There is an entry in this array for each glyph that is being measured.

The lsbArray parameter is of type FixedPtr. The FixedPtr data type is a pointer to an array, and each entry in the array is of type Fixed, which is 4 bytes in length. Multiply byteCount by 4 to calculate the memory you need in bytes.

Left-side bearing values are not rounded.

boundsArray

A pointer to an array that is, on output, filled with the bounding boxes for the glyphs being measured. Bounding boxes are the smallest rectangles that fit around the pixels of the glyph. There is an entry in this array for each glyph that is being measured.

The coordinate system used to describe the bounding boxes is in pixel units, centered at the glyph origin, and with a vertical positive direction upwards, which is the opposite of the QuickDraw vertical orientation.

The boundsArray parameter is of type RectPtr. The RectPtr data type is a pointer to QuickDraw's Rect data type, which is 8 bytes in length. Multiply byteCount by 8 to calculate the memory you need in bytes. Allocate the memory needed for the array and pass a pointer to the array in the boundsArray parameter.

DESCRIPTION

The OutlineMetrics function computes the maximum y-value, minimum y-value, advance widths, left-side bearings, and bounding boxes for a block of text. It uses the font, size, and style specified in the current graphics port. You can use these measurements when laying out text. You may need to adjust line spacing to accommodate exceptionally large glyphs.

The OutlineMetrics function works for outline fonts only and is the preferred method for measuring text that is drawn with an outline font.

When you are using OutlineMetrics to compute advance width values, left-side bearing values, or bounding boxes, you need to bear in mind that when a text block contains 2-byte characters, not every byte in the awArray, lsbArray, and boundsArray structures is used. Each of these arrays is indexed by the glyph index; thus, if you have five characters in a string and two of them are 2-byte characters, only the first five entries in each array contains a value. Call the CharByte function (described in the chapter "Script Manager" in this book) to determine how many characters there are in the text block, and ignore the unused array entries (which occur at the end of each array).

If you don't want OutlineMetrics to compute one of these three values, pass NIL in the applicable parameter. Otherwise, allocate the amount of memory needed for the array and pass a pointer to it in this parameter.

4

Font Manager

ASSEMBLY–LANGUAGE INFORMATION

The trap macro and selector for the `OutlineMetrics` procedure are

Trap macro	Selector
`_FontDispatch`	`$7008`

SEE ALSO

The terms used for measuring text, including advance width, left-side bearing, and bounding box, are described in the section "Font Measurements," which begins on page 4-8. Scaling of fonts and the use of the font scaling factors are described in the section "How the Font Manager Scales Fonts," which begins on page 4-19.

Enabling Fractional Glyph Widths

The `SetFractEnable` procedure enables or disables fractional glyph widths. When fractional glyph widths are enabled, the Font Manager can determine the locations of glyphs more accurately than is possible with integer widths, as described in the section "How the Font Manager Calculates Glyph Widths" on page 4-23.

SetFractEnable

The `SetFractEnable` procedure enables or disables fractional glyph widths.

```
PROCEDURE SetFractEnable (fractEnable: Boolean);
```

`fractEnable`
Specifies whether fractional widths or integer widths are to be used to determine glyph measurements. A value of `TRUE` indicates fractional glyph widths; a value of `FALSE` indicates integer glyph widths.

DESCRIPTION

The `SetFractEnable` procedure establishes whether or not the Font Manager provides fractional glyph widths to QuickDraw, which then uses them for advancing the pen during text drawing. If you set the `fractEnable` parameter to `TRUE`, the Font Manager provides fractional glyph widths. If you set it to `FALSE`, the Font Manager provides integer glyph widths.

The `SetFractEnable` procedure assigns the value that you specify in the `fractEnable` parameter to the global variable `FractEnable`.

The Font Manager defaults to integer widths to ensure compatibility with existing applications.

Disabling Font Scaling

The `SetFScaleDisable` procedure enables or disables font scaling of bitmapped glyphs. When font scaling is enabled, the Font Manager can scale a bitmapped glyph that is present in the System file to imitate the appearance of a bitmapped glyph in another point size that is not present. For more information about scaling of bitmapped fonts, see "The Scaling Process for a Bitmapped Font" on page 4-22.

SetFScaleDisable

The `SetFScaleDisable` procedure enables or disables the computation of font scaling factors by the Font Manager for bitmapped glyphs.

```
PROCEDURE SetFScaleDisable (fontScaleDisable: Boolean);
```

fontScaleDisable
> Specifies whether bitmapped fonts are to be scaled. A value of `TRUE` indicates that font scaling is disabled; a value of `FALSE` indicates that font scaling is enabled.

DESCRIPTION

The `SetFScaleDisable` procedure establishes whether or not the Font Manager computes font scaling factors for bitmapped fonts. If you set the `fontScaleDisable` parameter to `TRUE`, the Font Manager disables font scaling, which means it responds to a request for a font size that is not available by computing font scaling factors of 1/1 and returning a smaller, unscaled bitmapped font with the widths of the requested size. If you set the `fontScaleDisable` parameter to `FALSE`, the Font Manager computes scaling factors for bitmapped fonts.

QuickDraw performs the actual scaling of glyph bitmaps for bitmapped fonts by using the font scaling factors computed and returned by the Font Manager.

As a default, the Font Manager scales fonts to ensure compatibility with existing applications.

ASSEMBLY–LANGUAGE INFORMATION

The trap macro for the `SetFScaleDisable` procedure is

Trap macro

`_SetFScaleDisable`

Favoring Outline Fonts Over Bitmapped Fonts

The SetOutlinePreferred procedure causes either outline fonts or bitmapped fonts to be favored when the Font Manager receives a font request. You can use the GetOutlinePreferred function to find out whether outline or bitmapped fonts are currently favored. You can use the IsOutline function to find out if the font used in the current graphics port is an outline font.

SetOutlinePreferred

The SetOutlinePreferred procedure sets the preference for whether to use bitmapped or outline fonts when both kinds of fonts are available.

```
PROCEDURE SetOutlinePreferred (outlinePreferred: Boolean);
```

outlinePreferred
Specifies whether the Font Manager chooses an outline font or a bitmapped font when both are available to fill a font request. A value of TRUE indicates an outline font; a value of FALSE indicates a bitmapped font.

DESCRIPTION

If an outline font and a bitmapped font are both available for a font request, the default behavior for the Font Manager is to choose the bitmapped font, in order to maintain compatibility with documents that were created on computer systems on which outline fonts were not available. The SetOutlinePreferred procedure sets the Font Manager's current preference for either bitmapped or outline fonts when both are available. If you want the Font Manager to choose outline fonts over any bitmapped font counterparts, set the outlinePreferred parameter to TRUE; if you want it to choose bitmapped fonts, set the outlinePreferred parameter to FALSE.

If only outline fonts are available, the Font Manager chooses them regardless of the setting of outlinePreferred; if only bitmapped fonts are available, they are chosen. The Font Manager chooses bitmapped versus outline fonts on a size basis, before it takes stylistic variations into account, which can lead to unexpected results. For further information, see "How the Font Manager Responds to a Font Request," beginning on page 4-17.

The preference you set is valid only during the current session with your application. The outlinePreferred parameter does not set a global variable.

The trap macro and routine selector for the `SetOutlinePreferred` procedure are

Trap macro	Routine selector
_FontDispatch	$7001

GetOutlinePreferred

The `GetOutlinePreferred` function determines whether outline or bitmapped fonts are to be favored when the Font Manager receives a font request.

```
FUNCTION GetOutlinePreferred: Boolean;
```

DESCRIPTION

The `GetOutlinePreferred` function returns the value of the Font Manager's current preference for outline or bitmapped fonts. If `GetOutlinePreferred` returns `TRUE`, then the Font Manager chooses the outline font when both an outline font and a bitmapped font are available for a particular request. If `GetOutlinePreferred` returns `FALSE`, then the Font Manager chooses the bitmapped font when both types are available.

Use the `SetOutlinePreferred` procedure to change this preference.

ASSEMBLY–LANGUAGE INFORMATION

The trap macro and routine selector for the `GetOutlinePreferred` function are

Trap macro	Routine selector
_FontDispatch	$7009

IsOutline

The `IsOutline` function determines if the Font Manager chooses an outline font for the current graphics port to meet the specified scaling factors.

```
FUNCTION IsOutline (numer: Point; denom: Point): Boolean;
```

numer   The numerators of the vertical and horizontal scaling factors. The numer parameter is of type `Point`, and contains two integers: the first is the numerator of the ratio for vertical scaling, and the second is the numerator of the ratio for horizontal scaling.

denom   The denominators of the vertical and horizontal scaling factors. The
                 denom parameter is of type Point, and contains two integers: the first is
                 the denominator of the ratio for vertical scaling, and the second is the
                 denominator of the ratio for horizontal scaling.

DESCRIPTION

The IsOutline function returns TRUE if the Font Manager would choose an outline
font for the current graphics port. The Font Manager uses the font scaling factors
specified in the numer and denom parameters, as well as the current preference (as set
by the SetOutlinePreferred procedure) to make a decision as to which font to use.

ASSEMBLY–LANGUAGE INFORMATION

The trap macro and routine selector for the IsOutline function are

Trap macro	Routine selector
_FontDispatch	$7000

Scaling Outline Fonts

The SetPreserveGlyph procedure determines whether a glyph from an outline font is
displayed as designed or whether the Font Manager scales the glyph to fit between the
ascent and descent lines. These two behaviors are discussed in "Preserving the Shapes of
Glyphs" on page 4-35. You can use the GetPreserveGlyph function to find out
whether glyphs from outline fonts are to be scaled.

SetPreserveGlyph

The default behavior for the Font Manager is to scale a glyph from an outline font so that
it fits between the ascent and descent lines; however, this alters the appearance of the
glyph. The SetPreserveGlyph procedure changes this behavior temporarily so that
the Font Manager does not scale oversized glyphs.

PROCEDURE SetPreserveGlyph (preserveGlyph: Boolean);

preserveGlyph
                 Specifies whether or not glyphs from an outline font are scaled to fit
                 between the ascent and descent lines.

DESCRIPTION

The `SetPreserveGlyph` procedure establishes how the Font Manager treats glyphs that do not fit between the ascent and descent lines for the current font. If you set the value of the `preserveGlyph` parameter to `TRUE`, the measurements of all glyphs are preserved, which means that your application may have to alter the leading between lines in a document if some of the glyphs extend beyond the ascent or descent lines. If you set the value of the `preserveGlyph` parameter to `FALSE`, all glyphs are scaled to fit between the ascent and descent lines.

You can determine the current behavior of the Font Manager in this regard by calling the `GetPreserveGlyph` function. To ensure that documents have the same appearance whenever they are opened, you need to call `GetPreserveGlyph` and save the value that it returns with your documents and restore it each time a document is displayed by your application.

ASSEMBLY–LANGUAGE INFORMATION

The trap macro and routine selector for the `SetPreserveGlyph` procedure are

Trap macro	Routine selector
`_FontDispatch`	`$700A`

GetPreserveGlyph

The `GetPreserveGlyph` function determines whether the Font Manager preserves the shapes of glyphs from outline fonts.

```
FUNCTION GetPreserveGlyph: Boolean;
```

DESCRIPTION

The `GetPreserveGlyph` function returns a Boolean value indicating whether the Font Manager preserves the shapes of glyphs from outline fonts. Your application can set the value of this variable with the `SetPreserveGlyph` procedure. If `GetPreserveGlyph` returns `TRUE`, the Font Manager preserves glyph shapes; if `GetPreserveGlyph` returns `FALSE`, then the Font Manager scales glyphs to fit between the ascent and descent lines for the font in use.

ASSEMBLY–LANGUAGE INFORMATION

The trap macro and routine selector for the `GetPreserveGlyph` function are

Trap macro	Routine selector
`_FontDispatch`	`$700B`

Accessing Information About a Font

The `FMSwapFont` function gets a handle to a font, and some information about that font. It is used extensively by system software to access fonts.

FMSwapFont

The `FMSwapFont` function returns a handle to a font and information about that font. This function is used by QuickDraw and other parts of the system software to access font handles.

```
FUNCTION FMSwapFont (inRec: FMInput): FMOutPtr;
```

inRec   A font input record, which contains the font family ID, the style requested, scaling factors, and other information.

DESCRIPTION

The `FMSwapFont` function takes a font request and returns a pointer to a font output record. `FMSwapFont` is the heart of the Font Manager: it does all of the hard work of preparing font data for text measuring and text drawing.

The `inRec` parameter specifies the characteristics of the font that is requested. QuickDraw fills in the fields of the `CurFmInput` global variable and passes that record in this parameter.

The font output record contains a handle to a font resource that fulfills the font request, along with information about the font, such as the ascent, descent, and leading measurements. You supply the `FMSwapFont` function with the font request in the `inRec` parameter, using a font input record, and the Font Manager returns the font handle and the other information in a font output record.

QuickDraw calls the `FMSwapFont` function every time a QuickDraw text routine is used. If you want to call the `FMSwapFont` function in order to get a handle to a font resource or information about that font, you must build a font input record and then use the pointer returned to access the resulting font output record.

You cannot assume that the font resource pointed to by the `fontHandle` field of the font output record returned by this function is of any particular type, such as `'NFNT'` or `'sfnt'`. If you need to access specific information in the font resource, call the Resource Manager procedure `GetResInfo` with the handle returned in the font output record to determine the font resource type.

IMPORTANT

The pointer to the font output record returned as the value of `FMSwapFont` points to a record allocated in low memory by the Font Manager. The same record is reused for each call made to `FMSwapFont`. Do not free the memory allocated for this record. ▲

The trap macro for the FMSwapFont function is

Trap macro

_FMSwapFont

SEE ALSO

For more information about the font input record, see "How QuickDraw Requests a Font" on page 4-16. For more information about the font output record, see "How the Font Manager Responds to a Font Request" on page 4-17. For descriptions of the records themselves, see "The Font Input Record" on page 4-40 and "The Font Output Record" on page 4-41.

The GetResInfo procedure is described in the Resource Manager chapter in *Inside Macintosh: More Macintosh Toolbox.*

Handling Fonts in Memory

The Font Manager provides two routines that allow you to manipulate fonts in memory. The SetFontLock procedure makes a font resource, which is normally purgeable data in memory, unpurgeable. The FlushFonts function erases the Font Manager's memory caches, including resource data and any width tables the Font Manager may have built.

SetFontLock

The SetFontLock procedure makes the most recently used font unpurgeable. You can use this procedure when you want a font to remain in memory for the sake of efficiency.

```
PROCEDURE SetFontLock (lockFlag: Boolean);
```

lockFlag   Specifies whether or not the current font is considered purgeable.

DESCRIPTION

If you set the lockFlag parameter to TRUE, the SetFontLock procedure makes the most recently used font resource unpurgeable, and reads it into memory if it isn't already there. If you set the lockFlag parameter to FALSE, the SetFontLock procedure releases the memory occupied by the most recently used font by calling the ReleaseResource procedure.

The font considered to be the most recently used is the one referenced by the font output record in low memory, which is filled in by the FMSwapFont function. This is often, but not always, the font in which text has most recently been drawn. Since both QuickDraw and your application program can call FMSwapFont, you have to be careful about which font has most recently been used in a call to that function. To ensure that you are locking the font that you want to lock, explicitly call `FMSwapFont` immediately before calling `SetFontLock`.

ASSEMBLY–LANGUAGE INFORMATION

The trap macro for the `SetFontLock` procedure is

Trap macro

`_SetFontLock`

SEE ALSO

The `ReleaseResource` procedure is described in the chapter "Resource Manager" in *Inside Macintosh: More Macintosh Toolbox.*

FlushFonts

The `FlushFonts` function erases the Font Manager's memory caches.

```
FUNCTION FlushFonts: OSErr;
```

DESCRIPTION

The `FlushFonts` function erases all of the Font Manager's memory caches. Your application doesn't need this function unless it directly manipulates data in the outline font resource. Font Manager caches include the width tables, the bitmaps created from the outlines of the outline font resource, the calculations for the outlines, and a small cache of font family resources that have been read into memory.

ASSEMBLY–LANGUAGE INFORMATION

The trap macro and routine selector for the `FlushFonts` function are

Trap macro	Routine selector
`_FontDispatch`	`$700C`

The Bitmapped Font ('NFNT') Resource

The bitmapped font (`'NFNT'`) resource describes a bitmapped font—a font whose glyphs are represented by bit images. The structure of the bitmapped font resource is identical to that of the older `'FONT'` resource, which can be used for bitmapped fonts as well; however, the bitmapped font resource has a more flexible ID numbering scheme and is preferred over the `'FONT'` resource.

Font Manager

The bitmapped font resource consists of a header component, which describes the font, and a glyph data information component, which contains the definitions of the glyphs in the font. The header component of this resource is represented by the `FontRec` data type, the declaration of which is shown in the section "The Font Record," beginning on page 4-46. The structure of this resource is shown in Figure 4-16.

Figure 4-16   The bitmapped font (`'NFNT'`) resource

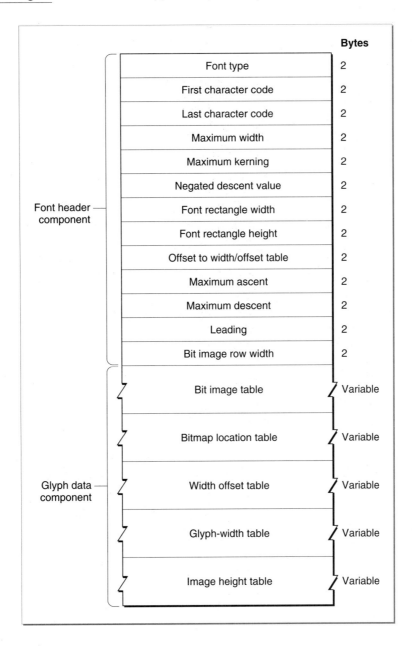

The bitmapped font header component consists of the elements listed below, each of which corresponds to a field in the FontRec data type.

■ Font type. An integer value that is used to specify the general characteristics of the font, such as whether it is fixed-width or proportional, whether the optional image-height and glyph-width tables are attached to the font, and information about the font depth and colors. This value is represented by the fontType field in the FontRec data type. For the meaning of the bits in this field, see "The Font Type Element" on page 4-70.

■ First character code. An integer value that specifies the ASCII character code of the first glyph in the font. This value is represented by the firstChar field in the FontRec data type.

■ Last character code. An integer value that specifies the ASCII character code of the last glyph in the font. This value is represented by the lastChar field in the FontRec data type.

■ Maximum width. An integer value that specifies the maximum width of the widest glyph in the font, in pixels. This value is represented by the widMax field in the FontRec data type.

■ Maximum kerning. An integer value that specifies the distance from the font rectangle's glyph origin to the left edge of the font rectangle, in pixels. If a glyph in the font kerns to the left, the amount is represented as a negative number. If the glyph origin lies on the left edge of the font rectangle, the value of the kernMax field is 0. This value is represented by the kernMax field in the FontRec data type.

■ Negated descent value. If this font has very large tables and this value is positive, this value is the high word of the offset to the width/offset table. For more information, see "The Offset to the Width/Offset Table" on page 4-71. If this value is negative, it is the negative of the descent and is not used by the Font Manager. This value is represented by the nDescent field in the FontRec data type.

■ Font rectangle width. An integer value that specifies the width, in pixels, of the image created if all the glyphs in the font were superimposed at their glyph origins. This value is represented by the fRectWidth field in the FontRec data type.

■ Font rectangle height. An integer value that specifies the height, in pixels, of the image created if all the glyphs in the font were superimposed at their glyph origins. This value equals the sum of the maximum ascent and maximum descent measurements for the font. This value is represented by the fRectHeight field in the FontRec data type.

■ Offset to width/offset table. An integer value that specifies the offset to the offset/width table from this point in the font record, in words. If this font has very large tables, this value is only the low word of the offset and the negated descent value is the high word, as explained in the section "The Offset to the Width/Offset Table" on page 4-71. This value is represented by the owTLoc field in the FontRec data type.

■ Maximum ascent. An integer value that specifies the maximum ascent measurement for the entire font, in pixels. The ascent is the distance from the glyph origin to the top of the font rectangle. This value is represented by the `ascent` field in the `FontRec` data type.

■ Maximum descent. An integer value that specifies the maximum descent measurement for the entire font, in pixels. The descent is the distance from the glyph origin to the bottom of the font rectangle. This value is represented by the `descent` field in the `FontRec` data type.

■ Leading. An integer value that specifies the leading measurement for the entire font, in pixels. Leading is the distance from the descent line of one line of single-spaced text to the ascent line of the next line of text. This value is represented by the `leading` field in the `FontRec` data type.

■ Bit image row width. An integer value that specifies the width of the bit image, in words. This is the width of each glyph's bit image as a number of words. This value is represented by the `rowWords` field in the `FontRec` data type.

The glyph data component of the bitmapped font resource consists of five tables that describe the glyphs in the font.

■ Bit image table. The bit image of the glyphs in the font. The glyph images of every defined glyph in the font are placed sequentially in order of increasing ASCII code. The bit image is one pixel image with no undefined stretches that has a height given by the value of the font rectangle element and a width given by the value of the bit image row width element. The image is padded at the end with extra pixels to make its length a multiple of 16.

■ Bitmap location table. For every glyph in the font, this table contains a word that specifies the bit offset to the location of the bitmap for that glyph in the bit image table. If a glyph is missing from the font, its entry contains the same value for its location as the entry for the next glyph. The missing glyph is the last glyph of the bit image for that font. The last word of the table contains the offset to one bit beyond the end of the bit image. You can determine the image width of each glyph from the bitmap location table by subtracting the bit offset to that glyph from the bit offset to the next glyph in the table.

■ Width/offset table. For every glyph in the font, this table contains a word with the glyph offset in the high-order byte and the glyph's width, in integer form, in the low-order byte. The value of the offset, when added to the maximum kerning value for the font, determines the horizontal distance from the glyph origin to the left edge of the bit image of the glyph, in pixels. If this sum is negative, the glyph origin is to the right of the glyph image's left edge, meaning the glyph kerns to the left. If the sum is positive, the origin is to the left of the image's left edge. If the sum equals zero, the glyph origin corresponds with the left edge of the bit image. Missing glyphs are represented by a word value of –1. The last word of this table is also –1, representing the end.

■ Glyph-width table. For every glyph in the font, this table contains a word that specifies the glyph's fixed-point glyph width at the given point size and font style, in pixels. The Font Manager gives precedence to the values in this table over those in the font family glyph-width table. There is an unsigned integer in the high-order byte and a fractional part in the low-order byte. This table is optional.

■ Image height table. For every glyph in the font, this table contains a word that specifies the image height of the glyph, in pixels. The image height is the height of the glyph image and is less than or equal to the font height. QuickDraw uses the image height for improved character plotting, because it only draws the visible part of the glyph. The high-order byte of the word is the offset from the top of the font rectangle of the first non-blank (or nonwhite) row in the glyph, and the low-order byte is the number of rows that must be drawn. The Font Manager creates this table.

The Font Type Element

The font type element of the bitmapped font resource is represented as the `fontType` field in the `FontRec` data type. This integer field defines the general characteristics of the font and records whether certain tables are present. Its bits are used as follows.

Bit	Meaning
0	This bit is set to 1 if the font resource contains an image height table.
1	This bit is set to 1 if the font resource contains a glyph-width table.
2–3	These two bits define the depth of the font. Each of the four possible values indicates the number of bits (and therefore, the number of colors) used to represent each pixel in the glyph images.

Value	Font depth	Number of colors
0	1-bit	1
1	2-bit	4
2	4-bit	16
3	8-bit	256

Normally the font depth is 0 and the glyphs are specified as monochrome images. If bit 7 of this field is set to 1, a resource of type 'fctb' with the same ID as the font can optionally be provided to assign RGB colors to specific pixel values.

If this font resource is a member of a font family, the settings of bits 8 and 9 of the `fontStyle` field in this font's association table entry should be the same as the settings of bits 2 and 3 in the `fontType` field. For more information, see "The Font Association Table" on page 4-95.

| 4–6 | Reserved. Should be set to 0. |
| 7 | This bit is set to 1 if the font has a font color table ('fctb') resource. The font is for color Macintosh computers only if this bit is set to 1. |

Bit	Meaning
8	This bit is set to 1 if the font is a synthetic font, created dynamically from the available font resources in response to a certain color and screen depth combination. The font is for color Macintosh computers only if this bit is set to 1.
9	This bit is set to 1 if the font contains colors other than black. This font is for color Macintosh computers only if this bit is set to 1.
10–11	Reserved. Should be set to 0.
12	Reserved. Should be set to 1.
13	This bit is set to 1 if the font describes a fixed-width font, and is set to 0 if the font describes a proportional font. The Font Manager does not check the setting of this bit.
14	This bit is set to 1 if the font is not to be expanded to match the screen depth. The font is for color Macintosh computers only if this bit is set to 1. This is for some fonts, such as Kanji, which are too large for synthetic fonts to be effective or meaningful, or bitmapped fonts that are larger than 50 points.
15	Reserved. Should be set to 0.

The Offset to the Width/Offset Table

The offset to the width/offset table element of the bitmapped font resource is represented as the `owtLoc` field in the `FontRec` data type. This field defines the offset from the beginning of the resource to the beginning of the width/offset table.

The value of `nDescent`, when positive, is used as the high-order 16 bits in the 32-bit value that is used to store the offset of the width table from the beginning of the resource. To compute the actual offset, the Font Manager uses this computation:

```
actualOffsetWord := BSHL(nDescent, 16) + owTLoc;
```

If the value of `nDescent` is negative, it is still the negative of the descent measurement, as it was in the original usage of these values; however, the Font Manager no longer uses this value.

Note

This field was originally defined as an integer value, because it was not foreseen that this value could exceed 32 KB. The negated descent element, represented in the `nDescent` field of the `FontRec` data type, was created purely for the convenience of the Font Manager. It stored the negative of the value of the descent field, which is always positive by QuickDraw convention. When the depth of fonts increased, the values of the `owTLoc` field had to increase, and the extra bits needed to be stored somewhere. Since the `nDescent` field was created as a convenience, it was a handy place to store more information. ◆

4

Font Manager

The Outline Font ('sfnt') Resource

The outline font (`'sfnt'`) resource, which describes a TrueType outline font, consists of a sequence of tables that contain the data necessary for drawing the glyphs of the font, measurement information about the font, and any instructions that the font designer might include. These tables can appear in any order in the resource. Some of the tables are required, such as the description of the font's glyphs, and others are optional, such as kerning information. TrueType outline fonts are available on platforms other than the Macintosh computer, and some tables reflect the variety of information needed for these different operating systems. A table directory at the beginning of the outline font resource contains a version number and keys to access the tables.

Note

There are no data type definitions of the outline font resource tables and there are no fields, although the divisions of the tables are referred to as *fields* in this chapter. You must access the data using the routines and data structures that are described in this chapter or write table-specific code. Listing 4-2 beginning on page 4-76 shows how to read the contents of the various tables. ◆

The Font Manager uses some of the tables defined for the outline font resource to construct the font's glyphs or to store the font designer's information about creating bitmaps from the font data. Developers of general-purpose applications do not need these tables; consequently, the internal specifications of these tables are not provided in this chapter, although descriptions of their functions are. The needs of platforms other than the Macintosh computer are also not discussed.

Some of the terms used in descriptions of these tables pertain solely to the font designer's creation of the font. The em square is the imaginary area on which the glyphs of the font are first designed. The term units per em describes the resolution of the grid; the greater the number of units per em, the finer the detail of design that the designer can achieve. Apple's TrueType fonts use a resolution of 2048 units per em. The measurement pixels per em describes the relationship of the point size to the em square; the units per em measurements of the font are translated, using this pixels per em measurement, into bitmaps. The Font Manager handles this translation for you.

Similarly, the instruction set is for the use of the font designer only and cannot be used or altered by the Font Manager routines, and so is not included in this chapter. If you want the complete description of all of the tables in the outline font resource, consult the *TrueType Font Format Specification*.

Each table in the outline font resource is aligned on a longword boundary in memory (long-aligned) and may have been padded when necessary to make it long-aligned. Each table is named with a four character identifier known as its tag name. The only table that does not have a tag name is the font directory table. This table is a guide to the contents of the resource and is mandatory in all outline font resources.

Note
Detailed descriptions of many of the values in the outline font resource tables are found in the *TrueType Font Format Specification* and are not repeated in this chapter. If you are designing a font editor or similar application that requires detailed knowledge of these tables, please refer to that book. ◆

These are the required tables in the outline font resource:

Tag name	Table
(none)	Font directory
'cmap'	Character code mapping table
'glyf'	Glyph data table
'head'	Font header table
'hhea'	Horizontal header table
'hmtx'	Horizontal metrics table
'loca'	Location table
'maxp'	Maximum profile table
'name'	Font-naming table
'post'	PostScript table

Some of the optional tables in the 'sfnt' resource are

Tag	Table
'cvt '	Control-value table
'fpgm'	Font program table
'hdmx'	Horizontal device metrics table
'kern'	Kerning table
'prep'	Preprogram (control value program) table

Font designers can define additional tables for the outline font resource to support other platforms where outline fonts are available or to provide for future expansion of a font. Tag names consisting of all lowercase letters are reserved for use by Apple Computer, Inc.

The Font Directory

The font directory is a guide to the tables in the outline font resource. It provides you with the information that is needed to efficiently find the other parts of the resource. Each table in the resource has a tag name, a checksum, a location that is defined as an offset in bytes from the first byte of the resource, and a length in bytes. To use the data in a table, you first find the table's tag name in the font directory and then access its data starting at the specified location.

The font directory consists of an offset component and a variable length array of directory entries, as shown in Figure 4-17.

Figure 4-17 The font directory

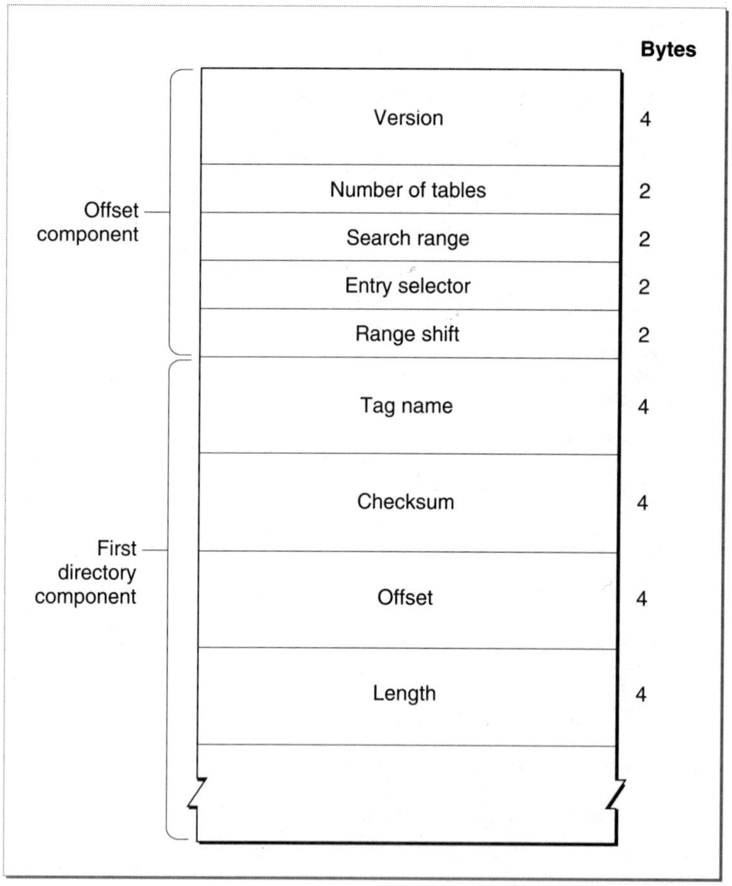

The font directory offset component specifies the number of tables in the resource (and thus in the directory component). It contains several values that you can use to optimize searching through the directory components for a tag name:

■ Version. The version number of the font, given as a 32-bit fixed point number. For version 1.0 of any font, this number is $00010000.

■ Number of tables. The number of tables in the outline font resource, not counting the font directory or any subtables in the font. This is an unsigned integer value.

■ Search range. An unsigned integer value that is used, along with the entry selector and range shift values, to optimize a binary search through the directory.

■ Entry selector. An unsigned integer value that is used, along with the search range and range shift values, to optimize a binary search through the directory.

■ Range shift. An unsigned integer value that is used, along with the search range and entry selector values, to optimize a binary search through the directory.

The search range, entry selector, and range shift values are used together to construct a binary search through the directory if it is too large for an efficient sequential search. Note, however, that most programs that access kerning data use a linear search and do not make use of these values.

If a font does contain a large number of tables, you can perform a binary search of the directory components. You use the range shift value as the initial position in the directory to examine. Compare the tag name of the component at this position with the one you are searching for. If the target tag name comes before the one you are searching for, search from the beginning of the directory to the range shift position. If the target name comes after the one you are searching for, search from that position to the end of the directory.

The font directory table entries are sorted alphabetically by tag name. Each component consists of the following elements:

■ Tag name. The identifying name for this table, such as 'cmap'.

■ Checksum. The checksum for this table, which is the unsigned sum of the long values in the table. This number can be used to verify the integrity of the data in the table.

■ Offset. The offset from the beginning of the outline font resource to the beginning of this table, in bytes.

■ Length. The length of this table, in bytes.

Listing 4-2 shows a function that determines the checksum of a given table.

| Listing 4-2 | Calculating the checksum of a given table |

```
TYPE
    LongPtr = ^LongInt;

FUNCTION MyCalcTableChecksum (table: LongPtr;
                                lngth: LongInt): LongInt;
VAR
    sum : LongInt;
    mask: LongInt;

BEGIN
    sum := 0;
    WHILE lngth > 0 DO BEGIN
        IF lngth > 3 THEN
            sum := sum + table^
        ELSE BEGIN
            mask := BitShift($FFFFFFFF, 8 * (4 - lngth));
            sum := sum + BitAnd(table^, mask);
            table := LongPtr(ord(table) + 4);
            lngth := lngth - 4;
        END;
    END;
    MyCalcTableChecksum := sum;
END;
```

The Character-Code Mapping Table

The character-code mapping table, with a tag name of 'cmap', maps character codes (like ASCII codes) to glyph indexes. The glyph repertoire of an outline font is indexed consecutively from zero to the number of glyphs in the font. The encoding method selected by the font designer depends on the conventions used by the intended platform and sometimes on other platform-specific selectors, such as which script system is in use. A font intended for use on multiple platforms with different conventions requires multiple encoding tables; however, double-byte fonts require various special formats for efficient encoding. As a result, the 'cmap' table may contain multiple encoding components, one for each supported encoding scheme, often in different formats.

Character codes that do not correspond to any glyph in the font should be mapped to glyph index 0. At this location in the font there should be a special glyph representing a missing character, which typically is a box (□). For more information on requirements for character-to-glyph mapping, see the *TrueType Font Format Specification*.

In the simplest case, the character-code mapping table consists of a header component and only one character-mapping format component, which includes an array of glyph indexes. In other cases, there are several character-mapping components in the table.

The Control-Value Table

The control-value table, with a tag name of `'cvt '`, is an optional table that can be used by fonts that contain instructions. This table contains data (control values) used by the instructions. Each entry in this table is 4 bytes long. The number of values in the table can be computed by dividing the length of the table by 4. The length of the table is found in the directory component for this table in the outline font resource directory.

The font directory is described in "The Font Directory," beginning on page 4-74.

The control-value program, which uses these values, is contained in the preprogram table, which is described on page 4-89.

The Font Program Table

The font program table, with a tag name of `'fpgm'`, is an optional table that contains the font program, a list of instructions that the Font Manager executes once, when it loads the font into memory. The font program is a variable length sequence of bytes that are interpreted by the Font Manager. The length of this table is found in the directory component for this table in the outline font resource directory.

The font directory is described in "The Font Directory," beginning on page 4-74.

The Glyph Data Table

The glyph data table, with a tag name of `'glyf'`, contains the data that defines the appearance of the glyphs in the font: the specification of points that make up the contours of a glyph and the instructions that help change the shape of the glyph under various conditions. Glyphs can be stored in any character-code mapping order, since the location of the data for each is specified separately, through the character-code mapping table, which is described beginning on page 4-76, and the location table, which is described on page 4-84.

Font Manager

The data for each glyph consists of some descriptive information, as shown in Figure 4-18, followed by the actual instructions and coordinate values that define the glyph. The format of the definition data for glyphs is described in the *TrueType Font Format Specification*. Note that the glyph data is compressed.

Figure 4-18   A glyph description

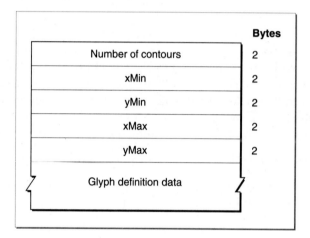

- Number of contours. If this integer value is positive, it specifies the number of closed curves defined in the outline data for the glyph. If it is −1, it indicates that the glyph is composed of other simple glyphs (see the explanation of component glyphs in the section "The Maximum Profile Table" beginning on page 4-84).

- xMin. The left edge of the glyph's bounding box, specified in units per em.

- yMin. The top edge of the glyph's bounding box, specified in units per em.

- xMax. The right edge of the glyph's bounding box, specified in units per em.

- yMax. The bottom edge of the glyph's bounding box, specified in units per em.

- Glyph definition data. The data that defines the appearance of the glyph, as described in the *TrueType Font Format Specification*.

The Horizontal Device Metrics Table

The horizontal device metrics table, with a tag name of 'hdmx', is an optional table that stores integer advance widths scaled to pixel-per-em sizes for the Macintosh computer's screen. The horizontal device metrics table is used only for certain screen sizes that are determined by the font's designer and only when fractional widths are disabled (as described in "SetFractEnable" on page 4-58). This table contains fine-tuned integer widths for the glyphs at low pixel-per-em values. These values can be used to reduce the unpleasant consequences of rounding the widths for small point sizes at low resolution.

The Font Header Table

The font header table, with a tag name of 'head', is shown in Figure 4-19. This table contains global information about the font: the font version number; creation and modification dates; revision number; basic typographic data that applies to the font as a whole, such as the direction in which the font's glyphs are most likely to be written; and other information about the placement of glyphs in the em square.

Figure 4-19   The font header table

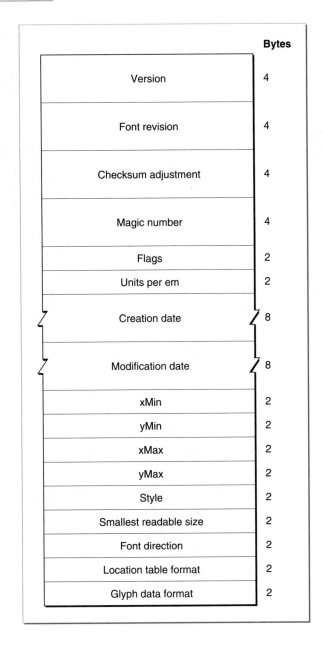

For a complete description of the individual fields in this table, see the *TrueType Font Format Specification*. Application developers may be interested in the following fields:

- Version. The version number of the table, as a fixed-point value. This value is $00010000 if the version number is 1.0.

- Font revision. A fixed-point value set by the font designer.

- Checksum adjustment. The checksum of the font, as an unsigned long integer.

- Units per em. This unsigned integer value represents a power of 2 that ranges from 64 to 16,384. Apple's TrueType fonts use the value 2048.

- Creation date. The date this font was created. This is a long date-time value of data type `LongDateTime`, which is a 64-bit, signed representation of the number of seconds since Jan. 1, 1904.

- Modification date. The date this font was last modified. This is a long date-time value of data type `LongDateTime`, which is a 64-bit, signed representation of the number of seconds since Jan. 1, 1904.

- Smallest readable size. The smallest readable size for the font, in pixels per em. The `RealFont` function, which is described in the section "RealFont" beginning on page 4-52, returns `FALSE` for a TrueType font if the requested size is smaller than this value.

- Location table format. The format of the location table (tag name: `'loca'`), as an signed integer value. The table has two formats: if the value is 0, the table uses the short offset format; if the value is 1, the table uses the long offset format. The location table is described in the section "The Location Table" on page 4-84.

You can use the value of the checksum adjustment element to verify the integrity of the data in the font, to confirm that no data has been changed, or to compare two similar fonts. This value is the designer's checksum value for the font. The checksum value is an unsigned long word that you compute as follows:

1. Set the value of the checksum word to 0 (so that it does not factor into the value that you are computing).

2. Calculate the checksum for each table in the outline font resource and store the table's checksum in the table directory.

3. Now sum the entire font as an unsigned, 32-bit value.

4. Subtract the sum from $B1B0AFBA, which is a magic number for this checksum computation. Store the result.

Listing 4-2 provides an example of a function to compute the checksum of a font. This example includes type declarations for the outline font header information and uses the `MyCalcTableChecksum` function (from Listing 4-2 on page 4-76) to compute the checksum for each table.

Listing 4-3   Calculating the checksum of a font

```
TYPE

DirectoryEntry =
RECORD
    tag: OSType;
    checksum: LongInt;
    offset: LongInt;
    lngth: LongInt;
END;

OffsetTable =
RECORD
    version: LongInt;
    numTables: Integer;
    searchRange: Integer;
    entrySelector: Integer;
    rangeShift: Integer;
    tableDir: ARRAY[1..1] OF DirectoryEntry;
                          { actually 1..numTables }
END;

SfntPtr = ^OffsetTable;
SfntHandle = ^SfntPtr;

HeaderTable =
RECORD
    version: LongInt;
    fontRevision: LongInt;
    checkSumAdjustment: LongInt;
    magicNumber: LongInt;
    flags: Integer;
    unitsPerEm: Integer;
    created: LongDateTime; { defined in Script.p }
    modified: LongDateTime;
    xMin: Integer;
    yMin: Integer;
    xMax: Integer;
    yMax: Integer;
    macStyle: Integer;
```

```
    lowestRecPPEM: Integer;
    fontDirectionHint: Integer;
    indexToLocFormat: Integer;
    glyphDataFormat: Integer;
END;


HeaderTablePtr = ^HeaderTable;


FUNCTION CalcSfntChecksum (sp: SfntPtr): LongInt;
CONST
    checkSumMagic = $B1B0AFBA;
VAR
    i: Integer;
    cs, sum, size: LongInt;
    htp: HeaderTableptr;

BEGIN
    sum := 0;
    FOR i := 1 TO sp^.numTables DO BEGIN
        IF sp^.tableDir[i].tag = 'head' THEN
            BEGIN
                htp := HeaderTablePtr(ord(sp) +
                                sp^.tableDir[i].offset);
                htp^.checkSumAdjustment := 0;
                cs := CalcTableChecksum(LongPtr(htp),
                                SizeOf(HeaderTable));
            END
        ELSE
            cs := MyCalcTableChecksum(
                    LongPtr(ord(sp) + sp^.tableDir[i].offset),
                    sp^.tableDir[i].lngth);

        sp^.tableDir[i].checksum := cs;
        sum := sum + cs;
    END;
    size := SizeOf(OffsetTable) +
            (sp^.numTables - 1) * SizeOf(DirectoryEntry);
    sum := sum + CalcTableChecksum(LongPtr(sp), size);
    CalcSfntChecksum := checkSumMagic - sum;
    { to be written into htp^.checkSumAdjustment }
END;
```

The Horizontal Header Table

The horizontal header table, with a tag name of 'hhea', contains information needed to lay out fonts whose glyphs are written horizontally (either left to right or right to left) across a page. This table contains information that pertains to the font as a whole. Information that pertains to specific glyphs is given in the horizontal metrics table, which is described in the next section "The Horizontal Metrics Table."

The Horizontal Metrics Table

The horizontal metrics table, with a tag name of 'hmtx', consists of arrays that contain metrics information—the advance widths and left-side bearings—for the horizontal layout of each glyph in the font. The horizontal metrics table structure is shown in Figure 4-20.

Figure 4-20   The horizontal metrics table

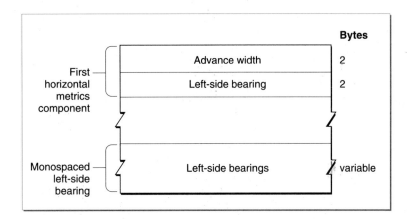

The first component of the horizontal metrics table contains two values for each entry: the advance width and the left-side bearing for the associated glyph. The number of value pairs in this component is specified in the number of advance widths element of the horizontal header table, which is described in the preceding section, "The Horizontal Header Table."

The horizontal metrics table may have a second component that is used for fixed-width glyphs. It contains the left-side bearings only. The advance width is the same as the last entry in the first component of this table.

The Kerning Table

The kerning table, with a tag name of 'kern', is an optional table that contains the values you can use to adjust the spacing between glyphs in a font. Kerning can be parallel to the flow of text or perpendicular to the flow of text. For example, if you specify perpendicular kerning and if text is normally read horizontally, the glyphs are kerned vertically. Kerning is always applied to pairs of glyphs.

The kerning table in the outline font resource consists of a header and a series of subtables. The *TrueType Font Format Specification* documents a basic set of kerning subtables.

The Location Table

The location table, with a tag name of 'loca', stores the offsets to the locations of actual glyph data in the outline font resource relative to the beginning of the glyph table. It provides quick access to the data for a particular glyph. The location table is an array of offset values, one for each glyph in the font, including the 0th or missing character glyph.

Offsets are stored in one of two forms: in the short format, each offset is a 16-bit unsigned integer value that specifies the number of words from the beginning of the glyph data table to the data for the glyph. In the long format, each offset is a 32-bit unsigned integer value that specifies the number of bytes from the beginning of the glyph data table to the data for the glyph. The format that is used for a font is specified in the location table format element of the font header table, whose description begins on page 4-79.

The Maximum Profile Table

The maximum profile table, with a tag name of 'maxp', establishes the memory requirements for a font. Most of the information in this table is for the use of the font's designer, a font editor that may alter the makeup of the resource, or the Font Manager itself.

Some of the elements in the maximum profile table refer to simple versus component glyphs. A simple glyph is one that is defined as a single equation, such as an "e". A component glyph is a design that the font designer builds by adding a simple glyph to another equation or by adding two glyphs together. For example, the glyph "ê" can be created as a single entity or as a component glyph: the simple glyph "e" plus the simple glyph "^". In this way, a small set of simple glyphs can create a much larger set of component glyphs. The font designer could also design the glyph "ê" as a simple glyph. However, this leads to separate designs for "â", "î", and so on. Some fonts distributed by Apple use component glyphs and some do not.

For more information about this table, see the *TrueType Font Format Specification*.

The Font Naming Table

The font naming table, with a tag name of 'name', is shown in Figure 4-21. This table contains multilingual strings associated with the outline font resource. These strings can represent copyright notices, font names, style names, and so on, and each string is stored in a separate record with some information about what kind of string it is. You may want to provide this information in your application for the user, or you may want to use it to check one version of a font against another.

Figure 4-21   The naming table

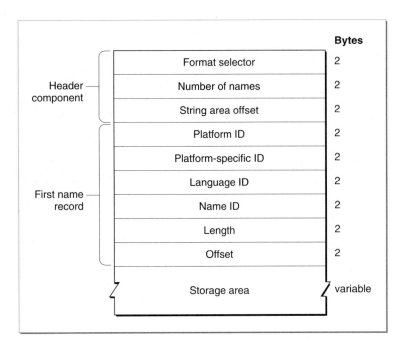

The header component of the font naming table consists of the following elements:

■ Format selector. The format selector (set to 0). This is an unsigned integer.

■ Number of names. The number of name records that follow. This is an unsigned integer.

■ String area offset. The offset from the start of the table to the start of string storage, in bytes. This is an unsigned integer.

Font Manager

Each name record contains information about the platform and language of the strings stored in the naming table.

- Platform ID. The platform identifier.

- Platform-specific ID. The platform-specific encoding identifier.

- Language ID. The language identifier.

- Name ID. The name identifier.

- Length. The length of the string, in bytes.

- Offset. The offset from the start of storage area, in bytes.

The storage area at the end of the naming table contains the actual string data.

There is no length limit for the strings contained in a name record, but font designers should not include empty strings (of byte length 0). The Font Manager sorts the entries in the naming table first by platform identifier, next by platform-specific identifier, next by language identifier, and last by name identifier.

To keep the size of this table small, a font designer may make a limited set of name records in a small set of languages, because the font can be localized and the existing strings translated or new strings added. Other parts of the outline font resource that need these strings can refer to them by their index number, and applications that need a particular string can look it up by its platform identifier, language identifier, and font name identifier. Platform IDs are shown in Table 4-2, language identifiers are shown in Table 4-4, and font name identifiers are shown in Table 4-5.

TrueType outline fonts are available on other platforms besides the Macintosh computer, which is why the font designer must specify the platform. There are only four predefined platform identifiers, listed in Table 4-2, and they use values 0 through 3.

Table 4-2   Platform identifiers

ID	Platform	Specific encoding
0	Unicode	Reserved (set to 0)
1	Macintosh	The Script Manager code
2	ISO	ISO encoding
3	Microsoft	Microsoft encoding
240–255	User-defined	Reserved for all nonregistered platforms

When the platform used is the Macintosh computer, the platform-specific identifier names the specific script code for this name record. The script codes defined for the Macintosh system software are listed in the chapter "Script Manager" in this book.

The platform-specific identifier encodings for the ISO platform are listed in Table 4-3.

Table 4-3   ISO platform-specific identifiers

Code	ISO encoding scheme
0	7-bit ASCII
1	ISO 10646
2	ISO 8859-1

The value of the language identifier specifies the language in which a particular string is written. The language identifiers available on the Macintosh platform are listed in Table 4-4.

Table 4-4   ISO language codes

Code	Language	Code	Language
0	English	12	Arabic
1	French	13	Finnish
2	German	14	Greek
3	Italian	15	Icelandic
4	Dutch	16	Maltese
5	Swedish	17	Turkish
6	Spanish	18	Yugoslavian
7	Danish	19	Chinese
8	Portuguese	20	Urdu
9	Norwegian	21	Hindi
10	Hebrew	22	Thai
11	Japanese		

Font Manager

The font name identifier values, listed in Table 4-5, contain the strings with information about the font.

Table 4-5   Font name identifiers

Code	Meaning	Description
0	Copyright notice	The copyright notice of the font—for example, "Copyright Apple Computer, Inc. 1992"
1	Font family name	The font family name, such as "New York"
2	Font style	The style of the font, such as "Bold"
3	Font identification	A unique identification string for the font—for example, "Apple Computer New York Bold version 1.0"
4	Full font name	The font family name combined with the font style name—for example, "New York Bold"
5	Version string	The version of the font, or when it was created—for example, "August 10, 1991, 1.08d21"
6	PostScript name of the font	A name of this font that the PostScript printer driver can recognize—for example, "Times-Bold"
7	Trademark	The trademark notice of the designer
8	Designer	Corporate name of the designer

The full font name for a font family, given in string 4 of Table 4-5, is most often the same as the family name, given in string 1. The default style for a family or the only font in a family should have "Regular" in the font style string. (Font designers use the term "Regular" to denote the plain style for a font, so as to reflect typographic terminology more accurately.) One exception, based on historical convention, is when the full name of a font includes the word "Roman" (e.g. Times Roman). In all other cases, the full name should be made up of the family name and the style name, as in Bookman Bold.

The unique font identification consists of the designer's name, followed by a space serving as a separator, followed by the full name of the font. For example, though there might be many Symbol fonts, the name "Apple Computer Symbol" is unique. The use of unique names allows applications to determine if the current system software has the fonts used in the original document.

The PostScript Table

The PostScript table, with a tag name of 'post', contains information needed to use an outline font on a PostScript printer. It contains the PostScript names for all of the glyphs in the font. It also contains memory information needed by the PostScript driver for memory management. The PostScript table consists of a header component and an optional format component, which is used only for two of the possible four PostScript format types.

The header component of the PostScript table contains the memory requirements. PostScript drivers can make better use of the Memory Manager if the virtual memory requirements of an outline font that can be downloaded to the printer are known beforehand. If the font designer does not know the virtual memory requirements, the values for the memory use requirements of this font are set to zero.

The memory use of a downloaded outline font varies depending on whether it is defined as a TrueType or Adobe™ Type 1 font on the printer. You can compute the minimum memory required for a font as follows:

1. Send the PostScript VMStatus call to the printer and store the result.

2. Download the font to the printer.

3. Send the VMStatus call again.

4. Subtract the first result from the second to calculate the amount of memory that the font requires.

The maximum memory required for a font is computed by adding the maximum run-time memory use to the minimum memory value. The maximum run-time memory use depends on the maximum band size of any bitmap that the outline font scaler might have to create from an outline description.

The Preprogram Table

The preprogram table, with a tag name of 'prep', is an optional table that stores the control value program. This is a set of outline font instructions that the Font Manager executes before it creates any glyph and again whenever the user changes the point size, the angle at which the font is being displayed, or the font itself. This table consists of an ordered list of instruction opcodes, each of which is one byte long. Control values for the instructions in the preprogram are found in the 'cvt ' table, which is described in "The Control-Value Table" on page 4-77.

The Font Family ('FOND') Resource

A font family contains references to the fonts (which can be bitmapped font ['NFNT'], outline font ['sfnt'], or 'FONT' resources) that make up the family and information that describes the family as a whole, such as a global width table for each available style.

The font family ('FOND') resource contains general information about the font family, the font association table, and a collection of optional tables: the family glyph-width table, the style-mapping table, the kerning table, the offset table, and the bounding-box table. Several data structures and routines use the font family resource. For example, the global width table can use the font family information to find the recommended glyph widths and the LaserWriter printer driver can use tables that contain information about kerning pairs and mapping of styles to printer fonts.

The font family resource consists of a header component, which contains general information about the font family, and a font family tables component, which consists of the font association table and some number (possibly zero) of the optional tables that provide measurement and naming information about the font family. The header component of this resource is represented by the FamRec data type, the declaration of which is shown in the section "The Font Family Record" on page 4-47. The structure of this resource is shown in Figure 4-22.

Figure 4-22 The font family ('FOND') resource

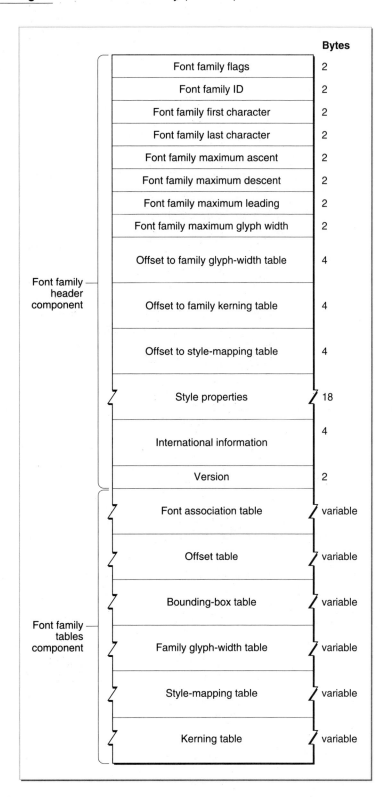

The header component of the font family resource consists of a number of elements that describe characteristics of the family. Each of the elements in this component is represented by a field in the `FamRec` data type.

■ Font family flags. An integer value, the bits of which specify general characteristics of the font family. This value is represented by the `ffFlags` field in the `FamRec` data type. The bits in the `ffFlags` field have the following meanings:

Bit	Meaning
0	This bit is reserved by Apple and should be cleared to 0.
1	This bit is set to 1 if the resource contains a glyph-width table.
2–11	These bits are reserved by Apple and should be cleared to 0.
12	This bit is set to 1 if the font family ignores the value of the `FractEnable` global variable when deciding whether to use fixed-point values for stylistic variations; the value of bit 13 is then the deciding factor. The value of the `FractEnable` global variable is set by the `SetFractEnable` procedure.
13	This bit is set to 1 if the font family should use integer extra width for stylistic variations. If not set, the font family should compute the fixed-point extra width from the family style-mapping table, but only if the `FractEnable` global variable has a value of `TRUE`.
14	This bit is set to 1 if the family fractional-width table is not used, and is cleared to 0 if the table is used.
15	This bit is set to 1 if the font family describes fixed-width fonts, and is cleared to 0 if the font describes proportional fonts.

■ Font family ID. An integer value that specifies the `'FOND'` resource ID number for this font family. This value is represented by the `ffFamID` field in the `FamRec` data type.

■ Font family first character. An integer value that specifies the ASCII character code of the first glyph in the font family. This value is represented by the `ffFirstChar` field in the `FamRec` data type.

■ Font family last character. An integer value that specifies the ASCII character code of the last glyph in the font family. This value is represented by the `ffLastChar` field in the `FamRec` data type.

■ Font family maximum ascent. The maximum ascent measurement for a one-point font of the font family. This value is in a 16-bit fixed-point format with an integer part in the high-order 4 bits and a fractional part in the low-order 12 bits. This value is represented by the `ffAscent` field in the `FamRec` data type.

■ Font family maximum descent. The maximum descent measurement for a one-point font of the font family. This value is in a 16-bit fixed-point format with an integer part in the high-order 4 bits and a fractional part in the low-order 12 bits. This value is represented by the `ffDescent` field in the `FamRec` data type.

■ Font family maximum leading. The maximum leading for a 1-point font of the font family. This value is in a 16-bit fixed-point format with an integer part in the high-order 4 bits and a fractional part in the low-order 12 bits. This value is represented by the ffLeading field in the FamRec data type.

■ Font family maximum glyph width. The maximum glyph width of any glyph in a one-point font of the font family. This value is in a 16-bit fixed-point format with an integer part in the high-order 4 bits and a fractional part in the low-order 12 bits. This value is represented by the ffWidMax field in the FamRec data type.

■ Offset to family glyph-width table. The offset to the family glyph-width table from the beginning of the font family resource to the beginning of the table, in bytes. The family glyph-width table is described in the section "The Family Glyph-Width Table," beginning on page 4-98. This value is represented by the ffTabOff field in the FamRec data type.

■ Offset to family kerning table. The offset to the beginning of the kerning table from the beginning of the 'FOND' resource, in bytes. The kerning table is described in the section "The Font Family Kerning Table," beginning on page 4-106. This value is represented by the ffKernOff field in the FamRec data type.

■ Offset to family style-mapping table. The offset to the style-mapping table from the beginning of the font family resource to the beginning of the table, in bytes. The style-mapping table is described in the section "The Style-Mapping Table," beginning on page 4-99. This value is represented by the ffStyleOff field in the FamRec data type.

■ Style properties. An array of 9 integers, each indicating the extra width, in pixels, that would be added to the glyphs of a 1-point font in this font family after a stylistic variation has been applied. This value is represented by the ffProperty field in the FamRec data type, which is an array with nine values. The Font Manager multiplies these values by the requested point size to get the correct width. Each value is in a 16-bit fixed-point format with an integer part in the high-order 4 bits and a fractional part in the low-order 12 bits. If the font with a given stylistic variation already exists as an intrinsic font, the Font Manager ignores the value in the ffProperty field for that style. The values in this array are used as follows:

Property index	Meaning
1	Extra width for plain text. Should be set to 0.
2	Extra width for bold text.
3	Extra width for italic text.
4	Extra width for underline text.
5	Extra width for outline text.
6	Extra width for shadow text.
7	Extra width for condensed text.
8	Extra width for extended text.
9	Not used. Should be set to 0.

■ International information. An array of 2 integers reserved for internal use by script management software. This value is represented by the ffIntl field in the FamRec data type.

■ Version. An integer value that specifies the version number of the font family resource, which indicates whether certain tables are available. This value is represented by the ffVersion field in the FamRec data type. Because this field has been used inconsistently in the system software, it is better to analyze the data in the resource itself instead of relying on the version number. The possible values are as follows:

Value	Meaning
$0000	Created by the Macintosh system software. The font family resource will not have the glyph-width tables and the fields will contain 0.
$0001	Original format as designed by the font developer. This font family record probably has the width tables and most of the fields are filled.
$0002	This record may contain the offset and bounding-box tables.
$0003	This record definitely contains the offset and bounding-box tables.

The font family tables component of the font family resource contains a number of tables. The font association table must be included in the resource, but the other tables are all optional. You can determine whether or not the glyph-width, kerning, or style-mapping tables are present by examining the offset value for each. Each offset value is a number of bytes from the beginning of the resource to the table; an offset of 0 means that the table is not present. For example, if the value of the ffWTabOff field is greater than 0, the glyph-width table is present in the resource data.

Additional tables, including the bounding-box table, can be added to the font family resource by a font designer. Whenever any table, including the glyph-width, kerning, and style-mapping tables, is included in the resource data, an offset table is included. The offset table contains a long integer offset value for each table that follows it.

The Font Style Code

A number of tables in the font family resource contain information that pertains only to a certain style. Actually, a style can be a combination of styles. The **style code** data type, which is used to represent a style in the tables in this resource, uses a single bit for each of the seven Macintosh character styles. You can set any of these bits to 1 in the style code element of a table to specify the unique style of the font to which that table applies. Although each table that contains a font style code allocates 2 bytes for the value, only the low-order byte of the value is used to specify the style code; the high-order byte is used internally by the Font Manager. The values of the bits in a style code element are shown in Figure 4-23.

Figure 4-23   Style codes

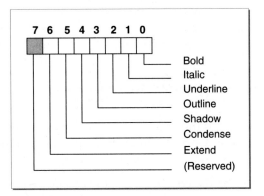

The Font Association Table

The font association table of the font family resource maps a point size and style into a specific font that is part of the family. This table is represented by the `fontAssoc` field of the font family resource. This table, which is shown in Figure 4-24, matches a given font size and style combination with the resource ID of a `'FONT'`, bitmapped, or outline resource.

Figure 4-24   The font association table

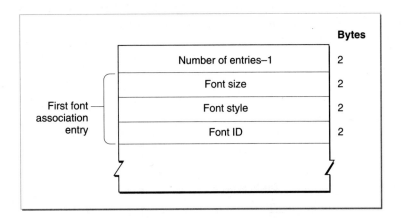

The font association table consists of an integer count and a variable number of font association entries. The table is represented by the `FontAssoc` data type, which is shown on page 4-47.

- Number of entries. An integer value that specifies the number of font association records in this table minus 1. This value is represented by the `numAssoc` field in the `FontAssoc` data type.

Each font association entry is represented by the AsscEntry data type, which is shown on page 4-48. The Font Manager looks first for outline font resources, then bitmapped font resources, then 'FONT' resources. Entries are sorted according to point size, with the smallest sizes coming first in the table. The font size value for outline font resources is 0, so they are always listed first. Plain fonts are sorted before styled fonts. The elements of each entry are:

- Font size. This integer value specifies the size of the font in points. This value is represented by the fontSize field of the AsscEntry data type.

- Font style. This integer value specifies the style code of the entry, as shown in Figure 4-23 on page 4-95. This value is represented by the fontStyle field of the AsscEntry data type.

- Font ID. This integer value specifies the resource ID of the related 'sfnt', 'NFNT', or 'FONT' resource. This value is represented by the fontID field of the AsscEntry data type.

Note
Bits 8 and 9 of the fontStyle field of the font association table entry specify the font depth. They need to contain the same values as bits 2 and 3 of the fontType field of the font resource that this entry describes. ◆

The Offset Table

The offset table is an optional table that is included in the font family resource whenever any of the other optional tables are included. This table, which is shown in Figure 4-25, allows the font designer to add more tables to the font family resource.

Figure 4-25   The offset table

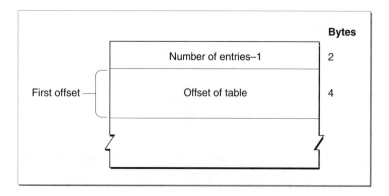

The offset table consists of an integer count and a variable number of table offset values, each of which is 4 bytes long. There is no data type defined for this table.

■ Number of entries. An integer value that specifies the number of offset values in this table minus 1.

■ Offset of table. A long integer value that specifies the number of bytes from the start of the offset table to the start of the table.

The Bounding-Box Table

The bounding-box table, shown in Figure 4-26, contains the bounding-box measurements for a 1-point font. The bounding boxes used in this table are similar to the font rectangle, since each describes the smallest rectangle that encloses the shape of each glyph in a given font. There are separate bounding-box entries in the table for different styles.

Figure 4-26   The bounding-box table

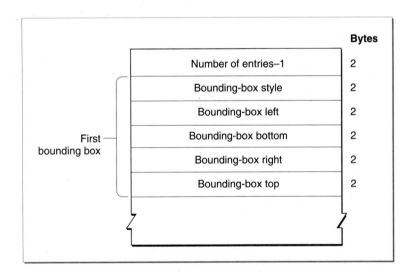

The bounding-box table consists of an integer count and a variable number of bounding-box entries, each of which is 10 bytes long. There is no data type defined for this table.

■ Number of entries. An integer value that specifies the number of bounding-box entries in this table minus 1.

Each bounding-box entry consists of the following elements. There is no data type defined for these entries, each of which is 10 bytes long.

■ Bounding-box style. An integer value that specifies the style code for this bounding-box entry. Style codes are shown in Figure 4-23 on page 4-95.

■ Bounding-box left. The coordinate value of the left edge of the bounding box, in 16-bit fixed-point format, with an integer part in the high-order 4 bits and a fractional part in the low-order 12 bits.

■ Bounding-box bottom. The coordinate value of the bottom edge of the bounding box, in 16-bit fixed-point format, with an integer part in the high-order 4 bits and a fractional part in the low-order 12 bits.

■ Bounding-box right. The coordinate value of the right edge of the bounding box, in 16-bit fixed-point format, with an integer part in the high-order 4 bits and a fractional part in the low-order 12 bits.

■ Bounding-box top. The coordinate value of the top edge of the bounding box, in 16-bit fixed-point format, with an integer part in the high-order 4 bits and a fractional part in the low-order 12 bits.

The Family Glyph-Width Table

The font family glyph-width table is used to specify glyph widths for the font family on a per-style basis. This table, which is shown in Figure 4-27, can contain a number of glyph-width subtables, with one subtable for each style in the family.

Figure 4-27   The font family glyph-width table

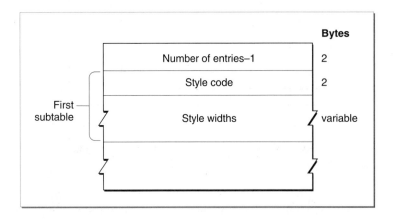

The family glyph-width table consists of an integer count and a variable number of glyph-width subtables. The table is represented by the `WidTable` data type, which is shown on page 4-48.

■ Number of entries. An integer value that specifies the number of bounding-box entries in this table minus 1. This value is represented by the `numWidths` field in the `WidTable` data type.

Each glyph-width subtable in the table is represented by the `WidEntry` data type, which is shown on page 4-48. Each subtable consists of the following elements.

■ Style code. An integer value that specifies the style code for this bounding-box entry. Style codes are shown in Figure 4-23 on page 4-95. This value is represented by the `widStyle` field in the `WidEntry` data type.

■ Style widths. A variable length array of integer values, with one entry in the array for each glyph in the font. Each width is in 16-bit fixed-point format, with the integer part in the high-order 4 bits and the fractional part in the low-order 12 bits.

The Style-Mapping Table

The printer driver uses *font classes* to differentiate among the different methods of implementing font styles. The style-mapping table provides a flexible way to assign font classes and to specify character-set encodings. The table contains the font class, information about the character-encoding scheme that the font designer used, and a mechanism for obtaining the name of the appropriate printer font. The style-mapping table is primarily used by drivers for high-resolution printers such as the LaserWriter.

The font name suffix subtable and the glyph-encoding subtable that are part of the style-mapping table immediately follow it in the resource data. The font name suffix subtable contains the base font name and the suffixes that can be added to the font family's name to produce a real PostScript name (one that is recognized by the PostScript LaserWriter printer driver). The style-mapping table uses the suffix table to build a font name for a PostScript printer. The glyph-encoding table allows character codes to be mapped to PostScript glyph names. Figure 4-28 shows the structure of the style-mapping table.

Figure 4-28   The style-mapping table

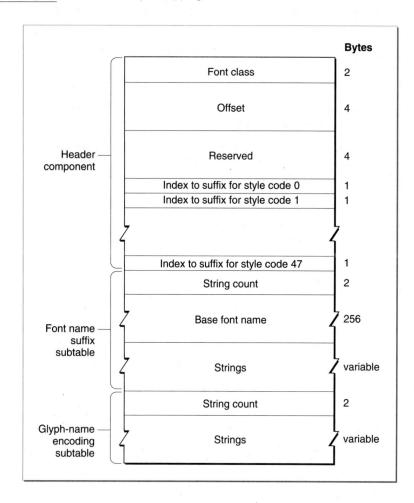

The header component of the style-mapping table contains a list of indexes into the font name suffix subtable, which is described below. The style-mapping table is represented by the `StyleTable` data type, which is shown on page 4-49. The elements of this table are as follows.

- Font class. An integer value that specifies a collection of flags that alert the printer driver to what type of PostScript font this font family is. This value is represented by the `fontClass` field of the `StyleTable` data type. For more information about how these flags are used, see the *LaserWriter Reference* book.

The default font class definition is 0, which has settings that indicate the printer driver should derive the bold, italic, condense, and extend styles from the plain font. Intrinsic fonts are assigned classes (bits 2 through 8) that prevent these derivations from occurring. The meanings of the 16 bits of the `fontClass` word are as follows:

Bit	Meaning
0	This bit is set to 1 if the font name needs coordinating.
1	This bit is set to 1 if the Macintosh vector reencoding scheme is required. Some glyphs in the Apple character set, such as the Apple glyph, do not occur in the standard Adobe character set. This glyph must be mapped in from a font that has it, such as the Symbol font, to a font that does not, like Helvetica.
2	This bit is set to 1 if the font family creates the outline style by changing PaintType, a PostScript variable, to 2.
3	This bit is set to 1 if the font family disallows simulating the outline style by smearing the glyph and whiting out the middle.
4	This bit is set to 1 if the font family does not allow simulation of the bold style by smearing the glyphs.
5	This bit is set to 1 if the font family simulates the bold style by increasing point size.
6	This bit is set to 1 if the font family disallows simulating the italic style.
7	This bit is set to 1 if the font family disallows automatic simulation of the condense style.
8	This bit is set to 1 if the font family disallows automatic simulation of the extend style.
9	This bit is set to 1 if the font family requires reencoding other than Macintosh vector encoding, in which case the glyph-encoding table is present.
10	This bit is set to 1 if the font family should have no additional intercharacter spacing other than the space character.
11–15	Reserved. Should be set to 0.

- Offset. A long integer value that specifies the offset from the start of this table to the glyph-encoding subtable component. This value is represented by the `offset` field of the `StyleTable` data type.

- Reserved. A long integer element reserved for use by Apple Computer, Inc.

- Index to font name suffix subtable. This is an array of 48 integer index values, each of which is a location in the naming table. The value of the first element is an index into the naming table for the string name for style code 0; the value of the forty-eighth element is an index into the naming table for the string name for style code 47. This array is represented by the `indexes` field of the `StyleTable` data type.

The Font Name Suffix Subtable

The font name suffix subtable is part of the style-mapping table. This subtable contains the base font name and the suffixes that can be added to the font family's name to produce a real PostScript name (that is, one that is recognized by the PostScript printer driver). This subtable is represented by the `NameTable` data type, which is described on page 4-49. It consists of the following elements:

- String count. An integer value that specifies the number of strings in the array of suffixes. This value is represented by the `stringCount` field of the `NameTable` data type.

- Base font name. The font family name in a 256 byte long Pascal string. This value is represented by the `baseFontName` field of the `NameTable` data type.

- Strings. A variable length array of Pascal strings, each of which contains the suffixes or numbers specifying which suffixes to put together to produce the real PostScript name. This array is represented by the `strings` field of the `NameTable` data type. This section describes the format of these strings and provides an example of using this subtable.

Each of the strings in the string list contains a sequence of one-byte values, the first of which specifies how many other bytes follow, and each of the following contains an index value. To form the complete name of a font, the base name is concatenated with each of the strings whose index is in the string.

For an example of how this table works, consider the PostScript name of the bold-italic version of the font ExampleFont. Here are the strings of the font name suffix subtable for this font:

Index	Contents
1	`'ExampleFont'`
2	`$02 $09 $0A`
3	`$02 $09 $0B`
4	`$03 $09 $0A $0B`
5	`$02 $09 $0C`
6	`$04 $09 $0C $09 $0A`
7	`$04 $09 $0C $09 $0B`
8	`$05 $09 $0C $09 $0A $0B`
9	–
10	`'Bold'`
11	`'Oblique'`
12	`'Narrow'`

QuickDraw has assigned the bold-italic style the number $03; since the base font name is the first entry in this array, you need to access the entry at *i*+1, where *i* is the style value. So, for the bold-italic style, you look at the fourth string. The first byte in this string is $03, which indicates that three string indexes follow.

- The first index is $09, which produces the string '-'.

- The second index is $0A, which produces the string 'Bold'.

- The third index is $0B, which produces the string 'Oblique'.

By concatenating them together with the base font name, you produce the font name string "ExampleFont-BoldOblique". If the LaserWriter printer driver cannot find the font on the printer, it looks for the font: in version 7.1 and later of system software, the driver looks in the "Fonts" folder; in earlier versions of system software, it first looks in the folder where the driver code is located, then in the System Folder. If the font is there, the driver sends it to the printer. If it is not, the driver sends a QuickDraw bitmap that has already been scaled to the correct size.

Listing 4-4 provides a function for using the style table to build a full PostScript font name.

Listing 4-4   Using the style-mapping table to build a PostScript font name

```
TYPE
    IntegerPtr = ^Integer;
    FamRecPtr = ^FamRec;
    FamRecHdl = ^FamRecPtr;
    StyleTablePtr = ^StyleTable;

FUNCTION MyCompressStyle (aStyle: Style): Integer;
    {A "Set of StyleItem" is mapped into [0..47],}
    {assuming that condense and extend are mutually exclusive}

VAR
    styleCode: Integer;

BEGIN
    styleCode := 0;
    IF bold IN aStyle THEN
        styleCode := styleCode + 1;
    IF italic IN aStyle THEN
        styleCode := styleCode + 2;
    IF outline IN aStyle THEN
        styleCode := styleCode + 4;
    IF shadow IN aStyle THEN
        styleCode := styleCode + 8;
```

```
        IF condense IN aStyle THEN
            styleCode := styleCode + 16
        ELSE IF extend IN aStyle THEN
            styleCode := styleCode + 32;
        MyCompressStyle := styleCode;
END;



FUNCTION MyNthStyleName (index: Integer; q: Ptr): Str255;

VAR
    s: Str255;

BEGIN
    WHILE index > 1 DO
        BEGIN
        q := Ptr(ord(q) + q^ + 1);
                        { assumes q^ = stringlength < 128 ...}
        index := index - 1;
        END;
    BlockMove(q, @s[0], q^ + 1);
                        { assumes q^ = stringlength < 127 ...}
    MyNthStyleName := s;
END;



FUNCTION MyPSFontName(fh: FamRecHdl; aStyle: Style): Str255;
VAR
    stp: StyleTablePtr;
    q: Ptr;     { pointer to Style-name table. }
                { This is not a Pascal structure. }
    PSName, suffixIndices: Str255;
    i, nbOfStrings, offset, whichIndex: Integer;

BEGIN
    PSName := '';
    offset := fh^^.ffStylOff;
    IF offset > 0 THEN
```

```
    BEGIN
    stp := StyleTablePtr(ord(fh^) + offset);
    q := Ptr(ord(stp) + SizeOf(StyleTable));
            { style-name table follows style-mappingTable}
    nbOfStrings := IntegerPtr(q)^;
        { for range checking below }
    q := Ptr(ord(q) + 2);
            { now pointing to basename of font }
    BlockMove(q, @PSName, q^ + 1);
            { basename of font; assumes length < 128 }
    whichIndex := stp^.indexes[MyCompressStyle(aStyle)];
    IF (whichIndex > 1) AND (whichIndex <= nbOfStrings) THEN
        BEGIN
        suffixIndices := MyNthStyleName(whichIndex, q);
        FOR i := 1 TO ord(suffixIndices[0]) DO
            PSName := concat(PSName,
                MyNthStyleName(ord(suffixIndices[i]), q));
        END
    ELSE { corrupted FOND };
    END
ELSE { no style mapping table in FOND };
MyBuildPSFontName := PSName;
END;
```

The Glyph-Name Encoding Subtable

The glyph-name encoding subtable of the style-mapping table allows the font family
designer to map 8-bit character codes to PostScript glyph names. This subtable is
required when the font family character set is not the Standard Roman character set or
the standard Adobe character set. Each entry in this table is a Pascal string, the first byte
of which is the character code that is being mapped, and the remaining bytes of which
specify the PostScript glyph name.

There is no data type defined to represent the glyph-encoding subtable. The elements of
this subtable are as follows:

- String count. An integer value that specifies the number of entries in the
  encoding subtable.

- Strings. A variable length array of Pascal strings. The first byte of each string is an
  eight-bit character code, and the remaining bytes are the name of a PostScript glyph.
  This section beginning on page 4-105, provides an example of using this table.

The following example demonstrates the use of an encoding table in a font resource:

Byte sequence	Use
$0002	The number of entries in this encoding table.
$A8	The character code of the first character that is being remapped.
'diamond'	The name of the PostScript character to be used for character code $A8.
$A9	The character code of the second (and last) character that is being remapped.
'heart'	The name of the PostScript character to be used for character code $A9.

The effect of this table is to assign the PostScript character named diamond to the character code $A8 and to assign the PostScript character named heart to the character code $A9. If either of these character codes has a character assigned to it in the font, that character is replaced by the PostScript character named in the table.

For more information about the font name suffix subtable and the glyph-name encoding table, please see the *LaserWriter Reference*.

The Font Family Kerning Table

The font family kerning table consists of a group of kerning subtable entries. Each subtable contains the measurements of a hypothetical 1-point font of this family with a different stylistic variation. The Font Manager multiplies these measurements by the requested font size. The structure of the font family kerning table is shown in Figure 4-29.

Figure 4-29   The font family kerning table

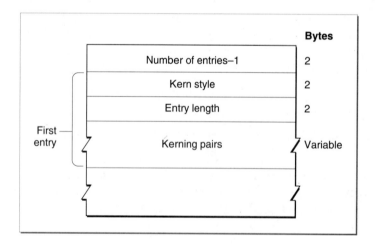

The font family kerning table is represented by the `KernTable` data type, which is shown on page 4-49. It consists of a count, followed by a variable number of kerning subtable entries.

■ Number of entries. This is an integer value that specifies the number of kerning subtable entries in this table minus 1. This value is represented by the `numKerns` field of the `KernTable` data type.

Each kerning subtable entry is represented by the `KernEntry` data type, which is described on page 4-50. Each subtable pertains to a specific style code and contains a variable number of kerning pair entries. The style code values are shown in Figure 4-23 on page 4-95. The elements of each subtable entry are as follows:

■ Kern style. This is an integer value that specifies the style code to which the kerning information in the subtable pertains. This value is represented by the `kernStyle` field of the `KernEntry` data type.

■ Entry length. This is an integer value that specifies the number of bytes in this kerning subtable. This value is represented by the `kernLength` field of the `KernEntry` data type.

Each kerning pair entry specifies a kerning distance in pixels for a pair of glyphs. Each glyph is specified by its character code. The structure of the kerning pair entry is shown in Figure 4-30.

Figure 4-30   A kerning pair entry

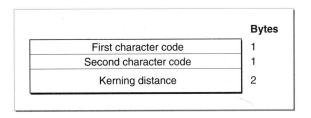

Each kerning pair entry is represented by the `KernPair` data type, which is shown on page 4-50. The elements of each entry are as follows:

■ First character code. The one-byte character code of the first glyph of the kerning pair. This value is represented by the `kernFirst` field of the `KernPair` data type.

■ Second character code. The one-byte character code of the second glyph of the kerning pair. This value is represented by the `kernSecond` field of the `KernPair` data type.

■ Kerning distance. The kerning distance, in pixels, for the two glyphs at a point size of 1. This is a 16-bit fixed point value, with the integer part in the high-order 4 bits, and the fractional part in the low-order 12 bits. The Font Manager measures the distance in pixels and then multiplies it by the requested point size. This value is represented by the `kernWidth` field of the `KernPair` data type.

Summary of the Font Manager

Pascal Summary

Constants

```
CONST
    systemFont = 0;
    applFont = 1;
    newYork = 2;
    geneva = 3;
    monaco = 4;
    venice = 5;
    london = 6;
    athens = 7;
    sanFran = 8;
    toronto = 9;
    cairo = 11;
    losAngeles = 12;
    times = 20;
    helvetica = 21;
    courier = 22;
    symbol = 23;
    mobile = 24;
```

Data Types

```
TYPE FMInput =
PACKED RECORD
    family:      Integer;    {font family ID}
    size:        Integer;    {requested point size}
    face:        Style;      {requested font style}
    needBits:    Boolean;    {if bitmaps need to be constructed}
    device:      Integer;    {device driver ID}
    numer:       Point;      {scaling factor numerators}
    denom:       Point;      {scaling factor denominators}
END;
```

```
TYPE FMOutput =
PACKED RECORD
    errNum:         Integer;        {reserved for internal use}
    fontHandle:     Handle;         {handle to font}
    bold:           Byte;           {for drawing of bold style}
    italic:         Byte;           {for drawing of italic style}
    ulOffset:       Byte;           {for drawing of underline style}
    ulShadow:       Byte;           {for drawing of underline shadow style}
    ulThick:        Byte;           {for drawing of underline thickness}
    shadow:         Byte;           {for drawing of shadow style}
    extra:          SignedByte;     {# of pixels added for styles}
    ascent:         Byte;           {ascent measurement of font}
    descent:        Byte;           {descent measurement of font}
    widMax:         Byte;           {maximum width of glyphs in font}
    leading:        SignedByte;     {leading value for font}
    fOutCurStyle:   Byte;           {actual output font style}
    numer:          Point;          {scaling factor numerators}
    denom:          Point;          {scaling factor denominators}
END;

Type WidthTable =
PACKED RECORD
    tabData:        ARRAY [1..256] OF Fixed;
                                    {character widths}
    tabFont:        Handle;         {font record used to build table}
    sExtra:         LongInt;        {extra line spacing}
    style:          LongInt;        {extra line spacing due to style}
    fID:            Integer;        {font family ID}
    fSize:          Integer;        {font size request}
    face:           Integer;        {style (face) request}
    device:         Integer;        {device requested}
    inNumer:        Point;          {scale factors requested}
    inDenom:        Point;          {scale factors requested}
    aFID:           Integer;        {actual font family ID for table}
    fHand:          Handle;         {family record used to build up table}
    usedFam:        Boolean;        {used fixed-point family widths}
    aFace:          Byte;           {actual face produced}
    vOutput:        Integer;        {vertical scale output value}
    hOutput:        Integer;        {horizontal scale output value}
    vFactor:        Integer;        {vertical scale output value}
    hFactor:        Integer;        {horizontal scale output value}
    aSize:          Integer;        {size of actual font used}
    tabSize:        Integer;        {total size of table}
END;
```

```
TYPE FontRec =
RECORD
    fontType:       Integer;        {font type}
    firstChar:      Integer;        {character code of first glyph}
    lastChar:       Integer;        {character code of last glyph}
    widMax:         Integer;        {maximum glyph width}
    kernMax:        Integer;        {negative of maximum glyph kern}
    nDescent:       Integer;        {negative of descent}
    fRectWidth:     Integer;        {width of font rectangle}
    fRectHeight:    Integer;        {height of font rectangle}
    owTLoc:         Integer;        {location of width/offset table}
    ascent:         Integer;        {ascent}
    descent:        Integer;        {descent}
    leading:        Integer;        {leading}
    rowWords:       Integer;        {row width of bit image / 2 }
END;

TYPE FamRec =
RECORD
    ffFlags:        Integer;        {flags for family}
    ffFamID:        Integer;        {family ID number}
    ffFirstChar:    Integer;        {ASCII code of 1st character}
    ffLastChar:     Integer;        {ASCII code of last character}
    ffAscent:       Integer;        {maximum ascent for 1 pt font}
    ffDescent:      Integer;        {maximum descent for 1 pt font}
    ffLeading:      Integer;        {maximum leading for 1 pt font}
    ffWidMax:       Integer;        {maximum widMax for 1 pt font}
    ffWTabOff:      LongInt;        {offset to width table}
    ffKernOff:      LongInt;        {offset to kerning table}
    ffStylOff:      LongInt;        {offset to style-mapping table}
    ffProperty:     ARRAY [1..9] OF Integer;
                                    {style property info}
    ffIntl:         ARRAY [1..2] OF Integer;
                                    {for international use}
    ffVersion:      Integer;        {version number}
END;

TYPE FontAssoc =
RECORD
    numAssoc:       Integer;        {number of entries - 1}
END;
```

```
TYPE AsscEntry =
RECORD
    fontSize:       Integer;            {point size of font}
    fontStyle:      Integer;            {style of font}
    fontID:         Integer;            {font resource ID}
END;

TYPE WidTable =
RECORD
    numWidths:      Integer;            {number of entries - 1}
END;

TYPE WidEntry =
RECORD
    widStyle:       Integer;            {style that entry applies to}
END;

TYPE StyleTable =
RECORD
    fontClass:      Integer;            {the font class of this table}
    offset:         LongInt;            {offset to glyph-encoding subtable}
    reserved:       LongInt;            {reserved}
    indexes:        PACKED ARRAY [0..47] OF SignedByte;
                                        {indexes into the font suffix name }
                                        { table that follows this table}
END;

TYPE NameTable =
RECORD
    stringCount:    Integer;            {number of entries}
    baseFontName:   Str255;             {font family name}
END;

TYPE KernTable =
RECORD
    numKerns:       Integer;        {number of subtable entries}
END;

TYPE KernEntry =
RECORD
    kernStyle:      Integer;        {style the entry applies to}
    kernLength:     Integer;        {length of this entry}
END;
```

```
TYPE KernPair =
RECORD
    kernFirst:      Char;        {Code of 1st character of kerned pair}
    kernSecond:     Char;        {Code of 2nd character of kerned pair}
    kernWidth:      Integer;     {kerning value in 1pt fixed format}
END;

Type FMetricRec =
RECORD
    ascent:         Fixed;       {baseline to top}
    descent:        Fixed;       {baseline to bottom}
    leading:        Fixed;       {leading between lines}
    widMax:         Fixed;       {maximum glyph width}
    wTabHandle:     Handle;      {handle to global width table}
END;
```

Routines

Initializing the Font Manager

```
PROCEDURE InitFonts;
```

Getting Font Information

```
PROCEDURE GetFontName        (familyID: Integer;VAR theName: Str255);
PROCEDURE GetFNum            (theName: Str255;VAR familyID: Integer);
FUNCTION RealFont            (fontNum: Integer;size: Integer): Boolean;
```

Using the Current, System, and Application Fonts

```
FUNCTION GetDefFontSize: Integer;
FUNCTION GetSysFont: Integer;
FUNCTION GetAppFont: Integer;
```

Getting the Characteristics of a Font

```
PROCEDURE FontMetrics        (theMetrics: FMetricRec);
FUNCTION OutlineMetrics      (byteCount: Integer; textPtr: UNIV Ptr;
                             numer: Point; denom: Point; VAR yMax: Integer;
                             VAR yMin: Integer; awArray: FixedPtr;
                             lsbArray: FixedPtr; boundsArray: RectPtr):
                             OSErr;
```

Enabling Fractional Glyph Widths

```
PROCEDURE SetFractEnable    (fractEnable: Boolean);
```

Disabling Font Scaling

```
PROCEDURE SetFScaleDisable  (fscaleDisable: Boolean);
```

Favoring Outline Fonts Over Bitmapped Fonts

```
PROCEDURE SetOutlinePreferred
                          (outlinePreferred: Boolean);
FUNCTION GetOutlinePreferred: Boolean;
FUNCTION IsOutline          (numer,denom: Point) : Boolean;
```

Scaling Outline Fonts

```
PROCEDURE SetPreserveGlyph  (preserveGlyph: Boolean);
FUNCTION GetPreserveGlyph: Boolean;
```

Accessing Information About a Font

```
FUNCTION FMSwapFont         (inRec: FMInput): FMOutPtr;
```

Handling Fonts in Memory

```
PROCEDURE SetFontLock       (lockFlag: Boolean);
FUNCTION FlushFonts: OSErr;
```

C Summary

Constants

```
enum {
   systemFont = 0,
   applFont = 1,
   newYork = 2,
   geneva = 3,
   monaco = 4,
   venice = 5,
   london = 6,
   athens = 7,
   sanFran = 8,
   toronto = 9,
```

```
    cairo = 11,
    losAngeles = 12,
    times = 20,
    helvetica = 21,
    courier = 22,
    symbol = 23,
    mobile = 24,
};
```

Data Types

```
struct FMInput {
    short           family;         /*font family ID*/
    short           size;           /*requested point size*/
    Style           face;           /*requested font style*/
    Boolean         needBits;       /*if bitmaps need to be constructed*/
    short           device;         /*device driver ID*/
    Point           numer;          /*scaling factor numerators*/
    Point           denom;          /*scaling factor denominators*/
};

typedef struct FMInput FMInput;

struct FMOutput {
    short           errNum;         /*reserved for internal use*/
    Handle          fontHandle;     /*handle to font*/
    unsigned char   bold;           /*for drawing of bold style*/
    unsigned char   italic;         /*for drawing of italic style*/
    unsigned char   ulOffset;       /*for drawing of underline style*/
    unsigned char   ulShadow;       /*for drawing of underline shadow style*/
    unsigned char   ulThick;        /*for drawing of underline thickness*/
    unsigned char   shadow;         /*for drawing of shadow style*/
    char            extra;          /*# of pixels added for styles*/
    unsigned char   ascent;         /*ascent measurement of font*/
    unsigned char   descent;        /*descent measurement of font*/
    unsigned char   widMax;         /*maximum width of glyphs in font*/
    char            leading;        /*leading value for font*/
    char            fOutCurStyle;   /*actual output font style*/
    Point           numer;          /*scaling factor numerators*/
    Point           denom;          /*scaling factor denominators*/
};

typedef struct FMOutput FMOutput;
```

```
struct WidthTable {
    Fixed           tabData[256];
                                    /*character widths*/
    Handle          tabFont;        /*font record used to build table*/
    long            sExtra;         /*extra line spacing*/
    long            style;          /*extra line spacing due to style*/
    short           fID;            /*font family ID*/
    short           fSize;          /*font size request*/
    short           face;           /*style (face) request*/
    short           device;         /*device requested*/
    Point           inNumer;        /*scale factors requested*/
    Point           inDenom;        /*scale factors requested*/
    short           aFID;           /*actual font family ID for table*/
    Handle          fHand;          /*family record used to build up table*/
    Boolean         usedFam;        /*used fixed-point family widths*/
    unsigned char   aFace;          /*actual face produced*/
    short           vOutput;        /*vertical scale output value*/
    short           hOutput;        /*horizontal scale output value*/

    short           vFactor;        /*vertical scale output value*/
    short           hFactor;        /*horizontal scale output value*/
    short           aSize;          /*size of actual font used*/
    short           tabSize;        /*total size of table*/
};

typedef struct WidthTable WidthTable;

struct FontRec {
    short           fontType;       /*font type*/
    short           firstChar;      /*character code of first glyph*/
    short           lastChar;       /*character code of last glyph*/
    short           widMax;         /*maximum glyph width*/
    short           kernMax;        /*negative of maximum glyph kern*/
    short           nDescent;       /*negative of descent*/
    short           fRectWidth;     /*width of font rectangle*/
    short           fRectHeight;    /*height of font rectangle*/
    short           owTLoc;         /*location of width/offset table*/
    short           ascent;         /*ascent*/
    short           descent;        /*descent*/
    short           leading;        /*leading*/
    short           rowWords;       /*row width of bit image / 2 */
};

typedef struct FontRec FontRec;
```

4

Font Manager

```
struct FamRec {
    short           ffFlags;        /*flags for family*/
    short           ffFamID;        /*family ID number*/
    short           ffFirstChar;    /*ASCII code of 1st character*/
    short           ffLastChar;     /*ASCII code of last character*/
    short           ffAscent;       /*maximum ascent for 1 pt font*/
    short           ffDescent;      /*maximum descent for 1 pt font*/
    short           ffLeading;      /*maximum leading for 1 pt font*/
    short           ffWidMax;       /*maximum widMax for 1 pt font*/
    long            ffWTabOff;      /*offset to width table*/
    long            ffKernOff;      /*offset to kerning table*/
    long            ffStylOff;      /*offset to style-mapping table*/
    short           ffProperty[9];  /*style property info*/
    short           ffIntl[2];      /*for international use*/
    short           ffVersion;      /*version number*/
};

typedef struct FamRec FamRec;

struct FontAssoc {
    short           numAssoc;       /*number of entries - 1*/
};

typedef struct FontAssoc FontAssoc;

struct AsscEntry {
    short           fontSize;       /*point size of font*/
    short           fontStyle;      /*style of font*/
    short           fontID;         /*font resource ID*/
};

typedef struct AsscEntry AsscEntry;

struct WidTable {
    short           numWidths;      /*number of entries - 1*/
};

typedef struct WidTable WidTable;

struct WidEntry {
    short           widStyle;       /*style that entry applies to*/
};

typedef struct WidEntry WidEntry;
```

```
struct StyleTable {
    short           fontClass;      /*the font class of this table*/
    long            offset;         /*offset to glyph-encoding subtable*/
    long            reserved;       /*reserved*/
    char            indexes[47];    /*indexes into the font suffix name table*/
};

typedef struct StyleTable StyleTable;

struct NameTable {
    short           stringCount;    /*number of entries*/
    Str255          baseFontName;   /*font family name*/
};

typedef struct NameTable NameTable;

struct KernTable{
    short           numKerns;       /*number of subtable entries*/
};

typedef struct KernTable KernTable;

struct KernEntry {
    short           kernLength;     /* length of this entry*/
    short           kernStyle;      /* style this entry applies to*/
}

typedef struct KernEntry KernEntry;

struct KernPair {
    char        kernFirst;      /*Code of 1st character of kerned pair*/
    char        kernSecond;     /*Code of 2nd character of kerned pair*/
    short       kernWidth;      /*kerning value in 1pt fixed format*/
};

typedef struct KernPair KernPair;

struct FMetricRec {
    Fixed           ascent;         /*baseline to top*/
    Fixed           descent;        /*baseline to bottom*/
    Fixed           leading;        /*leading between lines*/
    Fixed           widMax;         /*maximum glyph width*/
    Handle          wTabHandle;     /*handle to global width table*/
};

typedef struct FMetricRec FMetricRec;
```

Routines

Initializing the Font Manager

```
pascal void InitFonts        (void);
```

Getting Font Information

```
pascal void GetFontName      (short familyID, Str255 theName);
pascal void GetFNum          (ConstStr255Param name, short *familyID);
pascal Boolean RealFont      (short fontNum, short size);
```

Using the Current, System, and Application Fonts

```
pascal short GetDefFontSize (void);
pascal short GetSysFont      (void);
pascal short GetAppFont      (void);
```

Getting the Characteristics of a Font

```
pascal void FontMetrics      (const FMetricRec *theMetrics);
pascal OSErr OutlineMetrics (short byteCount, const void *textPtr,
                             Point numer, Point denom, short *yMax,
                             short *yMin, FixedPtr awArray,
                             FixedPtr lsbArray, RectPtr boundsArray);
```

Enabling Fractional Glyph Widths

```
pascal void SetFractEnable   (Boolean fractEnable);
```

Disabling Font Scaling

```
pascal void SetFScaleDisable (Boolean fscaleDisable);
```

Favoring Outline Fonts Over Bitmapped Fonts

```
pascal void SetOutlinePreferred
                             (Boolean outlinePreferred);
pascal Boolean GetOutlinePreferred
                             (void);
pascal Boolean IsOutline     (Point numer, Point denom);
```

Scaling Outline Fonts

```
pascal void SetPreserveGlyph
                        (Boolean preserveGlyph);
pascal Boolean GetPreserveGlyph
                        (void);
```

Accessing Information About a Font

```
pascal FMOutPtr FMSwapFont   (const FMInput *inRec);
```

Handling Fonts in Memory

```
pascal void SetFontLock      (Boolean lockFlag);
pascal OSErr FlushFonts      (void);
```

Assembly-Language Summary

Trap Macros

Trap Macros with Trap Words

Trap macro name	Trap word
_FMSwapFont	$A901
_FontMetrics	$A835
_GetFNum	$A900
_GetFontName	$A8FF
_InitFonts	$A8FE
_RealFont	$A902
_SetFontLock	$A903
_SetFScaleDisable	$A834

Trap Macros Requiring Routine Selectors

_FontDispatch

Selector	Routine
$7000	IsOutline
$7001	SetOutlinePreferred
$7008	OutlineMetrics
$7009	GetOutlinePreferred
$700A	SetPreserveGlyph
$700B	GetPreserveGlyph
$700C	FlushFonts

Global Variables

ApFontID	Font ID of application font.
CurFMInput	The current QuickDraw FMInput record for FMSwapFont.
FDevDisable	Disables device-defined extra spacing for styles.
FMDefaultSize	The default point size.
FMgrOutRecc	The current FMOutput record from FMSwapFont.
FONDID	The resource ID of the last font family resource used.
FractEnable	If nonzero, fractional widths are enabled.
FScaleDisable	If nonzero, scaling is disabled.
FScaleHFact	The current horizontal scale factor.
FScaleVFact	The current vertical scale factor.
IntlSpec	International software installed if the value of this is greater than zero.
LastFOND	Handle to last family record used.
LastSPExtra	The most recent value of extra spacing for styles.
ROMFont0	Handle to font record for system font.
SynListHandle	Handle to synthetic font list.
SysFontFam	If nonzero, the font ID to use for the system font.
SysFontSiz	If nonzero, the size of the system font.
UsedFWidths	A flag determining whether fractional widths were used for the most recent font request.
WidthListHand	Handle to a list of handles to recently used width tables (referred to in some places as jFontInfo).
WidthPtr	Pointer to global width table.
WidthTabHandle	Handle to global width table.

Text Utilities

Contents

The Text Utilities provide you with an integrated collection of routines for performing a variety of operations on textual information, ranging from modifying the contents of a string, to sorting strings from different languages, to converting times, dates, and numbers from internal representations to formatted strings and back. These routines work in conjunction with QuickDraw text drawing routines to help you display and modify text in applications that are distributed to an international audience.

Many of the Text Utilities routines were previously located in other managers in the Macintosh system software. Several of these have been replaced with new versions that take a script code as a parameter and others have been renamed. The appendix "Renamed and Relocated Text Routines" in this book shows the original names and locations of all of the text-handling routines.

You need to read this chapter if you are working with text in your application. This includes basic operations such as accessing a string resource and comparing two strings for equality. If you have used Macintosh text-processing routines in the past, you need to review the material in this chapter to understand the new capabilities that have been added to many of the routines.

To understand the material in this chapter, you need to have a basic understanding of the Macintosh script management system. Read this chapter after reading "Introduction to Text on the Macintosh." For parts that describe international resources, read the appendix "International Resources" along with this chapter. For parts that describe text layout, read "QuickDraw Text" along with this chapter.

This chapter describes the resources and text strings with which the Text Utilities interact, and discusses how to use the Text Utilities to compare, sort, modify, and find breaks in text strings, and to convert and format date, time, and numeric strings.

About the Text Utilities

The Text Utilities routines are used for numerous text-handling tasks, including

- defining strings—including functions for allocating strings in the heap and for loading strings from resources

- comparing and sorting strings—including functions for testing whether two strings are equal and functions for finding the sorting relationship between two strings

- modifying the contents of strings—including routines for converting the case of characters, stripping diacritical marks, replacing substrings, and truncating strings

- finding breaks and boundaries in text—including routines for finding word and line breaks, and for finding different script runs in a line of text

- converting and formatting date and time strings—including routines that convert numeric and string representations of dates and times into record format, and routines that convert numeric and record representations of dates and times into strings

- converting and formatting numeric strings—including routines that convert string representations of numbers into numeric representations, and routines that convert from numeric representations into formatted strings

The Text Utilities and the International Resources

Many of the Text Utilities routines script-aware, which means that you need to understand script systems and the international resources to use the routines properly. Each script system contains a collection of these resources, which contain data and routines that define how regional differences are handled. In particular, the international resources contain tables that define how different text elements are represented.

The resources used by the Text Utilities are

- the script-sorting ('itlm') resource, which defines the sorting order among scripts

- the numeric-format ('itl0') resource, which describes details of how time, numbers, and short dates are presented

- the long-date-format ('itl1') resource, which describes how long dates are presented

- the string-manipulation ('itl2') resource, which contains tables that define how strings are sorted and which characters cause breaks between words

- the tokens ('itl4') resource, which contains tables that define which sequences of characters create which tokens

The appendix "International Resources" in this book describes each international resource in detail.

Obtaining Resource Information

Many Text Utilities routines perform operations—such as modifying text or sorting strings—that require information from resources. Some routines determine which resources to use by checking a resource parameter; others check a script code parameter.

For a Text Utilities routine that uses a resource parameter, you can explicitly specify the resource you want to use, or you can specify NIL. The value NIL causes the routine to use the resources associated with the current script. The **current script** is either the system script (the script associated with the currently running version of Macintosh system software) or the font script (the script of the current font in the current graphics port), and is determined by the value of the international resources selection flag, which is represented by the global variable IntlForce. If the value of this flag is TRUE, the current script is the system script; if the value of the flag is FALSE, the current script is the font script. (See Figure 5-1.)

Figure 5-1 Determining the current script

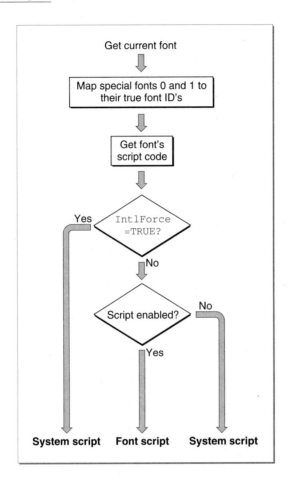

The international resources selection flag is initialized at startup from the system script configuration ('itlc') resource. For most system scripts, the international resources selection flag has a default value of TRUE. If you want to change its value, you can use the SetSMVariable function with the smIntlForce selector. If you want to test its values, you can use the GetSMVariable function with the same selector. The GetSMVariable and SetSMVariable functions are described in the chapter "Script Manager" in this book.

The value of the international resources selection flag actually controls the operation of the GetIntlResource function, which is used by other routines to access the international resources. The operation of GetIntlResource is described in detail in the chapter "Script Manager" in this book.

Other Text Utilities routines use a script code parameter, in which you specify the unique number that defines the script system whose resources you want to use.

Constants for all defined script codes are listed in the chapter "Script Manager" in this book. If you wish, you can specify the following two special constants in the script code parameter: smSystemScript, which indicates that the routine should use the international resources of the system script, and smCurrentScript, which indicates that the routine should use the font script.

Pascal Strings and Text Strings

This chapter describes many routines, almost all of which operate on strings that are specified in one of two forms: as Pascal strings or as text strings. These are two ways of representing text characters, each of which has advantages and disadvantages relative to the other.

A **Pascal string** is an array of characters, the first byte of which defines the number of bytes that follow. This is the standard representation of strings used in Pascal programming. Most of the Text Utilities routines that use Pascal strings use the Str255 or StringHandle type. An advantage of the Str255 type is that it can be passed directly as a single parameter on the stack. A disadvantage is that a Str255 value can hold only up to 255 bytes of character data. A typical Pascal string parameter declaration is as follows:

```
PROCEDURE MyUsePascalString (str: Str255);
```

The alternative representation for character data, a **text string**, can contain up to 32,767 bytes of character data and is specified by two parameters: a pointer to the first byte of character data and a 16-bit integer length value. A typical declaration of a routine that uses a text string parameter declaration is as follows:

```
PROCEDURE MyUseTextString (textPtr: Ptr; textLen: Integer);
```

Some of the Text Utilities routines have been modified to allow for even longer strings. These routines allow a 32-bit integer length value, which means that they can operate on text strings of up to approximately two billion bytes in length.

IMPORTANT

Length is specified in bytes, not characters, for both Pascal strings and text strings. In international text processing, two bytes are sometimes required to represent a single character in certain fonts, as illustrated in Figure 5-2. Because you have to accommodate both 1-byte and 2-byte characters in the same string, the length of each string cannot be specified as a number of characters. ▲

Figure 5-2   A string containing 1-byte and 2-byte characters

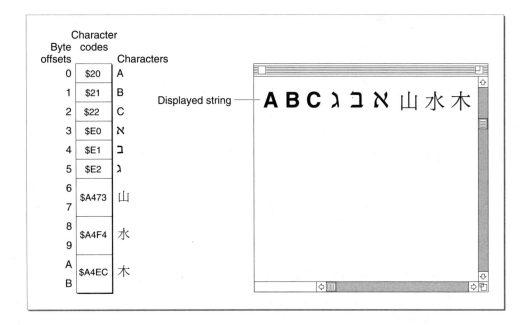

Using the Text Utilities

This section provides you with general information about how to use each group of Text Utilities routines. A description of the basic concepts that each group deals with is provided so that you can learn how to choose the appropriate function to meet your needs. The following areas are covered:

- how to define strings

- how to retrieve the values of string resources

- how to compare and sort strings, including how to sort strings in a multi-language environment

- how to modify strings by converting between uppercase and lowercase and stripping diacritical marks

- how to truncate strings to fit in specified screen areas

- how to search for and replace portions of strings

- how to find word, line, and script run boundaries in strings

- how to convert date and time values into strings, accommodating different international formats for the strings

- how to convert date and time strings into internal numeric representations

- how to convert numeric values into strings, accommodating different international formats for the numbers

Defining Strings

Before you use a string in your application, you must define it in some way. You can use a string variable to represent text characters, or you can allocate an object in the heap to represent those text characters. Many strings, including error messages and lists of input choices, originate in the resource fork of your application; you need access to these string resources before using any of the Text Utilities routines with the strings. This section describes several routines that you can use to allocate strings and to access string resources.

Working With String Handles

When you need to modify a string, it is useful to create a version of the string as an object in the heap. That way, you can increase or reduce the memory allocated for the string object as necessary. String handles provide a means for you to work with heap-oriented strings.

The Text Utilities include two routines that work with strings and string handles. The NewString function creates a copy of a specified string in the heap and returns a handle to that string. The SetString procedure changes the contents of the string referenced by a string handle by copying a specified string into its area of the heap. If you pass SetString a string that is longer than the one originally referenced by the handle, SetString automatically resizes the handle and copies in the contents of the specified string.

For example, suppose that you want to write a routine that creates both an uppercase and lowercase version of an input string. The MyUpperAndLower function shown in Listing 5-1 replaces the contents of the lowerStr parameter with a lowercase version of the str parameter, and returns a new string handle to the uppercase version.

Listing 5-1   Using the NewString and SetString routines

```
FUNCTION MyUpperAndLower (str: Str255;
                          VAR lowerStr: StringHandle): StringHandle;
VAR
   myStr: StringHandle;
   len: Integer;
BEGIN
   myStr := NewString(str);   {create string handle to be converted to upper}
   SetString( lowerStr, str); {set string handle to be converted to lower}
```

```
    len := ord(str[0]);

    HLock(Handle(myStr));          {UppercaseText can move memory}
    UppercaseText(@myStr^^[1], len, smSystemScript);
    HLock(Handle(myStr));

    HLock(Handle(lowerStr));        {LowercaseText can move memory}
    LowercaseText(@lowerStr^^[1], len, smSystemScript);
    HLock(Handle(lowerStr));
    MyUpperAndLower := myStr;
END;
```

Working With String Resources

Since many of the strings in your Macintosh applications are specified in resource files, you need access to those strings. Strings are defined by two different resource types: the string ('STR ') resource and the string list ('STR#') resource. To work with the string resource, you use the GetString function, and to work with a string list resource, you use the GetIndString procedure.

The GetString function reads a string resource into memory and returns the handle to the string resource as its result. GetString does not copy the string, so you must create your own copy if you are going to modify the string in your application. If the resource has already been read into memory, GetString simply returns a handle to the string.

If you use a number of strings in your application, it is more efficient to specify them in a string list resource rather than as individual resources. This is because the system software that reads in the resources can operate more efficiently when reading a collection of strings from a file than when reading and storing each individually.

To work with an element in a string list, use the GetIndString procedure. It reads the resource, locates the string, and copies the string into a Pascal string variable you supply. You can then use the NewString function to create a copy of the string in the heap, if you wish.

Sorting Strings in Different Languages

Strings in the same language must be sorted according to that language's sorting rules; information about these rules is found in resources that belong to that language's script system. [4]

However, if the strings are in two different languages or writing systems, sorting order is also governed by rules about the order among languages or writing systems. For example, an application might need to sort names in English, French, and German, or it might need to sort an index of English and Japanese names written in Roman and Katakana characters.

If you only need to sort strings from a single language in your application, you don't need to read this section or use the routines that are described here. You can skip ahead to the section "Sorting Strings in the Same Language," which begins on page 5-12.

When you sort strings in different languages, you must use routines that work with script-sorting and language-sorting information. The script-sorting ('itlm') resource contains tables that define the sorting order among the languages or writing systems in each script system and among the different script systems that are available. It also shows the parent script for each language, the parent language for each region, and the default language for each script. The ScriptOrder function, which determines the sorting relationship between two script systems, and the LanguageOrder function, which determines the sorting relationship between two languages, use the tables in the script-sorting resource to determine their results. For more information on the script-sorting resource, see the appendix "International Resources" in this book.

To sort two Pascal strings in different languages, you begin by calling the StringOrder function. (You can use the TextOrder function to compare two text strings; it operates in the same way as does StringOrder.) The StringOrder function first calls the ScriptOrder function; if the script codes of the two strings are different, then StringOrder returns a result indicating the sorting relationship between the two script codes. For example, if the first string is from a Japanese script system and the second is from a Thai script system, then the second string comes before the first according to the tables in the script-sorting resource.

If both strings come from the same script system, StringOrder then compares their language codes by calling the LanguageOrder function. If the language codes of the two strings are different, then StringOrder returns a result indicating the sorting relationship between the two language codes. For example, if the first string is in English and the second is in German, then the first string comes before the second according to the tables in the script-sorting resource.

Finally, if the script codes and language codes for both strings are the same, then StringOrder compares the two strings using one of the comparison functions described in the next section, "Sorting Strings in the Same Language."

If you need to sort a collection of strings, you can choose to implement your sorting algorithm so that it uses StringOrder or TextOrder, or you can build a list for each language and/or for each script system and sort each list independently. If you want to use StringOrder or TextOrder, you need to store each string so that you can easily access its script code and language code during the sort.

It is usually desirable to sort all strings from a script system together, using the sorting rules that are associated with the current language for that script on the machine (and ignoring the different sorting rules for the different languages). For example, if you are sorting German, French, and English strings together for a system in England, you usually want the English sorting rules to be applied to all of those strings. In some cases, it may be more efficient to build a list for each language by using the language code of each to determine to which list it belongs. After building a list for each language, you can sort each with an algorithm that uses one of the comparison functions described in the next section, "Sorting Strings in the Same Language."

Figure 5-3 shows a collection of strings from different languages that need to be sorted.

Figure 5-3   Strings in different languages in one list

Script	Language	String
Roman	English	love
	German	Liebe
Japanese	Japanese	愛
Roman	English	peace
	German	Frieden
Japanese	Japanese	平和
Roman	English	hope
	German	Hoffnung
Japanese	Japanese	希望

In Figure 5-4, the strings have been sorted into two lists: one for each script system. The Roman script system strings have been sorted according to the sorting rules for English, which is assumed to be the current language for the script in this example.

Figure 5-4   Strings in different languages sorted by script

Script	Strings
Roman	Frieden Hoffnung hope Liebe love peace
Japanese	希望 愛 平和

Figure 5-5 shows the same strings separated into three lists: one for each language. Each list has been sorted independently by applying the sorting rules for a language. The language lists in each script system have been ordered by calling the `LanguageOrder` function.

Figure 5-5   Strings in different languages sorted by language within script

Script	Language	Sorted strings
Roman	English	hope love peace
	German	Frieden Hoffnung Liebe
Japanese	Japanese	希望 愛 平和

Sorting Strings in the Same Language

The Text Utilities provide a number of routines that you can use to compare and sort strings in the same language. Some of these routines perform a comparison that assumes single-byte character codes in the strings; others take into account the sorting rules of the current script system, and still others allow you to explicitly specify the script system resource to use for sorting strings.

Comparing strings can be an extremely intricate operation, because in many languages you may have to account for subtleties such as complex characters, ignorable characters, and exceptional words. Even for a straightforward language such as English, you can't always determine the sorting order by a simple table lookup or character value comparison.

This section provides an introduction to some of the principles of text comparison and sorting used by the Macintosh script management system. It then describes the routines you can use for different comparison tasks.

Primary and Secondary Sorting Order

Sorting consists of two steps: determining primary sorting order and determining secondary sorting order.

What happens in primary sorting order and secondary sorting order depends on the language of the strings that are being sorted; however, there are two levels of importance in the sorting operation, with some sorting differences subordinate to others. In the primary sorting order for many Roman script system languages, uppercase and lowercase characters are equivalent and diacritical marks are ignored. Thus, after primary sorting, the two strings "The" and "thé" are considered equivalent. In the secondary sorting order, lowercase characters are ranked after uppercase characters and characters with diacritical marks are ranked individually. Thus, after secondary sorting, "The" would sort before "thé".

You can think of the character ranking that is used to determine sorting order as a two-dimensional table. Each row of the table is a class of all characters such as all *A*'s: uppercase and lowercase, with and without diacritical marks. The characters are ordered within each row to form a secondary sorting order, while the order within each column determines primary sorting order. Table 5-1 shows an example of such a table.

Table 5-1   Excerpt from the Standard Roman script system sorting order

Primary sorting order	Secondary sorting order
A	A À Á Â Ä Å Æ a à á â ä å æ
B	B b
C	C Ç c ç
D	D d
E	E È É Ê Ë e è é ê ë
F	F f

In primary sorting, each of the characters in the first row would be considered equivalent and sorted before characters in the second row. In secondary sorting, the order of the characters in each row would be taken into consideration. Another way of saying this is to say that primary sorting characteristics take precedence over secondary sorting characteristics: if any primary differences are present, all secondary differences are ignored. When the strings being compared are of different lengths, each character in the longer string that does not correspond to a character in the shorter one results in a "comes after" result. This takes precedence over secondary sorting order.

For example, here is a list of strings that have not yet been sorted:

Å ab Ác ac Ab àb Ac

After primary sorting, the list appears as follows

Å ab Ab àb Ác ac Ac

After secondary sorting, the list appears as follows

Å Ab ab àb ac Ác Ac

Expansion and Contraction of Characters

In some languages, a single character may be expanded—that is, sorted as a sequence of characters. First, the sorting routine expands the character, then it performs sorting on the expanded version. Next, the sorting routine recombines the character and then performs secondary sorting. For instance, the *ä* in German may be sorted as if it were the two characters *ae*: *Bäcker* would come after *Bad*, but before *Bahn*.

A sequence of characters may also be contracted—that is, sorted as a single character. For instance, *ch* in Spanish may be sorted as if it were one character that sorts after *c* but before *d*: *coche* comes after *coco* but before *codo*.

Ignorable Characters

Certain characters need to be ignored unless the strings are otherwise equal; that is, these characters have no effect on the primary sorting order, but they do influence the secondary sorting order. In English, hyphens, apostrophes, and spaces are ignorable characters. For instance, the hyphen is ignored in primary sorting order in English: *black-bird* would come after *blackbird*, but before *blackbirds*.

Converting and Stripping Characters

Sometimes you may want to strip out certain characters (notably diacritical marks) or convert the case of characters in a string to produce a different comparison result. For example, you may want to convert all alphabetic characters in two strings into uppercase before comparing the strings, rendering uppercase and lowercase characters equivalent. The Text Utilities provide a number of routines for converting the case of characters and for stripping diacritical marks. These routines are described in the section "Modifying Text," which begins on page 5-18.

Special Cases for Sorting

Sometimes the sorting order changes drastically for special cases. For instance, when words are understood to be abbreviations, the strings should be sorted as if they were spelled out in full, as in the following examples.

First string	Second string	Explanation
McDonald	Mary	*McDonald* is treated as *MacDonald*
St. James	Smith	*St.* is an abbreviation for *Saint*
Easy Step	Easy St.	*St.* is an abbreviation for *Street*

Cases such as these require a direct dictionary lookup and are not handled automatically by the Macintosh script management system. Note that some abbreviations are context-dependent, such as *St.*, which may denote *Saint* or *Street*, depending on the meaning of the adjacent text.

Variations in Sorting Behavior

Here are some examples of variations in sorting behavior in different writing systems of the world.

- Sorting in Japanese depends upon the subscript. Kana and Romaji sorting are complicated by the presence of both 1- and 2-byte character codes. Moreover, many Katakana symbols have diacritical marks indicating a sound modification. For example, the symbol for *ga* is formed from the symbol for *ka*. The secondary sorting order for *ga* includes the four combinations of 1-byte or 2-byte *ka* with the 1-byte or 2-byte diacritical mark, plus a 2-byte character that combines the character and diacritical into a single glyph.

  In the Japanese script system, Kanji is currently sorted by character code, which can produce unexpected results. Proper sorting in Kanji is commonly done using one of three methods:

  - First by a character's primary radical, then by the number of remaining strokes.
  - First by the number of total strokes, then by the primary radical.
  - By sound value.

- Sorting in Arabic is quite straightforward except that some characters are ignorable, such as vowels and the extension bar (used to lengthen the cursive connection between characters). Vowels in Arabic are also diacritical marks, overlapping over or under the previous character (the character to the right).

- The Thai script system currently provides for third-level sorting involving character clusters. For more on character clusters, see the chapter "Introduction to Text on the Macintosh" in this book.

Note

If you need to modify a script system's standard string comparison or replace it with your own version, you have to create your own string-manipulation (`'itl2'`) resource by following the guidelines described in the appendix "International Resources" in this book. ◆

Choosing a Comparison Routine

The Text Utilities include six different routines for comparing one string to another. Three of these routines test two strings for equality and the other three determine the ordering relationship between two strings. You can use these routines with Pascal strings and text strings, and they allow you to work with information from various resources or to ignore script and language information altogether.

Figure 5-6 provides you with convenient guidelines for choosing from among the comparison routines included in the Text Utilities. You first decide whether you are comparing two Pascal strings or two text strings, and then decide whether to unconditionally use the Macintosh file system string comparison rules or to explicitly specify a string-manipulation resource that defines such rules. If you use a routine that requires a parameter for a string-manipulation resource handle, you can specify NIL for the value of that parameter to indicate that you want the current script system's string-manipulation resource.

Text Utilities

The top routine names in the boxes in Figure 5-6 are used to test two strings for equality, and the bottom routine names in the boxes are used to compare two strings and determine their sorting order. The term script-aware is used in this figure to indicate that you must explicitly specify a string-manipulation resource as a parameter to a routine, rather than the routine automatically using the file system's string-manipulation rules.

Figure 5-6   Choosing a string comparison routine

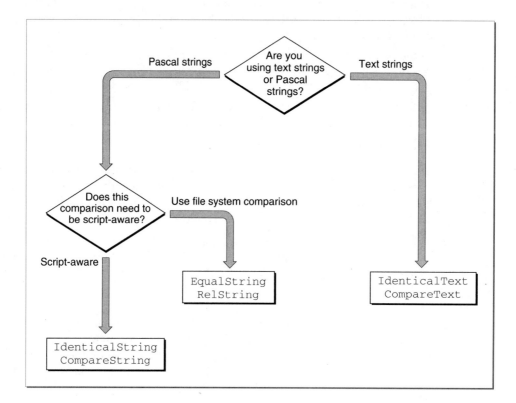

The Macintosh file system string comparison rules are a subset of the Roman script system comparison rules. These rules are used when the Macintosh file system compares filenames for sorting. Since the *Macintosh character set* only contains characters with codes from $0 to $D8, the file system comparison rules only work correctly for character codes through $D8. You should only use the routines that use these rules when you are trying to emulate the way that the Macintosh file system compares strings.

Table 5-2 describes the sorting behavior implemented by the routines that use the file system comparison rules.

Table 5-2   Sorting features of the Macintosh file system

Reordering of ligatures		Stripping of diacritical marks		Uppercase conversion	
Ligature	Falls between	Marked character	Stripped to	Lower	Upper
Æ	Å and a	Ä, Å, À, Ã	A	a–z	A–Z[*]
æ	å and B	Ç	C	à	À
Œ	Ø and o	É	E	ã	Ã
œ	ø and P	Ñ	N	ä	Ä
ß	s and T	Ö, Õ, Ø	O	å	Å
		Ü	U	æ	Æ
		á, à, â, ä, ã, å, [a]	a	ç	Ç
		ç	c	é	É
		é, è, ê, ë	e	ñ	Ñ
		í, ì, î, ï	i	ö	Ö
		ñ	n	õ	Õ
		ó, ò, ô, ö, õ, ø, [o]	o	ø	Ø
		ú, ù, û, ü	u	œ	Œ
		ÿ	y	ü	Ü

[*]All simple lowercase Roman characters are converted to their uppercase equivalents.

Testing Two Strings for Equality

To test whether two strings are equal, use `EqualString`, `IdenticalString`, or `IdenticalText`. You can use the first two functions with Pascal strings, and the last one with text strings.

The functions that work with Pascal strings—`EqualString` and `IdenticalString`—allow you to specify the kind of information you want to consider in your test. If you want to test two Pascal strings using the Macintosh file system comparison rules, use `EqualString`. If you want to consider the information from a string-manipulation resource, use the `IdenticalString` function. You can explicitly specify the handle of a string-manipulation resource or you can specify `NIL` as the value to indicate that you want the current script's string-manipulation resource used.

To test two text strings for equality, you use the `IdenticalText` function, which makes use of the information in a string-manipulation resource. You can explicitly specify the handle of a string-manipulation resource or you can specify `NIL` as the value to indicate that you want the current script's string-manipulation resource used.

Comparing Two Strings for Ordering

There are also three Text Utilities routines that compare two strings and return a value that indicates whether the first string is less than, equal to, or greater than the second string. Two of these routines take Pascal string parameters and the other takes text string parameters.

To compare one Pascal string to another, you have to choose either the `RelString` function or the `CompareString` function. If you want to compare two Pascal strings using the Macintosh file system comparison rules, use `RelString`. If you want to consider the information from a string-manipulation resource, use the `CompareString` function. You can explicitly specify the handle of a string-manipulation resource or you can specify `NIL` as the value to indicate that you want the current script's string-manipulation resource used.

To compare one text string to another, you use the `CompareText` function, which makes use of the information in a string-manipulation resource. You can explicitly specify the handle of a string-manipulation resource or you can specify `NIL` as the value to indicate that you want the current script's string-manipulation resource used.

Modifying Text

The Text Utilities include a number of routines that you can use to modify the contents of strings. Several of these routines operate on Pascal strings, while others operate on text strings.

Several of the text modification routines also take a script code parameter, which is used to indicate which script system's resources should be used to define the results of various character modifications. Script codes are described in the chapter "Script Manager" in this book.

There are three kinds of text modification routines:

- routines that convert the case of characters and strip diacritical marks from characters in a string

- routines that truncate a string to make it fit into a specified area on the screen

- routines that search for a character pattern in a string and replace it with a different character pattern

Converting Characters and Stripping Marks in Strings

Several Text Utilities routines allow you to convert the case of characters and strip diacritical marks from strings. They can be useful when you want to present strings in a simplified form or to store strings in a form that can increase the efficiency of a comparison.

You can use the `UpperString` procedure to convert any lowercase letters in a Pascal string into their uppercase equivalents; however, this procedure assumes that you are using the Macintosh file system conversion rules and does not use any of the information in the international resources to perform its conversion.

You can use the `UppercaseText` procedure to convert any lowercase letters in a text string into their uppercase equivalents. This procedure takes a script code parameter and uses the case conversion information in the string-manipulation resource for the indicated script system to convert the characters.

The `LowercaseText` procedure converts any uppercase letters in a text string into their lowercase equivalents. This procedure takes a script code parameter and uses the case conversion information in the string-manipulation resource for the indicated script system to convert the characters.

The `StripDiacritics` procedure removes any diacritical marks from a text string. This procedure takes a script code parameter and uses the information in the string-manipulation resource for the indicated script system to determine what character results when a diacritical mark is stripped.

The `UppercaseStripDiacritics` procedure combines the effects of the `UppercaseText` and `StripDiacritics` procedures: it converts any lowercase letters to their uppercase equivalents and strips any diacritical marks from characters in a text string. This procedure also takes a script code parameter, which specifies which script system's resources are used to determine conversion results.

Certain other routines in Macintosh system software convert characters in a text string. The `TransliterateText` function converts characters from one subscript into the closest possible approximation in a different subscript within the same script system. The `IntlTokenize` function converts text into language-independent tokens, for further processing by interpreters or compilers. `TransliterateText` and `IntlTokenize` are documented in the chapter "Script Manager" in this book.

Fitting a String Into a Screen Area

When you want to ensure that a string fits in a certain area of the screen, you can use either the `TruncString` or `TruncText` routine. Each performs the same operation: truncating the string (removing characters from it) so that it fits into a specified pixel width. The `TruncString` function truncates a Pascal string and the `TruncText` function truncates a text string.

Both of the truncation functions use the current font—the font currently in use in the current graphics port—and its script to determine where the string should be truncated. The font size is used to determine how many characters can completely fit in the number of pixels specified as a parameter to the function.

Both functions also take a parameter that specifies where any needed truncation is to occur. You can specify that characters are to be truncated from the end or from the middle of the string, as MPW does with pathnames, for example.

A truncation indicator is inserted into a string after characters are truncated; in the U.S. Roman script system, the ellipsis (…) is used for this purpose. You should specify the truncation indicator by token, rather than by specific character code, so that the proper indicator is applied to each script system's text. Specify a token from the untoken table of the tokens ('itl4') resource of the script system of the current font. The untoken table is described in the appendix "International Resources" in this book.

Truncating a string in its middle is commonly used on pathnames, where you want the user to see the beginning and end of the full path, but are willing to sacrifice some of the information in the middle, as shown in Figure 5-7.

Figure 5-7   Truncating a pathname in its middle

Pathname string
Mymac:myfolder: mysubfolder: myownfolder: myfile

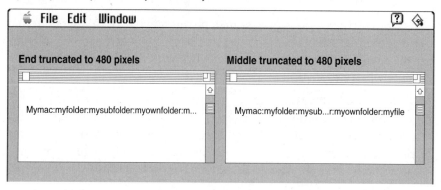

The code in Listing 5-2 performs the truncation that is illustrated in Figure 5-7. Assuming that each character in the string requires 12 pixels, then 480 pixels will be wide enough to hold 40 characters:

Listing 5-2   Truncating a pathname

```
str := "Mymac:myfolder:mysubfolder:myownfolder:myfile"
ans := TruncString( 480, str, truncEnd );    {480 pixels available}
   {str would be "Mymac:myfolder:mysubfolder:myownfolder:…"}
ans := TruncString( 480, str, truncMiddle );
   {str would now be "Mymac:myfolder:mysub…:myownfolder:myfile"}
```

Since the truncation functions can alter the length and contents of the string that you pass in, it is good practice to make a copy of a string before passing it to one of them.

Replacing a Portion of a String

The Text Utilities include two routines for replacing a portion of a string with another string. Each of these routines searches through a string looking for the pattern string. Whenever it finds an occurrence of the pattern string, the routine replaces it with the new string.

The `ReplaceText` function takes information about the current script system into account: it looks through the string character-by-character rather than byte-by-byte. Specifically, this means that `ReplaceText` properly examines strings that contain both 1-byte and 2-byte characters.

The `Munger` function searches for a sequence of bytes and replaces it with another sequence of bytes that you specify. It provides the same capability as `ReplaceText`, but searches for a byte pattern without regard to character length. In a string that contains a mixture of 1-byte and 2-byte characters, `Munger` can, under some conditions, wrongly find a pattern string. This is because the second byte in some 2-byte characters can be wrongly regarded as a 1-byte character.

For example, suppose that you want to search a string for the copyright ("©") character and replace each occurrence with the string "Registered". If you use `Munger` to search a string with Japanese characters in it, `Munger` will mistakenly find and replace the byte with value A9, which is really part of a 2-byte character in the Japanese script system. Figure 5-8 shows how the Japanese word for "morning sun" could be incorrectly identified as containing the copyright character.

Figure 5-8   Replacing a portion of a string with 1-byte and 2-byte characters

`Munger` provides a great deal of power, allowing you to perform many interesting substitutions; however, you need to limit your use of `Munger` in applications that are script-aware, or else do your own checking for 2-byte characters.

Text Utilities

Listing 5-3 uses the `ReplaceText` and `TruncText` functions. It assumes that you have `Str255` strings containing base text and substitution text and that you want the result to fit in a specified number of pixels.

Listing 5-3   Substituting and truncating text

```
CONST
   maxInt = 32767;
VAR
   baseString: Str255;
   subsString: Str255;
   baseHandle: Handle;
   subsHandle: Handle;
   keyStr: Str15;
   sizeL: LongInt;
   myWidth: Integer;
   length: Integer;
   result: Integer;
   myErr: OSErr;

BEGIN
   baseString:'abcdefghijklmnopqrstuvwxyzabcdefghijklmnopqrstuvwxyz';

   subsString := 'KILROY WAS HERE';     {insert this into baseString}
   keyStr := 'mnop';                    {replace this with subString}
   myWidth := 500;                      {truncate string at this width}
   sizeL := ord(baseString[0]);
   myErr := PtrToHand(@baseString[1], baseHandle, sizeL);
   IF myErr <> noErr
      THEN DoError(myErr);
   sizeL := ord(subsString[0]);
   myErr := PtrToHand(@subsString[1], subsHandle, sizeL);
   IF myErr <> noErr
      THEN DoError(myErr);
   result := ReplaceText(baseHandle, subsHandle, keyStr);
   IF result < 0
      THEN DoError(result);
   sizeL := GetHandleSize(baseHandle);
   IF MemError <> noErr
      THEN DoError(MemError);
   length := sizeL;
   HLock(baseHandle);
```

```
IF MemError <> noErr
    THEN DoError(MemError);                {Memory Manager error}
result := TruncText(myWidth, baseHandle^, length, TruncEnd);
IF result < 0
    THEN DoError(result);
DrawText(baseHandle^, 0, length);
HUnlock(baseHandle);
IF MemError <> noErr
    THEN DoError(myErr);                    {Memory Manager error}
END;
```

The code in Listing 5-3 first calls the `ReplaceText` function to replace a portion of the base string (the string initialized to contain the alphabet) with another string. Since two of the parameters to `ReplaceText` are string handles, the code first creates handles to the two strings and verifies that no errors occurred. It then calls the `TruncText` function to remove characters from the end of the modified base string so that the string can be displayed, using the text font, size, and style settings in the current graphics port, in an area 500 pixels wide. Once the string is truncated, the code calls the QuickDraw procedure `DrawText` to draw the string in the current graphics port on the screen.

Finding Word, Line, and Script Run Boundaries

This section describes the Text Utilities routines that you can use to determine where the boundaries of the current word in a text sequence are, where to break the line for drawing text, and where the end of the current subscript text run is. These routines are commonly used in word-processing applications.

Finding Word Boundaries

When working with text in your application, you sometimes need to process each word in the text. You can use the `FindWordBreaks` procedure to determine the starting and ending locations in a string of a word. You pass `FindWordBreaks` a string and a starting position, and it searches backward for the start of the word, then searches forward for the end of the word.

This procedure normally uses the string-manipulation (`'itl2'`) resource of the current script system in determining where the word boundaries are. Most string-manipulation resources include a word-selection break table of type `NBreakTable` that specifies what constitutes a word boundary in that script; however, some string-manipulation resources do not include such a table, in which case `FindWordBreaks` uses default definitions of word boundaries. Some script systems provide a separate extension that allows

FindWordBreaks to find word breaks in a more sophisticated fashion such as using a dictionary lookup. The format of the word-selection break table is described in the appendix "International Resources" in this book.

This procedure returns the beginning and ending of a word in a string. Theses values are returned in a table of type OffsetTable, which contains values that indicate the starting and ending positions in the string of the word. The OffsetTable data structure is described in the section "The Offset Table Record" on page 5-44.

You can also use FindWordBreaks to break lines of text, although the procedure is more complicated than using StyledLineBreak, as described in the next section. For more information, see the discussion of text drawing in the chapter "QuickDraw Text" in this book.

Finding Line Breaks

You display text on the Macintosh screen by calling the QuickDraw text routines. These routines handle text in different fonts, styles, and sizes, and even draw text that is displayed in different directions. However, the QuickDraw text display routines do not break lines for you to fit into screen areas of your own designation, which means that you have to display your text line-by-line. (The QuickDraw text routines are described in the chapter "QuickDraw Text" in this book.)

To draw a string line-by-line, you need to use the StyledLineBreak function. What you do is start at the first character in your text and use StyledLineBreak to search for the first line break, draw that portion of the string, and then start up again with the character that follows the line break. You continue this process until the remaining characters all fit on one line. The size and style of the glyphs are factors in determining how many characters fit onto a line, since they affect the number of pixels required for each glyph on the line. Another factor in breaking lines is that it is desirable to break a line on a word boundary whenever possible.

The StyledLineBreak function looks for the next line break in a string. It accommodates different fonts, styles, and glyph sizes, and accounts for complications such as the word boundary rules for the script system of the text. You usually call StyledLineBreak to traverse a line in memory order, which is not necessarily the same as display order for mixed-directional text. StyledLineBreak finds line breaks on word boundaries whenever possible. StyledLineBreak always chooses a line break for the last style run on the line as if all trailing whitespace in that style run would be stripped.

The StyledLineBreak function works on one style run at a time. To use StyledLineBreak, you must represent the text in your documents in a manner that allows you to quickly iterate through script runs in your text and style runs within each script run. Figure 5-9 shows an example of a line break in a text string with multiscript text runs.

Text Utilities

Figure 5-9   Finding line breaks in multiscript text

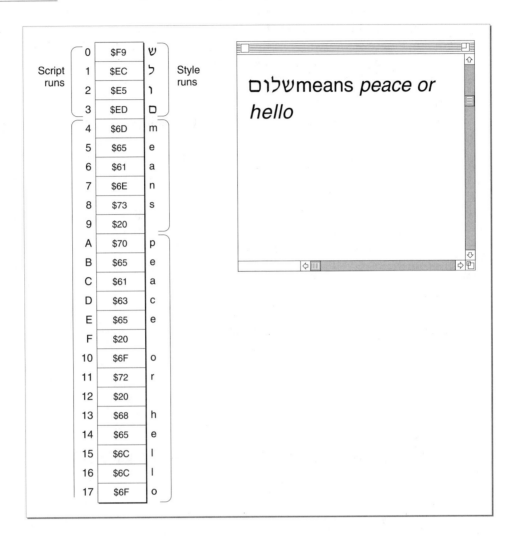

Use the `StyledLineBreak` function when you are displaying text in a screen area to determine the best place to break each displayed line. You can only use this function when you have organized your text in script runs and style runs within each script run. This type of text organization used by most text-processing applications that allow for multiscript text.

What you do is iterate through your text, a script run at a time, using `StyledLineBreak` to check each style run in the script run until the function determines that it has arrived at a line break. As you loop through each style run, before calling `StyledLineBreak`, you must set the text values in the current graphics port that are used by QuickDraw to measure the text. These include the font, font size, and font style of the style run. For details on these parameters, see the chapter "QuickDraw Text" in this book.

Once `StyledLineBreak` has arrived at a line break, you can display the line, advance the pointers into your text, and call the function again to find the next line break. You continue to follow this sequence until you've reached the end of your text. `StyledLineBreak` does not break on a space character, so a sequence of spaces of any length remains with the previous line.

The `StyledLineBreak` function uses a number of parameters; the value of some of these parameters must change for each style run, and the value of others must change for each script run. Figure 5-10 illustrates how the parameters of the `StyledLineBreak` function are used when finding a line break in text that contains a number of script and style runs.

Figure 5-10   Relationships of the parameters of `StyledLineBreak`

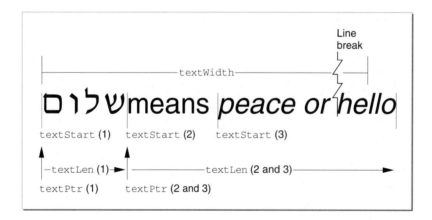

The `textPtr` parameter points to the start of the script run, the `textStart` parameter is the location of the start of the style run, and the `textLen` parameter is the number of bytes in the style run. The `textWidth` parameter specifies the number of pixels in the display line. Other parameters are `textEnd`, which specifies the number of bytes in the script run, and `textOffset`, in which the location of the break is returned. Declarations and descriptions of these parameters are found in the section "StyledLineBreak" beginning on page 5-79.

Note that the style runs in `StyledLineBreak` must be traversed in memory order, not in display order. For more information about this, read about the `GetFormatOrder` routine in the chapter "QuickDraw Text" in this book. It is also important to remember that word boundaries can extend across style runs, but cannot extend across script runs.

The `StyledLineBreak` function looks for a line break on a word boundary. The only time it cannot find such a break is when a word spans across an entire line. If such a word starts past the beginning of the line, `StyledLineBreak` determines that a break should occur before the start of the word; otherwise, it breaks the line in the middle of the word, at a character boundary instead of at a word boundary. `StyledLineBreak` uses the value of the `textOffset` parameter to differentiate between these two cases. The `textOffset` parameter must be nonzero for the first call on a line and zero for each subsequent call to the function on the line.

No matter which case occurs, `StyledLineBreak` returns a code that specifies whether or not it found a break and what kind of break (word or character boundary) it is. This value is one of the constants defines as the `StyledLineBreakCode` type:

StyledLineBreak constant	Value	Meaning
BreakOverflow	2	No break is necessary because the current style run fits on the line (within the width)
BreakChar	1	Line breaks on character boundary
BreakWord	0	Line breaks on word boundary

`StyledLineBreak` automatically decrements the `textWidth` variable by the width of the style run for use on the next call. You need to set the value of `textWidth` before calling it to process a line. Listing 5-4 shows a basic loop structure that you can use to call `StyledLineBreak` in your application.

Listing 5-4   Using the `StyledLineBreak` function

```
REPEAT                              {repeat for each line}
   textOffset := 1
   textWidth := number of display pixels available for line
   done := FALSE;
   WHILE not done DO
      BEGIN                         {for each script run}
      textPtr := the address of the first byte of the script run
      textLen := the number of bytes in the script run
      WHILE not done DO
         BEGIN                      {for each style run}
         textStart := byte offset within script run of the start
                  of the style run
         textEnd := byte offset within script run of the end
                  of the style run
         {Set up the QuickDraw font parameters for style run}
         ...
         ans := StyledLineBreak(textPtr, textLen, textStart,
                  textEnd, flags, textWidth, textOffset);
```

```
    if ans <> smBreakOverflow
        THEN done := TRUE;
        ELSE textOffset := 0;{always 0 after first call}
    END;
  END;
  {Display the text that starts at textPtr & continues }
  { for textOffset bytes}
  ...
UNTIL                                 {until no more text to process}
```

Finding Subscripts Within a Script Run

Some script systems include subscripts, which are character sets that are subsidiary to the main character set. One useful subscript is the set of all character codes that have the same meaning in Roman as they do in a non-Roman script. For other scripts such as Japanese, there are additional useful subscripts. For example, a Japanese script system might include some Hiragana characters that are useful for input methods.

When you are displaying or working with a string that contains subscript characters, it is often convenient to identify the subscript text runs so that you can treat those characters differently. You might, for instance, want to display the Roman subscript text in a different font, or apply different rules to it when searching for word boundaries. In Figure 5-11, the English words "Hebrew" and "Russian" are initially drawn in native language fonts from their script systems. Each of these words is then extracted and redrawn using a font from the Roman script system.

Figure 5-11   Extracting blocks of Roman text

The FindScriptRun function is used to identify blocks of subscript text in a string. FindScriptRun searches a string for such a block, and sets a VAR parameter to the length in bytes of the subscript run that begins with the first character in the string.

`FindScriptRun` also returns a script-run status record, which specifies the script code and subscript information for the block of text. The fields of the script-run status record are described in the section "FindScriptRun," beginning on page 5-81.

Working With Date and Time Strings

Applications that address international audiences must work with how the numeric-format (`'itl0'`) resource and long-date-format (`'itl1'`) resource handle the differences in date and time formats used in different countries and regions of the world.

The numeric-format resource contains general conventions for formatting numeric strings. It provides several different definitions, including separators for decimals, thousands, and lists; currency information; time values; and short date formats. Some of the variations in date and time formats are shown in Table 5-3.

Table 5-3   Variations in time and short date formats

Morning	Afternoon	Short date	System software
1:02 AM	1:02 PM	2/1/90	United States
1:02	13:02	02/01/90	Canadian French
1:02 AM	1:02 PM	90.01.02	Chinese
1:02	13:02	02-01-1990	Dutch
1:02 Uhr	13:02 Uhr	2.1.1990	German
1:02	13:02	2-01-1990	Italian
01.02	13.02	90-02-01	Swedish

For time and date values, the numeric-format resource includes values that specify this information:

- the order of the month, day, and year values in short date formats

- which separator to use in the short date format (for example, : or / or -)

- the trailing string to display for morning (for example, *A.M.*)

- the trailing string to display for evening (for example, *P.M.*)

- up to 4 trailing bytes to display for 24-hour times before noon, and another 4 bytes to display for 24-hour times at noon and after. For example, the German string *Uhr* is used for both purposes.

- whether or not to indicate leading zeros in each of the time elements (hours, minutes, and seconds)

The long-date-format resource includes conventions for long date formats, abbreviated date formats, and the regional version of the script the resource is associated with. Some of the variations in long and abbreviated date formats are shown in Table 5-4.

Table 5-4   Variations in long and abbreviated date formats

Long date	Abbreviated date	System software
Tuesday, January 2, 1990	Tue, Jan 2, 1990	United States
Tuesday, 2 January 1990	Tue, 2 Jan 1990	Australian
Mardi 02 janvier 1990	Mard 02 janv 1990	Canadian French
tirsdag 2. januar 1990	tir 2. jan 1990	Danish
Mardi 2 Janvier 1990	Mar 2 Jan 1990	French

The long-date-format resource includes values that specify this information:

- the names of the days
- the names of the months
- which punctuation to use for abbreviated day names and month names

You can optionally add an extension to a long-date-format resource that adds a number of other specification capabilities, including the following:

- a calendar code for the specification of calendars other than the standard Gregorian calendar, such as the Arabic calendar
- a list of extra day names for calendars with more than seven days
- a list of extra month names for calendars with more than twelve months
- a list of abbreviated day names
- a list of abbreviated month names
- a list of additional date separators

Many of the Apple-supplied long-date-format resources already include such extensions.

The Text Utilities routines that work with dates and times use the information in the long-date-format and numeric-format resources to create different string representations of date and time values. The Macintosh Operating System provides routines that return the current date and time to you in numeric format; you can then use the Text Utilities routines to convert those values into strings that can be presented in different international formats.

The Text Utilities also include routines that can parse date and time strings as entered by users and fill in the fields of a record with the components of the date and time, including the month, day, year, hours, minutes, and seconds.

For more details on the numeric-format (`'itl0'`) and long-date-format (`'itl1'`) resources, see the appendix "International Resources" in this book. For information on obtaining the current date and time values from the Macintosh Operating System, see *Inside Macintosh: Operating System Utilities*.

Converting Formatted Date and Time Strings Into Internal Numeric Representations

When your application works with date and time values, it must convert string versions of dates and times into internal numeric representations that it can manipulate. You might, for example, need to convert a date typed by the user into a numeric representation so that you can compute another date some number of days ahead. You can then format the new value for display as a formatted date string.

The Text Utilities contains two routines that you can use to parse formatted date and time values from input strings and create an internal numeric representation of the date and time. The `StringToDate` function parses an input string for a date, and the `StringToTime` function parses an input string (possibly the same input string) for time information.

Both of these functions pass a date cache record as one of the parameters. A date cache record is a data structure of type `DateCacheRec` that you must declare in your application. Because you must pass this record as a parameter, you must initialize it by calling the `InitDateCache` function before calling `StringToDate` or `StringToTime`. You need to call `InitDateCache` only once—typically in your main program initialization code. For more information about the date cache record and the `InitDateCache` function, see the section "InitDateCache" on page 5-83.

Both the `StringToDate` and the `StringToTime` functions fill in fields in a long date-time record, which is defined by a `LongDateRec` data structure. This data type is described in the book *Inside Macintosh: Operating System Utilities*.

You usually use `StringToDate` and `StringToTime` sequentially to parse the date and time values from an input string and fill in these fields. Listing 5-5 shows how to first call `StringToDate` to parse the date, then offset the starting address of the string, and finally, call `StringToTime` to parse the time.

Listing 5-5   Using `StringToDate` and `StringToTime`

```
str := "March 27, 1992 08:14 p.m.";

strPtr := ptr(ord(@str) + 1); {Pointer to 1st char of str}
strLen := length(str);
status := StringToDate(strPtr, strLen, myDateCache,
                                    numBytes, lDateRec);
strPtr := ptr(ord(@str)+numBytes+1);
strLen := strLen - numBytes;
status := StringToTime(strPtr, strLen, myDateCache,
                                    numBytes, lDateRec);
```

`StringToDate` parses the text string until it has finished finding all date information or until it has examined the number of bytes specified by `textLen`. It returns a status value that indicates the confidence level for the success of the conversion. `StringToDate` recognizes date strings in many formats, including "September 1, 1987," "1 Sept 1987," "1/9/1987," and "1 1987 sEpT."

Note that `StringToDate` fills in only the year, month, day, and day of the week; `StringToTime` fills in the hour, minute, and second. You can use these two routines sequentially to fill in all of the values in a `LongDateRec` record.

`StringToDate` assigns to its `lengthUsed` parameter the number of bytes that it uses to parse the date; use this value to compute the starting location of the text that you can pass to `StringToTime`.

`StringToDate` interprets the date and `StringToTime` interprets the time based on values that are defined in the long-date-format (`'itl1'`) resource. These values, which include the tokens used for separators and the month and day names, are described in the appendix "International Resources" in this book.

`StringToDate` uses the `IntlTokenize` function, as described in the chapter "Script Manager" in this book, to separate the components of the strings. It assumes that the names of the months and days, as specified in the international long-date-format resource, are single alphanumeric tokens.

When one of the date components is missing, such as the year, the current date value is used as a default. If the value of the input year is less than 100, `StringToDate` determines the year as follows.

1. If (current year) MOD 100 is greater than or equal to 90 and the input year is less than or equal to 10, the input year is assumed to be in the next century.

2. If (current year) MOD 100 is less than or equal to 10 and the input year is greater than or equal to 90, the input year is assumed to be in the previous century.

3. Otherwise, the input year is assumed to be in the current century.

If the value of the input year is between 100 and 1000, then 1000 is added to it. Thus the dates 1/9/87, 1/9/987, and 1/9/1987 are equivalent.

Both `StringToDate` and `StringToTime` return a value of type `StringToDateStatus`, which is a set of bit values that indicate confidence levels, with higher numbers indicating low confidence in how closely the input string matched what the routine expected. Each `StringToDateStatus` value can contain a number of the possible bit values that have been OR'ed together. For example, specifying a date with nonstandard separators may work, but it returns a message indicating that the separator was not standard.

The possible values of this type are described in Table 5-5.

Table 5-5   `StringToDateStatus` values and their meanings

`StringToDateStatus` value	Result of the conversion
`fatalDateTime`	A fatal error occurred during the parse.
`tokenErr`	The token processing software could not find a token.
`cantReadUtilities`	The resources needed to parse the date or time value could not be read.
`dateTimeNotFound`	A valid date or time value could not be found in the string.
`dateTimeInvalid`	The start of a valid date or time value was found, but a valid date or time value could not be parsed from the string.
`longDateFound`	A valid long date was found. This bit is not set when a short date or time was found.
`leftOverChars`	A valid date or time value was found, and there were characters remaining in the input string.
`sepNotIntlSep`	A valid date or time value was found; however, one or more of the separator characters in the string was not an expected separator character for the script system in use.
`fieldOrderNotIntl`	A valid date or time value was found; however, the order of the fields did not match the expected order for the script system in use.
`extraneousStrings`	A valid date or time value was found; however, one or more unparsable strings was encountered and skipped while parsing the string.
`tooManySeps`	A valid date or time value was found; however, one or more extra separator characters was encountered and skipped while parsing the string.
`sepNotConsistent`	A valid date or time value was found; however, the separator characters did not consistently match the expected separators for the script system in use.

For example, if `StringToDate` and `StringToTime` successfully parse date and time values from the input string and more characters remain in the string, then the function result will be the constant `leftOverChars`. If `StringToDate` discovers two separators in sequence, the parse will be successful and the return value will be the constant `tooManySeps`. If `StringToDate` finds a perfectly valid short date, it returns the value `noErr`; if `StringToDate` finds a perfectly valid long date, it returns the value `longDateFound`.

Date and Time Value Representations

The Macintosh Operating System provides several different representations of date and time values. One representation is the standard date-time value that is returned by the Macintosh Operating system routine `GetDateTime`. This is a 32-bit integer that represents the number of seconds between midnight, January 1, 1904 and the current time. Another is the date-time record, which includes integer fields for each date and time component value.

The Macintosh Operating System also provides two data types that allow for longer spans of time than do the standard date-time value and date-time record: the long date-time value and the long-date record. The long date-time value, of data type `LongDateTime`, is a 64-bit, signed representation of the number of seconds since Jan. 1, 1904, which allows for coverage of a much longer span of time (approximately 30,000 years) than does the standard date-time representation. The long date-time record, of data type `LongDateRec`, is similar to the date-time record, except that it adds several additional fields, including integer values for the era, the day of the year, and the week of the year.

The Macintosh Operating System provides four routines for converting among the different date and time data types:

- `DateToSeconds`, which converts a date-time record into a standard date-time value

- `SecondsToDate`, which converts a standard date-time value into a date-time record

- `LongDateToSeconds`, which converts a long-date record into a long date-time value

- `LongSecondsToDate`, which converts a long date-time value into a long-date record

The standard date-time value, the long date-time value, and each of the data structures and routines mentioned in this section are described in the book *Inside Macintosh: Operating System Utilities*.

Converting Standard Date and Time Values Into Strings

When you want to present a date or time value as a string, you need to convert from one of the numeric date-time representations into a formatted string. The Text Utilities include the `DateString` and `TimeString` procedures for converting standard date-time values into formatted strings, and the `LongDateString` and `LongTimeString` procedures for converting long date-time values into formatted strings. Each of these routines uses information from a long-date-format or numeric-format resource that you specify as a parameter.

When you use the `DateString` and `LongDateString` procedures, you can request an output format for the resulting date string. The output format can be one of the three values of the `DateForm` enumerated data type:

```
DateForm = (shortDate,longDate,abbrevDate);
```

Here are examples of the date strings that these specifications produce.

Value	Date string produced
shortDate	1/31/92
abbrevDate	Fri, Jan 31, 1992
longDate	Friday, January 31, 1992

When you request a long or abbreviated date format, the formatting information in a long-date-format resource is used. For short date formats, the information is found in a numeric-format resource. The `DateString` and `LongDateString` procedures use the long-date-format or numeric-format resource that you specify. If you request a long or abbreviated date format, you must include the handle to a long-date-format resource, and if you request a short date format, you must include the handle to a numeric-format resource. If you specify NIL for the value of the resource handle parameter, both routines uses the appropriate resource from the current script.

When you use the `TimeString` and `LongTimeString` procedures to produce a formatted time string, you can request an output format for the resulting string. You specify whether or not you want the time string to include the seconds by passing a Boolean parameter to these procedures.

Value	Time string produced
FALSE	03:24 P.M.
TRUE	03:24:17 P.M.

The `TimeString` and `LongTimeString` procedures use the time formatting information in the numeric-format resource that you specify. This information defines which separator to use between the elements of the time string, which suffix strings to use, and whether or not to add leading zeros in each of the time elements. If you specify NIL in place of a resource handle, these procedures use the numeric-format resource from the current script.

Working With Numeric Strings

When you present numbers to the user, or when the user enters input numbers for your application to use, you need to convert between the internal numeric representation of the number and the output (or input) format of the number. The Text Utilities provide several routines for performing these conversions. Some of these routines take into account the many variations in numeric string formats (output formats) of numbers in different regions of the world.

If you are converting integer values into numeric strings or numeric strings into integer values, and you don't need to take international number formats into account, you can use the two basic number conversion routines: `NumToString`, which converts an integer into a string, and `StringToNum`, which converts a string into an integer. These routines are described in the section "Converting Between Integers and Numeric Strings," which begins on page 5-38.

If you are working with floating-point numbers, or if you want to accommodate the possible differences in output formats for numbers in different countries and regions of the world, you need to work with number format specification strings. These are strings that specify the input and output formats for numbers and allow for a tremendous amount of flexibility in displaying numbers.

To use number format specification strings and convert numbers, you need to follow these steps:

1. You first define the format of numbers with a number format specification string. An example of such a string is `###,###.##;-###,###.##;0`. This string specifies three number formats: for positive number values, for negative number values, and for zero values. The section "Using Number Format Specification Strings," which begins on page 5-39, describes these definitions in detail.

2. You must also define the syntactic components of numeric string formats using a number parts table. This table is part of the tokens (`'itl4'`) resource for each script system. It includes definitions of which characters are used in numeric strings for displaying the percent sign, the minus sign, the decimal separator, the less than or equal sign, and other symbols. The number parts table is described with the tokens resource in the appendix "International Resources" in this book.

3. You then use Text Utilities routines to convert the number format specification string into an internal representation that is stored in a `NumFormatStringRec` record. This is a private data type that is used by the number conversion routines. You convert a number format specification string into a `NumFormatStringRec` record with the `StringToFormatRec` function, and you perform the opposite conversion with the `FormatRecToString` function. Both of these functions are described in the section "Converting Number Format Specification Strings Into Internal Numeric Representations," which begins on page 5-43.

4. Once you have a `NumFormatStringRec` record that defines the format of numbers for a certain country or region, you can convert floating-point numbers into numeric strings and numeric strings into floating-point numbers. The `StringToExtended` and `ExtendedToString` functions perform these conversions; these are described in the section "Using Number Format Specification Strings," which begins on page 5-39.

To accommodate all of the possibilities for the different number formats used in different countries and regions, you need to work with numeric strings, number parts tables, number format specification strings, and floating-point numbers. The Text Utilities include the routines shown in Figure 5-12 to make it possible for your application to accept and display numeric strings in many different formats. You can accept an input string in one format and create an output numeric string that is appropriate for an entirely different area of the world. Figure 5-12 summarizes the relationships among the different data and routines used for these conversions.

Figure 5-12   Using the number formatting routines

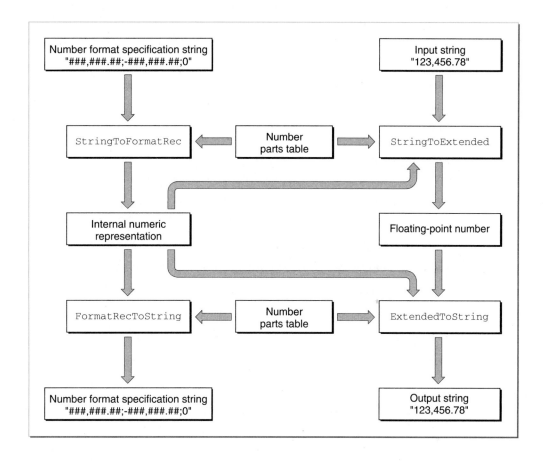

The number format specification string in the upper left box in Figure 5-12 defines how input and output numeric strings are formatted; in this case, they are formatted in the style most commonly used in the United States, with a comma as the thousand separator. The `StringToFormatRec` format takes the number format specification string as input, along with a number parts table, and creates an internal representation, which is stored in a record of data type `NumFormatStringRec`.

If you later want to create a number format specification string from the internal representation, you can call the `FormatRecToString` function. This function takes a record of type `NumFormatStringRec` and a parts table, and creates a string that you can display or edit.

Once you have an internal representation of your formatting specification, you can use it for converting between strings and floating-point numbers. The `StringToExtended` function takes an input string, a `NumFormatStringRec`, and a number parts table, and creates a floating-point number. The `ExtendedToString` function takes a floating-point number, a `NumFormatStringRec`, and a number parts table, and creates a string.

Each of the four functions shown in Figure 5-12 returns a result of type `FormatStatus`, which is an integer value. The low byte of the result is of type `FormatResultType`, the values of which are summarized in Table 5-6.

Table 5-6   `FormatResultType` values for numeric conversion functions

`FormatStatus` value	Result of the conversion
fFormatOK	The format of the input value is appropriate and the conversion was successful.
fBestGuess	The format of the input value is questionable; the result of the conversion may or may not be correct.
fOutOfSynch	The format of the input number string did not match the format expected in the number format specification string.
fSpuriousChars	There are extra characters in the input string.
fMissingDelimiter	A delimiter is missing in the input string.
fExtraDecimal	An extra decimal was found in the input number string.
fMissingLiteral	The close of a literal is missing in the input number string.
fExtraExp	There is an extra exponent in the input number string.
fFormatOverflow	The number in the input string exceeded the magnitude allowed for in the number format specification.
fFormStrIsNAN	The format specification string is not valid.
fBadPartsTable	The parts table is not valid.
fExtraPercent	There is an extra percentage symbol in the input number string.
fExtraSeparator	There was an extra separator in the input number string.
fEmptyFormatString	The format specification string was empty.

Converting Between Integers and Numeric Strings

The simplest number conversion tasks for your application involve integer values and do not take international output format differences into account. Text Utilities provides one routine to convert an integer value into a numeric string and another to convert a numeric string into an integer value.

The `NumToString` procedure converts a long integer value into a string representation of it as a base-10 value. The `StringToNum` procedure performs the opposite operation, converting a string representation of a number into a long integer value. For example, Listing 5-6 converts a number into a string and then back again.

Listing 5-6 Converting a long integer into a numeric string

```
VAR
    str: Str255;
    i,j: LongInt;
BEGIN
    i := 4329;
    NumToString(i, str);        {str is now "4329"}
    StringToNum(str, j);        {j is now 4329 }
END;
```

Using Number Format Specification Strings

When you want to work with floating-point values and numeric strings, you need to
take into account the different formats that are used for displaying numbers in different
countries and regions of the world. Table 5-7 shows some of the numeric string formats
that are used in different versions of system software.

Table 5-7 Numeric string formats

Numeric string	System software
1,234.56	All versions
1 234,56	French and others
1.234,56	Danish and others
1 234.56	Greek
1.234 56	Russian
1'234.56	Swiss French, Swiss German

You use number format specification strings to define the appearance of numeric strings
in your application. Each number format specification string contains up to three parts:
the positive number format, the negative number format, and the zero number format.
Each format is applied to a numeric value of the corresponding type: when a positive
value is formatted, the positive format is used, when a negative value is formatted, the
negative format is used, and when a zero value is formatted, the zero format is used.
When a number format specification string contains only one part, that part is used for
all values. When a number format specification string contains two parts, the first part is
used for positive and zero values, and the second part is used for negative values.

Text Utilities

Table 5-8 shows several different number format specification strings, and the output numeric string that is produced by applying each format to a numeric value.

Table 5-8 Examples of number format specification strings

Number format specification string	Numeric value	Output format
###,###.##;-###,###.##;0	123456.78	123,456.78
###,###.0##,###	1234	1,234.0
###,###.0##,###	3.141592	3.141,592
###;(000);^^^	–1	(001)
###.###	1.234999	1.235
###'CR';###'DB';''zero''	1	1CR
###'CR';###'DB';''zero''	0	'zero'
##%	0.1	10%

The three portions of a number format specification string (positive, negative, and zero formats) are separated by semicolons. If you do not specify a format for negative values, negative numbers are formatted using the positive format and a minus sign is inserted at the front of the output string. If you do not specify a format for zero values, they are presented as a single '0' digit.

These number format specification strings contain different elements:

■ number parts separators for specifying the decimal separator and the thousand separator

■ literals that you want included in the output formats

■ digit placeholders

■ quoting mechanisms for handling literals correctly

■ symbol and sign characters

Number parts separators come in two types: the decimal separator and the thousand separator. In the U.S. localized version of the Roman script system, the decimal separator is the '.' character and the thousand separator is the ',' character. Some script systems use other characters for these separators. The number conversion routines each take a number parts table parameter that includes definitions of the separator characters.

Text Utilities

Literals in your format strings can add annotation to your numbers. Literals can be strings or brackets, braces, and parentheses, and must be enclosed in quotation marks. Table 5-9 shows some examples of using literals in number format specification strings.

Table 5-9   Literals in number format strings

Number format specification string	Numeric value	Output format
###'CR';###'DB';\'"zero\'"	1	1CR
[###' Million '###' Thousand '###]	300	[300]
[###' Million '###' Thousand '###]	3210432	[3 Million 210 Thousand 432]

Digit placeholders that you want displayed in your numeric strings must be indicated by digit symbols in your number format specification strings. There are three possible digit symbols: zero digits (0), skipping digits (#), and padding digits (^). The format string in line 4 of Table 5-8 contains examples of each. The actual characters used for denoting each of these are defined in the tokens ('itl4') resource number parts table.

■ Zero digits add leading zeros wherever an input digit is not present. For example, –1 in line 4 of Table 5-8 produces (001) because the negative number format is specified as "(000)", meaning that the output is enclosed in parentheses and leading zeros are added to produce three digits.

■ Skipping digits only produce output characters when an input digit is present. For example, if the positive number format is "###" and the input string is "1", then the output format is "1" (not " 1" as you might expect. Each skipping digit in the number format specification string is replaced by a digit character if one is present, and is not replaced by anything (is skipped) if a digit character is not present.

■ Padding digits are like zero digits except that a padding character such as a nonbreaking space is used instead of leading zeros to "pad" the output string. You can use padding digits to align numbers in a column. The number conversion routines each take a number parts table parameter that includes definitions of padding characters.

You must specify the maximum number of digits allowed in your formats, as the number formatting routines do not allow extension beyond them. If the input string contains too many digits, an error (formatOverflow) will be generated. If the input string contains too many decimal places, the decimal portion is automatically rounded. For example, given the format of ###.###, a value of 1234.56789 results in an error condition, and a value of 1.234999 results in the rounded-off 1.235 value.

Text Utilities

The number formatting routines always fill in integer digits from the right and decimal places from the left. This can produce the results shown in Table 5-10, which includes a literal in the middle of the format strings to demonstrate this behavior.

Table 5-10   Filling digits in

Number format specification string	Numeric value	Output format
###'my'###	1	1
###'my'###	123	123
###'my'###	1234	1my234
0.###'my'###	0.1	0.1
0.###'my'###	0.123	1.123
0.###'my'###	0.1234	0.123my4

Quoting mechanisms allow you to enclose most literals in single quotation marks in your number format specification strings. If you need to include single quotation marks as literals in your output formats, you can precede them with the escape character (\). Table 5-11 shows several examples of using quoting mechanisms.

Table 5-11   Quoting mechanisms in number format strings

Number format specification string	Numeric value	Output format
###'CR';###'DB';''zero''	1	1CR
###'CR';###'DB';''zero''	-1	1DB
###'CR';###'DB';''zero''	0	'zero'

Symbol and sign characters in your number format specification strings allow you to display the percent sign, exponents, and numbers' signs. The actual glyphs displayed for these symbols depend on how they are defined in the number parts table of a tokens resource. The symbols that you can use and the characters used for them in the U.S. Roman script system are shown in Table 5-12.

Table 5-12   Symbols in number format strings

Symbol	U.S. Roman	Number format string	Example
Plus sign	+	+###	+13
Minus sign	–	-###	–243
Percent sign	%	##%	14%
EPlus	E+	##.####E+0	1.2344E+3
EMinus	E–	#.#E-#	1.2E–3

For more information about these symbols and the tokens defined for them, see the section on number parts tables in the appendix "International Resources" in this book.

Converting Number Format Specification Strings Into Internal Numeric Representations

To use a number format specification string in your application, you must first convert the specification string into an internal numeric representation that is independent of country, language, and other cultural considerations. This allows you to map the number into different output formats. This internal representation is sometimes called a canonical number format. The internal representation of format strings is stored in a `NumFormatStringRec` record.

You can use the `StringToFormatRec` function to convert a number format specification string into a `NumFormatStringRec` record. To perform this conversion, you must also specify a number parts table from a numeric-format resource. The number parts table defines which characters are used for certain purposes (such as separating parts of a number) in the format specification string.

You can use the `FormatRecToString` function to convert a `NumFormatStringRec` record back into a number format specification string, in which the three parts (positive, negative, and zero) are separated by semicolons. This function also uses a number parts table to define the components of numbers; by using a different table than was used in the call to `StringToFormatRec`, you can produce a number format specification string that specifies how numbers are formatted for a different region of the world. You use `FormatRecToString` when you want to display the number format specification string to a user for perusal or modification.

Converting Between Floating-Point Numbers and Numeric Strings

Once you have a `NumFormatStringRec` record that defines the format of numbers for a certain region of the world, you can convert between floating-point numbers and numeric strings.

You can use the `StringToExtended` function to convert a numeric string into an 80-bit floating-point value. `StringToExtended` uses a `NumFormatStringRec` record and a number parts table to examine and convert the numeric string into a floating-point value.

The ExtendedToString function performs the opposite conversion: it uses a NumFormatStringRec record and a number parts table to convert an 80-bit floating-point value into a numeric string that is formatted for output.

Text Utilities Reference

This section describes the data structures and routines that comprise the Text Utilities. The "Data Structures" section provides a description of the data structures that are used with certain of the Text Utilities routines. The "Routines" section describes the routines you can use in your applications to work with strings.

Data Structures

This section describes the data structures that are used with the Text Utilities routines. Each is used with one or more of the Text Utilities routines to pass information into or to receive information back from the routine.

The Offset Table Record

The FindWordBreaks procedure uses the offset table, which is defined by the OffsetTable data type. You pass a record of this type by VAR to FindWordBreaks, and it fills in the fields to specify the location of the next word in the input string. The FindWordBreaks procedure is described in the section "FindWordBreaks," which begins on page 5-77.

```
OffsetTable = ARRAY [0..2] of OffPair;

OffPair =
RECORD
    offFirst: Integer;    {offset of first word boundary}
    offSecond: Integer;   {offset of second word boundary}
END;
```

Field descriptions

offFirst   The offset in bytes from the beginning of the string to the first character of the word.

offSecond   The offset in bytes from the beginning of the string to the last character of the word.

Although the offset table contains three OffPair records, the FindWordBreaks procedure fills in only the first of these records with the offset values for the word that it finds. The other two entries are for use by the `HiliteText` procedure, which is described in the chapter "QuickDraw Text" in this book.

The Date Cache Record

The `StringToDate` and `StringToTime` functions use the date cache, defined by the `DateCacheRecord` data type, as an area to store date conversion data that is used by the date conversion routines. This record must be initialized by a call to the `InitDateCache` function, which is described in the section "InitDateCache" beginning on page 5-83. The data in this record is private—you should not attempt to access it.

```
DateCachePtr = ^DateCacheRecord;

DateCacheRecord =
PACKED RECORD
        hidden: ARRAY [0..255] OF INTEGER;{only for temporary use}
END;
```

Field descriptions

hidden   The storage used for converting dates and times.

The Number Format Specification Record

Four of the numeric string functions use the number formatting specification, defined by the `NumFormatStringRec` data type: `StringToFormatRec`, `FormatRecToString`, `StringToExtended`, and `ExtendedToString`. The number format specification record contains the data that represents the internal number formatting specification information. This data is stored in a private format.

```
NumFormatStringRec =
PACKED RECORD
    fLength: Byte;
    fVersion: Byte;
    hidden: ARRAY [0..253] OF INTEGER;{only for temporary use}
END;
```

Field descriptions

fLength	The number of bytes (plus 1) in the hidden data actually used for this number formatting specification.
fVersion	The version number of the number formatting specification.
hidden	The data that comprises the number formatting specification.

The Triple Integer Array

The `FormatRecToString` function uses the triple-integer array, defined by the `TripleInt` data type, to return the starting position and length in a string of three different portions of a formatted numeric string: the positive value string, the negative value string, and the zero value string. Each element of the triple integer array is an `FVector` record.

```
TripleInt =
ARRAY[0..2] OF FVector;     {indexed by fPositive..fZero}


FVector =
RECORD
    start: Integer;
    length: Integer;
END;
```

Field descriptions

start	The starting byte position in the string of the specification information.
length	The number of bytes used in the string for the specification information.

Each of the three `FVector` entries in the triple integer array is accessed by one of the values of the `FormatClass` type.

```
FormatClass = (fPositive,fNegative,fZero);
```

The Script Run Status Record

The `FindScriptRun` function returns the script run status record, defined by the `ScriptRunStatus` data type, when it completes its processing, which is to find a run of subscript text in a string. The `FindScriptRun` function is described in the section "FindScriptRun," which begins on page 5-81.

```
ScriptRunStatus =
RECORD
    script: SignedByte;   {script code of block}
    variant: SignedByte;  {additional CharacterType information}
END;
```

Field descriptions

script   The script code of the subscript run. Zero indicates the Roman
                script system.

variant   Script-specific information about the run, in the same format as that
                returned by the CharacterType function, described in the chapter
                "Script Manager" in this book. This information includes the type of
                subscript—for example, Kanji, Katakana, or Hiragana for a Japanese
                script system.

Routines

This section describes the routines that you use to work with strings in your application,
including sorting strings, modifying the contents of strings, converting dates and times
to and from strings, and converting numbers to and from strings.

Defining and Specifying Strings

This section describes two routines that you can use to work with string handles and two
routines for accessing string resources.

- The NewString function creates a copy of the specified string as a relocatable object
  in the heap.

- The SetString procedure changes the contents of a string that has already been
  allocated in the heap.

- The GetString function loads a string from a resource of type 'STR ', reading the
  string from the resource file if necessary.

- The GetIndString procedure copies a string from a string list that is contained in a
  resource of type 'STR#'.

NewString

The NewString function allocates memory in the heap for a string, copies its contents,
and produces a handle for the heap version of the string.

```
FUNCTION NewString (theString: Str255): StringHandle;
```

theString   A Pascal string that you want copied onto the heap.

DESCRIPTION

NewString returns a handle to the newly allocated string. If the string cannot be allocated, NewString returns NIL. The size of the allocated string is based on the actual length of theString, which may not be 255 bytes.

Note

Before using Pascal string functions that can change the length of the string, it is a good idea to maximize the size of the string object on the heap. You can call either the SetString procedure or the Memory Manager procedure SetHandleSize to modify the string's size. ◆

SPECIAL CONSIDERATIONS

NewString may move memory; your application should not call this function at interrupt time.

ASSEMBLY-LANGUAGE INFORMATION

The trap macro for the NewString function is

Trap macro

_NewString

SetString

The SetString procedure changes the contents of a string referenced by a string handle, replacing the previous contents by copying the specified string.

```
PROCEDURE SetString (h: StringHandle; theString: Str255);
```

h   A handle to the string in memory whose contents you are replacing.

theString   A Pascal string.

DESCRIPTION

The SetString procedure sets the string whose handle is passed in the h parameter to the string specified by the parameter theString. If the new string is larger than the string originally referenced by h, SetString automatically resizes the handle and copies in the contents of the specified string.

SPECIAL CONSIDERATIONS

SetString may move memory; your application should not call this procedure at interrupt time.

ASSEMBLY-LANGUAGE INFORMATION

The trap macro for the `SetString` procedure is

Trap macro

`_SetString`

GetString

The `GetString` function loads a string from a string (`'STR '`) resource into memory. It returns a handle to the string with the specified resource ID, reading it from the resource file if necessary.

```
FUNCTION GetString (stringID: Integer): StringHandle;
```

stringID   The resource ID of the string (`'STR '`) resource containing the string.

DESCRIPTION

The `GetString` function returns a handle to a string with the specified resource ID. If `GetString` cannot read the resource, it returns `NIL`.

`GetString` calls the `GetResource` function of the Resource Manager to access the string. This means that if the specified resource is already in memory, `GetString` simply returns its handle.

Like the `NewString` function, `GetString` returns a handle whose size is based upon the actual length of the string.

Note
If your application uses a large number of strings, it is more efficient to store them in a string list (`'STR#'`) resource than as individual resources in the resource file. You then use the `GetIndString` procedure to access each string in the list. ◆

SPECIAL CONSIDERATIONS

`GetString` does not create a copy of the string.

`GetString` may move memory; your application should not call this function at interrupt time.

ASSEMBLY-LANGUAGE INFORMATION

The trap macro for the `GetString` function is

Trap macro

`_GetString`

GetIndString

The GetIndString procedure loads a string from a string list ('STR#') resource into memory. It accesses the string by using the resource ID of the string list and the index of the individual string in that list. The list is read from the resource file if necessary.

```
PROCEDURE GetIndString (VAR theString: Str255; strListID: Integer;
                        index: Integer);
```

theString   On output, the Pascal string result.

strListID   The resource ID of the 'STR#' resource that contains the string list.

index   The index of the string in the list. This is a value from 1 to the number of strings in the list that is referenced by the strListID parameter.

DESCRIPTION

GetIndString returns in the parameter theString a copy of the string from a string list that has the resource ID provided in the strListID parameter. If the resource that you specify cannot be read or the index that you specify is out of range for the string list, GetIndString sets theString to an empty string.

If necessary, GetIndString reads the string list from the resource file by calling the Resource Manager function GetResource. GetIndString accesses the string specified by the index parameter and copies it into theString. The index can range from 1 to the number of strings in the list.

SPECIAL CONSIDERATIONS

GetIndString may move memory; your application should not call this procedure at interrupt time.

ASSEMBLY-LANGUAGE INFORMATION

There is no trap macro for the GetIndString procedure. Instead, you need to use the _GetResource trap macro with the resource type ('STR#') and string index.

Comparing Strings for Equality

This section describes text routines that you can use to determine whether two strings are equal.

Some of the routines operate on Pascal strings and others on text strings. Pascal strings are stored using standard Pascal string representation, which precedes the text characters with a length byte; these strings are limited to 255 bytes of data. Text strings do not use a length byte and can be up to 32 KB in length. Pascal strings are passed directly as parameters, while text strings are specified by an address value and an integer length value.

■ The EqualString function compares two Pascal strings using the comparison rules of the Macintosh file system. This function does not make use of any script or language information.

■ The IdenticalString function compares two Pascal strings for equality, making use of the string comparison information from a specified resource.

■ The IdenticalText function compares two text strings for equality, making use of the string comparison information from a specified resource.

EqualString

The EqualString function compares two Pascal strings for equality, using the comparison rules of the Macintosh file system. The comparison performed by EqualString is a simple, character-by-character value comparison. This function does not make use of any script or language information; it assumes the use of a Roman script system.

```
FUNCTION EqualString (aStr, bStr: Str255;
                      caseSens, diacSens: Boolean): Boolean;
```

aStr   One of the Pascal strings to be compared.

bStr   The other Pascal string to be compared.

caseSens   A flag that indicates how to handle case-sensitive information during the comparison. If the value of caseSens is TRUE, uppercase characters are distinguished from the corresponding lowercase characters. If it is FALSE, case information is ignored.

diacSens   A flag that indicates how to handle information about diacritical marks during the string comparison. If the value of diacSens is TRUE, characters with diacritical marks are distinguished from the corresponding characters without diacritical marks during the comparison. If it is FALSE, diacritical marks are ignored.

DESCRIPTION

EqualString returns TRUE if the two strings are equal and FALSE if they are not equal. If its value is TRUE, EqualString distinguishes uppercase characters from the corresponding lowercase characters. If its value is FALSE, EqualString ignores diacritical marks during the comparison.

SPECIAL CONSIDERATIONS

The EqualString function is not localizable.

ASSEMBLY-LANGUAGE INFORMATION

The trap macro and routine selector for the `EqualString` function are

Trap macro	Selector
_CmpString	$A03C

This trap macro can take optional arguments, each of which changes the default setting used by the macro when it is called without arguments. Each of these arguments corresponds to the Boolean parameters that are used with the Pascal function call. The various permutations of this trap macro are shown below; you must type each exactly as it is shown. The syntax shown here applies to the MPW Assembler; if you are using another development system, be sure to consult its documentation for the proper syntax.

Macro permutation		Value of diacSens	Value of caseSens
_CmpString		FALSE	FALSE
_CmpString	,MARKS	TRUE	FALSE
_CmpString	,CASE	FALSE	TRUE
_CmpString	,MARKS,CASE	TRUE	TRUE

The registers on entry and exit for this routine are

Registers on entry

A0	pointer to first character of the first string
A1	pointer to first character of the second string
D0	high-order word: number of bytes in the first string low-order word: number of bytes in the second string

Registers on exit

D0	long word result: 0 if strings are equal, 1 if strings are not equal

IdenticalString

The `IdenticalString` function compares two Pascal strings for equality, making use of the string comparison information from a resource that you specify as a parameter. `IdenticalString` uses only primary differences in its comparison.

```
FUNCTION IdenticalString (aStr, bStr: Str255;
                          itl2Handle: Handle): Integer;
```

aStr	One of the Pascal strings to be compared.
bStr	The other Pascal string to be compared.
itl2Handle	
	A handle to a string-manipulation ('itl2') resource that contains string comparison information.

DESCRIPTION

IdenticalString returns 0 if the two strings are equal and 1 if they are not equal. It compares the two strings without regard for secondary sorting order, the meaning of which depends on the language of the strings. For example, for the English language, using only primary differences means that IdenticalString ignores diacritical marks and does not distinguish between lowercase and uppercase. For example, if the two strings are 'Rose' and 'rosé', IdenticalString considers them equal and returns 0.

The itl2Handle parameter is used to specify a string-manipulation resource. If the value of this parameter is NIL, IdenticalString makes use of the resource for the current script. The string-manipulation resource includes tables for modifying string comparison and tables for case conversion and stripping of diacritical marks.

Specifying a resource as a parameter is described in the section "Obtaining Resource Information," which begins on page 5-4.

SPECIAL CONSIDERATIONS

IdenticalString may move memory; your application should not call this function at interrupt time.

ASSEMBLY-LANGUAGE INFORMATION

There is no trap macro for the IdenticalString function. Instead, you must convert the Pascal string into a text string by creating a pointer to its first character and finding its length, and then use the same macro as you do for the IdenticalText function, which is described next.

IdenticalText

The IdenticalText function compares two text strings for equality, making use of the string comparison information from a resource that you specify as a parameter. IdenticalText uses only primary sorting order in its comparison.

```
FUNCTION IdenticalText (aPtr, bPtr: Ptr; aLen, bLen: Integer;
                        itl2Handle: Handle): Integer;
```

aPtr   A pointer to the first character of the first text string.

bPtr   A pointer to the first character of the second text string.

aLen   The number of bytes in the first text string.

bLen   The number of bytes in the second text string.

itl2Handle
                A handle to a string-manipulation ('itl2') resource that contains string comparison information.

DESCRIPTION

IdenticalText returns 0 if the two text strings are equal and 1 if they are not equal. It compares the strings without regard for secondary sorting order, which means that it ignores diacritical marks and does not distinguish between lowercase and uppercase. For example, if the two text strings are 'Rose' and 'rosé', IdenticalText considers them equal and returns 0.

The itl2Handle parameter is used to specify a string-manipulation resource. If the value of this parameter is NIL, IdenticalText makes use of the resource for the current script. The string-manipulation resource includes routines and tables for modifying string comparison and tables for case conversion and stripping of diacritical marks.

Specifying a resource as a parameter is described in the section "Obtaining Resource Information," which begins on page 5-4.

SPECIAL CONSIDERATIONS

IdenticalText may move memory; your application should not call this function at interrupt time.

ASSEMBLY-LANGUAGE INFORMATION

The trap macro and routine selector for the IdenticalText function are

Trap macro	Selector
_Pack6	$001C

Determining Sorting Order for Strings in Different Languages

This section describes the Text Utilities routines available to help you sort strings in different languages. When strings from different languages occur in a single list, you must separate the strings so that all strings from each script system are contained in their own list. You then sort the list for each script system, using the sorting rules for that language and script system. You can then concatenate the individual language lists together, ordering the lists according to language and script ordering information that is found in the international script-sorting ('itlm') resource.

- The ScriptOrder function indicates the order in which text from two different script systems should be sorted.

- The LanguageOrder function indicates the order in which text from two different languages from the same script system should be sorted.

- The StringOrder function determines the appropriate sorting order for two Pascal strings, taking into account the script and language codes of each.

- The TextOrder function determines the appropriate sorting order for two text strings, taking into account the script and language codes of each.

Note

When determining the order in which text from two different script systems should be sorted, the system script always sorts first, and scripts that are not enabled and installed always sort last. Invalid script or language codes always sort after valid ones. ◆

Script systems and the enabling and installing of scripts are described in the chapter "Script Manager" in this book and the script-sorting resource is described in the appendix "International Resources" in this book.

Pascal strings are stored using standard Pascal string representation, which precedes the text characters with a length byte; these strings are limited to 255 characters. Text strings do not use a length byte and can be up to 32 KB in length. Pascal strings are passed directly as parameters, while text strings are specified by two parameters: an address value and an integer length value.

The functions `LanguageOrder`, `StringOrder`, and `TextOrder` accept as parameters the implicit language codes listed in Table 5-13, as well as the explicit language codes listed in the chapter "Script Manager."

Table 5-13   Implicit language codes

Constant	Value	Explanation
systemCurLang	–2	Current language for system script (from `'itlb'`)
systemDefLang	–3	Default language for system script (from `'itlm'`)
currentCurLang	–4	Current language for current script (from `'itlb'`)
currentDefLang	–5	Default language for current script (from `'itlm'`)
scriptCurLang	–6	Current language for specified script (from `'itlb'`)
scriptDefLang	–7	Default language for specified script (from `'itlm'`)

ScriptOrder

The `ScriptOrder` function determines the order in which strings in two different scripts should be sorted.

```
FUNCTION ScriptOrder (script1, script2: ScriptCode): Integer;
```

script1   The script code of the first script.

script2   The script code of the second script.

DESCRIPTION

`ScriptOrder` takes a pair of script codes and determines in which order strings from the first script system should be sorted relative to strings from the second script system.

It returns a value that indicates the sorting order: –1 if strings in the first script should be sorted before strings in the second script are sorted, 1 if strings in the first script should be sorted after strings in the second script are sorted, or 0 if the sorting order does not matter (that is, if the scripts are the same).

The script code values are listed in the chapter "Script Manager" in this book.

Note
Text of the system script is always first in a sorted list, regardless of the result returned by this function. ◆

SPECIAL CONSIDERATIONS

ScriptOrder may move memory; your application should not call this function at interrupt time.

ASSEMBLY-LANGUAGE INFORMATION

The trap macro and routine selector for the ScriptOrder function are

Trap macro	Selector
_Pack6	$001E

LanguageOrder

The LanguageOrder function determines the order in which strings in two different languages should be sorted.

```
FUNCTION LanguageOrder (language1, language2: LangCode): Integer;
```

language1   The language code of the first language.

language2   The language code of the second language.

DESCRIPTION

LanguageOrder takes a pair of language codes and determines in which order strings from the first language should be sorted relative to strings from the second language. It returns a value that indicates the sorting order: –1 if strings in the first language should be sorted before sorting text in the second language, 1 if strings in the first language should be sorted after sorting strings in the second language, or 0 if the sorting order does not matter (that is, if the languages are the same).

Explicit language code values are listed in the chapter "Script Manager"; implicit language codes are listed in Table 5-13 on page 5-55 of this chapter. The implicit language codes scriptCurLang and scriptDefLang are not valid for LanguageOrder because the script system being used is not specified as a parameter to this function.

SPECIAL CONSIDERATIONS

LanguageOrder may move memory; your application should not call this function at interrupt time.

ASSEMBLY-LANGUAGE INFORMATION

The trap macro and routine selector for the LanguageOrder function are

Trap macro	Selector
_Pack6	$0020

StringOrder

The StringOrder function compares two Pascal strings, taking into account the script system and language for each of the strings. It takes both primary and secondary sorting orders into consideration and returns a value that indicates whether the first string is less than, equal to, or greater than the second string.

```
FUNCTION StringOrder (aStr, bStr: Str255;
                      aScript, bScript: ScriptCode;
                      aLang, bLang: LangCode): Integer;
```

aStr   One of the Pascal strings to be compared.

bStr   The other Pascal string to be compared.

aScript   The script code for the first string.

bScript   The script code for the second string.

aLang   The language code for the first string.

bLang   The language code for the second string.

DESCRIPTION

StringOrder returns –1 if the first string is less than the second string, 0 if the first string is equal to the second string, and 1 if the first string is greater than the second string. The ordering of script and language codes, which is based on information in the script-sorting resource, is considered in determining the relationship of the two strings.

Script code values and explicit language code values are listed in the chapter "Script Manager"; implicit language codes are listed in Table 5-13 on page 5-55 of this chapter. Most applications specify the language code scriptCurLang for both the aLang and bLang values.

StringOrder first calls ScriptOrder; if the result of ScriptOrder is not 0 (that is, if the strings use different scripts), StringOrder returns the same result.

StringOrder next calls LanguageOrder; if the result of LanguageOrder is not 0 (that is, if the strings use different languages), StringOrder returns the same result.

At this point, StringOrder has two strings that are in the same script and language, so it compares them by using the sorting rules for that script and language, applying both the primary and secondary sorting orders. If that script is not installed and enabled (as described in the chapter "Script Manager" in this book), it uses the sorting rules specified by the system script or the font script, depending on the state of the international resources selection flag. See the section "Obtaining Resource Information," beginning on page 5-4.

The StringOrder function is primarily used to insert Pascal strings in a sorted list; for sorting, rather than using this function, it may be faster to sort first by script and language by using the ScriptOrder and LanguageOrder functions, and then to call the CompareString function, described on page 5-62, to sort strings within a script or language group.

SPECIAL CONSIDERATIONS

StringOrder may move memory; your application should not call this function at interrupt time.

TextOrder

The TextOrder function compares two text strings, taking into account the script and language for each of the strings. It takes both primary and secondary sorting orders into consideration and returns a value that indicates whether the first string is less than, equal to, or greater than the second string.

```
FUNCTION TextOrder (aPtr, bPtr: Ptr; aLen, bLen: Integer;
                    aScript, bScript: ScriptCode;
                    aLang, bLang: LangCode): Integer;
```

aPtr   A pointer to the first character of the first text string.

bPtr   A pointer to the first character of the second text string.

aLen   The number of bytes in the first text string.

bLen   The number of bytes in the second text string.

aScript   The script code for the first text string.

bScript   The script code for the second text string.

aLang   The language code for the first text string.

bLang   The language code for the second text string.

DESCRIPTION

TextOrder returns –1 if the first string is less than the second string, 0 if the first string is equal to the second string, and 1 if the first string is greater than the second string. The ordering of script and language codes, which is based on information in the script-sorting resource, is considered in determining the relationship of the two strings.

Script code values and explicit language code values are listed in the chapter "Script Manager"; implicit language codes are listed in Table 5-13 on page 5-55 of this chapter. Most applications specify the language code scriptCurLang for both the aLang and bLang values.

TextOrder first calls ScriptOrder; if the result of ScriptOrder is not 0 (that is, if the strings use different scripts), TextOrder returns the same result.

TextOrder next calls LanguageOrder; if the result of LanguageOrder is not 0 (that is, if the strings use different languages), TextOrder returns the same result.

At this point, TextOrder has two strings that are in the same script and language, so it compares them by using the sorting rules for that script and language, applying both the primary and secondary sorting orders. If that script is not installed and enabled (as described in the chapter "Script Manager" in this book), it uses the sorting rules specified by the system script or the font script, depending on the state of the international resources selection flag. See the section "Obtaining Resource Information," beginning on page 5-4.

The TextOrder function is primarily used to insert text strings in a sorted list; for sorting, rather than using this function, it may be faster to sort first by script and language by using the ScriptOrder and LanguageOrder functions, and then to call the CompareText function, described on page 5-63, to sort strings within a script or language group.

SPECIAL CONSIDERATIONS

TextOrder may move memory; your application should not call this function at interrupt time.

ASSEMBLY-LANGUAGE INFORMATION

The trap macro and routine selector for the TextOrder function are

Trap macro	Selector
_Pack6	$0022

Determining Sorting Order for Strings in the Same Language

This section describes text routines that you can use to determine the sorting order of two strings.

Some of the routines operate on Pascal strings and others on text strings. Pascal strings are stored using standard Pascal string representation, which precedes the text characters with a length byte; these strings are limited to 255 bytes of data. Text strings do not use a length byte and can be up to 32 KB in length. Pascal strings are passed directly as parameters, while text strings are specified by an address value and an integer length value.

- The `RelString` function compares two Pascal strings using the string comparison rules of the Macintosh file system. This function does not make use of any script or language information, assuming the use of a Roman script system.

- The `CompareString` function compares two Pascal strings, making use of the string comparison information from a specified resource.

- The `CompareText` function compares two text strings for equality, making use of the string comparison information from a specified resource.

RelString

The `RelString` function compares two Pascal strings using the string comparison rules of the Macintosh file system and returns a value that indicates the sorting order of the first string relative to the second string. This function does not make use of any script or language information; it assumes the original Macintosh character set only. `RelString` uses the sorting rules that are described in Table 5-2 on page 5-17.

```
FUNCTION RelString (aStr, bStr: Str255;
                    caseSens, diacSens: Boolean): Integer;
```

aStr   One of the Pascal strings to be compared.

bStr   The other Pascal string to be compared.

caseSens   A flag that indicates how to handle case-sensitive information during the comparison. If the value of `caseSens` is `TRUE`, uppercase characters are distinguished from the corresponding lowercase characters. If it is `FALSE`, case information is ignored.

diacSens   A flag that indicates how to handle information about diacritical marks during the string comparison. If the value of `diacSens` is `TRUE`, characters with diacritical marks are distinguished from the corresponding characters without diacritical marks during the comparison. If it is `FALSE`, diacritical marks are ignored.

DESCRIPTION

`RelString` returns –1 if the first string is less than the second string, 0 if the two strings are equal, and 1 if the first string is greater than the second string. It compares the two strings in the same manner as does the `EqualString` function, by simply looking at the ASCII values of their characters. However, `RelString` provides more information about the two strings—it indicates their relationship to each other, rather than determining if they are exactly equal.

If the value of the `diacSens` parameter is FALSE, `RelString` ignores diacritical marks and strips them as shown in the appendix "International Resources" in this book.

If the value of the `caseSens` parameter is FALSE, the comparison is not case-sensitive; `RelString` performs a conversion from lowercase to uppercase characters.

SPECIAL CONSIDERATIONS

The `RelString` function is not localizable and does not work properly with non-Roman script systems.

ASSEMBLY-LANGUAGE INFORMATION

The trap macro and routine selector for the `RelString` function are

Trap macro	Selector
_RelString	$A050

The trap macro for the `RelString` function can take optional arguments, each of which changes the default setting used by the macro when it is called without arguments. Each of these arguments corresponds to the Boolean parameters that are used with the Pascal function call. The various permutations of this trap macro are shown below; you must type each exactly as it is shown. The syntax shown here applies to the MPW Assembler; if you are using another development system, be sure to consult its documentation for the proper syntax.

Macro permutation	Value of diacSens	Value of caseSens
_RelString	FALSE	FALSE
_RelString ,MARKS	TRUE	FALSE
_RelString ,CASE	FALSE	TRUE
_RelString ,MARKS,CASE	TRUE	TRUE

The registers on entry and exit for this routine are

Registers on entry

A0   pointer to first character of the first string

A1   pointer to first character of the second string

D0   high-order word: number of bytes in the first string
      low-order word: number of bytes in the second string

Registers on exit

D0   long word result: –1 if first string is less than second,
      0 if equal, 1 if first string is greater than second

CompareString

The CompareString function compares two Pascal strings, making use of the string comparison information from a resource that you specify as a parameter. It takes both primary and secondary sorting orders into consideration and returns a value that indicates the sorting order of the first string relative to the second string.

```
FUNCTION CompareString(aStr, bStr: Str255;
                       itl2Handle: Handle): Integer;
```

aStr   One of the Pascal strings to be compared.

bStr   The other Pascal string to be compared.

itl2Handle
            The handle to the string-manipulation resource that contains string comparison information.

DESCRIPTION

CompareString returns –1 if the first string is less than the second string, 0 if the first string is equal to the second string, and 1 if the first string is greater than the second string.

The itl2Handle parameter is used to specify a string-manipulation resource. If the value of this parameter is NIL, CompareString makes use of the resource for the current script. The string-manipulation resource includes routines and tables for modifying string comparison and tables for case conversion and stripping of diacritical marks.

Specifying a resource as a parameter is described in the section "Obtaining Resource Information," beginning on page 5-4.

SPECIAL CONSIDERATIONS

CompareString may move memory; your application should not call this function at interrupt time.

ASSEMBLY-LANGUAGE INFORMATION

There is no trap macro for the CompareString function. Instead, you must convert the Pascal string into a text string by creating a pointer to its first character and finding its length, and then use the same macro as you do for the CompareText function, which is described next.

CompareText

The CompareText function compares two text strings, making use of the string comparison information from a resource that you specify as a parameter. It takes both primary and secondary sorting orders into consideration and returns a value that indicates the sorting order of the first string relative to the second string.

```
FUNCTION CompareText (aPtr, bPtr: Ptr; aLen, bLen: Integer;
                      itl2Handle: Handle): Integer;
```

aPtr   A pointer to the first character of the first text string.

bPtr   A pointer to the first character of the second text string.

aLen   The number of bytes in the first text string.

bLen   The number of bytes in the second text string.

itl2Handle

        A handle to a string-manipulation ('itl2') resource that contains string comparison information.

DESCRIPTION

CompareText returns –1 if the first string is less than the second string, 0 if the first string is equal to the second string, and 1 if the first string is greater than the second string.

The itl2Handle parameter is used to specify a string-manipulation resource. If the value of this parameter is NIL, CompareText makes use of the resource for the current script. The string-manipulation resource includes routines and tables for modifying string comparison and tables for case conversion and stripping of diacritical marks.

Specifying a resource as a parameter is described in the section "Obtaining Resource Information," beginning on page 5-4.

SPECIAL CONSIDERATIONS

CompareText may move memory; your application should not call this function at interrupt time.

ASSEMBLY-LANGUAGE INFORMATION

The trap macro and routine selector for the CompareText function are

Trap macro	Selector
_Pack6	$001A

Modifying Characters and Diacritical Marks

This section provides details on text routines that you can use to modify the characters in text:

- The UpperString procedure converts any lowercase letters in a Pascal string to their uppercase equivalents. UpperString uses the Macintosh file system string-manipulation rules, which means that it only works properly for Roman characters with codes through $D8.

The following four routines use tables in the string-manipulation ('itl2') resource to perform their character-mapping operations. This allows you to customize their operation for different countries.

- The LowercaseText procedure converts any uppercase characters in a text string into their lowercase equivalents, making use of the conversion rules for the specified script system.

- The UppercaseText procedure converts any lowercase characters in a text string into their uppercase equivalents, making use of the conversion rules for the specified script system.

- The StripDiacritics procedure strips diacritical characters from a text string, making use of the conversion rules for the specified script system.

- The UppercaseStripDiacritics procedure strips diacritical marks and converts lowercase characters into their uppercase equivalents in a text string, making use of the conversion rules for the specified script system.

UpperString

The UpperString procedure converts any lowercase letters in a Pascal string to their uppercase equivalents. This procedure converts characters using the Macintosh file system rules, which means that only a subset of the Roman character set (character codes with values through $D8) are converted. These rules are summarized in Table 5-2 on page 5-17. Use this procedure to emulate the behavior of the Macintosh file system.

```
PROCEDURE UpperString (VAR theString: Str255; diacSens: Boolean);
```

theString   On input, this is the Pascal string to be converted. On output, this contains the string resulting from the conversion.

diacSens   A flag that indicates whether the case conversion is to strip diacritical marks. If the value of this parameter is FALSE, diacritical marks are stripped.

DESCRIPTION

UpperString traverses the characters in theString and converts any lowercase characters with character codes in the range $0 through $D8 into their uppercase equivalents. If the diacSens flag is TRUE, diacritical marks are considered in the conversion; if it is `FALSE`, any diacritical marks are stripped. `UpperString` places the converted characters in `theString`.

The trap macro and routine selector for the `UpperString` procedure are

Trap macro	Selector
_UprString	$A054

The registers on entry and exit for this routine are

Registers on entry

A0	pointer to first character of string
D0	the length of the string (a word value)

Registers on exit

A0	pointer to first character of string

The trap macro for the `UpperString` procedure can take an optional argument, which changes the default setting used by the macro when it is called without arguments. This argument corresponds to the Boolean parameter `diacSens` that is used with the Pascal function call. The permutations of this trap macro are shown below; you must type each exactly as it is shown.

The syntax shown here applies to the MPW Assembler; if you are using another development system, be sure to consult its documentation for the proper syntax.

Macro permutation	Value of diacSens
_UprString	TRUE
_UprString ,MARKS	FALSE

LowercaseText

The `LowercaseText` procedure converts any uppercase characters in a text string into their lowercase equivalents. The text string can be up to 32 KB in length.

```
PROCEDURE LowercaseText (textPtr: Ptr; len: Integer;
                         script: ScriptCode);
```

textPtr	A pointer to the text string to be converted.
len	The number of bytes in the text string.
script	The script code for the script system whose resources are used to determine the results of converting characters.

DESCRIPTION

LowercaseText traverses the characters starting at the address specified by textPtr and continues for the number of characters specified in len. It converts any uppercase characters in the text into lowercase.

The conversion uses tables in the string-manipulation ('itl2') resource of the script specified by the value of the script parameter. The possible values for script codes are listed in the chapter "Script Manager" of this book. You can specify smSystemScript to use the system script and smCurrentScript to use the script of the current font in the current graphics port.

If LowercaseText cannot access the specified resource, it generates an error code and does not modify the string. You need to call the ResError function to determine which, if any, error occurred. ResError is described in the Resource Manager chapter of the book *Inside Macintosh: More Macintosh Toolbox*.

SPECIAL CONSIDERATIONS

LowercaseText may move memory; your application should not call this procedure at interrupt time.

ASSEMBLY-LANGUAGE INFORMATION

The trap macro for the LowercaseText procedure is

Trap macro

_LowerText

The registers on entry and exit for this routine are

Registers on entry

A0   pointer to first character of string

D0   length of string in bytes (word); must be less than 32 KB

Registers on exit

D0   result code

RESULT CODES

noErr	0	No error
resNotFound	–192	Can't get correct 'itl2' resource or resource is not in current format

UppercaseText

The `UppercaseText` procedure converts any lowercase characters in a text string into their uppercase equivalents. The text string can be up to 32 KB in length.

```
PROCEDURE UppercaseText (textPtr: Ptr; len: Integer;
                         script: ScriptCode);
```

textPtr   A pointer to the text string to be converted.

len   The number of bytes in the text string.

script   The script code of the script system whose case conversion rules are used for determining uppercase character equivalents.

DESCRIPTION

`UppercaseText` traverses the characters starting at the address specified by `textPtr` and continues for the number of characters specified in `len`. It converts any lowercase characters in the text into uppercase.

The conversion uses tables in the string-manipulation (`'itl2'`) resource of the script specified by the value of the `script` parameter. The possible values for script codes are listed in the chapter "Script Manager" of this book. You can specify `smSystemScript` to use the system script and `smCurrentScript` to use the script of the current font in the current graphics port.

If `UppercaseText` cannot access the specified resource, it generates an error code and does not modify the string. You need to call the `ResError` function to determine which, if any, error occurred. `ResError` is described in the Resource Manager chapter of the book *Inside Macintosh: More Macintosh Toolbox*.

SPECIAL CONSIDERATIONS

`UppercaseText` may move memory; your application should not call this procedure at interrupt time.

ASSEMBLY-LANGUAGE INFORMATION

The trap macro for the `UppercaseText` procedure is

Trap macro

`_UpperText`

The registers on entry and exit for this routine are

Registers on entry

A0   pointer to first character of string

D0   length of string in bytes (word); must be less than 32 KB

Registers on exit

D0   result code

RESULT CODES

noErr	0	No error
resNotFound	–192	Can't get correct 'itl2' resource or resource is not in current format

StripDiacritics

The StripDiacritics procedure strips any diacritical marks from a text string. The text string can be up to 32 KB in length.

```
PROCEDURE StripDiacritics (textPtr: Ptr; len: Integer;
                           script: ScriptCode);
```

textPtr   A pointer to the text string to be stripped.

len   The number of bytes in the text string.

script   The script code for the script system whose rules are used for determining which character results from stripping a diacritical mark.

DESCRIPTION

StripDiacritics traverses the characters starting at the address specified by textPtr and continues for the number of characters specified in len. It strips any diacritical marks from the text.

The conversion uses tables in the string-manipulation ('itl2') resource of the script specified by the value of the script parameter. The possible values for script codes are listed in the chapter "Script Manager" of this book. You can specify smSystemScript to use the system script and smCurrentScript to use the script of the current font in the current graphics port.

If StripDiacritics cannot access the specified resource, it generates an error code and does not modify the string. You need to call the ResError function to determine which, if any, error occurred. ResError is described in the Resource Manager chapter of the book *Inside Macintosh: More Macintosh Toolbox.*

SPECIAL CONSIDERATIONS

`StripDiacritics` may move memory; your application should not call this procedure at interrupt time.

ASSEMBLY-LANGUAGE INFORMATION

The trap macro for the `StripDiacritics` procedure is

Trap macro

`_StripText`

The registers on entry and exit for this routine are

Registers on entry

A0   pointer to first character of string

D0   length of string in bytes (word); must be less than 32 KB

Registers on exit

D0   result code

RESULT CODES

noErr	0	No error
resNotFound	–192	Can't get correct `'itl2'` resource or resource is not in current format

UppercaseStripDiacritics

The `UppercaseStripDiacritics` procedure converts any lowercase characters in a text string into their uppercase equivalents and strips any diacritical marks from the text. The text string can be up to 32 KB in length.

```
PROCEDURE UppercaseStripDiacritics (textPtr: Ptr; len: Integer;
                                    script: ScriptCode);
```

textPtr   A pointer to the text string to be converted.

len   The number of bytes in the text string.

script   The script code of the script system whose resources are used to determine the results of converting characters.

DESCRIPTION

UppercaseStripDiacritics traverses the characters starting at the address specified by textPtr and continues for the number of characters specified in len. It converts lowercase characters in the text into their uppercase equivalents and also strips diacritical marks from the text string. This procedure combines the effects of the UppercaseText and StripDiacritics procedures.

The conversion uses tables in the string-manipulation ('itl2') resource of the script specified by the value of the script parameter. The possible values for script codes are listed in the chapter "Script Manager" of this book. You can specify smSystemScript to use the system script and smCurrentScript to use the script of the current font in the current graphics port.

If UppercaseStripDiacritics cannot access the specified resource, it generates an error code and does not modify the string. You need to call the ResError function to determine which, if any, error occurred. ResError is described in the Resource Manager chapter of the book *Inside Macintosh: More Macintosh Toolbox*.

SPECIAL CONSIDERATIONS

UppercaseStripDiacritics may move memory; your application should not call this procedure at interrupt time.

ASSEMBLY-LANGUAGE INFORMATION

The trap macro for the UppercaseStripDiacritics procedure is

Trap macro

_StripUpperText

The registers on entry and exit for this routine are

Registers on entry

A0   pointer to first character of string

D0   length of string in bytes (word); must be less than 32 KB

Registers on exit

D0   result code

RESULT CODES

noErr	0	No error
resNotFound	–192	Can't get correct 'itl2' resource or resource is not in current format

Truncating Strings

This section describes two Text Utilities functions that you can use to truncate portions of strings. Each of these function can truncate characters from different locations in a string, and each makes use of the current script and font to perform its operation. The current script is defined on page 5-4. The current font is the font that is currently in use in the current graphics port.

■ The `TruncString` function ensures that a Pascal string fits into the specified pixel width, by truncating the string as necessary.

■ The `TruncText` function ensures that a text string fits into the specified pixel width, by truncating the string as necessary.

TruncString

The `TruncString` function ensures that a Pascal string fits into the specified pixel width, by truncating the string as necessary. This function makes use of the current script and font.

```
FUNCTION TruncString (width: Integer; VAR theString: Str255;
                      truncWhere: TruncCode): Integer;
```

width
The number of pixels in which the string must be displayed in the current script and font.

theString
The Pascal string to be displayed. On output, contains a version of the string that has been truncated (if necessary) to fit in the number of pixels specified by `width`.

truncWhere

A constant that indicates where the string should be truncated. You must set this parameter to one of the constants `truncEnd` or `truncMiddle`.

DESCRIPTION

The `TruncString` function ensures that a Pascal string fits into the pixel width specified by the `width` parameter by modifying the string, if necessary, through truncation. `TruncString` uses the font script to determine how to perform truncation. If truncation occurs, `TruncString` inserts a truncation indicator, which is the ellipsis (…) in the Roman script system. You can specify which token to use for indicating truncation as the `tokenEllipsis` token type in the untoken table of a tokens (`'itl4'`) resource.

The `truncWhere` parameter specifies where truncation is performed. If you supply the `truncEnd` value, characters are truncated off the end of the string. If you supply the `truncMiddle` value, characters are truncated from the middle of the string; this is useful when displaying pathnames.

The `TruncString` function returns a result code that indicates whether the string was truncated.

SPECIAL CONSIDERATIONS

`TruncString` may move memory; your application should not call this function at interrupt time.

ASSEMBLY-LANGUAGE INFORMATION

The trap macro and routine selector for the `TruncString` function are

Trap macro	Selector
_ScriptUtil	$8208 FFE0

RESULT CODES

Truncated	1	Truncation performed
NotTruncated	0	No truncation necessary
TruncErr	–1	Truncation necessary, but cannot be performed within the specified width
resNotFound	–192	Cannot get the correct 'itl4' resource or resource is not in current format

SEE ALSO

To determine the width of a string in the current font and script, use the QuickDraw `StringWidth` function, which is described in the chapter "QuickDraw Text" in this book.

TruncText

The `TruncText` function ensures that a text string fits into the specified pixel width, by truncating the string as necessary. This function makes use of the current script and font. The text string can be up to 32 KB long.

You can use the `TruncText` function to ensure that a string defined by a pointer and a byte length fits into the specified pixel width, by truncating the string in a manner dependent on the font script.

```
FUNCTION TruncText (width: Integer; textPtr: Ptr;
                    VAR length: Integer;
                    truncWhere: TruncCode): Integer;
```

width	The number of pixels in which the text string must be displayed in the current script and font.
textPtr	A pointer to the text string to be truncated.
length	On input, the number of bytes in the text string to be truncated. On output, this value is updated to reflect the length of the (possibly) truncated text.

truncWhere

A constant that indicates where the text string should be truncated. You must set this parameter to one of the constants `truncEnd` or `truncMiddle`.

DESCRIPTION

The `TruncText` function ensures that a text string fits into the pixel width specified by the `width` parameter by modifying the string, if necessary, through truncation. `TruncText` uses the font script to determine how to perform truncation. If truncation occurs, `TruncText` inserts a truncation indicator which is the ellipsis (…) in the Roman script system. You can specify which token to use for indicating truncation as the `tokenEllipsis` token type in the untoken table of a tokens resource.

The `truncWhere` parameter specifies where truncation is performed. If you supply the `truncEnd` value, characters are truncated off the end of the string. If you supply the `truncMiddle` value, characters are truncated from the middle of the string; this is useful when displaying pathnames.

The `TruncText` function returns a result code that indicates whether the string was truncated.

SPECIAL CONSIDERATIONS

`TruncText` may move memory; your application should not call this function at interrupt time.

ASSEMBLY-LANGUAGE INFORMATION

The trap macro and routine selector for the `TruncText` function are

Trap macro	Selector
_ScriptUtil	$820C FFDE

RESULT CODES

Truncated	1	Truncation performed
NotTruncated	0	No truncation necessary
TruncErr	−1	Truncation necessary, but cannot be performed within the specified width
resNotFound	−192	Cannot get the correct 'itl4' resource or resource is not in current format

SEE ALSO

To determine the width of a string in the current font and script, use the QuickDraw `StringWidth` function, which is described in the chapter "QuickDraw Text" in this book.

Searching for and Replacing Strings

This section describes two Text Utilities routines that you can use to search for and replace strings in larger strings:

■ The `ReplaceText` function searches a text string and replaces all instances of a target string with another string. `ReplaceText` uses the string-manipulation resource tables and works properly for all script systems, including 2-byte script systems.

■ The `Munger` function searches text for a specified target string and replaces it with another string. This function operates on a byte-by-byte basis; thus, it does not always work for 2-byte script systems.

ReplaceText

The `ReplaceText` function searches text, replacing all instances of a string in that text with another string. `ReplaceText` searches on a character-by-character basis (as opposed to byte-by-byte), so it works properly for all script systems.

```
FUNCTION ReplaceText (baseText, substitutionText: Handle;
                      key: Str15): Integer;
```

baseText   A handle to the string in which `ReplaceText` is to substitute text.

substitutionText
                A handle to the string that `ReplaceText` uses as substitute text.

key   A Pascal string of less than 16 bytes that `ReplaceText` searches for.

DESCRIPTION

`ReplaceText` searches the text specified by the `baseText` parameter for instances of the string in the `key` parameter and replaces each instance with the text specified by the `substitutionText` parameter. `ReplaceText` searches on a character-by-character basis. It recognizes 2-byte characters in script systems that contain them and advances the search appropriately after encountering a 2-byte character.

`ReplaceText` returns an integer value. If the returned value is positive, it indicates the number of substitutions performed; if it is negative, it indicates an error. The constant `noErr` is returned if there was no error and no substitutions were performed.

SPECIAL CONSIDERATIONS

`ReplaceText` may move memory; your application should not call this function at interrupt time.

ASSEMBLY-LANGUAGE INFORMATION

The trap macro and routine selector for the `ReplaceText` function are

Trap macro	Selector
`_ScriptUtil`	$820C FFDC

RESULT CODES

nilHandleErr	109	GetHandleSize fails on baseText or substitutionText
memFullErr	108	SetHandleSize fails on baseText
memWZErr	–111	GetHandleSize fails on baseText or substitutionText

Munger

The `Munger` function searches text for a specified string pattern and replaces it with another string.

```
FUNCTION Munger (h:  Handle; offset: LongInt; ptr1: Ptr;
                 len1: LongInt; ptr2: Ptr; len2: LongInt): LongInt;
```

h	A handle to the text string that is being manipulated.
offset	The byte offset in the destination string at which `Munger` begins its operation.
ptr1	A pointer to the first character in the string for which `Munger` is searching.
len1	The number of bytes in the string for which `Munger` is searching.
ptr2	A pointer to the first character in the substitution string.
len2	The number of bytes in the substitution string.

DESCRIPTION

`Munger` manipulates bytes in a string to which you specify a handle in the `h` parameter. The manipulation begins at a byte offset, specified in `offset`, in the string. Munger searches for the string specified by `ptr1` and `len1`; when it finds an instance of that string, it replaces it with the substitution string, which is specified by `ptr2` and `len2`.

IMPORTANT

`Munger` operates on a byte-by-byte basis, which can produce inappropriate results for 2-byte script systems. The `ReplaceText` function works properly for all languages. You are encouraged to use `ReplaceText` instead of `Munger` whenever possible. ▲

`Munger` takes special action if either of the specified pointer values is `NIL` or if either of the length values is `0`.

■ If `ptr1` is `NIL`, `Munger` replaces characters without searching. It replaces `len1` characters starting at the `offset` location with the substitution string.

■ If `ptr1` is `NIL` and `len1` is negative, `Munger` replaces all of the characters from the `offset` location to the end of the string with the substitution string.

■ If `len1` is `0`, `Munger` inserts the substitution string without replacing anything. `Munger` inserts the string at the `offset` location and returns the offset of the first byte past where the insertion occurred.

■ If `ptr2` is `NIL`, `Munger` searches but does not replace. In this case, `Munger` returns the offset at which the string was found.

■ If `len2` is `0` and `ptr2` is not `NIL`, `Munger` searches and deletes. In this case, `Munger` returns the offset at which it deleted.

■ If the portion of the string from the `offset` location to its end matches the beginning of the string that `Munger` is searching for, `Munger` replaces that portion with the substitution string.

`Munger` returns a negative value when it cannot find the designated string.

▲ **WARNING**

Be careful not to specify an offset with a value that is greater than the length of the destination string. Unpredictable results may occur. ▲

SPECIAL CONSIDERATIONS

`Munger` may move memory; your application should not call this function at interrupt time.

The destination string must be in a relocatable block that was allocated by the Memory Manager.

SEE ALSO

Munger calls the GetHandleSize and SetHandleSize routines to access or modify the length of the string it is manipulating. These routines are described in the book *Inside Macintosh: Memory Manager.*

ASSEMBLY-LANGUAGE INFORMATION

The trap macro for the Munger function is

Trap macro

_Munger

Working With Word, Script, and Line Boundaries

This section describes the text routines that you can use to edit and display formatted text. These functions all take into account script and language considerations, making use of tables in the string-manipulation ('itl2') resource in their computations.

- The FindWordBreaks procedure determines the beginning and ending boundaries of a word in a text string.

- The StyledLineBreak function determines the proper location at which to break a line of text that may contain multiple script runs, breaking it on a word boundary if possible.

- The FindScriptRun function finds the next boundary between main text and a specified subscript within a script run.

FindWordBreaks

The FindWordBreaks procedure determines the beginning and ending boundaries of a word in a text string.

```
PROCEDURE FindWordBreaks(textPtr: Ptr; textLength: Integer;
                offset: Integer; leadingEdge: Boolean;
                nbreaks: BreakTablePtr;
                VAR offsets: OffsetTable; script: ScriptCode);
```

textPtr   A pointer to the text string to be examined.

textLength
               The number of bytes in the text string.

offset   A byte offset into the text. This parameter plus the leadingEdge parameter determine the position of the character at which to start the search.

leadingEdge
>   A flag that specifies which character should be used to start the search. If leadingEdge is TRUE, the search starts with the character specified in the offset parameter; if it is FALSE, the search starts with the character previous to the offset.

nbreaks
>   A pointer to a word-break table of type NBreakTable or BreakTable. If the value of this pointer is 0, the default word-break table of the script system specified by the script parameter is used. If the value of this pointer is –1, the default line-break table of the specified script system is used.

offsets
>   On output, the values in this table indicate the boundaries of the word that has been found.

script
>   The script code for the script system whose tables are used to determine where word boundaries occur.

DESCRIPTION

FindWordBreaks searches for a word in a text string. The textPtr and textLength parameters specify the text string that you want searched. The offset parameter and leadingEdge parameter together indicate where the search begins.

If leadingEdge is TRUE, the search starts at the character at the offset. If leadingEdge is FALSE, the search starts at the character preceding the offset position.

FindWordBreaks searches backward through the text string for one of the word boundaries and forward through the text string for its other boundary. It uses the definitions in the table specified by nbreaks to determine what constitutes the boundaries of a word. Each script system's word-break table is part of its string-manipulation ('itl2') resource. The format of the NBreakTable record is described in the appendix "International Resources" in this book.

FindWordBreaks returns its results in an OffsetTable record, the format of which is described in the section "The Offset Table Record" on page 5-44. FindWordBreaks uses only the first element of this three-element table. Each element is a pair of integers: offFirst and offSecond.

FindWordBreaks places the offset from the beginning of the text string to just before the leading edge of the character of the word that it finds in the offFirst field.

FindWordBreaks places the offset from the beginning of the text string to just after the trailing edge of the last character of the word that it finds in the offSecond field. For example, if the text "This is it" is passed with offset set to 0 and leadingEdge set to TRUE, then FindWordBreaks returns the offset pair (0,4).

If leadingEdge is TRUE and the value of offset is 0, then FindWordBreaks returns the offset pair (0,0). If leadingEdge is FALSE and the value of offset equals the value of textLength, then FindWordBreaks returns the offset pair with values (textLength, textLength).

The trap macro and routine selector for the `FindWordBreaks` procedure are

Trap macro	Selector
`_ScriptUtil`	$C012 001A

StyledLineBreak

The `StyledLineBreak` function returns the proper location to break a line of text. It breaks the line on a word boundary if possible and allows for multiscript runs and style runs on a single line.

```
FUNCTION StyledLineBreak(textPtr: Ptr; textLen: LongInt;
                textStart, textEnd, flags: LongInt;
                VAR textWidth: Fixed;
                VAR textOffset: LongInt): StyledLineBreakCode;
```

textPtr   A pointer to the beginning of a script run on the current line to be broken.

textLen   The number of bytes in the script run on the current line to be broken.

textStart A byte offset to the beginning of a style run within the script run.

textEnd   A byte offset to the end of the style run within the script run.

flags   Reserved for future expansion; must be 0.

textWidth The maximum length of the displayed line in pixels. `StyledLineBreak` decrements this value for its own use. Your responsibility is to set it before your first call to `StyledLineBreak` for a line.

textOffset

Must be nonzero on your first call to `StyledLineBreak` for a line, and zero for subsequent calls to `StyledLineBreak` for that line. This value allows `StyledLineBreak` to differentiate between the first and subsequent calls, which is important when a long word is found (as described below).

On output, `textOffset` is the count of bytes from `textPtr` to the location in the text string where the line break is to occur.

DESCRIPTION

Use the `StyledLineBreak` function when you are laying out lines in an environment that may include text from multiple scripts. To use this function, you need to understand how QuickDraw draws text, which is described in the chapter "QuickDraw Text" in this book.

You can only use the `StyledLineBreak` function when you have organized your text in script runs and style runs within each script run. This type of text organization is used by most text-processing applications that allow for multiscript text. Use this function when you are displaying text in a screen area to determine the best place to break each displayed line. For an overview of how to use this function, read the section "Finding Line Breaks" beginning on page 5-24.

What you do is iterate through your text, a script run at a time starting from the first character past the end of the previous line. Use `StyledLineBreak` to check each style run in the script run (in memory order) until the function determines that it has arrived at a line break. As you loop through each style run, before calling `StyledLineBreak`, you must set the text values in the graphics port record that are used by QuickDraw to measure the text. These include the font, font size, and font style of the style run. An example of a loop that uses this function is found in Listing 5-4 on page 5-27.

When used with unformatted text, `textStart` can be 0, and `textEnd` is identical to `textLen`. With styled text, the interval between `textStart` and `textEnd` specifies a style run. The interval between `textPtr` and `textLen` specifies a script run. Note that the style runs in `StyledLineBreak` must be traversed in memory order, not in display order.

If the current style run is included in a contiguous sequence of other style runs of the same script, then `textPtr` should point to the start of the first style run of the same script on the line, and `textLen` should include the last style run of the same script on the line. This is because word boundaries can extend across style runs, but not across script runs.

`StyledLineBreak` automatically decrements the `textWidth` variable by the width of the style run for use on the next call. You need to set the value of `textWidth` before calling it to process a line.

The `textOffset` parameter must be nonzero for the first call on a line and zero for each call to the function on the line. This allows `StyledLineBreak` to act differently when a long word is encountered: if the word is in the first style run on the line, `StyledLineBreak` breaks the line on a character boundary within the word; if the word is in a subsequent style run on the line, `StyledLineBreak` breaks the line before the start of the word.

When `StyledLineBreak` finds a line break, it sets the value of `textOffset` to the count of bytes that can be displayed starting at `textPtr`.

IMPORTANT

When `StyledLineBreak` is called for the second or subsequent style runs within a script run, the `textOffset` value at exit may be less than the `textStart` parameter (that is, it may specify a line break before the current style run). ▲

Although the offsets are in long integer values and the widths are in fixed values for future extensions, in the current version the long integer values are restricted to the integer range, and only the integer portion of the widths is used.

StyledLineBreak always chooses a line break for the last style run on the line in memory order as if all whitespace in that style run would be stripped. The VisibleLength function, which is a QuickDraw function used to eliminate trailing spaces from a style run before drawing it, can be called for the style run that is at the display end of a line. This leads to a potential conflict when both functions are used with mixed-directional text: if the end of a line in memory order actually occurs in the middle of the displayed line, StyledLineBreak assumes that the whitespace is stripped from that run, but VisibleLength does not strip the characters. The VisibleLength function is described in the chapter "QuickDraw Text" in this book.

The StyledLineBreak result (defined by the StyledLineBreakCode data type) indicates whether the function broke on a word boundary or a character boundary, or if the width extended beyond the edge of the text.

ASSEMBLY-LANGUAGE INFORMATION

The trap macro and routine selector for the StyledLineBreak function are

Trap macro	Selector
_ScriptUtil	$821C FFFE

RESULT CODES

BreakOverflow	2	No line break is yet necessary, since the current style run still fits on the line
BreakChar	1	Line breaks on character boundary
BreakWord	0	Line breaks on word boundary

SEE ALSO

For details on the VisibleLength, TextWidth, and PortionText functions, see the chapter "QuickDraw Text" in this book.

FindScriptRun

The FindScriptRun function finds the next block of subscript text within a script run.

```
FUNCTION FindScriptRun (textPtr: Ptr;
                        textLen: LongInt;
                        VAR lenUsed: LongInt): ScriptRunStatus;
```

textPtr   A pointer to the text string to be analyzed.

textLen   The number of bytes in the text string.

lenUsed   On output, contains the length, in bytes, of the script run that begins with the first character in the string; this length is always greater than or equal to 1, unless the string passed in is of length 0.

DESCRIPTION

The `FindScriptRun` function is used to identify blocks of subscript text in a string. Some script systems include subscripts, which are character sets that are subsidiary to the main character set. One useful subscript is the set of all character codes that have the same meaning in Roman as they do in a non-Roman script. For other scripts such as Japanese, there are additional useful subscripts. For example, a Japanese script system might include some Hiragana characters that are useful for input methods.

`FindScriptRun` computes the length of the current run of subscript text in the text string specified by `textPtr` and `textLen`. It assigns the length, in bytes, to the `lenUsed` parameter and returns a status code. You can advance the text pointer by the value of `lenUsed` to make subsequent calls to this function. You can use this function to identify runs of subscript characters so that you can treat them separately.

The function result identifies the run as either native text, Roman, or one of the defined subscripts of the script system and returns a record of type `ScriptRunStatus`. This record is described in the section "The Script Run Status Record" on page 5-46.

Word processors and other applications can call `FindScriptRun` to separate style runs of native text from non-native text. You can use this capability to extract those characters and apply a different font to them. Figure 5-11 on page 5-28 provides an example of using the `FindScriptRun` routine.

ASSEMBLY-LANGUAGE INFORMATION

The trap macro and routine selector for the `FindScriptRun` function are

Trap macro	Selector
`_ScriptUtil`	$820C 0026

Converting Date and Time Strings Into Numeric Representations

This section describes the Text Utilities routines that you can use to convert date and time strings into numeric representations:

- The `InitDateCache` function initializes the date cache record, which is used by the `StringToDate` and `StringToTime` functions.

- The `StringToDate` function parses text for a date specification and fills in numeric date information in a `LongDateRec` record.

- The `StringToTime` function parses text for a time specification and fills in numeric time information in a `LongDateRec` record.

InitDateCache

The `InitDateCache` function initializes the date cache record, which is used to store data for use by the `StringToDate` and `StringToTime` functions.

```
FUNCTION InitDateCache(theCache: DateCachePtr): OSErr;
```

theCache   A pointer to a record of type `DateCacheRecord`. This parameter can be a local variable, a pointer, or a locked handle.

DESCRIPTION

You must call `InitDateCache` to initialize the date cache record before using either the `StringToDate` or `StringToTime` functions. You must pass a pointer to a date cache record. You have to declare the record as a variable or allocate it in the heap.

If you are writing an application that allows the use of global variables, you can make your date cache record a global variable and initialize it once, when you perform other global initialization.

SPECIAL CONSIDERATIONS

`InitDateCache` may move memory; your application should not call this function at interrupt time.

ASSEMBLY-LANGUAGE INFORMATION

The trap macro and routine selector for the `InitDateCache` function are

Trap macro	Selector
_ScriptUtil	$8204 FFF8

RESULT CODES

noErr	0	No error
fatalDateTime	–32768	A miscellaneous fatal error occurred, usually a failure in a call to get a resource

SEE ALSO

`InitDateCache` calls the `GetResource` and `LoadResource` routines and it can also return the error codes they produce. These routines and their return values are described in the book *Inside Macintosh: Operating System Utilities*.

StringToDate

The `StringToDate` function parses a string for a date and converts the date information into values in a date-time record. It expects a date specification, in a format defined by the current script, at the beginning of the string. It returns a status value that indicates the confidence level for the success of the conversion.

```
FUNCTION StringToDate(textPtr: Ptr; textLen: LongInt;
                theCache: DateCachePtr; VAR lengthUsed: LongInt;
                VAR dateTime: LongDateRec): StringToDateStatus;
```

textPtr   A pointer to the text string to be parsed.

textLen   The number of bytes in the text string.

theCache   A pointer to the date cache record initialized by the `InitDateCache` function with data that is used during the conversion process.

lengthUsed

On output, contains the number of bytes of the string that were parsed for the date.

dateTime   On output, this `LongDateRec` record contains the year, month, day, and day of the week parsed for the date.

DESCRIPTION

`StringToDate` parses the text string until it has finished finding all date information or until it has examined the number of bytes specified by `textLen`. It returns a status value that indicates the confidence level for the success of the conversion. For an overview of how this function operates, see the section "Converting Formatted Date and Time Strings Into Internal Numeric Representations" beginning on page 5-31.

Note that `StringToDate` fills in only the year, month, day, and day of the week; `StringToTime` fills in the hour, minute, and second. You can use these two routines sequentially to fill in all of the values in a `LongDateRec` record.

`StringToDate` assigns to its `lengthUsed` parameter the number of bytes that it uses to parse the date; use this value to compute the starting location of the text that you can pass to `StringToTime` (or you can use them in reverse order).

When one of the date components is missing, such as the year, the current date value is used as a default. If the value of the input year is less than 100, `StringToDate` determines the year as described on page 5-32.

`StringToDate` returns a value of type `StringToDateStatus`, which is a set of bit values that indicate confidence levels, with higher numbers indicating low confidence in how closely the input string matched what the routine expected. For example, specifying a date with nonstandard separators may work, but it returns a message indicating that the separator was not standard. The possible values of this type are described in Table 5-5 on page 5-33.

SPECIAL CONSIDERATIONS

`StringToDate` may move memory; your application should not call this function at interrupt time.

ASSEMBLY-LANGUAGE INFORMATION

The trap macro and routine selector for the `StringToDate` function are

Trap macro	Selector
_ScriptUtil	$8214 FFF6

StringToTime

The `StringToTime` function parses a string for a time specification and converts the date information into values in a date-time record. At the beginning of the string, it expects a time specification in a format defined by the current script. It returns a status value that indicates the confidence level for the success of the conversion.

```
FUNCTION StringToTime(textPtr: Ptr; textLen: LongInt;
                      theCache: DateCachePtr; VAR lengthUsed: LongInt;
                      VAR dateTime: LongDateRec): StringToDateStatus;
```

textPtr   A pointer to the text string to be parsed.

textLen   The number of bytes in the text string.

theCache   A pointer to the date cache record initialized by the `InitDateCache` function with data that is used during the conversion process.

lengthUsed
             On output, contains the number of bytes of the string that were parsed for the time.

dateTime   On output, this `LongDateRec` record contains the hour, minute, and second values that were parsed for the time.

DESCRIPTION

`StringToTime` parses the string until it has finished finding all time information or until it has examined the number of bytes specified by `textLen`. It returns a status value that indicates the confidence level for the success of the conversion.

Note that `StringToTime` fills in only the hour, minute, and second; `StringToDate` fills in the year, month, day, and day of the week. You can use these two routines sequentially to fill in all of the values in a `LongDateRec` record.

`StringToTime` assigns to its `lengthUsed` parameter the number of bytes that it used to parse the date.

StringToTime returns the same status value indicator type as does StringToDate: a set of bit values that indicate confidence levels, with higher numbers indicating low confidence in how closely the input string matched what the routine expected. The possible values of this type are described in Table 5-5 on page 5-33.

SPECIAL CONSIDERATIONS

StringToTime may move memory; your application should not call this function at interrupt time.

ASSEMBLY-LANGUAGE INFORMATION

The trap macro and routine selector for the StringToTime function are

Trap macro	Selector
_ScriptUtil	$8214 FFF4

Converting Numeric Representations Into Date and Time Strings

This section describes the routines that you can use to convert numeric representations of date and time values into formatted strings. The numeric representation used in these routines is the standard date-time representation: a 32-bit integer value that is returned by the GetDateTime routine. This is a long integer value that represents the number of seconds between midnight, January 1, 1904, and the time at which GetDateTime was called, as described in the book *Inside Macintosh: Operating System Utilities*.

■ The DateString procedure converts a date in the standard date-time representation into a string, making use of the date formatting information from a specified resource. If you specify NIL as the value of the resource handle parameter, DateString uses information from the current script.

■ The TimeString procedure converts a time in the standard date-time representation into a string, making use of the time formatting information from a specified resource. If you specify NIL as the value of the resource handle parameter, TimeString uses information from the current script.

DateString

The DateString procedure converts a date in the standard date-time representation into a Pascal string, making use of the date formatting information in the specified resource.

```
PROCEDURE DateString (dateTime: LongInt; longFlag: Boolean;
                      VAR result: Str255; intlParam: Handle );
```

dateTime   The date-time value in the representation returned by the GetDateTime procedure.

longFlag   A flag that indicates the desired format for the date string. This is one of the three values defined as the DateForm type.

result   On output, contains the string representation of the date in the format indicated by the longFlag parameter.

intlParam   A handle to a numeric-format or a long-date-format resource that specifies date formatting information for use in the conversion. The numeric-format ('itl0') resource specifies the short date formats and the long-date-format ('itl1') resource specifies the long date formats.

DESCRIPTION

DateString converts the long integer representation of date and time in the dateTime parameter into a Pascal string representation of the date. You can call the GetDateTime function to get the date-time value. GetDateTime is described in the book *Inside Macintosh: Operating System Utilities.*

The string produced by DateString is in one of three standard date formats used on the Macintosh, depending on which of the three DateForm values that you specify for the longFlag parameter: shortDate, abbrevDate, or longDate. The information in the supplied resource defines how month and day names are written and provides for calendars with more than 7 days and more than 12 months. For the Roman script system's resource, the date January 31, 1991, produces the following three strings:

Dateform value	Date string produced
shortDate	1/31/92
abbrevDate	Fri, Jan 31, 1992
longDate	Friday, January 31, 1992

DateString formats its data according to the information in the specified numeric-format resource (for short date formats) or long-date-format resource (for long date formats). If you specify shortDate, the intlParam value should be the handle to a numeric-format resource; if you specify abbrevDate or longDate, it should be the handle to a long-date-format resource. If the intlParam value is NIL, DateString uses the appropriate resource from the current script.

SPECIAL CONSIDERATIONS

DateString may move memory; your application should not call this procedure at interrupt time.

ASSEMBLY-LANGUAGE INFORMATION

The trap macro and routine selector for the DateString procedure are

Trap macro	Selector
_Pack6	$000E

TimeString

The TimeString procedure converts a time in the standard date-time representation into a string, making use of the time formatting information in the specified resource.

```
PROCEDURE TimeString (dateTime: LongInt; wantSeconds: Boolean;
                      VAR result: Str255; intlParam: Handle);
```

dateTime   The date-time value in the representation returned by the Operating System procedure GetDateTime.

wantSeconds
              A flag that indicates whether the seconds are to be included in the resulting string.

result   On output, contains the string representation of the time.

intlParam   A handle to a numeric-format ('itl0') resource that specifies time formatting information for use in the conversion.

DESCRIPTION

TimeString converts the long integer representation of date and time in the dateTime parameter into a Pascal string representation of the time. You can call the GetDateTime function to get the date-time value. GetDateTime is described in the book *Inside Macintosh: Operating System Utilities*.

TimeString produces a string that includes the seconds if you set the wantSeconds parameter to TRUE.

TimeString formats its data according to the information in the numeric-format resource specified in the intlParam parameter. If this value is NIL, TimeString uses the numeric-format resource from the current script. The numeric-format resource specifies whether or not to use leading zeros for the time values, whether to use a 12- or 24-hour time cycle, and how to specify morning or evening if a 12-hour time cycle is used.

SPECIAL CONSIDERATIONS

TimeString may move memory; your application should not call this procedure at interrupt time.

ASSEMBLY-LANGUAGE INFORMATION

The trap macro and routine selector for the TimeString procedure are

Trap macro	Selector
_Pack6	$0010

Converting Long Date and Time Values Into Strings

This section describes two procedures that use the LongDateTime data type in their conversions. This is a 64-bit, signed representation of the number of seconds since Jan. 1, 1904, which allows coverage of a much longer span of time (plus or minus approximately 30,000 years) than the standard, 32-bit representation. LongDateTime values are described in the book *Inside Macintosh: Operating System Utilities*.

■ The LongDateString procedure converts a date in LongDateTime representation into a string, making use of the date formatting information from a specified resource. If you specify NIL as the value of the resource handle parameter, LongDateString uses information from the current script.

■ The LongTimeString procedure converts a time in LongDateTime representation into a string, making use of the date formatting information from a specified resource. If you specify NIL as the value of the resource handle parameter, LongTimeString uses information from the current script.

LongDateString

The LongDateString procedure converts a date that is specified as a LongDateTime value into a Pascal string, making use of the date formatting information in the specified resource.

```
PROCEDURE LongDateString(VAR dateTime: LongDateTime;
                         longFlag: DateForm;
                         VAR result: Str255; intlParam: Handle);
```

dateTime   A 64-bit, signed representation of the number of seconds since Jan. 1, 1904.

longFlag   A flag that indicates the desired format for the date string. This is one of the three values defined as the DateForm type.

result   On output, contains the string representation of the date in the format indicated by the longFlag parameter.

intlParam   A handle to a numeric-format or long-date-format resource that specifies date formatting information for use in the conversion. The numeric-format ('itl0') resource specifies the short date formats and the long-date-format ('itl1') resource specifies the long date formats.

DESCRIPTION

LongDateString converts the LongDateTime value in the dateTime parameter into a Pascal string representation of the date. You can use the LongSecondsToDate and LongDateToSeconds procedures, which are described in the book *Inside Macintosh: Operating System Utilities*, to convert between the LongDateRec (as produced by the StringToDate function) and LongDateTime data types.

The string produced by LongDateString is in one of three standard date formats used on the Macintosh, depending on which of the three DateForm values that you specify for the longFlag parameter: shortDate, abbrevDate, or longDate. The information in the supplied resource defines how month and day names are written and provides for calendars with more than 7 days and more than 12 months. For the U.S. resource, the date January 31, 1991, produces the following three strings:

DateForm value	Date string produced
shortDate	1/31/92
abbrevDate	Fri, Jan 31, 1992
longDate	Friday, January 31, 1992

LongDateString formats its data according to the information in the specified numeric-format resource (for short date formats) or long-date-format resource (for long date formats). If you specify shortDate, the intlParam value should be the handle to a numeric-format resource; if you specify abbrevDate or longDate, it should be the handle to a long-date-format resource. If the intlParam value is NIL, LongDateString uses the resource from the current script.

SPECIAL CONSIDERATIONS

LongDateString may move memory; your application should not call this procedure at interrupt time.

ASSEMBLY-LANGUAGE INFORMATION

The trap macro and routine selector for the LongDateString procedure are

Trap macro	Selector
_Pack6	$0014

LongTimeString

The LongTimeString procedure converts a time that is specified as a LongDateTime value into a Pascal string, making use of the time formatting information in the specified resource.

```
PROCEDURE LongTimeString(VAR dateTime: LongDateTime;
                             wantSeconds: Boolean;
                             VAR result: Str255; intlParam: Handle);
```

dateTime   A 64-bit, signed representation of the number of seconds since Jan. 1, 1904.

wantSeconds

A flag that indicates whether the seconds are to be included in the resulting string.

result   On output, contains the string representation of the time.

intlParam

           A handle to a numeric-format (`'itl0'`) resource that specifies time formatting information for use in the conversion.

DESCRIPTION

LongTimeString converts the LongDateTime value in the dateTime parameter into a Pascal string representation of the time. You can use the LongSecondsToDate and LongDateToSeconds procedures, which are described in the book *Inside Macintosh: Operating System Utilities*, to convert between the LongDateRec (as produced by the StringToTime function) and LongDateTime data types.

LongTimeString produces a string that includes the seconds if you set the wantSeconds parameter to TRUE.

LongTimeString formats its data according to the information in the numeric-format resource specified in the intlParam parameter. If this value is NIL, LongTimeString uses the numeric-format resource from the current script. The numeric-format resource specifies whether or not to use leading zeros for the time values, whether to use a 12- or 24-hour time cycle, and how to specify morning or evening if a 12-hour time cycle is used.

SPECIAL CONSIDERATIONS

LongTimeString may move memory; your application should not call this procedure at interrupt time.

ASSEMBLY-LANGUAGE INFORMATION

The trap macro and routine selector for the LongTimeString procedure are

Trap macro	Selector
_Pack6	$0016

Converting Between Integers and Strings

This section describes routines that allow you to convert between string and numeric representations of numbers. Unless patched by a script system with different rules, these two routines assume that you are using standard numeric token processing, meaning that the Roman script system number processing rules are used.

- The NumToString procedure converts a long integer value to a string representation of it as a base-10 number.

- The StringToNum procedure converts a string representation of a base-10 number into a long integer value.

For routines that make use of the token-processing information that is found in the tokens ('itl4') resource of script systems for converting numbers, see the section "Using Number Format Specification Strings for International Number Formatting," which begins on page 5-94, and the section "Converting Between Strings and Floating-Point Numbers," which begins on page 5-98.

NumToString

The `NumToString` procedure converts a long integer value into a Pascal string.

```
PROCEDURE NumToString (theNum: LongInt; VAR theString: Str255);
```

theNum   A long integer value.

theString   On output, contains the Pascal string representation of the number.

DESCRIPTION

`NumToString` creates a string representation of `theNum` as a base-10 value and returns the result in `theString`.

If the value of the number in the parameter `theNum` is negative, the string begins with a minus sign; otherwise, the sign is omitted. Leading zeros are suppressed, except that a value of 0 produces the string "0". `NumToString` does not include thousand separators or decimal points in its formatted output.

SPECIAL CONSIDERATIONS

`NumToString` may move memory; your application should not call this procedure at interrupt time.

ASSEMBLY-LANGUAGE INFORMATION

The trap macro and routine selector for the `NumToString` procedure are

Trap macro	Selector
_Pack7	$0000

The registers on entry and exit for this routine are

Registers on entry

A0   pointer to the length byte that precedes `theString`

D0   the long integer value to be converted

Registers on exit

D0   pointer to the length byte that precedes `theString`

StringToNum

The StringToNum procedure converts the Pascal string representation of a base-10 number into a long integer value.

```
PROCEDURE StringToNum (theString: Str255; VAR theNum: LongInt);
```

theString   A Pascal string representation of a base-10 number.

theNum   On output, contains the numeric value.

DESCRIPTION

StringToNum converts the base-10 numeric string in the theString parameter to the corresponding long integer value and returns the result in the parameter theNum. The numeric string can be padded with leading zeros or with a sign.

The 32-bit result is negated if the string begins with a minus sign. Integer overflow occurs if the magnitude is greater than or equal to 2 raised to the 31st power. StringToNum performs the negation using the two's complement method: the state of each bit is reversed and then 1 is added to the result. For example, here are possible results produced by StringToNum:

Value of theString	Value returned in theNum
"–23"	–23
"–0"	0
"055"	55
"2147483648" (magnitude is 2^31)	–2147483648
"–2147483648"	–2147483648
"4294967295" (magnitude is 2^32–1)	–1
"–4294967295"	1

StringToNum does not check whether the characters in the string are between 0 and 9; instead, it takes advantage of the fact that the ASCII values for these characters are $30 through $39, and masks the last four bits for use as a digit. For example, StringToNum converts 2: to the number 30 since the character code for the colon (:) is $3A. Because StringToNum operates this way, spaces are treated as zeros (the character code for a space is $20), and other characters do get converted into numbers. For example, the character codes for 'C', 'A', and 'T' are $43, $41, and $54 respectively, producing these results:

Value of theString	Value returned in theNum
'CAT'	314
'+CAT'	314
'–CAT'	–314

Note

One consequence of this conversion method is that `StringToNum` does not ignore thousand separators (the "," character in the United States), which can lead to improper conversions. It is a good idea to ensure that all characters in `theString` are valid digits before you call `StringToNum`. ◆

SPECIAL CONSIDERATIONS

`StringToNum` may move memory; your application should not call this procedure at interrupt time.

ASSEMBLY-LANGUAGE INFORMATION

The trap macro and routine selector for the `StringToNum` procedure are

Trap macro	Routine selector
_Pack7	$0001

The registers on entry and exit for this routine are

Registers on entry

A0   pointer to the length byte that precedes `theString`

Registers on exit

D0   the long word value

Using Number Format Specification Strings for International Number Formatting

To allow for all of the international variations in numeric presentation styles, you need to include in your routine calls a number parts table from a tokens (`'itl4'`) resource. You can usually use the number parts table in the standard tokens resource that is supplied with the system. You also need to define the format of input and output numeric strings, including which characters (if any) to use as thousand separators, whether to indicate negative values with a minus sign or by enclosing the number in parentheses, and how to display zero values. These details are specified in number format specification strings, the syntax of which is described in the section "Using Number Format Specification Strings," beginning on page 5-39.

To make it possible to map a number that was formatted for one specification into another format, the Macintosh Operating System defines an internal numeric representation that is independent of region, language, and other multicultural considerations: the `NumFormatStringRec` record. This record is created from a number format specification string that defines the appearance of numeric strings. Its use is summarized in Figure 5-12 on page 5-37.

In brief, what you have to do is create a number format specification string that you want to use and convert that string into a `NumFormatStringRec` record. The Text Utilities include two routines for this purpose:

■ The `StringToFormatRec` function converts a number format specification string into a `NumFormatStringRec` record.

■ The `FormatRecToString` function converts the internal representation in a `NumFormatStringRec` record into a number format specification string, which can be viewed and modified.

StringToFormatRec

The `StringToFormatRec` function creates a number format specification string record from a number format specification string that you supply in a Pascal string.

```
FUNCTION StringToFormatRec(inString: Str255;
                partsTable: NumberParts;
                VAR outString: NumFormatStringRec): FormatStatus;
```

inString   A Pascal string that contains the number formatting specification.

partsTable

     A record usually obtained from the tokens (`'it14'`) resource that shows the correspondence between generic number part separators (tokens) and their localized version (for example, a thousand separator is a comma in the United States and a decimal point in France).

outString   On output, this `NumFormatStringRec` record contains the values that form the internal representation of the format specification. The format of the data in this record is private.

DESCRIPTION

`StringToFormatRec` converts a number format specification string into the internal representation contained in a number format string record. It uses information in the current script's tokens resource to determine the components of the number. `StringToFormatRec` checks the validity both of the input format string and of the number parts table (since this table can be programmed by the application). `StringToFormatRec` ignores spurious characters.

The `inString` parameter contains a number format specification string that specifies how numbers appear. This string contains up to three specifications, separated by semicolons. The positive number format is specified first, the negative number format is second, and the zero number format is last. If the string contains only one part, that is the format of all three types of numbers. If the string contains two parts, the first part is the format for positive and zero number values, and the second part is the format for negative numbers. The syntax for the number format specification strings is described in detail in "Using Number Format Specification Strings," which begins on page 5-39.

StringToFormatRec returns a value of type FormatStatus that denotes the confidence level for the conversion that it performed. The low byte of the FormatStatus value is of type FormatResultType, the values of which are described in Table 5-6 on page 5-38.

IMPORTANT

Be sure to cast the result of StringToFormatRec to a type FormatResultType before working with it. ▲

SPECIAL CONSIDERATIONS

StringToFormatRec may move memory; your application should not call this function at interrupt time.

ASSEMBLY-LANGUAGE INFORMATION

The trap macro and routine selector for the StringToFormatRec function are

Trap macro	Selector
_ScriptUtil	$820C FFEC

SEE ALSO

For comprehensive details on the number parts table, see the appendix "International Resources" in this book.

To obtain a handle to the number parts table from a tokens resource, use the GetIntlResourceTable procedure, which is described in the chapter "Script Manager" in this book.

FormatRecToString

The FormatRecToString function converts an internal representation of number formatting information into a number format specification string, which can be displayed and modified.

```
FUNCTION FormatRecToString(myFormatRec: NumFormatStringRec;
                partsTable: NumberParts; VAR outString: Str255;
                VAR positions: TripleInt): FormatStatus;
```

myFormatRec
The internal representation of number formatting information, as created by a previous call to the StringToFormatRec function.

partsTable

A record obtained from the tokens ('itl4') resource that shows the correspondence between generic number part separators (tokens) and their localized version (for example, a thousand separator is a comma in the United States and a decimal point in France).

outString   On output, contains the number format specification string.

positions   An array that specifies the starting position and length of each of the three possible format strings (positive, negative, or zero) in the number format specification string. Semicolons are used as separators in the string.

DESCRIPTION

FormatRecToString is the inverse operation of StringToFormatRec. The internal representation of the formatting information in myFormatRec must have been created by a prior call to the StringToFormatRec function. The information in the number parts table specifies how to build the string representation.

The output number format specification string in outString specifies how numbers appear. This string contains three parts, which are separated by semicolons. The first part is the positive number format, the second is the negative number format, and the third part is the zero number format. The syntax for this string is described in detail in "Using Number Format Specification Strings," which begins on page 5-39.

The positions parameter is an array of three integers (a TripleInt value), which specifies the starting position in outString of each of three formatting specifications:

Array entry	What its value specifies
positions[fPositive]	the index in outString of the first byte of the formatting specification for positive number values
positions[fNegative]	the index in outString of the first byte of the formatting specification for negative number values
positions[fZero]	the index in outString of the first byte of the formatting specification for zero number values

FormatRecToString returns a value of type FormatStatus that denotes the confidence level for the conversion that it performed. The low byte of the FormatStatus value is of type FormatResultType, the values of which are described in Table 5-6 on page 5-38.

IMPORTANT

Be sure to cast the result of FormatRecToString to a type FormatResultType before working with it. ▲

ASSEMBLY-LANGUAGE INFORMATION

The trap macro and routine selector for the FormatRecToString function are

Trap macro	Selector
_ScriptUtil	$8210 FFEA

For comprehensive details on the number parts table, see the appendix "International Resources" in this book.

To obtain a handle to the number parts table from a tokens resource, use the `GetIntlResourceTable` procedure, which is described in the chapter "Script Manager" in this book.

Converting Between Strings and Floating-Point Numbers

Once you have created a `NumFormatStringRec` record that specifies how numbers are represented, as described in "Using Number Format Specification Strings for International Number Formatting," which begins on page 5-94, you can use two other Text Utilities routines to convert between string and floating-point representations of numbers. Floating-point numbers are stored in standard Apple (SANE) format.

■ The `StringToExtended` function converts the string representation of a number into a floating-point number, using a `NumFormatStringRec` record to specify how the input number string is formatted.

■ The `ExtendedToString` function converts a floating-point number into a string that can be presented to the user, using a `NumFormatStringRec` record to specify how the output number string is formatted.

StringToExtended

The `StringToExtended` function converts a string representation of a number into a floating-point number.

```
FUNCTION StringToExtended(source: Str255;
                          myFormatRec: NumFormatStringRec;
                          partsTable: NumberParts;
                          VAR x: Extended80): FormatStatus;
```

source   A Pascal string that contains the string representation of a number.

myFormatRec
                The internal representation of the formatting information for numbers, as produced by the `StringToFormatRec` function.

partsTable
                A record obtained from the tokens (`'itl4'`) resource that shows the correspondence between generic number part separators (tokens) and their localized version (for example, a thousand separator is a comma in the United States and a decimal point in France).

x   On output, contains the 80-bit SANE representation of the floating-point number.

DESCRIPTION

`StringToExtended` uses the internal representation of number formatting information that was created by a prior call to `StringToFormatRec` to parse the input number string. It uses the number parts table to determine the components of the number string that is being converted. `StringToExtended` parses the string and then converts the string to a simple form, stripping nondigits and replacing the decimal point before converting it into a floating-point number. If the input string does not match any of the patterns, then `StringToExtended` parses the string as well as it can and returns a confidence level result that indicates the parsing difficulties.

`StringToFormatRec` returns a value of type `FormatStatus` that denotes the confidence level for the conversion that it performed. The low byte of the `FormatStatus` value is of type `FormatResultType`, the values of which are described in Table 5-6 on page 5-38.

IMPORTANT

Be sure to cast the result of `StringToExtended` to a type `FormatResultType` before working with it. ▲

SPECIAL CONSIDERATIONS

`StringToExtended` returns an 80-bit, not a 96-bit, representation.

ASSEMBLY-LANGUAGE INFORMATION

The trap macro and routine selector for the `StringToExtended` function are

Trap macro	Selector
`_ScriptUtil`	$8210 FFE6

SEE ALSO

For comprehensive details on the number parts table, see the description of the tokens (`'itl4'`) resource in the appendix "International Resources" in this book.

To obtain a handle to the number parts table from a tokens resource, use the `GetIntlResourceTable` procedure, which is described in the chapter "Script Manager" in this book.

ExtendedToString

The `ExtendedToString` function converts an internal floating-point representation of a number into a string that can be presented to the user.

```
FUNCTION ExtendedToString(x: Extended80;
                        myFormatRec: NumFormatStringRec;
                        partsTable: NumberParts;
                        VAR outString: Str255): FormatStatus;
```

x   A floating-point value in 80-bit SANE representation.

myFormatRec
                The internal representation of the formatting information for numbers, as produced by the `StringToFormatRec` function.

partsTable
                A record obtained from the tokens ('itl4') resource that shows the correspondence between generic number part separators (tokens) and their localized version (for example, a thousand separator is a comma in the United States and a decimal point in France).

outString   On output, contains the number formatted according to the information in `myFormatRec`.

DESCRIPTION

`ExtendedToString` creates a string representation of a floating-point number, using the formatting information in the `myFormatRec` parameter (which was created by a previous call to `StringToFormatRec`) to determine how the number should be formatted for output. It uses the number parts table to determine the component parts of the number string.

`StringToFormatRec` returns a value of type `FormatStatus` that denotes the confidence level for the conversion that it performed. The low byte of the `FormatStatus` value is of type `FormatResultType`, the values of which are described in Table 5-6 on page 5-38.

IMPORTANT

Be sure to cast the result of `ExtendedToString` to a type `FormatResultType` before working with it. ▲

ASSEMBLY-LANGUAGE INFORMATION

The trap macro and routine selector for the `ExtendedToString` function are

Trap macro	Selector
_ScriptUtil	$8210 FFE8

SEE ALSO

For comprehensive details on the number parts table, see the description of the tokens (`'itl4'`) resource in the appendix "International Resources" in this book.

To obtain a handle to the number parts table from a tokens resource, use the `GetIntlResourceTable` procedure, which is described in the chapter "Script Manager" in this book.

Summary of Text Utilities

Pascal Summary

Constants

```
CONST
        {StringToDate and StringToTime status values }
    longDateFound     = 1;      {mask to long date found}
    leftOverChars     = 2;      {mask to warn of left over chars}
    sepNotIntlSep     = 4;      {mask to warn of non-standard separators}
    fieldOrderNotIntl = 8;      {mask to warn of non-standard field order}
    extraneousStrings = 16;     {mask to warn of unparsable strings in text}
    tooManySeps       = 32;     {mask to warn of too many separators}
    sepNotConsistent  = 64;     {mask to warn of inconsistent separators}
    fatalDateTime     = $8000;  {mask to a fatal error}
    tokenErr = $8100;           {mask for 'tokenizer err encountered'}
    cantReadUtilities = $8200;  {mask for can't access needed resource}
    dateTimeNotFound = $8400;   {mask for date or time not found}
    dateTimeInvalid = $8800;    {mask for date/time format not valid}

        {Constants for truncWhere argument in TruncString and TruncText}
    truncEnd          = 0;      {truncate at end}
    truncMiddle       = $4000;  {truncate in middle}

        {Constants for TruncString and TruncText results}
    NotTruncated      = 0;      {no truncation was necessary}
    Truncated         = 1;      {truncation performed}
    TruncErr          = -1;     {general error}

        {Special language code values for Language Order}
systemCurLang  = -2; { current language for system script (from 'itlb')}
systemDefLang  = -3; { default language for system script (from 'itlm')}
currentCurLang = -4; { current language for current script (from 'itlb')}
currentDefLang = -5; { default language for current script (from 'itlm')}
scriptCurLang  = -6; { current lang for specified script (from 'itlb')}
scriptDefLang  = -7; { default language for specified script (from 'itlm')}
```

Data Types

```
TYPE

FormatStatus = Integer;

TruncCode = Integer;

DateForm = (shortDate,longDate,abbrevDate);

FormatResultType =
(fFormatOK,fBestGuess,fOutOfSynch,fSpuriousChars,fMissingDelimiter,
   fExtraDecimal,fMissingLiteral,fExtraExp,fFormatOverflow,fFormStrIsNAN,
   fBadPartsTable,fExtraPercent,fExtraSeparator,fEmptyFormatString);

FormatClass = (fPositive,fNegative,fZero);

StyledLineBreakCode = {BreakWord, BreakChar, BreakOverflow};

DateCacheRecord =
PACKED RECORD
   hidden: ARRAY [0..255] OF Integer;{only for temporary use}
END;

DateCachePtr = ^DateCacheRecord;

NumFormatStringRec =
PACKED RECORD
   fLength: Byte;
   fVersion: Byte;
   data: PACKED ARRAY [0..253] OF SignedByte;    {private data}
END;

FVector =
RECORD
   start: Integer;
   length: Integer
END;

TripleInt = ARRAY[0..2] OF FVector;                {index by [fPositive..fZero]}
```

Summary of Text Utilities

```
OffPair =
RECORD
   offFirst: Integer;
   offSecond: Integer;
END;

OffsetTable = ARRAY[0..2] OF OffPair;

ScriptRunStatus =
RECORD
   script: SignedByte;
   variant: SignedByte;
END;
```

Routines

Defining and Specifying Strings

```
FUNCTION NewString          (theString: Str255): StringHandle;
PROCEDURE SetString         (theString: StringHandle; strNew: Str255);
FUNCTION GetString          (stringID: Integer): StringHandle;
PROCEDURE GetIndString      (VAR theString: Str255; strListID: Integer;
                             index: Integer);
```

Comparing Strings for Equality

```
FUNCTION EqualString        (aStr, bStr: Str255;
                             caseSens, diacSens: Boolean): Boolean;
FUNCTION IdenticalString    (aStr, bStr: Str255;
                             itl2Handle: Handle): Integer;
FUNCTION IdenticalText      (aPtr, bPtr: Ptr; aLen, bLen: Integer;
                             itl2Handle: Handle): Integer;
```

Determining Sorting Order for Strings in Different Languages

```
FUNCTION ScriptOrder        (script1, script2: ScriptCode): Integer;
FUNCTION LanguageOrder      (lang1, lang2: LangCode): Integer;
FUNCTION StringOrder        (aStr, bStr: Str255; aScript, bScript:
                             ScriptCode; aLang, bLang: LangCode): Integer;
FUNCTION TextOrder          (aPtr, bPtr: Ptr; aLen, bLen: Integer;
                             aScript, bScript: ScriptCode;
                             aLang, bLang: LangCode): Integer;
```

Determining Sorting Order for Strings in the Same Language

```
FUNCTION RelString        (aStr, bStr: Str255;
                             caseSens, diacSens: Boolean): Integer;

FUNCTION CompareString    (aStr, bStr: Str255;
                             itl2Handle: Handle): Integer;

FUNCTION CompareText      (aPtr, bPtr: Ptr; aLen, bLen: Integer): Integer;
```

Modifying Characters and Diacritical Marks

```
PROCEDURE UpperString     (VAR theString: Str255; diacSens: Boolean);

PROCEDURE LowercaseText   (textPtr: Ptr; len: Integer;
                             script: ScriptCode);

PROCEDURE UppercaseText   (textPtr: Ptr; len: Integer;
                             script: ScriptCode);

PROCEDURE StripDiacritics (textPtr: Ptr; len: Integer;
                             script: ScriptCode);

PROCEDURE UppercaseStripDiacritics
                          (textPtr: Ptr; len: Integer;
                             script: ScriptCode);
```

Truncating Strings

```
FUNCTION TruncString      (width: Integer; VAR theString: Str255;
                             truncWhere: TruncCode): Integer;

FUNCTION TruncText        (width: Integer; textPtr: Ptr;
                             VAR length: Integer;
                             truncWhere: TruncCode): Integer;
```

Searching for and Replacing Strings

```
FUNCTION ReplaceText      (baseText, substitutionText: Handle;
                             key: Str15): Integer;

FUNCTION Munger           (h: Handle; offset: LongInt;
                             ptr1: Ptr; len1: LongInt;
                             ptr2: Ptr; len2: LongInt): LongInt;
```

Working With Word, Subscript, and Line Boundaries

```
PROCEDURE FindWordBreaks  (textPtr: Ptr; textLength: Integer;
                             offset: Integer; leadingEdge: Boolean;
                             nBreaks: NBreakTablePtr;
                             VAR offsets:OffsetTable );
```

```
FUNCTION StyledLineBreak      (textPtr: Ptr; textLen: LongInt;
                               textStart, textEnd, flags: LongInt;
                               VAR textWidth: Fixed;
                               VAR textOffset: LongInt): StyledLineBreakCode;
FUNCTION FindScriptRun        (textPtr: Ptr; textLen: LongInt;
                               VAR lenUsed: LongInt): ScriptRunStatus;
```

Converting Date and Time Strings Into Numeric Representations

```
FUNCTION InitDateCache        (theCache: DateCachePtr): OSErr;
FUNCTION StringToDate         (textPtr: Ptr; textLen: LongInt;
                               theCache: DateCachePtr;
                               VAR lengthUsed: LongInt;
                               VAR dateTime: LongDateRec): StringToDateStatus;
FUNCTION StringToTime         (textPtr: Ptr; textLen: LongInt;
                               theCache: DateCachePtr;
                               VAR lengthUsed: LongInt;
                               VAR dateTime: LongDateRec): StringToDateStatus;
```

Converting Numeric Representations Into Date and Time Strings

```
PROCEDURE DateString          (dateTime: LongInt; longFlag: DateForm;
                               VAR result: Str255; intlHandle: Handle);
PROCEDURE TimeString          (dateTime: LongInt; wantSeconds: Boolean;
                               VAR result: Str255; intlHandle: Handle);
```

Converting Long Date and Time Values Into Strings

```
PROCEDURE LongDateString      (VAR dateTime: LongDateTime; longFlag: DateForm;
                               VAR result: Str255; intlHandle: Handle);
PROCEDURE LongTimeString      (VAR dateTime: LongDateTime;
                               wantSeconds:Boolean; VAR result: Str255;
                               intlHandle: Handle);
```

Converting Between Integers and Strings

```
PROCEDURE NumToString         (theNum: LongInt; VAR theString: Str255);
PROCEDURE StringToNum         (theString: Str255; VAR theNum: LongInt);
```

Using Number Format Specification Strings for International Number Formatting

```
FUNCTION StringToFormatRec    (inString: Str255; partsTable: NumberParts;
                               VAR outString: NumFormatString): FormatStatus;
```

```
FUNCTION FormatRecToString    (myFormatRec: NumFormatString;
                               partsTable: NumberParts;
                               VAR outString: Str255;
                               VAR positions: TripleInt): FormatStatus;
```

Converting Between Strings and Floating-Point Numbers

```
FUNCTION StringToExtended     (source: Str255; myFormatRec: NumFormatString;
                               partsTable: NumberParts;
                               VAR x: Extended80): FormatStatus;
FUNCTION ExtendedToString     (x: Extended80; myFormatRec: NumFormatString;
                               partsTable: NumberParts;
                               VAR outString: Str255): FormatStatus;
```

C Summary

Constants

```
enum {       /*StringToDate and StringToTime status values*/
   longDateFound = 1;           /*mask to long date found*/
   leftOverChars = 2;           /*mask to warn of left over chars*/
   sepNotIntlSep = 4;           /*mask to warn of non-standard separators*/
   fieldOrderNotIntl = 8;       /*mask to warn of non-standard field order*/
   extraneousStrings = 16;      /*mask to warn of unparsable strings */
   tooManySeps = 32;            /*mask to warn of too many separators*/
   sepNotConsistent = 64;       /*mask to warn of inconsistent separators*/
   fatalDateTime = 0x8000;      /*mask to a fatal error*/
   tokenErr = 0x8100;           /*mask for 'tokenizer err encountered'*/
   cantReadUtilities = 0x8200;/*mask for can't access needed resource*/
   dateTimeNotFound = 0x8400;   /*mask for date or time not found*/
   dateTimeInvalid = 0x8800;    /*mask for date/time format not valid*/
};

enum {    /*constants for truncWhere argument in TruncString and TruncText*/
   truncEnd = 0,                /*truncate at end*/
   truncMiddle = 0x4000,        /*truncate in middle*/
};
```

```
enum {    /*constants for TruncString and TruncText results*/
    notTruncated = 0,          /*no truncation was necessary*/
    truncated = 1,             /*truncation performed*/
    truncErr = -1,             /*general error*/
};

enum {    /*special language code values for Language Order*/
    systemCurLang = -2,   /*current lang for system script (from 'itlb')*/
    systemDefLang = -3,   /*default lang for system script (from 'itlm')*/
    currentCurLang = -4,  /*current lang for current script (from 'itlb')*/
    currentDefLang = -5,  /*default lang for current script (from 'itlm')*/
    scriptCurLang = -6,   /*current lang for specified script (from 'itlb')*/
    scriptDefLang = -7,   /*default lang for specified script (from 'itlm')*/
};

enum {
    BreakWord,
    BreakChar,
    BreakOverflow
};

enum {
    fPositive,
    fNegative,
    fZero
};

enum{
    fFormatOK,
    fBestGuess,
    fOutOfSynch,
    fSpuriousChars,
    fMissingDelimiter,
    fExtraDecimal,
    fMissingLiteral,
    fExtraExp,
    fFormatOverflow,
    fFormStrIsNAN,
    fBadPartsTable,
    fExtraPercent,
    fExtraSeparator,
    fEmptyFormatString
};
```

```
enum {
    shortDate,
    longDate,
    abbrevDate
};
```

Types

```
typedef short StringToDateStatus;

typedef unsigned char StyledLineBreakCode;

typedef unsigned char FormatClass;

typedef short TruncCode;

typedef unsigned char FormatResultType;

typedef unsigned char DateForm;

struct DateCacheRecord {
    short hidden[256];              /*only for temporary use*/
};

typedef struct DateCacheRecord DateCacheRecord;
typedef DateCacheRecord *DateCachePtr;

struct NumFormatString {
    char fLength;
    char fVersion;
    char data[254];                /*private data*/
};

typedef struct NumFormatString NumFormatStringRec;
struct FVector {
    short start;
    short length;
};

typedef struct FVector FVector;
typedef FVector TripleInt[3];      /* index by [fPositive..fZero] */

struct ScriptRunStatus {
    char script;
    char variant;
```

```
};

typedef struct ScriptRunStatus ScriptRunStatus;

struct OffPair {
    short offFirst;
    short offSecond;
};

typedef struct OffPair OffPair;
typedef OffPair OffsetTable[3];
```

Routines

Defining and Specifying Strings

```
pascal StringHandle NewString
                            (ConstStr255Param theString);
pascal void SetString       (StringHandle theString,
                             ConstStr255Param strNew);
pascal StringHandle GetString
                            (short stringID);
pascal void GetIndString    (Str255 theString, short strListID,
                             short index);
```

Comparing Strings for Equality

```
pascal Boolean EqualString  (ConstStr255Param aStr, ConstStr255Param bStr,
                             Boolean caseSens, Boolean diacSens );
pascal short IdenticalString
                            (ConstStr255Param aStr, ConstStr255Param bStr,
                             Handle itl2Handle);
pascal short IdenticallText  (const void *aPtr, const void *bPtr,
                             short aLen, short bLen, Handle itl2Handle);
```

Determining Sorting Order for Strings in Different Languages

```
pascal short ScriptOrder    (ScriptCode script1, ScriptCode script2);
pascal short LanguageOrder   (LangCode language1, LangCode language2);
pascal short StringOrder      (ConstStr255Param aStr, ConstStr255Param bStr,
                             ScriptCode aScript, ScriptCode bScript,
                             LangCode aLang, LangCode bLang);
```

```
pascal short TextOrder        (const void *aPtr, const void *bPtr,
                               short aLen, short bLen,
                               ScriptCode aScript, ScriptCode bScript,
                               LangCode aLang, LangCode bLang);
```

Determining Sorting Order for Strings in the Same Language

```
pascal short RelString        (ConstStr255Param aStr, ConstStr255Param bStr,
                               Boolean caseSens, Boolean diacSens);
pascal short CompareString    (ConstStr255Param aStr, ConstStr255Param bStr,
                               Handle itl2Hande);
pascal short CompareText      (const void *aPtr, const void *bPtr,
                               short aLen, short bLen, Handle itl2Handle);
```

Modifying Characters and Diacritical Marks

```
pascal void UpperString       (Str255 theString, Boolean diacSens);
pascal void LowercaseText     (Ptr textPtr, short len, ScriptCode script);
pascal void UppercaseText     (Ptr textPtr, short len, ScriptCode script);
pascal void StripDiacritics   (Ptr textPtr, short len, ScriptCode script);
pascal void UppercaseStripDiacritics
                              (Ptr textPtr, short len, ScriptCode script);
```

Truncating Strings

```
pascal short TruncString      (short width, Str255 theString,
                               TruncCode truncWhere);
pascal short TruncText        (short width, Ptr textPtr, short *textLen,
                               TruncCode truncWhere);
```

Searching for and Replacing Strings

```
pascal short ReplaceText      (Handle baseText, Handle substitutionText,
                               Str15 key);
pascal long Munger            (Handle h, long offset, const void *ptr1,
                               long len1, const void *ptr2, long len2);
```

Working With Word, Subscript, and Line Boundaries

```
pascal void FindWordBreaks    (Ptr textPtr, short textLen, short offset,
                               Boolean leadingEdge, NBreakTablePtr breaks,
                               OffsetTable offsets);
pascal StyledLineBreakCode StyledLineBreak
                              (Ptr textPtr, long textLen, long textStart,
                               long textEnd, long flags, Fixed *textWidth,
                               long *textOffset);
```

```
pascal ScriptRunStatus FindScriptRun
                        (Ptr textPtr, long textLen, long *lenUsed);
```

Converting Date and Time Strings Into Numeric Representations

```
pascal OSErr InitDateCache  (DateCachePtr theCache);
pascal StringToDateStatus StringtoDate
                        (Ptr textPtr, long textLen,
                         DateCachePtr theCache, long *lengthUsed,
                         LongDateRec *dateTime);
pascal StringToDateStatus StringToTime
                        (Ptr textPtr, long textLen,
                         DateCachePtr theCache, long *lengthUsed,
                         LongDateRec *dateTime);
```

Converting Numeric Representations Into Date and Time Strings

```
pascal void DateString      (long dateTime, DateForm longFlag,
                             Str255 result, Handle intlHandle);
pascal void TimeString      (long dateTime, Boolean wantSeconds,
                             Str255 result, Handle intlHandle);
```

Converting Long Date and Time Values Into Strings

```
pascal void LongDateString  (LongDateTime *dateTime, DateForm longFlag,
                             Str255 result, Handle intlHandle);
pascal void LongTimeString  (LongDateTime *dateTime, Boolean wantSeconds,
                             Str255 result, Handle intlHandle);
```

Converting Between Integers and Strings

```
pascal void NumToString     (long theNum, Str255 theString);
pascal void StringToNum     (ConstStr255Param theString, long *theNum);
```

Using Number Format Specification Strings for International Number Formatting

```
pascal FormatStatus StringToFormatRec
                        (ConstStr255Param inString,
                         const NumberParts *partsTable,
                         NumFormatString *outString);
pascal FormatStatus FormatRecToStr
                        (const NumFormatString *myFormatRec,
                         const NumberParts *partsTable,
                         Str255 outString, TripleInt positions);
```

Converting Between Strings and Floating-Point Numbers

```
pascal FormatStatus StringToExtended
                        (ConstStr255Param source,
                         const NumFormatString *myFormatRec,
                         const NumberParts *partsTable, extended80 *x);
pascal FormatStatus ExtendedToString
                        (extended80 x,
                         const NumFormatString *myFormatRec,
                         const NumberParts *partsTable,
                         Str255 outString);
```

Assembly-Language Summary

Trap Macros

Trap Macro Names

Pascal name	Trap macro name
CompareText	_CompareText
DateString	_DateString
ExtendedToString	_ExtendedToString
FindScriptRun	_FindScriptRun
FindWordBreaks	_FindWordBreaks
FormatRecToString	_FormatRecToString
IdenticalText	_IdenticalText
InitDateCache	_InitDateCache
LanguageOrder	_LanguageOrder
LongDateString	_LongDateString
LongTimeString	_LongTimeString
NumToString	_NumToString
ReplaceText	_ReplaceText
ScriptOrder	_ScriptOrder
StringToDate	_StringToDate
StringToExtended	_StringToExtended
StringToFormatRec	_StringToFormatRec
StringToNum	_StringToNum
StringToTime	_StringToTime
StyledLineBreak	_StyledLineBreak

Pascal name	Trap macro name
TextOrder	_TextOrder
TimeString	_TimeString
TruncString	_TruncString
TruncText	_TruncText

Trap Macros With Trap Words

Trap macro name	Trap word
_CmpString	$A03C
_GetString	$A9BA
_LowerText	$A056
_Munger	$A9E0
_NewString	$A906
_RelString	$A050
_SetString	$A907
_StripText	$A256
_StripUpperText	$A656
_UpperText	$A456
_UprString	$A054

Trap Macros Requiring Routine Selectors

_PACK6

Selector	Routine
$000E	DateString
$0010	TimeString
$0014	LongDateString
$0016	LongTimeString
$001A	CompareText
$001C	IdenticalText
$001E	ScriptOrder
$0020	LanguageOrder
$0022	TextOrder

_PACK7

Selector	Routine
$0000	NumToString
$0001	StringToNum

_ScriptUtil

Selector	Routine
$8204 FFF8	InitDateCache
$8208 FFE0	TruncString
$820C 0026	FindScriptRun
$820C FFDC	ReplaceText
$820C FFEC	StringToFormatRec
$820C FFDE	TruncText
$8210 FFE6	StringToExtended
$8210 FFE8	ExtendedToString
$8210 FFEA	FormatRecToString
$8214 FFF6	StringToDate
$8214 FFF4	StringToTime
$821C FFFE	StyledLineBreak
$C012 001A	FindWordBreaks

Script Manager

Contents

This chapter describes the Script Manager, a core component of the Macintosh script management system. The Script Manager oversees script systems and gives you access to their features.

Read this chapter if you are writing a multiscript text-handling application and need access to the general settings and script-specific information provided by the Script Manager. Read this chapter also if you are writing a specialized application that parses source code or converts text among subscripts. Read this chapter also if you wish to modify the features or functions of an individual script system.

Before reading this chapter, you should be familiar with the Macintosh script management system, as described in the chapter "Introduction to Text on the Macintosh" in this book. Useful related information is found in the appendixes "International Resources," "Keyboard Resources," and "Built-in Script Support."

This chapter—and this book—do not catalog the features of individual script systems. More detailed information on the world's writing systems and the Macintosh script systems developed to support them can be found in *Guide to Macintosh Software Localization*.

The chapter gives a brief introduction to the Script Manager, and then shows how you can use the Script Manager to

- control default settings for text handling

- obtain information about a script system

- convert text through tokenization or transliteration

- modify a script system by replacing its resources or—in some cases—its routines

About the Script Manager

The Script Manager is at the center of the Macintosh script management system. It makes script systems available. It coordinates the interaction between many parts of Macintosh system software and those available script systems.

The Script Manager also provides several services directly to your application. Through them you can get information about the current text environment, modify that environment, and perform a variety of text-handling tasks.

The Script Manager has evolved through several versions. It started with sole responsibility for all international-compatibility and multilanguage text issues, but as more power and features have been added, many of its specific functions have been moved to the other parts of system software.

The Script Manager and the Script Management System

The Script Manager manages script systems. It monitors their initialization and maintains variables and data structures that affect their functioning. It makes sure that all initialized script systems are complete in terms of having the required international resources and fonts. It gives applications as well as other parts of system software their principal access to script systems' features.

The Script Manager works closely with the other managers that make up the Macintosh script management system, in particular the Text Utilities and QuickDraw. The Text Utilities include many script-aware routines that manipulate text, and QuickDraw provides script-aware measuring and drawing routines for text. When your program or a system routine makes a script-aware Text Utilities or QuickDraw call, it commonly results in an internal call to the Script Manager, to access a global setting or the data of a script system.

TextEdit also relies on the Script Manager, both directly and through the Text Utilities and QuickDraw, to make sure that it handles text correctly in any script system. The Font Manager, the Text Services Manager, and the Dictionary Manager use information maintained and provided by the Script Manager.

Other components of Macintosh system software also interact with the Script Manager. The Finder uses the Script Manager to correctly input, display, and sort file and folder names across all localized versions of system software. The Menu Manager, the Event Manager, the Process Manager, the Operating System Utilities, and the Component Manager all work with the Script Manager, directly or indirectly, to obtain the information necessary to properly handle multiscript text.

The Script Manager and Applications

The Script Manager is your application's principal interface—either direct or indirect—with any of the script systems that may be available on the user's computer. For many text-related tasks, the Script Manager's role is transparent; when you make a script-aware Text Utilities or QuickDraw call while processing text, that routine may get the information it needs through the Script Manager. For example, when you call the QuickDraw procedure `DrawText` to draw a line of text, `DrawText` in turn calls the Script Manager to determine which script system your text belongs to before drawing it.

In other situations you may need to call the Script Manager explicitly, to properly interpret the text you are processing. Those situations are the principal subject of this chapter.

The Script Manager provides services that fall into four general categories: controlling settings, obtaining information, modifying text, and modifying script systems. Any text-handling application that you write, unless it relies solely on TextEdit, will need to use some of those services. Almost any text application, for example, needs to call the

`GetScriptManagerVariable` function. Other calls are for specialized programs only. The `IntlTokenize` function, for example, is only for specialized programs that parse highly structured text such as source code, mathematical expressions, or formatted numbers.

These are the services provided by the Script Manager in each of the four categories:

- Controlling settings. The routines in this category are of general interest and are used by most text applications. With these routines you can
  - □ check and set the system direction, a global variable that controls the default alignment of text and can affect the order in which blocks of mixed-directional text are drawn.
  - □ check and set Script Manager variables, private variables used by the Script Manager to keep track of information that is general to the text environment.
  - □ check and set script variables, private variables used by script systems to keep track of their own configurations.
  - □ make keyboard settings that affect text input, so that users can enter text in any script system and you can display it properly.

- Obtaining information. Many of the routines in this category are of general interest and are used by most text applications. With these routines you can
  - □ determine script codes from font information. Most applications need this information.
  - □ analyze characters for size (in bytes) and type. Applications that work with 2-byte script systems need size information, and many applications need character-type information.
  - □ directly access a script system's international resources. Most applications need this information only to pass it to other routines. Some applications also use it to inspect or modify individual tables or other data within a resource.

- Converting text. The routines in this category are used by specialized applications only. (Text-modification routines of general interest to applications are described in the chapter "Text Utilities" in this book.) With these routines you can
  - □ tokenize text: convert source text from any script system into script-independent tokens.
  - □ transliterate text: phonetically convert text from one subscript to another within a script system.

- Modifying script systems. The routines in this category are used for specialized purposes, such as providing regional variants to existing script systems or assigning script-specific features to individual documents or applications. With these routines you can
  - □ replace or modify the default international resources of a script system.
  - □ replace individual text-handling routines in certain script systems.

Evolution of the Script Manager

The Script Manager is only one of several system software managers that make up the Macintosh script management system, but its position is central. That central position stems from the fact that, in previous versions, the Script Manager alone (including the International Utilities) was responsible for all international text processing.

The first version of the Script Manager was released with Macintosh System 4.1. Table 6-1 shows the routines and some of the features of Script Manager 1.0, and the additional routines and features that have marked each successive version of the Script Manager (and International Utilities). Some of the added routines rendered earlier ones obsolete, whereas others brought new capabilities.

Table 6-1 Evolution of the Script Manager

Version	New routines, other additions and enhancements
1.0	`Char2Pixel`, `CharByte`, `CharType`, `DrawJust`, `FindWord`, `Font2Script`, `FontScript`, `GetAppFont`, `GetDefFontSize`, `GetEnvirons`, `GetMBarHeight`, `GetScript`, `GetSysFont`, `GetSysJust`, `HiliteText`, `IntlScript`, `KeyScript`, `MeasureJust`, `Pixel2Char`, `SetEnvirons`, `SetScript`, `SetSysJust`, `Transliterate` introduced. New international resources defined.
2.0	`FindScriptRun`, `Format2Str`, `FormatStr2X`, `FormatX2Str`, `GetFormatOrder`, `InitDateCache`, `IntlTokenize`, `IULDateString`, `IULTimeString`, `LongDate2Secs`, `LongSecs2Date`, `LwrString`, `LwrText`, `ParseTable`, `PortionText`, `ReadLocation`, `Str2Format`, `String2Date`, `String2Time`, `StyledLineBreak`, `ToggleDate`, `ValidDate`, `VisibleLength`, `WriteLocation` added.
2.17/2.21[*]	Enhanced `'itl2'` resource. Full support for Standard Roman character set. New token types defined.
7.0	`IUClearCache`, `IUGetItlTable`, `IULangOrder`, `IUScriptOrder`, `IUStringOrder`, `IUTextOrder`, `LowerText`, `NChar2Pixel`, `NDrawJust`, `NFindWord`, `NMeasureJust`, `NPixel2Char`, `NPortionText`, `StripText`, `StripUpperText`, `TruncString`, `TruncText`, `UpperText` added. Support for scaled justified text layout. Implicit script codes, new selectors. New keyboard resources, enhanced U.S. `'KCHR'` resource.
7.1	`CharacterByteType`, `CharacterType`, `FillParseTable`, `GetQDPatchAddress`, `GetScriptUtilityAddress`, `SetQDPatchAddress`, `SetScriptUtilityAddress`, `TransliterateText` added to Script Manager; several existing routines renamed. Many additional new and renamed routines moved to other managers such as Text Utilities and QuickDraw. WorldScript extensions created.

[*] In hexadecimal, 2.17 is $211, and 2.21 is $215. See Table 6-2 on page 6-9.

The most extensive changes, in terms of how the Script Manager is documented, have been the most recent. Many of the routines described throughout *Inside Macintosh: Text* are previous Script Manager routines that have been relocated and possibly enhanced or renamed. They were moved to be documented alongside routines of similar purpose in other managers. Many of the early Script Manager routines listed in Table 6-1 are obsolete and are no longer documented at all. See the appendix "Renamed and Relocated Text Routines" in this book for information on the current status and location of any previous Script Manager or International Utilities routines not found in this chapter.

Using the Script Manager

This section explains how you can use the Script Manager in performing four types of text-related tasks. Script Manager routines can help you with

- accessing and controlling the configuration of the text-handling environment, by
  - □ determining the version of the Script Manager and the number of active script systems
  - □ checking and setting the system direction
  - □ checking and modifying Script Manager variables
  - □ checking and modifying script variables
  - □ making keyboard settings that affect text input

- obtaining script-related information to help you process text, by
  - □ determining script codes from font information
  - □ using character-type information for searching and analyzing text
  - □ directly accessing a script system's international resources
  - □ using specific tables within a script system's international resources

- converting text for specialized purposes, by
  - □ converting source text from any script system into script-independent tokens
  - □ transliterating text from one subscript to another within a script system

- modifying the features of a script system, by
  - □ replacing or modifying the default international resources of a script system
  - □ replacing individual text-handling routines in 1-byte complex script systems

Testing for the Script Manager and Script Systems

This section describes how to use the `Gestalt` function to test for the current version of the Script Manager and the number of active script systems. For details on the `Gestalt` function, see the Gestalt Manager chapter of *Inside Macintosh: Operating System Utilities*.

The Operating System initializes the Script Manager at startup. The Script Manager then initializes the Roman script system. Next the Script Manager initializes any other installed 1-byte simple script system whose `smsfAutoInit` bit (see page 6-69) is set. The Script Manager then allows the script extensions WorldScript I and WorldScript II (if present) to initialize all installed 1-byte complex and 2-byte script systems.

When initializing a script system, the Script Manager or script extension first checks to make sure that there is enough memory for the script system, and then checks that an international bundle resource is present in the System file and that at least one font in the proper ID range for that script system is present in the System file or in the Fonts folder. If these resources are present, the script system is considered to be **enabled** (available for use by the Script Manager and applications). If the required resources are not available, the script system remains disabled.

Note

The Script Manager is fully loaded and all script systems are enabled before any files of type `'INIT'` in the Extensions folder are launched. Thus, all Script Manager routines can be called from system extensions. ◆

Use `Gestalt` with the `gestaltScriptMgrVersion` selector to obtain a result in the response parameter that identifies the version number of the Script Manager. This is the same value returned by a call to the `GetScriptManagerVariable` function with the selector constant `smVersion`. Table 6-1 on page 6-6 lists some of the routines and features available with the principal versions of the Script Manager.

Table 6-2 gives more detail on the version numbers returned by `Gestalt` or by `GetScriptManagerVariable` with the selector `smVersion`, for all versions of system software and all versions of the Script Manager. It also shows the Roman script system versions returned by the `GetScriptVariable` function with the selector `smScriptVersion`.

Table 6-2   Version numbers for the Script Manager and Roman script system

System software version	Script Manager (newer ROMs)	Script Manager (older ROMs)[*]	Roman script system
6.0.3 and earlier	N.A.	<= $20F	<= $101
6.0.4 Roman	$215	$211	$101
6.0.4 non-Roman	$216	$212	$101
6.0.5 all	$217 (= 2.23)	$213	$101
Above this line, minor version numbers are binary; below, they are BCD:			
6.0.7 all[†]	$231 (= 2.3.1)	$230	$101
J-6.0.7.1 (Japanese)[‡]	$231	$230	$101
6.0.8 all	$231	$230	$101
6.1 (non-Roman)	$241	$240	$101
7.0	$700	$700	$700
7.0.1 Roman	$700	$700	$700
7.0.1 non-Rman	$701	$701	$701
7.1	$710	$710	$710

[*] On Macintosh Plus, Macintosh SE, Macintosh II, Macintosh IIx, Macintosh IIcx, Macintosh SE/30, Macintosh Classic. Other CPUs have newer ROMs.
[†] `Gestalt` actually returns $606 as the system version for non-Roman versions of system 6.0.7.
[‡] `Gestalt` actually returns $609 as the system version for system J-6.0.7.1.

Note

In versions of system software earlier than 6.0.7, the major and minor version numbers are each treated as if they were binary. Thus a result of $217 from `Gestalt` means a Script Manager version of 2.23 (in decimal). Starting with system 6.0.7, version numbers are returned as binary-coded decimal numbers, so a result of $710 means a Script Manager version of 7.10 (or 7.1.0). ◆

Use the `Gestalt` selector `gestaltScriptCount` to obtain a result in the response parameter that gives the number of active script systems. This is the same value returned by a call to the `GetScriptManagerVariable` function with the `smEnabled` selector.

Obtaining the number of active script systems is most useful for testing whether more than a single script system is present. If the result is 1, only the Roman script system is present and text-handling is simplest. If the result is greater than 1, at least one non-Roman script system is present, and your application needs to be able to handle its text.

Controlling Settings

The first principal use for the Script Manager is in controlling the settings that determine the current characteristics of the text-handling environment. The Script Manager gives you access to many variables, fields, flags, and files that affect how script systems function and how text is manipulated and displayed. The routines described in this section are of general interest and are used by most text applications. You can use these Script Manager routines to

■ set the system direction

■ access Script Manager variables

■ access script variables

■ determine the keyboard script, keyboard layout, and input method

Checking and Setting the System Direction

The **system direction** is a global setting that is commonly used to define the primary line direction for text display. The system direction is specified by the value of the global variable SysDirection. The value of SysDirection is 0 for a left-to-right primary line direction and –1 for a right-to-left primary line direction.

System direction always controls the alignment (right or left) of interface elements such as menu items and dialog box items that are drawn by the system. It can also affect caret placement and the order in which blocks of text are drawn or highlighted in bidirectional script runs and in multiscript lines.

QuickDraw, TextEdit, and other parts of system software that use TextEdit set the system direction before drawing text. Although applications can format and draw text independently of the current value of system direction, applications that follow suggested procedures for text layout typically set the system direction before laying out and drawing any text. See, for example, the description of the GetFormatOrder function in the chapter "QuickDraw Text" in this book.

The default value for SysDirection usually corresponds to the primary line direction of the system script; it is initialized from the system's international configuration ('itlc') resource at startup. The user can change the system direction from the Text control panel if a bidirectional script system is present.

If your application uses SetSysDirection to change the system direction in order to correctly order script runs in a line of text while drawing, be sure to first call GetSysDirection to save the original value. Then call SetSysDirection again at the appropriate time—such as when your application becomes inactive—to restore SysDirection to its original value.

Checking and Setting Script Manager Variables

The `GetScriptManagerVariable` and `SetScriptManagerVariable` functions let you check and set the values of the Script Manager variables, general environmental settings that the Script Manager maintains for all script systems.

These functions give you access to a large variety of general script-related information, including whether one or more bidirectional script systems is present, whether one or more 2-byte script systems is present, and what the states of the font force and international resources selection flags are.

You specify the variable you want to access with a **selector,** an integer constant that controls the function of a multipurpose routine. You pass a selector as a parameter to `GetScriptManagerVariable` or `SetScriptManagerVariable`. (The variables themselves are private and you cannot access them directly.) Table 6-3 lists the selector constants and the Script Manager variables they affect. See "Selectors for Script Manager Variables" beginning on page 6-61 for complete explanations of the selectors and variables.

Table 6-3 Script Manager variables accessed through
`GetScriptManagerVariable`/`SetScriptManagerVariable`

Selector constant	Explanation
`smVersion`	Script Manager version number
`smMunged`	Modification count
`smEnabled`	Script count (0 if Script Manager not enabled)
`smBidirect`	Bidirectional script present flag
`smFontForce`	Font force flag
`smIntlForce`	International resources selection flag
`smForced`	Script-forced result flag
`smDefault`	Script-defaulted result flag
`smPrint`	Print action vector
`smSysScript`	System script code
`smLastScript`	Previous keyboard script
`smKeyScript`	Current keyboard script
`smSysRef`	System Folder volume reference number
`smKeyCache`	(obsolete, not used)
`smKeySwap`	Handle to keyboard-swap (`'KSWP'`) resource
`smGenFlags`	Script Manager general flags

continued

Table 6-3 Script Manager variables accessed through
`GetScriptManagerVariable`/`SetScriptManagerVariable` (continued)

Selector constant	Explanation
smOverride	Script override flags (reserved)
smCharPortion	Intercharacter/interword spacing proportion
smDoubleByte	2-byte script present flag
smKCHRCache	Pointer to current keyboard-layout ('KCHR') data
smRegionCode	Region code for system script
smKeyDisableState	Current disable state for keyboards

The following code fragment shows how to use the `GetScriptManagerVariable` function to get the Script Manager version number. This is the same value as that returned by the `Gestalt` function using the `gestaltScriptMgrVersion` selector.

```
VAR
    selectorValue: LongInt;
BEGIN
    selectorValue := GetScriptManagerVariable(smVersion);
END;
```

The `SetScriptManagerVariable` function allows you to change many text-related settings, including

- the font force flag

- the international resources selection flag

- the current keyboard script

- the Script Manager general flags, which include control of the display of the keyboard icon and the dual caret in TextEdit

- the proportion of intercharacter versus interword spacing, when laying out lines of justified text (in non-Roman script systems)

Listing 6-1 shows how to use the `SetScriptManagerVariable` function to specify the display of a dual caret in mixed-directional text. You do this by setting the appropriate bit of the Script Manager general flags field after retrieving it with the `GetScriptManagerVariable` function.

Listing 6-1   Specifying a dual caret with `SetScriptManagerVariable`

```
FUNCTION MySetDualCaret: OSErr;
VAR
    myErr:          OSErr;
    selectorValue:  LongInt;
    flagValue:      LongInt;
BEGIN
    flagValue := BitShift($0001,smfDualCaret);
    selectorValue := GetScriptManagerVariable(smGenFlags);
    selectorValue := BitOr(selectorValue, flagValue);
    myErr := SetScriptManagerVariable(smGenFlags, selectorValue);
    MySetDualCaret := myErr;
END;
```

You can also use `SetScriptManagerVariable` to change the settings of the font force flag and the international resources selection flag, two flags that affect which script systems are used for text display and date/time/number formatting, respectively. See "Determining Script Codes From Font Information" beginning on page 6-21.

If you are using `SetScriptManagerVariable` to change the value of a variable for a specific task, first call `GetScriptManagerVariable` to retrieve the variable's original value, and save that value. Then call `SetScriptManagerVariable` and perform your task. Finally, restore the original value of the Script Manager variable with another call to `SetScriptManagerVariable` as soon as possible, so that other applications or software components that use the Script Manager will find the values they expect.

Checking and Setting Script Variables

The `GetScriptVariable` and `SetScriptVariable` functions let you retrieve and set script variables, local variables maintained for each script system by the Script Manager.

These functions give you access to a large variety of script-specific information, including the primary line direction for the script system, the default alignment for text in the script system, the script system's preferred system font and size, and its preferred application font and size.

You specify the script system whose variables you want to access with an explicit script code, or with an implicit script code specifying the system script or the font script. You specify the variable you want to access with a selector constant passed as a parameter to GetScriptVariable or SetScriptVariable. Table 6-3 lists the selector constants and the script variables they affect. See "Selectors for Script Variables" beginning on page 6-65 for complete explanations of the selectors and variables.

Table 6-4 Script variables accessed through GetScriptVariable/SetScriptVariable

Selector constant	Explanation
smScriptVersion	Script-system version number
smScriptMunged	Modification count
smScriptEnabled	Script-enabled flag
smScriptRight	Right-to-left line direction flag
smScriptJust	Default alignment (left or right)
smScriptRedraw	Amount of line to redraw when changing a character
smScriptSysFond	Preferred system font
smScriptAppFond	Preferred application font
smScriptNumber	Numeric-format ('itl0') resource ID
smScriptDate	Long-date-format ('itl1') resource ID
smScriptSort	String-manipulation ('itl2') resource ID
smScriptFlags	Script flags
smScriptToken	Tokens ('itl4') resource ID
smScriptEncoding	Encoding/rendering ('itl5') resource ID
smScriptLang	Language code for script
smScriptNumDate	Current numeral code and calendar code
smScriptKeys	Keyboard-layout ('KCHR') resource ID
smScriptIcon	Keyboard icon family ID
smScriptPrint	Print action routine for script
smScriptTrap	Pointer to script record dispatch routine entry point (for internal use)
smScriptCreator	Creator name for script file
smScriptFile	Filename for script file

Table 6-4 Script variables accessed through
GetScriptVariable/SetScriptVariable (continued)

Selector constant	Explanation
smScriptName	Name of script system
smScriptMonoFondSize	Preferred font and size for fixed-width font
smScriptPrefFondSize	(unused)
smScriptSmallFondSize	Preferred font family and size for small text
smScriptSysFondSize	Preferred system font family and size
smScriptAppFondSize	Preferred application font family and size
smScriptHelpFondSize	Preferred Balloon Help font family and size
smScriptValidStyles	Valid text styles for script
smScriptAliasStyle	Text styles to use for aliases

You can use the GetScriptVariable function to get, for example, the default
application font family ('FOND') ID and size. In the following code fragment, the
application uses the constant smSystemScript to specify that it is the system script
whose font ID is needed. The ID is returned in the high-order word and the size is
returned in the low-order word. The application then sets the appropriate graphics port
fields to those values.

```
VAR
    myAppFont: LongInt;
BEGIN
    myAppFont := GetScriptVariable(smSystemScript,
                                   smScriptAppFondSize);

    TextFont(HiWord(myAppFont));
    TextSize(LoWord(myAppFont));
END;
```

Listing 6-2 shows how to represent font names correctly using the proper script for that
font. First you call the Font Manager GetFNum procedure to get the font family ID using
the font name. You call the FontToScript function using that font family ID to get the
value of the associated script code. You then call GetScriptVariable with the
smScriptSysFond selector to determine the font family ID for the preferred system
font for the specified script. Finally, you call the QuickDraw TextFont procedure with
that font family ID to set the font ID of the current graphics port to the preferred system
font of the specified script.

6

Script Manager

Note

The Menu Manager `AddResMenu` procedure automatically represents
font names in their associated script for `'FOND'` resources. If you need
to display font names elsewhere than in the Font menu (for instance,
using the List Manager), be sure to use a technique such as that shown
in Listing 6-2. ◆

Listing 6-2   Representing font names correctly in the script for that font

```
PROCEDURE MySetTextFont(fontName: Str255);
VAR
    scriptFont: LongInt;
    scriptNum:  Integer;
    theNum:     Integer;

BEGIN
                                {from font name, get font ID}
    GetFNum(fontName, theNum); {use font ID to get script code, }
                                { then get preferred system font ID}

    scriptNum := FontToScript(theNum);
    scriptFont := GetScriptVariable(scriptNum, smScriptSysFond);

                                {now set the current grafPort's }
    TextFont(scriptFont);       { font ID to that font}
END;
```

The `SetScriptVariable` function allows you to change many script-specific
settings, including the default configuration settings for the script system, which
are initialized from a script system's international bundle (`'itlb'`) resource. You
call `SetScriptVariable` with the appropriate script constant and selector to
indicate the setting you want changed. Listing 6-3 shows how to use the
`SetScriptVariable` function to set the size of the Balloon Help font to the size
passed in the parameter `theSize`:

Listing 6-3   Setting the size of the Balloon Help font

```
PROCEDURE MySetHelpFontSize(theSize: LongInt);
VAR
    myErr:        OSErr;
    myHelpFont:   LongInt;

BEGIN
    theSize := BitAnd(theSize, $0000FFFF);
```

```
                                                {keep low word only}
   myHelpFont := GetScriptVariable(smSystemScript,
                                        smScriptHelpFondSize);
   myHelpFont := BitAnd(myHelpFont, $FFFF0000);
                                                {keep high word only}
   myErr := SetScriptVariable(smSystemScript,
                                  smScriptHelpFondSize,
                                  BitOr(myHelpFont,theSize));
   IF myErr <> noErr THEN DoError(myErr);
END;
```

If you are using `SetScriptVariable` to change the value of a variable for a specific task, first call `GetScriptVariable` to retrieve the variable's original value, and save it. Then call `SetScriptVariable` and perform your task. Finally, restore the original value of the script variable with another call to `SetScriptVariable` as soon as possible, so that other applications or software components using that script system will find the values they expect.

Making Keyboard Settings

The Script Manager `KeyScript` procedure lets you control the script system, keyboard layout, and input method used for text input. It also lets you make other settings related to text input.

You use the `KeyScript` procedure to change the keyboard script, the script system that controls text input. You also use it to switch among different keyboard layouts, resources that define the character sets and key positions for text input in a script system. You can also use it to switch among input methods, software facilities that allow text input in 2-byte script systems. If your application supports multiple languages, use `KeyScript` to change the keyboard script when the user changes the current font. For example, if the user selects Geezah as the current font or clicks the cursor within a run of text that uses the Geezah font, your application needs to set the keyboard script to Arabic. To do this, use the `FontToScript` function to find the script for the font, then use `KeyScript` to set the keyboard.

In addition, your application can check the keyboard script (using the `GetScriptManagerVariable` function) in its main event loop; if the keyboard script has changed, you can set the current font to the last-used font, application font, or system font of the new keyboard script (determined by a call to the `GetScriptVariable` function). This action saves the user from having to set the font manually after changing the keyboard script.

The system software performs the equivalent of calling `KeyScript` in response to the user selecting a keyboard layout or input method from the Keyboard menu. It also does the same when the user types Command–Option–Space bar (to select the next keyboard layout or input method within the same script system), or Command–Space bar (to select the next script system in the Keyboard menu).

When you call `KeyScript`, you pass it a `code` parameter that can explicitly specify a keyboard script by script code, or can implicitly specify a keyboard script, keyboard layout, input method, or other setting. Values for `code` equal to or greater than zero are interpreted as normal script codes. Several negative codes specify switching among keyboard scripts, keyboard layout, or input methods. Others toggle line direction or input method and are available only with certain script systems. Still others disable or enable keyboard layouts or keyboard scripts. Table 6-5 lists the valid constants for the `code` parameter.

Table 6-5   Constants for the code parameter in the `KeyScript` procedure

Constant	Value	Expanation
(any script code)	0…64	Switch to specified script
smKeyNextScript	−1	Switch to next script in Keyboard menu
smKeySysScript	−2	Switch to the system script
smKeySwapScript	−3	Switch to previously used script
smKeyNextKybd	−4	Switch to next keyboard layout or input method in Keyboard menu (within current script)
smKeySwapKybd	−5	(not implemented)
smKeyDisableKybds	−6	Disable keyboard layouts not in system script or Roman script
smKeyEnableKybds	−7	Enable keyboard layouts for all enabled scripts
smKeyToggleInline	−8	Toggle inline input for current script (available if 2-byte script present)
smKeyToggleDirection	−9	Toggle default line direction (available if bidirectional script present)
smKeyNextInputMethod	−10	(not implemented)
smKeySwapInputMethod	−11	(not implemented)
smKeyDisableKybdSwitch	−12	Disable switching out of current keyboard layout
smKeySetDirLeftRight	−15	Set primary line direction to left-to-right (available if bidirectional script present)
smKeySetDirRightLeft	−16	Set primary line direction to right-to-left (available if bidirectional script present)
smKeyRoman	−17	Set keyboard script to Roman (available only if multiple scripts present)

The `smKeyDisableKybds` selector is available for your use, although it is primarily used by the Finder or other parts of the system under special circumstances. For example, when the user enters the name of a file in a Standard-File dialog box, text input must be restricted to scripts that display correctly in the Finder and in dialog boxes, menus, and alert boxes. In that situation the system software calls `KeyScript` with the `smKeyDisableKybds` selector to disable keyboard input temporarily in any script system except Roman or the system script. Keyboards in other script systems then appear disabled in the Keyboard menu. When the user completes the filename entry, the system calls `KeyScript` again with a selector of `smKeyEnableKybds` to reenable keyboard input in all enabled script systems.

The `smKeyDisableKybdSwitch` selector is also available for your use, although it is primarily used by the Finder. When keyboard layouts and script systems are being moved into or out of the System file by the user, changing the current keyboard or keyboard script may corrupt files or cause other unpredictable results. To prevent all keyboard switching and to disable all the Keyboard menu items, the Finder calls `KeyScript` with the selector `smKeyDisableKybdSwitch`. When the move has been completed, the Finder again calls `KeyScript` with a selector of `smKeyEnableKybds` to reenable keyboard switching.

If you call `KeyScript` with `code = smKeyRoman` on a system in which only the Roman script system is enabled, nothing happens. However, if you call `KeyScript` with `code = 0` (to select the Roman script system), it forces an update that selects the current default Roman keyboard layout.

IMPORTANT

Although it is possible to change the keyboard script without changing the keyboard layout—by calling the `SetScriptManagerVariable` function with the `smKeyScript` selector—it violates the user interface paradigm and creates problems for other script management routines. ▲

Synchronizing the Font Script and Keyboard Script

To keep the user from accidentally entering meaningless characters, you must always keep the keyboard script synchronized with the font script, so that the glyphs displayed on the screen match the characters entered at the keyboard. You can synchronize the scripts in two ways: by setting the keyboard script when the font script changes, and by setting the font script when the keyboard script changes.

Setting the Keyboard Script From the Font Script

Set the keyboard script from the font script when the user selects a new font or when the user clicks in or selects text.

■ If the user selects a new font from the Font menu, call `TextFont` to set the current font to that font. Then set the keyboard script to the script system of that font.

■ If the user clicks in or selects a text area, set the current font to be the font, size, and style of the text where the click occurred. Then set the keyboard script to the script system of that font.

Listing 6-4 is an example of code to use for setting the keyboard script from the font script. Once you have obtained the script code value from the font family ID using the `FontToScript` function (see "Determining Script Codes From Font Information" beginning on page 6-21), you call the `GetScriptManagerVariable` function with the `smKeyScript` selector to determine the keyboard script. If the font script and the keyboard script are not the same, call the `KeyScript` procedure to change the keyboard script.

Listing 6-4   Setting the keyboard script from the font script

```
PROCEDURE MySetKeyboardFromFont(myFont: Integer);
VAR
    theFontScript: Integer;

BEGIN
                                {get script code from font ID.}

    theFontScript := FontToScript(myFont);
                            {compare with keyboard script, }
                            { change if necessary}
    IF (GetScriptManagerVariable(smKeyScript) <>
                                    theFontScript) THEN
        KeyScript(theFontScript);
END;
```

Setting the Font Script From the Keyboard Script

Each time the user types a character other than a control character, your application should check that the font script is still the same as the keyboard script. The user may have, for example, switched keyboard scripts since entering the last character. If the font script does not match the keyboard script, change the current font to correspond to the new keyboard script before displaying the character. Follow these guidelines:

- If possible, set the current font to the previous font that was used for that script (that is, the last font for that script preceding the current point in the document or text buffer).

- Otherwise, set the font to one of the preferred fonts for that script system. The preferred fonts are the preferred application font, the preferred system font, the preferred monospaced font, and the preferred small font. (The ID numbers of these fonts can be obtained through the `GetScriptVariable` function.)

Listing 6-5 is an example of setting the font (and therefore the font script) from the keyboard script. It calls `GetScriptManagerVariable` with the `smKeyScript` selector to determine the current keyboard script. It then calls `FontToScript` to determine whether the keyboard script differs from the font script. If it does, the routine calls `GetScriptVariable` with the `smScriptAppFond` selector to determine the application font for the script. Then it sets the current font based on that result.

Listing 6-5   Setting the font (script) from the keyboard script

```
PROCEDURE MySetFontFromKeyboard(VAR myFont: Integer);
VAR
    scriptNum:  LongInt;

BEGIN
    scriptNum := GetScriptManagerVariable(smKeyScript);
    IF (FontToScript(myFont) <> scriptNum) THEN
        myFont := GetScriptVariable(scriptNum, smScriptAppFond);
    TextFont(myFont)
END;
```

You can also use this code if your application does not have an interface that lets users change fonts but still needs to provide for different script systems.

Obtaining Information

The second principal use for the Script Manager is in obtaining script-specific information. Many of the routines described in this section are of general interest and are used by most text applications. You can use these Script Manager routines to

- determine script codes for the current script system or any other available script system, based on font information

- analyze characters in your text for size (in bytes) or other properties

- directly access the contents of a script system's international resources, to pass that information to other text-handling calls or to inspect or modify the information

Most text-processing applications need script-code information and character-type information, and may need to pass specific tables from international resources to some script-aware text routines. If you format currencies, you need access to the numeric-format resource. If you use special symbols or if you format numbers, you need access to the untoken table and perhaps the number parts table of the tokens resource. If your needs are more specialized, you can obtain the contents of other tables and other resources.

Determining Script Codes From Font Information

The script management system asssociates a script system with a sequence of text by examining the font of that text. Your application may also need the same information—to test for the presence of a particular script system, to load its resources, to pass its code as a parameter to a script-aware routine, or to execute script-specific conditional code. You may need to determine what script system is currently active for displaying text, what script system is being used to sort and format text, or what script system would be used if text of a particular font were to be displayed or formatted. The Script Manager provides three routines for that purpose: FontScript, FontToScript, and IntlScript.

The `FontScript` function tells you which script system the font of the current graphics port belongs to. The `FontToScript` function tells you which (available) script system a font of any ID number belongs to. The `IntlScript` function tells you which script system is used by the Text Utilities to determine the number, date, time, currency, and sorting formats.

The `FontToScript` function returns a script code for a specified font family ID, but the `FontScript` and `IntlScript` functions return the code for the **current script,** the presently active script system for text manipulation. Many script-aware routines in QuickDraw, Text Utilities, the Script Manager, and other parts of the Macintosh script management system need not take an explicit script code or international resource handle as a parameter; in that case they use the current script as the script system under which they are to function.

The current script for text display is normally the font script. The current script for date and time formatting and string sorting is by default the system script. However, the settings of two flags—the font force flag and the international resources selection flag—can affect which script system is considered current at any one moment. Furthermore, if the mapping from font to script results in a request for a script system that is not available, the result defaults to the system script.

The next subsection lists the steps taken by `FontScript`, `FontToScript`, and `IntlScript` to determine the script codes they return, and the following subsections discuss the font force flag and the international resources selection flag in more detail.

How a Script Code Is Determined

The `FontScript`, `FontToScript`, and `IntlScript` functions all use a font family ID to determine the script code they return. The formula they use is presented in the discussion of resource ID numbers and script codes in the appendix "International Resources" in this book. Fonts with IDs below 16384 ($4000) are all Roman; starting with 16384 each non-Roman script system has a range of 512 ($200) font IDs available.

Nevertheless, you should always call the functions instead of hardcoding any formula, because it may change in the future. Furthermore, the function results are influenced by the states of the font force flag and the international resources selection flag, and by the availability of the determined script. Figure 6-1 shows the method the functions follow:

1. The three functions initialize two result flags, the **script-forced result flag** and the **script-defaulted result flag,** to FALSE. These flags are Script Manager variables, accessed through the `GetScriptManagerVariable` function selectors `smForced` and `smDefault`.

2. The three functions map the two special font designations 0 and 1, meaning the system and application fonts, to their true font family ID numbers.

3. `FontScript` and `IntlScript` calculate the script code from the font family ID of the current font of the active port; `FontToScript` calculates the script code from the supplied font family ID. If the ID is in the range $4000 to $BFFF, it is a non-Roman font; otherwise, it is Roman.

4. Once the initial determination of the script code has been made, the three functions diverge:

□ If the font is Roman, `FontScript` and `FontToScript` examine the font force flag, which can be accessed through the `GetScriptManagerVariable` function selector `smFontForce`. If the flag is `TRUE`, the two functions substitute the system script for the font script, and set the script-forced result flag to `TRUE`. If the font is non-Roman, `FontScript` and `FontToScript` ignore the state of the font force flag.

□ Regardless of the font type (Roman or non-Roman), `IntlScript` examines the international resources selection flag, which can be accessed through the `GetScriptManagerVariable` function selector `smIntlForce`. If the flag is `TRUE` and the font script does not equal the system script, `IntlScript` substitutes the system script for the font script and sets the script-forced result flag to `TRUE`.

Figure 6-1   Determining script code from font family ID

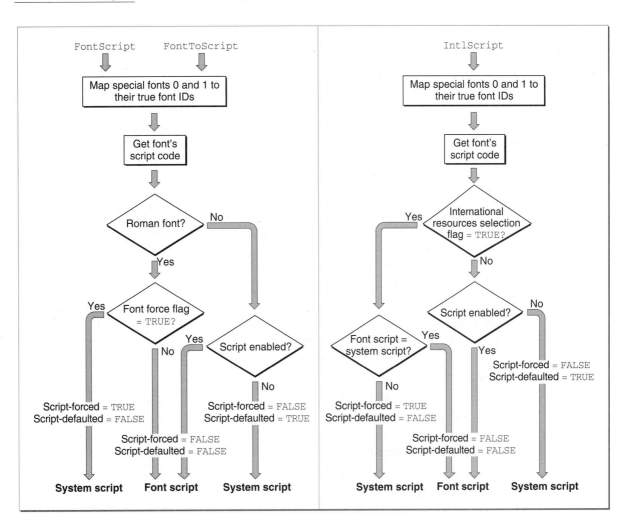

5. A final check is made to be sure that the resulting script is installed and enabled. If it is not, the three functions substitute the system script for the script code previously determined, set the script-forced result flag to FALSE, and set the script-defaulted result flag to TRUE.

6. The functions return the resulting script code in their function results.

Call FontScript when you want to know which script system will be used for text layout and display. The script code returned by FontScript tells you which script system controls the functioning of such calls as CharToPixel, CharacterType, FindWordBreaks, DrawText, and DrawJustified. Typically, FontScript returns the script code for the font script; in most situations the font force flag is FALSE, because applications usually expect to format and draw text according to the rules of the font script.

Call FontToScript when you want to know whether the script system for text of a particular font is available, or when you wish to manipulate text of a certain script system without setting the current font to that font's ID.

Note
Because a user can set the value of the font force flag from the Text control panel, the result returned from the FontToScript or FontScript function for a font whose ID number is in the Roman range can vary from call to call. ◆

Call IntlScript when you want to know which script system will be used for formatting dates and numbers, and for sorting strings. The script code returned by IntlScript tells you which script system controls the functioning of such calls as DateString, LongTimeString, and CompareText, when no explicit script code or resource handle is supplied to those calls. In many localized versions of sysem software, IntlScript by default returns the script code for the system script, because the international resources selection flag is by default TRUE. The Finder and other parts of system software usually expect to present dates, times, and lists of files according to the rules of the system script.

Because the two flags are independent of each other, two different meanings for current script can exist simultaneously. For example, your application might be sorting a set of strings by one script's rules, but displaying them by another's. If that is not appropriate, set the flags as needed before formatting or drawing. See the following discussion.

Using the Font Force Flag

You access and control the font force flag through the GetScriptManagerVariable and SetScriptManagerVariable functions, with the selector smfontForce. This flag directly affects the results of the FontScript and FontToScript functions, and indirectly affects the operation of script-aware text measuring and drawing routines.

At startup, the Script Manager sets the font force flag to the value specified in the system script's international configuration ('itlc') resource. Typically, that value is FALSE.

When the font force flag is set to `TRUE` and the system script is non-Roman, the script management system interprets font family ID numbers in the range of the Roman script system ($0002 to $3FFF) as belonging to the system script instead. Character codes representing non-Roman characters in the system script are drawn using the system font instead of in the specified Roman font. This feature exists to allow users to enter and read non-Roman text in those few applications that have hardcoded font numbers.

For example, an application may hardcode Geneva as its font; it may force the `txFont` field of its graphics ports to always have a value of 3. (Note that this is a violation of good programming practice.) If the application is running on a system with Hebrew as the system script, it would normally be impossible to write properly in Hebrew because the hardcoded font ID would require the font script to be Roman. However, if the font force flag is set to `TRUE`, the script management system notes that the current font has an ID number in the Roman range and draws glyphs from the Hebrew system font for any character codes that represent valid Hebrew characters.

Thus to enter or read non-Roman text in these applications, the user can set the font force flag to `TRUE` from the Text control panel. Setting the font force flag is only partially effective, because it cannot give users full control over fonts. The user cannot choose, for example, which font belonging to the system script is to be substituted for Roman.

The font force flag has no effect on non-Roman fonts and has no effect if the system script is Roman. It affects only Roman fonts when the system script is non-Roman.

You can determine the status of font forcing by inspecting the script-forced result flag and the script-defaulted result flag immediately after calling `FontScript` or `FontToScript`; see Figure 6-1.

Although the font force flag exists primarily to accommodate restrictions in certain existing applications, it is a user-changeable setting that your application should be aware of and accommodate. For example:

- If you are writing any application in which the user has control over fonts, you should always set the font force flag to `FALSE`. There is no need to force fonts if the user can choose them.

- If the user sets the font force flag to `TRUE`, you will get the system script when you call `FontScript` or `FontToScript` for fonts in the Roman range, even if your application allows mixed text. To preserve Roman text, you can change the setting of the font force flag before calling `FontScript` or `FontToScript`, or before calling any other script-aware text routine. If you do that, be sure to save the previous value and restore it when your application exits or becomes inactive.

Using the International Resources Selection Flag

You access and control the international resources selection flag through the `GetScriptManagerVariable` and `SetScriptManagerVariable` functions, with the selector `smIntlForce`. This flag directly affects the results of the `IntlScript` function, and indirectly affects the operation of the `GetIntlResource` function and the script-aware Text Utilities sorting and formatting routines.

At startup, the Script Manager sets the international resources selection flag to the value specified in the system script's international configuration ('itlc') resource. Typically, that value is TRUE.

The international resources selection flag affects the results of the GetIntlResource function (see page 6-90). GetIntlResource returns a handle to certain international resources, and the state of the international resources selection flag controls whether it is the system script or the font script whose international resources are loaded. When the flag is set to TRUE, GetIntlResource fetches the resources for the system script. When the flag is set to FALSE, GetIntlResource uses the current font in the active port to determine the script system whose resources will be fetched.

You can use the international resources selection flag to make sure that date formats, sorting, and so forth reflect the appropriate script in your application. Whenever you change the setting of the international resources selection flag, be sure to save the previous value and restore it when your application exits or becomes inactive.

Analyzing Characters

The Script Manager provides routines that let you analyze the size and type of individual characters. For example, with script systems that use 2-byte characters, you may need to determine what part of a character a single byte represents. In either 1-byte or 2-byte script systems, you may need to know whether a particular character is a letter or a punctuation mark, whether or not it is uppercase, or whether it is part of a subscript (Roman within Cyrillic, Hiragana within Japanese, and so on).

Searching Text With Mixed Character Sizes

When searching for a single 1-byte character in text that may contain 2-byte characters, your application must not mistake part of a 2-byte character for the character you are seeking. The CharacterByteType and FillParseTable functions tell you whether a given character is 1-byte or whether it is the first or second byte of a 2-byte character.

These functions use the fact that, in a 2-byte script system, only a restricted set of values within the high-ASCII range are used as the first bytes of 2-byte characters, and those values are never used for 1-byte characters in that script system. All other byte values represent single-byte characters, control characters, or the second bytes of 2-byte characters. The ranges reserved for initial bytes of 2-byte characters vary from script system to script system, but every font has a table that gives that information, and CharacterByteType and FillParseTable use those tables to perform their calculations. For an illustration of this concept, see the discussion of character encoding in the chapter "Introduction to Text on the Macintosh" in this book.

Listing 6-6 shows a search procedure that accounts for 2-byte characters. This routine uses the Text Utilities Munger function to find a match to a key string. Because Munger might find a match beginning at the second byte of a 2-byte character, the routine checks for this case (using the CharacterByteType function) and continues searching if it occurs.

The sample assumes two application global variables: gMainTextHandle, which is a handle to the application's text buffer, and gNewLocation, a long-integer offset into the buffer at which to start searching. The parameters keyPtr and keySize specify the string to be matched in the text buffer; scriptNum is an explicit script code. On return, the routine updates gNewLocation to point to the location at which the search string was found, or sets it to –1 if no match was found.

Listing 6-6   Handling 2-byte characters in a search procedure

```
PROCEDURE MySearch (keyPtr: Ptr; keySize: LongInt; scriptNum:
Integer);
VAR
    byteType: Integer;
BEGIN
    HLock(gMainTextHandle);      {CharacterByteType can move memory}
    REPEAT BEGIN
        gNewLocation := Munger(gMainTextHandle, gNewLocation,
                               keyPtr, keySize, NIL, 0);
                               {if we matched second byte of }
                               { 2-byte char in text, continue}
        IF (gNewLocation >= 0) AND (scriptNum > 0) THEN
            byteType := CharacterByteType(gMainTextHandle^,
                                        gNewLocation, scriptNum)
        ELSE
            byteType := smSingleByte;
    END UNTIL byteType <> smLastByte;
    HUnlock(gMainTextHandle);
    IF (gNewLocation >= 0) AND {range-check, update global}
        (gNewLocation + keySize > GetHandleSize(gMainTextHandle))
THEN
        gNewLocation := -1;
END;
```

The FillParseTable function is similar to CharacterByteType, in that it helps you find 2-byte characters. However, you don't send FillParseTable the character code to be analyzed. Instead, FillParseTable fills in an entire 256-byte table of information for you, showing every byte value that is the first byte of a 2-byte character for the current font. You can use the table filled out by FillParseTable to find 2-byte characters in a large body of text much more rapidly than you could by calling CharacterByteType for each byte value in the text.

6

Script Manager

Getting Character-Type Information

You may want to know more about a byte than whether it is part of a 2-byte character. If you are simply searching for sequences of Roman text in a buffer, or if you wish to divide a run of Japanese into Kanji, Katakana, Hiragana, and Romaji components, you can use the FindScriptRun function described in the chapter "Text Utilities" in this book. But if you have other reasons to isolate specific types of characters, you can use CharacterType.

The CharacterType function is similar to CharacterByteType, in that it tells you what kind of character occurs at a given offset in a text buffer. But the kind of information it returns is different. CharacterType tells you what the character's line direction is, whether it's uppercase, whether it belongs to a subscript within its script, whether it's a 2-byte character, and what the character's specific type and class are—letter or punctuation, low-ASCII or high-ASCII Roman letter, Katakana or Hiragana, Jamo or Hangul, and so on.

When you call the CharacterType function, you pass it a byte offset; it returns a value that is an integer bit field giving information about the character at that offset. See Figure 6-2. The paragraphs following the figure describe the fields.

Figure 6-2 Fields in the CharacterType return value

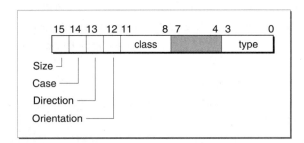

Bits 0–3 of the CharacterType function result describe the **character type** of the character in question.

■ The Roman script system recognizes three basic character types, defined by the following constants:

Character type	Hex. value	Explanation
smCharPunct	$0000	Punctuation (anything but a letter)
smCharAscii	$0001	ASCII letter (not a number or symbol, character code <= $7F)
smCharExtAscii	$0007	High-ASCII Roman letter (not a number or symbol, character code >= $80)

■ Additional character-type constants are provided for Japanese Katakana and Hiragana; the ideographic subscripts such as Hanzi, Kanji, and Hanja; 2-byte Cyrillic and Greek in 2-byte systems; bidirectional script systems such as Arabic and Hebrew; and Korean Hangul and Jamo subscripts:

Character type	Hex. value	Explanation
smCharKatakana	$0002	Japanese Katakana
smCharHiragana	$0003	Japanese Hiragana
smCharIdeographic	$0004	Hanzi, Kanji, Hanja
smCharTwoByteGreek	$0005	2-byte Greek in 2-byte scripts
smCharTwoByteRussian	$0006	2-byte Cyrillic in 2-byte scripts
smCharBidirect	$0008	Arabic, Hebrew
smCharContextualLR	$0009	Thai, Indic, etc.
smCharNonContextualLR	$000A	Cyrillic, Greek, etc.
smCharHangul	$000C	Korean Hangul
smCharJamo	$000D	Korean Jamo
smCharBopomofo	$000E	Chinese Bopomofo (Zhuyinfuhao)

Bits 8–11 of the CharacterType function result describe the **character class** of the character in question. Character classes can be considered as subtypes of character types; a given character type can have several classes that belong to it.

■ If the character type is smCharPunct, the following character classes are defined that include punctuation for both 1-byte and 2-byte script systems:

Character class	Hex. value	Explanation
smPunctNormal	$0000	Normal punctuation (such as ! , . ; ?)
smPunctNumber	$0100	Number character (such as 0–9)
smPunctSymbol	$0200	Nonpunctuation symbol (such as # $ &)
smPunctBlank	$0300	Blank character (such as ASCII $00, $0D, $20)
smPunctRepeat	$0400	Repeat marker in 2-byte script
smPunctGraphic	$0500	Line graphics in 2-byte script

■ In the Korean script system, if the character type is smCharJamo, the following character classes are defined. They determine whether a given byte contains a simple or complex consonant or a simple or complex vowel:

Character class	Hex. value	Explanation
smJamoJaeum	$0000	Simple consonant character
smJamoBogJaeum	$0100	Complex consonant character
smJamoMoeum	$0200	Simple vowel character
smJamoBogMoeum	$0300	Complex vowel character

The Jamo and Hangul subscripts of Korean are discussed briefly along with input methods in the chapter "Introduction to Text on the Macintosh" in this book.

■ In the Japanese script system, if the character type is smCharKatakana or smCharHiragana, the following character classes are defined:

Character class	Hex. value	Explanation
	$0000	(none of the following defined classes)
smKanaSmall	$0001	Small Kana character
smKanaHardOK	$0002	Can have dakuten
smKanaSoftOK	$0003	Can have dakuten or han-dakuten

A small Kana character is a special form of Kana used to modify the pronunciation of a previous (full-sized) Kana character. Dakuten and han-dakuten are pronunciation marks that soften consonant sounds in Kana.

■ In 2-byte script systems, if the character type is smCharIdeographic, the following character classes are defined:

Character class	Hex. value	Explanation
smIdeographicLevel1	$0000	Level 1 characters
smIdeographicLevel2	$0100	Level 2 characters
smIdeographicUser	$0200	User characters

The characters specified by the smIdeographicLevel1 constant are part of the level 1 Han character set specified by Japanese, Chinese, and Korean government standards. Approximately 90 percent of normal text consists of characters from the level 1 set.

The characters specified by the smIdeographicLevel2 constant are part of the level 2 Han character set, which includes obscure characters. The level 1 and level 2 character sets combined contain 98 percent of the character set used in the Kanji subscript.

The characters specified by smIdeographicUser represent custom characters created by the user.

Bits 12–15 of the CharacterType function result are the *character modifiers* of the character in question. One bit describes each modifier.

■ Bit 12 specifies the *orientation* of the character: whether it is intended for horizontal or vertical writing.

Character orientation	Hex. value	Explanation
smCharHorizontal	$0000	Character form is for horizontal writing, or for both horizontal and vertical
smCharVertical	$1000	Character form is for vertical writing only

■ Bit 13 specifies the *direction* of the character: whether its line direction is left-to-right or right-to-left.

Character direction	Hex. value	Explanation
smCharLeft	$0000	Character with left-to-right line direction
smCharRight	$2000	Character with right-to-left line direction

■ Bit 14 specifies the *case* of the character: whether it is lowercase or uppercase.

Character case	Hex. value	Explanation
smCharLower	$0000	Lowercase character
smCharUpper	$4000	Uppercase character

■ Bit 15 specifies the *size* of the character: whether it is 1 or 2 bytes long.

Character size	Hex. value	Explanation
smChar1byte	$0000	1-byte character
smChar2byte	$8000	2-byte character

You can describe individual characters with combinations of these constants. For example, if the byte being examined by CharacterType is a 1-byte English uppercase "A", then the value of the result could be expressed as smChar1Byte + smCharUpper + smCharLeft + smCharASCII. CharacterType indicates blank characters by a type smCharPunct and a class smCharBlank.

Some values are meaningful only in certain subscripts or script systems. The value smCharUpper is meaningless in a subscript that has no uppercase characters, for example; the value smIdeographicLevel is meaningless in 1-byte script systems.

You can use CharacterType for a variety of purposes—to validate input in numeric fields, to filter non-phonetic characters in an input method, or to search for punctuation, uppercase letters, and symbols. If you are breaking lines of text and are not using the Text Utilities StyledLineBreak function, you can use CharacterType to locate and skip whitespace characters at the ends of lines; see the description of text drawing in the chapter "QuickDraw Text" in this book.

The CharacterType function is described further on page 6-85.

Directly Accessing International Resources

This section shows how you can directly access the international resources of a script system. Such direct access can help you be more efficient in creating bilingual applications, formatting numbers in different scripts, accessing character information, and using tokens. Several script-aware Text Utilities calls can take a handle to an international resource as an input parameter; you can use the calls in this section to obtain those handles.

Your application can examine the international resources that determine numeric formats, date formats, string sorting, conversion to tokens, and character encoding or rendering by making the calls described here. You can also retrieve individual tables from some of the resources.

This access also helps you to provide your own versions or regional variations of certain international resources. See "Replacing a Script System's Default International Resources" beginning on page 6-48 for more information.

Note
Although you can access the international resources independently through the Resource Manager function `GetResource` and related calls, you can be sure to get the preferred resource of the current script system by using the calls described here. ◆

The calls you make to access the international resources are `ClearIntlResourceCache`, `GetIntlResource`, and `GetIntlResourceTable`. With them, you have access to the contents of a script system's numeric-format (`'itl0'`), long-date-format (`'itl1'`), string-manipulation (`'itl2'`), tokens (`'itl4'`), and encoding/rendering (`'itl5'`) resources.

To access one of these resources for the current script, follow these steps:

1. Make sure the current script is the script system containing the international resource you want to access. See "Determining Script Codes From Font Information" on page 6-21. You may need to verify the settings of the font script, the system script, and the international resources selection flag. See "Using the International Resources Selection Flag" on page 6-25.

2. If you need access to any version of the current script's string-manipulation or tokens resources other than its default version, call `ClearIntlResourceCache` first. See "Replacing a Script System's Default International Resources" on page 6-48.

3. Call `GetIntlResource`, specifying the type of resource you need. `GetIntlResource` returns a handle to the resource.

For an example of using `GetIntlResource` to extract information from an international resource, see the next section, "Using Currency, Number, and Date Formats."

To access a specific table within a string-manipulation or tokens resource, follow these steps:

1. If you don't already have it, determine the script code of the script system containing the international resource you want to access. See "Determining Script Codes From Font Information" on page 6-21.

2. If you need access to any other than the script's default version of that resource, call `ClearIntlResourceCache` first. See "Replacing a Script System's Default International Resources" on page 6-48.

3. Call `GetIntlResourceTable` to get the specified table within the specified resource belonging to the specified script system. Depending on the resource, you can get its number-parts, untoken, word-selection, line-break, or whitespace table.

For more information about these tables, see the following sections: "Using Number Parts," "Retrieving Text From Tokens," "Using Word-Break Tables," and "Using Whitespace Information."

IMPORTANT

Any time you replace the default international resources for a script system, whether or not you subsequently call `GetIntlResource` or `GetIntlResourceTable`, you need to call `ClearIntlResourceCache`, to make sure that the replacements are used by all script-aware calls. See "Replacing a Script System's Default International Resources" beginning on page 6-48. ▲

Using Currency, Number, and Date Formats

In general, you should use the Text Utilities routines for date, time, and number formatting. See the chapter "Text Utilities" in this book. If, however, you need to directly access fields in the numeric-format (`'itl0'`) and long-date-format (`'itl1'`) resources to find the characters, separators, strings, and orders for formatting numbers, dates, and times, you can do so with `GetIntlResource`.

Listing 6-7 shows how to determine the decimal, thousands, and list separators for number formatting in the current script. To access the numeric-format resource, the routine specifies a resource selector of 0 (for `'itl0'`) in the parameter `theID` of the `GetIntlResource` function. It then extracts the values it wants from the `decimalPt`, `thousSep`, and `listSep` fields.

Listing 6-7   Determining the number separators for the current script

```
PROCEDURE MyGetNumberSeparators (VAR myDecimal:Char;
                                 VAR myThousands:Char;
                                 VAR myListSep:Char);
VAR
    myHandle:      Intl0Hndl;
                            {make sure the desired script is set }
                            { before calling this routine}
BEGIN
    myHandle := Intl0Hndl(GetIntlResource(0));{Get 'itl0' resource}
    myDecimal := myHandle^^.decimalPt;   {for example, 1.234}
    myThousands := myHandle^^.thousSep; {for example, 1,234,567}
    myListSep := myHandle^^.listSep;    {for example, 1;2;3}
END;
```

IMPORTANT

Do not assume that the components of dates and times are always
ordered in a left-to-right direction when displayed. If you are drawing
individual time components, be careful not to simply draw them from
left to right in all cases. For instance, the AM/PM characters in an
English time string are on the right, whereas in an Arabic time string the
equivalent characters may be on the left or right, depending on the
primary line direction—even though in both cases these characters are at
the end of the time string in memory. ▲

Using Number Parts

You can access information on how separators and other parts of formatted numbers are
represented in a particular script system by examining the **number parts table** in the
script's tokens ('itl4') resource. Unlike the numeric-format resource, the number parts
table supports 2-byte characters; it also contains more information, especially for
complicated number formats such as scientific notation.

Your most common reason for obtaining the number parts table may be to pass it as a
parameter to the Text Utilities functions StringToFormatRec, FormatRecToString,
StringToExtended, and ExtendedToString. But you can also examine its contents.
Listing 6-8 shows how to call the GetIntlResourceTable procedure, with a table
selector of smNumberPartsTable, to obtain the number parts table associated with a
given script. The routine obtains the character associated with the number part specified
by thePart and saves it as a wide character, which is a character of either 1 or 2 bytes.
(See the discussion of the tokens resource in the appendix "International Resources" for
a definition of the WideChar data type.) To specify the system script, the parameter
theScript would have the value smSystemScript. The parameter thePart can
have such values as tokDecPoint and tokThousands. For a complete list of
number-parts constants, see the description of the tokens resource in the appendix
"International Resources" in this book.

Listing 6-8 Getting number parts from a script system's number parts table

```
PROCEDURE MyMapNumPartToWideChar(theScript: ScriptCode;
                                 thePart: Integer;
                                 VAR theWChar: WideChar);
VAR
    itlHandle: Handle;
    numpartsOffset: Longint;
    numpartsLength: LongInt;
    numpartsPtr: NumberPartsPtr;
```

```
BEGIN
    GetIntlResourceTable(theScript, smNumberPartsTable,
                        itlHandle, numpartsOffset,
                        numpartsLength);

    IF itlHandle = NIL THEN      {handle errors, }
        theWChar.b := 0          { return null WideChar}
    ELSE BEGIN                   {make numpartsPtr point to }
                                 { beginning of number parts table}

        numpartsPtr := NumberPartsPtr(LongInt(itlHandle^) +
                        numpartsOffset);
        IF thePart > tokMaxSymbols THEN   {invalid number part-- }
                                          { handle  error, }
            theWChar.b := 0               { return null WideChar}
        ELSE BEGIN
            theWChar := numpartsPtr^.data[thePart];
        END;
    END;
END;
```

Retrieving Text From Tokens

Tokens are abstract entities that stand for classes of text items such as alphanumeric strings, various symbols, and quoted literals. The Script Manager `IntlTokenize` function converts programming-language text into script-independent tokens useful to compilers or interpreters. See "Tokenization" on page 6-38. The **untoken table** in a script system's tokens (`'itl4'`) resource has the opposite purpose; it helps you convert script-independent tokens into the text of a given script system.

The untoken table lists the characters associated with each fixed (invariant) token defined by that script. (An invariant token is one that, like `tokenColon`, represents a unique symbol. Other types of tokens, like `tokenAlpha`, represent an arbitrary sequence of characters.) If you need to find out, for example, how a given script system represents the "less than or equal to" symbol (is it the 1-byte character "≤", a 2-byte encoding of the character "≤", the 2-byte, 2-character sequence "<=", or something else altogether?), you can look up the values of `tokenLessEqual1` and `tokenLessEqual2` in that script's untoken table.

The untoken table is most useful for obtaining script-specific forms for individual common symbols, such as the ellipsis or center dot. If you truncate strings with the ellipsis character (…) or use the center dot (•) such as AppleShare does for echoing passwords, don't hardcode their character codes; they may not be valid in some script systems. Instead, specify `tokenEllipsis` or `tokenCenterDot`, and use the untoken table of the current script system to obtain the proper text for those tokens.

Note

If a script system has no defined character or string that corresponds to a particular token, the untoken table contains either a null string or the string "??" for that token. ◆

You access the untoken table by calling the `GetIntlResourceTable` procedure with a table selector of `smNumberPartsTable`. Listing 6-9 provides an example of how to access the untoken table in the tokens resource. This code sample extracts the canonical string associated with a token. It sets the parameter `theString` to the string that corresponds to the token `theToken`. (Usually, this string is 4 bytes or less.) To specify the system script, the parameter `theScript` would have the value `smSystemScript`. The parameter `theToken` can have such values as `tokenNoBreakSpace`, `tokenEllipsis`, and `tokenCenterDot`. For a complete list of defined constants for tokens, see "Token Codes" beginning on page 6-58.

Listing 6-9   Getting a token string from the untoken table

```
PROCEDURE MyMapTokenToString(theScript: ScriptCode; theToken:
Integer; VAR theString: Str255);

VAR
    itlHandle:        Handle;
    untokenOffset:    LongInt;
    untokenLength:    LongInt;
    untokenPtr:       UntokenTablePtr;
    untokenStringPtr: StringPtr;

BEGIN
    GetIntlResourceTable(theScript, smUnTokenTable, itlHandle,
                    untokenOffset, untokenLength);

    IF itlHandle = NIL THEN      {handle errors, return null string}
        theString := ''
    ELSE BEGIN                      {make untokenPtr point to the }
                                    { beginning of the untoken table}
        untokenPtr := UntokenTablePtr(LongInt(itlHandle^) +
                    untokenOffset);
        IF theToken > untokenPtr^.lastToken THEN  {this token is }
                                            { not in table-- }
            theString := ''                 { return null string}
        ELSE BEGIN                   {index[theToken] is the offset }
                                    { of the desired string from the }
                                    { beginning of the untoken table}
            untokenStringPtr := StringPtr(LongInt(untokenPtr) +
```

```
untokenPtr^.index[theToken]);
        theString := untokenStringPtr^;
    END;
  END;
END;
```

Even though using the untoken table is conceptually the converse of calling the IntlTokenize function, their purposes are different. IntlTokenize is used as a first step toward compiling or interpreting programming-language source text, and its results are rarely returned or reconverted to source text. The untoken table is most commonly used to supply localized text for individual common tokens.

Using Word-Break Tables

If you use the Text Utilities FindWordBreaks procedure to determine the boundaries of a word, you normally do not need to pass it an explicit pointer to a word-break table. However, if you want to use a custom word-break table you can pass FindWordBreaks a pointer to that table. Word-break tables are in a script system's string-manipulation ('itl2') resource; you can gain access to them by calling the GetIntlResourceTable procedure with a table selector of smWordSelectTable or smWordWrapTable.

There are two possible table selectors because a script system may have different word breaks for word selection than it does for line breaking. If you are using FindWordBreaks to select an individual word, use smWordSelectTable when you call GetIntlResourceTable to obtain the word-break table. If you are using FindWordBreaks to find line breaks, use smWordWrapTable when you call GetIntlResourceTable.

Using Whitespace Information

Most applications that need whitespace information, such as when eliminating extra spaces in text or searching for non-space characters, can get it by calling the CharacterType function. However, if your application needs a listing of all valid whitespace characters in a script system, you can call GetIntlResourceTable with a table selector of smWhiteSpaceList. GetIntlResourceTable returns the whitespace table from the script system's tokens resource.

Converting Text

The third principal use for the Script Manager is in converting text from one form to another, for two specific purposes: tokenization and transliteration. The routines described in this section are used by specialized applications only. You can use these Script Manager routines to

- lexically convert text of the current script system into a series of language-independent tokens (tokenization)
- phonetically convert text of one subscript into text of another subscript within the same script system (transliteration)

Most text-processing applications have no need to perform either of these tasks. However, if your program needs to evaluate programming statements or logical or mathematical expressions in a script-independent fashion, you may want to use the Script Manager's tokenization facility. If your program performs phonetic conversion, for text input or for any other purpose, you may want to use the Script Manager's transliteration facility.

Tokenization

Programs that parse structured text expressions (such as compilers, assemblers, and scripting-language interpreters) usually assign sequences of characters to categories called **tokens.** Tokens are abstract entities that stand for names, operators, and quoted literals without making assumptions that depend on a particular writing system.

The Script Manager provides support for this conversion, called **tokenization.** Each script system's international tokens resource (type `'itl4'`) contains tables of token information used by the Script Manager's `IntlTokenize` function to identify the elements in an arbitrary string of text and convert them to tokens. The token stream created by `IntlTokenize` can be used as input to a compiler or interpreter, or to an expression evaluator such as might be used by a spreadsheet or database program.

The `IntlTokenize` function allows your application to create a common set of tokens from text in any script system. For example, a whitespace character might have different character-code representations in different script systems. The `IntlTokenize` function can assign the token `tokenWhite` to any whitespace character, thus removing dependence on any character-encoding scheme.

When you call `IntlTokenize`, you pass it the source text to interpret. `IntlTokenize` parses the text and returns a list of the tokens that make up the text. Among the token types that it recognizes are whitespace characters; newline or return characters; sequences of alphabetic, numeric, and decimal characters; the end of a stream of characters; unknown characters; alternate digits and decimals; and many fixed token symbols, such as open parentheses, plus and minus signs, commas, and periods. See page 6-58 for a complete list of recognized tokens and their defined constants.

`IntlTokenize` can return not only a list of the token types found in your text but also a normalized copy of the text of each of the tokens, so that the content of your source text is preserved along with the tokens generated from it.

Figure 6-3 illustrates the process that occurs when `IntlTokenize` converts text into a sequence of tokens. It shows that very different text from two separate script systems can result in the same set of tokens.

Figure 6-3   The action of `IntlTokenize`

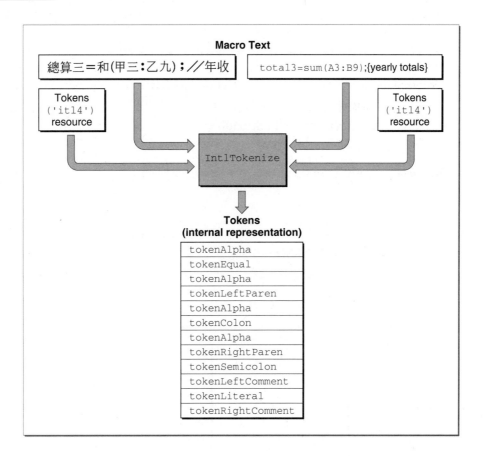

Because it uses the tokens resource belonging to the script system of the text being analyzed, `IntlTokenize` works on only one script run at a time. However, one way to process multiscript text is to make successive calls to `IntlTokenize` and append the results of each to the token list, thus building a single token stream from multiple calls.

Note

The `IntlTokenize` function does not provide complete lexical analysis; it returns a simple, sequential list of tokens. If necessary, your application can then process the output of `IntlTokenize` at a more sophisticated lexical or syntactic level. ◆

The rest of this section introduces the data structures used by `IntlTokenize`, discusses specific features and how it handles specific types of text, and gives an example.

Data Structures

When you call `IntlTokenize`, you supply it with a pointer to a **token block record,** a data structure that you have allocated. The token block record has a pointer to your source text and pointers to two other buffers you have allocated—one to hold the list of **token records** that `IntlTokenize` generates and the other to hold the string representations of those tokens, if you choose to have strings generated. See Figure 6-4.

`IntlTokenize` fills in the token list and the string list, updates information in the token block record, and returns the information to you.

Figure 6-4   `IntlTokenize` data structures (simplified)

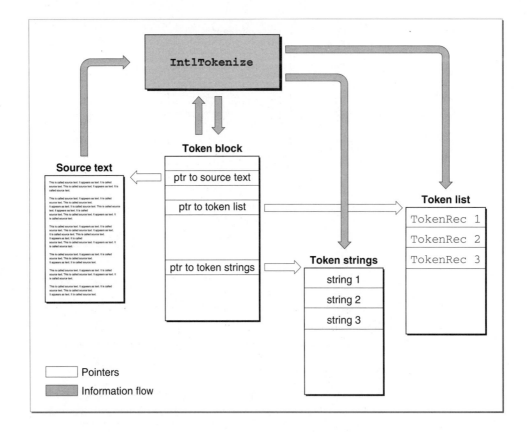

Delimiters for Literals and Comments

Your application may specify up to two pairs of delimiters each for quoted literals and for comments. Quoted literal delimiters consist of a single symbol, and comment delimiters may be either one or two symbols (including the newline character for notations whose comments automatically terminate at the end of a line). Each delimiter is represented by a token, as is the entire literal between the opening and closing delimiters—except when the literal contains an escape character; see "Escape Character" (next).

Limited support exists for nested comments. Comments may be nested if so specified by the doNest flag, with one restriction that must be strictly observed to prevent IntlTokenize from malfunctioning: nesting is legal only if both the left and right delimiters for the comment token are composed of two symbols each. If your application specifies two different sets of comment delimiters, then the doNest flag always applies to both.

IMPORTANT

When using nested comments specified by the doNest flag, test thoroughly to ensure that the requirements of IntlTokenize are met. ▲

Escape Character

The characters that compose literals within quotations and comments are normally defined to have no syntactic significance; however, the escape character within a quoted literal signals that the following character should not be treated as the closing delimiter. Outside of the limits of a quoted literal, the escape character has no significance and is not recognized as an escape character.

For example, if the backslash "\" (token type = tokenBackSlash) is defined as the escape character, the IntlTokenize function would consider it to be an escape character in the following string, and would not consider the second quotation mark to be a closing delimiter:

```
"This is a quote \" within a quoted literal"
```

In the following string, however, IntlTokenize would not consider the backslash to be an escape character, and therefore would consider the first quotation mark to be an opening delimiter:

```
This is a backslash \" preceding a quoted literal"
```

Alphanumeric Tokens

The `IntlTokenize` function allows you to specify that numeric characters do not have to be considered numbers when mixed with alphabetic characters. If a flag is set, alphabetic sequences may include digits, as long as first character is alphabetic. In that case the sequence `Highway61` would be converted to a single alphabetic token, instead of the alphabetic token `Highway` followed by the number `61`.

Alternate Numerals

Some script systems have not only Western digits (that is, the standard ASCII digits, the numerals 0 through 9), but also their own numeral codes. `IntlTokenize` recognizes these alternate numerals and constructs tokens from them, such as `tokenAltNum` and `tokenAltReal`.

String Generation

To preserve the content of your source text as well as the tokens generated from it, your application may instruct `IntlTokenize` to generate null-terminated, even-byte-boundaried Pascal strings corresponding to each token. `IntlTokenize` constructs the strings according to these rules:

- If the token is anything but alphabetic or numeric, `IntlTokenize` copies the text of the token verbatim into the Pascal string.

- If the token represents non-Roman alphanumeric characters, `IntlTokenize` copies the characters verbatim into the Pascal string.

- If the token represents Roman alphabetic characters, `IntlTokenize` normalizes them to standard ASCII characters (such as by changing 2-byte Roman to 1-byte Roman) and writes them into the Pascal string.

- If the token represents numeric characters—even if the script system uses an alternate set of digits—`IntlTokenize` normalizes them into standard ASCII numerical digits, with a period as the decimal separator, and creates a string from the result. This allows users of other script systems to transparently use their own numerals or Roman characters for numbers or keywords.

The tokens resource includes a string-copy routine that performs the necessary string normalization.

Appending Results

You can make a series of calls to `IntlTokenize` and append the results of each call to the results of previous calls. You can instruct `IntlTokenize` to use the output values for certain parameters from each call as input values to the next call. At the end of your sequence of calls you will have—in order—all the tokens and strings generated from the calls to `IntlTokenize`.

Appending results is the only way to use `IntlTokenize` to parse a body of text that has been written in two or more different script systems. Because `IntlTokenize` can operate only on a single script run at a time, you must first divide your text into script runs and pass each script's character stream separately to `IntlTokenize`.

Example

Here is an example of how the `IntlTokenize` function breaks text into segments that that can be processed in a way that is meaningful in a particular script system. The source text is identical to that shown in Figure 6-3 on page 6-39. Assume that you send this programming-language statement to `IntlTokenize`:

```
total3=sum(A3:B9);{yearly totals}
```

`IntlTokenize` might convert that into the following sequence of tokens and token strings:

Token	Token string
tokenAlpha	'total3'
tokenEqual	'='
tokenAlpha	'sum'
tokenLeftParen	'('
tokenAlpha	'A3'
tokenColon	':'
tokenAlpha	'B9'
tokenRightParen	')'
tokenSemicolon	';'
tokenLeftComment	'{'
tokenLiteral	'yearly totals'
tokenRightComment	'}'

This token sequence could then be processed meaningfully by an expression evaluator. If the statement had been created under a different script system, in which comment delimiters, semicolons, or equality were represented with different character codes, the resulting token sequence would still be the same and could be evaluated identically—although the strings generated from the tokens would be different.

The `IntlTokenize` function is described further on page 6-92.

Transliteration

The Script Manager provides support for **transliteration,** the automatic conversion of text from one form to another within a single script system. In the Roman script system, transliteration simply means case conversion. In Japanese, Chinese, and Korean script systems, it means the phonetic conversion of characters from one subscript to another.

The `TransliterateText` function performs the conversions. Tables that control transliteration for a 1-byte script system are in its international string-manipulation (`'itl2'`) resource; the tables for a 2-byte script system are in the script's transliteration (`'trsl'`) resource. This illustrates the difference in the meaning of transliteration for the two types of script systems: case conversion information is in the string-manipulation resource, whereas information needed for phonetic conversion is in the transliteration resource. The transliteration resource is available to all script systems, although currently no 1-byte script systems make use of it.

Transliteration here does not mean translation; the Macintosh script management system cannot translate text from one language to another. Nor does it include context-sensitive conversion from one subscript to another; that can be accomplished with an input method. See, for example, the discussions of input methods in the chapters "Introduction to Text on the Macintosh" and "Text Services Manager" in this book. Transliteration can, however, be an initial step for those more complex conversions:

■ Within the Japanese script system, you can transliterate from Hiragana to Romaji (Roman) and from Romaji to Katakana, and vice versa. You cannot transliterate from Hiragana to Kanji (Chinese characters). However, transliteration from Romaji to Katakana or Hiragana could be an initial step for an input method that would complete the context-sensitive conversion to Kanji.

■ Within the (traditional) Chinese script system, you can transliterate from the Bopomofo or Zhuyinfuhao (phonetic) subscript to Roman, and vice versa. You cannot transliterate from Zhuyinfuhao to Hanzi (Chinese characters). However, transliteration from Zhuyinfuhao to Pinyin could be an initial step for an input method that would complete the context-sensitive conversion to Hanzi.

■ Within the Korean script system, you can transliterate from Roman to Jamo, from Jamo to Hangul, from Hangul to Jamo, and from Jamo to Roman. It is therefore possible to transliterate from Hangul to Roman and from Roman to Hangul by a two-step process. It is not possible to transliterate from Hangul into Hanja (Chinese characters). Transliteration from Jamo to Hangul is used by the input method supplied with the Korean script system; that transliteration is sufficient when Hanja characters are not used. To include Hanja characters requires additional context-sensitive processing by the input method.

The Script Manager defines two basic types of transliteration you can perform: conversion to Roman characters, and conversion to a native subscript within the same non-Roman script system. Within those categories there are subtypes. For instance, in Roman text, case conversion can be either to uppercase or to lowercase; in Japanese text, native conversion can be to Romaji, Hiragana, or Katakana.

You can specify which types of text can undergo conversion. For example, in Japanese text you can, if you want to, limit transliteration to Hiragana characters only. Or you can restrict it to case conversion of Roman characters only.

Not all combinations of transliteration are possible, of course. Case conversion cannot take place in scripts or subscripts that do not have case; transliteration from one subscript to another cannot take place in scripts that do not have subscripts.

Transliteration is not perfect. Typically, it gives a unique result within a 2-byte script, although it may not always be the most phonetic or natural result. Transliterations may be incorrect in ambiguous situations; by analogy, in certain transliterations from English "th" could refer to the sound in *the*, the sound in *thick*, or the sounds in *boathouse*.

Figure 6-5 shows some of the possible effects of transliteration. Each string on the right side of the figure is the transliterated result of its equivalent string on the left.

- Roman characters can be transposed from uppercase to lowercase and vice versa—even if they are embedded in text that also contains Kanji.

- One-byte Roman characters can be converted to 2-byte Roman characters. (The glyphs for 2-byte Roman characters are typically larger and spaced farther apart, for better appearance when interspersed with ideographic glyphs.)

- Katakana can be converted to Hiragana.

- Hiragana can be converted to 1-byte Roman characters.

Figure 6-5   The effects of transliteration

to uppercase	**TO UPPERCASE**
TO LOWERCASE	**to lowercase**
Mixed 漢字	**MIXED 漢字**
romaji[*]	**r o m a j i**[*]
ニホン	にほん
にほん	**nihonn**

[*] 1-byte Romaji converted to 2-byte Romaji

When you call `TransliterateText`, you specify a **source mask,** a **target format,** and a **target modifier.** The source mask specifies which subscript or subscripts represented in the source text should be converted to the target format. The target modifier provides additional formatting instructions. For example, in Japanese text that contains Roman, Hiragana, Katakana, and Kanji characters, you could use the source mask to limit transliteration to Hiragana characters only. You could then use the target format to specify conversion to Roman, and you could use the target modifier to further specify that the converted text become uppercase.

For all script systems, there are three currently defined values for source mask, with the following assigned constants:

Source mask constant	Value	Explanation
smMaskAscii	1	Convert from Roman text
smMaskNative	2	Convert from text native to current script
smMaskAll	–1	Convert from all text

To specify that you want to convert only Roman characters, use smMaskAscii. To convert only native characters, use smMaskNative. Use the smMaskAll constant to specify that you want to transliterate all text. "Roman text" is defined as any Roman characters in the character set of a given script system. In most cases, this means the low-ASCII Roman characters, but—depending on the script system—it may also include certain characters in the high-ASCII range whose codes are not used for the script system's native character set, and it may include 2-byte Roman characters in 2-byte script systems. The definition of "native text" is also script-dependent.

The 2-byte script systems recognize the following additional values for source mask:

Source mask constant	Hex. value	Explanation
All 2-byte scripts:		
smMaskAscii1	$04	Convert from 1-byte Roman text
smMaskAscii2	$08	Convert from 2-byte Roman text
Japanese:		
smMaskKana1	$10	Convert from 1-byte Katakana text
smMaskKana2	$20	Convert from 2-byte Katakana text
smMaskGana2	$80	Convert from 2-byte Hiragana text
Korean:		
smMaskHangul2	$100	Convert from 2-byte Hangul text
smMaskJamo2	$200	Convert from 2-byte Jamo text
Chinese:		
smMaskBopomofo2	$400	Convert from 2-byte Zhuyinfuhao text

The low-order byte of the target parameter is the format; it determines what form the text should be transliterated to. For all script systems, there are two currently supported values for target format, with the following assigned constants:

Target format constant	Hex. value	Explanation
smTransAscii	$00	Convert to Roman
smTransNative	$01	Convert to a subscript native to current script
smTransCase	$FE	Convert case for all text (obsolete)
smTransSystem	$FF	Convert to system script (obsolete)

The 2-byte script systems recognize the following additional values for target format:

Target format constant	Value	Explanation
All 2-byte scripts:		
smTransASCII1	2	Convert to 1-byte Roman text
smTransASCII2	3	Convert to 2-byte Roman text
Japanese:		
smTransKana1	4	Convert to 1-byte Katakana text
smTransKana2	5	Convert to 2-byte Katakana text
smTransGana2	7	Convert to 2-byte Hiragana text
Korean:		
smTransHangul2	8	Convert to 2-byte Hangul text
smTransJamo2	9	Convert to 2-byte Jamo text
Chinese:		
smTransBopomofo2	10	Convert to 2-byte Zhuyinfuhao text

The high-order byte of the `target` parameter is the target modifier; it provides additional formatting instructions. All script systems recognize these values for target modifier, with the following assigned constants:

Target modifier constant	Hex. value	Explanation
smTransLower	$4000	Target becomes lowercase
smTransUpper	$8000	Target becomes uppercase

For example, for `TransliterateText` to convert all the characters in a block of text to 1-byte Roman uppercase, the value of `srcMask` is `smMaskAll` and the target value is `smTransAscii1+smTransUpper`. To convert only those characters that are already (1-byte or 2-byte) Roman, the value of `srcMask` is `smMaskAscii1+smMaskAscii2`.

The `TransliterateText` function is described further on page 6-98.

Note

For uppercasing or lowercasing Roman text in general, use `UppercaseText` or `LowercaseText`. Because the performance of `TransliterateText` is slower, you may rarely want to use its case-changing capabilities in Roman text. ◆

Modifying Script Systems

The fourth principal use for the Script Manager is in modifying the contents of script systems themselves. The routines described in this section are for specialized purposes, such as providing regional variants to existing script systems or assigning script-specific features to individual documents or applications. You can use these Script Manager routines to

■ replace one or more of a script system's international resources (this replacement occurs within the context of your application only)

■ replace one or more of an individual script system's routines (for 1-byte complex scripts only)

Most text-processing applications need not perform either of these replacements. However, if your program has special needs or if you are implementing a specific regional variation of a script system with unusual text-handling features, you can use these Script Manager calls.

Replacing a Script System's Default International Resources

In certain situations, you may want to replace the script-system-supplied international resources with some of your own. For example, your application might create documents containing currency amounts and get the currency format from the numeric-format resource. You may then want the unit of currency to remain the same, even if the document is displayed on a Macintosh with system software localized for another region.

You can store your own versions of some of the international resources in your application's or document's resource file, to override those in the System file. In this case, documents that your application creates could have their own copy of the numeric-format resource that was used to create them.

To replace the numeric-format (`'itl0'`) or long-date-format (`'itl1'`) resource, follow these two steps:

1. When your application starts up or when your document is opened, call the `GetScriptVariable` function for your target script system to get the ID number of the current default version of the resource you are replacing. Save that ID number for later.

2. Call the `SetScriptVariable` function to set the script's default ID number to the ID of the resource that you are supplying.

If your replacement resource is attached to your application or document, it will override the script system's default version. When a call for a resource is made, the Resource Manager searches first in the resource fork of the open document, then in the resource fork of the active application, and then in the System file. This search sequence is described in the chapter "Resource Manager" in *Inside Macintosh: More Macintosh Toolbox*.

To substitute the string-manipulation ('itl2') or tokens ('itl4') resources, you must take an additional step. If you want to replace the default resource currently used by a script system, you must first clear your application's **international resources cache.** The cache is part of an application's context as handled by the Process Manager; it is initialized when the application is launched, and is switched in and out with the application. It contains the resource ID numbers of the default string-manipulation and tokens resources for all installed script systems. Once the cache is set up, access to string-manipulation and tokens resources is exclusively through the ID numbers in the cache.

Therefore, to replace a string-manipulation or tokens resource, it is not enough to attach the resource to your document and call the SetScriptVariable function; this alone does not affect any cached ID numbers. In addition, add this third step:

3. After calling SetScriptVariable as described in step 2, call ClearIntlResourceCache. That will cause the cache to be reloaded with the current default resource ID numbers, including your override of the previous default, as each resource is called.

In this case, when a call for a resource is made, the Script Manager looks first in the cache for the resource ID to use. If the cache has been cleared, the Script Manager gets the ID from the script variables (and updates the cache with the new ID). The Script Manager then calls the Resource Manager, requesting a resource with that ID. The Resource Manager searches for the resource as described previously, taking it from your document or application.

Because the system maintains a separate international resources cache for each application's context, your application can provide its own string-manipulation and tokens resources without affecting the use of those resources by other applications or by the system. When the Process Manager switches in another application, that application's international resources cache has the defaults needed by that application.

No matter which international resource you have replaced, there is one final step to take:

4. When your application exits or is switched out, be sure to call SetScriptVariable once again to reset the script system's default ID number to what it was before you replaced it.

IMPORTANT

If the international resources selection flag is TRUE when a call to access your supplied resources is made, the ID numbers of your supplied resources must be within the system script range; if it is FALSE, the IDs must be in the range of the current script. Otherwise, your resources will not be found. See the appendix "International Resources" for a list of script codes and their resource ID ranges. ▲

Replacing a Script System's Default Routines

Applications do not normally need to modify a script system's text-handling routines. For 1-byte complex script systems and for 2-byte script systems, most script-specific behavior is built into tables in the script's international resources. Text-handling code is in Macintosh system software: in ROM, in the System file, or in one of two system extensions—WorldScript I and WorldScript II. WorldScript I and WorldScript II handle text for 1-byte complex and 2-byte script systems, respectively. They are described in the appendix "Built-in Script Support" in this book. For most needs the table-driven behavior is adequate, and you can access many of the tables through the Script Manager calls described in the previous section.

Even so, for 1-byte complex script systems, the Script Manager offers you the ability to modify or enhance the routines contained in WorldScript I. If you need specific script-based behavior that is not currently supported, you can replace one or more **script utilities** (low-level text-handling routines that employ the _ScriptUtil trap) or QuickDraw patches for your target script system. You can create a patch and install it with a System extension file (type 'INIT') that is executed at system startup.

IMPORTANT

Because this capability affects WorldScript I only, it is available only for 1-byte complex script systems. ▲

In every script system that uses WorldScript I, the dispatch-table element for every script utility and QuickDraw patch consists of two pointers: one to the WorldScript I implementation of the routine and one to the original (built-in Roman) routine. In all cases, the WorldScript I routine executes first. In some cases, WorldScript I calls the original routine after its own; in other cases, the pointer to the original routine is NIL and the WorldScript I routine is all that executes. See Figure 6-6. This design allows you to place a patched routine so that it executes before, in place of, or after the WorldScript I routine.

Figure 6-6   Dispatch table entry for script utilities and QuickDraw patches

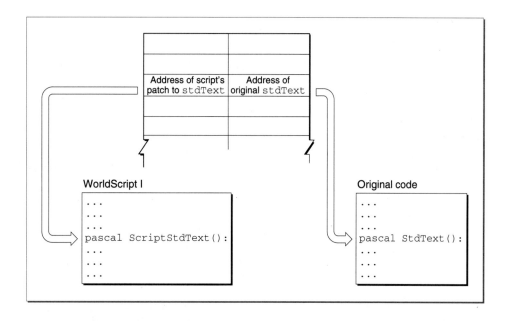

The script-based dispatch table design gives you a simple, flexible way to replace individual routines without having to patch out all of `_ScriptUtil` or any of the QuickDraw low-level routines in their entirety. Furthermore, in a multiscript environment each patch applies only to its own script system. You can, for example, patch **stdText** for the Thai script system only, leaving it unchanged for all other script systems.

To replace only the WorldScript I implementation of a routine, replace its pointer in the dispatch table; to keep the WorldScript I routine while replacing or patching the original routine, replace the original-routine pointer in the dispatch table. The four Script Manager routines that allow you to make those patches are `GetScriptUtilityAddress`, `SetScriptUtilityAddress`, `GetScriptQDPatchAddress`, and `SetScriptQDPatchAddress`. Either pointer in the dispatch table may be `NIL`, meaning that WorldScript I either (1) doesn't patch the original routine or (2) doesn't call the original routine.

For additional information on how to use these four Script Manager routines to customize a script's behavior, see the appendix "Built-in Script Support."

Script Manager Reference

This section describes the constants, data structures, and routines that are specific to the Script Manager.

Constants

The Script Manager defines a large number of constants. This section lists and describes the constants with which you can specify

- script codes, language codes, and region codes
- token codes
- selectors for Script Manager variables
- selectors for script variables

There are many other constants defined for other purposes that are listed with the routines that use them. In addition, all constants are listed in the section "Summary of the Script Manager" beginning on page 6-107.

Script Codes

You can specify script systems with implicit and explicit script code constants in the `script` parameter of the `GetScriptVariable` and `SetScriptVariable` functions. The implicit script codes `smSystemScript` and `smCurrentScript` are special negative values for the system script and the font script, respectively.

Script constant	Value	Explanation
smSystemScript	–1	System script
smCurrentScript	–2	Font script
smRoman	0	Roman
smJapanese	1	Japanese
smTradChinese	2	Traditional Chinese
smKorean	3	Korean
smArabic	4	Arabic
smHebrew	5	Hebrew
smGreek	6	Greek
smCyrillic	7	Cyrillic
smRSymbol	8	Right-to-left symbols
smDevanagari	9	Devanagari

Script constant	Value	Explanation (continued)
smGurmukhi	10	Gurmukhi
smGujarati	11	Gujarati
smOriya	12	Oriya
smBengali	13	Bengali
smTamil	14	Tamil
smTelugu	15	Telugu
smKannada	16	Kannada/Kanarese
smMalayalam	17	Malayalam
smSinhalese	18	Sinhalese
smBurmese	19	Burmese
smKhmer	20	Khmer
smThai	21	Thai
smLaotian	22	Laotian
smGeorgian	23	Georgian
smArmenian	24	Armenian
smSimpChinese	25	Simplified Chinese
smTibetan	26	Tibetan
smMongolian	27	Mongolian
smGeez	28	Geez/Ethiopic
smEthiopic	28	= smGeez
smEastEurRoman	29	Extended Roman for Slavic and Baltic languages
smVietnamese	30	Extended Roman for Vietnamese
smExtArabic	31	Extended Arabic for Sindhi
smUninterp	32	Uninterpreted symbols

Note

The script code represented by the constant smUninterp is available for representation of special symbols, such as items in a tool palette, that must not be considered as part of any actual script system. For manipulating and drawing such symbols, the smUninterp constant should be treated as if it indicated the Roman script system rather than the system script; that is, the default behavior of uninterpreted symbols should be Roman. ◆

Note

The script code represented by the constant smRSymbol is available as an alternative to smUninterp, for representation of special symbols that have a right-to-left line direction. Note, however, that the script management system provides no direct support for representation of text with this script code. ◆

6

Script Manager

Language Codes

Language codes have the following defined values. Note that each language is associated with a script code.

Language constant	Value	Language	(Script code)
langEnglish	0	English	(smRoman)
langFrench	1	French	(smRoman)
langGerman	2	German	(smRoman)
langItalian	3	Italian	(smRoman)
langDutch	4	Dutch	(smRoman)
langSwedish	5	Swedish	(smRoman)
langSpanish	6	Spanish	(smRoman)
langDanish	7	Danish	(smRoman)
langPortuguese	8	Portuguese	(smRoman)
langNorwegian	9	Norwegian	(smRoman)
langHebrew	10	Hebrew	(smHebrew)
langJapanese	11	Japanese	(smJapanese)
langArabic	12	Arabic	(smArabic)
langFinnish	13	Finnish	(smRoman)
langGreek	14	Greek	(smGreek)
langIcelandic	15	Icelandic	(smRoman)
langMaltese	16	Maltese	(smRoman)
langTurkish	17	Turkish	(smRoman)
langCroatian	18	Croatian	(smRoman)
langTradChinese	19	Chinese (traditional chars.)	(smTradChinese)
langUrdu	20	Urdu	(smArabic)
langHindi	21	Hindi	(smDevanagari)
langThai	22	Thai	(smThai)
langKorean	23	Korean	(smKorean)
langLithuanian	24	Lithuanian	(smEastEurRoman)
langPolish	25	Polish	(smEastEurRoman)
langHungarian	26	Hungarian	(smEastEurRoman)
langEstonian	27	Estonian	(smEastEurRoman)
langLettish	28	Lettish	(smEastEurRoman)
langLatvian	28	= langLettish	
langSaamisk	29	(language of Lapps/Sami)	(smRoman)
langLappish	29	= langSaamisk	
langFaeroese	30	Faeroese	(smRoman)

Language constant	Value	Language	(Script code) (continued)
langFarsi	31	Farsi	(smArabic)
langPersian	31	= langFarsi	
langRussian	32	Russian	(smCyrillic)
langSimpChinese	33	Chinese (simplified chars.)	(smSimpChinese)
langFlemish	34	Flemish	(smRoman)
langIrish	35	Irish	(smRoman)
langAlbanian	36	Albanian	(smRoman)
langRomanian	37	Romanian	(smEastEurRoman)
langCzech	38	Czech	(smEastEurRoman)
langSlovak	39	Slovak	(smEastEurRoman)
langSlovenian	40	Slovenian	(smEastEurRoman)
langYiddish	41	Yiddish	(smHebrew)
langSerbian	42	Serbian	(smCyrillic)
langMacedonian	43	Macedonian	(smCyrillic)
langBulgarian	44	Bulgarian	(smCyrillic)
langUkrainian	45	Ukrainian	(smCyrillic)
langByelorussian	46	Byelorussian	(smCyrillic)
langUzbek	47	Uzbek	(smCyrillic)
langKazakh	48	Kazakh	(smCyrillic)
langAzerbaijani	49	Azerbaijani	(smCyrillic)
langAzerbaijanAr	50	Azerbaijani	(smArabic)
langArmenian	51	Armenian	(smArmenian)
langGeorgian	52	Georgian	(smGeorgian)
langMoldovan	53	Moldovan	(smCyrillic)
langMoldavian	53	= langMoldovan	(smCyrillic)
langKirghiz	54	Kirghiz	(smCyrillic)
langTajiki	55	Tajiki	(smCyrillic)
langTurkmen	56	Turkmen	(smCyrillic)
langMongolian	57	Mongolian	(smMongolian)
langMongolianCyr	58	Mongolian	(smCyrillic)
langPashto	59	Pashto	(smArabic)
langKurdish	60	Kurdish	(smArabic)
langKashmiri	61	Kashmiri	(smArabic)
langSindhi	62	Sindhi	(smExtArabic)
langTibetan	63	Tibetan	(smTibetan)

continued

6

Script Manager

Language constant	Value	Language	(Script code) (continued)
langNepali	64	Nepali	(smDevanagari)
langSanskrit	65	Sanskrit	(smDevanagari)
langMarathi	66	Marathi	(smDevanagari)
langBengali	67	Bengali	(smBengali)
langAssamese	68	Assamese	(smBengali)
langGujarati	69	Gujarati	(smGujarati)
langPunjabi	70	Punjabi	(smGurmukhi)
langOriya	71	Oriya	(smOriya)
langMalayalam	72	Malayalam	(smMalayalam)
langKannada	73	Kannada	(smKannada)
langTamil	74	Tamil	(smTamil)
langTelugu	75	Telugu	(smTelugu)
langSinhalese	76	Sinhalese	(smSinhalese)
langBurmese	77	Burmese	(smBurmese)
langKhmer	78	Khmer	(smKhmer)
langLao	79	Lao	(smLaotian)
langVietnamese	80	Vietnamese	(smVietnamese)
langIndonesian	81	Indonesian	(smRoman)
langTagalog	82	Tagalog	(smRoman)
langMalayRoman	83	Malay	(smRoman)
langMalayArabic	84	Malay	(smArabic)
langAmharic	85	Amharic	(smEthiopic)
langTigrinya	86	Tigrinya	(smEthiopic)
langGalla	87	Galla	(smEthiopic)
langOromo	87	= langGalla	
langSomali	88	Somali	(smRoman)
langSwahili	89	Swahili	(smRoman)
langRuanda	90	Ruanda	(smRoman)
langRundi	91	Rundi	(smRoman)
langChewa	92	Chewa	(smRoman)
langMalagasy	93	Malagasy	(smRoman)
langEsperanto	94	Esperanto	(mod. smRoman)
langWelsh	128	Welsh	(smRoman)
langBasque	129	Basque	(smRoman)
langCatalan	130	Catalan	(smRoman)
langLatin	131	Latin	(smRoman)

Language constant	Value	Language	(Script code) (continued)
langQuechua	132	Quechua	(smRoman)
langGuarani	133	Guarani	(smRoman)
langAymara	134	Aymara	(smRoman)
langTatar	135	Tatar	(smCyrillic)
langUighur	136	Uighur	(smArabic)
langDzongkha	137	Bhutanese	(smTibetan)
langJavaneseRom	138	Javanese	(smRoman)
langSundaneseRom	139	Sundanese	(smRoman)

Region Codes

Region codes have the following defined values. Each region is associated with a particular language code and script code (not shown). Note that the existence of a defined region code does not necessarily imply the existence of a version of Macintosh system software localized for that region.

Region constant	Value	Explanation
verUS	0	United States
verFrance	1	France
verBritain	2	Great Britain
verGermany	3	Germany
verItaly	4	Italy
verNetherlands	5	Netherlands
verFrBelgiumLux	6	French for Belgium and Luxembourg
verSweden	7	Sweden
verDenmark	9	Denmark
verPortugal	10	Portugal
verFrCanada	11	French Canada
verIsrael	13	Israel
verJapan	14	Japan
verAustralia	15	Australia
verArabia	16	the Arabic world
verArabic	16	= verArabia
verFinland	17	Finland
verFrSwiss	18	French for Switzerland
verGrSwiss	19	German for Switzerland

continued

Region constant	Value	Explanation (continued)
verGreece	20	Greece
verIceland	21	Iceland
verMalta	22	Malta
verCyprus	23	Cyprus
verTurkey	24	Turkey
verYugoCroatian	25	Croatian system for Yugoslavia
verIndiaHindi	33	Hindi system for India
verPakistan	34	Pakistan
verLithuania	41	Lithuania
verPoland	42	Poland
verHungary	43	Hungary
verEstonia	44	Estonia
verLatvia	45	Latvia
verLapland	46	Lapland
verFaeroeIsl	47	Faeroe Islands
verIran	48	Iran
verRussia	49	Russia
verIreland	50	Ireland
verKorea	51	Korea
verChina	52	People's Republic of China
verTaiwan	53	Taiwan
verThailand	54	Thailand
minCountry		The lowest defined region code (for range-checking); currently = verUS
maxCountry		The highest defined region code (for range-checking); currently = verThailand

Token Codes

The following constants define the types of tokens recognized by the `IntlTokenize` function and specified in the field `theToken` of the token record (type `TokenRec`):

Constant	Value	Explanation
delimPad	–2	Delimiter pad (special code)
tokenEmpty	–1	Empty flag
tokenUnknown	0	Has no existing token type
tokenWhite	1	Whitespace character
tokenLeftLit	2	Opening literal marker

Constant	Value	Explanation (continued)
tokenRightLit	3	Closing literal marker
tokenAlpha	4	Alphabetic
tokenNumeric	5	Numeric
tokenNewLine	6	New line
tokenLeftComment	7	Opening comment marker
tokenRightComment	8	Closing comment marker
tokenLiteral	9	Literal
tokenEscape	10	Escape character
tokenAltNum	11	Alternate number (such as at $B0–$B9)
tokenRealNum	12	Real number
tokenAltReal	13	Alternate real number
tokenReserve1	14	(reserved 1)
tokenReserve2	15	(reserved 2)
tokenLeftParen	16	Opening parenthesis
tokenLeftBracket	18	Opening square bracket
tokenRightBracket	19	Closing square bracket
tokenLeftCurly	20	Opening curly bracket
tokenRightCurly	21	Closing curly bracket
tokenLeftEnclose	22	Opening European double quote
tokenRightEnclose	23	Closing European double quote
tokenPlus	24	Plus
tokenMinus	25	Minus
tokenAsterisk	26	Times/multiply
tokenDivide	27	Divide
tokenSlash	29	Slash
tokenBackSlash	30	Backslash
tokenLess	31	Less than
tokenGreat	32	Greater than
tokenEqual	33	Equal
tokenLessEqual2	34	Less than or equal to (2 symbols)
tokenLessEqual1	35	Less than or equal to (1 symbol)
tokenGreatEqual2	36	Greater than or equal to (2 symbols)
tokenGreatEqual1	37	Greater than or equal to (1 symbol)
token2Equal	38	Double equal
tokenColonEqual	39	Colon equal

continued

6

Script Manager

Constant	Value	Explanation (continued)
tokenNotEqual	40	Not equal
tokenLessGreat	41	Less/greater (not equal in Pascal)
tokenExclamEqual	42	Exclamation equal (not equal in C)
tokenExclam	43	Exclamation point
tokenTilde	44	Centered tilde
tokenComma	45	Comma
tokenPeriod	46	Period
tokenLeft2Quote	47	Opening double quote
tokenRight2Quote	48	Closing double quote
tokenLeft1Quote	49	Opening single quote
tokenRight1Quote	50	Closing single quote
token2Quote	51	Double quote
token1Quote	52	Single quote
tokenSemicolon	53	Semicolon
tokenPercent	54	Percent
tokenCaret	55	Caret
tokenUnderline	56	Underline
tokenAmpersand	57	Ampersand
tokenAtSign	58	At sign
tokenBar	59	Vertical bar
tokenQuestion	60	Question mark
tokenPi	61	Pi
tokenRoot	62	Square root
tokenSigma	63	Capital sigma
tokenIntegral	64	Integral
tokenMicro	65	Micro
tokenCapPi	66	Capital pi
tokenInfinity	67	Infinity
tokenColon	68	Colon
tokenHash	69	Pound sign (U.S. weight)
tokenDollar	70	Dollar sign
tokenNoBreakSpace	71	Nonbreaking space
tokenFraction	72	Fraction
tokenIntlCurrency	73	International currency
tokenLeftSingGuillemet	74	Opening single guillemet
tokenRightSingGuillemet	75	Closing single guillemet

Constant	Value	Explanation (continued)
tokenPerThousand	76	Per thousands
tokenEllipsis	77	Ellipsis character
tokenCenterDot	78	Center dot

Selectors for Script Manager Variables

This section lists and describes the selector constants for accessing the Script Manager variables through calls to the GetScriptManagerVariable and SetScriptManagerVariable functions. In every case the variable parameter passed to or from the function is a long integer (4 bytes); the column "Size of variable" indicates how many of the 4 bytes are necessary to hold the input or return value for that variable. If fewer than 4 bytes are needed, the low byte or low word contains the information.

Descriptions of all the variables accessed by these constants follow the list.

Selector constant	Value	Size of variable (bytes)
smVersion	0	2
smMunged	2	2
smEnabled	4	1
smBidirect	6	1
smFontForce	8	1
smIntlForce	10	1
smForced	12	1
smDefault	14	1
smPrint	16	4
smSysScript	18	2
smLastScript	20	2
smKeyScript	22	2
smSysRef	24	2
smKeyCache	26	4
smKeySwap	28	4
smGenFlags	30	4
smOverride	32	4
smCharPortion	34	2
smDoubleByte	36	1
smKCHRCache	38	4
smRegionCode	40	2
smKeyDisableState	42	1

Selector constant	Variable description
smVersion	The Script Manager version number. This variable has the same format as the version number obtained from calling the Gestalt function with the Gestalt selector gestaltScriptMgrVersion. The high-order byte contains the major version number, and the low-order byte contains the minor version number.
smMunged	The modification count for Script Manager variables. At startup, smMunged is initialized to 0, and it is incremented when the KeyScript procedure changes the current keyboard script and updates the variables accessed via smKeyScript and smLastScript. The smMunged selector is also incremented when the SetScriptManagerVariable function is used to change a Script Manager variable. You can check this variable at any time to see whether any of your own data structures that may depend on Script Manager variables need to be updated.
smEnabled	The script count; the number of currently enabled script systems. At startup time, the Script Manager initializes the script count to 0, then increments it for each installed and enabled script system (including Roman). You can use smEnabled to determine whether more than one script system is installed—that is, whether your application needs to handle non-Roman text.

IMPORTANT

Never call SetScriptManagerVariable with the smEnabled selector. It could result in inconsistency with other script system values. ▲

smBidirect	The bidirectional flag, which indicates when at least one bidirectional script system is enabled. This flag is set to TRUE ($FF) if the Arabic or Hebrew script system is enabled.
smFontForce	The font force flag. At startup, the Script Manager sets its value from the system script's international configuration ('itlc') resource. The flag returns 0 for FALSE and $FF for TRUE. If the system script is non-Roman, the font force flag controls whether a font with ID in the Roman script range is interpreted as belonging to the Roman script or to the system script. See "Using the Font Force Flag" on page 6-24.

IMPORTANT

When you call SetScriptManagerVariable with the smFontForce selector, be sure to pass only the value 0 or $FF, or a later call to GetScriptManagerVariable may return an unrecognized value. ▲

smIntlForce	The international resources selection flag. At startup, the Script Manager sets its value from the system script's international configuration ('itlc') resource. The flag returns 0 for FALSE and $FF for TRUE. This flag controls whether international resources of the font script or the system script are used for string manipulation. See "Using the International Resources Selection Flag" on page 6-25.

IMPORTANT

When you call `SetScriptManagerVariable` with the
`smIntlForce` selector, be sure to pass only the value 0 or $FF, or a
later call to `GetScriptManagerVariable` may return an
unrecognized value. ▲

`smForced`   The script-forced result flag. If the current script has been forced to
the system script, this flag is set to TRUE. Use the `smForced`
selector to obtain reports of the actions of the `FontScript`,
`FontToScript`, and `IntlScript` functions. This variable is for
information only; never set its value with
`SetScriptManagerVariable`.

`smDefault`   The script-defaulted result flag. If the script system corresponding
to a specified font is not available, this flag is set to TRUE. Use this
selector to obtain reports of the actions of the `FontScript`,
`FontToScript`, and `IntlScript` functions. This variable is for
information only; never set its value with
`SetScriptManagerVariable`.

`smPrint`   The print action routine vector, set up by the Script Manager at
startup. See *Inside Macintosh: Devices* for information on the print
action routine.

`smSysScript`   The system script code. At startup, the Script Manager initializes
this variable from the system script's international configuration
(`'itlc'`) resource. This variable is for information only; never set
its value with `SetScriptManagerVariable`. Constants for all
defined script codes are listed on page 6-52.

`smLastScript`   The previously used keyboard script. When you change keyboard
scripts with the `KeyScript` procedure, the Script Manager moves
the old value of `smKeyScript` into `smLastScript`. `KeyScript`
can also swap the current keyboard script with the previous
keyboard script, in which case the contents of `smLastScript` and
`smKeyScript` are swapped. Constants for all defined script codes
are listed on page 6-52. Never set the value of this variable with
`SetScriptManagerVariable`.

`smKeyScript`   The current keyboard script. The `KeyScript` procedure tests and
updates this variable. When you change keyboard scripts with the
`KeyScript` procedure, the Script Manager moves the old value of
`smKeyScript` into `smLastScript`. `KeyScript` can also swap the
current keyboard script with the previous keyboard script, in which
case the contents of `smLastScript` and `smKeyScript` are
swapped. The Script Manager also uses this variable to get the
proper keyboard icon and to retrieve the proper keyboard-layout
(`'KCHR'`) resource. Constants for all defined script codes are listed
on page 6-52. Never set the value of this variable directly with
`SetScriptManagerVariable`; call `KeyScript` to change
keyboard scripts.

`smSysRef`   The System Folder volume reference number. Its value is initialized
from the system global variable `BootDrive` at startup.

smKeyCache An obsolete variable. This variable at one time held a pointer to the keyboard cache. The value it provided was not correct and should not be used.

smKeySwap A handle to the keyboard-swap ('KSWP') resource. The Script Manager initializes the handle at startup. The keyboard-swap resource controls the key combinations with which the user can invoke various actions with the KeyScript procedure, such as switching among script systems. This resource is described in the appendix "Keyboard Resources" in this book.

smGenFlags The general flags used by the Script Manager. The Script Manager general flags is a long word value; its high-order byte is set from the flags byte in the system script's international configuration ('itlc') resource. The following constants are available to designate bits in the variable accessed through smGenFlags:

Constant	Value	Explanation
smfNameTagEnab	29	(reserved for internal use)
smfDualCaret	30	Use dual caret for mixed-directional text.
smfShowIcon	31	Show keyboard menu even if only one keyboard layout or one script (Roman) is available. (This bit is checked only at system startup.)

smOverride The script override flags. At present, these flags are not set or used by the Script Manager. They are, however, reserved for future use.

smCharPortion A value used by script systems to allocate intercharacter and interword spacing when justifying text. It denotes the weight allocated to intercharacter space versus interword space. The value of this variable is initialized to 10 percent by the Script Manager, although it currently has no effect on text of the Roman script system. The variable is in 4.12 fixed-point format, which is a 16-bit signed number with 4 bits of integer and 12 bits of fraction. (In that format, 10 percent has the hexadecimal value $0199.)

smDoubleByte The 2-byte flag, a Boolean value that is TRUE if at least one 2-byte script system is enabled.

smKCHRCache A pointer to the cache that stores a copy of the current keyboard-layout ('KCHR') resource. The keyboard-layout resource is described in the appendix "Keyboard Resources" in this book.

smRegionCode The region code for this localized version of system software, obtained from the system script's international configuration ('itlc') resource. This variable identifies the localized version of the system script. Constants for all defined region codes are listed starting on page 6-57.

smKeyDisableState

The current disable state for keyboards. The Script Manager disables some keyboard scripts or keyboard switching when text input must be restricted to certain script systems or when script systems are being moved into or out of the System file.

See "Making Keyboard Settings" beginning on page 6-17. These are the possible values for the variable accessed through `smKeyDisableState`:

Value	Explanation
0	All keyboards are enabled, switching is enabled
1	Keyboard switching is disabled
$FF	Keyboards for all non-Roman secondary scripts are disabled

The script management system maintains the keyboard disable state separately for each application. Never set the value of this variable directly with `SetScriptManagerVariable`; call `KeyScript` to change the keyboard disable state for your application.

Selectors for Script Variables

This section lists and describes the selector constants for accessing script variables through calls to the `GetScriptVariable` and `SetScriptVariable` functions. In every case the variable parameter passed to or from the function is a long integer (4 bytes); the column "Size of variable" indicates how many of the 4 bytes are necessary to hold the input or return value for that variable. If fewer than 4 bytes are needed, the low byte or low word contains the information.

In many cases the value of a script variable is taken from the script system's international bundle (`'itlb'`) resource. See the appendix "International Resources" for a description of the international bundle resource.

Descriptions of all the variables accessed by these constants follow the list.

Selector constant	Value	Size of variable (bytes)
smScriptVersion	0	2
smScriptMunged	2	2
smScriptEnabled	4	1
smScriptRight	6	1
smScriptJust	8	1
smScriptRedraw	10	1
smScriptSysFond	12	2
smScriptAppFond	14	2
smScriptNumber	16	2
smScriptDate	18	2
smScriptSort	20	2
smScriptFlags	22	2

continued

Selector constant	Value	Size of variable (bytes) (continued)
smScriptToken	24	2
smScriptEncoding	26	2
smScriptLang	28	2
smScriptNumDate	30	2
smScriptKeys	32	2
smScriptIcon	34	2
smScriptPrint	36	4
smScriptTrap	38	4
smScriptCreator	40	4
smScriptFile	42	4
smScriptName	44	4
smScriptMonoFondSize	78	4
smScriptPrefFondSize	80	4
smScriptSmallFondSize	82	4
smScriptSysFondSize	84	4
smScriptAppFondSize	86	4
smScriptHelpFondSize	88	4
smScriptValidStyles	90	1
smScriptAliasStyle	92	1

Selector constant	Variable description
smScriptVersion	The script system's version number. When the Script Manager loads the script system, the script system puts its current version number into this variable. The high-order byte contains the major version number, and the low-order byte contains the minor version number.
smScriptMunged	The modification count for this script system's script variables. The Script Manager increments the variable accessed by the smScriptMunged selector each time the SetScriptVariable function is called for this script system. You can check this variable at any time to see whether any of your own data structures that depend on this script system's script variables need to be updated.
smScriptEnabled	The script-enabled flag, a Boolean value that indicates whether the script has been enabled. It is set to $FF when enabled and to 0 when not enabled. Note that this variable is not equivalent to the Script Manager variable accessed by the smEnabled selector, which is a count of the total number of enabled script systems.

smScriptRight   The right-to-left flag, a Boolean value that indicates whether the primary line direction for text in this script is right-to-left or left-to-right. It is set to $FF for right-to-left text (used in Arabic and Hebrew script systems) and to 0 for left-to-right (used in Roman and other script systems).

smScriptJust   The script alignment flag, a byte that specifies the default alignment for text in this script system. It is set to $FF for right alignment (common for Arabic and Hebrew), and it is set to 0 for left alignment (common for Roman and other script systems). This flag usually has the same value as the smScriptRight flag.

smScriptRedraw

The script-redraw flag, a byte that provides redrawing recommendations for text of this script system. It describes how much of a line should be redrawn when a user adds, inserts, or deletes text. It is set to 0 when only a character should be redrawn (used by the Roman script system), to 1 when an entire word should be redrawn (used by the Japanese script system), and to –1 when the entire line should be redrawn (used by the Arabic and Hebrew script systems). The following constants are available for the script-redraw flag:

Constant	Value	Explanation
smRedrawChar	0	Redraw character only
smRedrawWord	1	Redraw entire word
smRedrawLine	–1	Redraw entire line

smScriptSysFond

The preferred system font, the font family ID of the system font preferred for this script. In the Roman script system, this variable specifies Chicago font, whose font family ID is 0 if Roman is the system script. The preferred system font in the Japanese script system is 16384, the font family ID for Osaka.

This variable holds similar information to the variable accessed through the smScriptSysFondSize selector. However, changing the value of this variable has no effect on the value accessed through smScriptSysFondSize.

Note
Remember that in all localized versions of system software the special value of 0 is remapped to the system font ID. Thus, if an application running under Japanese system software specifies a font family ID of 0 in a routine or in the txFont field of the current graphics port, Osaka will be used. However, the variable accessed by smScriptSysFond will still show the true ID for Osaka (16384). ◆

smScriptAppFond

The preferred application font; the font family ID of the application font preferred for this script. In the Roman script system, the value of this variable is the font family ID for Geneva.

This variable holds similar information to the variable accessed through the `smScriptAppFondSize` selector. However, changing the value of this variable has no effect on the value accessed through `smScriptAppFondSize`.

Note

Remember that in all localized versions of system software the special value of 1 is remapped to the application font ID. For example, if an application running under Arabic system software specifies a font family ID of 1 in a routine, Nadeem will be used. However, the variable accessed by `smScriptSysFond` will still show the true ID for Nadeem (17926). ◆

`smScriptNumber`   The resource ID of the script's numeric-format (`'itl0'`) resource. The numeric-format resource includes formatting information for the correct display of numbers, times, and short dates. The value of this variable is initialized from the script system's international bundle resource. See the appendix "International Resources" for a description of the numeric-format resource.

`smScriptDate`   The resource ID of the script's long-date-format (`'itl1'`) resource. The long-date-format resource includes formatting information for the correct display of long dates (dates that include month or day names). The value of this variable is initialized from the script system's international bundle resource. See the appendix "International Resources" for a description of the long-date-format resource.

`smScriptSort`   The resource ID of the script's string-manipulation (`'itl2'`) resource. The string-manipulation resource contains routines for sorting and tables for word selection, line breaks, character types, and case conversion of text. The value of this variable is initialized from the script system's international bundle resource. See the appendix "International Resources" for a description of the string-manipulation resource.

`smScriptFlags`   The script flags word, which contains bit flags specifying attributes of the script. The value of this variable is initialized from the script system's international bundle resource. The following constants are available for examining attributes in the script flags word. Bits above 8 are nonstatic, meaning that they may change during program execution. (Note that the constant values represent bit numbers in the flags word, not masks.)

Constant	Value	Explanation
`smsfIntellCP`	0	Can support intelligent cut and paste (uses spaces as word delimiters)
`smsfSingByte`	1	Has only 1-byte characters
`smsfNatCase`	2	Has both uppercase and lowercase native characters
`smsfContext`	3	Is contextual

Constant	Value	Explanation (continued)
smsfNoForceFont	4	Does not support font forcing (ignores the font force flag)
smsfB0Digits	5	Has alternate digits at $B0–$B9; Arabic and Hebrew, for example, have their native numeric forms at this location in their character sets
smsfAutoInit	6	Is intialized by the Script Manager; 1-byte simple script systems can set this bit to avoid having to initialize themselves
smsfUnivExt	7	Uses the WorldScript I extension
smsfSynchUnstyledTE	8	Synchronizes keyboard with font for monostyled TextEdit
smsfForms	13	Use contextual forms if this bit is set; do not use them if it is cleared
smsfLigatures	14	Use contextual ligatures if this bit is set; do not use them if it is cleared
smsfReverse	15	Reverse right-to-left text to draw it in (left-to-right) display order if this bit is set; do not reorder text if this bit is cleared

The smsfIntellCP flag is set if this script system uses spaces as word delimiters. In such a script system it is possible to implement intelligent cut and paste, in which extra spaces are removed when a word is cut from text, and any needed spaces are added when a word is pasted into text. *Macintosh Human Interface Guidelines* recommends that you implement intelligent cut and paste in script systems that support it.

If you use the CharToPixel function to determine text widths, such as for line breaking, you need to clear the smsfReverse bit first. For more information, see the chapter "QuickDraw Text" in this book.

smScriptToken   The resource ID of the script's tokens ('itl4') resource. The tokens resource contains information for tokenizing and number formatting. The value of this variable is initialized from the script system's international bundle resource. See the appendix "International Resources" in this book for a description of the tokens resource.

smScriptEncoding

The resource ID of the script's (optional) encoding/rendering ('itl5') resource. For 1-byte scripts, the encoding/rendering resource specifies text-rendering behavior; for 2-byte scripts, it specifies character-encoding information. The value of this variable is taken from the script system's international bundle resource. See the appendix "International Resources" for a description of the encoding/rendering resource.

smScriptLang

The language code for this version of the script. A language is a specialized variation of a specific script system. Constants for all defined language codes are listed on page 6-54. The value of this variable is initialized from the script system's international bundle resource.

smScriptNumDate

The numeral code and calendar code for the script. The numeral code specifies the kind of numerals the script uses, and is in the high-order byte of the word; the calendar code specifies the type of calendar it uses and is in the low-order byte of the word. The value of this variable is initialized from the script system's international bundle resource. It may be changed during execution when the user selects, for example, a new calendar from a script system's control panel.

The following numeral-code constants are available for specifying numerals. Note that they are bit numbers, not masks:

Constant	Value	Explanation
intWestern	0	Western numerals
intArabic	1	Native Arabic numerals
intRoman	2	Roman numerals
intJapanese	3	Japanese numerals
intEuropean	4	European numerals
intOutputMask	$8000	Output mask

The following calendar-code constants are available for specifying calendars. Note that they are bit numbers, not masks:

Constant	Value	Explanation
calGregorian	0	Gregorian calendar
calArabicCivil	1	Arabic civil calendar
calArabicLunar	2	Arabic lunar calendar
calJapanese	3	Japanese calendar
calJewish	4	Jewish calendar
calCoptic	5	Coptic calendar
calPersian	6	Persian calendar

smScriptKeys   The resource ID of the script's current keyboard-layout ('KCHR') resource. The keyboard-layout resource is used to map virtual key codes into the correct character codes for the script; it is described in the appendix "Keyboard Resources" in this book. The value of this variable is initialized from the script system's international bundle resource. It is updated when the user selects a new keyboard layout, or when the application calls the KeyScript procedure. You can force a particular keyboard layout to be used with your application by setting the value of this variable and then calling KeyScript.

smScriptIcon   The resource ID of the script's keyboard icon family (resource types 'kcs#', 'kcs4', and 'kcs8'). The keyboard icon family consists of the keyboard icons displayed in the keyboard menu; it is described in the appendix "Keyboard Resources" in this book. The value of this variable is initialized from the script system's international bundle resource. Note that, unlike smScriptKeys, the value of this variable is *not* automatically updated when the keyboard layout changes. (System software assumes that the icon family has an identical ID to the keyboard-layout resource, and usually ignores this variable.)

smScriptPrint   The print action routine vector, set up by the script system (or by the Script Manager if the smsfAutoInit bit is set) when the script is initialized. See *Inside Macintosh: Devices* for information on the print action routine.

smScriptTrap   A pointer to the script's script-record dispatch routine (for internal use only).

smScriptCreator
                The 4-character creator type for the script system's file, that is, the file containing the script system. For the Roman script system, it is 'ZSYS', for WorldScript I it is 'univ', and for World Script II it is 'doub'.

smScriptFile   A pointer to the Pascal string that contains the name of the script system's file, that is, the file containing the script system. For the Roman script system, the string is 'System'.

smScriptName   A pointer to a Pascal string that contains the script system's name. For the Roman script system and 1-byte simple script systems, the string is 'Roman'. For 1-byte complex script systems, this name is taken from the encoding/rendering ('itl5') resource. For 2-byte script systems, it is taken from the WorldScript II extension and is 'WorldScript II'.

smScriptMonoFondSize
                The default font family ID and size (in points) for monospaced text. The ID is stored in the high-order word, and the size is stored in the low-order word. The value of this variable is taken from the script system's international bundle resource. Note that not all script systems have a monospaced font.

Script Manager

`smScriptPrefFondSize`

> Currently not used.

`smScriptSmallFondSize`

> The default font family ID and size (in points) for small text, generally the smallest font and size combination that is legible on screen. The ID is stored in the high-order word, and the size is stored in the low-order word. Sizes are important; for example, a 9-point font may be too small in Chinese. The value of this variable is taken from the script system's international bundle resource.

`smScriptSysFondSize`

> The default font family ID and size (in points) for this script system's preferred system font. The ID is stored in the high-order word, and the size is stored in the low-order word. The value of this variable is taken from the script system's international bundle resource.

> This variable holds similar information to the variable accessed through the `smScriptSysFond` selector. If you neeed font family ID only and don't want size information, it is simpler to use `smScriptSysFond`. Note, however, that changing the value of this variable has no effect on the value accessed through `smScriptSysFond`.

`smScriptAppFondSize`

> The default font family ID and size (in points) for this script system's preferred application font. The ID is stored in the high-order word, and the size is stored in the low-order word. The value of this variable is taken from the script system's international bundle resource.

> This variable holds similar information to the variable accessed through the `smScriptAppFond` selector. If you neeed font family ID only and don't want size information, it is simpler to use `smScriptAppFond`. Note, however, that changing the value of this variable has no effect on the value accessed through `smScriptAppFond`.

`smScriptHelpFondSize`

> The default font family ID and size (in points) for Balloon Help. The ID is stored in the high-order word, and the size is stored in the low-order word. Sizes are important; for example, a 9-point font may be too small in Chinese. The value of this variable is taken from the script system's international bundle resource.

`smScriptValidStyles`

> The set of all valid styles for the script. For example, the Extended style is not valid in the Arabic script. When the `GetScriptVariable` function is called with the `smScriptValidStyles` selector, the low-order byte of the returned value is a style code that includes all of the valid styles for

the script (that is, the bit corresponding to each QuickDraw style is set if that style is valid for the specified script). See Figure 6-7. The value of this variable is taken from the script system's international bundle resource.

Figure 6-7   Style code format

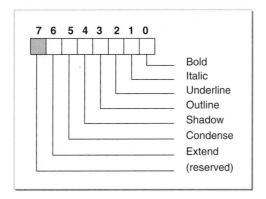

`smScriptAliasStyle`

The style to use for indicating aliases. When the `GetScriptVariable` function is called with `smScriptAliasStyle`, the low-order byte of the returned value is the style code (see Figure 6-7) that should be used in that script for indicating alias names (for example, in the Roman script system, alias names are indicated in italics). The value of this variable is taken from the script system's international bundle resource.

Note
Some script systems, such as Arabic and Hebrew, have private script-system selectors that are unique to those scripts. Those private selectors are negative, whereas selectors that extend across script systems are positive. ◆

Data Structures

This section presents the following types and data structures used by the Script Manager: the token block record and the token record. Other data type definitions are in the section "Summary of the Script Manager" beginning on page 6-107.

The Script Manager also makes use of many of the types and data structures defined in the appendix "International Resources" in this book.

Token Block Record

The token block record, of data type `TokenBlock`, is a parameter block used to pass information to the `IntlTokenize` function and to retrieve results from it.

```
TYPE
   TokenBlock =
   RECORD
       source:          Ptr;              {pointer to source text to be tokenized}
       sourceLength:    LongInt;          {length of source text in bytes}
       tokenList:       Ptr;              {pointer to array of token records}
       tokenLength:     LongInt;          {maximum size of TokenList}
       tokenCount:      LongInt;          {number of tokens currently in TokenList}
       stringList:      Ptr;              {pointer to list of token strings}
       stringLength:    LongInt;          {length available for string list}
       stringCount:     LongInt;          {current length of string list}
       doString:        Boolean;          {make strings & put into StringList?}
       doAppend:        Boolean;          {append to--not replace--TokenList?}
       doAlphanumeric:  Boolean;          {identifiers may include numerics?}
       doNest:          Boolean;          {do comments nest?}
       leftDelims:      ARRAY [0..1] OF TokenType;
                                          {opening delimiters for literals}
       rightDelims:     ARRAY [0..1] OF TokenType;
                                          {closing delimiters for literals}
       leftComment:     ARRAY [0..3] OF TokenType;
                                          {opening delimiters for comments}
       rightComment:    ARRAY [0..3] OF TokenType;
                                          {closing delimiters for comments}
       escapeCode:      TokenType;        {escape symbol code}
       decimalCode:     TokenType;        {decimal symbol code}
       itlResource:     Handle;           {'itl4' resource of script for this text}
       reserved:        ARRAY [0..7] OF LongInt;
                                          {must be zero!}
   END;


   TokenBlockPtr = ^TokenBlock;
```

The fields in the token block record are described under the routine description for `IntlTokenize`, beginning on page 6-92.

Token Record

The token record (data type `TokenRec`) holds the results of the conversion of a sequence of characters to a token by the `IntlTokenize` function. When it analyzes text, `IntlTokenize` generates a token list, which is a sequence of token records.

```
TYPE
   TokenRec =
   RECORD
      theToken:          TokenType;   {numeric code for token}
      position:          Ptr;         {pointer to source text from }
                                      { which token was generated}
      length:            LongInt;     {length of source text from }
                                      { which token was generated}
      stringPosition:    StringPtr;   {pointer to Pascal string }
                                      { generated from token}
   END;
   TokenRecPtr = ^TokenRec;
```

The fields in the token record are described under the routine description for
IntlTokenize, on page 6-95.

Routines

The Script Manager routines documented in this section allow you to

- control the system direction

- access Script Manager variables

- access script variables

- control the keyboard and keyboard script

- determine script codes

- obtain character-type information

- directly access a script system's international resources

- tokenize text

- transliterate text

- replace the default routines for a 1-byte complex script system

Throughout these routine descriptions, unless otherwise noted, the Script Manager
expects that

- there is a buffer containing text characters only; font and style information are stored
  separately

- the storage order of the characters—the order in which character codes are stored in
  memory—is their logical order, the order in which they would most naturally be
  entered from the keyboard

- all offsets within text buffers are zero-based and specified in bytes, not characters

- a valid graphics port exists, and the font of the port is set correctly; all text-related
  fields in the graphics port record reflect the characteristics of the text being
  manipulated

6

Script Manager

Assembly-language note
You can invoke each of the Script Manager routines that uses the `_ScriptUtil` trap with a macro that has the same name as the routine, preceded by an underscore. See "Summary of the Script Manager" at the end of this chapter for a list of the routines that use the `_ScriptUtil` trap. ◆

Checking and Setting the System Direction

The `GetSysDirection` routine returns the value of `SysDirection`, the global variable that represents the system direction. A value of 0 for `SysDirection` means that the primary line direction is left-to-right; a value of –1 means that the primary line direction is right-to-left. The value of `SysDirection` is initialized from the system's international configuration resource, and may be controlled by the user. Your application can use the `SetSysDirection` procedure to change `SysDirection` while drawing, but should restore it when appropriate (such as when your application becomes inactive).

GetSysDirection

The `GetSysDirection` function returns the current value of `SysDirection`, the global variable that determines the system direction (primary line direction).

```
FUNCTION GetSysDirection: Integer;
```

DESCRIPTION

There are two possible return values from `GetSysDirection`:

0 = left-to-right line direction

–1 = $FFFF = right-to-left line direction

SetSysDirection

The `SetSysDirection` procedure sets the value of `SysDirection`, the global variable that determines the system direction (primary line direction).

```
PROCEDURE SetSysDirection (newDirection: Integer);
```

newDirection
　　　　The desired value for `SysDirection`.

DESCRIPTION

There are two valid input values for `newDirection`:

  0 = left-to-right line direction

 –1 = $FFFF = right-to-left line direction

Checking and Setting Script Manager Variables

The Script Manager maintains a set of variables that control general settings of the text environment, including the identity of the system script and the keyboard script, and the settings of the font force flag and the international resources selection flag.

You may want access to the Script Manager variables in order to understand the current environment or to modify it. The `GetScriptManagerVariable` function retrieves the values of the Script Manager variables, and the `SetScriptManagerVariable` function sets their values. (The variables themselves are private and you cannot access them directly.) When you call either routine, you use a selector to describe the variable that interests you. The integer constants for all defined `GetScriptManagerVariable`/`SetScriptManagerVariable` selectors are described beginning on page 6-61.

GetScriptManagerVariable

The `GetScriptManagerVariable` function retrieves the value of the specified Script Manager variable.

```
FUNCTION GetScriptManagerVariable (selector: Integer): LongInt;
```

selector   A value that specifies a particular Script Manager variable.

DESCRIPTION

Although `GetScriptManagerVariable` always returns a long integer, the actual value may be a long integer, standard integer, or signed byte. If the value is not a long integer, it is stored in the low-order word or byte of the long integer returned by `GetScriptManagerVariable`; the remaining bytes are set to 0.

The `GetScriptManagerVariable` function returns 0 if the selector is invalid.

Note

For some valid selectors, 0 may also be a valid return value. For example, when you call `GetScriptManagerVariable` with a selector value of `smRegionCode` on a version of Macintosh system software that has been localized for the United States, it returns 0. ◆

To specify the Script Manager variable whose value you need, use one of the selector constants listed on page 6-61.

SetScriptManagerVariable

The `SetScriptManagerVariable` function sets the specified Script Manager variable to the value of the input parameter.

```
FUNCTION SetScriptManagerVariable (selector: Integer;
                                   param: LongInt): OSErr;
```

selector   A value that specifies a particular Script Manager variable.

param   The new value for the specified Script Manager variable.

DESCRIPTION

The actual values to be assigned may be long integers, standard integers, or signed bytes. If the value is other than a long integer, you must store it in the low-order word or byte of the `param` parameter and set the unused bytes to 0.

The `SetScriptManagerVariable` function returns the value `smBadVerb` if the selector is not valid. Otherwise, it returns 0 (`noErr`).

To specify the Script Manager variable whose value you wish to change, use one of the selector constants listed on page 6-61.

RESULT CODES

noErr	0	No error
smBadVerb	−1	Invalid selector passed to the routine

Checking and Setting Script Variables

Each enabled script system maintains a set of variables that control the current settings of that script system, including the ID numbers of its international resources, its preferred fonts and font sizes, and its primary line direction.

You may want access to the script variables in order to conform to the script's current settings or to modify them. The `GetScriptVariable` function retrieves the values of the script variables, and the `SetScriptVariable` function sets their values. (The variables themselves are private and you cannot access them directly.) When you call either routine, you use a selector to describe the variable that interests you. The integer constants for all defined `GetScriptVariable`/`SetScriptVariable` selectors are described on page 6-65.

GetScriptVariable

The `GetScriptVariable` function retrieves the value of the specified script variable from the specified script system.

```
FUNCTION GetScriptVariable (script: ScriptCode;
                            selector: Integer): LongInt;
```

script   A value that specifies the script system whose variable you are accessing.

selector   A value that specifies a particular script variable.

DESCRIPTION

Although `GetScriptVariable` always returns a long integer, the actual value may be a long integer, standard integer, or signed byte. If the value is not a long integer, it is stored in the low-order word or byte of the long integer returned by `GetScriptVariable`; the remaining bytes are set to 0.

Valid selector values are defined by each script system. `GetScriptVariable` returns 0 if the selector value is invalid or if the specified script system is not installed.

Note

For some valid selectors, 0 may also be a valid return value.
For example, calling `GetScriptVariable` with a selector of
`smScriptLang` on a version of Macintosh system software that has
been localized for the United States returns 0. ◆

To specify the script variable whose value you need, use one of the selector constants listed on page 6-65. To specify the script system, use one of the script-code constants listed on page 6-52.

SetScriptVariable

The `SetScriptVariable` function sets the specified script variable for the specifed script system to the value of the input parameter.

```
FUNCTION SetScriptVariable (script: ScriptCode; selector: Integer;
                            param: LongInt): OSErr;
```

script   A value that specifies the script system whose variable you are setting.

selector   A value that specifies a particular script variable.

param   The new value for the specified script variable.

DESCRIPTION

The actual values to be assigned may be long integers, standard integers, or signed bytes. If the value is not a long integer, you must store it in the low-order word or byte of the `param` parameter and set the unused bytes to 0.

The `SetScriptVariable` function returns the value `smBadVerb` if the selector is not valid, and `smBadScript` if the script is invalid. Otherwise, it returns 0 (`noErr`).

To specify the script variable whose value you wish to change, use one of the selector constants listed on page 6-65. To specify the script system, use one of the script-code constants listed on page 6-52.

RESULT CODES

`noErr`	0	No error
`smBadVerb`	–1	Invalid selector passed to the routine
`smBadScript`	–2	Invalid script code passed to the routine

Making Keyboard Settings

The Script Manager provides the `KeyScript` procedure to let you specify the current keyboard script (the script system used for keyboard input), keyboard layout (the mapping of keys to characters), or input method (a facility for entering 2-byte characters), and to make various settings related to text input.

For the purposes of `KeyScript`, *keyboard layout* means a keyboard-layout (`'KCHR'`) resource, plus optionally a key-remap (`'itlk'`) resource. To change keyboard layouts means to change the current keyboard-layout resource.

KeyScript

The `KeyScript` procedure uses the supplied value to change the keyboard script, to change the keyboard layout or input method within the current keyboard script, or to make a setting related to text input. If the Keyboard menu is displayed, `KeyScript` also updates the Keyboard menu.

```
PROCEDURE KeyScript (code: Integer);
```

code   If 0 or positive, directly specifies a script system (that is, it is read as a script code). Negative values have special meanings.

DESCRIPTION

The `Keyscript` procedure makes the change based on the selector with which it is called. If more than one script system is enabled or if the `smfShowIcon` bit flag is set in the Script Manager variable accessed by the `GetScriptManagerVariable` selector `smGenFlags`, `Keyscript` also updates the Keyboard menu by changing the icon displayed on the menu bar and placing a check beside the appropriate keyboard menu item.

The `code` parameter is a selector that can *explicitly* specify a keyboard script by script code. Script code constants are listed on page 6-52. If the selector specifies a script, then the current default keyboard layout (`'KCHR'` resource) for that script, as specified in the script's international bundle resource, becomes the current keyboard layout.

The selector can also *implicitly* specify a keyboard script (for example, the next script), a keyboard layout (for example, the previously used keyboard layout in the current script), or an input method (for example, inline input versus window-based input). It can also specify settings that enable or disable keyboard layouts and keyboard scripts, and toggle among input options or line direction. The valid constants for the `code` parameter are listed in Table 6-5 on page 6-18.

If you call `KeyScript` and explicitly specify a script system that is not available, `KeyScript` does nothing. The current keyboard script remains unchanged.

SPECIAL CONSIDERATIONS

`KeyScript` operates only on those keyboard-layout and key-remap resources that are present in the System file.

Your application's keyboard-menu setting is not maintained by the Process Manager; if the state of the keyboard menu is changed while you are switched out, the Process Manager does not restore your setting when you are switched back in. However, the Process Manager does maintain the keyboard disable state (Script Manager variable `smKeyDisableState`) for your application. See "Selectors for Script Manager Variables" beginning on page 6-61 for a description of the `smKeyDisableState` variable.

`KeyScript` may move memory; your application should not call this procedure at interrupt time.

SEE ALSO

The Process Manager is described in *Inside Macintosh: Processes.*

Determining Script Codes From Font Information

The `FontScript`, `FontToScript`, and `IntlScript` functions give you ways to determine a script code from font information. This information is subject to two control flags—the font force flag and the international resources selection flag. You can test and set these flags with the `GetScriptManagerVariable` and `SetScriptManagerVariable` selectors `smFontForce` and `smIntlForce`. For more information on the font force flag, see "Using the Font Force Flag" on page 6-24. For more information on the international resources selection flag, see "Using the International Resources Selection Flag" on page 6-25.

The routines start by initializing two result flags, the script-forced result flag and the script-defaulted result flag, to FALSE. These flags are Script Manager variables, accessed through the GetScriptManagerVariable function selectors smForced and smDefault.

FontScript

The FontScript function returns the script code for the current script. The current script is usually the font script.

```
FUNCTION FontScript: Integer;
```

DESCRIPTION

The FontScript function returns a script code. All recognized script codes and their defined constants are listed on page 6-52. FontScript returns only explicit script codes (≥ 0).

If the font of the active graphics port is Roman and the font force flag is TRUE, the script code returned is that of the system script and the script-forced result flag is set to TRUE.

If the font of the active graphics port is non-Roman, the state of the font force flag is ignored.

If the script system corresponding to the font of the active graphics port is not installed and enabled, the script code returned is that of the system script and the script-defaulted result flag is set to TRUE.

SPECIAL CONSIDERATIONS

FontScript may move memory; your application should not call this function at interrupt time.

FontToScript

The FontToScript function translates a font family ID number into its corresponding script code, if that script system is currently enabled.

```
FUNCTION FontToScript (fontNumber: Integer): Integer;
```

fontNumber
        A font family ID number.

DESCRIPTION

The `FontToScript` function returns a script code. All recognized script codes and their defined constants are listed on page 6-52. `FontToScript` returns only explicit script codes (≥ 0).

If `fontNumber` is in the Roman range and the font force flag is `TRUE`, the script code returned is that of the system script and the script-forced result flag is set to `TRUE`.

If `fontNumber` is in the non-Roman range, the state of the font force flag is ignored.

If the script system corresponding to `fontNumber` is not enabled, the script code returned is that of the system script and the script-defaulted result flag is set to `TRUE`.

SPECIAL CONSIDERATIONS

`FontToScript` may move memory; your application should not call this function at interrupt time.

IntlScript

The `IntlScript` function identifies the script system used by the Text Utilities date-formatting, time-formatting, and string-sorting routines. It also identifies the script system whose resources are returned by the Script Manager function `GetIntlResource`. It is either the font script—the script system corresponding to the current font of the active graphics port—or the system script.

```
FUNCTION IntlScript: Integer;
```

DESCRIPTION

The `IntlScript` function returns a script code. All recognized script codes and their defined constants are listed on page 6-52. `IntlScript` returns only explicit script codes (≥ 0).

If the international resources selection flag is `TRUE`, the script code returned is that of the system script.

If the identified script system is not enabled, the script code returned is that of the system script and the script-defaulted result flag is set to `TRUE`.

SPECIAL CONSIDERATIONS

`IntlScript` may move memory; your application should not call this function at interrupt time.

Analyzing Characters

This section describes the functions `CharacterByteType`, `CharacterType`, and `FillParseTable`, which give you information about a character or group of characters, specified by character code:

■ The `CharacterByteType` function identifies a byte in a text buffer as a 1-byte character or as the first or second byte of a 2-byte character.

■ The `CharacterType` function returns specific information about the character at a particular byte offset.

■ The `FillParseTable` function fills a 256-byte table that indicates, for each possible byte value, whether it is the first byte of a 2-byte character.

The script system associated with the character you wish to examine must be enabled in order for any of these three routines to provide useful information. For example, if only the Roman script system is available and you attempt to identify a byte in a run of 2-byte characters, the `CharacterByteType` function returns 0, indicating that the byte is a 1-byte character.

1-byte script systems

For 1-byte script systems, the character-type tables reside in the string-manipulation (`'itl2'`) resource and reflect region-specific or language-specific differences in uppercase conventions. The `CharacterType` function gets the tables from the string-manipulation resource using the `GetIntlResource` function. ◆

2-byte script systems

For 2-byte script systems, the character-type tables reside in the encoding/rendering (`'itl5'`) resource, not the string-manipulation resource. Whenever you call `CharacterByteType`, `CharacterType`, or `FillParseTable`, the necessary character-set encoding information is taken from the encoding/rendering resource. You cannot use the `GetIntlResource` function to access 2-byte character-type tables directly. ◆

CharacterByteType

The `CharacterByteType` function identifies a byte in a text buffer as a 1-byte character or as the first or second byte of a 2-byte character.

```
FUNCTION CharacterByteType (textBuf: Ptr; textOffset: Integer;
                                script: ScriptCode): Integer;
```

textBuf   A pointer to a text buffer containing the byte to be identified.

textOffset
            The offset to the byte to be identified. Offset is measured in bytes; the first byte has an offset of 0.

script   A value that specifies the script system of the text in the buffer. Constants
                for all defined script codes are listed on page 6-52. To specify the font
                script, pass `smCurrentScript` in this parameter.

DESCRIPTION

`CharacterByteType` returns one of three identifications: a 1-byte character, the first
byte of a 2-byte character, or the second byte of a 2-byte character. The first byte of a
2-byte character—the one at the lower offset in memory—is the high-order byte; the
second byte of a 2-byte character—the one at the higher offset—is the low-order byte.
This is the same order in which text is processed and numbers are represented.

From byte value alone, it is not possible to distinguish the second byte of a 2-byte
character from a 1-byte character. See the discussion of character encoding in the chapter
"Introduction to Text on the Macintosh" in this book. `CharacterByteType`
differentiates the second byte of a 2-byte character from a 1-byte character by assuming
that the byte at offset 0 is the first byte of a character. With that assumption, it then
sequentially identifies the size and starting position of each character in the buffer up to
`textOffset`.

SPECIAL CONSIDERATIONS

If you specify `smCurrentScript` for the `script` parameter, the value returned by
`CharacterByteType` can be affected by the state of the font force flag. It is unaffected
by the state of the international resources selection flag.

RESULT CODES

smFirstByte	–1	First byte of a 2-byte character
smSingleByte	0	1-byte character
smLastByte	1	Second byte of 2-byte character

CharacterType

The `CharacterType` function returns a variety of information about the character
represented by a given byte, including its type, class, orientation, direction, case, and size
(in bytes).

```
FUNCTION CharacterType (textBuf: Ptr; textOffset: Integer;
                        script: ScriptCode): Integer;
```

textBuf   A pointer to a text buffer containing the character to be examined.

textOffset
                The offset to the location of the character to be examined. (It can be an
                offset to either the first or the second byte of a 2-byte character.) Offset is
                in bytes; the first byte of the first character has an offset of 0.

script   A value that specifies the script system the byte belongs to. Constants for
                all defined script codes are listed on page 6-52. To specify the font script,
                pass smCurrentScript in this parameter.

DESCRIPTION

The CharacterType return value is an integer bit field that provides information about
the requested character. The field has the following format:

Bit range	Name	Explanation
0–3	Type	Character types
4–7		(reserved)
8–11	Class	Character classes (= subtypes)
12	Orientation	Horizontal or vertical
13	Direction	Left or right*
14	Case	Uppercase or lowercase
15	Size	1-byte or 2-byte

* In 2-byte script systems, bit 13 indicates whether or not the character is part of the main
  character set (not a user-defined character).

The Script Manager defines the recognized character types, character classes, and
character modifiers (bits 12–15), with constants to describe them. All of the constants are
listed and described in the section "Getting Character-Type Information" beginning on
page 6-28.

The Script Manager also defines a set of masks with which you can isolate each of the
fields in the CharacterType return value. If you perform an AND operation with the
CharacterType result and the mask for a particular field, you select only the bits in
that field. Once you've done that, you can test the result, using the constants that
represent the possible results.

The CharacterType field masks are the following:

Mask	Hex. value	Explanation
smcTypeMask	$000F	Character-type mask
smcReserved	$00F0	(reserved)
smcClassMask	$0F00	Character-class mask
smcOrientationMask	$1000	Character orientation (2-byte scripts)
smcRightMask	$2000	Writing direction (bidirectional scripts) Main character set or subset (2-byte scripts)
smcUpperMask	$4000	Uppercase or lowercase
smcDoubleMask	$8000	Size (1 or 2 bytes)

The character type of the character in question is the result of performing an AND
operation with smcTypeMask and the CharacterType result. Constants for the
defined character types are listed on page 6-28.

The character class of the character in question is the result of performing an AND operation with smcClassMask and the CharacterType result. Character classes can be considered as subtypes of character types. Constants for the defined character classes are listed on page 6-29.

The orientation of the character in question is the result of performing an AND operation with smcOrientationMask and the CharacterType result. The orientation value can be either smCharHorizontal or smCharVertical.

The direction of the character in question is the result of performing an AND operation with smcRightMask and the CharacterType result. The direction value can be either smCharLeft (left-to-right) or smCharRight (right-to-left).

The case of the character in question is the result of performing an AND operation with smcUpperMask and the CharacterType result. The case value can be either smCharLower or smCharUpper.

The size of the character in question is the result of performing an AND operation with smcDoubleMask and the CharacterType result. The size value can be either smChar1byte or smChar2byte.

Note

CharacterType calls CharacterByteType to determine whether the byte at textOffset is a 1-byte character or the first byte or second byte of a 2-byte character. The larger the text buffer, the longer CharacterByteType takes to execute. To be most efficient, place the pointer textBuf at the beginning of the character of interest before calling CharacterType. (If you want to be compatible with older versions of CharacterType, also set textOffset to 1, rather than 0, for 2-byte characters.) ◆

SPECIAL CONSIDERATIONS

CharacterType may move memory; your application should not call this function at interrupt time.

If you specify smCurrentScript for the script parameter, CharacterType always assumes that the text in the buffer belongs to the font script. It is unaffected by the state of the font force flag or the international resources selection flag.

For 1-byte script systems, the character-type tables are in the string-manipulation ('itl2') resource. For 2-byte script systems, they are in the encoding/rendering ('itl5') resource. If the appropriate resource does not include these tables, CharacterType exits without doing anything.

Some Roman fonts (for example, Symbol) substitute other characters for the standard characters in the Standard Roman character set. Since the Roman script system CharacterType function assumes the Standard Roman character set, it may return inappropriate results for nonstandard characters.

In versions of system software earlier than 7.0, the textOffset parameter to the CharacterType function must point to the second byte of a 2-byte character.

RESULT CODES

The complete set of `CharacterType` return values is found in the section "Getting Character-Type Information" beginning on page 6-28.

FillParseTable

The `FillParseTable` function helps your application to quickly process a buffer of mixed 1-byte and 2-byte characters. It returns a 256-byte table that distinguishes the character codes of all possible 1-byte characters from the first (high-order) byte values of all possible 2-byte characters in the specified script system.

```
FUNCTION FillParseTable (VAR table: CharByteTable;
                              script: ScriptCode): Boolean;
```

table   A 256-byte table to be filled in by `FillParseTable`.

script   A value that specifies the script system the parse table belongs to. Constants for all defined script codes are listed on page 6-52. To specify the font script, pass `smCurrentScript` in this parameter.

DESCRIPTION

Before calling `FillParseTable`, allocate space for a 256-byte table to pass to the function in the `table` parameter.

The information returned by `FillParseTable` is a packed array defined by the `CharByteTable` data type as follows:

```
CharByteTable = PACKED ARRAY[0..255] OF SignedByte;
```

In every script system, 2-byte characters have distinctive high-order (first) bytes that allow them to be distinguished from 1-byte characters. `FillParseTable` fills a 256-byte table, conceptually equivalent to a 1-byte character-set table, with values that indicate, byte-for-byte, whether the character-code value represented by that byte index is the first byte of a 2-byte character. An entry in the `CharByteTable` is 0 for a 1-byte character and 1 for the first byte of a 2-byte character.

If your application is processing mixed characters, it can use the table to identify the locations of the 2-byte characters as it makes a single pass through the text, rather than having to call `CharacterByteType` or `CharacterType` for each byte of the text buffer in turn. `CharacterByteType` and `CharacterType` start anew at the beginning of the text buffer each time they are called, tracking character positions up to the offset of the byte to be analyzed.

`FillParseTable` may move memory; your application should not call this function at interrupt time.

The table defined by `CharByteTable` is not dynamic; it does not get updated when the current font changes. You need to call it separately for each script run in your text.

The return value from `FillParseTable` is always `TRUE`.

If you specify `smCurrentScript` for the `script` parameter, the value returned by `FillParseTable` can be affected by the state of the font force flag. It is unaffected by the international resources selection flag.

Directly Accessing International Resources

You can access the International resources (resource types `'itl0'`, `'itl1'`, `'itl2'`, `'itl4'`, and `'itl5'`) with the `GetIntlResource` function. You can access specific tables within an international resource with the `GetIntlResourceTable` procedure. If your application provides its own `'itl2'` or `'itl4'` resources, it should call the `ClearIntlResourceCache` procedure before accessing those resources.

ClearIntlResourceCache

The `ClearIntlResourceCache` procedure clears the application's international resources cache, which contains the resource ID numbers of the string-manipulation (`'itl2'`) and tokens (`'itl4'`) resources for the current script.

```
PROCEDURE ClearIntlResourceCache;
```

At application launch, the script management system sets up an international resources cache for the application. The cache contains the resource ID numbers of the string-manipulation and tokens resources for all enabled scripts.

If you provide your own string manipulation or tokens resource to replace the default for a particular script, call `ClearIntlResourceCache` at launch to ensure that your supplied resource is used instead of the script system's `'itl2'` or `'itl4'` resource.

The current default ID numbers for a script system's `'itl2'` and `'itl4'` resources are stored in its script variables. You can read and modify these values with the `GetScriptVariable` and `SetScriptVariable` functions using the selectors `smScriptSort` (for the `'itl2'` resource) and `smScriptToken` (for the `'itl4'` resource). Before calling `ClearIntlResourceCache`, you should set the script's default ID number to the ID of the resource that you are supplying.

6

Script Manager

If the international resources selection flag is TRUE, the ID numbers of your supplied resources must be in the system script range. Otherwise, the IDs must be in the range of the current script.

IMPORTANT

If you use the SetScriptVariable function to change the value of the 'itl2' or 'itl4' resource ID and then call ClearIntlResourceCache to flush the cache, be sure to restore the original resource ID before your application quits. ▲

SPECIAL CONSIDERATIONS

ClearIntlResourceCache may move memory; your application should not call this procedure at interrupt time.

GetIntlResource

The GetIntlResource function returns a handle to one of the following international resources: numeric-format ('itl0'), long-date-format ('itl1'), string-manipulation ('itl2'), tokens ('itl4'), or encoding/rendering ('itl5'). GetIntlResource selects the resource of the requested type for the current script.

```
FUNCTION GetIntlResource (theID: Integer) :Handle;
```

theID   Contains an integer (0, 1, 2, 4, or 5 respectively for the 'itl0', 'itl1', 'itl2', 'itl4', and 'itl5' resources) to identify the type of the desired international resource.

DESCRIPTION

The GetIntlResource function returns a handle to the correct resource of the requested type. The resource returned is that of the current script, which is either the font script or the system script. See "Determining Script Codes From Font Information" on page 6-21.

If GetIntlResource cannot return the requested resource, it returns a NIL handle and sets the global variable resErr to the appropriate error code.

SPECIAL CONSIDERATIONS

GetIntlResource may move memory; your application should not call this function at interrupt time.

SEE ALSO

See the Resource Manager chapter in *Inside Macintosh: More Macintosh Toolbox* for information on `resErr` and how to get its value.

GetIntlResourceTable

The `GetIntlResourceTable` procedure gives you access to a specific word-selection, line-break, number-parts, untoken, or whitespace table from the appropriate international resource.

```
PROCEDURE GetIntlResourceTable (script: ScriptCode;
                                tableCode: Integer;
                                VAR itlHandle: Handle;
                                VAR offset: LongInt;
                                VAR length: LongInt);
```

script   A script code, the value that specifies a particular script system. Constants for all defined script codes are listed on page 6-52.

tableCode   A number that specifies which table is requested.

itlHandle   Upon completion of the call, contains a handle to the string-manipulation (`'itl2'`) or tokens (`'itl4'`) resource containing the table specified in the `tableCode` parameter.

offset   Upon completion of the call, contains the offset (in bytes) to the specified table from the beginning of the resource.

length   Upon completion of the call, contains the size of the table (in bytes).

DESCRIPTION

When you provide a script code in the `script` parameter, and a table code in the `tableCode` parameter, `GetIntlResourceTable` returns a handle to the string-manipulation resource or tokens resource containing that table, the offset of the specified table from the beginning of the resource, and the length of the table.

If the script system whose table is requested is not available, `GetIntlResourceTable` returns a `NIL` handle.

Constants for all defined script codes are listed on page 6-52.

Script Manager

These are the defined constants for `tableCode`:

Constant	Value	Explanation
smWordSelectTable	0	Word-break table
smWordWrapTable	1	Line-break table
smNumberPartsTable	2	Number-parts table
smUnTokenTable	3	Untoken table
smWhiteSpaceList	4	Whitespace table

If you wish to manipulate the contents of the table you have requested, use the size returned in the `length` parameter to allocate a buffer, and perform a block move of the table's contents into that buffer.

SPECIAL CONSIDERATIONS

`GetIntlResourceTable` may move memory; your application should not call this procedure at interrupt time.

SEE ALSO

Block moves are described in the Memory Manager chapter of *Inside Macintosh: Memory.*

Tokenization

The Script Manager provides a way to take programming-language text in an arbitrary script system and break it into tokens: language-independent symbols that can be used as input to a parser. The `IntlTokenize` function uses information in a script system's tokens (`'itl4'`) resource to convert text to tokens that stand for names, symbols, comments, and quoted literals.

IntlTokenize

The `IntlTokenize` function allows your application to convert text into a sequence of language-independent tokens. It returns a list of tokens that correspond to the text that you pass it.

```
FUNCTION IntlTokenize (tokenParam: TokenBlockPtr): TokenResults;
```

tokenParam
> A pointer to a token block record. The record specifies the text to be converted to tokens, the destination of the token list, a handle to the tokens (`'itl4'`) resource, and a set of options.

The token block record is a parameter block and a data structure of type `TokenBlock`, described on page 6-74. You specify input values and receive return values in as shown here:

Parameter block

→	source	Ptr	A pointer to the beginning of the source text (not a Pascal string) to be converted.
→	sourceLength	LongInt	The number of bytes in the source text.
↔	tokenList	Ptr	A pointer to a buffer you have allocated, into which the `IntlTokenize` function places the list of token records it generates.
→	tokenLength	LongInt	The maximum size of token list (in number of tokens, not bytes) that will fit into the buffer pointed to by the `tokenList` field.
↔	tokenCount	LongInt	On input: If doAppend = TRUE, must contain the correct number of tokens currently in the token list. (Ignored if doAppend = FALSE.) On output: The number of tokens currently in the token list.
↔	stringList	Ptr	If doString = TRUE, must contain a pointer to a buffer into which `IntlTokenize` can place a list of strings it generates. (Ignored if doString = FALSE.)
→	stringLength	LongInt	If doString = TRUE, must contain the size in bytes of the string list buffer pointed to by the `stringList` field. (Ignored if doString = FALSE.)
↔	stringCount	LongInt	On input: If doString = TRUE and doAppend = TRUE, must contain the correct current size in bytes of the string list. (Ignored if doString = FALSE or doAppend = FALSE.) On output: The current size in bytes of the string list. (Indeterminate if doString = FALSE.)
→	doString	Boolean	If TRUE, instructs `IntlTokenize` to create a Pascal string representing the contents of each token it generates. If FALSE, `IntlTokenize` generates a token list without an associated string list.
→	doAppend	Boolean	If TRUE, instructs `IntlTokenize` to append tokens and strings it generates to the current token list and string list. If FALSE, `IntlTokenize` writes over any previous contents of the buffer pointed to by `tokenList` and `stringList`.

6

Script Manager

→	doAlphanumeric	Boolean	If TRUE, instructs IntlTokenize to interpret numeric characters as alphabetic when mixed with alphabetic characters. If FALSE, all numeric characters are interpreted as numbers.
→	doNest	Boolean	If TRUE, instructs IntlTokenize to allow nested comments (to any depth of nesting). If FALSE, comment delimiters may not be nested within other comment delimiters.
→	leftDelims	DelimType	An array of two integers, each of which contains the token code of the symbol that may be used as an opening delimiter for a quoted literal. If only one opening delimiter is needed, the other must be specified to be delimPad.
→	rightDelims	DelimType	An array of two integers, each of which contains the token code of the symbol that may be used as the matching closing delimiter for the corresponding opening delimiter in the leftDelims field.
→	leftComment	CommentType	An array of two pairs of integers, each pair of which contains codes for the two token types that may be used as opening delimiters for comments.
→	rightComment	CommentType	An array of two pairs of integers, each pair of which contains codes for the two token types that may be used as closing delimiters for comments.
→	escapeCode	TokenType	A single integer that contains the token code for the symbol that may be an escape character within a quoted literal.
→	decimalCode	TokenType	A single integer that contains the token type of the symbol to be used for a decimal point.
→	itlResource	Handle	A handle to the tokens ('itl4') resource of the script system under which the source text was created.
→	reserved	ARRAY [0..7] OF LongInt	Must be set to 0.

DESCRIPTION

The IntlTokenize function returns a list of tokens that correspond to the input text. The token list is an array of token records (type TokenRec). Each token record describes the token generated, specifies the part of the source text it came from, and optionally provides a character string that is a normalized version of the text that generated the token.

IntlTokenize also returns a result code that specifies the type of error that occurred, if any.

Before calling the IntlTokenize function, allocate memory for and set up the following data structures:

- A token block record (data type TokenBlock). The token block record is a parameter block that holds both input and output parameters for the IntlTokenize function.

- A token list to hold the results of the tokenizing operation. To set up the token list, estimate how many tokens will be generated from your text, multiply that by the size of a token record, and allocate a memory block of that size in bytes. An upper limit to the possible number of tokens is the number of characters in the source text.

- A string list, if you want the IntlTokenize function to generate character strings for all the tokens. To set up the string list, multiply the estimated number of tokens by the expected average size of a string, and allocate a memory block of that size in bytes. An upper limit is twice the number of tokens plus the number of bytes in the source text.

IntlTokenize creates tokens based on information in the tokens ('itl4') resource of the script system under which the source text was created. You must load the tokens resource and place its handle in the token block record before calling the IntlTokenize function.

The token block record contains both input and output values. At input, you must provide values for the fields that specify the source text location, the token list location, the size of the token list, the tokens ('itl4') resource to use, and several options that affect the operation. You must set reserved locations to 0 before calling IntlTokenize.

On output, the token block record specifies how many tokens have been generated and the size of the string list (if you have selected the option to generate strings).

The results of the tokenizing operation are contained in the token list, an array of token records. A token record (data type TokenRec) consists of a token code, a pointer to a location in the source text, the length of a character sequence in the source text, and an optional pointer to a Pascal string:

```
TYPE
   TokenRec =
   RECORD
      theToken:        TokenType;   {numeric code for token}
      position:        Ptr;         {pointer to source text from }
                                    { which token was generated}
      length:          LongInt;     {length of source text from }
                                    { which token was generated}
      stringPosition:  StringPtr;   {pointer to Pascal string }
                                    { generated from token}
   END;
   TokenRecPtr = ^TokenRec;
```

6

Script Manager

Field descriptions

theToken	The token code that specifies the type of token (such as whitespace, opening parenthesis, alphabetic or numeric sequence) described by this token record. Constants for all defined token codes are listed on page 6-58.
position	A pointer to the first character in the source text that caused this particular token to be generated.
length	The length in bytes of the source text that caused this particular token to be generated.
stringPosition	If doString = TRUE, a pointer to a null-terminated Pascal string, padded if necessary so that its total number of bytes (length byte + text + null byte + padding) is even. If doString = FALSE, this field is NIL.

Note

The value in the length byte of the null-terminated Pascal string does not include either the terminating zero byte or the possible additional padding byte. There may be as many as two additional bytes beyond the specified length. ◆

Pascal strings are generated if the doString parameter in the token block record is set to TRUE. The string is a normalized version of the source text that generated the token; alternate digits are replaced with ASCII numerals, the decimal point is always an ASCII period, and 2-byte Roman letters are replaced with low-ASCII equivalents.

To make a series of calls to IntlTokenize and append the results of each call to the results of previous calls, set doAppend to FALSE and initialize tokenCount and stringCount to 0 before making the first call to IntlTokenize. (You can ignore stringCount if you set doString to FALSE.) Upon completion of the call, tokenCount and stringCount will contain the number of tokens and the length in bytes of the string list, respectively, generated by the call. On subsequent calls, set doAppend to TRUE, reset the source and sourceLength parameters (and any other parameters as appropriate) for the new source text, but maintain the output values for tokenCount and stringCount from each call as input values to the next call. At the end of your sequence of calls, the token list and string list will contain, in order, all the tokens and strings generated from the calls to IntlTokenize.

If you are making tokens from text that was created under more than one script system, you must load the proper tokens resource and place its handle in the token block record separately for each script run in the text, appending the results each time.

Delimiters for quoted literals are passed to IntlTokenize in a two-integer array:

```
TYPE DelimType = ARRAY[0..1] OF TokenType;
```

The individual delimiters, as specified in the leftDelims and rightDelims parameters, are paired by position. The first (in storage order) opening delimiter in leftDelims is paired with the first closing delimiter in rightDelims.

Comment delimiters may be 1 or 2 tokens each and there may be two sets of opening and closing pairs. They are passed to `IntlTokenize` in a `commentType` array:

```
TYPE CommentType = ARRAY[0..3] OF TokenType;
```

If only one token is needed for a delimiter, the second token must be specified to be `delimPad`. If only one delimiter of an opening-closing pair is needed, then both of the tokens allocated for the other symbol must be `delimPad`. The first token of a two-token sequence is at the higher position in the `leftComment` or `rightComment` array. For example, if the two opening (in this case, left) delimiters were "(*" and "{", they would be specified as follows:

```
leftComment[0] := tokenAsterisk;      (*asterisk*)
leftComment[1] := tokenLeftParen;     (*left parenthesis*)
leftComment[2] := delimPad ;          (*nothing*)
leftComment[3] := tokenLeftCurly;     (*curly brace*)
```

When `IntlTokenize` encounters an escape character within a quoted literal, it places the portion of the literal before the escape character into a single token (of type `tokenLiteral`), places the escape character into another token (`tokenEscape`), places the character following the escape character into another token (whatever token type it corresponds to), and places the portion of the literal following the escape sequence into another token (`tokenLiteral`). Outside of a quoted literal, the escape character has no special significance.

`IntlTokenize` considers the character specified in the `decimalCode` parameter to be a decimal character only when it is flanked by numeric or alternate numeric characters, or when it follows them.

SPECIAL CONSIDERATIONS

`IntlTokenize` may move memory; your application should not call this function at interrupt time.

Because each call to `IntlTokenize` must be for a single script run, there can be no change of script within a comment or quoted literal.

Comments and quoted literals must be complete within a single call to `IntlTokenize` in order to avoid syntax errors.

`IntlTokenize` always uses the tokens resource whose handle you pass it in the token block record. Therefore, it is not directly affected by the state of the font force flag or the international resources selection flag. However, if you use the `GetIntlResource` function to get a handle to the tokens resource to pass to `IntlTokenize`, remember that `GetIntlResource` is affected by the state of the international resources selection flag. See "Determining Script Codes From Font Information" beginning on page 6-21.

RESULT CODES

tokenOK	0	Valid token
tokenOverflow	1	Number of tokens exceeded maximum specified in tokenList field of token block record
stringOverflow	2	Size of string list larger than maximum specified in stringList field of token block record
badDelim	3	Invalid delimiter
badEnding	4	(currently unused)
crash	5	Unknown error

SEE ALSO

See the appendix "International Resources" in this book for a description of the tokens ('itl4') resource.

Transliteration

Transliteration is the conversion of text from one form or subscript to another within a single script system. In the Roman script system, transliteration means case conversion. In 2-byte script systems, it is the automatic conversion of characters from one subscript to another. One common use for transliteration is as an initial stage of text conversion for an input method.

TransliterateText

The TransliterateText function converts characters from one subscript to the closest possible approximation in a different subscript within the same 2-byte script system. TransliterateText also performs uppercasing and lowercasing, with consideration for regional variants, in the Roman script system and on Roman text within 2-byte script systems.

```
FUNCTION TransliterateText (srcHandle: Handle;
                            dstHandle: Handle;
                            target: Integer; srcMask: LongInt;
                            script: ScriptCode): OSErr;
```

srcHandle   A handle to the source text to be transliterated.

dstHandle   A handle to a buffer that, upon completion of the call, contains the transliterated text.

target   A value that specifies what kind of text the source text is to be transliterated into. The low byte of the target is the format to convert to. The high byte contains modifiers, whose meanings depend on the script code.

srcMask   A bit array that specifies which parts of the source text are to be
               transliterated. A bit is set for each script system or subscript that should
               be converted.

script   A value that specifies the script system of the text to be transliterated.
               Constants for all defined script codes are listed on page 6-52. To specify
               the font script, pass smCurrentScript in this parameter.

DESCRIPTION

The types of conversions TransliterateText performs are described in the section
"Transliteration" beginning on page 6-43.

The TransliterateText function converts all of the text that you pass it in the
srcHandle parameter. It determines the length of the source text (in bytes) from the
handle size.

Before calling TransliterateText, allocate a handle (of any size) to pass in the
dstHandle parameter. The length of the transliterated text may be different (as when
converting between 1-byte and 2-byte characters), and TransliterateText sets the
size of the destination handle as required. It is your responsibility to dispose of the
destination handle when you no longer need it.

The srcMask parameter is the source mask; it specifies which subscript(s) represented in
the source text should be converted to the target format. In all script systems, the
srcMask parameter may have the following values: smMaskAscii, smMaskNative,
and smMaskAll, as described on page 6-46. In 2-byte script systems, additional values
are recognized, as described on page 6-46.

The low-order byte of the target parameter is the target format; it determines what
form the the text should be transliterated to. In all script systems, there are two currently
supported values for target format: smTransAscii and smTransNative, as described
on page 6-46. In 2-byte script systems, additional values are recognized, as described
on page 6-47.

The high-order byte of the target parameter is the target modifier; it provides
additional formatting instructions. In all script systems, there are two values for target
modifer: smTransLower and smTransUpper, as described on page 6-47.

Note
Because the low-ASCII character set (character codes $20–$7F) is present
in all script systems, you could theoretically use the
TransliterateText function to convert characters from one script
system into another completely different script system. You could
transliterate from a native subscript into ASCII under one script system,
and then transliterate from that ASCII into a native subscript under a
different script system. Such a procedure is not recommended, however,
because of the imperfect nature of phonetic translation. Furthermore,
many script systems do not support transliteration from native
subscripts to ASCII. ◆

SPECIAL CONSIDERATIONS

`TransliterateText` may move memory; your application should not call this function at interrupt time.

If you pass `smCurrentScript` in the `script` parameter, the conversion performed by `TransliterateText` can be affected by the state of the font force flag. It is unaffected by the international resources selection flag.

Transliteration of a block of text does not work across script-run boundaries. Because the `TransliterateText` function requires transliteration tables that are in a script system's international resources, you need to call it anew for each script run in your text.

Currently, the Roman version of `TransliterateText` checks the source mask only to ensure that at least one of the bits corresponding to the `smMaskAscii` and `smMaskNative` constants is set.

The Arabic and Hebrew versions of `TransliterateText` perform case conversion only. They allow the target values `smTransAscii` and `smTransNative` only; otherwise, they behave like the Roman version.

The `TransliterateText` tables for 1-byte script systems reside in the script's string-manipulation (`'itl2'`) resource, so they can reflect region-specific or language-specific differences in uppercase conventions. If the string-manipulation resource does not include these tables, `TransliterateText` exits without doing anything.

The `TransliterateText` tables for 2-byte script systems reside in the script's transliteration (`'trsl'`) resource. If the `'trsl'` resource does not include these tables, `TransliterateText` exits without doing anything.

The Japanese, Traditional Chinese, and Simplified Chinese versions of `TransliterateText` have two modes of operation:

- If either `smMaskAscii` or `smMaskNative` is specified in the source mask, and if the target is `smTransAscii`, and if either of the target modifiers is specified, `TransliterateText` performs the specified case conversion on both 1-byte and 2-byte Roman letters.

- Otherwise, `TransliterateText` performs conversions according to the target format values defined on page 6-47. Any combination of source masks and target format is permitted.

RESULT CODES

In addition to Memory Manager errors, `TransliterateText` can return the following results:

noErr	0	No error
	−1	Illegal source or target, or `'itl2'` could not be loaded

Replacing a Script System's Default Routines

The four Script Manager routines described in this section allow you to access or replace the text-manipulation and text-display routines in WorldScript I, the system extension for 1-byte complex script systems. The function `GetScriptUtilityAddress` and the procedure `SetScriptUtilityAddress` work with the script utilities routines. The function `GetScriptQDPatchAddress` and the procedure `SetScriptQDPatchAddress` work with patches of the QuickDraw routines `StdText`, `StdTxMeas`, and `MeasureText`, and the Font Manager routine `FontMetrics`.

For more information on how to use these calls, see the appendix "Built-in Script Support" in this book.

For `GetScriptUtilityAddress` and `SetScriptUtilityAddress`, these are the valid values for the `selector` parameter:

Script utility	Selector value
GetScriptVariable	$000C
SetScriptVariable	$000E
CharacterByteType	$0010
CharacterType	$0012
TransliterateText	$0018
FindWordBreaks	$001A
HiliteText	$001C
FillParseTable	$0022
FindScriptRun	$0026
VisibleLength	$0028
PixelToChar	$002E
CharToPixel	$0030
DrawJustified	$0032
Measurejustified	$0034
PortionLine	$0036

For `GetScriptQDPatchAddress` and `SetScriptQDPatchAddress`, these are the valid values for the `trapNum` parameter:

QuickDraw patch	trapNum value
_StdText	$A882
_StdTxMeas	$A8ED
_MeasureText	$A837
_FontMetrics	$A835

GetScriptUtilityAddress

The `GetScriptUtilityAddress` function returns a pointer to the specified 1-byte script utility—or the original Roman utility—for the given script system.

```
FUNCTION GetScriptUtilityAddress (selector: Integer;
                                  before: Boolean;
                                  script: ScriptCode): Ptr;
```

selector   A value that specifies the name of the utility routine whose address is needed.

before   A Boolean that specifies which of two routines is needed. If TRUE, the address returned is that of the WorldScript I implementation of the utility. If FALSE, the address returned is that of the original routine (usually the built-in Roman version).

script   The numeric code that specifies the script system whose dispatch table contains the pointers to the utility routines. Constants for all defined script codes are listed on page 6-52.

DESCRIPTION

The `GetScriptUtilityAddress` function examines the specified script's dispatch table and returns a pointer to the desired routine.

Because each element in the dispatch table consists of a pair of addresses, one for the WorldScript I implementation of the utility, and another for the original (Roman) version of the utility, you can get the address of either routine. Either routine can then be replaced, using the `GetScriptUtilityAddress` call.

This function can return NIL for the pointer if, for example, either the WorldScript I implementation or the original Roman routine is not used by the script system.

Valid values for the `selector` parameter are listed on page 6-101.

If the specified script system is not enabled, `GetScriptUtilityAddress` returns a NIL pointer.

SEE ALSO

WorldScript I is described in the appendix "Built-in Script Support" in this book.

SetScriptUtilityAddress

The `SetScriptUtilityAddress` procedure replaces the specified 1-byte script utility—or the original Roman utility—for the given script.

```
PROCEDURE SetScriptUtilityAddress (selector: Integer;
                                   before: Boolean;
                                   routineAddr: Ptr;
                                   script: ScriptCode);
```

selector A value that specifies the name of the utility routine to be replaced.

before A Boolean that specifies which of two routines is to be replaced. If TRUE, the WorldScript I implementation of the utility is replaced. If FALSE, the original routine (usually the built-in Roman version) is replaced.

routineAddr
A pointer to the routine that is to replace the script utility.

script The numeric code that specifies the script system whose dispatch table contains the pointers to the utility routines. Constants for all defined script codes are listed on page 6-52.

DESCRIPTION

The `SetScriptUtilityAddress` procedure replaces the pointer to the desired routine in the specified script's dispatch table.

Several of the WorldScript I utilities call the original Roman routine after they execute. Each element in the dispatch table consists of a pair of addresses: one for the WorldScript I implementation of the utility, and another for the original (Roman) version of the utility. With `SetScriptUtilityAddress` you can replace either routine. Thus you can insert your patch code either before (or in place of) the WorldScript I version of the utility, or before (or in place of) the original Roman routine.

IMPORTANT

When you patch a script system's script utility, you alter that script's behavior for as long as it remains enabled. Therefore, be sure to restore the pointer to its original state whenever your application quits or is switched out by the Process Manager. ▲

Valid values for the `selector` parameter are listed on page 6-101.

SEE ALSO

WorldScript I is described in the appendix "Built-in Script Support" in this book.

6

Script Manager

GetScriptQDPatchAddress

The `GetScriptQDPatchAddress` function returns a pointer to the specified WorldScript I QuickDraw patch—or the built-in QuickDraw call—for the given script system.

```
FUNCTION GetScriptQDPatchAddress (trapNum: Integer;
                                  before: Boolean;
                                  forPrinting: Boolean;
                                  script: ScriptCode): Ptr;
```

trapNum   A value that specifies the name of the QuickDraw routine whose address is needed.

before   A Boolean that specifies which of two routines is needed. If `TRUE`, the address returned is that of the WorldScript I patch to the QuickDraw routine. If `FALSE`, the address returned is that of the original routine (usually the built-in QuickDraw routine).

forPrinting

A Boolean that specifies whether the desired routine is for printing. If `TRUE`, the address returned is that of a QuickDraw patch that is specifically for printing; if `FALSE`, the address returned is that of a QuickDraw patch that is not specifically for printing.

script   The numeric code that specifies the script system whose dispatch table contains the pointers to the QuickDraw routines. Constants for all defined script codes are listed on page 6-52.

DESCRIPTION

The `GetScriptQDPatchAddress` function examines the specified script's dispatch table and returns a pointer to the desired routine.

Because each element in the dispatch table consists of a pair of addresses, one for the WorldScript I patch to the QuickDraw routine, and another for the original QuickDraw version of the routine, you can get the address of either routine. Either routine can then be replaced, using the `SetScriptQDPatchAddress` call.

Some printers perform their own text layout on text that is passed to them. Therefore, each QuickDraw patch has two entry points: one for screen display and printing, and one for printing only. By specifying either `TRUE` or `FALSE` in the `forPrinting` parameter, the pointer you obtain is to either the "for printing only" or the "not for printing only" entry point. For example, some script systems might use the "for printing only" entry point to perform extra-fine justification of text on a PostScript printer.

Valid values for the `trapNum` parameter are listed on page 6-101.

If the specified script system is not enabled, `GetScriptQDPatchAddress` returns a `NIL` pointer.

WorldScript I is described in the appendix "Built-in Script Support" in this book.

In order to handle contextual formatting appropriately for each script system, printer drivers should call the Script Manager's print action routine, described in *Inside Macintosh: Devices*.

SetScriptQDPatchAddress

The `SetScriptQDPatchAddress` procedure replaces the WorldScript I specified QuickDraw patch—or the built-in QuickDraw call—for the given script.

```
PROCEDURE SetScriptQDPatchAddress (trapNum: Integer;
                                   before: Boolean;
                                   forPrinting: Boolean;
                                   routineAddr: Ptr;
                                   script: ScriptCode);
```

trapNum
: A value that specifies the name of the QuickDraw routine that is to be replaced.

before
: A Boolean that specifies which of two routines is to be replaced. If TRUE, the WorldScript I patch of the QuickDraw routine is replaced. If FALSE, the original routine (usually the built-in QuickDraw routine) is replaced.

forPrinting
: A Boolean that specifies whether the replacement routine is for printing. If TRUE, the new QuickDraw patch is specifically for printing; if FALSE, the new QuickDraw patch is not specifically for printing.

routineAddr
: A pointer to the routine that is to replace the existing QuickDraw routine.

script
: The numeric code that specifies the script system whose dispatch table contains the pointers to the QuickDraw routines. Constants for all defined script codes are listed on page 6-52.

DESCRIPTION

The `SetScriptQDPatchAddress` procedure replaces the pointer to the desired routine in the specified script's dispatch table.

All of the WorldScript I patches call the original QuickDraw routine after they execute. Each element in the dispatch table consists of a pair of addresses: one for the WorldScript I patch, and another for the original (built-in QuickDraw) version of the routine. With `SetQDPatchAddress` you can replace either routine. Thus you can insert your patch code either before (or in place of) the WorldScript I QuickDraw patch, or before (or in place of) the original QuickDraw routine.

Some printers perform their own text layout on text that is passed to them. Therefore, each QuickDraw patch has two entry points: one for screen display and one for printing only. By specifying either TRUE or FALSE in the `forPrinting` parameter, you specify whether you are passing the "for printing only" or the "not for printing only" entry point. For example, some script systems might use the "for printing only" entry point to perform extra-fine justification of text on a PostScript printer.

IMPORTANT

When you patch a script system's QuickDraw call, you alter that script's behavior for as long as it remains enabled. Therefore, be sure to restore the pointer to its original state whenever your application quits or is switched out by the Process Manager. ▲

Valid values for the `trapNum` parameter are listed on page 6-101.

SEE ALSO

WorldScript I is described in the appendix "Built-in Script Support" in this book.

In order to handle contextual formatting appropriately for each script system, printer drivers should call the Script Manager's print action routine, described in *Inside Macintosh: Devices.*

Summary of the Script Manager

Pascal Summary

Constants

```
{Script system constants}

{Implicit script codes}
smSystemScript = -1;          {designates system script.}
smCurrentScript = -2;         {designates font script.}
smAllScripts = -3;            {designates any script}
{Explicit script codes}
smRoman = 0;                  {Roman}
smJapanese = 1;               {Japanese}
smTradChinese = 2;            {Traditional Chinese}
smKorean = 3;                 {Korean}
smArabic = 4;                 {Arabic}
smHebrew = 5;                 {Hebrew}
smGreek = 6;                  {Greek}
smCyrillic = 7;              {Cyrillic}
smRSymbol = 8;                {Right-left symbol}
smDevanagari = 9;             {Devanagari}
smGurmukhi = 10;              {Gurmukhi}
smGujarati = 11;              {Gujarati}
smOriya = 12;                 {Oriya}
smBengali = 13;               {Bengali}
smTamil = 14;                 {Tamil}
smTelugu = 15;                {Telugu}
smKannada = 16;               {Kannada/Kanarese}
smMalayalam = 17;             {Malayalam}
smSinhalese = 18;             {Sinhalese}
smBurmese = 19;               {Burmese}
smKhmer = 20;                 {Khmer/Cambodian}
smThai = 21;                  {Thai}
smLaotian = 22;               {Laotian}
```

```
smGeorgian = 23;              {Georgian}
smArmenian = 24;              {Armenian}
smSimpChinese = 25;           {Simplified Chinese}
smTibetan = 26;               {Tibetan}
smMongolian = 27;             {Mongolian}
smGeez = 28;                  {Geez/Ethiopic}
smEthiopic = 28;              {Synonym for smGeez}
smEastEurRoman = 29;          {Synonym for smSlavic}
smVietnamese = 30;            {Vietnamese}
smExtArabic = 31;             {extended Arabic}
smUninterp = 32;              {uninterpreted symbols, e.g. palette symbols}

{Language Codes}
langEnglish = 0;              { smRoman script }
langFrench = 1;               { smRoman script }
langGerman = 2;               { smRoman script }
langItalian = 3;              { smRoman script }
langDutch = 4;                { smRoman script }
langSwedish = 5;              { smRoman script }
langSpanish = 6;              { smRoman script }
langDanish = 7;               { smRoman script }
langPortuguese = 8;           { smRoman script }
langNorwegian = 9;            { smRoman script }
langHebrew = 10;              { smHebrew script }
langJapanese = 11;            { smJapanese script }
langArabic = 12;              { smArabic script }
langFinnish = 13;             { smRoman script }
langGreek = 14;               { smGreek script }
langIcelandic = 15;           { extended Roman script }
langMaltese = 16;             { extended Roman script }
langTurkish = 17;             { extended Roman script }
langCroatian = 18;            { Serbo-Croatian in extended Roman script }
langTradChinese = 19;         { Chinese in traditional characters }
langUrdu = 20;                { smArabic script }
langHindi = 21;               { smDevanagari script }
langThai = 22;                { smThai script }
langKorean = 23;              { smKorean script }
langLithuanian = 24;          { smEastEurRoman script }
langPolish = 25;              { smEastEurRoman script }
langHungarian = 26;           { smEastEurRoman script }
langEstonian = 27;            { smEastEurRoman script }
langLettish = 28;             { smEastEurRoman script }
```

```
langLatvian = 28;              { Synonym for langLettish }
langSaamisk = 29;              { extended Roman script }
langLappish = 29;              { Synonym for langSaamisk }
langFaeroese = 30;             { smRoman script }
langFarsi = 31;                { smArabic script }
langPersian = 31;              { Synonym for langFarsi }
langRussian = 32;              { smCyrillic script }
langSimpChinese = 33;          { Chinese in simplified characters }
langFlemish = 34;              { smRoman script }
langIrish = 35;                { smRoman script }
langAlbanian = 36;             { smRoman script }
langRomanian = 37;             { smEastEurRoman script }
langCzech = 38;                { smEastEurRoman script }
langSlovak = 39;               { smEastEurRoman script }
langSlovenian = 40;            { smEastEurRoman script }
langYiddish = 41;              { smHebrew script }
langSerbian = 42;              { Serbo-Croatian in smCyrillic script }
langMacedonian = 43;           { smCyrillic script }
langBulgarian = 44;            { smCyrillic script }
langUkrainian = 45;            { smCyrillic script }
langByelorussian = 46;         { smCyrillic script }
langUzbek = 47;                { smCyrillic script }
langKazakh = 48;               { smCyrillic script }
langAzerbaijani = 49;          { Azerbaijani in smCyrillic script }
langAzerbaijanAr = 50;         { Azerbaijani in smArabic script (Iran) }
langArmenian = 51;             { smArmenian script }
langGeorgian = 52;             { smGeorgian script }
langMoldovan = 53;             { smCyrillic script }
langMoldavian = 53;            { Synonym for langMoldovan }
langKirghiz = 54;              { smCyrillic script }
langTajiki = 55;               { smCyrillic script }
langTurkmen = 56;              { smCyrillic script }
langMongolian = 57;            { Mongolian in smMongolian script }
langMongolianCyr = 58;         { Mongolian in smCyrillic script }
langPashto = 59;               { smArabic script }
langKurdish = 60;              { smArabic script }
langKashmiri = 61;             { smArabic script }
langSindhi = 62;               { smExtArabic script }
langTibetan = 63;              { smTibetan script }
langNepali = 64;               { smDevanagari script }
langSanskrit = 65;             { smDevanagari script }
langMarathi = 66;              { smDevanagari script }
```

Script Manager

```
langBengali = 67;              { smBengali script }
langAssamese = 68;             { smBengali script }
langGujarati = 69;             { smGujarati script }
langPunjabi = 70;              { smGurmukhi script }
langOriya = 71;                { smOriya script }
langMalayalam = 72;            { smMalayalam script }
langKannada = 73;              { smKannada script }
langTamil = 74;                { smTamil script }
langTelugu = 75;               { smTelugu script }
langSinhalese = 76;            { smSinhalese script }
langBurmese = 77;              { smBurmese script }
langKhmer = 78;                { smKhmer script }
langLao = 79;                  { smLaotian script }
langVietnamese = 80;           { smVietnamese script }
langIndonesian = 81;           { smRoman script }
langTagalog = 82;              { smRoman script }
langMalayRoman = 83;           { Malay in smRoman script }
langMalayArabic = 84;          { Malay in smArabic script }
langAmharic = 85;              { smEthiopic script }
langTigrinya = 86;             { smEthiopic script }
langGalla = 87;                { smEthiopic script }
langOromo = 87;                { synonym for langGalla }
langSomali = 88;               { smRoman script }
langSwahili = 89;              { smRoman script }
langRuanda = 90;               { smRoman script }
langRundi = 91;                { smRoman script }
langChewa = 92;                { smRoman script }
langMalagasy = 93;             { smRoman script }
langEsperanto = 94;            { extended Roman script }
langWelsh = 128;               { smRoman script }
langBasque = 129;              { smRoman script }
langCatalan = 130;             { smRoman script }
langLatin = 131;               { smRoman script }
langQuechua = 132;             { smRoman script }
langGuarani = 133;             { smRoman script }
langAymara = 134;              { smRoman script }
langTatar = 135;               { smCyrillic script }
langUighur = 136;              { smArabic script }
langDzongkha = 137;            { (lang of Bhutan) smTibetan script }
langJavaneseRom = 138;         { Javanese in smRoman script }
langSundaneseRom = 139;        { Sundanese in smRoman script }
```

```
{ Region codes }
verUS = 0;
verFrance = 1;
verBritain = 2;
verGermany = 3;
verItaly = 4;
verNetherlands = 5;
verFrBelgiumLux = 6;              {French for Belgium & Luxembourg}
verSweden = 7;
verSpain = 8;
verDenmark = 9;
verPortugal = 10;
verFrCanada = 11;
verNorway = 12;
verIsrael = 13;
verJapan = 14;
verAustralia = 15;
verArabia = 16;
verArabic = 16;                   {synonym for verArabia}
verFinland = 17;
verFrSwiss = 18;                  {Swiss French}
verGrSwiss = 19;                  {Swiss German}
verGreece = 20;
verIceland = 21;
verMalta = 22;
verCyprus = 23;
verTurkey = 24;
verYugoCroatian = 25;             {Croatian system}
verIndiaHindi = 33;               {Hindi system for India}
verPakistan = 34;
verLithuania = 41;
verPoland = 42;
verHungary = 43;
verEstonia = 44;
verLatvia = 45;
verLapland = 46;
verFaeroeIsl = 47;
verIran = 48;
verRussia = 49;
verIreland = 50;                  {English-language version for Ireland}
```

```
verKorea = 51;
verChina = 52;
verTaiwan = 53;
verThailand = 54;
minCountry = verUS;
maxCountry = verThailand;

{Calendar codes}
calGregorian = 0;
calArabicCivil = 1;
calArabicLunar = 2;
calJapanese = 3;
calJewish = 4;
calCoptic = 5;
calPersian = 6;

{Numeral codes}
intWestern = 0;
intArabic = 1;
intRoman = 2;
intJapanese = 3;
intEuropean = 4;
intOutputMask = $8000;

{ CharacterByteType byte types }
smSingleByte = 0;
smFirstByte = -1;
smLastByte = 1;
smMiddleByte = 2;

{CharacterType field masks}
smcTypeMask = $000F;
smcReserved = $00F0;
smcClassMask = $0F00;
smcOrientationMask = $1000;    {2-byte script glyph orientation}
smcRightMask = $2000;
smcUpperMask = $4000;
smcDoubleMask = $8000;

{Basic CharacterType character types}
smCharPunct = $0000;
smCharAscii = $0001;
smCharEuro = $0007;
smCharExtAscii = $0007;        {more correct synonym for smCharEuro}
```

```
{Additional CharacterType character types for script systems}
smCharKatakana = $0002;              {Japanese Katakana}
smCharHiragana = $0003;              {Japanese Hiragana}
smCharIdeographic = $0004;           {Hanzi, Kanji, Hanja}
smCharTwoByteGreek = $0005;          {2-byte Greek in Far East systems}
smCharTwoByteRussian = $0006;        {2-byte Cyrillic in Far East systems}
smCharBidirect = $0008;              {Arabic/Hebrew}
smCharContextualLR = $0009;          {contextual left-right: Thai, Indic scripts}
smCharNonContextualLR = $000A;       {noncontextual left-right: Cyrillic, Greek}
smCharHangul = $000C;                {Korean Hangul}
smCharJamo = $000D;                  {Korean Jamo}
smCharBopomofo = $000E;              {Chinese Bopomofo (Zhuyinfuhao)}

{CharacterType classes for punctuation (smCharPunct)}
smPunctNormal = $0000;
smPunctNumber = $0100;
smPunctSymbol = $0200;
smPunctBlank = $0300;

{Additional CharacterType classes for punctuation in two-byte systems}
smPunctRepeat = $0400;               {repeat marker}
smPunctGraphic = $0500;              {line graphics}

{CharacterType Katakana and Hiragana classes for 2-byte systems}
smKanaSmall = $0100;                 {small Kana character}
smKanaHardOK = $0200;                {can have dakuten}
smKanaSoftOK = $0300;                {can have dakuten or han-dakuten}

{CharacterType ideographic classes for 2-byte systems}
smIdeographicLevel1 = $0000;    {level 1 char}
smIdeographicLevel2 = $0100;    {level 2 char}
smIdeographicUser = $0200;      {user char}

{CharacterType Jamo classes for Korean systems}
smJamoJaeum = $0000;                 {simple consonant char}
smJamoBogJaeum = $0100;              {complex consonant char}
smJamoMoeum = $0200;                 {simple vowel char}
smJamoBogMoeum = $0300;              {complex vowel char}

{CharacterType glyph orientation for 2-byte systems}
smCharHorizontal = $0000;            {horizontal character form, or for both}
smCharVertical = $1000;              {vertical character form}
```

```
{CharacterType directions}
smCharLeft = $0000;
smCharRight = $2000;

{CharacterType case modifers}
smCharLower = $0000;
smCharUpper = $4000;

{CharacterType character size modifiers (1 or multiple bytes)}
smChar1byte = $0000;
smChar2byte = $8000;

{TransliterateText target types for Roman}
smTransAscii = 0;               {convert to ASCII}
smTransNative = 1;              {convert to font script}
smTransCase = $FE;             {convert case for all text}
smTransSystem = $FF;           {convert to system script}

{TransliterateText target types for 2-byte scripts}
smTransAscii1 = 2;             {1-byte Roman}
smTransAscii2 = 3;             {2-byte Roman}
smTransKana1 = 4;             {1-byte Japanese Katakana}
smTransKana2 = 5;             {2-byte Japanese Katakana}
smTransGana2 = 7;             {2-byte Japanese Hiragana (no 1-byte Hiragana)}
smTransHangul2 = 8;           {2-byte Korean Hangul}
smTransJamo2 = 9;             {2-byte Korean Jamo}
smTransBopomofo2 = 10;        {2-byte Chinese Bopomofo (Zhuyinfuhao)}

{TransliterateText target modifiers}
smTransLower = $4000;         {target becomes lowercase}
smTransUpper = $8000;         {target becomes uppercase}

{TransliterateText resource format numbers}
smTransRuleBaseFormat = 1;    {rule-based trsl resource format }
smTransHangulFormat = 2;      {table-based Hangul trsl resource format}

{TransliterateText property flags}
smTransPreDoubleByting = 1;   {convert all text to 2-byte }
                              { before transliteration}
smTransPreLowerCasing = 2;    {convert all text to lowercase }
                              { before transliteration}

{TransliterateText source mask - general}
smMaskAll = $FFFFFFFF;         {convert all text}
```

```
{TransliterateText source masks}
smMaskAscii = $00000001;        {2^smTransAscii}
smMaskNative = $00000002;       {2^smTransNative}

{TransliterateText source masks for 2-byte scripts}
smMaskAscii1 = $00000004;       {2^smTransAscii1}
smMaskAscii2 = $00000008;       {2^smTransAscii2}
smMaskKana1 = $00000010;        {2^smTransKana1}
smMaskKana2 = $00000020;        {2^smTransKana2}
smMaskGana2 = $00000080;        {2^smTransGana2}
smMaskHangul2 = $00000100;      {2^smTransHangul2}
smMaskJamo2 = $00000200;        {2^smTransJamo2}
smMaskBopomofo2 = $00000400;    {2^smTransBopomofo2}

{Result values from GetScriptManagerVariable, SetScriptManagerVariable, }
{ GetScriptVariable, and SetScriptVariable}
smNotInstalled = 0;             {routine not available in specified script}
smBadVerb = -1;                 {bad selector passed to a routine}
smBadScript = -2;               {bad script code passed to a routine}

{Values for script redraw flag}
smRedrawChar = 0;               {redraw character only}
smRedrawWord = 1;               {redraw entire word (2-byte systems)}
smRedrawLine = -1;              {redraw entire line (bidirectional systems)}

{GetScriptManagerVariable and SetScriptManagerVariable selectors}
smVersion = 0;                  {Script Manager version number}
smMunged = 2;                   {Globals change count}
smEnabled = 4;                  {Count of enabled scripts, incl Roman}
smBidirect = 6;                 {At least one bidirectional script}
smFontForce = 8;                {Force font flag}
smIntlForce = 10;               {Intl resources selection flag}
smForced = 12;                  {Script was forced to system script}
smDefault = 14;                 {Script was defaulted to Roman script}
smPrint = 16;                   {Printer action routine}
smSysScript = 18;               {System script}
smLastScript = 20;              {Last keyboard script}
smKeyScript = 22;               {Keyboard script}
smSysRef = 24;                  {System folder refNum}

smKeyCache = 26;                {obsolete}
smKeySwap = 28;                 {Swapping table handle}
smGenFlags = 30;                {General flags long}
smOverride = 32;                {Script override flags}
```

```
smCharPortion = 34;              {Ch vs SpExtra proportion}
smDoubleByte = 36;               {Flag for double-byte script installed}
smKCHRCache = 38;                {Returns pointer to KCHR cache}
smRegionCode = 40;               {Returns current region code (verXxx)}
smKeyDisableState = 42;          {Returns current keyboard disable state}

{ GetScriptVariable and SetScriptVariable selectors.}
smScriptVersion = 0;             {Script software version}
smScriptMunged = 2;              {Script entry changed count}
smScriptEnabled = 4;             {Script enabled flag}
smScriptRight = 6;               {Right to left flag}
smScriptJust = 8;                {Justification flag}
smScriptRedraw = 10;             {Word redraw flag}
smScriptSysFond = 12;            {Preferred system font}
smScriptAppFond = 14;            {Preferred Application font}
smScriptBundle = 16;             {Beginning of itlb verbs}
smScriptNumber = 16;             {Script itl0 id}
smScriptDate = 18;               {Script itl1 id}
smScriptSort = 20;               {Script itl2 id}
smScriptFlags = 22;              {flags word}
smScriptToken = 24;              {Script itl4 id}
smScriptEncoding = 26;           {id of optional itl5, if present}
smScriptLang = 28;               {Current language for script}
smScriptNumDate = 30;            {Script Number/Date formats.}
smScriptKeys = 32;               {Script KCHR id}
smScriptIcon = 34;               {ID # of SICN or kcs#/kcs4/kcs8 family}
smScriptPrint = 36;              {Script printer action routine}
smScriptTrap = 38;               {Trap entry pointer}
smScriptCreator = 40;            {Script file creator}
smScriptFile = 42;               {Script file name}
smScriptName = 44;               {Script name}
smScriptMonoFondSize = 78;       {default monospace FOND (hi) & size (lo)}
smScriptPrefFondSize = 80;       {preferred FOND (hi) & size (lo)}
smScriptSmallFondSize = 82;      {default small FOND (hi) & size (lo)}
smScriptSysFondSize = 84;        {default system FOND (hi) & size (lo)}
smScriptAppFondSize = 86;        {default app FOND (hi) & size (lo)}
smScriptHelpFondSize = 88;       {default Help Mgr FOND (hi) & size (lo)}
smScriptValidStyles = 90;        {mask of valid styles for script}
smScriptAliasStyle = 92;         {style (set) to use for aliases}

{ Negative selectors for KeyScript }
smKeyNextScript = -1;            { Switch to next available script }
smKeySysScript = -2;             { Switch to the system script }
smKeySwapScript = -3;            { Switch to previously-used script }
```

```
smKeyNextKybd = -4;        { Switch to next keyboard in current keyscript }
smKeySwapKybd = -5;        { Switch to previous keyboard in current keyscript }
smKeyDisableKybds = -6;  { Disable keyboards not in system or Roman script }
smKeyEnableKybds = -7;   { Re-enable keyboards for all enabled scripts }
smKeyToggleInline = -8;  { Toggle inline input for current keyscript }
smKeyToggleDirection = -9;   {Toggle default line direction (TESysJust)}
smKeyNextInputMethod = -10;   {Switch to next input method in current script}
smKeySwapInputMethod = -11;   {Switch to prev. input method in curr. script}
smKeyDisableKybdSwitch = -12; {Disable switching from current keyboard}
smKeySetDirLeftRight = -15;   {Set default line dir. left-right,align left}
smKeySetDirRightLeft = -16;   {Set default line dir. right-left,align right}
smKeyRoman = -17;          { Set keyscript to Roman. Does nothing if Roman-only}

{ Bits in the smScriptFlags word
(bits above 8 are non-static) }
smsfIntellCP = 0;              {Script has intelligent cut & paste}
smsfSingByte = 1;              {Script has only single bytes}
smsfNatCase = 2;              {Native chars have upper & lower case}
smsfContext = 3;              {Script is contextual}
smsfNoForceFont = 4;          {Script will not force characters}
smsfB0Digits = 5;             {Script has alternate digits at B0-B9}

smsfAutoInit = 6;             {Auto initialize the script}
smsfUnivExt = 7;             {Script is handled by WorldScript I}
smsfSynchUnstyledTE = 8;     {Synchronize keyboard and chartype in unstyled TE}
smsfForms = 13;              {Uses contextual forms for letters}
smsfLigatures = 14;          {Uses contextual ligatures}
smsfReverse = 15;            {Reverses native text, right-left}

{ Bits in the smGenFlags long.}
{First (high-order) byte is set from itlc flags byte. }
smfShowIcon = 31;            {Show icon even if only one script}
smfDualCaret = 30;           {Use dual caret for mixed direction text}
smfNameTagEnab = 29;         {Reserved for internal use}

{ Script Manager font equates. }
smFondStart = $4000;        {start from 16K}
smFondEnd = $C000;          {past end of range at 48K}

{ Miscellaneous font equates. }
smUprHalfCharSet = $80;     {first char code in top half of std char set}

{ Character Set Extensions }
diaeresisUprY = $D9;
fraction = $DA;
```

```
intlCurrency = $DB;
leftSingGuillemet = $DC;
rightSingGuillemet = $DD;
fiLigature = $DE;
flLigature = $DF;
dblDagger = $E0;
centeredDot = $E1;
baseSingQuote = $E2;
baseDblQuote = $E3;
perThousand = $E4;
circumflexUprA = $E5;
circumflexUprE = $E6;
acuteUprA = $E7;
diaeresisUprE = $E8;
graveUprE = $E9;
acuteUprI = $EA;
circumflexUprI = $EB;
diaeresisUprI = $EC;

graveUprI = $ED;
acuteUprO = $EE;
circumflexUprO = $EF;
appleLogo = $F0;
graveUprO = $F1;
acuteUprU = $F2;
circumflexUprU = $F3;
graveUprU = $F4;
dotlessLwrI = $F5;
circumflex = $F6;
tilde = $F7;
macron = $F8;
breveMark = $F9;
overDot = $FA;
ringMark = $FB;
cedilla = $FC;
doubleAcute = $FD;
ogonek = $FE;
hachek = $FF;

{ TokenType values }
tokenIntl = 4;          {the itl resource number of the tokenizer}
tokenEmpty = -1;        {used internally as an empty flag}
tokenUnknown = 0;       {chars that do not match a defined token type}
tokenWhite = 1;         {whitespace}
```

```
tokenLeftLit = 2;            {literal begin}
tokenRightLit = 3;           {literal end}
tokenAlpha = 4;              {alphabetic}
tokenNumeric = 5;            {numeric}
tokenNewLine = 6;            {new line}
tokenLeftComment = 7;        {open comment}
tokenRightComment = 8;       {close comment}
tokenLiteral = 9;            {literal}
tokenEscape = 10;            {character escape (e.g. '\' in "\n", "\t")}
tokenAltNum = 11;            {alternate number (e.g. $B0-B9 in Arabic,Hebrew)}
tokenRealNum = 12;           {real number}
tokenAltReal = 13;           {alternate real number}
tokenReserve1 = 14;          {reserved}
tokenReserve2 = 15;          {reserved}
tokenLeftParen = 16;         {open parenthesis}
tokenRightParen = 17;        {close parenthesis}

tokenLeftBracket = 18;       {open square bracket}
tokenRightBracket = 19;      {close square bracket}
tokenLeftCurly = 20;         {open curly bracket}
tokenRightCurly = 21;        {close curly bracket}
tokenLeftEnclose = 22;       {open guillemet}
tokenRightEnclose = 23;      {close guillemet}
tokenPlus = 24;
tokenMinus = 25;
tokenAsterisk = 26;          {times/multiply}
tokenDivide = 27;
tokenPlusMinus = 28;         {plus or minus symbol}
tokenSlash = 29;
tokenBackSlash = 30;
tokenLess = 31;              {less than symbol}
tokenGreat = 32;             {greater than symbol}
tokenEqual = 33;
tokenLessEqual2 = 34;        {less than or equal, 2 characters (e.g. <=)}
tokenLessEqual1 = 35;        {less than or equal, 1 character}
tokenGreatEqual2 = 36;       {greater than or equal, 2 characters (e.g. >=)}
tokenGreatEqual1 = 37;       {greater than or equal, 1 character}
token2Equal = 38;            {double equal (e.g. ==)}

tokenColonEqual = 39;        {colon equal}
tokenNotEqual = 40;          {not equal, 1 character}
tokenLessGreat = 41;         {less/greater, Pascal not equal (e.g. <>)}
tokenExclamEqual = 42;       {exclamation equal, C not equal (e.g. !=)}
tokenExclam = 43;            {exclamation point}
```

```
tokenTilde = 44;              {centered tilde}
tokenComma = 45;
tokenPeriod = 46;
tokenLeft2Quote = 47;         {open double quote}
tokenRight2Quote = 48;        {close double quote}
tokenLeft1Quote = 49;         {open single quote}
tokenRight1Quote = 50;        {close single quote}
token2Quote = 51;             {double quote}
token1Quote = 52;             {single quote}
tokenSemicolon = 53;
tokenPercent = 54;
tokenCaret = 55;
tokenUnderline = 56;
tokenAmpersand = 57;
tokenAtSign = 58;
tokenBar = 59;                {vertical bar}
tokenQuestion = 60;
tokenPi = 61;                 {lower-case pi}
tokenRoot = 62;               {square root symbol}
tokenSigma = 63;              {capital sigma}
tokenIntegral = 64;           {integral sign}
tokenMicro = 65;
tokenCapPi = 66;              {capital pi}
tokenInfinity = 67;
tokenColon = 68;
tokenHash = 69;               {e.g. #}
tokenDollar = 70;
tokenNoBreakSpace = 71;       {non-breaking space}
tokenFraction = 72;
tokenIntlCurrency = 73;
tokenLeftSingGuillemet = 74;
tokenRightSingGuillemet = 75;
tokenPerThousand = 76;
tokenEllipsis = 77;
tokenCenterDot = 78;
tokenNil = 127;
delimPad = -2;

{ Table selectors for GetIntlResourceTable }
smWordSelectTable = 0;        { get word break table from 'itl2' }
smWordWrapTable = 1;          { get line break table from 'itl2' }
smNumberPartsTable = 2;       { get number parts table from 'itl4' }
smUnTokenTable = 3;           { get unToken table from 'itl4' }
smWhiteSpaceList = 4;         { get whitespace table from 'itl4' }
```

Data Types

```
TYPE  TokenResults =
      (tokenOK,tokenOverflow,stringOverflow,badDelim,
      badEnding,crash);

      CharByteTable = PACKED ARRAY[0..255] OF SignedByte;

      TokenType = Integer;

      DelimType = ARRAY[0..1] OF TokenType;

      CommentType = ARRAY[0..3] OF TokenType;

      TokenRec =
      RECORD
         theToken:          TokenType;
         position:          Ptr;         {pointer into original source}
         length:            LongInt;     {length of text in original source}
         stringPosition:    StringPtr;   {Pascal/C string copy of identifier}
      END;
      TokenRecPtr = ^TokenRec;

      TokenBlock =
      RECORD
         source:            Ptr;       {pointer to stream of characters}
         sourceLength:      LongInt;   {length of source stream}
         tokenList:         Ptr;       {pointer to array of tokens}
         tokenLength:       LongInt;   {maximum length of TokenList}
         tokenCount:        LongInt;   {number tokens generated by tokenizer}
         stringList:        Ptr;       {pointer to stream of identifiers}
         stringLength:      LongInt;   {length of string list}
         stringCount:       LongInt;   {number of bytes currently used}
         doString:          Boolean;   {make strings & put into StringList}
         doAppend:          Boolean;   {append to TokenList rather than replace}

         doAlphanumeric:    Boolean;   {identifiers may include numeric}
         doNest:            Boolean;   {do comments nest?}
         leftDelims:        DelimType;
         rightDelims:       DelimType;
         leftComment:       CommentType;
         rightComment:      CommentType;
         escapeCode:        TokenType;{escape symbol code}
         decimalCode:       TokenType;
```

```
    itlResource:       Handle;  {handle to current script itl4 resource}
    reserved:          ARRAY [0..7] OF LongInt;    {must be zero!}
END;
TokenBlockPtr = ^TokenBlock;
```

Routines

Checking and Setting the System Direction

```
FUNCTION GetSysDirection: Integer;

PROCEDURE SetSysDirection    (newDirection: Integer);
```

Checking and Setting Script Manager Variables

```
FUNCTION GetScriptManagerVariable
                        (selector: Integer): LongInt;
FUNCTION SetScriptManagerVariable
                        (selector: Integer; param: LongInt): OSErr;
```

Checking and Setting Script Variables

```
FUNCTION GetScriptVariable   (script: ScriptCode;
                             selector: Integer): LongInt;
FUNCTION SetScriptVariable   (script: ScriptCode; selector: Integer;
                             param: LongInt): OSErr;
```

Making Keyboard Settings

```
PROCEDURE KeyScript          (code: Integer);
```

Determining Script Codes From Font Information

```
FUNCTION FontScript: Integer;

FUNCTION FontToScript        (fontNumber: Integer): Integer;

FUNCTION IntlScript: Integer;
```

Analyzing Characters

```
FUNCTION CharacterByteType    (textBuf: Ptr;textOffset: Integer;
                             script: ScriptCode): Integer;

FUNCTION CharacterType        (textBuf: Ptr; textOffset: Integer;
                             script: ScriptCode): Integer;

FUNCTION FillParseTable       (VAR table: CharByteTable;
                             script: ScriptCode): Boolean;
```

Directly Accessing International Resources

```
PROCEDURE ClearIntlResourceCache;
FUNCTION GetIntlResource      (theID: Integer): Handle;
PROCEDURE GetIntlResourceTable
                        (script: ScriptCode;tableCode: Integer;VAR
                         itlHandle: Handle; VAR offset: LongInt;VAR
                         length: LongInt);
```

Tokenization

```
FUNCTION IntlTokenize      (tokenParam: TokenBlockPtr): TokenResults;
```

Transliteration

```
FUNCTION TransliterateText (srcHandle: Handle; dstHandle: Handle;
                           target: Integer; srcMask: LongInt;
                           script: ScriptCode): OSErr;
```

Replacing a Script System's Default Routines

```
FUNCTION GetScriptUtilityAddress
                        (selector: Integer; before: Boolean;
                         script: ScriptCode): Ptr;
PROCEDURE SetScriptUtilityAddress
                        (selector: Integer; before: Boolean;
                         routineAddr: Ptr; script: ScriptCode);
FUNCTION GetScriptQDPatchAddress
                        (trapNum: Integer;
                         before: Boolean; forPrinting: Boolean;
                         script: ScriptCode): Ptr;
PROCEDURE SetScriptQDPatchAddress
                        (trapNum: Integer;before: Boolean;
                         forPrinting: Boolean; routineAddr: Ptr;
                         script: ScriptCode);
```

6

Script Manager

C Summary

Constants

Please see page 6-107 for a listing of constants defined in Pascal by the Script Manager.
The constants as defined in C are identical to them.

Data Types

```
typedef unsigned char TokenResults;

typedef char CharByteTable[256];

typedef short TokenType;

typedef TokenType DelimType[2];

typedef TokenType CommentType[4];

struct TokenRec {
 TokenType theToken;
 Ptr position;                /*pointer into original source*/
 long length;                 /*length of text in original source*/
 StringPtr stringPosition;    /*Pascal/C string copy of identifier*/
};
typedef struct TokenRec TokenRec;
typedef TokenRec *TokenRecPtr;

struct TokenBlock {
 Ptr source;                  /*pointer to stream of characters*/
 long sourceLength;           /*length of source stream*/
 Ptr tokenList;               /*pointer to array of tokens*/
 long tokenLength;            /*maximum length of TokenList*/
 long tokenCount;             /*number tokens generated by tokenizer*/
 Ptr stringList;              /*pointer to stream of identifiers*/
 long stringLength;           /*length of string list*/
 long stringCount;            /*number of bytes currently used*/
 Boolean doString;            /*make strings & put into StringList*/
 Boolean doAppend;            /*append to TokenList rather than replace*/
 Boolean doAlphanumeric;      /*identifiers may include numeric*/
 Boolean doNest;              /*do comments nest?*/
```

```
TokenType leftDelims[2];
TokenType rightDelims[2];
TokenType leftComment[4];
TokenType rightComment[4];
TokenType escapeCode;            /*escape symbol code*/
TokenType decimalCode;
Handle itlResource;             /*handle to itl4 resource of current script*/
long reserved[8];               /*must be zero!*/
};
typedef struct TokenBlock TokenBlock;
typedef TokenBlock *TokenBlockPtr;
```

Routines

Checking and Setting the System Direction

```
#define GetSysDirection()    (* (short*) 0x0BAC);
pascal void SetSysDirection (short newDirection);
```

Checking and Setting Script Manager Variables

```
pascal long GetScriptManagerVariable
                    (short selector);
pascal OSErr SetScriptManagerVariable
                    (short selector, long param);
```

Checking and Setting Script Variables

```
pascal long GetScriptVariable
                    (ScriptCode script, short selector);
pascal OSErr SetScriptVariable
                    (ScriptCode script, short selector, long param);
```

Making Keyboard Settings

```
pascal void KeyScript       (short code);
```

Determining Script Codes From Font Information

```
pascal short FontScript     (void);
pascal short FontToScript   (short fontNumber);
pascal short IntlScript     (void);
```

Analyzing Characters

```
pascal short CharacterByteType
                        (Ptr textBuf, short textOffset,
                         ScriptCode script);
pascal short CharacterType   (Ptr textBuf, short textOffset,
                         ScriptCode script);
pascal Boolean FillParseTable
                        (CharByteTable table, ScriptCode script);
```

Directly Accessing International Resources

```
pascal void ClearIntlResourceCache
                        (void);
pascal Handle GetIntlResource
                        (short theID);
pascal void GetIntlResourceTable
                        (ScriptCode script, short tableCode,
                         Handle *itlHandle, long *offset, long *length);
```

Tokenization

```
pascal TokenResults IntlTokenize
                        (TokenBlockPtr tokenParam);
```

Transliteration

```
pascal OSErr TransliterateText
                        (Handle srcHandle, Handle dstHandle,
                         short target, long srcMask, ScriptCode script);
```

Replacing a Script System's Default Routines

```
pascal Ptr GetScriptUtilityAddress
                        (short selector, Boolean before,
                         ScriptCode script);
pascal void SetScriptUtilityAddress
                        (short selector, Boolean before,
                         Ptr routineAddr, ScriptCode script);
pascal Ptr GetScriptQDPatchAddress
                        (short trapNum, Boolean before,
                         Boolean forPrinting, ScriptCode script);
pascal void SetScriptQDPatchAddress
                        (short trapNum, Boolean before,
                         Boolean forPrinting, Ptr routineAddr,
                         ScriptCode script);
```

Assembly-Language Summary

Trap Macros

Trap Macro Names

Pascal name	Trap macro name
FontScript	_FontScript
IntlScript	_IntlScript
KeyScript	_KeyScript
FontToScript	_FontToScript
GetScriptManagerVariable	_GetScriptManagerVariable
SetScriptManagerVariable	_SetScriptManagerVariable
GetScriptVariable	_GetScriptVariable
SetScriptVariable	_SetScriptVariable
CharacterByteType	_CharacterByteType
CharacterType	_CharacterType
TransliterateText	_TransliterateText
FillParseTable	_FillParseTable
GetScriptUtilityAddress	_GetScriptUtilityAddress
SetScriptUtilityAddress	_SetScriptUtilityAddress
GetScriptQDPatchAddress	_GetScriptQDPatchAddress
SetScriptQDPatchAddress	_SetScriptQDPatchAddress
IntlTokenize	_IntlTokenize
GetIntlResource	_GetIntlResource
ClearIntlResourceCache	_ClearIntlResourceCache
GetIntlResourceTable	_GetIntlResourceTable

Global Variables

SysDirection	System direction; the primary line direction and alignment for text
BootDrive	The drive number of the startup volume

Text Services Manager

Contents

Contents

This chapter describes how text-processing applications can communicate flexibly and efficiently with utilities that provide services to those applications. Applications that need input methods, spell-checking, hyphenation, and so forth can use the Text Services Manager to search for, obtain information about, and communicate with those utilities. Utilities can use the Text Services Manager to request actions and information from applications, and to send data to them.

Read this chapter if you are developing or enhancing an application to use text services. In particular, if you want your application to support text input in a 2-byte script system, you should use the Text Services Manager. Your application will then work with multiple script systems and many input methods.

Read this chapter if you are writing or adapting a utility that provides a text service such as text input. Utilities that work with the Text Services Manager are called *text service components*. If your utility is a text service component, it will be able to communicate with a wide range of applications.

Before reading this chapter, read the chapter "Introduction to Text on the Macintosh" in this book. To use this chapter, you should also be familiar with the Apple Event Manager and the Component Manager. For details on the Apple Event Manager, see *Inside Macintosh: Interapplication Communication*. For more on the Component Manager, see *Inside Macintosh: More Macintosh Toolbox*.

This chapter refers to routines, constants, and data structures from QuickDraw, the Event Manager, the Window Manager, the Menu Manager, and the Process Manager. For details on QuickDraw, see *Inside Macintosh: Imaging*. For more on the Event Manager, Window Manager, and Menu Manager, see *Inside Macintosh: Macintosh Toolbox Essentials*. For information on the Process Manager, see *Inside Macintosh: Processes*.

This chapter first provides a brief introduction to text services in general, input methods in particular, and the Text Services Manager itself. If you are writing an application, it then discusses how you can

- use the Text Services Manager routines for client applications, to send information to text service components

- implement the text-service Apple event handlers in your client application, to receive information from text service components

- communicate directly with the Component Manager and text service components, if your application's special needs require you to bypass the Text Services Manager

If you are writing a text service component, this chapter discusses how you can

- implement the text service component routines, so that the Text Services Manager and client applications can request the text services you provide

- use the Text Services Manager routines for text service components, to send information to client applications and the Text Services Manager

About Text Services

The Text Services Manager is the part of Macintosh system software that maintains communication between applications that need text services and utility programs that provide them. The Text Services Manager exists so that these two types of programs can work together without needing to know anything about each others' internal structures or identities.

A **text service** is a specific text-handling task such as spell-checking, hyphenation, and handling input of complex text. A **text service component** is a utility program that uses the Text Services Manager to provide a text service to an application. Text service components are registered components with the Component Manager, as described in the Component Manager chapter of *Inside Macintosh: More Macintosh Toolbox*.

A **client application** is a text-processing program that uses the Text Services Manager to request a service from a text service component. To accomplish this, a client application needs to make the Text Services Manager aware of its existence and needs to make specific Text Services Manager calls during execution.

In principle, text services can include many different types of tasks. However, only one type of text service is currently defined: text input. This chapter describes how to work with any type of text service component, and how to create any type of text service component, but it emphasizes input methods. It also points out the ways in which input methods are handled differently from other types of text service components.

About Input Methods

An **input method** is a facility that automatically converts phonetic or syllabic characters into ideographic or other complex representations. It permits use of a standard keyboard to generate the thousands to tens of thousands of different characters needed by some languages. Text input in Japanese, Chinese, and Korean usually requires an input method.

For example, text input in the Japanese script system requires software for transcribing Romaji (phonetic Japanese using Roman characters) or Hiragana (syllabic Japanese) into ideographic Kanji (Chinese characters). Each Kanji character may correspond to more than one possible Hiragana sequence, and vice versa. The input method must grammatically parse sentences or clauses of Hiragana text (which has no word separations) and select the best combination of Kanji and Hiragana characters to represent that text.

Chinese text input is similar to Japanese, in that a conversion from Pinyin (Roman) or Zhuyinfuhao (phonetic) to ideographic Hanzi (Chinese characters) is required. Korean text input requires conversion from Jamo (phonetic) to non-ideographic Hangul (complex clusters of Jamo).

Text Services Manager

Bottomline input allows the user to type text into a special **floating input window**—usually displayed in the lower portion of the screen—where conversion is to take place. The floating input window typically appears whenever the user starts typing characters. See Figure 7-1.

Figure 7-1   Bottomline input with a floating input window

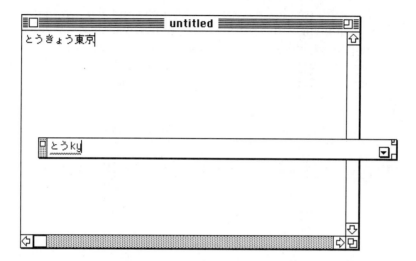

Inline input is an input method in which conversion of characters takes place at the current line position in the application where the text is intended to appear. This allows the user to type text directly into the application window and requires no separate input window. Inline input is the principal example of the kind of text service supported by the Text Services Manager. See Figure 7-2.

Figure 7-2   Inline input

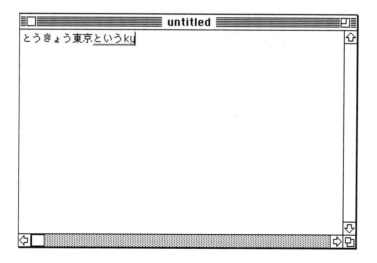

About Input Methods

With either bottomline input or inline input, the user can usually type Roman characters or characters of another subscript. Figure 7-3 shows an example of a floating palette, with which the user can select whether text entry is to be in 1-byte or 2-byte Romaji, Katakana, or Hiragana. The user presses a key such as the Space bar to initiate conversion from the input characters to the final characters.

The input method is often extended so that characters may be converted in extremely precise ways. For example, in the Japanese script system, when Hiragana text is converted to Kanji, the user has the option of changing any individual phrase: lengthening it, shortening it, or selecting different possible interpretations. Figure 7-3 shows a scrolling list of additional conversion options displayed next to the converted text in a floating input window. Only after the user is satisfied with the conversion and presses the Return key is the text actually sent to the application.

Figure 7-3   Displaying conversion options for bottomline input

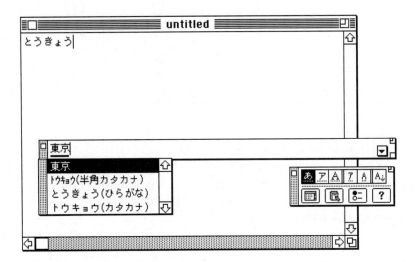

Input methods commonly rely upon one or more dictionaries to perform conversion. The main dictionary lists all standard conversion options for any valid syllabic or phonetic input. Besides using the main dictionary, users can add specialized dictionaries, such as legal or medical dictionaries, to extend the range of the input method. See the chapter "Dictionary Manager" in this book for more information.

About the Text Services Manager

The Text Services Manager links text service components to client applications that use text services. When a client application requests a service from the Text Services Manager, the Text Services Manager routes the request to a text service component associated with that application. The text service component processes the request and may send text or other information back to the Text Services Manager, which passes it on to the client application through an Apple event.

An application that explicitly uses the Text Services Manager is called a **TSM-aware application.** An application that does not make calls to the Text Services Manager is called non-TSM-aware. A non-TSM-aware application can still make indirect use of some services of the Text Services Manager; see "Floating Input Windows" on page 7-13.

The Text Services Environment

The text services environment is a structure for the efficient flow of information between client applications and text service components. It allows client applications to obtain text services without having to know anything about the specific text service components performing them. Likewise, it allows text service components to perform their services without having to know anything about the specific client applications making the requests.

The text services environment consists of a client application, a text service component, the Apple Event Manager, the Component Manager, and the Text Services Manager. For a client application to work within the text services environment, it must

- call the routines of the Text Services Manager application interface described under "Text Services Manager Routines for Client Applications" on page 7-48. By using these application-level routines, a client application becomes TSM-aware and communicates with other parts of the environment.

- implement handlers for the Apple events described under "Apple Event Handlers Supplied by Client Applications" on page 7-65. A client application receives text and other information from a text service component through Apple events.

For a text service component to work within the text services environment, it must

- register as a component with the Component Manager

- call the routines of the Text Services Manager component interface described under "Text Services Manager Routines for Components" on page 7-77

- implement the component-level text service component routines described under "Text Service Component Routines" on page 7-84

Figure 7-4 shows some of the flow of information in the text services environment when a TSM-aware application uses a text service component. Application-level calls that an application makes to the Text Services Manager application interface are converted to component-level calls that are passed to an individual text service component. The text service component in turn makes calls to the Text Services Manager component interface; those calls are converted to Apple events that are passed on to the application.

The Text Services Manager controls the overall process by keeping track of which text service components are available to a given application and which application is to receive data from a given text service component. The Text Services Manager communicates with text service components through the Component Manager; applications that have special needs can likewise communicate directly with individual text service components by calling the text service component routines.

Figure 7-4   How a TSM-aware client application uses the Text Services Manager

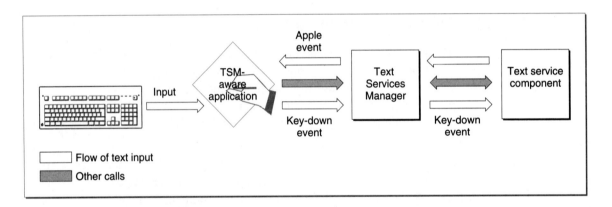

IMPORTANT

The event-handling structure of the Text Services Manager requires that the low-memory global variable `SEvtEnb` be nonzero. If your application sets `SEvtEnb` to 0 to force the Event Manager function `SystemEvent` to always return a value of `FALSE`, text service components do not function correctly. See *Inside Macintosh: Macintosh Toolbox Essentials* for more information on the `SystemEvent` function and the `SEvtEnb` global variable. ▲

The Text Services Manager and Input Methods

Although the Text Services Manager can work with any type of text service component, it provides several features specific to input methods for 2-byte script systems. The Text Services Manager synchronizes the current input method with the current keyboard script. For example, if the user changes from a Japanese to a Chinese font, the application changes the keyboard script to Chinese and the Text Services Manager then switches the current input method from Japanese to Chinese as well. Unlike with other text services, the Text Services Manager opens and closes input methods, and takes care of their menu handling.

Inline Input

A principal feature of the Text Services Manager is its support for inline input. Figure 7-4 shows how information flows through the Text Services Manager when a TSM-aware application uses it for inline input. The application passes key-down events to the text service component; the text service component sends text and messages back to the application with Apple events. Events, messages, and requests for service between the application and the text service component all pass through the Text Services Manager.

For inline input, the Text Services Manager offers routines that let client applications and text service components communicate about what happens in the **active input area**—the portion of the screen in which the user enters text and where the text service component displays converted text. The client application and the text service component share control over the active input area.

The active input area is almost like a small window with invisible borders inside of the application's document window. It replaces the insertion point in the document, but it can be any width; it can even occupy more than one entire line of text. Text within the active input area can have its own font and size, different from that of body text. Text within the active input area can even scroll out of sight if there is more text than can fit in the space allotted for it in the active input area.

The application is responsible for determining the location and size of the active input area, and for drawing and highlighting all text within it. The text service component is responsible for accepting user input (as key-down events), for converting input text to final text, and for telling the application what characters to draw—and what characters to accept as confirmed—at every step of the way. The text service component can also instruct the application to scroll certain parts of the active input area into view, if necessary.

The text service component processes the user input, called **raw text,** as it is entered. The text service component first has the application draw the text on the screen as entered. Then it **converts** the raw text, translating it from phonetic or syllabic to ideographic or complex syllabic characters. Finally, it **confirms** the converted text upon user approval of the conversion. By convention in some script systems, a text service component converts text when the user presses the Space bar after entering a sequence of characters, and confirms the converted text when the user presses Return to accept the conversion. See Figure 7-5. (In Korean, conversion happens continuously and automatically, and confirmation happens by convention when the user presses either Return or the Space bar.)

Figure 7-5   Entering, converting, and confirming text in an active input area

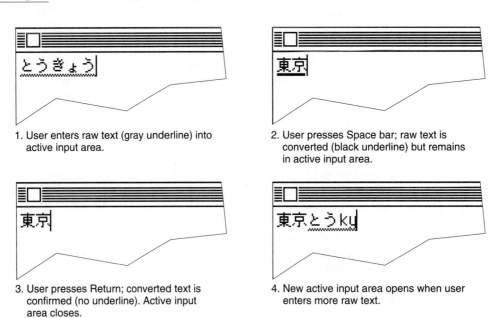

1. User enters raw text (gray underline) into active input area.

2. User presses Space bar; raw text is converted (black underline) but remains in active input area.

3. User presses Return; converted text is confirmed (no underline). Active input area closes.

4. New active input area opens when user enters more raw text.

The text service component continually removes the confirmed input from the active input area and sends it to the application for storage in its text buffer. The text service component uses Apple events for this purpose, and for notifying the application of every character (raw, converted, or confirmed) that needs to be drawn or highlighted within the active input area.

In a number of situations, a client application may need to initiate the confirmation of input in progress. For example, if a user switches input methods, makes a menu selection, or selects text outside the active input area, the user has implicitly requested confirmation of the existing text. The client application needs to inform the text service component so it can confirm all text, whether raw or converted, in the active input area. The client application can make that request through a call to the Text Services Manager.

Floating Input Windows

The Text Services Manager also provides a service to facilitate the use of an input window for text entry and conversion when inline input is not supported by the application or not desired by the user. This floating input window is a standard bottomline input window: it usually appears in the lower portion of the screen, although the user can drag it to any location. Once the user's text has been converted correctly in the window, it is sent to the application.

The Text Services Manager's floating input window is mainly for use with applications that are not TSM-aware. See Figure 7-4. The input window uses the **floating window service,** a part of the Text Services Manager. It works this way:

1. The Process Manager intercepts key-down events and passes them to the Text Services Manager.

2. The Text Services Manager passes them to the appropriate input method for processing.

3. The input method then passes the processed text back to the Text Services Manager. The floating window service displays the text in a floating input window.

4. When the user is finished with the text, the floating window service passes the processed text back to the client application through standard key-down events (not Apple events).

Figure 7-6   How a non-TSM-aware application uses the Text Services Manager

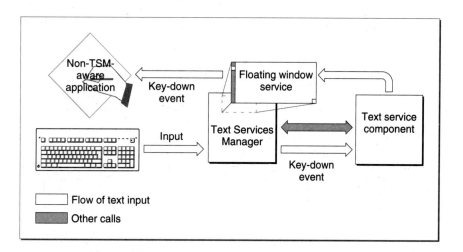

In this way the Text Services Manager can provide an input method text service component for applications that have no knowledge of the text services environment.

TSM-aware applications should normally use inline input. However, the Text Services Manager does allow TSM-aware applications to use a floating input window. Users may prefer bottomline input if the size of the text displayed in the document makes reading the characters difficult.

Floating Utility Windows

Floating windows are useful for more than just text entry. Input methods can use the Text Services Manager floating window service to create utility windows—floating windows that display palettes or present lists of choices to the user. For example, most Japanese input methods let a user set the input mode to either 2-byte Hiragana, 1-byte Hiragana, 2-byte Romaji, or 1-byte Romaji. In the past, users selected these modes from controls inside the input method's input window. Now, since the system provides a standard floating input window for non-TSM-aware applications as well as for TSM-aware applications that request it, input methods should offer mode selection in a separate floating palette. Figure 7-3 on page 7-8 shows an example of a floating palette window used with bottomline input; Figure 7-9 on page 7-33 shows the same palette used with inline input.

Figure 7-7 illustrates the window-layer organization provided by the Text Services Manager. A floating window, whether an input window or a utility window, is always in front of all application windows but behind any help balloons.

Figure 7-7   Floating window service layer

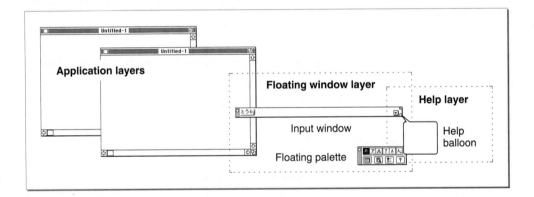

About Text Service Components

Text service components are components as defined and used by the Component Manager. They have a specific structure, interface, and manner of execution. For more information on components, see the chapter "Component Manager" in *Inside Macintosh: More Macintosh Toolbox*. This section briefly describes the component description record, a data structure associated with a text service component.

The *component description record,* maintained by the Component Manager for each registered component, identifies the characteristics of the component, including the nature of services provided by the component and the manufacturer of the component. It is filled out by the text service component at initialization.

The `ComponentDescription` data type defines the format of the component description record:

```
TYPE ComponentDescription =
    RECORD
        componentType:      OSType;   {command set ID}
        componentSubType:   OSType;   {specifies flavor}
        componentManufacturer:
                            OSType;   {vendor ID}
        componentFlags:     OSType;   {control flags}
        componentFlagsMask: OSType;   {mask for control flags}
    END;
```

Field descriptions

componentType   For text service components, this field contains the interface type. The **interface type** specifies the set of Apple events and component commands associated with the text service component. Currently, all text service components have the same interface type, `kTextService`, whose associated 4-character tag is `'tsvc'`. To obtain a list of all available text service components, a client application can specify the value `kTextServices` in the `componentType` field when calling the Component Manager routine `GetServiceList`.

componentSubType

     For text service components, this field contains the text service component type. The **text service component type** specifies the function and optionally a set of additional routines and data structures associated with that particular kind of text service component. Currently, only one text service component type is defined, `'inpm'`, specifying an inline input method.

componentManufacturer

     The identification number of the manufacturer of this particular text service component.

componentFlags   Four bytes that contain component-specific information. See
                  Figure 7-8:

                  Bits 0–7 contain the language code (as unsigned 8 bits).

                  Bits 8–14 contain the script code (as unsigned 7 bits).

                  Bit 15 indicates whether the text service component takes active
                  events. When bit 15 = 1, the text service component is interactive
                  and accepts user events. When bit 15 = 0, the text service
                  component is not interactive—that is, it only supplies batch services.

                  Apple has reserved bits 16–23, so text services must set them to 0.

                  The Component Manager defines bits 24–31.

Figure 7-8   The format of the componentFlags field of the component description record

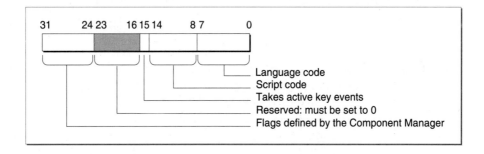

componentFlagsMask

                  Four bytes that contain values used to affect the componentFlags
                  field. This field should be 0 in the component description record for
                  any text service component.

For example, an input method for the Japanese script system might assign the following
values to the componentType, componentSubType, and componentFlags fields of
component description record.

```
cd: ComponentDescription;
cd.componentType      := kTextService;          {'tsvc'}
cd.componentSubType   := kInputMethodService; {'inpm'}
cd.componentFlags     := $0000810B;   {Japanese script & language }
                                      { --takes user events}
```

Using the Text Services Manager (for Client Applications)

This section describes how your client application can use the Text Services Manager application interface to communicate with text service components, how it can use Apple event handlers to receive information from text service components, and how it can communicate directly with text service components—bypassing the Text Services Manager altogether—for special purposes.

Testing for the Availability of the Text Services Manager

Use the `Gestalt` environmental selector `gestaltTSMgrVersion` to determine whether the Text Services Manager is available. The `Gestalt` function returns a 32-bit value indicating which version of the Text Services Manager is installed.

For more information on the `Gestalt` function, see the Gestalt Manager chapter in *Inside Macintosh: Operating System Utilities*.

Calling the Text Services Manager

The application interface to the Text Services Manager consists of application-level calls that your client application uses to send information to text service components by way of the Text Services Manager. They are documented in detail under "Text Services Manager Routines for Client Applications" on page 7-48. The Text Services Manager maps many of those calls to equivalent component-level calls to text service components. Those text service component routines are described under "Text Service Component Routines" on page 7-84.

This section describes how your client application can use the application interface to the Text Services Manager to

- prepare for communication with the Text Services Manager

- create an internal record called a TSM document

- make text services other than text input available to the user

- activate and deactivate a TSM document

- give text service components a chance to handle events, respond to menu selections, and set the shape of the cursor

- explicitly confirm text within the active input area

- terminate communication with the Text Services Manager

Initializing as a TSM-Aware Application

If your client application plans to use any of the Text Services Manager application-interface routines, it must call `InitTSMAwareApplication` at startup, immediately after calling the rest of the Toolbox initialization routines. See Listing 7-1.

Listing 7-1   Initializing as a TSM-aware application

```
FUNCTION Initialize: OSErr;
VAR
   myErr:    OSErr;
BEGIN
   InitGraf(@thePort);
   InitFonts;
   InitWindows;
   InitMenus;
   TEInit;
   InitDialogs(NIL);
   InitCursor;

   IF (InitTSMAwareApplication = noErr) THEN
      Initialize := DoNew;          {application routine that }
                                    { creates window & TSM document}
END;
```

The Text Services Manager records the fact that your client application is TSM-aware, and allocates any private data storage as necessary.

Creating a TSM Document

Your client application needs to create an internal record called a **TSM document** (defined by the `TSMDocument` data type) before it can use any services provided through the Text Services Manager. A TSM document is a private data structure that is associated with each of your application's documents that use a text service. You cannot access the TSM document record directly. You call the `NewTSMDocument` function to instruct the Text Services Manager to create the TSM document. The Text Services Manager returns a TSM document ID, an identifier that you supply in subsequent calls to the Text Services Manager.

Typically, you create a TSM document for each window that your application uses. Use the `supportedInterfaceTypes` array to indicate which text service interfaces you support. Currently only one interface is defined—`'tsvc'`, the component type for text services components. Pass any data you like in the `refcon` parameter to the call. The Text Services Manager returns the `refcon` value in the `keyAETSMDocumentRefcon` parameter of any Apple event sent to your application. You can then use the `refcon` value to determine which TSM document and window the Apple event belongs to.

Listing 7-2 shows the sample application's DoNew function, which is called from the initialization routine presented in Listing 7-1. The call to NewTSMDocument specifies that the application supports one interface type (kTextService). NewTSMDocument opens the default input method for the current keyboard script, assigns it to this document, and returns the TSM document ID in the idocID parameter. The routine makes use of a modified window record (type MyWindowRecord) that is a standard window record with an additional field for holding the TSM document ID.

Listing 7-2   Creating a new TSM document and associating it with a window

```
FUNCTION DoNew: OSErr;
VAR
    wRecordPtr:         myWindowPtr;
    window:             WindowPtr;
    supportedTypes:     InterfaceTypeList;
    myErr:              OSErr;
BEGIN
    supportedTypes[0] := kTextService;
                                    {allocate storage for window record}
    wRecordPtr := myWindowPtr(NewPtr(sizeof(myWindowRecord)));
    IF wRecordPtr <> NIL THEN
    BEGIN
        IF gColorQDAvailable THEN
            window := GetNewCWindow(kWINDResID, Ptr(wRecordPtr),
                                    WindowPtr(-1))
        ELSE
            window := GetNewWindow(kWINDResID, Ptr(wRecordPtr),
                                    WindowPtr(-1));
        IF window = NIL THEN                     {couldn't get window}
        BEGIN
            DisposePtr(Ptr(wRecordPtr));                     {clean up}
            DoNew := kWindowFailed;
            Exit(DoNew);
        END;
        myErr := NewTSMDocument(1, supportedTypes,
                                wRecordPtr^.idocID,
                                LongInt(wRecordPtr));
    END;
    {do other window intialization, like creating scroll bars}
    DoNew := myErr;
END;
```

Making Text Services Available to the User

Text services that are input methods are always displayed in the keyboard menu. System software takes care of that; your application does not need to list input methods. However, your application may wish to provide a menu or scrolling list to display other types of available text services. (Note that, currently, no text services other than input methods are available. This capability is provided for future extensibility.)

To obtain a list of the available text services on the user's system, call the GetServiceList function. You pass it an array of interface types (to indicate the types of services you want returned in the list) and a pointer to a data structure (to hold the list). The function returns the number of available components, and a name and component identifier for each one.

Because text service components can be registered or unregistered at any time, your client application should periodically call either GetServiceList or the Component Manager function GetComponentListModSeed to see if the list of registered text service components may have changed.

IMPORTANT

If your client application displays a list or menu of text service components, do not show input methods. They are already displayed in the Keyboard menu. To show them in two places would be confusing to users. ▲

The Text Services Manager automatically opens input methods; your client application does not have to open them. You do have to explicitly open all other types of text services, however. If the user chooses a text service from a menu or list that you have displayed, you need to open that text service.

You call the OpenTextService function to associate the text service component with the current TSM document. OpenTextService then returns a valid component instance to indicate that the text service component has been opened and initialized.

Whenever a user wishes to close a text service component that you have opened, call the CloseTextService function.

Activating and Deactivating a TSM Document

To notify the Text Services Manager that a window in your client application associated with a TSM document has been activated, and that you are ready to use a text service component, use the ActivateTSMDocument function.

Listing 7-3 shows how to handle activating and deactivating a TSM document. You specify the document using the ID assigned to it when it was created (with the NewTSMDocument function). This routine, like the previous samples, assumes that the application has an extended window record with a field, idocID, that contains the TSM document ID.

Listing 7-3   Activating and deactivating a TSM document

```
PROCEDURE DoActivate(window: WindowPtr; becomingActive: Boolean);
VAR
    myErr:    OSErr;
BEGIN
    IF becomingActive THEN
        myErr := ActivateTSMDocument(MyWindowPtr(window)^.idocID)
    ELSE
        myErr := DeactivateTSMDocument(MyWindowPtr(window)^.idocID);
END;
```

When the Text Services Manager receives an `ActivateTSMDocument` call, it deactivates the currently active TSM document (if it hasn't already been explicitly deactivated) and stores the new document as the currently active TSM document. If the specified text service component for the document has a menu, the Text Services Manager inserts the menu into the menu bar as an application or system menu.

When a window in your client application associated with a TSM document has been deactivated, you should call the `DeactivateTSMDocument` function. The Text Services Manager in turn calls the text service component function `DeactivateTextService` for any text service components associated with the TSM document being deactivated.

Input-method text services are handled in a special way: the identity of the input method of the deactivated document is retained by the Text Services Manager, and compared with the input method used by the next *activated* document. If the newly active document uses the same input method, the Text Services Manager will simply activate the new instance of the same input method. If the documents use different input methods, the previous input method is then closed, and any windows belonging to it are closed and menus are removed. The new input method is then activated. Not closing an input method until it is actually unneeded avoids extra removal and immediate redisplay of input method palettes and menus.

Passing Events, Menu Selections, and Cursor Setting

Whenever your client application receives an event from the Event Manager function `WaitNextEvent`, you need to give each text service component an opportunity to handle that event, if appropriate. Use the `TSMEvent` function to let the Text Services Manager dispatch the events to the correct text service component. You provide a pointer to the event record containing the event. The Text Services Manager passes the event in turn to each component associated with the currently active TSM document, starting with input methods. If the event is handled by a component, `TSMEvent` returns `TRUE` and the event is changed to a null event. If the event is not handled, `TSMEvent` returns `FALSE` and you are responsible for handling the event.

Listing 7-4 is a partial example of an event handler in which the application passes events to the Text Services Manager for routing to text service components. If no text service component handles an event, the application handles it. The global variable gUsingTSM is TRUE if the Text Services Manager is present and the application is making use of it.

Listing 7-4   Passing events to a text service component

```
PROCEDURE MyDoEvent(event: eventRecord);
VAR
    handledByTS:    Boolean;
    gotEvent:       Boolean;
BEGIN
    WHILE TRUE DO
    BEGIN
      IF gHasWaitNextEvent THEN
      BEGIN
         gotEvent := WaitNextEvent(everyEvent, event,
                                      kSleep, NIL);
         handledByTS := FALSE;
         IF (gUsingTSM AND gotEvent) THEN
            handledByTS := TSMEvent(event);
      END;
      IF gotEvent AND (NOT handledByTS) THEN

         {process event in normal way}
         ;
    END;
END;
```

Whenever a user chooses a menu item, it may be from a text service component's menu; your application must therefore give the text service component a chance to respond. (This situation occurs only with text service components that are not input methods.) To do this, use the TSMMenuSelect function with the result from the Menu Manager function MenuSelect in the menuResult parameter. If TSMMenuSelect returns TRUE, then the text service component has handled the menu selection, so your client application does not need to do so. However, your application is still responsible for removing the highlighting from the menu title after the selection has been handled.

Your client application is generally responsible for setting the cursor to an appropriate shape. However, the text service component may have its own cursor requirements when the cursor is within the boundaries of its windows or palettes. To allow a text service component to set the cursor, use the SetTSMCursor function. Call it whenever you would normally set the cursor yourself. If SetTSMCursor returns TRUE, the cursor is either on a text service component window or on the active input area and a text service component has set the cursor. In this case, you should not set the cursor.

Confirming Active Text Within a TSM Document

Normally, an input method text service component ejects finished input from the active input area continually as it processes user events, sending the confirmed text to your application with the Update Active Input Area Apple event.

Circumstances may arise in which you need to confirm input in progress before the text service component ejects it (that is, before the user presses Return). If, for example, the user clicks the mouse in text outside the active input area, that constitutes an implicit user acceptance of the text in the active input area. You should explicitly terminate any active input and save the text that is in the active input area by calling the FixTSMDocument function. The text service component sends the confirmed text to your application and empties the active input area.

Listing 7-5 shows what happens when the user clicks the go-away box of the active document window after entering some text in the active input area. The global variable gIDocID represents the ID of the active TSM document.

Listing 7-5   Confirming text in an active input area

```
PROCEDURE DoMouseDown (event: EventRecord);
VAR
    part:        Integer;
    theWindow:   WindowPtr;
    myErr:       OSErr;
BEGIN
    part := FindWindow(event.where, theWindow);
    CASE part OF
        inContent:
            DoContentClick(theWindow, event);

        inDrag:
            DragWindow(theWindow, event.where,
                            theWindow^.portRect);

        inGoAway:
            IF TrackGoAway(theWindow, event.where) THEN
            BEGIN
                myErr := FixTSMDocument(gIDocID);   {confirm text}
                DoActivate(theWindow, FALSE);     {deactivate window}
                HideWindow(theWindow);               {put it away}
                gVisible := FALSE;
            END;
    END;
END;
```

Deleting a TSM Document

When your client application closes a document window and no longer needs its associated TSM document, it needs to call the `DeleteTSMDocument` function to inform the Text Services Manager that the TSM document should be deleted.

The Text Services Manager closes the text service components for the specified TSM document by calling the Component Manager `CloseComponent` function for each open text service component. It then disposes of the internal TSM document record for the specified TSM document.

Closing Down as a TSM-Aware Application

To let the Text Services Manager perform needed housekeeping chores when your application has closed, your client application needs to call `CloseTSMAwareApplication` just before quitting, as shown in Listing 7-6.

Listing 7-6   Closing a TSM-aware application

```
FUNCTION DoQuitApplication: OSErr;
VAR
    myErr:    OSErr;
BEGIN

    {app-specific clean up}

    myErr := CloseTSMAwareApplication;   {ignore the error}
    ExitToShell;
END;
```

Requesting a Floating Input Window for Text Entry

Your client application may need to provide for users who prefer to enter text using a floating input window instead of entering text directly in the line of a document. For example, when the text font size is too small for reading ideographic characters, too big for convenient entry directly into the document window, or is being greeked, users may prefer a floating input window.

Your client application calls the `UseInputWindow` function with the `useInputWindow` parameter set to `TRUE` to display a floating input window for the TSM document you specify in the `idocID` parameter to the call. To display floating input windows for all documents associated with your application, you set the `idocID` parameter to `NIL` and the `useInputWindow` parameter to `TRUE`. To return to inline input, call `UseInputWindow` with the `useInputWindow` parameter set to `FALSE`.

Associating Input Methods With Scripts and Languages

If you use the application-interface routines, the Text Services Manager automatically associates a default input method with your TSM document every time the current script and language change. Although it is unlikely that it would ever need to, your client application can use Text Services Manager routines to control that automatic association.

The Operating System uses the GetDefaultInputMethod and SetDefaultInputMethod functions to associate an input method with a given script and language. When the user uses the Keyboard menu, Keyboard control panel, or other device for controlling input method preferences, these functions establish permanent associations (they last across restarts).

The Text Services Manager maintains a current text service language that it uses to synchronize input methods to the current script system and language. The Operating System calls the SetTextServiceLanguage function when the user switches the keyboard script, and the floating window service calls the GetTextServiceLanguage function to determine the text service language.

These routines make use of the script-language record, described under "Identifying the Supported Scripts and Languages" on page 7-42.

If your client application uses the Text Services Manager application-interface routines, the Text Services Manager automatically synchronizes the input method to the current text service language and there is no need to make the calls described here. If your client application bypasses the Text Services Manager and uses the text service component routines, the Text Services Manager does not provide automatic input method synchronization and you may have to make some of these calls yourself. See "Direct Access to Text Service Components" on page 7-36 for more information on the Component Manager and on how to communicate directly with text service components.

Handling Text Service Apple Events

Text service components send information to your client application through Apple events. To communicate with an input method text service component, you need to implement Apple event handlers that

- receive raw, converted, or confirmed text from the input method, update the active input area, and highlight text appropriately

- convert screen location (in global coordinates) to text offset (in the active input area or in the application's text buffer), so that the input method can, for example, adjust the caret position or cursor display to reflect the text beneath the cursor

- convert text offset to screen location, so that the input method can, for example, place a list of conversion options next to a particular section of raw text

- respond to the input method's request to show or hide a floating input window

Each Apple event contains two required parameters:

■ The `keyAETSMDocumentRefcon` parameter is filled in by the Text Services Manager. It tells the application which TSM document is affected by the Apple event.

■ The `keyAEServerInstance` parameter is filled in by the text service component, and identifies the component that is sending the Apple event.

Other parameters are specific to each Apple event, and are described under "Apple Event Handlers Supplied by Client Applications" on page 7-65.

For general rules for writing Apple event handlers, see the discussion of the Apple Event Manager in *Inside Macintosh: Interapplication Communication.*

Receiving Text and Updating the Active Input Area

The text service component uses the Update Active Input Area Apple event to request that your client application create and update an active input area, including drawing text in the active input area, and accepting confirmed text. For details on active input areas, see "Inline Input" on page 7-11. This Apple event also asks the client application to update a range of text in the active input area and highlight appropriately.

Because your application is responsible for all drawing in the active input area, it receives an Update Active Input Area Apple event whenever the user enters raw text (for example, Romaji for Japanese input), whenever that raw text is converted to an intermediate form (for example, Hiragana), whenever the text is converted (for example, to Kanji), and whenever the converted text is confirmed. The input method also uses this Apple event to instruct your application in how to highlight the various types of text (raw, converted, and so on) within the active input area.

The input method uses the Update Active Input Area Apple event to send additional information to your application, such as current caret position, a range of text that should be scrolled into view if it is not visible, and boundaries of clauses (language-specific groupings of text) that may exist in the active input area.

Listing 7-7 shows a sample handler for the Update Active Input Area Apple event. The handler first receives the input parameters, including the text and the ranges of text to highlight and update. The handler then puts any confirmed text into the application's text buffer.

Listing 7-7 A sample handler for the Update Active Input Area Apple event

```
FUNCTION MyHandleUpdateActive(theAppleEvent: AppleEvent;
                              reply: AppleEvent;
                              handlerRefCon: LongInt): OSErr;
VAR
    theHiliteDesc: AEDesc;
    theUpdateDesc: AEDesc;
    theTextDesc:   AEDesc;
    myErr:         OSErr;
```

```
      returnedType:    DescType;
      script:          ScriptLanguageRecord;
      fixLength:       LongInt;
      refcon:          LongInt;
      textSize:        LongInt;
      actualSize:      LongInt;
      thePinRange:     TextRange;

BEGIN
   {Get the required parameter keyAETSMDocumentRefcon}
   myErr := AEGetParamPtr(theAppleEvent, keyAETSMDocumentRefcon,
                          typeLongInteger, returnedType, @refcon,
                          sizeof(refcon), actualSize);
   IF myErr = noErr THEN
   BEGIN
      {Get the required parameter keyAETheData}
      theTextDesc.dataHandle := NIL;
      myErr := AEGetParamDesc(theAppleEvent, keyAETheData,
                              typeChar, theTextDesc);
   END;
   IF myErr <> noErr THEN
   BEGIN
      MyHandleUpdateActive := myErr;
      Exit(MyHandleUpdateActive);
   END;


   {Get the required parameter keyAEScriptTag}
   myErr := AEGetParamPtr(theAppleEvent, keyAEScriptTag,
                          typeIntlWritingCode, returnedType,
                          @script, sizeof(script), actualSize);
   IF myErr = noErr THEN
      {Get the required parameter keyAEFixLength}
      myErr := AEGetParamPtr(theAppleEvent, keyAEFixLength,
                             typeLongInteger, returnedType,
                             @fixLength, sizeof(fixlength),
                             actualSize);
   IF myErr = noErr THEN
   BEGIN
      {Get the optional parameter keyAEHiliteRange}
      theHiliteDesc.dataHandle := NIL;
      myErr := AEGetParamDesc(theAppleEvent, keyAEHiliteRange,
                              typeTextRangeArray, theHiliteDesc);
   END;
```

```
IF myErr <> noErr THEN
BEGIN
   MyHandleUpdateActive := myErr;
   myErr := AEDisposeDesc(theTextDesc);    {ignore the error}
   Exit(MyHandleUpdateActive);
END;

{Get the optional parameter keyAEUpdateRange}
theUpdateDesc.dataHandle := NIL;
myErr := AEGetParamDesc(theAppleEvent, keyAEUpdateRange,
                        typeTextRangeArray, theUpdateDesc);
IF myErr <> noErr THEN
BEGIN
   MyHandleUpdateActive := myErr;
   myErr := AEDisposeDesc(theTextDesc);    {ignore the error}
   myErr := AEDisposeDesc(theHiliteDesc);
   Exit(MyHandleUpdateActive);
END;

{Get the optional parameter keyAEPinRange}
myErr := AEGetParamPtr(theAppleEvent, keyAEPinRange,
                       typeTextRange, returnedType,
                       @thePinRange, sizeof(thePinRange),
                       actualSize);

MyHandleUpdateActive := myErr;
IF myErr = noErr THEN
BEGIN
   textSize := GetHandleSize(theTextDesc.dataHandle);
   MyHandleUpdateActive := MemError;
   IF MemError = noErr THEN
   BEGIN
      {if the value of keyAEFixLength is -1, the text }
      { contained in the keyAETheData parameter should }
      { completely replace the active input area in }
      { the application window}

      IF fixLength = -1 THEN fixLength := textSize;

      {the application procedure SetNewText handles }
      { updating and confirming the text in the active }
      { input area, highlighting, and scrolling the }
      { specified offsets into view}
```

```
        SetNewText(refcon, script, theTextDesc.dataHandle,
                textSize, fixLength,
                TextRangeArrayHandle(theUpdateDesc.dataHandle),
                TextRangeArrayHandle(theHiliteDesc.dataHandle) );
      END;
    END;
    myErr := AEDisposeDesc(theTextDesc);        {ignore the errors}
    myErr := AEDisposeDesc(theHiliteDesc);
    myErr := AEDisposeDesc(theUpdateDesc);
END;
```

Converting Screen Position to Text Offset

An input method text service component uses the Position To Offset Apple event when it needs to know the byte offset in a text buffer (usually the buffer corresponding to the active input area) corresponding to a given screen position. An input method typically sends the Position To Offset Apple event to your application in response to a mouse-down event. If the event location is in the application window (including the active input area), the input method may want to know which character the event corresponds to, in order to locate the caret or define highlighting.

An input method may also send Position To Offset in response to SetTSMCursor, so that it can modify the appearance of the cursor depending on the type of text the cursor passes over.

Your application's handler returns a byte offset and a value indicating whether the screen position is within the active input area. If it is, the offset is measured from the start of the active input area (the leading edge of the first character on the first line). If it is not, the offset is measured from the beginning of the application's body text. The definition of *body text* and the significance of measurements within it are specific to your application; here it means any application text outside of the active input area.

To help the input method more specifically define individual characters, your application can optionally return an indication as to whether the position corresponds to the leading edge or the trailing edge of the glyph corresponding to the character at the indicated offset.

The Position To Offset Apple event is similar in function to the QuickDraw PixelToChar function, and returns similar results. Your handler may use PixelToChar to get the information it returns to the text service component, or it may use a TextEdit call, as shown in the following code sample.

Listing 7-8 shows a sample handler for the Position To Offset Apple event. The handler first receives the input parameters, then uses the TextEdit function TEGetOffset to convert a screen location to text offset. The TEGetOffset function is described in the chapter "TextEdit" in this book.

Text Services Manager

Listing 7-8   A sample handler for the Position To Offset Apple event

```pascal
FUNCTION MyHandlePos2Offset(theAppleEvent: AppleEvent;
                                reply: AppleEvent;
                                handlerRefCon: LongInt): OSErr;
VAR
    myErr:         OSErr;
    returnedType:  DescType;
    refcon:        LongInt;
    currentPoint:  Point;
    clickWindow:   WindowPtr;
    where, part:   Integer;
    oldPort:       GrafPtr;
    offset:        LongInt;
    te:            TEHandle;
    actualSize:    LongInt;
    bodyRect:      Rect;
    dragging:      Boolean;
    isMatch:       Boolean;

BEGIN
    {Get the required parameter TSMDocumentRefcon}
    myErr := AEGetParamPtr (theAppleEvent, keyAETSMDocumentRefcon,
                        typeLongInteger, returnedType, @refcon,
                        sizeof(refcon), actualSize);
    IF myErr = noErr THEN
        {Get the required parameter keyAECurrentPoint}
        myErr := AEGetParamPtr (theAppleEvent, keyAECurrentPoint,
                        typeQDPoint, returnedType,
                        @currentPoint,
                        sizeof(currentPoint), actualSize);
    IF myErr <> noErr THEN
    BEGIN
        MyHandlePos2Offset := myErr;
        Exit(MyHandlePos2Offset);
    END;

    where := kTSMOutsideOfBody;
    part  := FindWindow(currentPoint, clickWindow);

    {the application function IsWindowForTheAE returns TRUE}
    {if the refcon is associated with the window}

    isMatch := IsWindowForTheAE(refcon, clickWindow);
```

```
IF ((clickWindow = FrontWindow) AND
      isMatch AND (part = inContent)) THEN
BEGIN
   GetPort(oldPort);
   SetPort(clickWindow);

   {convert currentPoint into the local }
   { coordinates of the current grafport}

   GlobalToLocal(currentPoint);

   {the application function GetTheBodyRect returns the}
   {body rect of the window}

   bodyRect := GetTheBodyRect(clickWindow);
   IF PtInRect(currentPoint, bodyRect) THEN
   BEGIN
      where  := kTSMInsideOfBody;


   {the application function FindTheTEHandle returns the }
   { window's TEHandle. Then the TextEdit function }
   { TEGetOffset returns the offset corresponding to the point}

      te := FindTheTEHandle (clickWindow);
      offset := TEGetOffset(currentPoint, te);

      {The application function IsInsideInputArea returns }
      { TRUE if offset is within the active input area. }
      { It is application's responsibility to remember }
      { the range of the input area.}

      IF IsInsideInputArea(offset, clickWindow) THEN
         where  := kTSMInsideOfActiveInputArea;
   END;

   {get the optional parameter: keyAEDragging}
   dragging := FALSE;
   myErr := AEGetParamPtr (theAppleEvent, keyAEDragging,
                           typeBoolean, returnedType,
                           @dragging, sizeof(dragging),
                           actualSize);
END;
IF myErr <> noErr THEN
```

```
BEGIN
   MyHandlePos2Offset := myErr;
   Exit(MyHandlePos2Offset);
END;


{if the parameter keyAEdragging is TRUE and the mouse}
{ position is outside the body text, the application }
{ can scroll the text within the active input area, }
{ rather than returning kTSMOutsideOfBody. The application }
{ procedure HandleScroll is handling the scrolling.}

IF (dragging = TRUE) AND (where = kTSMOutsideOfBody) THEN
BEGIN
   HandleScroll(te, offset);
   where := kTSMInsideOfActiveInputArea;
END;
SetPort(oldPort);

{Construct the return parameter keyAEOffset}
myErr := AEPutParamPtr(reply, keyAEOffset, typeLongInteger,
                       @offset, sizeof(offset));
IF myErr = noErr THEN
   {Construct the return parameter keyAERegionClass}
   MyHandlePos2Offset := AEPutParamPtr(reply, keyAERegionClass,
                                       typeShortInteger,
                                       @where, sizeof(where))
   ELSE MyHandlePos2Offset := myErr;
END;
```

Converting Text Offset to Screen Position

An input method text service component uses the Offset To Position Apple event when it needs to know the screen position corresponding to a given byte offset in the text buffer for the active input area. An input method typically sends the Offset To Position Apple event to your application when it needs to draw something in a specific spatial relationship with a given character in the active input area. For example, it may need to draw a floating window containing suggested conversion options beside a particular range of raw or converted text. See Figure 7-9.

The text service component supplies a byte offset, measured from the character at the start of the active input area. The application returns a point designating the global coordinates of the caret position corresponding to that offset. Your application may optionally return information about the font, size, and other measurements of the text in the active input area, so that the text service component can more precisely locate the elements it is to draw.

Figure 7-9 Drawing a window with conversion options next to the active input area

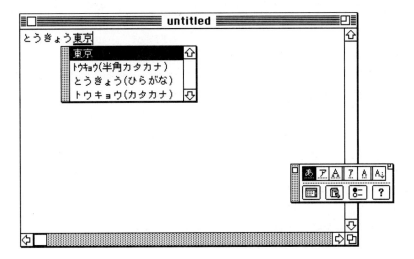

The Offset To Position Apple event is similar in function to the QuickDraw `CharToPixel` function, and it returns similar results. Your handler may use `CharToPixel` to get the information it returns to the text service component, or it may use a TextEdit call, as shown in the following code sample.

Listing 7-9 shows a sample handler for the Offset To Position Apple event. The handler first receives the input parameters, then uses the TextEdit function `TEGetPoint` to convert a text offset to a screen location. The `TEGetPoint` function is described in the chapter "TextEdit" in this book.

Listing 7-9 A sample handler for the Offset To Position Apple event

```
FUNCTION MyHandleOffset2Pos(theAppleEvent: AppleEvent;
                            reply: AppleEvent;
                            handlerRefCon: LongInt): OSErr;
VAR
    myErr:          OSErr;
    rtErr:          OSErr;
    returnedType:   DescType;
    offSet:         LongInt;
    refcon:         LongInt;
    actualSize:     LongInt;
    theWindow:      WindowPtr;
    te:             TEHandle;
    oldPort:        GrafPtr;
    thePoint:       Point;
    theFixed:       Fixed;
BEGIN
```

```
{Get the required parameter keyAEOffset}
myErr := AEGetParamPtr(theAppleEvent, keyAEOffset,
                        typeLongInteger, returnedType, @offSet,
                        sizeof(offSet), actualSize);
IF myErr = noErr THEN
   {Get the required parameter TSMDocumentRefcon}
   myErr := AEGetParamPtr(theAppleEvent,
                        keyAETSMDocumentRefcon,
                        typeLongInteger, returnedType,
                        @refcon, sizeof(refcon),
                        actualSize);
IF myErr <> noErr THEN
BEGIN
   MyHandleOffset2Pos := myErr;
   Exit(MyHandleOffset2Pos);
END;
{the application function GetWindowFromRefcon returns the }
{ window which is associated with the refcon}

rtErr := noErr;                                  {initialize rtErr}
theWindow := GetWindowFromRefcon(refcon);
IF theWindow = NIL THEN
   rtErr := errOffsetInvalid
ELSE
BEGIN
   {the application function FindTheTEHandle returns the }
   { TEHandle for the window}

   te := FindTheTEHandle(theWindow);

   {the TextEdit function TEGetPoint returns the point }
   { corresponding to the given offset}

   thePoint := TEGetPoint(offSet, te);
   IF (offSet > te^^.teLength) OR (offSet < 0) THEN
      rtErr := errOffsetInvalid
   ELSE IF(PtInRect(thePoint,theWindow^.portRect) = FALSE) THEN
      rtErr := errOffsetIsOutsideOfView
   ELSE
   BEGIN
      GetPort(oldPort);
      SetPort(theWindow);
```

```
      {Convert thePoint into global coordinates}

      LocalToGlobal(thePoint);
      SetPort(oldPort);
   END;


   {construct the return parameter keyAEPoint}
   myErr := AEPutParamPtr(reply, keyAEPoint, typeQDPoint,
                          @thePoint, sizeof(thePoint));
   IF myErr = noErr THEN
      {construct the optional return parameter keyAETextFont}
      myErr := AEPutParamPtr(reply, keyAETextFont,
                             typeLongInteger, @te^^.txFont,
                             sizeof(longInt));
   IF myErr = noErr THEN
   BEGIN
      {construct optional return parameter keyAETextPointSize}
      theFixed := BSL(Fixed(te^^.txSize), 16);
      myErr := AEPutParamPtr(reply, keyAETextPointSize,
                             typeFixed, @theFixed,
                             sizeof(theFixed));
   END;
   IF myErr = noErr THEN
      {construct optional return parameter keyAETextLineHeight}
      myErr := AEPutParamPtr(reply, keyAETextLineHeight,
                             typeShortInteger, @te^^.lineHeight,
                             sizeof(Integer));
   IF myErr = noErr THEN
      {construct optional return parameter keyAETextLineAscent}
      myErr := AEPutParamPtr(reply, keyAETextLineAscent,
                             typeShortInteger, @te^^.fontAscent,
                             sizeof(Integer));
   IF myErr = noErr THEN
   BEGIN
      {construct the optional return parameter keyAEAngle-- }
      {90 = horizontal direction, 180 = vertical direction}
      theFixed := Fixed(90);
      myErr := AEPutParamPtr(reply, keyAETextPointSize,
                             typeFixed, @theFixed,
                             sizeof(Fixed));
   END;
   IF myErr <> noErr THEN
   BEGIN
```

```
        MyHandleOffset2Pos := myErr;
        Exit(MyHandleOffset2Pos);
    END;
END;
{Construct the return parameter keyErrorNumber}
MyHandleOffset2Pos := AEPutParamPtr(reply, keyErrorNumber,
                              typeShortInteger, @rtErr,
                              sizeof(rtErr));
END;
```

Showing or Hiding the Input Window

Input methods that work with a floating input window often offer options to the user for either (1) continually displaying the input window, (2) displaying it only as text is being typed in and hiding it immediately after the user confirms it, or (3) leaving the window up for a specified amount of time after confirmation. The Show/Hide Input Window Apple event requests that your client application make the bottomline floating input window either visible or not visible. An input method text service component sends this Apple event whenever it needs to know or change the current state of the window.

This Apple event is for use only by applications that display their own input windows. If your application does not itself control the display of a floating input window, you can ignore this Apple event. If your application uses the Text Services Manager floating window service for bottomline input (by calling `UseInputWindow`), you do not receive this Apple event because it is handled by the Text Sevices Manager.

Direct Access to Text Service Components

Your client application can bypass the Text Services Manager and communicate with text service components directly. Many of the text service component routines correspond in function to the Text Services Manager application-interface routines. It is therefore possible for a client application to use the text service component routines if it needs to exert finer control over its interaction with text service components or if it requires specific kinds of text services or server-specific knowledge. It is not recommended in most cases, because the Text Services Manager is not available to help with dispatching and housekeeping chores.

Calling the Component Manager

If your client application does not use the Text Services Manager, it has to communicate with the Component Manager directly to identify and initialize individual text service components. You can use Component Manager calls to find components, set a default component, get information about components, and open components. See the chapter "Component Manager" in *Inside Macintosh: More Macintosh Toolbox* for more information.

Calling Text Service Components

If your client application calls text service components directly, it uses the text service component routines, a component-level interface described under "Text Service Component Routines" on page 7-84.

After opening a text service component with the `OpenComponent` or `OpenDefaultComponent` function, your client application calls `InitiateTextService` function to instruct the text service component to commence its operations.

To inform a text service component that its associated document window is becoming active or inactive, call the `ActivateTextService` or `DeactivateTextService` function.

You are responsible for adding the text service component menu to your application's menu bar. Furthermore, you are responsible for either disabling the menu or removing it from your menu bar when the text service component becomes inactive. Call the `GetTextServiceMenu` function to obtain menus from each open text service component.

To pass events to text service components, call the `TextServiceEvent` function. You are also responsible for allowing the text service components to control the cursor. Use the `SetTextServiceCursor` function to give the text service component a chance to set the cursor.

When a user makes a selection from the menu for a text service component, call the `TextServiceMenuSelect` function. You should call `TextServiceMenuSelect` right after the Menu Manager routines `MenuSelect` or `MenuKey`.

Before closing the component, call the `TerminateTextService` function to tell the text service component to finish its operations. You should remove the text service component's menu from the menu bar when the text service component is deactivated.

Using the Text Services Manager (for Text Service Components)

This chapter does not describe how to write a text service component. It describes only the interface between text service components and the Text Services Manager. Each text service component has several functions; it must be able to

- perform the tasks for which it was created
- communicate with the Component Manager
- receive calls from the Text Services Manager (or client applications), through the Component Manager
- send calls to the Text Services Manager

How components perform their specific text-handling tasks is beyond the scope of *Inside Macintosh*. How components communicate with the Component Manager is described in the chapter "Component Manager" in *Inside Macintosh: More Macintosh Toolbox*. How text service components communicate with the Text Services Manager is described in this section.

The text service component routines are the component-level calls that the Text Services Manager makes to text service components through the Component Manager. See "Text Service Component Routines" on page 7-84 for detailed descriptions of the calls. If you are writing a text service component, it must implement the text service component routines.

Text service components also make calls to the Text Services Manager, to send Apple events to client applications and to request the use of a floating window when needed. See "Text Services Manager Routines for Components" on page 7-77 for detailed descriptions of those component-interface calls.

For a brief discussion of some of the data types associated with text service components, see "About Text Service Components" beginning on page 7-14.

Providing Menus and Icons

If you are writing a text service component, you can have it display its own menu, provide an icon for the title of that menu, and provide icons for the Keyboard menu.

Providing a Text Service Component Menu

Although most user selections and configurations are best made with floating palettes, a text service component may put one menu into the menu bar. For input-method text service components, the menu cannot be hierarchical. Input-method menus appear on the right (system) side of the menu bar, between the Help menu and the Keyboard menu. Menus for non-input-method text service components appear on the left (application) side of the menu bar. See Figure 7-10 on page 7-40.

To create the menu, follow the standard procedures as described in the Menu Manager chapter of *Inside Macintosh: Macintosh Toolbox Essentials*. The Text Services Manager installs the menu in the menu bar whenever your component is opened or activated. The application (through the Text Services Manager) passes the menu commands to you for handling when appropriate.

All instances of an input-method text service component must share one menu handle. Therefore, make sure to allocate the handle in the System heap. You can store the menu handle in your component's `refcon` field. See the discussion of the Component Manager `SetComponentRefcon` routine in *Inside Macintosh: More Macintosh Toolbox*.

IMPORTANT

An input-method text service component should never dispose of its menu handle in response to a `TerminateTextService` call (see page 7-86). Any other kind of text service component should always dispose of its menu handle in response to a `TerminateTextService` call. ▲

Using an icon for the menu title

If you wish to have an icon instead of text as the title of your text service component menu, first create a small-icon suite (such as `'kcs#'`, `'kcs4'`, and `'kcs8'`) to represent your menu title. Then, in your menu resource, make the menu title a 5-byte Pascal string (6 bytes total size), with this format:

Byte	Value
0	$05 (length byte for menu string)
1	$01 (invalid character code)
2–5	Handle to icon suite

When the menu is created, the menu bar definition procedure knows from the values of the first 2 bytes that the final 4 bytes are a handle to an icon suite, and the procedure will put the icon in the menu bar. For more on creating icon suites and drawing icons, see the Finder Interface chapter of *Inside Macintosh: Macintosh Toolbox Essentials*. See also *Macintosh Human Interface Guidelines* for design suggestions for color icon families. ◆

Remember these limitations when considering an input-method menu: an input method can put up only one menu, the menu cannot be hierarchical, and the menu can be removed from the menu bar if there is insufficient room for it (on a small screen). It may be more appropriate to use palettes.

Providing Input Method Icons for the Keyboard Menu

Any text service component that provides an input method must supply the following keyboard icon resources to display an icon for the input method in the Keyboard menu: `'kcs#'`, `'kcs4'`, and `'kcs8'`. The resource ID number of the keyboard icon resources must equal the script code of the script system that the input method supports. If your input method supports more than one script system, you can have more than one icon suite, each with the appropriate resource IDs.

Figure 7-10 shows a Keyboard menu displaying a Japanese input method and a Korean input method, as well as keyboard layouts from several other script systems. The Japanese input method is active; its icon is checked in the menu and appears highlighted on the menu bar.

Figure 7-10   Input method icons in the Keyboard menu and menu bar

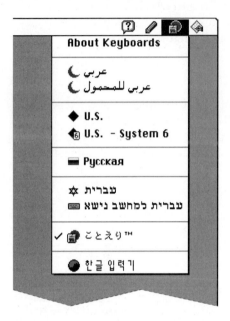

The pencil icon between the Keyboard menu and the Help menu in Figure 7-10 is the title for the menu belonging to the active input method.

For more information on keyboard icon suites, see the appendix "Keyboard Resources" in this book. For information on script codes, see the chapter "Script Manager" in this book.

Responding to Calls

When a client application makes certain calls to the Text Services Manager application interface, the Text Services Manager in turn calls your text service component. Your text service component responds to these calls by initiating or closing a text service, manipulating text service windows, responding to events or menu commands, and confirming text input.

Initiating a Text Service

When your text service component receives the `InitiateTextService` call, it can commence its operations to provide its text service. That may include opening windows or palettes, initializing data structures, communicating with the user or application, or otherwise getting started with its tasks.

The Text Services Manager may call `InitiateTextService` on its own or in response to receiving the application-interface call `OpenTextService`.

Activating Text Service Component Windows

If a window associated with a TSM document associated with your text service is being activated, your text service component receives the `ActivateTextService` call. You should show floating windows associated with your component instance and prepare to receive and handle events.

If the window is being deactivated, your text service component receives the `DeactivateTextService` call. You should perform any necessary cleanup or other tasks associated with deactivating your current component instance. If your text service component is not an input method, you should also hide all floating windows associated with the document being deactivated. If your text service component is an input method and if the newly activated document does *not* use your text services, you will receive the `HidePaletteWindows` call. At that point you should hide all floating windows associated with the component instance being deactivated.

The Text Services Manager calls `ActivateTextService` and `DeactivateTextService` in response to receiving the application-interface calls `ActivateTSMDocument` and `DeactivateTSMDocument`, respectively.

Responding to Events and Updating the Cursor and Menu

The Text Services Manager (or a client application) is responsible for adding your text service component's menu to the menu bar. When your text service component receives a `GetTextServiceMenu` call, it needs to return a menu handle. The section "Providing Menus and Icons" on page 7-38 gives instructions for creating text service menus and icons.

When your text service component receives the call `TextServiceEvent`, `TextServiceMenuSelect`, or `SetTextServiceCursor`, it should handle the event, menu command, or cursor-drawing if appropriate. For example, when the user enters text, you receive and handle the key-down events; you in turn inform the application what characters to draw in the active input area. When the user makes a menu selection, you are given an opportunity to check whether it is from your menu and then to act on it. You are regularly given the opportunity to redraw the cursor, in case it may be over an area under your control (such as a palette window or the active input area).

The Text Services Manager may call `GetTextServiceMenu` on its own or in response to receiving the application-interface call `OpenTextService`. The Text Services Manager calls `TextServiceEvent`, `TextServiceMenuSelect`, and `SetTextServiceCursor` in response to receiving the application-interface calls `TSMEvent`, `TSMMenuSelect`, and `SetTSMCursor`, respectively.

Confirming Active Text Input

A client application may need your input method text service component to terminate input immediately and confirm any text currently in the active input area. When your text service component receives the call `FixTextService`, it should confirm all text in the active input area, just as if the user had pressed Return. It should send the confirmed text to the client application through the Update Active Input Area Apple event.

The Text Services Manager calls `FixTextService` in response to receiving the application-interface call `FixTSMDocument`.

Closing a Text Service

When your text service is no longer needed, the Text Services Manager calls your text service component's `TerminateTextService` function before calling the Component Manager to close the component. Your text service component should use this time to confirm any active input in progress and then dispose of memory as needed.

The Text Services Manager may call `TerminateTextService` on its own or in response to receiving the application-interface call `CloseTextService`.

Identifying the Supported Scripts and Languages

The Operating System, the Text Services Manager, or a client application may need to determine which scripts and languages your text service component supports. When you receive the `GetScriptLanguageSupport` call, you return that information in a script-language support record.

The `GetScriptLanguageSupport` function and several Text Services Manager application-interface routines use the **script-language record**—and the **script-language support record**—to pass information about the scripts and languages associated with text service components.

The script-language record provides a script code and language code for the script system and the language associated with a given text service component. The script-language record is defined by the `ScriptLanguageRecord` data type as follows:

```
TYPE ScriptLanguageRecord =
    RECORD
        fScript:    ScriptCode;
        fLanguage:  LangCode;
    END;
```

Field descriptions

`fScript`	The number that identifies a script system supported by the text service component
`fLanguage`	The number that identifies a language associated with the script supported by the text service component

For a list of constants for all defined script and language codes, see the chapter "Script Manager" in this book.

The script-language support record consists of an array of script-language records. It is defined by the `ScriptLanguageSupport` data type as follows:

```
TYPE ScriptLanguageSupport =
    RECORD
        fScriptLanguageCount:   Integer;
        fScriptLanguageArray:   ARRAY[0..0] of ScriptLanguageRecord;
    END;
```

Field descriptions

`fScriptLanguageCount`

> The number of script-language records in this script-language support record.

`fScriptLanguageArray`

> A variable-length array of script-language records.

The Text Services Manager can call `GetScriptLanguageSupport` on its own or in response to receiving the application-interface call `GetTextServiceLanguage`.

Listing 7-10 gives an example of the response to the `GetScriptLanguageSupport` call by a Chinese input method.

Listing 7-10 Determining the script and language for a text service component

```
TYPE
    scriptHandlePtr= ^ScriptLanguageSupportHandle;

VAR
    scriptHdlPtr:scriptHandlePtr;

{The following is part of the case statement that dispatches }
{ text service component routines. It is the component's }
{ response to receiving a GetScriptLanguageSupport call}

kCMGetScriptLangSupport:
    BEGIN
        scriptHdlPtr := (scriptHandlePtr) @(cmParams^.params[0]);
        IF scriptHdlPtr^ = NIL THEN
```

```
                  scriptHdlPtr^ := (ScriptLanguageSupportHandle)NewHandle
                                       (sizeof(ScriptLanguageSupport));
          IF scriptHdlPtr^ <> NIL THEN
              WITH scriptHdlPtr^^^ DO BEGIN
                  fScriptLanguageCount := 1;
                  fScriptLanguageArray[0].fScript:= smTradChinese;
                  fScriptLanguageArray[0].fLanguage:=
                                               langTradChinese;
                  result := noErr;
              END;
          ELSE
              result := memFullErr;
      END;
```

Making Calls

Your text service component needs to make two kinds of calls to the Text Services Manager: calls that cause the sending of an Apple event to a client application, and calls that request a floating window from the Text Services Manager.

Sending Apple Events to Client Applications

Apple events allow text service components to send information to and request specific services of client applications. It is the responsibility of the client application to install Apple event handlers for these Apple events. Using these events, the text service component controls the text services environment by requesting a variety of services from the client application.

Your text service component can send Apple events to request that a client application perform the following actions:

- create or update text in an active input area

- help you track cursor movements by converting global coordinates to the byte offset of characters in the active input area

- help you position items on the screen by converting the byte offset of characters in the active input area to global coordinates

- show or hide a floating input window

Note
Your text service component must always use the kCurrentProcess constant as the target address when it creates an Apple event to send to the Text Services Manager. ◆

To send Apple events to a client application, your text service component calls the Text Services Manager `SendAEFromTSMComponent` function. The Text Services Manager then completes the Apple event and sends it to the application. For general information on constructing and sending Apple events, see the discussion of the Apple Event Manager in *Inside Macintosh: Interapplication Communication.*

Listing 7-11 shows an example of a text service component preparing and sending an Update Active Input Area Apple event. The component creates the Apple event and constructs the required parameters, including the text to be sent to the application. It also constructs the optional parameters that specify highlighting and update ranges in the text. It then calls `SendAEFromTSMComponent` to send the Apple event. In this listing, `globalHandle` is a handle to a data structure in which the text service component maintains all information about the text in the active input area.

Listing 7-11   Constructing and sending an Update Active Input Area Apple event

```
FUNCTION MyCreateUpdateInlineAreaAE(globalHandle: TglobalHandle)
: OSErr;
VAR
    psnRecord:              ProcessSerialNumber;
    myErr:                  OSErr;
    addrDescriptor:         AEAddressDesc;
    theAEvent:              AppleEvent;
    theReply:               AppleEvent;
    slRecord:               ScriptLanguageRecord;
    theRangeTableSize:      LongInt;
    theTextData:            Handle;
    theUpdateRangeTable:    TextRangeArray;
    theHiliteRangeTable:    TextRangeArray;
BEGIN
    {Apple event must go to the current process }
    psnRecord.highLongOfPSN := 0;
    psnRecord.lowLongOfPSN  := kCurrentProcess;
    myErr := AECreateDesc(typeProcessSerialNumber, @psnRecord,
                          sizeof(psnRecord), addrDescriptor);
    IF myErr <> noErr THEN
    BEGIN
        MyCreateUpdateInlineAreaAE := myErr;
        Exit(MyCreateUpdateInlineAreaAE);
    END;
```

```
{create the Apple event record}
myErr := AECreateAppleEvent(kTextServiceClass,
                            kUpdateActiveInputArea,
                            addrDescriptor,
                            kAutoGenerateReturnID,
                            kAnyTransactionID, theAEvent);
IF myErr <> noErr THEN
BEGIN
   MyCreateUpdateInlineAreaAE := myErr;
   myErr := AEDisposeDesc(addrDescriptor);    {ignore the error}
   Exit(MyCreateUpdateInlineAreaAE);
END;

{construct the required parameter keyAEServerInstance-- }
{ globalHandle^^.fSelf = global containing component instance}
myErr := AEPutParamPtr(theAEvent, keyAEServerInstance,
                       typeComponentInstance,
                       @globalHandle^^.fSelf,
                       sizeof(ComponentInstance));
IF myErr = noErr THEN
BEGIN
   {construct required parameter keyAEScriptTag }
   { --Korean in this case}
   slRecord.fScript := smKorean;
   slRecord.fLanguage := langKorean;
   myErr := AEPutParamPtr(theAEvent, keyAEScriptTag,
                          typeIntlWritingCode,
                          @slRecord, sizeof(slRecord));
END;
IF myErr = noErr THEN
BEGIN
   {construct required parameter keyAETheData. globalHandle }
   { is a handle to component's data structure describing }
   { all text in the active inline area}
   theTextData := globalHandle^^.fTextData;
   HLock(theTextData);
   myErr := AEPutParamPtr(theAEvent, keyAETheData, typeChar,
                          theTextData^,
                          globalHandle^^.fTextDataLength);
   HUnlock(theTextData);
END;
```

```
    IF myErr = noErr THEN
        {construct the required parameter keyAEFixLength}
        myErr := AEPutParamPtr(theAEvent, keyAEFixLength,
                            typeInteger,
                            @globalHandle^^.fFixedLength,
                            sizeof(LongInt));

    IF myErr = noErr THEN
    BEGIN
        {construct the optional parameter UpdateRangeTable}
        theUpdateRangeTable := globalHandle^^.fUpdateRangeTable;
        theRangeTableSize := sizeof(TextRangeArray)
                            + theUpdateRangeTable.fNumOfRanges
                            * sizeof(TextRange);
        myErr := AEPutParamPtr(theAEvent, keyAEFixLength,
                            typeInteger,
                            @theUpdateRangeTable,
                            theRangeTableSize);
    END;
    IF myErr = noErr THEN
    BEGIN
        {construct the optional parameter HiliteRangeTable}
        theHiliteRangeTable := globalHandle^^.fHiliteRangeTable;
        theRangeTableSize := sizeof(TextRangeArray)
                            + theHiliteRangeTable.fNumOfRanges
                            * sizeof(TextRange);
        myErr := AEPutParamPtr(theAEvent, keyAEFixLength,
                            typeInteger,
                            @theHiliteRangeTable,
                            theRangeTableSize)
    END;
    IF myErr <> noErr THEN
    BEGIN
        MyCreateUpdateInlineAreaAE := myErr;
        myErr := AEDisposeDesc(theAEvent);      {ignore the errors}
        myErr := AEDisposeDesc(addrDescriptor);
        Exit(MyCreateUpdateInlineAreaAE);
    END;

    {send the Apple event}
    myErr := SendAEFromTSMComponent(theAEvent, theReply,
                            kAEWaitReply + kAENeverInteract,
                            kAENormalPriority, 120, NIL, NIL);
    MyCreateUpdateInlineAreaAE := myErr;
```

```
    myErr := AEDisposeDesc(theAEvent);        {ignore the errors}
    myErr := AEDisposeDesc(addrDescriptor);
    myErr := AEDisposeDesc(theReply);
END;
```

Opening Floating Utility Windows

To open a floating utility window in front of the current client application, you use the `NewServiceWindow` function. If the call is successful, `NewServiceWindow` allocates a floating window in the floating window service layer, and returns a pointer to the window. See "Floating Input Windows" on page 7-13 and "Floating Utility Windows" on page 7-14 for a discussion of the Text Services Manager floating window service and the floating window service layer.

Your text service component can open multiple floating windows. When your component receives an event, you must determine if the event belongs to one of your text service floating windows. To get a pointer to the frontmost window in the floating window service layer, call the `GetFrontServiceWindow` function. To find out which part of your floating window an event occurred in, call the `FindServiceWindow` function. Your text service component can close the floating window you originally allocated by using the `CloseServiceWindow` function.

Text Services Manager Reference

This section describes four categories of routines and handlers, and their related constants and data structures:

- Text Services Manager routines called by client applications (the application interface to the Text Services Manager)

- application-supplied handlers for Apple events initiated by text service components

- Text Services Manager routines called by text service components (the component interface to the Text Services Manager)

- text service component routines, called by the Text Services Manager and possibly by client applications

Text Services Manager Routines for Client Applications

The Text Services Manager provides an application interface that allows client applications to use text service components independently of any specific knowledge of those components. Your client application makes these application-level calls to the Text Services Manager, which in turn calls the text service component using the component-level routines described in the section "Text Service Component Routines" on page 7-84.

The routines in the application interface let you

- initialize and close your TSM-aware application
- use TSM documents
- pass events, menu items, and cursor control to text service components
- confirm active input in TSM documents that use input methods
- provide text services to the user
- request a floating input window instead of inline input
- associate scripts and languages with text service components

Initializing and Closing as a TSM-Aware Application

If your client application uses any of the application-level Text Services Manager routines, call the `InitTSMAwareApplication` function immediately after you have called the other Toolbox initialization routines.

The Text Services Manager needs to perform some housekeeping when your client application is closed. To expedite this process, call the `CloseTSMAwareApplication` function when you quit.

InitTSMAwareApplication

The `InitTSMAwareApplication` function informs the Text Services Manager that your application is TSM-aware.

```
FUNCTION InitTSMAwareApplication: OSErr;
```

DESCRIPTION

The Text Services Manager notes that your application is TSM-aware by allocating the necessary data in its internal data structures.

RESULT CODES

noErr	No error
memFullErr	Insufficient memory to initialize
tsmAlreadyRegisteredErr	Application is already TSM-initialized
tsmNotAnAppErr	The caller is not an application

SEE ALSO

For sample code that uses the `InitTSMAwareApplication` function, see Listing 7-1 on page 7-18.

CloseTSMAwareApplication

The CloseTSMAwareApplication function informs the Text Services Manager that you have closed your application.

```
FUNCTION CloseTSMAwareApplication: OSErr;
```

DESCRIPTION

The Text Services Manager performs necessary housekeeping when your application closes.

Before you call the CloseTSMAwareApplication function, be sure that your application disposes of all open TSM documents by calling the DeleteTSMDocument function (see page 7-53).

RESULT CODES

noErr	No error
tsmNeverRegisteredErr	Application was never TSM-initialized

SEE ALSO

For sample code that uses the CloseTSMAwareApplication function, see Listing 7-6 on page 7-24.

Creating and Activating TSM Documents

This section describes the functions that let you create, activate, deactivate, and dispose of a TSM document (for details on the contents of a TSM document, see the section "Creating a TSM Document" on page 7-18).

NewTSMDocument

The NewTSMDocument function creates a TSM document and returns a handle to the document's ID.

```
FUNCTION NewTSMDocument (numOfInterface: Integer;
                         VAR supportedInterfaceTypes:
                         InterfaceTypeList;
                         VAR idocID: TSMDocumentID;
                         refCon: LongInt): OSErr;
```

numOfInterface

> The number of supported text service interface types. Currently, this number must be 1.

supportedInterfaceTypes

> A list of supported interface types. This list helps the Text Services Manager to locate the text services that have the correct interface type. Currently, the Text Services Manager has defined one interface type: kTextService (= 'tsvc'). The data type InterfaceTypeList is a simple array of 4-character (OSType) tags.

idocID

> Upon successful completion of the call, contains the document identification number of the TSM document created.

refCon

> A reference constant to store in the TSM document record. It may have any value you wish.

DESCRIPTION

Each time your client application calls the NewTSMDocument function, the Text Services Manager creates an internal record called a TSM document and returns its ID.

If the call is successful, NewTSMDocument opens the default input method text service component of the current keyboard script and assigns it to this document. If NewTSMDocument returns tsmScriptHasNoIMErr, it has still created a valid TSM document, but has not associated an input method with it.

If NewTSMDocument fails to create a new TSM document, it returns an error and sets idocID to NIL.

RESULT CODES

noErr	No error
memFullErr	Insufficient memory to open document
tsmUnsupportedTypeErr	Supported type was not 'tsvc'
tsmNeverRegisteredErr	Application is not TSM-aware
tsmScriptHasNoIMErr	Current script does not use input methods
tsmCantOpenComponentErr	Cannot open default input of current script

SEE ALSO

For sample code that uses the NewTSMDocument function, see Listing 7-2 on page 7-19.

ActivateTSMDocument

The ActivateTSMDocument function instructs the Text Services Manager to mark the TSM document associated with a newly active window as active.

```
FUNCTION ActivateTSMDocument (idocID: TSMDocumentID): OSErr;
```

idocID   A TSM document identification number created by a prior call to the
                NewTSMDocument function (see page 7-50).

DESCRIPTION

When a window that has an associated TSM document becomes active, your client
application must call the ActivateTSMDocument function to inform the Text Services
Manager that the document is activated and is ready to use text service components.

ActivateTSMDocument calls the equivalent text service component routine
ActivateTextService (see page 7-85) for all open text service components associated
with the TSM document.

If a text service component has a menu, the Text Services Manager inserts the menu into
the menu bar.

RESULT CODES

noErr   No error
tsmInvalidDocIDErr   Document is not a valid TSM document

SEE ALSO

For sample code that uses the ActivateTSMDocument function, see Listing 7-3 on
page 7-21.

DeactivateTSMDocument

The DeactivateTSMDocument function instructs the Text Services Manager to mark
the TSM document as inactive.

```
FUNCTION DeactivateTSMDocument (idocID: TSMDocumentID): OSErr;
```

idocID   A TSM document identification number created by a prior call to the
                NewTSMDocument function (see page 7-50).

DESCRIPTION

The DeactivateTSMDocument function lets you inform the Text Services Manager that
a TSM document in your client application is no longer active and must temporarily stop
using text service components.

The Text Services Manager calls the equivalent text service component function
DeactivateTextService (see page 7-85) for any text service component associated
with the TSM document being deactivated.

IMPORTANT

Once your application is initialized as a TSM-aware application, at least one TSM document must always be active when your application is active. If a situation arises in which you are a TSM-aware application but all of your TSM documents are inactive, any text service component that has a menu or palette windows will be unable to communicate with the user. The best policy is to always create a TSM document, even if only a dummy document, immediately after initializing as a TSM-aware application. ▲

RESULT CODES

`noErr`	No error
`tsmInvalidDocIDErr`	Document is not a valid TSM document

SEE ALSO

For sample code that uses the `DeactivateTSMDocument` function, see Listing 7-3 on page 7-21.

DeleteTSMDocument

The `DeleteTSMDocument` function closes all opened text service components for the TSM document.

```
FUNCTION DeleteTSMDocument (idocID: TSMDocumentID): OSErr;
```

idocID   A TSM document identification number created by a prior call to the `NewTSMDocument` function (see page 7-50).

DESCRIPTION

When your application disposes of a TSM document, it must call the `DeleteTSMDocument` function to inform the Text Services Manager that the document is no longer using text service components. `DeleteTSMDocument` invokes the Component Manager `CloseComponent` function for each open text service component associated with this document. It also disposes of the internal data structure for the TSM document.

RESULT CODES

`noErr`	No error
`tsmInvalidDocIDErr`	Document is not a valid TSM document
`tsmNeverRegisteredErr`	Application is not TSM-aware

Passing Events to Text Service Components

This section describes a function that lets you instruct the Text Services Manager to pass certain events to the appropriate text service component.

TSMEvent

The `TSMEvent` function passes all events obtained from the `WaitNextEvent` function, including null events, to the Text Services Manager.

```
FUNCTION TSMEvent (VAR event: EventRecord): Boolean;
```

event   The event record for the event that has been obtained from
               `WaitNextEvent`.

DESCRIPTION

Your client application regularly obtains events such as key-down events from the Toolbox Event Manager function `WaitNextEvent`. Some of these events may need to be handled by text service components. The `TSMEvent` function lets you pass those events to the Text Services Manager. The Text Services Manager dispatches the passed events to the appropriate text service components by calling the `TextServiceEvent` function for each component (see page 7-87).

If `TSMEvent` returns `FALSE`, you need to process the event as you normally do. If `TSMEvent` returns `TRUE`, the event has been handled by a text service component and is now a null event. You should process the null event as you normally do.

Note
The way the Text Services Manager uses and dispatches Apple events creates the potential for a reentrance situation that your client application should know about and be prepared to handle. When your application calls `TSMEvent`, the Text Services Manager uses the Apple Event Manager function `AESend` to pass data to your application through an Apple event. Your Apple event handler is thus invoked before the `TSMEvent` trap has returned. ◆

SEE ALSO

The `WaitNextEvent` function is described in the Event Manager chapter of *Inside Macintosh: Macintosh Toolbox Essentials*.

For sample code that uses the `TSMEvent` function, see Listing 7-4 on page 7-22.

Passing Menu Selections and Cursor Setting

This section describes two functions, `TSMMenuSelect` and `SetTSMCursor`, that let you instruct the Text Services Manager to pass menu commands and cursor control to the appropriate text service component.

TSMMenuSelect

The `TSMMenuSelect` function gives the specified text service component a chance to reply to a menu selection.

```
FUNCTION TSMMenuSelect (menuResult: LongInt): Boolean;
```

menuResult
> The result from the Menu Manager `MenuSelect` function.

DESCRIPTION

When the user chooses a menu item, the item may belong to a text service component's menu. To provide an opportunity for the text service component to reply to its menu selections, your application should call `TSMMenuSelect` with the result from the Menu Manager `MenuSelect` function.

`TSMMenuSelect` returns `FALSE` if a text service component did not handle the menu selection. In this case, your client application should process the menu selection normally. `TSMMenuSelect` returns `TRUE` when a text service component handled the menu selection. In this case, you should take no action.

After `TSMMenuSelect` returns, your application should—as usual—call the Menu Manager function `HiliteMenu` with the `menuID` parameter set to 0 to remove the highlighting from the menu title.

SEE ALSO

The Menu Manager is described in *Inside Macintosh: Macintosh Toolbox Essentials*.

SetTSMCursor

The `SetTSMCursor` function provides an opportunity for the text service component to set the shape of the cursor. If the text service component does not respond, your application may set the cursor.

```
FUNCTION SetTSMCursor (mousePos: Point): Boolean;
```

mousePos   A QuickDraw point indicating the position (in global coordinates) of the cursor in your application.

DESCRIPTION

Your client application is responsible for setting the cursor to an appropriate shape as it passes over your various user interface elements. It is also necessary to provide an opportunity for a text service component to set the cursor over its own user interface elements. The SetTSMCursor function allows the text service component to control the shape of the cursor if appropriate.

Call SetTSMCursor whenever you would normally call the QuickDraw SetCursor procedure. When SetTSMCursor returns TRUE, the cursor is positioned in a text service component window or in the active input area and it has been set by a text service component. Your client application should not set the cursor in this case. When SetTSMCursor returns FALSE, the cursor has not been set, and your client application may set it.

SetTSMCursor calls the equivalent text service component function SetTextServiceCursor (page 7-88) for each open text service component to provide an opportunity for each one to set shape of the cursor. If a text service component actually changes the shape of the cursor, the Text Services Manager does not call SetTextServiceCursor for the rest of the text service components and returns TRUE. If none of the text service components sets the cursor, then SetTSMCursor returns FALSE.

SEE ALSO

The SetCursor procedure is described in the QuickDraw chapters of *Inside Macintosh: Imaging*.

Confirming Active Input in a TSM Document

This section describes the FixTSMDocument function, which allows you to explicitly confirm text in the active input area.

FixTSMDocument

The FixTSMDocument function informs the Text Services Manager that input in the active input area of a specified TSM document has been interrupted, and that the text service component must confirm the text and terminate user input.

```
FUNCTION FixTSMDocument (idocID: TSMDocumentID): OSErr;
```

idocID   The identification number of a TSM document created by a prior call to the NewTSMDocument function (see page 7-50).

DESCRIPTION

Typically, an inline input text service component removes confirmed input from the active input area each time the user presses the Return key, and passes the confirmed text to your application through an Apple event.

In certain situations, however, your client application may need to inform the text service component that there has been an interruption in user input for a specific TSM document. In this case you call the FixTSMDocument function to give the input method text service component the opportunity to confirm any input in progress.

For instance, if the user clicks in the close box of the window in which active input is taking place, call FixTSMDocument before you close the window. The text service component will pass you the current contents (both converted and unconverted) of the active input area as confirmed text.

For simple activating and deactivating of your application's window, it is not necessary to confirm the text in the active inline area. The input method saves the text and restores it when your window is reactivated.

RESULT CODES

noErr	No error
tsmInvalidDocIDErr	The document is not a valid TSM document
tsmDocNotActiveErr	The TSM document is not active
tsmTSNotOpenErr	The default input method is not open

SEE ALSO

For sample code that uses the FixTSMDocument function, see Listing 7-5 on page 7-23.

Making Text Services Available to the User

This section describes functions that let you provide ways for the user to choose, open, and close text service components that are not input methods.

Your client application is responsible for providing a way—usually a menu—for the user to choose from among all available text service components. To get a list of available text service components to display in a menu, call the GetServiceList function. Be sure to filter out input methods, because the Keyboard menu already displays them.

When the user chooses a text service component that is not an input method, call the OpenTextService function to add the text service component to the TSM document. The OpenTextService and CloseTextService functions let you inform the Text Services Manager that a user of your client application has chosen to open or close a text service component. The Text Services Manager then opens or closes the component and associates it with a TSM document or ends the association as appropriate.

GetServiceList

The `GetServiceList` function obtains a complete list of text service components of a given kind available to the user of your client application.

```
FUNCTION GetServiceList (numOfInterfaceTypes: Integer;
                         supportedInterfaceTypes:
                         InterfaceTypeList;
                         VAR serviceInfo: TextServiceListHandle;
                         VAR seedValue: LongInt): OSErr;
```

numOfInterfaceTypes
: The number of interface types supported by your client application.

supportedInterfaceTypes
: A list of the interface types supported by your client application. The data type `InterfaceTypeList` is a simple list of 4-character (`OSType`) tags.

serviceInfo
: A handle to the text service component list data structure. If the handle is `NIL`, the Text Services Manager allocates the handle; otherwise, it assumes the handle is a valid text service component list handle, as defined by the `TextServiceListHandle` data type.

seedValue
: A value that indicates whether the list of text service components returned by `GetServiceList` may have been modified. This value is returned in this parameter after the Text Services Manager calls the Component Manager `GetComponentListModSeed` function.

DESCRIPTION

When your client application calls `GetServiceList`, the Text Services Manager locates all the text service components that support the specified interface and text service component types and creates a text service component list, defined by the `TextServiceList` data type, that contains an entry for each of the text service components.

It is possible to register text service components or withdraw them from registration at any time. Once it has compiled a list of text services, the Text Services Manager invokes the `GetComponentListModSeed` function and returns the value in the `modseed` parameter. You can save that value and, the next time you need to draw or regenerate the list of services, call the Component Manager `GetComponentListModSeed` function. If the seed value differs from the one you received from your last call to `GetServiceList`, you need to call `GetServiceList` once more to update the information. Alternatively, you can simply call `GetServiceList` each time you need to update the list, although that may be less efficient.

`GetServiceList` uses the text service component information record, defined by the `TextServiceInfo` data type, and the text service component list record, defined by the `TextServiceList` data type.

```
TYPE TextServiceInfo =
    RECORD
        fComponent: Component;
        fItemName:  Str255;
    END;
    TextServicesInfoPtr = ^TextServiceInfo;
```

Field descriptions

fComponent	A component identifier for this text service component. You can use the component identifier in Text Services Manager functions that open or obtain information about a text service component.
itemName	A Pascal string with the name of a text service component. (The script system to use for displaying the string is specified in the `componentFlags` field of the component description record. See page 7-15.)

```
TYPE TextServiceList =
    RECORD
        fTextServiceCount:   Integer;
        fServices:           ARRAY[0..0] of TextServiceInfo;
    END;
    TextServiceListPtr = ^TextServiceList;
    TextServiceListHandle = ^TextServiceListPtr;
```

Field descriptions

fTextServiceCount	An integer that provides the number of text service components in the text service component list.
fServices	A variable-length array of text service component information records.

RESULT CODES

noErr	No error
memFullErr	Insufficient memory
tsmUnsupportedTypeErr	Supported type was not 'tsvc'

OpenTextService

The `OpenTextService` function instructs the Text Services Manager to open a text service component that a user has chosen and to associate it with a TSM document.

```
FUNCTION OpenTextService (idocID: TSMDocumentID;
                          aComponent: Component;
                          VAR aComponentInstance:
                          ComponentInstance): OSErr;
```

idocID   The identification number of a TSM document created by a prior call to the `NewTSMDocument` function (see page 7-50).

aComponent
                A component identifier for this text service component.

aComponentInstance
                Upon completion of the call, contains a component instance. This value identifies your application's connection to a text service component. You must supply this value whenever you call the text service functions provided by the component directly.

DESCRIPTION

You can obtain the component identifier to pass in `aComponent` by comparing the menu item name selected by the user with the component item names in the `TextServiceList` record obtained by calling `GetServiceList`.

The Text Services Manager opens the requested component by calling the Component Manager `OpenComponent` function.

If the specified text service component is already open, the Text Services Manager does not open it again and the `tsmComponentAlreadyOpenErr` error message is returned as a result code. Whether or not the text service is open, the Text Services Manager calls the functions `InitiateTextService` (see page 7-84) and `ActivateTextService` (see page 7-85) for the given text service and returns a valid component instance. Upon completion of the `OpenTextService` call, the selected text service component is initialized and active.

Note
This function is for opening text service components other than input methods. Your application does not need to open or close input methods. ◆

RESULT CODES

noErr	No error
tsmInvalidDocIDErr	The document is not a valid TSM document
tsmComponentAlreadyOpenErr	Component is already open for this document
tsmCantOpenComponentErr	Component doesn't exist or won't open

CloseTextService

The `CloseTextService` function deactivates the active TSM document's association with the specified text service and closes the service component.

```
FUNCTION CloseTextService (idocID: TSMDocumentID;
                           aComponentInstance: ComponentInstance):
                           OSErr;
```

idocID   The identification number of a TSM document created by a prior call to the `NewTSMDocument` function (see page 7-50).

aComponentInstance
                The component instance created by a prior call to `OpenTextService`.

DESCRIPTION

When a user wants to close an opened text service component, your client application should call `CloseTextService`.

If the text service component displays a menu, the Text Services Manager removes the menu from the menu bar.

Note
This function is for closing text service components other than input methods. Your application does not need to open or close input methods. ◆

RESULT CODES

noErr	No error
tsmInvalidDocIDErr	The document is not a valid TSM document
tsmNoOpenTSErr	The component for this document is not open

Requesting a Floating Input Window

In certain situations, bottomline input with a floating input window is preferable to inline input for text input users. The Text Services Manager provides two ways to control how the floating input window is used: with a single specified TSM document or with all documents of a given application.

UseInputWindow

The `UseInputWindow` function associates a floating input window with a particular TSM document or with all TSM documents of an application.

```
FUNCTION UseInputWindow (idocID: TSMDocumentID;
                         useWindow: Boolean): OSErr;
```

idocID   The TSM document ID of the particular TSM document to be associated with the floating input window. If NIL, this call affects all your application's TSM documents.

useWindow   A Boolean value that indicates whether to use the floating input window. Set it to TRUE if you want to use a floating window; set it to FALSE if you do not want to use a floating window.

DESCRIPTION

The Text Services Manager provides a floating input window for your application's use if you call `UseInputWindow` with a value of TRUE in the `useWindow` parameter. To specify inline input instead, call `UseInputWindow` with a value of FALSE in the `useWindow` parameter.

The default value for `useWindow` is FALSE; if you do not call `UseInputWindow`, the Text Services Manager assumes that your application wants to use inline input. If your application wants to save the user's choice, it can put the last-used value for `useWindow` in a preferences file before quitting.

If you pass a valid TSM document ID for the `idocID` parameter, the `useWindow` parameter affects only that TSM document. If you pass NIL for the `idocID` parameter, the `useWindow` parameter affects all your application's TSM documents, including documents you create after making this call.

RESULT CODES

noErr	No error
tsmInvalidDocIDErr	The document is not a valid TSM document
tsmNeverRegisteredErr	Application is not TSM-aware

Associating Scripts and Languages With Components

The utility routines described in this section allow you to

- assign a particular text service component as the default component to be associated with a given script system and language

- determine which text service component is the default component associated with a given script system and language

■ determine the script system and language combination for the currently active text service component

■ assign a script system and language combination to the currently active text service component

In addition to these routines, you can use the text service component function `GetScriptLanguageSupport` (described on page 7-90) to determine which additional scripts and languages a text service component supports.

These routines make use of the script-language record, described under "Identifying the Supported Scripts and Languages" on page 7-42.

SetDefaultInputMethod

The operating system uses the `SetDefaultInputMethod` function to assign a default (input method) text service component to a given script and language.

```
FUNCTION SetDefaultInputMethod (ts: Component;
                                VAR slRecord: ScriptLanguageRecord):
                                OSErr;
```

ts   The component identifier of the input method text service component to be associated with the script and language combination given in the `slRecord` parameter.

slRecord   A script-language record that describes the script and language combination to be associated with the input method text service component specified in the `ts` parameter.

DESCRIPTION

The operating system uses `SetDefaultInputMethod` to associate an input method text service component with a given script and language. The operating system calls this function when the user expresses input method preferences through the Keyboard menu, Keyboard control panel, or other device. The associations made with this function are permanent; that is, they persist after restart.

If the script code and language code specified in the script-language record are incompatible, `SetDefaultInputMethod` returns the error `paramErr`.

RESULT CODES

noErr	No error
paramErr	The script does not match the language
tsmScriptHasNoIMErr	Current script does not use input methods
tsmCantOpenComponentErr	Cannot open default input of current script

GetDefaultInputMethod

The GetDefaultInputMethod function returns the default (input method) text service component for a given script and language.

```
FUNCTION GetDefaultInputMethod (VAR ts: Component;
                                VAR slRecord: ScriptLanguageRecord):
                                OSErr;
```

ts   The component identifier of the input method text service component
            that is associated with the script and language combination given in the
            slRecord parameter.

slRecord   A script-language record that describes the script and language
            combination that is associated with the input method text service
            specified in the ts parameter.

DESCRIPTION

The operating system uses GetDefaultInputMethod to find out which input method to activate when the user selects a new keyboard script from the Keyboard menu or by Command-key combination, or when an application calls KeyScript to change keyboard scripts.

In versions of Japanese system software starting with KanjiTalk 7.0, if the default input method is an old (pre-KanjiTalk 7.0) non-TSM-aware method, GetDefaultInputMethod returns the error tsmInputMethodIsOldErr. In that case the ts parameter contains the script code of the old input method in its high-order word, and the reference ID of the old input method in its low-order word.

RESULT CODES

noErr	No error
paramErr	The script does not match the language
tsmScriptHasNoIMErr	The script does not use input methods
tsmInputMethodIsOldErr	The default input method is old-style

SetTextServiceLanguage

The SetTextServiceLanguage function changes the current input script and language.

```
FUNCTION SetTextServiceLanguage (VAR slRecord:
                                 ScriptLanguageRecord): OSErr;
```

slRecord   A script-language record for the current text service component.

DESCRIPTION

The operating system calls this Text Services Manager function when the user switches the keyboard script, so that the Text Services Manager can synchronize the input method with the current keyboard script.

RESULT CODES

noErr	No error
paramErr	The script does not match the language
tsmCantOpenComponentErr	Cannot open default input of the script

GetTextServiceLanguage

The `GetTextServiceLanguage` function returns the language supported by the default (current) input method text service component for the current keyboard script.

```
FUNCTION GetTextServiceLanguage (VAR slRecord:
                                   ScriptLanguageRecord): OSErr;
```

slRecord   A script-language record that, upon completion of the call, describes the language supported by the current text service component.

RESULT CODES

noErr   No error

Apple Event Handlers Supplied by Client Applications

This section describes the Apple events for which client applications must install handlers. Text service components request action from and send information to client applications through these Apple events.

Your application uses these Apple events to receive text from text service components, to show or hide input windows, and to convert screen positions to text offsets—and vice versa—for text service components. The conversion operations are used to track mouse events and determine screen locations of text in the active input area.

The Apple events described in this section are all organized under the `kTextServiceClass` constant with a value of `'tsvc'`.

lists the Apple event ID constants for the Apple events described in this section.

Table 7-1   Apple event ID constants

Constant	Value	Explanation
kUpdateActiveInputArea	'updt'	Update Active Input Area
kPos2Offset	'p2st'	Position To Offset
kOffset2Pos	'st2p'	Offset To Position
kShowHideInputWindow	'shiw'	Show/Hide Input Window

Table 7-2 shows the Apple event keyword constants used in the Apple events described in this section.

Table 7-2   Apple event keyword constants

Constant	Value	Meaning
keyAETSMDocumentRefcon	'refc'	TSM document reference constant
keyAEServerInstance	'srvi'	Component instance
keyAETheData	'kdat'	Text from active input area
keyAEScriptTag	'sclg'	Script-language record
keyAEFixLength	'fixl'	Length of confirmed text
keyAEHiliteRange	'hrng'	Highlight range in text
keyAEUpdateRange	'udng'	Update range in text
keyAEClauseOffsets	'clau'	Clause offsets array
keyAECurrentPoint	'cpos'	Current point
keyAEDragging	'bool'	Dragging flag
keyAEOffset	'ofst'	Byte offset in text
keyAERegionClass	'rgnc'	Region class
keyAEPoint	'gpos'	Calculated point
optional keyword for Update Active Input Area		
keyAEPinRange	'pnrg'	Range for scrolling
optional keywords for Offset To Position		
keyAETextFont	'ktxf'	Text font
keyAETextPointSize	'ktps'	Text size
keyAETextLineHeight	'ktlh'	Text line height
keyAETextLineAscent	'ktas'	Font ascent

Table 7-2   Apple event keyword constants (continued)

Constant	Value	Meaning
keyAEAngle	'kang'	Text angle
optional keyword for Position To Offset		
keyAELeadingEdge	'klef'	Leading-edge Boolean

Table 7-3 lists the Apple event descriptor types discussed in this section.

Table 7-3   Apple event descriptor types

Constant	Value	Meaning
typeComponentInstance	'cmpi'	Server instance
typeTextRangeArray	'tray'	Text range array
typeOffsetArray	'ofay'	Offset array
typeIntlWritingCode	'intl'	Script-language record
typeQDPoint	'QDpt'	QuickDraw point
typeAEText	'tTXT'	Apple event text
typeText	'TEXT'	Plain text
typeTextRange	'txrn'	A text range record
typeTSMDocumentRefcon	'refc'	TSM document reference constant
typeFixed	'fixd'	Fixed 16.16 format

Table 7-4 lists the Apple event descriptor type constants for region class discussed in this section.

Table 7-4   Apple event descriptor type constants for the Apple event region class

Constant	Value
kTSMOutsideOfBody	1
kTSMInsideOfBody	2
kTSMInsideOfActiveInputArea	3

For the values of standard Apple event constants used in the following section not listed in these tables, see the *Apple Event Registry: Standard Suites*.

Creating and Updating an Active Input Area

The text service component uses the Update Active Input Area Apple event to request that your client application create and update an active input area, and accept confirmed text. For details on active input areas, see "Inline Input" on page 7-11.

Update Active Input Area—Creating and Updating an Active Input Area

Event class   `kTextServiceClass`

Event ID   `kUpdateActiveInputArea`

Requested action   Update a range of text. Specify any necessary highlighting with offsets in the optional `keyAEHiliteRange` parameter.

Required parameters

Keyword: `keyAETSMDocumentRefcon`

Descriptor type: `typeLongInteger`

Data: A TSM document specifier (reference constant) supplied by the application in a prior call to the `NewTSMDocument` function (see page 7-50). This value is associated with the TSM document whose active input area is to be updated.

Keyword: `keyAEServerInstance`

Descriptor type: `typeComponentInstance`

Data: A component instance value created by a prior call to the Component Manager `OpenComponent` function. This value identifies the text service component.

Keyword: `keyAETheData`

Descriptor type: `typeChar`

Data: Text data that has been processed in some way by a text service component.

Keyword: `keyAEScriptTag`

Descriptor type: `typeIntlWritingCode`

Data: The script code and language code associated with the text returned in the `keyAETheData` parameter. The information is passed in a script-language record, as defined on page 7-42.

Update Active Input Area—Creating and Updating an Active Input Area (continued)

Required parameters

Keyword:	`keyAEFixLength`
Descriptor type:	`typeLongInteger`
Data:	The length of the confirmed text in the active inline area.

If the value of `keyAEFixLength` is –1, the text contained in the `keyAETheData` parameter is to completely replace the current selection in the application window. In this case, there is to be no active input area, the text is all considered to be confirmed, and is to be made part of the body text of the client application.

If the value is 0, an active input area is in process, but there is no completely confirmed text being sent.

If the value is greater than 0, the text specified in the `keyAETheData` parameter up to the indicated offset is confirmed data and should be consumed by the application. The Text Services Manager considers any text beyond the offset specified by the `keyAEFixLength` parameter to be inside the active input area with the starting point of the active input area at that offset. This is illustrated in Figure 7-11.

Figure 7-11   Updating text in an active input area

Update Active Input Area—Creating and Updating an Active Input Area (continued)

Optional parameters

Keyword:	`keyAEHiliteRange`
Descriptor type:	`typeTextRangeArray`
Data:	An array that specifies the ranges of text to be highlighted in the active input area. It also specifies caret position. There are 5 types of highlighting:

Constant	Applies to
`kCaretPosition`	The caret position only
`kRawText`	All of the unconverted text
`kSelectedRawText`	Part of the unconverted text
`kConvertedText`	All of the converted text
`kSelectedConvertedText`	Part of the converted text

For instance, the input method may have the application highlight all raw text with a gray underline; but if it needs to further highlight a selection within that raw text, it may specify a different underline for the selected raw text. The text range array is an array of text-range records, each of which has this form:

```
TYPE TextRange =
  RECORD
    fStart:        LongInt;
    fEnd:          LongInt;
    fHiliteStyle:  Integer;
  END;
```

For the text-range record whose highlight style is `kCaretPosition`, both `fStart` and `fEnd` are the same and denote the position of the caret.

Negative values for a text range mean that the specified range only adds to, rather than replaces, any current highlighting for the specified type of text.

Update Active Input Area—Creating and Updating an Active Input Area (continued)

Optional parameters

Keyword:	keyAEUpdateRange
Descriptor type:	typeTextRangeArray

Data: An array of text-range records that indicates the update range of the active input area (in many circumstances, not all of the active input area needs updating). Update Active Input Area always uses the text-range records in the text range array in pairs. The first record (0) specifies a range of old text (text in the inline buffer) to be updated; the second record (1) specifies the range of text in keyAETheData that is to replace that old text. In general, the record n ($n >= 0$, n is an even number) specifies the range of old text to be updated and the record $n + 1$ specifies the range of new text to replace the corresponding old text. (The fHiliteStyle field is ignored.)

Keyword:	keyAEPinRange
Descriptor type:	typeTextRange

Data: A text range record that specifies a start offset and and an end offset that should be scrolled into view if the text specified by these offsets is not already in view. (The fHiliteStyle field is ignored.)

Keyword:	keyAEClauseOffsets
Descriptor type:	typeOffsetArray

Data: An offset array (defined by the OffsetArray data type) that specifies offsets of word or clause boundaries of the new text. Offsets are from the start of the active input area. Applications can use this information for word selection or other purposes.

```
TYPE OffsetArray =
  RECORD
    fNumOfOffsets: Integer;
    fOffset: ARRAY[0..0] of LongInt;
  END;
```

The numOfOffsets field contains an integer that specifies the number of offsets in the offset array. The fOffset field is an array of long integers with the number of entries specified in the numOfOffsets field.

Return parameter

Keyword:	keyErrorNumber
Descriptor type:	typeShortInteger

Data: Any errors that the application needs to return to the text service component. The application must pass Memory Manager, TextEdit, or other errors that it receives through to the component; otherwise, it should pass 0 (noErr).

The text range array data structure used in the `keyAEHiliteRange` and `keyAEUpadateRange` parameters described above is defined by the `TextRangeArray` data type:

```
TYPE TextRangeArray =
    RECORD
        fNumOfRanges:   Integer;
        fRange:         ARRAY[0..0] of TextRange;
    END;
```

The `fNumOfRanges` field contains an integer that indicates how many text ranges this array holds. The `fRange` field contains a series of text-range records. (If the array consists of more than one text-range record, the size of the array must be calculated as `fNumOfRanges * SizeOf(fRange)`.)

For sample code that handles the Update Active Input Area Apple event, see Listing 7-7 on page 7-26.

Converting Global Coordinates to Text Offsets

The Position To Offset Apple event requests a client application to convert specified global coordinates to byte offsets in text. The text service component uses this Apple event for mouse tracking, in order to draw the caret, highlight text, or adjust the cursor appearance.

Position To Offset—Converting Global Coordinates to Text Offset

Event class	`kTextServiceClass`
Event ID	`kPos2Offset`
Requested action	Convert global coordinates specified in the `keyAECurrentPoint` parameter to a byte offset. If the click is within the limits of the active input area, the offset is relative to the start of the active input area. Otherwise, the offset is relative to the start of the application's body text. The client application specifies the classification of the location of the offset in the `keyAERegionClass` return parameter.

Required parameters

Keyword:	`keyAETSMDocumentRefcon`
Descriptor type:	`typeLongInteger`
Data:	A TSM document specifier (reference constant) supplied by the application in a prior call to the `NewTSMDocument` function (see page 7-50). This value is associated with the TSM document affected by this event.

Position To Offset—Converting Global Coordinates to Text Offset (continued)

Required parameters

Keyword:	`keyAEServerInstance`
Descriptor type:	`typeComponentInstance`
Data:	A component instance value created by a prior call to the Component Manager `OpenComponent` function. This value identifies the text service component.
Keyword:	`keyAECurrentPoint`
Descriptor type:	`typePoint`
Data:	A point that contains the global coordinates that describe the current mouse position.

Optional parameter

Keyword:	`keyAEdragging`
Descriptor type:	`typeBoolean`
Data:	A Boolean value that indicates whether the input method is currently tracking the mouse—that is, whether the user is dragging the current selection. If it is TRUE, the application should pin the cursor to the limits of the active input area (to avoid highlighting beyond the limits of the active input area).

Return parameters

Keyword:	`keyAEOffset`
Descriptor type:	`typeLongInteger`
Data:	A byte offset that specifies the character corresponding to the current mouse position (`keyAECurrentPoint`). If the click is within the limits of the active input area, the offset is relative to the start of the active input area. Otherwise, the offset is relative to the start of the application's body text.
Keyword:	`keyAERegionClass`
Descriptor type:	`typeShortInteger`
Data:	The classification of the position specified in the `keyAEOffset` parameter. Three constants define the classification:

Constant	Value
`kTSMOutsideOfBody`	1
`kTSMInsideOfBody`	2
`kTSMInsideOfActiveInputArea`	3

A value of `kTSMOutsideOfBody` means that the offset is outside the application's body text. A value of `kTSMInsideOfBody` means that the offset is inside the body text. `kTSMInsideOfActiveInputArea` means that the offset is inside the active input area.

continued

Position To Offset—Converting Global Coordinates to Text Offset (continued)

Return parameters

Keyword:	`keyErrorNumber`
Descriptor type:	`typeShortInteger`
Data:	Any errors that the application needs to return to the text service component. The application must pass Memory Manager, TextEdit, or other errors that it receives through to the component; otherwise, it should pass 0 (`noErr`).

Optional return parameter

Keyword:	`keyAELeadingEdge`
Descriptor type:	`typeBoolean`
Data:	A Boolean value that is equivalent to the `leadingEdge` parameter of the QuickDraw `PixelToChar` function. It is `TRUE` if the specified point corresponds to the leading edge of the character whose offset is returned; it is `FALSE` if the specified point corresponds to the trailing edge of the character.

For sample code that handles the Position To Offset Apple event, see Listing 7-8 on page 7-30.

Converting Text Offsets to Global Coordinates

The Offset To Position Apple event requests that a client application convert byte offsets in text to global coordinates. The text service component uses this Apple event to determine where in the active input area to draw an element (such as the caret or a palette of conversion choices) that relates to a particular character.

Offset To Position—Converting Text Offsets to Global Coordinates

Event class	`kTextServiceClass`
Event ID	`kOffset2Pos`
Requested action	Convert a specified byte offset into global coordinates. The offset value passed to the client application is relative to the start of the active input area. If there is no active input area, the offset is relative to the start of the current text body.

Required parameters

Keyword:	`keyAETSMDocumentRefcon`
Descriptor type:	`typeLongInteger`
Data:	A TSM document specifier (reference constant) supplied by the application in a prior call to the `NewTSMDocument` function (see page 7-50). This value is associated with the TSM document affected by this event.

Offset To Position—Converting Text Offsets to Global Coordinates (continued)

Required parameters

Keyword:	`keyAEServerInstance`
Descriptor type:	`typeComponentInstance`
Data:	A component instance value returned by a prior call to the Component Manager `OpenComponent` function. This value identifies the text service component.
Keyword:	`keyAEOffset`
Descriptor type:	`typeLongInteger`
Data:	The text offset to be converted into a global point. Offset is in terms of bytes from the start of the active input area.

Return parameters

Keyword:	`keyAEPoint`
Descriptor type:	`typePoint`
Data:	A point that contains the global coordinates obtained by converting the byte offset passed in the `keyAEOffset` parameter.
Keyword:	`keyErrorNumber`
Descriptor type:	`typeShortInteger`
Data:	`errOffsetInvalid` indicates that there is no text at the offset. `errOffsetIsOutsideOfView` indicates that the text offset is out of view.
	The application must pass Memory Manager, TextEdit, or other errors that it receives through to the component; otherwise, it should pass 0 (`noErr`).

Optional return parameters

Keyword:	`keyAETextFont`
Descriptor type:	`typeLongInteger`
Data:	The font of the text in the active input area. The application can send this information to the input method to help the input method position the active input area.
Keyword:	`keyAETextPointSize`
Descriptor type:	`typeFixed`
Data:	The size of the text in the active input area. The application can send this information to the input method to help the input method position the active input area.
Keyword:	`keyAETextLineHeight`
Descriptor type:	`typeShortInteger`
Data:	The line height of the text in the active input area. The application can send this information to the input method to help the input method position the active input area.

continued

Offset To Position—Converting Text Offsets to Global Coordinates (continued)

Optional return parameters

Keyword:	`keyAETextLineAscent`
Descriptor type:	`typeShortInteger`
Data:	The ascent height of the text in the active input area. The application can send this information to the input method to help the input method position the active input area.
Keyword:	`keyAEAngle`
Descriptor type:	`typeFixed`
Data:	The orientation of the text in the active input area. The value 90 specifies a horizontal line direction and 180 specifies a vertical line direction. The application can send this information to the input method to help the input method position the active input area.

For sample code that handles the Offset To Position Apple event, see Listing 7-9 on page 7-33.

Showing or Hiding the Floating Input Window

Input methods that supply floating input windows for bottomline input may need to show or hide the input window at various times. The Show/Hide Input Window Apple event requests the client application to make the floating input window either visible or not visible, so that an input method can offer any of the above options.

Note
If your application is not displaying its own floating input window, you can ignore this Apple event. ◆

Show/Hide Input Window—Showing or Hiding the Floating Input Window

Event class	`kTextServiceClass`
Event ID	`kShowHideInputWindow`
Requested action	Make the bottomline floating input window either visible or not visible, depending on the value of the `keyAEShowHideInputWindow` parameter.

Required parameters

Keyword:	`keyAETSMDocumentRefcon`
Descriptor type:	`typeLongInteger`
Data:	A TSM document specifier (reference constant) supplied by the application in a prior call to the `NewTSMDocument` function (see page 7-50). This value is associated with the TSM document for the window being shown or hidden.
Keyword:	`keyAEServerInstance`
Descriptor type:	`typeComponentInstance`

Show/Hide Input Window—Showing or Hiding the Floating Input Window (continued)

Data: A component instance value returned by a prior call to the Component Manager `OpenComponent` function. This value identifies the text service component.

Optional parameter

Keyword: `keyAEShowHideInputWindow`

Descriptor type: `typeBoolean`

Data: If `TRUE`, the bottomline input window should be shown; if `FALSE`, it should be hidden. This parameter is not needed if the input method is simply inquiring about the state of the input window.

Return parameter

Keyword: `keyAEShowHideInputWindow`

Descriptor type: `typeBoolean`

Data: The current state of the input window: `TRUE` if the window is shown; `FALSE` if it is hidden. If the optional parameter `keyAEShowHideInputWindow` is included, this return parameter should show the state of the window *before* it was set to the state requested in the optional parameter.

Text Services Manager Routines for Components

This section describes the Text Services Manager component interface—the routines and related data structures that are for the use of text service components. These functions let your text service component

■ send Apple events to a client application to request specific information about the active input area in a TSM document

■ put up a floating window for various purposes

Sending Apple Events to a Client Application

This section describes the `SendAEFromTSMComponent` function, with which your text service component sends Apple events to a client application.

SendAEFromTSMComponent

The `SendAEFromTSMComponent` function sends Apple events from a text service component to a client application.

```
FUNCTION SendAEFromTSMComponent (VAR theAppleEvent: AppleEvent;
                                 VAR reply: AppleEvent;
                                 sendMode: AESendMode;
```

```
                                    sendPriority: AESendPriority;
                                    timeOutInTicks: LongInt;
                                    idleProc: IdleProcPtr;
                                    filterProc: EventFilterProcPtr):
                                    OSErr;
```

theAppleEvent
: The Apple event to be sent.

reply
: The reply Apple event returned by SendAEFromTSMComponent.

sendMode
: The value that lets you specify one of the following modes specified by corresponding constants: the reply mode for the Apple event, the interaction level, the application switch mode, the reconnection mode, and the return receipt mode. To obtain the value for this parameter, add the appropriate constants. Comprehensive details about these constants are provided in the description of the Apple Event Manager AESend function in *Inside Macintosh: Interapplication Communication*.

sendPriority
: The value that specifies whether to put the Apple event at the back of the event queue (set with the kAENormalPriority flag) or at the front of the queue (kAEHighPriority flag).

timeOutInTicks
: The length of time (in ticks) that the client application is willing to wait for the reply or return receipt from the server application before it times out. If the value of this parameter is kNoTimeOut, the Apple event never times out.

idleProc
: A pointer to a function for any tasks (such as displaying a globe, a wristwatch, or a spinning beach ball cursor) that the application performs while waiting for a reply or a return receipt.

filterProc
: A pointer to a routine that accepts certain incoming Apple events that are received while the handler waits for a reply or a return receipt and filters out the rest.

DESCRIPTION

The SendAEFromTSMComponent function is essentially a wrapper routine for the Apple Event Manager function AESend. See the description of AESend for additional necessary information, including constants for the sendMode parameter and result codes.

SendAEFromTSMComponent identifies your text service component from the keyAEServerInstance parameter in the Apple event specified in the theAppleEvent parameter. If a reference constant (refcon) in a TSM document that corresponds to this parameter is found in the internal data structures of the Text Services Manager, SendAEFromTSMComponent adds the reference constant as the keyAETSMDocumentRefcon parameter to the given Apple event before sending it to the application.

If the client application is not TSM-aware, `SendAEFromTSMComponent` routes the Apple events to the floating input window to allow bottomline input.

IMPORTANT

If your text service component changes the environment in any way— such as by modifying the A5 world or changing the current zone—while constructing an Apple event, it must restore the previous settings before sending the Apple event. ▲

Note

Your text service component should always use the `kCurrentProcess` constant as the target address when it creates an Apple event to send to the Text Services Manager. ◆

SEE ALSO

The `AESend` function is described with the Apple Event Manager in *Inside Macintosh: Interapplication Communication*.

The `kCurrentProcess` constant is described in *Inside Macintosh: Processes*.

For sample code showing how a text service component calls the `SendAEFromTSMComponent` function, see Listing 7-11 on page 7-45.

Opening Floating Utility Windows

In conjunction with the Process Manager, the Text Services Manager maintains the floating window service, whose windows occupy a special layer called the floating window service layer. See Figure 7-7 on page 7-14.

The Text Services Manager uses the floating window service to provide a standard floating input window when needed. Text service components can use the service to create, close, and find floating windows used for various other user-interface purposes. You can manipulate the service windows with these calls:

■ The `NewServiceWindow` function lets you open a floating window in front of the current application.

■ The `CloseServiceWindow` function lets you close a previously allocated floating window.

■ The `GetFrontServiceWindow` function helps you find out which is the frontmost window in the floating window service layer.

■ The `FindServiceWindow` function helps you find out which part of a text service component's floating window a mouse-down event has occurred in.

Client applications

These calls may be made by client applications also. See the following description of `NewServiceWindow` for special instructions for client applications. ◆

NewServiceWindow

The NewServiceWindow function opens a floating utility window in the floating
window service layer, in front of the current application. The text service component
may use the window for interaction with the user or other purposes.

```
FUNCTION NewServiceWindow (wStorage: Ptr; boundsRect: Rect;
                           title: Str255; visible: Boolean;
                           theProc: Integer; behind: WindowPtr;
                           goAwayFlag: Boolean;
                           ts: ComponentInstance;
                           VAR window: WindowPtr): OSErr;
```

wStorage   A pointer to the location in memory of the window record. Do not
              allocate the window record on the stack. Always be sure to allocate the
              window in the heap, or else pass NIL for this parameter.

boundsRect
              A rectangle given in global coordinates that determines the size and
              location of the new floating window. This rectangle becomes the
              portRect field of the graphics port record (defined by the QuickDraw
              GrafPort data type) for this window.

title   A Pascal string that contains the title of the window.

visible   A Boolean value to determine whether the window is to be drawn. If
              TRUE, NewServiceWindow draws the window. First it calls the window
              definition procedure defined in the theProc parameter to draw the
              window frame. Then it generates an update event for the entire window
              contents.

theProc   The window definition procedure for the floating window.

behind   A window pointer (defined by the Window Manager WindowPtr data
              type) that determines the plane of the floating window.
              NewServiceWindow inserts the new window behind the window
              pointed to by this parameter. To put the new window behind all other
              windows, use behind = NIL. To place it in front of all other windows,
              use behind = POINTER(-1).

goAwayFlag
              A Boolean value that determines whether the go-away region should be
              drawn in the window. If this parameter is TRUE and the window is
              frontmost (as specified by the behind parameter), NewServiceWindow
              draws a go-away region in the frame.

ts   A component instance returned by a prior call to the Component
              Manager OpenComponent function. This value is stored in the refcon
              field of the window record; text service components should not change
              the value of the window's refcon field.

Client applications

If you are a client application making this call, pass the Process Manager constant `kCurrentProcess` in this parameter so that events in the new window will be forwarded to you. After you have created the window, you can use its `refcon` field for private storage as usual. ◆

`window`   A pointer to the newly allocated floating window.

DESCRIPTION

This function calls the Window Manager `NewWindow` function. If a floating window is successfully allocated, `NewServiceWindow` returns a pointer to that window as the function result. Otherwise, it returns `NIL`.

A text service component can open multiple windows in this layer. When a text service component receives an event, it determines whether the event belongs to one of its text service component windows by calling `FindServiceWindow`.

If you are an application that uses `NewServiceWindow` to open a floating window, be sure to hide the floating window when you are switched out; that is, when another application's windows become active.

Balloon Help

If you are writing a text service component and want the service window to have custom Balloon Help, place an `'hwin'` resource (with references to `'hcrt'` and `'STR#'` resources) in your component resource fork, with a name equal to the window title. The Text Services Manager will then open the resources automatically when needed. If you are writing a client application, you need not follow anything other than normal procedures to have Balloon Help. ◆

RESULT CODES

`noErr`	No error
`memFullErr`	Insufficient memory to open the window

SEE ALSO

Window definition procedures and the `NewWindow` function are described in the Window Manager chapter of *Inside Macintosh: Macintosh Toolbox Essentials*.

Balloon Help is described in the Help Manager chapter of *Inside Macintosh: More Macintosh Toolbox*.

CloseServiceWindow

The `CloseServiceWindow` function closes a previously allocated floating input window.

```
FUNCTION CloseServiceWindow (window: WindowPtr): OSErr;
```

window   A pointer to the service window to close. This function calls the Window Manager `CloseWindow` procedure.

DESCRIPTION

If the window pointer is `NIL` or if it points to a non-floating window, `CloseServiceWindow` returns `paramErr`.

RESULT CODES

noErr   No error
paramErr   Parameter error

SEE ALSO

The `CloseWindow` procedure is described in the Window Manager chapter of *Inside Macintosh: Macintosh Toolbox Essentials.*

GetFrontServiceWindow

The `GetFrontServiceWindow` function determines which is the frontmost window in the floating window service layer.

```
FUNCTION GetFrontServiceWindow (VAR window: WindowPtr): OSErr;
```

window   A pointer to the frontmost window in the service layer.

DESCRIPTION

This function calls the Window Manager `FrontWindow` function. The `GetFrontServiceWindow` function returns a pointer to the frontmost window in the service layer. If there is no window in the service layer, it returns `NIL`.

SEE ALSO

The `FrontWindow` function is described in the Window Manager chapter of *Inside Macintosh: Macintosh Toolbox Essentials.*

FindServiceWindow

The `FindServiceWindow` function determines which part of a text service component's floating window a mouse-down event has occurred in.

```
FUNCTION FindServiceWindow (thePoint: Point;
                            VAR theWindow: WindowPtr): Integer;
```

thePoint   The point where the mouse button was pressed (in global coordinates, as stored in the `where` field of the Event Manager event record).

theWindow   A pointer to a Window Manager window pointer (defined by the `WindowPtr` data type) that identifies the floating window in which the mouse-down event occurred. If the mouse-down event did not occur in a text service component floating window, this parameter is set to `NIL`.

DESCRIPTION

The `FindServiceWindow` function is similar to the Window Manager `FindWindow` function, except that `FindServiceWindow` searches the floating window service layer only.

`FindServiceWindow` calls the Window Manager `FindWindow` function. It returns one of the following predefined constants to identify the location of the mouse-down event.

Constant	Value	Explanation
inDesk	0	None of the following
inMenuBar	1	In menu bar
inSysWindow	2	In system window
inContent	3	In content region (except grow, if active)
inDrag	4	In drag region
inGrow	5	In grow region (active window only)
inGoAway	6	In go-away region (active window only)
inZoomIn	7	In zoom-in region
inZoomOut	8	In zoom-out region

It the mouse position is not over a floating window, `FindServiceWindow` returns `inDesk` (0) as its function result, and sets the return parameter `theWindow` to `NIL`.

SEE ALSO

The `FindWindow` function is described in the Window Manager chapter of *Inside Macintosh: Macintosh Toolbox Essentials*.

Event records are described in the Event Manager chapter of *Inside Macintosh: Macintosh Toolbox Essentials*.

The Process Manager is described in *Inside Macintosh: Processes*.

Text Service Component Routines

This section describes the component-level routines and related data structures and constants through which the Text Services Manager communicates with text service components. The Text Services Manager uses the Component Manager to dispatch the text service component routines to specific text service components.

Client applications also may make the calls described in this section, but the Text Services Manager does not play a role in the connection between the client application making the call and the text service component receiving it. If you are an application making these calls, you need to know the component instance of the component whose routine you are calling.

If you are writing a text service component, it must implement routines for the calls described in this section. With these routines, your component

- provides a text service

- accepts events and updates its cursor and menu (if any)

- confirms active input when requested (if it is an input method)

- identifies the scripts and languages it supports

Providing a Text Service

This section describes the functions a text service component supports to initiate, activate, deactivate, and terminate a text service. The Text Services Manager makes these calls to components either on its own or in response to application-interface calls it receives from client applications.

InitiateTextService

The `InitiateTextService` function instructs a specified text service component to do whatever it needs to set up its operations and commence its performance.

```
FUNCTION InitiateTextService (ts: ComponentInstance):
                              ComponentResult;
```

ts   A component instance created by a prior call to the Component Manager `OpenComponent` function.

DESCRIPTION

The Text Services Manager can call `InitiateTextService` to any component that it has already opened with the Component Manager `OpenComponent` or `OpenDefaultComponent` functions. Text service components should be prepared to handle `InitiateTextService` calls at any time.

Any text service component can receive multiple `InitiateTextService` calls. The Text Services Manager calls `InitiateTextService` each time the user adds a text service to a TSM document, even if the text service component has already been opened. This provides an opportunity for the component to restart or to display user interface elements that the user may have closed.

This function should return a `ComponentResult` value of zero if there is no error, and an error code if there is one.

ActivateTextService

The `ActivateTextService` function notifies a text service component that its associated document window is becoming active. This allows the text service component to display any associated floating windows.

```
FUNCTION ActivateTextService (ts: ComponentInstance):
                                  ComponentResult;
```

ts   A component instance created by a prior call to the Component Manager `OpenComponent` function.

DESCRIPTION

The appropriate response to `ActivateTextService` is for the text service component to restore its active state, including displaying all floating windows if they have been hidden. If it is an input method, it should specify the redisplay of any unconfirmed text currently in the active input area.

DeactivateTextService

The `DeactivateTextService` function lets a text service component know that its associated document window is becoming inactive. This allows time for the text service component to prepare for deactivation.

```
FUNCTION DeactivateTextService (ts: ComponentInstance):
                                  ComponentResult;
```

ts   A component instance created by a prior call to the Component Manager `OpenComponent` function.

DESCRIPTION

When it receives a `DeactivateTextService` call, the text service component is responsible for saving whatever state information it needs to save, so that it can restore the proper information when it becomes active again. A component other than an input method should also hide all its floating windows and menus. However, an input-method component should *not* hide its windows in response to this call. If the subsequent document being activated is using the same component's service, it would be irritating to the user to hide and then immediately redisplay the same windows. An input-method component should hide its windows only in response to a `HidePaletteWindows` call.

An input method should not confirm any unconfirmed text in the active input area, but should save it until reactivated.

HidePaletteWindows

The `HidePaletteWindows` function instructs an input method to hide its floating windows because another input method is becoming active.

```
FUNCTION HidePaletteWindows (ts: ComponentInstance):
                            ComponentResult;
```

ts   A component instance created by a prior call to the Component Manager `OpenComponent` function.

DESCRIPTION

The `HidePaletteWindows` function is not called every time a component's document becomes inactive; it is called by the Text Services Manager only if the new document that is becoming active does not use the same text service component as the document last deactivated. When it receives a `HidePaletteWindows` call, the text service component should hide all its floating and nonfloating windows. Its menus, if any, will be removed from the menu bar by the Text Services Manager.

If the text service component has no palettes, it should return a `ComponentResult` value of `noErr`.

TerminateTextService

The `TerminateTextService` function terminates the operations of a text service in preparation for closing the text service component.

```
FUNCTION TerminateTextService (ts: ComponentInstance):
                              ComponentResult;
```

ts   A component instance created by a prior call to the Component Manager
            OpenComponent function.

DESCRIPTION

The Text Services Manager calls TerminateTextService before closing the
component instance. A text service component must use this opportunity to confirm any
inline input in progress.

If the text service component needs to remain open, it should return an OSErr value in
the component result return value. This could happen, for example, if the user chooses
Cancel in response to a text service component dialog box.

If this call is made to the *last* open instance of a text service component, the component
should hide any open palette windows. If it is an input method, the component should
not dispose of its menu handle if it has a menu.

Responding to Events and Updating the Cursor and Menu

To pass events to text service components, the Text Services Manager calls the
TextServiceEvent function. To allow components to handle menu commands, it calls
TextServiceMenuSelect. To allow components to set the shape of the cursor, it calls
SetTextServiceCursor. To allow components to add their menus to the menu bar, it
calls GetTextServiceMenu.

TextServiceEvent

The TextServiceEvent function routes an event to a specified text service component.

```
FUNCTION TextServiceEvent (ts: ComponentInstance;
                           numOfEvents: Integer;
                           VAR event: EventRecord):
                           ComponentResult;
```

ts   A component instance created by a prior call to the Component Manager
            OpenComponent function.

numOfEvents
            The number of events being passed.

event   The Event Manager event record (defined by the EventRecord data
            type) for the event being passed.

DESCRIPTION

If the text service component handles the event, it should return a nonzero value for `componentResult` and it should change the event to a null event. If it does not handle the event, it should return 0.

TextServiceMenuSelect

The `TextServiceMenuSelect` function lets a text service component handle commands from its menus.

```
FUNCTION TextServiceMenuSelect (ts: ComponentInstance;
                                serviceMenu: MenuHandle;
                                item: Integer): ComponentResult;
```

ts   A component instance created by a prior call to the Component Manager `OpenComponent` function.

serviceMenu
                A Menu Manager menu handle (defined by the `MenuHandle` data type) to a specific text service component menu.

item   The text service component menu item that the user has selected.

DESCRIPTION

When the user makes a menu selection, the client application calls `TSMMenuSelect`; the Text Services Manager in turn calls `TextServiceMenuSelect` to all active components. The text service component receiving this call should return 0 for `componentResult` if it did not handle the menu selection, and 1 if it did.

After the text service component performs the chosen task, it is not responsible for removing the highlighting from the menu title.

SetTextServiceCursor

The `SetTextServiceCursor` function lets the text service component control the shape of the cursor.

```
FUNCTION SetTextServiceCursor (ts: ComponentInstance;
                               mousePos: Point): ComponentResult;
```

ts   A component instance created by a prior call to the Component Manager `OpenComponent` function.

mousePos   A location (specified as a QuickDraw point) that specifies the global
            coordinates for the vertical and horizontal position of the mouse.

DESCRIPTION

The text service component must return a nonzero value for `ComponentResult` if it has
set the cursor, and 0 if it has not.

GetTextServiceMenu

The `GetTextServiceMenu` function returns a handle to a menu belonging to a text
service component.

```
FUNCTION GetTextServiceMenu (ts: ComponentInstance;
                             VAR serviceMenu: MenuHandle):
                             ComponentResult;
```

ts   A component instance created by a prior call to the Component Manager
            `OpenComponent` function.

serviceMenu
            A menu handle (defined by the Menu Manager `MenuHandle` data type)
            for the text service component that is to be updated.

DESCRIPTION

The Text Services Manager calls `GetTextServiceMenu` to a text service component
when the component is opened or activated, so that it can put the component's menu on
the menu bar.

The menu handle passed in `serviceMenu` may be preallocated or it may be `NIL`. If
the menu handle is `NIL`, the text service component should allocate a new menu and
return it.

Note
All instances of an input-method component must share a single menu
handle, allocated in the system heap. ◆

If the text service component does not have a menu, it should return a
`ComponentResult` value of `TSMHasNoMenuErr`.

Confirming Active Input in a TSM Document

To stop active input in a text service component, the Text Services Manager calls the
`FixTextService` function described in this section.

FixTextService

The `FixTextService` function explicitly terminates any input that is in progress in a specified text service component.

```
FUNCTION FixTextService (ts: ComponentInstance): ComponentResult;
```

ts   A component instance created by a prior call to the Component Manager `OpenComponent` function.

DESCRIPTION

This function is equivalent to the user explicitly confirming text, but the request comes instead from the application or from the Text Services Manager. The text service component must stop accepting further input and confirm the current input, as appropriate.

Identifying the Supported Scripts and Languages

The Text Services Manager or a client application may call the `GetScriptLanguageSupport` function to find out all the scripts and languages supported by your text service component.

GetScriptLanguageSupport

The `GetScriptLanguageSupport` function determines which languages and scripts a specified text service component supports, including its primary language and script.

```
FUNCTION GetScriptLanguageSupport (ts: ComponentInstance;
                                   VAR scriptHandle:
                                   ScriptLanguageSupportHandle):
                                   ComponentResult;
```

ts   A component instance created by a prior call to the Component Manager `OpenComponent` function.

scriptHandle
                A handle to a script-language support record. The handle must be either NIL or a valid handle. If it is NIL, the text service component allocates a new handle. If it is already a valid handle, the text service component resizes it as necessary.

DESCRIPTION

The GetScriptLanguageSupport function lets a caller find out all scripts and languages that your text service component supports. GetScriptLanguageSupport should return a list of scripts and languages in the scriptHandle return parameter. The ComponentResult return value should contain 0 if the list is correct, or an error value if an error occurred.

The component should list all its supported scripts and languages, starting with the primary script and language as specified in the componentFlags field of its component description record. See page 7-15.

The result is returned in a handle to a script-language support record. See "Identifying the Supported Scripts and Languages" on page 7-42 for a description of the script-language support record.

SEE ALSO

For sample code that shows a text service component responding to the GetScriptLanguageSupport function, see Listing 7-10 on page 7-43.

Summary of the Text Services Manager

Pascal Summary

Constants

```
CONST

    kTSMVersion = 1;                 {Version of Text Services Manager}
    kTextService = 'tsvc';           {Component type for component description}
    kInputMethodService = 'inpm';    {Component subtype for component desc.}

    bTakeActiveEvent = 15;           {Bit set if component takes activate events}
    bScriptMask = $00007F00;                                   {Bits 8 - 14}
    bLanguageMask = $000000FF;                                 {Bits 0 - 7}
    bScriptLanguageMask = ScriptMask + bLanguageMask;          {Bits 0 - 14}

{Hilite styles}
    kCaretPosition = 1;              {specify caret position}
    kRawText = 2;                    {specify range of raw text}
    kSelectedRawText = 3;            {specify range of selected raw text}
    kConvertedText = 4;              {specify range of converted text}
    kSelectedConvertedText = 5;      {specify range of selected converted text}

{Apple Event constants}

    kTextServiceClass = kTextService;    {Event class}
    kUpdateActiveInputArea = 'updt';     {Update active inline area}
    kPos2Offset = 'p2st';                {Convert global coordinates to }
                                         { character position}
    kOffset2Pos = 'st2p';                {Convert character position to }
                                         { global coordinate}
    kShowHideInputWindow = 'shiw';       {show or hide the input window}

    {Event keywords}
    keyAETSMDocumentRefcon = 'refc'; {TSM document refcon}

    keyAEServerInstance = 'srvi'; {Server instance}
    keyAETheData = 'kdat';           {typeText}
```

```
   keyAEScriptTag = 'sclg';          {Script tag}
   keyAEFixLength = 'fixl';
   keyAEHiliteRange = 'hrng';        {Hilite range array}
   keyAEUpdateRange = 'udng';        {Update range array}
   keyAEClauseOffsets = 'clau';      {Clause offsets array}
   keyAECurrentPoint = 'cpos';       {Current point}
   keyAEDragging = 'bool';           {Dragging flag}
   keyAEOffset = 'ofst';             {Offset}
   keyAERegionClass = 'rgnc';        {Region class}
   keyAEPoint = 'gpos';              {Current point}
   keyAEBufferSize = 'buff';         {Buffer size to get the text}
   keyAERequestedType = 'rtyp';      {Requested text type}
   keyAEMoveView = 'mvvw';           {Move view flag}
   keyAELength = 'leng';             {Length}
   keyAENextBody = 'nxbd';           {Next or previous body}

{optional keywords for Offset2Pos}
   keyAETextFont = 'ktxf';
   keyAETextPointSize = 'ktps';
   keyAETextLineHeight = 'ktlh';
   keyAETextLineAscent = 'ktas';
   keyAEAngle = 'kang';

{optional keyword for Pos2Offset}
   keyAELeftSide = 'klef';           {type Boolean}

{optional keyword for kShowHideInputWindow}
   keyAEShowHideInputWindow = 'shiw';  {type Boolean}

{keyword for PinRange}
   keyAEPinRange = 'pnrg';

{Desc type ...}
   typeComponentInstance = 'cmpi';   {component instance}
   typeTextRange = 'txrn';           {text range}
   typeTextRangeArray = 'tray';      {text range array}
   typeOffsetArray = 'ofay';         {offset array}
   typeIntlWritingCode = 'intl';     {script code}
   typeQDPoint = 'QDpt';             {QuickDraw point}
   typeAEText = 'tTXT';              {Apple event text}
   typeText = 'TEXT';                {plain text}

{Apple event descriptor type constants}
   kTSMOutsideOfBody = 1;
   kTSMInsideOfBody = 2;
```

```
    kTSMInsideOfActiveInputArea = 3;

    kNextBody = 1;
    kPreviousBody = 2;

{Apple event error constants}
    errOffsetInvalid = -1800;
    errOffsetIsOutsideOfView = -1801;
    errTopOfDocument = -1810;
    errTopOfBody = -1811;
    errEndOfDocument = -1812;
    errEndOfBody = -1813;
```

Data Types

```
TYPE TextRange =
    RECORD
        fStart:        LongInt;
        fEnd:          LongInt;
        fHiliteStyle:  Integer;
    END;
    TextRangePtr = ^TextRange;
    TextRangeHandle = ^TextRangePtr;

    TextRangeArray =
    RECORD
        fNumOfRanges:  Integer;
        fRange:        ARRAY [0..0] of TextRange;
    END;
    TextRangeArrayPtr = ^TextRangeArray;
    TextRangeArrayHandle = ^TextRangeArrayPtr;

    OffsetArray =
    RECORD
        fNumOfOffsets: Integer;
        fOffset:       ARRAY [0..0] of LongInt;
    END;
    OffsetArrayPtr = ^OffsetArray;
    OffsetArrayHandle = ^OffsetArrayPtr;

    TextServiceInfo =
    RECORD
        fComponent: Component;
```

```
      fItemName:   Str255;
END;
TextServicesInfoPtr = ^TextServiceInfo;

TextServiceList =
RECORD
   fTextServiceCount:   Integer;
   fServices:           ARRAY [0..0] of TextServiceInfo;
END;
TextServiceListPtr = ^TextServiceList;
TextServiceListHandle = ^TextServiceListPtr;

ScriptLanguageRecord =
RECORD
   fScript:    ScriptCode;
   fLanguage:  LangCode;
END;

ScriptLanguageSupport =
RECORD
   fScriptLanguageCount:   Integer;
   fScriptLanguageArray:   ARRAY [0..0] of ScriptLanguageRecord;
END;
ScriptLanguageSupportPtr = ^ScriptLanguageSupport;
ScriptLanguageSupportHandle = ^ScriptLanguageSupportPtr;

InterfaceTypeList = ARRAY [0..0] of OSType;

TSMDocumentID = Ptr;
```

Text Services Manager Routines for Client Applications

Initializing and Closing as a TSM-Aware Application

```
FUNCTION InitTSMAwareApplication: OSErr;
FUNCTION CloseTSMAwareApplication: OSErr;
```

Creating and Activating TSM Documents

```
FUNCTION NewTSMDocument     (numOfInterface: Integer;
                            VAR supportedInterfaceTypes: InterfaceTypeList;
                            VAR idocID: TSMDocumentID;
                            refCon: LongInt): OSErr;
FUNCTION ActivateTSMDocument
                            (idocID: TSMDocumentID): OSErr;
```

```
FUNCTION DeactivateTSMDocument
                            (idocID: TSMDocumentID): OSErr;
FUNCTION DeleteTSMDocument   (idocID: TSMDocumentID): OSErr;
```

Passing Events to Text Service Components

```
FUNCTION TSMEvent            (VAR event: EventRecord): Boolean;
```

Passing Menu Selections and Cursor Setting

```
FUNCTION TSMMenuSelect       (menuResult: LongInt): Boolean;
FUNCTION SetTSMCursor        (mousePos: Point): Boolean;
```

Confirming Active Input in a TSM Document

```
FUNCTION FixTSMDocument      (idocID: TSMDocumentID): OSErr;
```

Making Text Services Available to the User

```
FUNCTION GetServiceList      (numOfInterfaceTypes: Integer;
                             supportedInterfaceTypes: InterfaceTypeList;
                             VAR serviceInfo: TextServiceListHandle;
                             VAR seedValue: LongInt): OSErr;
FUNCTION OpenTextService     (idocID: TSMDocumentID; aComponent: Component;
                             VAR aComponentInstance: ComponentInstance):
                             OSErr;
FUNCTION CloseTextService    (idocID: TSMDocumentID; aComponentInstance:
                             ComponentInstance): OSErr;
```

Requesting a Floating Input Window

```
FUNCTION UseInputWindow      (idocID: TSMDocumentID; useWindow: Boolean):
                             OSErr;
```

Associating Scripts and Languages With Components

```
FUNCTION SetDefaultInputMethod
                            (ts: Component;
                             VAR slRecord: ScriptLanguageRecord): OSErr;
FUNCTION GetDefaultInputMethod
                            (VAR ts: Component;
                             VAR slRecord: ScriptLanguageRecord): OSErr;
FUNCTION SetTextServiceLanguage
                            (VAR slRecord: ScriptLanguageRecord): OSErr;
FUNCTION GetTextServiceLanguage
                            (VAR slRecord: ScriptLanguageRecord): OSErr;
```

Text Services Manager Routines for Components

Sending Apple Events to a Client Application

```
FUNCTION SendAEFromTSMComponent
                        (VAR theAppleEvent: AppleEvent;
                         VAR reply: AppleEvent; sendMode: AESendMode;
                         sendPriority: AESendPriority;
                         timeOutInTicks: LongInt;
                         idleProc: IdleProcPtr;
                         filterProc: EventFilterProcPtr): OSErr;
```

Opening Floating Utility Windows

```
FUNCTION NewServiceWindow   (wStorage: Ptr; boundsRect: Rect;
                             title: Str255; visible: Boolean;
                             theProc: Integer; behind: WindowPtr;
                             goAwayFlag: Boolean; ts: ComponentInstance;
                             VAR window: WindowPtr): OSErr;
FUNCTION CloseServiceWindow (window: WindowPtr): OSErr;
FUNCTION GetFrontServiceWindow
                            (VAR window: WindowPtr): OSErr;
FUNCTION FindServiceWindow  (thePoint: Point; VAR theWindow: WindowPtr):
                             Integer;
```

Text Service Component Routines

Providing a Text Service

```
FUNCTION InitiateTextService
                        (ts: ComponentInstance): ComponentResult;
FUNCTION ActivateTextService
                        (ts: ComponentInstance): ComponentResult;
FUNCTION DeactivateTextService
                        (ts: ComponentInstance): ComponentResult;
FUNCTION HidePaletteWindows (ts: ComponentInstance): ComponentResult;
FUNCTION TerminateTextService
                        (ts: ComponentInstance): ComponentResult;
```

Responding to Events and Updating the Cursor and Menu

```
FUNCTION TextServiceEvent   (ts: ComponentInstance; numOfEvents: Integer;
                             VAR event: EventRecord): ComponentResult;
```

```
FUNCTION TextServiceMenuSelect
                        (ts: ComponentInstance; serviceMenu:
                         MenuHandle; item: Integer): ComponentResult;
FUNCTION SetTextServiceCursor
                        (ts: ComponentInstance; mousePos: Point):
                         ComponentResult;
FUNCTION GetTextServiceMenu (ts: ComponentInstance;
                         VAR serviceMenu: MenuHandle): ComponentResult;
```

Confirming Active Input in a TSM Document

```
FUNCTION FixTextService        (ts: ComponentInstance): ComponentResult;
```

Identifying the Supported Scripts and Languages

```
FUNCTION GetScriptLanguageSupport
                        (ts: ComponentInstance; VAR scriptHandle:
                         ScriptLanguageSupportHandle): ComponentResult;
```

C Summary

Constants

```
#define   kTSMVersion          1                 /* Version of the
                                                     Text Services Manager */
#define   kTextService         'tsvc'            /* component type for
                                                     the component description */
#define   kInputMethodService  'inpm'            /* component subtype for
                                                     the component description */

#define   bTakeActiveEvent     15                /* bit set if the component
                                                      takes active event */
#define   bScriptMask          0x00007F00        /* bit 8 - 14 */
#define   bLanguageMask        0x000000FF        /* bit 0 - 7  */
#define   bScriptLanguageMask  bScriptMask+bLanguageMask    /* bit 0 - 14  */

/* Hilite styles ... */
typedef enum {
   kCaretPosition        = 1,     /* specify caret position */
   kRawText              = 2,     /* specify range of raw text */
   kSelectedRawText      = 3,     /* specify range of selected raw text */
   kConvertedText        = 4,     /* specify range of converted text */
```

```
    kSelectedConvertedText  =  5        /* specify range of selected
                                           converted text */

} HiliteStyleType;

/* Apple Event constants ... */

/* Event class ... */
#define    kTextServiceClass          kTextService

/* event ID ... */
#define    kUpdateActiveInputArea     'updt'    /* update active Inline area */
#define    kPos2Offset                'p2st'    /* converting global coordinates
                                                   to char position */
#define    kOffset2Pos                'st2p'    /* converting char position
                                                   to global coordinates */
#define    kShowHideInputWindow       'shiw'    /* show or hide bottomline
                                                   input window */

/* Event keywords ... */
#define    keyTSMDocumentRefcon       'refc'    /* TSM document refcon */
#define    keyAEServerInstance        'srvi'    /* component instance */
#define    keyAETheData               'kdat'    /* typeText */
#define    keyAEScriptTag             'sclg'    /* script tag */
#define    keyAEFixLength             'fixl'    /* fix len ?? */
#define    keyAEHiliteRange           'hrng'    /* hilite range array */
#define    keyAEUpdateRange           'udng'    /* update range array */
#define    keyAEClauseOffsets         'clau'    /* Clause Offsets array */
#define    keyAECurrentPoint          'cpos'    /* current point */
#define    keyAEDragging              'bool'    /* dragging flag */
#define    keyAEOffset                'ofst'    /* offset */
#define    keyAERegionClass           'rgnc'    /* region class */
#define    keyAEPoint                 'gpos'    /* current point */
#define    keyAEBufferSize            'buff'    /* buffer size to get text */
#define    keyAERequestedType       . 'rtyp'    /* requested text type */
#define    keyAEMoveView              'mvvw'    /* move view flag */
#define    keyAELength                'leng'    /* length */
#define    keyAENextBody              'nxbd'    /* next or previous body */

/* optional keyword for UpdateActiveInputArea */
#define    keyAEPinRange              'pnrg'

/* optional keywords for Offset2Pos */
#define    keyAETextFont              'ktxf'
#define    keyAETextPointSize         'ktps'
```

```
#define   keyAETextLineHeight      'ktlh'
#define   keyAETextLineAscent      'ktas'
#define   keyAEAngle               'kang'

/* optional keywords for Pos2Offset */
#define   keyAELeadingEdge         'klef'

/* Apple event descriptor type ... */
#define   typeComponentInstance    'cmpi'      /* server instance */
#define   typeTextRange            'txrn'      /* text range record */
#define   typeTextRangeArray       'tray'      /* text range array */
#define   typeOffsetArray          'ofay'      /* offset array */
#define   typeIntlWritingCode      'intl'      /* script code */
#define   typeQDPoint              'QDpt'      /* QuickDraw Point */
#define   typeAEText               'tTXT'      /* Apple Event text */
#define   typeText                 'TEXT'      /* Plain text */
#define   typeFixed                'fixd'      /* Fixed number 16.16 */

/* Apple event descriptor type constants */
typedef enum {
   kTSMOutsideOfBody            = 1,
   kTSMInsideOfBody             = 2,
   kTSMInsideOfActiveInputArea  = 3
} AERegionClassType;

typedef enum {
   kNextBody                    = 1,
   kPreviousBody                = 2
} AENextBodyType;

/* Apple Event error definitions */
typedef enum {
   errOffsetInvalid          = -1800,
   errOffsetIsOutsideOfView  = -1801,
   errTopOfDocument          = -1810,
   errTopOfBody              = -1811,
   errEndOfDocument          = -1812,
   errEndOfBody              = -1813
} AppleEventErrorType;
```

Data Types

```
struct TextRange {                          /* typeTextRange  'txrn' */
   long  fStart;
   long  fEnd;
   short fHiliteStyle;
};
typedef struct TextRange        TextRange;
typedef         TextRange        *TextRangePtr;
typedef         TextRangePtr     *TextRangeHandle;

struct TextRangeArray {              /* typeTextRangeArray   'txra' */
   short       fNumOfRanges;         /* specify the size of the fRange array */
   TextRange   fRange[1];            /* when fNumOfRanges > 1, the size of this
                                        array has to be calculated */
};
typedef struct TextRangeArray        TextRangeArray;
typedef         TextRangeArray       *TextRangeArrayPtr;
typedef         TextRangeArrayPtr *TextRangeArrayHandle;

struct OffsetArray {                 /* typeOffsetArray'offa' */
   short fNumOfOffsets;              /* specify the size of the fOffset array */
   long  fOffset[1];                 /* when fNumOfOffsets > 1, the size of
                                        this array has to be calculated */
};
typedef struct OffsetArray      OffsetArray;
typedef         OffsetArray     *OffsetArrayPtr;
typedef         OffsetArrayPtr *OffsetArrayHandle;

/* extract Script/Language code from Component flag ... */
#define  mGetScriptCode(cdRec)    ((ScriptCode) (cdRec.componentFlags &
                                                    bScriptMask) >> 8)

#define  mGetLanguageCode(cdRec) ((LangCode)    cdRec.componentFlags &
                                                    bLanguageMask)


typedef  void  *TSMDocumentID;

/* text service component information list */
struct TextServiceInfo {
   Component    fComponent;
   Str255       fItemName;
};
typedef struct TextServiceInfo     TextServiceInfo;
typedef         TextServiceInfo    *TextServiceInfoPtr;
```

```
/*text service component list*/
struct TextServiceList {
    short               fTextServiceCount;   /* number of entries in the
                                                 'fServices' array */
    TextServiceInfo     fServices[1];        /* Note: array of 'TextServiceInfo'
                                                 records follows */
};
typedef struct TextServiceList      TextServiceList;
typedef         TextServiceList     *TextServiceListPtr;
typedef         TextServiceListPtr  *TextServiceListHandle;

/*script and language record*/
struct ScriptLanguageRecord {
    ScriptCode  fScript;
    LangCode    fLanguage;
};
typedef struct ScriptLanguageRecord ScriptLanguageRecord;

/*script and language support record*/
struct ScriptLanguageSupport {
    short                   fScriptLanguageCount; /* number of entries in the
                                                     'fScriptLanguageArray'
                                                     array */
    ScriptLanguageRecord    fScriptLanguageArray[1]; /* Note: array of
                                                        'ScriptLanguageRecord'
                                                        records follows */
};
typedef struct ScriptLanguageSupport        ScriptLanguageSupport;
typedef         ScriptLanguageSupport       *ScriptLanguageSupportPtr;
typedef         ScriptLanguageSupportPtr    *ScriptLanguageSupportHandle;
```

Text Services Manager Routines for Client Applications

Initializing and Closing as a TSM-Aware Application

```
pascal OSErr InitTSMAwareApplication ();
pascal OSErr CloseTSMAwareApplication ();
```

Creating and Activating TSM Documents

```
pascal OSErr NewTSMDocument (short numOfInterface,
                             OSType supportedInterfaceTypes[],
                             TSMDocumentID *idocID, long refCon);
```

```
pascal OSErr ActivateTSMDocument
                             (TSMDocumentID idocID);
pascal OSErr DeactivateTSMDocument
                             (TSMDocumentID idocID);
pascal OSErr DeleteTSMDocument
                             (TSMDocumentID idocID);
```

Passing Events to Text Service Components

```
pascal Boolean TSMEvent        (EventRecord *event);
```

Passing Menu Selections and Cursor Setting

```
pascal Boolean TSMMenuSelect (long menuResult);
pascal Boolean SetTSMCursor  (Point mousePos);
```

Confirming Active Input in a TSM Document

```
pascal OSErr FixTSMDocument  (TSMDocumentID idocID);
```

Making Text Services Available to the User

```
pascal OSErr GetServiceList (short numOfInterfaceTypes,
                            OSType supportedInterfaceTypes[],
                            TextServiceListHandle *serviceInfo,
                            long *seedValue);
pascal OSErr OpenTextService
                            (TSMDocumentID idocID, Component aComponent,
                             ComponentInstance *aComponentInstance);
pascal OSErr CloseTextService
                            (TSMDocumentID idocID,
                             ComponentInstance aComponentInstance)
```

Requesting a Floating Input Window

```
pascal OSErr UseInputWindow (TSMDocumentID idocID, Boolean useWindow);
```

Associating Scripts and Languages With Components

```
pascal OSErr SetDefaultInputMethod
                            (Component  ts,
                             ScriptLanguageRecord *slRecordPtr);
pascal OSErr GetDefaultInputMethod
                            (Component *ts,
                             ScriptLanguageRecord *slRecordPtr);
```

```
pascal OSErr SetTextServiceLanguage
                        (ScriptLanguageRecord *slRecordPtr);

pascal OSErr GetTextServiceLanguage
                        (ScriptLanguageRecord *slRecordPtr);
```

Text Services Manager Routines for Components

Sending Apple Events to a Client Application

```
pascal OSErr SendAEFromTSMComponent
                        (AppleEvent *theAppleEvent,
                         AppleEvent *reply, AESendMode sendMode,
                         AESendPriority sendPriority,
                         long timeOutInTicks, IdleProcPtr idleProc,
                         EventFilterProcPtr filterProc);
```

Opening Floating Utility Windows

```
pascal OSErr NewServiceWindow
                        (void *wStorage, const Rect *boundsRect,
                         ConstStr255Param title, Boolean visible,
                         short theProc, WindowPtr behind,
                         Boolean goAwayFlag, ComponentInstance ts,
                         WindowPtr *window);

pascal OSErr CloseServiceWindow
                        (WindowPtr window);

pascal OSErr GetFrontServiceWindow
                        (WindowPtr *window);

pascal short FindServiceWindow
                        (Point thePoint, WindowPtr *theWindow);
```

Text Service Component Routines

Providing a Text Service

```
pascal ComponentResult InitiateTextService
                        (ComponentInstance ts);

pascal ComponentResult ActivateTextService
                        (ComponentInstance ts);

pascal ComponentResult DeactivateTextService
                        (ComponentInstance ts);
```

```
pascal ComponentResult HidePaletteWindows
                            (ComponentInstance ts);
pascal ComponentResult TerminateTextService
                            (ComponentInstance ts);
```

Responding to Events and Updating the Cursor and Menu

```
pascal ComponentResult TextServiceEvent
                            (ComponentInstance ts,
                             short numOfEvents, EventRecord *event)
pascal ComponentResult TextServiceMenuSelect
                            (ComponentInstance ts,
                             MenuHandle serviceMenu, short item);
pascal ComponentResult SetTextServiceCursor
                            (ComponentInstance ts, Point mousePos);
pascal ComponentResult GetTextServiceMenu
                            (ComponentInstance ts, MenuHandle *serviceMenu);
```

Confirming Active Input in a TSM Document

```
pascal ComponentResult FixTextService
                            (ComponentInstance ts);
```

Identifying the Supported Scripts and Languages

```
pascal ComponentResult GetScriptLanguageSupport
                            (ComponentInstance ts,
                             ScriptLanguageSupportHandle *scriptHdl);
```

Assembly-Language Summary

Trap Macros

Trap Macro Names for Text Services Manager Routines

Pascal name	Trap macro name
NewTSMDocument	_NewTSMDocument
DeleteTSMDocument	_DeleteTSMDocument
ActivateTSMDocument	_ActivateTSMDocument
DeactivateTSMDocument	_DeactivateTSMDocument
TSMEvent	_TSMEvent
TSMMenuSelect	_TSMMenuSelect

Pascal name	Trap macro name
SetTSMCursor	_SetTSMCursor
FixTSMDocument	_FixTSMDocument
GetServiceList	_GetServiceList
OpenTextService	_OpenTextService
CloseTextService	_CloseTextService
SendAEFromTSMComponent	_SendAEFromTSMComponent
SetDefaultInputMethod	_SetDefaultInputMethod
GetDefaultInputMethod	_GetDefaultInputMethod
SetTextServiceLanguage	_SetTextServiceLanguage
GetTextServiceLanguage	_GetTextServiceLanguage
UseInputWindow	_UseInputWindow
NewServiceWindow	_NewServiceWindow
CloseServiceWindow	_CloseServiceWindow
GetFrontServiceWindow	_GetFrontServiceWindow
InitTSMAwareApplication	_InitTSMAwareApplication
CloseTSMAwareApplication	_CloseTSMAwareApplication
FindServiceWindow	_FindServiceWindow

Trap Macro Names for Text Service Component Routines

Pascal name	Trap macro name
GetScriptLanguageSupport	_GetScriptLanguageSupport
InitiateTextService	_InitiateTextService
TerminateTextService	_TerminateTextService
ActivateTextService	_ActivateTextService
DeactivateTextService	_DeactivateTextService
TextServiceEvent	_TextServiceEvent
GetTextServiceMenu	_GetTextServiceMenu
TextServiceMenuSelect	_TextServiceMenuSelect
FixTextService	_FixTextService
SetTextServiceCursor	_SetTextServiceCursor
HidePaletteWindows	_HidePaletteWindows

7

Text Services Manager

Result Codes

`tsmComponentNoErr`	0	Component result: no error
`tsmUnsupScriptLanguageErr`	–2500	Specified script and language are not supported
`tsmInputMethodNotFoundErr`	–2501	Specified input method cannot be found
`tsmNotAnAppErr`	–2502	The caller was not an application
`tsmAlreadyRegisteredErr`	–2503	The caller is already TSM-initialized
`tsmNeverRegisteredErr`	–2504	The caller is not TSM-aware
`tsmInvalidDocIDErr`	–2505	Invalid TSM document ID
`tsmTSMDocBusyErr`	–2506	Document is still active
`tsmDocNotActiveErr`	–2507	Document is not active
`tsmNoOpenTSErr`	–2508	There is no open text service component
`tsmCantOpenComponentErr`	–2509	Can't open the component
`tsmTextServiceNotFoundErr`	–2510	No text service component found
`tsmDocumentOpenErr`	–2511	There are open documents
`tsmUseInputWindowErr`	–2512	An input window is being used
`tsmTSHasNoMenuErr`	–2513	The text service component has no menu
`tsmTSNotOpenErr`	–2514	Text service component is not open
`tsmComponentAlreadyOpenErr`	–2515	Text service component already open for document
`tsmInputMethodIsOldErr`	–2516	The default input method is old-style
`tsmScriptHasNoIMErr`	–2517	Script has no (or old) input method
`tsmUnsupportedTypeErr`	–2518	Unsupported interface type
`tsmUnknownErr`	–2519	Any other error

Dictionary Manager

Contents

This chapter describes how you can use the Dictionary Manager to create and work with dictionaries for input methods or other text services. The Dictionary Manager supplies a uniform and public dictionary format that lets you perform searching, insertion, and deletion.

Read this chapter if you are developing or enhancing an input method or other text service component that uses dictionaries.

To use this chapter, you should be familiar with the Macintosh script management system, the Text Services Manager, and parts of the File Manager. The script management system is described in the chapter "Introduction to Text on the Macintosh" in this book. The Text Services Manager is described in the chapter "Text Services Manager" in this book. The organization of the Dictionary Manager is based on B*-trees, used by the File Manager and the Finder. For more on the B*-trees, see the File Manager chapter of *Inside Macintosh: Files*.

This chapter presents a brief introduction to dictionaries and then discusses how you can make, access, locate records in, and modify them.

About Dictionaries for Input Methods

Input methods for 2-byte script systems use *dictionaries,* data files with information essential to the text conversions they perform. An input method uses its dictionary to convert the raw text entered by the user. For a discussion of raw text, conversion, and input methods, see the chapter "Text Services Manager" in this book.

Input methods commonly rely upon two or more dictionaries to perform conversion most efficiently. The **main dictionary** lists all standard conversion options for any valid syllabic or phonetic input. A main dictionary may have thousands to tens of thousands of entries, and is usually fixed in content. The **user dictionary,** also called an *editable dictionary,* is a complementary file in which users can add specialized or custom information that does not exist in the main dictionary. Because the main dictionaries of many input methods have only about 80 percent of the needed conversion options, a user dictionary is extremely valuable to users who customize the input process to improve its precision.

Users can also set dictionary learning. This allows the input method to incorporate frequency information as the user works, so that the frequency of combinations *in a particular grammatical context i*s taken into account in doing conversions. This makes a user dictionary even more valuable to the individual that has worked with it for a long time.

In principle, the dictionaries for different input methods of a given writing system should be very similar. For instance, most Japanese dictionaries contain information relevant to the conversion of Hiragana to Kanji. Korean dictionaries consist of data necessary for the conversion of Hangul to Hanja. Chinese dictionaries have entries relevant to the conversion of radical to Hanzi, Zhuyinfuhao to Hanzi, or Pinyin to Hanzi.

In practice, however, many currently available Chinese, Japanese, and Korean input methods use their own dictionary formats. Each input method has independently implemented operations to insert, delete, and search for the entries in its own dictionaries.

Input methods that use their own dictionary formats can understand only the dictionaries they create. This may be desirable for main dictionaries, because the features of a main dictionary can distinguish the quality of one input method from another; input method developers may be hesitant to share such dictionaries with other vendors. But for user dictionaries, incompatible formats create serious difficulties for users—particularly when a user dictionary contains many entries.

Consider the following situation. A user purchases an input method and uses it for perhaps a year, making numerous entries in the user dictionary. Then a new and better input method is introduced, but the new input method cannot understand the customized user dictionary. Because there is no general dictionary format, the user is forced to choose between two undesirable alternatives: creating an entirely new user dictionary by manually keying in thousands of previous entries, or continuing to use the old input method, forgoing the benefits of the new one.

This chapter describes a dictionary format that allows user dictionaries to be carried over from one input method to another, to avoid the difficulty just described. And although dictionaries are primarily of use to input methods, and are discussed in that context here, other text services such as thesauri or spelling checkers can also benefit from using dictionaries with this format.

About the Dictionary Manager

The Dictionary Manager supplies a uniform and public dictionary format and a set of operations that allows you to manipulate data in a dictionary file. This standard dictionary format helps to make the insertion, deletion, and searching operations in a dictionary available for all input methods.

This section describes the format and content of the data in a dictionary file, discusses the concept of garbage data and how the Dictonary Manager handles it, and presents some of the limitations you should be aware of before planning to use the Dictionary Manager.

Dictionary file types and Finder routing

Dictionaries belong in the Extensions folder within the user's System Folder. If your dictionary has a file type of `'dict'`, `'dic0'`, `'dic1'`, or `'dic2'`, the Finder automatically routes it to the Extensions folder if the user drops it on the System Folder. ◆

The Structure of a Dictionary

A **dictionary** is a collection of dictionary records. Each **dictionary record** consists of a key and some associated *data* referenced by that key. A **key** is a Pascal search string with a maximum length of 129 bytes (including the length byte). The data associated with a key has a maximum length of 4096 bytes.

The key for a dictionary record is stored separately from its data. The key, an offset to the data, and the length of the data make up the record's **index** entry. The index entry is stored as a **B*-tree** structure in the data fork of the dictionary file. The data is stored in the resource fork of the file; the Dictionary Manager accesses the data with Resource Manager partial resource routines. When a dictionary lookup is needed, the Dictionary Manager uses the key to find the location and size of the data in the resource fork. Then, it uses a partial resource reading to read the data into memory. (Routines for reading partial resources are described in the Resource Manager chapter of *Inside Macintosh: More Macintosh Toolbox*.) Figure 8-1 shows the general format of a dictionary record.

Note

Always use Dictionary Manager functions to gain access to records in the resource fork rather than examining them directly with Resource Manager routines. ◆

Figure 8-1   General format of a dictionary record

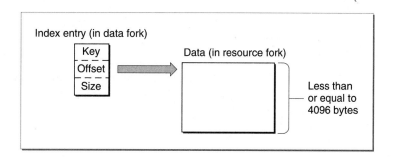

Each key-data pair is unique in a dictionary. No two keys in a single dictionary are identical.

Figure 8-2 shows the format of the data associated with a dictionary key. The first byte, which specifies the total number of entries in the data, is followed by a series of entries. Each entry has a maximum length of 256 bytes.

Figure 8-2   Format of data associated with a key

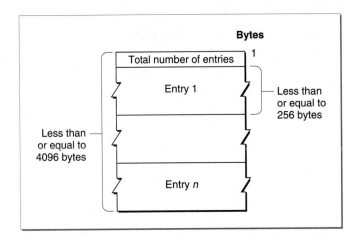

A **dictionary entry** in the data associated with a key contains raw data plus optional attributes. **Raw data** consists of any information related to the key entry. In a general dictionary it might be an explanation of the key; in a given East Asian dictionary it might be all the Chinese characters with the pronunciation of the key. A **data attribute** contains some information about the raw data—for example, grammatical or context-sensitive details, plus an attribute type. The **attribute type** is an integer constant in the range –128 to 127. The currently defined attribute types are listed on page 8-27.

Note

Apple reserves all negative attribute types. Positive attribute types are available for the use of developers of applications and text service components. ◆

Figure 8-3 shows the format of an entry. If data attributes are present, the first two bytes in each data attribute are the attribute size and the attribute type.

Figure 8-3   Format of an entry in the data associated with a key

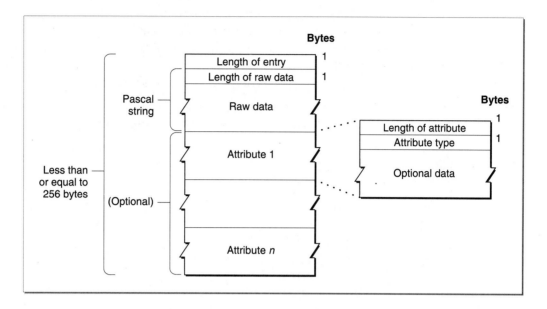

Depending on the script system, the key, raw data, and attributes may differ.

- In a record in an English dictionary, a key is any word; raw data is one or more definitions of the word; and a data attribute is the type of speech of the key—for example—verb, noun, adverb, adjective, or a combination of these.

- In a record in a Japanese dictionary, a key is a symbol of the phonetic subscript Hiragana; the associated raw data are the Kanji (ideographic characters); and the data attributes include the parts of speech or input method–specific attributes such as homonyms or groupings (clauses) of Kanji.

- In a record in a Chinese phonetic dictionary, a key is one of the phonetic symbols of Bopomofo; raw data is one or more Chinese words with the same pronunciation as the key; and there may be no associated data attributes.

- In a record in a Korean dictionary, a key may be a syllable or word in the Hangul subscript; associated raw data may be one or more Chinese words with the pronunciation of the key; and there may be no associated data attributes.

Garbage Data

In an editable dictionary, information is continually being added, deleted, or altered. Because it is too time-consuming to regenerate the entire dictionary each time a change is made, unused information called **garbage data** builds up over time. Garbage data is created whenever the size of the information associated with a key increases or decreases, or if the information is deleted. The data is no longer used by the dictionary.

Consider the simple dictionary file in Figure 8-4. It has only two dictionary records; each record has two entries. There is no garbage data in either record.

Figure 8-4   A simple dictionary with no garbage data

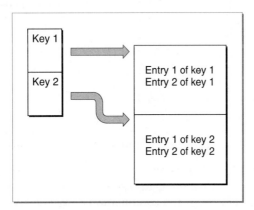

With the addition of one entry to the first record, the Dictionary Manager allocates a new block at the end of the dictionary's resource fork to hold all the entries in the first record, and creates a new index entry that points to the new block. The data the old index entry points to is no longer accessible and becomes garbage data. See Figure 8-5.

Figure 8-5   Creating garbage data in a dictionary

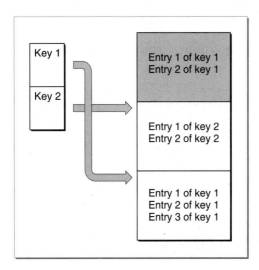

As the records in a dictionary file are modified, the size of the garbage data continues to increase. The Dictionary Manager keeps track of the amount of garbage data in a dictionary; to obtain the current size of garbage data in a dictionary, you can use the `GetDictionaryInformation` function (see page 8-24).

At some point, you may want to get rid of the garbage data permanently. The `CompactDictionary` function (see page 8-33) instructs the Dictionary Manager to create a new copy of the dictionary file, containing only valid entries. Once the new dictionary is constructed, the Dictionary Manager deletes the old one. (If the new dictionary fails to build properly, the original dictionary is preserved intact.) Note that `CompactDictionary` does not actually compress any data; it simply removes unusable information.

Figure 8-6 illustrates the structure of the simple dictionary built in Figure 8-4 and Figure 8-5 after the compaction process. Note that the order of the records in the resource fork may be different from what it was before compaction.

Figure 8-6   Deleting garbage data from a dictionary

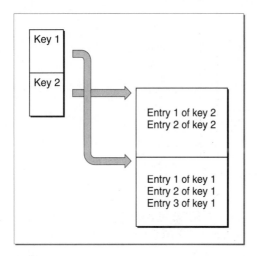

Note

The Dictionary Manager creates new garbage data only if the size of the associated data is enlarged or reduced or if the associated data is deleted altogether. If you simply rearrange the order of the entries within a single record, without changing the size of the associated data, the Dictionary Manager does not create any garbage data. This feature is especially useful for input methods that support dictionary learning, in which the entries require constant rearrangement according to their frequency of use. ◆

Dictionary Manager Limitations

Consider these limitations before using the Dictionary Manager:

■ The Dictionary Manager does not perform data compression. Your input method can compress part of the information before submitting it to the Dictionary Manager—but such compression would make your dictionary nontransferable and thus defeat a major purpose of using the Dictionary Manager.

■ The Dictionary Manager utilizes partial resource reading and writing to manipulate the actual data in a dictionary. Hence, each dictionary may not exceed 16 MB, a Resource Manager limitation.

- The user cannot edit an active dictionary (one currently being used by an input method). This also is a Resource Manager limitation.

- If you are developing a sophisticated input method, you may decide not to convert your main dictionaries into the Dictionary Manager format, because you may not want to publicize the keys and associated data in your main dictionaries.

- It may not even be practical to convert your main dictionaries. For example, several input methods contain gigantic—and significantly compressed—main dictionaries. In such cases, the conversion and decompression of dictionaries into Dictionary Manager format might greatly increase the size of your dictionary.

In summary, the Dictionary Manager is best for constructing user dictionaries of moderate size. Nevertheless, it is possible and in some cases it may be practical to use the Dictionary Manager for a main dictionary also.

Using the Dictionary Manager

This section tells how to use the Dictionary Manager to create and manipulate dictionaries. Using Gestalt Manager, Dictionary Manager, and File Manager calls, you can

- determine whether the Dictionary Manager is present and what attributes it has

- make a new dictionary (create a file and initialize the dictionary)

- gain access to a dictionary (open it, close it , and get information about it)

- locate records in a dictionary (by key or by index)

- modify the contents of a dictionary (insert, replace, or delete information)

- compact a dictionary

Testing for the Presence of the Dictionary Manager

Use `Gestalt` with the `gestaltDictionaryMgrAttr` environment selector to obtain a result in the response parameter that identifies the attributes of the Dictionary Manager. A result of `gestaltDictionaryMgrPresent` (= 0) means that the Dictionary Manager is present.

For details on the `Gestalt` function, see the Gestalt Manager chapter in *Inside Macintosh: Operating System Utilities*.

Making a Dictionary

You make a new dictionary by first creating a file and then initializing it as a Dictionary Manager dictionary.

Creating the File

To create a dictionary file, you first use a File Manager function such as `FSpCreate` or `HCreate` to create a file. Listing 8-1 is a sample routine that creates a file for a user dictionary.

Listing 8-1   Creating a dictionary file

```
FUNCTION CreateUserDictionary (VAR dictionaryFSSpec: FSSpec;
                                  creator, fileType: OSType;
                                  script: ScriptCode): OSErr;
VAR
   err: OSErr;
   fileReply: StandardFileReply;
BEGIN
   err := noErr;

   {get dictionary name and filespec}
   StandardPutFile('Create empty dictionary as...',
                'UserDictionary', fileReply);

   {delete existing dictionary if user OKs it}
   IF fileReply.sfGood THEN BEGIN
      dictionaryFSSpec := fileReply.sfFile;
      IF fileReply.sfReplacing THEN
         err := FSpDelete(dictionaryFSSpec);

      {create the empty dictionary file}
      IF err = noErr THEN BEGIN
         err := FSpCreate(dictionaryFSSpec, creator,
                        fileType, script);
         IF err <> noErr THEN
            DebugErrStr(err, 'FSpCreate');{handle error here}
      END
      ELSE
         DebugErrStr(err, 'FSpDelete');   {handle error here}
   END
   ELSE
      err := fnfErr;                           {assign error}
   CreateUserDictionary := err;
END;      {CreateUserDictionary}
```

Constructing the Dictionary

To make the internal structure of your newly created dictionary file, you use the `InitializeDictionary` function. You provide a file system specification pointer to the file you just created, you specify what maximum size the dictionary keys can have, and you can specify what search criteria—such as case-sensitivity—the dictionary will support.

The following code is a statement that initializes a dictionary file. It uses an application-defined constant (`kMaximumKeyLength`) to specify key length, an application-defined global (`gDictionaryScriptID`) to specify the script system for the dictionary, and the `kIsCaseSensitive` constant to specify that searches are to be case-sensitive.

```
err := InitializeDictionary(dictionaryFile, kMaximumKeyLength,
                    $1000 + kIsCaseSensitive,
                    gDictionaryScriptID);
```

Accessing a Dictionary

Before you can use a dictionary you must first open it. Once it is open, you can get information about it and you can use it. When you are finished with the dictionary, you must close it.

Opening and Closing the Dictionary

To open and use a dictionary, you must create an access path to the dictionary file using the `OpenDictionary` function. You provide a pointer to the file system specification record that defines the file, and you specify the read and write permission for the access path.

The `OpenDictionary` function returns a long integer, called a *dictionary reference number,* that specifies the open dictionary. You use that same dictionary reference number whenever you use the dictionary, and finally when you close the dictionary with the `CloseDictionary` function.

Listing 8-2 gives an example of how to create and close this access path. It consists of portions of the `CASE` statement from a sample application's menu-dispatching routine.

Listing 8-2   Opening and closing a dictionary file

```
{if user selects "Open dictionary" menu item:}
iOpenDictionary:
    IF gDictionaryReference = 0 THEN BEGIN
        {only open my own dictionary file types}
        fileTypes[0] := kMyDictionaryFileType;
```

```
StandardGetFile(NIL, 1, fileTypes, fileReply);
IF fileReply.sfGood THEN BEGIN
    gDictionaryFile := fileReply.sfFile;
    {open file with read-write permission}
    err := OpenDictionary(@gDictionaryFile,
                          fsRdWrPerm,
                          gDictionaryReference);
END;
    END;

{if user selects "Close dictionary" menu item:}
iCloseDictionary:
    IF gDictionaryReference <> 0 THEN BEGIN
        err := CloseDictionary(gDictionaryReference);
        gDictionaryReference := 0;
    END;
```

Obtaining Information About the Dictionary

You can use the GetDictionaryInformation function to obtain the following information about a dictionary file:

- its file system specification record

- the number of records it contains

- the current size in bytes of its unused (garbage) data

- the script code of the script system it belongs to

- its maximum key length

- its search criteria

To identify the desired dictionary file, you use the dictionary reference number obtained when you open a dictionary file with the OpenDictionary function.

The GetDictionaryInformation function returns its information in a dictionary information record. The dictionary information record is defined by the DictionaryInformation data type as follows:

```
TYPE DictionaryInformation =
    RECORD
        dictionaryFSSpec:    FSSpec;        {file system spec}
        numberOfRecords:     LongInt;       {total no. of records}
        currentGarbageSize:  LongInt;       {size of unusable data}
        script:              ScriptCode;    {script system}
        maximumKeyLength:    Integer;       {maximum length of keys}
        keyAttributes:       UnsignedByte;  {key search criteria}
    END;
```

See page 8-25 for a complete description of these fields. Listing 8-3 shows a call to `GetDictionaryInformation` to obtain the number of records in a dictionary.

Listing 8-3   Obtaining information about a dictionary

```
FUNCTION GetNumberOfRecordsInDictionary(dictionaryReference:
                                        LONGINT): INTEGER;
VAR
   err:              OSErr;
   dictionaryInfo:   DictionaryInformation;
   numRecords:       Integer;
BEGIN
   numRecords := -1;              {return result in case of error}
   IF dictionaryReference <> 0 THEN BEGIN
      {get the dictionary information record}
      err := GetDictionaryInformation(gDictionaryReference,
                                      dictionaryInfo);
      IF err <> noErr THEN
         numRecords := dictionaryInfo.numberOfRecords
      ELSE
         DebugErrStr(err, 'GetDictionaryInformation');   {error}
   END;
   GetNumberOfRecordsInDictionary := numRecords;
END;  {GetNumberOfRecordsInDictionary}
```

Locating Records in a Dictionary

This section tells you how to use a dictionary—that is, how to extract records from it. You can obtain records from a dictionary in two general ways: by key (search string) and by index (position in the file).

Locating Records by Key

You can use the `FindRecordInDictionary` function to search for dictionary records that match specified keys. Matching keys is perhaps the most standard dictionary search method: the user types in a key, and you search the dictionary for the data associated with that key.

You can provide a *requested attributes table* to narrow the search to only certain types of entries within the record that matches the search key. Figure 8-7 shows its format. You can request

■ only the entries with the specified attributes

■ the raw data of all the entries in the record without any attributes

■ everything in the record

Figure 8-7   The requested attributes table

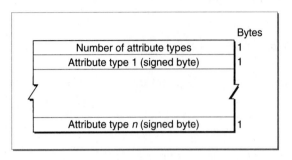

For example, you can use the requested attributes table to select only the verbs or nouns in the dictionary that match a key. The currently defined attribute types and their constants are listed in Table 8-2 on page 8-27.

Here is an example of how to use `FindRecordInDictionary`. Suppose the following entries are all the entries that match the key "hunch" in a dictionary record:

Raw data	Attribute type	Value	Optional attribute data
'guess'	kNoun	−1	
	kVerb	−2	
'push'	kVerb	−2	
	kMyType1	127	MyType1Data
'bend'	kMyType2	126	MyType2Data

Now suppose you call `FindRecordInDictionary` and pass a pointer to a requested attributes table that specifies two types: kNoun (−1) and kMyType1 (127). `FindRecordInDictionary` returns the data shown in Table 8-1.

Table 8-1   Sample data returned by `FindRecordInDictionary`

Offset	Value	Explanation
00	2	Number of entries found
(first entry starts here)		
01	8	Length of entry
02	5	Length of raw data
03	'guess'	The raw data
08	1	Length of first attribute
09	−1	Attribute type (= kNoun)
(second entry starts here)		
10	18	Length of entry

Table 8-1   Sample data returned by `FindRecordInDictionary` (continued)

Offset	Value	Explanation
11	4	Length of raw data
12	`'push'`	The raw data
16	12	Length of first attribute
17	127	Attribute type (= kMyType1)
18	`'MyType1Data'`	Optional data for first attribute

Locating Records by Index

You can use the `FindRecordByIndexInDictionary` function to retrieve record data within a dictionary file by index rather than by matching key strings. In this way you can examine a specific record or sequence of records, to look for the information you need.

As with `FindRecordInDictionary`, you can provide a requested attributes table to narrow the search to certain types of entries. If you want to get all records with entries of a particular attribute type, you can call `FindRecordByIndexInDictionary` repeatedly. In Listing 8-4, the routine loops through the entire dictionary, displaying the key and the raw data of the first entry of each record in turn. (The application routine `GetIndexedDataStringFromRecord` converts the raw data from each record into a string for display.)

Listing 8-4   Displaying all records in a dictionary by index

```
PROCEDURE ShowAllEntries (dictionaryReference: LONGINT);
VAR
    err:                        OSErr;
    dictionaryInfo:             DictionaryInformation;
    index:                      Integer;
    keyString, descriptionStr:  Str255;
    entriesHandle:              Handle;
    txtDialog:                  DialogPtr;
    finalTick:                  LongInt;
BEGIN
    IF dictionaryReference <> 0 THEN BEGIN
        {first find out how many records there are}
        err := GetDictionaryInformation(gDictionaryReference,
                                        dictionaryInfo);
        IF err = noErr THEN BEGIN
            entriesHandle := NewHandle(0);
            IF entriesHandle <> NIL THEN BEGIN
                descriptionStr := 'Displaying names in dictionary';
```

```
        txtDialog := ShowTextDialog(@descriptionStr[1],
                                LENGTH(descriptionStr));
        Delay(60, finalTick);

        FOR index := 1 TO dictionaryInfo.numberOfRecords
        DO BEGIN
            {return raw data for all entries of each record}
            err := FindRecordByIndexInDictionary
                                (dictionaryReference,
                                index - 1, NIL,
                                keyString, entriesHandle);

            {we only care about the first description string }
            GetIndexedDataStringFromRecord(entriesHandle, 1,
                                descriptionStr);

            {format as "key: description"}
            keyString := CONCAT(keyString, ': ');
            keyString := CONCAT(keyString, descriptionStr);
            SetTextDialog(txtDialog, @keyString[1],
                        LENGTH(keyString));
            Delay(60, finalTick);
        END;
        CloseTextDialog(txtDialog);
        DisposeHandle(entriesHandle);
      END;
    END;
  END;
END;   {ShowAllEntries}
```

Modifying a Dictionary

This section tells you how to use the Dictionary Manager routines to add, replace, or delete dictionary records.

You can use the InsertRecordToDictionary function to add or replace a record in a specified dictionary. Because there cannot be two separate records with the same key value in a dictionary, adding a new record may nullify an existing one. To avoid such a problem, you can specify the **insertion mode,** which notifies the Dictionary Manager how you want the new record treated. The insertion mode determines whether to put the record into the dictionary

■ only if it does *not* replace an existing record with the same key

■ only if it *does* replace an existing record with the same key

■ regardless of whether it adds a record or replaces another record

You can effectively insert and replace individual entries in records, in that you can obtain a record from a dictionary (with FindRecordInDictionary or FindRecordByIndexInDictionary), modify parts of the record, and then put the record back into the dictionary with InsertRecordToDictionary.

In Listing 8-5, the routine prompts the user for a key word and data for a new dictionary record. It then constructs the new record—in proper dictionary format—by calling the application routine NewDictionaryEntry. Finally, it calls InsertRecordToDictionary, providing a dictionary reference number to the desired dictionary file, a Pascal string representing the key, a handle to the new record, and a specification of how to insert the record into the dictionary.

Listing 8-5   Inserting a record into a dictionary

```
PROCEDURE AddNewRecord (dictionaryReference: LongInt);
VAR
    keyStr, descriptionStr: Str255;
    descriptionHandle:      Handle;
    err:                    OSErr;
BEGIN
    IF dictionaryReference <> 0 THEN BEGIN
        keyStr := Ask('Enter key:', '<key word>');
        IF keyStr <> '' THEN BEGIN
            descriptionStr := Ask(CONCAT(CONCAT
                                    ('Enter description for "',
                                    keyStr), '"'), '<record data>');

            IF descriptionStr <> '' THEN BEGIN
                descriptionHandle := NewDictionaryEntry
                                    (descriptionStr, 128, '');
                IF descriptionHandle <> NIL THEN BEGIN
                    err := InsertRecordToDictionary
                                    (dictionaryReference,
                                    keyStr, descriptionHandle,
                                    kInsertOrReplace);

                    IF err <> noErr THEN
                        DebugErrStr(err, 'InsertRecordToDictionary');
                    DisposeHandle(descriptionHandle);
                END;
            END;
        END;
    END;
END;    {AddNewRecord}
```

To remove a record from a dictionary, call the `DeleteRecordFromDictionary` function. When you call `DeleteRecordFromDictionary` you specifiy the key of the record to be deleted and the dictionary reference number of the dictionary file that contains the record.

Remember that deleting records from a dictionary, or replacing them with shorter records, does not make the dictionary file any smaller. It simply creates garbage data.

Compacting a Dictionary

You can use the `CompactDictionary` function to reduce the size of the dictionary by removing garbage data from the dictionary file.

IMPORTANT

Before compacting a dictionary, be aware that the operation may require considerable time to complete. You should notify the user of this. Avoid the compaction operation unless it is absolutely necessary or is mandated by the user. ▲

Dictionary Manager Reference

This section describes the routines and related data structures and constants that are specific to the Dictionary Manager.

Data Structures

The `DictionaryInformation` data type, which defines the dictionary information record, is described with the `GetDictionaryInformation` function on page 8-24.

Routines

This section shows the functions for making, accessing, using, and modifying dictionaries.

Making a Dictionary

To make a dictionary file, first create a file with a File Manager function such as `FSpCreate` or `HCreate`, and then call the `InitializeDictionary` function described in this section.

InitializeDictionary

The `InitializeDictionary` function constructs, for the specified file, the internal B*-tree structure that makes it a dictionary file.

```
FUNCTION InitializeDictionary (theFSSpecPtr: FSSpecPtr;
                               maximumKeyLength: Integer;
                               keyAttributes: Byte;
                               script: ScriptCode): OSErr;
```

theFSSpecPtr
: A pointer to a file system specification record. This record contains the filename, directory, and volume associated with this dictionary file.

maximumKeyLength
: The maximum length of the keys in the dictionary, including the length byte. The length must be less than or equal to 129.

keyAttributes
: The search criteria for the keys in the dictionary.

script
: The number that specifies the script system this dictionary supports.

DESCRIPTION

`InitializeDictionary` does not open the dictionary file after the Dictionary Manager initializes it. To open and use a dictionary file, use the `OpenDictionary` function (see page 8-22).

You can set the maximum key length of a dictionary only once; you cannot change it after the dictionary has been created. To maximize efficiency, keep the length to a minimum.

The `keyAttributes` parameter allows you to specify search criteria. For example, in one script system, it might be desirable to design the search to disregard case and be sensitive to diacritical marks, whereas in another script system these preferences might be reversed in keeping with the character encoding. Two predefined constants are available for the key attributes: the `kIsCaseSensitive` constant indicates that search procedures are to be case sensitive, and the `kIsNotDiacriticalSensitive` constant specifies that the search procedures are to ignore diacritical marks. To specify a combination of the different attributes, you add the constants together.

Constant	Value	Explanation
kIsCaseSensitive	16	Search is case-sensitive
kIsNotDiacriticalSensitive	32	Search is not diacritical-sensitive

SPECIAL CONSIDERATIONS

`InitializeDictionary` may move memory; your application should not call this function at interrupt time.

RESULT CODES

In addition to the standard File Manager, Memory Manager, and Resource Manager error codes, `InitializeDictionary` may return any of the following result codes.

noErr	0	No error
btNoSpace	–413	Insufficient disk space to store dictionary information
keyLenErr	–416	Maximum key length too great or equal to zero
keyAttrErr	–417	No such key attribute

SEE ALSO

Constants for all defined script codes are listed in the chapter "Script Manager" in this book.

File system specification records and File Manager error codes are described in *Inside Macintosh: Files*. Memory Manager error codes are described in *Inside Macintosh: Memory*. Resource Manager error codes are described in *Inside Macintosh: More Macintosh Toolbox*.

Accessing a Dictionary

Once you have created and initialized a dictionary file, you can use the `OpenDictionary` and `CloseDictionary` functions to open and close the dictionary. Once the dictionary is open, you can get information about it with the `GetDictionaryInformation` function.

OpenDictionary

The `OpenDictionary` function creates an access path to the specified dictionary file.

```
FUNCTION OpenDictionary (theFSSpecPtr: FSSpecPtr;
                         accessPermission: SignedByte;
                         VAR dictionaryReference: LongInt)
                         : OSErr;
```

theFSSpecPtr
:   A pointer to the file system specification record for the file to open. This record contains the filename, directory, and volume associated with this dictionary file.

accessPermission
:   The read and write permission for the access path. This permission must follow the File Manager access permission conventions.

dictionaryReference
:   A number that specifies a particular open dictionary.

DESCRIPTION

The OpenDictionary function returns, in the dictionaryReference parameter, a dictionary reference number—an identifying value that you use to specify the dictionary in subsequent calls to the Dictionary Manager.

The data structures accessed through the dictionaryReference parameter are allocated in the current heap. If the same dictionary is to be shared across applications, make sure the current zone is the system zone, so the data structures will be allocated in the system heap.

The following constants define the allowed values for the accessPermission parameter:

Constant	Value	Explanation
fsRdPerm	1	Request read permission only
fsWrPerm	2	Request write permission only
fsRdWrPerm	3	Request exclusive read/write permission

If the requested permission is not granted, OpenDictionary returns a result code that specifies the type of error.

SPECIAL CONSIDERATIONS

OpenDictionary may move memory; your application should not call this function at interrupt time.

RESULT CODES

In addition to the standard File Manager, Memory Manager, and Resource Manager errors, OpenDictionary may return any of the following result codes.

noErr	0	No error
notBTree	–410	File is not a dictionary

SEE ALSO

File system specification records, File Manager access permissions, and File Manager error codes are described in *Inside Macintosh: Files*. Memory Manager error codes are described in *Inside Macintosh: Memory*. Resource Manager error codes are described in *Inside Macintosh: More Macintosh Toolbox*.

For sample code that uses the OpenDictionary function, see Listing 8-2 on page 8-13.

CloseDictionary

The `CloseDictionary` function closes the specified open dictionary.

```
FUNCTION CloseDictionary (dictionaryReference: LongInt)
                        : OSErr;
```

dictionaryReference
            A number that specifies a particular open dictionary.

RESULT CODES

In addition to the standard File Manager and Resource Manager errors,
`CloseDictionary` may return any of the following result codes.

noErr   0   No error
notBTree   –410   File is not a dictionary

SEE ALSO

File Manager error codes are described in *Inside Macintosh: Files*. Resource Manager error
codes are described in *Inside Macintosh: More Macintosh Toolbox*.

For sample code that uses the `CloseDictionary` function, see Listing 8-2 on page 8-13.

GetDictionaryInformation

The `GetDictionaryInformation` function returns, in a dictionary information
record, information about the specified dictionary.

```
FUNCTION GetDictionaryInformation
                (dictionaryReference: LongInt;
                VAR theDictionaryInformation:
                DictionaryInformation): OSErr;
```

dictionaryReference
            A number that specifies a particular open dictionary.
theDictionaryInformation
            Upon completion of the call, contains a filled-out dictionary information
            record that describes the dictionary.

DESCRIPTION

The `GetDictionaryInformation` function returns data about a dictionary in a
dictionary information record in the `dictionaryInformation` parameter. The
`DictionaryInformation` data type defines this record as follows:

```
TYPE DictionaryInformation =
    RECORD
        dictionaryFSSpec:      FSSpec;
        numberOfRecords:       LongInt;
        currentGarbageSize:    LongInt;
        script:                ScriptCode;
        maximumKeyLength:      Integer;
        keyAttributes:         UnsignedByte;
    END;
```

Field descriptions

dictionaryFSSpec

>The file system specification record for this particular dictionary.

numberOfRecords

>The number of records in the dictionary.

currentGarbageSize

>The current size of unusable (garbage) information in the dictionary. For a discussion of garbage in a dictionary, see "Garbage Data" on page 8-8.

script   The number that specifies the script system this dictionary supports.

maximumKeyLength

>The maximum length of any key in the dictionary.

keyAttributes   A value that specifies the criteria for key searching. For a description of the key attribute constants, see the description of the InitializeDictionary function on page 8-21.

SPECIAL CONSIDERATIONS

>GetDictionaryInformation may move memory; your application should not call this function at interrupt time.

RESULT CODES

>In addition to the standard File Manager and Resource Manager errors, GetDictionaryInformation may return any of the following result codes.

noErr   0   No error
notBTree   –410   File is not a dictionary

SEE ALSO

>Constants for all defined script codes are listed in the chapter "Script Manager" in this book.

>File Manager error codes are described in *Inside Macintosh: Files*. Resource Manager error codes are described in *Inside Macintosh: More Macintosh Toolbox*.

For sample code that uses the `GetDictionaryInformation` function, see Listing 8-3 on page 8-15.

Locating Records in a Dictionary

The following section describes the Dictionary Manager functions that let you

- locate a record within a dictionary by its key

- locate a record within a dictionary by its index

You can constrain both key and index searches to include only entries with certain attributes.

FindRecordInDictionary

The `FindRecordInDictionary` function searches a dictionary for a record that matches the specified key, and returns entries with the specified attributes.

```
FUNCTION FindRecordInDictionary
                        (dictionaryReference: LongInt;
                         key: Str255;
                         requestedAttributeTablePointer: Ptr;
                         recordDataHandle: Handle): OSErr;
```

`dictionaryReference`
A number that specifies a particular open dictionary.

`key`   A Pascal string that denotes the key to be matched.

`requestedAttributeTablePointer`
A pointer to a table with attributes that you can request. This parameter provides a way for you to narrow the search to specified types of entries in the record. For instance, you could use the requested attributes table to specify only the verbs in the record that matches the key.

`recordDataHandle`
On entry, any valid handle. Upon completion, a handle to the requested data.

DESCRIPTION

The `FindRecordInDictionary` function returns, in the `recordDataHandle` parameter, a handle to the record data: a collection of entries matching the key and the requested attributes. `FindRecordInDictionary` returns the data in standard Dictionary Manager data format—as shown in Figure 8-2 on page 8-6 and Figure 8-3 on page 8-7.

The Dictionary Manager uses the Memory Manager procedure SetHandleSize to set the size of the recordDataHandle parameter correctly. If the Dictionary Manager cannot change the size of the handle to accommodate the returned matched data, it returns a Memory Manager error.

To limit the search to specific types of attributes, you construct a requested attributes table and pass a pointer to that table to FindRecordInDictionary. The requested attributes table consists of a byte which specifies the number of attributes, followed by a list of attribute types, as shown in Figure 8-7 on page 8-16.

■ If the requestedAttributeTablePointer parameter is Ptr(-1), FindRecordInDictionary returns everything in the matching record (that is, both raw data and attributes for all entries in the record).

■ If the requestedAttributeTablePointer parameter is NIL, FindRecordInDictionary returns the raw data of all the entries in the matching record, without any attached attributes.

■ If the requestedAttributeTablePointer parameter is a valid pointer, FindRecordInDictionary returns only those entries in the matching record whose attributes match those in the requested attributes table. In this case, if a record in the dictionary has a key that matches the search key but no entries in the record possess the requested attributes, the returned recordDataHandle parameter references a data buffer one byte in length that contains a value of 0.

Table 8-2 lists constants for the currently defined attribute types.

Table 8-2   Defined attribute types for dictionary entries

Constant	Value	Explanation
kNoun	−1	Noun
kVerb	−2	Verb
kAdjective	−3	Adjective
kAdverb	−4	Adverb

SPECIAL CONSIDERATIONS

FindRecordInDictionary may move memory; your application should not call this function at interrupt time.

RESULT CODES

In addition to the standard File Manager, Memory Manager, and Resource Manager errors, FindRecordInDictionary can return any of the following result codes.

noErr	0	No error
notBTree	−410	File is not a dictionary
btRecNotFnd	−415	Record cannot be found
btKeyLenErr	−416	Key length too great or equal to zero

SEE ALSO

File Manager error codes are described in *Inside Macintosh: Files*. Memory Manager error codes are described in *Inside Macintosh: Memory*. Resource Manager error codes are described in *Inside Macintosh: More Macintosh Toolbox*.

FindRecordByIndexInDictionary

The `FindRecordByIndexInDictionary` function locates a record in a dictionary by index, and returns entries with the specified attributes.

```
FUNCTION FindRecordByIndexInDictionary
                        (dictionaryReference: LongInt;
                         recordIndex: LongInt;
                         requestedAttributeTablePointer: Ptr;
                         VAR recordKey: Str255;
                         recordDataHandle: Handle): OSErr;
```

dictionaryReference
:   A number that specifies a particular open dictionary.

recordIndex
:   The index for the record to be searched; its position in the dictionary. The index range for `FindRecordByIndexInDictionary` is from 0 to one less than the maximum number of records in a dictionary. To obtain the maximum index range of a dictionary, you can use the `GetDictionaryInformation` function (see page 8-24).

requestedAttributeTablePointer
:   A pointer to a table with attributes that you can request. This parameter provides a way for you to narrow the search to specified types of entries in the record. For instance, you could use the requested attributes table to specify only the verbs in the record at that index.

recordKey   Upon succcessful completion, contains the key of the indexed record.

recordDataHandle
:   A handle that contains a collection of entries in the indexed record that match the requested attributes.

DESCRIPTION

The `FindRecordByIndexInDictionary` function returns, in the `recordDataHandle` parameter, a handle to the record data: a collection of entries from the specified record matching the requested attributes.
`FindRecordByIndexInDictionary` returns the data in standard Dictionary Manager data format—as shown in Figure 8-2 on page 8-6 and Figure 8-3 on page 8-7.

The Dictionary Manager uses the Memory Manager procedure `SetHandleSize` to set the size of the `recordDataHandle` parameter correctly. If the Dictionary Manager cannot change the size of the handle to accommodate the returned matched data, it returns a Memory Manager error.

To limit the search to specific types of attributes, you construct a requested attributes table and pass a pointer to that table to `FindRecordByIndexInDictionary`. The requested attributes table and a list of defined attribute types are described with the `FindRecordInDictionary` function, on page 8-26.

- If the `requestedAttributeTablePointer` parameter is `Ptr(-1)`, `FindRecordByIndexInDictionary` returns everything in the matching record (that is, both raw data and attributes for all entries in the record).

- If the `requestedAttributeTablePointer` parameter is `NIL`, `FindRecordByIndexInDictionary` returns the raw data of all the entries in the matching record, without any attached attributes.

- If the `requestedAttributeTablePointer` parameter is a valid pointer, `FindRecordByIndexInDictionary` returns only those entries in the matching record whose attributes match those in the requested attributes table. In this case, if a record in the dictionary has a key that matches the search key but no entries in the record possess the requested attributes, the returned `recordDataHandle` parameter references a data buffer 1 byte in length that contains a value of 0.

SPECIAL CONSIDERATIONS

`FindRecordByIndexInDictionary` may move memory; your application should not call this function at interrupt time.

RESULT CODES

In addition to the standard File Manager, Memory Manager, and Resource Manager errors, `FindRecordByIndexInDictionary` may return any of the following result codes.

noErr	0	No error
notBTree	–410	File is not a dictionary
btRecNotFnd	–415	Record cannot be found

SEE ALSO

File Manager error codes are described in *Inside Macintosh: Files*. Memory Manager error codes are described in *Inside Macintosh: Memory*. Resource Manager error codes are described in *Inside Macintosh: More Macintosh Toolbox*.

For sample code that uses the `FindRecordByIndexInDictionary` function, see Listing 8-4 on page 8-17.

Modifying a Dictionary

The routines described in this section allow you to modify the contents of a dictionary by adding, replacing, or deleting records.

InsertRecordToDictionary

The `InsertRecordToDictionary` function inserts a dictionary record into the specified dictionary file.

```
FUNCTION InsertRecordToDictionary
                        (dictionaryReference: LongInt;
                         key: Str255;
                         recordDataHandle: Handle;
                         whichMode: InsertMode): OSErr;
```

dictionaryReference
: A number that specifies a particular open dictionary.

key
: A Pascal string that denotes the key of the record to be inserted.

recordDataHandle
: A handle containing the data for the new record.

whichMode
: A value that determines whether the inserted record is to replace a record in the dictionary whose key matches the `key` parameter.

DESCRIPTION

The `InsertRecordToDictionary` function places the specified record into the specified dictionary. The `recordDataHandle` parameter must be a handle to data formatted like the data of a dictionary record, as shown in Figure 8-2 on page 8-6. Each entry in the data must be formatted as shown in Figure 8-3 on page 8-7. If the data size referenced by the `recordDataHandle` parameter exceeds the maximum of 4096 bytes, `InsertRecordToDictionary` returns a `recordDataTooBigErr` result code.

The `whichMode` parameter controls the insertion mode, the manner in which the insertion can take place. There are three possibilities, for which the Dictionary Manager defines three constants:

Constant	Value	Description
kInsert	0	Insert the record only if no existing record has a matching key. If a record with a matching key already exists in the dictionary, this function returns the result code btDupRecErr.
kReplace	1	Insert the record only if it replaces an existing record with a matching key. If no existing record in the dictionary has a matching key, this function returns the result code btRecNotFnd.
kInsertOrReplace	2	Insert the new record either way. Add it if no existing record in the dictionary has a matching key; replace the existing record if there is a match.

If `InsertRecordToDictionary` returns one of the errors listed in "Result Codes," the specified record was not inserted or replaced.

SPECIAL CONSIDERATIONS

`InsertRecordToDictionary` may move memory; your application should not call this function at interrupt time.

RESULT CODES

In addition to the standard File Manager, Memory Manager, and Resource Manager errors, `InsertRecordToDictionary` can return one of the following result codes.

noErr	0	No error
notBTree	–410	File is not a dictionary
btNoSpace	–413	Insufficient disk space to store dictionary
btDupRecErr	–414	Record already exists
btRecNotFnd	–415	Record cannot be found
btKeyLenErr	–416	Key length too great or equal to zero
unknownInsertModeErr	–20000	No such insertion mode
recordDataTooBigErr	–20001	Entry data bigger than buffer size

SEE ALSO

File Manager error codes are described in *Inside Macintosh: Files*. Memory Manager error codes are described in *Inside Macintosh: Memory*. Resource Manager error codes are described in *Inside Macintosh: More Macintosh Toolbox*.

For sample code that uses the `InsertRecordToDictionary` function, see Listing 8-5 on page 8-19.

DeleteRecordFromDictionary

The `DeleteRecordFromDictionary` function removes a record from the specified dictionary file.

```
FUNCTION DeleteRecordFromDictionary
                (dictionaryReference: LongInt;
                    key: Str255): OSErr;
```

dictionaryReference
: A number that specifies a particular open dictionary.

key
: A Pascal string that denotes the key of the record to be deleted.

DESCRIPTION

If `DeleteRecordFromDictionary` returns any of the errors listed in "Result Codes," it did not remove any records from the specified dictionary.

SPECIAL CONSIDERATIONS

`DeleteRecordFromDictionary` may move memory; your application should not call this function at interrupt time.

RESULT CODES

In addition to the standard File Manager, Memory Manager, and Resource Manager errors, `DeleteRecordFromDictionary` may return any of the following result codes.

noErr	0	No error
notBTree	−410	File is not a dictionary
btRecNotFnd	−415	Record cannot be found
btKeyLenErr	−416	Key length too great or equal to zero

SEE ALSO

File Manager error codes are described in *Inside Macintosh: Files*. Memory Manager error codes are described in *Inside Macintosh: Memory*. Resource Manager error codes are described in *Inside Macintosh: More Macintosh Toolbox*.

Compacting a Dictionary

The routine described in this section allows you to compact a dictionary file.

CompactDictionary

The CompactDictionary function compacts the specified dictionary file by removing all garbage data from it.

```
FUNCTION CompactDictionary (dictionaryReference:LongInt)
                              : OSErr;
```

dictionaryReference
          A number that specifies a particular open dictionary.

DESCRIPTION

The CompactDictionary function removes garbage data by creating a new copy of the dictionary file that contains only valid entries. Once the new dictionary is constructed, the Dictionary Manager deletes the old one.

If there is insufficient disk space to build the new dictonary, CompactDictionary returns the btNoSpace error message, and the original dictionary is preserved intact.

Note that CompactDictionary makes a dictionary file smaller by removing unusable information. It does not actually compress any data.

SPECIAL CONSIDERATIONS

CompactDictionary may move memory; your application should not call this function at interrupt time.

RESULT CODES

In addition to the standard File Manager, Memory Manager, and Resource Manager errors, CompactDictionary may return any of the following result codes.

noErr	0	No error
notBTree	–410	File not a dictionary
btNoSpace	–413	Insufficient disk space to store dictionary information

SEE ALSO

File Manager error codes are described in *Inside Macintosh: Files*. Memory Manager error codes are described in *Inside Macintosh: Memory*. Resource Manager error codes are described in *Inside Macintosh: More Macintosh Toolbox*.

Summary of the Dictionary Manager

Pascal Summary

Constants

```
CONST     {Data Insertion Modes}
   kInsert                 = 0;  {only insert input entry if nothing in }
                                 { dictionary matches key}
   kReplace                = 1;  {only replace entries that match key with }
                                 { input entry}
   kInsertOrReplace        = 2;  {insert entry if nothing in the dictionary }
                                 { matches key; if already matched }
                                 { entries exist, replace them with the }
                                 { input entry}

CONST {Key Attribute Constants}
   kIsCaseSensitive           = 16;     {diacritical mark is case sensitive}
   kIsNotDiacriticalSensitive = 32;     {diacritical mark not case sensitive}

CONST {Registered Attribute Types}
   kNoun       =  -1;   {noun}
   kVerb       =  -2;   {verb}
   kAdjective  =  -3;   {adjective}
   kAdverb     =  -4;   {adverb}
```

Data Types

```
TYPE
   InsertMode = Integer;

   AttributeType = Integer:
```

```
DictionaryInformation =
   RECORD
      dictionaryFSSpec:      FSSpec;          {file system specification }
                                              { record for this dictionary}
      numberOfRecords:       LongInt;         {number of records in }
                                              { this dictionary}
      currentGarbageSize:    LongInt;         {current size of garbage }
                                              { (unusable) data in dictionary}
      script:                ScriptCode;      {script system supported by }
                                              { this dictionary}
      maximumKeyLength:      Integer;         {maximum length of any key }
                                              { in this dictionary}
      keyAttributes:         UnsignedByte;    { key search criteria}
   END;
```

Routines

Making a Dictionary

```
FUNCTION InitializeDictionary
                          (theFSSpecPtr: FSSpecPtr;
                           maximumKeyLength: Integer;
                           keyAttributes: Byte;
                           script: ScriptCode): OSErr;
```

Accessing a Dictionary

```
FUNCTION OpenDictionary          (theFSSpecPtr: FSSpecPtr;
                                  accessPermission: SignedByte;
                                  VAR dictionaryReference: LongInt):
                                  OSErr;

FUNCTION CloseDictionary          (dictionaryReference: LongInt):
                                  OSErr;

FUNCTION GetDictionaryInformation
                                  (dictionaryReference: LongInt;
                                  VAR theDictionaryInformation:
                                  DictionaryInformation): OSErr;
```

Locating Records in a Dictionary

```
FUNCTION FindRecordInDictionary
                          (dictionaryReference: LongInt;
                           key: Str255;
                           requestedAttributeTablePointer: Ptr;
                           recordDataHandle: Handle): OSErr;
```

```
FUNCTION FindRecordByIndexInDictionary
                        (dictionaryReference: LongInt;
                         recordIndex: LongInt;
                         requestedAttributeTablePointer: Ptr;
                         VAR recordKey: Str255;
                         recordDataHandle: Handle): OSErr;
```

Modifying a Dictionary

```
FUNCTION InsertRecordToDictionary
                        (dictionaryReference:LongInt;
                         key: Str255;
                         recordDataHandle: Handle;
                         whichMode: InsertMode): OSErr;
FUNCTION DeleteRecordFromDictionary
                        (dictionaryReference: LongInt;
                         key: Str255): OSErr;
```

Compacting a Dictionary

```
FUNCTION CompactDictionary   (dictionaryReference:LongInt)
                         OSErr;
```

C Summary

Constants

```
/* Dictionary data insertion modes. */
enum {
  kInsert = 0,             /* Only insert the input entry if there is nothing
                              in the dictionary that matches the key. */
  kReplace = 1,            /* Only replace the entries which match the key
                              with the input entry. */

  kInsertOrReplace = 2     /* Insert the entry if there is nothing in the
                              dictionary which matches the key. If there are
                              already matched entries, replace the existing
                              matched entries with the input entry. */
};

/* Key attribute constants. */
#define kIsCaseSensitive 0x10            /* case-sensitive = 16 */
#define kIsNotDiacriticalSensitive 0x20  /* non-diac-sensitive = 32 */
```

```
/* Registered attribute type constants.*/
enum {
 kNoun = -1,
 kVerb = -2,
 kAdjective = -3,
 kAdverb = -4
};
```

Data Types

```
typedef short InsertMode;

typedef short AttributeType;

/* Dictionary information record.*/
struct DictionaryInformation{
    FSSpec          dictionaryFSSpec;
    long            numberOfRecords;
    long            currentGarbageSize;
    ScriptCode      script;
    short           maximumKeyLength;
    unsigned char   keyAttributes;
};
typedef struct DictionaryInformation DictionaryInformation;
```

Routines

Making a Dictionary

```
pascal OSErr InitializeDictionary
                        (FSSpecPtr theFsspecPtr,
                         short maximumKeyLength,
                         unsigned char keyAttributes,
                         ScriptCode script)
```

Accessing a Dictionary

```
pascal OSErr OpenDictionary (FSSpecPtr theFsspecPtr,
                         char accessPermission,
                         long *dictionaryReference)
pascal OSErr CloseDictionary
                        (long dictionaryReference)
```

```
pascal OSErr GetDictionaryInformation
                        (long dictionaryReference,
                         DictionaryInformation
                         *theDictionaryInformation)
```

Locating Records in a Dictionary

```
pascal OSErr FindRecordInDictionary
                        (long dictionaryReference, ConstStr255Param key,
                         Ptr requestedAttributeTablePointer,
                         Handle recordDataHandle)
pascal OSErr FindRecordByIndexInDictionary
                        (long dictionaryReference,
                         long recordIndex,
                         Ptr requestedAttributeTablePointer,
                         Str255 recordKey, Handle recordDataHandle)
```

Modifying a Dictionary

```
pascal OSErr InsertRecordToDictionary
                        (long dictionaryReference,
                         ConstStr255Param key, Handle recordDataHandle,
                         InsertMode whichMode)
pascal OSErr DeleteRecordFromDictionary
                        (long dictionaryReference, ConstStr255Param key)
```

Compacting a Dictionary

```
pascal OSErr CompactDictionary
                        (long dictionaryReference)
```

Assembly-Language Summary

Trap Macros

Trap Macro Names

Pascal name	Trap macro name
InitializeDictionary	_InitializeDictionary
OpenDictionary	_OpenDictionary
CloseDictionary	_CloseDictionary
InsertRecordToDictionary	_InsertRecordToDictionary
DeleteRecordFromDictionary	_DeleteRecordFromDictionary
FindRecordInDictionary	_FindRecordInDictionary
FindRecordByIndexInDictionary	_FindRecordByIndexInDictionary
GetDictionaryInformation	_GetDictionaryInformation
CompactDictionary	_CompactDictionary

Result Codes

notBTree	–410	File not a dictionary
btNoSpace	–413	Insufficient disk space to store dictionary information
btDupRecErr	–414	Record already exists
btRecNotFnd	–415	Record cannot be found
btKeyLenErr	–416	Key length too great or equal to zero
btKeyAttrErr	–417	Dictionary Manager doesn't understand an attribute
unknownInsertModeErr	–20000	No such insertion mode
recordDataTooBigErr	–20001	Entry data bigger than buffer size
invalidIndexErr	–20002	Invalid index

Appendixes

Built-in Script Support

Contents

This appendix describes support for script-specific behavior that is built into Macintosh system software. The code and data described here can work with the resources of many script systems to give the script systems their unique behaviors.

For historical reasons, much of the behavior of the Roman script system is built into Macintosh system software code resources and ROM. The rest of its behavior is expressed in international and keyboard resources that are installed in every version of Macintosh system software. This appendix summarizes that behavior, which represents the default set of Macintosh text-handling features.

WorldScript I is a script extension, consisting of code that implements table-driven measuring and drawing behavior for all 1-byte complex script systems. Using tables in each script system's international resources, WorldScript I properly performs caret placement, hit-testing, justification, text layout, and drawing for all supported scripts. This appendix describes how WorldScript I works and how you can replace some of its individual routines.

WorldScript II is another script extension that implements table-driven measuring and drawing behavior for all 2-byte script systems. Like WorldScript I, WorldScript II uses tables in each script system's international resources to perform text manipulation properly for all supported scripts. This appendix describes how WorldScript II works; note, however, that you cannot replace any of its routines.

Read this appendix for information on Roman character encoding, U.S. Roman keyboard-layout resource features, and the default Roman sorting routines. Read this appendix also if you wish to understand how the WorldScript extensions work, and especially if you intend to replace or modify any of the WorldScript I routines.

Before reading this appendix, read the chapter "Introduction to Text on the Macintosh" in this book. If you intend to modify WorldScript I, read also the discussion on replacing a script system's default routines in the chapter "Script Manager" in this book. Additional information on sorting behavior can be found in the description of the string-manipulation resource in the appendix "International Resources" in this book. Additional information on the keyboard-layout resource can be found in the appendix "Keyboard Resources" in this book.

The Roman Script System

The Roman script system is available on all localized versions of Macintosh system software throughout the world. It is not entirely uniform; in different localized systems, the Roman script may have different features. Nevertheless, its character set and its sorting and formatting rules provide baselines that non-Roman script systems adopt, modify, or replace as their needs align with or diverge from Roman conventions.

The Standard Roman character set is implemented by the U.S. keyboard-layout ('KCHR') resource—included with every Macintosh system—and by the keyboard-layout resources of other localized versions of the Roman script system (such as French or Spanish).

The standard U.S. Roman sorting routines are the basis for sorting strings composed of characters from the Standard Roman character set. The routines can be modified with code in a script system's string-manipulation resource; many non-U.S. Roman script systems and many non-Roman script systems override the standard U.S. routines.

The Standard Roman Character Set

The **Standard Roman character set** is an extended version of the **Macintosh character set**, documented in Volume I of the original *Inside Macintosh*. The Macintosh character set is itself an extended version of the **ASCII character set.** The conventional ASCII character set, also called *low ASCII,* defines control codes, symbols, numbers, and letters, assigning them character codes from $00 through $7F. The Macintosh character set adds codes from $80 through $D8, representing accented characters and additional symbols. Current Macintosh file-system sorting, as well as the sorting order used by several Text Utilities routines such as RelString, is based on the Macintosh character set.

The Standard Roman character set adds more accented forms, symbols, and diacritical marks, assigning them character codes from $D9 through $FF. It thus consists of all the character codes from $00–$FF, and it includes uppercase versions of all of the lowercase accented forms, a number of symbols, and other forms. See Figure A-1.

The Standard Roman character set is the closest to a universal character encoding that exists in the Roman script system. The Standard Roman characters are available in most Roman outline fonts, but not all are available in the Apple bitmapped versions of Chicago, Geneva, New York, and Monaco.

Figure A-1   The Standard Roman character set

	0x	1x	2x	3x	4x	5x	6x	7x	8x	9x	Ax	Bx	Cx	Dx	Ex	Fx
x0	nul	dle	sp	0	@	P	`	p	Ä	ê	†	∞	¿	–	‡	(apple)
x1	soh	DC1	!	1	A	Q	a	q	Å	ë	°	±	¡	—	·	Ò
x2	stx	DC2	"	2	B	R	b	r	Ç	í	¢	≤	¬	"	‚	Ú
x3	etx	DC3	#	3	C	S	c	s	É	ì	£	≥	√	"	„	Û
x4	eot	DC4	$	4	D	T	d	t	Ñ	î	§	¥	ƒ	'	‰	Ù
x5	enq	nak	%	5	E	U	e	u	Ö	ï	•	µ	≈	'	Â	ı
x6	ack	syn	&	6	F	V	f	v	Ü	ñ	¶	∂	Δ	÷	Ê	ˆ
x7	bel	etb	'	7	G	W	g	w	á	ó	ß	Σ	«	◊	Á	˜
x8	bs	can	(	8	H	X	h	x	à	ò	®	Π	»	ÿ	Ë	¯
x9	ht	em	)	9	I	Y	i	y	â	ô	©	π	…	Ÿ	È	˘
xA	lf	sub	*	:	J	Z	j	z	ä	ö	™	∫	nbsp	/	Í	˙
xB	vt	esc	+	;	K	[	k	{	ã	õ	´	ª	À	¤	Î	˚
xC	ff	fs	,	<	L	\	l	|	å	ú	¨	º	Ã	‹	Ï	¸
xD	cr	gs	-	=	M	]	m	}	ç	ù	≠	Ω	Õ	›	Ì	˝
xE	so	rs	.	>	N	^	n	~	é	û	Æ	æ	Œ	fi	Ó	˛
xF	si	us	/	?	O	_	o	del	è	ü	Ø	ø	œ	fl	Ô	ˇ

Nonprinting Characters

Table A-1 lists the nonprinting characters in the Standard Roman character set. The Unicode 1.0 name and the Macintosh character code (in hexadecimal and decimal) are provided also. **(Unicode** is an ISO standard for 16-bit universal worldwide character encoding.)

Table A-1   Nonprinting characters in the Standard Roman character set

Unicode name	Hexadecimal	Decimal
NULL	$00	0
START OF HEADING	$01	1
START OF TEXT	$02	2
END OF TEXT	$03	3
END OF TRANSMISSION	$04	4
ENQUIRY	$05	5
ACKNOWLEDGE	$06	6
BELL	$07	7
BACKSPACE	$08	8
HORIZONTAL TABULATION	$09	9
LINE FEED	$0A	10
VERTICAL TABULATION	$0B	11
FORM FEED	$0C	12
CARRIAGE RETURN	$0D	13
SHIFT OUT	$0E	14
SHIFT IN	$0F	15
DATA LINK ESCAPE	$10	16
DEVICE CONTROL ONE	$11	17
DEVICE CONTROL TWO	$12	18
DEVICE CONTROL THREE	$13	19
DEVICE CONTROL FOUR	$14	20
NEGATIVE ACKNOWLEDGE	$15	21

Table A-1   Nonprinting characters in the Standard Roman character set (continued)

Unicode name	Hexadecimal	Decimal
SYNCHRONOUS IDLE	$16	22
END OF TRANSMISSION BLOCK	$17	23
CANCEL	$18	24
END OF MEDIUM	$19	25
SUBSTITUTE	$1A	26
ESCAPE	$1B	27
FILE SEPARATOR	$1C	28
GROUP SEPARATOR	$1D	29
RECORD SEPARATOR	$1E	30
UNIT SEPARATOR	$1F	31
DELETE	$7F	127

Using Roman Character Codes as Delimiters

Your application may need to use a character code or range of codes to represent noncharacter data (such as field delimiters). Character codes below $20 are never affected by the script system. Some of these character codes can be used safely for special purposes. Note, however, that most characters in this range are already assigned special meanings by parts of Macintosh system software, such as TextEdit, or by programming languages like C. Table A-2 lists the low-ASCII characters to avoid in your application.

Table A-2   Low-ASCII characters to avoid as delimiters

Character	Hexadecimal representation
Null	$00
Home	$01
Enter	$03
End	$04
Help	$05
Backspace	$08
Tab	$09

continued

Table A-2   Low-ASCII characters to avoid as delimiters (continued)

Character	Hexadecimal representation
Page up	$0B
Page down	$0C
Carriage return	$0D
F1 through F15	$10
System characters	$11, $12, $13, $14[*]
Clear	$1B
Arrow keys	$1C, $1D, $1E, $1F

[*] System fonts use these codes for the printing characters PROPELLER, LOZENGE , RADICAL, and APPLE LOGO, respectively.

For certain writing systems, font layouts (tables that map glyph codes to glyphs) may use some of these character codes internally, for ligatures or other contextual forms. Also, as noted in Table A-2, system fonts use codes $11 through $14 for printing special symbols such as the Apple logo. Thus in unusual situations font changes may have an impact on the glyph representation of stored character codes with values less than $20, even though a user cannot generate those codes directly.

Printing Characters

Table A-3 shows the printing characters that exist in the Standard Roman character set. Macintosh applications can assume that glyphs for these characters exist in every Roman font. (However, see also the discussion of Roman fonts on page A-18.) The Unicode 1.0 and PostScript names and Macintosh character code (in hexadecimal and decimal) are provided along with a glyph example for printable characters. Modified versions of the Standard Roman character set exist for Croatian, Romanian, Turkish, and Icelandic/ Faroese, with different character assignments for the same codes. See Table A-4 through Table A-7.

Table A-3   Printing characters in the Standard Roman character set

Glyph	Unicode name	PostScript name	Hexadecimal	Decimal
	SPACE	space	$20	32
!	EXCLAMATION MARK	exclam	$21	33
"	QUOTATION MARK	quotedbl	$22	34
#	NUMBER SIGN	numbersign	$23	35
$	DOLLAR SIGN	dollar	$24	36
%	PERCENT SIGN	percent	$25	37
&	AMPERSAND	ampersand	$26	38
'	APOSTROPHE-QUOTE	quotesingle	$27	39
(	OPENING PARENTHESIS	parenleft	$28	40
)	CLOSING PARENTHESIS	parenright	$29	41
*	ASTERISK	asterisk	$2A	42
+	PLUS SIGN	plus	$2B	43
,	COMMA	comma	$2C	44
-	HYPHEN-MINUS	hyphen	$2D	45
.	PERIOD	period	$2E	46
/	SLASH	slash	$2F	47
0	DIGIT ZERO	zero	$30	48
1	DIGIT ONE	one	$31	49
2	DIGIT TWO	two	$32	50
3	DIGIT THREE	three	$33	51
4	DIGIT FOUR	four	$34	52
5	DIGIT FIVE	five	$35	53
6	DIGIT SIX	six	$36	54
7	DIGIT SEVEN	seven	$37	55
8	DIGIT EIGHT	eight	$38	56
9	DIGIT NINE	nine	$39	57
:	COLON	colon	$3A	58
;	SEMICOLON	semicolon	$3B	59
<	LESS-THAN SIGN	less	$3C	60
=	EQUALS SIGN	equal	$3D	61

continued

Built-in Script Support

Table A-3   Printing characters in the Standard Roman character set (continued)

Glyph	Unicode name	PostScript name	Hexadecimal	Decimal
>	GREATER-THAN SIGN	greater	$3E	62
?	QUESTION MARK	question	$3F	63
@	COMMERCIAL AT	at	$40	64
A	LATIN CAPITAL LETTER A	A	$41	65
B	LATIN CAPITAL LETTER B	B	$42	66
C	LATIN CAPITAL LETTER C	C	$43	67
D	LATIN CAPITAL LETTER D	D	$44	68
E	LATIN CAPITAL LETTER E	E	$45	69
F	LATIN CAPITAL LETTER F	F	$46	70
G	LATIN CAPITAL LETTER G	G	$47	71
H	LATIN CAPITAL LETTER H	H	$48	72
I	LATIN CAPITAL LETTER I	I	$49	73
J	LATIN CAPITAL LETTER J	J	$4A	74
K	LATIN CAPITAL LETTER K	K	$4B	75
L	LATIN CAPITAL LETTER L	L	$4C	76
M	LATIN CAPITAL LETTER M	M	$4D	77
N	LATIN CAPITAL LETTER N	N	$4E	78
O	LATIN CAPITAL LETTER O	O	$4F	79
P	LATIN CAPITAL LETTER P	P	$50	80
Q	LATIN CAPITAL LETTER Q	Q	$51	81
R	LATIN CAPITAL LETTER R	R	$52	82
S	LATIN CAPITAL LETTER S	S	$53	83
T	LATIN CAPITAL LETTER T	T	$54	84
U	LATIN CAPITAL LETTER U	U	$55	85
V	LATIN CAPITAL LETTER V	V	$56	86
W	LATIN CAPITAL LETTER W	W	$57	87
X	LATIN CAPITAL LETTER X	X	$58	88
Y	LATIN CAPITAL LETTER Y	Y	$59	89
Z	LATIN CAPITAL LETTER Z	Z	$5A	90
[	OPENING SQUARE BRACKET	bracketleft	$5B	91
\	BACK SLASH	backslash	$5C	92

Table A-3   Printing characters in the Standard Roman character set (continued)

Glyph	Unicode name	PostScript name	Hexadecimal	Decimal
]	CLOSING SQUARE BRACKET	bracketright	$5D	93
^	SPACING CIRCUMFLEX	asciicircum	$5E	94
_	SPACING UNDERSCORE	underscore	$5F	95
`	SPACING GRAVE	grave	$60	96
a	LATIN SMALL LETTER A	a	$61	97
b	LATIN SMALL LETTER B	b	$62	98
c	LATIN SMALL LETTER C	c	$63	99
d	LATIN SMALL LETTER D	d	$64	100
e	LATIN SMALL LETTER E	e	$65	101
f	LATIN SMALL LETTER F	f	$66	102
g	LATIN SMALL LETTER G	g	$67	103
h	LATIN SMALL LETTER H	h	$68	104
i	LATIN SMALL LETTER I	i	$69	105
j	LATIN SMALL LETTER J	j	$6A	106
k	LATIN SMALL LETTER K	k	$6B	107
l	LATIN SMALL LETTER L	l	$6C	108
m	LATIN SMALL LETTER M	m	$6D	109
n	LATIN SMALL LETTER N	n	$6E	110
o	LATIN SMALL LETTER O	o	$6F	111
p	LATIN SMALL LETTER P	p	$70	112
q	LATIN SMALL LETTER Q	q	$71	113
r	LATIN SMALL LETTER R	r	$72	114
s	LATIN SMALL LETTER S	s	$73	115
t	LATIN SMALL LETTER T	t	$74	116
u	LATIN SMALL LETTER U	u	$75	117
v	LATIN SMALL LETTER V	v	$76	118
w	LATIN SMALL LETTER W	w	$77	119
x	LATIN SMALL LETTER X	x	$78	120
y	LATIN SMALL LETTER Y	y	$79	121
z	LATIN SMALL LETTER Z	z	$7A	122

continued

Table A-3   Printing characters in the Standard Roman character set (continued)

Glyph	Unicode name	PostScript name	Hexadecimal	Decimal
{	OPENING CURLY BRACKET	braceleft	$7B	123
|	VERTICAL BAR	bar	$7C	124
}	CLOSING CURLY BRACKET	braceright	$7D	125
~	TILDE	asciitilde	$7E	126
	DELETE (nonprinting)		$7F	127
Ä	LATIN CAPITAL LETTER A DIAERESIS	Adieresis	$80	128
Å	LATIN CAPITAL LETTER A RING	Aring	$81	129
Ç	LATIN CAPITAL LETTER C CEDILLA	Ccedilla	$82	130
É	LATIN CAPITAL LETTER E ACUTE	Eacute	$83	131
Ñ	LATIN CAPITAL LETTER N TILDE	Ntilde	$84	132
Ö	LATIN CAPITAL LETTER O DIAERESIS	Odieresis	$85	133
Ü	LATIN CAPITAL LETTER U DIAERESIS	Udieresis	$86	134
á	LATIN SMALL LETTER A ACUTE	aacute	$87	135
à	LATIN SMALL LETTER A GRAVE	agrave	$88	136
â	LATIN SMALL LETTER A CIRCUMFLEX	acircumflex	$89	137
ä	LATIN SMALL LETTER A DIAERESIS	adieresis	$8A	138
ã	LATIN SMALL LETTER A TILDE	atilde	$8B	139
å	LATIN SMALL LETTER A RING	aring	$8C	140
ç	LATIN SMALL LETTER C CEDILLA	ccedilla	$8D	141
é	LATIN SMALL LETTER E ACUTE	eacute	$8E	142
è	LATIN SMALL LETTER E GRAVE	egrave	$8F	143
ê	LATIN SMALL LETTER E CIRCUMFLEX	ecircumflex	$90	144
ë	LATIN SMALL LETTER E DIAERESIS	edieresis	$91	145
í	LATIN SMALL LETTER I ACUTE	iacute	$92	146
ì	LATIN SMALL LETTER I GRAVE	igrave	$93	147
î	LATIN SMALL LETTER I CIRCUMFLEX	icircumflex	$94	148
ï	LATIN SMALL LETTER I DIAERESIS	idiaresis	$95	149
ñ	LATIN SMALL LETTER N TILDE	ntilde	$96	150
ó	LATIN SMALL LETTER O ACUTE	oacute	$97	151
ò	LATIN SMALL LETTER O GRAVE	ograve	$98	152

Table A-3   Printing characters in the Standard Roman character set (continued)

Glyph	Unicode name	PostScript name	Hexadecimal	Decimal
ô	LATIN SMALL LETTER O CIRCUMFLEX	ocircumflex	$99	153
ö	LATIN SMALL LETTER O DIAERESIS	odieresis	$9A	154
õ	LATIN SMALL LETTER O TILDE	otilde	$9B	155
ú	LATIN SMALL LETTER U ACUTE	uacute	$9C	156
ù	LATIN SMALL LETTER U GRAVE	ugrave	$9D	157
û	LATIN SMALL LETTER U CIRCUMFLEX	ucircumflex	$9E	158
ü	LATIN SMALL LETTER U DIAERESIS	udieresis	$9F	159
†	DAGGER	dagger	$A0	160
°	DEGREE SIGN	degree	$A1	161
¢	CENT SIGN	cent	$A2	162
£	POUND SIGN	sterling	$A3	163
§	SECTION SIGN	section	$A4	164
•	BULLET	bullet	$A5	165
¶	PARAGRAPH SIGN	paragraph	$A6	166
ß	LATIN SMALL LETTER SHARP S	germandbls	$A7	167
®	REGISTERED TRADEMARK SIGN	registered	$A8	168
©	COPYRIGHT SIGN	copyright	$A9	169
™	TRADEMARK	trademark	$AA	170
´	SPACING ACUTE	acute	$AB	171
¨	SPACING DIAERESIS	dieresis	$AC	172
≠	NOT EQUAL TO	notequal	$AD	173
Æ	LATIN CAPITAL LETTER AE	AE	$AE	174
Ø	LATIN CAPITAL LETTER O SLASH	Oslash	$AF	175
∞	INFINITY	infinity	$B0	176
±	PLUS-OR-MINUS SIGN	plusminus	$B1	177
≤	LESS THAN OR EQUAL TO	lessequal	$B2	178
≥	GREATER THAN OR EQUAL TO	greaterequal	$B3	179
¥	YEN SIGN	yen	$B4	180
µ	MICRO SIGN	mu	$B5	181
∂	PARTIAL DIFFERENTIAL	partialdiff	$B6	182

continued

Built-in Script Support

Table A-3   Printing characters in the Standard Roman character set (continued)

Glyph	Unicode name	PostScript name	Hexadecimal	Decimal
Σ	N-ARY SUMMATION	summation	$B7	183
∏	N-ARY PRODUCT	product	$B8	184
π	GREEK SMALL LETTER PI	pi	$B9	185
∫	INTEGRAL	integral	$BA	186
ª	FEMININE ORDINAL INDICATOR	ordfeminine	$BB	187
º	MASCULINE ORDINAL INDICATOR	ordmasculine	$BC	188
Ω	OHM	Omega	$BD	189
æ	LATIN SMALL LETTER AE	ae	$BE	190
ø	LATIN SMALL LETTER O SLASH	oslash	$BF	191
¿	INVERTED QUESTION MARK	questiondown	$C0	192
¡	INVERTED EXCLAMATION MARK	exclamdown	$C1	193
¬	NOT SIGN	logicalnot	$C2	194
√	SQUARE ROOT	radical	$C3	195
ƒ	LATIN SMALL LETTER SCRIPT F	florin	$C4	196
≈	ALMOST EQUAL TO	approxequal	$C5	197
Δ	INCREMENT	Delta	$C6	198
«	LEFT POINTING GUILLEMET	guillemotleft	$C7	199
»	RIGHT POINTING GUILLEMET	guillemotright	$C8	200
…	HORIZONTAL ELLIPSIS	ellipsis	$C9	201
	NON-BREAKING SPACE		$CA	202
À	LATIN CAPITAL LETTER A GRAVE	Agrave	$CB	203
Ã	LATIN CAPITAL LETTER A TILDE	Atilde	$CC	204
Õ	LATIN CAPITAL LETTER O TILDE	Otilde	$CD	205
Œ	LATIN CAPITAL LETTER O E	OE	$CE	206
œ	LATIN SMALL LETTER O E	oe	$CF	207
–	EN DASH	endash	$D0	208
—	EM DASH	emdash	$D1	209
"	DOUBLE TURNED COMMA QUOTATION MARK	quotedblleft	$D2	210
"	DOUBLE COMMA QUOTATION MARK	quotedblright	$D3	211
'	SINGLE TURNED COMMA QUOTATION MARK	quoteleft	$D4	212

Table A-3   Printing characters in the Standard Roman character set (continued)

Glyph	Unicode name	PostScript name	Hexadecimal	Decimal
'	SINGLE COMMA QUOTATION MARK	quoteright	$D5	213
÷	DIVISION SIGN	divide	$D6	214
◊	LOZENGE	lozenge	$D7	215
ÿ	LATIN SMALL LETTER Y DIAERESIS	ydieresis	$D8	216
Ÿ	LATIN CAPITAL LETTER Y DIAERESIS	Ydieresis	$D9	217
⁄	FRACTION SLASH	fraction	$DA	218
¤	CURRENCY SIGN	currency	$DB	219
‹	LEFT POINTING SINGLE GUILLEMET	guilsingleleft	$DC	220
›	RIGHT POINTING SINGLE GUILLEMET	guilsingleright	$DD	221
fi	(no Unicode designation)	fi	$DE	222
fl	(no Unicode designation)	fl	$DF	223
‡	DOUBLE DAGGER	daggerdbl	$E0	224
·	MIDDLE DOT	periodcentered	$E1	225
‚	LOW SINGLE COMMA QUOTATION MARK	quotesinglbase	$E2	226
„	LOW DOUBLE COMMA QUOTATION MARK	quotedblbase	$E3	227
‰	PER MILLE SIGN	perthousand	$E4	228
Â	LATIN CAPITAL LETTER A CIRCUMFLEX	Acircumflex	$E5	229
Ê	LATIN CAPITAL LETTER E CIRCUMFLEX	Ecircumflex	$E6	230
Á	LATIN CAPITAL LETTER A ACUTE	Aacute	$E7	231
Ë	LATIN CAPITAL LETTER E DIAERESIS	Edieresis	$E8	232
È	LATIN CAPITAL LETTER E GRAVE	Egrave	$E9	233
Í	LATIN CAPITAL LETTER I ACUTE	Iacute	$EA	234
Î	LATIN CAPITAL LETTER I CIRCUMFLEX	Icircumflex	$EB	235
Ï	LATIN CAPITAL LETTER I DIAERESIS	Idieresis	$EC	236
Ì	LATIN CAPITAL LETTER I GRAVE	Igrave	$ED	237
Ó	LATIN CAPITAL LETTER O ACUTE	Oacute	$EE	238
Ô	LATIN CAPITAL LETTER O CIRCUMFLEX	Ocircumflex	$EF	239
	APPLE LOGO	Apple	$F0	240
Ò	LATIN CAPITAL LETTER O GRAVE	Ograve	$F1	241
Ú	LATIN CAPITAL LETTER U ACUTE	Uacute	$F2	242
Û	LATIN CAPITAL LETTER U CIRCUMFLEX	Ucircumflex	$F3	243

continued

Built-in Script Support

Glyph	Unicode name	PostScript name	Hexadecimal	Decimal
Ù	LATIN CAPITAL LETTER U GRAVE	Ugrave	$F4	244
ı	LATIN SMALL LETTER DOTLESS I	dotlessi	$F5	245
ˆ	MODIFIER LETTER CIRCUMFLEX	circumflex	$F6	246
˜	SPACING TILDE	tilde	$F7	247
¯	SPACING MACRON	macron	$F8	248
˘	SPACING BREVE	breve	$F9	249
˙	SPACING DOT ABOVE	dotaccent	$FA	250
°	SPACING RING ABOVE	ring	$FB	251
¸	SPACING CEDILLA	cedilla	$FC	252
˝	SPACING DOUBLE ACUTE	hungarumlaut	$FD	253
˛	SPACING OGONEK	ogonek	$FE	254
ˇ	MODIFIER LETTER HACEK	caron	$FF	255

Variations in the Character Set

Two types of variations from the Standard Roman character set can occur. First, several languages and regional variations of Roman reassign parts of the character set; second, many specialized Roman fonts completely override the character set to provide other types of symbols.

Table A-4 shows the glyph assignments in the Croatian version of the Roman character set that diverge from the Standard Roman character set, their Unicode and PostScript names, and their Macintosh character codes in hexadecimal and decimal. For example, the code (hexadecimal $A9) that is assigned to the copyright sign in the Standard Roman character set is replaced by the Scaron (that is, the Roman capital letter "S" with a hacek). The copyright sign appears later at position $D9, which is assigned to the Latin capital letter "Y" diaeresis in the Standard Roman character set.

Table A-4   Croatian variations from the Standard Roman character set

Glyph	Unicode name	PostScript name	Hexadecimal	Decimal
Š	LATIN CAPITAL LETTER S HACEK	Scaron	$A9	169
Ž	LATIN CAPITAL LETTER Z HACEK	Zcaron	$AE	174
Δ	INCREMENT	Delta	$B4	180
š	LATIN SMALL LETTER S HACEK	scaron	$B9	185
ž	LATIN SMALL LETTER Z HACEK	zcaron	$BE	190

Table A-4   Croatian variations from the Standard Roman character set (continued)

Glyph	Unicode name	PostScript name	Hexadecimal	Decimal
Ć	LATIN CAPITAL LETTER C ACUTE	Cacute	$C6	198
Č	LATIN CAPITAL LETTER C HACEK	Ccaron	$C8	200
Đ	LATIN CAPITAL LETTER D BAR	Dmacron	$D0	208
⌘	APPLE LOGO	apple	$D8	216
©	COPYRIGHT SIGN	copyright	$D9	217
Æ	LATIN CAPITAL LETTER A E	AE	$DE	222
»	RIGHT POINTING GUILLEMET	guillemotright	$DF	223
–	EN DASH	endash	$E0	224
ć	LATIN SMALL LETTER C ACUTE	cacute	$E6	230
č	LATIN SMALL LETTER C HACEK	ccaron	$E8	232
đ	LATIN SMALL LETTER D BAR	dmacron	$F0	240
π	GREEK SMALL LETTER PI	pi	$F9	249
Ë	LATIN CAPITAL LETTER E DIAERESIS	Edieresis	$FA	250
Ê	LATIN CAPITAL LETTER E CIRCUMFLEX	Ecircumflex	$FD	253
æ	LATIN SMALL LETTER A E	ae	$FE	254

Table A-5 shows the glyph assignments in the Romanian version of the Roman character set that diverge from the Standard Roman character set, their Unicode and PostScript names, and their Macintosh character codes in hexadecimal and decimal.

Table A-5   Romanian variations from the Standard Roman character set

Glyph	Unicode name	PostScript name	Hexadecimal	Decimal
Ă	LATIN CAPITAL LETTER A BREVE	Abreve	$AE	174
Ș	LATIN CAPITAL LETTER S CEDILLA (COMMA VARIANT)	Scedilla	$AF	175
ă	LATIN SMALL LETTER A BREVE	abreve	$BE	190
ș	LATIN SMALL LETTER S CEDILLA (COMMA VARIANT)	scedilla	$BF	191
Ț	LATIN CAPITAL LETTER T CEDILLA (COMMA VARIANT)	Tcedilla	$DE	222
ț	LATIN SMALL LETTER T CEDILLA (COMMA VARIANT)	tcedilla	$DF	223

Built-in Script Support

Table A-6 shows the glyph assignments in the Turkish version of the Roman character set that diverge from the Standard Roman character set, their Unicode and PostScript names, and their Macintosh character codes in hexadecimal and decimal.

Table A-6   Turkish variations from the Standard Roman character set

Glyph	Unicode name	PostScript name	Hexadecimal	Decimal
Ğ	LATIN CAPITAL LETTER G BREVE	Gbreve	$DA	218
ğ	LATIN SMALL LETTER G BREVE	gbreve	$DB	219
İ	LATIN CAPITAL LETTER I DOT	Idot	$DC	220
ı	LATIN SMALL LETTER DOTLESS I	dotlessi	$DD	221
Ş	LATIN CAPITAL LETTER S CEDILLA	Scedilla	$DE	222
ş	LATIN SMALL LETTER S CEDILLA	scedilla	$DF	223

Table A-7 shows the glyph assignments in the Icelandic and Faroese versions of the Roman character set that diverge from the Standard Roman character set, their Unicode and PostScript names, and their Macintosh character codes in hexadecimal and decimal.

Table A-7   Icelandic and Faroese variations from the Standard Roman character set

Glyph	Unicode name	PostScript name	Hexadecimal	Decimal
Ý	LATIN CAPITAL LETTER Y ACUTE	Yacute	$A0	160
Ð	LATIN CAPITAL LETTER ETH	Eth	$DC	220
ð	LATIN SMALL LETTER ETH	eth	$DD	221
Þ	LATIN CAPITAL LETTER THORN	Thorn	$DE	222
þ	LATIN SMALL LETTER THORN	thorn	$DF	223
ý	LATIN SMALL LETTER Y ACUTE	yacute	$E0	224

In addition to regional variations in the character set, the Roman script system in particular contains many fonts with unique glyphs. Since the character encoding is limited to 256 values, specialized fonts such as Symbol and ITC Zapf Dingbats override the Standard Roman character encoding. For example, in the Standard Roman character set $70 corresponds to lowercase "p", but it is the numeric symbol for pi (π) in the Symbol font, an outlined square (❑) in Zapf Dingbats, and the musical symbol pianissimo for *play quietly* in the Sonata font. Hence, there is no guarantee that a Roman character code will always represent the same character in every font.

The U.S. Keyboard-Layout ('KCHR') Resource

The U.S. system software keyboard-layout resource (resource type 'KCHR', ID = 0) is included with every Macintosh system. It implements the Standard Roman character set shown in Figure A-1 on page A-5. The structure of the keyboard-layout resource is documented in the appendix "Keyboard Resources" in this book. This section describes in general how the U.S. 'KCHR' resource handles key combinations and dead keys.

The U.S. system software's keyboard-layout resource makes it possible to enter accented forms in the Standard Roman character set with **dead keys,** designated keys or modifier-plus-key combinations that produce no immediate effect when pressed but instead affect the character or characters produced by the next keys typed, called **completer keys.** Users can enter all the accented forms in the Standard Roman character set with dead keys. For example, pressing Option-E on the U.S. keyboard produces nothing (no event is posted), but subsequently typing "e" produces "é".

Note
Other keyboard layouts may produce accented characters in other ways.
On the French keyboard ('KCHR' resource ID = 1), for example,
pressing Option-E directly produces "é". ◆

The U.S. keyboard-layout resource provides the following key-combination features for consistency:

- Because the Shift key is ignored if the Command key is pressed, the Caps Lock key is also ignored if the Command key is pressed.

- Handling of the Option-Shift and Option–Caps Lock key combinations is based on the following principles:
  □ If either the Option or the Option-Shift key combination produces a letter, then the Option–Caps Lock key combination produces the same character as the Option, not the Option-Shift, key combination.
  □ If the Option key combination is a dead key for a particular accent, then the Option-Shift key combination produces the accent directly.

A **no-match character** (also called a *default completion character*) is the character that is produced when the keystroke following a dead key is either a space or a key for a character that cannot take the accent corresponding to the dead key. In system software versions 7.0 and later, default completion characters are "real" accent characters instead of low-ASCII approximations.

Standard Sorting Routines

The standard Macintosh sorting routines are contained in the Pack 6 resource, a system code resource (type = 'PACK', ID = 6) initialized at startup. As they process each character or sorting unit, the standard routines first call equivalent routines in the current script system's string-manipulation ('itl2') resource. Those routines, called **sorting hooks,** are described with the string-manipulation resource in the appendix "International Resources" in this book.

The U.S. string-manipulation ('itl2') resource contains only empty sorting hooks. Other localized versions of the Roman script system—and non-Roman script systems—provide their own string-manipulation resources that may have nonempty routines to modify or replace any of the standard routines, on a character-by-character basis.

Table A-8 describes the sorting behavior implemented by the standard Macintosh sorting routines. All characters of the Standard Roman character set are sorted. Primary sorting is shown in vertical order; secondary sorting is horizontal. This is the default sorting behavior used by the Text Utilities, and is appropriate for U.S. and similar localized versions of the Roman script system. All Text Utilities sorting routines (other than RelString and EqualString) use the sorting behavior specified in the string-manipulation resource, which may or may not be identical to the standard behavior. (RelString and EqualString use an invariant sorting behavior that is described in the chapter "Text Utilities" in this book.)

Table A-8   Standard sorting order (for Standard Roman character set)

Primary	Secondary
$00	NUL
…	
$1F	US
$20	space ($20) non-breaking space ($CA)
$21	!
$22	" « ($C7) » ($C8) " ($D2) " ($D3)
$23	#
$24	$
$25	%
$26	&

Table A-8   Standard sorting order (for Standard Roman character set) (continued)

Primary	Secondary
$27	' ´ ($D4) ´ ($D5)
$28	(
…	
$40	@
$41	A Á À Â Ä Ã Å a á à â ä ã å
$42	B b
$43	C Ç c ç
$44	D d
$45	E É È Ê Ë e é è ê ë
…	
$49	I Í Ì Î Ï i ı í ì î ï
…	
$4E	N Ñ n ñ
$4F	O Ó Ò Ô Ö Õ Ø o ó ò ô ö õ ø
…	
$55	U Ú Ù Û Ü u ú ù û ü
…	
$59	Y y ÿ Ÿ
$5A	Z z
$5B	[
…	
$60	`
$7B	{
…	
$7F	DEL
$A0	†
…	

Low-ASCII characters (other than letters) not listed in Table A-8 have primary sorting only and are sorted according to numeric code. Low-ASCII letters not listed in Table A-8 have a primary sorting order that is alphabetical and a secondary sorting order of uppercase followed by lowercase (like "B b"). All characters with codes above $A0 that are not listed in Table A-8 are sorted after $A0 according to numeric character code (except for ligatures; see note on sorting of ligatures).

Note the following details and anomalies in the standard Macintosh sorting order:

- The symbols ª ($BB) and º ($BC) are explicitly treated as symbols, not as letters, and their primary sorting positions are not respectively the same as A and O.

- The en-dash ($D0) and em-dash ($D1) do not have the same primary sorting position as hyphen-minus ($2D).

- The double low quotation mark „ ($E3) does not have the same primary sorting position as quotation " ($22).

- The single low quotation mark , ($E2), and the left and right single guillemet ‹ › ($DC, $DD) do not have the same primary sorting position as apostrophe ' ($27).

- The secondary sorting position for dotless-lower-i ı ($F5) is indeterminate. It sorts at exactly the same place (primary and secondary order) as regular lower i ($69).

- The character Ÿ does not sort between Y and y.

Sorting of ligatures

For a ligature, the primary sorting position is equivalent to the separate characters that make up the ligature. The secondary sorting position is just following the equivalent separate characters. Ligatures are sorted by the following first and second characters:

Ligature	First character	Second character
Æ	A	E
æ	a	e
fi	f	i
fl	f	l
Œ	O	E
œ	o	e
ß	s	s

Diacritical Stripping and Case Conversion

The Text Utilities routines `LowercaseText`, `UppercaseText`, `StripDiacritics`, and `UppercaseStripDiacritics` use information in a script system's string-manipulation (`'itl2'`) resource to perform their tasks. A Roman string-manipulation resource is included with every Macintosh system; the U.S. version of the Roman string-manipulation resource converts case and strips diacritical marks according to the following rules:

■ The unaccented letters A–Z and a–z are converted to unaccented a–z and A–Z, respectively, by case conversion. They are unaffected by stripping.

■ Accented versions (Å, ê, Ñ) are converted to equivalent unaccented versions (A, e, N) by stripping.

■ Accented versions (Å, ê, Ñ) are converted to identically accented case-changed versions (å, Ê, ñ) by case conversion.

■ Ligatures are unaffected by stripping, but are converted as appropriate by case conversion. Only the ligatures ß, fi, and fl, which have no uppercase versions, are unaffected by case conversion as well as by stripping.

U.S. International Resources and Keyboard Resources

When Macintosh system software is localized for a non-U.S. market, its system script may be Roman or non-Roman. In either case, it contains replacements for or modifications to the U.S. international resources and keyboard resources. Any U.S. Roman resource that is not replaced is included with the localized system.

Table A-9 shows which international resources are included in the U.S. system software, and how localized versions of the system software (and secondary scripts) add resources or replace them in the System file. Note that all non-Roman script systems and most localized versions of system software include localized versions of the `'itl0'`, `'itl1'`, `'itl2'`, and `'itl4'` resources. (Not all non-U.S. Roman script systems add a non-U.S. `'itl4'`.) Some non-Roman systems may also use optional `'itl5'` or `'trsl'` resources.

Table A-9   International resources in U.S. system software

Resource type	U.S. system software including Roman script system	Localized versions of system software or other script systems
`'itlc'`	Roman `'itlc'`	May replace `'itlc'`
`'itlm'`	Default `'itlm'`	May replace `'itlm'`
`'itlb'`	Roman `'itlb'`	May add non-Roman `'itlb'`

continued

Built-in Script Support

Table A-9 International resources in U.S. system software (continued)

Resource type	U.S. system software including Roman script system	Localized versions of system software or other script systems
'itl0'	U.S. 'itl0'	Adds non-U.S. 'itl0'
'itl1'	U.S. 'itl1'	Adds non-U.S. 'itl1'
'itl2'	U.S. 'itl2'	Adds non-U.S. 'itl2'
'itl4'	U.S. 'itl4'	May add non-U.S. 'itl4'
'itl5'	(none)	May add non-Roman 'itl5'
'trsl'	(none)	May add non-Roman 'trsl'

Table A-10 lists the keyboard resources that are included in the U.S. system software and shows how localized versions of the system software (and auxiliary scripts) add resources or replace them in the System file. Note that all localized versions of system software and all non-Roman script systems include at least one keyboard-layout resource and keyboard icon family; some provide a key-remap resource; and none need provide a key-map resource or key-caps resource.

Table A-10 Keyboard resources in U.S. system software

Resource type	U.S. system software including Roman script system	Localized versions of system software or other script systems
'itlk'	(none)	May add an 'itlk'[*]
'KCHR'	U.S. 'KCHR'	Adds non-U.S. 'KCHR'
'KSWP'	Standard 'KSWP'	May replace 'KSWP'
'KMAP'	All necessary 'KMAP's	(none)
'kcs#'	U.S. 'kcs#'	Adds non-U.S. 'kcs#'[*]
'kcs4'	U.S. 'kcs4'	Adds non-U.S. 'kcs4'[*]
'kcs8'	U.S. 'kcs8'	Adds non-U.S. 'kcs8'[*]
'KCAP'	All necessary 'KCAP's	(none)

[*] ID number equal to corresponding 'KCHR' ID number

For more information on these resources, see the appendixes "International Resources" and "Keyboard Resources" in this book.

WorldScript I

WorldScript I is a system extension, available with system software version 7.1 and later, that can support all types of 1-byte complex script systems. It contains code that implements many script-aware text-manipulation routines, eliminating the need for each script to maintain its own code extensions.

WorldScript I is a single file located in the Extensions folder within the System Folder on the user's Macintosh computer. It installs and initializes all compatible script systems present in the System Folder, and provides each with a set of standard routines. Script systems compatible with WorldScript I are called *universal scripts,* because they make use of the universally applicable WorldScript I routines.

About WorldScript I

Script systems developed prior to system software version 7.1 contain their own code to handle language-specific text processing. Each script system also has its own initialization and configuration code, installing itself at startup and adding its own modifications to the system. This process can result in a layering of patches to the same traps, inconsistent behavior, and inefficient use of memory.

WorldScript I redefines what a script system consists of by combining the executable code for many routines for all 1-byte script systems. It includes initialization and formatting routines that support all contextual forms required by all 1-byte scripts; script-specific behavior is encoded in resource-based tables. This approach reduces memory requirements for multiscript systems and avoids layering of patches.

WorldScript I routes script-aware calls through each universal script's own *dispatch table;* the dispatch table initially points back to the *script utility* routines in WorldScript I. This indirection allows your application to add to or replace existing routines on a script-by-script basis. Script Manager calls allow you to modify or add to any script's utility routine or patch. You can even replace an individual script system's routine completely if you need features significantly different from those provided by WorldScript I. Script utilities and dispatch tables are described in the next section and under "Flexible Dispatching Method" beginning on page A-28.

Shared Script Utilities and QuickDraw Patches

The **script utilities** are the low-level routines through which an individual script system implements script-aware Text Utilities, QuickDraw, and Script Manager routines. When an application makes a script-aware call, the script management system converts it to a script utility call and passes it on to the appropriate script system. Previous to system software version 7.1, individual script systems provided their own script utilities. With WorldScript I, a single set of script utilities can work with all 1-byte complex scripts.

Two Script Manager routines, `GetScriptUtilityAddress` and `SetScriptUtilityAddress`, allow you to access and override a script's utility routines.

Table A-11 lists the script utilities implemented by WorldScript I, along with the chapters in this book that describe their corresponding high-level routines.

Table A-11   Script utilities supported by WorldScript I

Script utility	Chapter in this book
CharacterByteType	Script Manager
CharacterType	Script Manager
CharToPixel	QuickDraw Text
DrawJustified	QuickDraw Text
FillParseTable	Script Manager
FindScriptRun[*]	Text Utilities
FindWordBreaks[*]	Text Utilities
GetScriptQDPatchAddress	Script Manager
GetScriptUtilityAddress	Script Manager
GetScriptVariable[†]	Script Manager
HiliteText	QuickDraw Text
MeasureJustified	QuickDraw Text
PixelToChar	QuickDraw Text
PortionLine	QuickDraw Text
SetScriptQDPatchAddress	Script Manager
SetScriptUtilityAddress	Script Manager
SetScriptVariable	Script Manager
TransliterateText	Script Manager
VisibleLength	QuickDraw Text

NOTE WorldScript I supports the following script utilities for backward compatibility. They call newer versions of themselves to handle their tasks. They are: `Pixel2Char` (calls `PixelToChar`), `Char2Pixel` (calls `CharToPixel`), `DrawJust` (calls `DrawJustified`), `MeasureJust` (calls `MeasureJustified`), `PortionText` (calls `PortionLine`), `CharByte` (calls `CharacterByteType`), `CharType` (calls `CharacterType`), `ParseTable` (calls `FillParseTable`), `Transliterate` (calls `TransliterateText`).

[*] The Script Manager handles these routines directly if the necessary tables are in the script's `'itl2'` resource. Otherwise, they are passed to WorldScript I.
[†] The Script Manager handles these routines directly if the standard selectors documented in this book are used. The routines are passed to WorldScript I if private selectors are used.

WorldScript I also patches four standard QuickDraw text-handling routines: `StdText`, `StdTxMeas`, `MeasureText`, and `FontMetrics`. (`FontMetrics` is a Font Manager routine, but for simplicity all four routines and patches are referred to in this appendix as QuickDraw routines and patches.) The purpose of the QuickDraw patches is to lay out text according to context and line direction. The original QuickDraw routine is called after the text is laid out properly. The QuickDraw dispatch table has special entries to support developer patching of routines for printing as well as for display.

Two Script Manager routines, `GetScriptQDPatchAddress` and `SetScriptQDPatchAddress`, allow you to access and override a script's QuickDraw patches.

Table A-12 lists the QuickDraw patches implemented by WorldScript I, along with the chapters in this book that describe the original routines.

Table A-12   QuickDraw patches supported by WorldScript I

QuickDraw patch	Chapter in this book
FontMetrics	Font Manager
MeasureText	QuickDraw Text
StdText	QuickDraw Text
StdTxMeas	QuickDraw Text

Table-Based Script Behavior

The shared script utilities determine script-specific characteristics from the tables in each script system's international resources.

WorldScript I uses tables in a script system's string-manipulation (`'itl2'`) resource for analyzing character types, finding word breaks, and performing case conversion. This use of tables predates the existence of WorldScript I, but WorldScript I extends the use of tables to all routines for 1-byte complex script systems. New tables that are required are put in the script's encoding/rendering (`'itl5'`) resource, using a tagged-table index for storage and retrieval. For example, the contextual formatting routines (described in the next section) uses tables in the encoding/rendering resource.

The international resources are described in the appendix "International Resources" in this book.

Contextual Formatting Routines

WorldScript I uses a set of table-driven routines to format text according to each script's requirements and attributes. The WorldScript I script utilities and QuickDraw patches that perform text formatting and layout rely on these table-driven routines. Each script has several tables in its encoding/rendering (`'itl5'`) resource to specify the display characteristics of its text.

Flexible Dispatching Method

Each enabled script system has a **script record,** a private data structure that holds information and addresses pertinent to that script. When an application makes a script-aware call, the script management system determines the current script and consults that script's script record for the address of the script's **dispatch routine** (which is actually part of WorldScript I). It passes the call to the dispatch routine, which uses the script's **dispatch table** to execute the proper script utility. Every script system has its own pointer to the dispatch routine and its own dispatch table, separate from other scripts. When the application makes a script-aware QuickDraw call, WorldScript I uses the script's QuickDraw dispatch table to execute the proper QuickDraw patch.

At run time, the application call has been converted to a lower-level script utility call or QuickDraw call. Each script utility call includes a *script utility selector*, a number that the dispatch routine uses to select the proper routine from the dispatch table.

Initialization Sequence

The startup code for enabling all available 1-byte complex script systems and script utility routines is in WorldScript I. WorldScript I is located in the Extensions folder; its file type is `'scri'` and its creator is `'univ'`.

At startup, WorldScript I does the following:

1. It checks for a valid machine configuration. WorldScript I works on Macintosh Plus models and later; it requires Script Manager version 2.0 or later and system software version 7.1 or later.

2. WorldScript I gets the number of valid 1-byte script bundles in the System file. A valid script bundle consists of a set of international resources (`'itlb'` and `'itl5'` required, `'itl0'`, `'itl1'`, `'itl2'`, and `'itl4'` optional) and at least one font in the script system's ID range. The `smsfSingByte` bit in the international bundle (`'itlb'`) resource must also be set to indicate that the script is 1-byte.

   If no 1-byte script bundles are present, WorldScript I does not load any of its script utilities or QuickDraw patches. It exits without signaling an error.

3. If one or more valid script bundles are present, WorldScript I does the following for each script:

   1. It checks for enough memory to load the script.

   2. It checks the `smsfUnivExt` bit in the script's international bundle resource. If the flag is set, the script system is a universal script system, and WorldScript I proceeds. If the flag is clear, WorldScript I goes on to the next script.

   3. It creates a script record and initializes the record with the script's values.

   4. If this is the first universal 1-byte script allocated, WorldScript I loads its script utilities and QuickDraw patches into the system heap.

5. WorldScript I allocates the script's dispatch table and sets the table's elements to point to the WorldScript I script utilities and QuickDraw patches or to the original Roman script utilities and QuickDraw calls, as appropriate for the script.

6. WorldScript I makes default settings for the script system based on information from the configuration table in the script's encoding/rendering ('itl5') resource. It then looks in the Preferences folder for a script preferences file. If one is found, and if the file contains a configuration resource (type 'CNFG') for this script system, WorldScript I uses that resource to reinitialize the script record's fields. If no preferences file is available, WorldScript I keeps the default settings loaded from the encoding/rendering resource.

7. WorldScript I initializes Script Manager data structures that point to this script record.

Any initialization errors that occur are reported to the user via the Notification Manager.

How Calls Are Dispatched

In every script system that is compatible with WorldScript I, the dispatch-table element for every script utility and QuickDraw patch consists of two pointers: one to the WorldScript I implementation of the routine and one to the original routine. In all cases, the WorldScript I routine executes first. In some cases, WorldScript I calls the original routine after its own; in other cases, the pointer to the original routine is NIL and the WorldScript I routine is all that executes. See Figure A-2. This design allows you to place a patched routine so that it executes either before, in place of, or after the WorldScript I routine and allows you to either call the original routine or not call it.

Figure A-2   Dispatch table entry for script utilities and QuickDraw patches

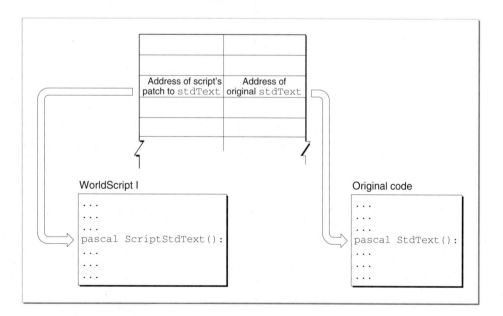

Every script-aware call to system software that executes as a script utility goes through the _ScriptUtil trap ($A8B5). The script management system handles some of those calls, such as GetSMVariable, itself; other calls, such as DrawJustified, it passes to a script system through the script system's script record. Those calls are listed in Table A-11 on page A-26. The script system uses its script utility dispatch table to call the right script utility. See Figure A-3.

When it receives a script utility call, a script's dispatch routine does the following:

1. It checks to see if the call (as defined by the script utility selector) is within the range of routines handled by the script.

2. It gets the address of the script utility from the script's dispatch table, using the script utility selector.

3. It replaces the selector on the stack with the address of its own script record.

4. It jumps into the WorldScript I routine obtained in step 2. As the routine executes, it obtains script-specific characteristics from the script record passed to it in step 3.

5. The WorldScript I routine gets the address of the original (Roman) routine from the dispatch table and, if it is not NIL, jumps to that routine upon completion.

Figure A-3   How calls are dispatched to the 1-byte script utilities

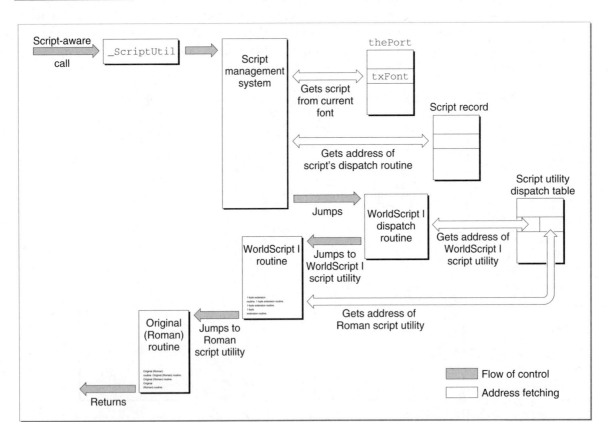

A patched low-level QuickDraw call follows a similar path, except that it goes through a QuickDraw trap that has been patched to execute code in WorldScript I instead of passing through the script management system. After determining which script should handle this call (by examining the current font), WorldScript I uses the script's QuickDraw dispatch table to jump to the proper routine. See Figure A-4.

Figure A-4   How calls are dispatched to the 1-byte QuickDraw patches

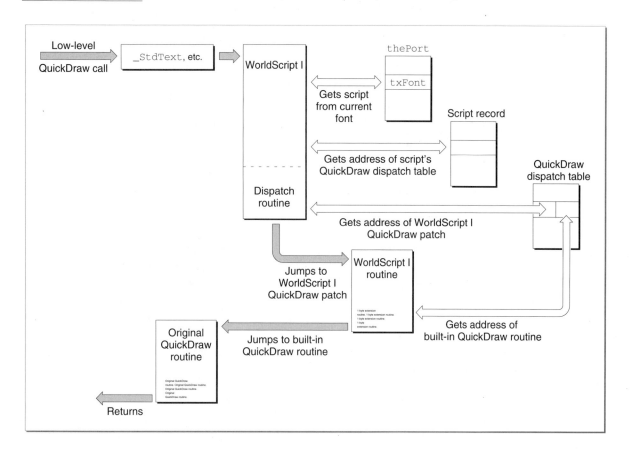

Saving User Preferences

The Operating System and some individual script systems use control panels to let users change text-related system settings, such as line direction, associated font, kashida preferences, and caret style. Script systems may store these settings in a script preferences file in the Extensions folder. This file contains resources of type `'CNFG'`, whose resource ID numbers are equal to the script codes of the script systems they represent.

As noted under "Initialization Sequence" on page A-28, when installing a script system WorldScript I looks for a script preferences file in the Preferences folder. For each script system it initializes, WorldScript I loads the 'CNFG' resource for that script from the script preferences file and uses it to reconfigure the script.

Note

The 'CNFG' resource in the script preferences file has exactly the same format as the script configuration table in the encoding/rendering resource. However, it may not have exactly the same elements. The types of configuration settings specified in the 'itl5' resource may be different from those settable by the user through a control panel. ◆

See the discussion of the encoding/rendering resource in the appendix "International Resources" in this book for a description of the script configuration table.

Replacing a Script Utility or QuickDraw Patch

Developers of 1-byte complex script systems should be able to specify most of their script system's behavior in tables in the script system's encoding/rendering ('itl5') resource. In cases where the WorldScript I routines are insufficient to handle the script's specific needs, the developers may create patches and install them as described here. The patches may be installed by an extensions file that is executed at system startup.

Application developers who need specific script-based behavior for their programs should not alter the tables in a 1-byte script's encoding/rendering ('itl5') resource. However, they can replace one or more 1-byte script utilities or QuickDraw patches for their target script system, as described here.

IMPORTANT

When you patch a script system's script utility or QuickDraw call, you alter that script's behavior for as long as it remains enabled. Therefore, be sure to restore the patches to their original state whenever your application quits or is switched out by the Process Manager. ▲

The script-based dispatch table design gives you a simple, flexible way to replace individual routines without having to patch out all of the _ScriptUtil trap or any of the QuickDraw low-level routines in their entirety. Furthermore, in a multiscript environment each patch of this type applies only to its own script system. A developer might, for example, patch StdText for the Thai script system only, leaving all the other scripts unchanged.

In addition, you can choose the point at which your patched routine executes: either before (which also means *in place of* if your routine does not call the WorldScript I routine at all) or after the WorldScript I routine executes. For example, the WorldScript I version of `StdText` works by first performing contextual analysis and reordering of characters on the supplied text, and then calling the original version of `StdText`. Suppose you want to keep the WorldScript I contextual analysis and reordering of characters, but you want to do some additional processing before calling the original `StdText`. To do that, just patch out the WorldScript I routine's call to the original `StdText`, instead of patching out the entire WorldScript I routine. Then do your own processing and call `StdText` yourself.

Because you can patch at two points, and because you can perform your own processing either before or after a patch, your flexibility is great. To replace only the WorldScript I routine, replace its pointer in the dispatch table; to keep the WorldScript I routine while replacing or patching the original routine, replace the original-routine pointer in the dispatch table. The four Script Manager routines that allow you to make those patches are `GetScriptUtilityAddress`, `SetScriptUtilityAddress`, `GetScriptQDPatchAddress`, and `SetScriptQDPatchAddress`. Either pointer in the dispatch table may be `NIL`, meaning that WorldScript I either doesn't patch the original routine or doesn't call the original routine.

Patching Script Utilities

In terms of how to patch them, the script utilities can be divided into different groups, depending on whether or not WorldScript I performs contextual formatting and whether or not it subsequently calls the original Roman version of the utility. See Table A-13. For utilities that perform contextual formatting, keep in mind that if you replace them you will have to handle formatting yourself. For utilities that subsequently call their original Roman version, you can replace either the WorldScript I version of the call or the Roman version or both, depending on what your needs are.

Table A-13   Classification of 1-byte script utilities by function

No formatting, do not call original Roman routine	No formatting, do call original Roman routine	May do formatting, do not call original Roman routine
CharacterByteType	CharacterType	HiliteText
GetScriptVariable	TransliterateText	VisibleLength
SetScriptVariable	FindWordBreaks	PixelToChar
FillParseTable	FindScriptRun	CharToPixel
PortionLine		DrawJustified
		MeasureJustified

Note that those script utilities that do not call their equivalent Roman routine nevertheless call QuickDraw `StdText` or `StdTxMeas` *if* the `grafProcs` field in the graphics port has been changed. Thus, if you have changed (patched) either of those QuickDraw routines, your patch will still be called. Conversely, if the `grafProcs` field is `NIL`, The WorldScript I script utilities do not necessarily call `StdText` or `StdTxMeas`.

If you are replacing a script utility, remember that its interface is similar to that of its equivalent high-level call as described in *Inside Macintosh*. The utility takes the same parameters in the same order, except that it gets one additional last parameter on the stack: a pointer to the script record. For example, if you are replacing `VisibleLength`, whose high-level interface is

```
FUNCTION VisibleLength (textPtr: Ptr;
                        textLen: LongInt): LongInt;
```

your patch to the equivalent script utility should expect to receive parameters as if the high-level interface were

```
FUNCTION VisibleLength (textPtr: Ptr;
                        textLen: LongInt;
                        scriptRecord: Ptr): LongInt;
```

Also, if your replacement calls the original routine, don't forget to pass the extra parameter to it.

Patching QuickDraw Routines

WorldScript I patches the low-level QuickDraw text-handling routines `StdText` and `StdTxMeas`, the high-level QuickDraw routine `MeasureText`, and the Font Manager routine `FontMetrics`.

The QuickDraw patches lay out lines of text according to the context and line-direction rules for a script system. In each case (except for `MeasureText`) the patch calls the original QuickDraw routine after performing the contextual formatting. The contextual formatting routines are called only for contextual scripts.

Table A-14 lists the patches and what they do. For those patches that perform contextual formatting, if you replace them you will have to handle formatting for line layout yourself. For all of them, you can replace either the WorldScript I patch or the standard QuickDraw call or both, depending on your needs.

Table A-14   Classification of 1-byte QuickDraw patches by function

Call	Function
FontMetrics	Returns font measurements
MeasureText	Calls MeasureJustified (with slop = 0)
StdText	Does formatting, then calls original routine
StdTxMeas	Does formatting, then calls original routine

Issues in Designing a Script Utility or QuickDraw Patch

Keep the following points in mind if you plan to replace one or more script utilities or QuickDraw patches in WorldScript I:

■ In script systems compatible with WorldScript I, text handling typically involves WorldScript I contextual analysis followed by a call to the original Roman version of the routine. You need to know whether it is the WorldScript I functionality or the original functionality that you want your routine to replace, and you need to be sure that your routine is called only at the correct points in the process. More detailed information on text layout is found in the chapter "QuickDraw Text" in this book.

■ Script utilities process text in individual style runs, whose boundaries are defined by the application. If your application supports styled text, each script utility will need to handle only individual style runs. But if your application supports unstyled text only, there may be mixed Roman and non-Roman characters in a single font. Before performing text layout, your script utility will have to separate the Roman characters into their own style runs, and assign them to an associated font, if your script system uses associated fonts.

■ If you provide your own script utility, you need to be sure that text is not formatted more than once. Because script utilities might be called reentrantly during printing, you may want to save the port for each contextual analysis. Check this port against the current port for each possible contextual analysis request, so you can prevent the text from being formatted twice.

■ Printing adds another level of complexity to the WorldScript I QuickDraw patches and your ability to patch out those patches. The QuickDraw dispatch table has special entries to support developer patching of routines in printing as well as for display. See the descriptions of the routines GetScriptQDPatchAddress and SetScriptQDPatchAddress in the chapter "Script Manager" in this book for more information. See also Macintosh Technical Note #174 for additional information on printing.

WorldScript II

WorldScript II is a system extension, available with system software versions 7.1 and later, that can support 2-byte script systems: Chinese (traditional and simplified characters), Japanese, and Korean. It contains code that implements script-aware text-manipulation routines, eliminating the need for each script to maintain its own code extensions. WorldScript II supports the input, display, and printing of the thousands of characters needed by the 2-byte script systems.

WorldScript II is a single file located in the Extensions folder within the System Folder on the user's Macintosh. It installs all compatible 2-byte script systems that are present in the System Folder and provides each with a set of standard routines.

Note
Unlike WorldScript I, WorldScript II does not support the Script Manager routines (such as `SetScriptUtilityAddress`) that allow replacement of script utilities or QuickDraw calls. ◆

About WorldScript II

The 2-byte script systems developed prior to system software version 7.1 contain their own code to handle language-specific text processing. Each also has its own initialization and configuration code, installing itself at startup and adding its own modifications to the system. Each script system patches three different areas of system software: QuickDraw, the Event Manager, and the script management system. This can result in a layering of patches to the same traps, inconsistent behavior, and inefficient use of memory.

WorldScript II, working with the Text Services Manager and other parts of system software, eliminates code duplication and provides for the special text-input needs of the 2-byte systems:

■ Enhancements to QuickDraw and the Font Manager now support the display of the thousands of Chinese, Korean, and Japanese characters. To handle a character set that is larger than the 256-character ASCII range, the Font Manager and other parts of system software contain the code necessary to retrieve and render the characters.

■ The Text Services Manager, using enhancements to the Event Manager, provides broad support for input methods. Input methods that employ the Text Services Manager intercept every key-down event, map the event to a character code, and pass the result to the application.

■ WorldScript II provides language-specific capabilities for script-aware text-handling routines called **script utilities.** For instance, WorldScript II provides routines that tell whether a byte in a string is a 1-byte or 2-byte character.

WorldScript II redefines what a 2-byte script system consists of. WorldScript II combines the executable code for many routines for all 2-byte script systems. Script-specific behavior is encoded in resource-based tables. This reduces memory requirements for multiscript systems and avoids layering of patches.

Shared Script Utilities

WorldScript II contains the code for all script utilities. Script-specific behavior is determined by tables in each script's international resources. In a multiscript environment, WorldScript II loads only one copy of its code into memory. Furthermore, the user needs only the WorldScript II file in the Extensions folder, rather than one extension file per script system. This eases memory requirements and saves disk space.

Table A-11 lists the script utilities implemented by WorldScript II, along with the chapters in this book that describe their corresponding high-level routines.

Table A-15   Script utilities supported by WorldScript II

Script utility	Chapter in this book
CharacterByteType	Script Manager
CharacterType	Script Manager
CharToPixel	QuickDraw Text
DrawJustified	QuickDraw Text
FillParseTable	Script Manager
FindScriptRun[*]	Text Utilities
FindWordBreaks[*]	Text Utilities
GetScriptVariable[†]	Script Manager
HiliteText	QuickDraw Text
MeasureJustified	QuickDraw Text
PixelToChar	QuickDraw Text
PortionLine	QuickDraw Text
SetScriptVariable[†]	Script Manager
TransliterateText	Script Manager
VisibleLength	QuickDraw Text

NOTE   WorldScript II supports the following script utilities for backward compatibility. They call newer versions of themselves to handle their tasks. They are: Pixel2Char (calls PixelToChar), Char2Pixel (calls CharToPixel), DrawJust (calls DrawJustified), MeasureJust (calls MeasureJustified), PortionText (calls PortionLine), CharByte (calls CharacterByteType), CharType (calls CharacterType), ParseTable (calls FillParseTable), Transliterate (calls TransliterateText).

[*]   The Script Manager handles these routines directly if the necessary tables are in the script's 'itl2' resource. Otherwise, they are passed to WorldScript II.
[†]   The Script Manager handles these routines directly if the standard selectors documented in this book are used. The routines are passed to WorldScript II if private selectors are used.

Table-Based Script Behavior

Script-specific text behavior is controlled by tables in each script system's international resources. The encoding/rendering resource (type 'itl5') contains character encoding information, and the transliteration resource (type 'trsl') contains information for character conversion among subscripts of a 2-byte script.

For example, the byte-type table in a script's encoding/rendering resource typically contains information about the type of a specific byte in the range of $00–$FF—whether it can be the high-order byte of a 2-byte character, the low-order byte of a 2-byte character, or a 1-byte character. The character-type table in the same resource gives more detailed information about a character in a particular coding scheme.

Currently, there are two transliteration formats used by WorldScript II and supported by tables in a script's transliteration resource. One of them is used to transliterate Jamo to Hangul (and Hangul to Jamo) in the Korean system. The other is a more general rule-based transliteration. You cannot customize the Jamo-to-Hangul transliteration. You can customize the rule-based transliteration by supplying the proper tables in a transliteration resource.

The encoding/rendering resource and the transliteration resource are described in the appendix "International Resources" in this book.

Initialization Sequence

The startup code for enabling all available 2-byte script systems and script utility routines is in WorldScript II. WorldScript II is located in the Extensions folder; its file type is 'scri' and its creator is 'doub'.

At system startup, all extension files in the Extensions folder are executed; script files are executed before all other extensions.

At startup, WorldScript II does the following:

1. It gets the total number of international bundle ('itlb') resources from the System Folder.

2. For each bundle resource that belongs to a 2-byte script, WorldScript II
   - creates a script record and copies the byte-type table from the script's encoding/rendering ('itl5') resource into the script record
   - gets handles to all transliteration resources for that script and adds them to the script record
   - initializes the script's script record, a private data structure that holds information and addresses pertinent to that script

How Calls Are Dispatched

WorldScript II does not implement all of the script utilities because some of them (such as `GetScriptManagerVariable`) are handled by the script management system itself. The script utilities that the script management system does not handle are listed in Table A-11 on page A-26. For those, the script management system passes execution to the WorldScript II dispatch routine, which in turn uses the script system's dispatch table to call the appropriate utility routine in WorldScript II.

When the WorldScript II dispatch routine calls a script utility, it replaces the selector of a normal script utility call with the address of the script record of the font script. It then calls the script utility. For instance:

1. In assembly language, when you call `CharacterByteType`, you typically call it through a macro in the following way:

```
subq.w   #2, sp              ; room for result.
   move.l   textPtr,-(sp)    ; push text pointer.
   clr.w    -(sp)            ; push text offset.
   CharacterByteType         ; find out whether it is 1-byte or
                             ; 2-byte character.
   tst.w    (sp)+            ; is it 1-byte?
```

2. The `CharacterByteType` macro expands into

```
move.l   $82060010,-(sp)     ; push the selector.
ScriptUtil                   ; call Script Manager trap.
```

3. For this example, the stack looks like the following when the trap has been called:

return address   (long) <-- top of stack

routine selector   (long)

text offset   (word)

text pointer   (long)

result   (word)

4. If the Script Manager does not handle the call, it passes the call to the current script's dispatch routine. The dispatch routine figures out by the value of the routine selector whether the call is in the range of calls it handles. If it is not, the dispatch routine strips the stack and returns without doing anything.

5. If the call is in the valid range, the dispatch routine performs these tasks:

   1. It gets the address of the WorldScript II version of the script utility from the script's dispatch table.

   2. It gets the address of the script record and replaces the selector on the stack with the address of the script record.

   3. It jumps into the routine.

6. So the stack becomes

return address	(long) <-- top of stack
address of script record	(long)
text offset	(word)
text pointer	(long)
result	(word)

The script's dispatch routine passes the script record to the WorldScript II script utilities so that they can use the script-specific information (such as the byte-type tables) in the script's international resources.

International Resources

Contents

This appendix describes the international resources, which constitute the major portion of each Macintosh script system. The international resources define how a script system implements its particular writing system and how it allows for language or regional variations within a writing system.

The Script Manager, the Text Utilities, QuickDraw, and the Font Manager all use the international resources directly to handle text in various script systems. TextEdit makes indirect use of information in the international resources through calls to the Script Manager and other managers.

A text application uses the international resources indirectly whenever it makes a call to a script-aware routine in QuickDraw, the Text Utilities, or the Script Manager. It can also access the international resources directly through Script Manager calls, in order to

- pass a resource handle or pointer as a parameter to a text-handling routine

- extract formatting information from a table within a resource

- modify the contents of a resource, to customize text handling

Your most common reason to access the international resources may be to get a handle or pointer to pass to a text-handling routine. For that task, you do not need the information in this appendix.

Read this appendix if your application needs information about the internal structure of one or more international resources. If you need a particular resource table to perform a specific operation, such as formatting currencies or dates, extracting number parts, or converting script-independent tokens to the text of a particular script system, this appendix shows you where to get the information you need.

Read this appendix also if your application requires a custom localized version of some text-handling feature. To provide that feature, you can modify one or more of the international resources and supply that modified version with your application or its documents. In this way, you can localize the formats of numbers, currency, time, dates, and measurement; you can localize string comparison and word selection; you can modify the conversion of strings to tokens; you can specify custom character-rendering behavior; and you can specify custom transliteration rules.

Read this appendix also if you are creating a new script system. A complete script system requires a full set of the appropriate international resources, certain keyboard resources (as described in the appendix "Keyboard Resources" in this book), and one or more fonts.

Before reading this appendix, read the chapter "Introduction to Text on the Macintosh" in this book. The parts of the Macintosh script management system that make use of the resources documented here are described in the chapters "QuickDraw Text," "Text Utilities," and especially "Script Manager," in this book. The Resource Manager, which manages all Macintosh resources, is described in *Inside Macintosh: More Macintosh Toolbox*.

This appendix describes the international resources in general, shows the relationship between resource ID and script code, shows how to gain access to international resources and use them, and then describes each resource in detail.

About the International Resources

This section introduces the international resources, describes how the set of international resources varies among script systems and among different localized versions of Macintosh system software, and gives a table showing the relationship between script code and resource ID number used by fonts and by specific types of international resources and keyboard resources.

What the International Resources Are

Each script system consists of a set of international resources and a set of keyboard resources. These resources, possibly in conjunction with the WorldScript I or WorldScript II extension—and with the use of the proper font—completely specify a script's behavior. Because script-specific behavior is segregated into resources that are customizable and replaceable, your software can potentially use the same routines to handle text in any language, even one that is not curently supported.

The international resources that define individual script systems can include all but two in the following table. Two of the international resources, the international configuration resource and the script-sorting resource, are unique to each Macintosh System file; they do not belong to any script system.

Table B-1 lists the international resources and their resource types, and gives a capsule description of their contents. More complete descriptions follow.

Table B-1   The international resources

Name	Resource type	Partial contents
International configuration	`'itlc'`	Configuration of the system
Script sorting	`'itlm'`	Sorting order among scripts
International bundle	`'itlb'`	IDs of all resources for a script system
Numeric format	`'itl0'`	Number, time, and short-date formats
Long-date format	`'itl1'`	Long date formats
String manipulation	`'itl2'`	Sorting order, word breaks
Tokens	`'itl4'`	Tables of tokens, number parts
Encoding/rendering	`'itl5'`	Character encoding or rendering
Transliteration	`'trsl'`	Tables for phonetic conversion

■ International configuration resource. Sets up the basic configuration for the system, including the system script. Specifies the system script code and the region code that identifies the regional version of the system script; initializes the states of the system direction, the font force flag, the international resources selection flag, the international keyboard flag (used for the Macintosh Plus), and the Script Manager general flags. There is only one `itlc` resource for each localized version of system software.

■ Script-sorting resource. Specifies the preferred sorting order for script codes, language codes, and region codes. Also specifies the default language for each script, the parent script for each language, and the parent language for each region. There is only one `itlm` resource for each localized version of system software.

■ International bundle resource. Sets up the basic configuration for an individual script system. The international bundle resource specifies the resource IDs for the script's resources. It also initializes many script variables, such as the script flags, the default language code, and the numeral and calendar representation codes for the script. The international bundle resource also specifies font information, script initialization data, valid styles for the script, and the style to use for designating aliases. Each script system has one `itlb` resource.

■ Numeric-format resource. Contains short date and time formats, and formats for currency and numbers and the preferred unit of measurement. It also contains the region code for this particular resource. A script system can have one or more `itl0` resources.

■ Long-date-format resource. Specifies the long date format for a particular region, including the names of days and months. Each long-date-format resource contains the region code for this particular resource. A long-date-format resource can have an optional extension for additional month and day names as well as abbreviated month and day names. A script system can have one or more `itl1` resources.

■ String-manipulation resource. Contains routines that control text-sorting behavior, and tables for character type, case conversion, and word breaks. A script system can have one or more `itl2` resources.

■ Tokens resource. Contains tables and code for converting text to tokens. It also has tables for formatting numbers, for converting tokens to text, and for determining whitespace characters. A script system can have one or more `itl4` resources.

■ Encoding/rendering resource. Contains either information related to character encoding, or information controlling text-rendering behavior, in a script-specific format. This is an optional resource; a script system can have zero or more `itl5` resources.

■ Transliteration resource. Specifies how to convert characters from one subscript to another within a script system. This is an optional resource; a script system can have zero or more `trsl` resources.

International resources and localized system software

When Macintosh system software is localized for a non-U.S. market, it contains replacements for or modifications to some of the U.S. versions of the international resources. See the discussion of U.S. international resources and keyboard resources in the appendix "Built-in Script Support" for a list of resources that may be replaced during localization. ◆

Script Codes and Resource ID Ranges

Fonts, international resources, and keyboard resources that are related to a particular script system have resource ID numbers in a range specific to that script. The script management system uses this relationship between resource ID and script code to assign the proper resources for displaying and formatting text. For example, the Script Manager `FontScript`, `IntlScript`, and `FontToScript` functions all use a font family ID to determine the script code that they return. Many other Script Manager, Text Utilities, and QuickDraw routines that load and use international resources take an explicit or implicit script code parameter; they will load only resources with ID numbers in the proper range for the supplied script code.

This numbering convention applies to font family IDs, and to the ID numbers of the following international and keyboard resources: `'itl0'`, `'itl1'`, `'itl2'`, `'itl4'`, `'itl5'`, `'trsl'`, `'KCHR'`, `'itlk'`, `'kcs#'`, `'kcs4'`, and `'kcs8'`.

Resources with ID numbers below 16384 ($4000) belong to the Roman script system. Currently, the script management system uses the following formula to calculate the script code for resources with ID numbers of 16384 and over:

```
scriptCode = ((resourceID - 16384) DIV 512) + 1
```

The formula allots half of the range of nonnegative ID values to the Roman script system, and 512 ID numbers (for each resource type) to each other script system, as shown in Table B-2. Please note that this formula may change in the future; note also that future script systems may possibly use negative ID values.

Table B-2   Resource ID ranges for each script system

Script system	Script code	Resource ID range	
		Decimal	Hexadecimal
Roman	0	2–16383	$0000–$3FFF
Japanese	1	16384–16895	$4000–$41FF
Chinese (Traditional)	2	16896–17407	$4200–$43FF
Korean	3	17408–17919	$4400–$45FF

Table B-2   Resource ID ranges for each script system (continued)

Script system	Script code	Resource ID range	
		Decimal	Hexadecimal
Arabic	4	17920–18431	$4600–$47FF
Hebrew	5	18432–18943	$4800–$4FF9
Greek	6	18944–19455	$4A00–$4BFF
Russian	7	19456–19967	$4C00–$4DFF
Right-left symbols	8	19968–20479	$4E00–$4FFF
Devanagari	9	20480–20991	$5000–$51FF
Gurmukhi	10	20992–21503	$5200–$53FF
Gujarati	11	21504–22015	$5400–$55FF
Oriya	12	22016–22527	$5600–$57FF
Bengali	13	22528–23039	$5800–$5FF9
Tamil	14	23040–23551	$5A00–$5BFF
Telugu	15	23552–24063	$5C00–$5DFF
Kannada	16	24064–24575	$5E00–$5FFF
Malayalam	17	24576–25087	$6000–$61FF
Sinhalese	18	25088–25599	$6200–$63FF
Burmese	19	25600–26111	$6400–$65FF
Cambodian	20	26112–26623	$6600–$67FF
Thai	21	26624–27135	$6800–$6FF9
Laotian	22	27136–27647	$6A00–$6BFF
Georgian	23	27648–28159	$6C00–$6DFF
Armenian	24	28160–28671	$6E00–$6FFF
Chinese (Simplified)	25	28672–29183	$7000–$71FF
Tibetan	26	29184–29695	$7200–$73FF
Mongolian	27	29696–30207	$7400–$75FF
Ethiopian	28	30208–30719	$7600–$77FF
Non-Cyrillic Slavic	29	30720–31231	$7800–$79FF
Vietnamese	30	31232–31743	$7A00–$7BFF
Sindhi	31	31744–32255	$7C00–$7DFF
Uninterpreted symbols	32	32256–32767	$7E00–$7FFF

Starting with a script code, you can back-calculate resource ID ranges as follows:

- Scripts with script codes in the range 1–32 have a range of 512 resource ID numbers, beginning with a number calculated according to this formula:

```
firstID = 16384 + 512 * (script code — 1)
```

- Scripts with script codes in the range 33–64 have a range of 512 resource ID numbers, beginning with a number calculated according to this formula:

```
firstID = —32768 + 512 * (script code —33)
```

Note

Some script codes above 32 are not usable because they correspond to resource ID ranges that are reserved for other purposes. Script codes 33 through 40 are invalid; furthermore, script codes above 48 are currently unavailable and may become invalid. ◆

Constants for all defined script codes are listed in the chapter "Script Manager" in this book.

Using the International Resources

The Script Manager and the other managers that make up the Macintosh script management system use the information in the international resources to format dates and times, find word boundaries, transliterate text, and determine character type, among other tasks. Your application indirectly accesses that information when it makes script-aware calls that rely on the current script system. In addition, you can directly access an international resource in order to

- pass a resource handle or pointer as a parameter to a text-handling routine. Many text-handling calls may take an explicit handle to an international resource; you first load the resource with calls to the Script Manager, and then pass its handle as a parameter to the call.

- extract formatting information from a table within a resource. If you are formatting currencies, dates, or numbers (without calling the Text Utilities routines that do formatting for you) , or if you are converting script-independent tokens to the text of a particular script system, you can load the appropriate resource with calls to the Script Manager, and then examine its contents for the information you need.

- provide a modified version of a resource, to customize text handling. You can load the appropriate resource with calls to the Script Manager, change it, and then save the changed resource in such a manner that it is used in place of the original resource.

Keep these points in mind when using a script system's international resources:

- You can load the international resources `'itl0'`, `'itl1'`, `'itl2'`, or `'itl4'` directly with `GetResource` or other related Resource Manager routines, but it is not recommended. If you use a Script Manager call such as `GetIntlResource` instead, the Script Manager determines which particular instance of an international resource to load, given the current font script, the script system's default preferences, and the current state of the international resources selection flag.

- Remember that most of the script-specific international resources have ID numbers within a range unique to their script system. If you are providing resources that add to or replace a script system's default resources, make sure that your resources have resource IDs in the proper range.

- If the international resources selection flag is set to TRUE, the international resources used by several script-aware Text Utilities routines are those of the system script. However, you can force those routines to use the international resources of the font script instead by clearing the international resources selection flag to FALSE. You can set and clear the international resources selection flag by using the Script Manager SetScriptManagerVariable function. See the discussion on determining script codes in the chapter "Script Manager" in this book.

- You can use multiple formats for different languages or regions with the same script system by adding multiple versions of international resources, each having a different resource ID within the script's range. You store those international resources in your application's or document's resource fork, where they can override those in the System file.

For more information, see the discussions of direct access to international resources and replacing default international resources in the chapter "Script Manager" in this book.

Note

Several international resources have type definitions that give you direct access to their components from high-level languages. These definitions are documented in this appendix. For other international resources high-level types are not defined, and graphic figures show the structures instead. ◆

International Configuration Resource (Type 'itlc')

The international configuration resource (resource type 'itlc') contains script-related configuration information for the currently executing version of system software. Only one 'itlc' resource is provided with each localized version of Macintosh system software. It is in the System file. Its resource ID is 0.

The Script Manager uses the international configuration resource at startup to configure the system and the system script. The resource includes fields that specify these attributes:

- script code for the system script

- region code for this localized version of system software and the system script

- initial values for the Script Manager general flags

- initial value for the system direction

Several Script Manager variables are initialized from this resource. Selectors for the Script Manager variables are listed in the chapter "Script Manager" in this book.

The ItlcRecord Data Type

The international configuration record (data type `ItlcRecord`) describes the contents of the international configuration resource.

```
TYPE ItlcRecord =
    RECORD
        itlcSystem:      Integer;      {system script}
        itlcReserved:    Integer;      {reserved}
        itlcFontForce:   SignedByte;   {initial font force flag}
        itlcIntlForce:   SignedByte;   {initial int'l res. flag}
        itlcOldKybd:     SignedByte;   {old keyboard}
        itlcFlags:       SignedByte;   {Script Mgr. general flags}
        itlcIconOffset:  Integer;      {reserved}
        itlcIconSide:    SignedByte;   {reserved}
        itlcIconRsvd:    SignedByte;   {reserved}
        itlcRegionCode:  Integer;      {preferred region code}
        itlcSysFlags:    Integer;      {flags for system globals}
        itlcReserved4:   ARRAY [0..31] OF SignedByte;  {reserved}
    END;
```

Field descriptions

`itlcSystem`   The script code defining the system script. The system script affects system default settings, such as the default font and the text that appears in dialog boxes and menu bars, and so forth. Script codes and their constants are listed in the chapter "Script Manager" in this book. At startup, this value is copied into the Script Manager variable accessed through the selector `smSysScript`.

`itlcReserved`   Reserved.

`itlcFontForce`   The initial setting for the font force flag. A value of TRUE ($FF) forces Roman fonts to be interpreted as belonging to the system script. The font force flag is described in the chapter "Script Manager" in this book. At startup, this value is copied into the Script Manager variable accessed through the selector `smFontForce`.

`itlcIntlForce`   The initial setting for the international resources selection flag. A value of TRUE ($FF) forces Text Utilities routines to use the international resources for the system script, rather than the font script. The international resources selection flag is described in the chapter "Script Manager" in this book. At startup, this value is copied into the Script Manager variable accessed through the selector `smIntlForce`.

itlcOldKybd	The initial setting for the international keyboard flag for use by the Macintosh Plus computer. In addition to the standard Macintosh Plus keyboard (keyboard type 11), two types of smaller keyboard without numeric keypad are available: a U.S. version and an international version. Both have a keyboard type of 3, and the user uses the Keyboard control panel to indicate which is being used; the user's selection is saved in this field. When TRUE ($FF), this flag indicates that the international keyboard is being used. When FALSE, this flag indicates that the U.S. keyboard is being used.
itlcFlags	The initial settings for the Script Manager general flags. At startup, this value is copied into the first (high-order) byte of the Script Manager variable accessed through the selector smGenFlags.
itlcIconOffset	(reserved).
itlcIconSide	(reserved).
itlcIconRsvd	(reserved).
itlcRegionCode	The region code for this version of system software. It specifies the region for which the system and system-script resources were localized. The constants that define region codes are also described in the chapter "Script Manager" in this book. At startup, this value is copied into the Script Manager variable accessed through the selector smRegionCode.
itlcSysFlags	Flags for setting system global variables. Currently only one bit is defined; it allows the configuration resource to set the system direction (left-to-right or right-to-left) at startup. It is bit 15, defined by the following constant:

```
CONST
    itlcSysDirection    = 15;
```

The system global SysDirection is initialized from this value. A value of 0 for bit 15 sets a system direction of left-to-right (SysDirection = 0) at startup, whereas a value of 1 for the bit sets a system direction of right-to-left (SysDirection = $FFFF). You can access SysDirection through the Script Manager routines GetSysDirection and SetSysDirection. System direction may be initially localized to a value appropriate for the system script, but the user can reset its value at any time if a bidirectional script system is present.

Note

The itlcSysFlags field was formerly the itlcReserved3 field. ◆

itlcReserved4	An array of 32 bytes that is reserved for future use.

Script-Sorting Resource (Type 'itlm')

The script-sorting resource (resource type 'itlm') lists, in preferred sorting order, a set of script codes, language codes, and region codes. For each listed script system it defines the default language; for each listed language it defines the script system that language belongs to; and for each listed regional version it describes the language that region belongs to. The listing may be sparse; not all defined script, language, and region codes need appear in the resource. Only one script-sorting resource is provided with each localized version of Macintosh system software. It is in the System file. Its resource ID is 0.

One purpose of the script-sorting resource is to aid the sorting of multilanguage lists. Each individual script system defines, in its string-manipulation ('itl2') resource, how its own strings are sorted; the script-sorting resource defines how strings in two or more different scripts (or languages or regions) are ordered. For example, the string-manipulation resource for the Japanese script system defines the order in which Japanese strings appear in a sorted list. The script-sorting resource, on the other hand, defines whether Japanese strings appear before or after Roman strings in a sorted list.

IMPORTANT

Regardless of the sorting order presented in the script-sorting resource, text in the system script is always sorted to appear ahead of text in any other script system. ▲

Another purpose of the script-sorting resource is to provide a mapping among scripts, languages, and regions. From information in the resource you can determine all the languages of a listed script system, and all the regional variations of a listed language.

The script-sorting resource consists of a resource header followed by three tables. Figure B-1 shows the format of the resource header.

Figure B-1   Format of the script-sorting resource header

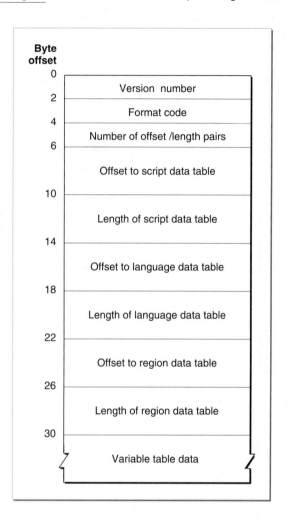

The resource header contains these elements:

- Version number. The version number of this resource.

- Format code. A number that identifies the format of this resource.

- Number of offset/length pairs. The number of data tables in the resource.

- Offsets to, and lengths of, the defined tables for this resource. Offsets are measured from the beginning of the resource.

Currently there are three defined tables in the script-sorting resource: the script data table, the language data table, and the region data table. The formats of the three tables are similar, as shown in Figure B-2.

Figure B-2   Script, language, and region data tables in the script-sorting resource

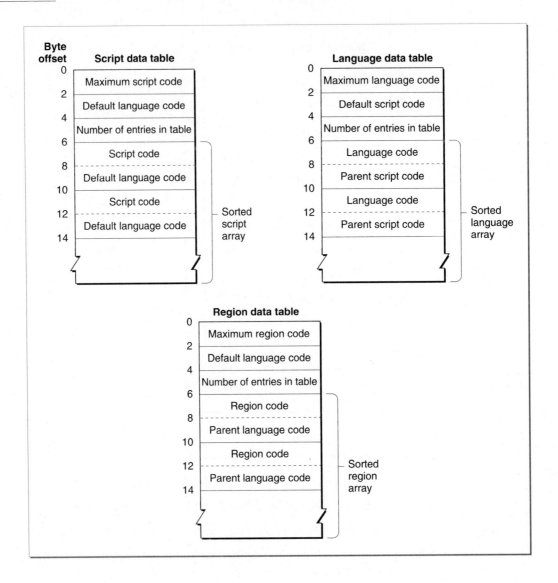

Each table consists of a header, followed by an array of paired integers. These are the fields in the script data table, language data table, and region data table, respectively:

- Maximum code. The maximum defined value for script, language, or region code listed in this table. Because entries in the table may be sparse (incomplete), this value is useful for defining the maximum size of table to construct to hold the information. For example, a maximum script code of `smUninterp` means the script data table might cover any subset of the scripts with codes 0 through 32, but the table does not contain any script codes above 32.

- Default code. The default language code for unlisted script codes, the default script code for unlisted language codes, or the default language code for unlisted region codes. This assures a defined sorting position for any script, language, or region code, whether or not it is listed in the resource.

- Number of entries in table. The number of script codes, language codes, or region codes in this table.

- Sorted array. A list of paired integers, in sorting order:
  - □ For the script data table, it is a script array: a list of script codes in their preferred sorting order, each paired with (followed by) its default language code.
  - □ For the language data table, it is a language array: a list of language codes in their preferred sorting order, each paired with (followed by) the code for its parent script.
  - □ For the region data table, it is a region array: a list of region codes in their preferred sorting order, each paired with (followed by) the code for its parent language.

Constants for all defined script codes, language codes, and region codes are listed in the chapter "Script Manager" in this book.

Table B-3 lists a sorting hierarchy of scripts, languages, and regions generated from a sample script-sorting resource. Not all scripts and languages are represented in this list because region codes do not currently exist for all language codes and script codes.

Table B-3   Sorted scripts, languages, and regions from a script-sorting resource

Script code	Language code	Region code
smRoman	langEnglish	verUS
		verBritain
		verAustralia
		verIreland
	langFrench	verFrance
		verFrBelgiumLux
		verFrCanada
		verFrSwiss

continued

Table B-3   Sorted scripts, languages, and regions from a script-sorting resource (continued)

Script code	Language code	Region code
	langGerman	verGermany
		verGrSwiss
	langItalian	verItaly
	langDutch	verNetherlands
	langSwedish	verSweden
	langSpanish	verSpain
	langDanish	verDenmark
	langPortuguese	verPortugal
	langNorwegian	verNorway
	langFinnish	verFinland
	langIcelandic	verIceland
	langMaltese	verMalta
	langTurkish	verTurkey
	langLithuanian	verLithuania
	langEstonian	verEstonia
	langLettish	verLatvia
	langSaamisk	verLapland
	langFaeroese	verFaeroeIsl
	langCroatian	verYugoCroatian
smEastEurRoman	langPolish	verPoland
	langHungarian	verHungary
smGreek	langGreek	verGreece
smCyrillic	langRussia	verRussia
smArabic	langArabic	verArabic
	langUrdu	verPakistan
	langFarsi	verIran
smHebrew	langHebrew	verIsrael
smDevanagari	langHindi	verIndiaHindi

Table B-3 Sorted scripts, languages, and regions from a script-sorting resource (continued)

Script code	Language code	Region code
smThai	langThai	verThailand
smTradChinese	langTradChinese	verTaiwan
smSimpChinese	langSimpChinese	verChina
smJapanese	langJapanese	verJapan
smKorean	langKorea	verKorea

International Bundle Resource (Type 'itlb')

The international bundle resource (resource type 'itlb') has two purposes. First, it is the **bundle resource** for a particular script system: by analogy with the Finder bundle resource type, it specifies the resource IDs for the other international resources and keyboard resources used by that script. (See the Finder Interface chapter of *Inside Macintosh: Macintosh Toolbox Essentials* for a description of Finder bundle resources.) Second, the 'itlb' resource contains configuration information for the script.

Several script variables are initialized from this resource. Selectors for the script variables are listed in the chapter "Script Manager" in this book. If you need to change the initial values of those variables, you need to change the content of the international bundle resource itself. For example, to change the initial keyboard layout (script variable smScriptKeys) for a script system, you would change the value of the itlbKeys field of the international bundle resource. The user can makes this change from the Keyboard control panel; the user can make other changes to the 'itlb' resource from other control panels, as described under user control of script systems in the chapter "Introduction to Text on the Macintosh" in this book.

Each script system has one and only one international bundle resource. The resource ID of the resource is that script system's script code. Therefore, once you know the script code for a particular script system, you can find all of the script's default international and keyboard resources by examining the international bundle resource whose ID equals that script code. For a list of defined script codes, see the chapter "Script Manager" in this book.

The original international bundle resource, defined by the ItlbRecord data type, was defined for system software versions earlier than 7.0. The extended 'itlb' record, defined by the ItlbExtRecord data type, is defined for system software versions 7.0 and later. It includes the standard international bundle resource and adds extensions.

The ItlbRecord Data Type

The structure of the standard international bundle resource, defined by the `ItlbRecord` data type, is as follows:

```
TYPE ItlbRecord =
    RECORD
        itlbNumber:     Integer;        {'itl0' ID number}
        itlbDate:       Integer;        {'itl1' ID number}
        itlbSort:       Integer;        {'itl2' ID number}
        itlbFlags:      Integer;        {script flags}
        itlbToken:      Integer;        {'itl4' ID number}
        itlbEncoding:   Integer;        {'itl5' ID number (optional)}
        itlbLang:       Integer;        {current language for script}
        itlbNumRep:     SignedByte;     {current numeral code}
        itlbDateRep:    SignedByte;     {current calendar code}
        itlbKeys:       Integer;        {'KCHR' ID number}
        itlbIcon:       Integer;        {ID of keyboard icon family}
    END;
```

Field descriptions

itlbNumber
The resource ID of the numeric-format (`'itl0'`) resource to be used by this script. The Script Manager initializes the script variable accessed through the selector `smScriptNumber` from this field.

itlbDate
The resource ID of the long-date-format (`'itl1'`) resource to be used by this script. The Script Manager initializes the script variable accessed through the selector `smScriptDate` from this field.

itlbSort
The resource ID of the string-manipulation (`'itl2'`) resource to be used by this script system. The Script Manager initializes the script variable accessed through the selector `smScriptSort` from this field.

itlbFlags
The bit flags that describe the features of this script system. The Script Manager initializes the script flags variable, accessed through the selector `smScriptFlags`, from this field. For example, you can set the `smsfAutoInit` bit in the `itlbFlags` field to instruct the Script Manager to initialize the script system automatically. For definitions of the constants that specify the components of the script flags word, see the list of selectors for script variables in the chapter "Script Manager" in this book.

`itlbToken`	The resource ID of the tokens (`'itl4'`) resource to be used by this script. The Script Manager initializes the script variable accessed through the selector `smScriptToken` from this field.
`itlbEncoding`	The resource ID of the encoding/rendering (`'itl5'`) resource to be used by this script system. The Script Manager initializes the script variable accessed through the selector `smScriptEncoding` from this field. If there is no encoding/rendering resource for this script, this field is set to 0. This field was reserved in versions of system software prior to 7.0.
`itlbLang`	The language code specifying the default language for this script. The Script Manager initializes the script variable accessed through the selector `smScriptLang` from this field. See the chapter "Script Manager" in this book for a list of defined language codes.
`itlbNumRep`	The numeral code to be used by this script system. This byte specifies which types of numerals the script supports. The Script Manager initializes the high-order byte of the script variable accessed through the selector `smScriptNumDate` from this field. For definitions of the constants that specify numeral codes, see the list of selectors for script variables in the chapter "Script Manager" in this book.
`itlbDateRep`	The calendar code to be used by this script system. This byte specifies which types of calendars the script supports. The Script Manager initializes the low-order byte of the script variable accessed through the selector `smScriptNumDate` from this field. For definitions of the constants that specify calendar codes, see the list of selectors for script variables in the chapter "Script Manager" in this book.
`itlbKeys`	The resource ID of the preferred keyboard-layout (`'KCHR'`) resource to be used by this script system. The Script Manager initializes the script variable accessed through the selector `smScriptKeys` from this field.
`itlbIcon`	The resource ID of the keyboard icon family (resource types `'kcs#'`, `'kcs4'`, and `'kcs8'`) for the default keyboard layout to be used with this script. The Script Manager initializes the script variable accessed through the selector `smScriptIcon` from this field. (When loading a keyboard-layout resource, the Script Manager in fact ignores that variable and looks only for a keyboard icon suite whose ID matches that of the keyboard-layout resource being loaded.)

The ItlbExtRecord Data Type

The extended `'itlb'` record adds font and style information to the standard `'itlb'` record. Its structure, defined by the `ItlbExtRecord` data type, is as follows:

```
TYPE ItlbExtRecord =
    RECORD
        base:            ItlbRecord;    {standard ItlbRecord}
        itlbLocalSize:   LongInt;       {size of script variables}
        itlbMonoFond:    Integer;       {default monospaced font}
        itlbMonoSize:    Integer;       {default monospaced size}
        itlbPrefFond:    Integer;       {not used}
        itlbPrefSize:    Integer;       {not used}
        itlbSmallFond:   Integer;       {default small font}
        itlbSmallSize:   Integer;       {default small font size}
        itlbSysFond:     Integer;       {default system font}
        itlbSysSize:     Integer;       {default system font size}
        itlbAppFond:     Integer;       {default application font}
        itlbAppSize:     Integer;       {default appl. font size}
        itlbHelpFond:    Integer;       {default Help font}
        itlbHelpSize:    Integer;       {default Help font size}
        itlbValidStyles: Style;         {valid styles for script}
        itlbAliasStyle:  Style;         {styles to mark aliases}
    END;
```

Field descriptions

`base`	The standard `'itlb'` record for this script.
`itlbLocalSize`	The size of the record of script variables for this script system. (A script system whose `smsfAutoInit` bit in its `itlbFlags` field is set needs to provide this information for the Script Manager.)
`iltbMonoFond`	The font family ID for the preferred font for monospaced text in this script system. The Script Manager initializes the high-order word of the script variable accessed through the selector `smScriptMonoFondSize` from this field.
`itlbMonoSize`	The default size for monospaced text in this script system. The Script Manager initializes the low-order word of the script variable accessed through the selector `smScriptMonoFondSize` from this field.
`itlbPrefFond`	This field is currently unused.
`itlbPrefSize`	This field is currently unused.

`itlbSmallFond`	The font family ID for the default font to display small text in this script system. The Script Manager initializes the high-order word of the script variable accessed through the selector `smScriptSmallFondSize` from this field.
`itlbSmallSize`	The default size for small text in this script system. The Script Manager initializes the low-order word of the script variable accessed through the selector `smScriptSmallFondSize` from this field.
`itlbSysFond`	The font family ID for the preferred system font in this script system. The Script Manager initializes the high-order word of the script variable accessed through the selector `smSysFondSize` from this field.
`itlbSysSize`	The default size for the system font in this script system. The Script Manager initializes the script variable accessed through the selector `smScriptSysFond`, and the low-order word of the script variable accessed through the selector `smSysFondSize`, from this field.
`itlbAppFond`	The font family ID for the preferred application font in this script system. The Script Manager initializes the script variable accessed through the selector `smScriptAppFond`, and the high-order word of the script variable accessed through the selector `smScriptAppFondSize`, from this field.
`itlbAppSize`	The default size for the application font in this script system. The Script Manager initializes the low-order word of the script variable accessed through the selector `smScriptAppFondSize` from this field.
`itlbHelpFond`	The font family ID for the preferred font for Balloon Help in this script system. The Script Manager initializes the high-order word of the script variable accessed through the selector `smScriptHelpFondSize` from this field.
`itlbHelpSize`	The default size for the Balloon Help font in this script system. The Script Manager initializes the low-order word of the script variable accessed through the selector `smScriptHelpFondSize` from this field.
`itlbValidStyles`	A style code that defines all of the valid styles for this script system. (In a style code, the bit corresponding to each QuickDraw style is set if that style is valid for the specified script. For example, the extend style is not valid in the Arabic script system.) The Script Manager initializes the script variable accessed through the selector `smScriptValidStyles` from this field.
`itlbAliasStyle`	A style code that defines the styles to use for displaying alias names in this script system. For example, in the Roman script system, alias names are displayed in italics. The Script Manager initializes the script variable accessed through the selector `smScriptAliasStyle` from this field.

Numeric-Format Resource (Type 'itl0')

The numeric-format resource (resource type 'itl0') contains general conventions for formatting numeric strings. It provides separators for decimals, thousands, and lists; it determines currency symbols and units of measurement; it specifies formats for currency, times, and short dates (the specification of dates in purely numeric representation—for example, in the U.S. Roman script system the short date for Tuesday, December 3, 1946, is 12/3/46). It also contains the region code for this particular instance of the 'itl0' resource.

Each enabled script system has one or more numeric-format resources. The resource ID for each one is within the range of resource ID numbers for that script system. The default numeric-format resource for a script is specified in the itlbNumber field of the script's international bundle ('itlb') resource.

The Text Utilities routines TimeString, LongTimeString, and StringToTime use information in the numeric-format resource to create time strings and to convert time strings to internal numeric representations. See the chapter "Text Utilities" in this book. The Operating System Utilities function IsMetric examines the numeric-format resource to determine the result it returns. See *Inside Macintosh: Operating System Utilities*.

Each numeric-format resource specifies the following:

- Number format. The characters to use as the decimal separator, thousands separator, and list separator.

- Currency format. The currency symbol and its position; whether or not to include leading unit zero or trailing decimal zero; how to show negative values.

- Short date format. The order of presentation of the day, month, and year elements; whether or not to include the century and a leading zero for month or days; the separator for the elements.

- Time format. Whether or not to present leading zeros for hours, minutes, and seconds; whether to use a 24-hour time cycle or a 12-hour A.M./P.M. cycle; how to specify a trailing string (such as a morning or an evening string if a 12-hour time cycle is being used).

- Unit of measure. Whether or not the metric system should be used.

Table B-4 lists constants that you can use in the numeric-format and long-date-format resources to specify separators for standard international formats. For example, in the U.S., slashSymbol is the separator for the short date 12/3/46, but in Germany periodSymbol is the separator for the short date 3.12.1946.

Table B-4   Constants for specifying numeric separators

Constant	Symbol
periodSymbol	.
commaSymbol	,
semicolonSymbol	;
dollarsignSymbol	$
slashSymbol	/
colonSymbol	:

IMPORTANT

When it specifies the order of elements, the numeric-format resource describes them in terms of *storage order*, not display order. Using the information in a numeric-format resource frees you from assuming a particular memory order for the components of numbers and short dates. However, the resource does not necessarily specify the left-to-right order for displaying the components. ▲

The Intl0Rec Data Type

You can access the numeric-format resource through the `Intl0Rec` data type.

```
TYPE  Intl0Rec =
   PACKED RECORD
        decimalPt:    Char;      {decimal point character}
        thousSep:     Char;      {thousands separator}
        listSep:      Char;      {list separator}
        currSym1:     Char;      {currency symbol}
        currSym2:     Char;
        currSym3:     Char;
        currFmt:      Byte;      {currency format flags}
        dateOrder:    Byte;      {order of short date elements}
        shrtDateFmt:  Byte;      {short date format flags}
        dateSep:      Char;      {date separator}
        timeCycle:    Byte;      {time cycle:0-23, 0-11, or 12-11}
        timeFmt:      Byte;      {time format flags}
        mornStr:      PACKED ARRAY[1..4] OF Char;   {trailing }
                                 { string for first 12-hour cycle}
        eveStr:       PACKED ARRAY[1..4] OF Char;   {trailing }
                                 { string for last 12-hour cycle}
        timeSep:      Char;      {time separator}
        time1Suff:    Char;      {trailing string for morning }
        time2Suff:    Char;      { part of 24-hour cycle}
```

```
        time3Suff:      Char;
        time4Suff:      Char;
        time5Suff:      Char;      {trailing string for afternoon }
        time6Suff:      Char;      { part of 24-hour cycle}
        time7Suff:      Char;
        time8Suff:      Char;
        metricSys:      Byte;      {255 if metric, 0 if not}
        intl0Vers:      Integer;  {version information}
    END;
    Intl0Ptr        = ^Intl0Rec;
    Intl0Hndl       = ^Intl0Ptr;
```

Note

A NULL character (ASCII code 0) in a field of type Char means that no such character exists. The currency symbol and the trailing string for the 24-hour cycle are separated into individual Char fields because of Pascal packing conventions. All strings include any required spaces. ◆

Field descriptions

decimalPt   Part of the number format definition. The1-byte character that appears before the decimal representation of a fraction with a denominator of 10. In the United States, this format is a period. In several European countries, it is a comma.

thousSep   Part of the number format definition. The 1-byte character that separates every three digits to the left of the decimal point. In the United States, this format is a comma. In several European countries, it is a period.

listSep   Part of the number format definition. The 1-byte character that separates numbers, as when a list of numbers is entered by the user; it must be different from the decimal point character. If it's the same as the thousands separator, the user must not include the latter in entered numbers. In the United States, this format is a semicolon. In the United Kingdom, it is a comma.

currSym1   Part of the currency format definition. The initial byte used to indicate currency. One character is sufficient for the United States ($) and United Kingdom (£).

currSym2   Part of the currency format definition. The second byte used to indicate currency. Two characters are required for France (Fr).

currSym3   Part of the currency format definition. The third byte used to indicate currency. Three characters are required for Italy (Li.) and Germany (DM.).

`currFmt`	Part of the currency format definition. The four least significant bits are unused. The four most significant bits are Boolean values. Bit 7 determines whether there is a leading integer zero; for example, a 1 in this field specifies a format like 0.23, whereas a 0 specifies .23. Bit 6 determines whether there are trailing decimal zeros; for example, a 1 in this field specifies a format like 325.00, whereas a 0 specifies 325. Bit 5 determines whether to use a minus sign or parentheses to denote a negative currency amount; for example, a 1 in this field specifies a format like –0.45, whereas a 0 specifies (0.45). Bit 4 determines whether the currency symbol trails or leads; for example, a value of 1 in this field specifies a format like the $3.00 used in the United States, whereas a value of 0 specifies the 3 DM. used in Germany.

You can use the following predefined constants as masks to set or test the bits in the `currFmt` field:

Constant	Value	Explanation
`currSymLead`	16	Currency symbol leads
`currNegSym`	32	Use minus sign for negative
`currTrailingZ`	64	Use trailing decimal zeros
`currLeadingZ`	128	Use leading integer zero

Note

You can also apply the currency format's leading-zero and trailing-zero indicators to the number format if desired. ◆

`dateOrder`	Part of the short date format definition. Defines the order of the elements (month, day, and year) of the short date format. The order varies from region to region—for example, 12/29/72 is a common order in the United States, whereas 29.12.72 is common in Europe.

You can indicate the order of the day, month, and year with the following constants:

Constant	Value	Explanation
`mdy`	0	Month-day-year
`dmy`	1	Day-month-year
`ymd`	2	Year-month-day
`myd`	3	Month-year-day
`dym`	4	Day-year-month
`ydm`	5	Year-day-month

shrtDateFmt   Part of the short date format definition. The five least significant bits are unused. The three most significant bit fields are Boolean values that determine whether to show the century, and whether to show leading zeros in month and day numbers. For example, if the first bit is set to 1 it specifies a date format like 10/21/1917, and set to 0 specifies the format 10/21/17. The second bit set to 1 specifies a format like 05/23/84, and set to 0 specifies the format 5/23/84. The third bit set to 1 specifies a format like 12/03/46, and set to 0 specifies the format 12/3/46.

To set or test the bits in the shrtDateFmt field, you can use the following predefined constants as masks:

Constant	Value	Explanation
dayLdingZ	32	Show leading zero for day
mntLdingZ	64	Show leading zero for month
century	128	Show century

dateSep   Part of the short date format definition. The 1-byte character that separates the different parts of the date. For example, in the United States this character is a slash (12/3/46), in Italy it is a hyphen (3-12-46), and in Japan it is a decimal point (46.12.3).

timeCycle   Part of the time format definition. Indicates the time cycle—that is, whether to use 12 or 24 hours as the basis of time, and whether to consider midnight and noon to be 12:00 or 0:00. You can use the following predefined constants to specify the time cycle:

Constant	Value	Explanation
timeCycle24	0	Use 24-hour format (midnight = 0:00)
timeCycleZero	1	Use A.M./P.M. format (midnight and noon = 0:00)
timeCycle12	255	Use A.M./P.M. format (midnight and noon = 12:00)

timeFmt   Part of the time format definition. Indicates whether to show leading zeros in time representation. Bit 5 determines whether there are leading zeros in seconds; for example, a value of 1 in this field specifies a format like 11:15:05, whereas a 0 specifies the format 11:15:5. Bit 6 determines whether there are leading zeros in minutes; for example, a value of 1 in this field specifies a format like 10:05, whereas a 0 specifies the format 10:5. Bit 7 determines whether there are leading zeros in hours; for example, a value of 1 in this field specifies a format like 09:15, whereas a 0 specifies the format 9:15.

You can use the following predefined constants as masks for setting or testing bits in the time format field:

Constant	Value	Explanation
secLeadingZ	32	Use leading zero for seconds
minLeadingZ	64	Use leading zero for minutes
hrLeadingZ	128	Use leading zero for hours

mornStr
: Part of the time format definition. A string of up to 4 bytes to follow the time to indicate morning (for example, " AM"). Typically, the string includes a leading space.

eveStr
: Part of the time format definition. A string of up to 4 bytes to follow the time to indicate evening (for example, " PM"). Typically, the string includes a leading space.

timeSep
: Part of the time format definition. The 1-byte character that is the time separator (for example, the colon).

time1Suff, time2Suff, time3Suff, time4Suff
: Part of the time format definition. A trailing string of up to 4 bytes for the morning part of the 24-hour cycle. For example, the German string "uhr" can be stored here.

time5Suff, time6Suff, time7Suff, time8Suff
: Part of the time format definition. A trailing string of up to 4 bytes for the evening part of the 24-hour cycle. Typically, this string duplicates the string contained in time1Suff through time4Suff. For example, the German string "uhr" can be stored here.

metricSys
: The unit-of-measure definition. Indicates whether to use the metric system. If 255, the metric system is used; if 0, metric is not used.

intl0Vers
: Region code and version number. The code number of the region that this resource applies to is in the high-order byte, and the version number of this numeric-format resource is in the low-order byte.

Long-Date-Format Resource (Type 'itl1')

The long-date-format resource (resource type `'itl1'`) contains the long date format for a particular region, including the names of days and months, the exact order of presentation of the elements, and the specification of whether or not to suppress any element. (For example, in U.S. format, the long date for 12/3/46 without the name of the day suppressed is Tuesday, December 3, 1946.) The long-date-format resource also has an optional extension for additional month and day names as well as abbreviated month and day names and separators. The extension also specifies the calendar code (for example, Arabic lunar) to use for long dates.

Each enabled script system has one or more long-date-format resources. The resource ID for each one is within the range of resource ID numbers for that script system. The default long-date-format resource for a script system is specified in the `itlbDate` field of the script's international bundle (`'itlb'`) resource.

The Text Utilities routines `DateString`, `LongDateString`, and `StringToDate` use information in the long-date-format resource to create date strings and to convert date strings to internal numeric representations. See the chapter "Text Utilities" in this book.

The basic (unextended) long-date-format resource specifies

- The long date format. Month and day names, order of elements, and which elements to suppress.

- Separator strings. What characters (commonly punctuation) appear between elements of the date.

- Region code. The number that identifies the regional version of the script system that this long-date-format resource applies to.

IMPORTANT

When it specifies the order of elements, the long-date-format resource describes them in terms of *storage order,* not display order. Using the information in a long-date-format resource frees you from assuming a particular memory order for the components of long dates. However, the resource does not necessarily specify the left-to-right order for displaying the components. ▲

The Intl1Rec Data Type

You can access the contents of the long-date-format resource through the `Intl1Rec` data type.

```
TYPE Intl1Rec =
PACKED RECORD
    days:          ARRAY[1..7] OF Str15;       {day names}
    months:        ARRAY[1..12] OF Str15;      {month names}
    suppressDay:   Byte;                       {elements to suppress}
    lngDateFmt:    Byte;                       {order of elements}
    dayLeading0:   Byte;                       {leading 0 in day no.?}
    abbrLen:       Byte;                       {abbreviation length}
    st0:           PACKED ARRAY[1..4] OF Char; {separator string}
    st1:           PACKED ARRAY[1..4] OF Char; {separator string}
    st2:           PACKED ARRAY[1..4] OF Char; {separator string}
    st3:           PACKED ARRAY[1..4] OF Char; {separator string}
    st4:           PACKED ARRAY[1..4] OF Char; {separator string}
    intl1Vers:     Integer;                    {version & region}
    localRtn:      ARRAY[0..0] OF Integer; {flag for extended itl1}
END;
TYPE Intl1Ptr = ^Intl1Rec;
TYPE Intl1Hndl = ^Intl1Ptr;
```

Field descriptions

days
: An array of 7 day names (ordered for days corresponding to Sunday through Saturday). Each day name may consist of a maximum of 15 characters.

months
: An array of 12 month names (ordered for months corresponding to January through December). Each month name may consist of a maximum of 15 characters.

suppressDay
: A byte that lets you omit any element in the long date. To include the day name in the long date, you set the field to 0. To suppress the day name, set the field to 255 ($FF).

  If the value does not equal 0 or $FF, this field is treated as bit flags. You can use the following predefined constants as masks to set the appropriate bits in the suppressDay byte.

Constant	Value	Explanation
supDay	1	Suppress day of month
supWeek	2	Suppress day name
supMonth	4	Suppress month
supYear	8	Suppress year

  Note that a value of 2 is same as a value of $FF in this field.

lngDateFmt

The byte that indicates the order of long date elements. If the byte value of the field is neither 0 (which specifies an order of day/month/year) nor $FF (which specifies an order of month/day/year), then its value is divided into 4 fields of 2 bits each. The least significant bit field (bits 0 and 1) corresponds to the first element in the long date format, whereas the most significant bit field (bits 6 and 7) specifies the last (fourth) element in the format. You can use the following predefined constants to set each bit field to the appropriate value.

Constant	Value	Explanation
longDay	0	Day of the month
longWeek	1	Day of the week
longMonth	2	Month
longYear	3	Year

Note that these constants represent values for the 2-bit field, and are neither masks nor bit numbers. For example, suppose you wanted long dates to appear in this order: day of the week, day of the month, month, and year. You would set the value of longDateFmt like this:

```
longDateFmt :=
    longWeek*1      {sets bits 0 and 1}
    + LongDay*4     {sets bits 2 and 3}
    + longMonth*16  {sets bits 4 and 5}
    + longYear*64;  {sets bits 6 and 7}
```

dayLeading0

If 255 ($FF), specifies a leading zero in a day number. If 0, no leading zero is included in the day number.

abbrLen

The number of characters to which month and day names should be abbreviated when abbreviation is desired.

st0

String that precedes (in memory) the first element in a long date. See Table B-5 and Figure B-3.

st1

String that separates the first and second elements in a long date. See Table B-5 and Figure B-3. This string is suppressed if the first element in the long date is suppressed.

st2

String that separates the second and third elements in a long date. See Table B-5 and Figure B-3. This string is suppressed if the second element in the long date is suppressed.

st3

String that separates the third and fourth elements in a long date. See Table B-5 and Figure B-3. This string is suppressed if the third element in the long date is suppressed.

st4   String that follows the fourth element in a long date. See Table B-5
                    and Figure B-3. This string is suppressed if the fourth element in the
                    long date is suppressed.

Table B-5   Separator positions in long date format

lngDateFmt	Long date format				
0	st0 *day name*	st1 *day*	st2 *month*	st3 *year*	st4
255	st0 *day name*	st1 *month*	st2 *day*	st3 *year*	st4

intl1Vers   Region code and version number. The code number of the region
                    that this resource applies to is in the high-order byte, and the
                    version number of this long-date-format resource is in the
                    low-order byte.

localRtn   Originally designed to contain a routine that localizes sorting order;
                    now unused for that purpose. If an extended long-date-format
                    resource is available (see the next section), this field contains the
                    hexadecimal value $A89F as the first word.

Figure B-3 gives two examples of how the Text Utilities routines format dates based on
the fields in the numeric-format resource. The examples assume that the suppressDay
and dayLeading0 fields contain 0. If the SuppressDay field contains a value of 255,
the formatting routines omit the day and the punctuation indicated in the st1 field. If
the dayLeading0 field contains a value of 255, the Text Utilities place a 0 before day
numbers less than 10.

Figure B-3   Examples of long date formatting

lngDateFmt	st0	st1	st2	st3	st4	Sample result
0	"	', '	'. '	' '	"	Mittwoch, 2. February 1985
255	"	' '	' '	' '	"	Wednesday February 1 1985

The Itl1ExtRec Data Type

The standard long-date-format resource has several limitations. First, it assumes that
seven day names and 12 month names are sufficient, which is not true for some
calendars. For example, the Jewish calendar can have 13 months in some years. Second,
it assumes that day and month names can be abbreviated by simply truncating them to a
fixed length, but this not true in many languages.

International Resources

An optional extension to the long-date-format resource provides additional information that solves these problems. The Text Utilities routines that generate date strings use information in the 'itl1' extension if it is present.

The standard long-date-format resource ends with a variable-length field (localRtn) originally intended to be used for code that alters the built-in U.S. sorting behavior. This field is no longer needed, because code for changing the sorting behavior is now in the string-manipulation ('itl2') resource.

In existing unextended long-date-format resources, the localRtn field contains a single RTS instruction (hexadecimal $4E75). In extended long-date-format resources, the hexadecimal value $A89F is the first word in thelocalRtn field. (This is the unimplemented trap instruction, which could not have been the first word of any valid local routine.) The resource extension follows immediately after that word.

You can access the contents of the 'itl1' resource extension through the Itl1ExtRec data type.

```
TYPE Itl1ExtRec =
RECORD
    base:                    Itl1Rec;{un-extended Itl1Rec}
    version:                 Integer; {version number}
    format:                  Integer; {format code}
    calendarCode:            Integer; {calendar code for 'itl1'}
    extraDaysTableOffset:    LongInt; {offset to extra days table}
    extraDaysTableLength:    LongInt; {length of extra days table}
    extraMonthsTableOffset:  LongInt; {offset to extra months table}
    extraMonthsTableLength:  LongInt; {length of extra months table}
    abbrevDaysTableOffset:   LongInt; {offset to abbrev. days table}
    abbrevDaysTableLength:   LongInt; {length of abbrev. days table}
    abbrevMonthsTableOffset:LongInt; {offset to abbr. months table}
    abbrevMonthsTableLength:LongInt; {length of abbr. months table}
    extraSepsTableOffset:    LongInt; {offset to extra seps table}
    extraSepsTableLength:    LongInt; {length of extra seps table}
    tables:                  ARRAY[0..0] OF Integer;
                                     {the tables; variable-length}
END;
```

Field descriptions

base   A standard (unextended) long-date-format resource.

version   The version number of this extension. Unlike the itl1Vers field in the unextended 'itl1' resource, this field contains nothing but the version number.

format
: A number that identifies the format of this resource. The current extended long-date-format resource format has a format code of 0.

calendarCode
: Multiple calendars may be available on some systems, and it is necessary to identify the particular calendar for use with this long-date-format resource. Constants for the currently defined calendars are as follows:

Constant	Value	Explanation
calGregorian	0	Gregorian calendar
calArabicCivil	1	Arabic civil calendar
calArabicLunar	2	Arabic lunar calendar
calJapanese	3	Japanese calendar
calJewish	4	Jewish calendar
calCoptic	5	Coptic calendar
calPersian	6	Persian calendar

The Script Manager initializes part of the script variable accessed through the selector smScriptNumDate with the value in this field.

extraDaysTableOffset
: The offset from the beginning of the long-date-format resource to the extra days table.

extraDaysTableLength
: The length in bytes of the extra days table.

extraMonthsTableOffset
: The offset from the beginning of the long-date-format resource to the extra months table.

extraMonthsTableLength
: The length in bytes of the extra months table.

abbrevDaysTableOffset
: The offset from the beginning of the long-date-format resource to the abbreviated days table.

abbrevDaysTableLength
: The length in bytes of the abbreviated days table.

abbrevMonthsTableOffset
: The offset from the beginning of the long-date-format resource to the abbreviated months table.

abbrevMonthsTableLength
: The length in bytes of the abbreviated months table.

extraSepsTableOffset
: The offset from the beginning of the long-date-format resource to the extra separators table.

extraSepsTableLength
: The length in bytes of the extra separators table.

tables
: The tables that make up the rest of the 'itl1' resource extension.

Each table in the `'itl1'` resource extension is an array consisting of an integer count followed by a list of Pascal strings specifying names of days, names of months, or separators.

- Extra days table. A list of names. This format is for those calendars with more than 7 day names.

- Extra months table. A list of names. This format is for those calendars with more than 12 months.

- Abbreviated days table. A table of abbreviations. If the header specifies an offset to and length of the abbreviated days table, the Text Utilities routines that create date strings use this table instead of truncating day names to the number of characters specified in the `abbrevLen` field of the standard `'itl1'` resource.

- Abbreviated months table. A table of abbreviations. If the header specifies an offset to and length of the abbreviated months table, the Text Utilities routines that create date strings use this table instead of truncating month names to the number of characters specified in the `abbrevLen` field of the standard `'itl1'` resource.

- Extra separators table. A list of additional date separators. When parsing date strings, the Text Utilities `StringToDate` and `StringToTime` functions permit the separators in this list to be used in addition to the date separators specified elsewhere in the numeric-format and long-date-format resources.

String-Manipulation Resource (Type 'itl2')

The string-manipulation resource (resource type `'itl2'`) is used by the Text Utilities and the Script Manager for defining and comparing text elements.

The string-manipulation resource contains routines, called sorting hooks, that perform string sorting; it also contains tables that define character type, case conversion, and word boundaries. The Text Utilities routines `IdenticalString`, `IdenticalText`, `CompareString`, and `CompareText` call the Text Utilities sorting hooks. The Text Utilities routines `CharacterType`, `FindWordBreaks`, `LowercaseText`, `UppercaseText`, `StripDiacritics`, and `UppercaseStripDiacritics`, and the Script Manager function `TransliterateText`, may make use of tables in the string-manipulation resource.

By replacing the sorting hooks, you can modify the way string comparisons are made; by replacing tables in the string-manipulation resource, you can modify how word boundaries are determined. See the sections "Supplying Custom Sorting Routines" on page B-43, and "Supplying Custom Word-Break Tables" on page B-44, for more information.

Each enabled script system has one or more string-manipulation resources. The resource ID for each one is within the range of resource ID numbers for that script system. The default `'itl2'` resource for a script is specified in the `itlbSort` field of the script's international bundle resource (type `'itlb'`).

Note

The resource template used by `Rez` and `DeRez` specifies a particular ordering of code and tables in the string-manipulation resource, although that order is not required for the resource to be used correctly. ◆

Each string-manipulation resource contains the following elements:

- header

- string comparison routines (sorting hooks)

- character-type tables (optional)

- case-conversion and stripping tables (optional)

- word break tables

- subscript table (optional)

The string-manipulation resource described in this section is sometimes called the *extended `'itl2'` resource*. Prior to Macintosh system software version 6.0.4, a more abbreviated `'itl2'` version was supported. That original `'itl2'` resource consisted of the header and sorting hooks only. The full resource as documented here is supported by system software versions 7.0 and later.

Resource Header

The string-manipulation resource header allows you to access the code segments and tables that make up the resource. All fields in the header are 16-bit words. Each field designated as an offset contains the signed offset, in bytes, from the beginning of the resource to the specified code block or table. The header is followed by the actual code segments and tables, which may be in any order. Figure B-4 shows the structure of the header.

Figure B-4   Format of the string-manipulation resource header

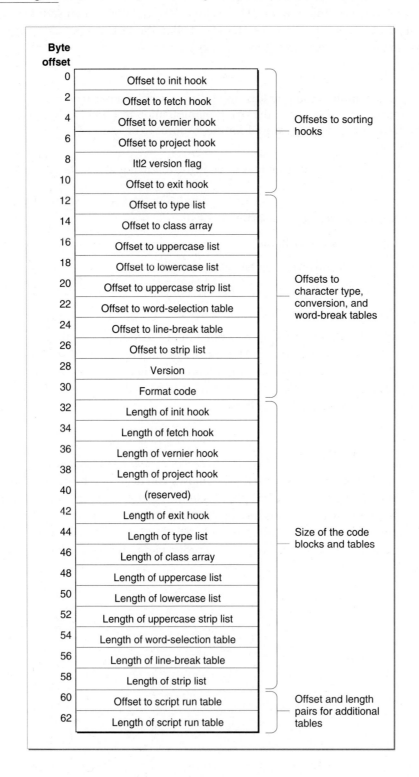

The header consists of four sections. The first section contains offsets to the sorting hooks; the second section contains offsets to tables for character type, case conversion and diacritical stripping, and word break; the third section contains the lengths of all of the code blocks and tables; the fourth section contains offset and length pairs for tables to be added in the future.

■ The first section of the header contains a version flag and five offsets to the sorting hooks: init hook, fetch hook, vernier hook, project hook, and exit hook. The sorting hooks are string-comparison routines, code segments that control sorting behavior. The hooks can replace or modify the built-in U.S. sorting behavior, on a character-by-character basis.

The Itl2 version flag is a long integer value that describes the format of this string-manipulation resource. A value of –1 indicates that this string-manipulation resource is in the system software version 6.0.4 (or newer) format. In versions previous to 6.0.4, this element contains the offset to the reserved hook, another sorting hook. In versions previous to 6.0.4, the string-manipulation resource header stops at this point.

■ The second section of the resource header contains the following elements:

□ Offsets to the character-type tables: type list, class array.

□ Offsets to the case conversion and diacritical stripping lists: uppercase list, lowercase list, uppercase strip list, strip list.

□ Offsets to the word-break tables: word-selection table, line-break table.

□ Version number. The version number of this string-manipulation resource.

□ Format code. Contains 0 if the string-manipulation resource header stops at this point (true for system software version 6.0.4); contains 1 if the string-manipulation resource header has the format shown in Figure B-4 (true for system software version 7.0 and later).

■ The third section of the header contains the lengths of all of the code blocks and tables for which there are offsets in the first two sections. The Script Manager requires valid length values in this section only for those tables that can be accessed through the `GetIntlResourceTable` procedure (the word-selection and line-break tables).

■ The fourth section contains offset and length pairs for additional tables. The first pair in this section is used for an optional table (`findScriptTable`) defining characters of a subscript within a non-Roman script system. It is used by the Script Manager `FindScriptRun` function. See "Script Run Table Format" beginning on page B-40. If this table is not present, the offset and length are 0.

The 'itl2' Sorting Hooks

The string-manipulation resource contains five sorting hooks, each of which can modify the functioning of its equivalent default sorting routine that is built into Text Utilities. If the sorting hooks are all empty, the default U.S. Roman sorting behavior results. For example, the `'itl2'` resource in the version of the Roman script system that has been localized for the United States contains the built-in sorting behavior and empty hooks. For other script systems, one or more of the hooks are replaced with actual routines, to handle characters that need to be sorted differently from the default—for example, the

International Resources

Spanish character combination "rr" or the Norwegian "ñ". Most of the sorting routines are called in turn for each character in each string of a pair that are being compared. Here is what each of the routines does:

- Init routine. The init routine prepares two strings for comparison. The Text Utilities sorting routines compare a pair of strings byte for byte, and pass control to the init routine as soon as a pair of unequal byte values occur. All the init routine does is check to see if either of the byte values is the second byte of a 2-byte character (or other sorting unit, such as "rr" in Spanish). If it is, the init routine backs up one byte in the string, and passes control to the fetch routine.

- Fetch routine. The fetch routine fetches the next sorting unit from each string, taking into account whether the unit is composed of one or two bytes. Many, though not all, characters in 2-byte script systems are 2 bytes long. Character combinations in 1-byte scripts can also be considered as single sorting units during sorting—such as "ch" in Spanish and "dz" in Croatian. For example, consider the second characters in these two strings:

b c h a
b c a d

In analyzing the second sorting unit of each string, English versions of the fetch routine would return "c" in each case. Spanish versions, which combine "c" and "h" into a singular sorting unit "ch", would return "ch" for the upper string and "c" for the lower string.

- Project routine. The project routine defines the primary sorting position for the individual sorting unit passed to it. In the example just presented, the English version of the project routine would give the same result for the second sorting unit of each string, whereas the Spanish version would give them different values.

Where secondary sorting exists, the project routine "projects" each character into the sorting position of its equivalent primary character (perhaps uppercase with diacritical marks stripped). For example, consider the following two strings:

b C a d f
B c å d g

The project routine would give identical results for all the character pairs until passed the "f" and "g". In terms of the project routine, the strings would be sorted as if they were

B C A D F
B C A D G

The Text Utilities use the project routine to establish decision characters to be used later if a primary difference is not available. The first pair of sorting units that have the same projected position but are not byte-for-byte identical is saved from this. Those decision characters are acted upon by the vernier routine.

- Vernier routine. The vernier routine is the tie breaker that determines the sorting order for strings that are equivalent in terms of primary sorting. It defines the secondary sorting position for the sorting unit passed to it. Suppose, in the previous example, that the strings were

b c a d f
b c å d f

Primary equivalence exists between the two strings. The decision characters "a" and "å" are passed in turn to the vernier routine; the vernier routine passes back a sorting position for each one. The return values determine whether "a" sorts before or after "å", and thus establish the sorting order for the strings.

- Exit routine. This sorting hook exists to allow for any needed post-processing after the sorting order for a pair of strings has been determined. It is called just before the Text Utilities string-comparison routine returns to the caller.

For information on providing custom versions of the sorting hooks, see "Supplying Custom Sorting Routines" on page B-43.

The 'itl2' Tables

The following tables in the string-manipulation resource define character and word features for processing strings.

- Type list. Contains character-type information for each class of character (as specified by the class array) in the script system's character set. The Script Manager `CharacterType` function uses this table. The type list is used by 1-byte script systems only; character-type information for a 2-byte script system is in that script's encoding/rendering ('itl5') resource.

- Class array. Maps each character in the script system's character set to a *class*, which is used to index into the other character tables in the string-manipulation resource. The Script Manager `CharacterType` function uses this table. The class array is used by 1-byte script systems only; character-class information for a 2-byte script system is in that script's encoding/rendering ('itl5') resource.

- Uppercase list. Used to generate uppercase equivalents for all lowercase characters in the script system's character set. For each character class, contains a value to be added to the character code to convert all characters to uppercase. The Text Utilities `UppercaseText` procedure uses this table. The uppercase list is used by 1-byte script systems only.

- Lowercase list. Used to generate lowercase equivalents for all uppercase characters in the script system's character set. For each character class, contains a value to be added to the character code to convert all characters to lowercase. The Text Utilities `LowercaseText` procedure uses this table. The lowercase list is used by 1-byte script systems only.

- Uppercase strip list. Used to generate uppercase equivalents—without diacritical marks—for all characters in the script system's character set. For each character class, contains a value to be added to the character code to convert all characters to uppercase versions without diacritical marks. The Text Utilities `UppercaseStripDiacritics` procedure uses this table. The uppercase strip list is used by 1-byte script systems only.

- Strip list. Used to generate equivalents—without diacritical marks—for all characters in the script system's character set. For each character class, contains a value to be added to the character code to strip diacritical marks. The Text Utilities `StripDiacritics` procedure uses this table. The strip list is used by 1-byte script systems only.

■ Word-selection table. A table of data type `NBreakTable` or `BreakTable`, used by the Text Utilities `FindWordBreaks` procedure to find word boundaries for the purposes of word selection. See "Supplying Custom Word-Break Tables" on page B-44 for a description of the break-table formats.

■ Line-break table. A table of data type `NBreakTable` or `BreakTable`, used by theText Utilities `FindWordBreaks` procedure to find word boundaries for breaking lines of text. The rules governing word boundaries for line breaking are generally somewhat different from those for word selection.

■ Script run table. A data structure used by the Text Utilities `FindScriptRun` function. It is used to find runs of a subscript, such as Roman, within text of a non-Roman script system. See the next section.

Script Run Table Format

The script run table is used by the Text Utilities `FindScriptRun` function. `FindScriptRun` locates runs of text that belong to a subscript, such as Roman, within a single script run. The `FindScriptRun` function is described in the chapter "Text Utilities" in this book.

There are two formats of script run table. The original format, used in versions of system software earlier than 7.1, consists of a series of byte pairs with the format *character code, script code*. The character code is the final character code in a range of characters that belongs to the script specified by the script code. (The table contains only final character codes; the initial character code of a range is assumed to be one greater than the final character code in the previous range—or 0 for the first range.) The last pair must have character code $FF. For example, if the character set encoding for script `smSample` were defined such that $00–7F and $A0 were Roman characters and the remaining characters were native characters in `smSample`, the table would appear as follows:

Character code	Script code
$7F	smRoman
$9F	smSample
$A0	smRoman
$FF	smSample

This simple format is appropriate for script systems whose text can be separated into Roman or native characters based purely upon character code, and for which other subscript information (returned in the `variant` field of the `ScriptRunStatus` record by `FindScriptRun`) is always 0. For 2-byte script systems, or when the same character could be designated as either Roman or native (depending on its context), this simple format is insufficient.

The newer format for the script run table is used in versions of system software starting with 7.1. It consists of a header, a state table, and a set of associated tables, similar in structure to the word-break table of type `NBreakTable` (described on page B-44). It is more flexible than the old format: for example, it can consider punctuation marks such as the period (ASCII code $2E) to be either to Roman or non-Roman, depending upon whether they are associated with Roman or non-Roman characters in the text. The script run table format is shown in Figure B-5.

Figure B-5   Format of the script run table header (new format)

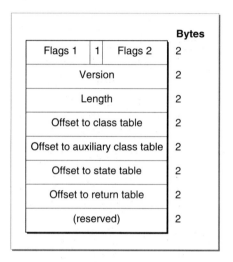

The table header has these elements:

■ Flags 1 and flags 2. The flags are not defined and should be 0, except that the high-order bit of the second byte (flags 2) must be 1 to mark this as a new-format script run table.

■ Version. The version number of this script run table format.

■ Length. The length in bytes of this script run table.

■ Offset to class table. The offset in bytes from the beginning of the script run table to the beginning of the class table.

■ Offset to auxiliary class table. The offset in bytes from the beginning of the script run table to the beginning of the auxiliary class table.

■ Offset to state table. The offset in bytes from the beginning of the script run table to the beginning of the state table.

■ Offset to return table. The offset in bytes from the beginning of the script run table to the beginning of the return table.

■ (reserved). Reserved.

The header is immediately followed by the data of the class table, auxiliary class table, state table, and return table. The tables have this format and content:

■ The class table is an array of 256 signed bytes. It assigns class values to 1-byte characters and works with the auxiliary class table to assign class values for 2-byte characters. It has the same format as the class table used by the word-break table described under "NBreakTable Format" beginning on page B-44.

■ The auxiliary class table assigns character classes to 2-byte characters. It has the same format as the auxiliary class table used by the word-break table described under "NBreakTable Format" beginning on page B-44.

■ The state table is used by `FindScriptRun` to determine the subscript assignment for a given character class, accounting for its context. Using the state table, `FindScriptRun` starts at a specified character, moving forward through the text until it encounters a subscript boundary.

The state table is shown in Figure B-6. The table begins with a list of words containing byte offsets from the beginning of the state table to the rows of the state table; this is followed by a *c*-by-*s* byte array, where *c* is the number of classes (columns) and *s* is the number of states (rows). The bytes in this array are stored with the column index varying most rapidly—that is, the bytes for the state 0 row precede the bytes for the state 1 row. There is a maximum of 128 classes and 64 states (including the start and exit states).

Figure B-6   Script run table state table

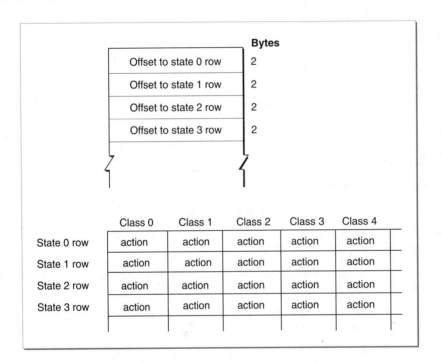

Each entry in this array is an action code, which specifies

■ whether to mark the current offset

■ whether to exit

■ the next state or (if exiting) the exit code

The format of an action code is shown in Figure B-7.

Figure B-7   Format of a script run table action code

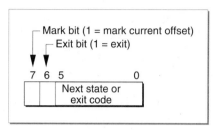

The return table is a list of script code–variant pairs, as shown in Figure B-8. The table lists possible return values for the FindScriptRun function. Each pair in the table is a ScriptRunStatus record, as described in the chapter "Text Utilities" in this book. The variant associated with each script code gives subscript information for 2-byte script systems. When FindScriptRun exits the state table, it has encountered a subscript boundary; it uses the exit code to index into the return table and determine the script code of the subscript run it has just exited from.

Figure B-8   Format of the script run table return table

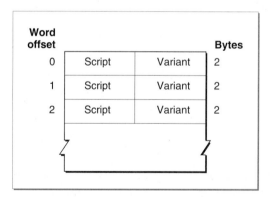

Supplying Custom Sorting Routines

String comparison in a given script system is controlled by routines accessed through the sorting hooks in the string-manipulation resource. However, there is also a default sorting behavior built into the Text Utilities, and the sorting hooks are designed to allow a given script system to use, modify, or replace parts of that default behavior, on a character-by-character basis. The U.S. version of the Roman script system, for example, uses the built-in sorting behavior exclusively; its 'itl2' resource has only nonfunctional (empty) sorting hooks. The built-in sorting behavior used by the Text Utilities is described in the appendix "Built-in Script Support" in this book.

The sorting hooks are described under "The 'itl2' Sorting Hooks" on page B-37. You can supply a replacement string-manipulation resource with nonempty versions of any sorting hooks, to create sorting behavior more appropriate for your target region.

Note
Even "empty" sorting hooks cannot be completely empty. All 'itl2' sorting hooks are responsible for setting the condition codes that indicate whether or not they have taken any sorting action. If these condition codes have not been set, the Text Utilities uses the default Roman sorting behavior. ◆

For more information on replacing any or all of the sorting hooks, see Macintosh Technical Note #178, available from Macintosh Developer Technical Support.

Supplying Custom Word-Break Tables

The Text Utilities `FindWordBreaks` procedure uses state machines and associated tables in a script's string-manipulation resource to determine word boundaries and line breaks.

The `FindWordBreaks` procedure examines a block of text to determine the boundaries of the word that includes a specified character in the block. Usually, `FindWordBreaks` uses different state tables to define words for word selection than it does for line breaking.

To replace the word-selection criteria, you can supply a replacement string-manipulation resource with a modified break table. This section describes the break table and how `FindWordBreaks` uses it.

NBreakTable Format

`FindWordBreaks` uses word-break tables of type `NBreakTable`, defined for system software version 7.0 and later:

```
TYPE     NBreakTable =
   RECORD
         flags1:              SignedByte;   {break table format flags}
         flags2:              SignedByte;   {break table format flags}
         version:             Integer;      {version no. of break table}
         classTableOff:       Integer;      {offset to ClassTable array}
         auxCTableOff:        Integer;      {offset to auxCTable array}
         backwdTableOff:      Integer;      {offset to backwdTable array}
         forwdTableOff:       Integer;      {offset to forwdTable array}
         doBackup:            Integer;      {skip backward processing?}
         length:              Integer;      {length of the break table}
```

```
        charTypes:          ARRAY[0..255] OF SignedByte;
        tables:             ARRAY[0..0] OF Integer;
                                    {break tables}

END;


TYPE NBreakTablePtr = ^NBreakTable;
```

Field descriptions

flags1
: The high-order byte of the break table format flags. If the high-order bit of this byte is set to 1, this break table is in the format used by FindWordBreaks.

flags2
: The low-order byte of the break table format flags. If the value in this byte is 0, the break table belongs to a 1-byte script system; in this case FindWordBreaks does not check for 2-byte characters.

version
: The version number of this break table.

classTableOff
: The offset in bytes from the beginning of the break table to the beginning of the class table.

auxCTableOff
: The offset in bytes from the beginning of the break table to the beginning of the auxiliary class table.

backwdTableOff
: The offset in bytes from the beginning of the break table to the beginning of the backward-processing table.

forwdTableOff
: The offset in bytes from the beginning of the break table to the beginning of the forward-processing table.

doBackup
: The minimum byte offset into the buffer for doing backward processing. If the selected character for FindWordBreaks has a byte offset less than doBackup, FindWordBreaks skips backward processsing altogether and starts from the beginning of the buffer.

length
: The length in bytes of the entire break table, including all the individual tables.

charTypes
: The class table. See explanation below.

tables
: The data of the auxiliary class table, backward table, and forward table.

The tables have this format and content:

■ The class table is an array of 256 signed bytes. Offsets into the table represent byte values; if the entry at a given offset in the table is positive, it means that a byte whose value equals that offset is a single-byte character, and the entry at that offset is the class number for the character. If the entry is negative, it means that the byte is the first byte of a 2-byte character code, and the auxiliary class table must be used to determine the character class. Odd negative numbers are handled differently from even negative numbers.

■ The auxiliary class table assigns character classes to 2-byte characters. It is used when the class table determines that a byte value represents the first byte of a 2-byte character.

□ Here is how the auxiliary class table handles odd negative values from the class table. If the first word of the auxiliary class table is equal to or greater than zero, it represents the default class number for 2-byte character codes—the class assigned to every odd negative value from the class table. If the first word is less than zero, it is the negative of the offset from the beginning of the auxiliary class table to a first-byte class table (a table of 2-byte character classes that can be determined from just the first byte). The value from the class table is negated, 1 is subtracted from it to obtain an even offset, and the value at that offset into the first-byte class table is the class to be assigned.

□ Here is how the auxiliary class table handles even negative values from the class table. The auxiliary class table begins with a variable-length word array. The words that follow the first word are offsets to row tables. Row tables have the same format as the class table, but are used to map the second byte of a 2-byte character code to a class number. If the entry in the class table for a given byte is an even negative number, FindWordBreaks negates this value to obtain the offset from the beginning of the auxiliary class table to the appropriate word, which in turn contains an offset to the appropriate row table. That row table is then used to map the second byte of the character to a class number.

■ The backward-processing table is a state table used by FindWordBreaks for backward searching. Using the backward-processing table, FindWordBreaks starts at a specified character, moving backward as necessary until it encounters a word boundary.

■ The forward-processing table is a state table used by FindWordBreaks for forward searching. Using the forward-processing table, FindWordBreaks starts at one word boundary and moves forward until it encounters another word boundary.

The backward-processing table and the forward-processing table have the same format, as shown in Figure B-9. The table begins with a list of words containing byte offsets from the beginning of the state table to the rows of the state table; this is followed by a c-by-s byte array, where c is the number of classes (columns) and s is the number of states (rows). The bytes in this array are stored with the column index varying most rapidly—that is, the bytes for the state 1 row precede the bytes for the state 2 row.

Note
There is a maximum of 128 classes and 64 states (including the start and exit states). ◆

Figure B-9   `NBreakTable` state table

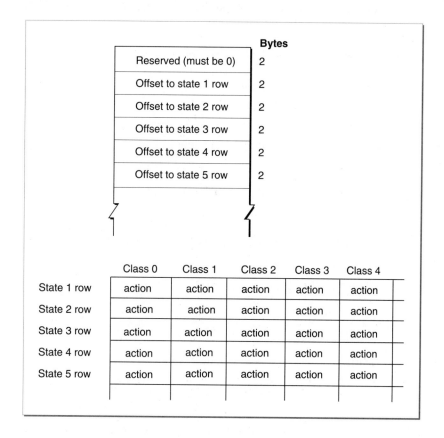

Each entry in this array is an action code, which specifies

- whether to mark the current offset
- the next state, which may be the exit state (state 0)

The format of an action code is shown in Figure B-10.

Figure B-10   Format of an `NBreakTable` action code

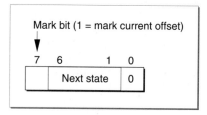

International Resources

Table B-6 shows an example of the classes used in a state table. It is taken from the word-selection table of the U.S. localized version of the Roman script system.

Table B-6   Example of classes for an `NBreakTable` state table

Class number	Class name	Used for
0	break	Everything not included below
1	nonBreak	Nonbreaking spaces
2	letter	Letters, ligatures, and accents
3	number	Digits
4	midLetter	Hyphen
5	midLetNum	Apostrophe (vertical or right single quote)
6	preNum	$ £ ¥ ¤
7	postNum	% ‰ ¢
8	midNum	, /
9	preMidNum	.
10	blank	Space, tab, null
11	cr	Return

Table B-7 shows an example of the defined states for a state table. It is taken from the forward-processing table of the word-selection table of the U.S. localized version of the Roman script system.

Table B-7   Example of states for an `NBreakTable` state table

State number	Explanation
0	Exit
1	Start, or has detected initial *nonBreak* sequence
2	Has detected a *letter*
3	Has detected a *number*
4	Has detected a non-whitespace character that should stand alone; now anything but *nonBreak* generates an exit
5	Has detected *preMidNum* or *preNum*; now anything but *number* or *nonBreak* generates an exit
6	Has detected a *blank*

Table B-7   Example of states for an `NBreakTable` state table (continued)

State number	Explanation
7	Has detected *letter* followed by *midLetter, midLetNum,* or *preMidNum*; now anything but *letter* generates an exit
8	Has detected a non-whitespace character followed by *nonBreak* (the *nonBreak* should be treated as non-whitespace)
9	Has detected *number* followed by *midNum, midLetNum,* or *preMidNum*; now anything but *number* generates an exit
10	Marks current offset, then exits
11	Has detected *blank* followed by *nonBreak* (the *nonBreak* should be treated as a blank)

How FindWordBreaks Uses the Break Table

`FindWordBreaks` uses a state machine to determine the word boundaries on either side of a given character in a text buffer. The state machine must start at a point in the buffer at or before the beginning of the word that includes that character. If the specified character is sufficiently close to the beginning of the text buffer (controlled by the `doBackupMin` parameter in the break table), the state machine simply starts from the beginning of the buffer. Otherwise, `FindWordBreaks` uses the backward-processing table to work backwards from the specified character, analyzing characters until it encounters a word boundary.

Once determined, this starting location is saved as an initial word boundary. From this point the `FindWordBreaks` state machine moves forward using the forward-processing table until it encounters another word boundary. If that word boundary is still before the specified character, its location is saved as the starting point and the state machine is restarted from that location. This process repeats until the state machine finds a word boundary that is after the specified character. At that point, `FindWordBreaks` returns the location of the previously saved word boundary and the current word boundary as the offset pair defining the word.

The state machine operates in a similar manner whether moving backward or forward; any differences in behavior are determined by the tables. The machine begins in the start state (state 1). It then cycles one character at a time until it finds a boundary break and exits. In each cycle, the current character is mapped to a class number, and the character class and the current state are used as indices into the array of action codes in the state table. Each action code specifies the next state and whether to mark the current offset. When the state machine exits, it has encountered a word boundary. The location of the word boundary is the last character offset that was marked.

Figure B-11 gives two examples of the forward operation of the state machine for word selection. It shows that an exit may or may not be generated at a hyphen, depending on the character that follows. It also shows that the marked offset on exit may or may not include the last character before the exit was generated.

Figure B-11   Forward operation of the state machine for word selection

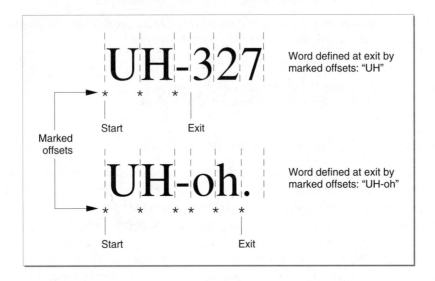

Tokens Resource (Type 'itl4')

The tokens resource (resource type 'itl4') contains information needed to convert text into a series of language-independent tokens. Compilers, interpreters, and other expression evaluators convert source text to tokens as an initial step in their processing. The Script Manager IntlTokenize function uses information in the tokens resource to produce tokens from source text.

The tokens resource also contains tables for converting tokens into text, for formatting numbers, and for determining whitespace characters.

Each enabled script system has one or more tokens resources. The resource ID for each one is within the range of resource ID numbers for that script system. The default 'itl4' resource for a script is specified in the itlbToken field of the script's international bundle ('itlb') resource.

Each tokens resource contains the following:

- Header
- Tokenizing tables and code
- Untoken table

■ Number parts table

■ Whitespace table

The tokenizing tables and code are used by the `IntlTokenize` function. The untoken table is used by the `IntlTokenize` function and by applications that want to convert tokens to strings. The number parts table is used by the Text Utilities number-formatting routines and by applications that do their own number formatting. The whitespace table is available for application use.

The NItl4Rec Data Type

The tokens resource is defined by the `NItl4Rec` data type as follows:

```
TYPE  NItl4Rec =
   RECORD
        flags:            Integer;     {reserved}
        resourceType:     LongInt;     {contains 'itl4'}
        resourceNum:      Integer;     {resource ID}
        version:          Integer;     {version number}
        format:           Integer;     {format code}
        resHeader:        Integer;     {reserved}
        resHeader2:       LongInt;     {reserved}
        numTables:        Integer;     {number of tables}

        mapOffset:        LongInt;     {offset to token table}
        strOffset:        LongInt;     {offset to string-copy rtn.}
        fetchOffset:      LongInt;     {offset to ext. fetch routine}
        unTokenOffset:    LongInt;     {offset to untoken table}
        defPartsOffset:   LongInt;     {offset to number parts table}
        whtSpListOffset:  LongInt;     {offset to whitespace table}

        resOffset7:       LongInt;     {reserved}
        resOffset8:       LongInt;     {reserved}
        resLength1:       Integer;     {reserved}
        resLength2:       Integer;     {reserved}
        resLength3:       Integer;     {reserved}
        unTokenLength:    Integer;     {length of untoken table}
        defPartsLength:   Integer;     {length of number parts table}
        whtSpListLength:  Integer;     {length of whitespace table}
        resLength7:       Integer;     {reserved}
        resLength8:       Integer;     {reserved}
   END;

TYPE NItl4Ptr    = ^NItl4Rec;
TYPE NItl4Handle = ^NItl4Ptr;
```

Field descriptions

flags	(reserved)
resourceType	'itl4' (the resource type of the tokens resource).
resourceNum	The resource ID number of this tokens resource.
version	The version number of this tokens resource.
format	The format code, a number that identifies the format of this tokens resource.
resHeader	(reserved)
resHeader2	(reserved)
numTables	The number of tables in this tokens resource.
mapOffset	The offset in bytes from the beginning of the resource to the token table, an array that maps each byte to a token type.
strOffset	The offset in bytes from the beginning of the resource to the token-string copy routine, a code segment that creates strings that correspond to the text that generated each token.
fetchOffset	The offset in bytes from the beginning of the resource to the extension-fetching routine, a code segment that fetches the second byte of a 2-byte character for the IntlTokenize function.
unTokenOffset	The offset in bytes from the beginning of the resource to the untoken table, an array that maps token types back to the canonical strings that represent them.
defPartsOffset	
	The offset in bytes from the beginning of the resource to the number parts table, an array of characters that correspond to each part of a number format (used primarily by the FormatRecToString and StringToExtended functions).
whtSpListOffset	
	The offset in bytes from the beginning of the resource to the whitespace table, a list of all the characters that should be treated as whitespace—for example, blank and tab for the Roman script system.
resOffset7	(reserved)
resOffset8	(reserved)
resLength1	(reserved)
resLength2	(reserved)
resLength3	(reserved)
unTokenLength	The length in bytes of the untoken table.
defPartsLength	
	The length in bytes of the number parts table.
whtSpListLength	
	The length in bytes of the whitespace table.
resLength7	(reserved)
resLength8	(reserved)

The Token Table

The 'itl4' resource includes the token table, an array of type mapCharTable. The token table, also called the character-mapping table, maps each possible byte value in a 1-byte character set into a token type. Its format is shown in Figure B-12.

Figure B-12   Format of the token table

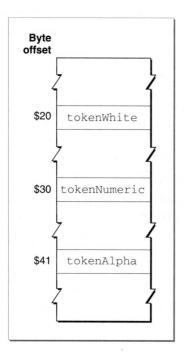

The table consists of 256 bytes. The byte offset of each location in the table represents a character code: location 0 represents a character code of 0, location 255 represents a character code of 255. Each location in the table contains a token code that represents the type of token corresponding to that character code. Constants for all defined token codes are listed in the chapter "Script Manager" in this book.

The token table is used to define tokens in 2-byte script systems also. Any location in the table that has a value of –1 represents the first byte of a 2-byte character. When it encounters such a byte, the IntlTokenize function calls the extension-fetching routine, described next, which analyzes that byte and the subsequent byte in the source text to determine what type of token is represented.

The Extension-Fetching Routine

The `IntlTokenize` function uses the extension-fetching routine to retrieve the second byte of a 2-byte character and determine what type of token should represent it. When `IntlTokenize` encounters a byte value in the source text that is represented by a –1 in the token table, `IntlTokenize` calls the extension-fetching routine with register A0 pointing to the second byte of the 2-byte character.

The extension-fetching routine consults internal, script-specific tables and returns the token code associated with the byte pair. `IntlTokenize` adds that token to the token list, and continues processing with the first byte following the byte pair.

The Token-String Copy Routine

When it creates a token list, the `IntlTokenize` function offers the option of also returning Pascal strings that are the normalized equivalents of the tokens it generates. `IntlTokenize` uses the token-string copy routine to create those strings and store them in a canonical format in a string list.

Canonical format means that the string-copy routine converts all numerals into standard ASCII numbers and converts the decimal separator to a period. For example, it would convert the Thai number "๒๔๘" into one token, `tokenAltNum`, with an associated Pascal string of `'248'`.

The Untoken Table

The **untoken table** provides a Pascal string for any type of fixed token. A **fixed token** is a token whose representation is unvarying, like punctuation. Alphabetic and numeric tokens are not fixed; specifying the token does not specify the string it represents.

The untoken table contains standard representations for the fixed tokens. You can use it to display the canonical format for any fixed token in the script system of the tokens resource.

The `unTokenTable` data type describes the format of the untoken table:

```
TYPE
    UntokenTable =
    RECORD
        len:         Integer;          {length of untoken table}
        lastToken:   Integer;          {maximum token code to be used}
        index:       ARRAY[0..255] OF Integer;
                                       {offsets to Pascal strings for }
                                       { tokens; last entry = lastToken}
    END;


    UntokenTablePtr        =   ^UntokenTable;
    UntokenTableHandle     =   ^UntokenTablePtr;
```

Field descriptions

`len`	The length in bytes of the untoken table.
`lastToken`	The highest token code used in this table (for range-checking).
`index`	An array of byte offsets from the beginning of the untoken table to Pascal strings—one for each possible token type—that give the canonical format for each fixed token type. The entries in the array correspond, in order, to token code values from 0 to `lastToken`. For example, the offset to the Pascal string for `tokenColonEqual` (token code = 39) is found at offset 39 in the array.

The string data directly follows the `index` array. It is a simple concatenation of Pascal strings; for example, the Pascal string for the token type `tokenColonEqual` may consist of a length byte (of value 2) followed by the characters ":=".

The Number Parts Table

The **number parts table** contains standard representations for the components of numbers and numeric strings. The Text Utilities number-formatting routines `StringToExtended` and `ExtendedToString` use the number parts table, along with a number-format string created by the `StringToFormatRec` and `FormatRecToString` routines, to create number strings in localized formats.

The `NumberParts` data type defines the number parts table:

```
TYPE NumberParts =
    RECORD
        version:        Integer;              {version of this table}
        data:           ARRAY[1..31] OF WideChar;
                                              {2-byte number parts}
        pePlus:         WideCharArr;          {positive exp. notation}
        peMinus:        WideCharArr;          {negative exp. notation}
        peMinusPlus:    WideCharArr;          {neg. or pos. exp.}
        altNumTable:    WideCharArr;          {alternate digits}
        reserved: PACKED ARRAY[0..19] OF Char;
                                              {reserved}
    END;
TYPE NumberPartsPtr = ^NumberParts;
```

`version`	An integer that specifies which version of the number parts table is being used. A value of 1 specifies the first version.
`data`	An array of 31 wide characters (2 bytes each), indexed by a set of constants. Each element of the array, accessed by one of the constants, contains 1 or 2 bytes that make up that number part. (If the element contains only one 1-byte character, it is in the low-order byte and the high-order byte contains 0.) Each number part, then, may consist of one or two 1-byte characters, or a single 2-byte character.

Of the 31 allotted spaces, 15 through 31 are reserved for up to 17 unquoted characters—special literals that do not need to be enclosed in quotes in a numeric string. See the discussion of number formatting in the chapter "Text Utilities" in this book for more information.

These are the defined constants for accessing number parts in the data array:

Constant	Value	Explanation
tokLeftQuote	1	Left quote
tokRightQuote	2	Right quote
tokLeadPlacer	3	Spacing leader format marker
tokLeader	4	Spacing leader character
tokNonLeader	5	No leader format marker
tokZeroLead	6	Zero leader format marker
tokPercent	7	Percent
tokPlusSign	8	Plus
tokMinusSign	9	Minus
tokThousands	10	Thousands separator
	11	(reserved)
tokSeparator	12	List separator
tokEscape	13	Escape character
tokDecPoint	14	Decimal separator
tokUnquoteds	15	(first unquoted character)
		(15 through 31 reserved)
tokMaxSymbols	31	Maximum symbol (for range check)

IMPORTANT

Note that these constants are unrelated to the token-type constants defined for the IntlTokenize function. ▲

pePlus

An array that specifies how to represent positive exponents for scientific notation. It is a wide character array, an 11-word data structure defined by the WideCharArr data type. It contains up to ten 1-byte or 2-byte number parts for representing positive exponents.

peMinus

An array that specifies how to represent negative exponents for scientific notation. It is a wide character array, an 11-word array defined by the WideCharArr data type. It contains up to ten 1-byte or 2-byte number parts for representing negative exponents.

International Resources

peMinusPlus	An array that specifies how to represent positive exponents for scientific notation when the format string exponent is negative. Symbols from this array can be used with the input number string to the `StringToExtended` function; they are not for use with the `StringToFormatRec` function. The array is a wide character array, an 11-word array defined by the `WideCharArr` data type. It contains up to ten 1-byte or 2-byte number parts for representing positive exponents.
altNumTable	A wide character array that specifies the alternate representation of numerals. The array contains ten character codes, each of which represents an alternate numeral. If the `smsfB0Digits` bit of the script-flags word is set, you should substitute the characters in this array for the character codes $30–$39 (regular ASCII numerals) in a string whose token code is `tokenAltNum` or `tokenAltReal`. Alternate numerals and the script flags word are described with the list of selectors for script variables in the chapter "Script Manager" in this book.
reserved	(reserved for future expansion)

The wide character (data type `WideChar`) is a format for representing a character that may be either 1 or 2 bytes long. For a 1-byte character, the high-order (first) byte in the record is 0, and the low-order (second) byte contains the character code. For a 2-byte character, the high-order byte is nonzero.

```
TYPE
    WideChar = RECORD
    CASE BOOLEAN OF
        TRUE:
            (a: PACKED ARRAY[0..1] OF Char);     {0 = high-order char}
        FALSE:
            (b: INTEGER);
    END;
```

The wide character array (data type `WideCharArr`) consists of an integer count followed by a packed array of wide characters.

```
TYPE
    WideCharArr = RECORD
        size: INTEGER;                               {no. of entries -1}
        data: PACKED ARRAY[0..9] OF WideChar;
    END;
```

Field descriptions

size	The number of items in the table minus 1.
data	Up to ten wide characters. If the number part is only a single 1-byte character, that character is in the low-order byte of the word.

The Whitespace Table

The whitespace table contains characters that may be used to indicate white space, such as blanks, tabs, and carriage returns. Figure B-13 shows the format of the whitespace table. Each entry pointed to by the table is a Pascal string specifying a single whitespace character (which may be 1 or 2 bytes long). The strings immediately follow the offset fields.

Figure B-13   Format of the whitespace table

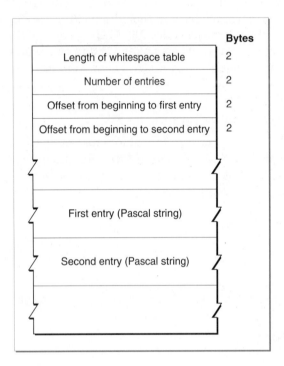

Encoding/Rendering Resource (Type 'itl5')

The encoding/rendering resource (resource type 'itl5') specifies character encoding or display behavior in a given script system. The resource has different formats and functions for 1-byte and 2-byte script systems. In 1-byte script systems, it specifies character rendering behavior. In 2-byte script systems, it contains byte-type and character-type information.

The encoding/rendering resource is optional; it does not exist for all script systems. The Roman script system does not include an 'itl5' resource.

The resource ID of an encoding/rendering resource is within the range of resource ID numbers for that script system. Although more than one encoding/rendering resource may be associated with a given script system, the script by default uses the resource specified in the itlbEncoding field of its international bundle ('itlb') resource.

Resource Header

The header for the encoding/rendering resource is the same for 1-byte and 2-byte script systems. Its format is general enough to allow new tables to be added in the future. This is the definition of the resource-header format:

```
TYPE   Itl5Record =
   RECORD
       versionNumber:     Fixed;
       numberOfTables:    Integer;
       reserved:          ARRAY[0..2] OF Integer;
       tableDirectory:    ARRAY[0..0] OF TableDirectoryRecord;
   END;
```

Field descriptions

versionNumber The version of this 'itl5' resource.

numberOfTables

The number of tables this resource contains.

reserved   (for internal use)

tableDirectory

A directory of all the tables in the resource. Each entry in the directory is a table directory record, with this format:

```
TYPE   TableDirectoryRecord =
   RECORD
       tableSignature:   OSType ;
       reserved:         LongInt;
       tableStartOffset: LongInt;
       tableSize:        LongInt;
   END;
```

Field descriptions

tableSignature

A 4-byte tag (of type OSType) that identifies the kind of table this record refers to.

reserved   (for internal use)

tableStartOffset

The number of bytes from the beginning of the resource to the beginning of the table.

tableSize   The length of the table, in bytes.

Tables for 1-Byte Script Systems

In 1-byte script systems, the encoding/rendering resource specifies character-rendering behavior. In general, only 1-byte complex script systems—those that work with the WorldScript I script extension—include an encoding/rendering resource. The defined table types at this time are

- Script configuration table

- Line-layout metamorphosis table

- Line-layout glyph-properties table

- Character-expansion table

- Glyph-to-character table

- Break-table directory

- `FindScriptRun` tables

- Feature-list table

- Kashida priorities table

- Reordering table

Script Configuration Table

The script configuration table (`OSType = 'info'`) defines certain settings that affect the characteristics of a script system. The table exists so that user preferences for script configuration can be saved in a preferences file, called the script preferences file, between system restarts.

The script configuration table consists of a 6-byte header followed by a set of table entries, each of which contains a `SetScriptVariable` selector. The table entries correspond to script settings that the user can make, typically through a script-system control panel.

The format of the script configuration table is shown in Figure B-14.

Figure B-14   Format of the script configuration table

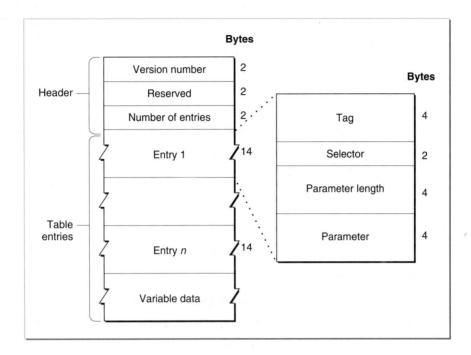

The resource header consists of three elements:

■ Version number. The version number of this resource. The major version number is in the high-order byte; the minor version number is in the low-order byte.

■ Reserved. A 2-byte reserved element.

■ Number of entries. The number of entries in the script configuration table.

The entries immediately follow the header. Each entry has four elements:

■ Tag. A 4-byte identifier of type OSType.

■ Selector. A selector to access a script variable through the Script Manager SetScriptVariable function.

■ Parameter length. The length of the parameter to pass to the SetScriptVariable function. This value always equals 4, unless this entry refers to variable-length data. See below.

■ Parameter. This element contains the parameter to pass to the SetScriptVariable function, unless this entry refers to variable-length data. See below.

For most entries in the script configuration table, the tag is 'long', the parameter length is 4 (the length of a SetScriptVariable parameter), and the parameter element contains the SetScriptVariable parameter. However, a table entry may reference variable-length data, such as a string representing the name of a script system.

Such data follows the last entry in the table, and its location is specified—as an offset from the beginning of the table—in the parameter element of the table entry that references it. The data length in bytes is specified in the parameter length element of that table entry.

For example, a Hebrew encoding/rendering resource might have a script configuration table with the information shown in Table B-8.

Table B-8   A script configuration table for a Hebrew encoding/rendering resource

Offset	Value	Explanation
00	0x0100	Version number (first release = 1.0)
02	0x0000	(reserved)
04	0x0004	Four tables follow

(The table entries start here)

Offset	Value	Explanation
06	'long'	The data type is a long
10	0x006	SetScriptVariable selector smScriptRight
12	0x0004	Four bytes follow
16	0xFFFF	–1 = right-to-left line direction
20	'long'	The data type is a long
24	0x0008	SetScriptVariable selector smScriptJust
26	0x0004	Four bytes follow
30	0xFFFF	–1 = right-aligned
34	'long'	The data type is a long
38	0x000A	SetScriptVariable selector smScriptRedraw
40	0x0004	Four bytes follow
44	0xFFFF	–1 = redraw entire line for each character
48	'pstr'	The data type is a Pascal string
52	0x002C	SetScriptVariable selector smScriptName
54	0x0008	The string is 8 bytes long (with length byte and pad)
58	62	Offset from beginning of table to data
62	0x6,'Hebrew'	The data string

In this case, the script configuration table causes the execution of four `SetScriptVariable` calls, to set the script's line direction, alignment, redraw characteristics, and name.

Each script system generally has two versions of the script configuration table: one in the encoding/rendering resource and one in a script preferences file in the Preferences folder within the user's System Folder. The table in the encoding/rendering resource has an `OSType` tag of `'info'`; the corresponding table in the preferences file is a resource of type `'CNFG'`. The script preferences file is a file of type `'pref'` with creator `'univ'`.

Both script configuration tables are used at startup. When installing a 1-byte complex script system, WorldScript I locates the script configuration table in the script's encoding/rendering resource, and loops through the table for as many times as there are entries in it, making a `SetScriptVariable` call for each entry. WorldScript I then looks for a `'CNFG'` resource for that script system in the script preferences file, and loops through that table. Thus a script system is always configured to its default settings at initialization, and then those settings are modified to reflect any user changes that have been saved. WorldScript I is described in the appendix "Built-in Script Support" in this book.

Line-Layout Metamorphosis Table

The line-layout metamorphosis table (`OSType = 'mort'`) specifies a set of transformations that the WorldScript I contextual formatting routines can apply to the glyphs of a font. WorldScript I is described in the appendix "Built-in Script Support" in this book.

A transformation can be something simple, such as a ligature, or something complex, such as a number of changes (ligatures plus ornateness of style plus positioning of glyphs in a word). These transformations are called text features in the context of the metamorphosis table. Each text feature can have different settings, or levels of operation.

These are the text features and settings currently supported by the contextual formatting routines in WorldScript I:

- Ligature formation. Whether to form ligatures and to what extent.

- Contextual ornateness. Whether to use contextual glyphs and which set of them to use.

- Noncontextual ornateness. Which of various style and case-substitution options to use.

- Character reordering. Whether or not to reorder characters.

- Diacritical marks. Whether to show diacritical marks, hide them, or make them separate glyphs.

The line-layout metamorphosis table is identical in format to the "glyph metamorphosis table" described in the currently unpublished document *TrueType GX Font Table Formats*, available from Macintosh Developer Technical Support.

Line-Layout Glyph-Properties Table

The line-layout glyph properties table (OSType = 'prop') defines the properties associated with each glyph in a font. Examples of a glyph's properties are its line direction and whether or not it is a space character.

The line-layout glyph properties table is identical in format to the "glyph properties table" described in the currently unpublished document *TrueType GX Font Table Formats*, available from Macintosh Developer Technical Support.

Character Expansion Table

The character expansion table (OSType = 'c2c#') gives multiple-character equivalents to compound characters in a script system's character set. This table expands ligatures into their component characters, analogous to expanding the Roman ligature "fi" into "f" and "i". The contextual formatting routines need the character expansion table because they are specifically designed to work with a script system's fundamental character codes.

Figure B-15 shows the format of the character expansion table.

Figure B-15   Format of the character expansion table

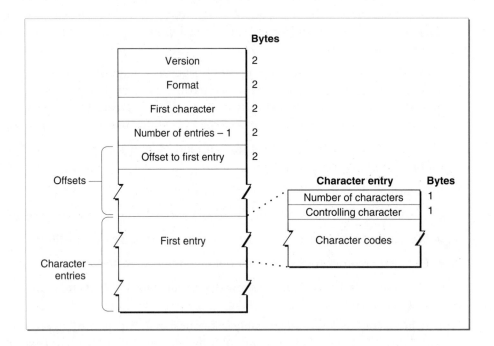

The table has these elements:

■ Version. The version number of this table. A value of $0100 means version 1.

■ Format. The format code, a number that identifies the format of this table.

- First character. The character code of the first character to be expanded.

- Number of entries – 1. The number of entries in this table, as a zero-based count.

- Offsets to entries. The offset from the beginning of the table to each character entry.

The character entries immediately follow the offsets. Because the table always covers a continuous range of a character set, the character code corresponding to each character entry is calculated as (first character) + (entry number), where the first character entry is numbered 0. Each character entry has these elements:

- The total number of (expanded) characters in this entry.

- The *controlling character,* the character whose position is considered equivalent to the position of the ligature as a whole. By analogy with Roman, the controlling character in the "fi" ligature might be considered the "f", so that a mouse-down event on the leading edge of the ligature would translate, after expansion, to a mouse-down event on the leading edge of the "f".

- The character codes of the characters that are the expanded equivalent to the character code for this entry.

Any character within the range of character codes for this table that does not have an expanded equivalent has a value of 0 for its offset.

Glyph-to-Character Table

The glyph-to-character table (OSType = 'pamc') maps 2-byte glyph indexes to 1-byte character codes, or to 1-byte glyph codes in bitmapped fonts whose font layouts do not exactly correspond to their script system's character encoding. The glyph-to-character table is conceptually the opposite of the TrueType character-code mapping table (type 'cmap'). It is used by the WorldScript I contextual formatting routines.

Figure B-16 shows the format of the glyph-to-character table.

Figure B-16   Format of the glyph-to-character table

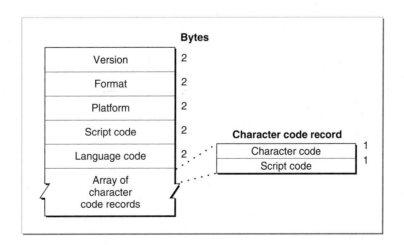

The table header has these elements:

■ Version. The version number of this table. A value of $0100 means version 1.

■ Format. The format code, a number that identifies the format of this table.

■ Platform. The computer system this table is designed for. A value of 1 means Macintosh.

■ Script code. The script system of this glyph set.

■ Language code. The language of this glyph set.

The table header is followed by an array of character code records. There is one record for each glyph index, which ranges from zero to a maximum value that can be greater than $FF. Each character code record has two elements:

■ Character code. The character code corresponding to this glyph code.

■ Script code. The script system of the character. For example, most glyphs that map to low-ASCII characters have a script code of smRoman in their character code record.

Break-Table Directory

The break-table directory (OSType = 'fwrd') provides access to one or more break tables (of type NBreakTable) for use by the Text Utilities FindWordBreaks procedure. It consists of a header, followed by entries that give offsets to the break tables, followed by the break tables themselves. Figure B-17 shows the format of the break-table directory.

Figure B-17   Format of the break-table directory

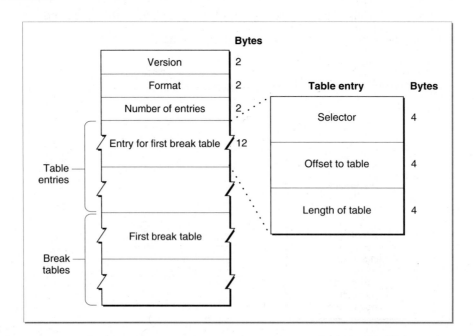

The directory header has these elements:

■ Version. The version number of this directory. A value of $0100 means version 1.

■ Format. Another type of version number.

■ Number of entries. The number of entries, and therefore the number of break tables, in this directory.

The table entries consist of three elements each:

■ Selector. A number that designates the specific type of break table referenced by this entry. The currently defined values are 0, signifying a table for word selection, and –1, signifying a table for line-breaking. These are the same default values that may be passed as break-table pointers to the `FindWordBreaks` procedure.

■ Offset to table. The byte offset from the beginning of the directory to the break table referenced by this entry.

■ Length of table. The length in bytes of the break table referenced by this entry.

The break tables themselves follow the table entries.

Most script systems' break tables are in their string-manipulation (`'itl2'`) resources. For some 1-byte complex script systems, break tables are in the encoding/rendering resource so that the Script Manager routines for replacing the WorldScript I script utilities will function correctly. See the discussions of the `GetScriptUtilityAddress` and `SetScriptUtilityAddress` routines in the chapter "Script Manager" in this book, and the discussion of WorldScript I in the appendix "Built-in Script Support."

Script Run Tables

Typically, tables to control the Text Utilities `FindScriptRun` function are in a script system's string-manipulation (`'itl2'`) resource. For some 1-byte complex script systems, the script run tables (`OSType = 'fstb'`) are in the encoding/rendering resource so that the Script Manager routines for replacing the WorldScript I script utilities will function correctly.

The set of script run tables in the encoding/rendering resource consists of a header followed by one or more tables. The header has this format:

■ Version number (2 bytes).

■ Format code (2 bytes).

■ Chain header (12 bytes). This part of the header is identical in format to the chain header in the line-layout metamorphosis table (see page B-63).

The header is followed by one or more tables. Each script run table consists of a table flags element (4 bytes), followed by a table identical to the new-format script run table in the string-manipulation resource. See "Script Run Table Format" beginning on page B-40.

For more information, see the discussions of the `GetScriptUtilityAddress` and `SetScriptUtilityAddress` routines in the chapter "Script Manager" in this book, and the discussion of WorldScript I in the appendix "Built-in Script Support."

Kashida Preferences Table

The kashida preferences table (OSType = 'kash'), used in Arabic versions of the encoding/rendering resource, maps each glyph code to a kashida priority class. It specifies which glyphs can have kashida inserted between them, in what priority, when justifying Arabic text.

Feature List Table

The feature list table (OSType = 'flst') contains information used to override default line-layout behaviors (features) specified in the metamorphosis table (page B-63). It includes an array of feature entries, each of which specifies a feature type and a setting for that feature.

Reordering Table

The reordering table (OSType = 'reor') is a state table that specifies the classes and states used to reorder glyphs for contextual formatting. The reordering table contains offsets to three state tables and two arrays of level adjustments. The WorldScript I contextual formatting routine makes a first pass to resolve ordering of numbers, a second pass to resolve neutrals (whitespace, number separators, and terminators), and a third pass (using the values in the level adjustments arrays) to adjust nesting levels for each glyph. Finally, the routine reorders the line according to the resolved nesting levels.

Tables for 2-Byte Script Systems

In 2-byte script systems, the encoding/rendering resource contains byte-type and character-type information. The tables immediately follow the directory in the 'itl5' header.

A byte-type table contains character-size information about a specific byte in the range of $00 to $FF. A character-type table contains detailed information about the character represented by a specific byte, given a particular character-encoding scheme.

Table B-9 shows the general structure of a typical encoding/rendering resource for a 2-byte script system.

Table B-9   Sample encoding/rendering resource for a 2-byte script system

Offset	Value	Explanation
0	$00010000	Version number (first release = 1.0)
4	2	Two tables in this resource
6	$000000000000	(reserved)
12	'btyp'	Tag for byte-type table
16	$00000000	(reserved)
20	30	Offset to the byte-type table

Table B-9   Sample encoding/rendering resource for a 2-byte script system (continued)

Offset	Value	Explanation
24	256	Length of the byte-type table
28	`'ctyp'`	Tag for the character-type table
32	$00000000	(reserved)
36	286	Offset to the character-type table
40	variable	Length of the character-type table
44		Start of byte-type table (256 bytes long)
300		Start of character-type table

Byte-Type Table

A byte-type table has 256 integer entries, one for each possible byte value in the range
$00 to $FF. Each byte value is an index into the table. At each byte value, the table entry
can have one of three values, specifying what kind of character or part of a character that
byte value can represent.

- 1 = 1-byte character only

- 0 = 1-byte character or low-order byte of a 2-bye character

- –1 = high-order or low-order byte of a 2-byte character

When processing text sequentially in a buffer, you encounter a 2-byte character's
high-order byte before its low-order byte. Thus you can determine the character
relationship of a given byte (1-byte or 2-byte, high-order or low-order byte) by
determining its byte type and, if necessary, comparing it with the byte type of the
previous byte in the buffer.

Character-Type Table

The character-type table consists of one high-order byte table and a series of low-order
byte tables.

The high-order byte table contains 256 word-length entries. The index position of each
entry represents a high-order byte value. Nonzero entries mark valid high-order bytes of
a 2-byte character. If a given entry is nonzero, it specifies which low-order byte table to
consult to get character-type information.

There are one or more low-order byte tables, each of which can contain either a single
entry or 256 word-length entries. If all low-order bytes for a given high-order byte have
the same character type, the low-order byte "table" for that high-order byte consists of a
single character-type value. Otherwise, every possible low-order byte is represented by
an index into the table, with an appropriate character-type value at each valid index
position.

For example, to find character-type information for the Japanese character with character code $EA40, you would examine location $EA in the high-order byte table; it would indicate the existence of a low-order byte table, and in that table you would examine location $40. That location would contain information showing that the character is a 2-byte JIS level-2 ideographic character that is part of the main character set.

Character types are discussed under the description of the `CharacterType` function in the chapter "Script Manager" in this book.

Transliteration Resource (Type 'trsl')

The transliteration resource (resource type `'trsl'`) contains information used by the Script Manager `TransliterateText` function, which performs phonetic conversion among subscripts in 2-byte script systems.

The transliteration resource is optional. Currently, no 1-byte script systems, including the Roman script system, have transliteration resources. All 2-byte script systems have transliteration resources.

The resource ID for a transliteration resource is within the range of resource ID numbers for its script system. There is one transliteration resource for each kind of transliteration supported by the script system. The name of an individual `'trsl'` resource, such as "Jamo to Hangul", specifies the kind of transliteration that the resource performs.

There are two formats for the transliteration resource: one supplies table-based transliteration from Jamo and Hangul, and vice versa, in the Korean script system; the other provides a more general rule-based transliteration.

Note
In the Roman script system, and for Roman text within other script systems, the `TransliterateText` function performs case conversion. The tables that control case conversion are in a script system's string-manipulation (`'itl2'`) resource, not in a transliteration resource. ◆

Resource Header

Figure B-18 shows the format of the transliteration resource header.

Figure B-18   Format of the transliteration resource header

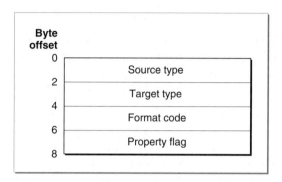

The resource header is the same for both the table-based and the rule-based formats:

■ Source type. The type of text to perform the transliteration on. Specified by an integer; the currently defined mask constants for source type are listed under the discussion of the `TransliterateText` function in the chapter "Script Manager" in this book.

■ Target type. The type of text to convert to. Specified by an integer; the currently defined target format constants are listed under the discussion of the `TransliterateText` function in the chapter "Script Manager" in this book.

■ Format code. A number that identifies the format of this transliteration resource.

■ Property flag. A bit field that specifies the kinds of operations to perform on a piece of text before or after transliteration. These are the currently defined bits of the property flag:

Bit number	Operation
1	Convert all 1-byte characters into 2-byte characters before performing the transliteration.
2	Convert all Roman characters to uppercase before performing the transliteration.

The property flag is needed because of the complex nature of the Chinese, Japanese, and Korean character sets, which include 1-byte and 2-byte characters as well as lowercase and uppercase characters. For example, to transliterate the Roman string "ki" into 2-byte Hiragana characters, the two-character string could be interpreted with as many as eight combinations of 1-byte Roman, 2-byte Roman, uppercase, and lowercase characters.

To simplify matters the transliteration resource allows you to convert your source text into a common set of characters before it matches them against the transliteration rules. So, to translate the Roman string "ki" into Hiragana, you can first convert the characters into their 2-byte equivalents, then convert them into uppercase, and then perform the transliteration.

Note

In most 2-byte transliteration resources, bits 1 and 2 in the property flag are set (= 1). The reason for the preliminary conversion of all source text to 2 bytes is that 2-byte Katakana is a superset of all the Katakana characters; thus, it is possible to convert all the 1-byte Katakana characters to 2-byte characters but not vice versa. ◆

Rule-Based Format

In the rule-based version of the transliteration resource, the header is followed immediately by a 2-byte field containing a count of the number of rules in the resource; the rules immediately follow the count field and constitute the remainder of the resource. This is the definition of the rule-based resource header:

```
TYPE  RuleBasedTrslRecord =
    RECORD
        sourceType:    Integer; {target type for left side of rule}
        targetType:    Integer; {target type for right side of rule}
        formatNumber:  Integer; {format of this resource}
        propertyFlag:  Integer; {transliteration property flags}
        numberOfRules: Integer; {number of rules that follow}
    END;
```

Figure B-19 shows the format of a rule.

Figure B-19   Format of a transliteration rule

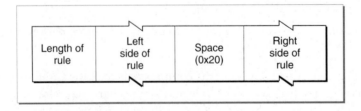

- The length of the rule is a byte that specifies the actual number of bytes in the rule, excluding the length byte itself.

■ The left side of the rule contains the source pattern, a sequence of one or more character codes that the `TransliterateText` function compares to the source string. If it finds a match, it returns the right side of the rule (the target pattern). The rules are organized to implement the *longest match* algorithm, meaning that the longest source pattern that matches a particular target pattern is the one that is converted. For instance, the rule

abb → hello

takes precedence over the rule

ab → hello

Some rules in some versions of the transliteration resource incorporate a look-ahead feature, in which a particular source pattern is converted to its target pattern only if it is followed by other specific characters. For example, if "[" represents the look-ahead symbol, the characters preceding it in the left side of the rule are converted to the right side of the rule only if the characters following "[" in the left side of the rule match the subsequent characters in the input string.

If these are the matching rules:

Left side	Rignt side
a[bc	A
b	B
c	C
d[ef	D
f	F

Then if we have the input string

abcdf

the output string will be:

ABCdF

because, in the input string, the characters "bc" follow "a", but the characters "ef" do not follow "d".

Table-Based Format

The Jamo-to-Hangul transliteration resource contains a set of conversion tables. The structure of the tables is private.

Jamo-to-Hangul transliteration is used by the input method supplied with the Korean script system; see the discussion of input methods in the chapter "Introduction to Text on the Macintosh" in this book.

Summary of the International Resources

Pascal Summary

Constants

```
{ Bits in the itlcFlags byte.}
itlcShowIcon = 7;                    {show icon even if only one script}
itlcDualCaret = 6;                   {use dual caret for mixed direction text}

{ Bits in the itlcSysFlags word.}
itlcSysDirection = 15;            {system direction - left/right or right/left}

{ the NumberParts indices }
tokLeftQuote = 1;
tokRightQuote = 2;
tokLeadPlacer = 3;
tokLeader = 4;
tokNonLeader = 5;
tokZeroLead = 6;
tokPercent = 7;
tokPlusSign = 8;
tokMinusSign = 9;
tokThousands = 10;
tokSeparator = 12;                   {11 is a reserved field}
tokEscape = 13;
tokDecPoint = 14;
tokUnquoteds = 15;
tokMaxSymbols = 31;

curNumberPartsVersion = 1; {current version of NumberParts record}

currSymLead = 16;
currNegSym = 32;
currTrailingZ = 64;
currLeadingZ = 128;
```

```
zeroCycle = 1;                {0:00 AM/PM format}
longDay = 0;                  {day of the month}
longWeek = 1;                 {day of the week}
longMonth = 2;                {month of the year}
longYear = 3;                 {year}
supDay = 1;                   {suppress day of month}
supWeek = 2;                  {suppress day of week}
supMonth = 4;                 {suppress month}
supYear = 8;                  {suppress year}
dayLdingZ = 32;
mntLdingZ = 64;
century = 128;
secLeadingZ = 32;
minLeadingZ = 64;
hrLeadingZ = 128;

{ Date Orders }
mdy = 0;
dmy = 1;
ymd = 2;
myd = 3;
dym = 4;
ydm = 5;
```

Data Types

```
TYPE   ItlcRecord =
       RECORD
           itlcSystem:        Integer;     {default system script}
           itlcReserved:      Integer;     {reserved}
           itlcFontForce:     SignedByte;  {default font force flag}
           itlcIntlForce:     SignedByte;  {default intl force flag}
           itlcOldKybd:       SignedByte;  {MacPlus intl keybd flag}
           itlcFlags:         SignedByte;  {general flags}
           itlcIconOffset:    Integer;     {reserved}
           itlcIconSide:      SignedByte;  {reserved}
           itlcIconRsvd:      SignedByte;  {reserved}
           itlcRegionCode:    Integer;     {preferred verXxx code}
           itlcSysFlags:      Integer;     {flags for setting system globals}
           itlcReserved4:     ARRAY[0..31] OF SignedByte;    {for future use}
       END;
```

```
ItlbRecord =
RECORD
    itlbNumber:      Integer;      {itl0 id number}
    itlbDate:        Integer;      {itl1 id number}
    itlbSort:        Integer;      {itl2 id number}
    itlbFlags:       Integer;      {Script flags}
    itlbToken:       Integer;      {itl4 id number}
    itlbEncoding:    Integer;      {itl5 ID # (optional; char encoding)}
    itlbLang:        Integer;      {current language for script }
    itlbNumRep:      SignedByte;   {number representation code}
    itlbDateRep:     SignedByte;   {date representation code }
    itlbKeys:        Integer;      {KCHR id number}
    itlbIcon:        Integer;      {ID# of SICN or kcs#/kcs4/kcs8 family}
END;

ItlbExtRecord =
RECORD
    base:             ItlbRecord;   {unextended ItlbRecord}
    itlbLocalSize:    LongInt;      {size of script's local record}
    itlbMonoFond:     Integer;      {default monospace FOND ID}
    itlbMonoSize:     Integer;      {default monospace font size}
    itlbPrefFond:     Integer;      {preferred FOND ID}
    itlbPrefSize:     Integer;      {preferred font size}
    itlbSmallFond:    Integer;      {default small FOND ID}
    itlbSmallSize:    Integer;      {default small font size}
    itlbSysFond:      Integer;      {default system FOND ID}
    itlbSysSize:      Integer;      {default system font size}
    itlbAppFond:      Integer;      {default application FOND ID}
    itlbAppSize:      Integer;      {default application font size}
    itlbHelpFond:     Integer;      {default Help Mgr FOND ID}
    itlbHelpSize:     Integer;      {default Help Mgr font size}
    itlbValidStyles:  Style;        {set of valid styles for script}
    itlbAliasStyle:   Style;        {style (set) to mark aliases}
END;

Intl0Rec =
PACKED RECORD
    decimalPt:    Char; {decimal point character}
    thousSep:     Char; {thousands separator character}
    listSep:      Char; {list separator character}
    currSym1:     Char; {currency symbol}
    currSym2:     Char;
    currSym3:     Char;
    currFmt:      Byte; {currency format flags}
```

```
     dateOrder:        Byte; {order of short date elements: mdy, dmy, etc.}
     shrtDateFmt:      Byte; {format flags for each short date element}
     dateSep:          Char; {date separator character}
     timeCycle:        Byte; {specifies time cycle: 0..23, 1..12, or 0..11}
     timeFmt:          Byte; {format flags for each time element}
     mornStr:          PACKED ARRAY[1..4] OF Char;
                             {trailing string for AM if 12-hour cycle}
     eveStr:           PACKED ARRAY[1..4] OF Char;
                             {trailing string for PM if 12-hour cycle}
     timeSep:          Char; {time separator character}
     time1Suff:        Char; {trailing string for AM if 24-hour cycle}
     time2Suff:        Char;
     time3Suff:        Char;
     time4Suff:        Char;
     time5Suff:        Char; {trailing string for PM if 24-hour cycle}
     time6Suff:        Char;
     time7Suff:        Char;
     time8Suff:        Char;
     metricSys:        Byte; {255 if metric, 0 if inches etc.}
     intl0Vers:        Integer;
                             {region code (hi byte) and version (lo byte)}
END;
Intl0Ptr = ^Intl0Rec;
Intl0Hndl = ^Intl0Ptr;

Intl1Rec =
PACKED RECORD
     days:             ARRAY[1..7] OF Str15;       {day names}
     months:           ARRAY[1..12] OF Str15;      {month names}
     suppressDay:      Byte;
                            {255 for no day, or flags to suppress any element}
     lngDateFmt:       Byte;        {order of long date elements}
     dayLeading0:      Byte;        {255 for leading 0 in day number}
     abbrLen:          Byte;        {length for abbreviating names}
     st0:              PACKED ARRAY[1..4] OF Char;
                             {separator strings for long date format}
     st1:              PACKED ARRAY[1..4] OF Char;
     st2:              PACKED ARRAY[1..4] OF Char;
     st3:              PACKED ARRAY[1..4] OF Char;
     st4:              PACKED ARRAY[1..4] OF Char;
     intl1Vers:        Integer;
                             {region code (hi byte) and version (lo byte)}
     localRtn:         ARRAY[0..0] OF Integer;
                             {a flag for optional extension}
```

```
END;
Intl1Ptr = ^Intl1Rec;
Intl1Hndl = ^Intl1Ptr;

Itl1ExtRec =
RECORD
    base:                      Intl1Rec; {un-extended Intl1Rec}
    version:                   Integer; {version number}
    format:                    Integer; {format code}
    calendarCode:              Integer; {calendar code for 'itl1'}
    extraDaysTableOffset:      LongInt; {offset to extra days table}
    extraDaysTableLength:      LongInt; {length of extra days table}
    extraMonthsTableOffset:    LongInt; {offset to extra months table}
    extraMonthsTableLength:    LongInt; {length of extra months table}
    abbrevDaysTableOffset:     LongInt; {offset to abbrev. days table}
    abbrevDaysTableLength:     LongInt; {length of abbrev. days table}
    abbrevMonthsTableOffset:   LongInt; {offset to abbr. months table}
    abbrevMonthsTableLength:   LongInt; {length of abbr. months table}
    extraSepsTableOffset:      LongInt; {offset to extra seps table}
    extraSepsTableLength:      LongInt; {length of extra seps table}
    tables:                    ARRAY[0..0] OF Integer;
                                   {the tables; variable-length}
END;

NItl4Rec =
RECORD
    flags:          Integer; {reserved}
    resourceType:   LongInt; {contains 'itl4'}
    resourceNum:    Integer; {resource ID}
    version:        Integer; {version number}
    format:         Integer; {format code}
    resHeader:      Integer; {reserved}
    resHeader2:     LongInt; {reserved}
    numTables:      Integer; {number of tables, one-based}
    mapOffset:      LongInt; {table that maps byte to token}
    strOffset:      LongInt; {routine that copies string}
    fetchOffset:    LongInt; {routine to get next byte of character}
    unTokenOffset:  LongInt; {table that maps token to string}
    defPartsOffset: LongInt; {offset to default number parts table}
    whtSpListOffset: LongInt; {offset to whitespace table}
    resOffset7:     LongInt; {reserved}
    resOffset8:     LongInt; {reserved}
    resLength1:     Integer; {reserved}
    resLength2:     Integer; {reserved}
```

```
            resLength3:         Integer; {reserved}
            unTokenLength:      Integer; {length of untoken table}
            defPartsLength:     Integer; {length of number parts table}
            whtSpListLength:    Integer; {length of whitespace table}
            resLength7:         Integer; {reserved}
            resLength8:         Integer; {reserved}
        END;
        NItl4Ptr = ^NItl4Rec;
        NItl4Handle = ^NItl4Ptr;

        UntokenTable =
        RECORD
            len:        Integer;
            lastToken:  Integer;
            index:      ARRAY[0..255] OF Integer;  {index table; last=lastToken}
        END;
        UntokenTablePtr = ^UntokenTable;
        UntokenTableHandle = ^UntokenTablePtr;


WideChar = RECORD
    CASE Boolean OF
        TRUE:
          (a: PACKED ARRAY[0..1] OF Char);{0 is the high order character}
        FALSE:
          (b: Integer);
    END;


WideCharArr = RECORD
    size: Integer;
    data: PACKED ARRAY[0..9] OF WideChar;
    END;

    NumberParts =
    RECORD
        version:        Integer;
        data:           ARRAY[1..31] OF WideChar;
        pePlus:         WideCharArr;
        peMinus:        WideCharArr;
        peMinusPlus:    WideCharArr;
        altNumTable:    WideCharArr;
        reserved:       PACKED ARRAY[0..19] OF Char;
    END;
    NumberPartsPtr = ^NumberParts;
```

```
    Itl5Record =
    RECORD
        versionNumber:     Fixed;               {itl5 resource version number}
        numberOfTables:    Integer;             {number of tables it contains}
        reserved:          ARRAY[0..2] OF Integer;
                                                {reserved for internal use}
        tableDirectory:    ARRAY[0..0] OF TableDirectoryRecord;
                                                {table directory records}
    END;

    TableDirectoryRecord =
    RECORD
        tableSignature:    OSType ;     {4 byte long table name}
        reserved:          LongInt;     {reserved for internal use}
        tableStartOffset:  LongInt ;    {table start offset in bytes}
        tableSize:         LongInt;     {table size in bytes}
    END;

    RuleBasedTrslRecord =
    RECORD
        sourceType:     Integer;     {target type for left side of rule}
        targetType:     Integer;     {target type for right side of rule}
        formatNumber:   Integer;     {transliteration resource format number}
        propertyFlag:   Integer;     {transliteration property flags}
        numberOfRules:  Integer;     {Number of rules following this field}
    END;
```

C Summary

Constants

```
enum {

/* Bits in the itlcFlags byte. */
  itlcShowIcon = 7,              /*show icon even if only one script*/
  itlcDualCaret = 6,             /*use dual caret for mixed direction text*/

/* Bits in the itlcSysFlags word. */
  itlcSysDirection = 15,         /*System direction--left/right or right/left*/
```

```
/* the NumberParts indices */
 tokLeftQuote = 1,
 tokRightQuote = 2,
 tokLeadPlacer = 3,
 tokLeader = 4,
 tokNonLeader = 5,

tokZeroLead = 6,
 tokPercent = 7,
 tokPlusSign = 8,
 tokMinusSign = 9,
 tokThousands = 10,
 tokSeparator = 12,                 /*11 is a reserved field*/
 tokEscape = 13,
 tokDecPoint = 14,
 tokUnquoteds = 15,
 tokMaxSymbols = 31,

    curNumberPartsVersion = 1       /*current version of NumberParts record*/
};

enum {
 currSymLead = 16,
 currNegSym = 32,
 currTrailingZ = 64,
 currLeadingZ = 128,
};

enum {mdy,dmy,ymd,myd,dym,ydm};

enum {
 zeroCycle = 1,                     /*0:00 AM/PM format*/
 longDay = 0,                       /*day of the month*/
 longWeek = 1,                      /*day of the week*/
 longMonth = 2,                     /*month of the year*/
 longYear = 3,                      /*year*/
 supDay = 1,                        /*suppress day of month*/
 supWeek = 2,                       /*suppress day of week*/
 supMonth = 4,                      /*suppress month*/
 supYear = 8,                       /*suppress year*/
 dayLdingZ = 32,
 mntLdingZ = 64,
 century = 128,
 secLeadingZ = 32,
```

```
 minLeadingZ = 64,
 hrLeadingZ = 128
};
```

Data Types

```
typedef unsigned char DateOrders;

struct ItlcRecord {
  short itlcSystem;           /*default system script*/
  short itlcReserved;         /*reserved*/
  char itlcFontForce;         /*default font force flag*/
  char itlcIntlForce;         /*default intl force flag*/
  char itlcOldKybd;           /*MacPlus intl keybd flag*/
  char itlcFlags;             /*general flags*/
  short itlcIconOffset;       /*reserved*/
  char itlcIconSide;          /*reserved*/
  char itlcIconRsvd;          /*reserved*/
  short itlcRegionCode;       /*preferred verXxx code*/
  short itlcSysFlags;         /*flags for setting system globals*/
  char itlcReserved4[32];     /*for future use*/
};
typedef struct ItlcRecord ItlcRecord;

struct ItlbRecord {
  short itlbNumber;           /*itl0 id number*/
  short itlbDate;             /*itl1 id number*/
  short itlbSort;             /*itl2 id number*/
  short itlbFlags;            /*Script flags*/
  short itlbToken;            /*itl4 id number*/
  short itlbEncoding;         /*itl5 ID # (optional; char encoding)*/
  short itlbLang;             /*current language for script */
  char itlbNumRep;            /*number representation code*/
  char itlbDateRep;           /*date representation code */
  short itlbKeys;             /*KCHR id number*/
  short itlbIcon;             /*ID # of SICN or kcs#/kcs4/kcs8 family.*/
};
typedef struct ItlbRecord ItlbRecord;

/* New ItlbExtRecord structure for System 7 */
struct ItlbExtRecord {
  ItlbRecord base;            /*unextended ItlbRecord*/
  long itlbLocalSize;         /*size of script's local record*/
```

```
   short itlbMonoFond;          /*default monospace FOND ID*/
   short itlbMonoSize;          /*default monospace font size*/
   short itlbPrefFond;          /*preferred FOND ID*/

short itlbPrefSize;            /*preferred font size*/
   short itlbSmallFond;         /*default small FOND ID*/
   short itlbSmallSize;         /*default small font size*/
   short itlbSysFond;           /*default system FOND ID*/
   short itlbSysSize;           /*default system font size*/
   short itlbAppFond;           /*default application FOND ID*/
   short itlbAppSize;           /*default application font size*/
   short itlbHelpFond;          /*default Help Mgr FOND ID*/
   short itlbHelpSize;          /*default Help Mgr font size*/
   Style itlbValidStyles;       /*set of valid styles for script*/
   Style itlbAliasStyle;        /*style (set) to mark aliases*/
};
typedef struct ItlbExtRecord ItlbExtRecord;

struct Intl0Rec {
 char decimalPt;/*decimal point character*/
 char thousSep;/*thousands separator character*/
 char listSep; /*list separator character*/
 char currSym1;/*currency symbol*/
 char currSym2;
 char currSym3;
 unsigned char currFmt;         /*currency format flags*/
 unsigned char dateOrder;       /*order of short date elements:mdy,dmy,etc.*/
 unsigned char shrtDateFmt;     /*format flags for each short date element*/
 char dateSep;                  /*date separator character*/
 unsigned char timeCycle;       /*specifies time cycle:0..23,1..12,or 0..11*/
 unsigned char timeFmt;         /*format flags for each time element*/
 char mornStr[4];               /*trailing string for AM if 12-hour cycle*/
 char eveStr[4];                /*trailing string for PM if 12-hour cycle*/
 char timeSep;                  /*time separator character*/
 char time1Suff;                /*trailing string for AM if 24-hour cycle*/
 char time2Suff;
 char time3Suff;
 char time4Suff;
 char time5Suff;                /*trailing string for PM if 24-hour cycle*/
 char time6Suff;
 char time7Suff;
 char time8Suff;
 unsigned char metricSys;       /*255 if metric, 0 if inches etc.*/
 short intl0Vers;               /*region code (hi byte) and version (lo byte)*/
```

```
};
typedef struct Intl0Rec Intl0Rec;
typedef Intl0Rec *Intl0Ptr, **Intl0Hndl;

struct Intl1Rec {
 Str15 days[7];                  /*day names*/
 Str15 months[12];               /*month names*/
 unsigned char suppressDay;      /*255 = no day, or flags to suppress elements*/
 unsigned char lngDateFmt;       /*order of long date elements*/
 unsigned char dayLeading0;      /*255 for leading 0 in day number*/
 unsigned char abbrLen;          /*length for abbreviating names*/
 char st0[4];                    /*separator strings for long date format*/
 char st1[4];
 char st2[4];
 char st3[4];
 char st4[4];
 short intl1Vers;                /*region code (hi byte) and version (lo byte)*/
 short localRtn[1];              /*now a flag for opt extension*/
};
typedef struct Intl1Rec Intl1Rec;
typedef Intl1Rec *Intl1Ptr, **Intl1Hndl;

struct Itl1ExtRec {                     /*fields for optional itl1 extension*/
 Intl1Rec base;                         /*un-extended Intl1Rec*/
 short version;
 short format;
 short calendarCode;                    /*calendar code for this itl1 resource*/
 long extraDaysTableOffset;             /*offset in itl1 to extra days table*/
 long extraDaysTableLength;             /*length of extra days table*/
 long extraMonthsTableOffset;           /*offset in itl1 to extra months table*/
 long extraMonthsTableLength;           /*length of extra months table*/
 long abbrevDaysTableOffset;            /*offset in itl1 to abbrev days table*/
 long abbrevDaysTableLength;            /*length of abbrev days table*/
 long abbrevMonthsTableOffset;          /*offset in itl1 to abbrev months table*/
 long abbrevMonthsTableLength;          /*length of abbrev months table*/
 long extraSepsTableOffset;             /*offset in itl1 to extra seps table*/
 long extraSepsTableLength;             /*length of extra seps table*/
 short tables[1];                       /*now a flag for opt extension*/
};
typedef struct Itl1ExtRec Itl1ExtRec;

struct UntokenTable {
 short len;
 short lastToken;
```

```
  short index[256];              /*index table; last = lastToken*/
};
typedef struct UntokenTable UntokenTable;
typedef UntokenTable *UntokenTablePtr, **UntokenTableHandle;

union WideChar {
 char a[2];                      /*0 is the high-order character*/
 short b;
};
typedef union WideChar WideChar;

struct WideCharArr {
 short size;
 WideChar data[10];
};
typedef struct WideCharArr WideCharArr;

struct NumberParts {
 short version;
 WideChar data[31];             /*index by [tokLeftQuote..tokMaxSymbols]*/
 WideCharArr pePlus;
 WideCharArr peMinus;
 WideCharArr peMinusPlus;
 WideCharArr altNumTable;
 char reserved[20];
};
typedef struct NumberParts NumberParts;
typedef NumberParts *NumberPartsPtr;

/* New NItl4Rec for System 7.0: */
struct NItl4Rec {
 short flags;           /*reserved*/
 long resourceType;     /*contains 'itl4'*/
 short resourceNum;     /*resource ID*/
 short version;         /*version number*/
 short format;          /*format code*/
 short resHeader;       /*reserved*/
 long resHeader2;       /*reserved*/
 short numTables;       /*number of tables, one-based*/
 long mapOffset;        /*offset to table that maps byte to token*/
 long strOffset;        /*offset to routine that copies canonical string*/
 long fetchOffset;      /*offset to routine that gets next byte of char.*/
 long unTokenOffset;    /*offset to table that maps token to canon. string*/
 long defPartsOffset;   /*offset to number parts table*/
```

```
long whtSpListOffset;   /*offset to whitespace table*/
long resOffset7;        /*reserved*/
long resOffset8;        /*reserved*/
short resLength1;       /*reserved*/
short resLength2;       /*reserved*/
short resLength3;       /*reserved*/
short unTokenLength;    /*length of untoken table*/
short defPartsLength;   /*length of default number parts table*/
short whtSpListLength;  /*length of whitespace table*/
short resLength7;       /*reserved*/
short resLength8;       /*reserved*/
};
typedef struct NItl4Rec NItl4Rec;
typedef NItl4Rec *NItl4Ptr, **NItl4Handle;

struct TableDirectoryRecord {
 OSType tableSignature;          /*4 byte long table name */
 unsigned long reserved;         /*reserved for internal use */
 unsigned long tableStartOffset; /*table start offset in byte*/
 unsigned long tableSize;        /*table size in byte*/
 };
typedef struct TableDirectoryRecord TableDirectoryRecord;

struct Itl5Record {
 Fixed versionNumber;                      /*itl5 resource version number */
 unsigned short numberOfTables;            /*number of tables it contains */
 unsigned short reserved[3];               /*reserved for internal use */
 TableDirectoryRecord tableDirectory[1];   /*table directory records */
 };
typedef struct Itl5Record Itl5Record;

struct RuleBasedTrslRecord {
 short sourceType;      /*target type for left side of rule */
 short targetType;      /*target type for right side of rule */
 short formatNumber;    /*transliteration resource format number */
 short propertyFlag;    /*transliteration property flags */
 short numberOfRules;   /*number of rules following this field */
 };
typedef struct RuleBasedTrslRecord RuleBasedTrslRecord;
```

Keyboard Resources

Contents

This appendix describes the Macintosh keyboard resources. The keyboard resources make text input possible; they provide a hardware interface to different types of keyboards and a software interface to different script systems. Some of the keyboard resources belong to an individual script system and are independent of any particular keyboard; others belong to a type of keyboard and are independent of any script system.

By installing the appropriate keyboard resources, you can perform text input in any script system, from any Macintosh-supported keyboard. By modifying the keyboard resources, you can localize or customize text input by changing keyboard layouts, remapping key combinations, creating keyboard icons, modifying the keyboard-layout display in the Key Caps desk accessory, and changing the way the user switches among keyboard layouts and keyboard scripts.

Most text-processing applications have no need for direct access to keyboard resources. You may need to read this appendix, however, if you are

■ using the Event Manager `KeyTranslate` function to get specific information from a custom keyboard-layout resource or to make Command-key handling more script-independent

■ creating your own localized version of a script system

■ designing a new type of keyboard

Before reading this appendix, read the chapter "Introduction to Text on the Macintosh" in this book. The keyboard resources are used by the Script Manager, described in this book, and by the Event Manager and Menu Manager, described in *Inside Macintosh: Macintosh Toolbox Essentials*. Resources in general are described in the Resource Manager chapter of *Inside Macintosh: More Macintosh Toolbox*. Additional information on keyboards themselves can be found in *Inside Macintosh: Devices* and in *Guide to the Macintosh Family Hardware*.

This appendix starts with a brief discussion of keyboards. It then lists the keyboard resources, shows how they may differ in different versions of localized software, and presents the concept of key translation. It then discusses each keyboard resource in detail.

Note
All keyboard information that relates to virtual key codes and their relation to raw key codes is discussed under "Key-Map Resource (Type 'KMAP')" beginning on page C-11, even if it is not specifically related to the key-map resource. ◆

About Keyboards

The Macintosh computer supports over 12 separate physical types of keyboards. Your application needs to be able to handle text input from the domestic and ISO layouts of all Apple keyboards. It also needs to be able to distinguish multiple keyboards and to use the modifier flag that detects the state of the **modifier keys** (Shift, Caps Lock, Command, Option, and Control) on keyboards.

Table C-1 lists the keyboard types. These type values are used in some of the keyboard resources discussed later in this appendix.

Table C-1   The keyboard types

Keyboard type[*]	Keyboard
1	Apple Keyboard and Apple Keyboard II (domestic layout)
2	Apple Extended Keyboard and Apple Extended Keyboard II (domestic layout)
3	Small Macintosh 512K Keyboard (no keypad; domestic layout)
4	Apple Keyboard (ISO layout)
5	Apple Extended Keyboard II (ISO layout)
6	Apple Macintosh Portable Keyboard (domestic layout)
7	Apple Macintosh Portable Keyboard (ISO layout)
8	Apple Macintosh Keyboard II (domestic layout)
9	Apple Macintosh Keyboard II (ISO layout)
11	Macintosh Plus Keyboard with the built-in keypad
12	Macintosh PowerBook Keyboard (domestic layout)
13	Macintosh PowerBook Keyboard (ISO layout)
259	Small Macintosh 512K Keyboard (no keypad; ISO layout)

[*] Keyboard type is also the resource ID of the corresponding 'KMAP' or 'KCAP' resource. The KbdType low-memory global variable contains the low byte of this value for the last keyboard used.

Figure C-1 and Figure C-2 show the U.S. layout of the Apple Keyboard II and Apple Extended Keyboard II and the virtual key codes produced by each key. The codes are the values that result after the raw key codes produced by the hardware have been mapped through the key-map resource. See "Key Translation" on page C-8. Other keyboards can produce different virtual key codes; some produce raw key codes only.

The Apple Extended Keyboard may be connected to the Apple Desktop Bus (ADB) of any computer in the Macintosh II or Macintosh SE family. It contains duplicated Shift, Option, and Control keys to the right of the Space bar. Other keyboards have different physical layouts.

Figure C-1   Apple Keyboard II (domestic layout)

Figure C-2   Apple Extended Keyboard II (domestic layout)

Table C-2 shows the keyboard modifier bits in the high byte of the modifiers field of an event record (defined by the EventRecord data type). The byte consisting of these bits is used to control the selection of tables in the keyboard-layout resource. See "Keyboard-Layout Resource (Type 'KCHR')" beginning on page C-18.

Table C-2   The keyboard modifier bits in an event record

Bit	Key
7	(Right Control if used)[*]
6	(Right Option if used)[*]
5	(Right Shift if used)[*]
4	Control (Left Control if different from Right Control)
3	Option (Left Option if different from Right Option)
2	Caps Lock
1	Shift (Left Shift if different from Right Shift)
0	Command

[*] See "Reassigning Right-Hand Key Codes" beginning on page C-14.

About the Keyboard Resources

The keyboard resources are Macintosh resources that facilitate worldwide keyboard handling and support the Macintosh script management system. They specify how keyboard input is converted to text for a particular writing system, language, or region. The Event Manager, the Script Manager, and the Menu Manager use the information in these resources to convert keystrokes to character codes, to switch input among different script systems, and to display the icon of the current keyboard in the Keyboard menu.

Note
Other Apple publications use the term *ASCII code* for **character code** (the 8-bit integer representing a text character generated by a key or a combination of keys on the keyboard or keypad) and the terms *key-down transition code* and *response code* for **virtual key code** (the key code that actually appears in keyboard events—that is, the value produced after a **raw key code** [the original value generated by a keyboard] has been mapped through the key-map resource). The terms *character code, raw key code*, and *virtual key code* are preferred in this book. *ASCII code* is limited here to the 7-bit code representing a character from the lower half of the Standard Roman character set. ◆

What the Keyboard Resources Are

The keyboard resources fall into two categories: those that are hardware-dependent (and script-independent) and those that are script-dependent (and hardware-independent). It is this division that allows many different physical keyboards to work correctly with many different script systems. Table C-3 lists the keyboard resources and their resource types, and gives a capsule description of their contents. More complete descriptions follow.

Table C-3   The keyboard resources

Name	Resource type	Contents
Key map	`'KMAP'`	Tables to map raw key codes to virtual key codes
Key remap	`'itlk'`	Tables to remap virtual key codes for certain key combinations
Keyboard layout	`'KCHR'`	Tables to map virtual key codes to character codes
Keyboard icons	`'kcs#'`	Keyboard icon (1-bit; black-and-white)
	`'kcs4'`	Keyboard icon (4-bit)
	`'kcs8'`	Keyboard icon (8-bit)
Keyboard swap	`'KSWP'`	Table specifying key combinations for changing keyboard script or input method
Key caps	`'KCAP'`	Data that determines keyboard display

- Key-map resource. Maps the raw key codes that have been generated by a specific keyboard microprocessor into hardware-independent standard virtual key codes. There is a maximum of one key-map resource per physical keyboard (several keyboards can share a single key-map resource).

- Key-remap resource. Remaps the virtual key codes for certain key combinations on certain keyboards to other virtual key codes, to allow a single keyboard-layout resource to work with all keyboards. This resource is optional; it is provided with certain keyboard-layout resources.

- Keyboard-layout resource. Maps virtual key codes to character codes. The keyboard-layout resource implements the character set for a script system. It is with different keyboard-layout resources that text input for different script systems and localized versions of system software is enabled. A script system has one or more keyboard-layout resources.

- Keyboard icon family. Implements keyboard icons—small icons that represent a keyboard script or input method—for screens of different bit depths (black-and white, 4-bit, and 8-bit, respectively). These icons are used in the Keyboard menu and in the Keyboard control panel. There is one icon family per keyboard-layout resource (or input method).

- Keyboard-swap resource. Lists modifier-plus-key combinations that can be used to change the keyboard script, or the keyboard layout or input method within a script. There is one keyboard-swap resource per version of system software.

- Key-caps resource. Specifies the physical arrangement of keys on a keyboard and is used to display the characters produced by each keypress. The key-caps resource is independent of any script system, but the Key Caps desk accessory uses it along with the keyboard-layout resource of the current script system—and a font in the current script system—to display the characters corresponding to each keypress or combination of keypresses.There is one key-caps resource per physical keyboard.

Keyboard resources and localized system software
When Macintosh system software is localized for a non-U.S. market, it contains replacements for or modifications to some of the U.S. versions of the keyboard resources. See the discussion of U.S. international resources and keyboard resources in the appendix "Built-in Script Support" for a list of resources that may be replaced during localization. ◆

Key Translation

Key translation is the conversion of keystrokes to character codes. In early versions of the Macintosh, keyboard translation was simple and direct: two low-memory pointers in the System file (accessed through global variables `Key1Trans` or `Key2Trans`) pointed to the translation routines. Those pointers are still available and are called by the Macintosh Plus but are not called by newer systems. The pointers are preserved so that applications that call them can still function correctly. However, they now point to a routine that implements a new standard mechanism.

The standard mechanism was developed with the advent of ADB keyboards; it was needed to map the different sets of raw key codes to a standard set of virtual key codes, which could in turn be mapped to character codes. In the standard method, a keystroke generates an interrupt; the keyboard driver maps the raw key code to a virtual key code, which it sends to the Event Manager; the Event Manager maps the virtual key code to a character code, and returns the character code to the driver. The driver in turn posts the key-down event. This method has two advantages:

- The mapping from raw key code to virtual key code achieves keyboard hardware independence. The raw mapping routine uses the table of a key-map resource for the keyboard, in the System file or in ROM.

- The mapping from virtual key code to character code allows support of multiple character sets. It is performed by the Event Manager `KeyTranslate` function, which is accessed through the `_KeyTrans` trap (not to be confused with the `Key1Trans` or `Key2Trans` pointers). `KeyTranslate` maps the virtual key code (plus modifiers, if any) to a character code, using tables in a keyboard-layout resource, also in the System file or in ROM. (`KeyTranslate` also handles *dead keys;* see page C-19.)

The Macintosh keyboard routines handle the keyboard properly for all script systems. Except for purely hardware-specific characteristics such as controlling lights on the keyboard, the function of the keyboard is completely determined by character-encoding tables in the keyboard-layout resource (with an optional associated key-remap resource). For each virtual key code and each possible modifier-key state, the character-encoding tables specify the equivalent character code. Figure C-3 summarizes the key translation process:

1. A keystroke initially produces a raw key code.

2. The keyboard driver uses the hardware-dependent key-map resource to map that raw key code into a hardware-independent virtual key code, and to set bits indicating the state of the modifier keys.

3. It then calls the Event Manager `KeyTranslate` function. The optional key-remap resource specifies how `KeyTranslate` should remap certain key combinations on certain keyboards before it performs its mapping. The key-remap resource reintroduces hardware dependence because certain scripts, languages, and regions need subtle differences in layout for specific keyboards. Generally, the key-remap resource affects only a few keys.

4. `KeyTranslate` uses the keyboard-layout resource to map a modifier state and a virtual key code into a character code, such as an ASCII code.

5. `KeyTranslate` returns the character code, and if the character code is nonzero the keyboard driver posts the key-down event into the event queue.

The net result of the process of key translation is a virtual key code and a character code in the `message` field of an event record, and modifier-key information in the `modifiers` field of the event record.

Note

On the Macintosh Plus, the event record contains raw key codes, not virtual key codes. However, except in the case of the small Macintosh 512K Keyboard with ISO layout, the Macintosh Plus raw key codes are identical to the virtual key codes that would have been produced. ◆

Figure C-3 The key translation process

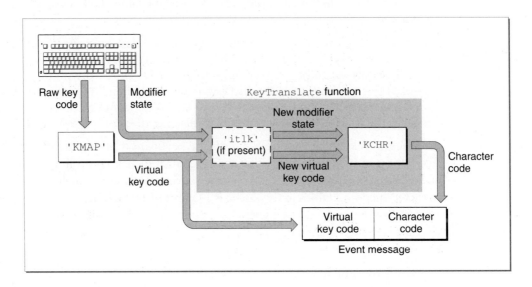

Using the Keyboard Resources

The Operating System, along with the Script Manager and other Macintosh system software managers, uses information in the keyboard resources to convert keystrokes into character codes; to display keyboard icons; to change the current keyboard script, keyboard layout, or input method when the user enters Command-key combinations; and to properly display keyboard layout with the Key Caps desk accessory.

Most applications do not handle any of these tasks and therefore have no need for direct access to any of the keyboard resources. However, if you have the following special software needs related to text input, you can use the keyboard resources to help meet them:

■ If your application needs to provide better international support for Command-key equivalents or a custom keyboard-layout resource, you can use the Event Manager `KeyTranslate` function to get the information you need from the appropriate keyboard-layout resource. See "Special Uses for the KeyTranslate Function" beginning on page C-22.

■ If you are creating your own localized version of a script system and need to allow text input in that script system, you may need to create or modify a keyboard-layout resource, and possible a key-remap resource. If you do make a new keyboard-layout resource, you also need to create a keyboard icon family to accompany it. To do that you will need the information in "Keyboard-Layout Resource (Type 'KCHR')" beginning on page C-18, "Key-Remap Resource (Type 'itlk')" beginning on page C-16, and "Keyboard Icon Family (Types 'kcs#', 'kcs4', 'kcs8')" beginning on page C-25.

■ If you are designing a new type of keyboard, you need to make sure it produces the appropriate raw key codes. See the next section. Each new keyboard also needs to work correctly with the Key Caps desk accessory; see "Key-Caps Resource (Type 'KCAP')" beginning on page C-28. Note that hardware development is beyond the scope of *Inside Macintosh*. See *Guide to the Macintosh Family Hardware* and contact Macintosh Developer Technical Support for more information.

Key-Map Resource (Type 'KMAP')

The key-map resource (resource type 'KMAP') is used for converting the raw key codes produced by a keyboard's microprocessor into hardware-independent virtual key codes. There is one key-map resource per physical keyboard on a Macintosh; it belongs to the Operating System, not to any script system.

The key-map resource ID number equals the ID number of the type of keyboard it is associated with. See Table C-1 on page C-4. If a matching key-map resource cannot be found for the keyboard in use, the Operating System substitutes the 'KMAP' resource whose ID is 0; on all Macintosh systems later than the Macintosh Plus, the key-map resource with ID = 0 is in ROM.

Note
Most current keyboards use the key-map resource with ID = 0. However, keyboard types 2 and 5, for example, require their own key-map resources. ◆

The key-map resource contains a 128-byte table that provides a one-to-one mapping of raw key codes to virtual key codes—the first byte contains the virtual key code for a raw key code of $00, the second for $01, and so forth. The table is followed by an array of exceptions. The high bit of the byte containing the virtual key code signals an exception entry in the exception array. (Virtual key codes themselves are only 7 bits long.)

The exception array lets the device driver initiate communication with the device, usually to perform a state change—for example, to send codes to the keyboard that instruct it to turn on lights when a given key such as Caps Lock is down. The exception array begins with a 2-byte record count followed by that many records. The format of the key-map resource and its exception array is shown in Figure C-4.

Figure C-4   Format of the key-map resource

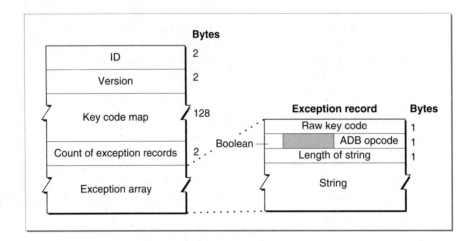

The elements in the resource have these meanings:

- ID. The resource ID for this particular key-map resource.

- Version. The version number of this key-map resource format.

- Key code map. A 128-byte table that contains virtual key codes. At each byte offset into the table, the entry is the virtual key code (plus possibly an exception entry flag) for the raw key code whose value equals that offset.

- Count of exception records. The number of entries in the exception array.

- Exception array. An array of exception records, which map raw key codes to communication instructions.

Each exception record has these elements (see also Figure C-4):

- A raw key code.

- One byte containing the following elements:
  - A Boolean (Xor or noXor) field that determines whether to instruct the driver to invert the state of the key instead of using the state provided by the hardware.
  - Filler (3 bits in length).
  - The ADB opcode, an instruction to the keyboard to perform some task. ADB opcodes are described in *Inside Macintosh: Devices*.

■ A variable length Pascal data string that is passed to the ADB op trap along with the ADB opcode. The first byte in the string is the length byte.

The following is an example of the exception array used to turn the Caps Lock light of the Apple Extended Keyboard II on and off, to match the state of the Caps Lock key.

```
    {
            $39, noXor, $E, "\$00\$02";
            $B9, noXor, $E, "\$00\$02";
    }
```

Note

Do not change the key-map resource. Everything your application needs to support any kind of text input is in the keyboard-layout and key-remap resources. You need to work with the key-map resource only if you are making your own keyboard. ◆

Apple Extended Keyboard

With the Apple Extended Keyboard (and Apple Extended Keyboard II, shown in Figure C-2), the standard key-map resource that is supplied with the system converts the following raw key codes to virtual key codes, as listed in Table C-4.

Table C-4   Key-map resource assignment of raw key codes to virtual key codes

Key	Raw key code	Virtual key code
Control	$36	$3B
Left Arrow	$3B	$7B
Right Arrow	$3C	$7C
Down Arrow	$3D	$7D
Up Arrow	$3E	$7E

The standard key-map resource leaves all other virtual key codes identical to the raw key codes they are generated from.

Reassigning Right-Hand Key Codes

It is possible to reassign the standard raw key codes and virtual key codes for the Shift, Option, and Control keys on the right side of the Apple Extended Keyboard, in order to distinguish right-side keystrokes from left-side keystrokes for those keys. To do so, you need to obtain the special values listed in Table C-5.

Table C-5   Reassigning right key codes for Shift, Option, and Control keys

Right key	Normal raw	Normal virtual	Special raw	Special virtual
Shift	$38	$38	$7B	$3C
Option	$3A	$3A	$7C	$3D
Control	$36	$3B	$7D	$3E

The normal raw and virtual key codes for Right-Shift, Right-Option, and Right-Control keys correspond to the left versions of these keys. You can obtain the special raw and virtual key codes only by changing the value of the device handler ID field in the Apple Extended Keyboard's register 3 from 2 to 3. For details about the device handler ID field, see *Inside Macintosh: Devices*.

▲ **WARNING**
This capability is included for compatibility with certain existing operating systems that distinguish between the left and right versions of these keys. Its use by new applications violates the Apple human interface guidelines and is strongly discouraged. ▲

Other Hardware Dependencies

The principle underlying virtual key codes is to have a single unique code per character code, regardless of the keyboard used. Nevertheless, some hardware dependencies remain:

■ The small Macintosh 512K Keyboard with ISO layout and the ISO ADB keyboards have an extra key not present on domestic keyboards. This key produces a virtual key code of $0A.

- There is a different virtual key code for the Enter key, depending on whether it is on the keypad ($4C on the Macintosh Plus keyboard and most ADB keyboards), or on the main section of the keyboard ($34 on the original Macintosh keyboard and the Macintosh Portable and PowerBook keyboards).

- Virtual key codes for cursor keys and some keypad operator keys differ between ADB keyboards and non-ADB (Macintosh Plus) keyboards, as shown in Table C-6. Note that on Macintosh Plus keyboards, the virtual key codes for keypad operators are the same as the virtual key codes for cursor keys. The Shift modifier controls which character code is generated. On these keyboards, for example, holding down the Shift key and pressing the Left Arrow key produces the plus character (+).

Table C-6   ADB and non-ADB virtual key codes for cursor keys and keypad keys

Key	ADB code	Non-ADB code (Macintosh Plus)
Left Arrow	$7B	$46
Right Arrow	$7C	$42
Down Arrow	$7D	$48
Up Arrow	$7E	$4D
Keypad Plus (+)	$45	$46 (with Shift bit set in modifiers)
Keypad Asterisk (*)	$43	$42 (with Shift bit set in modifiers)
Keypad Equal (=)	$51	$48 (with Shift bit set in modifiers)
Keypad Slash (/)	$4B	$4D (with Shift bit set in modifiers)

Virtual Key Codes for Non-ADB Keyboards

The original Macintosh keyboard (for both the 128K and 512K versions) and the Macintosh Plus keyboard produce event records with raw key codes rather than virtual key codes, because there is no key-map resource for them. For domestic versions of these keyboards it is not a problem, because the raw key codes are identical to the virtual key codes expected by the U.S. keyboard-layout resource. The international version of the Macintosh Plus keyboard, however, and the ISO layout of the small Macintosh 512K keyboard, produce raw key codes that cannot be treated as virtual.

When a keypress from the international version of the Macintosh Plus keyboard occurs, the interrupt handler calls the _Key1Trans hook, which translates the raw key codes to virtual key codes before calling KeyTranslate. Thus your application normally receives the correct character codes even if an international version of the Macintosh Plus keyboard is attached. However, the raw key code is what is placed in the event record. Therefore, if you need to explicitly convert raw key codes to virtual key codes, you can use the values in Table C-7. Raw key codes are offsets into the table; the byte at each offset represents the virtual key code for that raw key code. (The keyboard produces raw key codes up to $3F only; key codes above that value are generated by an optional keypad.)

Table C-7 Virtual key codes for the international Macintosh Plus keyboard

Raw codes	Virtual codes							
$00–$07	$00	$01	$02	$03	$04	$05	$32	$06
$08–$0F	$07	$08	$2C	$09	$0C	$0D	$0E	$0F
$10–$17	$10	$11	$12	$13	$14	$15	$16	$17
$18–$1F	$18	$19	$1A	$1B	$1C	$1D	$1E	$1F
$20–$27	$20	$21	$22	$23	$2A	$25	$26	$27
$28–$2F	$28	$29	$24	$2E	$2F	$0B	$2D	$2B
$30–$37	$30	$34	$0A	$33	$31	$35	$36	$37
$38–$3F	$38	$39	$3A	$3B	$3C	$3D	$3E	$3F

The domestic and ISO layouts of the small Macintosh 512K keyboard have keyboard types of 3 and 259, respectively. However, in both cases the low-memory global that specifies current keyboard type (KbdType) holds the value 3. The user indicates which keyboard is in use through a control in the Keyboard control panel that appears only on non-ADB systems. The user's selection is kept in the itlcOldKeyboard field of the system script's international configuration ('itlc') resource. You can examine that field if you need to know whether the ISO or domestic layout of the small Macintosh 512K keyboard is in use.

Key-Remap Resource (Type 'itlk')

The key-remap resource (resource type 'itlk') is used by the KeyTranslate function to ensure that all international keyboard layouts work on all Macintosh keyboards. The key-remap resource specifies how to remap the virtual key codes produced by certain key combinations before KeyTranslate converts the virtual key codes to character codes with a keyboard-layout ('KCHR') resource. KeyTranslate is described in the chapter "Event Manager" in *Inside Macintosh: Macintosh Toolbox Essentials*.

There is one key-remap resource per keyboard-layout resource that needs it. The `'itlk'` resource has the same resource ID as the keyboard-layout resource with which it is associated. The Operating System loads key-remap resources from the System file only.

The key-remap resource consists of an integer count of entries followed by a set of 8-byte entries. Figure C-5 shows the format of an entry.

Figure C-5   Format of an entry in the key-remap resource

Keyboard type (integer)	Current modifiers (byte)	Current key code (byte)	Modifiers mask (byte)	Key code mask (byte)	New modifiers (byte)	New key code (byte)

Before the KeyTranslate function begins processing with the keyboard-layout resource, it determines which entry in the key-remap resource to use. It tests each entry in the key-remap resource to see whether

- the actual keyboard type matches the keyboard type element

- the product of an AND operation on the actual virtual key code with the key code mask matches the current key code element

- the product of an AND operation on the actual modifiers with the modifiers mask matches the current modifiers element

If all three match, KeyTranslate substitutes the new modifiers and virtual key code from that entry before applying them to the keyboard-layout resource.

To allow for a more compact table when several virtual key codes produced from one key (using different modifiers) are all mapped together to a different key, an additional step is taken. KeyTranslate uses the modifiers mask and key-code mask in the key-remap entry to produce a number of new modifiers and virtual key codes. Here is how a single entry can remap all modifier combinations for a given key:

1. An AND operation is performed on the new modifiers and new virtual key code with the modifiers mask and the key-code mask from the entry.

2. An AND operation is performed on the actual modifiers and actual virtual key code with the 1's complement of the modifiers mask and key code mask from the entry.

3. The OR of these two operations is the final result that is used for key translation.

Note
If the keyboard type is 259 (the ID for the ISO layout of the small Macintosh 512K Keyboard), the third field in the key-remap resource (which usually contains the current virtual key code) consists of the raw key code. See Table C-1 on page C-4 of this appendix for a list of the keyboard types. ◆

Keyboard-Layout Resource (Type 'KCHR')

The keyboard-layout resource (resource type 'KCHR') specifies the mapping of virtual key codes to character codes. Each installed script system has one or more keyboard-layout resources; there may be one or more for each language or region to suit the preference of the user. The resource ID for each keyboard-layout resource is within the range of resource ID numbers for its script system. The ID number of the default 'KCHR' resource for a script system is specified in the itlbKeys field of the script's international bundle ('itlb') resource.

U.S. keyboard-layout resource
Specific features of the U.S. keyboard-layout resource (ID = 0) are described in the appendix "Built-in Script Support" in this book. ◆

Keyboard-layout resources for 2-byte script systems
Keyboard-layout resources for 2-byte script systems have the same size and function as those for 1-byte script systems; they generate 1-byte character codes only. It is the input method that is responsible for producing the final 1-byte or 2-byte character codes. ◆

Resource Format

Figure C-6 shows the format of the keyboard-layout resource. Its header consists of a version number only. The header is followed by a 256-byte table-selection index that is used to access character-mapping tables. The index is followed by the character-mapping tables, a series of 128-byte tables that map virtual key codes to character codes, depending on what modifier keys are pressed. The final part of the resource is a dead-key table, a series of records that define dead keys and completers. The dead-key records allow the user to enter special character forms, such as accented characters, from the keyboard. How dead keys are processsed is described under "The KeyTranslate Function and the Keyboard-Layout Resource" beginning on page C-19.

The dead-key table consists of a 2-byte count of dead-key records, followed by that many records. A dead key record consists of a 1-byte table number (corresponding to a character-mapping table), a 1-byte virtual key code (without up/down bit), a completion table, and a no-match character.

Each completion table in a dead-key record consists of a count of completion records, followed by that number of completion records. A completion record is simply a substitution pair for character codes. If the character code matches the first byte in the completion record, the second byte is substituted for it.

Figure C-6   Format of the keyboard-layout resource

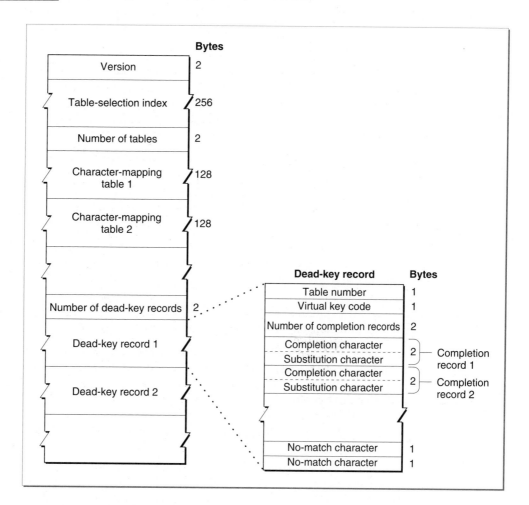

The KeyTranslate Function and the Keyboard-Layout Resource

During the process of key translation, the Event Manager `KeyTranslate` function applies the virtual key code and the state of the modifier keys to the keyboard-layout resource to determine a character code. Table C-2 on page C-6 shows the meanings of the keyboard modifier bits in the high-order byte of the `modifiers` field of an event record (defined by the `EventRecord` data type). The `KeyTranslate` function uses the byte value determined by the settings of these bits to control the selection of tables in the keyboard-layout resource.

Figure C-7 gives an overview of how the parts of the keyboard-layout resource are used. It starts when the user presses a key or combination of keys, and the Event Manager passes the virtual key code and the state of the modifier keys to the `KeyTranslate` function:

1. First, `KeyTranslate` treats the modifier state information—8 bits, each bit indicating the state of one modifier key—as a byte whose value is used as an index into the 256-byte table-selection index to get a table code. The table code specifies which of the 128-byte character-mapping tables to use to map the virtual key code to a character code.

2. `KeyTranslate` uses the virtual key code as an index into the selected character-mapping table. If the table has a nonzero entry for the virtual key code, that entry is the desired character code. `KeyTranslate` returns that character code and the Event Manager posts a key-down event—*unless* the previous keypress had been a dead key. See step 4.

3. If the entry in the character-mapping table is 0, `KeyTranslate` searches the dead-key table. It looks for a match with both the virtual key code and the table number fields in a dead-key record. If there is no match, `KeyTranslate` returns 0. If there is a match, the dead-key information is preserved in the `state` parameter of the `KeyTranslate` function. `KeyTranslate` returns 0, so no event is posted, but the state information affects how the next virtual key code is to be processed.

4. If the previous key was a dead key, `KeyTranslate` searches the completion table in the dead-key record corresponding to the previous keypress. If the character code of the current keypress matches the first byte of any completion record in the completion table, the second byte in the record is substituted for it. If it does not match any first bytes in the completion table, the current character code is preceded by the no-match character found at the end of the dead key record and `KeyTranslate` returns both characters.

   For instance, in the U.S. keyboard-layout resource the Option-E combination is a dead key. When pressed, no character appears on the screen, but the `state` parameter of `KeyTranslate` is modified to hold the information that the dead key for the acute accent (´) has been pressed. If the next character is a valid completer key (such as a, e, i, o, or u), `KeyTranslate` returns the equivalent substitution character (á, é, í, ó, ú), an event is posted, and the character appears on the screen. If the next character is not a valid completer (for example, x), `KeyTranslate` returns *both* the no-match character (typically the accent character by itself) and the current character code; two events are posted, and both characters appear on the screen (´x).

As far as your application is concerned, no event is generated by pressing a dead key. The only information you receive regarding the dead key is after the fact. When the user produces "Á" by pressing Option-E followed by "A", you receive a single event containing a virtual key code corresponding to "A", no modifiers, and a character code of "Á".

Figure C-7   Inside the keyboard-layout resource

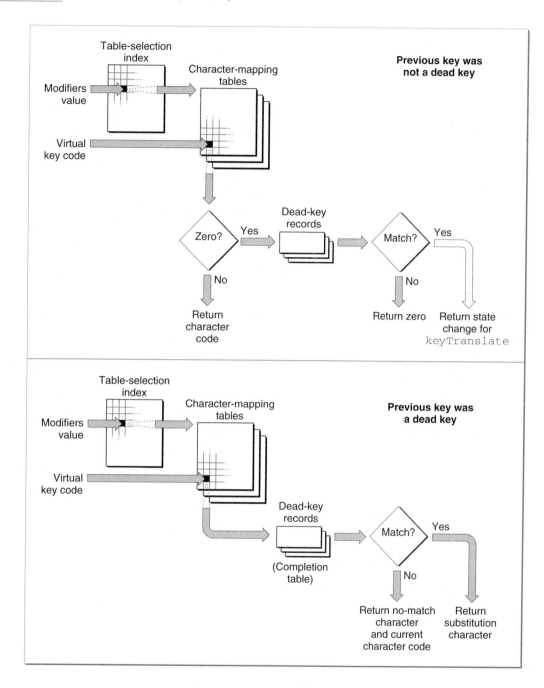

Special Uses for the KeyTranslate Function

In normal key translation, the Event Manager `KeyTranslate` function performs the conversion from virtual key code to character code and passes the result to your application in the `message` field of the event record for a key-down event. The script management system provides `KeyTranslate` with a pointer to the proper keyboard-layout resource to use, based on the current script.

There may be situations, however, in which you may want to explicitly call `KeyTranslate`, either to install your own keyboard layout or to perform special processing.

Installing a Custom Keyboard-Layout Resource

The script management system loads and uses only those keyboard-layout resources that are installed in the System file. It cannot load a keyboard-layout resource that is, for example, in the resource fork of your application. However, if your application needs to modify the keyboard layout temporarily without forcing users to install a new keyboard layout, you can load a keyboard-layout resource from your own application resource fork and call `KeyTranslate` directly after each key-down event, passing it a pointer to that keyboard-layout resource and using the same virtual key code and modifiers that you received in the event message.

To more permanently replace a script system's keyboard layout, you can have the user install a keyboard-layout resource and a keyboard-icon family in the System file. Both resources must have identical ID numbers, in the range for the script system for which they will be used. You call the Script Manager `SetScriptVariable` procedure twice, to make those IDs the defaults for the given script system. You then call the Script Manager `KeyScript` procedure to load the resources and make them available to the system. Listing C-1 demonstrates the calls for a Dvorak keyboard layout in the Roman script system.

Listing C-1   Loading a non-system keyboard-layout resource

```
CONST
    DvorakID =  500;

VAR
    err:  OSErr;

BEGIN
    err    := SetScriptVariable(smRoman, smScriptKeys, DvorakID);
    err    := SetScriptVariable(smRoman, smScriptIcon, DvorakID);
    KeyScript(smRoman);
END;
```

In this example you do not need to call `KeyTranslate` to get character codes for the new keyboard layout, and the new keyboard layout will be in effect until the system is restarted or until your application restores the original keyboard layout.

The most permanent way to replace the keyboard layout is to make the system use your keyboard layout as its default. To do that you must modify the `itlbKeys` field of the target script system's international bundle (`'itlb'`) resource. The international bundle resource is described in the appendix "International Resources" in this book.

IMPORTANT

Apple Computer's system software licensing policy forbids shipping a modified System file. If you want to modify the System file, it is best to have the user either run the Installer to install your resources, or drag a file consisting of those resources onto the System Folder. Contact Macintosh Developer Technical Support for information on the Installer. ▲

You can inspect and edit any keyboard-layout resource by using a resource editor such as ResEdit.

Using KeyTranslate for Command-Key Equivalents

In some cases you may need to call `KeyTranslate` to regenerate a different character code using the same keyboard-layout resource. For example, the U.S. `'KCHR'` and some other Roman keyboard layouts ignore the Shift modifier key if the Command modifier key is also pressed. That means you cannot directly use uppercase characters or shifted symbols as Command equivalents. Furthermore, for those keyboard layouts where the period is a shifted key, it means that the standard Macintosh command to cancel an operation (Command-period) cannot be generated. As another example, some applications that accept Command-? as a request for Help simply assume that "?" is a shifted version of "/", and thus bring up a Help window whenever the Command key and "/" are pressed simultaneously. This gives incorrect behavior on keyboards in which "?" is not generated by Shift-/.

To overcome this and similar difficulties, you can use the virtual key code you receive in the key-down event record, and call `KeyTranslate` to run it back through the same keyboard-layout resource, but without the modifier(s) that applied when the character code was first generated. If the resulting character code is one that is significant for a command equivalent, you can use it plus the modifier state that originally applied to decide what action to take.

Listing C-2 is a routine that removes the Command-key bit from the modifiers field of an event record and runs the same virtual key code through `KeyTranslate`, using the same keyboard-layout resource, to see if a different character code results.

Listing C-2   Regenerating a character code with `KeyTranslate`

```
FUNCTION TryAgain(myEvent: EventRecord): LongInt;

CONST
    newModifierMask = $FE00;                    {turn off cmdKey bit}

VAR
    Modifiers:      Integer;
    VirtualCode:    Integer;
    KeyCode:        Integer;
    someState:      LongInt;
    KCHRPtr:        Ptr;

BEGIN
                                    {don't keep cmdKey bit}
    Modifiers := BAnd(myEvent.modifiers, newModifierMask);
                                    {keep virtual key code, put in low byte}
    VirtualCode := BSR(BAnd(myEvent.message, keyCodeMask), 8);
                                    {assemble new key code for KeyTranslate}
    KeyCode := BOr(Modifiers, VirtualCode);
                                    {get pointer to current 'KCHR'}
    KCHRPtr := Ptr(GetScriptManagerMVariable(smKCHRCache));
    someState := 0;                 {initialize KeyTranslate dead-key state}
                                    {see what ascii code is returned}
    TryAgain := KeyTranslate(KCHRPtr, KeyCode, someState);
                                    {look for returned values in both }
                                    { high and low word of result}
END;
```

In designing Command equivalents for your application, keep in mind that there may be less chance of inconsistency and confusion if you present Command equivalents to the user—and interpret them yourself—as grouped modifiers applied to the basic (unshifted) character you want to use for the command. (Note, however, that to do so you would have to write your own custom menu-definition resource.) For example, you might show "Command-Option-P" in the menu rather than "Command-π"; when interpreting it, you could use `KeyTranslate` and the virtual key code in the event record to make sure that the key for "p" was pressed, rather than just assuming that "π" is produced by Option-P.

Another possibility is to define few Commmand-key equivalents yourself, and to let the user create as many equivalents as desired.

Keyboard Icon Family (Types 'kcs#', 'kcs4', 'kcs8')

The keyboard icon family is a set of resources (resource types 'kcs#', 'kcs4', and 'kcs8') that specify a family of small icons representing a keyboard layout. They define black-and-white, 4-bit, and 8-bit small color icons, respectively. There is one keyboard icon family per keyboard-layout resource; each of the keyboard icon resources has the same resource ID as the keyboard-layout resource with which it is associated.

The Operating System loads keyboard icon resources from the System file only. The ID number of the default keyboard icon family for a script system is specified in the itlbIcon field of the script's international bundle ('itlb') resource. However, the Operating System ignores this value and instead looks for a keyboard icon family whose resource ID matches the ID of the keyboard-layout resource it is loading. If it cannot find an icon family with that ID, the Operating System loads the default keyboard icon suite (ID = –16491).

Some differences exist between the keyboard icon family and the color icon families used elsewhere in the Macintosh Operating System. First, only small icons (16-by-16 pixels) are supplied; there are no large keyboard icons (32-by-32 pixels). Second, the resource type for keyboard small color icons is different from the resource type used elsewhere for small color icons ('ics#', 'ics4', and 'ics8'). This difference is to avoid resource ID conflicts with those icon resources, because the keyboard color icons may have IDs anywhere in the range 0–32767, and certain negative ranges as well. The keyboard icon types and the equivalent standard color icon types are shown in Table C-8.

Table C-8   Keyboard color icon types and standard icon equivalents

Keyboard icon type	Standard icon equivalent	Bit depth
'kcs#'	'ics#'	1
'kcs4'	'ics4'	4
'kcs8'	'ics8'	8

Note

If the 4-bit and 8-bit icons (resources 'kcs4' and 'kcs8') in your application have exactly the same appearance and colors, then you only need to provide a 4-bit icon. ◆

Keyboard Resources

The keyboard icons are used in the Keyboard control panel and in the Keyboard menu when it is displayed. In Macintosh system software versions 7.0 and later, the Keyboard menu always appears when more than one script system is enabled, and may be forced to appear even if only one script system is present (if the smfShowIcon flag in the Script Manager general flags is set at startup).

Figure C-8   Sample keyboard icons

See the Finder Interface chapter of *Inside Macintosh: Macintosh Toolbox Essentials* for additional information on color icons and icon families. See also *Macintosh Human Interface Guidelines* for design suggestions for color icon families.

Keyboard-Swap Resource (Type 'KSWP')

The keyboard-swap resource (resource type 'KSWP') specifies the modifier-plus-key combinations with which the user can change keyboard scripts, keyboard layouts within scripts, and input methods. For example, the standard keyboard-swap resource specifies that pressing Command–Space bar changes the keyboard to the default keyboard for the next script. (In this case, *next* means next in the Keyboard menu.)

There is one keyboard-swap resource per localized version of system software. A localized system may either use the standard 'KSWP' resource or replace it with one of its own. The keyboard-swap resource is in the System file; its resource ID is 0.

The keyboard-swap resource consists of an array with series of entries, each of which specifies modifier-plus-key combinations that can be used to change keyboard layouts and scripts. Figure C-9 shows the format of entries in the 'KSWP' resource.

Figure C-9   Format of entries in the keyboard-swap resource

Script code or special negative code (integer)	Virtual key code (byte)	Modifier state (byte)

The elements of the entry have these meanings:

- Script code or negative code. The code number of a script system—such as 0 (smRoman)—or a special negative code for switching. The special negative codes are identical to the selectors for the Script Manager KeyScript procedure. The selectors are listed and described along with the KeyScript procedure in the chapter "Script Manager" in this book.

- Virtual key code. The virtual key code (for example, $31 for Space bar) required to generate the script code or special negative code of this element.

- Modifier state. The modifier-key setting (for example, Command key down) that must accompany the virtual key code.

Listing C-3 is a Rez-format definition of a hypothetical keyboard-swap resource.

Listing C-3   A hypothetical keyboard-swap resource

```
resource 'KSWP' (0, sysheap) {
      {/* array: 2 elements */
          /* [1] = smKeyNextScript */
          -1, $31, controlOff, optionOff, shiftOff, commandOn,
          /* [2] = smKeyNextKybd */
          -4, $31, controlOff, optionOn, shiftOff, commandOn,
      }
};
```

This resource defines a rotation to the next script system on Command–Space bar, and a rotation to the next keyboard layout on Command–Option–Space bar.

Note

The expression that evaluates the size of a keyboard-swap resource is complicated. If you need to perform a DeRez operation on a keyboard-swap resource, contact Macintosh Developer Technical Support for details. ◆

IMPORTANT

The Script Manager removes from the event queue any Command-key combinations involving the Space bar if that Command-key combination indicates feature supported by the current script system. For example, if multiple script systems are installed, the Script Manager strips the Command–Space bar combination (which specifies changing script systems) from the event queue. If multiple script systems are not installed, this event is not removed, so users can use it in Command-key macros. Applications, however, should never depend on Command-key combinations involving the Space bar. ▲

Key-Caps Resource (Type 'KCAP')

The key-caps resource (resource type 'KCAP') reflects the physical layout of a particular keyboard and is used by the Key Caps desk accessory. The resource indicates the shapes and positions of all keys, and defines the virtual key codes that correspond to each physical key. Key Caps uses this resource to draw a representation of the current keyboard layout—using the current keyboard-layout resource—for the current physical keyboard. If you are creating a new keyboard, you can define its physical layout in a key-caps resource.

For system software versions 7.0 and later, the key-caps resource is located in the System file. There is one 'KCAP' resource per physical keyboard on a Macintosh; it belongs to the Operating System, and not to any script system. The resource ID for each key-caps resource is equal to the keyboard type of the keyboard it is associated with. See Table C-1 on page C-4 for a list of keyboard types. For ADB keyboards, the ID of the key-caps resource is the same as the keyboard handler ID.

IMPORTANT

The key-caps resource should never require localization. The only time a key-caps resource needs to be added is for a keyboard that has a new physical arrangement (or a new keyboard handler ID). ▲

Resource Format

Figure C-10 shows the format for the key-caps resource.

Figure C-10 Format of the key-caps resource

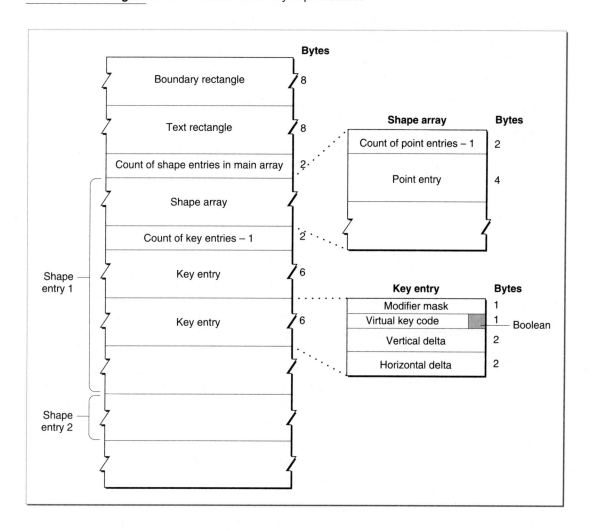

Keyboard Resources

The key-caps resource has these elements:

■ Boundary rectangle. The position of the content region of the Key Caps window.

■ Text rectangle. The position of the text box within the Key Caps window.

■ Main array. The remainder of the resource. It consists of an array of one shape entry for each key shape.

Each shape entry in the main array has two components:

■ Shape array. A (zero-based) count of entries followed by one or more entries. Each entry is a point, representing the relative pixel offset from the origin of the key, that define a particular key shape. The shape array is a single point for rectangular keys. More complex keys, like the Return key, need two points in their shape array.

■ Key array. A set of key entries, describing all the keys with that shape.

Each key entry in a shape entry specifies the following information:

■ Vertical delta and horizontal delta. Vertical and horizontal values to move the pen before drawing the current key. For each shape (that is, for each shape entry in the main array), the pen starts out at the upper-left corner of the content region of the Key Caps window, so the vertical and horizontal delta values for the first key in the key array for that shape are distances from the upper-left corner to the origin of the first key. For subsequent keys in the key array, the deltas are distances from the origin of the previous key to the origin of the current key. Each key is drawn with the shape defined by the shape array for that shape.

■ Virtual key code. The virtual key code for the current key. Because it uses virtual key codes, each key-caps resource is tied directly to a particular key-map resource and hardware keyboard but can work with any keyboard-layout resource.

■ Modifier mask and Boolean. A modifier mask and a Boolean flag for how to use it. When Key Caps draws the current key, it retrieves the byte that represents the real modifier key state, combines it with this mask performing an OR or AND operation as specified, calls the `KeyTranslate` function with the resulting modifier byte and the virtual key code from the key-caps resource, and draws the resulting character or characters in the current key's location. The modifier mask is only required for non-ADB keyboards, which use artificial modifier key states to overlap the key codes for arrow keys and keypad operator keys. For other keyboards, the mask is 0 and the flag is set to specify an OR operation.

Listing C-4 is an abridged example of the data in a key-caps resource, shown in Rez format.

Listing C-4   Sample key-caps resource data in Rez format

```
resource 'KCAP' ($01) {
         {60, 45, 220, 455},                  /* boundsRect */
         {12, 42, 36, 368},                   /* textRect */
         {
             { {21, 21} }, {                  /* Shape No. 1 */
                0, or, $35, 50, 10;              /* escape */
                0, or, $12, 0, 20;              /* 1 ! */
                0, or, $13, 0, 20;              /* 2 @ */
                ...
                0, or, $7D, 0, 20;             /* Down arrow */
                0, or, $7E, 0, 20;             /* Up arrow */
                0, or, $41, 0, 80;             /* Keypad . */
                0, or, $55, -20, 0;            /* Keypad 3 */
                ...
         };
             { {21, 31} }, {                  /* Shape No. 2 */
                0, or, $30, 70, 10;             /* Tab */
                0, or, $33, -20, 260            /* Backspace */
         };
             ...
             {  {-21, 36}; {-41, 15} }, {  /* Shape No. 3 */
                0, or, $24, 111, 265           /* Return */
         };
             ...
         }
};
```

The basic square key has a shape array of { {21, 21} }, which puts the origin in the upper-left corner of the key. The first key in the key array for this shape is the Escape key (key code $35) in the upper-left corner of the keyboard; this key is at vertical and horizontal delta offsets of (50, 50) from the upper-left corner of the window's content region. The next key with this shape is immediately to the right, with its origin at delta offsets of (0, 20) from the origin of the previous key.

The next shape is the slightly wider key with a shape array of { {21, 31} }, used for the Tab and Backspace keys. The origin of the Tab key is at offsets (70, 10) from the upper-left corner of the window's content region (which puts the Tab key one row below the Escape key).

The shape array for the Return key is { {-21, 36}; {-41, 15} }, which means that it is the union of two rectangles: the first rectangle is from the origin of the key to the first point, and the second rectangle is from the first point to the second point. (Both points are measured relative to the key origin, however.) This shape array puts the Return key's origin in the lower-left corner of the key. See Figure C-11. The origin is at offsets (111, 265) from the upper-left corner of the window's content region.

Figure C-11   Shape array and resulting region for the Return key

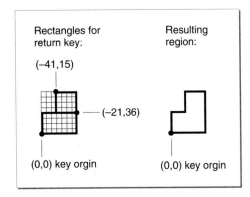

Key Caps Desk Accessory

This section discusses how the Key Caps desk accessory uses information in its key-caps resource to represent the physical layout of a keyboard. It also describes how the Key Caps desk accessory provides feedback to the user on how dead keys produce accented characters.

Listing C-4 on page C-31 is a portion of the data from the key-caps resource ('KCAP' ID = 1), which is used with the standard ADB keyboard (keyboard type 1, the domestic layout of the Apple Keyboard II). Working with that resource, the Key Caps desk accessory produces the display shown in Figure C-12 when it is used with the standard U.S. keyboard-layout resource ('KCHR' ID = 0).

Figure C-12 Key Caps display with key origins

The Key Caps desk accessory provides feedback on using dead keys to produce accented characters. It indicates dead keys with dotted borders, as shown in the Key Caps window in Figure C-13, which shows the U.S. keyboard layout with the Option key pressed.

Figure C-13 Key Caps display of dead keys with Option key pressed

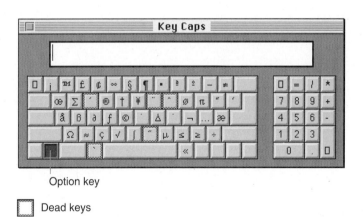

Option key

☐ Dead keys

If a dead key is entered, such as the circumflex dead-key combination (Option-I), the display changes to highlight the completer keys for this dead key. The user can press any completer key to generate valid accented character combinations, as shown in Figure C-14. If your application displays keyboards, you should use a similar method of indicating dead keys and completers.

Figure C-14   Key Caps display of completer keys after circumflex dead key has been pressed

☐ Completer keys

Summary of the Keyboard Resources

Assembly-Language Summary

Global Variables

KbdType	The keyboard type of the most recently used keyboard
Key1Trans	Pointer to key-translation routine (for non-ADB keyboards)
Key2Trans	Pointer to key-translation routine (for non-ADB keyboards)

Renamed and Relocated Text Routines

Renamed and Relocated Text Routines

This appendix lists, in Table D-1, those Macintosh system software routines that have been renamed or relocated from one manager to another during the reorganization necessary for the creation of *Inside Macintosh: Text*. It also lists those calls that have been rendered obsolete by newer versions of themselves and are therefore removed from documentation.

Most of the changes have been to text-related routines: the International Utilities Package and the Binary-Decimal Conversion Package have been replaced by a new manager called Text Utilities. The Text Utilities include most of their routines and also several text-related routines that were formerly part of the Toolbox Utilities and Operating System Utilities.

Many text-related routines that were formerly part of the Script Manager have been moved to other managers, such as QuickDraw, the Font Manager, the Text Utilities, or the Menu Manager, to be documented alongside existing routines with similar capabilities. For example, all routines that measure and draw justified text have been moved from the Script Manager to QuickDraw, to be with the existing QuickDraw text-measuring and drawing routines.

Many other routines have not been moved, but their names have been changed to more clearly reflect their functions, to minimize ambiguous interpretations, and to expand abbreviations.

Some routines that are not related to text handling are listed here. They are former Script Manager or International Utilities routines dealing with international issues, such as `IUMetric` and `WriteLocation`. Those routines now belong to other managers, as noted in Table D-1.

Note

Although obsolete routines are no longer documented, they may remain in system software and their declarations may be maintained in the interface files for backward compatibility. Renamed routines are no longer documented under their old names, other than within the table in this appendix. ◆

Table D-1   Renamed, relocated, and obsolete text and international routines

Old name	New name	Old location	New location
Char2Pixel	(obsolete; use CharToPixel)		QuickDraw
CharByte	(obsolete; use CharacterByteType)		Script Manager
CharType	(obsolete; use CharacterType)		Script Manager
Date2Secs	DateToSeconds	O.S. Utilities	(not moved)
DrawJust	(obsolete; use DrawJustified)		QuickDraw
EqualString	(unchanged)	O.S. Utilities	Text Utilities
FindScriptRun	(unchanged)	Script Manager	Text Utilities
FindWord	(obsolete; use FindWordBreaks)		Text Utilities
Font2Script	FontToScript	Script Manager	(not moved)
Format2Str	FormatRecToString	Script Manager	Text Utilities
FormatStr2X	StringToExtended	Script Manager	Text Utilities
FormatX2Str	ExtendedToString	Script Manager	Text Utilities
GetAppFont	(unchanged)	Script Manager	Font Manager
GetDefFontSize	(unchanged)	Script Manager	Font Manager
GetEnvirons	GetScriptManagerVariable	Script Manager	(not moved)
GetFormatOrder	(unchanged)	Script Manager	QuickDraw
GetIndString	(unchanged)	Toolbox Utilities	Text Utilities
GetMBarHeight	(unchanged)	Script Manager	Menu Manager
GetScript	GetScriptVariable	Script Manager	(not moved)
GetString	(unchanged)	Toolbox Utilities	Text Utilities
GetStylHandle	TEGetStyleHandle	TextEdit	(not moved)
GetStylScrap	TEGetStyleScrapHandle	TextEdit	(not moved)
GetSysFont	(unchanged)	Script Manager	Font Manager
GetSysJust	GetSysDirection	Script Manager	(not moved)
HiliteText	(unchanged)	Script Manager	QuickDraw
InitDateCache	(unchanged)	Script Manager	Text Utilities
IUClearCache	ClearIntlResourceCache	Intl. Utilities	Script Manager
IUCompPString	CompareString	Intl. Utilities	Text Utilities
IUCompString	(obsolete; use CompareString)		Text Utilities
IUDatePString	DateString	Intl. Utilities	Text Utilities

Table D-1   Renamed, relocated, and obsolete text and international routines (continued)

Old name	New name	Old location	New location
IUDateString	(obsolete; use DateString)		Text Utilities
IUEqualPString	IdenticalString	Intl. Utilities	Text Utilities
IUEqualString	(obsolete; use IdenticalString)		Text Utilities
IUGetIntl	GetIntlResource	Intl. Utilities	Script Manager
IUGetItlTable	GetIntlResourceTable	Intl. Utilities	Script Manager
IULangOrder	LanguageOrder	Intl. Utilities	Text Utilities
IULDateString	LongDateString	Intl. Utilities	Text Utilities
IULTimeString	LongTimeString	Intl. Utilities	Text Utilities
IUMagIDPString	IdenticalText	Intl. Utilities	Text Utilities
IUMagIDString	(obsolete; use IdenticalText)		TextUtilities
IUMagPString	CompareText	Intl. Utilities	Text Utilities
IUMagString	(obsolete; use CompareText)		Text Utilities
IUMetric	IsMetric	Intl. Utilities	O.S. Utilities
IUScriptOrder	ScriptOrder	Intl. Utilities	Text Utilities
IUSetIntl	(obsolete; for 'INTL' resources)	Intl. Utilities	Text Utilities
IUStringOrder	StringOrder	Intl. Utilities	Text Utilities
IUTextOrder	TextOrder	Intl. Utilities	Text Utilities
IUTimePString	TimeString	Intl. Utilities	Text Utilities
IUTimeString	(obsolete; use TimeString)		Text Utilities
KeyTrans	KeyTranslate	Event Manager	(not moved)
LongDate2Secs	LongDateToSeconds	Script Manager	O.S. Utilities
LongSecsToDate	LongSecondsToDate	Script Manager	O.S. Utilities
LowerText	(obsolete; use LowercaseText)		Text Utilities
MeasureJust	(obsolete; use MeasureJustified)		QuickDraw
Munger	(unchanged)	Toolbox Utilities	Text Utilities
NChar2Pixel	CharToPixel	Script Manager	QuickDraw
NDrawJust	DrawJustified	Script Manager	QuickDraw
NewString	(unchanged)	Toolbox Utilities	Text Utilities
NFindWord	(obsolete; use FindWordBreaks)		Text Utilities
NMeasureJust	MeasureJustified	Script Manager	QuickDraw

continued

Table D-1   Renamed, relocated, and obsolete text and international routines (continued)

Old name	New name	Old location	New location
NPixel2Char	PixelToChar	Script Manager	QuickDraw
NPortionText	PortionLine	Script Manager	QuickDraw
NumToString	(unchanged)	Binary-Dec. Conv.	Text Utilities
ParseTable	(obsolete; use FillParseTable)		Script Manager
Pixel2Char	(obsolete; use PixelToChar)		QuickDraw
PortionText	(obsolete; use PortionLine)		QuickDraw
ReadLocation	(unchanged)	Script Manager	O.S. Utilities
RelString	(unchanged)	O.S. Utilities	Text Utilities
ReplaceText	(unchanged)	Script Manager	Text Utilities
Secs2Date	SecondsToDate	O.S. Utilities	(not moved)
SetClikLoop	TESetClickLoop	TextEdit	(not moved)
SetEnvirons	SetScriptManagerVariable	Script Manager	(not moved)
SetScript	SetScriptVariable	Script Manager	(not moved)
SetString	(unchanged)	Toolbox Utilities	Text Utilities
SetStylHandle	TESetStyleHandle	TextEdit	(not moved)
SetStylScrap	TEUseStyleScrap	TextEdit	(not moved)
SetSysJust	SetSysDirection	Script Manager	(not moved)
SetWordBreak	TESetWordBreak	TextEdit	(not moved)
Str2Format	StringToFormatRec	Script Manager	Text Utilities
String2Date	StringToDate	Script Manager	Text Utilities
String2Time	StringToTime	Script Manager	Text Utilities
StringToNum	(unchanged)	Binary-Dec. Conv.	Text Utilities
StripText	(obsolete; use StripDiacritics)		Text Utilities
StripUpperText	(obsolete; use UppercaseStripDiacritics)		Text Utilities
StyledLineBreak	(unchanged)	Script Manager	Text Utilities
TEGetScrapLen	TEGetScrapLength	TextEdit	(not moved)
TESetJust	TESetAlignment	TextEdit	(not moved)
TESetScrapLen	TESetScrapLength	TextEdit	(not moved)
TEStylInsert	TEStyleInsert	TextEdit	(not moved)
TEStylNew	TEStyleNew	TextEdit	(not moved)

Renamed and Relocated Text Routines

Table D-1   Renamed, relocated, and obsolete text and international routines (continued)

Old name	New name	Old location	New location
TeStylPaste	TEStylePaste	TextEdit	(not moved)
TextBox	TETextBox	TextEdit	(not moved)
ToggleDate	(unchanged)	Script Manager	O.S. Utilities
Transliterate	(obsolete; use TransliterateText)		Script Manager
TruncString	(unchanged)	Script Manager	Text Utilities
TruncText	(unchanged)	Script Manager	Text Utilities
UpperText	(obsolete; use UppercaseText)		Text Utilities
UprString	UpperString	O.S. Utilities	Text Utilities
ValidDate	(unchanged)	Script Manager	O.S. Utilities
VisibleLength	(unchanged)	Script Manager	QuickDraw
WriteLocation	(unchanged)	Script Manager	O.S. Utilities

Glossary

active input area   In inline input, the area of the application window in which the user enters text for conversion by a text service component. The application and the text service component share responsibility for the active input area.

advance width   The full width of a glyph, measured from the **glyph origin** to the other side of the glyph, including any white space on either side.

alignment   The horizontal placement of lines of text with respect to the left and right edges of the text area. Alignment can be left, right, centered, or **justified** (flush on both left and right edges). Not to be confused with **line direction.**

alphabet   The set of letters, or **characters,** used to write a language. The alphabet used by the Roman script consists of 26 letters.

Apple event   A high-level event that is used for communication and data sharing among applications.

Apple event handler   An application-defined function that extracts pertinent data from an Apple event, performs the action requested by the Apple event, and returns a result.

application font   The default font for use by applications. The application font is defined by each script system.

Arabic calendar   A lunar calendar used in much of the Arabic world. There are two Arabic calendars supported by the Arabic script system: the astronomical lunar calendar, based on the moon's phases as actually observed at each location around the world; and the civil lunar calendar, a statutory version of the astronomical calendar. In both versions, the positions in time of each month vary from year to year.

Arabic numerals   In the Macintosh script management system, numerals native to the Arabic writing system and not used in the Roman writing system. Compare **western numerals.**

ascent line   An imaginary horizontal line that coincides with the tops of the tallest characters in a font. See also **base line, descent line, x-height.**

ASCII character set   The standard set of Roman characters, with character-code values from $00 to $7F. Also called **low ASCII,** to distinguish them from character codes with values from $80 to $FF, which are sometimes called *high ASCII* or *extended ASCII.* The Roman characters that are part of each non-Roman character set are the low ASCII set only. Compare **Macintosh character set** and **Standard Roman character set.**

associated font   A Roman font whose glyphs are automatically substituted for glyphs of a non-Roman font, for characters in the Roman range. For example, the Arabic script system uses an associated font to display all Roman characters, even within script runs of Arabic text.

attribute type   An integer constant describing a data attribute of a dictionary entry.

auxiliary script   A script system other than the system script that is available for application use. An auxiliary script can be used in documents, but it does not affect the default behavior of the system software.

background   The part of a glyph bitmap that surrounds the pixels that constitute the glyph itself. Compare **foreground.**

background color   The color that QuickDraw applies to the background parts of a glyph; specified by the `bkColor` field of the current graphics port.

base line   An imaginary horizontal line that coincides with the bottom of each character in a font, excluding descenders (tails on letters such as p).

Bézier curve   A curve, used for defining character shapes in outline fonts, defined by three outline points: two on-curve points that serve as endpoints and one off-curve point that determines the degree of curvature.

bidirectional script system   A script system where text is generally right-aligned with most characters written from right to left, but with some left-to-right text as well. Arabic and Hebrew are bidirectional script systems.

bitmapped font   A font made up of bitmapped glyphs. Compare **outline font.**

bitmapped glyph   A bitmap of a character designed for display at a fixed point size for a particular display device.

Bopomofo   Chinese phonetic characters. Also called **Zhuyinfuhao.**

bottomline input   A type of input method in which the user enters text in a small window, called a **floating input window,** that appears near the bottom of the screen.

B*-tree   A data structure used by the Dictionary Manager to organize dictionary index entries for fast searching.

bundle resource   (1) A resource of type `'BNDL'` that is used by the Finder to associate an application and its files and icons. (2) A script system's **international bundle resource.**

byte offset   The indexed position of a byte in a text buffer, starting at zero for the first byte. In 1-byte script systems, byte offset is the same as **character offset,** and sequential values for byte offset correspond to the **storage order** of the characters. In 2-byte script systems, byte offset and character offset are different.

canonical string   The preferred representation of a character or string in a particular writing system, language, or region, often corresponding to a token type defined by the Script Manager `IntlTokenize` function. For example, the left literal double curly quotes (") can, in the appropriate context, also be represented as double straight quotes ("). This stored preference is the canonical string.

caret   A vertical blinking bar within a line of displayed text that marks the insertion point. Compare **cursor.**

caret position   A location (on the screen) corresponding to the offset (in memory) of the current text insertion point. At the boundary between a right-to-left and left-to-right direction run on a line, one character offset may correspond to two caret positions, and one caret position may correspond to two offsets.

case   Uppercase or lowercase, an attribute of the characters of some writing systems such as Roman.

character   A symbol standing for a sound, syllable, or notion used in a script; one of the simple elements of a written language, for example, the lowercase letter "a" or the number "1". Compare **character code, glyph.**

character attribute   The font, size, style, or color of text. Text of a single style run has uniform character attributes.

character class   A return value of the `CharacterType` function. Character class is a subtype of **character type.**

character cluster   A collection of characters treated as individual components of a whole, including a principal character plus attachments in memory. For example, in Hebrew, a cluster may be composed of a consonant, a vowel, a dot to soften the pronunciation of the consonant, and a cantillation mark.

character code   An 8-bit or 16-bit value representing a text character. Text is stored in memory as character codes. Each script system's keyboard-layout (`'KCHR'`) resource converts the virtual key codes generated by the keyboard or keypad into character codes; each script system's fonts convert the character codes into glyphs for display or printing.

character-code mapping table   A table in a font that matches character codes to glyph indexes.

character encoding   The organization of the numeric codes that represent the characters of a character set in memory.

character key   A key that generates a keyboard event when pressed (any key but Shift, Caps Lock, Command, Control, or Option).

character offset   (1) The indexed position of a character in a text buffer, starting at zero for the first character. Sequential values for character offset correspond to the **storage order** of the characters. In 1-byte script systems, character offset is equivalent to **byte offset;** in 2-byte systems it is not. (2) The horizontal separation between a character rectangle and a font rectangle—that is, the position of a given character within the font's bit image.

character origin   See **glyph origin.**

character type   A return value of the `CharacterType` function. Character type describes the features of a given character, such as whether it is a letter, number, or subscript character.

character width   The distance from one character's origin to the next character's origin. It is how far QuickDraw moves the pen after drawing a character.

client application   A program that requests text services such as input methods, spell-checking, and hyphenation from the Text Services Manager. Client applications use the Text Services Manager to search for, obtain information about, and communicate with **text service components.**

completer key   A keypress, following a **dead key,** that generates a character. The key *e* is a completer key for the dead-key combination *Option-E.*

completion character   The character produced by a completer key. The completion character for the completer key *e* pressed after the dead-key combination *Option-E* is *é.*

component   A software module of the specific type managed by the Component Manager. See also **text service component.**

component instance   A single executing version of a component. There can be more than one instance of a given component running at one time.

Component Manager   The part of system software that allows applications to find and use at runtime predefined classes of software objects called **components.**

configuration resource   See **international configuration resource.**

confirm   To accept converted text in an active input area or floating input window as final and send it to the application. Compare **convert, raw text.**

context dependence   In text, when the glyph corresponding to a character may be modified depending on the preceding or following characters in the text.

contextual script system   A script system, such as Arabic, in which the displayed glyph for a character may be context-dependent. It may be modified based on the characters it is adjacent to.

continuous style   In TextEdit, a style value that is constant over an entire selection range.

convert   To change the text entered in an active input area or floating input window into an ideographic or other complex form. An input method converts **raw text,** such as Hiragana, into converted text, such as Kanji. See also **confirm.**

current font The current font for drawing text; the font specified in the `txFont` field of the current graphics port.

current port The graphics port to which the next drawing or measuring operation applies. The current port is specified by the global variable `thePort`, and changed by the QuickDraw `SetPort` procedure.

current script The script system currently used for text manipulation or display. It is the script system used by a script-aware text-handling routine when the identity of the script or its resources is not an explicit parameter of the call. The current script can be either the **font script** or the **system script.**

cursive font A set of characters in one typeface in which letters are connected together as in cursive handwriting.

cursor An arrow, I-beam marker, spinning disk, or other small icon that marks a screen location and moves with the mouse. Compare **caret.**

data attribute In a dictionary, some information about raw data—for example, grammatical or context-sensitive details.

Date & Time control panel A control panel that allows the user to set the current date and time and to specify formatting preferences for both.

date cache A temporary storage area used to convert strings to date and time values.

dead key A keypress or modifier-plus-keypress combination that produces no immediate effect, but instead affects the character or characters produced by the next key (called the **completer key**) that is pressed. For example, in the U.S. Roman system *Option-E* has no effect; however, when you type *e* after pressing *Option-E,* the accented form appears: *é.*

derived font A font whose characteristics are partially determined by modifying an **intrinsic font.** A derived font might be one whose characters are scaled from an intrinsic font to achieve a desired size or are slanted to achieve an italic style.

descent line An imaginary horizontal line that coincides with the bottoms of character descenders (such as the tail on a lowercase p) extending farthest below the **base line.** See also **ascent line.**

destination rectangle In TextEdit, the rectangle defining the area in which the text is drawn. Text drawn in the destination rectangle is made visible to the application user in the **view rectangle.**

diacritic or **diacritical mark** A sign that modifies the implicit sound or value of the character with which it is associated. For example, in the Roman system, the acute accent (´) is a diacritical mark.

dictionary A collection of records used by input methods and other software modules that let the user enter, format, and process text. See also **main dictionary, user dictionary.**

dictionary entry An item associated with a dictionary key. Each entry consists of raw data plus optional data attributes.

dictionary key A Pascal search string that may have a maximum length of 129 bytes. Data associated with the key may consist of one or more dictionary entries.

Dictionary Manager The part of Macintosh system software that makes dictionaries available to input methods.

dictionary record In a dictionary, a key and one or more entries (data associated with the key).

direction See **line direction.**

direction boundary A point between offsets in memory or glyphs on a display, at which the direction of the stored or displayed text changes.

direction run A contiguous (in memory) sequence of characters having the same right-to-left or left-to-right **line direction.**

discontinuous highlighting A highlighting effect that can occur when a selection range crosses one or more direction boundaries.

discontinuous selection   A type of **selection range** in which the selected characters themselves are not contiguous in memory. Not to be confused with **discontinuous highlighting.**

dispatch routine   A routine in a script system that dispatches script utility calls. WorldScript I and WorldScript II each contain a single dispatch routine that works for all compatible 1-byte and 2-byte scripts, respectively.

dispatch table   A table that is part of a script system's script record; it contains the addresses of the script utilities for that script system.

display line   The horizontal extent of an area for drawing text on a display device. The left and right ends of the display line are the text area's left and right margins.

display order   The left-to-right order in which glyphs are drawn on a screen by QuickDraw. Because not all text is read left-to-right, the display order of glyphs may be different from the **storage order** of their corresponding character codes in memory.

dithering   A technique of mixing existing colors to create the effect of additional colors. Used by QuickDraw to draw dimmed text on the screen.

dual caret   A high caret and a low caret, each measuring half the line's height. The dual caret appears only when the text insertion point is at the boundary between two direction runs in a line of text. The high (primary) caret is displayed at the **primary caret position,** corresponding to the character offset in the direction run that corresponds to the **system direction.** The low (secondary) caret is displayed at the **secondary caret position,** corresponding to the character offset in the direction run that is counter to the system direction. When the caret position is unambiguous (not on a direction boundary), the primary and secondary carets are at the same position, so the user sees one caret. Compare **single caret.**

enable   To make a script system available. The Script Manager and the script extensions enable only those script systems that have a required set of resources and fonts. Compare **install, initialize.**

encoding/rendering resource   An international resource of type `'itl5'`. The encoding/rendering resource specifies character encoding or rendering information for a particular script system. The encoding/rendering resource is optional and has different formats in 1-byte and 2-byte script systems.

entry   See **dictionary entry.**

explicit scaling   Scaling performed by the Font Manager when an application specifically asks QuickDraw to change text from a particular size or shape to another. Compare **implicit scaling.**

fixed input   In **inline input,** text that has already been converted from phonetic to ideographic representation, and thus can be removed from the active input area. Usually, the text service component continually gets rid of fixed input. In certain situations, a client application may need to explicitly fix input, if for example it must suspend input in progress.

fixed token   A token associated with a single, invariant set of characters. The token `tokenPeriod` is a fixed token; it represents a period (.). The token `tokenNumeric` is not fixed; it could represent any number.

fixed-width font   A font whose characters all have the same width. Compare **proportional font.**

floating input window   A floating window used for text entry by an input method.

floating window   A window that is similar to a standard Window Manager window except that it occupies a special layer so that it always remains in front of any application windows.

floating window service   A service, managed by the Text Services Manager and the Process Manager, that provides floating windows for text service components.

font   (1) For bitmapped fonts, a complete set of glyphs in one typeface, size, and style. (2) For outline fonts, a complete set of glyphs in one typeface and style. A font also has a table that associates those glyphs with their equivalent character codes.

font characterization table   A table of parameters in a device driver that specifies how best to adapt fonts to that device.

font family   A complete set of fonts for one typeface including all available styles and sizes of the glyphs in that typeface. A font family may include both bitmapped and outline fonts. Font families are defined by resources of type `'FOND'`.

font-family ID   The number that identifies the resource file (of type `'FOND'`) that specifies the font family. Every font family has a unique font-family ID, in a range of values that determines the script system to which the font family belongs.

font force flag   A Script Manager variable that forces text whose font has an ID in the range of the Roman script system to be interpreted as belonging to the system script instead.

font height   The vertical distance from a font's ascent line to its descent line.

font ID   (1) Font-family ID. (2) The number that identifies the resource file of a particular individual font, of type `'FONT'`, `'nfnt'`, or `'sfnt'`.

font layout   (1) The mapping of character codes to the glyphs of one typeface. (2) The mapping of glyph indexes to the glyphs of one typeface.

Font Manager   The part of the Toolbox that supports the use of various fonts for QuickDraw when it draws text.

font name   The name, such as Geneva or Kyoto, given to a font family to distinguish it from other font families.

font number   See **font ID.**

font rectangle   The smallest rectangle enclosing all the glyphs in a font if the images are all superimposed over the same glyph origin.

font run   A sequence of text that is contiguous in memory and in which all characters are in the same font.

font scaling   The process of changing a glyph from one size or shape to another. The Font Manager can scale bitmapped and outline fonts by changing both sizes and shapes of glyphs.

font scaling factors   Ratios that indicate how the Font Manager should scale a glyph in the vertical and horizontal directions.

font script   The script system that corresponds to the current font (the font specified in the `txFont` field of the current graphics port), hence the script that determines in which writing system to display text characters in the window.

font size   The size of the glyphs in a font in points; nominally a measure of the distance from the base line of one line of text to the base line of the next line of single-spaced text.

foreground   The part of a glyph bitmap that constitutes the glyph itself. Compare **background.**

foreground color   The color that QuickDraw applies to the foreground parts of a glyph; specified by the `fgColor` field of the current graphics port.

full justification   See **justification.**

garbage data   A type of data in a dictionary that exists if the size of the information associated with a key increases or decreases or if the information is deleted. This data is no longer used by the dictionary.

global width table   A data structure used by the Font Manager to communicate character widths to QuickDraw.

glyph   The distinct visual representation of a character in a form that a screen or printer can display. A glyph may represent one character (the lowercase *a*), more than one character (the *fi* ligature, two characters but one glyph), or a nonprinting character (the space character).

glyph index   A number that specifies a particular glyph in a font. Some fonts directly specify glyphs with character codes, whereas others map character codes to glyph indexes, which in turn specify the glyphs.

glyph origin   The point on a base line used as a reference location for drawing a glyph. QuickDraw draws a glyph so that the glyph origin corresponds to the current **pen position.**

graphics port   A complete drawing environment in QuickDraw, including such elements as a bitmap, a subset of it in which to draw, a character font, patterns for drawing and erasing, and other graphics characteristics. Graphics ports can be either black-and-white (data type `grafPort`) or color (data type `CgrafPort`).

greeked   Said of text that is drawn so that its individual characters are replaced with shading or illegible marks. Text at very small point sizes is often greeked when drawn to the screen.

Gregorian calendar   The calendar used in Europe and America. It is not universally accepted—for example, different calendar systems are often used in Japan, China, and the Middle East.

Han   A general term for Chinese-derived ideographic characters. Includes **Hanzi, Kanji,** and **Hanja.**

Hangul   A Korean subscript which consists of blocks of component glyphs called **Jamo** that are arranged and transformed into boxes. Hangul characters differ from typical **character clusters** in that they are treated as singular units in memory; there are no principal characters and attachments.

Hanja   Korean ideographic characters borrowed from Chinese.

Hanzi   Native Chinese ideographic characters.

high caret   See **primary caret.**

highlighting   The display of text in inverse video or with a colored background, to designate a **selection range.**

Hiragana   A cursive, phonetic subscript of the Japanese writing system, with 50 syllables that represent all sounds of the Japanese language. Compare **Katakana.**

ideographic   A type of character representation in which characters do not represent pronunciation alone, but are also related to the component meanings of words; for example, Japanese Kanji, Chinese Hanzi, and Korean Hanja.

implicit scaling   Scaling performed by the Font Manager when an application asks QuickDraw to draw text in a size that is not represented by the available fonts. Compare **explicit scaling.**

index   (1) The part of a dictionary through which records are retrieved. Each index entry contains a **key.** (2) A zero-based, ordinal position in a buffer or data structure.

initialize   For a script system, to create and set up a script record at system startup. Script systems either initialize themselves or are initialized by the Script Manager. Only script systems that are **installed** can be initialized.

inline input   An input method that allows the user to enter text directly into a document. In inline input, entry and conversion of characters take place at the current line position—where the converted text is intended to appear—rather than in a separate window. Inline input is the principal example of the kind of text service supported by the Text Services Manager.

input method   A software facility for 2-byte script systems that converts phonetic or syllabic characters, entered from a keyboard, into ideographic or other complex representations of text. Because 2-byte script systems have too many characters to be entered directly from a keyboard, the input method uses a conversion technique, such as translating sequences of phonetic characters that are typed into a special input window. For example, the Japanese script system provides software for transcribing Kana (phonetic Japanese) into ideographic Kanji.

insertion mode   For a dictionary, the manner in which insertion of a new record occurs—for example, whether its data adds to or replaces data of an existing matching key.

insertion point   A location (offset) in a text buffer at which the next insertion or deletion of text is to take place. An insertion point is equivalent to a **selection range** of zero characters.

install   To place (the resources of a script system) in the System file.

intercharacter spacing   Extra pixels that are added between glyphs, in addition to the space surrounding the glyph as defined by the font, in formatting or justifying text.

interface type   A specification of the set of Apple events and component commands associated with a component; part of the component description record. Currently, all text service components have the same interface type: kTextService, whose associated 4-character tag is 'tsvc'.

international bundle resource   An international resource of type 'itlb'. The international bundle resource identifies the complete set of international resources and keyboard resources used by a script system. It also specifies some of the script's default behavior. Every script system has one international bundle resource.

international configuration resource   An international resource of type 'itlc'. The international configuration resource identifies and configures the system script. There is only one international configuration resource for each Macintosh System file, regardless of the number of script systems it supports.

international resources   A specific set of resources used by the Script Manager, the Text Utilities, and TextEdit. The international resources contain information specific to language or region, such as date and time formats, sorting order, and word-break rules.

international resources cache   A cache that holds resource IDs of international resources used by an application.

international resources selection flag   A Script Manager variable that determines which set of international resources are to be used for text processing operations. When the flag is set, the resources belonging to the system script are used. When the flag is clear, the resources belonging to the font script are used.

interword spacing   Extra pixels that are added to word delimiters—whether white space or extension bars—when formatting or justifying text.

intrinsic font   A font whose characteristics are entirely defined in a 'FONT' or 'NFNT' resource. The plain-style font of any family is an intrinsic font. Other styles may or may not be intrinsic. Compare **derived font.**

'itl0' resource   See **numeric-format resource.**

'itl1' resource   See **long-date-format resource.**

'itl2' resource   See **string-manipulation resource.**

'itl4' resource   See **tokens resource.**

'itl5' resource   See **encoding/rendering resource.**

'itlb' resource   See **international bundle resource.**

'itlc' resource   See **international configuration resource.**

'itlk' resource   See **key-remap resource.**

'itlm' resource   See **script-sorting resource.**

Jamo   An individual phonetic glyph in the Korean script that is transformed and combined into clusters called **Hangul.**

jumping caret   See **single caret.**

justification   A type of **alignment** that involves the spreading or compressing of printed text to fit into a given line width so that it is flush on both left and right edges of the text area (destination rectangle).

Kana   A collective term for the Japanese subscripts **Hiragana** and **Katakana.**

Kanji   Japanese ideographic characters borrowed from Chinese.

kashida   Extension bars drawn between specific Arabic characters to create justified text.

Katakana   An angular, phonetic subscript of the Japanese writing system, with 50 syllables that represent all sounds of the Japanese language. Compare **Hiragana.**

'KCAP' resource   See **key caps resource.**

'KCHR' resource   See **keyboard-layout resource.**

`'kcs#'` resource   See **keyboard icons family.**

`'kcs4'` resource   See **keyboard icons family.**

`'kcs8'` resource   See **keyboard icons family.**

kern   To draw part of a glyph so that it overlaps the space of an adjacent glyph.

key   See **dictionary key.**

keyboard   (1) A hardware input device consisting of an array of keys that the user presses in order to enter text into the computer. (2) For the Macintosh script management system, a keyboard-layout resource that provides for keyboard input in a given script system. In this sense, to change keyboards means to activate a different keyboard layout, rather than physically switching keyboards.

Keyboard control panel   A control panel that allows the user to switch among available keyboard layouts.

keyboard equivalent   The combination of the Command key and another key, used to invoke a menu item from the keyboard.

keyboard icon   A small icon associated with each keyboard through its keyboard-layout (`'KCHR'`) resource. Keyboard icons are used in the Keyboard menu and the Keyboard control panel.

keyboard icon family   A set of keyboard resources, of types `'kcs#'`, `'kcs4'`, and `'kcs8'`. The keyboard icon family specifies keyboard icons for screens of different bit depth (black-and white, 4-bit, and 8-bit, respectively). There is one keyboard icon family for every keyboard-layout (`'KCHR'`) resource.

keyboard layout   (1) The specification of the physical arrangement of keys on a keyboard and the characters produced when those keys are pressed. (2) The keyboard-layout resource.

keyboard-layout resource   A keyboard resource of type `'KCHR'`. The keyboard-layout resource defines a particular character set by associating a character code with each virtual key code produced by a keystroke or combination of keystrokes on the keyboard or keypad. Each script system has one or more `'KCHR'` resources.

Keyboard menu   A menu on the right side of the menu bar that appears when more than one script system is enabled. The Keyboard menu is managed by the Operating System and permits the user to change keyboard layouts, input methods, and script systems for text input.

keyboard resources   A specific set of resources used by the Script Manager, the Text Utilities, and TextEdit for text input. The keyboard resources provide for text input in any language from any keyboard, for convenient switching from one input language to another on a single keyboard, and for simultaneous input from multiple keyboards.

keyboard script   The script system for keyboard input. It determines the character input method and the mapping of keystrokes to character codes. The keyboard script may be different from the font script, which determines how text is displayed.

keyboard swap resource   A keyboard resource of type `'KSWP'`. The keyboard swap resource specifies key combinations that can be used to change the keyboard script and the current keyboard layout. There is one `'KSWP'` resource per system.

Key Caps   A desk accessory that displays the keyboard layout for a given keyboard and a specified font.

key caps resource   A keyboard resource of type `'KCAP'`. The key caps resource specifies the physical arrangement of keys on a keyboard and is used by the Key Caps desk accessory. There is one `'KCAP'` resource for each physical keyboard supported.

key code   An integer representing a key on the keyboard or keypad, without reference to the character the key stands for. See also **raw key code** and **virtual key code.**

key entry   In a Dictionary Manager dictionary, contains raw data and optional attributes. Each entry may have a maximum length of 256 bytes. The maximum length of the associated data is 1024 bytes.

key-map resource   A keyboard resource of type `'KMAP'`. The key-map resource takes the raw key codes that have been generated by the keyboard microprocessor and maps them into standard virtual key codes. There is exactly one `'KMAP'` resource for each physical keyboard on a Macintosh system.

key-remap resource   A keyboard resource of type `'itlk'`. The key-remap resource provides hardware-specific modifications for certain keyboards. It remaps a few key combinations into the virtual key codes needed for input to certain versions of the keyboard-layout (`'KCHR'`) resource. There is one `'itlk'` resource for every `'KCHR'` resource that needs one.

key translation   The process of converting raw key codes to virtual key codes, and thence to character codes, during text input.

`'KMAP'` resource   See **key-map resource.**

`'KSWP'` resource   See **keyboard swap resource.**

language   For the Macintosh script management system, a particular implementation of a writing system. Languages within a writing system usually share a character set but differ in rules of composition. For example, English and Spanish are two languages within the Roman writing system.

language code   A number used to indicate a particular written version of a language on the Macintosh. Constants are defined for each of the language codes recognized by the Macintosh script management system.

large character set   A character set with more than 256 characters. Japanese, Chinese, and Korean writing systems have large character sets. The script system for such a writing system requires 2-byte **character codes,** and is therefore called a **2-byte script system.**

leading (pronounced "LED-ing")   The amount of blank vertical space between the descent line of one line of text and the ascent line of the next line of single-spaced text. In early typesetting, strips of lead were placed between lines of type for spacing, hence the term. See also **line spacing.**

leading edge   The edge of a glyph that is encountered first when reading text of that glyph's script system. Compare **trailing edge.**

ligature   A glyph that is created when two or more characters are combined to create a new character.

line breaking   The automatic continuation of text from the end of one line to the beginning of the next without ending the line in the middle of a word.

line direction   Also called *text direction, character direction,* or simply *direction.* The direction in which text in a particular language is written and read. The English language has a left-to-right line direction; Arabic and Hebrew have a (primarily) right-to-left line direction. See also **system direction.** Line direction is not the same as **alignment.**

line spacing   The vertical distance between two lines of type, measured from base line to base line. For example, 10/12 indicates 10-point type with 12 points base to base (that is, with 2 points of **leading**).

localization   The adaptation of system software or applications to a particular language or region. Localization involves translating strings and providing proper conventions for sorting, date and time formats, currency and measurement units, calendars, numbers, and other culturally specific items such as icons.

localized system software   Macintosh system software that has been adapted to a particular language or region. Localization may involve adding a second script system, as in the case of Japanese system software; or it may simply require modifying the U.S. Roman script system, as in the case of French or Turkish system software.

long-date-format resource   An international resource of type `'itl1'`. The long-date-format resource defines conventions for formatting long dates, including names of days and months. Each installed script system has one or more long-date-format resources.

low ASCII character set   Same as **ASCII character set;** the standard set of Roman characters with character-code values from $00 to $7F.

low caret   See **secondary caret.**

Macintosh character set   The characters and character codes originally defined for the Macintosh computer. The Macintosh character set consists of the **ASCII character set,** plus additional characters (sometimes called *high ASCII* or *extended ASCII*) with character codes between $80 and $D8. Compare **Standard Roman character set.**

Macintosh script management system   The Script Manager, the script-aware parts of other text managers, the WorldScript extensions, and one or more Macintosh script systems.

main dictionary   A dictionary that contains most of the information used by an input method for its conversion operations. Compare **user dictionary.**

missing character glyph   The glyph in a font that is drawn when no glyph is defined for a character code in a font.

mixed-directional text   The combination of writing systems with left-to-right and right-to-left directions—within a single line of text.

modifier key   Any of the following keys on a Macintosh keyboard: Option, Caps Lock, Shift, Command, Control.

monospaced font   See **fixed-width font.**

monostyled edit record   A TextEdit record used to contain text that is set in a single font, size, and face.

mouse-down region   The region between the caret position and the middle of an adjacent character that maps unambiguously to a single character offset.

moving caret   See **single caret.**

multistyled edit record   A TextEdit record that contains text with style information that can vary from character to character. A multistyled edit record contains a number of additional subsidiary data structures that support the text styling information.

native   Characters in a character set that belong to the character set traditionally defined for the writing system of that font. For example, a Hebrew font can display both Hebrew characters and Roman characters. The Hebrew characters are native to the font and the script system; the Roman characters are not.

neighborhood base font   The font with the lowest font family ID for a particular script system.

no-match character   The character produced when the keystroke that follows a dead key is a space character or is not a valid completer key. The no-match character is usually a stand-alone accent form; for example, the no-match character for the dead-key combination Option-E is ´.

null scrap   A scrap that is created and initialized for a TextEdit **multistyled edit record** to store style information associated with an insertion point.

number parts table   A table in the tokens resource that contains number-formatting information.

Numbers control panel   A control panel that allows the user to specify default number and currency formats for text of the system script.

numeric-format resource   An international resource of type `'itl0'`. The numeric-format resource defines conventions for formatting numeric strings. Each installed script system has one or more numeric-format resources.

off-curve point   An **outline point** between two **on-curve points** that determines the curve of the line between the two on-curve points. A **Bézier curve** is defined by all three points.

on-curve point   One of the **outline points** that determines the shape of a **Bézier curve.** Two on-curve points and one off-curve point are required to define the curve.

1-byte complex script system   A script system that supports a writing system with a small character set (requires only 1-byte characters), but that is characterized by bidirectional or contextual text. Arabic and Hebrew are examples of complex 1-byte script systems.

1-byte extension   See **WorldScript I.**

1-byte simple script system   A script system that supports a writing system with a small character set (requires only 1-byte characters), has a left-to-right text direction only, and that is non-contextual. The Roman script system is an example of a 1-byte simple script system.

Operating System   A specific installation of Macintosh system software. The Operating System (or *system*) consists of the System file and its associated resources, and the Operating System components of the ROM-based Macintosh Toolbox.

outline font   A font made up of outline glyphs in a particular typeface and style, with no size restriction. The Font Manager can generate thousands of point sizes from the same outline font.

outline highlighting   The highlighting of a selection range by drawing an outline around the selected characters. Typically used to show a selection range in an inactive window.

outline point   A point used by the Font Manager to calculate the lines and curves that constitute an outline glyph. See also **on-curve point** and **off-curve point.**

Pascal string   An array of characters, consisting of a length byte followed by up to 255 bytes of data. Compare **text string.**

pen position   The screen position where QuickDraw begins to draw a character, as specified by the `penLoc` field of the active graphics port.

Pinyin   A system for writing Chinese ideographs by using Roman letters to represent the sounds.

point   A QuickDraw data structure that defines a screen location.

port   See **graphics port.**

port font   The font for drawing text in a graphics port, as specified in the `txFont` field of the graphics port record.

primary caret   The high caret that is displayed at the **primary caret position;** part of a **dual caret.**

primary caret position   When a dual caret appears, the screen location that marks the insertion point for text whose line direction matches the **primary line direction.**

primary line direction   The dominant line direction (right-to-left or left-to-right) of the current text. The primary line direction is typically specified by the value of the system direction global variable, `SysDirection`.

private scrap   A scrap used exclusively by TextEdit.

proportional font   Any font in which different characters have different widths; thus, the space taken up by words having the same number of letters can vary.

raw data   In a dictionary, any information related to the key entry. The information can be the explanation of the key in a general dictionary, or perhaps all the Han characters with the pronunciation of the key entry in an East Asian dictionary.

raw key code   A key code generated by a keyboard prior to any processing by the `'KMAP'` resource. See also **virtual key code.**

raw text   Characters in an active input area or floating input window that have not yet been converted to ideographic or other final form. Compare **convert, confirm.**

region   For the Macintosh script management system, a particular subset of a language. A region can represent a linguistic or cultural entity, not necessarily corresponding to a nation, whose language is different enough from other versions of the same language that it merits a specific localized version of Macintosh system software. For example, U.S. and British are two regional variations that are subsets of the English language.

region code   A number indicating the Macintosh version of the written language of a particular region. Constants are defined for each of the region codes recognized by the Macintosh script management system.

Roman character set   A set of characters used for the Roman writing system. Roman character sets include the **Standard Roman character set, Macintosh character set,** and **ASCII character set.**

Roman writing system   The visual representation of words and letters based on the Roman alphabet (a, b, c, and so forth). Developed during the Roman empire, Roman is the most widely used writing system in the world today. For example, Roman is used in most countries of Europe, the Americas, Africa, Oceania, and some Asian nations.

run   A sequence of characters that are contiguous in memory and share a set of common attributes. See, for example, **direction run, script run, font run,** and **style run.**

scaling   The adjustment in size or shape of the glyphs of a font. The Font Manager performs both **implicit scaling** and **explicit scaling,** at the request of QuickDraw.

script   See **script system.**

script-aware   Said of a routine or system-software manager that takes the current script system into account when manipulating or displaying text.

script code   A number indicating a particular script system on the Macintosh. Constants are defined for each of the script codes recognized by the Macintosh script management system.

script-defaulted result flag   A Script Manager variable that indicates whether the system script has replaced the font script due to the unavailability of the font script.

script extension   A part of the Macintosh script management system that allows for convenient and efficient creation of new script systems. Each script system provides tables in its international resources that specify the proper text-manipulation and formatting behavior; the script extension interprets those tables when an application makes a text-related call. There are two script extensions: **WorldScript I,** the universal 1-byte script system extension, and **WorldScript II,** the universal 2-byte script system extension.

script-forced result flag   A Script Manager variable that indicates whether the system script has replaced the font script due to font forcing.

script-language record   A record that defines a script and language supported by a text service component.

script-language support record   An array of script-language records that defines all the scripts and languages supported by a text service component.

script record   A private data structure, maintained by the script management system, that defines each enabled script system, and through which calls to that script system are dispatched.

script run   A sequence of text that is contiguous in memory and belongs to a single script system.

script-sorting resource   An international resource, of type `'itlm'`. The script-sorting resource lists all defined script codes, language codes, and region codes, in proper sorting order. It also maps each region to its parent language, and each language to its parent script. An application uses the script-sorting resource to sort multiple-language lists. There is only one script-sorting resource for each version of the Macintosh system software.

script system   A collection of software facilities that provides for the representation of a specific writing system. It consists of a set of keyboard resources, a set of international resources, one or more fonts, and possibly a script system extension (1-byte or 2-byte). Script systems include Roman, Japanese, Arabic, Traditional Chinese, Simplified Chinese, Hebrew, Greek, Thai, and Korean. Types of script systems include 1-byte simple, 1-byte complex, and 2-byte.

script utility   The low-level equivalent to one of a large group of script-aware Script Manager, Text Utilities, or QuickDraw text routines. Some script utilities are handled by the script management system; others are passed on to script systems. Script utilities all use the `_ScriptUtil` trap.

secondary caret   The low caret that is displayed at the **secondary caret position;** part of a **dual caret.**

secondary caret position   The screen location (denoted by the secondary caret) associated with the character that has an opposing direction from the primary line direction.

secondary script   See **auxiliary script.**

selection range   The series of characters in memory where the next editing operation is to occur. The onscreen glyphs of those characters are commonly highlighted. The characters in a selection range are always contiguous in memory, but their glyphs are not necessarily so on screen.

selector   An integer value that controls the function of a multipurpose routine. For example, the Script Manager uses selectors to figure out which variable you want to read when calling `GetScriptManagerVariable`.

simple script system   See **1-byte simple script system.**

single caret   In unidirectional text, the standard text-insertion caret. In mixed-directional text, one caret that appears at the place where the user will insert the next character, given the current keyboard script. At a boundary between two direction runs, the single caret can correspond to either the primary line direction or the secondary line direction. Because changing the keyboard script in that situation changes the caret location, the single caret is also called a *moving caret* or *jumping caret.* Compare **dual caret.**

slop   In justified text, the amount of space (in pixels) that must be added to a line of text to make it exactly fit the desired line length. The slop value for a line is to be distributed among the style runs, words, and characters on the line.

small character set   A character set with no more than 256 characters. Roman, Hebrew, and Arabic have small character sets. The script system for such a writing system needs only 1-byte **character codes,** and is therefore called a 1-byte script system.

sorting hook   A routine in the string-manipulation (`'itl2'`) resource that controls sorting behavior for a particular script system.

source mask   A value that specifies which of a script system's subscripts the `TransliterateText` function is to operate on.

split caret   See **dual caret.**

Standard Roman character set   The 256 characters and character codes that are supplied with the Macintosh Roman script system. The Standard Roman character set consists of the **Macintosh character set** plus additional defined characters with character codes between $D9 and $FF.

storage order   The order in which character codes are stored in memory. Storage order may be different from **display order.**

string-manipulation resource   An international resource of type `'itl2'`. The string-manipulation resource defines conventions for comparing text elements, including sorting order, character types, case conversion, and word breaks. Each installed script system has one or more string-manipulation resources.

style   A visual attribute, other than size, applied as a systematic variation to the plain (unstyled) characteristics of a font's glyphs. The set of styles supported by QuickDraw consists of bold, italic, underline, outline, shadow, condense, and extend.

style code   A byte-length mask with one bit set for each QuickDraw-supported style to be applied.

styled text   Text that is displayed in multiple styles.

style run   A sequence of text that is contiguous in memory and in which all the characters are in the same font, size, style, color, and script system.

style scrap   A TextEdit scrap that stores style information associated with text that is cut or copied.

subscript   A distinguishable subset of characters included within a script—for example, Japanese Hiragana, Katakana, Kanji, and Romaji.

synthetic font   A font created by the Font Manager from a **bitmapped font** resource by expanding the 1-bit font into a font that matches the current screen depth.

system direction   The horizontal placement of interface elements, including the default line direction (left-to-right or right-to-left) for text in the system script. System direction is specified by the global variable `SysDirection`.

System file   A file, located in the System Folder, that contains the basic system software plus some system resources, such as international and keyboard resources of installed script systems.

system font   The font used to display text in menus, dialog boxes, alert boxes, and so forth in a given script system. For example, in the Roman script system, the system font is Chicago.

system script   The primary script system used by various parts of the Operating System, such as in dialog boxes and menu bars. The system script affects system defaults, such as the system font, line direction, and text-formatting rules. All other scripts are secondary to the system script. The system script is specified in the system software's configuration resource (`'itlc'`).

target format   A value that specifies what format the `TransliterateText` function is to convert text into.

target modifier   A value that provides formatting information beyond that specified in the **target format**, for use by the `TransliterateText` function.

text   The written representation of language. Text is a sequence of symbols that conveys meaning to its reader. The set of symbols used, and the most basic rules for their presentation, constitute the writing system of the text. The lexical, grammatical, and semantic significance of combinations of the symbols constitute the language of the text.

Text control panel   A control panel, available on non-U.S. versions of system software, that allows the user to set aspects of the text behavior of any enabled script system.

text rendering   The process of preparing characters that are stored in memory for display as glyphs.

text segment   For text layout, the portion of a style run (it may be the entire style run) that falls on a single text line. Most text measuring and drawing routines work on a single text segment at a time.

text service   A text-entry or text-processing function provided by a text service component. Inline input is one example of a text service.

text service component   A software module that is a registered component with the Component Manager, and that is used for entry, processing, or formatting of text. Text service components use the Text Services Manager to request action from and send information to client applications.

text service component type   A specification of the function associated with a particular kind of text service component; part of its component description record. Currently, only one text service component type is defined: `'inpm'`, specifying an inline input method.

Text Services Manager   The part of system software that manages the interactions between applications that request text services and text service components that provide them.

text string   An array of characters referenced by a pointer and a length word. A text string may contain up to 32,767 bytes of character data. Compare **Pascal string.**

text style   See **style.**

token   An abstract category of text element that stands for a name, symbol, punctuation, quoted literal, or other sequence of characters.

token block record   A parameter block used by the `IntlTokenize` function. The token block record contains, among other information, a pointer to a list of **token records.**

tokenization   A function provided by the Script Manager and individual script systems. Tokenization identifies the different lexical elements in an arbitrary string of text by using localized information from the tokens resource (`'itl4'`), and converts the string to a series of **tokens.**

token record   A data structure, used by the `IntlTokenize` function, that describes an individual token.

tokens resource   An international resource of type `'itl4'`. The tokens resource contains information needed to convert text in a particular language into a series of tokens. Each installed script system has one or more tokens resources.

trailing edge   The edge of a glyph that is encountered last when reading text of that glyph's script system. Compare **leading edge.**

trailing spaces   White space characters occurring at the end of the last style run in a line of text.

transcription   The representation of sound sequences in phonetic symbols.

transfer mode   A specification of which Boolean operation to perform when drawing. In drawing text, QuickDraw uses transfer mode, along with foreground and background color, to determine how the text to be drawn (called the *source*) interacts with anything already drawn in the current graphics port, called the *destination*.

transliteration   For the Macintosh script management system, the conversion of characters that are phonetic representations of the same sound sequence between subscripts within a script. In the Roman script system, this means case conversion. For Japanese, Chinese, and Korean, transliteration refers to the conversion, without linguistic or semantic considerations, of characters from one subscript to another subscript within a script. Examples include the transliteration of Japanese Hiragana to Katakana, and the transliteration of Korean Jamo to Hangul.

transliteration resource   An international resource of type `'trsl'`. The transliteration resource provides rules for converting text phonetically from one subscript to another within a script system. The transliteration resource is optional; it is used only by 2-byte script systems.

`'trsl'` resource   See **transliteration resource.** See also **international resources.**

TSM-aware application   An application that makes calls to the Text Services Manager. A TSM-aware application can use a variety of text services such as inline input.

TSM document   A private data structure maintained by the Text Services Manager that relates one or more text service components to a particular application window.

2-byte extension   See **WorldScript II.**

2-byte script system   A script system that supports a writing system with a large character set (requires 2-byte characters) and requires sophisticated procedures for character input. Japanese, Chinese, and Korean are examples of 2-byte script systems.

Unicode   A standard for a universal character set now under development. Unicode assigns two bytes per character code, and includes all the characters of all the world's major writing systems in one character set.

unidirectional text   A sequence of text that has a single direction. Compare **mixed-directional text.**

universal script   A 1-byte complex script system that is compatible with WorldScript I.

untoken table   A table in the tokens resource that converts script-independent tokens to text of a given script system.

user dictionary   Also called an *editable dictionary.* A file, complementary to the **main dictionary** used by input methods, in which users can add information that does not exist in the main dictionary.

verb   See **selector.**

view rectangle   In TextEdit, the rectangle defining the portion of the window within which text is actually displayed. Text drawn in the **destination rectangle** is made visible to the application user in the view rectangle.

virtual key code   The key code that an application receives in keyboard events. It is the value produced after a **raw key code** has been mapped through the key-map (`'KMAP'`) and key-remap (`'itlk'`) resources.

western numerals   For the Macintosh script management system, the numerical symbols 1, 2, 3, 4, 5, 6, 7, 8, 9, and 0. Sometimes known as *Arabic numerals,* but not to be confused with the numerals native to the Arabic writing system.

word wrap   See **line breaking.**

WorldScript I   A script extension used for all 1-byte complex script systems. Code in the extension reads tables in the script system's international resources in order to provide the proper text manipulation and formatting for that script. Simple 1-byte script systems do not need to use WorldScript I.

WorldScript II   A script extension used for all 2-byte script systems. Code in the extension reads tables in the script system's international resources in order to provide the proper text manipulation and formatting for that script.

writing system   A set of characters and the basic rules for their use in creating a visual depiction of language. Writing systems may differ in the direction in which their characters and lines run, the size of the character set used, and the context sensitivity of character selection. Writing systems include Roman, Japanese, Arabic, and Hebrew. Compare **script system.** See also **language, region.**

x-height   The height of a lowercase *x* in a given font. It is the height, measured from the base line, of the main portion of most lowercase letters (excluding ascenders and descenders). See also **ascent line, base line, descent line.**

Zhuyinfuhao   Chinese phonetic characters. Also called **Bopomofo.**

Index

O

U

X

Xor transfer mode. *See* transfer modes

Y

year, determining in date conversion 5-32, 5-84
y-values, minimum and maximum 4-10

Z

zero digits. *See* number format specification strings
zero-width characters 1-73, 3-10
Zhuyinfuhao 1-93, 7-6

THE APPLE PUBLISHING SYSTEM

This Apple manual was written, edited, and composed on a desktop publishing system using Apple Macintosh computers and FrameMaker software. Proof pages were created on an Apple LaserWriter IINTX printer. Final page negatives were output directly from text files on an AGFA ProSet 9800 imagesetter. Line art was created using Adobe™ Illustrator. PostScript™, the page-description language for the LaserWriter, was developed by Adobe Systems Incorporated.

Text type is Palatino® and display type is Helvetica®. Bullets are ITC Zapf Dingbats®. Some elements, such as program listings, are set in Apple Courier.

WRITERS
David Bice, Gary Hillerson, Judy Melanson

LEAD WRITER
David Bice

DEVELOPMENTAL EDITORS
Sanborn Hodgkins, Anne Szabla, Jeanne Woodward

ILLUSTRATOR
Sandee Karr

PRODUCTION EDITOR
Teresa Lujan

FORMATTER
Judith Radin

PROJECT MANAGER
Patricia Eastman

COVER DESIGN
Barbara Smyth, Sandee Karr

CHIEF TECHNICAL ADVISOR
Peter Edberg

Special thanks to Jens Peter Alfke, Sue Bartalo, Patria Brown, Ray Chiang, John Harvey, Hae-Sung Kim, Don Louv, Joseph Maurer, Linda Pan, Diane Patterson, Yishai Steinhart, Forrest Tanaka, Kenny Tung, and Andrew Wilson.

Acknowledgments to Hani Abdelazim, Joel Cannon, Rob Dearborn, Chris Derossi, Sharon Everson, Martin Gannholm, Shannon Holland, Norbert Lindenberg, Brian McGhie, Tim Monroe, Mimi Obinata, Dana Rader, Jim Reekes, Gidi Shalom-Bendor, Eric Soldan, Joan Trainer, Celia Vigil, Essam Zaky, Mark Zeren, and the entire *Inside Macintosh* team.

Inside Macintosh

Imaging
How to create images, display them in black-and-white or color, and print them. Includes descriptions of QuickDraw, its associated graphics managers, and the Printing Manager.

Overview
A general introduction to *Inside Macintosh* and to programming for Macintosh computers. Describes the look and feel of Macintosh applications and describes how to implement that interface.

Files
The parts of the Operating System that allow you to manage files. How to handle File menu commands and perform other file-related operations.

Processes
The parts of the Operating System that allow you to control processes and tasks. How to launch processes and to install interrupt-level tasks (such asTime Manager tasks and VBL tasks).

Memory
The parts of the Operating System that allow you to allocate, release, and otherwise manipulate memory. How to use temporary memory and interact with virtual memory.

Text
How to draw characters and lines of text in any font, size, and style. How to write applications that can format, sort, search, display, print, and accept input of text in any language supported by the Macintosh.

Macintosh Toolbox Essentials
How to create and manage
• menus
• windows
• dialog boxes
• alert boxes
• controls
Also, how your application interacts with the Finder.

More Macintosh Toolbox
More about the Macintosh Toolbox, including how to
• provide support for copy and paste
• provide help balloons
• use resources
• gain access to or write a component

Operating System Utilities
The parts of the Operating System that perform various low-level utility operations. Includes descriptions of the Gestalt Manager, Queue Utilities, Date and Time Utilities, and others.

Guide to Software Localization*

Macintosh Human Interface Guidelines*

QuickTime
How to integrate time-based data (such as video and sounds) into your application and compress and decompress image sequences. Includes the Movie Toolbox and the Image Compression Manager.

QuickTime Components
How to use and develop QuickTime components, such as image compressors, movie controllers, sequence grabbers, and video digitizers.

Devices
How to write a device driver, plus
• Device Manager
• Apple Desktop Bus
• Disk Driver
• Power Manager
• SCSI Manager
• Serial Driver
• Slot Manager

Interapplication Communication
How applications can work together. How your application can
• share data
• request information or services
• allow the user to automate tasks
• communicate with remote databases

Networking
The components and organization of AppleTalk. How to select an AppleTalk protocol. Application interfaces to all AppleTalk protocols and to the LAP Manager.

Designing Cards and Drivers for the Macintosh Family*

Communications Toolbox
How to use the Communications Toolbox to write protocol-independent communications software and modular communications tools.

Inside AppleTalk*

Key

Books that every Macintosh programmer needs.

Books that Macintosh programmers need for specialized tasks.

*Not part of *Inside Macintosh*, but contains related information.

Please keep me informed about future volumes in
New Inside Macintosh.

Name   _____

Company   _____

Address   _____

  _____

City   _____

State   _____

Zip   _____

Please tear out card, put in an envelope, and mail to:
Chris Platt
Addison-Wesley Publishing Company
One Jacob Way
Reading, MA   01867

APDA
Your main source for Apple development products

Get easy access to *New Inside Macintosh* and over 300 other programming products through APDA, Apple's worldwide source for Apple and third-party development products. Ordering is easy. APDA offers convenient payment and shipping options.

Call today for your FREE APDA Tools Catalog

1-800-282-2732	U.S.
1-800-637-0029	Canada
(716) 871-6555	International

Site licensing is available for many of the development tools. For information, contact Apple Software Licensing at (408) 974-4667.

apda
tools for developers